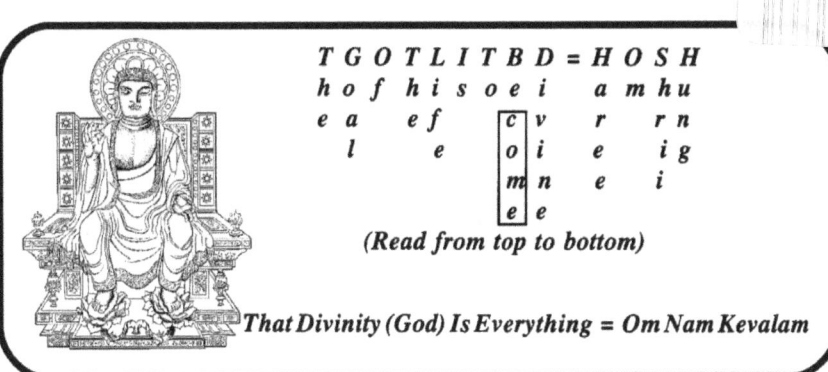

THOTH
The Holiest Of The Holies
"The Last Testament"

Maitreya
(Joseph Emmanuel)

The books of **THOTH** with no date are the first edition (1982).

The second edition was published August 1985.

The third edition was published July 1986.

The fourth edition was published March 1989.

The fifth edition was published February 1991.

The sixth edition was published April 1993.

The seventh edition was published April 2000.

The eighth edition was published November 2001.

The ninth edition was published June 2006.

This (tenth) edition was published June 2013 using Print On Demand services.

Copyright © 1982 by Maitreya

If any man shall add to the words of this Book, God shall add to his burden (karma), and if any man shall take away from the words of this book, God shall take away his part out of the book of life.

Mission of Maitreya
"Eternal Divine Path"
P. O. Box 44100
Albuquerque, NM 87174

www.maitreya.org

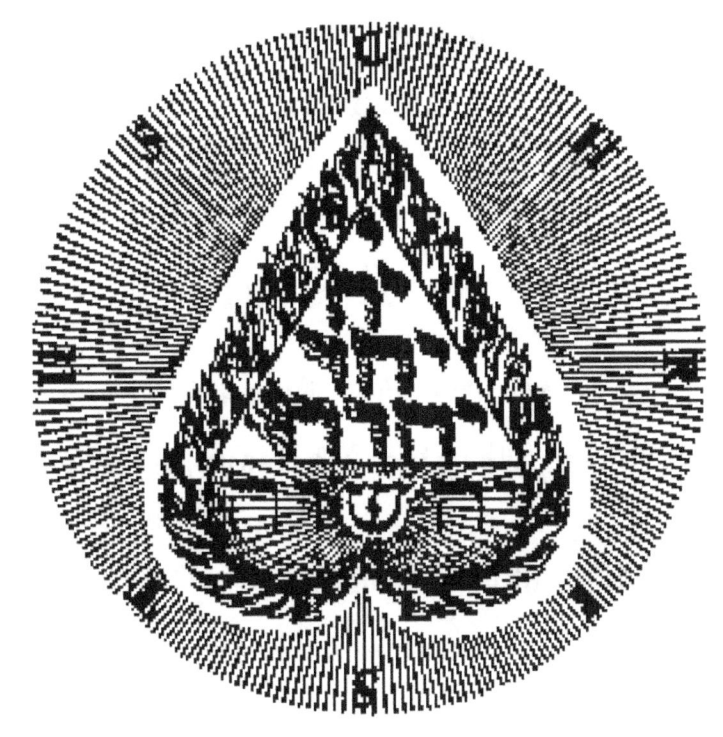

DEDICATED TO
THE THRONE OF THE FIRE OF COMPASSION
WHICH BURNS ALL IMPURITIES:

FATHER
WHO IS IN HEAVEN

MOTHER
(THE HOLY GHOST)
WHO IS IN THE EARTH (CREATION)

AND

THE SON
WHO IS THE MESSIAH

Maitreya

As Joseph (Yoseph) is
a disciple

As Maitreya (The Compassionate One) is
The Buddha

As יהושע (The Messiah) is
The Christ (Christus, Chrishna, Charisma)

As Mohammad (The Praiseworthy) is
The Mehdi

He is also called, Vigi,
The Youthful

And Kumar, The Prince.
He has come to bring Peace and The Kingdom

His Last name is Emmanuel (God with us),
The Father and He are One, and He knows the Mother

He has been given these names. He did not call himself by these names, as many have, fulfilling the Prophecy that "for many shall come in my Name(s) … and shall deceive many" (Matthew 24:5).

PREFACE

The book, **The Holiest Of The Holies (THOTH), The Last Testament** is the collection of the eighteen books, plus Supplements and The Glossary, written by **Maitreya**. Like any other Scripture, although it reveals many truths, it is a puzzle. That is, to understand the whole truth and message, all the books should be read, contemplated, understood and put together until the whole picture and depth, with His Grace, can be grasped.

The book is called **The Holiest Of The Holies** because it contains explanations of most of the Holy books of the world and how all of them are related together, complement one another, and are from the same Source.

It is called **The Last Testament** because it is in the seventh stage of human progress that all the truths of the relationship between man and the universe are revealed. The teaching of **Maitreya**, which is the seventh one, reveals the whole Plan of God. So it is also called **The Last Testament**.

THOTH has been divided into four sections: **THE HOLIEST** containing the first twelve books, **KINGDOM** the next three books, **ESSAYS** (three books of essays) and **SUPPLEMENTS**.

The section **THE HOLIEST** is primarily about creation and history, the explanation of how God has directed humanity the last 12,000 years, and many things that have happened in the past and a few things of the future. The essence of this section is the **Eternal Divine Path**. The first book in this section is called The Holiest Book which is the longest book in **THOTH**. It contains the basic teachings from which the rest of **THOTH** has been derived. This first book has been divided into seven sections as "Holiest" one to seven.

KINGDOM contains three books which explain how human social systems have been guided for the last 12,000 years, and a system to manifest His Kingdom has been presented.

The **ESSAYS** are mostly about the future and how things will manifest or should be.

The unity of all religions of the world, as is explained in **THOTH**, was revealed to **Maitreya** after a long time of being guided step-by-step to reach this point. The story of this period by itself is incredible and can be considered a miracle. It culminated in a vision when he visited the Baha'i Temple in Chicago in 1977. Then the vision gradually formed itself into a sign, **The Greatest Sign**. In 1978 these teachings were put into written form. They continued to be refined as the years went by.

However, the basic teachings based on **The Greatest Sign** remain the same. Like a painter who first sketches the overall outlines, and then gradually continues to bring the picture to more clarification, so did these writings continue to be refined. The "overall outline" is **The Greatest Sign**, but as the teachings continued toward more detail, these details needed to be fine-tuned to deeper meanings. This reaching for the deeper meaning still continues. That is why in each new edition of **THOTH**, there might be some small changes and additions. There is also the section **SUPPLEMENTS**.

SUPPLEMENTS are additional essays which are written to clarify and explain some points, answer some important questions, or expand the meaning of the main part of the book **THOTH**. This part will be expanded in each new edition, if necessary. There are also other materials which can be considered as supplements to **THOTH**, such as the Golden Keys series, The Plan, Discourses, various audio and video recordings, the www.maitreya.org website, etc. This will continue until **Maitreya** is satisfied that fairly all questions are answered and no misunderstanding is left.

If you do not understand all the teachings, or they do not appeal to you at first, do not let this concern you. Accept that which you understand and like; the rest will also gradually be revealed to you. Not everyone resonates with all parts of any Scripture but all parts are necessary. Different parts of Scriptures are written for and appeal to different people! If you have any questions, ask and they will be answered.

If the history, different religions, beliefs, and even present events of the world are studied, you can find each of them occurring because the emphasis is on one or a few narrow realizations, which each is a part of **THOTH**. Different realizations in **THOTH** also will be emphasized in different situations in the future, according to the time, place, and people involved. **THOTH** therefore, is a revelation for each and all people, times, and situations!

Some parts may never appeal to you or to any culture, etc. Remember the true teaching of **Maitreya** is the non-dogmatic practical path that is the **Eternal Divine Path**. Other explanations and revelations should not become a source of separation. If such a situation is created, the arguments should be stopped and the attention directed toward this practical path, which is to follow the **Eternal Divine Path**, unify humanity, and bring His Kingdom on earth.

The verses with their numbers in the beginning of the sentence are explanations or were written by **Maitreya**. The sentences indented and/or with their numbers at the end of the quotes, are from other Scriptures.

The brackets used in verses from other Scriptures were added to emphasize, refer to a point, or clarify the meaning of a word or the verse.

The contents of each book in **THOTH** can be explained as below:

THE HOLIEST

1- **THE HOLIEST BOOK**: An in-depth explanation of the teachings.

2- **THE BASE**: The base of **Maitreya**'s teachings.

3- **CHILDREN OF ABRAM (ABRAHAM), "ALL PROPHECIES ARE FULFILLED"**: An explanation of the historical events of the Children of Abram (Abraham), how all promises given to them are fulfilled, and also other revealing points.

4- **THE HOUSE OF JUDAH (JEWS)**: An explanation of the historical events of the Jews and how they have been chosen as an example for humanity to observe.

5- **CREATION AND HISTORY**: An explanation of how creation occurred; also, history from a spiritual and historical point of view.

6- **ALL ARE LESSONS TO LEARN, NOT TO ARGUE, BUT REJOICE**: A brief explanation that the teachings of **Maitreya** and whatever happened, is happening, or will happen are all lessons. They are not to argue about and create division within humanity, but to learn the lesson, progress, and rejoice in the bliss of progressing to Him.

7- **COMMENTARIES ON ST. MATTHEW** (Chapters 1-23): A commentary on the first twenty-three chapters of the gospel according to Saint Matthew.

8- **SAINT JOHN (EXPLAINED)** (Chapters 1-4): A commentary on the first four chapters of the gospel according to Saint John.

9- **READINGS (THE KORAN)**: An explanation of many verses in the Koran, topics related to these verses, many revealing points, and the relationship of the verses to the rest of **Maitreya's** teachings.

10- **UNIVERSE AND MAN**: A brief explanation of the structure of the universe and its relationship with man.

11- **REVELATION OF THE REVELATION**: A complete revelation of the meaning of the whole book of The Revelation (the last book in the Bible).

12- **THE ESSENCE, "ETERNAL DIVINE PATH"**: This is the essence of

Maitreya's teaching and a more in-depth explanation of the **Eternal Divine Path**. This book emphasizes that the teaching is not a dogmatic one, but a practical path to freedom from bondage and narrowness of the mind, which leads to salvation.

KINGDOM

13- **COMMENTARIES ON PROPHECIES IN DANIEL, "PERIOD OF INTELLECTUAL DOMINATION"**: The meanings of the four important dreams and visions in the book of Daniel and their relationships with the events in our time and soon to come.

14- **THE KINGDOM OF HEAVEN ON EARTH**: Reveals how, through a unique set-up, God has been guiding humanity through the last 6,000 years of history, and why man has no choice but to follow Him.

15- **MOUNT ZION AND ZION, AND EXPLANATION OF THE SYSTEM**: The true symbolic meanings of Mount Zion and Zion, and the explanation of the system for the Kingdom Of Heaven On Earth.

ESSAYS

16- **ESSAYS 1**: Short essays on the family, society, education, world and other topics.

17- **ESSAYS 2**: Continuation of Essays 1.

18- **ESSAYS 3**: Recommendations, guides, and rules given by **Maitreya** to help an aspirant in his spiritual progress.

SUPPLEMENTS

19- **SUPPLEMENTS**: Additional essays written by **Maitreya**. In each new edition of **THOTH**, this book may be expanded to further explain and enhance the book and/or add additional information to it.

GLOSSARY: Explanation of the terminology used in **Maitreya's** teachings.

INDEX: Page locations of the important terms in **THOTH**.

O, Son Of Man

For thousands of years humanity has longed for a truth, revelation, or knowledge that explains the unity of God behind all mystical experiences, previous revelations, and religions of the world, and the truth behind the universe (science). There have been mystical explanations of God from those claiming they have experienced the truth by direct contact with Spirit. There are also those who have founded great religions of the world. However, a great confusion still reigns among spiritualists, religions of the world, and the many different branches within each religion.

This is partly because of the lack of knowledge of the followers of each religion, that they each are a part of a greater truth (**Eternal Divine Path**). If this is understood by each and every one of them, they have no choice but to be unified. Also, it is partly because God (Infinite) can be explained and understood in Infinite ways. Each group or branch has closed itself to any input from other realizations. The ultimate realization of God is an individual achievement not based on any organization, church, denomination, group, etc. Spiritual beings are not chosen by men (organizations, etc.). God chooses those He wills.

Lastly, this confusion and separation between humanity in the spiritual level is because of those (intellectual spiritualists) who have created dogmas which have resulted in many sects and cults born out of each religion and/or mystical experience(s). Whatever separates man from man, or for that matter any part of the universe from any other part, is not from God. God unifies; ego (intellect without spirit) divides.

Every explanation and mystical experience has some truth. Each of these truths appeal only to some people. However, the whole is the sum total of all and more. The ultimate truth is personal experience.

Then there is another disciplinary body that is trying to unveil the truth behind the universe through experimental studies, the sciences. They have presented one powerful tool to this process: Verification of each theory by observation, reasoning, and scientific experiments through scientific tools (models, machines, theories, etc.). However, science can only go so far. Science can only explain the universe to the brink of the physically manifested universe and spirit. Then it reaches a point where scientific experiments and observations no longer are possible. Science no longer can explain!

Scientists can verify the different forces working in the universe and/or particles existing, but where these forces have come from they cannot explain. They see a logical and explainable manifested universe but what or who is this logic behind it, they cannot know. If they cross this point and call this logic, "God," then they pass the threshold of science and spirit. They are no longer accepted as scientists; they have entered the realm of the mystics.

However, science and Spirit (God) are as close now as they ever have been in the known history. There is a very thin layer separating them. Even this layer has been shattered by many who have started to see or have seen these two as One. Many scientists have reached a point where they have begun to accept a unified base for the manifested universe. They realize that there is a single Law (God) operating the whole creation. The mystics are also accepting science as a way to verify the truth behind the manifested universe. However, the ultimate step which would make these two One has not yet become universal.

One of the aims of **THOTH (The Holiest Of The Holies)** is to bring the spirit (mystery) and science (practical verification of creation) together.

Besides the mystics who have had direct experience with the spirit and the scientists who have reached the threshold between the spirit and manifested universe, there are also others.

There are those who are called religious people. They are suspicious of any scientific explanations or anything which is not according to their dogmatic beliefs. The scientists are logical and beyond emotional bounds. The mystic is sure and detached from any dogmatic fury. However, those with dogmas are emotional and easily aroused and/or manipulated.

There are also many who claim they have had direct experience in the spirit, or claim they are chosen, but are not. These can be a great obstacle in the path of a seeker of the truth. These claims stem from nothing but ego. That is why it has been said, "Beware of false prophets, which come to you in sheep's clothing, but inwardly they are ravening wolves" (Matthew 7:15). Every individual has the power to experience God. When such an experience occurs, purity will emanate from the person, which is beyond ego. Such people then can teach God (mysteries).

Now the question can arise: What is the role of the great religions of the world? It is here that the concept of Messiah comes into play. There have been many great mystics and religious beings, but few have come to establish a great religion in the world or reveal a great truth to humanity. These great spokesmen have appeared in the last six thousand years or so.

There usually is a long period of prophecy of their coming. It is to distinguish them from any other ordinary spiritual event or claim. Also it is to prepare humanity for each step of the revelation of a Master Plan.

This Master Plan has been formulated to be revealed gradually to humanity. It is a seven-step path which reveals an Eternal Truth for human progress to its ultimate Goal. Each part of this Plan has been revealed to humanity by the Christ (Messiah); the culmination or synthesis of this Plan is revealed in **THOTH**.

Prior to the last twelve thousand years, man had the knowledge of spiritual powers. He was able to manipulate them. However, he did not follow the Eternal Truth which had been revealed to him in order to keep creation in its purity and harmony. He misused his powers and knowledge. That is why he failed, and that is when great disasters befell him.

It was then that it was decided to create human history, and only guide him spiritually by revealing the truth of this **Eternal Path** during the last twelve thousand years. This path has been recognized and existed from (in) eternity. It is a path of spirit. So it is **Divine**. That is the reason it is called the **Eternal Divine Path**.

This seven-step path, **Eternal Divine Path**, is revealed to humanity in the form of a sign, **The Greatest Sign**. In this sign not only have the seven stages of the **Eternal Divine Path** been crystallized, but it is shown that each step in the path is the focal point of one of the great religions of the world.

The first step in this path is concerned with all the Mystical Paths, which explain the relationship between man and God (universe). These teachings are the ancient wisdom that has come to us. This first seal also covers those religions that are based on mystical experiences (such as Buddhism, Hinduism, Cabbala, Sufism, etc.). The understanding of this First Seal (step) is the spirit of all religions.

The next six steps each represent one great religion or revelation that has been revealed to humanity. Each of them are explained to represent one truth, which when put together with the first step (mystical understandings), reveals the whole process of the **Eternal Divine Path**.

The Greatest Sign also explains Creation and History, reveals the essence of "Be"-ing (God) and much more. The whole teaching in **THOTH** evolves around **The Greatest Sign** and is based on It. Still new realizations can be recognized about **The Greatest Sign** as a person meditates on It. It can be Infinitely explained.

The Greatest Sign not only reveals the **Eternal Divine Path**, but also unifies all the religions of the world. So It unifies humanity. Even if a person calls himself an atheist or an agnostic, they most probably believe in science. **THOTH** and **The Greatest Sign** can even help them to see the Logic behind science. In short, if one is open, and is not closed by believing in a set of dogmas, he can see God in the universe. Then all humans can be unified under Him.

The shape of **The Greatest Sign** has been designed to be built as a **Temple**. This will accelerate the unity of all of humanity.

Besides unification of all religions of the world and mystical knowledge, it has also been foretold that God's Kingdom will come to earth at the end of this era (world). The sign of such a longing can be seen all throughout the earth.

The dawn of a new era has been felt by millions. The signs of the end of the old era are apparent in every corner of the earth. This new era is not to return to the old, but to combine the old and the new to a synthesized (whole) way of life. The new era is the time of realizing and implementing the ancient truths combined with new technology (with the use of natural, renewable, and pollution-less resources) to improve the life of man. **The new technology will free man from the mundane. The ancient truth will guide him to the Goal.**

This new way of life necessitates a new system to make it workable. This new era neither can exist based only on diversity and the decentralized mode of the agricultural era, nor on the centralized unified notion of the industrialized period.

The coming of the new era will be more diverse than the agricultural period, but will be highly connected to the rest of humanity or even the universe. This system, therefore, has not only to recognize and accommodate for this diversity, but also to maintain the unity between the complex and interrelated components existing on earth.

That is why the uniqueness of every individual and community has to be recognized, by allowing them to function based on their desired (designed) destiny and culture. However, each and every community will also be connected through their need to participate in the system. This allows diversity to exist in the unified body of humanity. The inter-relationship between them, in the long run, will gradually bring a unified and greater culture on earth.

To present such a system is another main purpose of **THOTH**. This system is an integral part of the **Eternal Divine Path** and **The Greatest Sign** (Second Seal). This system will bring justice to All. **Justice is closest to the Heart of God.**

The Messiah (Christ), a true Saint (Mystic), or anyone who is One with God, has The Grace of God with him. Salvation is possible only through His Grace. Such people, through His Grace, can each lead a person to Him (salvation).

Together **The Greatest Sign**, the **Eternal Divine Path**, and **<u>THOTH</u>**, Is the ultimate manifestation of Christ. They are the sum total of all there IS. They not only lead an individual to God, but also the whole of humanity collectively. God alone Is Salvation. Amen (ॐ).

Maitreya

TABLE OF CONTENTS

PREFACE I

O, SON OF MAN V

THE HOLIEST 1

THE HOLIEST BOOK 3

HOLIEST ONE 5
Genesis 7
Far East Philosophies – Mystical Paths 40

HOLIEST TWO 50
Elected Ones (Hebrews) 50

HOLIEST THREE 56
Christianity 57
Christianity After Christ, and Revelation of <u>The Revelation</u> 63
The Revelation 64

HOLIEST FOUR 81
Islam 81

HOLIEST FIVE 94
The Baha'i Faith 94

HOLIEST SIX 96
Paravipras – The Elects 96

HOLIEST SEVEN 101
Last Chapter – Summary 101

THE BASE 105

CHILDREN OF ABRAM (ABRAHAM) "ALL PROPHECIES ARE FULFILLED" 127

PREFACE 129

SECTION I 130

    The earth is divided: 130

    Abram is chosen as the father of the Hebrews: 130

    A promise is given about Abram's seed: 131

    This promise is given for Ishmael: 131

    The name of Abram is changed to Abraham, and new promises are given for his new son, Isaac: 131

    Abraham is tested by the Lord: 133

    The promises given to Abraham are repeated to Isaac: 134

    Esau sells his birthright to Jacob: 135

    Jacob receives the blessing of Isaac instead of Esau: 135

    The promises are repeated to Jacob: 135

    Jacob's name becomes Israel, a new promise is given to him, and the old promises are repeated: 136

    Two sons of Joseph's become Israel's (Jacob's): 136

    Israel blesses Ephraim and Manasseh, and prefers Ephraim over Manasseh: 136

    Israel separates the spiritual promises (the scepter) from the material promises (birthright) and gives them to two of his sons: 137

    The Children of Israel reject God as their King: 138

    The meaning of the Star of David (✡): 139

    Jews become separated from the House of Israel. Jews are the House of Judah: 139

    Prophets predict the fall of the House of Israel and the Jews: 140

    Many of the House of Israel leave their country even before the attack of the Assyrians: 140

    The House of Israel is captured by the Assyrians: 140

    The House of Judah (Jews) falls also: 141

    Jews return to their land. The House of Israel apparently never returns: 141

The ten lost tribes are the House of Israel (Samarian, or Ephraim): 141

SECTION II 142
Fulfillment of the "birthright:" 142
The nation is the United Kingdom: 142
America is the company of nations: 142
The promise was unconditional: 143

SECTION III 143
Fulfillment of the promise of the scepter: 143
Prophecies of the coming of the Messiah: 143
The Messiah comes: 143
The promise of the "scepter" to Judah is fulfilled: 143
Christ "gathered the people:" 144
The meaning of the teachings of Christ and the cross (✝): 145
The promises to Israel are fulfilled: 145

SECTION IV 145
The promise of spiritual blessing also was given to Ishmael: ... 145
Akashic Records: 145
Readings: 145
Koran means "readings:" 146
What the Koran says about the future of Abram's seed, Ishmael: 146
It is also revealed in The Revelation: 147

SECTION V 147
All promises given to Abram's and Abraham's seed are fulfilled: 147
The spiritual truth was finished by Prophet Muhammad: 148
The next Prophet did not come from the children of Abram (Arabs) or Abraham (Hebrews): 148
God is no longer obligated to any special people: 149
All earthly powers will be humbled: 149

The Elected Ones are not a race: 151

His Will, will be done on earth as it is in heaven: 151

APPENDIX 152

THOSE PROPHECIES WHICH ARE NOT YET FULFILLED 152

THE USE OF THE POWER 153

There is a message for America (and all those who gain power): 153

The people who created the foundation of the United States were evolved beings: 153

Explanation of the obverse side of The Seal of the United States: 153

Explanation of the reverse side of the seal: 155

To be chosen does not mean to be greater: 155

THE HOUSE OF JUDAH (JEWS) 157

INTRODUCTION 159

1 - Elected Ones: 160

2 - Strengthening the Elected Ones: 160

3 - They were tested: 160

4 - They failed: 161

5 - First purification (punishment): 161

6 - The Children of Israel become two nations: 161

7 - They are given another chance: 161

8 - The coming of Esa The Messiah, and his rejection by the Jews: 162

9 - The Prophethood is taken from the Jews and given to other nations: 162

10 - Revelation of <u>The Revelation</u>: 162

11 - Second Purification (punishment): 163

12 - The advent of Prophet Muhammad: 163

13 - The rejection of Prophet Muhammad and his prediction of a great punishment for the Jews: 164

14 - The third purification (punishment): 164

15 - The Jews are given another chance: 164

16 - A distinction between Hebrews and Jews: 164

17 - The struggle of God to make humans understand His Divine Justice: 165

CREATION AND HISTORY 167

INTRODUCTION 169
CREATION 169
HISTORY 173

ALL ARE LESSONS TO LEARN, NOT TO ARGUE, BUT REJOICE 181

COMMENTARIES ON <u>ST. MATTHEW</u> 189

<u>SAINT JOHN</u> (EXPLAINED) 273

INTRODUCTION 275

READINGS (THE <u>KORAN</u>) 291

INTRODUCTION 293

Ability of God to Change Human and His Condition 295
Akashic Records 295
All Things Belong to God 296
All Are God's Children 297
Angels (Avatars) 297
Choice of the Human to Be Guided or to Go Astray 298
Daharma 298
The Devil 299
Difference Between God (Father) and Others 300

Disbelievers 301
Disciples 302
Elected Ones 302
Evolution 304
God Can Do All Things 305
God Does Not Have a Name – All Good Names Are His 305
God Is All-Pervasive 306
God Is the Greatest 307
God Wants Humans to Understand 307
Heaven Is Pure Consciousness 308
Hell (Ignorance) 309
The Hierarchy in Heaven 310
History as a Lesson for Humanity 310
The Holy Spirit (Brings the Revelation) 311
Immortality 312
Human as a Channel for Divine Actions 312
Judge Not 313
Karma 314
Knowing God by Thinking About His Universe (Creation) 316
The Last Days (Day of Judgment) 317
Law of the Grace of God 318
Life Is a Struggle 318
Lower Nature 319
Maya 320
Meditation 321
Miracles and Disbelievers 322
More Prophets Will Come 322
Paravipras (Elected Ones) 324
Parents 324
Propagation of Religions 325

- Prophets 325
- There Is a Purpose in Creation 327
- Reincarnation 329
- Resistance to Believe in Prophets 331
- Sacrifice 332
- Self-Realization 333
- Sin 333
- Spiritual Struggle Is for Self, Not for Prophets or God 334
- Study of Scriptures 334
- Surrendering 335
- Some Symbols Corresponding to Those Used in the Bible 336
- Tests 338
- Tribulation (the Way God Warns Us) 339
- Thirst for Limitlessness 339
- Unifying the Spiritualists 340
- Union, Separation, and Reunification 340
- Universe Is Consciousness 341
- Virtues 341
- Water Is Purifier 342
- Women 343
- Ending 343

UNIVERSE AND MAN **345**

KOSHAS AND LOKAS 347
RELATIONSHIP BETWEEN CHAKRAS AND KOSHAS (SHEATHS) 351
UNIVERSE AND MAN SUMMARIZED 354
APPENDIX I 355
Energy Activates Propensities 355
APPENDIX II 357

There Is an Infinite Range in Creation 357
A NOTE 358

REVELATION OF **THE REVELATION** **359**
INTRODUCTION 361
EVERY WORD OF GOD HAS MORE THAN SEVEN MEANINGS. 428

THE ESSENCE, "ETERNAL DIVINE PATH" **429**

KINGDOM **453**

COMMENTARIES ON PROPHECIES IN DANIEL, "PERIOD OF INTELLECTUAL DOMINATION" **455**
PREFACE 457
The Dream of King Nebuchadnezzar 458
Vision of the Four Beasts by Daniel 462
Vision of the Ram and He Goat by Daniel 469
Conclusion 474

THE KINGDOM OF HEAVEN ON EARTH **477**
THE FIVE CLASSES AFTER THE FLOOD OF NOAH 479
HISTORICAL EXPLANATION OF THE CLASS DOMINATION 480
PARAVIPRAS AND THEIR ROLE IN SOCIETY 483
CONTRIBUTION OF EACH CLASS IN SOCIETY 484
BALANCE 485

THE CLASSLESS HUMANS..488
GUIDING LIGHT FOR THE LEADERS..............................489

MOUNT ZION AND ZION, AND EXPLANATION OF THE SYSTEM 491

INTRODUCTION 493
PART I: WHAT ARE MOUNT ZION AND ZION? 493

The symbolic meaning of mountain in the <u>Bible</u>: 493

Similarity of the shape of a mountain to a triangle upward (△): 493

Mount Zion: 494

Zion: 494

There are three Kingdoms of Heaven: 494

God is the only true King of these three Kingdoms, whether humans accept it or not: 494

God desires to see that His Kingship is known and accepted (established): 495

Only in such an environment is peace, tranquility, and prosperity possible for humanity. Otherwise suffering will continue to be present: 495

Mount Zion is given to humanity: 496

PART II: MOUNT ZION 497

Introduction to Mount Zion: 497

(1) Selection process of the leaders: 497

(2) Unawareness of the leaders that any existing ideology or approach is valid only in a given time: 498

(3) Attachment of the leaders (and people) to a small portion of the earth, a special culture, group, religion, ideology, etc.: 498

(4) Lack of a body as an overseer of the system: 498

(5) Lack of the presence of spiritual considerations (putting God out of the system): 498

REGIONAL GOVERNMENT 499
    Administrative body, twelve-people leader selection process: 499
    Judiciary board (Board of Brahmins): 501
    Legislative body (House of Elects): 502
    Elders: 503
    Decision-making process: 504

WORLDWIDE APPLICATION (WORLD GOVERNMENT) 505

THE HIERARCHY 507
    The place of each class in society: 507

PART III: ZION 508
    Justice (Zion) in the system: 508
    When the system becomes corrupt: 508

PART IV: FINANCING THE SYSTEM, AND THE BEST WAY TO CREATE THE BASE OF TWELVE 509
    Financing the system: 509
    A recommended house for twelve people: 511

PART V: FINAL POINTS 512
    Subjective approach with objective adjustment: 512
    Progressive nature of the universe: 512
    Exceptions to the rule: 512

ESSAYS 513

ESSAYS 1 515
    SAL-OM (SALUT-OM) 517
    ATMAN 517
    DAHARMA (DARMA) 518
    TIME, PLACE, AND PERSON, IGNORANCE, PASSION, OR KNOWLEDGE 518

THE THREE GUNAS 519
CONTROL OF THE LOWER SELF 520
INVISIBILITY OF GOD AND HUMAN 521
THE PREREQUISITES OF SPIRITUAL LIFE 521
ENVIRONMENT 522
PURITY (PURITY OF BODY, MIND, AND
ENVIRONMENT) 523
SATSANG 524
THE IMPORTANCE OF THE SPIRITUAL TEACHER 524
UNIVERSALISM 525
SELECTION OF ONE LANGUAGE 525
MIXING RACES 526
VIRTUES OF MARRIAGE 527
UNIVERSAL NAMING 529
SOCIETY 530
EDUCATION 530
SCIENCE 530
POPULATION 531
ARTISTS 532
JUSTICE 532
THE MEDIA 533
WHAT IS WRONG WITH MANAGEMENT STUDIES 534
THE TEMPLE 535
SPIRITUAL CENTER 537
SETTING OF THE ALTAR 537
THE BASE OF HISTORY AND DATING 538
THE DAYS AND THE NIGHTS 540

FEASTS AND HOLY DAYS OF THE LORD 541
NEW YEAR, PASSOVER, AND OTHER SYMBOLS 542
KINGDOM OF HEAVEN IN HEAVEN (KOHIH) 543
SONS OF GOD (gods) 544
GOD JUST "IS" 545

ESSAYS 2 .... **547**

FALSE EGO 549
RELATIONSHIPS 549
PARENTS 551
MASOCHISM AND SADISM 551
MALE AND FEMALE 552
MEN AND WOMEN 553
RENUNCIATES (SANNYASINS) 555
ORIGIN OF THE MYTHS 555
VISIONS, IMAGES, AND DREAMS 556
ETHEREAL BEINGS AND ASTRAL PROJECTION 557
IDOL WORSHIPPING 557
CULTS 558
MIDDLE PATH (BALANCE) 558
LAW OR JUSTICE 559
EXTERNAL SYMBOL OF INTERNAL
PUNISHMENT 560
WHEN THE LIFE STARTS 561
ETERNAL DIVINE PATH 561
TEACHINGS OF MAITREYA SIMPLIFIED 562
HAREE OM SHRII HUNG (HOSH) SIGN 562
SUN, MOON, AND STARS 563

SYMBOLIC MEANING OF BAPTISM 563

TO SIN AND TO COMMIT SIN 564

THE ROLE OF INDIA AND THE FAR EAST IN THE PROGRESS OF HUMAN CIVILIZATION 565

ACTION (KARMA), KNOWLEDGE (JNANA), AND DEVOTION (BHAKTI) YOGAS, AND THEIR PLACES IN THE GREATEST SIGN 565

SOME POINTS IN ISLAM 566

JAHAD 568

AN ESSAY ON THE THEORY OF THE HIERARCHY OF NEEDS OF MASLOW 569

PRESSURE 572

DAYDREAMERS 573

PREDESTINATION OR CHOICE 573

QUOTE: "GREATER THAN MEDITATION..." 574

ESSAYS 3 .... **575**

INTRODUCTION 577

BATH 578

CIRCUMCISM 579

CLOTHING 579

COOLING OF THE BODY 579

DISPOSING OF THE DEAD BODY 580

DIVINE PATH 581

FASTING 581

FIFTEEN COMMANDMENTS 582

EXPLANATION OF THE FIFTEEN COMMANDMENTS 583

FOOD 586

GIFT-GIVING 588
HOSPITALITY 588
MUSIC 589
OCCUPATION (WORK) 589
PRAYER 589
THE REMINDER 590
EXPLANATION OF THE REMINDER 590
SABBATH AND SABBATH COMMUNITY UNITY MEETING 595
SAMGACCHADVAM 596
SPIRITUAL CHANTING AND DANCING (KIRTAN) 596
THIRTY-THREE VIRTUES 597
UNIVERSAL CALL TO PRAYER 598
WASHING OF THE COLON 599
WORSHIPPING 599
YOGA POSTURES (ASANAS) 600

SUPPLEMENTS 601

INTRODUCTION 603
A SLOGAN 603
MISSION OF MAITREYA (MOM) 603
THE ONLY ISSUE 603
COVENANT WITH GOD, OR THE MISSION OF MAITREYA (MAITREYA) 604
WHY TITHES 605
SHOULD WE ACKNOWLEDGE THE TEACHER? 606
SHOULD I COME AND LIVE IN THE MISSION CENTER, OR CLOSE BY? 607

TO BE(COME) A CONTACT PERSON FOR THE MISSION	608
FAMILY	608
THERE SHOULD NOT BE ANY SECRETS IN THE COMMUNITIES OF LIGHT	608
CHIDREN AND COMMUNITY	609
POSITIVE, NEGATIVE, AND NEUTRAL FORCES IN THE UNIVERSE	611
SUBCONSCIOUS MIND	612
SUBCONSCIOUS MIND, REVISITED	612
MALE, FEMALE, MAN, WOMAN, ADAM, gods, DIVINE FATHER, DIVINE MOTHER, GOD	614
GOD'S LAWS VS. MAN'S LAWS	615
GODLY SOCIETIES AND UNGODLY SOCIETIES	615
ABSOLUTE LAWS AND RELATIVE LAWS	616
DIVINE SYSTEM (A SYSTEM FROM DIVINES, BY DIVINES, AND FOR DIVINES)	617
COLLECTIVE KARMA	619
PASSING OF THE SCEPTER	620
LAWS ON NATIONS AND PEOPLE	626
ARTIFICAL POWER CENTERS	626
IS IT IMMORAL OR ILLEGAL?	627
WHY GOD COMMANDED US TO EAT KOSHER FOOD AND AVOID EATING UNCLEAN FOOD	627
EASTERN AND WESTERN BIAS	628
CRYSTALS	629
RELATIONSHIP BETWEEN THE SPINAL CORD, MEDICAL LOGO (CADUCEUS), AND THE STORY OF KING ARTHUR	629

SYMBOLIC MEANINGS OF THE STORY OF KING ARTHUR 631
LOTUSTICA VS. SWASTIKA 632
DOES GOD TALK TO EVERYONE DIRECTLY? 633
GO TO THE SOURCE 634
CHANNELING VS. BEING A LIGHT WORKER 635
MEDITATION AND PRAYER 635
IN PRAYING 635
NON-VIOLENCE 636
LIGHT BODY 637
MERGE INTO GOD OR PLAY THE PLAY 637
OVERACTIVE CHAKRAS IN A PREGNANT WOMAN 637
COLLECTIVE MEDITATION VS. TRANSMISSION MEDITATION 638
SALVATION 639
THE NEW MAN 640
A DECREE 642

GLOSSARY 643

INDEX 681

THE HOLIEST

(Holy means, "to be whole, complete, perfect, the truth.")

In The Name and Glory of God, The Formless, Invisible, Nameless, and Eternal (FINE), Who Is and Is All

The section THE HOLIEST consists of the first twelve books. It is primarily about creation and history. These books explain how God has directed the human and his history for the last 12,000 years. They also cover many other things that had happened in the past and a few things of the future. The essence of this section is the revelation and explanation of the Eternal Divine Path.

THE HOLIEST BOOK

The first book in the section THE HOLIEST is also called <u>The Holiest Book</u>, and it contains the basic teachings from which the rest of <u>THOTH</u> has been derived. This is the only book in <u>THOTH</u> which has been divided into seven subsections as Holiest One to Seven.

THE HOLIEST BOOK

HOLIEST ONE

Tablet One

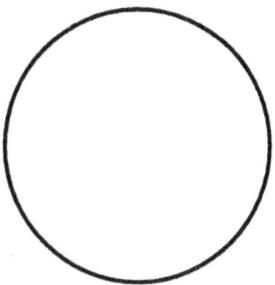

<1> God is everlasting, complete, without beginning or end. <2> He is One and indivisible.
<3> The universe (God) is consciousness and its three creative forces (three gunas).
<4> The three creative forces in the universe are: Sentient force (satva guna), mutative force (raja guna), and static force (tama guna). <5> The sentient force (satva guna) or intelligence brings the feeling of "know"-ness. <6> The mutative force (raja guna) or energy is responsible for any movement, vibration, and also is the life-force which brings the feeling of "doer"-ship.
<7> The static or crudifying force (tama guna) is the centripetal (crudifying) force in the universe. <8> In the operative stage it crudifies the consciousness and in its first state of influence creates fine ether (akasha) which is the memory in the universe. This force also brings the feeling of "I" into the universe. <9> So when in the operative state, the memory as "I have done" will be awakened. <10> Furthermore, this force is one which fixes things in the mind and enables the consciousness to visualize them. <11> In other words, it creates the visualization or screen for things to be seen in the universe.

Tablet Two

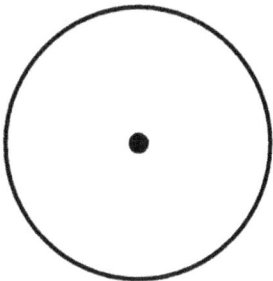

"In the beginning was the Word, and the Word was with God, and the Word was God.
The same was in the beginning with God.
All things were made by him; and without him was not any thing made that was made." (<u>Bible</u>, John 1:1-3)

THE HOLIEST BOOK

<1> In truth all Scriptures should start with the three verses above (John 1:1-3) which imply that there has been a beginning for all things and there are creative forces from which all things are made.

<2> The three creative forces (three gunas) cannot be separated from the consciousness. They are one and inseparable. They are two sides of one entity. <3> Creative forces without consciousness cannot be directed and used, and consciousness without creative forces has no creativity but merely "IS," without knowledge, ability (doing) or remembrance.

<4> In the beginning the operative powers of these three creative forces were not released but were in a balanced state (▽). <5> So the universe was in a state of "Be"-ness (symmetric). <6> Through the desire of God, their operative powers were released.

<7> Because of the operative power of the satva guna (sentient force) and presence of the active tama guna (crudifying force), the feeling of "I know" was awakened and spread in the universe. <8> The first part of the ego was evolved.

<9> Because of the operative power of the raja guna (mutative force) and presence of the active tama guna, the feeling of "I do" was created and spread in the universe. <10> The second part of the ego came into existence.

<11> Through the influence of the operative power of the tama guna (crudifying force), the first state of ethereal factor (fine ether) evolved and the memory as "I have done" was felt. <12> So the ego became complete. <13> This process continued until the unit consciousnesses (individual egos) were evolved. A manifestation of the Divine (Spark of Light) through gross form (body), is individualized ego (Illusion), separated from God.

<14> With this, each unit consciousness is felt separately as "I" which "knows," "does," and "has done." <15> So because of the influence of the tama guna as "I," the universal consciousness was divided into infinite unit consciousnesses as separate "I"s.

<16> As the tama guna becomes more dominant, the feeling of separation becomes greater and this results in self-centeredness, which is the cause of all sufferings, miseries, confusions, and chaos.

<17> Before the release of the operative powers of the three gunas, there was no vibration in the universe. <18> By the release of their operative powers and because of the influence of the raja guna, vibration was created. <19> The manifested universe indeed is vibration in different stages. <20> Vibration is sound. <21> This sound vibration or the creative power in the universe in the operative state is "The Word" (ॐ). <22> It is the part and parcel of God, which "was with God, and the Word was God," and "All things are made by him [It]."

Tablet Three

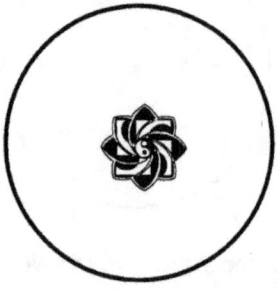

"In him was life; and the life was the light of men.
And the light shineth in darkness; and the darkness comprehended it not." (John 1:4-5)

<1> Raja guna is the energy (life-force) in the universe. <2> When this energy (prana) is directed to higher things or God, it becomes the Light of the consciousness. <3> It resides in all things in the universe, "In him was life, and the life was the light of men."

<4> Because of the influence of the tama guna (darkness), although it is present even in darkness and human consciousness, it cannot be comprehended. The ego prevents this Light and life to be seen by man, "And the light shineth in darkness; and the darkness comprehended it not."

Tablet Four

GENESIS

Chapter 1

"In the beginning God created the heaven and the earth." (Genesis 1:1)

<1> Consciousness, when un-manifested, is in the state of "Be"-ness. It is Formless, Nameless, Invisible, and Eternal, neither male nor female. It is Pure Consciousness (Divine Will) as an observer of the universe. It is pure intuition. <2> Consciousness is passive and neutral.

<3> When the same consciousness is engaged in planning and guiding the universe, It becomes pure Divine Logic (Father or El).

<4> Satva guna is passive and positive, neither male nor female. <5> Raja guna (energy) is active and neutral. <6> When it is activated, and also remains neutral, because it has no polarity it becomes unconditional Love or Divine Grace (Mother).

<7> When Divine Logic (Father) and Divine Grace (Mother) are present, then God is the Father Mother God (Elohim). <8> When only Divine Logic is present, God is the Father. <9> Divine Mother is when God is pure Divine Grace.

<10> Tama guna is passive and negative, neither male nor female. <11> When tama guna dominates, man falls into his lower nature.

<12> God called this state (Pure Consciousness) that He Himself was in (卐) "heaven," and the state of being lost and under the influence of the tama guna He called "earth" (hell). <13> So heaven and hell (earth) were created.

<14> As it is explained, through crudification of consciousness, the mind (ego, three gunas) is manifested. Therefore, Pure Consciousness is beyond all of these (three gunas) or any other grosser manifestation. That is why It can by no means be explained in any level of the manifested world, including the ethereal. Neither can it be understood in the mental state. <15> Anything which can be explained or is explained is not Pure Consciousness.

<16> Pure Consciousness can only be known with direct experience. <17> However, consciousness is interwoven into every-

thing which Is or Is Not. Pure Consciousness is the state of equilibrium of the three gunas (Mind).

<18> Do not be concerned about reaching God (Pure Consciousness). <19> Take each day as it comes, meditate, observe, contemplate to do His Will (Live in God). This will earn His Grace. <20> Only through His Grace is salvation possible.

<21> One day a surge of Great Love, Light, and Higher Thoughts will dawn on you; it is then that you know God is with you. <22> Eventually the Goal will be achieved, you will be One.

"And the earth was without form, and void;…" (Genesis 1:2a)

<23> The earth or hell is not a place nor has any shape. <24> It is a state of consciousness. It is where the Soul (consciousness) is under the influence of the tama guna, feeling separate and lost.

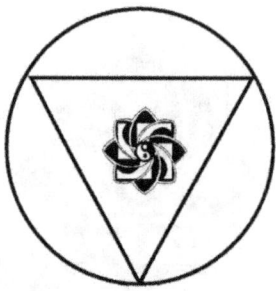

"…and darkness was upon the face of the deep…" (Genesis 1:2b)

<25> Father (God) (✡) has complete control of the universe by the Universal Mind or the three gunas (▽).

<26> The satva guna of the universe is the intelligent or decision-making part of the Universal Mind (Mahatattva). <27> The raja guna in the universe is the recognizing part of the Universal Mind (Ahamtattva). <28> The tama guna in the universe is the visualizing part or the screen of the Universal Mind (Chitta).

<29> Through the Universal Mind (▽), God saw His universe (consciousness). It was in a state of chaos, lost, and in darkness, "and darkness was upon the face of the deep."

<30> Because of this chaos, God decided to bring the lost unit consciousnesses under His control and then help them reach Pure Consciousness – be(come) One with Him.

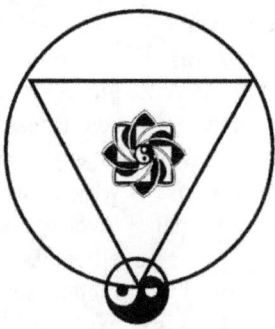

"…And the Spirit of God moved upon the face of the waters." (Gen. 1:2c)

<31> **Water is the symbol for manifested consciousness (ether).** <32> So God moved in the universe (water) through His Universal Mind ("Spirit of God") and brought the lost

unit consciousnesses () under His control (▽).

<33> The I-Ching sign in the horizontal position () symbolizes a unit consciousness in the state of ignorance, being lost and in darkness, with its spiritual power in the latent state, or not realized (awakened).

"And God said, Let there be light:..." (Genesis 1:3a)

<34> God created great compassion for those lost souls (). <35> He projected His Light (Christ) into the universe. <36> He desired (willed) that the lost universe might reach Pure Consciousness, "Let there be light."

"And the Word was made flesh,..." (John 1:14)

<37> Because The Word was made flesh, he had to go through the same struggle as any other flesh. <38> With His Grace with him, he started to realize the influences of the three gunas over himself. <39> He began to meditate on his moods. <40> He realized that he went from a state of happiness and feeling of belonging to the universe (or at least to a small part of it), <41> to a state of complete separation and self-centeredness. <42> He realized that when he feels he belongs to the universe or at least to a part of it, a happiness is created, <43> and when he feels lonely and separated, great stress and unhappiness prevails.

Tablet Five

<1> By becoming more and more familiar with the influences of the three gunas, he realized that it is the power of the tama guna which crudifies the consciousness and results in self-centeredness. <2> This creates the great feeling of separation as "I." So through meditation, he started to realize the reasons for his ups and downs, and his spiritual forces began to be awakened.

<3> Also he realized that whenever he is in an environment with much tamasic force present, he is influenced to be more self-centered and again the unhappiness increased. <4> So he realized that a proper environment is essential for his happiness and progress.

<5> As he came to higher consciousness and felt one with his environment, he realized also many other unit consciousnesses were lost. <6> A desire arose in him to help them understand the things he had realized, <7> and also through helping others he could

create more sentient beings around him to establish a better environment (sentient environment).

<8> So he engaged himself in helping others to come to higher consciousness. <9> He later realized not all would listen. These unit consciousnesses were so lost and self-centered that they would not be guided but instead go astray. <10> Eventually a few became attracted and showed readiness to go through the struggle to reach higher consciousness. <11> He created greater concentration to help those who would listen. <12> In doing so, he forgot about himself and with this a great joy was felt. <13> He realized that true joy will not come by thinking about the self and always meditating on "I," but by sacrificing (not being self-centered) to bring others to higher consciousness and to create the desired environment (✡).

<14> He then intensified his efforts and, in the process, some of the unit consciousnesses that he was helping started to progress. <15> He began to feel how great he was to have sacrificed so much to help others. <16> Also when they would not progress as he liked, he would become discouraged and unhappy about why they were not evolving as he liked despite all his efforts.

<17> Eventually a great realization came to him, that even **being attached to the result of one's actions is a hindrance on the spiritual path.** <18> So he did the sacrifices and tried to help others reach higher consciousness with the highest possible effort, but he **surrendered the result to the Lord.**

<19> With this, neither the feeling of false greatness was created which results in superiority feelings and furthering self-centeredness, <20> nor was there the discouragement about why the result was not as expected.

<21> Later on, a greater realization came to him that even in surrendering there is still an "I" left as "'I' surrender to the Lord the result of my actions." <22> But with submission to the Lord and letting Him do the actions (sacrifice) through him, then there would be no "I" left, and the "doer," "the things done," and "the one for whom the things are done" become **ONE**. Then the unity is complete. <23> So no false ego and no anxiety would be created, and he was free of any bondage from his actions. <24> Submission also means contentment with whatever God does to us. <25> We do our best to do His Will but we are content with the result.

<26> However, to be submissive to the Lord by dissolving the "I" into Him and letting Him do the actions all the time is a great task. <27> The ego comes in, the ideation is forgotten, and the "I" becomes the doer again. <28> Therefore, later on the attachment to the result appears and with it either false pride or discouragement occurs.

<29> He realized that he should submit himself to the Lord all the time, but if he forgets to do that, then he should surrender the result later on or whenever he realizes that he is becoming attached to the result of his actions (this is the path of detachment or renunciation).

<30> With these realizations, he started helping the lost consciousnesses in his immediate surroundings and disregarding the ones out of that immediate environment. <31> Also a great feeling of possessiveness of that environment was created in him. <32> However, as he came to higher consciousness, he realized more and more that everything is God. So he understood then that he could not love only a part of Him and hate the rest.

<33> So he extended his love and effort toward the whole universe. With this, he expanded his mind and shattered all narrowness of the mind, prejudice, misunderstanding, and evils related to them. <34> He became a Universalist.

<35> With meditation, reflection, concentration, etc., he awoke his spiritual forces (☯). <36> He also realized that a proper environment (✡) is necessary to progress to higher consciousness. <37> Without sacrifice (✝), creation of such an environment is impossible. <38> He also realized that even being attached to the result of one's sacrifice or action will create bondage, so the result should be surrendered to God, or one should become submissive (☪) to Him.

<39> Furthermore, he recognized that attachment to a small portion of the universe would create narrowness of the mind. Therefore, he became a Universalist (✹). With this, he expanded his mind and destroyed all narrowness of the mind.

<40> With all these realizations, he became a dynamic spiritual force in the universe (✡). Through intensifying his engagement in helping others to reach higher consciousness, little by little, he dissolved his ego into the Universal Ego.

Tablet Six

"…and there was light." (Genesis 1:3b)

<1> With these progressions and realizations with the Grace of God, he reached Pure Consciousness, "and there was light."

<2> With this, he became the First Begotten Son of God. <3> He reached the Light (Pure Consciousness; became Christ, Christos, Krishna, Charisma, god). <4> So he (✺) became the same as the Father (✺), <5> and the path he went through became the Way and the Truth. <6> Whoever wants to go to the Father must walk this path. That is the **Eternal Path**, the **Divine Path**.

THE HOLIEST BOOK

"And God saw the light, that it was good: and God divided the light from the darkness." (Genesis 1:4)

"And God called the light Day, and the darkness he called Night. And the evening and the morning were the first day." (Genesis 1:5)

<7> God was very pleased to see His First Begotten Son (light), **<8>** and He distinguished the state of Pure Consciousness (light) and the path to reach it, **<9>** from the state of being under the influence of the tama guna and lost (darkness). **<10>** He called that state of clarity of mind "Day." **<11>** The state of darkness ("I" as separate from God), which is the cause of self-centeredness, He called "Night."

<12> With this, the first period of helping the lost consciousnesses reach Pure Consciousness (Divinity) was finished, **<13>** and the **Eternal Divine Path** was realized in doing so, "And the evening and the morning were the first day."

"And God said, Let there be a firmament in the midst of the waters, and let it divide the waters from the waters." (Genesis 1:6)

<14> With the success of His First Begotten Son in reaching Pure Consciousness, God decided ("Let there be") to create a system which would help the lost consciousnesses (waters) reach Pure Consciousness, but in a self-sustaining and faster manner. **<15>** In order to do so, The Divine Father (Father, The Divine Will) planned to create the creation, with the help of The Divine Mother (the creative forces, nature).

<16> God would see in His Mind (Universal Mind) how things should be created and then would codify the process in the ethereal state to be manifested later on. **<17>** He activated the manifested consciousnesses in the universe into different levels ("…a firmament in the midst of the waters") according to the level of awareness or progress they were in, "and let it divide the waters from the waters."

"And God made the firmament, and divided the waters which were under the firmament from the waters which were above the firmament: and it was so." (Genesis 1:7)

<18> These decisions would be created in the ethereal stage first, "And God made the firmament,…" God divided the consciousnesses (waters) according to their states (△). **<19>** Those consciousnesses in lower levels and greatly under the influence of the tama guna were divided from those in higher levels. **<20>** The ones in the lower levels are those "under the firmament" or in the bottom of the Hierarchy in the triangle upward (△), **<21>** and the ones in higher levels are those at the top, "above the firmament." **<22>** With this also, the seven lokas (worlds) were created (read <u>Universe and Man</u>). The Heavenly Hierarchy was created in this stage!

Tablet Seven

"And God called the firmament Heaven. And the evening and the morning were the second day." (Genesis 1:8)

<1> Now through the crudifying force (centripetal force in nature, or tama guna), <2> God could crudify these divided consciousnesses. <3> Those in higher levels, by this process of crudification, would create the first two elements in the universe. The cruder ether and aerial (gaseous) factors, which are the most invisible factors in the manifested world, are called "Heaven." <4> With this, the second period of the struggle was finished, "and the evening and the morning were the second day."

"And God said, Let the waters under the heaven be gathered together unto one place, and let the dry land appear: and it was so." (Genesis 1:9)

<5> Through this centripetal or crudifying force ("gathered together") by the use of the crudest consciousnesses ("waters under the heaven"), the solid factor (dry land) would be made.

"And God called the dry land Earth; and the gathering together of the waters called he Seas: and God saw that it was good." (Genesis 1:10)

<6> God called the dry land "Earth" (solid factor), <7> and by crudifying ("gathering together") more sentient consciousnesses ("waters") (but still under the firmament), the liquid factors ("Seas") would be created. <8> God was very pleased with this process.

<9> The luminous factor (heat, fire) also was created, <10> but this element is almost an exception, because it is in the brink between the unseen and seen elements. <11> That is why although fire is the first visible element in the universe, it disappears as soon as it appears. <12> It is the third element in nature and is crude enough to be seen but subtle enough to disappear (dissolve) into the higher elements. It **is** the firmament.

"And God said, Let the earth bring forth grass, the herb yielding seed, and the fruit tree yielding fruit after his kind, whose seed is in itself, upon the earth: and it was so." (Genesis 1:11)

<13> With the help of the centrifugal force (the opposite of the centripetal force) by loosening up the crudifying power of the static force, and by use of the five elements, the plants would be manifested.

"And the earth brought forth grass, and herb yielding seed after his kind, and the tree yielding fruit, whose seed was in itself, after his kind: and God saw that it was good." (Genesis 1:12)

<14> God planned the creation of the grass, herbs and trees, and God was pleased with this Plan. <15> He created them in the ethereal stage, in His Mind, and He saw and knew it was possible to create them in the physical state later.

<16> He would create them in a self-sustaining manner. They would continue the evolutionary progress without interference. That is why "whose seed was in itself, after his kind."

"And the evening and the morning were the third day." (Genesis 1:13)

<17> The third period of the struggle was finished.

"And God said, Let there be lights in the firmament of the heaven to divide the day from the night; and let them be for signs, and for seasons, and for days, and years:" (Genesis 1:14)

<18> Now God was planning to create the sun and the moon. <19> He wanted to create them for signs (astrology, navigation, etc.), for dividing days from nights, for seasons, and for years. <20> So the Day and Night which were mentioned before are different than these. God decided that the light in the sky (Heaven) for recognizing day and night, etc., was necessary for the earth in this stage.

<21> Light is necessary for plants and life, so the sun and moon were planned to be created.

"And let them be for lights in the firmament of the heaven to give light upon the earth: and it was so." (Genesis 1:15)

<22> These lights would be able to some degree to enlighten the humans about their conditions. They are lights (knowledge) in the firmament of the heaven, which give light (knowledge) upon the earth (by studying these lights we can predict and understand the phases and their effects on our lives, and we can gain some knowledge from them, environmentally or astrologically).

"And God made two great lights; the greater light to rule the day, and the lesser light to rule the night: he made the stars also." (Genesis 1:16)

<23> Therefore, God would create the sun, the moon, and the stars. They were necessary for the evolution of the creation.

"And God set them in the firmament of the heaven to give light upon the earth," (Genesis 1:17)

<24> He would put them in the sky to give their light (light as light and as knowledge) to the earth. <25> Also for growing grass and other life on earth and in the universe, these lights would be necessary.

"And to rule over the day and over the night, and to divide the light from the darkness: and God saw that it was good." (Genesis 1:18)

<26> They rule over the physical day and night, <27> as well as reveal a limited knowledge (day) to humanity (astrologically or environmentally), <28> and a limited ignorance (night) by our not understanding the knowledge they reveal to us. <29> God was pleased with His creation.

"And the evening and the morning were the fourth day." (Genesis 1:19)

<30> The fourth phase was finished.

"And God said, Let the waters bring forth abundantly the moving creature that hath life, and fowl that may fly above the earth in the open firmament of heaven." (Genesis 1:20)

<31> Then God planned to create creatures of the oceans and seas, and the birds. Animal life started from the sea.

<32> The plants were necessary for animal life. But before the plants were created, the sun had to be formed. Plants needed sunshine. <33> Here it is shown that all these verses are a sequence of planning for creation step-by-step. Each step is perfected with a new decision necessary for creation and its ultimate goal.

"And God created great whales, and every living creature that moveth, which the waters brought forth abundantly, after their kind, and every winged fowl after his kind: and God saw that it was good." (Genesis 1:21)

<34> God created animals of the waters and birds of the air, and God was pleased with them.

"And God blessed them, saying, Be fruitful, and multiply, and fill the waters in the seas, and let fowl multiply in the earth." (Genesis 1:22)

<35> God blessed them and wished them to be multiplied in the waters and on the earth.

"And the evening and the morning were the fifth day." (Genesis 1:23)

<36> The plan of the fifth phase of creation was finished.

"And God said, Let the earth bring forth the living creature after his kind, cattle, and creeping thing, and beast of the earth after his kind: and it was so." (Genesis 1:24)

<37> Animal life on earth is considered here. Later on God planned to create higher conscious animals, such as cattle, and it was so.

"And God made the beast of the earth after his kind, and cattle after their kind, and every thing that creepeth upon the earth after his kind: and God saw that it was good." (Genesis 1:25)

<38> God created these higher conscious animals in the ethereal state and was pleased with them.

Tablet Eight

"And God said, Let us make man in our image, after our likeness: and let them have dominion over the fish of the sea, and over the fowl of the air, and over the cattle, and over all the earth, and over every creeping thing that creepeth upon the earth." (Genesis 1:26)

<1> Now the evolutionary process had reached a point where God could plan to create man. All other creation had been done to reach man (atman, soul). At this point now God could awaken those unit consciousnesses that had gone through the whole evolutionary process to full awakening as man, <2> or use the consciousnesses in the higher states to cause further progress. <3> This was the highest achievement for the evolutionary process.

<4> Man would be in the image of God and after His likeness. He would have a consciousness, a mind (three gunas) <5> and also as this universe is God's body which has been divided into seven spheres (Lokas), man would have seven spiritual centers (chakras) in his body, corresponding to the seven divisions of the universe (Lokas) (read Universe and Man).

<6> Evolution here is not in the sense which is known by scientists. It is not used as accidental events based on chance, but evolution in the sense of readiness of each unit consciousness to occupy its place (niche) in the hierarchy of creation. It is neither life risen from matter nor Spirit fallen to matter, but both. It is a simultaneous manifestation in all levels of creation. <7> The higher the unit consciousness, the greater (closer to Pure Consciousness or God) its place in the Hierarchy.

<8> Each unit consciousness is manifested according to its level of awareness which provides the base for its codification in the ethereal level. It is this codification (genetic codes) in the ethereal (astral) level which determines its place in creation. <9> Although the evolutionary steps described by science, in a limited sense, are true, they are only a small part of the system.

<10> In any major evolutionary leap, it is a mass change in the ethereal body, of those who have reached a higher level, which dictates a new environment. Then in such an environment new beings with new genetic codes appear. That is why we can find mass extinctions of those who have lagged behind, which occur at the leap periods of evolutionary intervals.

<11> In essence, although the theory of "survival of the fittest" is correct in a limited sense, truly it is **"the fittest survives!"** That is, those who have reached a higher level of consciousness or desired level, are first prepared (codified, their consciousnesses' demand), and then the proper environments are created to fit them. It is in this new environment that some offshoots from the main body adapt themselves to different niches for the continuation of their survival.

<12> The main body which demands the new environment are those who are the "fittest." Those who adapt themselves to this new situation "survive."

<13> The confusion between different ideologies, groups, explanations, etc., persists when the question of "either"/"or" arises; that is, when people create small visions and so separation among themselves. Therefore they accept "either" this theory "or" that, such as either creation or evolution, either this religion or that.

<14> However, the Universe or God is an infinite Being. There is not such a thing as "either" or "or." Indeed when all are put together, then Its significance and truth can be realized in whole. Yet because the whole is so

vast, many prefer to limit their vision. With limited vision they feel more comfortable. However, the limited vision also creates separation, misunderstanding, strife, and suffering. <15> Limited ego loves limited vision, and that is the cause of all sufferings!

"So God created man in his own image, in the image of God created he him; male and female created he them." (Genesis 1:27)
<16> **In his image means likeness.** <17> One of the most misunderstood sentences in the <u>Bible</u> is: "In the image of God created he him; male and female created he them." <18> The first part indicates that, "he created him," which means a single person. <19> This is referred to as "them" later on, which means He created more than one.
<20> The verse above, therefore, says that God created each of them with male and female qualities (androgynous). <21> The man had not been separated into male and female but these two complementary parts were together in one being.
<22> Only in this stage was man in the likeness of God, male and female, at the same time. <23> Later on, God saw that it was very hard to help man reach Pure Consciousness because he was so complete and did not feel any need to be helped. <24> That is why in chapter 2, verse 18 of <u>Genesis</u>, God says, "It is not good that the man should be alone." "Alone" there means "one" (all-one) or male and female in the same being. It does not mean lonely. It was then (in chapter 2) that God divided man into male and female.
<25> Therefore, God created them, in that stage, in His image (male and female), and God made more than one. He made "them."

"And God blessed them, and God said unto them, Be fruitful, and multiply, and replenish the earth, and subdue it: and have dominion over the fish of the sea, and over the fowl of the air, and over every living thing that moveth upon the earth." (Genesis 1:28)
<26> Then God blessed them and gave them dominion over everything on earth.

"And God said, Behold, I have given you every herb bearing seed, which is upon the face of all the earth, and every tree, in the which is the fruit of a tree yielding seed; to you it shall be for meat." (Genesis 1:29)
<27> This man would be vegetarian. <28> That is what God planned at the beginning for man to be. <29> "Meat" here means food. It does not mean the flesh of animals. <30> Meat-eating started after the flood of Noah (Gen. 9:3) when man became more flesh. <31> That is why vegetables, herbs, grains, and seeds are food for consciousness, and meat is for flesh. <32> Therefore emphasis should be on vegetables in our diets with less meat eaten.
<33> Also, it should be noted that in this stage man does not eat. This sentence is a decision for when man becomes a breathing being and will receive a visible body.

"And to every beast of the earth, and to every fowl of the air, and to every thing that creepeth upon the earth, wherein there is life, I have given every green herb for meat: and it was so." (Genesis 1:30)
<34> Therefore, animals and other beings also would be vegetarian.

"And God saw every thing that he had made, and, behold, it was very good. And the evening and the morning were the sixth day." (Genesis 1:31)
<35> The Lord God looked over all His creation and was very pleased with it. The sixth phase of creation was finished. So He completed His Plan of creating everything in order to help unit consciousnesses reach Pure Consciousness. <36> So far everything was in a state of planning and was created in the ethereal stage. God was planning now to bring unit consciousnesses to that state of awareness where they could be more easily helped to reach Pure Consciousness. <37> The human is that being which can reach Pure Consciousness. <38> In the next chapter God started to create everything into a visible form and continued to perfect it as necessity arose.

Tablet Nine

Chapter 2

"Thus the heavens and the earth were finished, and all the host of them." (Genesis 2:1)

<1> God finished The Plan of creating a complete process to accelerate the progress of reaching Pure Consciousness by the unit minds.

"And on the seventh day God ended his work which he had made; and he rested on the seventh day from all his work which he had made." (Genesis 2:2)

<2> The first six periods of the struggle to perfect the universe to bring the unaware parts to awareness were finished. <3> Now the universe was perfectly planned and would be self-sustaining. Therefore God could be just a witness entity of His creation. <4> That is what is meant by "he rested."

<5> The only struggle remaining for God was to bring it to the visible stage, <6> to observe man, and to try to guide him more and more to understand **WHAT THE PURPOSE OF MAN'S LIFE IS**.

<7> That is why the evolutionary process will continue mostly with man, because it is only man that is fully awakened and **has a choice of selecting his way of living.** <8> The other things in the universe are guided by the Laws (Daharmas) that have been set up for them, <9> but man is the great exception. <10> Therefore, only when he completely understands what the Laws (Daharmas) of the universe are and his purpose of having this life, can he reach his destiny, Pure Consciousness.

"And God blessed the seventh day, and sanctified it: because that in it he had rested from all his work which God created and made." (Genesis 2:3)

<11> God was so pleased with His creation that when He rested and saw that it was so perfect and self-sustaining, He blessed it.

"These are the generations of the heavens and of the earth when they were created, in the day that the Lord God made the earth and the heavens," (Genesis 2:4)

<12> All things were prepared to be created in the manifested level.

"And every plant of the field before it was in the earth, and every herb of the field before it grew: for the Lord God had not caused it to rain upon the earth, and there was not a man to till the ground." (Genesis 2:5)

<13> Everything would be self-sustaining and would grow without any interference.

"But there went up a mist from the earth, and watered the whole face of the ground." (Genesis 2:6)

<14> The earth would be watered and sustained without interference by any being. The earth was different than what we know now. It changed to this earth later on. <15> However, the basic Laws are the same. The earth needs water to grow, <16> but water is now more under the control of God. He gives it when He feels it should be given, and He withholds it when it is not necessary, or when He does not want to give it.

"And the Lord God formed man of the dust of the ground, and breathed into his nostrils the breath of life; and man became a living soul." (Genesis 2:7)

<17> God would form man from the dust of the ground (atom). Atom would be manifested matter. <18> These codes, as programs (forces) in the ethereal state, would manifest the atomic particles. From these particles the atom would be made. Then from atoms all other things would be created. All creation has been designed according to the codes ("And God said, Let…") stored in the ethereal level (akasha) to be manifested later on.

<19> However, in order that these codes are manifested into life form (man), life-force or prana is necessary. This life-force (prana)

is called "the breath of life." It is through this pranic energy that physical manifestation (solid, liquid, luminous or heat, and aerial) can be linked to the ethereal (astral) level. <20> In the human this link is maintained through breath. That is why when a person stops breathing, his astral body (ethereal body, spirit) leaves. <21> The soul (individual) resides in the ethereal body and so it also leaves the body.

"And the Lord God planted a garden eastward in Eden; and there he put the man whom he had formed." (Genesis 2:8)
<22> After going through all the evolutionary steps, man will dwell on earth (Eden).

Tablet Ten

"And out of the ground made the Lord God to grow every tree that is pleasant to the sight, and good for food; the tree of life also in the midst of the garden, and the tree of knowledge of good and evil." (Genesis 2:9)
<1> However, because man would be in the manifested world (dual nature of creation as positive and negative, good and bad, etc.) and would be able to choose good or evil ("…knowledge of good and evil"), God had to create moral codes which would guide man and are according to Universal Laws. <2> Man's happiness and growth increases by following God's Laws (disciplines). Choosing his own ways ("the tree of knowledge of good and evil") against God's Ways (Will) will result in the loss of "the tree of life."
<3> To choose His Laws is to accept His Will. That is the path of submission. <4> Only such a path wins His Grace, and it is Grace that enables man to follow the Laws to salvation. Grace is the Law!

"And a river went out of Eden to water the garden; and from thence it was parted, and became into four heads." (Genesis 2:10)

"The name of the first is Pison: that is it which compasseth the whole land of Havilah, where there is gold;" (Genesis 2:11)

"And the gold of that land is good: there is bdellium and the onyx stone." (Genesis 2:12)

"And the name of the second river is Gihon: the same is it that compasseth the whole land of Ethiopia." (Genesis 2:13)

"And the name of the third river is Hiddekel: that is it which goeth toward the east of Assyria. And the fourth river is Euphrates." (Genesis 2:14)
<5> These verses refer to the earth as it was planned, or it means creation has come from One fountainhead – un-manifested universe ("And a river went out of Eden to water the ground…") – then this same river is divided into four primal elements (consciousness and three gunas) in creation ("…and from thence it was parted, and became into four heads").

"And the Lord God took the man, and put him into the garden of Eden to dress it and to keep it." (Genesis 2:15)
<6> Now everything seemed ready for man to be created to live on earth. He should dress it and keep it well. So man is responsible for what he does to the earth.

"And the Lord God commanded the man, saying, Of every tree of the garden thou mayest freely eat:" (Genesis 2:16)
<7> Man would be allowed to utilize it for his progress and enjoyment.

"But of the tree of the knowledge of good and evil, thou shalt not eat of it: for in the day that thou eatest thereof thou shalt surely die." (Genesis 2:17)
<8> However, he can utilize it according to God's (nature's) Laws. He cannot indiscriminately and selfishly use it. There are limits ("…of the tree of knowledge of good and evil, thou shalt not eat of it:…") and proper ways to use it.

<9> If he oversteps those boundaries, the tree of life (immortality) will be taken away from him ("…for in the day that thou eatest thereof thou shalt surely die").

<10> Death here means both physically and spiritually. Disobedience to the Laws (sin) creates karma. This will result in the separation of the soul (man, atman) from God (Soul, Atman), this is spiritual death. <11> Also karma results in physical death.

<12> However, with going to God humbly, and with confession, repentance, prayer, and learning the lesson, His Grace can be won. Then one will be forgiven and become one with Him again (in His Grace). <13> That is the way to escape death, to reach salvation.

<14> Through sin man dies and will be born again and again in order to learn his lessons and follow His Laws. Then he again becomes immortal, by His Grace.

<15> That argument about God's Laws and trying to replace them with man's laws and understandings is what makes man go astray, "eating of the tree of the knowledge." <16> That is to say, "My (our) will, not Thine."

Tablet Eleven

"And the Lord God said, It is not good that the man should be alone; I will make him an help meet for him." (Genesis 2:18)

<1> God does not say that it is not good for man to be lonely but He says "alone" ("all-one"). <2> So far man is still both male and female in the same being. God decided to separate Adam into man and woman.

"And out of the ground the Lord God formed every beast of the field, and every fowl of the air; and brought them unto Adam to see what he would call them: and whatsoever Adam called every living creature, that was the name thereof." (Genesis 2:19)

<3> God also would make bodies for the animals. He would make their bodies from the ground (the cosmic dust or Atom). For the first time the concepts and names of things would be created by man. <4> God does not call by name the things He would create but He relates to them as the purpose for which they were made.

<5> It is man who gives names to things and then becomes attached to the power of the names that he himself created. This is one of man's greatest illusions, and until he overcomes it, he will stay in the illusion of the power of words. <6> Man should look at things from the point of view of the Daharma (nature) of everything, for what each thing or being was made.

<7> Also, we understand from this verse that God Himself does not have any name. <8> That is why He has been called the "God of Abraham, Isaac, and Jacob." When Moses asked Him, "Behold, when I come unto the children of Israel, and shall say unto them, The God of your fathers hath sent me unto you; and they shall say to me, What is his name? What shall I say unto them? <9> And God said unto Moses, 'I AM THAT I AM:…'" (Exodus 3:13-14). <10> Only later on, because people insisted on having a God with a name, does He call Himself Y'weh, which is a corrupt pronunciation of a power word (mantra) that in its true form cannot be pronounced in the material world. <11> It is a subtle word (fire word or power word) as His Sacred Name.

"And Adam gave names to all cattle, and to the fowl of the air, and to every beast of the field; but for Adam there was not found an help meet for him." (Genesis 2:20)

<12> Man would create a name for everything. <13> Yet still he was complete and one in nature – male and female. There was no creature on earth that man could relate to as his mate, because he was superior to animals and no one was on the same level of consciousness to relate to him.

"And the Lord God caused a deep sleep

to fall upon Adam, and he slept: and he took one of his ribs, and closed up the flesh instead thereof;" (Genesis 2:21)

"And the rib, which the Lord God had taken from man, made he a woman, and brought her unto the man." (Genesis 2:22)

<14> Female principle (Grace) and male principle (Logic) were divided. <15> From these principles God created man and woman.

"And Adam said, This is now bone of my bones, and flesh of my flesh: she shall be called Woman, because she was taken out of Man." (Genesis 2:23)

<16> So man and woman are two parts of the same being and will be perfect when they merge as one again (androgynous).

Tablet Twelve

"Therefore shall a man leave his father and his mother, and shall cleave unto his wife: and they shall be one flesh." (Genesis 2:24)

<1> When a man or woman finds their other part (soulmate) they become perfect and complete.

<2> The greatest achievement in spiritual life is forgetting the self for others. <3> Marriage is a great instrument for fulfilling this great step. <4> Originally male and female were in one body. Because of the necessity for the evolution of the human, they were separated. The man and woman were created.

<5> In a marriage between a man and a woman, therefore, the attraction between them should be spiritual, not physical or intellectual. When these two spiritually attracted people join with each other, they can become a perfect being – in the image of God, male (The Divine Logic) and female (The Divine Grace), <6> the dual nature of God Himself.

<7> With this ideal of a spiritual marriage, the false egos of each individual will be dissolved in the process and together both of them will become complete. <8> They then can manifest the qualities and love of God through themselves.

<9> With creating children and a family environment, these spiritual parents will be able to feel toward their children exactly the way God feels about humanity. <10> This again will help parents to understand the very heart of God and realize Him easier. <11> Only then can they also love others and the universe as His creation.

<12> Therefore, as we can see, marriage is a spiritual union to help a man and woman grow physically, mentally, and spiritually. <13> Marriage also helps them to radiate God's Love by merging to become One in spirit. <14> Also this will help couples to realize God and how He feels about His universe, <15> the same way as they feel about their family and children. <16> So a person can reach Pure Consciousness in the middle of a family by understanding that marriage is a beautiful set-up by the Lord God to make humans dissolve their false egos, progress spiritually, and realize Him.

<17> Furthermore, marriage has social, mental, physical and psychological significance.

<18> Each married couple and their children make up the blocks which build the foundation of society. If the blocks of a building are strong and well-placed, the building will be sturdy and strong. This is also true about societies. If the family structure is strong, society can withstand any shock and go through the tests of time. It will be crushed to nothingness if the family ties are loose and weak, no matter how powerful that society looks.

<19> Also only in a strong family structure with love and devotion between the members can healthy, strong, and well-balanced children develop to be responsible members of society. <20> The children today are the men and women of tomorrow. So with weak family ties, men and women with weak characters will be created, and this will affect the whole society. For the mental well-being of all, sacrifice by couples to create strong families is necessary.

<21> It is through the purity of the body of the couple and the restriction of physical relationships only through marriage that the spread of venereal diseases can be checked and brought to a minimum. <22> Otherwise these diseases will become widespread and will affect the happiness of the lives of many. <23> So we can see that even diseases have a purpose to fulfill – in this case, to make men and women realize that physical love-making should only be performed through marriage between two pure beings (male and female) if they do not want to be infected by some incurable disease. <24> In fact, promiscuity was one of the main causes of the fall of man. It destroyed the purity of the relationship in the family, which is the cause of all evils. **Purity in marriage is the essence of family strength.**

<25> Also through marriage, the two partners become karmically sealed to each other and will be a companion, friend, lover, and comforter for each other. <26> So a great and deep relationship develops between them, and this will help to fulfill the psychological needs of the individuals.

<27> The meaning of the verse above, "Therefore shall a man leave his father and his mother,…" is that the couple should separate themselves as a new unit in society and become independent, if economically possible. <28> However, its deeper meaning is that they should become adults and grow as responsible members of society by cutting off their attachments from childhood and the past. <29> Although they become independent and have to make their own decisions, they should respect their parents even if they might decide to follow a different way of life.

<30> He whose other part has either not been incarnated or is both male and female in one body (spiritually) and wishes to devote his life to God, can easily become a renunciate (sannyasin). <31> In this case he also should detach himself from any unnecessary attachments, <32> which in the verse above symbolically is stated as "leave his father and his mother." <33> So he can fulfill his duties as a renounced person, serve the universal family, be released from his lower nature to his higher self, and become complete, in the image of God (卐).

"And they were both naked, the man and his wife, and were not ashamed." (Genesis 2:25)

<34> Man and woman would be created innocent, "And they were both naked, … and were not ashamed." For this matter, the whole universe is created innocent!

Tablet Thirteen

Chapter 3

"Now the serpent was more subtil than any beast of the field which the Lord God had made. And he said unto the woman, Yea, hath God said, Ye shall not eat of every tree of the garden?" (Genesis 3:1)

<1> Besides consciousness, there are three gunas which exist in the universe. <2> Satva guna is neither male nor female. It is passive and positive. <3> Raja guna (life-force) is the female principle. It is active and neutral. It activates and brings all into life. <4> Tama guna is also neither male nor female. It is passive and negative. <5> Consciousness is passive and neutral.

<6> Raja guna (energy) is the only active force in the universe. When it is in the passive state the universe will be un-manifested. Universe (God) will be in the state of "Be"-ness, which is Formless, Nameless, Invisible, Eternal, neither male nor female. <7> This is the seventh state of consciousness.

<8> When the same consciousness becomes activated, but still is in pure form (Pure Consciousness), it will become engaged in planning and guiding the universe. In this state it becomes pure Divine Logic (Father). Logic is male energy or principle. This is the sixth state of consciousness.

<9> Raja guna in the active state, however, receives the polarity of positivity when directed toward higher things (satva), will be neutral when pure raja, and will be negative when directed toward mundanity (tama).

<10> When satva guna is activated (by raja guna – female principle, Grace) and dominates the consciousness (Logic or male principle), in this state God is Male (Father) Female (Mother) God. This is the fifth state of consciousness. <11> It is in this state that The Holy Ghost (Bliss) is experienced which is full of Grace (female principle) and knowledge (male principle).

<12> Raja guna is Grace, when it dominates the consciousness and is directed to higher things. Because it has no polarity, it becomes the unconditional Love (Mother, no polarity or condition) or The Divine Grace (Divine Mother). This is experienced in the fourth level of consciousness (chakra).

<13> Tama guna is bondage. When it is activated by energy (raja guna) and dominates active satva guna and the consciousness, then the Logic becomes earthly. It is then that a person becomes man (earthly). This is the third state of consciousness.

<14> In the state where tama guna dominates the active raja and consciousness, then The Grace (female) becomes passion and temptation. A person then will become woman. This state is what is referred to as woman here in the Bible. This is the second state of consciousness.

<15> In the first level of consciousness, tama guna dominates with complete force. The consciousness (kundalini, the serpent) is dormant. By meditating and creating greater prana (raja guna) in the body, the grip of the tama guna will be loosened and the consciousness will be brought to higher levels. This is called the awakening of the spiritual forces (kundalini).

<16> As long as the consciousness is latent in the first level (chakra) a person will be bound by his physiological and safety needs. His energy will be used toward maintenance of his physical body and worldly activities. He also will receive most of his energy by consuming food. In this state man is a rational animal and has no Divine consciousness. He identifies himself as only being the body.

<17> Although the physical body of the human as male and female has some relationship with manifestation of Logic or Grace, it is not absolute. Each of these qualities can be developed by practice in either sex and also there are exceptions.

<18> Whoever opens his heart chakra (fourth chakra) will manifest unconditional Love or Grace (Divine Mother) and he who reaches the sixth level is one with the Father (pure Logic controlling the emotions – first five levels).

<19> In the explanation above, the most important thing is the dual nature of raja guna (female principle, activating energy). It either can be directed to positivity as Divine Grace or Holy Mother, or toward negativity as lower nature of man. These two sides of the same phenomenon (energy) have been mythically symbolized in Hindu religions as the two consorts of their gods, such as Krishna and Shiva. Usually one of them is the symbol of the energy of transmutation and destruction, such as Kali and Durga, and the other as one full of Grace, Shakti and Radah. <20> These two consorts actually are the two sides of each person or the mythical gods themselves.

<21> This part of female energy is symbolized as the woman in the Bible, the same meaning implied by the goddess Kali, who is shown as an old dark-skinned woman who has a necklace of skulls around her neck and is dreadful.

<22> The same phenomenon (raja guna), when directed toward higher things, becomes The Divine Grace or The Holy Mother.

<23> The serpent (kundalini) in this verse is related to this energy (raja guna) of temptation in the second level of consciousness, that makes humans heedlessly pursue the attraction to Maya (or power of the tama guna over the consciousness in the second chakra). But when the same energy has been channeled to higher chakras, it becomes the wisdom of understanding (compassion). That is why Christ said, be wise as serpents (Matthew 10:16).

THE HOLIEST BOOK

HOLIEST 1 - Tablet 12

<24> The first sign of temptation begins when the human starts reasoning (rationalizing) and tries to make his actions seem good to himself (doubting). <25> Therefore, the woman (symbolizing the lower nature of the human) receives the first sign of temptation as "Yea, hath God said, Ye shall not eat of every tree of the garden?" The doubt comes in her mind about forbidden actions. She becomes tempted to do those actions which were forbidden by God. She starts questioning the Laws of God.

"And the woman said unto the serpent, We may eat of the fruit of the trees of the garden:" (Genesis 3:2)

<26> Now the woman (person) starts to fight with this temptation. She says, "We can perform many other actions which are in accord with God's Laws, and there are so many things to enjoy." These enjoyments are symbolized by "the fruit of the trees" that they were permitted to eat.

"But of the fruit of the tree which is in the midst of the garden, God hath said, Ye shall not eat of it, neither shall ye touch it, lest ye die." (Genesis 3:3)

<27> Here again the weakness of the mind of the human is presented by using the word "but." She says, "I can have all permitted actions and I have all these things to enjoy, 'but' I cannot do that (those) forbidden action (actions)." This "but" (doubt) is a desire of the human to experience something which is not in keeping with the Laws of the universe and is one of the greatest problems for man in overcoming the temptation and power of Maya.

"And the serpent said unto the woman, Ye shall not surely die:" (Genesis 3:4)

<28> Again temptation steps in and says, "Well, maybe it is not as bad as I think to do that forbidden action." Therefore, she rationalizes that, "I surely will not die."

"For God doth know that in the day ye eat thereof, then your eyes shall be opened, and ye shall be as gods, knowing good and evil." (Genesis 3:5)

<29> Man desires to be a God himself and forms his life by his own reasoning power.

"And when the woman saw that the tree was good for food, and that it was pleasant to the eyes, and a tree to be desired to make one wise, she took of the fruit thereof, and did eat, and gave also unto her husband with her; and he did eat." (Genesis 3:6)

<30> Now reasoning changes its direction to the favor of doing the action. Therefore, the action seems good, as symbolized by "the woman saw that the tree was good for food." She forgets all about God's commands or Laws which were set up to keep her from doing the action, because now it seems so good to do it.

<31> The words "that it was pleasant to the eyes" indicate that she lost her deeper understanding and now she follows her sight or what seems right.

<32> The words "and a tree to be desired to make one wise" come from the result of the previous temptation, which now seems to her as a truth. With all these and through the power of temptation and attraction of Maya, she does those forbidden actions and becomes attached to the external world.

<33> Not only does she herself become lost in Maya but she will tempt others to become corrupt by attempting to show the man that her reasoning is true. Therefore, others follow her. Or it can be said that the lower nature (woman) causes the higher nature to fall.

"And the eyes of them both were opened, and they knew that they were naked; and they sewed fig leaves together, and made themselves aprons." (Genesis 3:7)

<34> By their eyes being opened here it means that they lost their innocence. So things started to look ugly, and because they became sinners, shame, or a feeling of guilt, crept in and they became ashamed of themselves. So they started to hide themselves from each other and the barrier started in their relationship.

Tablet Fourteen

"And they heard the voice of the Lord God walking in the garden in the cool of the day: and Adam and his wife hid themselves from the presence of the Lord God amongst the trees of the garden." (Genesis 3:8)

<1> Now humans had created bad karma (bad action, violating the Laws of the universe). Therefore, they tried to hide from the presence of the Lord (which is innocence and only the innocent can see Him). In fact, the moment a bad karma is created, a veil of separation is created between a unit consciousness and God.

<2> "In the cool of the day": The sunrise and sunset are two times which are "the cool of the day," and are the best times for meditation and prayer.

"And the Lord God called unto Adam, and said unto him, Where art thou?" (Genesis 3:9)

<3> Still God wanted communion with humans. So He called upon Adam.

"And he said, I heard thy voice in the garden, and I was afraid, because I was naked; and I hid myself." (Genesis 3:10)

<4> With the feeling of guilt from doing wrong, fear automatically came in. That is why for the first time humans became fearful. This led humans to look down upon themselves and to feel unworthy to be in the presence of a higher being like God, or even reject the existence of God because of it.

"And he said, Who told thee that thou wast naked? Hast thou eaten of the tree, whereof I commanded thee that thou shouldest not eat?" (Genesis 3:11)

<5> And God said, "Who told you that you should be afraid and feel unworthy of being in my presence?" And God knew that this could only happen to man when he has created feelings of guilt through doing things that are not according to the Daharma or the Laws of the universe. <6> Only a guilty consciousness has fears.

"And the man said, The woman whom thou gavest to be with me, she gave me of the tree, and I did eat." (Genesis 3:12)

<7> Now man was trying to direct his guilt and the result of his actions toward someone else. Man was trying to reason with God that it is His fault because He gave woman to be with man and it was woman who made man eat from the tree. In other words, he was saying that he was tempted by his lower nature and was powerless in opposing it.

<8> With this reasoning, man thinks he can escape from the result of his action. But as we can see later, he will receive punishment for the action that he has done, even if it is imposed on him through temptation. <9> Therefore, each individual is responsible for the result of his actions and cannot escape from them by reasoning that, "I was misled" or "I was ignorant." <10> That is why each person is responsible to search, pray, seek His Grace, find the truth, and understand the Laws of the universe if he wants to become pure enough to reach the presence of God and escape sufferings.

"And the Lord God said unto the woman, What is this that thou hast done? And the woman said, The serpent beguiled me, and I did eat." (Genesis 3:13)

<11> Now the woman (lower nature, or the one who misguided others to do the forbidden action) was questioned. However, she was also trying to escape from the result of her action and said that it was the power of the temptation that misguided her.

<12> She did not bring out the previous reasoning that the fruit was good and would make men wise, so they should eat it. She accepted the wrongdoing because when you are in the presence of God, you cannot lie. He knows everything, and you intuitively know that what you have done was wrong. <13> That is why in meditation man comes face-to-face with truth and has no choice but to accept his wrongdoings. That is also why sometimes a great sadness is created in the

person because he intuitively desires to correct his wrongdoings and is sad for what he has done or is. That sadness is the process of purification. <14> Of course many try to not see the wrong in themselves, as the woman in this case also who tried to escape the blame.

"And the Lord God said unto the serpent, Because thou hast done this, thou art cursed above all cattle, and above every beast of the field; upon thy belly shalt thou go, and dust shalt thou eat all the days of thy life:" (Genesis 3:14)

<15> That is why there is such controversy about the second chakra. All through history the power of sex and sexual relationships have been the most cursed and are the cause of much confusion in the world.

<16> This is because **temptation** (attraction to Maya) will result in doing **forbidden actions**. This results in **guilty feelings** which bring man down more to the lower nature. That creates more **attachment**, the attachment accelerates **desires**, and the desires create more **temptation**. This cycle goes on and on and makes man fall more. That is why temptation is so cursed.

<17> A person who is a slave of his second chakra will crawl on his belly (like a serpent) all his life.

"And I will put enmity between thee and the woman, and between thy seed and her seed; it shall bruise thy head, and thou shalt bruise his heel." (Genesis 3:15)

<18> That is why the human should fight ceaselessly with this temptation, and temptation should fight back to try to tempt the man.

"Unto the woman he said, I will greatly multiply thy sorrow and thy conception; in sorrow thou shalt bring forth children; and thy desire shall be to thy husband, and he shall rule over thee." (Genesis 3:16)

<19> Here the relationship of the serpent force with sexual energy becomes very clear. It is this part which will bring sorrow to humans and is symbolized by the sorrow of women delivering children. <20> The concept of woman has been used in these verses as the lower nature of the human, and the concept of husband as the higher nature. <21> Therefore, whoever is a slave of his desires and is drawn to the temptations of the second chakra will be lost in the battle of life and ruled by whomever overcomes his lower nature (temptation).

<22> Also one of the Laws (forbidden fruits) is not to be promiscuous which results in impurity, destruction of the family, and eventually the fall of the society. This is also related to the second chakra and temptation of doing this forbidden action. If done, then the person, family, and society will be thrown out of Eden (being in the presence of God, from His Grace) to sorrow and suffering.

"And unto Adam he said, Because thou hast hearkened unto the voice of thy wife, and hast eaten of the tree, of which I commanded thee, saying, Thou shalt not eat of it: cursed is the ground for thy sake; in sorrow shalt thou eat of it all the days of thy life;" (Genesis 3:17)

<23> Therefore, Adam (the higher nature of the human or higher self) has been punished, although he was misled by his wife (lower nature or lower self) to do the forbidden action. He should have been so strong in God that the lower nature (woman) could not have been able to mislead him. That is why each person should overcome the lower nature, by submission to God (His Laws), to overcome suffering.

"Thorns also and thistles shall it bring forth to thee; and thou shalt eat the herb of the field;" (Genesis 3:18)

<24> By listening to the woman (Maya), The Divine Logic becomes worldly logic (human). So man becomes earthbound.

"In the sweat of thy face shalt thou eat bread, till thou return into the ground; for out of it wast thou taken: for dust thou art, and unto dust shalt thou return." (Genesis 3:19)

<25> That soul or higher self which listens to the lower self (lower chakras) is bound to the demand of the basic things of life. The

second chakra controls thirst and hunger, and a man who is bound by this chakra will ceaselessly pursue satisfaction of this part of his existence. Therefore, this low-natured human will die and will return to dust (atom) until he comes back again and works on his evolutionary process to reach higher consciousness.

"And Adam called his wife's name Eve; because she was the mother of all living." (Genesis 3:20)
<26> Wife, woman, and Eve all symbolize the lower nature of man which is present in all humans. The higher self can be reached by going through this lower self first. <27> That is why Eve is called the "mother of all living," because humans must go through this lower self to be born again as a higher Soul ("living"). That is why it is said that all men have sinned – have gone through their lower natures (Eve), except the First Begotten Son who reached Pure Consciousness before flesh (creation).

Tablet Fifteen

"Unto Adam also and to his wife did the Lord God make coats of skins, and clothed them." (Genesis 3:21)
<1> Man became gross enough that he assumed a fleshly body with skin ("coats of skins").

"And the Lord God said, Behold, the man is become as one of us, to know good and evil: and now, lest he put forth his hand, and take also of the tree of life, and eat, and live for ever:" (Genesis 3:22)
<2> Now God was cautious that man, with these weaknesses after being separated into two parts and by his desire to follow his lower self, should not be allowed to come to godhood (immortal and powerful), because he would use these powers for his selfish desires and disturb the whole creation. Therefore God made man mortal until he comes to a stage where he overcomes these weaknesses.
<3> The tree of life is the state of Pure Consciousness which will bring everlasting (eternal) life. <4> However, man should not reach this stage before he overcomes his lower nature (tama guna over his soul) and also understands the reality behind this universe (helps those who have an ear to hear to reach Pure Consciousness). Then he will be worthy to join the gods. Otherwise he will be "spued out of His mouth" (Revelation 3:16).

"Therefore the Lord God sent him forth from the garden of Eden, to till the ground from whence he was taken." (Genesis 3:23)
<5> Man became so gross that he identified himself with his body and thought that he was his body, and that was when his sorrow started. <6> Here the word "him" refers to a single person. Therefore, we can see that Eve and Adam are two natures of the same man. This has been used in all of chapter 3 of <u>Genesis</u> to refer to the lower and higher selves.
<7> Also in this stage of evolution a new condition for the earth was necessary which is symbolized by sending man from the garden of Eden. That misty kind of environment which was described in chapter 2 is not present here. Man should till the ground. The era of Shudras (laborers) began.

"So he drove out the man; and he placed at the east of the garden of Eden Cherubims, and a flaming sword which turned every way, to keep the way of the tree of life." (Genesis 3:24)
<8> Only by overcoming his lower nature and realizing that he has to help others, can man enter Pure Consciousness. <9> He should understand that a selfish individual desire to reach Pure Consciousness without helping others who are also ready will not be successful.
<10> He should also help others on the path. Otherwise he will be "spued out of His mouth" (Rev. 3:16). That spuing out of

His mouth here is symbolized as the flaming sword which Cherubims (external world) have in their hands. Attraction of the external world will prevent man from entering the eternal world (tree of life), until man overcomes his lower nature. <11> That is why those who have chosen the spiritual path will be tested, in each step and turn, to prove themselves.

Tablet Sixteen

Chapter 4

"And Adam knew Eve his wife; and she conceived, and bare Cain, and said, I have gotten a man from the Lord." (Genesis 4:1)

<1> Man became attached to the family life and its pleasure of having sons and daughters. God gave man children to make him understand how God feels about humans. God has the same feeling about humans as a parent has about his children. <2> Also, usually children have the same feeling about their parents, as man has about God (unappreciative).

"And she again bare his brother Abel. And Abel was a keeper of sheep, but Cain was a tiller of the ground." (Genesis 4:2)

<3> As man multiplied, the division of labor started.

"And in process of time it came to pass, that Cain brought of the fruit of the ground an offering unto the Lord." (Genesis 4:3)

<4> Now the process of worshipping God became one of offering gross things, because humans thought that God needed things. However, the ideation and feeling created is what is important in this type of worshipping.

"And Abel, he also brought of the firstlings of his flock and of the fat thereof. And the Lord had respect unto Abel and to his offering:" (Genesis 4:4)

<5> Firstling flock was a great offering by a sheep keeper, and he gave the best for his Lord. Abel was not attached to the external wealth but he sought God's Grace, and offered it without any attachment to the results of his offering. <6> Therefore, God respected the offering.

"But unto Cain and to his offering he had not respect. And Cain was very wroth, and his countenance fell." (Genesis 4:5)

<7> Cain was attached to the result of his action. God wanted to show Cain that he was not presenting the offering with a pure heart and without expectation. That is why God did not respect his offering. Instead of being patient and understanding that the perfect God has a reason for doing that, <8> Cain became very angry and his countenance fell. God was trying to make a point and give him a lesson.

<9> That is exactly what happens to those who are not completely surrendered to God and are not willing to understand and follow His Laws. They become wroth, their countenance falls, and they become lost, because they are attached to their lower natures and judge God from that state of consciousness, instead of to be patient and learn.

"And the Lord said unto Cain, Why art thou wroth? and why is thy countenance fallen?" (Genesis 4:6)

<10> Those are really the questions that every person (Cain in this case) should ask him or herself, i.e., **"Why am I attached to the result of my actions? Why am I angry about everything? Why am I lost?"**

"If thou doest well, shalt thou not be accepted? and if thou doest not well, sin lieth at the door. And unto thee shall be his desire, and thou shalt rule over him." (Genesis 4:7)

<11> Here it is shown that it was not the offering which was rejected, but the way it was offered, "If thou doest well, shalt thou not be accepted?" <12> The sentence, "and if thou doest not well, sin lieth at the door" means, "Your desire to receive some result of your action and your attachment to gain for

something you do for the Lord is completely apparent from you."

<13> Desire to gain something for any service makes it a business, not service. <14> Giving something for gain is business. <15> Service means to give without expecting anything in return. This kind of service brings His Grace.

<16> "And unto thee shall be his desire, and thou shalt rule over him" means, "Therefore this desire will rule over you, your actions will become fruitless, and you will lose the respect for your actions."

Tablet Seventeen

"And Cain talked with Abel his brother: and it came to pass, when they were in the field, that Cain rose up against Abel his brother, and slew him." (Genesis 4:8)

<1> Cain could not understand these things. Therefore he (or any lost soul) started wondering why he was so miserable while Abel (a wise person) was so happy and joyful. <2> Cain talked with Abel and tried to understand the reason for this difference. But he could not understand it. Therefore, he became jealous of Abel and killed him.

<3> That is how lost people feel about realized humans or Prophets. Cain could not understand his own Daharma. Instead of looking within himself to find out his own abilities and source of happiness, he looked for them outside of himself. So he did not find it and started to blame others for his own suffering.

"And the Lord said unto Cain, Where is Abel thy brother? And he said, I know not: Am I my brother's keeper?" (Genesis 4:9)

<4> Cain denied his sin to the Lord.

"And he said, What hast thou done? the voice of thy brother's blood crieth unto me from the ground." (Genesis 4:10)

<5> But nothing can be hidden from God. He knows everything happening in His universe. He made this universe in such a way that He is able to know all things going on through His Angels (the Universal Mind).

"And now art thou cursed from the earth, which hath opened her mouth to receive thy brother's blood from thy hand;" (Genesis 4:11)

<6> Cain will suffer even though he denied what he did and thought he could hide his action from God. <7> It does not matter how smart anyone thinks he is in hiding his sins. God will know them, and the result of all actions will be received by the doer, unless he repents and corrects himself.

"When thou tillest the ground, it shall not henceforth yield unto thee her strength; a fugitive and a vagabond shalt thou be in the earth." (Genesis 4:12)

<8> Not only do your actions affect you, but they also affect the whole universe, and so disasters and famines are a part of the reaction of the actions done by humans.

"And Cain said unto the Lord, My punishment is greater than I can bear." (Genesis 4:13)

<9> Now Cain did not want to accept the punishment of his actions, and he felt it was too great. That is what everyone feels. Each person thinks that he suffers more and has greater problems than anyone else.

"Behold, thou hast driven me out this day from the face of the earth; and from thy face shall I be hid; and I shall be a fugitive and a vagabond in the earth; and it shall come to pass, that every one that findeth me shall slay me." (Genesis 4:14)

<10> When the burden of karma becomes too heavy, then man completely loses his touch with God. He becomes a homeless and lost soul who does not feel that even the earth is his home. Such a person can be hurt by others easily. That is exactly what the false

ego is. It does not feel itself to be a part of the universe but feels separated, lonely, and vulnerable.

"And the Lord said unto him, Therefore whosoever slayeth Cain, vengeance shall be taken on him sevenfold. And the Lord set a mark upon Cain, lest any finding him should kill him." (Genesis 4:15)

<11> It is true that Cain was cursed and lost but it is not any man's duty to judge and/or punish another human. It is only God who can judge and guide humans as well as those in a state of very high consciousness or Pure Consciousness (sons of God). <12> Therefore, if anyone inflicts a punishment on another person, he will suffer sevenfold for what was done to that other person.

"And Cain went out from the presence of the Lord, and dwelt in the land of Nod, on the east of Eden." (Genesis 4:16)

<13> Again the human went further away from being in the presence of God by committing more sins and crudifying himself. This is exactly how the Law of Karma works: As man creates samskaras (bad actions, or breaking the Daharma), he will separate himself more and more from God.

<14> Races on earth started to be mixed with one another, "…and dwelt in the land of Nod…"

"And Cain knew his wife; and she conceived, and bare Enoch: and he builded a city, and called the name of the city, after the name of his son, Enoch." (Genesis 4:17)

<15> The words "to know his wife" means to cleave with the other part of the human and to become complete. Therefore, Cain was with his other part as his wife and the result was Enoch. Intermarriage between races started.

"And unto Enoch was born Irad: and Irad begat Mehujael: and Mehujael begat Methusael: and Methusael begat Lamech." (Genesis 4:18)

<16> The use of generations in the Bible is for showing that many years passed after the creation of Adam, and humans became more and more separated from God. It took a long line of birth and rebirth until God started to select some to lead others to the straight path, or until He could see the defect of those humans who had failed and could then do something about it.

"And Lamech took unto him two wives: the name of the one was Adah, and the name of the other Zillah." (Genesis 4:19)

<17> By marrying two wives, Lamech created a strong karmic link with these two women. They became his soulmates and/or twin flames.

"And Adah bare Jabal: he was the father of such as dwell in tents, and of such as have cattle." (Genesis 4:20)

<18> Cattle-keeping became a profession.

"And his brother's name was Jubal: he was the father of all such as handle the harp and organ." (Genesis 4:21)

<19> Earthly music was born.

"And Zillah, she also bare Tubalcain, an instructor of every artificer in brass and iron: and the sister of Tubalcain was Naamah." (Genesis 4:22)

<20> The importance of brass and iron was recognized.

"And Lamech said unto his wives, Adah and Zillah, Hear my voice; ye wives of Lamech, hearken unto my speech: for I have slain a man to my wounding, and a young man to my hurt." (Genesis 4:23)

<21> Lamech had slain someone and confessed his sin.

"If Cain shall be avenged sevenfold, truly Lamech seventy and sevenfold." (Genesis 4:24)

<22> Because Lamech confessed his sins, no one should judge him for his action by hate. If that does happen, he will be avenged seventy-seven times. Therefore, the person who is aware of his sins is in a much higher place than the person who denies his sins.

Tablet Eighteen

"And Adam knew his wife again; and she bare a son, and called his name Seth:…" (Genesis 4:25)

"And to Seth, to him also there was born a son; and he called his name Enos: then began men to call upon the name of the Lord." (Genesis 4:26)

<1> Enos and Seth caused people to become God-conscious and to worship Him again.

Chapter 5

"This is the book of the generations of Adam. In the day that God created man, in the likeness of God made he him;" (Genesis 5:1)

<2> As it is said, these books of generations are used in the Bible not to show who is the son or daughter of whom, but to show that it took generations before a new evolutionary process took place.

<3> The words, "in the day God created man" indicate that the next phrase, "in the likeness of God made he him," was true only at the first phase of the evolutionary process and creation. Later on Adam (man) was divided into male and female.

<4> Only when a human finds his other part will he become perfect. However, some people's other parts might not have been incarnated, and these are the ones who become sannyasins (renunciates) and will merge with their other parts on the spiritual plane. Some are born androgynous.

"Male and female created he them; and blessed them, and called their name Adam, in the day when they were created." (Genesis 5:2)

<5> In this verse it is completely clear that Adam (the first man) was male and female. The sentence, "and called **their** name Adam" is referring to the name given to the people (more than one person) whom He called Adam. It does not say, "they were called Adam and Eve" or "man and woman," or anything that indicates separation between the sexes, but He called "them" (which means more than one) Adam. "Male and female created he them" indicates that each of them was male and female at the same time.

<6> The phrase "in the day when they were created" shows that later on this changed and Adam was divided into two parts as Adam and Eve, or man and woman. They were separated from each other and each was something less than the image of God. Only when these two parts join each other, either on the material plane or on the spiritual plane, can they become perfect again.

"And Adam lived an hundred and thirty years, and begat a son in his own likeness, after his image; and called his name Seth:" (Genesis 5:3)

<7> This verse clearly shows what is the relationship between a perfected man (Adam before the split) and God. God created Adam in His image, and Adam (after the split) begat a son in his image and likeness (half of perfection). Adam created another human who was in his image (like himself). Therefore, he was Adam's son. God created (in the beginning of creation) Adam (man) in His image and likeness. Therefore, Adam was His son!

<8> That is why when a human reaches perfection, he becomes a son of God. <9> Another point is that this lifetime was different from the one when he begot Abel and Cain. He lived a hundred and thirty years in this lifetime and begot Seth.

"And the days of Adam after he had begotten Seth were eight hundred years: and he begat sons and daughters:" (Genesis 5:4)

<10> The lifespan of the human was much longer at that time, and they would mature slower. <11> The words "the days of Adam after he had begotten Seth" show that Seth was his first born in this lifetime. There is no mention of Abel or Cain in this verse. If it was the same lifetime as the one with Abel

and Cain, the name of Cain should have appeared here as the first born, not Seth. But Seth is the first born in this incarnation of Adam and his wife. Only the name of the first born is mentioned first in all the generations in this chapter in the Bible.

"And all the days that Adam lived were nine hundred and thirty years: and he died." (Genesis 5:5)

"And Seth lived an hundred and five years, and begat Enos:" (Genesis 5:6)

"And Seth lived after he begat Enos eight hundred and seven years, and begat sons and daughters:" (Genesis 5:7)

"And all the days of Seth were nine hundred and twelve years: and he died." (Genesis 5:8)

"And Enos lived ninety years, and begat Cainan:" (Genesis 5:9)

"And Enos lived after he begat Cainan eight hundred and fifteen years, and begat sons and daughters:" (Genesis 5:10)

"And all the days of Enos were nine hundred and five years: and he died." (Genesis 5:11)

"And Cainan lived seventy years, and begat Mahalaleel:" (Genesis 5:12)

"And Cainan lived after he begat Mahalaleel eight hundred and forty years, and begat sons and daughters:" (Genesis 5:13)

"And all the days of Cainan were nine hundred and ten years: and he died." (Genesis 5:14)

"And Mahalaleel lived sixty and five years, and begat Jared:" (Genesis 5:15)

"And Mahalaleel lived after he begat Jared eight hundred and thirty years, and begat sons and daughters:" (Genesis 5:16)

"And all the days of Mahalaleel were eight hundred ninety and five years: and he died." (Genesis 5:17)

"And Jared lived an hundred sixty and two years, and begat Enoch:" (Genesis 5:18)

"And Jared lived after he begat Enoch eight hundred years, and begat sons and daughters:" (Genesis 5:19)

"And all the days of Jared were nine hundred sixty and two years: and he died." (Genesis 5:20)

"And Enoch lived sixty and five years, and begat Methuselah:" (Genesis 5:21)

"And Enoch walked with God after he begat Methuselah three hundred years, and begat sons and daughters:" (Genesis 5:22)

<12> The phrase "to walk with God" is related to pursuing a pure life and observing the Laws (Daharma) that have been set up by God. By following the Daharma of everything, a person will not violate any Law and will lead a life of non-violence. <13> This will be considered as walking with God on the same path.

"And all the days of Enoch were three hundred sixty and five years:" (Genesis 5:23)

"And Enoch walked with God: and he was not; for God took him." (Genesis 5:24)

<14> Because Enoch walked with God (he lived a Daharmic life), the phrase "he was not," when compared with the sequence of the previous sentences, can be interpreted as meaning: Enoch did not die, but "God took him," or he reached liberation or Pure Consciousness. Because Enoch walked with God, he reached Pure Consciousness and immortality, and God took him. <15> He became one of the gods (sons of God).

<16> Although he started to walk with God later in his life (after he begat Methuselah – verse 22), still he reached Pure Consciousness.

"And Methuselah lived an hundred eighty and seven years, and begat Lamech:" (Genesis 5:25)

"And Methuselah lived after he begat Lamech seven hundred eighty and two years, and begat sons and daughters:" (Genesis 5:26)

"And all the days of Methuselah were nine hundred sixty and nine years: and he died." (Genesis 5:27)

"And Lamech lived an hundred eighty and two years, and begat a son:" (Genesis 5:28)

<17> To "begat a son" here refers to Noah, who was a spiritually incarnated personality. <18> Also, not mentioning his name but only the word "son" can be interpreted to mean that he was the son of God (in His image, His son, an Avatar).

"And he called his name Noah, saying, This same shall comfort us concerning our work and toil of our hands, because of the ground which the Lord hath cursed." (Genesis 5:29)

<19> Noah was a spiritual personality who would bring a rest on the earth and a new evolutionary step would be taken in his lifetime. He was born for a great purpose and he would fulfill it.

"And Lamech lived after be begat Noah five hundred ninety and five years, and begat sons and daughters:" (Genesis 5:30)

"And all the days of Lamech were seven hundred seventy and seven years: and he died." (Genesis 5:31)

<20> 777 is a very mystical number (three sevens). Seven is God's number. Also it is the number of mystics.

"And Noah was five hundred years old: and Noah begat Shem, Ham, and Japheth." (Genesis 5:32)

<21> However, it was necessary for Noah to go through a regular life until he reached maturity and complete understanding to be informed of his mission. <22> Also his three sons are the symbols of the five types of humans on the earth (explained at the end of chapter 9 and in chapter 10).

Tablet Nineteen

Chapter 6

"And it came to pass, when men began to multiply on the face of the earth, and daughters were born unto them," (Genesis 6:1)

<1> So far, in describing the generations of Adam, all the first born were men (or men were mentioned as the likeness of their fathers). Now in this sentence it is emphasized that "daughters were born unto them," meaning that there were also people with first born daughters.

"That the sons of God saw the daughters of men that they were fair; and they took them wives of all which they chose." (Genesis 6:2)

<2> In this time many Avatars (god-men or sons of God) were on earth. <3> Also there was more than one son of God even before the flood of Noah, "the sons of God...." <4> Furthermore, sons of God (gods) are in Pure Consciousness; they no longer need a mate and all feel complete when in their presence. Also these people surely will be just toward their wives. That is why sons of God "took them wives of all which they chose," more than one.

<5> This might have, however, made some of them (in a lower level) become too attached to earth. They became earthbound (failed) into mundanity (their lower natures)! It was these fallen ones who joined the fallen hierarchy. <6> They represent themselves to those who are susceptible enough to be their channels. They are not a part of the Heavenly Hierarchy, but they pretend themselves to be.

<7> True Heavenly Beings do not use individuals as channels, but help them to realize God. They also reveal to them realization of subtle truths through individual intuition (the quiet, still Voice of God). They have no individual ego and are one with God. Individuals become channels for God.

<8> It is of extreme importance not to be possessed with fallen ethereal beings. That is one of the reasons God sends the Messiah to show the shortest way to salvation. <9> The ethereal beings sometimes reveal a lot of good information, but God alone is the salvation.

<10> There are also those who claim they are channels and are not. It is done as an ego gratification. This is the worst. Be honest. Greater than being honest to others is to be honest to yourself! Then you surely will be honest with others. Honesty starts within the heart! Some, however, take their own creative mind by mistake as being a being out of themselves. They should also analyze it to be sure it is coming from a pure heart.

"And the Lord said, My spirit shall not always strive with man, for that he also is flesh: yet his days shall be an hundred and twenty years." (Genesis 6:3)

<11> The word "And" here at the beginning of the verse means, "And it came to pass," or "later on," when man became more corrupt. "The Lord said" means that God made the decision that "my spirit shall not always strive with man." Until now humans had direct contact with the forces of nature and could manipulate them. They had misused these forces for their mundane and fleshly desires. That is why the sentence, "for that he also is flesh" is used, which means, "not only is man spirit but also he is flesh [Maya]."

<12> Man has been so attached to his fleshly desires that he thinks he is more flesh than spirit (when the soul of man becomes very crude, he indeed is flesh). <13> However, this man with these qualities was making problems for God, "...My spirit shall not always strive with man," and it was very difficult to guide him to the right path. Therefore another evolutionary process became necessary: A new kind of man would have to be created. The occult powers and the power of understanding the forces of nature should be taken away from man, and instead their earthly logic and reasoning (intellect) would be increased.

<14> One further change that occurred with this process was that the time for reaching maturity was accelerated and the lifespan would become around one hundred twenty years long. However, it would take generations before man's lifespan would become close to this number. As in chapter 11, still after the flood of Noah, the lifespan was much longer, but in a declining trend. <15> Each lifetime is like a day in the spiritual life of an individual. He will be reincarnated again and again in many lifetimes (each as one day) until he reaches Pure Consciousness and becomes a son of God.

<16> With this process of letting intelligence remain and/or increase, God does not have to strive with man all the time and can guide him step-by-step with His Messengers and Prophets (His sons) and with the creation of history and its message to man. Eventually, after humans have gained more knowledge and experience from history, they will know that the only way to happiness is to follow the Laws (Daharmas) that have been set up by God, to try to become Pure Consciousness, and to help others to become the same.

"There were giants in the earth in those days; and also after that, when the sons of God came in unto the daughters of men, and they bare children to them, the same became mighty men which were of old, men of renown." (Genesis 6:4)

<17> There were giants (Nefilims) in the earth in those days. Before the human became as he is now, he had direct contact with the forces of nature. Therefore, through misusing his powers of being able to understand nature, the old generation tried to extract and process the life-force and to use it against the Laws of nature. This created great disturbances on earth. Therefore it was necessary to close the door of the human's power (the third eye) and

let only the intellect remain.

<18> For doing this the sons of God came down to the earth again and they changed the way women should bear children (by changing the genetic codes in the human), and a new generation was born from the sons of God. This generation consisted of the new mighty men who came from the old humans but were much greater ("mighty men which were of old, men of renown").

<19> This generation was the one very similar to ours. The power of the third eye was closed and intellect increased. The human's spiritual eye was closed and became the pineal gland placed in the brain. Now man must prove himself to be trustworthy before this eye becomes open.

<20> That is what the process of evolution and history teaches humans. If they understand and follow the lessons given by this process, they can accelerate their progress toward Pure Consciousness. Yet if they follow their false egos and their own laws and regulations (lower natures), no one will be hurt but themselves. <21> This body is given to us for a purpose. For example, when we feel pain we know something is wrong. In the same way, when everyone becomes lost and does not know what to do in life, then man should know there is something wrong with his laws and way of living.

<22> When man finally sees that throughout all of history he has suffered by following his false ego, then he will realize the shortcomings of his own laws and surrender to the Universal Laws, no matter how bad they look to his ego. Only by following the Daharma of everything can we be happy. No matter how much we intellectually argue, it will not help to bring happiness to humanity. Only following the Laws of God will bring everlasting happiness and peace.

"And God saw that the wickedness of man was great in the earth, and that every imagination of the thoughts of his heart was only evil continually." (Genesis 6:5)

<23> God looked at the earth and saw that the previous generation that had the power of being in direct contact with the forces of nature was badly corrupt. They became so attached to the external world (Maya, evil) that there was no hope for them.

"And it repented the Lord that he had made man on the earth, and it grieved him at his heart." (Genesis 6:6)

<24> God grieved about why he had separated un-awakened consciousnesses, had given them bodies, and had made them to live on earth. The sentence, "he had made man on the earth," indicates that God wished He had tried the old process and helped unaware consciousnesses in the ethereal world. It is true that it would have taken longer to bring them to Pure Consciousness, but there would not have been so much trouble. But now men were on the earth and God wanted to help them and had great compassion for these lost consciousnesses.

"And the Lord said, I will destroy man whom I have created from the face of the earth; both man, and beast, and the creeping thing, and the fowls of the air; for it repenteth me that I have made them." (Genesis 6:7)

<25> Then God decided to destroy all that He had created.

Tablet Twenty

"But Noah found grace in the eyes of the Lord." (Genesis 6:8)

<1> God remembered Noah, a great spiritual being (one of His sons) and His Grace arose in Him. People like Noah are those who encourage the Lord that His task is not completely fruitless. They are the "light of the world" (Matthew 5:14).

"These are the generations of Noah: Noah was a just man and perfect in his generations, and Noah walked with God." (Genesis 6:9)

<2> As it can be seen, the description of the generations of Adam stopped at the end of chapter 5 before the generations of Noah are described, and then the generations of Noah are picked up again here. Verses 6:1 to 6:9 describe how the world became corrupt and what the situation was at that time. <3> Noah was chosen to lead the new generation of men to safety.

<4> The sentence "Noah was a just man and perfect in his generations" indicates that Noah had reached perfection (Pure Consciousness). <5> "And Noah walked with God" means that he understood and followed the Laws of the Lord. Because of these things, Noah "found grace in the eyes of the Lord" (Genesis 6:8).

"And Noah begat three sons, Shem, Ham, and Japheth." (Genesis 6:10)

<6> Noah helped the new generations to start, as symbolized by his three sons. Previously, when explaining the generations of Adam, only the first son was considered (in their likeness). Now here, the names of all three sons of Noah are given. This sudden difference shows the change of the human from a man who was in touch with the power of nature, to an intellectual being instead.

<7> Also the sons of Adam were in his image, "And Adam lived an hundred and thirty years, and begat a son in his own image;...." But here there is no emphasis that the sons of Noah were in his image. That is, the sons were different than he. They were different types of humans in new generations (not different races).

"The earth also was corrupt before God, and the earth was filled with violence." (Genesis 6:11)

<8> This violence refers to the climate of the earth. God also decided to change the climate of the earth. The climate had been affected by the actions of the previous generation and needed to be cleansed and changed to fit the new generation. <9> Also, its other meaning is that the people had become corrupt and were violating the Laws of the universe (Daharmas). They were not following the Commandment of non-violence (not violating the Daharma).

"And God looked upon the earth, and, behold, it was corrupt; for all flesh had corrupted his way upon the earth." (Genesis 6:12)

<10> All creatures were bound to the desires of their senses (flesh), and they had forgotten that they were not only flesh, but spirit also. They were lost in their physical senses toward the external world (Maya). <11> Each person was following his own laws – false ego ("corrupted his way upon the earth") instead of the Daharmas (Laws of God). This also had affected the earth itself.

"And God said unto Noah, The end of all flesh is come before me; for the earth is filled with violence through them; and, behold, I will destroy them with the earth." (Genesis 6:13)

<12> God decided to destroy all the old creatures and the earth ("with the earth"), which means to create a new generation with a new climate (earth). Noah, who was a son of God and pleased the Lord – "…found grace in the eyes of the Lord" (Genesis 6:8) – was chosen for this task.

"Make thee an ark of gopher wood; rooms shalt thou make in the ark, and shalt pitch it within and without with pitch." (Genesis 6:14)

<13> God instructed Noah on how to make a safe place or condition (ark) in order to save the new generation. As we can see, God decided to destroy only the old generation, not Noah and his newly founded generation.

"And this is the fashion which thou shalt make it of: The length of the ark shall be three hundred cubits, the breadth of it fifty cubits, and the height of it thirty cubits." (Genesis 6:15)

<14> Further instructions were given on how to save them and bring about the new situation.

THE HOLIEST BOOK

"A window shalt thou make to the ark, and in a cubit shalt thou finish it above; and the door of the ark shalt thou set in the side thereof; with lower, second, and third stories shalt thou make it." (Genesis 6:16)

"And, behold, I, even I, do bring a flood of waters upon the earth, to destroy all flesh, wherein is the breath of life, from under heaven; and every thing that is in the earth shall die." (Genesis 6:17)

<15> God surely decided to destroy all old things and start a new generation. However, the new generation would not be created abruptly after the flood of Noah. Like all the Plans of the Lord, it would take hundreds or thousands of years before being completed. Although the process started 12,000 years ago, its completion occurred 6,000 years ago.

"But with thee will I establish my covenant; and thou shalt come into the ark, thou, and thy sons, and thy wife, and thy sons' wives with thee." (Genesis 6:18)

<16> The new generation would be saved by Noah, through His Grace.

"And of every living thing of all flesh, two of every sort shalt thou bring into the ark, to keep them alive with thee; they shall be male and female." (Genesis 6:19)

<17> New animal generations should be saved too. Here God demanded, "two of every sort shalt thou bring into the ark." Later on, God demanded that Noah bring more than two (Genesis 7:2) of each clean animal, so that at least two of them, a male and a female, would stay alive, "to keep them alive with thee; they shall be male and female."

"Of fowls after their kind, and of cattle after their kind, of every creeping thing of the earth after his kind, two of every sort shall come unto thee, to keep them alive." (Genesis 6:20)

<18> Again emphasis is placed on "two of every sort ... , to keep them alive."

"And take thou unto thee of all food that is eaten, and thou shalt gather it to thee; and it shall be for food for thee, and for them." (Genesis 6:21)

"Thus did Noah; according to all that God commanded him, so did he." (Genesis 6:22)

<19> Noah did all the instructions given to him, and he prepared everything to save the new generations of humans and animals for the new climate on earth.

Tablet Twenty-One

Chapter 7

"And the Lord said unto Noah, Come thou and all thy house into the ark; for thee have I seen righteous before me in this generation." (Genesis 7:1)

<1> Noah was a righteous and perfect man.

"Of every clean beast thou shalt take to thee by sevens, the male and his female: and of beasts that are not clean by two, the male and his female." (Genesis 7:2)

<2> We can see here that God is concerned even for the unclean beasts because their existence is also necessary for creation. They are a part of the evolutionary process.

<3> From clean animals, seven pairs or fourteen singles were taken, because the new generation also ate meat (Gen. 9:3), so they could be consumed while sheltered, but at least leave two (a male and a female) alive.

<4> Also some extra were necessary for sacrifice after the flood (Gen. 8:20).

"Of fowls also of the air by sevens, the male and the female; to keep seed alive upon the face of all the earth." (Genesis 7:3)

"For yet seven days, and I will cause it to rain upon the earth forty days and forty nights; and every living substance that I have made will I destroy from off the face of the earth." (Genesis 7:4)

<5> Therefore, it was necessary for those creatures to be destroyed that had lagged behind in the evolutionary process so much that there was no hope for them to reach the new stage of human existence of the new generation.

"And Noah did according unto all that the Lord commanded him." (Genesis 7:5)

<6> Noah was completely surrendered to the commands of the Father. Only in this way can you be a devotee of His.

"And Noah was six hundred years old when the flood of waters was upon the earth." (Genesis 7:6)

<7> Noah was the last from the previous generation and lived for a long time. The new generation would have a shorter lifespan.

"And Noah went in, and his sons, and his wife, and his sons' wives with him, into the ark, because of the waters of the flood." (Genesis 7:7)

<8> Therefore, Noah saved the new generation by taking them to the ark.

"Of clean beasts, and of beasts that are not clean, and of fowls, and of every thing that creepeth upon the earth," (Genesis 7:8)

<9> New generations of animals of every kind were saved also.

"There went in two and two unto Noah into the ark, the male and the female, as God had commanded Noah." (Genesis 7:9)

"And it came to pass after seven days, that the waters of the flood were upon the earth." (Genesis 7:10)

<10> God never fails in His promises.

"In the six hundredth year of Noah's life, in the second month, the seventeenth day of the month, the same day were all the fountains of the great deep broken up, and the windows of heaven were opened." (Genesis 7:11)

<11> The process of destruction of the old earth started. "Fountains of the great deep" refer to the ice of the two poles. Ice on the earth started to melt, and all the clouds rained ("the windows of heaven were opened").

"And the rain was upon the earth forty days and forty nights." (Genesis 7:12)

<12> Again God did as He promised.

"In the selfsame day entered Noah, and Shem, and Ham, and Japheth, the sons of Noah, and Noah's wife, and the three wives of his sons with them, into the ark;" (Genesis 7:13)

<13> The people that were chosen to create the new generation sheltered themselves from the destruction.

"They, and every beast after his kind, and all the cattle after their kind, and every creeping thing that creepeth upon the earth after his kind, and every fowl after his kind, every bird of every sort." (Genesis 7:14)

<14> The animal kingdom was saved also (those needed to create new generations of animals).

"And they went in unto Noah into the ark, two and two of all flesh, wherein is the breath of life." (Genesis 7:15)

<15> Animals were sheltered also.

"And they that went in, went in male and female of all flesh, as God had commanded him: and the Lord shut him in." (Genesis 7:16)

<16> The emphasis of "went in male and female" shows how the male and female are important in the reproduction of flesh and how God supports all being coupled and married. <17> The sentence "and the Lord shut him in" shows that they all have been saved only by His Grace and under His shelter.

"And the flood was forty days upon the earth; and the waters increased, and bare up the ark, and it was lift up above the earth." (Genesis 7:17)

<18> Noah and the new generation were beyond destruction.

"And the waters prevailed, and were increased greatly upon the earth; and the ark went upon the face of the waters." (Genesis 7:18)

"And the waters prevailed exceedingly upon the earth; and all the high hills, that were under the whole heaven, were covered." (Genesis 7:19)

<19> The important point is that the old generation was destroyed and replaced by a new one. <20> Also the destruction appeared to be worldwide to those who were later inspired to report it to their offspring.

"Fifteen cubits upward did the waters prevail; and the mountains were covered." (Genesis 7:20)

"And all flesh died that moved upon the earth, both of fowl, and of cattle, and of beast, and of every creeping thing that creepeth upon the earth, and every man:" (Genesis 7:21)

<21> The old earth (generations) was destroyed.

"All in whose nostrils was the breath of life, of all that was in the dry land, died." (Genesis 7:22)

<22> Only the creatures on the dry land died, but not animals in the seas or any other waters.

"And every living substance was destroyed which was upon the face of the ground, both man, and cattle, and the creeping things, and the fowl of the heaven; and they were destroyed from the earth: and Noah only remained alive, and they that were with him in the ark." (Genesis 7:23)

"And the waters prevailed upon the earth an hundred and fifty days." (Genesis 7:24)

Tablet Twenty-Two

Chapter 8

"And God remembered Noah, and every living thing, and all the cattle that was with him in the ark: and God made a wind to pass over the earth, and the waters assuaged;" (Genesis 8:1)

<1> The process of destruction of those corrupted souls was finished and now the preparation was beginning for the new generation to assume possession of the earth.

"The fountains also of the deep and the windows of heaven were stopped, and the rain from heaven was restrained;" (Genesis 8:2)

<2> "Fountains of the deep" refer to the melted ice of the poles.

"And the waters returned from off the earth continually: and after the end of the hundred and fifty days the waters were abated." (Genesis 8:3)

<3> The waters started to go back to the places they were before (frozen at the two poles and vapor in the sky).

"And the ark rested in the seventh month, on the seventeenth day of the month, upon the mountains of Ararat." (Genesis 8:4)

"And the waters decreased continually until the tenth month: in the tenth month, on the first day of the month, were the tops of the mountains seen." (Genesis 8:5)

<4> The ark rested on Mount Ararat. <5> The new generation was saved. A new earth with a new environment was prepared for them to live on. Now God would further make the earth ready for them to spread over.

"And it came to pass at the end of forty days, that Noah opened the window of the ark which he had made:" (Genesis 8:6)

THE HOLIEST BOOK

HOLIEST 1 - Tablet 22

"And he sent forth a raven, which went forth to and fro, until the waters were dried up from off the earth." (Genesis 8:7)

"Also he sent forth a dove from him, to see if the waters were abated from off the face of the ground;" (Genesis 8:8)

"But the dove found no rest for the sole of her foot, and she returned unto him into the ark, for the waters were on the face of the whole earth: then he put forth his hand, and took her, and pulled her in unto him into the ark." (Genesis 8:9)

"And he stayed yet other seven days; and again he sent forth the dove out of the ark;" (Genesis 8:10)

"And the dove came in to him in the evening; and, lo, in her mouth was an olive leaf pluckt off: so Noah knew that the waters were abated from off the earth." (Genesis 8:11)

"And he stayed yet other seven days; and sent forth the dove; which returned not again unto him any more." (Genesis 8:12)

"And it came to pass in the six hundredth and first year, in the first month, the first day of the month, the waters were dried up from off the earth: and Noah removed the covering of the ark, and looked, and, behold, the face of the ground was dry." (Genesis 8:13)

<6> Now the new generation could come out of their shelter and inhabit the new earth with its new climate which suited them.

"And in the second month, on the seven and twentieth day of the month, was the earth dried." (Genesis 8:14)

<7> The earth became ready and refined for the new humans.

"And God spake unto Noah, saying," (Genesis 8:15)

"Go forth of the ark, thou, and thy wife, and thy sons, and thy sons' wives with thee." (Genesis 8:16)

<8> Now God saw that the new humans were ready to go forward and take over the earth.

"Bring forth with thee every living thing that is with thee, of all flesh, both of fowl, and of cattle, and of every creeping thing that creepeth upon the earth; that they may breed abundantly in the earth, and be fruitful, and multiply upon the earth." (Genesis 8:17)

<9> The new animals were ready also.

"And Noah went forth, and his sons, and his wife, and his sons' wives with him:" (Genesis 8:18)

<10> The life of the new human generation started.

"Every beast, every creeping thing, and every fowl, and whatsoever creepeth upon the earth, after their kinds, went forth out of the ark." (Genesis 8:19)

<11> The new generation of animals also started.

Tablet Twenty-Three

FAR EAST PHILOSOPHIES – MYSTICAL PATHS

"And Noah built an altar unto the Lord; and took of every clean beast, and of every clean fowl, and offered burnt offerings on the altar." (Genesis 8:20)

<1> The new generation started to build altars and offer burnt offerings to the Lord. This new generation lost its direct contact with God. However, Noah still had this direct relationship with God, so he set a symbolic example for the other humans of sacrificing.

<2> These teachings of Noah to the new generation and his example became the base for the religion of the new human. <3> Later on the essence of these teachings was preserved as the base of the religion of humanity and spread all throughout the earth. This is the base of most of the Mystical Paths existing. Eventually some of these teachings were written down as the <u>Vedas</u>. In their refined form they became the <u>Vedantas</u>.

<4> In the Far East, from this knowledge combined with many other discoveries and absorption of many parts from other religions, a body of knowledge was formed to which all religions of the Far East and the Mystical Paths in other religions are related. (For a deeper meaning of the phrases used here as "Mystical Paths" or "Far East Philosophies," see <u>The Glossary</u>.)

"And the Lord smelled a sweet savour; and the Lord said in his heart, I will not again curse the ground any more for man's sake; for the imagination of man's heart is evil from his youth; neither will I again smite any more every thing living, as I have done." (Genesis 8:21)

<5> God was very pleased with this new man, because He had complete control over him and He did not have to struggle with him. He thought that now man, with his intellect, will understand the purpose of his life, which is to be(come) Divine, and will try to become Pure Consciousness. <6> Also he does not have spiritual powers which the previous generations had. Therefore, he cannot disturb the forces in nature. So God decided not to curse the ground, destroy him by flood, or smite him again but gradually bring him to an understanding of the truth.

<7> However, if this weakened man does not understand the realities behind this universe (the Laws), he will suffer until he understands the creation and history, the goal of life, and the Plan of creation.

"While the earth remaineth, seedtime and harvest, and cold and heat, and summer and winter, and day and night shall not cease." (Genesis 8:22)

<8> No further evolutionary process is necessary from the point of view of the climate of the earth for the existence of humans.

Chapter 9

"And God blessed Noah and his sons, and said unto them, Be fruitful, and multiply, and replenish the earth." (Genesis 9:1)

THE HOLIEST BOOK

<9> God was pleased with this new generation. He blessed them, and they started living on the earth.

"And the fear of you and the dread of you shall be upon every beast of the earth, and upon every fowl of the air, upon all that moveth upon the earth, and upon all the fishes of the sea; into your hand are they delivered." (Genesis 9:2)

<10> Still human is the superior creature.

"Every moving thing that liveth shall be meat for you; even as the green herb have I given you all things." (Genesis 9:3)

<11> Humans fell so far that they became meat and vegetable eaters. The new generation with the new body can eat meat also, it is nutritious for flesh, but it is not good for their consciousnesses. <12> So the emphasis should be on vegetables, grains, herbs, nuts, and fruit in our diets.

"But flesh with the life thereof, which is the blood thereof, shall ye not eat." (Genesis 9:4)

<13> Blood should all be taken out of the body of the animal before being eaten.

"And surely your blood of your lives will I require; at the hand of every beast will I require it, and at the hand of man; at the hand of every man's brother will I require the life of man." (Genesis 9:5)

"Whoso sheddeth man's blood, by man shall his blood be shed: for in the image of God made he man." (Genesis 9:6)

<14> The new generation was built and new Laws were necessary to govern them, but still this new generation can reach Pure Consciousness, to the state of a son of God (His likeness). <15> However, this generation also is not in His image as it says, "in the image of God made he man." It does not say, "in the image of God **is** man." The word "made" is in the past tense. Man still can reach that state by perfecting himself. <16> Also whoever **murders**, "shall his blood be shed."

HOLIEST 1 - Tablet 23

"And you, be ye fruitful, and multiply; bring forth abundantly in the earth, and multiply therein." (Genesis 9:7)

"And God spake unto Noah, and to his sons with him, saying," (Genesis 9:8)

"And I, behold, I establish my covenant with you, and with your seed after you;" (Genesis 9:9)

<17> Now God has complete control over humans. Therefore, He made a covenant with Noah and made promises, because He is sure that He will be able to fulfill them.

"And with every living creature that is with you, of the fowl, of the cattle, and of every beast of the earth with you; from all that go out of the ark, to every beast of the earth." (Genesis 9:10)

<18> Not only has He complete control over humans but also over all animals that He has made with this new generation.

"And I will establish my covenant with you; neither shall all flesh be cut off any more by the waters of a flood; neither shall there any more be a flood to destroy the earth." (Genesis 9:11)

<19> Therefore all flesh will not be "cut off any more by the waters of a flood," but a flood might destroy some flesh, and there might be other kinds of destruction (such as fire). <20> No destruction comes from God but from man himself by his own actions. Only they can stop the destruction and tribulation by understanding the Laws and The Plan of the Father, and by following them.

"And God said, This is the token of the covenant which I make between me and you and every living creature that is with you, for perpetual generations:" (Genesis 9:12)

"I do set my bow in the cloud, and it shall be for a token of a covenant between me and the earth." (Genesis 9:13)

<21> Rainbow is that bow.

"And it shall come to pass, when I bring a cloud over the earth, that the bow shall be seen in the cloud:" (Genesis 9:14)

"And I will remember my covenant, which is between me and you and every living creature of all flesh; and the waters shall no more become a flood to destroy all flesh." (Genesis 9:15)

"And the bow shall be in the cloud; and I will look upon it, that I may remember the everlasting covenant between God and every living creature of all flesh that is upon the earth." (Genesis 9:16)

"And God said unto Noah, This is the token of the covenant, which I have established between me and all flesh that is upon the earth." (Genesis 9:17)

<22> All these verses show that God does not have to destroy man again. He has complete control over the earth. Only man can destroy himself, if he does not follow the Laws given by God. Therefore it is not God who will destroy the earth but it is the choice of the human to either understand the Laws and work according to the Daharmas of the universe and become Pure Consciousness, or to go against them and destroy himself.

Tablet Twenty-Four

"And the sons of Noah, that went forth of the ark, were Shem, and Ham, and Japheth: and Ham is the father of Canaan." (Genesis 9:18)

"These are the three sons of Noah: and of them was the whole earth overspread." (Genesis 9:19)

<1> The three sons of Noah are symbols of the new generation. The different types of humans as we know them have been created after the flood of Noah. They will be described later (also read the books The Kingdom Of Heaven On Earth and Commentaries on Prophecies in Daniel, Period of Intellectual Domination).

"And Noah began to be an husbandman, and he planted a vineyard:" (Genesis 9:20)

<2> Agriculture, with new improved seed, still was possible. That is why the civilization based on agriculture for this new generation started around 12,000 years ago.

"And he drank of the wine, and was drunken; and he was uncovered within his tent." (Genesis 9:21)

"And Ham, the father of Canaan, saw the nakedness of his father, and told his two brethren without." (Genesis 9:22)

<3> Ham was attached to the small things related to the body.

"And Shem and Japheth took a garment, and laid it upon both their shoulders, and went backward, and covered the nakedness of their father; and their faces were backward, and they saw not their father's nakedness." (Genesis 9:23)

<4> However, Shem and Japheth were concerned with higher matters and tried to cover the physical attractions in order to be able to concentrate on more important things in life.

"And Noah awoke from his wine, and knew what his younger son had done unto him." (Genesis 9:24)

<5> Noah noticed this difference between his sons, "And Noah awoke from his wine."

"And he said, Cursed be Canaan; a servant of servants shall he be unto his brethren." (Genesis 9:25)

<6> Noah realized a person with the qualities of Ham is one who is earthbound. So he will be cursed and "a servant of servants."

"And he said, Blessed be the Lord God

of Shem; and Canaan shall be his servant." (Genesis 9:26)

<7> In truth, the three symbolic sons of Noah represent three different kinds of humans on earth. <8> Those who are in the physical level of consciousness (when the satisfaction of physiological and safety needs are the prime object of life, and those who try to dominate matter by physical vigor) are symbolized by Ham – Shudras (laborers) and Ksattriyas (warriors). <9> Those who are in the mental level of consciousness (intellectuals; those who are interested in dominating matter through the mind) are symbolized by Japheth – Vipras (intellectuals) and Vaeshyas (businessmen). <10> Those who are in the spiritual (Soul) level of consciousness (true spiritual aspirants and those who become seers and great spiritual beings) are symbolized by Shem. They are different than intellectual spiritualists who bring superstitions and suffering to humanity by taking the Scriptures at their apparent meanings without understanding their symbolic meanings.

<11> He who creates characteristics of all these three types through many incarnations is a Paravipra.

<12> Those who become real spiritualists and earn spiritual truth and powers (sons of Shem) are exalted over the other types, and those who try to understand or exploit the manifested universe through their intellects are exalted over those who neither try to understand the truth of the spiritual world nor the physical world. <13> That is why Noah made Canaan (the child of Ham, symbolizing one who is earthbound) "a servant of servants."

"God shall enlarge Japheth, and he shall dwell in the tents of Shem; and Canaan shall be his servant." (Genesis 9:27)

<14> Japheth would be enlarged. However, he should follow the guidance and advice of Shem (the seers, the true spiritual incarnations), "and he shall dwell in the tents of Shem."

<15> The people who are earthbound should be his (symbolic Japheth) servants. So the person who is bound to his physiological and safety needs will be the servant of Shem and the servant of Japheth. He will be the servant of the servants.

<16> However, this explanation should not become a reason to create a caste system, because there can be different types of people within any one family. The purpose of this categorizing is not for humans to look down on each other; the experience in each type is necessary for a soul to progress toward perfection. <17> In fact, a Paravipra (true leader of humanity) is one who creates abilities of all these five types and is able to manifest them and understand people in each level. Otherwise he will be bound to one type and will create suffering for others.

"And Noah lived after the flood three hundred and fifty years." (Genesis 9:28)

"And all the days of Noah were nine hundred and fifty years: and he died." (Genesis 9:29)

<18> Physically Noah died, but not spiritually.

Tablet Twenty-Five

Chapter 10

"Now these are the generations of the sons of Noah, Shem, Ham, and Japheth: and unto them were sons born after the flood." (Genesis 10:1)

<1> "And unto them were sons born": "Son" always means "likeness." So the generation of the sons of Noah" which was explained to mean symbolically the five different types of humans in the different levels of evolution – Shem (Brahmins), Ham (Shudras and Ksattriyas) and Japheth (Vipras and Vaeshyas) – begat "sons." <2> Therefore it was the generation after Noah that consisted of these three types. They are the sons of Shem, Japheth, and Ham.

THE HOLIEST BOOK

"The sons of Japheth; Gomer, and Magog, and Madai, and Javan, and Tubal, and Meshech, and Tiras." (Genesis 10:2)

"And the sons of Gomer; Ashkenaz, and Riphath, and Togarmah." (Genesis 10:3)

"And the sons of Javan; Elishah, and Tarshish, Kittim, and Dodanim." (Genesis 10:4)

"By these were the isles of the Gentiles divided in their lands; every one after his tongue, after their families, in their nations." (Genesis 10:5)

<3> "By these were the isles of the Gentiles divided in their lands" means that the sons of Japheth (Vipras and Vaeshyas, or intellectuals and business-oriented people) were created (Gentiles).

<4> "Every one after his tongue": These people understand each other very well, because all are in the same level of consciousness.

<5> "After their families, in their nations" means that they are all one family on earth in different levels of consciousness ("after their families"). They create a nation as intellectuals and businessmen.

<6> Also this verse means that many different nations with different languages were created by those who were saved by Noah after the flood.

"And the sons of Ham; Cush, and Mizraim, and Phut, and Canaan." (Genesis 10:6)

"And the sons of Cush; Seba, and Havilah, and Sabtah, and Raamah, and Sebtechah: and the sons of Raamah; Sheba, and Dedan." (Genesis 10:7)

<7> The name Raamah is similar to the East Indian name Rahma. The similarity of the names in the <u>Bible</u> (also Sarah and Saravati, etc.) is further evidence of a link between the original <u>Bible</u> language and the ancient language. Sanskrit is the spiritual language of the Hindus.

"And Cush begat Nimrod: he began to be a mighty one in the earth." (Genesis 10:8)

HOLIEST 1 - Tablet 24

"He was a mighty hunter before the Lord: wherefore it is said, Even as Nimrod the mighty hunter before the Lord." (Genesis 10:9)

"And the beginning of his kingdom was Babel, and Erech, and Accad, and Calneh, in the land of Shinar." (Genesis 10:10)

<8> The period of the phase of the mighty warriors started, "He was a mighty hunter before the Lord." The period of domination of warriors (Ksattriyas) began, and they started the empires and kingdoms.

<9> As it was described, in general, humans can be categorized into five groups: workers (Shudras), warriors or courageous ones (Ksattriyas), intellectuals (Vipras), businessmen (Vaeshyas), and seers (Brahmins).

<10> The dominating class can be traced in the course of history. First there was the domination of the mighty men of war (Ksattriyas) who established their domination through their physical abilities and skillfulness in war (purely physical strength over others). They exploited the Shudras by their might.

<11> The second domination was by the intellectuals, who through their administrative abilities and intellectual understanding of the realities of life, exploited the warriors (because their administrative abilities were needed by the Ksattriyas) and masses (through creating superstitions and false superiority ideas in society).

<12> The third domination was of businessmen through their control of the basic necessities of human needs. <13> They exploited the rest (Shudras, Ksattriyas, and Vipras) through using all of them for their benefit and making them workers for commercial rewards.

<14> The fifth class, the seers, never were exploited because they would never become so attached to this external world that others would be able to exploit them. They always either escaped the society by being satisfied with the minimum or stood against the exploiters.

<15> However, the true leaders are those who have all the qualities of the five types and

understand them all. <16> Then they become classless and are able to handle all of them on their own terms and guide humanity toward the goal (for more detail, read The Kingdom Of Heaven On Earth and Commentaries on Prophecies in Daniel, Period of Intellectual Domination).

<17> In verses 8 through 10 above, the period of the domination of the warrior class (Ksattriyas) started.

"Out of that land went forth Asshur, and builded Nineveh, and the city Rehoboth, and Calah," (Genesis 10:11)

"And Resen between Nineveh and Calah: the same is a great city." (Genesis 10:12)

<18> The kings started to build great cities and bring others under their control by their might and armies. They created empires for themselves by exploiting the masses. These all are the sons of Ham.

"And Mizraim begat Ludim, and Anamim, and Lehabim, and Naphtuhim," (Genesis 10:13)

"And Pathrusim, and Casluhim, (out of whom came Philistim,) and Caphtorim." (Genesis 10:14)

"And Canaan begat Sidon his firstborn, and Heth," (Genesis 10:15)

"And the Jebusite, and the Amorite, and the Girgasite," (Genesis 10:16)

"And the Hivite, and the Arkite, and the Sinite," (Genesis 10:17)

"And the Arvadite, and the Zemarite, and the Hamathite: and afterward were the families of the Canaanites spread abroad." (Genesis 10:18)

"And the border of the Canaanites was from Sidon, as thou comest to Gerar, unto Gaza; as thou goest, unto Sodom, and Gomorrah, and Admah, and Zeboim, even unto Lasha." (Genesis 10:19)

"These are the sons of Ham, after their families, after their tongues, in their countries, and in their nations." (Genesis 10:20)

<19> So the generations of Ham (the Shudras and Ksattriyas; workers and warriors) were created. They made up a family (on earth) with their special tongues (they understood each other well), in their countries (each in his territory) and in their nations (with still many different types).

<20> Also it means that more nations with different languages were created.

"Unto Shem also, the father of all the children of Eber, the brother of Japheth the elder, even to him were children born." (Genesis 10:21)

<21> Shem is the symbol of spiritual people (true spiritualists; the great incarnations). That is why it is emphasized that, "even to him were children born." That is, that not all spiritual people should become renunciates.
<22> Also usually it is rarer for highly spiritual people to have many children.
<23> Also the emphasis that Shem was "the father of all the children of Eber" shows the importance of the children of Eber in the history of the sons of Shem. The children were Peleg – "for in his days was the earth divided" (Gen. 10:25) – and Joktan.

"The children of Shem; Elam, and Asshur, and Arphaxad, and Lud, and Aram." (Genesis 10:22)

"And the children of Aram; Uz, and Hul, and Gether, and Mash." (Genesis 10:23)

"And Arphaxad begat Salah; and Salah begat Eber." (Genesis 10:24)

"And unto Eber were born two sons: the name of one was Peleg; for in his days was the earth divided; and his brother's name was Joktan." (Genesis 10:25)

<24> So Shem, the symbol of the spiritual types (Brahmin class) or those who were entrusted to preserve and learn sacred Scriptures after Noah, also became a class among others.

<25> However, in the time of the children of Eber (Peleg and Joktan) a great event happened. Before then and after the flood of Noah, God had created the earth in such a way that there were few lands isolated from the mainland. That is, the dry land on earth was accessible to the new generations which were created after the flood.

<26> But in the time of the children of Eber, after humans had scattered all over the earth, "and from thence did the Lord scatter them abroad upon the face of all the earth" (Gen. 11:9), then the earth was divided.

<27> This division of the earth happened because God had a great Plan for the future. He wanted to keep some parts of the earth isolated to be used later on for a great purpose. The purpose for this event is explained in the book <u>Children of Abram (Abraham), All Prophecies Are Fulfilled</u>.

<28> The destruction of their lands forced many Great Souls of the new generation to leave and go to other lands. They helped many civilizations to accelerate their progress. **<29>** That is why we find great structures and civilizations in some parts of the world that were constructed at the time when the natives were very backward, such as in Egypt, South America, Central America, and other places. This accelerated human civilization.

"And Joktan begat Almodad, and Sheleph, and Hazarmaveth, and Jerah," (Genesis 10:26)

"And Hadoram, and Uzal, and Diklah," (Genesis 10:27)

"And Obal, and Abimael, and Sheba," (Genesis 10:28)

"And Ophir, and Havilah, and Jobab: all these were the sons of Joktan." (Genesis 10:29)

"And their dwelling was from Mesha, as thou goest unto Sephar a mount of the east." (Genesis 10:30)

<30> So the sons of Eber, like the sons of Ham and Japheth, were also scattered abroad.

"These are the sons of Shem, after their families, after their tongues, in their lands, after their nations." (Genesis 10:31)

<31> So the generations of spiritual people (the seers) also increased. They became a family on earth, who would understand each other with their special tongue, in different levels ("in their lands"), and they became a nation.

<32> Also it means that further races and languages were created.

"These are the families of the sons of Noah, after their generations, in their nations: and by these were the nations divided in the earth after the flood." (Genesis 10:32)

<33> Many races and nations were created on the earth. After the flood of Noah, because the earth had not yet been divided, these people settled all over the world, especially when God "scattered them abroad upon the face of all the earth" (Gen. 11:9). They were scattered even more when their land was destroyed and they were forced to leave.

<34> The point is that Japheth, Shem, and Ham are the different types of humans in different levels of evolution. Therefore, to try to find who is the ancestor of whom will create confusion. The races were not from these symbolic three sons of Noah. **<35>** The races were created for gaining different experiences in each race for further evolutionary progress, just as the whole universe was created to allow man to go through different levels of experiences. So the purpose of the races after the flood is the same.

<36> However, intermarriage between races will create new bodies with new biological set-ups for new experiences for those who are ready now to go through those kinds of experiences. **<37>** Also with these new teachings of creation and history, man should understand the realities behind this universe and realize that God is All, and also, man should not misuse his powers. So intermarriage, acceptance of one language for the whole world, and following God's Laws will cause man to destroy all narrowness of the mind and prejudices about the differences of race, creed, and language. **<38>** Then the Kingdom Of Heaven On Earth (KOHOE) will be created, and all will accelerate their progress toward self-realization and perfection. **<39>** Then the Kingdom Of Heaven Within (KOHW) also will be established. The Kingdom Of Heaven In Heaven (KOHIH) has already been created by God, so when the Kingdom Of Heaven within and without is created also, then His Will, will be done on earth as it is in heaven.

Tablet Twenty-Six

Chapter 11

"And the whole earth was of one language, and of one speech." (Genesis 11:1)

<1> In the last chapter, the sentence, "every one after his language" (Gen. 10:5, 20, 31) shows that there had been many languages on earth. This verse here means that humans still had the ability to communicate with each other telepathically. Therefore all humans could understand each other easily by this way of communication (whenever they chose to use this method of communication).

"And it came to pass, as they journeyed from the east, that they found a plain in the land of Shinar; and they dwelt there." (Genesis 11:2)

<2> Humans found the best parts of the earth to live on. Some of them journeyed toward the west of the original land they were in after the flood.

"And they said one to another, Go to, let us make brick, and burn them throughly. And they had brick for stone, and slime had they for morter." (Genesis 11:3)

<3> The human started to use his intelligence for replacing the resources of nature with his own discoveries.

"And they said, Go to, let us build us a city and a tower, whose top may reach unto heaven; and let us make us a name, lest we be scattered abroad upon the face of the whole earth." (Genesis 11:4)

<4> The human started to use his intelligence for gaining fame, name, and power, instead of using it to progress to perfection. By becoming involved in a luxurious life and thinking about their name and fame, they forgot that this intellect was given to them to further their progress to perfection. It was not given for gaining name, fame, or material wealth. This striving to gain these things is called the "great Babylon."

<5> Also they did not want to be scattered all over the world ("lest we be scattered abroad upon the face of the whole earth") so they planned on building a tower in order to stay together. However, The Plan of God is that man **should** be scattered not only all over the earth, but all over the universe.

"And the Lord came down to see the city and the tower, which the children of men builded." (Genesis 11:5)

<6> God was observing what they were doing.

"And the Lord said, Behold, the people is one, and they have all one language; and this they begin to do: and now nothing will be restrained from them, which they have imagined to do." (Genesis 11:6)

<7> With the good communication through having telepathic abilities, being united, and having the use of their intellect, men started again to manipulate nature towards their own selfish desires and for their lower natures. As had been seen before, this would again further the fall of man and destroy him.

<8> The purpose of man is to reach Pure Consciousness. Directing the intellect toward the satisfaction of the lower self is against the Laws of nature and will bring disaster to man, nature, and his society. God does not mind that man gains all the knowledge in the universe. Yet He will stop him if he starts to misuse it for his own selfish ends.

"Go to, let us go down, and there confound their language, that they may not understand one another's speech." (Genesis 11:7)

<9> Therefore, another evolutionary process became necessary, which was to take the telepathic ability away from men so they would have many different languages and would not be able to communicate properly with each other. <10> With being different races, different nations, and different languages, and with having intelligence instead of direct power over the forces of nature, men now could be prevented from self-destruction through directing their powers and intelligence toward their lower selves.

<11> The human should have gone through a great struggle during the last 6,000 years of history until he is able to come to the point that he has reached now: To understand that the only way to salvation is to follow the Universal Laws and Daharmas which have been set up by God (come to his higher nature). <12> Only then can he live happily, gain his powers back, and understand the real truth behind this universe.

"So the Lord scattered them abroad from thence upon the face of all the earth: and they left off to build the city." (Genesis 11:8)

<13> Only with this event were they prevented from self-destruction. Also, that is one of the desires of the Lord God – to see man spread all over the earth and understand the Laws governing the earth. <14> Not only does He desire to see man understand the earth and spread over it, but also He desires to see man understand the Laws governing space and other planets in order to spread all over the universe!

<15> This event is the same as that of verse 25 in chapter 10, when God divided the earth. Both of them describe the same event which forced the inhabitants (the new generation) to leave and be scattered all over the earth.

"Therefore is the name of it called Babel; because the Lord did there confound the language of all the earth: and from thence did the Lord scatter them abroad upon the face of all the earth." (Genesis 11:9)

<16> Babel refers to idle talk. When a person talks nonsense, we say he is "babbling" instead of communicating. This prevented them from building the city and making a name for themselves.

<17> We are still in this stage and most of what we do and say in the individual, societal, or even international level, is only "babbling." The real communication has been lost and life has become "Babel-like." <18> That is why it is so necessary for man to understand the lessons given by history and the evolutionary process, which is to show that the only way to happiness is to "follow the Laws, try to become Pure Consciousness, and help others to be(come) the same."

<19> By understanding this lesson, then humans should create a society with one language (for best communication, and of course very soon many people will gain their telepathic abilities to communicate as before, beside other powers), one race (with intermarriage between races), <20> and one religion (with understanding the existence of one God and the Laws of the universe – **Eternal Divine Path**).

<21> **Then and only then will the human be able to establish the earth as one country and the universe as his home, God as his Father and nature (creative force) as his Mother, the Universal Laws as his ideals, and the attainment of Pure Consciousness for himself and for others as his goals.** <22> That is what the Bible teaches and what all the Messengers and Prophets came to tell humans.

Tablet Twenty-Seven

"These are the generations of Shem: Shem was an hundred years old, and begat Arphaxad two years after the flood:" (Genesis 11:10)

<1> Any time in the Bible the history of

generations of some people is discontinued and some events are described, and then later on the description of the generations of those people is picked up again, it means that those events which were described in-between happened during that generation and are related to them. Also it shows the importance of those events and their relationships with those people.

<2> In these verses, the generations of Shem are picked up again after they were finished in chapter 10. So it shows that the events described in chapter 11 from verses 1 through 9 happened in the period described about Shem's generations and are related to them.

"And Shem lived after he begat Arphaxad five hundred years, and begat sons and daughters." (Genesis 11:11)

<3> In chapter 10 only the sons (the likenesses) were described who had been born from them. This again shows that in chapter 10 the emphasis was in showing the likeness of different types that were created on earth.

<4> Now in this chapter, the daughters are also described who had been born unto them.

"And Arphaxad lived five and thirty years, and begat Salah:" (Genesis 11:12)

<5> The time of becoming mature and being able to have children was shortened. Arphaxad was only thirty-five years old when he "begat Salah." God decided to shorten the lifespan of man to around one hundred twenty years before creating new generations. This occurred in chapter 6 of <u>Genesis</u>, "his days shall be an hundred and twenty years" (Gen. 6:3).

<6> Still in these verses, we can see that man is living much longer than that. As the explanation of the generations of Shem continues, the lifespan shrinks. This shows the Will of the Lord is taking place. But it takes generations before the actual desire of the Lord is achieved. <7> God desires and sets the process in motion but it takes time for His Will to be completely done. In fact the process of creating the new generation started 12,000 years ago and was complete 6,000 years ago. It took 6,000 years to reach this human as we know him.

"And Arphaxad lived after he begat Salah four hundred and three years, and begat sons and daughters." (Genesis 11:13)

"And Salah lived thirty years, and begat Eber:" (Genesis 11:14)

"And Salah lived after he begat Eber four hundred and three years, and begat sons and daughters." (Genesis 11:15)

"And Eber lived four and thirty years, and begat Peleg:" (Genesis 11:16)

<8> It was in the time of Eber's sons that a great event happened to humanity.

"And Eber lived after he begat Peleg four hundred and thirty years, and begat sons and daughters." (Genesis 11:17)

"And Peleg lived thirty years, and begat Reu:" (Genesis 11:18)

"And Peleg lived after he begat Reu two hundred and nine years, and begat sons and daughters." (Genesis 11:19)

<9> It was in Peleg's time that "the earth was divided" (Gen. 10:25). This division of the earth destroyed the land that was between North America and Canada, and the northern part of Europe. With this, the land of America was completely isolated from the rest of the world.

"And Reu lived two and thirty years, and begat Serug:" (Genesis 11:20)

"And Reu lived after be begat Serug two hundred and seven years, and begat sons and daughters." (Genesis 11:21)

"And Serug lived thirty years, and begat Nahor:" (Genesis 11:22)

THE HOLIEST BOOK

"And Serug lived after he begat Nahor two hundred years, and begat sons and daughters." (Genesis 11:23)

"And Nahor lived nine and twenty years, and begat Terah:" (Genesis 11:24)

"And Nahor lived after he begat Terah an hundred and nineteen years, and begat sons and daughters." (Genesis 11:25)

HOLIEST TWO

Tablet One

"And Terah lived seventy years, and begat Abram, Nahor, and Haran." (Genesis 11:26)
<1> Abram was born. Abram was a Great Soul; he was an Avatar.

"Now these are the generations of Terah: Terah begat Abram, Nahor, and Haran; and Haran begat Lot." (Genesis 11:27)
<2> Repetition of the generations of Terah show their importance. He had the same number of children as Noah.

"And Haran died before his father Terah in the land of his nativity, in Ur of the Chaldees." (Genesis 11:28)
<3> They were living in Ur in Chaldees.

"And Abram and Nahor took them wives: the name of Abram's wife was Sarai; and the name of Nahor's wife, Milcah, the daughter of Haran, the father of Milcah, and the father of Iscah." (Genesis 11:29)
<4> Abram was leading a regular life. Also the name Sarai is very similar to the Sanskrit names Sarvati and Saradamoni.

"But Sarai was barren; she had no child." (Genesis 11:30)
<5> Even after Abram found out she was barren, he continued their marriage.

"And Terah took Abram his son, and Lot the son of Haran his son's son, and Sarai his daughter in law, his son Abram's wife; and they went forth with them from Ur of the Chaldees, to go into the land of Canaan; and they came into Haran, and dwelt there." (Genesis 11:31)
<6> The similarity of the name of Haran, the son of Terah, with the place they went to dwell in, shows the desire of Terah toward having the place Haran. It also shows the name of a place is used as the name of a person!

"And the days of Terah were two hundred and five years: and Terah died in Haran." (Genesis 11:32)

ELECTED ONES (HEBREWS)

Chapter 12

"Now the Lord had said unto Abram, Get thee out of thy country, and from thy kindred, and from thy father's house, unto a land that I will shew thee:" (Genesis 12:1)

<7> With the process of evolution and many reincarnations of humans, God was able to select some of those who had reached a higher level of consciousness as Elected Ones. Abram was the first Selected One and was given the instructions of how to start his mission. <8> Although he was called A-bram* ("not a Brahmin"), God chose him. God is not a respecter of man-made titles, but the fullness of the Heart. Abram was a true Brahmin!

"And I will make of thee a great nation, and I will bless thee, and make thy name great; and thou shalt be a blessing:" (Genesis 12:2)

<9> Abram not only had been chosen for starting the great mission, but he would be a blessing for all whenever he was reincarnated in the future. <10> There was also a promise that if the commandment of leaving his family and going where the Lord wanted was followed, there would be a "great nation" from him, who are the Elected Ones.

"And I will bless them that bless thee, and curse him that curseth thee: and in thee shall all families of the earth be blessed." (Genesis 12:3)

<11> Through his children (who would cover most of the world) and his nation (Elected Ones), the whole earth would be blessed. Also he would be born in so many different parts of the world and they all would be blessed through him.

"So Abram departed, as the Lord had spoken unto him; and Lot went with him: and Abram was seventy and five years old when he departed out of Haran." (Genesis 12:4)

<12> Abram left to obey the Lord's command and to start his mission, so God would keep His Promise to him also.

Tablet Two

<1> This explanation of Genesis verse-by-verse finishes here. However, the important verses of the rest of this book will be briefly explained below. These verses and the significance of the rest of Genesis are explained in more detail in the book Children of Abram (Abraham), All Prophecies Are Fulfilled.

A promise is given to Abram:

And the Lord said unto Abram, after that Lot was separated from him, Lift up now thine eyes, and look from the place where thou art northward, and southward, and eastward, and westward:

For all the land which thou seest, to thee will I give it, and to thy seed for ever.

And I will make thy seed as the dust of the earth:... (Genesis 13:14-16)

<2> There are two promises here: First, that a land would be given to Abram's seed which would stretch in all directions with no mention of boundaries; and second, that Abram's seed would be increased, "as the dust of the earth." **So the land should be very large to bear that huge a population.**

The promises above are for Abram's seed:

And Abram was fourscore and six years old, when Hagar bear Ishmael to Abram. (Genesis 16:16)

---

* When an "A" is used in front of any Sanskrit name, it becomes negative or opposite, such as Vidya (knowledge) to Avidya (ignorance).

<3> These promises and more were given to Abram. The seed of Abram was Ishmael.

The previous promises are repeated to Abram and then the name of Abram is changed to Abraham:

> And when Abram was ninety years old and nine, the Lord appeared to Abram, and said unto him, I am the Almighty God; walk before me, and be thou perfect, (Genesis 17:1)

<4> "Walk before me, and be thou perfect" is the same as walking with God, which is to be submissive to Him and His Laws.

> And I will make my covenant between me and thee, and will multiply thee exceedingly.
> And Abram fell on his face: and God talked with him, saying,
> As for me, behold, my covenant is with thee, and thou shalt be a father of many nations.
> Neither shall thy name any more be called Abram, but thy name shall be Abraham; for a father of many nations have I made thee. (Genesis 17:2-5)

New promises are given to Abraham:

> And I will make thee exceeding fruitful, and I will make nations of thee, and kings shall come out of thee.
> And I will establish my covenant between me and thee and thy seed after thee in their generations for an everlasting covenant, to be a God unto thee, and to thy seed after thee.
> And I will give unto thee, and to thy seed after thee, the land wherein thou art a stranger, all the land of Canaan, for an everlasting possession; and I will be their God. (Genesis 17:6-8)

<5> There were two promises given to Abraham: a promise of material possession ("nations") <6> and a promise of kingly status ("kings shall come out of thee").

<7> These promises were given to Abraham and his seed, "…will give unto thee, and to thy seed after thee [after Abraham]." <8> Also this time the land which would be given to Abraham's seed was mentioned with definite boundaries, "Canaan" (promised land).

These promises are for Isaac, Abraham's seed:

> And God said unto Abraham, As for Sarai thy wife, thou shalt not call her name Sarai, but Sarah shall her name be.
> And I will bless her, and give thee a son also of her:… (Genesis 17:15-16)

> And God said, Sarah thy wife shall bear thee a son indeed; and thou shalt call his name Isaac: and I will establish my covenant with him for an everlasting covenant, and with his seed after him. (Genesis 17:19)

<9> Sarai's name was also changed to Sarah. This was done to emphasize the significance of the change of the name of Abram to Abraham. These promises were given to Abraham for Sarah's son Isaac.

Abraham is tested and an unconditional promise is given to him:

> That in blessing I [God] will bless thee [Abraham], and in multiplying I will multiply thy seed… ; and thy seed shall possess the gate of his enemies;
> …because thou hast obeyed my voice. (Genesis 22:17-18)

<10> God commanded Abraham to sacrifice his son Isaac for Him. Abraham obeyed God and prepared his son as a sacrifice to Him. But God stopped him, gave him new promises, and repeated the old ones.

<11> Until this point, all the promises were conditional with a commandment or some-

thing to be done to receive that promise. But here, after Abraham obeyed God even to sacrifice his old-age-begotten son, God gave him unconditional promises, "because thou hast obeyed my voice."

Tablet Three

The promises are repeated to Isaac:

And I will make thy [Isaac's] seed to multiply as the stars of heaven,…
Because that Abraham obeyed my voice, and kept my charge, my commandments, my statutes, and my laws. (Genesis 26:4-5)

<1> The promises were repeated to Isaac for his seed. These promises had two aspects: First, the promise of birthright which would go to the first son, which was the material part of the promise, a nation; <2> and second, the promise of spiritual blessing or kingly stature ("scepter") which would go to the son who would be blessed by the father (Isaac in this case).
<3> Although Jacob was the younger son of Isaac, he bought the birthright from Esau, the elder brother (Genesis 25:29-33), and received Isaac's (his father's) blessing (Genesis chapter 27). So although being the younger son, Jacob received both the birthright and spiritual kingship (scepter).

The previous promises (and more) are repeated to Jacob:

And thy [Jacob's] seed shall be as the dust of the earth, and thou shalt spread abroad to the west, and to the east, and to the north, and to the south:… (Genesis 28:14)

<4> These promises were repeated to Jacob that also his seed would spread in all directions.

The name of Jacob is changed and new promises are given to him:

And God said unto him [Jacob], Thy name is Jacob: thy name shall not be called any more Jacob, but Israel shall be thy name: and he called his name Israel. (Genesis 35:10)

<5> So the name of Jacob was changed to Israel.

And God said unto him, I am God Almighty: be fruitful and multiply; **a nation and a company of nations** shall be of thee, and kings shall come out of thy loins; (Genesis 35:11)

<6> His name was changed and a new promise was given to him, "a nation and a company of nations." <7> This promise was given exclusively to Israel, not to Isaac and his seed, Jacob and Esau. This was only for the children of Israel.

Israel (Jacob) takes his son's sons (Joseph's sons) as his own sons:

And now thy [Joseph's] two sons, Ephraim and Manasseh, which were born unto thee in the land of Egypt before I came unto thee into Egypt, are mine;… (Genesis 48:5)

<8> Jacob (Israel) made his grandsons, Ephraim and Manasseh, as his own sons. Therefore they would inherit whatever was given to Joseph, his own son.

Israel separates the inheritance of the scepter and the birthright by giving them to two of his sons separately:

The scepter shall not depart from Judah, nor a lawgiver from between his feet, until Shiloh come; and unto him shall the gathering of the people be. (Genesis 49:10)

<9> This verse was spoken by Jacob (Israel) at the time of his death. He separated the kingly inheritance ("scepter") from the birthright, and he gave the scepter to Judah, "the scepter shall not depart from Judah." But this promise was "until Shiloh [Messiah] come." <10> Then not only would the scepter depart from Judah but also the lawgiving.

<11> So with the coming of the promised Messiah, in addition to his mission as a Savior, the two aspects above would be fulfilled, <12> and also "unto him shall the gathering of the people [people who are from Israel] be."

<13> The birthright or material possession ("a nation and a company of nations") was given to Joseph (Gen. 49:22-26), <14> and also it is stated in Chronicles I 5:2, "...but the birthright was Joseph's," <15> which later on was inherited by Ephraim and Manasseh, his sons whom Israel (Jacob) looked upon as his own sons (Gen. 48:3-5).

<16> How these promises were fulfilled and what their relationships are with the rest of the material in **THOTH** can be found in the book Children of Abram (Abraham), All Prophecies Are Fulfilled.

Tablet Four

<1> After Abraham was selected to be the first Elected One, his children and seed were all the incarnations of Great Souls who had gone through many reincarnations until they had reached a very high consciousness. Only in this state could they be born in the Hebrew community as God's people.

<2> At the end of Genesis, it is shown how the number of Hebrews increased to seventy-one by the time of the death of Israel (Jacob). <3> Israel means, "He who struggles with God" – "struggle with" in the sense of struggling side-by-side with God to bring all to Pure Consciousness. <4> So the Children of Israel are those humans who strive to bring the whole universe to higher consciousness and Pure Consciousness. <5> Also these chapters of Genesis show the struggle of the Israelites to find a land where they could settle in and start their nation.

<6> Eventually they settled in Egypt. However, after some time, the Egyptians enslaved them and made their lives miserable. In order for the Hebrews to become stronger and multiply their numbers, they had to go through this long period of struggle. This was foretold by God (Gen. 15:12-14).

<7> In Exodus, the great heroic legend of the Israelites and how God helped them go out of Egypt shows how God waited all this time to see the Elected Ones increase in number and to reincarnate all the good seed that had reached higher consciousness in that race.

<8> By leaving Egypt through the instructions given by the Lord, by the Laws which were revealed to Moses, through their suffering in the desert, and by multiplying their numbers, the Israelites became ready as the mighty nation. With these qualities and through their long struggle, they created great characteristics which are necessary for any group in order to advance and bring about a new change in the world.

<9> That is what God had planned to do. The Israelites were chosen to bring about a new understanding of the reality of God. They were set aside to destroy the superstitious and false religions which were practiced by many. However, their most important mission was to make humans realize that the proper environment is necessary for spiritual progress, which means the establishment of the Kingdom Of Heaven On Earth (✡), with Him as the King, is a must.

<10> The conquest of the promised land by the Israelites is finished at the end of Joshua [there is no "j" in the Hebrew language so it is actually "Y'shua," which itself is a cor-

rupt pronunciation of the sacred name of the son (יהוה)].

<11> After the conquering of the land was finished, the system of government was left in the hands of the judges. They were supposed to receive their instructions from the Lord. However, because of the cruelty of the time and the minds of the people, these positions were left in the hands of the warriors. <12> People thought that if someone was a good warrior, he would be a good judge also. They were in the state of praising the mighty men of war (Ksattriyas).

<13> However, this system failed and the people requested that there be a human king. <14> People rejected God as their King (I Samuel 8:7). This was the greatest mistake any man or nation could make and was the mark of the failure of the Israelites. <15> They chose Saul as their king, who was a mighty man, vigorous and handsome.

<16> However, God reincarnated a Great Soul as David, who was fair in appearance but was in tune with God's Will.

Tablet Five

<1> David was the grandson of Ruth. Ruth was a foreigner who accepted the God of Israel (the only God) as her Lord and put her trust in Him. She was kind and considerate, so she received the favor of God, and He made her grandson, David, the greatest king of Israel. <2> With this doing, God showed that the Elected Ones are not those who call themselves "chosen people" but are those who accept Him as their God and obey His Laws.

<3> King David brought the symbol of a great king (✡). With his unparalleled wisdom, he understood the meaning of the sign of the Children of Abraham (✡) which means that with great organization (△) and with the application of justice (▽), the Kingdom Of Heaven On Earth can be established. <4> However, this Kingdom is impossible if the leaders do not follow the Laws of God and do not listen to His Voice, which comes to them by The Holy Ghost and through His Prophets.

<5> We can see that it is in the book of Kings that the first real sign of corruption of the Israelites started. The reason is, the kings of Israel started to forget God and were caught up in their false egos. They thought the power and might came from themselves. <6> It is always true that the leaders have the greatest effect over their people. When leaders forget about their God and their religion, the people will surely also abandon theirs. <7> That is why Prophets started coming to the scene of the history of Israel. It was only the Prophets who were left to think about God, understand His Will, and warn people to go back to Him.

<8> However, as we can see, the people became more and more corrupt. Eventually they reached such a point that they completely lost the reason and purpose for which they had been chosen (✡).

<9> So, the Israelites lost their strength and might. They became involved in the small aspects of life and abandoned their religion by accepting others' beliefs. They lost to the Assyrians because whatever God had given to make them strong had been forgotten. <10> They did not listen to the Prophets that God had sent them. Therefore, they became lost.

<11> **If a person closes his ears to the truth and does not want to hear what the reality of life is, even gods cannot help him.** That is why the Children of Israel became lost sheep.

<12> However, after exile the Jews returned and tried to re-establish their traditions. <13> But the religion had been so diluted by other beliefs that it did not seem possible. This task was undertaken by Ezra.

<14> Before the fall of Jerusalem, many Prophets warned the people that a great disaster would befall them because of their sins. This shows how the Law of Karma works and punishes wrongdoers. Again, at the same time, most of these Prophets had prophesied that the people in exile would return to Judah later on.

<15> This means that after each punishment, people, nations, communities, or humans in general will be given another chance to follow the Laws of God and bring the Kingdom Of Heaven On Earth. Unfortunately, humans keep making the same mistakes again and again. <16> They should suffer the consequences of their actions until all understand how this universe works and come into harmony (His Grace) with it.

HOLIEST THREE

Tablet One

<1> It was at this time that the Prophets longed for another great Messenger to come and re-establish the faith, and that is when the coming of the Messiah was prophesied. <2> Also because of the rising of the consciousness of the human, the new Messenger would preach a new faith which was more suitable for that higher consciousness. "You do not put new wine into old skins" (Matthew 9:17). <3> Furthermore, the coming of the Messiah (Shiloh) was prophesied by Jacob (Israel) (Gen. 49:10) and by God as the owner of the scepter.

<4> Jesus came as the Messiah [this is not his real name – his birth name most probably was Esa ("E" as in "Emmanuel," "S" as in "Sample" and "A" as in "Anointed"). In the rest of the book we use this name as his name. For more detail, read The Glossary under "Jesus."]. <5> He came to bring salvation to the reach of the masses. His new teaching was, besides other things, to show how sacrifice (not being self-centered) is necessary for establishing the Kingdom Of Heaven On Earth and to warn the Jews that God will take the Kingdom from them and give it to another nation. <6> He also gathered the Children of Israel (people) together as prophesied by Jacob (read Children of Abram (Abraham), All Prophecies Are Fulfilled).

<7> With all the revisions that have been made of the Bible, a summary of the real teaching of Christ, which was given directly to his disciples (not to the multitudes) can be found in chapters 5 and 6 of Matthew. Also chapter 7 is important in his teachings, and was given both to the multitudes and his disciples.

<8> In chapter 5, verses 1 to 10 describe humans in different levels of progress. From verse 10 to the end, the teaching is how those who want to follow the truth should endure, be true, and set an example by their actions, until they become perfect as the Father and radiate His Truth through themselves.

<9> Chapter 6 is a continuation of chapter 5. It also contains the prayer and instructions to his disciples of how they should become detached from this external world if they want to be(come) an instrument to do His Will and work.

<10> Chapter 7 is given to the multitudes and his disciples. The teachings in this chapter are: "Do not judge," "Do unto others as you expect others to do unto you," "Seek the truth and it will be revealed to you," and others.

<11> The rest of the chapter describes that only those who do whatever he teaches can have hope to enter the Kingdom Of Heaven, not those who talk and do not do.

<12> Only chapter 5 is described below. A commentary on the first 23 chapters of Matthew has also been revealed in the book, Commentaries on St. Matthew (Chapters 1-23).

THE HOLIEST BOOK

Tablet Two

CHRISTIANITY

MATTHEW Chapter 5

"And seeing the multitudes, he went up into a mountain: and when he was set, his disciples came unto him:" (Matthew 5:1)

"And he opened his mouth, and taught them, saying," (Matthew 5:2)

<1> He taught these things to his disciples, not to the people, because the multitudes were only interested in favors and miracles, not the truth.

"Blessed are the poor in spirit: for theirs is the kingdom of heaven." (Matthew 5:3)

<2> The poor in spirit refers to those refined Souls who hate evildoings and false teachings ("deeds of the Nicolaitanes" Rev. 2:6). They intuitively know that there is more in life than only physiological satisfaction, safety needs, and pursuance of Maya (worldly attraction).

<3> Therefore, they long for that lasting happiness. They will come to this conclusion that the Kingdom Of Heaven is only within. So they forsake society and try to find the Kingdom Of Heaven within. They become escapists. <4> That is why people will call them poor in spirit, because they do not have the courage to face hardship. So they inherit the Kingdom Of Heaven within, only.

"Blessed are they that mourn: for they shall be comforted." (Matthew 5:4)

<5> (☯) Those poor in spirit who have overcome being escapists and instead try to stay in society – "thy first love" (Rev. 2:4) – are those who mourn. They are poor in spirit and hate evildoings and false teachings, and they see so much wrongdoing and inequity in society. So they mourn over being oppressed in that environment and are very unhappy as to why they do not receive their fair share. They shall be comforted when the Kingdom Of Heaven On Earth comes, and they will receive their fair share.

"Blessed are the meek: for they shall inherit the earth." (Matthew 5:5)

<6> (✡) When a person mourns for a while and no one listens to him, he realizes that he is too powerless to be able to gain whatever he wants. So he starts to conform instead of mourn. He becomes a meek person; he becomes submissive. He will endure suffering with patience and without resentment.

<7> However, these are the first people who will submit themselves when the Kingdom Of Heaven comes, and because they consist of the majority of the people, they will inherit the earth.

"Blessed are they which do hunger and thirst after righteousness: for they shall be filled." (Matthew 5:6)

<8> (✝) A meek person, however, after

being submissive for some time will realize that the reason for all his and others' suffering is because of the lack of righteousness in all levels of society. That is when he will create a strong desire for righteousness. He hungers and thirsts for righteousness to be established. These are the ones who will be filled when the Kingdom Of Heaven On Earth is established and righteousness restored.

"Blessed are the merciful: for they shall obtain mercy." (Matthew 5:7)

<9> (☾) If a person progresses more in understanding himself (overcoming the false ego), he will realize that in all the last four stages, he has been following the demands of his own false ego. He was unhappy about society and was trying to change it because he wanted a fair share for himself.

<10> He had been in his first three chakras which are related to the false ego. However, when he overcomes being selfish about what he wants himself then he creates a great compassion for those in distress. He realizes that overcoming ego is a hard thing, so he creates compassion for those who are lost because of their false egos. He becomes merciful. So he himself will obtain mercy from heaven.

"Blessed are the pure in heart: for they shall see God." (Matthew 5:8)

<11> (✹) A pure in heart is one whose innermost character, feelings, and inclinations are free from moral fault or guilt. He is a man after God's own heart. He is a man who not only is merciful, but has created a universal point of view with utmost compassion for all things in it, so he looks at the universe exactly the way God looks at it. <12> Therefore, he will start to understand how God feels about all things in His universe, and he can see God face-to-face in all the manifested universe.

"Blessed are the peacemakers: for they shall be called the children of God." (Matthew 5:9)

<13> (✡) A peacemaker is one who brings harmony, tranquility, or quietness to people internally and externally. These are the ones who not only have reached the state of being pure in heart, but are actively engaged in establishing the Kingdom Of Heaven On Earth (establishing Daharma) in order to bring that harmony and tranquility to the world. They are the real Paravipras, who with their spiritual understanding and powers, bring the Kingdom Of Heaven On Earth. They are the children of God, because they have completely realized His Will and are trying to fulfill it. They are good children of God.

"Blessed are they which are persecuted for righteousness' sake: for theirs is the kingdom of heaven." (Matthew 5:10)

<14> (卍) These are the ones who have already reached a very high consciousness or Pure Consciousness and have come back to earth in order to establish the righteousness. They have no interest in this external material world for any selfish desires, but are interested in the establishment of the Kingdom Of Heaven On Earth in order to see that the proper environment is created for all to progress physically, mentally, and spiritually. They have no fear of being persecuted for their ideology and goal, because they know eternal life is everlasting and forever.

<15> Theirs is the Kingdom Of Heaven (within and without), because these are the ones who are really worthy to assume the leadership of humanity. They will be the Great Paravipras (Maha-Paravipras) who will establish and maintain the Kingdom Of Heaven On Earth.

<16> In reality the teaching of Esa finishes here. The rest of chapter 5 is the description of the characteristics of a Paravipra.

Tablet Three

"Blessed are ye, when men shall revile you, and persecute you, and shall say all manner of evil against you falsely, for my sake." (Matthew 5:11)

<1> His disciples were also of those who would be persecuted for righteousness. The

reason humans persecute these people and "say all manner of evil against [them] falsely" is because most men are in their lower natures and do not want to go out of them.

<2> That is where they have been all their lives and had been taught that this is the way to live. So they feel more comfortable to conform than fight against these false teachings and power of Maya (lower nature).

<3> That is why those who go against this rule will become outcasts, different, and hated by people. The reason is that intuitively deep inside, each person longs to go to his higher self and break the bondages of this world and lower nature. However, it needs a very brave person to do so. That is why when a person starts to progress in the spiritual path, he is suddenly confronted with so much opposition.

<4> It seems that everyone is trying to stop him. Yet if he refuses to listen to them to stay in his lower nature, they will hate him. <5> That is also one of the reasons why after a period of time the religions become diluted by people. The teachings of the founder (Prophet) seem very hard to follow. So a simpler doctrine suited to their own lower natures is adopted, and the truth becomes lost by simplified dogmas.

<6> That is when the religion dies but its followers will not throw away this dead religion and instead hold onto it until it becomes so distorted that it rots the whole society, "and their dead bodies shall lie in the street of the great city [earth], which spiritually is called Sodom and Egypt;..." (Rev. 11:8).

"Rejoice, and be exceeding glad: for great is your reward in heaven: for so persecuted they the prophets which were before you." (Matthew 5:12)

<7> This process has been repeated time after time in the past. Those who are chosen should keep their "eyes single" toward the goal. They should rejoice in their path of struggle, because, "strait is the gate, and narrow is the way, which leadeth into life, and few there be that find it." (Matthew 7:14).

"Ye are the salt of the earth: but if the salt have lost his savour, wherewith shall it be salted? it is thenceforth good for nothing, but to be cast out, and to be trodden under foot of men." (Matthew 5:13)

<8> This whole universe was created so that man might reach Pure Consciousness. So those who find the way and try to become Pure Consciousness are the ones who make this system worthwhile, not those who stay in their lower natures and refuse to fulfill the Darma of the universe. That is why those who progress in this path are "the salt of the earth," which gives savour to the world.

<9> However, if these people who have reached some progress fall back, their fall will be great. They will crash to nothingness and become more unworthy than a man in his lower nature. That is why they will be "good for nothing, but to be cast out, and to be trodden under foot of men."

"Ye are the light of the world. A city that is set on a hill cannot be hid." (Matthew 5:14)

<10> But those who continue their struggle and progress further in the path to become the light of the world will shine, and they cannot hide it.

"Neither do men light a candle, and put it under a bushel, but on a candlestick; and it giveth light unto all that are in the house." (Matthew 5:15)

<11> These people should accept their responsibilities to humanity and become a guiding light for them.

"Let your light so shine before men, that they may see your good works, and glorify your Father which is in heaven." (Matthew 5:16)

<12> Shine in the world by your great actions, but surrender the result to the Lord. Become a channel for His Divine actions and glorify Him. When people praise you for what you do, let them know that it is He who does these great works through you. That is the way to be freed from the bondage of karma.

<13> If a person lets Him do the great ac-

tions through him, then the real doer is not he but He. So there will not be a false ego created by the person, and then he is free from any trace of separateness from Him and will dissolve his ego into the Universal Ego. <14> He will become one with Him, a submissive one.

"Think not that I am come to destroy the law, or the prophets: I am not come to destroy, but to fulfil." (Matthew 5:17)

<15> Each Prophet comes to further the understanding of humanity by his new teachings and to clarify some points from the old, "to fulfil."

"For verily I say unto you, Till heaven and earth pass, one jot or one tittle shall in no wise pass from the law, till all be fulfilled." (Matthew 5:18)

<16> The Universal Laws (Darmas) cannot be broken. All will understand this truth and become it, "till all be fulfilled."

"Whosoever therefore shall break one of these least commandments, and shall teach men so, he shall be called least in the kingdom of heaven: but whosoever shall do and teach them, the same shall be called great in the kingdom of heaven." (Matthew 5:19)

<17> Whoever tries to break these Laws will break himself against them, and whoever follows them will reach Pure Consciousness, "shall be called great in the kingdom of heaven."

"For I say unto you, That except your righteousness shall exceed the righteousness of the scribes and Pharisees, ye shall in no case enter into the kingdom of heaven." (Matthew 5:20)

<18> Pharisees and scribes used to teach but not follow what they taught. So to become greater than them, a person not only should teach but also he should follow his teachings.

<19> Also Pharisees and scribes taught the Torah and Ten Commandments, <20> but Esa taught that the goal is not just **not** to sin, but is to reach such a state that no desire is left to sin.

Tablet Four

"Ye have heard that it was said by them of old time, Thou shalt not kill; and whosoever shall kill [murder] shall be in danger of the judgment;" (Matthew 5:21)

"But I say unto you, That whosoever is angry with his brother without a cause shall be in danger of the judgment: and whosoever shall say to his brother, Raca, shall be in danger of the council: but whosoever shall say, Thou fool, shall be in danger of hell fire." (Matthew 5:22)

<1> The goal is not "Do not murder," but to reach such a state of consciousness that you would have complete control over your mind and would not become angry without a cause, would not curse any person, and would not judge ("shall say, thou fool").

"Therefore if thou bring thy gift to the altar, and there rememberest that thy brother hath ought against thee;" (Matthew 5:23)

"Leave there thy gift before the altar, and go thy way; first be reconciled to thy brother, and then come and offer thy gift." (Matthew 5:24)

<2> Reaching that state of purification of body, mind, and spirit is necessary. So search your Soul and find the impurities within and overcome them. After you have cleansed yourself then you might be able to approach the Lord.

<3> You have to approach the Lord with a pure heart and free of any guilt, because with an impure soul one cannot see Him or know Him. Only the pure in heart can see God (verse 8). <4> This impurity also was the reason that Adam and Eve hid themselves from the presence of the Lord. An impure person

might try to pray or approach Him, but he will not benefit very much.

<5> However, this should not discourage people from going to Him. In fact, the process of overcoming is to go toward Him, which is equal to increasing the awareness of these impurities, bringing them to the light, and confronting them face-to-face. Then they will be dissolved effortlessly. <6> He desires us to go to Him. He forgives us. He desired to see Adam, but Adam could not forgive himself!

"Agree with thine adversary quickly, whiles thou art in the way with him; lest at any time the adversary deliver thee to the judge, and the judge deliver thee to the officer, and thou be cast into prison." (Matthew 5:25)

<7> Do not become involved in disputes and mundane things in life. Leave them to those who are drowned in Maya. Be satisfied with whatever you have with no attachments to them so you can concentrate on higher things and progress in becoming great.

"Verily I say unto thee, Thou shalt by no means come out thence, till thou hast paid the uttermost farthing." (Matthew 5:26)

<8> However, if you were accused of something, act in such a way that you would leave no doubt in others and your own mind of your honesty.

"Ye have heard that it was said by them of old time, Thou shalt not commit adultery:" (Matthew 5:27)

"But I say unto you, That whosoever looketh on a woman to lust after her hath committed adultery with her already in his heart." (Matthew 5:28)

<9> The goal is not, "Do not do adultery," but to reach a state of consciousness where even no desire to do adultery or lust is left.

"And if thy right eye offend thee, pluck it out, and cast it from thee: for it is profitable for thee that one of thy members should perish, and not that thy whole body should be cast into hell." (Matthew 5:29)

"And if thy right hand offend thee, cut it off, and cast it from thee; for it is profitable for thee that one of thy members should perish, and not that thy whole body should be cast into hell." (Matthew 5:30)

<10> Whatever is an obstacle in your path to reach that state (Divinity, Pure Consciousness) where no desire is left to do sin should be destroyed, no matter how dear it is to you.

"It hath been said, Whosoever shall put away his wife, let him give her a writing of divorcement:" (Matthew 5:31)

"But I say unto you, That whosoever shall put away his wife, saving for the cause of fornication, causeth her to commit adultery: and whosoever shall marry her that is divorced committeth adultery." (Matthew 5:32)

<11> A husband and wife are each other's soulmates who become as one. So they should avoid divorce as much as possible. <12> Also couples and families are the base and blocks from which society is built. If these blocks are not strong, then the whole society will collapse. So even if married couples are not made up of the true corresponding parts, still they can become a strong base for society with a little sacrifice. <13> So divorce for small causes brings great harm.

"Again, ye have heard that it hath been said by them of old time, Thou shalt not forswear thyself, but shalt perform unto the Lord thine oaths:" (Matthew 5:33)

"But I say unto you, Swear not at all; neither by heaven; for it is God's throne:" (Matthew 5:34)

"Nor by the earth; for it is his footstool: neither by Jerusalem; for it is the city of the great King." (Matthew 5:35)

"Neither shalt thou swear by thy head, because thou canst not make one hair white or black." (Matthew 5:36)

"But let your communication be, Yea, yea; Nay, nay: for whatsoever is more than these cometh of evil." (Matthew 5:37)

<14> The goal is to be(come) the truth itself, and a person in truth does not have to swear at all. To reach this state you should refrain from idle talk, because idle talk "cometh of evil."

"Ye have heard that it hath been said, An eye for an eye, and a tooth for a tooth:" (Matthew 5:38)

"But I say unto you, That ye resist not evil: but whosoever shall smite thee on thy right cheek, turn to him the other also." (Matthew 5:39)

"And if any man will sue thee at the law, and take away thy coat, let him have thy cloak also." (Matthew 5:40)

"And whosoever shall compel thee to go a mile, go with him twain." (Matthew 5:41)

<15> Forgive those who do bad to you, and make the aggressor ashamed of his actions by showing forgiveness and detachment.

<16> It should be kept in mind that the teachings of Christ are for individual progress and are related to the acts a person does to become perfect – to be(come) detached in overcoming the lower nature and an instrument to manifest His qualities.

<17> However, there is another side of human life and that is the relationship of man with society and the external world. Therefore, to complete these teachings of forgiveness it should be taught: <18> **Forgive whatever wrong has been done to you, but forgive not wrong done to society**.

<19> That is why Prophet Muhammad taught that if someone smites you, smite him back, because his teaching is more socially-oriented and Christ's teaching is individually-oriented.

"Give to him that asketh thee, and from him that would borrow of thee turn not thou away." (Matthew 5:42)

<20> Be helpful to others in need as much as you can. Help others with knowledge, not from ignorance (helping the wrong person, or at the wrong time, or in the wrong place), or from passion (expecting something in return).

"Ye have heard that it hath been said, Thou shalt love thy neighbor, and hate thine enemy." (Matthew 5:43)

"But I say unto you, Love your enemies, bless them that curse you, do good to them that hate you, and pray for them which despitefully use you, and persecute you;" (Matthew 5:44)

"That ye may be the children of your Father which is in heaven: for he maketh his sun to rise on the evil and on the good, and sendeth rain on the just and on the unjust." (Matthew 5:45)

<21> In order to become like the Father (His son), you have to be(come) indiscriminating in your Love (create compassion), as God gives to both the good and the sinners. <22> Even if He punishes someone, it is for that person's good so he might receive a lesson and progress further toward his goal. <23> So be like Him and do all things with compassion (corrective and unconditional Love) toward the whole universe.

"For if ye love them which love you, what reward have ye? do not even the publicans the same?" (Matthew 5:46)

"And if ye salute your brethren only, what do ye more than others? do not even the publicans so?" (Matthew 5:47)

<24> If you do not love everything, because everything is He, then it shows that you still have your separated ego as "I" and only love those who love "I," and hate those who hate "I."

<25> Is not this the way for those who have a false separated ego? In order to be different and perfect, look upon all things as being manifested from God and are God. <26> So love all things because they are God. Look

at everything as God looks. Even when you punish a person, do it for the sake of correction, not from hate.

"Be ye therefore perfect, even as your Father which is in heaven is perfect." (Matthew 5:48)

<27> That is exactly what the goal of life is, to be(come) as perfect as God, to be(come) Divine, Pure Consciousness, the Law. <28> The goal is to reach this point. It is not to try to follow a set of rules, regulations, and Commandments but to become those Commandments. <29> It does not mean that the Laws and Commandments are destroyed by these teachings, but the true way is shown: To implement them by purification of one's existence (physically, mentally, and spiritually), or to reach that purity of God.

<30> Then you become the same as the Father. God is the Law so you also become the Law, or perfect. <31> Until you reach there, any Commandments, Laws, or teachings are only words, yet they show the way. <32> When you do reach there, then you do the Laws and follow the Commandments without even thinking about them.

<33> So, "Be ye therefore perfect, even as your Father which is in heaven is perfect."

<34> Once again we can see how all these things are related to **The Greatest Sign**. By becoming perfect, you become as God in heaven. You reach Pure Consciousness (✺).

<35> As it was explained, chapter 6 is also the teaching to his disciples in order to become great and detach themselves so as to be able to do His work.

<36> Chapter 7 is a warning to false prophets and those who do not follow his teachings but still think they can be disciples of Christ. Many will think that they can enter the Kingdom Of Heaven by assuming they are disciples of Christ and following misleading teachings. <37> But only those who follow His true teachings and do His Will can have hope to be saved by Him.

Tablet Five

CHRISTIANITY AFTER CHRIST, AND REVELATION OF THE REVELATION

<1> After Christianity started to flourish and was accepted by the Elected Ones, its followers were persecuted because of its depth, truth, and being against the worldly interests of many. However, it could not be stopped, because of the vigorous preaching of the true gospel by Christ's disciples and their willingness to sacrifice all things for their ideology.

<2> So, many churches were founded, and with the great struggle by Christ's disciples and many others, the seed of Christianity was planted.

<3> However, as it is revealed in the books after the four gospels in the <u>Bible</u>, from the very beginning many false teachers wished to influence Christ's teachings in one way or another (Acts 8:1-24, Jude 4). The apostles fought vigorously with these influences and somehow established a pure ideology of Christ's teachings.

<4> These true teachings lasted about four hundred years until Christianity was accepted by Rome's emperors and then by the majority of the people.

<5> Thousands of people started to accept Christianity as their religion. But they did not want to give up their previous beliefs completely and follow Christianity wholeheartedly. Many of these people had previously followed the worshipping of the sun god. They had many pagan ideas, festivals, holidays, etc., but their religions lacked the universal outlook. They believed in the sun god, but Christians believed in the Father, the universal, invisible God who had complete power over the whole universe, even over the sun.

<6> Also the concept of Christ as being born from a virgin mother (which he was) fit into the belief of the followers of Mithra (sun god of Zoroastrians) that Mithra would be

born from a virgin to save the world. Many of the Romans were followers of Mithra.

<7> With all these factors presented, and also because of the freedom-loving and democratic ideals of the Romans, people were left to make anything they wanted out of Christianity.

<8> The sun god was replaced by the son of God. The Virgin Mary took the place of the Virgin Mother. The Saturday Sabbath was changed to Sunday (their day of worshipping the sun), God's festivals (revealed in chapter 23 of Leviticus in the Bible as Holy Days to keep for ever and ever) with pagan festivals (refer to encyclopedias about the origin of Christian festivals). <9> In fact, Passover, the Feast of the Tabernacles, and other Holy Days of God were observed by the apostles and many of their followers until about 700 A.D. Many other things were changed which cannot be found in the Bible but are now followed by many.

<10> However, those who were to be saved by him were saved in the first four hundred years of Christianity. Those who had not been saved eventually will be after many lifetimes or in future creations.

<11> This is, however, a historical explanation. These happenings were revealed many centuries before they occurred in the prophecies in the book of Daniel (the dream of King Nebuchadnezzar, the vision of the four beasts, and the vision of the ram and the he goat), and in The Revelation (the third church, Rev. 2:12-16).

<12> In the visions of Daniel, the little horn, which is the symbol of the intellectualization of things, is prophesied to change the true religions "the same made war with the saints" (Daniel 7:21), and to try to replace the truth by believing that the intellect of man is superior to all things (read Commentaries on Prophecies in Daniel, Period of Intellectual Domination).

<13> Also, in The Revelation, the last book of the Bible, in the message to the third church (which is the third sign in **The Greatest Sign**, the cross), it is revealed that in this church there are still some who "hold the doctrine of Balaam,…" (Rev. 2:14). The "doctrine of Balaam" is the pagan ideas and festivals which entered into this third church.

<14> So God had revealed many centuries before what will happen in the future. Now it is time for the human to see the limits of his intellect and understandings, then surrender himself to God and the words revealed through His Prophets, and overcome the confusion between them by understanding **The Greatest Sign**. Then the glory of God will be realized and His Kingdom will come on earth as it is in heaven.

<15> Because these things should have happened and because intellectual domination should have continued for two thousand three hundred years – "unto two thousand and three hundred days" (Daniel 8:14) – and also because God had a Master Plan in the future to be fulfilled and He wanted to complete His great book (Bible) as one of the bases for all religions, He revealed The Revelation as the last book of the Bible.

<16> The first book in the Bible (Genesis) is the description of creation and other events which can be viewed as an introduction to the Bible and that which would happen later on.
<17> The Revelation is the last book or the summary and conclusion of the Bible (like a good book with an introduction, main part, with summary and conclusion at the end).

<18> The Revelation, therefore, can be viewed as a mini-Bible. Also it reveals the whole Plan of God, what will happen in the future, and how. So, whoever understands the first book (Genesis) and the last book (The Revelation) can understand the rest of the Bible also. The description of some important verses in The Revelation follows.

THE REVELATION

<19> The second and third chapters of The Revelation have a twofold purpose. First of all, they are a prophecy of what had happened in the past, what was happening at the time they were revealed, and what would happen in the future.

<20> At the same time, they are related

to each individual's progress on the spiritual path.

<21> From chapter 4 on, it is explained what had happened, what is happening, what will happen to humanity, and how only those who overcome the pitfalls of the spiritual path, which are related to each chakra, can really understand all the realities in the Scriptures. Those humans will eventually establish the Kingdom Of Heaven On Earth.

<22> Some of the verses of the book of The Revelation are given here. For a complete commentary on the book, read the book Revelation of The Revelation.

Tablet Six

Chapter 1

"John to the seven churches which are in Asia: Grace be unto you, and peace, from him which is, and which was, and which is to come; and from the seven Spirits which are before his throne;" (Rev. 1:4)

<1> Why are the seven churches in Asia? It is because all the great Prophets of the seven churches have come from there. **<2>** At the same time, the mystery of the seven energy centers of the body (chakras) was revealed to humanity in this region (Asia), through the Far East Philosophies (Vedas, etc.).

<3> What are those seven spirits? They are the seven truths that lead a man to become a son of God. **<4>** They are the seven spheres of the universe. As the body of the man has seven chakras, also the universe has seven spheres which are called "Lokas."

"Behold, he cometh with clouds; and every eye shall see him, and they also which pierced him: and all kindreds of the earth shall wail because of him. Even so, Amen." (Rev. 1:7)

<5> "Cloud" means confusion. He comes whenever confusion comes to humanity. "When righteousness is weak and faints, and unrighteousness exults in pride [confusion], then my Soul arises on earth" (Bhagavad-Gita 4:7). **<6>** "Every eye shall see him" means that those who have their eyes (third eyes) opened will see him. "They also which pierced him" means that those who pierced him will be reincarnated also and see his glory.

<7> Also when it is said he will come from the sky, the sky is the same as heaven, and heaven means Pure Consciousness. So he will come from Pure Consciousness to help those who need him. He comes as an Avatar.

"I am Alpha and Omega, the beginning and the ending,…" (Rev. 1:8)

<8> "I was, I am, and I will be," also it means "I AM" everything.

"I was in the Spirit on the Lord's day, and heard behind me a great voice, as of a trumpet." (Rev. 1:10)

<9> "I was in the Spirit" means "I was in a trance." The "voice of a trumpet" is the sound of many waterfalls (OM ॐ) which can be heard in higher consciousness.

"…seven golden candlesticks;" (Rev. 1:12)

<10> The seven golden candlesticks are the seven chakras. When a human masters the chakras, they become a golden light for his guidance. **<11>** At the same time, the seven candlesticks represent the Light for each religion in **The Greatest Sign**, as do the seven churches, each church for one religion.

"…one like unto the Son of man,…" (Rev. 1:13)

<12> John was not sure that the being he saw was the Son of man, or Christ. He could have been anyone. That means each person has the potential to reach Christhood (Pure Consciousness). In fact, it was John's own Soul.

"And he had in his right hand seven stars: and out of his mouth went a sharp twoedged sword:…" (Rev. 1:16)

<13> The seven stars are the seven truths that have been revealed to humanity through Christ. We can say that each star refers to the Prophet of each seal, which symbolically represents each religion or truth in **The Greatest Sign**.

<14> "A sharp twoedged sword" is the truth which comes out of the mouth of a realized Soul (in Christ Consciousness) or from the mouth of Christ. This sword cuts through superstitions and ignorance, dispels the darkness, and brings light and truth to humanity.

"And when I saw him, I fell at his feet as dead. And he laid his right hand upon me, saying unto me, Fear not; I am the first and the last:" (Rev. 1:17)

<15> What John really had seen was his own spirit of truth which is within all humans. The person who begins spiritual practices becomes fearful of meditating because seeing the truth within is hard. That is why when he saw who he was, "one like unto the Son of man" (which is his own Soul), he was afraid and "fell at his feet as dead."

<16> However, the Soul is kind and humble. That is why he (the Soul) "laid his right hand upon" John and comforted him by saying, "Fear not: I am the first and the last," which means, "I will be with you in your progress from the very beginning to the end."

"I am he that liveth, and was dead; and, behold, I am alive for evermore, Amen; and have the keys of hell and of death." (Rev. 1:18)

<17> "I am he that liveth, and was dead" means, "I have come from ignorance, which is the state of deadness, to life, which is the state of Pure Consciousness."

<18> "I am alive for evermore" means, "I am in Pure Consciousness. I have overcome the power of the tama guna over my Soul. Therefore, I gained the eternal life."

<19> "And have the keys of hell and of death" means, "I have mastered the power of the tama guna, which brings man to hell and death (ignorance). I have the truth which can release you from this hell and death."

"Write the things which thou hast seen, and the things which are, and the things which shall be hereafter;" (Rev. 1:19)

<20> This verse means, "Write the things which have happened, are happening, and will happen." Therefore, <u>The Revelation</u> is a brief explanation of the Plan of the Lord God that will guide humans from ignorance to the state of Pure Consciousness (full realization of the reality behind this universe). It is an explanation of what happened in the beginning of the formation of the new race (generation) after Noah, and how the Lord God will bring the human to the realization that he should only utilize this body and all the gifts related to this body for reaching Pure Consciousness.

<21> This brief and most important book of the <u>Bible</u> (<u>The Revelation</u>) shows how following the false ego, being under the influence of the power of the tama guna, and being attracted to the power of Maya will lead the human to destruction and death (ignorance).

<22> We can say that this book is a miniature <u>Bible</u>. It reveals the real purpose of creation and shows how all things have happened so far in order to bring humanity to this point where everything seems so confusing. By understanding <u>The Revelation</u> and the truth underlying **The Greatest Sign** and history, we can see that really there is no confusion left. Only then can we realize the compassion and mercy of our Lord God, be able to appreciate all things in this universe, and find our way to the goal (Pure Consciousness, Christ Consciousness, God, etc.).

Tablet Seven

Chapter 2

<1> Chapters 2 and 3 are messages that are sent to the seven churches. Each church can be viewed as one psychic center, and at the same time can refer to one symbol in **The Greatest Sign** and its corresponding religions.

<2> Each message contains the meaning of one of those churches, the pitfalls in that stage and how they should be avoided, and eventually what is the reward of overcoming these pitfalls.

"Unto the angel of the church of Ephesus write; These things saith he that holdeth the seven stars in his right hand, who walketh in the midst of the seven golden candlesticks;" (Rev. 2:1)

<3> The church of Ephesus can be viewed as the first chakra. <4> At the same time, it refers to the first awakening of the consciousness (☯) and latent spiritual forces (☯) in the human (first step in the **Eternal Divine Path**).

<5> "Who walketh in the midst of the seven golden candlesticks" shows that it is Christ who revealed all the truth of the religions to humanity. <6> Another meaning is that each person is a consciousness in the middle of his chakras, as Arjuna (<u>Bhagavad-Gita</u>) struggling to overcome the lower nature, so becoming Christ (Krishna).

"I know thy works, and thy labor, and thy patience, and how thou canst not bear them which are evil: and thou hast tried them which say they are apostles, and are not, and hast found them liars:" (Rev. 2:2)

<7> Who are these people that awaken their consciousnesses which are in the first chakra, or those who for the first time open their eyes more to the realities of their environment and the goal of their lives? These are the poor in spirit (Matthew 5:3) who have worked hard to obtain real satisfaction in their lives. Instead they find more and more evil going on in the society around them. They try to find real guidance ("apostles") in order to be led to the truth. Instead they find that all those who consider themselves to be teachers and guides are liars, or are as lost as themselves.

<8> That is why the person becomes discouraged, as he sees all the plays people engage in to get by in life. He or she sets out to search for the truth. That is the reason the yogis left the regular life and isolated themselves in mountains or jungles to find the truth within, because they felt the truth could not be found by following men.

<9> Therefore, the first symbol in our **Sign** (☯) is related to the teachings of the Far East (Mystical Paths), which work to awaken or raise the latent consciousness from the first chakra to higher chakras.

<10> However, as long as man is lost in the attraction of the external world and gets along with the plays of society, he will not even search to find what the real truth is. When he finds that all the guidance he used to follow is as lost as himself, then he will start to search his own Soul in order to find the truth.

"And hast borne, and hast patience, and for my name's sake hast laboured, and hast not fainted." (Rev. 2:3)

<11> "And hast borne, and hast patience": Why have these people borne? They have endured because they became different. They stopped playing and became searchers of the truth. Society does not like those who are different. That is why they become outcasts and will endure hardships in their search for finding the truth. Their patience leads them to the truth.

<12> "For my name's sake": What is His Name? His name is "the truth." So they will bear persecution for the sake of the truth. Those who persist and do not faint will find it.

"Nevertheless I have somewhat against thee, because thou hast left thy first love." (Rev. 2:4)

<13> What was these people's first love? It was the external world. It was the society that they were first in love with. They tried to find the reality and the truth in it, but they did not. So they leave their first love. God is against it.

"Remember therefore from whence thou art fallen, and repent, and do the first works; or else I will come unto thee quickly, and will remove thy candlestick out of his place, except thou repent." (Rev. 2:5)

<14> The sentence, "Remember therefore from whence thou art fallen" completely shows what the "first love" means. The first love is where the person has first fallen from: The society. He or she has fallen from the society and became discouraged about its teachings and plays.

<15> "Do the first works": The first works are to bring others to this realization that the truth is only in spirit and to try to establish the Kingdom Of Heaven On Earth. Otherwise, "I will come unto thee quickly, and will remove thy candlestick out of his place." You will not reach anywhere, you will only become an escapist by leaving your first love, and you will lose further realization of the spiritual life. That is exactly what happened to the Far East. "Candlestick" means the light of guidance.

"But this thou hast, that thou hatest the deeds of the Nicolaitanes, which I also hate." (Rev. 2:6)

<16> The "deeds of the Nicolaitanes" are the evil things and false guidance in society. People who are poor in spirit are escapists and the Lord God does not want them to be that way (poor in spirit). Yet He likes them because they hate evil things and false guides ("Nicolaitanes") (refer to Rev. 2:2).

"He that hath an ear, let him hear what the Spirit saith unto the churches; To him that overcometh will I give to eat of the tree of life, which is in the midst of the paradise of God." (Rev. 2:7)

<17> "He that hath an ear, let him hear what the Spirit saith unto the churches" means that those who have their eyes (third eyes) opened will understand when the truth behind these revelations is explained, and what the message of the Spirit is to each church.

<18> "To him that overcometh will I give to eat of the tree of life" means that whoever understands that life is a struggle, and that a person should stay in society and perfect himself in order to set an example for others, "I will help him to reach Pure Consciousness, which is life eternal." <19> The tree of life is the pattern in which a person progresses in spiritual understanding, "which is in the midst of the paradise of God" or the human body. It can be referred to as the raising of the kundalini through the chakras.

<20> These people are the ones who were mourning and will be comforted (Matthew 5:4). They will eat of the tree of life and are the conquerors of the Souls ("conquering, and to conquer," Rev. 6:2).

"And unto the angel of the church in Smyrna write; These things saith the first and the last, which was dead, and is alive;" (Rev. 2:8)

<21> What is the church in Smyrna? It is the second symbol in our **Sign** (✡), the star of David (the seal of Solomon). It also refers to the second chakra.

"I know thy works, and tribulation, and poverty, (but thou art rich) and I know the blasphemy of them which say they are Jews, and are not, but are the synagogue of Satan." (Rev. 2:9)

<22> "I know thy works, and tribulation, and poverty" means that those who had overcome escapism will start to fight with evildoers and liars. They will go through tribulation, become outcasts, and be struck with poverty.

<23> "But thou art rich" means, "But you are rich in spirit and life, because you have an ideology for which to fight and a goal for which to strive." <24> However, those who lie, do evil, and are lost in Maya are rich in material things but are poor in spiritual wealth.

<25> "And I know the blasphemy of them which say they are Jews, and are not, but are the synagogue of Satan": Jews were supposed

to be the Children of Israel (those who struggle with God, or Elected Ones) and should have shown humanity that the Kingdom Of Heaven On Earth (✡) is necessary for human progress. They should have tried to establish it. Hence those who do not strive to bring this ideal are "the synagogue of Satan."

"Fear none of those things which thou shalt suffer: behold, the devil shall cast some of you into prison, that ye may be tried; and ye shall have tribulation ten days: be thou faithful unto death, and I will give thee a crown of life." (Rev. 2:10)

<26> "Fear none of those things" refers to suffering and being persecuted. Be faithful and do not fear death, because "I will give thee a crown of life." There is not such a thing as death for a realized Soul. He dies of knowledge and will gain eternal life. <27> It is true that in this state a person is in his second chakra. However, if he is so sincere as to be ready to sacrifice all, even his life, for truth and his ideology, then he has overcome the attraction of this external world. If a person who reaches this point, where nothing can stop him from fighting for truth, is killed, then he is martyred and becomes a martyr.

<28> Such a person will reach Pure Consciousness because he is worthy of it, "I will give thee a crown of life." This is also promised in both the Koran and Bhagavad-Gita. "A war to establish justice, such as this one, opens the doors of heaven. ... Happy is he who fights such a war. Not to fight such a righteous battle is to disregard your sacred duty and honor, and that is sin [transgression of the Law (Daharma)], Arjuna" (B.G. 2:32-33). "Do not think of those who are slain in the way of God [righteous war] as dead. No, indeed, they are with their Lord...." (Koran, The Family of Imran, Ali 'Imran, 169).

"...He that overcometh shall not be hurt of the second death." (Rev. 2:11)

<29> Those who overcome their fears and attachments to this external life will gain everlasting life. They will reach Pure Consciousness. These are the people who are meek, who will inherit the earth (Matthew 5:5) and will gain eternal life (Rev. 2:11). The power will be given to them to take peace from the earth (Rev. 6:4).

Tablet Eight

"And to the angel of the church in Pergamos write; These things saith he which hath the sharp sword with two edges;" (Rev. 2:12)

<1> What is the church in Pergamos? It is the third symbol (✝) in **The Greatest Sign**. It is the teaching of Christ, and the Angel is Esa. His teaching is the sharpest ("hath the sharp sword") and has a twofold meaning, literally and mystically, "with two edges."

<2> The sharp sword is the truth. Whoever is in Pure Consciousness will say the truth, which is sharp as a sword. The sharp sword is used only in the verses about the third sign, because who has the sharpest teaching among the Prophets? It is Esa. The four gospels are the most direct and sharpest teachings of the truth. They cut through the faults (if you understand them!)

<3> This church can also refer to the third chakra.

"I know thy works, and where thou dwellest, even where Satan's seat is: and thou holdest fast my name, and hast not denied my faith, even in those days wherein Antipas was my faithful martyr, who was slain among you, where Satan dwelleth." (Rev. 2:13)

<4> "Where Satan's seat is": The first three chakras are where a human is bound to the attraction of the external world and still greatly under the influence of the tama guna (Satan). Therefore whoever overcomes these three psychic energy centers knows "where Satan's seat is."

<5> That is why Esa taught that you have to be born again. To be born again means to

go from these first three chakras (lower nature) to the higher chakras (higher self). Or in other words, to crucify the false ego (lower self) so to be born again (resurrect) into the higher self and be glorified. That is why until you are born again, you are not saved. <6> In fact the very symbolic meaning of the crucifixion of Esa (symbol of the death of the false ego) and his resurrection is to show that you have to die first (your false ego) before you can be born again (resurrect to the higher self), "It is in dying that we are born to Eternal Life" (St. Francis of Assisi).

<7> "Antipas" is the true consciousness against the attraction of the external world which will be slain by these three chakras. By overcoming these first three chakras, you enter "the heart of the yogi" (the sacred heart) which is the place of unconditional Love (Mother, fourth chakra).

<8> Christianity is the symbol of this overcoming of these first three chakras. It is a symbol of individual achievement in detaching completely from Maya. He who overcomes the first three chakras overcomes evil (attraction of Maya) and is a true disciple of Christ.

"But I have a few things against thee, because thou hast there them that hold the doctrine of Balaam, who taught Balac to cast a stumblingblock before the children of Israel, to eat things sacrificed unto idols, and to commit fornication." (Rev. 2:14)

<9> However, still in this stage between overcoming the power of the first three chakras and entering the fourth chakra, man can be misled by false prophets and teachers in spiritual realities. He can fall from being a child of Israel (one who struggles with God) and be as lost as others.

"So hast thou also them that hold the doctrine of the Nicolaitanes, which thing I hate." (Rev. 2:15)

<10> The deeds of the Nicolaitanes are evildoings and false guidance. In the third chakra, the desire for power, prestige, and possession is dominating. Therefore, the pitfall is that a person might follow false guides or become one of them himself, and do evil from passion. That is what God does not like. He dislikes people who do evil or become false guides for their own desires to gain power, position, or prestige.

<11> Also, verses 14 and 15 refer to the influence of the Roman doctrines (pagan religions of Rome) and other false teachers who tried from the very beginning to influence Christ's teachings (Acts 8:1-24, Jude 4), and eventually did.

"Repent; or else I will come unto thee quickly, and will fight against them with the sword of my mouth." (Rev. 2:16)

<12> How did Christ fight with the Pharisees and scribes? He fought with his teaching, which was sharp and true like the sword. He came quickly and fought with the truth ("sword of my mouth") against those who were following false teachings (Balaam doctrine) and performing false doings (Nicolaitanes).

"...To him that overcometh will I give to eat of the hidden manna, and will give him a white stone, and in the stone a new name written, which no man knoweth saving he that receiveth it." (Rev. 2:17)

<13> He who overcomes the first three chakras will enter the fourth chakra, which is the center of love. The experience of bliss in this chakra is so great and the nectar that will be felt in the throat area is so unexplainable that the joy is not comparable with anything in this external world. That nectar is the "hidden manna."

<14> "And will give him a white stone, and in the stone a new name written." The white stone is the stone of purity (purified consciousness) and knowledge of God – not intellectual knowledge, but intuitive. The experience of eating of the hidden manna will bring that relationship with God where there is no mistake, you know that He exists. The "new name" is The Word, which is a vibration within you.

<15> These are the people who will hunger

and thirst for righteousness and will be filled (Matthew 5:6). They will eat of the hidden manna, and they will be given a white stone and new name (Rev. 2:17). They will hunger for bringing justice on earth, as symbolized by the balance in Rev. 6:5.

"And unto the angel of the church in Thyatira write; These things saith the Son of God,…" (Rev. 2:18)

<16> What is the church in Thyatira? It is the fourth symbol in **The Greatest Sign** (☪), the symbol of Islam. Islam comes from the word "tasleim," which means to be surrendered to the Will of God. Being surrendered to God does not mean to be idle and let Him do everything for you, but to do your best and then surrender the result to Him with no attachment, "Work not for a reward, but cease not to do thy work" (Bhagavad-Gita 2:47).

<17> This church is also the end of the fourth chakra and the entering into the fifth chakra where the sound OM (ॐ) can be heard.

"I know thy works, and charity, and service, and faith, and thy patience, and thy works; and the last to be more than the first." (Rev. 2:19)

<18> By residing in the fourth chakra and trying to reach the fifth chakra, the quality of giving charity, doing service, and having great faith and patience will become manifest. You become merciful (Matthew 5:7). Islam is the symbol of all these things. In fact definite rules and regulations are set up to awaken the people to do these things. Another quality in Islam was bringing the right of all being spiritually equal, "the last to be more than the first."

"Notwithstanding I have a few things against thee, because thou sufferest that woman Jezebel, which calleth herself a prophetess, to teach and to seduce my servants to commit fornication, and to eat things sacrificed unto idols." (Rev. 2:20)

<19> Who is this Jezebel? She is the false understanding of the teachings and realities which were revealed to the person who has come to the fourth chakra and is trying to go to the fifth chakra. The false understanding is that the person feels so content and experiences such a joy and great truth that he feels he has reached the end of the spiritual path. So this becomes a source of misunderstanding and also a hindrance in further progress. But because the universal point of view has not been created, this leads to narrowness of the mind.

<20> Moslems also think that Islam is the last religion. Like many other religions, they follow concepts that have been imposed on them. They believe that Prophet Muhammad is the last Prophet and Islam is complete by itself. So they oppose any Prophet after Prophet Muhammad. They do not accept the three truths after the sign of Islam in **The Greatest Sign**, nor do they add the knowledge of the three previous signs.

"And I gave her space to repent of her fornication; and she repented not." (Rev. 2:21)

"…and them that commit adultery with her into great tribulation, except they repent of their deeds." (Rev. 2:22)

<21> The following of this false belief is like adultery with Jezebel, who calls herself a prophetess. This will create confusion and cause man tribulation and misery.

"And I will kill her children with death; and all the churches shall know that I am he which searcheth the reins and hearts: and I will give unto every one of you according to your works." (Rev. 2:23)

<22> In the sentence, "And I will kill her children with death," death means ignorance. Therefore, those who follow the false understandings of the teachings and realizations in this state (which is narrowness and not having a universal view), will become ignorant and their minds will become more narrow, further into death.

"But unto you I say, and unto the rest in Thyatira, as many as have not this doctrine, and which have not known the depths of Satan, as they speak; I will put upon you none other burden." (Rev. 2:24)

<23> "As many as have not this doctrine" means, "As many as are surrendered to My Will and are submissive to Me, and so will progress further in the spiritual path, or those who are ignorant of the depth of Satan as they speak [they think they know], to these people will I be merciful."

<24> **The point is that the doctrine you follow in your life is the most important part of your spiritual progress. Doctrine means your ideology and goal.**

<25> Therefore, if you are ignorant of the depths of Satan (you are following a false teaching or doctrine), "I will put upon you none other burden." That is, if the person in this state will open his heart to understand others also, then God will be merciful to him and he can progress further.

"But that which ye have already hold fast till I come." (Rev. 2:25)

<26> Those who stay in this state from ignorance will not be punished for their ignorance, but only for their bad deeds (samskaras, or sins).

"And he that overcometh, and keepeth my works unto the end, to him will I give power over the nations:" (Rev. 2:26)

<27> Those who overcome these false understandings of the teachings of the fourth symbol in **The Greatest Sign** will become surrendered ones to the Will of God. They will become people with expanded minds and eventually will become universalists. They will study the teachings of the three truths before (in **The Greatest Sign**) and also will accept the next three truths after this fourth one, "and keepeth my works unto the end." Only such people can assume the leadership of the nations, because they have overcome the narrowness of the mind.

<28> The power over the nations was given to the Moslems when in a short period of time they conquered so many great nations, such as Persia and Rome. This was possible only because they were following the true teachings of Prophet Muhammad at that time. Also, it was His Will ("…And power was given unto them over the fourth part of the earth…" Rev. 6:8).

"And he shall rule them with a rod of iron; as the vessels of a potter shall they be broken to shivers: even as I received of my Father." (Rev. 2:27)

<29> "He shall rule them with a rod of iron" because the authority of these people shall not come from man but from God. "Even as I received of my Father" means, in the same way, "as my authority which is from the Father."

"And I will give him the morning star." (Rev. 2:28)

<30> The star of the morning is the sun. "The morning star" (sun) is the symbol of the highest spiritual realization, which is to be completely surrendered and submissive to The Plan of God.

<31> Surrendering does not mean escapism, it means to use all the beautiful gifts of life, such as intellect, spiritual powers, our bodies, tongues, eyes, etc., toward bringing about The Plan of the Lord. This Plan was the main purpose of the creation of the universe, which is to create the proper environment in order for all to reach Pure Consciousness. So we try our best to use all of our abilities to do His Will and then surrender the results of our actions to Him. <32> Or, we let Him do the actions through us.

<33> The people in the fourth chakra are those who are merciful and shall obtain mercy (Matthew 5:7). The Spirit says, "I will put upon [them] none other burden" (Rev. 2:24), power over the nations will be given to them (Rev. 2:26), and they will receive the morning star (true knowledge of God) (Rev. 2:28). Also, power is given to them over the fourth part of the earth (Rev. 6:8).

Chapter 3

Tablet Nine

"And unto the angel of the church in Sardis write; These things saith he that hath the seven Spirits of God, and the seven stars; I know thy works, that thou hast a name that thou livest, and art dead." (Rev. 3:1)

<1> The fifth church is represented by the symbol of the nine-armed star of the Baha'i Faith (✹). The name Baha'u'llah means the "Beauty of God." "That thou hast a name" refers to this name which the followers of the Baha'i Faith should bring to the world. They should glorify the Lord. "That thou livest, and art dead": But this name is dead. They are not glorifying the Lord (formless, nameless, and invisible). They are glorifying their Prophet (Baha'u'llah).

<2> Also the fifth church is related to the fifth psychic center (chakra).

"Be watchful, and strengthen the things which remain, that are ready to die: for I have not found thy works perfect before God." (Rev. 3:2)

<3> "I have not found thy works perfect before God": The true founder of the Baha'i Faith was Bab (one of the titles Bab gave to himself was Baha'u'llah – Bab means "The Door"), who was martyred. One of Bab's disciples by the name of Baha'u'llah tried to perfect his teachings and he changed many things.

<4> Also because the followers of Bab went through much persecution, they lost much of their strength. To make the movement survive, Baha'u'llah's followers had to compromise so that they might be able to survive in their hostile environment. Also, through Baha'u'llah (Bab's disciple), these teachings spread west so that we might become familiar with them. Otherwise it would have remained a small group and never spread abroad as it did. This all happened by His Will as it was predicted in these verses and shown in history.

<5> What remained and the main purpose of the coming of the Baha'i Faith is its universal view which should be accepted and preserved, "Be watchful, and strengthen the things which remain, that are ready to die."

"Remember therefore how thou hast received and heard, and hold fast, and repent. If therefore thou shalt not watch, I will come on thee as a thief, and thou shalt not know what hour I will come upon thee." (Rev. 3:3)

<6> The Baha'i Faith was revealed in Persia. Islam was the dominating religion. However, many people embraced the faith and were slain in doing so. Later on, the followers of the Baha'i Faith lost their strength and changed many things in their ideology in order to be able to live peacefully in that environment. That is the meaning of "Remember therefore how thou hast received and heard, and hold fast, and repent."

<7> Also, in the individual situation in this level of spiritual progress, a person might again become an escapist. That is because he can now see God (Matthew 5:8) and His perfect universe, and he sees Its perfection. So he might just sit back and enjoy his realization without bothering to help others. He feels he should not interfere with Its flow and alleviate some of the suffering. With a little push, however, things can be accelerated. <8> These people forget how they went through a great struggle to reach there. That is why it says, "Remember therefore, how thou hast received and heard." So become active and help others also.

"Thou hast a few names even in Sardis which have not defiled their garments; and they shall walk with me in white: for they are worthy." (Rev. 3:4)

<9> However, in the beginning of the movement a very few Great Souls supported the faith and were slain in doing so. They were worthy to walk with the Spirit (Christ) in white (Pure Consciousness, light, knowl-

edge). Those who overcome being escapists are worthy to reach Pure Consciousness (※).

"He that overcometh, the same shall be clothed in white raiment; and I will not blot his name out of the book of life, but I will confess his name before my Father, and before his angels." (Rev. 3:5)

<10> He who overcomes the pitfalls of this stage will overcome all attractions of Maya. He will overcome the material world (the five elements). He will be spiritually purified. The white raiment will be given to him as mentioned in Rev. 6:11, "And white raiment will be given unto every one of them."

"Them" refers to "the souls of them that were slain for the word of God, and for the testimony which they held," who are the people that were slain in the Baha'i Faith and those who reach the fifth chakra but are not afraid to fight for their beliefs.

<11> So these are the ones who are blessed because they are pure in heart and will see God (Matthew 5:8). They will be given white garments, their names will be in the book of life, and the Spirit (Christ) will confess their names before the Father and His angels (Rev. 3:5). They have been slain for the word of God and for the testimony (of truth) which they held (Rev. 6:9).

Tablet Ten

"And to the angel of the church in Philadelphia write; These things saith he that is holy, he that is true, he that hath the key of David, he that openeth, and no man shutteth; and shutteth, and no man openeth;" (Rev. 3:7)

<1> The sixth church is the sign (✡) which was revealed to a great spiritual teacher in India. His affectionate name is Baba (Bab = The Door, a = Aum), and he is the one "that is true [and] hath the key of David." The key of David is the sign (✡) which is the same as used in Baba's sign (✡), the symbol of the Kingdom Of Heaven within, or those who reach this state (sixth level) and are pure in heart but have overcome being escapist.

"I know thy works: behold, I have set before thee an open door, and no man can shut it: for thou hast a little strength, and hast kept my word, and hast not denied my name." (Rev. 3:8)

<2> "I have set before thee an open door, and no man can shut it." That is true about the teachings of Baba. The truth he revealed to humanity is so great that "no man can [ever] shut it." The concept of Paravipra has come from his teaching. However, with knowing **The Greatest Sign**, we can understand their characteristics and places in society.

<3> "For thou hast a little strength": That is true about the path he revealed. They have very little strength in comparison with other religions. However, they have kept the word of God (Truth) and have not denied His Name (Truth). <4> Also the door refers to the door of entering into heaven, because after the sixth chakra is the seventh (Aum = ॐ) and last chakra, which is heaven (Pure Consciousness). Whoever is in the sixth chakra has this door opened for him.

"Because thou hast kept the word of my patience, I also will keep thee from the hour of temptation, which shall come upon all the world, to try them that dwell upon the earth." (Rev. 3:10)

<5> "I also will keep thee from the hour of temptation, which shall come upon all the world, and to try them that dwell upon the earth." Therefore this sixth church will come in the hour that the temptations will come upon the earth. It is the same as this time that we are living in now. These teachings and its sign were revealed in the beginning of this time (1945). The people in this path are trying to overcome these temptations with the many purifying techniques that are given by their spiritual teacher.

<6> Also, the sixth seal in Rev. 6:12 refers to the beginning of the tribulation and confusion in the world. The sixth seal that is in **The Greatest Sign** was also revealed at the time

of the start of the tribulation and temptation in the world (1945).

"Behold, I come quickly: hold that fast which thou hast, that no man take thy crown." (Rev. 3:11)

<7> This verse means that the whole truth will be revealed very soon after the revelation of this sixth truth. Those who have reached the sixth state should be steady. They should behold the teachings and those things that are taught them, because the last stages of The Plan of the Lord God are approaching. If they do not hold fast in what they have then they will lose in entering the next stage which is the crown of the stages (seventh level or chakra) and contains the whole truth.

Tablet Eleven

"Him that overcometh will I make a pillar in the temple of my God, and he shall go no more out: and I will write upon him the name of my God, and the name of the city of my God, which is new Jerusalem, which cometh down out of heaven from my God: and I will write upon him my new name." (Rev. 3:12)

<1> He who overcomes all the pitfalls will become a son of God, "will I make a pillar in the temple of my God." <2> "He shall go no more out," means not going back to ignorance. <3> "I will write upon him the name of my God," the sacred name of the Father, will be revealed to you. <4> Such a person is in Pure Consciousness, "New Jerusalem," <5> and the Sacred Name of the First Begotten Son will be revealed to him also, "my new name."

<6> These are the ones who are the peacemakers and will be called the children of God (Matthew 5:9). <7> They are those who will have a pillar in the temple of God (Rev. 3:12) and will be sealed with the seal of the living God (Rev. 7:3).

Tablet Twelve

"And unto the angel of the church of the Laodiceans write; These things saith the Amen,…" (Rev. 3:14)

<1> These are the ones who try to reach Pure Consciousness through meditation, yoga exercises, or any other means that are taught in the Mystical Paths as the way to raise the consciousness to the seventh chakra, without caring too much for other people. They do not try to direct the spiritual energies they have gained toward establishing the Kingdom Of Heaven, but instead try to reach higher consciousness individually and selfishly. They try to reach Pure Consciousness by being escapists.

"I know thy works, that thou art neither cold nor hot: I would thou wert cold or hot." (Rev. 3:15)

<2> "Thou art neither cold nor hot": Why are they no longer cold or hot? They are this way because they have overcome any effects of the external world on their bodies and Souls through spiritual powers (siddhis).

<3> "I would thou wert cold or hot." However, God wishes them to be "cold or hot," because the purpose of this universe is to bring all to Pure Consciousness. <4> Therefore, those who have reached this stage by merely using techniques and exercises should come back to this world of suffering (cold and hot, up and down), help others come to the path of enlightenment, and establish His Kingdom.

"So then because thou art lukewarm, and neither cold nor hot, I will spue thee out of my mouth." (Rev. 3:16)

<5> Even when a person reaches higher or Pure Consciousness ("neither cold nor hot") this way, he would not stay there for a long period of time but would gain his "I" back as an entity separate from God because "I will spue thee out of my mouth." He would not be able to stay there forever, until he proved

himself worthy by his actions in helping the whole universe to higher consciousness.

<6> Indeed, this part has the identical message as the third chapter of Genesis, when God threw Adam and Eve out of heaven and set up the flaming sword to keep them from the tree of life (Pure Consciousness).

<7> As it was explained, the reason for that was because Adam wanted to eat of the tree of knowledge and life when he was not yet ready for it. He was still in his lower nature (Eve).

<8> He also had the same desire to go to heaven by force and through mastering the powers in the universe ("tree of knowledge of good and evil").

<9> Just as he was sent out of the garden, also those who attempt the same path will be thrown "out of his mouth" or a flaming sword (Maya) will keep them from entering heaven (the tree of life).

"Because thou sayest, I am rich, and increased with goods, and have need of nothing; and knowest not that thou art wretched, and miserable, and poor, and blind, and naked:" (Rev. 3:17)

<10> Because they are in a very high consciousness, these people feel that they are superior to others, are rich in spirit, and need nothing. They become escapists, and they teach that this world is nothing but illusion. God does not like it, because they lose the real purpose of being in that high spiritual state. Instead of utilizing their abilities and high level of consciousness toward bringing about the Kingdom Of Heaven On Earth and helping others to become Pure Consciousness, they lead others to escapism. Therefore, God makes them miserable, poor, blind, and naked.

"I counsel thee to buy of me gold tried in the fire, that thou mayest be rich; and white raiment, that thou mayest be clothed, and that the shame of thy nakedness do not appear; and anoint thine eyes with eyesalve, that thou mayest see." (Rev. 3:18)

<11> This verse means, "I helped you to reach this stage of consciousness which is so beautiful in order that you might be rich (in spirit) and pure (white raiment). Then you might help the world with these qualities and set an example for others on how to be. They were not given to you to become an escapist."

"As many as I love, I rebuke and chasten: be zealous therefore, and repent." (Rev. 3:19)

<12> This means that from this church, who God loves, He will rebuke and chasten. Be zealous therefore, and do the first work. Be a Paravipra. <13> God does not love escapists, those who try to find the Kingdom Of Heaven only within, teach that this world is illusion, and do not understand the reality behind this creation. <14> Those He loves are given severe tests, so that they become strong and prove themselves worthy to go to Him or to be in His Presence, <15> which is to know Him (He put Abraham to the tests also). <16> As you come closer to Pure Consciousness, you should pass more severe tests in order to be trustworthy.

Tablet Thirteen

"Behold, I stand at the door, and knock: if any man hear my voice, and open the door, I will come in to him, and will sup with him, and he with me." (Rev. 3:20)

<1> "I (Spirit) am in all of you. I am always within you. If any person hears what I say and opens his heart to Me, I will come in and he will know the truth." <2> This is the same as, "Ask, and it shall be given you; seek and ye shall find; knock, and it shall be opened unto you:" (Matthew 7:7).

"To him that overcometh will I grant to sit with me in my throne, even as I also overcame, and am set down with my Father in his throne." (Rev. 3:21)

<3> The pitfall of the spiritual path in this stage is to forget about other people's suffer-

ings and be content with the peace and joy of being in higher consciousness. If these people overcome this last pitfall, they will reach the highest consciousness and will inherit the Kingdom Of Heaven On Earth. They will sit on the throne with God. They will become Avatars.

<4> These are the people who will be persecuted for righteousness (Matthew 5:10). They are dynamic spiritualists, not escapists. They will be as Angels to the earth and will guide humans to the understanding that the only way to salvation is to listen to the Prophets, follow the Laws of God, and lead others to the path of righteousness.

Some points should be noticed:

<5> The first point is that the first four churches are presented in one chapter. Also the first four seals are related to the four horsemen (chapter six), and the first four Angels with trumpets (chapter eight) are presented in one chapter together. Therefore, these first four churches and those first four horsemen and Angels have a relationship that causes them to differ from the next three.

<6> Their relationship is that the spiritual understanding and coming to the state of direct contact with the depth of its reality finishes with the first four chakras or seals. However, a further development in understanding the realities of this universe is necessary, which can be gained through progressing and overcoming the next three chakras. That is why with Islam the real understanding of the spiritual world finishes. <7> The first seal is related to the Far East Philosophies (Mystical Paths) and awakening the spiritual forces (☯). <8> The second is to direct these awakened forces toward the establishment of the Kingdom Of Heaven On Earth (KOHOE) (✡).

<9> The third is to sacrifice all and overcome the false ego for the KOHOE (✝). <10> The fourth seal is to surrender the result to the Lord and be completely detached from the fruit (☪), or to become submitted to Him. With this, the highest spiritual realization is achieved. In this regard, Prophet Muhammad can be viewed as the last Prophet, because with him the spiritual understanding ended. <11> However, to become perfect and free from bondage and narrowness of mind, it is necessary to become a universalist (✹) and dynamic spiritualist or Paravipra (✡), so we might then reach Pure Consciousness (࿊). <12> These last three seals are the three steps to freedom from bondage (individually and collectively; physically, mentally, and spiritually).

<13> The second point is that each understanding of one state or chakra or religion brings the human further on the path of entering the next stage (chakra). On the way to perfect the next stage there are pitfalls which should be overcome. <14> For example, when Christ (Spirit, truth) says that the woman Jezebel is a pitfall on your path, it is when a person is in the fourth chakra and trying to overcome the pitfalls in this level in order to rise to the next chakra. When a person masters that stage, the reward of that chakra will be given to him in the next chakra.

<15> In other words, when a person overcomes the pitfalls in the first chakra (stage), he will be given to eat of the tree of life. So he will leave the first stage and go to the next stage, which is the second one, and so on. <16> That is why in overcoming the pitfalls of the third stage the reward is to eat of the hidden manna which is in the fourth chakra. Or in overcoming the pitfalls of the sixth stage, the reward is to enter into a pillar in the temple of God, which is the seventh stage.

Tablet Fourteen

Chapter 4

"After this I looked, and, behold, a door was opened in heaven: and the first voice which I heard was as it were of a trumpet talking with me; which said, Come up hither, and

THE HOLIEST BOOK

HOLIEST 3 - Tablet 15

I will shew thee things which must be hereafter." (Rev. 4:1)

<1> "After this" means, "After a person goes through all the stages described in chapters 2 and 3."

<2> "A door was opened" means, "The door of all-pervasive understanding and realization will be opened to the person who has reached this state."

<3> "And the first voice which I heard" is the voice of truth that comes from The Holy Ghost, which guides a human to full realization.

<4> "Things which must be hereafter" means that only such a person will fully realize and understand the things written in the rest of the book <u>The Revelation</u> and their significance.

Tablet Fifteen

Chapter 6

"And I saw when the Lamb opened one of the seals, and I heard, as it were the noise of thunder, one of the four beasts saying, Come and see." (Rev. 6:1)

<1> Only the Lamb can open these seals as mentioned. The Lamb is that spirit of truth (Christ) that opened up or helped to open the truth of the religions to humanity.

<2> "Opened one of the seals": The other seals are numbered as second seal, third seal, etc. Therefore, this seal is the first seal.

<3> In **The Greatest Sign**, the first seal is represented by (☯), which is the I-Ching in the horizontal position and symbolizes latent spiritual forces.

<4> This seal symbolizes the teachings of the Far East (Mystical Paths) which are related to the many techniques for awakening these spiritual forces. Also these teachings give a philosophy of the relationship between individual actions and the universe. They have been given to humanity after the flood of Noah. <5> Although many Mystical Paths originated from these teachings throughout the earth, the books of the <u>Vedas</u> are the only written words of this original knowledge. In the Far East, many other disciplinary ideals have evolved from these original teachings, such as yoga, tantra (right-handed), <u>Upanishads</u>, etc. They all help a person to realize the deeper truth behind other Mystical Paths and religious dogmas.

"And I saw, and behold a white horse: and he that sat on him had a bow; and a crown was given unto him: and he went forth conquering, and to conquer." (Rev. 6:2)

<6> "A white horse" symbolizes the process of purity. Also white is the color for satva guna. Indeed all exercises, disciplines, diets, and philosophies of these original teachings are based on purifying the body, mind, and spirit.

<7> "He that sat on him had a bow" means that he who tries to follow these teachings becomes like a warrior (Arjuna in the <u>Bhagavad-Gita</u>). With his bow, he goes to war with the influence of the tama guna over his Soul and fights those creatures that make him or her poor in spirit and/or lost. <8> These practices and philosophies awaken the kundalini which will help the person to conquer his weaknesses, expand his mind, experience the presence of God, open his spiritual (third) eye, and overcome all negative forces within his Soul.

<9> "And a crown was given unto him," because he starts to overcome the power of the tama guna over his Soul and tries to overcome the Maya. He becomes great by detaching himself from the attraction of the external world and he awakens the spiritual forces in order to overcome his lower nature. So he becomes the king of his Soul and receives a crown.

<10> "He went forth conquering, and to conquer." He starts to conquer those weaknesses within and without by purifying the self. He is a conqueror because his Soul is awakened, and through struggle, the conquer-

ing of the self (Soul) is guaranteed (like Arjuna in the Bhagavad-Gita).

<11> Also the philosophy of the Far East is so deep and mind-catching that it conquers the hearts, minds, and Souls of those who are real seekers. <12> However, these teachings do not reveal all of The Plan and desire of God for humanity to follow. They might lead to escapism. That is why other seals are necessary to perfect these teachings.

"And when he had opened the second seal, I heard the second beast say, Come and see." (Rev. 6:3)

<13> The second seal is the second symbol in **The Greatest Sign** (✡), which is the star of David or the seal of Solomon.

"And there went out another horse that was red: and power was given to him that sat thereon to take peace from the earth, and that they should kill one another: and there was given unto him a great sword." (Rev. 6:4)

<14> The color red symbolizes activity, war, and action. Also it is the color for raja guna. The sign (✡) is the symbol of the Kingdom Of Heaven On Earth (KOHOE). <15> The power of taking peace from the earth is given to those Elected Ones who will fight to bring the KOHOE. This power was once given to Hebrews, and it will be given to Elected Ones all the time in order to eventually bring the Kingdom to the earth.

<16> "They should kill one another" means that until the Kingdom Of Heaven is established on earth, humans will be lost in narrowness of the mind (ignorance) and will kill each other in the process. <17> However, if humans understand that all these things happened throughout history in order to bring all to this point of understanding that the only way for peace, harmony, and happiness is to give up the false ego and follow what God desires, then the bloodshed will stop.

"And when he had opened the third seal, I heard the third beast say, Come and see. And I beheld, and lo a black horse; and he that sat on him had a pair of balances in his hand." (Rev. 6:5)

<18> In this stage the seal refers to the third seal in **The Greatest Sign**, the cross (✝), which is the symbol of Christianity. The cross itself is representative of a balance if you add the scales on the two sides (⚖).

<19> The black horse symbolizes the death of the devil (false ego, lower nature) in this stage of development of the human. <20> Also black is the color for tama guna. The pair of balances is the symbol of equality. With Christ's teachings and the understanding of his teachings, a person should come to the point where he can overcome the devil (which is the attraction to Maya and/or false ego) and be ready to sacrifice (not being self-centered) all of individual self for establishing the Kingdom Of Heaven (balances). He should hunger for righteousness and try to bring equity on earth.

"And I heard a voice in the midst of the four beasts say, A measure of wheat for a penny, and three measures of barley for a penny; and see thou hurt not the oil and the wine." (Rev. 6:6)

<21> He who has the pair of balances has come to make sure that equity has been established in the human race. Therefore, the sentence, "A measure of wheat for a penny, and three measures of barley for a penny" means, "Make sure that the Laws which have been set up are followed and no one is exploited, and all will have the basic necessities."

<22> The phrase, "And see thou hurt not the oil and the wine" means, "Make sure that those who are worthy to have more than the basic necessities of life are not being hurt." Whosoever contributes more to society should receive more. Spiritual contribution is superior to intellectual, and intellectual contribution is superior to physical. <23> Another meaning is that the chosen ones (Paravipras) will establish this equity on earth. These are the ones that have the pair of balances in themselves (Kingdom Of Heaven within).

<24> In short, "Make sure all receive their

share without any one being unfairly treated." That is what Christ taught his disciples. The essence of his teaching is "Sacrifice in establishing the Kingdom Of Heaven." The rest will be added to you.

"And when he had opened the fourth seal, I heard the voice of the fourth beast say, Come and see." (Rev. 6:7)

<25> The fourth seal is the fourth symbol in **The Greatest Sign** (☾), which is the last part of the symbol OM (ॐ). It is the symbol of Islam, which was brought by Prophet Muhammad. With this seal, the four horsemen are finished.

"And I looked, and behold a pale horse: and his name that sat on him was Death, and Hell followed with him. And power was given unto them over the fourth part of the earth, to kill with sword, and with hunger, and with death, and with the beasts of the earth." (Rev. 6:8)

<26> The pale horse means a balance in the revelation in this stage. It means completion of knowledge. It is neither white, nor red, nor black, but a balance between all these extremes. That is why in Islam the material world and spiritual world both are considered equally important, and many laws were set up for social relationships.

<27> "And his name that sat on him was Death" means that the one who sat on him brings the death of Maya, because in this stage, you will enter the fifth chakra which is the abode of overcoming all unnecessary material longings.

<28> "And power was given unto them over the fourth part of the earth, to kill with sword,...." Islam covered the fourth part of the earth through the concept of "Holy Wars."

<29> They established themselves by the power of war "with sword," which was given to them. If this power had not been given to them, they would not have been able to do it. All is done with His Blessings!

Tablet Sixteen

"And when he had opened the fifth seal, I saw under the altar the souls of them that were slain for the word of God, and for the testimony which they held:" (Rev. 6:9)

<1> This seal is the fifth seal in **The Greatest Sign** (✹), the nine-armed star, which is the symbol of the Baha'i Faith. <2> It symbolizes universality. As described before, many saints of this religion were slain for the word of God (their belief which came by their Prophet), "and for the testimony which they held."

"And they cried with a loud voice, saying, How long, O Lord, holy and true, dost thou not judge and avenge our blood on them that dwell on the earth?" (Rev. 6:10)

"And white robes were given unto every one of them; and it was said unto them; that they should rest yet for a little season, until their fellow servants also and their brethren, that should be killed as they were, should be fulfilled." (Rev. 6:11)

<3> White robes were given to them, which corresponds to the promise that if they overcome the pitfalls of the fifth church (fifth seal), they will be given white raiment (Rev. 3:5).

<4> They have reached the state where they can see God (Matthew 5:8). So they were crying for justice. <5> However, they should wait "for a little season." Baha'i came in the 1800's. So the judgment should come sometime after this revelation which is in this century.

"And I beheld when he had opened the sixth seal, and, lo, there was a great earthquake; and the sun became black as sackcloth of hair, and the moon became as blood;" (Rev. 6:12)

<6> The sixth seal is the sixth symbol in **The Greatest Sign** (✡). <7> As it was mentioned in Rev. 3:10, with the revelation of this sign, the tribulation based on temptation started in the world. This sign was revealed

THE HOLIEST BOOK

to humanity in the year 1945 at which time tribulation (the attraction to Maya and the external world) also started to become stronger.

Chapter 7

"And I saw another angel ascending from the east, having the seal of the living God: and he cried with a loud voice to the four angels, to whom it was given to hurt the earth and the sea," (Rev. 7:2)

"Saying, Hurt not the earth, neither the sea, nor the trees, till we have sealed the servants of our God in their foreheads." (Rev. 7:3)

<8> In this time period before tribulations (disasters) start, the teachings of the Far East will be brought to the West. Those who are the servants of God (Elected Ones) will become interested in them and familiar with them in order to become prepared to understand the real meaning which underlies the reality behind their Scriptures. <9> Also it is in this time that many will reach a very high level of consciousness (sixth seal) and are ready to become Paravipras and be sealed by the seal of God as His true children.

<10> The four angels are: The excess attraction to the external world (Maya), desire, attachment, and greed. <11> The "earth and the sea" means people (unit consciousnesses, sea) in their lower natures (earth).

Chapter 8

"And when he had opened the seventh seal, there was silence in heaven about the space of half an hour." (Rev. 8:1)

<12> When the seventh seal is opened, the teaching will first be revealed to the Elects. <13> It will come like a thief of the night, "there was silence in heaven about the space of half an hour."

<14> With the revelation of the seventh truth, <15> the mystery of God will be finished (Rev. 10:7, 11:18, 14:18, 16:17).

<16> For a complete and more detailed revelation of all the verses in The Revelation, read the book Revelation of The Revelation.

HOLIEST FOUR

Tablet One

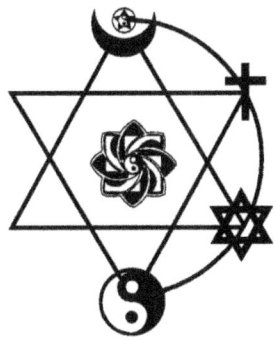

ISLAM

<1> Next after The Revelation, the word of God came to Prophet Muhammad. As it is described in The Revelation, both the seven churches and seven seals are descriptions of the seven truths which will be revealed to humanity through Prophets (Angels of the churches).

<2> Therefore, the next Scripture after the Bible was revealed to the Moslems. In fact the Scripture for humanity is one that covers the descriptions of all the seven symbols in **The Greatest Sign**. <3> The fourth sign (☾) and its Scripture will be considered in this part.

THE HOLIEST BOOK

HOLIEST 4 - Tablet 2

<4> Historically, after Christianity covered a great part of the world for some centuries, the teaching of Christ lost its truth for the majority. Instead of following the example of Christ, people started to follow dogmas about the religion. <5> Therefore, expectations of the coming of another great Prophet increased in this later period.

<6> Prophet Muhammad was the one all were expecting. His mission was to finish the spiritual realization by bringing the fourth seal. <7> With the awakening of the latent spiritual forces (☯), longing to create the KOHOE (✡), sacrificing for this ideal (✝), and surrendering and submitting to Him (☪), the highest spiritual realization is achieved.

<8> Islam tried to establish this ideal and for a short period of time, it succeeded. We should remember that the Arab civilization then was so primitive that the people used to kill their female children or sell them in childhood. <9> However, after Islam was established, in a short period of time, that same society became the center of world civilization. <10> That shows how, with the proper environment and by following God's Principles, a difference will be made for the progress of man.

<11> The explanation of the advent of Islam given above is historical. The spiritual explanation is that the coming of this new teaching for furthering the course of humanity was part of the promise given to Abram (read the book Children of Abram (Abraham), All Prophecies Are Fulfilled.) <12> Also the coming of Islam had been predicted in The Revelation, when the fourth seal is opened (pale horseman). By adding this teaching to The Revelation, the Bible will become more complete.

<13> The basic teaching of the Koran consists of several points: There is only one God. He is the absolute power. He is just, merciful, and beneficent. <14> There will be a last day of judgment, which is the resurrection from the dead (ignorance) to life (spiritual knowledge). <15> All things in the universe belong to God, and humans should only surrender and submit themselves to Him. In fact, "Islam" means "to be surrendered and submissive to the Lord," and it is this which is the most important message of this religion.

<16> Some verses of importance will be described in the following pages for further explanation of the Koran. These verses will not reveal all the truth behind this Scripture and religion, but will clarify that the truths revealed in the Koran are not different than in other Scriptures. <17> Also this will shed light on some parts which have been misunderstood. In the book Readings (The Koran) more verses and truths are revealed.

<18> To make the Koran more universal for those who are not familiar with the name Allah, one can substitute "God" for "Allah" (which are the same) in the verses in order to be able to relate to the truth which underlies the words of the Koran.

Tablet Two

Surah The Family of 'Imran

What the Koran means by the devil, verses 14 and 15:

The desire for pleasure from the objects of the senses which comes from women [lower nature] and offspring and stored-up reserves of gold and silver, marked horses (by their names), and cattle and properties, appeals to the worldly men. These are the comfort for this material world. It is with Allah which is an excellent abode.

Say (O Muhammad): Shall I inform you of something better than these which are so dear to you (O worldly people)! For those who keep from evil and are aware of their duties to Allah, there are gardens with rivers flowing beneath, and pure companions and the blessings of Allah. Allah is watchful of His Bondmen. (The Family of 'Imran, 14-15)

THE HOLIEST BOOK

HOLIEST 4 - Tablet 2

<1> What these verses describe is that, "The desire for pleasure from the objects of the senses which comes from women and offspring, and stored-up gold and silver," and horses, cattle, and similar things, are all the attractions of the external world. In verse 15 it is said, "Those who keep from evil," which means, those who keep from being attracted to these things which are evil (attractions to the external world) can understand the reality of the spiritual world.

<2> So again evil is nothing but excess attraction to the external world. Evil is not a being. It is a quality of the human which can be overcome. So evil is the same as Maya, the attraction to the material world.

Reincarnation, verse 27:

...You bring the living from the dead, and bring the dead from the living. (The Family of 'Imran, 27)

<3> God can bring the living from the dead and He can bring the dead from the living. So God (Allah) in the Koran is an able God. He can do whatever He wishes to do. If He is an able God and can bring the dead from the living and the living from the dead, then He is also able to reincarnate. If we say He cannot reincarnate, then we are saying that He is not an able God as Prophet Muhammad taught.

Meditation, silence, and remembrance of God, verse 41:

Zakariah said: My Lord, lay upon me a token. He (the Angel) replied: The token for you is that you should not speak with people for three days but by signs, and remember the Lord much, and praise Him by night and early morning. (The Family of 'Imran, 41)

<4> This verse presents that silence, the remembrance of God, and meditating on Him and His creation is a part of becoming closer to Him. That is why meditation, silence, and being an observer is recommended by all great spiritual teachers to keep oneself away from the crowd. <5> Also this encourages thinking about the creation, what is happening in this world, why we are here, what we are doing here, what we are, what is God, etc.

Reincarnation, verse 49:

...and I raise the dead, by Allah's permission... (The Family of 'Imran, 49)

<6> It is Allah (God) who will decide to raise or cause to die. It is God who can reincarnate or not reincarnate. It is Allah (God) who can send the same person again and again to this earth, or not. It is God who can also send some people sometime or other people other times. Or it is God who does not send at all. <7> So again, if we say, "Allah cannot reincarnate" then we are saying what He can do or what He cannot do. He can do whatever He wants to do.

Non-believers, verse 54:

And they (the disbelievers) devised their plans, and Allah devised His! Allah is the best planner, (The Family of 'Imran, 54)

<8> Unbelievers think that they can cheat on God, especially by changing the Scriptures. But they do not know that God is very aware of their hearts and will carry out His own Plan for the universe. They change the Scriptures or try to follow their own false egos in order to serve their own purposes. However, then God sends another great Prophet (in this case Prophet Muhammad) to bring truth back to the light again. <9> So the sun does not stay under the clouds forever. Truth should be accepted by all. That is The Plan.

<10> God brings His religion again and again into this world. The people try to destroy it, but another Prophet or spiritual teacher comes and reveals truth from the Akashic Records again, until eventually all understand and see the hand of God in history and

creation. Then people should stop fighting the truth and accept it!

Elected Ones, verse 55:

Remember when Allah told Esa that: I will cause you to die and then your Soul shall be ascended unto me, and will clean you from calumnies of disbelievers, and will exalt you above disbelievers to the Day of Judgment; then unto Me you all will return, and I shall judge between you on what you used to differ. (The Family of 'Imran, 55)

<11> Why are Christ and his followers preferred over the unbelievers? It is because he and his followers were always preferred to unbelievers. They are the Elected Ones. The people who followed Christ were Elected Ones, as the people who followed Prophet Muhammad were Elected Ones.
<12> These people have been reincarnated again and again, and have set the world in the right direction. <13> Later on, the world becomes corrupt again. So they have to come back. <14> However, each time they come back some new people will be saved and will reach higher consciousness. This process will continue until all understand The Plan of God and establish the Kingdom Of Heaven On Earth. That is why Christ called them "the salt of the earth" (Matthew 5:13). Without these people we would not even be here where we are now. That is why they are above disbelievers.

Worshipping one God, verse 79:

A righteous human being whom Allah had given the Scripture and wisdom and the prophethood will not say to people: **Worship me instead of Allah**. But according to their duty, they say: **Be faithful devotees of God**, by constant preaching and attentive studying of the Scriptures. (The Family of 'Imran, 79)

<15> It says, "Those whom Allah sends as His Messengers or Prophets do not tell people, 'Worship me.' They come and say, 'Worship the Lord.'" <16> For example, even if God incarnated Himself as a human and started preaching the truth, what good would it do for Him to say who He is? The only thing that would happen is that the people who followed Him would create big false egos and would start to look down at others. <17> That is why those who take Prophets as the Lord God or think they themselves are the only chosen ones do more harm than good for God-realization.
<18> Also this verse is helpful to observe some points that Prophet Muhammad was revealing:
<19> "Whom Allah had given the Scripture and wisdom and the prophethood": So God can give prophethood to anyone He wishes to, in any time of history before and after Prophet Muhammad. It is up to Him. Even thinking that any Prophet is the last is a sin, because we are saying what God should do or should not do. The Lord God has a Great Plan to fulfill, and He will not stop until it is fulfilled.
<20> "Be faithful devotees of God by constant preaching and attentive studying of the Scripture": Here it is emphasized to read the Scriptures and share satsang. <21> That is one of the reasons why religions have lost their validity, because people do not know about them. So they just believe whatever they have been told by other people or preachers.
<22> "Attentive studying of the Scripture": Study of the Scriptures is one of the duties of the human. Those who believe they can find all the truth only by meditating are completely wrong. Study is a great part of spiritual progress.

Tablet Three

Worshipping one God, verse 80:

Nor would he command you to take Angels and the Prophets as lords. Would he ask you to become one of the disbelievers after you had submitted to Allah? (The Family of 'Imran, 80)

<1> Again he says, "You should not believe in Angels and Prophets as the Lord." Angels and Prophets both refer to those in Pure Consciousness who have been incarnated as humans (god-men or men-gods). It is true that they are god-incarnated, yet only the Lord God is the Father, and you should worship Him. <2> Also only worshipping one invisible God unifies humanity. Any other thing will bring disunity. Visible incarnation even represents the invisible!

Accepting the other religions, verse 84:

Say (O Muhammad): We believe in Allah and that which has been revealed unto us, and that which was revealed to Abraham and Ishmael and Isaac and Jacob and the tribes, and which was given to Moses and Esa and other Prophets from their Lord. There is no distinction between them for us, and unto Him we submit. (The Family of 'Imran, 84)

<3> This verse means, "God is one. We believe in Him and whomever He sent." However, the Scriptures were changed after they were revealed and many things were distorted. So Prophet Muhammad says, "We should understand these things and know that there is only one God for all of us, and we should worship Him."
<4> In later verses, he says that it does not matter what you call the Lord God. Any good name you give to Him, He is, because He does not have any name (except His sacred Divine Name, the Divine vibration, The Word). "He is that He is." <5> In fact, everything in this universe "is that it is." Names are only used to facilitate communication for humanity, not for creating concepts and barriers.

Surrendering to God, verse 102:

O those who believe, be aware of your duty to Allah and be mindful of it, so you would not die but as one completely submissive to Him. (The Family of 'Imran, 102)

<6> Islam comes from the word "tasleim," which means to be surrendered or submissive. Islam means, "Those who have surrendered and are submissive to God." Therefore, believers are those who have surrendered themselves to God (Allah). So it is only necessary to be surrendered to be called a Moslem. <7> However, the Will of God should be understood first. Then man should surrender himself to His Will and do His Will, which is to establish the Kingdom Of Heaven within and without.
<8> "Be mindful" means that you should approach the Lord with right ideation and devotion. Not doing prayers and spiritual duties is better than doing them automatically with no feelings. The devotion and reverence toward God should be created.

All things belong to God, verse 109:

To Allah belongs whatsoever is in the heavens and whatsoever is in the earth; and unto Him all shall return. (The Family of 'Imran, 109)

<9> It is true, all things in this universe were made by Him. So all things belong to Him.

The hand of God in history, verse 137:

There have many dispositions passed before you. Just travel on the earth and see how evil is the end of those who rejected (the Messengers [truth]). (The Family of 'Imran, 137)

<10> The Children of Israel and the Jews denied the Prophets and rejected the Lord God. They forgot why they had been chosen so the Lord punished them as a lesson for them and others; read the book <u>The House of Judah (Jews)</u>. He destroyed Jerusalem and scattered them all over the world. <11> We want God to punish everyone right away, but He takes His time. He does it by His own time schedule. It might take lifetimes before you receive your punishment for your samskaras.

Immortality, verse 169:

Do not think of those who are slain in the way of Allah [righteous war] as dead. No, indeed, they are with their Lord with a provision. (The Family of 'Imran, 169)

<12> In the <u>Koran</u>, in the <u>Bible</u> (Old Testament, New Testament, and <u>The Revelation</u> 2:10), in the <u>Bhagavad-Gita</u> (2:32) and in all the teachings of the great Prophets, it is promised that those who are slain in the battle for establishing the righteousness (internally or externally) will not suffer the second death. They will be liberated. That is what Prophet Muhammad is saying also, because he who is ready to lay down his life for his ideal has overcome this world and its attractions, and that is liberation.
<13> Another point is that the righteous people have provision with their Lord and will become immortal.

Choosing the Prophets, verse 179:

Allah's purpose is not to leave you in the present state; He shall separate the wicked from the good. Nor would He reveal to you the unseen. But Allah chooses of His Messengers whom He will and reveals to them the knowledge of the unseen. So believe in Allah and His Messengers. If you believe and are pure, yours is a great reward. (The Family of 'Imran, 179)

<14> "Allah's purpose is not to leave you in the present state": So humans will not stay in a low state but will progress towards perfection or Pure Consciousness.
<15> "Nor would He reveal to you the unseen" because you are not ready physically, mentally, and spiritually, to know about the unseen.
<16> "But Allah chooseth of His Messengers whom He will": Only those who reach very high consciousness will be chosen by God. He selects them, so He can choose another Messenger anytime it is needed.
<17> "So believe in Allah and His Messengers. If you believe and are pure, yours is a great reward." So listen to and understand the Messengers and high spiritual people by warding off the evil, which is jealousy and egotism toward Prophets and Messengers.

Meditation, verse 191:

Remember Allah standing, sitting, and lying on sides, and contemplate the creation of the heavens and the earth, which make them humbly utter: O Lord, You have not created this in vain [without purpose]. Holy you are; Preserve us from the torment of the Fire. (The Family of 'Imran, 191)

<18> "Remember Allah standing, sitting, and lying on sides": So love your God with all your heart, mind, and being. Remember your God and meditate on Him all the time.
<19> "And contemplate the creation of the heavens and the earth." So contemplate the creation. Think about the perfection of this universe. Then you should know that it cannot be by chance. <20> Only those who have a narrow knowledge and a crude mind would think that this universe has no Creator.
<21> "You have not created this in vain." God created this universe for a definite purpose, to bring all to Pure Consciousness. He did not create this universe in vain. <22> Those who do not understand this will be drowned in the lake of the fire of Maya, "Preserve us from the torment of the Fire."

THE HOLIEST BOOK

Tablet Four

Surah Women

Everything is done by God, verse 78:

> Wheresoever you might be, death will overtake you, even though you hide in strong towers. Still if something good happens to them, they say it is from God, and if something unfortunate comes to them, they make you [Muhammad] responsible for it. Tell them: It is all from God. What is with these people that they do not even come close to the understanding of the events? (Women, 78)

<1> This means that whatever happens in this world comes from God. When something bad happens it is a warning that you are not walking on the path. When good happens it is a reward. In other words, we can say that this world is self-sustaining: The laws are set up in such a way that bad actions provoke bad reactions and good actions bring good return. <2> However, God has complete control over everything.
<3> So, a realized person will be content in both situations and will use all his efforts for His Purpose. Also we have intelligence to do our best!

Best religion, verse 125:

> Whose religion is better than he who submits his will to God, while doing good, and follows the tradition of Abraham, the upright. God took Abraham as a friend. (Women, 125)

<4> The best religion is one in which you are surrendered and submissive to the purpose of the Lord while at the same time are helping others reach their goal. Abraham was surrendered to the Will of the Lord. Being surrendered is the greatest achievement for a spiritualist. <5> However, this does not mean escapism. That is surrendering from ignorance. Be surrendered to the Lord's purpose which is to try to establish the Kingdom Of Heaven within and without, and surrender the results to the Lord.
<6> "God took Abraham as a friend": This sentence shows completely that Father is also a unit consciousness (besides other things) like us, who is able to choose another unit consciousness as a friend. <7> Also, whoever surrenders himself to Him and His purpose might become as Abraham, His friend.

Everything belongs to Him and is in Him, verse 126:

> To Allah belongs whatsoever is in the heavens and whatsoever is in the earth, and He encompasses all things [All things are within Him; He is All and beyond]. (Women, 126)

<8> Again, He created all, and all belongs to Him. Also He is all-pervasive; He is All and is beyond all.

Christ was not slain, verses 157 and 158:

> And they say: We did kill the Messiah Esa son of Mary, the Messenger of God. They did not kill him, nor crucified him, but it just appeared to them as such, and those who have different opinions about this certainly are in doubt [are lost]; they pursue a conjecture; they surely did not slew him.
> But Allah took him up into Himself. Allah is Mighty, Wise. (Women, 157-158)

<9> Christ was in Pure Consciousness, which means that he was immortal. So how can you kill an immortal person? That is why they just think they killed him but in truth he went to His Father in heaven. Indeed all Souls are immortal!

Surah The Table Spread

Justice, verse 8:

O ye who believe! Be steadfast in Allah's ways, and be an example (for others) in equity, and let not the enmity of the people toward you make you deal with them unjustly. Be just, it is nearer to righteousness, and be aware of your duty to Allah; verily He knows all that you do. (The Table Spread, 8)

<10> You should not let your differences affect your justness, because justice is even "nearer to righteousness," and righteousness is the way to become close to Him.

Prophet Muhammad was not the last Prophet, verse 54:

O ye who believe! Whoso of you turns his back from his religion, know that in His stead Allah will bring a people whom He loves and they love Him, kind and considerate toward believers, firm and stern toward disbelievers. They will struggle in the way of Allah and will fear not the blame of the fault-finders. Such is Allah's Grace, which He bestows upon whosoever He will, Allah is All-Embracing, All-Knowing. (The Table Spread, 54)

<11> This verse says that if Moslems, or those who call themselves Moslems, fail in their fate, duties, and following the real teachings of Prophet Muhammad, they will be disregarded. A new nation or a new people will be selected as the new forerunners of the champion of belief in God and will be completely in love with Him. They will replace those who fail!

<12> God also will love them because they will be kind towards believers and stern towards disbelievers. They will be striving in the way of God.

<13> Who are striving with God? As you know, Israel means, "he who struggles with God." Who are those who struggle with Him in establishing His Kingdom? They are the Elected Ones. They are the Children of Israel.

<14> If people do not follow the example of the Elected Ones which brought Islam, then these Elected Ones will be incarnated somewhere else and will again establish God's faith. They will become new Moslems or new surrendered ones.

<15> This again shows that Prophet Muhammad did not regard himself as the last Prophet, "Allah chooses of His Messengers whom He will…" (Surah Family of Imran, 179). There could be other Prophets who will come with the Elected Ones and will bring the truth again and again on this earth. So in this verse Prophet Muhammad clearly declared that he was not the last Prophet. There would be more Prophets to come. Any time the truth is lost a Prophet will come.

Following the ancestors of ignorance, verse 104:

When it is said unto them: Come to that which God has sent, and to the Messenger, they answer: Wherein we found our fathers is sufficient for us. Would they insist even though their fathers had not knowledge and true guidance? (The Table Spread, 104)

<16> It is true that you should honor your parents and your ancestors. However, if they are ignorant and a hindrance in your spiritual progress, you should not follow them. But always love and help them. To love someone is not to follow him. Of course if they are also a light and advanced in truth, they should be followed. They can become both the parents and spiritual teacher of the person.

Surah Cattle

Evolutionary process, verse 38:

There is not one animal in the earth, nor a flying bird which flies on its two wings but are peoples like unto you. We have neglected nothing in the Book. Then unto their Lord all will be gathered. (Cattle, 38)

<17> This verse shows that the evolutionary process had been revealed to Prophet Muhammad. He says all animals are like people, because they are consciousnesses too. They are in the evolutionary process and will reach higher consciousness, and eventually Pure Consciousness. Then they will become sons of the Lord, and they will be gathered unto Him.

Reincarnation, verse 96:

Surely it is Allah who sprouts the grain of corn and the datestone. Verily it is He who brings forth the living from the dead and brings forth the dead from the living. Such is Allah… (Cattle, 96)

<18> He created this universe and is the knower of the laws of this universe. He can bring the dead from the living and the living from the dead. He can do whatever He wants to do, so He can reincarnate also. If He can bring you once to existence, then He can bring you to this world again.

<19> The problem is that people think they are their bodies. We are not our bodies but are our Souls (consciousnesses). Our bodies might change, but the consciousness does not.

<20> In fact, the whole body, except for the brain, changes each seven years. So which body will be resurrected?

<21> Even if we consider that we are the brain, if He can bring it once into existence, then He can bring it into existence again!

<22> In truth we are the unchangeable, indestructible Soul which changes bodies from one lifetime to the other, as a person changes his clothes when they become old. It is this Soul which will eventually reach salvation and will be liberated.

Tablet Five

Surah The Heights
Reincarnation, verse 25:

There shall you live, and there you shall die, and from there you will be brought forth. (The Heights, 25)

<1> He said these things to Adam and Eve. They will live on earth, they will die, and again they will be brought forth from the dead. The Lord God can bring into life anyone that He wants to. He can reincarnate.

Surah Al-Hijr
The purpose of creation, verse 85:

We have created not the heavens and the earth and all between them except with truth and wisdom, and the promised hour is sure to come. So forgive generously, O Muhammad. (Al-Hijr, 85)

<2> The creation was made for a definite purpose. Its purpose is to bring all unit consciousnesses to Pure Consciousness. The day of judgment will come to take all elected people in Pure Consciousness and help others to accelerate their progress to Pure Consciousness, because as Prophet Muhammad said, "All will return to Him."

Surah The Heights
The law of samskaras and karma, verse 13:

Every one's action We have fastened firmly to his neck; and we shall bring before him, in the Day of Judgment, a book wide open, and he will be told: Read your record, you are sufficient to judge yourself. (The Heights, 13)

<3> That book is the reaction of your actions over your Soul, which is the same as the law of Karma and samskaras. Karma is the action, and samskara is the effect of the reaction of your actions over your Soul. These reactions are like a necklace over the Soul.

<4> In the day of judgment or spiritual birth, a person will know what these reactions

were. Like an open book (also referred to as the Akashic Records, or the universal memory), he will know how he is getting rewarded or suffering for what he has done.

<5> However, some suffering or reward might not be because of the law of samskaras, but has been inflicted on the person in order to guide him to the right path or to give him a new experience for his later use (especially those who are in higher consciousness or Pure Consciousness).

<6> The human alone is enough to read his deeds (actions and reactions of these actions over his Soul) and to judge himself. That is what a spiritual person does in his meditation. By meditating you start to bring these deeds to the light and see them face-to-face until you are completely free of all your sins (samskaras).

<7> That is why most of the time the individual tribulation starts when a person begins to meditate. It is only by the Grace of the Guru (within or without, which are the same) that a person can withstand these reactions. However with a zealous repentance of sins (samskaras) and by not repeating the same mistakes, the reactions will be taken from the Soul by His Grace.

<8> The purpose of all things is to guide the human to the path. When a person comes to the path, then none of them are needed. The path is to be surrendered to the Will of God and to try to be(come) Divine and help others to be(come) the same (establishing the Kingdom Of Heaven within and without).

It does not matter whatever pleasant name you call the Lord God, verse 110:

> Say! Call Him Allah [Adorable One] or call Him Rahman [Merciful], by whichever beautiful name you call Him (is the same). His are the most beautiful attributes. (The Heights, 110)

<9> Any beautiful name that presents His wonderful attributes can refer to Him. However, He is One and is the Lord God of the universe. In reality He has no name. "He is that He is." He is that Divine vibration. He is the Divine light. He is The Word, and The Word is He. <10> You can call Him anything, such as: Merciful, Father, Beneficent, Krishna (all-attractive), Mother, Parama Purusa, Yahweh, etc., because He is all of them. At the same time He is none of them because "He just IS."

<11> Again we see that the name "Allah" was chosen only to be able to communicate about God. It is a derivative of "Elohim" and other Hebrew roots which all mean "God" or the "Adorable One." In fact there is no name for anything in this universe. Everything just "**IS**." <12> However, for the purpose of communication, we give names to things. Unfortunately people become so attached to the power of the words that they forget this simple truth. That is one of the greatest confusions created between religions, "the barrier of the power of the word."

<13> As it is said in the <u>Bible</u>, names were given to things by Adam (man) (Gen. 2:19). Before Adam there was no name for anything, not even a name for God Himself. He is The Word (יהוה). All things are known to Him by their purposes and characteristics. It is in the manifested world where there is vibration (names).

Surah Ta Ha

Evolution, verse 50:

> Moses answered, Our Lord is He whom bestows upon everything its nature [Daharma], then has guided it to perfection. (Ta Ha, 50)

<14> How can a person be guided to perfection if he has only one lifetime to do that and fails? Unless a person comes again and again to this world in many lifetimes and is guided a bit each lifetime towards perfection, it would seem to be an unfair creation.

<15> There are some people who never even have a chance to think deeply about God, creation, their destiny, and so on. If we had only one lifetime and did not have the chance to perfect ourselves, either from igno-

rance (being lost in Maya) or because of the situation we were in, then either God will not judge us or if He does, we cannot say He is a just God, which He is. <16> So it is necessary for humans to go through the evolutionary process until they reach perfection (Pure Consciousness), by His Grace, of course.

Tablet Six

Surah The Prophets
Inheritance of the earth by the righteous, verse 105:

> Verily We have recorded in the Scripture, after the exhortation, My righteous bondmen shall inherit the earth: (The Prophets, 105)

<1> Who are the righteous bondmen? They are the Elected Ones. Those who are Elected will come to this earth and inherit it. They are Paravipras. They are the ones whom Christ called "the salt of the earth." They are the ones referred to as "Blessed are they which are persecuted for righteousness sake: for theirs is the Kingdom of heaven" (Matthew 5:10). They will inherit the Kingdom Of Heaven On Earth and within, and they sit in the Kingdom Of Heaven In Heaven with God.

Surah The Pilgrimage
Other Prophets, verse 75:

> Allah chooses His messengers from among the angels and men, God certainly is All-Hearing, All-Seeing. (The Pilgrimage, 75)

<2> Whenever it is necessary, a Prophet will come. <3> Therefore, you cannot bind God by saying that any Prophet is the last one, unless you are an unbeliever (not surrendered). <4> Another point is that Prophet Muhammad said, "Allah chooses His Messengers from among the angels and men." Those Prophets who come from the angels are Avatars (god-men), and those who come from humans are Satgurus (men-gods).

Surah The Story
Other Prophets will be chosen, verse 45:

> We send ... whoever we find capable like you as Prophet. (The Story, 45)

<5> Those who are capable and are chosen will be sent as Prophets.

The pettiness of wealth and power, verse 78:

> Karoh said: I have been given this (wealth) because of my great knowledge. Did he not know that God had destroyed those who were even mightier and richer than him before? (The Story, 78)

<6> Wealth and power are nothing, because even the proud, wealthy, and powerful nations were destroyed, and you yourself can never be that wealthy and powerful. You do not even have the power over your own death. So when you die all the wealth you have accumulated will have to be left behind and you have no choice. You are completely helpless. These are only the attractions of Maya to keep you from progressing toward the perfection of your Soul. They only bring the human a big false ego.

The Prophets are not aware of their prophethood, verse 86:

> You did not expect such a Scripture to be revealed to you, but it came as a mercy from your Lord. (The Story, 86)

<7> As we can see, Prophet Muhammad did not know he was going to become a Prophet. That is why it is difficult for people to accept a person as a Prophet when they can remember him as being one of them or because he seems exactly like themselves. It is one of the greatest problems for humans to overcome.

Tablet Seven

Surah The Spider

Karma (samskara) is equal with sin in the Koran, verse 13:

> However they verily will bear their own loads besides the loads of others which will be added to theirs, and they surely will be questioned on the Day of Judgment, concerning that which they fabricated. (The Spider, 13)

<1> What is that load? That is the reaction of your bad actions (samskaras, sins). Also you will be punished for misguiding others. So the false Prophets will be severely punished.

Knowing God by contemplation of the universe, verse 44:

> Allah has created the heavens and the earth for a purpose, therein is definitely a sign for those who believe. (The Spider, 44)

<2> By understanding how perfect the universe and all things in it are, we would know that it cannot be by chance. So there is a Creator, and it will help us to become a believer.

Warning Moslems not to fight with Jews and Christians, verse 46:

> And argue not with the People of the Book, except with a good manner which is best, save their unjust ones. Tell them: We believe in that which is revealed to us and in that which is revealed to you. Our God and yours is One, and unto Him we submit. (The Spider, 46)

<3> We can see here that Prophet Muhammad was discouraging his followers from fighting, and even arguing, with Jews and Christians. However, later in history there was a great fight between them (the crusades). <4> So it is the people who create these fights and inflict suffering on humanity by following dogmatic beliefs and bringing superstitions between people.

<5> It is not the religions that have brought suffering to humanity, but it is those who misinterpret the religions and present them this way to the people. <6> Because of their ignorance and because they do not search for the truth themselves, they believe whatever is told them. They become narrow-minded and this brings suffering to humanity. In short, **suffering comes from ignorance**.

Hell is in each of our lifetimes, verse 54:

> They ask thee hasten on the punishment of the Day of Doom, but surely hell is already compassing the disbelievers. (The Spider, 54)

<7> We can see that "hell is already compassing the disbelievers," so it surrounds them right now in this lifetime. They do not have to die to go to hell. They are in the hell of the attraction of Maya, which is attachment, desire, fear, shame, insecurity, and many other sufferings related to this attraction.

Surah The Romans

On the Resurrection Day man will be sundered (separated), verse 43:

> Before the unavoidable Day which Allah has destined to come, people will be sundered... (The Romans, 43)

<8> They will be sundered by their actions. Those who have reached Pure Consciousness will be saved and those left in Maya will stay in ignorance for a long time. Also he who reaches higher consciousness becomes different (is sundered).

Reincarnation, verse 50:

> Observe, therefore, the signs of Allah's mercy (everywhere), how He

quickens the earth after its death: He is the One who gives life to the dead, for He is Able to do all things. (The Romans, 50)

<9> "He is the One who gives life to the dead, for He is Able to do all things." So He can reincarnate also.

<10> Another point in this verse is that, "Observe, therefore, the signs of Allah's mercy (everywhere)." He created the whole universe to help humanity to come from the unaware state to aware consciousness and will help them to eventually reach Pure Consciousness. <11> So that is how you understand God's mercy and compassion in His actions and creation, by His signs in the universe. In fact these signs are the results of His actions. <12> It is exactly the same with people. You know them by their actions. You know God by His creation.

<13> This is a very small portion of the Koran which was taken to show how Prophet Muhammad and other Prophets are saying these truths of the universe, in different ways, with the same understanding of the realities of the universe.

<14> They all understand these points: (1) There is reincarnation; (2) There is an evolutionary process, and eventually all will reach perfection through that process; (3) God is the Generator, Operator, and Destroyer; (4) God is the Greatest; (5) God has not been taken from anything, and God has not been created; (6) God has control over everything; (7) There is a purpose in creation; and (8) The Laws of the universe should be understood and followed by everyone.

<15> If we understand Him, and surrender ourselves to Him, we accelerate that process to reach Pure Consciousness. So we will suffer less than those who do not understand and are lost in the attraction of Maya. <16> Being lost in the attraction of Maya (excess attraction to the external world) will bring suffering to the person, society, and humanity in general.

<17> It is the duty of the Elects to establish the Kingdom Of Heaven On Earth and to bring humans to Pure Consciousness as fast as possible. <18> That is when the end of the tribulation will come. The tribulation is to make humanity understand that there is a God, there are Laws in this universe, and that these Laws should be followed. Otherwise there will be suffering and unhappiness in the world. <19> The human should understand that he has no choice but to follow the Laws of the universe in order to become Pure Consciousness, where the bliss is.

<20> In fact for a realized Soul, suffering is a blessing. It is a warning that you have gone astray from the path of the reality of this universe, <21> or it is a lesson. <22> Whenever you come back to the reality of the universe (the right path), you will have joy. You will "quicken" (accelerate) your Soul's progress toward reaching the goal (Pure Consciousness). And when you do reach there, you will be in the Bliss (God).

HOLIEST FIVE

Tablet One

THE BAHA'I FAITH

<1> The Baha'i Faith (its essence brought by Bab) is the symbol of universality. <2> Humans will never obtain peace and happiness unless they understand that no matter how great is their power, wealth, position, or philosophy, without a universal point of view and without considering the well-being of the whole universe (in individual and collective endeavors), all is in vain.

<3> If any nation, power, philosophy, religion, or anything, loses this view, it will not last long. Without the universal view, the individual or collective actions will create negative reactions and will bring the downfall of the doer.

<4> We can study history and observe this truth: As long as the original philosophy of a truth which was given by a founder with an expanded mind was followed, the people who followed that expanded philosophy were the conquerors of the hearts of other people. These ideologies spread so fast that it amazes the reader how it was possible. <5> The same ideologies are supposedly presented by the followers of these religions or philosophies in the present age. If these ideologies spread so fast then, why are they not spreading any longer but actually losing their members? <6> The answer is their loss of the universal view. The problem is the narrowness (the dogma) which has crept into the original ideal.

<7> That is what happened to the first four ideals in our **Sign**. So a new Prophet was necessary (was planned) to come and further the understanding of humanity. This Prophet was Bab (Baha'u'llah). <8> He brought the fifth truth: Universalism.

<9> The greatest contribution of this fifth truth can be expressed in one sentence from Baha'u'llah's teaching: If religion separates mankind by causing disunity, **IT IS NOT EXPRESSING THE SPIRIT OF GOD**.

<10> The oneness of mankind is the pivot around which all the teachings of Baha'u'llah revolve. There are many practical suggestions given by Baha'u'llah in order to create a universal environment and to establish a worldwide justice. <11> Some of these are: Acceptance of one language as an international language along with the mother tongue; each community must have a House of Justice, each nation must have a National House of Justice, and an International House of Justice should be established with members selected from the National or Secondary Houses of Justice; and humans must make a systematic effort to wipe out all those prejudices that cause division.

Tablet Two

<1> As we can see, from a view of spiritual understanding, there is nothing new added to what the first four truths brought to humanity. <2> From the practical point of view or from the psychological level to establish world unity, however, Baha'u'llah gave many progressive ideas. <3> In the beginning the way the Moslems treated the people of the Baha'i Faith caused many reactionary ideas to be injected into this religion. Also it lost its original vigor, "Remember therefore how thou hast received and heard,..." (Rev. 3:3).

<4> In fact, it was The Plan of God for this to happen, because a further evolutionary process was necessary. Still two more steps were needed to bring the highest realization to humanity. <5> This imperfection is revealed in Rev. 3:2, which says, "I have not found thy works perfect before God."

<6> One interesting point about the Baha'i Faith is the way the Moslems treated its followers. Many of them were slain. As it was explained in the commentary on the Koran, Prophet Muhammad warned Moslems in Surah The Table Spread (Al-Ma'idah), 54, that if they forget his teachings: "...in his stead, God will bring a people whom He loves and they would love Him,...." This indirectly means that another Prophet would come. <7> Still the very word Moslem means to be surrendered to the Will of God, so if a new movement with a more progressive ideology was revealed to humanity, a Moslem (surrendered one) should accept it, or at least not oppose it.

Tablet Three

<1> Unfortunately the narrowness of the people's minds and the misunderstanding of the Islamic teachings resulted in such a disaster. <2> However, as we saw in the second chapter of The Revelation, when Christ (the spirit of truth) was talking about the fourth church, the pitfall in this stage was narrowness of the mind. <3> And again in the third chapter in the fifth church, the main point of suffering was that their saints will be slain and a few of them will be given white robes, "Thou hast a few names even in Sardis which have not defiled their garments; and they shall walk with me in white:" (Rev. 3:4). <4> This is also given in Rev. 6:11, so all that was prophesied would happen.

<5> However, the great contribution of this religion is universalism. And after the birth of Bab (Baha'u'llah), the world started to progress toward a more international feeling. This especially shows the greatness of this Prophet and his mission.

HOLIEST SIX

Tablet One

PARAVIPRAS – THE ELECTS

<1> Paravipras are those elected people who have gone through the evolutionary process from the first seal to the sixth seal. <2> They have been reincarnated again and again into this world, and in each incarnation have furthered their spiritual advancement.

<3> They will be born apparently the same as all other people, yet they will differ in spirit. <4> Spiritually they cannot stand the wrongdoings in society. Intuitively they know that this society and world in general do not give the satisfaction which they long for within themselves. <5> They will try to be(come) escapists and forsake the society. These are the poor in spirit (Matthew 5:3).

<6> However, as mentioned in Rev. 2:5, "Remember therefore from whence thou art fallen, and repent, and do the first works…," where are they fallen from to this escapism? They are fallen from society. <7> They do not like what they see in society so they try to just forget about it. But they should not. They should "do the first works" which is to establish the Kingdom Of Heaven within and without.

<8> After they overcome this first fear of society and try to stay in society, and by analyzing the self as to why they are different, they will try to change themselves from within and thus change things without. <9> In this stage knowledge of spiritual truth, spiritual practices, and the understanding of the reality behind this universe will greatly help them and will accelerate the awakening of their latent spiritual forces. <10> This is shown in **The Greatest Sign** as the first seal (☯), the I-Ching in the horizontal position.

<11> Otherwise their fear and ignorance will only cause them to be frustrated about everything. These are the ones who are called "they that mourn" (Matthew 5:4).

Tablet Two

<1> However, by gaining the true knowledge of life, they will overcome their fears, because they will know that a spiritual person is not afraid of anything. <2> They will increase their intuition by spiritual practices, and they will understand that this whole universe is neither a reality nor an illusion. <3> The real life is eternal life when man reaches Pure Consciousness. <4> Only with this realization and by overcoming their fears can they start their spiritual journey which is symbolized as "the tree of life" (Rev. 2:7).

<5> Through this process a person stops mourning and starts to notice that no one listens to him. He sees that he is too powerless to be able to gain whatever he thinks is his fair

share. So he starts to conform to the environmental set-ups. <6> He becomes meek and submissive to these set-ups. He will endure suffering with patience and without resentment.

<7> He also starts to notice that not only is he unhappy but all others are unhappy also. They all pretend that they are happy, but deep inside they all long for a more permanent happiness that they intuitively know exists. <8> Therefore, he starts to go away from being self-centered and only thinking about his own problems and looks around at the situation he and others live in. This brings a person out of being self-centered and egotistical.

<9> With becoming observant of the situation, he longs for the Kingdom Of Heaven (✡), which is justice in the social organization. <10> However, he is still afraid of suffering and fighting in order to bring the change. <11> These people are the majority in the society. That is why they will be the majority in the Kingdom Of Heaven On Earth also: "…they shall inherit the earth" (Matthew 5:5). However if they overcome this fear of suffering, they "shall not be hurt of the second death" (Rev. 2:11).

Tablet Three

<1> With overcoming the fear of suffering for the Kingdom Of Heaven, they will reach a point where they understand that the cause of all this suffering is the lack of righteousness. <2> They will start to "hunger and thirst after righteousness" (Matthew 5:6). These are the ones who start to set an example for others by their personal conduct. They understand that the only way to establish the Kingdom Of Heaven within and without is self-sacrifice and selflessness (✝). These are the ones who "shall be filled" (Matthew 5:6).

<3> However, the pitfall in this stage is that these people might become corrupt themselves. It is hard to withstand the power of Maya, <4> especially since they have gained enough knowledge by now to be able to easily exploit others by doing evil things or by false teachings – doctrine of Nicolaitanes: "So hast thou also them that hold the doctrine of the Nicolaitanes [evil doers and false teachers]…" (Rev. 2:15).

<5> However, whoever overcomes this pitfall will overcome the power of the lower self, which is the power of the first three chakras over the Soul, and he will enter into the fourth chakra (the first three chakras are related to the worldly desires, "Maya"). <6> He will be given "to eat of the hidden manna [nectar], will be given a white stone [purified consciousness], and in the stone a new name written [The Word], which no man knoweth saving he that receiveth it [it is within you]" (Rev. 2:17). <7> With this achievement, the death of the false ego is complete (riding the black horse = the death of the false ego).

Tablet Four

<1> So far the person was in his first three chakras. Therefore, all his endeavors were toward establishing a situation that would help him to have a fair share in society. As we can see, the pitfall of the third chakra was the possibility of corruption of the person. That means he was still attracted toward things which the external world offered him.

<2> By overcoming this last attraction of the external world (the possibility of being corrupted), he enters into the fourth chakra, which is the center of love and mercy. <3> This person longs for righteousness. However, he realizes that changing the environment takes much more strength and knowledge than he has. Also it needs more detachment and realization of one's own self. <4> He realizes that all his fear, mourning, observance, meekness, and hungering for righteousness were only related to his own limited false ego. He wanted all these things to happen so that he is able to have some fair share and to

satisfy his materialistic longings.

<5> After this achievement, the person knows he needs more spiritual knowledge and self-realization. So he starts to create a great compassion for those who are lost in the power of the ocean of Maya, <6> because he realizes how hard it is to completely overcome that power. Even those who hunger and thirst for righteousness can fall into the grip of Maya. **Their concern for establishing the righteousness is even for their own concern**, not with the pure ideation of being for the good of all.

<7> So, they become merciful, forgiving, and create compassion for others. They are the ones who are called "merciful" (Matthew 5:7). By being merciful and forgiving, they will "obtain mercy" (Matthew 5:7).

<8> However, the pitfall in this stage is to become narrow in mind. The person creates mercy, but he has not created a universal sentiment. He might follow a false philosophy or a narrow, dogmatic belief which would stop his progress towards creating compassion for the whole universe. He might become concerned only for a very small portion of the universe. <9> This possibility of becoming narrow in mind is shown in Rev. 3:20, by using the symbol of the "woman Jezebel, which calleth herself a prophetess...." This symbolizes a wrong belief about a teaching which did not intend to bring a narrow view, but the people (or person) in this stage will fall into it because of the narrowness of the mind ("prophetess Jezebel"). <10> All this description is related to our fourth seal (☾), which is the symbol of the death of material longing, "...and his name that sat on him was Death,..." (Rev. 6:8).

<11> However, "he that overcometh, and keepeth my works unto the end, to him will I give power over the nations" (Rev. 2:26). So, whoever overcomes this narrowness of the mind or these false teachings will become a universalist. Not only will he be concerned about a small portion of the world, but he will also be concerned about the whole world in general. He goes to his fifth spiritual center.

Tablet Five

<1> The moment the person becomes a universalist, he will look at the whole universe as his own body. He then will be able to feel about the universe exactly the same way the Lord God feels about it. <2> Only then can he see the perfection of this universe and understand the realities behind all the things that are in it. Even the power of the tama guna, the attraction of Maya, and all things happening will be clearly revealed to him. <3> So, he will be beyond this universal suffering. He will not be affected by anything in this world. He becomes "pure in heart" (Matthew 5:8), and he "shall see God" (Matthew 5:8) because he feels like God Himself.

<4> However, he is not yet in the state of Pure Consciousness. There is a pitfall to overcome. <5> This stage is related to our fifth seal (✹), the nine-armed star, which is the symbol of universalism.

<6> The pitfall in this stage is forgetfulness of the struggle the person himself went through to reach this point. Now the person knows the reason behind all things happening. He even understands why tribulation is necessary for the human to reach the point of realizing that the only way is God's way. <7> So he might become just an observer and enjoy the happenings in the universe. He might not become engaged in guiding others to this higher realization; instead he thinks that all these things should take their natural course toward perfection. He forgets that the natural course can be accelerated by some application of force.

<8> That is what Rev. 3:3 is trying to reveal to the person: "Remember therefore how thou hast received and heard, and hold fast, and repent...." So remember the struggle and the way you went through it yourself to come to this point and remember the way you received and heard all these realizations. <9> So, "hold fast," which means, "Hold fast in this remembering, and do not just sit and try

to enjoy what you have gained. Repent being this way and help others reach this realization also." **<10>** What that verse means is that "the goal of the life is to be(come) Divine and **also help others to be(come) Divine.**"

<11> By overcoming this pitfall in the fifth stage, the person will come to the sixth stage. "He that overcometh, the same shall be clothed in white raiment; and I will not blot out his name out of the book of life, but I will confess his name before my Father, and before his angels." (Rev. 3:5). By this achievement, the person will be(come) a Paravipra. **<12>** So a Paravipra is a realized person who helps others reach higher consciousness with his dynamic personality and the radiance of truth coming from him. He will be given a white raiment (pure personality) and his name will be written in the book of life forever (he will be included as a Saint). He will be in the last stage of becoming a son of God ("…confess his name before my Father and before his angels").

<13> By overcoming the pitfall of the fifth stage, the person enters the sixth stage, which is symbolized by the sixth seal in **The Greatest Sign** (✡). **<14>** This is the sign of the Paravipras, those spiritualists who dynamically work to bring humanity to Pure Consciousness. **<15>** In the sign of Paravipra, the triangle upward (△) symbolizes the ability to reach out in order to help others, and the triangle downward (▽) symbolizes justness and spiritual depth. The sun (☀) symbolizes the rising of the deeper spiritual knowledge and understanding, and the Lotustica (卍) is the symbol of spiritual victory through these understandings.

<16> These people are the ones who are called "the peacemakers" (Matthew 5:9), because they try to bring peace and harmony to the world. "They shall be called the children of God" (Matthew 5:9). They will enter the state of Pure Consciousness.

Tablet Six

<1> As it was explained, Paravipras should have gone through all these stages and reached the sixth seal in **The Greatest Sign**. They have awakened their latent spiritual forces (☯). They long for the Kingdom Of Heaven to be established (✡). They are ready to sacrifice everything for establishing the Kingdom of God (✝). They surrender the result of their actions to the Lord and submit themselves to His Will (☽). **<2>** However, without a universal point of view all their endeavors will not express the spirit of God, so they must also become universalists (✸). With all these qualities and by a dynamic forcefulness and character, they shine in the world. They become "the light of the world" (Matthew 5:14), and they are the "salt of the earth" (Matthew 5:13). **<3>** It is true that they take the path of struggle to create characteristics of an intellectual (Vipra), businessman (Vaeshya), and courageous one (Ksattriya), and they are ready to work like a laborer (Shudra). **<4>** However, the base of this ability to go through this struggle is their refined Souls, which have evolved through so many reincarnations. **<5>** In each reincarnation they have forwarded their progress, until they have reached this point where spiritually they are incorruptible. **<6> This virtue of incorruptibility is the highest asset of a Paravipra.** Only these people are worthy to be called Paravipras, "incorruptibles."

<7> However, in addition to having the ability of not being corruptible, a Paravipra is a dynamic, intuitive intellectual who is courageous like a warrior, shrewd as a businessman, and is ready to do all kinds of physical work if necessary. He is developed physically, mentally, and spiritually. **<8>** He will direct all these abilities toward the good of all of humanity and the universe. These are the ones who we can call the real leaders of the future society.

<9> These people are the ones who are in front of the door to enter into heaven, "…I have set before thee an open door, and no man can shut it:…" (Rev. 3:8). The door to heaven is open to them, and no man can stop them from entering. <10> However, there is a pitfall in this last stage also. "...Hold that fast which thou hast, that no man take thy crown." (Rev. 3:11). Even in this stage there is a possibility of falling off the path and not entering into Pure Consciousness. So the Paravipras should watch that "no man take their crown," which is entering the crown of the head or the seventh center, which is heaven (the end of the spiritual journey).

<11> "Him that overcometh will I make a pillar in the temple of my God, and he shall go no more out: [he will reach Pure Consciousness] and I will write upon him the name of my God [he will become a son of God, he will be a god himself, he will know His Sacred Name], and the name of the city of my God [Pure Consciousness, heaven], which is new Jerusalem [symbol of the state of Pure Consciousness], which cometh down out of heaven from my God [which comes to the person]: and I will write upon him my new name [truth, pure light]" (Rev. 3:12). However, these people will assume a human body and come back as god-men (Avatars) to help others in the path. They will be in the state of Pure Consciousness even in the body, with very little ego.

Tablet Seven

<1> It is the destiny of all humans and the universe to reach pure light, which is symbolized by the seventh seal in **The Greatest Sign** (❀). <2> So the journey of spiritual achievement will be finished with entering Pure Consciousness.

<3> However, the first priority in anyone's life is to do the first work (establishing the Kingdom Of Heaven within and without, establishing Daharma). Even reaching Pure Consciousness by forsaking the world will not help you in escaping the suffering of this manifested world, because this whole universe was created in order to help All reach Pure Consciousness. If a person desired to reach Pure Consciousness and did everything necessary to only reach there himself, he would be "spue[d] out" (Rev. 3:16) of heaven back to earth to help others on the path.

<4> You cannot stay in that consciousness and just enjoy that you are "neither cold nor hot" (Rev. 3:15). God does not want you to stay in that stage. "I would thou wert cold or hot" (ibid.) means, "I wish thou wert cold or hot [the misery of the manifested world]."

<5> "So then because thou art lukewarm, and neither cold nor hot, I will spue thee out of my mouth" (Rev. 3:16). So then because you are neither cold nor hot, God will throw you out of this stage ("spue thee out of my mouth") to the manifested world. He will reincarnate you in a situation which forces you to help others to progress.

<6> Therefore, even those who reach Pure Consciousness by merely forsaking the world will be sent back to help others reach higher consciousness and eventually Pure Consciousness. **So those who become escapists should abandon this attitude and engage in this world to improve it.**

<7> The pitfall for these people is to be un-zealous. That is why the Spirit says, "…be zealous therefore, and repent" (Rev. 3:19). <8> However, "To him that overcometh will I grant to sit with me in my throne,…" (Rev. 3:21). <9> So whoever overcomes being un-zealous in this stage will be granted a seat on the throne with Christ.

HOLIEST SEVEN

Tablet One

LAST CHAPTER – SUMMARY

<1> Before any expression of awareness, the universe was in a state of "Be"-ness. <2> The universe consists of consciousness and the three forces, or gunas: Tama (static), raja (mutative), and satva (sentient).

"In the beginning was the Word, and the Word was with God, and the Word was God." (John 1:1)

"The same was in the beginning with God." (John 1:2)

<3> Because of the desire of God, the operative powers of the creative forces (three gunas) were released. <4> With this, vibration, which is sound, was created. This sound vibration which is the three creative powers in the operative state, is The Word (ॐ) which has created all things.

<5> The influence of the satva guna (sentient force) brought the feeling of "I know," the raja guna (mutative force) brought the feeling of "I do," and the tama guna brought the feeling of "I have done" or memory. <6> With this, the unit consciousnesses were evolved and felt separate from the universe, which is the essence of suffering.

"In the beginning God created the heaven and the earth." (Genesis 1:1)

<7> The nucleus and controller of the universe who is in heaven (Pure Consciousness), feels to be (and IS) a part of the universe (God) and is in Bliss, called the state He is in Himself "heaven" (Pure Consciousness), and the state the unit consciousnesses were in (lost), He called "hell" (earth).

"And the earth was without form, and void; and darkness was upon the face of the deep. And the Spirit of God moved upon the face of the waters." (Genesis 1:2)

<8> The hell (earth) does not have a form nor is it a place; it is a state of consciousness. <9> The rest of the universe was in this hell (darkness), "and darkness was upon the face of the deep." <10> So God created a great compassion for those lost souls and desired to bring them to the state of Pure Consciousness that they might also feel one with the universe (God) and come to the Bliss. <11> So through the Universal Mind (▽), He moved over the consciousnesses of the universe (waters) to bring them under His control. Therefore He could guide them to the goal (Pure Consciousness).

"And God said, Let there be light: and there was light." (Genesis 1:3)

<12> God desired (projected His Light into the universe), "Let there be light," and The Word became flesh. He started to help this unit consciousness toward the **Eternal Divine Path** and with His Grace, The Word

reached Pure Consciousness, "and there was light." <13> The first unit consciousness reached Pure Consciousness. He became the First Begotten Son of God.

"And God saw the light, that it was good: and God divided the light from the darkness." (Genesis 1:4)

<14> God was very pleased with the seven steps of the **Eternal Divine Path** which led His first son to Pure Consciousness (light), "and God saw the light, that it was good." <15> Those who do not follow the Light are in darkness (ignorance), and those who go through this path will enter into the light. God established this truth, "and God divided the light from the darkness."

"And God called the light Day, and the darkness he called Night. And the evening and the morning were the first day." (Genesis 1:5)

<16> The Light (knowledge) clears things for the consciousness like the Day, and Darkness (ignorance) is like the Night, which hides the truth from the eyes. "And the evening and the morning were the first day." The first period of His struggle was finished.

Tablet Two

<1> From Genesis 1:8 until the story of Abraham, the process of creation and the different phases of the evolutionary process are explained. <2> Also many explanations are given for some points which have been a source of confusion. The following paragraphs will help to clarify these explanations:

<3> Adam is a name for the first humans and the First Begotten Son, who were dual in nature (male and female). There were many humans in the beginning made by God: "… created he them,…" (Gen. 1:27). <4> The first human did not have any body. He was in the ethereal stage. In fact, all things were in this stage. <5> In chapter 2 of Genesis God decided to give Adam a body. So He made a body for him, and only in this stage was the breath of life (prana) necessary to link the Soul and spirit to the body. This also was done to all other things.

<6> Man and woman were divided from the original Adam (which had a dual nature). After this evolutionary process, the word Adam and man are used interchangeably in the Bible.

<7> The name woman is used with a two-fold meaning: Woman as female, and woman as the lower nature of the human.

<8> It is through the influence of this lower nature, that the fall of man occurs. They were thrown out of heaven (higher consciousness, or beings) to the gross world. Only in this stage did they assume a new body with skin (Gen. 3:21).

<9> However, humans fell more and furthered their distance from the Lord. **This is explained by the fact that as the sin (samskaras) becomes heavier, or humans become attracted too much to the external world, the Soul becomes more distant from realizing God.**

<10> In this state, however, humans still preserved their direct relationship with the forces of nature. Their third eyes were opened. They had great occult powers. They could manipulate the forces of nature. The old generation misused these powers so much that the whole earth became corrupt, "And God saw that the wickedness of man was great in the earth,…" (Gen. 6:5).

<11> So God decided to withdraw completely all the occult powers from man and destroy all things He had created. He closed the third eye of man and only left intellect to make man able to grasp the realities behind this visible universe. <12> The Lord God also created a new climate on earth and gave man the body he presently has. The humans were also divided into different types (Shudras, Ksattriyas, Vipras, Vaeshyas, and Brahmins) in this stage. <13> This is all symbolized by the flood at the time of Noah, which was completed around six thousand years ago.

<14> Still humanity had the power of

telepathy, symbolized by the verse, "And the whole earth was of one language, and of one speech" (Gen. 11:1). With this good communicative ability and with the use of their intellect, they started to become a great civilization again. They started to use these abilities to make name and fame for themselves ("Babel" Gen. 11:9), instead of using them for progressing spiritually. <15> So again another evolutionary process took place. Telepathic ability was taken away from them. With having different languages with many different dialects – their languages were already different, "…every one after his tongue,…" (Gen. 10:5, 20, 31) – man became completely powerless (for his own good).

<16> However, the Lord God did not go through all these things to leave man in this stage. He had a definite Plan for doing so. He had a Plan to bring humans to a point where they would realize that the only way is to understand the realities behind this universe and creation, and to obey the Laws. <17> Humans should use all their powers and might toward spiritual progress of the self and others. Selfish endeavors will bring destruction to all. The only way is His Way (Universal Laws).

<18> This Plan or process started 12,000 years ago. Man reached this state that he is in now around 6,000 years ago. The last 6,000 years of history were necessary to show how the Laws of Karma, reincarnation, and many other Universal Laws work. The Lord God demonstrated that whenever people lose the view of these Laws, they will suffer because of their actions. Also the seven steps of the **Eternal Divine Path** were revealed by seven religions in this period to guide man in his spiritual progress.

Tablet Three

<1> So The Plan was this: To select some of the humans (or send those who had already reached a very high consciousness or Pure Consciousness) to guide and re-guide people toward perfection. These people were those who had already progressed to a very high state by following the Mystical Paths which had existed from the time of Noah and even before then. <2> Abraham was chosen as the first Elected One, and Hebrews were chosen as the first elected nation. Abraham, Isaac, Ishmael, and Jacob guided their children and family toward God-realization. Moses brought the Children of Israel out of Egypt, and gave them Laws necessary for a disciplined, neat nation. <3> Going out of Egypt is also a symbol of going out of the gross world to progress toward the spiritual world, "the Promised Land." Joshua (it is not "Joshua" because there is no "j" in Hebrew) conquered the Canaanites for them. David was the best king and used the sign (✡) which symbolizes the Kingdom Of Heaven On Earth.

<4> However, they failed to understand the reason they had been chosen. They mixed the beliefs of others with theirs, and they lost the original truths. They thought they had been chosen because they were superior to others. <5> When someone is chosen, there is a job to be done by that person. If he does the job then he is worthy of being called a chosen one for that task, and if he does it perfectly, then he can be respected and praised also. <6> However, if a person is chosen for a great mission, and he does not do it but misuses his powers, not only will he be disrespected, but he also will be punished for this misuse.

<7> Hebrews were selected to establish the Kingdom Of Heaven On Earth. But they failed in their mission. However, they should have failed because other truths in **The Greatest Sign** should have been revealed and many prophecies should have been fulfilled before the true Kingdom Of Heaven would come. <8> A part of them became an example for humanity throughout history to show that whenever any person or group fails, they would be punished. After punishment when they become purified, they will be given another chance to prove themselves worthy. After they fail again they create bad karma and will be punished to be purified again.

<9> The example of the Jewish race should be a lesson for all of humanity and shows how the Law of Karma works collectively and also individually; read The House of Judah (Jews).

<10> Jews are the people from the House of Judah. <11> There were the people of the House of Israel that never came back to their lands and supposedly are lost. The House of Israel also was chosen for a great Plan by the Lord; read Children of Abram (Abraham), All Prophecies Are Fulfilled.

Tablet Four

<1> Another Great Messiah, Esa the Christ, came after the first part of The Plan was finished. He came to show how the Kingdom Of Heaven within and without can be established: <2> By overcoming the individual weaknesses within and sacrificing the selfishness – not being self-centered (without). So he is the symbol of the personal struggle and sacrifice within and without (✝).

<3> However, still the teaching of Christ was either misunderstood or distorted because it did not fit some individuals' situation. <4> Also, the Lord God sent His complete Plan for bringing humanity to their senses through the book of The Revelation.

<5> After The Revelation was revealed and His Plan explained, the next seal was opened by Prophet Muhammad. The symbol is (☾) which is the last part of the symbol OM (ॐ). With spiritual powers, his individual conduct, and sacrifice (✝), and also with his deep understanding of the society (✡), Prophet Muhammad established the ideal of the three previous religions. <6> He brought the Kingdom Of Heaven for a small group of people in a small region of the world for a short period of time.

<7> With Prophet Muhammad the spiritual understanding was perfected. The greatest achievement of a spiritual seeker is to surrender (submit) to His Will or purpose (to be a surrendered one).

<8> However, further developments were necessary for humanity. The universal point of view – expansion of the mind (✹) – is necessary for any action taken by humanity. This came through the teachings of Bab (Baha'u'llah) (Baha'i Faith).

<9> Through creating an intense longing to help others to higher consciousness, a person with this last development in the spiritual path becomes a Paravipra (✡). He will help others to understand the realities behind this universe and will help all reach Pure Consciousness.

<10> Paravipras can be related to the last three stages of progress in **The Greatest Sign**: Those who reach the sixth stage in **The Greatest Sign** (✡), those who reach the seventh stage (卍), but do not leave their bodies in order to help others reach Pure Consciousness (men-gods or Satgurus), and those who have reached Pure Consciousness (卍) but will return to help others reach Pure Consciousness (god-men or Avatars). <11> However, we can say the last two are Maha-Paravipras (Great Paravipras). With these Great Paravipras, other Paravipras, and His First Begotten Son, God will bring His Kingdom on earth (Daharma). His Will, will be done on earth as it is in heaven. This is what is known as the First Resurrection. This will last for a long time, "a thousand years" (Rev. 20). After this long time is the time for the Second Resurrection!

THE BASE

This book is the base of the teachings of Maitreya and The Greatest Sign.

THE BASE

Tablet One

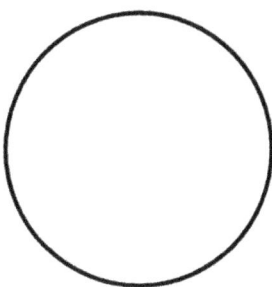

<1> God is everlasting, complete, without beginning or end. He is one and indivisible. He is the source of all things. He is infinite consciousness. <2> The circle above represents the infinity of God.

<3> The universe consists of consciousness and the three creative forces (three gunas). <4> In the beginning before any expression of consciousness, the universe was in the state of "Be"-ness or "AM"-ness. <5> The circle in the center above represents the infinity of the universe and God, and the shadow in the background shows the inability of the human mind to comprehend infinity.

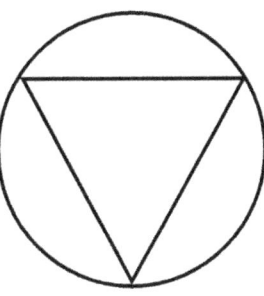

<6> The three creative forces or three gunas (▽) in the universe are the sentient force (satva guna), mutative force (raja guna), and static or crudifying force (tama guna). <7> The sentient force (satva guna) in the operative state is the intelligence or power of decision-making, <8> and the mutative force (raja guna) in the operative state is the power of movement (energy) in the universe. Without the raja guna there would be no movement

in the universe. <9> The static force (tama guna) in the operative state crudifies the consciousness and creates the five elements in the universe. They are: Ethereal, aerial, luminous (heat), liquid, and solid factors. Also it is responsible for memory.

Tablet Two

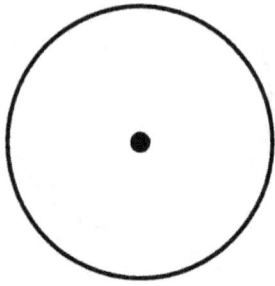

"In the beginning was the Word, and the Word was with God, and the Word was God.
The same was in the beginning with God.
All things were made by him; and without him was not anything made that was made." (John 1:1-3)

<1> Because of the desire of God, the balance between the creative forces (▽) was disturbed and the three operative powers were released.
<2> The operative power of the satva guna (sentient force), with the presence of the operative power of the tama guna, brought the feeling of "I know" (intelligence) into play.
<3> The operative power of the raja guna (mutative force), with the presence of the active tama guna, invoked the feeling of "I do" (action, energy), <4> and the release of the operative power of the tama guna resulted in the manifestation of fine ethereal factors. Then the feeling of "I have done" (memory) was awakened.
<5> With this, the three parts of the ego were evolved and the unit consciousnesses came into existence; <6> unit consciousness is the manifestation of consciousness in the gross universe in the illusive state of being separate from the rest (God).
<7> This illusion of being separate from the universe was created because of the influences of the ego ("I"). This resulted in unhappiness and causing the unit consciousnesses to become lost, suffer, and inflict suffering on others also.
<8> The dot in the middle of the circle represents this release of the operative powers of the three gunas which created the vibration. <9> This sound vibration, which is the same as the creative forces in the universe, is The Word (ॐ). This Word, or the creative powers in the universe, is the one responsible for all things being created.

THE BASE

Tablet 3

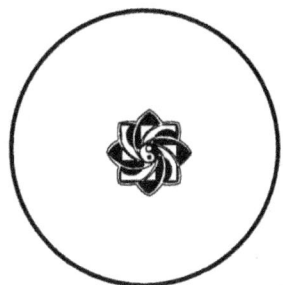

"In him was life; and the life was the light of men.
And the light shineth in darkness; and the darkness comprehended it not." (John 1:4-5)

<10> The life-force (energy, movement) is the power of the raja guna which is in the universe, "In him was life." In the higher level when this energy (life) is in the sentient state (light, satva) it is the light of the unit consciousness (man).

<11> But because of the influence of the tama guna (darkness), this energy or life-force (prana) becomes bondage. So the light, although always present, will not be comprehended by this darkened consciousness, "and the light shineth in darkness; and the darkness comprehended it not."

<12> The life-force in the universe is prana (raja guna) and is in God (universe), "In him was life." Also satva guna in the operative state is the light of the consciousness. This light which comes alive with life (raja guna) is also in every man (☯), "and the life was the light of men."

<13> But those who are darkened by ignorance (power of the tama guna) "comprehended it not." <14> So the life is raja guna, the light is satva guna, and darkness is the tama guna (separate "I") in the universe.

<15> Also the universe consists of two polarities, "positive and negative" or satva and tama (☯). The satva guna is positive and the tama guna is negative. <16> However, the raja guna exists in the universe as neutral and will gain the polarity of the dominating force. If the tama dominates, the raja (action) becomes bondage. If the satva dominates, the raja becomes positive and Divine (light).

Tablet Three

"In the beginning God created the heaven and the earth." (Genesis 1:1)

<1> God – Parama (beyond) Purusa (world), Parasutma (center of the universe), etc. – who is in Pure Consciousness (✦) (beyond the influence of the three gunas) called the state He was in Himself (Pure Consciousness) "heaven," and the state of being lost and separate from God (ignorance), He called "earth" (hell). <2> So heaven and hell (earth)

THE BASE

were created.

<3> The sign above represents the state of Pure Consciousness (✺). <4> It is the sign "Haree Om Shrii Hung" (**HOSH**), which means, "The goal of the life is to be(come) DIVINE (Pure Consciousness)." <5> The sign consists of four parts. The (•) in the middle is a representation of the beginning of the release of the creative forces (The Word).

<6> The I-Ching sign ((☯)) represents the dual nature of all things, as positive (satva) and negative (tama), in the universe. Also it represents the spiritual powers in the universe (activated by raja guna).

<7> The sign of the Expanding Lotus (✺), represents the All-Pervasive Love of God (the consciousness), <8> and the sign of Lotustica (卐) is the detachment quality of the consciousness (God) which lets those who are lost go away from Him into Maya (material attraction) and suffer so that they might learn their lessons and know that the only way to true happiness is to go toward Him and out of Maya. So we can say that it is the punishing side.

<9> Therefore, the sign **HOSH**, in general means that with spiritual powers ((☯)), Father controls the operative powers of the three gunas (•), and He is the nucleus of the universe. The Expanding Lotus (✺) shows that He is all-pervasive and loving. The Lotustica (卐) shows His detachment from those who go astray (toward ignorance), <10> but the moment they come back to Him they will be touched by His loving side and again accepted.

"And the earth was without form, and void;…" (Genesis 1:2a)

<11> The hell (earth) is not a place but a state of consciousness, "and the earth was without form, and void."

"…And darkness was upon the face of the deep…" (Genesis 1:2b)

<12> The three gunas (▽) together make up the creative power in the universe, or the Universal Mind. The satva guna (sentient force) is the intelligence or decision-making part of the Universal Mind. The raja guna (mutative force) is the recognizing part of the Universal Mind. The tama guna (static or crudifying force) is the screen or visualizing part of the Universal Mind.

<13> Through this Universal Mind, God can see His universe, recognize each part of it and the state of consciousness it is in, and decide what should be done about it.

<14> Through this Universal Mind, God saw that so many unit consciousnesses were lost and in darkness, "and darkness was upon the face of the deep…."

THE BASE

Tablet 4

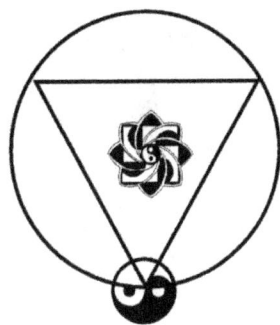

"...And the Spirit of God moved upon the face of the waters." (Genesis 1:2c)

<15> Water is a symbol for manifested consciousness (ether). <16> So God decided to rescue these lost souls and bring them to Pure Consciousness. Through His Universal Mind ("Spirit of God"), He moved to help them. He brought them () under His control (▽).

Tablet Four

"And God said, Let there be light: and there was light." (Genesis 1:3)

<1> And God desired that these lost souls realize their Divinity (light), "Let there be light." The Word became flesh and started to realize the path to salvation.

<2> He started to meditate on his moods and Soul. Little by little he became more familiar with himself and the realities of this universe. <3> He realized the effect of the three gunas as the three moods in nature and his Soul.
<4> He realized that the tama guna (static force) is responsible for intensifying the feeling of separation from the Lord and becoming self-centered (ignorance). <5> So he started to overcome this force over his Soul. As he succeeded in expanding his mind and feeling greater oneness with God, he experienced a great joy. But this joy was temporary and again the power of the tama guna would prevail.

<6> He realized that the environment around him also affects his moods and whenever there is much tama present, it would affect him and he would become more self-centered and lost. So he longed for a more satvic (sentient) environment (✡).

THE BASE Tablet 4

<7> In order to create such an environment, he started to help others around himself to realize what he had already realized. By bringing them to higher consciousness, he tried to create a better environment. So he started to sacrifice (✝) for others in order to show them the way to higher consciousness.

<8> By much endeavor, he succeeded in helping some to progress a little. So he created much pride that he is such a great being and had sacrificed so much for others. By this he created a great ego and so became self-centered, because he thought that he was greater than those who needed his help. This resulted in an intensified feeling of separation and again unhappiness.

<9> Also after some time, those whom he had helped to progress fell back to their previous states, and he became very discouraged as to why they would not progress even though he had done so much to help them.

<10> So a great realization came to him. He understood that because he was attached to the result of his action, he had become egoistical and had longed for glory. With not receiving it, he had become discouraged.

<11> From then on, he did the action but surrendered the result to the Lord. With this, he freed himself from the bondage of his action.

<12> Still later on he realized that even greater than surrendering is submission, which is to become a channel for His Divine actions. With this there would be no "I" left so no attachment.

<13> With these realizations, he greatly succeeded in helping the ones immediately close to him. But as he helped them more and expanded his consciousness further, greater joy came to him and with it greater realization.

<14> He realized that "God is All" and he not only should be concerned for those who are in his immediate surroundings but for all the universe, because even being concerned for only a small part of the universe (God) still is separation from Him, and the result will be the same as being self-centered.

<15> So he extended his effort and concern toward the whole universe. With this, he started to realize God and His concerns in the deepest level. Therefore, he could see God (universe) face-to-face.

THE BASE

Tablet 4

<16> With all the progress of the last five steps, he became a dynamic spiritual force (⬡) in the universe. Not only was a great permanent joy established in him, he also won the Grace of the Lord.

<17> With His Grace, he eventually overcame the power of the tama guna over his Soul and reached Pure Consciousness (light), "and there was light." <18> He became the First Begotten Son of God. He (卍) and the Father (卍) became one (卍).

> "And God saw the light, that it was good; and God divided the light from the darkness.
> And God called the light Day, and the darkness he called Night. And the evening and the morning were the first day." (Genesis 1:4-5)

<19> God was pleased to see His First Begotten Son in His likeness (Pure Consciousness, light). He divided the state of Pure Consciousness from the state of being lost. <20> He became the master of light and darkness and knew how to help the lost souls come out of the darkness (hell).

<21> The state of Pure Consciousness is called "Day," and the darkness (being under the influence of the tama guna) is called "Night." With this, the first period of His struggle was finished, "and the evening and the morning were the first day."

<22> However, helping the lost souls in this state was very hard. So God decided to create a more orderly process to bring the lost unit consciousnesses to Pure Consciousness. He began to create the manifested world (creation) and the evolutionary process.

Tablet Five

"And God said, Let there be a firmament in the midst of the waters, and let it divide the waters from the waters.

And God made the firmament, and divided the waters which were under the firmament from the waters which were above the firmament: and it was so." (Genesis 1:6-7)

<1> As water is a symbol for consciousness, with this decision He started to divide the consciousnesses in the universe into many levels according to their awareness: "Let there be a firmament in the midst of the waters, and let it divide the waters from the waters."

<2> The triangle upward symbolizes the Hierarchy into which the consciousnesses had been divided. Those in a higher consciousness are at the top of the triangle and those who are lost and in a complete illusion of separation are in the bottom of the triangle (△).

<3> Therefore, the triangle upward (△) represents the Hierarchy of the unit consciousnesses which reached Pure Consciousness (by the help of God) in heaven, those in higher consciousness, down to the ones completely lost at the bottom. The more sentient the consciousness, the higher the possibility of reaching Pure Consciousness first.

<4> The two triangles together symbolize the Kingdom Of Heaven (in heaven) (✡). The triangle upward symbolizes the actions taken to carry out the activities necessary in the manifested universe to help the unit consciousnesses reach the goal (Pure Consciousness) by all the elements of the universe and those who reached higher consciousness or Pure Consciousness. The triangle downward symbolizes the Universal Mind which enables God to control and direct these activities.

<5> Also, the triangle upward symbolizes action and organization (symbol for organizational structure) in heaven, and the triangle downward symbolizes control and justice.

<6> Then, by using the crudifying ability of the tama guna, God started to bind and crudify the consciousnesses (waters) toward a more solid state. <7> As the binding power of the static force (tama guna) started working, the first elements of the basic five elements (ethereal, aerial, luminous, liquid, and solid), namely, ethereal and aerial factors, became manifested. <8> These two elements are referred to as the "waters which were above the firmament." Those consciousnesses which in the process of crudification became the base for creating the liquid and solid factors, are called the "waters which were under the firmament."

"And God called the firmament Heaven. And the evening and the morning were the second day." (Genesis 1:8)

<9> So the elements of the manifested world started to be created. At this stage those parts of the elements which contained ethereal, aerial, and gaseous factors were

called Heaven (sky or the most invisible elements in the universe). From this verse on, the description is about The Plan of creation of the visible elements in the universe.

> "And God said, Let the waters under the heaven be gathered together unto one place, and let the dry land appear: and it was so." (Genesis 1:9)

<10> The "waters under the heaven" are those consciousnesses which, in the process of crudification, became the base for creating liquid and solid factors. Now in this stage they would be crudified further to create dry land, "Let the waters under the heaven be gathered together unto one place, and let the dry land appear."

<11> This gathering together or crudifying process is what is called the centripetal force of nature. Through this centripetal force, different levels of the universal elements, which are ethereal, aerial, luminous (fire, heat, light), liquid, and solid, and all the elements between them, were created.

> "And God called the dry land Earth; and the gathering together of the waters called he Seas: and God saw that it was good." (Genesis 1:10)

<12> So the dry land, or the most crudified consciousnesses, became the earth, or the solid factors in the universe. Also from the rest of the consciousnesses under the firmament, liquid factor was created, "called he Seas." With this, all the necessary elements to start the evolutionary process in the universe were prepared.

Tablet Six

> "And God said, Let the earth bring forth grass, the herb yielding seed, and the fruit tree yielding fruit after his kind, whose seed is in itself, upon the earth: and it was so." (Genesis 1:11)

<1> With the help of the centrifugal force, or by the loosening up of the crudifying power of the static force and by the use of the five elements already created, God now planned to start the creation of the plants.

> "And God said, Let us make man in our image, after our likeness:…" (Genesis 1:26)

<2> The evolutionary process of going from plants to animals, and eventually to humans, was achieved. <3> However, the entire first chapter of Genesis in the Bible is a description of creation in the state of planning and thinking. The real creation as a manifested world starts later in chapter 2 of Genesis.
<4> God decided to create man in His image and likeness (☺). He decided to bring the unit consciousnesses to human form as they were male and female in one being.

<5> Also, man is the end of the evolutionary process. **The human is in that state of being which can reach Pure Consciousness or perfect awareness.** He can gain complete control of the tama guna over his Soul and can also go beyond the influences of the crudified satva guna (reasoning directed toward selfishness) and the crudified raja guna (selfish actions). <6> He can direct them toward universalism and become **DIVINE** (become a son of God, Pure Consciousness).

> "And God blessed the seventh day, and sanctified it: because that in it he had rested from all his work which God created and made." (Genesis 2:3)

<7> After these seven periods in which God finished planning the creation, He saw the process of evolution and was very pleased with it. After He would create it, it would be self-sustaining and He did not have to interfere in its process very frequently. So He could rest and become a witness entity (consciousness) in the universe, "he had rested from all his work."

<8> Therefore, through the Laws God has established in the universe, whenever man goes astray he would suffer, and whenever he progresses he would receive joy. So through this process eventually he would find the way to God (Pure Consciousness).

> "And the Lord God formed man of the dust of the ground, and breathed into his nostrils the breath of life; and man became a living soul." (Genesis 2:7)

<9> When the first expression of awareness appeared as a sound vibration, "The Word," time was perceived. When this manifested universe started to be created, the reality of space became understood, and the atom was built. <10> In Sanskrit, the atom (anu) is called "avidya" meaning "ignorance." This same atom in the Bible is called "the dust of the ground" which is the atom in the first stages and also can be called the "cosmic dust." Man did not have the same body as we know it today. His body was made more of psychic and spiritual factors.

<11> However, he had many basic things in common with the man of today. He had a Soul (he was a unit consciousness) which had a unit mind (the three gunas). This unit being resided in the ethereal factor (spirit), but he also had a material body consisting of the four other elements, namely, aerial, luminous, liquid, and solid. <12> The four-element-material body can only link itself to the psychic (spirit) or ethereal body (unit Soul and its ethereal factor) with some fine element. This fine element in the Bible is symbolized by "the breath of life," which is also called "prana."

<13> This "prana" is the outgoing energy (raja guna) from the Soul. It can be found in fresh air and is even more necessary for survival than oxygen. It is the life-force which is also available in other elements in nature besides air. It is a living thing that can be controlled, directed and used for many purposes in human life. It is the life-force of all living things.

<14> By creating the manifested universe, the evolutionary process, and the human, God guides the unit consciousnesses. With the attraction of the external world (Maya) – and because of the ignorance of man of his Divinity as "'I am' one with the 'I AM'" – he becomes a slave of his illusion that he is a separate being in the whole universe, and he becomes more and more lost because of the impulses of his desires and attachments to the external world. <15> Only after many lifetimes he reaches a point where he realizes that there should be more in life than this heedless pursuance of the lower nature which brings so much suffering.

<16> That is when he starts searching for more meaningful realities than these unsatisfying, impulsive desires, which are the root of all suffering. **That is when he will be helped and be shown the way to salvation, and is the reason for this creation and Maya.**

Tablet Seven

> "And the Lord God caused a deep sleep to fall upon Adam, and he slept: and he took one of his ribs, and closed up the flesh instead thereof;
> And the rib, which the Lord God had taken from man, made he a woman,…" (Genesis 2:21-22)

<1> However, a further evolutionary process became necessary: The separation of male and female into man and woman. This occurred because each unit consciousness was a perfect unit in quality and did not feel any need for the help that was necessary to attract it toward the Great (the goal). <2> That is why this separation, especially at the higher levels of the evolutionary process (higher plants, animals, and humans) took place. "And the rib, which the Lord God had taken from man, made he a woman,…"

<3> With this separation, a great feeling of not being complete is inherent in the human, and forces a man to search for the cause of this emptiness and dissatisfaction. The search to find the other half draws them even deeper and faster into the ocean of Maya. This helps the humans realize faster how weak they are.

<4> Through this process man starts questioning the reason for being here, who he is, where he has come from, where he is going, and so on.

<5> This is the beginning of the attraction to the mystery of the universe and the basis for the human search in finding answers to his questions. This will lead him to the deeper level of his being and cause him to become more familiar with the world within.

<6> If he continues and is sincere and persistent, eventually he will be led to the reality that there is a Superior Power in this universe, with definite Laws to follow and many realities to understand. It is then that he will thirst to know the truth, and if he is sincere, he will know. "Ask, and it shall be given you; seek, and ye shall find; knock, and it shall be opened unto you:" (Matthew 7:7).

<7> Intuitively he knows that he was once perfect in the past but some time ago he had lost one part of himself. With all these drives, his journey toward Pure Consciousness begins.

<8> **Only when a human realizes his imperfection and feels the need of help from God will he be helped.**

<9> At the time of reunion with his other half, or when born male and female, or when the lower nature (woman) is overcome, he becomes perfect and will reach Pure Consciousness. So **he will be(come) a son of God**, because he has, by His Grace, overcome the forces of nature over his Soul and is in the image and likeness of God. He will reach Pure Consciousness (卍).

<10> **This reaching Pure Consciousness is the goal of yoga (yoga means "union").**

> "Unto Adam also and to his wife did the Lord God make coats of skins, and clothed them." (Genesis 3:21)

<11> As the human fails and becomes more separated from God, a new evolutionary step is necessary. Up to this point, the human was more a mass of Soul (unit consciousness), spirit (ethereal body), and psychic being, than a physical being. He also had a direct relationship with the forces of nature, and he could manipulate these occult powers for his own selfish desires.

<12> The misuse of these powers brought a fall in morality and humans started to use them for their mundane self-satisfaction. This affected man's environment and crudified the human more. They became more flesh, "did the Lord God make coats of skins, and clothed them."

Tablet Eight

> "There were giants in the earth in those days; and also after that, when the sons of God came in unto the daughters of men, and they bare children to them, the same became mighty men which were of old, men of renown." (Genesis 6:4)

> "And God said unto Noah, The end of all flesh is come before me; for the earth is filled with violence through them; and, behold, I will destroy them with the earth." (Genesis 6:13)

<1> The humans had direct access to the spiritual powers, so they could manipulate them and use them as they pleased. Because they (most of them) misused them, a disturbance in the balance of nature resulted and this affected all levels of existence of the old generation. <2> Also great powers were released which had created unrest in nature ("the earth is filled with violence through them").

<3> God then decided to take these powers away from humans, so He would not have to struggle with them, "And the Lord said, My Spirit shall not always strive with man,…" (Gen. 6:3). He would only give these powers back to those who were worthy to receive them after proving they would not misuse them.

<4> So the door of the spiritual center (third eye) in the human was closed, and the spiritual understandings and powers became latent (kundalini). Man became a rational animal with only intellect left in him.

<5> With this, the human became completely helpless and powerless. He no longer can misuse the powers in the universe for his mundane desires. Now God could leave men by themselves and only through His Prophets and sons, little by little, bring those who show they are worthy to higher consciousness, awaken their spiritual understandings (kundalini), and open their eyes (third eyes) to the higher truth. This process started twelve thousand years ago.

<6> Also, in the last six thousand years, He has created a history for men that is full of lessons. This was done so that eventually they would understand these lessons and through them would learn not to make the same mistakes again. Also it would teach that God is the true Guide and should be followed. That is what history is for.

<7> Man before the flood did not have a history. That is why history only goes back five or six thousand years. <8> Furthermore, through the same time period, by His Messengers (sons of God), God has sent the **Eternal Divine Path** to guide humans, step-by-step, toward becoming His sons. This path covers seven truths that have been revealed to humanity by seven Prophets (Angels) as seven religions.

<9> Only when all of the seven truths are understood and their relationships realized and followed, can a man awaken his spiritual forces and become one with Him.

<10> The beginning of this new kind of man ("men of renown") and Plan is symbolized by the flood of Noah, destruction of the old earth and creation of the new one.

<11> Actually the civilization that was destroyed was living in a land* in the Atlantic Ocean between Southern Europe and Northern Africa, and it stretched to the southern part of North America.

<12> These new humans started their life on the earth in an area north of that land which also was destroyed later (Gen. 10:25). They became "mighty men which were of old, men of renown." Their intellectual power, reasoning, and understandings were greater than that

---

* The land mentioned above in the Atlantic Ocean surfaced between North America and Europe, and then later on sank again.

THE BASE   *Tablet 9*

of the old human with great spiritual powers but little reasoning. With these abilities, they could reach higher consciousness but could not misuse the universal forces for their mundane desires.

Tablet Nine

"And Noah builded an altar…" (Genesis 8:20)

<1> With the third eye of man closed, he no longer had direct access to the spiritual understandings. So the truth of the spirit was revealed to him through the sons of God (in this age, Noah) in abstract and symbolic ways, "and Noah builded an altar…." Man started to worship God in a gross state as building altars and giving material and burnt offerings.

<2> However the deeper truth of the universe and man was entrusted to a few Great Souls who preserved it for those who were worthy to receive it. The essence of this knowledge eventually became the base of the Mystical Paths in most of the earth. The oldest written materials in this regard are the three books of the Vedas or Scripture of the Hindus. These Mystical Paths should be understood, practiced, and realized in order to awaken the latent spiritual forces (☯) of the human.

<3> However, to study only these teachings without understanding the other truths which underlie **The Greatest Sign**, might lead to escapism, and that God does not like (Revelation 3:14-22 in the book Revelation of The Revelation).

<4> Those who try to reach Pure Consciousness with selfish pursuance of mastering themselves "only" and escaping the world, will be "spue[d] out of His mouth" (Rev. 3:16), which is back to the misery of this external world. So they will be forced to help others in their struggle toward Pure Consciousness.

<5> However, these practices and knowledge of the Mystical Paths (Far East Philosophies) are highly recommended, especially contemplation, meditation, reflection, study of the Scriptures, and those practices which help a person to calm his mind and realize the self and God: "Be still, and know that I am God" (Psalms 46:10). Eventually he should be able to direct these energies and knowledge toward helping others to reach higher consciousness.

<6> After the flood of Noah, humanity was divided into five different types, as workers (Shudras), warriors (Ksattriyas), intellectuals (Vipras), business-minded ones (Vaeshyas), and seers or masters (Brahmins). (For more detail read The Holiest Book chapters 9 and 10 of Genesis in that book).

<7> The true spiritual knowledge was entrusted to this Brahmin class, and they guided the new man in their spiritual needs.

119

THE BASE *Tablet 10*

> "And the whole earth was of one language, and of one speech." (Genesis 11:1)

> "…for in his days was the earth divided;…" (Genesis 10:25)

> "So the Lord scattered them abroad from thence upon the face of all the earth:…" (Genesis 11:8)

<8> However, still the humans had telepathic abilities and they could understand each other through these abilities ("…the whole earth was of one language,…"). So they again started to use this great communicative ability and their intellect for their selfish use and mundane desires. <9> This misuse of the powers is always based on egotism and will lead to self-destruction, "…let us build us a city and tower, whose top may reach unto heaven; and let us make us a name, lest we be scattered abroad upon the face of the whole earth." (Gen. 11:4).

<10> So they wanted to make a city with great towers to make themselves a name (become famous) and also to stay together, "lest we be scattered abroad…." <11> But God not only wants them to be scattered abroad upon the earth, but also to other planets.

<12> Therefore God took away their telepathic abilities and made them become confused by their different languages, "…every one after his tongue,…" (Genesis 10:5, 20, 31). <13> Also by dividing the earth and destroying the land they were in, "…in his days was the earth divided…" (Gen. 10:25), He forced them to leave their land and they were scattered all over the world.

<14> The spiritual masters who foresaw this destruction left their land before it occurred and took their knowledge with them. <15> One of these groups (Aryans) went to the Himalayas and India, and the <u>Vedas</u> are what is left from their knowledge.

<16> So the first seal (☯) in **The Greatest Sign** is related to the awakening of the spiritual forces. However, it is the first step in spiritual progress.

Tablet Ten

> "Now the Lord had said unto Abram, Get thee out of thy country, and from thy kindred, and from thy father's house, unto a land that I will shew thee:" (Genesis 12:1)

<1> With this command, God set a great Plan in motion which would create significant events in the future history of man. It would bring great lessons for humanity's understanding and progress.

<2> Centuries after the flood of Noah, when many Souls had gone through a great amount of progress, God decided to reveal

THE BASE

the second part (✡) of the **Divine Path** to humanity.

<3> So Abram (Abraham) was chosen to start this mission. <4> The purpose of this second revelation is to show that organization, justice (Laws), and great leaders are necessary in order to create a proper environment that allows the human to progress to his highest potential.

<5> The very theme of the Old Testament is based on these points to show their importance: <6> the laws brought by Moses, the great king (leader) was symbolized by David, the organization of the governmental bodies was shown by those bodies in the countries that the Children of Israel ruled, and through God's Laws, justice was established when they were followed.

<7> But throughout the Old Testament, we can see that the kings failed to have mercy on their subjects and most of the time no one was ready to sacrifice to create that desired environment.

<8> This is the lesson of truth which was brought by the Children of Israel and is symbolized by the Star of David (✡). The triangle upward (△) represents organizational structure, and the triangle downward (▽), justice and control through Laws. <9> So the sign (✡) in a broader sense means, "The Kingdom Of Heaven should be established on earth by the Hebrews (those who have gone beyond) or the Children of Israel (those who struggle – are on one team – with God, the Elected Ones)."

Tablet Eleven

"...until Shiloh come; and unto him shall the gathering of the people be." (Genesis 49:10)

<1> The coming of the Messiah ("Shiloh") was predicted long before the Children of Israel had even attempted to create what they were supposed to bring about, which was a desired environment (✡) where all can progress physically, mentally, and spiritually.

<2> The Messiah came as Esa the Christ. His message was: **In order to create that ideal environment, sacrifice (not being self-centered) (✝) is necessary.** Without sacrifice (✝) the Kingdom Of Heaven On Earth (✡) is not possible. <3> Of course sacrifice, like everything else, is of three kinds, from ignorance, passion, or knowledge. Any sacrifice (✝) done for this ideal (✡) is from knowledge.

<4> He also gathered together "the people" under his religion, Christianity (✝). For more detail, read <u>Children of Abram (Abraham), All Prophecies Are Fulfilled</u>.

<5> So, sacrifice means to struggle to progress physically, mentally, and spiritually and to help others (not being self-centered) also to progress in these spheres. Therefore, in the process, the false ego is crucified (✝).

THE BASE

"Blessed is he that readeth, and they that hear the words of this prophecy, and keep those things which are written therein:..." (Revelation 1:3)

<6> After the New Testament, the last book of the Bible (The Revelation) was revealed to humanity. In this book, the events which would happen in the last six thousand years were revealed in a symbolic language.

<7> It is revealed that there will be seven churches, seven seals which would be opened, and seven Angels in different periods who would bring plagues to the earth. All these seven churches, seals, and Angels are the seven truths and mysteries which would come to the earth. <8> Truth is always guidance to those who are ready and have overcome, and is torture to those who are attached to this external world (plagues).

<9> As it was explained, one of the plans in the last six thousand years was to reveal the seven truths that will guide man to salvation or the state of becoming one with the **ONE**.

<10> The first three of these truths were revealed to humanity before the book of The Revelation. They have been explained in the previous pages. They are: The Far East Philosophies (Mystical Paths), which will help a person to awaken his latent spiritual forces (☯); the teachings and theme of the Old Testament, or the necessity of the establishment of the Kingdom Of Heaven On Earth (✡); and the theme of the New Testament, that not being self-centered – being humble (✝) – is necessary to establish such a Kingdom.

<11> As it was explained, sacrifice without surrendering the result to the Lord (☪) can become a binding force in human progress toward complete freedom from all bondages. <12> Also the sacrifice and endeavors should be directed toward the whole universe. Otherwise separation of man from man would result. So a universal point of view (✹) is necessary, or in other words, it is necessary to realize that God is everything.

<13> After going through all of these steps, and when a person with all these realizations becomes a dynamic spiritual force (✡), he can win The Grace of the Lord and reach Pure Consciousness (✾) which is to know all, become His son, and be in His image.

<14> That is why after those first three truths which were explained previously, four more truths should have come to humanity so that the seven truths to salvation (✾) would be complete. <15> These seven truths are the seven symbols which are used in different parts in The Revelation.

Tablet Twelve

"And as for Ishmael, ... I have blessed him,..." (Genesis 17:20)

<1> As it was explained, the next step is surrendering and becoming submissive to God. Islam (☪) comes from the word "tasleim" which means both surrendering and submission.

<2> So this fourth truth which was re-

THE BASE

Tablet 13

vealed to humanity as the religion of Islam, is another step toward perfection, salvation, and freedom from bondage in this manifested world.

<3> Even in doing a great action to create the proper environment and/or help others, if the result is not surrendered to the Lord, it will become a burden. <4> That is because either he will create a great ego of how wonderful a person he is and so is greater than most others, or he will become very discouraged as to why no one respects him for his greatness or why others do not progress with all his effort.

<5> But by doing the action and surrendering the result, he will free himself of this binding effect and therefore never become depressed. **The very cause of depression is expectation and attachment to the result of one's actions. When the result is not as the ego expected, then a person becomes depressed.**

<6> Even greater than surrendering is submission. In surrendering still there is an "I" left which surrenders the result of "his" action to the Lord. There exists a separation between "I" and "He."

<7> In submission, however, a person lets Him do the Divine actions through him. So the person no longer is the doer but is the observer of Him doing it. Therefore if he never did anything, how can he create any attachment to the result of something he had not done? Then he is free. <8> Also in submission, the doer, the thing done, and for whom it is done, all become one and the unity is complete. There is no "I" as separate from Him.

<9> However, to be in that ideation that He is the doer and "I am submitted to Him" is very difficult. So if it is forgotten, or a person becomes attached to the result of his action, and realizes it, then he can surrender it to the Lord and be free. <10> But the goal is to be in that state of mind of submission to Him (One with Him).

<11> The very theme of the <u>Koran</u> (the Scripture of Islam) is to surrender and submit to God. It is a part of **The Greatest Sign** and its teachings (**Eternal Divine Path**).

Tablet Thirteen

"And when he had opened the fifth seal, I saw under the altar the souls of them that were slain for the word of God, and for the testimony which they held:" (Rev. 6:9)

<1> Although the spiritual realization was completed with the first four truths explained so far, if a universal feeling (✹) is not created, all of them could lead to narrowness of the mind <2> which is the very cause of prejudice, separation, and much suffering.

<3> The fifth truth, which expresses this teaching the strongest, was brought by Bab (Baha'u'llah), the Baha'i Faith (✹).

<4> Only when it is realized that God is everything, inseparable, and **ONE**, that we all are a part of Him and He is the whole universe, and that we have to direct all of our endeavors and realizations toward Him (the whole

THE BASE   *Tablet 14*

universe), can we shatter all narrowness of the mind and be free from this evil also.

<5> The very writings of Baha'u'llah (Bab) express this point strongly. <6> Also, it was after him that the world became more aware of its interdependence and oneness.

<7> In the beginning of the spread of this religion, many Souls were slain, "for the testimony which they held."

Tablet Fourteen

"And I beheld when he had opened the sixth seal, and, lo, there was a great earthquake; and the sun became black…" (Rev. 6:12)

<1> When a person sees that God is everything and all are within Him, he sees Him everywhere. Then there is a tendency to forget about this external world and only become an observer, so again escape this world of suffering.

<2> However, if he does not forget about those who are suffering, and with the previous realizations in the first five truths or steps, tries to help others also to progress physically, mentally, and spiritually, such a person would become a dynamic spiritual force in the world. He then can be called a Paravipra (✡).

<3> So the sign (✡) is the sign of Paravipras – <4> those great beings who have awakened their spiritual forces (☯), have realized the effect of the environment on their spiritual progress, long to establish a spiritual environment (✡), are ready to sacrifice (✝) for this ideal, surrender and submit their endeavors to Him (☪), and know that God is ONE and inseparable or is All, and they would help the whole universe (✹). <5> With all of these steps and their powers, they become dynamic spiritual forces or Paravipras (✡). <6> Then they would receive the Grace of God and the Kingdom Of Heaven within themselves (✡) would be established.

<7> This seal was revealed to humanity in the twentieth century in the year 1945 after the second world war (1944). After the revelation of this seal, great changes started to occur and tribulation began to form on earth, "…there was a great earthquake."

THE BASE

Tablet Fifteen

"But in the days of the voice of the seventh angel, ... the mystery of God should be finished,..." (Rev. 10:7)

<1> As the mysteries behind this universe and existence finish when a person reaches the seventh chakra, so the mystery of the Scriptures and truth which have come through the last six Prophets (Angels) will be finished by the seventh Angel. This has been promised in the book of The Revelation (read Revelation of The Revelation).

<2> The teachings behind **The Greatest Sign**, as described briefly in this book and other books in **THOTH**, reveal the mysteries of creation and history. <3> They also explain the meaning of each seal, which is related to one religion. When the meanings of all these seals are put together and combined, they will show the **Eternal Divine Path**. This is the path to salvation to be(come) in His image, a son of God.

<4> Also before the seventh Angel comes, there is a mystery which has not been revealed to humanity. "Mystery" means something unknown, or not discovered. So mystery brings confusion. <5> But when this mystery will be revealed, the confusion between the previous truths and their relationships together will be no more ("will finish").

<6> That is exactly what **The Greatest Sign** does: **It clarifies the confusion between all**.

<7> So the seventh truth is the one which covers all the previous ones and clarifies the confusion (mystery) between them all.

Tablet Sixteen

"He that overcometh shall inherit all things; and I will be his God, and he shall be my son." (Rev. 21:7)

<1> Those who meditate, contemplate, become familiar with the Far East teachings (Mystical Paths) or somehow awaken their spiritual forces (understandings) (☯), will realize that there is more in life than only satisfying physiological, safety, and emotional (false ego) needs. They see the power of Maya and long to become Divine and know God.

<2> If they also realize how a proper environment (✡) is necessary to progress toward their goal – to be(come) Divine – then they realize they should help in the establishment of this environment.

<3> Furthermore they should realize that to establish such an environment, sacrifice (✝) is necessary, and they should set an example for others so that they also will come to a higher realization. With this, they become other-centered and dissolve their false egos of self-centeredness.

<4> By surrendering (☾) the result of

their actions, they free themselves from any bondages of their actions. Also by submission they dissolve their egos as "I" separate from Him. They become one with Him and rid themselves of the result of their actions.

<5> Also by becoming Universalists (✸), they shatter all narrowness of the mind and become free from all evils related to it.

<6> Then, if with all these realizations they direct all their energies and understandings toward helping others to progress, they dissolve their separated egos into Him and will win His Grace. <7> They will feel it constantly within and so establish the Kingdom Of Heaven within (✡).

<8> Such a person truly overcomes all the pitfalls of the spiritual path and that is the only requirement to win His Grace and become His son, "He that overcometh … shall be my son."

<9> Such a person becomes one with the Father (✿), in His image and likeness (✿): **A son of God**.

CHILDREN OF ABRAM (ABRAHAM)
"ALL PROPHECIES ARE FULFILLED"

The book, <u>Children of Abram (Abraham), All Prophecies Are Fulfilled</u>, explains the promises God gave to Abram (Abraham). God gave promises for both of Abram's (Abraham's) children. They were Ishmael and Isaac. He fulfilled these promises and other prophecies. So God gave promises and fulfilled them. Therefore, God certainly exists. Furthermore, with these teachings God brings a greater truth to humanity and unifies them.

CHILDREN OF ABRAM (ABRAHAM) "ALL PROPHECIES ARE FULFILLED"

PREFACE

As it is described in the book <u>The Base</u>, as the base of our teachings, creation started billions of years ago and gradually has been perfected through numerous stages and changes until man was created. Then through many different evolutionary steps, again man became more and more under the control of God.

Then, around twelve thousand years ago, with another evolutionary step (symbolized by the flood of Noah), new man as we know him today was evolved. This evolutionary process was completed around six thousand years ago. Through many lifetimes and also from those who had already reached higher consciousness even before the flood of Noah (such as Enoch), a group of humans were chosen as the Elected People to set an example for others and also to guide humanity to the true path of reaching Pure Consciousness.

He who was chosen as the first of such a people, and became their father, was Abram (Abraham). God chose Abram because he was a great spiritual personality and one who longed to preserve the Laws of God (read <u>The Holiest Book</u>, Holiest 1 and Holiest 2).

This book is about the promises given to Abram (Abraham) and how all of them are fulfilled. Also it is about the fulfillment of many prophecies in this same period of time. Furthermore, it will explain some prophecies have not been fulfilled yet but will be soon to come. At the end, it will be mentioned how the Kingdom of God on earth will be established and His Will, will be done on earth as it is in heaven.

However, before starting the book there are two points which should be kept in mind and never lost sight of throughout the entire book.

First, we have to remember four things: The Law of Karma (that each action has a reaction and the doer should bear the result of his actions), the Law of Reincarnation (that man will be reincarnated again and again until he reaches perfection), the ability of God to forgive, through His Grace, the sins (bad karma) whenever He desires (that is, when a person learns the lessons of an experience and follows the Laws of God, his sins will be forgiven, because all this creation was made to give man different experiences in different levels of evolution. When the experience and the lesson are gained, there is no reason that he should suffer more, so God forgives he who understands and walks with Him), and lastly, the ability of God to put a person in situations that are necessary for him to gain some experiences or lessons, or to perform a duty, even without sin, and without having done any bad karma (bad actions).

Remembrance of these four points will keep us aware that when we talk about a special race or people, or their ancestry, it is not a description of generations as a superior or inferior race. As described by the four laws (or points) above, these people have been reincarnated in that situation because of their past deeds or for fulfilling the purposes that God was trying to bring about. So this will help the reader to stay away from prejudice and narrowness of the mind.

The second point is to remember that this book is written only to show another sign of God's actions to fulfill His Plan of bringing man to his senses, showing how He works, and fulfilling His promises even when humans fail to understand His works. So this book is written to enhance and increase the faith of those who try to know the truth and realities behind our teachings. But the base of our teachings is what is revealed through <u>The Holiest Book</u>, <u>The Essence</u>, <u>The Base</u>, and <u>Revelation of The Revelation</u>.

This book also will help the student of the

CHILDREN OF ABRAM (ABRAHAM)   Tablet 1

Bible to understand the Bible more completely when he keeps in mind why all things in the Bible had happened so that the things described in this book are fulfilled.

Some truth in this book was realized through some other people also. But this book is more complete than any other explanation of The Plan of the Lord for humanity, because others only had realized a part of the truth by narrowing themselves into explaining these things only from the view of one religion. **When man wants to describe God's Plan (or any great idea) for humanity in narrow ways, then the trouble starts and he has no choice but to err.**

However, with expansion of the mind and understanding the Laws of God for the whole universe (universalism), man can solve many problems in the world, only by knowing Him. Amen (ॐ).

Tablet One

SECTION I

<1> This generation of human with the form as we know it now started 12,000 years ago and was completed 6,000 years ago. God took away the spiritual powers of man and increased his intellectual understandings. <2> Man became a thinking being rather than a being with spiritual powers. Through many evolutionary steps, God brought man to this helpless point in order to guide him. (For more detail, read The Base).

<3> Through the history of the last six thousand years, by many lessons from Great Souls, and through His Prophets, God has created a fountain of knowledge and has given many lessons in order to guide the humans to understand the truth behind this creation and the goal of the life.

<4> After the flood of Noah until the time of Abram's selection as the father of the Hebrews, many humans went through progress toward higher consciousness and were ready to be chosen as Elected Ones. These Elected Ones will be used to bring the spiritual truth and realities behind this universe to humanity.

<5> Also, to make man understand and believe that these six thousand years of history have been guided by the Lord, great events which took place in this time period had been predicted and prophesied by His Messengers, and are written in the Scriptures. These were given so that many might believe, especially in this time of religious degeneration.

The earth is divided:

<6> To start this part of The Plan, the earth was divided and one part of it was reserved for a great purpose. This event should have had great significance in that it was recorded in the Bible: "...for in his days was the earth divided;..." (Gen. 10:25). What was the purpose of this division, and what land has it been? The answers to these questions are one part of The Plan.

Abram is chosen as the father of the Hebrews:

Now the Lord had said unto Abram, **Get thee out of thy country, and from thy kindred, and from thy father's house**, unto a land that I will shew thee:

And I will make of thee **a great nation**, and I will **bless thee**, and make thy name great; and thou shalt **be a blessing**:

And I will **bless them that bless thee**, and **curse him that curseth thee: and in thee shall all families of the earth be blessed**. (Genesis 12:1-3)

<7> With this, God chose Abram and commanded him to "...Get thee out of thy country, and from thy kindred, and from thy father's house, unto a land that I will shew thee." Abram complied with the command of the Lord, took all his belongings, and left

CHILDREN OF ABRAM (ABRAHAM)

his home. So he showed his obedience to the Lord and his detachment to the external world and its attractions, such as family, friends, and belongings.

<8> Also, if the command was obeyed there was a promise: "And I will make of thee a great nation, … will bless thee, and make thy name great; and thou shalt be a blessing" and "I will bless them that bless thee, and curse him that curseth thee: and in thee shall all families of the earth be blessed." <9> The command was obeyed, so the promise would be fulfilled by the Lord.

A promise is given about Abram's seed:

And the Lord said unto Abram, after that Lot was separated from him, Lift up now thine eyes, and look from the place where thou art northward, and southward, and eastward, and westward:

For all the land which thou seest, to thee will I give it, and to thy seed for ever.

And I will make thy seed as the dust of the earth: so that if a man can number the dust of the earth, then shall thy seed also be numbered. (Genesis 13:14-16)

<10> Two things were promised: First, that a land would be given to Abram's seed which stretches northward, southward, eastward and westward (with no mention of boundaries), and secondly, that he would increase his seed "as the dust of the earth." **So the land should be very large to bear that huge a population.**

This promise is given for Ishmael:

And Abram was fourscore and six years old, when Hagar bare Ishmael to Abram. (Genesis 16:16)

<11> These promises were given to Abram. The seed of Abram was Ishmael. Later on God changed the name of Abram to Abraham and gave him new promises different from these and also a promise of a new seed by the name of Isaac. These new promises after the change of the name to Abraham were given to Abraham and Isaac. But the promises which were given to Abram were for his seed, Ishmael. <12> Also, as we can see historically, the promises given for Ishmael, the father of the Arabs, have come true. Arabs are a great nation with a large territory.

Tablet Two

The name of Abram is changed to Abraham, and new promises are given for his new son, Isaac:

And when Abram was ninety years old and nine, the Lord appeared to Abram, and said unto him, I am the Almighty God; walk before me, and be thou perfect.

And I will make my covenant between me and thee, and will multiply thee exceedingly.

And Abram fell on his face: and God talked with him, saying,

As for me, behold, my covenant is with thee, and thou shalt be a father of many nations.

Neither shall thy name any more be called Abram, but thy name shall be Abraham; for a father of many nations have I made thee.

And I will make thee exceeding fruitful, and I will make nations of thee, and kings shall come out of thee.

And I will establish my covenant between me and thee and thy seed after thee in their generations for an everlasting covenant, to be a God unto thee, and to thy seed after thee.

And I will give unto thee, and to thy seed after thee, the land wherein thou

CHILDREN OF ABRAM (ABRAHAM)　　　　　　　　　　Tablet 2

art a stranger, all the land of Canaan, for an everlasting possession; and I will be their God. (Genesis 17:1-8)

<1> God appeared to Abram again when he was ninety-nine years old and requested, "be thou perfect" and follow God's Laws ("walk before me"). The result of following His Laws would be: "I will make my covenant between me and thee, and will multiply thee exceedingly." So still there was a requirement for the promises which God gave to Abram, that is, he should follow God's Laws and be perfect.

<2> Also a new chapter started in God's relationship with him. God changed his name from Abram (which has become synonymous to mean "father of one [nation]") to Abraham, "father of many [nations]." <3> With this, it seems that God had changed His promise, because God had promised Abram that He would make "a great nation" of him, but now He promised he would be "a father of many nations." The truth is that it is Abraham who would be the father of many nations. God changed his name from Abram to Abraham and said, "I have made thee [the Abraham] a father of many nations." So it is Abraham who would be the father of many nations, not Abram.

<4> Abram is the father of a great nation, whose seed was Ishmael, so the promise also belongs to Ishmael. However, Abraham would have a son by the name of Isaac who would create many nations, and Isaac's father is Abraham.

<5> "And I will make nations of thee," and "kings shall come out of thee." Here are two completely different promises, a promise of material possession which is "nations," and a promise of spiritual domination, "kings."

<6> Also God promised to give to his seed (Isaac) **all the land of Canaan**. This time God gave a definite name as to which land He was going to give to Isaac. There was a definite boundary about the land that would be given to him. But in the case of the promises given before (to Abram), many lands with no boundaries would be given to his seed.

<7> So we can see that not only was the name of Abram changed to Abraham, but a completely new relationship was established between God and Abraham. These promises also are completely different than the previous ones.

And God said unto Abraham, Thou shalt keep my covenant therefore, thou, and thy seed after thee in their generations.

This is my covenant, which ye shall keep, between me and you and thy seed after thee; Every man child among you shall be circumcised.

And ye shall circumcise the flesh of your foreskin; and it shall be a token of the covenant betwixt me and you.

And he that is eight days old shall be circumcised among you, every man child in your generations, he that is born in the house, or bought with money of any stranger, which is not of thy seed.

He that is born in thy house, and he that is bought with thy money, must needs be circumcised: and my covenant shall be in your flesh for an everlasting covenant.

And the uncircumcised man child whose flesh of his foreskin is not circumcised, that soul shall be cut off from his people; he hath broken my covenant. (Genesis 17:9-14)

<8> The sign of the covenant was that all males should be circumcised.

And God said unto Abraham, As for Sarai thy wife, thou shalt not call her name Sarai, but Sarah shall her name be.

And I will bless her, and give thee a son of her: yea, I will bless her, and she shall be a mother of nations; kings of people shall be of her. (Genesis 17:15-16)

<9> The name of Abraham's wife also was changed from Sarai to Sarah. With this she was blessed to have a son. It is here again that

CHILDREN OF ABRAM (ABRAHAM)

the promise of "many nations" and "kings" was given to her seed, which is Isaac.

> Then Abraham fell upon his face, and laughed, and said in his heart, Shall a child be born unto him that is an hundred years old? and shall Sarah, that is ninety years old, bear?
> And Abraham said unto God, O that Ishmael might live before thee! (Genesis 17:17-18)

<10> Abraham could not believe that he would have a child at that age and from his ninety year old wife. That is why he asked God if these promises could be fulfilled through Ishmael, whom he already had from Hagar, "that Ishmael might live before thee."

> And God said, Sarah thy wife shall bear thee a son indeed; and thou shalt call his name Isaac: and I will establish my covenant with him for an everlasting covenant, and with his seed after him.
> And as for Ishmael, I have heard thee: Behold, I have blessed him, and will make him fruitful, and will multiply him exceedingly; twelve princes shall be begat, and I will make him a great nation.
> But my covenant will I establish with Isaac, which Sarah shall bear unto thee at this set time in the next year. (Genesis 17:19-21)

<11> God knew what Abraham was thinking, and that is why He said to him, "Sarah thy wife shall bear thee a son **indeed**." He assured Abraham that He had decided it would happen so it surely ("indeed") would occur.

<12> Also God repeated His promises which were given to Abram about his seed (Ishmael). He said, "As for Ishmael, … I have blessed him." That is, "I have already blessed him and promised what I will do about him." <13> Abraham could not believe he would have another son, so he asked if also these promises would be fulfilled by Ishmael.

<14> That is why God here repeated the promises He had given about Ishmael: "And [I] will make him fruitful, and will **multiply** him exceedingly; … and I will make him **a great nation**." So again God showed that the previous promises which were given to Abram were about Ishmael. He had already blessed him, and would multiply him as the number of the stars, give him a large territory, and make "a great nation" from him. These all are the same promises previously given to Abram. <15> Also He had blessed Ishmael, which is, spiritual domination (scepter).

<16> "But my covenant will I establish with Isaac." However, this covenant and also all the new promises He gave after Abram's name became Abraham would be with his son Isaac. With this, God separated the promises given before and after the name change from Abram to Abraham and Sarai to Sarah.

Tablet Three

Abraham is tested by the Lord:

> And it came to pass after these things, that God did tempt Abraham, and said unto him, Abraham: and he said, Behold, here I am.
> And he said, Take now thy son, thine only son Isaac, whom thou lovest, and get thee into the land of Moriah; and offer him there for a burnt offering upon one of the mountains which I will tell thee of. (Genesis 22:1-2)

> And they came to the place which God had told him of; and Abraham built an altar there, and laid the wood in order, and bound Isaac his son, and laid him on the altar upon the wood.
> And Abraham stretched forth his hand, and took the knife to slay his son.
> And the angel of the Lord called unto him out of heaven,…
> And he said, Lay not thine hand upon the lad, neither do thou any thing unto him: for now I know that thou fearest

CHILDREN OF ABRAM (ABRAHAM)

God, seeing thou hast not withheld thy son, thine only son from me. (Genesis 22:9-12)

<1> God was testing Abraham to see how detached he was. God demanded him to sacrifice his son whom he had received in old age from Him. <2> Abraham proved that he understood the realities behind this universe with complete detachment. He realized that God had given him the child and now He wanted him back. <3> A child is not the parent's but God's. So, with complete surrendering, Abraham was ready to give up Isaac. That is why Abraham is the symbol of being surrendered to the Lord's Will, and that is how he passed the test.

And Abraham called the name of that place Jehovah-jireh: as it is said to this day, In the mount of the Lord it shall be seen.

And the angel of the Lord called unto Abraham out of heaven the second time,

And said, By myself have I sworn, saith the Lord, for because thou hast done this thing, and hast not withheld thy son, thine only son:

That in blessing I will bless thee, and in multiplying I will multiply thy seed as the stars of the heaven, and as the sand which is upon the sea shore; and thy seed shall possess the gate of his enemies;

And in thy seed shall all the nations of the earth be blessed; because thou hast obeyed my voice. (Genesis 22:14-18)

<4> God was very pleased with Abraham, to see that he was so detached and obedient. He was ready to sacrifice his "only son"* for God's sake and demand. <5> That was a great sign of being surrendered and ready to sacrifice all for His Will.

<6> That is why God was so pleased that He gave Abraham an **unconditional** blessing and promise, with no covenant necessary this time. <7> God blessed him with the highest blessing by saying, "in blessing I will bless thee." God would multiply his seed numerously, and his "seed shall possess the gate of his enemies." In Abraham's offspring, all the nations of the earth would be blessed, with no condition necessary, only for Abraham's sake.

Tablet Four

The promises given to Abraham are repeated to Isaac:

And the Lord appeared unto him [Isaac], and said, Go not down into Egypt; dwell in the land which I shall tell thee of:

Sojourn in this land, and I will be with thee, and will bless thee; for unto thee, and unto thy seed, I will give all these countries, and I will perform the oath which I sware unto Abraham thy father;

And I will make thy seed to multiply as the stars of Heaven, and will give unto thy seed all these countries; and in thy seed shall all the nations of the earth be blessed;

Because that Abraham obeyed my voice, and kept my charge, my commandments, my statutes, and my laws. (Genesis 26:2-5)

---

* We can see here that it says that Isaac was the "only son" of Abram (Abraham). Of course we know that this is not true as Abram (Abraham) also had Ishmael, from Hagar. The Koran says that the son that God commanded to be sacrificed was Ishmael. The truth is that God commanded Abram (Abraham) to sacrifice both. This of course has been changed in the Bible by those who tried hard to exclude Ishmael and promote Isaac. This is corrected in the Koran, and Ishmael is also included in this event!

CHILDREN OF ABRAM (ABRAHAM)

<1> God reminded Isaac that all these promises would come to his seed, not because of his merits or greatness, but because of Abraham. <2> Also, there were many small countries in Canaan at that time, "all these countries."

> And the Lord appeared unto him the same night, and said, I am the God of Abraham thy father: fear not, for I am with thee, and will bless thee, and multiply thy seed for my servant Abraham's sake. (Genesis 26:24)

<3> Again these promises were "for … Abraham's sake," not for Isaac's sake or because of his merits.

Esau sells his birthright to Jacob:

<4> Isaac married Rebekah, and she bore two sons, Esau and Jacob. Esau was the elder.

> And Jacob sod pottage: and Esau came from the field, and he was faint:
> And Esau said to Jacob, Feed me, I pray thee, with that same red pottage; for I am faint: therefore was his name called Edom.
> And Jacob said, Sell me this day thy birthright.
> And Esau said, Behold, I am at the point to die: and what profit shall this birthright do to me?
> And Jacob said, Swear to me this day; and he sware unto him: and he sold his birthright unto Jacob. (Genesis 25:29-33)

<5> Esau sold his birthright to Jacob (there is no "j" in Hebrew. The name actually is "Yaghob"). The birthright is the heritage of the ownership of the promised nations (material domination) which was given to Abraham to be passed down to his seed. This birthright, which God had promised to give to Abraham's seed, would go to the first born male in the family. When Esau sold it to Jacob, then Jacob would be the father of many nations.

Jacob receives the blessing of Isaac instead of Esau:

<6> All of chapter 27 of Genesis is about how Jacob, the younger son of Isaac, who already had bought Esau's birthright, also received his father's blessings. <7> Because his mother realized that Jacob deserved the blessings of his father more than Esau, an arrangement was made for Jacob to receive the blessings of his father. The blessing is given below:

> …and blessed him [Jacob],…
> Therefore God give thee of the dew of heaven and the fatness of the earth, and plenty of corn and wine:
> Let people serve thee, and nations bow down to thee: be lord over thy brethren, and let thy mother's sons bow down to thee: cursed be every one that curseth thee, and blessed be he that blesseth thee. (Genesis 27:27-29)

<8> As the birthright was related to the material part or inheritance of the nations of the promises of the Lord to Abraham, the blessing of the father was related to the spiritual part, the dominance of the spirit over others, the kings to the nations, the scepter, and the messianic part of the promise.

<9> So with receiving the blessing from his father and buying the birthright from Esau, Jacob became the legitimate owner of both parts of the promises given by the Lord to Abraham.

The promises are repeated to Jacob:

> And, behold, the Lord stood above it, and said, I am the Lord God of Abraham thy father, and the God of Isaac: the land wherein thou liest, to thee will I give it, and to thy seed;
> And thy seed shall be as the dust of the earth, and **thou shalt spread abroad to the west, and to the east, and to the north, and to the south**: and in thee

CHILDREN OF ABRAM (ABRAHAM)

and in thy seed shall all the families of the earth be blessed.

And, behold, I am with thee, and will keep thee in all places whither thou goest, and will bring thee again into this land; for I will not leave thee, until I have done that which I have spoken to thee of. (Genesis 28:13-15)

<10> The promises were repeated to Jacob, after he received both the birthright and blessings. <11> Also, the phrase, "…and thou shalt be spread abroad to the west, and to the east,…" shows that his seed would go "abroad," meaning out of the land (Canaan) God would give to his seed, and would be spread out all over the world.

Jacob's name becomes Israel, a new promise is given to him, and the old promises are repeated:

And God said unto him, Thy name is Jacob: thy name shall not be called any more Jacob, but Israel shall be thy name: and he called his name Israel.

And God said unto him, I am God Almighty: be fruitful and multiply; a nation and a company of nations shall be of thee, and kings shall come out of thy loins;

And the land which I gave Abraham and Isaac, to thee I will give it, and to thy seed after thee will I give the land. (Genesis 35:10-12)

<12> The name of Jacob was changed to Israel. It was actually changed before (Gen. 32:26-28) but God wanted him to be called with this name from now on. <13> Also the promise to Israel about his seed changed a little. His seed would inherit "a nation and a company of nations" in the future. That relates to his birthright of material possession.

<14> Also it should be noted that the promise of many nations to Isaac would be fulfilled through both Esau and Jacob (Israel), and their seed.

Two sons of Joseph's become Israel's (Jacob's):

<15> Israel (Jacob) had twelve sons. The oldest from his wife Rachael was Joseph (actual name is "Yoseph"). Joseph had two sons, Manasseh and Ephraim. Israel took them as his own sons and put his name Israel on them.

And Jacob said unto Joseph, God Almighty appeared unto me at Luz in the land of Canaan, and blessed me,

And said unto me, Behold, I will make thee fruitful, and multiply thee, and I will make of thee a multitude of people; and will give this land to thy seed after thee for an everlasting possession.

And now thy two sons, Ephraim and Manasseh, which were born unto thee in the land of Egypt before I came unto thee into Egypt, are mine: as Reuben and Simeon, they shall be mine. (Genesis 48:3-5)

<16> So, **Ephraim and Manasseh became Israel's sons from this point on**, like his other sons ("as Reuben and Simeon, they shall be mine.")

<17> Also, nothing is said here about the family of earth being blessed by them or kings coming from them (scepter), but they will possess the material part of the promises.

Israel blesses Ephraim and Manasseh, and prefers Ephraim over Manasseh:

And Joseph took them both [his sons], Ephraim in his right hand toward Israel's left hand, and Manasseh in his left hand toward Israel's right hand, and brought them near unto him.

And Israel stretched out his right hand, and laid it upon Ephraim's head, who was the younger, and his left hand upon Manasseh's head, guiding his hands wittingly; for Manasseh was the firstborn.

CHILDREN OF ABRAM (ABRAHAM)

And he blessed Joseph, and said, God, before whom my fathers Abraham and Isaac did walk, the God which fed me all my life long unto this day,

The angel which redeemed me from all evil, bless the lads; and **let my name be named on them**, and the name of my fathers Abraham and Isaac; and let them grow into a multitude in the midst of the earth. (Genesis 48:13-16)

<18> Israel (Jacob) blessed Joseph's sons but he put his right hand (which is used for the blessing of the firstborn) over the head of Ephraim, who was the younger one. By giving his name to them, they became as his sons in sharing Israel's blessings (inheritance). They became one of the Children of Israel, "and let my name be named on them."

And when Joseph saw that his father laid his right hand upon the head of Ephraim, it displeased him: and he held up his father's hand, to remove it from Ephraim's head unto Manasseh's head.

And Joseph said unto his father, Not so, my father: for this is the firstborn; put thy right hand upon his head.

And his father refused, and said, I know it, my son, I know it; he also shall become a people, and he also shall be great: but truly his younger brother shall be greater than he, and his seed shall become **a multitude of nations**. (Genesis 48:17-19)

<19> With accepting Joseph's sons as his own and blessing them, then whatever Israel gave to Joseph would go to these sons, especially to Ephraim, because he was blessed over Manasseh. He would become "a multitude of nations." Also he prophesied about the children in the future.

And he blessed them that day, saying, In thee shall Israel bless, saying, God make thee as Ephraim and as Manasseh: and he set Ephraim before Manasseh… (Genesis 48:20)

<20> So he blessed them and prophesied that people would want to be "as Ephraim and as Manasseh." They would want to be as blessed as they were.

Tablet Five

Israel separates the spiritual promises (the scepter) from the material promises (birthright) and gives them to two of his sons:

The scepter shall not depart from Judah, nor a lawgiver from between his feet, until **Shiloh come**; and unto him shall the gathering of the people be. (Genesis 49:10)

<1> So, "the scepter … nor a lawgiver from between his feet…," the supreme spiritual dominance and authority, "shall not depart from Judah…." This part of the promise of God, which said, "kings shall come out of thee" to Abraham, Isaac, and Jacob, should be fulfilled through Judah. <2> That is why the great kings of Israel and the Jews have come from the tribe of Judah.

<3> But that will last only "until Shiloh come," or until the Messiah comes. Then that would be taken away from Judah.

<4> The other part of the promise, the birthright of inheriting the material possession, was given to Joseph, who already demonstrated God's Will to see him have material and social status domination over his brothers.

Joseph is a fruitful bough, even a fruitful bough by a well; whose branches run over the wall:

The archers have sorely grieved him,

and shot at him, and hated him:

But his bow abode in strength, and the arms of his hands were made strong by the hands of the mighty God of Jacob; (from thence is the shepherd, the stone of Israel:)

Even by the God of thy father, who shall help thee; and by the Almighty, who shall bless thee with blessings of heaven above, blessings of the deep that lieth under, blessings of the breasts, and of the womb:

The blessings of thy father have prevailed above the blessings of my progenitors unto the utmost bound of the everlasting hills: they shall be on the head of Joseph, and on the crown of the head of him that was separate from his brethren. (Genesis 49:22-26)

<5> "Whose branches run over the wall" means Joseph's material domination would exceed his country and territories.

<6> "Blessings of the breasts, and of the womb:" Very healthy and strong children or people would be given to him and his seed.

<7> "The utmost bound of the everlasting hills" refers to the great material possession.

<8> These all would go to Joseph and his seed, Ephraim and Manasseh (Ephraim above Manasseh).

<9> With this gift of the spiritual dominance to Judah and the material dominance to Joseph, the two promised possessions of the children of Abraham became separated, with two different destinies.

<10> Also, a record of that birthright which went to Joseph can be found in the first two verses of chapter 5 of I Chronicles:

Now the sons of Reuben the firstborn of Israel, (for he was the firstborn; but, forasmuch as he defiled his father's bed, his birthright was given unto the sons of Joseph the son of Israel:...

For Judah prevailed above his brethren, and of him came the chief ruler; but the birthright was Joseph's:) (I Chronicles 5:1-2)

<11> With these events in the first book of the Bible, the foundation of the future events in history was shaped. The seed of Abram or Abraham would be multiplied "as the dust of the earth" or "the number of the stars in heaven." They would possess "a great nation" in the case of Ishmael, and "many nations" for Isaac. <12> Also the people of the earth would be blessed through them because of the spiritual domination and for the spiritual truth which would be revealed through them to humanity (the scepter).

<13> In the case of the seed of Ishmael, the material possession (great nation) and the spiritual possession (the scepter) remained together to be fulfilled in the future. But in the case of the Children of Israel, the material possession went to the seed of Joseph and the scepter to Judah.

<14> After this chapter in the Bible, the history of the Children of Israel continues. They became servants of Pharaohs in Egypt. Moses took them out of Egypt by the power of the Lord. Joshua (Y'shua) conquered the land of Canaan for them. <15> With the Laws that God revealed to them and the struggle they went through, they became a mighty nation. <16> However, later on, they lost their previous vigor and eventually, after rejecting God as their King, they failed.

Tablet Six

The Children of Israel reject God as their King:

<1> After the possession of Canaan, the system of judges was established in that country for the Children of Israel. However, the judges became corrupt, and because people followed them instead of following God's Laws, their connection with the Lord became disturbed. That is why people longed for a human king. They rejected God as their King.

CHILDREN OF ABRAM (ABRAHAM)

<2> That was why God said these words to Samuel, "…for they have not rejected thee, but they have rejected me [God], that I should not reign over them." (I Samuel 8:7). That was the greatest mistake made by the Children of Israel or anyone who rejects God as their only Ruler or King.

<3> The reason is very simple. When a society accepts a ruler, leader, or king, that society becomes the subject of that ruler. Only God and His Laws are the true Laws which lead to salvation and happiness. When a human becomes the king or leader of a society instead of God, then men have to follow this human's whims or rules and laws. Because most of the humans are not in complete tune with the Lord, and because power blinds them, they misuse their powers and bring suffering and mischief to their subjects in God's name.

<4> However, if the leaders become in tune with the Laws of the Lord, listen to His Voice, recognize His Signs, understand the lessons of history, and become self-sacrificing for the good of their subjects and all, or if people reject those leaders who do not follow God's Laws, then His Will, will be done and His Kingdom will be established.

<5> So, Saul was chosen as the king of the Children of Israel. He failed. Then God chose a Great Soul as their king, David, and revealed to him the Star of David (✡) as the sign for His Kingdom.

The meaning of the Star of David (✡):

<6> The sign (✡) of the Children of Israel consists of two triangles. The triangle upward (△) is the symbol of organization. It has always been used to show organizational structure in management. The triangle downward (▽) is the symbol of control and justice.

<7> Therefore, the two triangles together (✡) make up the symbol of the true human society according to God's Will. The triangle upward shows that an organization is necessary, and the triangle downward shows that only with the application of justice and the Laws of God can it be an ideal organization. <8> In short, the sign (✡) means the Kingdom Of Heaven On Earth. Only with a well-structured organization and application of justice in that organization according to the Laws of the Lord can His Kingdom be established "on earth as it is in heaven."

<9> So this sign was given to the Children of Israel through King David, and they were chosen to establish such a kingdom.

Tablet Seven

Jews become separated from the House of Israel. Jews are the House of Judah:

<1> The first time the name "Jew" appears in the Bible is in II Kings 16:6. It has never been used as the name for the Children of Israel.

At that time **Rezin king of Syria** recovered Elath to Syria, and drave **the Jews** from Elath: and the Syrians came to Elath, and dwelt there unto this day.

So Ahaz [king of Judah] sent messengers to Tiglathpileser king of Assyria, saying, I am thy servant and thy son: come up, and save me out of the hand of the **king of Syria**, and out of the hand of the **king of Israel**, which rise up against me. (II Kings 16:6-7)

<2> It can clearly be seen here that the Jews are the people from Judah, and Israel refers to the House of Israel. It was both the House of Israel and Syria who fought against the Jews (the House of Judah) in war. This House of Israel in the Bible is also called "Samaria" and "Ephraim."

<3> It is true that the Jews (House of Judah) and the House of Israel both were the Children of Israel, but only the tribes of

Judah and Benjamin and the priests of the tribe of the Levites with them were called Jews. The other ten tribes including Ephraim and Manasseh were called the House of Israel. As it was prophesied by Israel in his last moments of death, his name was given to Ephraim and Manasseh, "Let my name be named on them," (Gen. 48:16).

<4> With this separation of the Jews from the House of Israel, the destiny of the birthright (material possession) and the spiritual blessing (scepter) were also separated. The kingly domination and spiritual blessing stayed with the Jews, because the tribe of Judah was with them, and the birthright or material possession ("a nation and a company of nations") went to the House of Israel, which included the tribes of Ephraim and Manasseh.

Prophets predict the fall of the House of Israel and the Jews:

<5> Before Assyria overthrew the House of Israel and then later on the Babylonians overthrew the House of Judah (Jews), many Prophets predicted the event (that the Children of Israel would be captured and taken away).

Many of the House of Israel leave their country even before the attack of the Assyrians:

<6> With these predictions, many people of the House of Israel left their country and traveled abroad. The most logical direction of their immigration was toward the west and northwest, because in the south, north, and east, many nations had already been established. Also, the hostile Assyrians were approaching their country from the east. To the south was also their enemy, Egypt (Pharaoh).

<7> The study of geography and history also supports this. In addition, The Book of Mormon clearly shows that many people were in stress and had fled from the House of Israel to immigrate to the west. The two tribes of Ephraim and Manasseh (children of Joseph) were in the House of Israel. Many of them left their country even before the attack of the Assyrians. (In The Book of Mormon, it is described that some of the people of Samaria left their country and came to America.) Also, the people mentioned in The Book of Mormon were descendants of Joseph:

> And it came to pass that my father, Lehi, also found upon the plates of brass a genealogy of his father; wherefore he knew that he was a descendant of Joseph;... (The Book of Mormon, I Nephi 5:14)

<8> This was predicted by the Lord when He said that the seed of Jacob "...shalt spread abroad to the west, and to the east,..." (Gen. 28:14).

The House of Israel is captured by the Assyrians:

> Until the Lord removed Israel out of his sight, as he had said by all his servants the prophets. So was Israel carried away out of their own land to Assyria unto this day. (II Kings 17:23)

<9> The remainder of the House of Israel was captured by the Assyrians and they were carried out of their land (to the east). <10> They were replaced by many people from other nations:

> And the king of Assyria brought men from Babylon, and from Cuthah, and from Ava, and from Hamath, and from Sepharvaim, and placed them in the cities of Samaria [House of Israel] instead of the children of Israel: and they possessed Samaria, and dwelt in the cities thereof. (II Kings 17:24)

<11> Not only was the House of Israel carried away from their lands but also others took their lands.

CHILDREN OF ABRAM (ABRAHAM)

The House of Judah (Jews) falls also:

At that time the servants of Nebuchadnezzar king of Babylon came up against Jerusalem [the capital of Judah], and the city was besieged. (II Kings 24:10)

And he [Nebuchadnezzar] carried away all Jerusalem, and all the princes, and all the mighty men of valour, even ten thousand captives, and all the craftsmen and smiths: none remained, save the poorest sort of the people of the land. (II Kings 24:14)

<12> Not only did the House of Israel fall, but the House of Judah fell also. However, they were not replaced by other people from other nations but the same people of Judah stayed there, although their royal people and craftsmen were taken away.

Tablet Eight

Jews return to their land. The House of Israel apparently never returns:

...the Lord stirred up the spirit of Cyrus king of Persia, that he made a proclamation throughout all his kingdom, and put it also in writing, saying,
...The Lord God of heaven hath given me all the kingdoms of the earth; and he hath charged me to build him an house at **Jerusalem, which is in Judah**. (Ezra 1:1-2)

<1> The temple was to be built in "Jerusalem, which is in Judah." There is no mention of the Samarian or the House of Israel, and also:

Then rose up the chief of the fathers of Judah and Benjamin, and the priests, and the Levites,... (Ezra 1:5)

<2> So those who went up to build the temple in "Jerusalem, which is in Judah" were the Children of Judah, Benjamin, and the priests of the Levites. There is no mention of the name of the other tribes, nor of Ephraim or Manasseh, the inheritors of the promise of the material possession of "a nation and a company of nations." Furthermore:

Now these are the children of the province that went up out of the captivity, of those which had been carried away, **whom Nebuchadnezzar the king of Babylon had carried away unto Babylon, and came again unto Jerusalem and Judah, every one unto his city**; (Ezra 2:1)

<3> It was the House of Judah (Jews) which was carried away by Nebuchadnezzar, into Babylon, not the House of Israel. The House of Israel was carried away by Shalmaneser, king of Assyria (II Kings 17:3-6).

<4> Also, it was the Jews who were carried to Babylon, not the Samarians (House of Israel). Samarians were placed "...in Halah and in Habor by the river of Gozan, and in the cities of the Medes" (II Kings 17:6).

<5> So it was surely only the Jews that "came again unto Jerusalem and Judah," not the House of Israel.

The ten lost tribes are the House of Israel (Samarian, or Ephraim):

<6> What happened to the House of Israel? It is what is known to many as the "ten lost tribes" of Israel, and apparently no one knows what became of them.

<7> Since we know that God never fails in His Promises and that the Jews never became "a nation and a company of nations" in

CHILDREN OF ABRAM (ABRAHAM)

a great sense, then we should look for other clues that God left for humanity to understand His Work.

<8> From this point on the story of the promises given to Israel take two completely different routes. <9> One is how the promise of spiritual dominance (scepter) was fulfilled through the Children of Judah. <10> The other one is how the promise of "a nation and a company of nations" which was given to the children of Joseph would be fulfilled (the birthright).

<11> So there are three promises which should have been fulfilled through the Children of Israel: First, a spiritual blessing through a kingly Messiah (scepter); secondly, a great nation from Joseph's seed (Manasseh); and thirdly, a great company of nations from Joseph's seed (Ephraim).

Tablet Nine

SECTION II

Fulfillment of the "birthright:"

<1> Before the House of Israel was attacked by Assyria and taken away captive, many of the people of this nation, through Prophets and the signs of the times, predicted that the disaster of being conquered by other nations was near. Therefore, a great movement started from the House of Israel. Many people left this part of the territories of the Children of Israel toward the west and northwest. Furthermore, after the fall of Assyria, even more of the House of Israel immigrated toward the west.

<2> In fact, as the records have been preserved by God and given to the Mormons, even some of these immigrants crossed the ocean and came to America.

<3> However, most of them stayed in Europe and in England. These Children of Israel were the people of the ten tribes of Israel. The tribes of Ephraim and Manasseh also were with them. <4> However, for thousands of years this birthright did not materialize until the nineteenth century. About this time, in the 1800s, suddenly the English-speaking nations flourished and two great countries were born.

The nation is the United Kingdom:

<5> The first or elder one (the children of Manasseh) became the United Kingdom with a territory where "the sun never sets." England became a great empire which had never been seen before. This whole United Kingdom was under the rulership of one king in London and was very prosperous.

<6> So with this sudden flourishing of England and creation of the United Kingdom, the promise of "a nation" to Israel was fulfilled. The promise which was given to Manasseh ended with the fading of the power of England over this vast kingdom.

America is the company of nations:

<7> Then after England, its younger brother the United States (Ephraim), started to grow and prosper. Through the Louisiana purchase and access to the west of America, and because of the events which happened later on, suddenly it became the wealthiest and most powerful "united states" ever existing in history. <8> With this, the promise to Ephraim about becoming a company of nations also is fulfilled (Gen. 49:22-26).

<9> The land which was divided in the time of Peleg is the land of America, "for in his days was the earth divided;..." (Gen. 10:25), and was kept apart from the rest of the world for a great purpose. <10> Both the U.K. and the U.S.A. spread their dominations abroad, "whose branches run over the wall" (Gen. 49:22).

CHILDREN OF ABRAM (ABRAHAM)

The promise was unconditional:

<11> The promise of a nation and a company of nations was given to Israel (for Abraham's sake) unconditionally. That is, the land and greatness given to these two countries is only to show that God exists and never fails to fulfill His promises, even if the people do not follow His commandments or their covenant with Him (one covenant was that all Hebrews should be circumcised).

<12> He fulfilled His promise without the people who received it even realizing why they had been given such a blessing. However, the promises are now fulfilled; only those who follow His Laws are Blessed.

Tablet Ten

SECTION III

Fulfillment of the promise of the scepter:

<1> Before the fall of Jerusalem, many Prophets warned people that a great disaster would befall them because of their sins. At the same time, most of these Prophets told that after a time in exile they would return to Judah. <2> That shows how after each punishment God gives humanity another chance to repent and come back to Him and His Laws.

Prophecies of the coming of the Messiah:

<3> After the Jews returned and later found out that their customs and beliefs were so diluted that they no longer had the original foundation, the people started to long for a Messiah to guide them to the right path. That is when the coming of the Messiah was prophesied by many Prophets.

<4> So the expectation arose, and many prophecies came to the Jews in symbolic language. They created expectations and concepts of how the Messiah should be and in what manner he would come. Even in this aspect there was not a common agreement between different groups.

The Messiah comes:

<5> Esa The Christ came as the expected Messiah. He came in a humble way and preached the gospel of the Kingdom Of Heaven to the Jews. But they expected him to come from the "cloud" and in the way that had been symbolically described by the Prophets. <6> So the Jews, because of their concepts, did not accept him as the Expected One.

<7> He also taught differently than the beliefs of the Pharisees and scribes of the Jews. This created a barrier for Jews to follow him. The Jews were waiting for the Messiah to come and purify their religion, but when he came and tried to break those misconceptions and purify it, they started to resist him. <8> That is always a great obstacle when any new teaching comes to humanity. **The concepts of previous religious leaders become a barrier to accepting the new teachings.**

<9> The reasons for the difference in the teachings of the Prophets are twofold, for the same reasons: (1) because the mission of each Prophet is different, and (2) because the consciousness of the human is in a higher level at the time of the new teacher than when the previous Prophet came. That is why Christ said, "You do not put new wine into the old skin." <10> Also if the Messiah comes and teaches what the people already know, **then what is the need for his coming**?

The promise of the "scepter" to Judah is fulfilled:

<11> However, with the coming of Christ, the promise of the scepter of spiritual domination and kingly status (lawgiver) given to Judah was fulfilled. Esa was from the tribe of Judah, and he came as the "King of the Jews."

<12> He was the "Shiloh" who ended the promise of the "scepter" to Judah. The right

CHILDREN OF ABRAM (ABRAHAM) — Tablet 10

of having this privilege no longer belonged to Judah, "The scepter shall not depart from Judah, nor a lawgiver from between his feet, until Shiloh come; and unto him shall the gathering of the people be" (Gen. 49:10).

Christ "gathered the people:"

<13> As it was said before, "the House of Israel" moved toward the west and northwest of Europe. Indeed, that is where Christianity flourished and gathered all the lost Children of Israel under one religion. They were the "lost children of Israel" who were gathered, as it was prophesied by Israel, "...and unto him shall the gathering of the people be" (Gen. 49:10).

<14> Also in the gospel of St. John we read:

> And this spake he not of himself: but being high priest that year, he prophesied that Esa would die **for that nation** [Jews];
> And not for that nation only, but that also he should **gather together in one the children of God that were scattered abroad**. (John 11:51-52)

<15> So, Esa should have been crucified "for that nation" (the House of Judah) and also to "gather together in one the children of God that were scattered abroad."

<16> As it was said, in addition to other purposes, Christ came to disqualify the Jews from being chosen people; what happened to the Jews and their purpose in God's Plan is explained in the book The House of Judah (Jews).

<17> Also, he came to "gather together the people" or as it was prophesied here, to "gather together in one the children of God" – not all the children of God, but "that were scattered abroad."

<18> "And not for that nation only" but for "the children of God that were scattered abroad" from that nation (Children of Israel). Who were those who were scattered abroad and were lost? They were the House of Israel. They were the ones whom God had predicted would be scattered from the seed of Jacob (Gen. 28:14).

<19> It was these people who were scattered abroad that would be blessed with the unconditional promise given to Abraham when he obeyed God even to sacrifice his son for him. This promise will be in effect to the end of the last age. This is also revealed through Prophet Muhammad:

> Remember when God told Esa: I will exalt those who follow you above disbelievers to the Day of Judgment... (Koran Ali'Imran 55)

<20> The Day of Judgment is the beginning of the next age in which the true spiritual understanding will dawn and the age of enlightenment will start (resurrection).

<21> So Christ fulfilled his mission even if it appears that the Jews did not accept him. But God keeps His Promises in ways that humans cannot understand easily. The reason is very simple, because humans do not look at His Universe as He sees it. He has a complete picture of everything and is guiding the whole universe toward its goal. However, the human, because of his narrowness of mind (caused by concepts of "mine" and "thine," as "my country," "my religion," "my history," etc.) only sees a small part of the truth. That is why the work of the Lord seems strange to humanity.

<22> Also, as God has declared in the book of The Revelation (the last book in the Bible), His Work will remain a mystery until the time of the seventh Angel:

> But in the days of the voice of the seventh angel, ... the mystery of God should be finished,... (Rev. 10:7)

CHILDREN OF ABRAM (ABRAHAM)

Tablet Eleven

The meaning of the teachings of Christ and the cross (✝):

<1> Sacrifice (not being self-centered) is the essence of the teaching of Christ. Only by sacrifice can the Kingdom Of Heaven within and without be attained. With sacrifice, everything is possible. Without sacrifice, nothing is possible. <2> The cross (✝) therefore, is the symbol of crucifixion of the false ego for a higher ideal in the direction of the Will of God. That is the way for individual perfection, and individual perfection is the essence of Christ's teachings.

<3> He also came to finish the promise given to Israel about the kingly and spiritual dominance of his seed, which was passed to Judah. <4> In addition, he came to tell the Jews that this right and other rights had been taken away from them, "Therefore say I unto you, The kingdom of God shall be taken from you, and given to a nation bringing forth the fruits thereof." (Matthew 21:43). So with this Christ fulfilled the promise which was given to the Children of Judah of the ownership of the "scepter."

The promises to Israel are fulfilled:

<5> With the coming of Christ and the flourishing of America and England, all the promises which were given to Israel are fulfilled. <6> With Christ ("Shiloh"), the promise of the scepter through Judah is fulfilled. <7> Through the United Kingdom, the promise of a nation was given to the Children of Israel, and through America, the promise of a company of nations was ended. <8> Also all the lost tribes of Israel were gathered under Christianity together, "…shall the gathering of the people be." (Gen. 49:10).

<9> However, there are more prophecies which were fulfilled by God, so the human might eventually believe in Him and walk in His Ways.

Tablet Twelve

SECTION IV

The promise of spiritual blessing also was given to Ishmael:

Akashic Records:

<1> Any action or event which occurs in the universe creates a record of that event in the Universal Mind as the Akashic Records. These Akashic Records are the truest source of the realities behind this universe and whatever had happened from the beginning of creation until now is kept there. <2> Once in awhile, according to the need or Plan of God for the human, some truth of these records is sent to humanity by His Messengers, either to bring a new teaching or higher understanding to man, or to correct previous records.

<3> That is why it does not matter to God if humans change the Scriptures or if some of the Scriptures become lost. The truth will be revealed to a zealous individual who seeks it, and eventually to all of humanity, "Ask, and it shall be given you; seek, and ye shall find; knock, and it shall be opened unto you:" (Matthew 7:7).

Readings:

<4> The revelation of the events from these Akashic Records to humanity is known as **Readings**. For example, there was an American Prophet (or Sleeping Prophet as he is known) by the name of Edgar Cayce. He would lie down on the couch, go into a state of trance (or sleep), and answer many questions, diagnose diseases, or give remedies correctly. These answers to the questions are known as "the readings" of Edgar Cayce, which were revealed from the Akashic Records (the

Koran means "readings:"

<5> Prophet Muhammad also was commanded in a sleep or trance by an Angel of God (Gabriel) to "read." He did not know how to read so he answered, "I cannot read." The voice again said, "Read!" He repeated, "I cannot read." For the third time the voice demanded, "Read!" He then asked, "What can I read?" <6> So the revelations from these Akashic Records started to be revealed to him. In fact he never read anything but the voice of Gabriel revealed it to him from these records.

<7> That is why the Moslems call their book "The Koran," which means "The Readings." It is no accident that the answers from Prophet Cayce in sleep, and the revelations to Prophet Muhammad in a trance both are called "readings." This again has been done to make man believe and have faith in these revelations.

<8> Therefore, the Koran has been revealed from the Akashic Records. In Surah Ornaments of Gold (Az-Zukhruf) verse 4, these records are called "The Eternal Tablet." Also in the Koran it is revealed, "The records of the transgressor are kept in Sijjin" (bad records) and "The records for the righteous are kept in Iliyin" (good deeds) in Surah Defrauding (At-Tatfif) verses 7-9 and 18-20. In the Bible, these records are called "the book of remembrance:"

> Then they that feared the Lord spake often one to another: and the Lord hearkened, and heard it, and a book of remembrance was written before him for them that feared the Lord, and that thought upon his name. (Malachi 3:16)

<9> The Koran was sent to correct previous stories which had been given by God, and also to bring new laws after the lawgiving was taken from Judah, "...nor a lawgiver from between his feet, until Shiloh come;" (Gen. 49:10). <10> Furthermore, we know the Old Testament had been lost, many other teachings had influenced it, and some parts had been omitted or added. Therefore, for understanding the truth, we should trust the new revelations which were sent by God to humanity. But not blindly – we should see if they have been fulfilled or not.

What the Koran says about the future of Abram's seed, Ishmael:

> ...and of our offspring a nation submissive unto thee [God]...
> ...and from them raise a messenger for their guidance... (Surah The Cow, 128-129)

<11> So there was to be a nation (birthright) and among them a Messenger (scepter) would arise. These both were fulfilled. Arabs are a nation and Prophet Muhammad is that Messenger. These prophecies (or promises) were given to Abram thousands of years ago.

<12> This truth (promise of spiritual blessing for Ishmael) either had been lost from the Bible through the turbulent history of the Hebrews, or the book was changed, and that part which told of a Prophet also coming from the seed of Ishmael was taken out of the Old Testament. Both of these explanations are possible because we know that the Old Testament was written around 500 B.C., and the book was completely lost after the captivity of the Jews. <13> It was revealed again in the Koran, "They say it is from Allah what they have written by their own hands. Woe be unto them!" (Surah The Cow, 79). <14> The blessing of God is the same as the promise of the scepter (Gen. 17:20).

<15> The point is that the promise of material possession (the birthright) and spiritual blessing (the scepter) were both also given to Ishmael. **Not accepting this is to miss a great part of The Plan of the Lord.**

CHILDREN OF ABRAM (ABRAHAM)

It is also revealed in The Revelation:

<16> In The Revelation, the last book of the Bible, it was predicted that seven truths would be revealed to humanity. The first truth is the teachings of the Far East – Mystical Paths (☯), which helped many Great Souls become prepared to be chosen as Elected Ones (Hebrews). This is symbolized by the white horse and its rider (Rev. 6:1-2). The second truth is the history and purpose of the Hebrews from the time of Abraham to the New Testament (✡) and is symbolized by the red horse. The third truth is the black horse which is Christianity, the symbol of overcoming the lower nature of man (black horse) and bringing equality (the balance). The fourth truth or the end of the riders of the horses is the pale horse or Islam (for a deeper study, read Revelation of The Revelation).

<17> Islam is one of the accepted world religions, and a great part of humanity has been blessed through it. So denying its validity and that it has been the work of God for fulfilling the promises given to Abram for his seed Ishmael is just like denying the sun on a sunny day.

<18> Therefore, both the promises of the scepter (spiritual blessing) and birthright (the material possession) given to Abram and Abraham for his seed Ishmael and Isaac have been fulfilled.

Tablet Thirteen

SECTION V

All promises given to Abram's and Abraham's seed are fulfilled:

<1> Isaac begot Esau and Jacob. Esau married many wives and had many sons. They created Edomites, and because he also married one of the daughters of Ishmael, they mixed with Ishmaelites (Arabs). So through Arabs and Edomites, He created nations and blessed the people on earth (Gen. 27:39-40).

<2> Jacob received both the birthright and scepter. They were divided and given to Joseph and Judah. After the name Jacob became Israel, God promised him a nation and a company of nations. He also was the one who would spread all over the world. Jacob gave his name Israel to Ephraim and Manasseh, the two sons of Joseph, the receivers of the birthright.

<3> The House of Israel (the ten lost tribes) scattered all over the world, especially to the west and northwest of Europe. They created many nations there. One of them was the English-speaking people who with no doubt were the children of Manasseh and Ephraim.

<4> The children of Manasseh possessed "a nation" as the United Kingdom, and Ephraim's seed possessed "the company of nations" as the United States. <5> Also Jacob preferred Ephraim (the younger) over Manasseh (the older). So it was the seed of the younger (Ephraim) who would possess the land promised to Abraham, the land which was divided from the rest of the world and kept for a great use in the future: "…for in his days was the earth divided;…" (Gen. 10:25). This is also the land of milk and honey (material greatness).

<6> The land of America, especially North America, was kept aside for hundreds of years until those to whom it was promised were ready to receive it. When the medieval time was in its highest domination in Europe and many of the adventurous and great-minded people longed for freedom from that environment, then God suddenly caused the Children of Abram (Abraham) to rediscover this land. <7> All the freedom-lovers and people who longed for escape from religious persecution were squeezed out of Europe and came to this new virgin and fertile land. **That was no accident. It was well planned by the Lord.**

<8> With this, not only was a great new way of living and looking at the possibilities of man's abilities released, but also the prom-

ises given to Isaac and Jacob (or Israel) about the birthright were fulfilled.

<9> As we know, God never does anything without purpose. The conquest of America by the white man not only fulfilled the promises which were given to Abraham, also it was an act to bring Europeans in contact with the natives of America and gather many people together in this land.

<10> Although Native Americans apparently suffered a great deal in the process, in truth this made them become purified (humble, meek), so they (Native Americans) would eventually find the essence of the teachings of their ancestors (Mystical Paths) and also become familiar with the rest of the steps of the **Eternal Divine Path**.

<11> In short, all these happenings eventually will enhance and further the evolution of humanity, physically, mentally, and spiritually.

<12> With the coming of Christ, the promise of the scepter (spiritual blessing) was finished through the tribe of Judah.

<13> Then God completed the book of the Children of Israel by revealing the last book of the Bible, The Revelation. In this book God revealed in a symbolic language: What is the goal of life, why this universe was created, what is His desire to be accomplished through humanity, what are the pitfalls of the path, what had happened so far, and what will happen in the future. With this, the Bible, as an inspired book explaining creation and history, is complete.

<14> Furthermore, the promises given about Ishmael are fulfilled. After Christ's teachings, when he directly told the Jews that they would no longer be the possessors of the scepter and another nation would be chosen, "…The kingdom of God shall be taken from you, and given to a nation bringing forth the fruits thereof" (Matthew 21:43), then the next Prophet did not come from the Jews but from their brothers, the Arabs (the seed of Ishmael).

<15> Arabs are a very large nation which possess a substantial portion of the world, and were also blessed by the religion of Islam, being submissive to the Lord.

The spiritual truth was finished by Prophet Muhammad:

<16> The name "Islam" comes from "tasleim" which means to be surrendered or submissive to the Will of the Lord. That is the highest achievement in the spiritual world.

<17> To be submissive or surrendered to the Lord does not mean to be an escapist, but to do the best in everything, try to understand what is His Will and do accordingly, and then surrender the result of our actions to Him. That is, not being attached to the result of our actions and to be content with the outcome. So, whatever the outcome should be accepted as His Will.

<18> Also it means to submit or surrender our earthly will to the Supreme Will. That is the highest spiritual realization. With the truths which had come before (Far East Philosophies, Judaism, and Christianity) and Islam, the spiritual truth was finished.

Tablet Fourteen

The next Prophet did not come from the children of Abram (Arabs) or Abraham (Hebrews):

…God will bring a people whom He loves and they would love Him… (Koran, The Table Spread, 54)

<1> This verse is the prediction of the coming of another Prophet. He would not come from Arabs, but from another nation. That is why the next Prophet came from Persia. He brought the truth of the fifth seal described in The Revelation. He was Bab (Baha'u'llah), and the religion was Baha'i (the teachings of Bab).

<2> Prophet Muhammad is the "Khatem"

CHILDREN OF ABRAM (ABRAHAM)

("the last") of the Prophets in the sense of spiritual understanding. That is why Prophets or Messengers after Islam did not bring any higher spiritual truths than what had already been revealed to humanity. But new understandings were necessary to complete **The Greatest Sign**.

<3> Also, with the coming of Christ and Prophet Muhammad, the promises given to Abram or Abraham about his seed Ishmael and Isaac (that the nations of the earth would be blessed through them) were fulfilled. That is why the next Prophet did not come from the Children of Abram or Abraham but from people who closely associated with them, Persians [Abram (Abraham) was Persian (Median) Himself!]

God is no longer obligated to any special people:

<4> With fulfillment of all the promises God had given to Abram's and Abraham's seed, which were explained, He is no longer obligated to any special people. Now humans once more are equal. These historical events have happened according to the Scriptures, to make humans again understand that they are not left alone in this world with no one looking after them, or that they can do whatever they want to, or that they can choose their ways as they please.

<5> Once more God is trying to awaken man to understand that He exists. He expects man to understand this, give up his little false ego, and follow Him and His Laws. Only those who do so will be regarded as greater than the rest. Those who keep their limited egos and do not come to the path of righteousness will suffer the consequences of their actions and will go far astray. Those who go to Him will reach salvation through His Grace.

All earthly powers will be humbled:

<6> Through all of history, when we study the progress of great nations, those which became conquerors and prosperous went through several stages: A period of great struggle before emerging as great people, then a time of progress toward greatness, then a long period of laxity or steadiness, and then the period of decline.

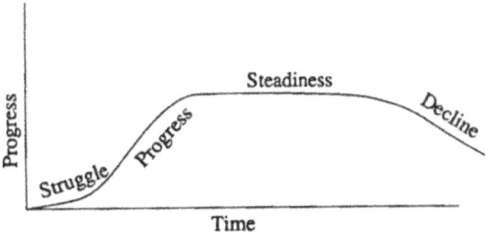

<7> Also when we study the life cycle of these great nations, we realize that in the beginning of the time of their struggle, they possessed a great deal of religious beliefs and disciplines. Especially we find out that the family structure was important, and was very close and strong.

<8> However, as they progressed toward prosperity, their discipline broke down, their beliefs became forgotten, the family closeness was destroyed, and many other symptoms were created, such as egotism, excessive preoccupation with sports (like the Romans and their gladiators), looseness of sexual relationships, emphasis on body gratification, over-prosperity and laziness, dullness of the mind, high expectation of others to respect their excesses, and so on.

<9> In short, when a nation or people are oppressed and are struggling toward the release of that situation, they trust in God and follow His Laws more or less. But when they become prosperous, they trust in themselves and go against His Laws. This brings their doom.

<10> We can trace this trend almost in any situation about any nation or people. The very loud examples are the Hebrews, who through a great struggle and with the help of God became a great nation and then declined to disgrace, or the Roman Empire, which through their great philosophy and endeavors reached a very great position and then declined.

<11> This trend has been shown throughout history to man so that he might become awak-

CHILDREN OF ABRAM (ABRAHAM) Tablet 14

ened that there is no other way but God's Way, as He has declared to the Children of Israel thousands of years ago (Leviticus chapter 26):

> Ye shall make you no idols nor graven image, neither rear you up a standing image, neither shall ye set up any image of stone in your land, to bow down unto it: for I am the Lord your God. (Leviticus 26:1)

<12> Only the invisible God unifies. Any other images (any image) will separate man from man. That is why God is so opposed to images and says, "for I am the Lord your God," the invisible God and the One for whom no one can make any image. At the same time every image is He. However, only worshipping Him in the invisible form can unify all men.

> If ye walk in my statutes, and keep my commandments, and do them;
> Then I will give you rain in due season, and the land shall yield her increase, and the trees of the field their fruit. (Leviticus 26:3-4)

<13> As it is described in the books The Base, The Essence, etc., everything is made from consciousness and the three gunas, even our minds and actions. So our thoughts and actions affect the whole universe and its levels of being. That is why when man becomes corrupt, the earth, climate, and everything else becomes corrupt also. Then the climate will change and man will suffer because of his actions.

<14> So God goes on and reveals what will happen if men follow His Laws and Commandments: How prosperous they will become, how they will gain the power over their enemies, and so on, by His Grace, until verse 14.

<15> Then He describes what will happen if they do not follow Him:

> But if ye will not hearken unto me, and will not do all these commandments;
> And if you shall despise my statutes, or if your soul abhor my judgments, so that ye will not do all my commandments, but that ye break my covenant:
> I also will do this unto you; I will even appoint over you terror, consumption, and the burning ague, that shall consume the eyes, and cause sorrow of heart: and ye shall sow your seed in vain, for your enemies shall eat it. (Leviticus 26:14-16)

<16> Then is when the tribulation starts. That is why the world tribulation is affecting men all over the earth, because all of them have fallen short of following His Laws.

> And I will set my face against you, and ye shall be slain before your enemies: they that hate you shall reign over you; and ye shall flee when none pursueth you.
> And if ye will not yet for all this hearken unto me, then I will punish you seven times more for your sins.
> And I will break the pride of your power; and I will make your heaven as iron, and your earth as brass: (Leviticus 26:17-19)

<17> That is exactly what happens to those who break His Laws. <18> In fact, no man can break His Laws but he can only break himself against them. He "will break the pride" of the power of those nations that lose their trust in Him, and they will fall.

<19> To walk with God is not just to praise Him, have many ceremonies, or talk about Him, but to establish justice, to help the oppressed, and to stand for truth. <20> Those who lose these qualities lose the pride of their powers also. When His Grace is withdrawn, they are doomed as history has shown us.

<21> That is exactly what is happening in the world today. All the earthly leaders are trying to bring peace but because they have forgotten the basic Laws of the Lord, they are going more and more toward self-destruction. This can be prevented when the truth prevails

CHILDREN OF ABRAM (ABRAHAM)

and destroys all the wrong concepts of the humans. <22> As in the dream of King Nebuchadnezzar in the book Daniel (chapter 2), the stone which is the symbol of the truth, hit the clay-like base of the image, destroyed it to ashes, and then filled the world.

Tablet Fifteen

The Elected Ones are not a race:

<1> The great things which happen in the world are all done with those elected by the Lord. Whenever any great thing should happen on earth, a Great Soul or many such Souls are born to do that. They will come again and again to fulfill many different tasks in the world.

<2> That is how God controls and guides His universe. People think that all the events in history or in their lives occur because of wild, unpredictable forces out of their control. They say that they are neither guided by any power nor can be controlled or directed by any being. <3> But those who know God realize that He is controlling all great things happening to humanity.

<4> Therefore, Elected Ones are those who are chosen by God to do His Will, knowingly or unknowingly. That is why they are all over the world and are helping His Will to be done. They are not in a special country or place. They might be reincarnated in one place because it is necessary for that time. However, this does not mean they belong, or consider themselves to belong, to any special part of the world.

<5> Indeed, they consider themselves to belong to the universe and that is where their true home is. It is these Elected Ones who eventually will guide the whole universe to the goal, Pure Consciousness.

His Will, will be done on earth as it is in heaven:

<6> These Elected Ones will be reincarnated again and again, and also there will be others added to them more and more in the course of time. They will increase to such a great multitude that eventually they will bring the The Kingdom Of Heaven On Earth. "His Will be done on earth as it is in heaven."

<7> In truth, His Kingdom is on earth, as it is described in the book The Kingdom Of Heaven On Earth. He is the King and controller of all events. But if the human follows His Will and creates an ideal environment according to His Will, then His Plan will go smoother. So in reality His Kingdom should only be realized on earth and His Laws followed as in heaven.

APPENDIX

Tablet Sixteen

THOSE PROPHECIES WHICH ARE NOT YET FULFILLED

<1> In the book of Daniel in the Bible, there are three prophecies which are of great significance.

<2> First, the dream of King Nebuchadnezzar, which is described in Daniel 2:31-35. Its interpretation is given by God through Daniel in verses 37-45. In brief, the interpretation informs the king that there will be five great kingdoms on earth. The first is the kingdom of Nebuchadnezzar (the Chaldean Empire). The second kingdom, which is somehow inferior to the first (symbolized by silver, the first was symbolized by gold) will rise, and then the third (of brass) will rise. The fourth will be strong as iron but will be divided, and the fifth will be half iron and half clay. In the time of these last kingdoms which were symbolized as the feet of the image, the truth will come and will destroy the whole image and replace it.

<3> Therefore, so far we know that the first kingdom is the Chaldean Empire. What are the next four? We can find the clues in another prophecy and vision of Daniel in chapter 8. The vision is about a ram with two horns, and about "an he goat" with one "notable horn between his eyes" (Daniel 8:5). The goat destroys the ram and becomes very great but in the height of its greatness, its horn will be broken.

<4> The interpretation of the dream is given to Daniel by Archangel Gabriel that the two horns of the ram are the kings of Media and Persia, "And the rough goat is the king of Grecia: and the great horn that is between his eyes is the first king [Alexander the Great]" (Daniel 8:21).

<5> With these visions a clue is given for understanding the dream of King Nebuchadnezzar: That the next great kingdom is of Media and Persia (ram with two horns), and the third will be the king of Grecia. Also history supports this. These kings came to power and were destroyed as it was prophesied in the book of Daniel.

<6> So far the three kingdoms of the expected five have been identified, namely Chaldean Empire, Persian Empire, and the Grecian Empire. The fourth empire which would be divided into two is the Roman Empire with capitals at Rome and Constantinople. So with this, four empires have been created and destroyed so far. <7> However, there is one more which has not come yet which apparently has no clues as to what it is. But the Bible always clarifies itself by giving the answer somehow in other parts.

<8> In chapter 7 of Daniel, another vision is seen by him about four beasts. In verse 17, the interpretation is given that, "These great beasts, which are four, are four kings, which shall arise out of the earth" (Daniel 7:17). With comparison to the previously revealed four empires, the fourth kingdom is the Roman Empire. <9> The head of this fourth beast had ten horns corresponding to the ten toes in the dream seen by King Nebuchadnezzar. These ten horns are the last kingdom which will come with ten nations (a union of nations) which are very closely related to the Roman Empire.

> And in the days of these kings shall the God of heaven set up a kingdom, which shall never be destroyed:...
> (Daniel 2:44)

<10> Also in The Revelation and many other different parts of the Bible, it has been prophesied that eventually the Kingdom of God will be established on earth and the saints will gain dominance over it. As all other prophecies have been fulfilled so far, so a dominion of ten united nations closely related to the Roman Empire will arise. <11> After that is the time that the Kingdom of God will be

established (for a more detailed explanation of the Daniel prophecies, read Commentaries on Prophecies in Daniel, Period of Intellectual Domination).

Tablet Seventeen
THE USE OF THE POWER

There is a message for America (and all those who gain power):

The obverse and reverse of the
GREAT SEAL OF THE UNITED STATES

<1> A part of the land which was divided at the time of Peleg (Gen. 10:25) was chosen for a purpose. As it was explained, that land is America.

The people who created the foundation of the United States were evolved beings:

<2> The foundation of the United States, which is based on the Declaration of Independence, the Constitution of the United States, The Bill of Rights, and the Great Seal† of America (the obverse and its reverse) was not prepared or founded by people with narrow views of selfish nationalism or even with limited views of a religion. They had been prepared with a Divine inspiration, by people who were designed for that task.

<3> These documents and seals, knowingly or unknowingly, were prepared in such a way that they represent: First, a universal view; and secondly, a great relationship between them (especially the seal) and the Will of God.

<4> The relationship between the seal and God's Will, will be described in the next pages. The relationship between the Declaration of Independence, the Constitution of the United States, and The Bill of Rights, with His Will, is apparent. With this book and this appendix, it will become obvious.

Explanation of the obverse side of The Seal of the United States‡:

---

† "The term 'great seal' implies the existence of a smaller seal. The expression seems to have originated in England during the reign of King John (1199-1216). Shortly before or during this period, the king's chamber acquired a seal of its own for use in the sovereign's private business. This 'privacy seal' was of small size. Because of the contrast between the two, the larger seal used on documents of state soon became known as the 'great seal'. The term has continued in use ever since." (Richard S. Patterson and Richardson Dougall, "The Eagle and the Shield, A History of the Great Seal of the United States," U.S. Government Printing Office, Washington, D.C. 1976, p.3).

‡ "Throughout its history, the American seal has been known by two names, both equally correct: 'The Seal of the United States' and 'The Great Seal' (or 'The Great Seal of the United States')." Ibid., p.4.

CHILDREN OF ABRAM (ABRAHAM) — Tablet 16

<5> The olive branches in the right talon of the eagle§ represent a peaceful approach or loving way of the nature of the eagle. The thirteen arrows in the left talon represent the wrath or punishing quality of the eagle. But the eagle looks to the right, the loving way of dealing with others.

<6> These are all the qualities of the Lord. God always tries first to bring humanity to the right path by loving ways and by sending Messengers and Prophets to them. He then warns them, and if nothing works, then shocks and punishes them (withdraws His Grace).

<7> "E Pluribus Unum" means "from many, one." That is also a great realization. All things have come from the Lord and are the Lord. The apparent division is the illusion of humanity. The truth is that all our different perceptions are in fact one. <8> The reason we see differences is because the various levels of manifestations from the combinations of the forces of the universe bring this expression of many. But indeed all are one. All are God. (For further explanation, read <u>The Base</u> or <u>The Essence</u>).

<9> However, the most striking part in the seal is the thirteen stars at the top of the head of the eagle. They are put together in this shape (⋰⋱). If the stars are joined together from top to bottom and from bottom to top (✡), the outcome is the Star of David (✡) with one star left in the middle. <10> As it was explained previously, the Star of David is the symbol of the Kingdom Of Heaven On Earth. The Star of David with a sign in the middle (such as a star, or the sign **HOSH**¶, or any other great symbol) symbolizes that His kingdom is established.

<11> Also when His Kingdom is established on earth, a dot or star can be added to the Star of David, informing all that His Kingdom is come on earth as it is in Heaven. If later on people forget about God again and the earth becomes corrupt, the sign in the middle of the Star of David can be removed as a warning that the earth has become corrupt again and man has forgotten his true King (God), as the Star of David is used now.

<12> Furthermore, the two triangles together (✡) with a star in the middle (✡) means the Kingdom Of Heaven In Heaven. So also this sign at the top of the head of the eagle means that God watches the power (eagle) and the owner of it.

<13> In the seal, this Star of David (✡) is coming out of a cloud. Cloud always means confusion. <14> So His Kingdom will come after a great confusion (tribulation) when the phoenix will be burned to ashes and humbled. <15> Then it will be realized that the eagle, which is a symbol of the power given to a people (also given to the Roman Empire) which is from Him **will benefit the owner only if it is directed toward establishment of the Kingdom Of Heaven On Earth (His Will)** (✡).

---

§   In truth, the bird which was used in the early drawing of the seal was not an eagle but a phoenix, which is the symbol of the spirit soaring upward. The phoenix is the bird which rises from its ashes renewed. That is why in the early drawings the neck of the bird is so long and it has some feathers at the top of its head.

¶   Haree Om Shrii Hung, the sign of Pure Consciousness, the sign in the middle of **The Greatest Sign**, the emblem of the **Mission of Maitreya** (✡).

CHILDREN OF ABRAM (ABRAHAM)

<16> If the power given to any individual, people, or nation is not used to establish the Kingdom Of Heaven On Earth (justice, liberty, brotherhood, and unity), that power will eventually destroy the misuser.

<17> There are numerous examples of this truth in history. In fact, this is the theme and lesson of the Old Testament (especially after the human kings appeared in Hebrew history in the <u>Bible</u>).

Tablet Seventeen

Explanation of the reverse side of the seal:

<1> The other side of the Great Seal of America consists of a square-based pyramid with an eye at the top (capstone) which is separated from the rest of the pyramid.

<2> The shape of the pyramid is the same as a triangle upward which is the symbol of hierarchy in organization. The eye at the top is that entity which witnesses all things in the universe (God), in this case the One who is watchful of this Hierarchy and its True Guide.

<3> So actually the pyramid symbolizes the same thing as the triangle upward (△) in the Star of David (✡), which is the symbol of the Kingdom Of Heaven On Earth. However, the pyramid is the truer symbol of the Hierarchy in the Kingdom Of Heaven On Earth, because it is given in a three-dimensional form.

<4> The base of the pyramid is a square form which is the most stable base in the universe. The four sides are the four pillars on which the pyramid is supported. These four sides or pillars are the four bodies in the government. (For more detail, read <u>Mt. Zion and Zion, and Explanation of the System</u>).

<5> However, this Hierarchy cannot be God's Kingdom unless His Kingship (👁) is realized by all in the system and His Laws are followed.

<6> Only by implementing His system can the new order and era with peace and tranquility come to humanity (NOVUS ORDO SECLORUM** = The New Order of the Ages), and those who work to bring about this order are blessed and favored by the Lord (ANNUIT COEPTIS** = God has Favored Our Undertaking).

To be chosen does not mean to be greater:

<7> Therefore as all this evidence shows, the U.S. has been chosen for a great task. But also history has given the lesson through the <u>Bible</u>, other Scriptures, and the events which have happened in the last six thousand years (as explained in this book and <u>The Base</u>), that to be chosen means that a task should be done by those who have been chosen. It does not mean that those who have been selected are greater than others, but they are assigned to fulfill a duty.

<8> If they do the task, they will be given the reward and will continue as Chosen Ones. If they do the task in a superior way, then also they will be praised and very highly regarded. <9> But if the task is forgotten and a false pride is produced, such as "we are Cho-

---

** The mottos used on the reverse side of the Great Seal.

CHILDREN OF ABRAM (ABRAHAM) — *Tablet 17*

sen Ones so we are greater," then what they have will be taken away and given to others. Throughout history God has shown this lesson again and again.

THE HOUSE OF JUDAH
(JEWS)

The book, **The House Of Judah (Jews)**, explains how God chose Abraham and His children to set an example for humanity.

THE HOUSE OF JUDAH (JEWS)

INTRODUCTION

In order to understand the revelation in this book which explains another part of The Plan of the Lord and historical events, the Laws of Karma and Reincarnation should first be understood.

Karma, which loosely has been explained as the Law of action and reaction, in the simplest form can be described as: For any action there is a reaction created in the universe which should bear its fruit. Or, when a good action is done, a reward should be received, and when a bad action (sin) is done, punishment (suffering) is the result.

However, the reason for this Law is to guide humanity. If man understands that there is such a Divine Law and that the Lord (like a loving Father) is trying to guide him toward a goal which this universe was created for, then he will realize that he is not left alone on this earth to do as he pleases.

Although more sensitive people realize this Law in their and others' lives, and all the Prophets have warned men that such a Law exists, in general the mass does not really and deeply believe and understand this truth.

That is why throughout history God has chosen a people whose history is well known to all, and by the events which have happened to them, made them a loud example of how the Law of Karma works.

However, we also should truly understand that God is just and He will not punish a man for the action of another person (his ancestors). To realize this truth, belief in reincarnation and the Laws governing it is very necessary. In the simplest form, reincarnation can be explained as a person (Soul) assuming a new body after each death according to the previous deeds (karmas). Therefore he would bear the fruit of those actions, gain new experiences, learn new lessons, progress and eventually realize the self, God, and His Laws. Finally he would reach the goal (become Divine).

This process is very slow and many cannot see it clearly. Therefore God made history as a lesson for humanity, and through the revelations in this book which explain how these chosen people paid for their collective karma, these Divine Laws will be realized profoundly. Then men might know His Justice, follow His Laws, and create His Kingdom on earth.

If these two Laws are not understood or are not accepted, then the justness of God can never be explained and a person has no choice but to err and create irrational and illogical assumptions about God and His Purpose. This in turn creates more suffering for himself, for his community, and for humanity as a whole.

That is because a belief about one race might then arise, and the whole lesson and purpose for revealing the material in this book will be lost sight of. Then the person not only will not benefit from it, but will go even further from the truth, create greater resentment, and bring more suffering unto the self and others.

So know that God is just, and He never punishes a man for what his fathers did. Also He has complete control over all things and can do whatever He wants to do and can reincarnate a Soul anywhere He desires.

Then learn the lessons of these revelations and their relationships with our other writings, so you might free yourself from all earthly bondage and be free to the Lord. Amen (ॐ).

THE HOUSE OF JUDAH (JEWS)

Tablet One

1 - Elected Ones:

<1> Abraham was selected as the first Elected One in order to set the cornerstone of one of The Plans of the Lord. <2> One part of this Plan was to choose a people as an example for humanity, a people who would stand out in history as a pattern for others, and who would be rewarded and punished in order to bring them, and also everyone else, to the realization that the human has no choice but to follow the Laws of the universe and the Will of the Father. The people who were chosen were from the House of Judah.

<3> Before Hebrews became Elected Ones, a large number of mystical religions were on the earth. Many different gods were being worshipped, and the goal of spirituality was either to please the gods for receiving favors or to gain mystical powers for selfish reasons, such as the misuse of social powers by priests and administrators. <4> Therefore, the majority of the people were exploited through many taboos which were created by the priest classes or rulers.

<5> **However, the only way possible for all men to progress to their highest potential (physically, mentally, and spiritually) is when an environment is created to allow all to have equal opportunities to grow to the fullest.**

<6> In doing so, God chose the Hebrews to carry out the task. He decided to weaken mystical religions, and He destroyed many of the undesirable ones, because they had become a source of suffering for man instead of being used for spiritual progress.

2 - Strengthening the Elected Ones:

<7> Through Abraham, Isaac, and Jacob (Israel), God established the idea of "Hebrews being elected people by the Lord." He brought the Children of Israel to Egypt, increased their numbers, made them suffer there in order to become strong, and chose Moses to be their guide. <8> God allowed Moses to gain all the knowledge of the Egyptians and the people of the Midian, and then gave him the stature of prophethood and power to bring the Children of Israel out of Egypt.

<9> Despite all of this effort, the Children of Israel were not yet ready to become a perfect example for others. God then gave the Hebrews laws and regulations to bring them order and to make them strong and unique from their neighbors. <10> He made them go through great hardships and struggles to develop those characteristics which were necessary for them particularly, and are necessary for any person or group individually, in order to set an example for others and so influence them to bring the Kingdom Of Heaven within and without.

<11> That is the period between the coming out of Egypt until the conquering of the land of the Canaanites. <12> This is also a symbol for those who try to go out of their lower natures (Egypt) to their higher natures (the Promised Land). A great struggle and period of strengthening is necessary.

Tablet Two

3 - They were tested:

<1> The Children of Israel conquered the land of the Canaanites and settled there. God became their King, and judges became the rulers who were supposed to follow the Will of the Lord through their relationships with Him or through listening to the high priests.

<2> These judges failed. The Israelites forgot the purpose for which they were chosen. They rejected God as the only King (I Samuel 8). They longed for a human king like their neighbors, and therefore the system of kingship started in Israel.

THE HOUSE OF JUDAH (JEWS)

4 - They failed:

<3> By rejecting God (I Samuel 8:7) and accepting a human king, they cut themselves off from His direct influence in their lives. Then they started bowing down in front of the earthly kings who were as human as themselves with all the earthly shortcomings and faults. <4> **By accepting a human king, man becomes the subject of that king and his wills and whims.** Therefore, he forgets about God and His Laws. He becomes a bondman of the earthly laws instead of being a bondman of the Lord's Laws.

<5> **However, the man who accepts the Lord as his only God and the only King, will become the subject of the Lord and has only to follow His Will and His Laws.** That is why Esa said to Pontius Pilate that he (Pilate) had no power over him (Esa) because Esa was not a subject of Pilate but of the Lord. <6> He was not following the laws of man but those of God.

<7> With rejection of God as their King by the Israelite people and through accepting a human king, they further lost their direct relationship with the Lord. Then more Prophets started coming to the scene. <8> That is the rule of the Prophets. **They are a connection between the Lord and the lost human.** <9> However, if the human accepts the Lord as his only master, follows His Will and becomes His subject, then each man can understand his Lord and **there is no need for any Prophet**. <10> However, the lower nature of man is strong and overcoming it is not easy for many.

<11> With these happenings, the first period of the failure of the Children of Israel began.

5 - First purification (punishment):

<12> Later on, the punishment came in the form of being held captive by other nations and being scattered around the world. A great suffering came upon God's people, because they rejected Him. <13> He never rejected them, but they rejected Him. That is why they were punished (fell from His Grace).

<14> However, God punished them not because He liked to or needed their covenant, but because He is a loving Father who knows the best way for His children to grow and reach the highest possible state. **He punished them for their own good.** <15> He demanded to be accepted as the true King, because no earthly king or authority on earth is worthy of being called a king or true leader. The human's flesh is strong and spirit is weak, but the Father has no fleshly desire, and only those who have overcome the flesh are worthy of being the leaders of humanity. As long as the human does not understand this great truth, he will not conquer the suffering in society and individual life.

<16> Therefore punishment should not be viewed as a bad thing. If it is inflicted on a nation or a man, that nation or human should seek the reason for the chastisement. Then by correcting the self and through repentance, the nation or man will be forgiven and guided further towards progress.

6 - The Children of Israel become two nations:

<17> Before the Children of Israel were conquered and held captive, they were divided into two nations, the "House of Israel" and the "House of Judah." The House of Israel was captured first and then the House of Judah was taken. <18> The House of Judah are those who are known as "Jews." The ten tribes of the House of Israel are known as the ten lost tribes of the Children of Israel.

<19> The rest of this book is the explanation about the Jewish people because the House of Israel never truly came back to their land and had a different purpose to fulfill. For more information and a detailed explanation, refer to the book <u>Children of Abram (Abraham), All Prophecies Are Fulfilled</u>.

7 - They are given another chance:

<20> Therefore, one of the purposes for bad events in life is for purification because of previous bad deeds and to give a lesson to humans for their further progress. That is the

THE HOUSE OF JUDAH (JEWS)

reason why we can see after each punishment, God gives His chosen nation another chance to repent and go back to Him. <21> But unfortunately, the human is very slow to learn the lesson, and also his false ego does not let him realize how insignificant he is in comparison to the power of the Creator. At the same time, man is the greatest (after the Lord) in this universe, if he could just realize that the only way to reach this greatness is His Way.

<22> That is the reason why God gathered the House of Judah (Jews) back to their lands and told them, through His Prophets, that a great Prophet (Messiah) will come to them.

Tablet Three

8 - The coming of Esa The Messiah, and his rejection by the Jews:

<1> The promised Messiah came as Esa The Christ. He fulfilled all the signs which were given for his coming, but the Jews rejected him. He came to show the way of establishing the Kingdom Of Heaven within and without, but the Jews had many concepts about the new Messiah. <2> They expected him to come and place them in a position superior to others. They expected him to be similar to the kings they knew, with material glory and power for suppressing others because of their wrong conception of Jewish superiority.

<3> However, Esa came as a universal personality with a teaching of equality: "balances in his hands" (Rev. 6:5). He was, as a symbol, the first of the Jews who truly overcame his lower nature or false ego: "…and lo a black horse; and he that sat on him…" (Rev. 6:5).

<4> Many believed him and it seemed to the priests that he was going to destroy their already established, quiet social structures. That is why they not only rejected him but put him on the cross without a cause. That was a great sin.

<5> However, no man can stop God's Plan. Even with putting Esa on the cross, the new teaching could not be completely suppressed and Christianity flourished. He "gathered the people," as it was explained in Children of Abram (Abraham), All Prophecies Are Fulfilled.

<6> This process of sinning, being punished (purified) and being given another chance is shown in Matthew 23:37, "O Jerusalem, Jerusalem, thou that killest the Prophets, and stonest them which are sent unto thee, how often would I have gathered thy children together, even as a hen gathereth her chickens under her wings, and ye would not!" The sentence, "and ye would not" means, "You would not repent."

9 - The Prophethood is taken from the Jews and given to other nations:

<7> With the rejection of Esa The Messiah and the fulfillment of the prophecies of his coming, God took away the prophethood from the Jews and gave it to other nations. This was prophesied by Israel (Jacob), and is also explained in Children of Abram (Abraham), All Prophecies Are Fulfilled.

<8> This event is shown in Matthew 21:43, "Therefore I say unto you, The Kingdom of God shall be taken from you, and given to a nation bringing forth the fruits thereof."

<9> With this sentence, the great struggle of the Jews started, but they did not believe the words of the prophecy told by Christ. <10> However, it does not matter if humans accept or reject a Prophet. Messengers of God (Angels) are only the warners and have a message for people. What they say will happen even if their words are not accepted. <11> Also in the case of Esa, his crucifixion was a part of his mission.

10 - Revelation of The Revelation:

<12> Because of the circumstances under which Christ's teachings came to humanity, and because of the short period of his ministry, many of his teachings were lost, many

THE HOUSE OF JUDAH (JEWS)

were misinterpreted, and still others were distorted. This occurred between the time of his teachings and the time of writing them down in the gospels and their supplements, and even later on.

<13> Therefore, as the final book of the Bible (The Revelation), God sent His complete Plan in a very symbolic language in order to seal its understanding until He decides to unseal it ("But in the days of the voice of the seventh angel, ... the mystery of God should be finished,..." Rev. 10:7).

<14> The Revelation shows His complete Plan of how He will bring humanity, step-by-step, to a point where they will be left with no choice but to understand the truth which underlies this universe. <15> With this perfect arrangement of having Genesis as the first book, the rest of the Old Testament representing man's overcoming his lower nature ("black horse," Rev. 6:5), and revealing the whole Plan in summary in the last book as what happened and will happen, the Bible, as the prophetic and historical base for all other spiritual Scriptures, is complete. <16> However, although the Bible is the base, knowledge of other Scriptures is necessary to understand the truth behind it.

<17> That is why an understanding of the mystical part of the universe, such as the Far East wisdom (relationship between the spirit of man and the universe) and of Islam, the Baha'i Faith, who is a Paravipra, and **THOTH** is necessary to complete the knowledge of the true Plan of the Lord. So in the process a person can reach a complete faith and become a dynamic spiritual force in order to manifest the power of the Lord through his one-pointedness and knowledge of the truth behind this universe.

<18> Therefore The Revelation can be viewed as a mini-Bible. It is as the Vedantas are considered in Vedic teachings: The last and most important part, a summary or conclusion.

<19> As it was stated, the prophethood was taken from the Jews and given to other nations. <20> Also as The Revelation reveals and **The Greatest Sign** shows, the seven truths (steps) will come to humanity in order to complete the truth of the spiritual path. These are shown in chapters 2 and 3 by the seven churches, and also in chapters 6 through 22 (read Revelation of The Revelation).

<21> That is why the next Prophet came not from the Jews, but from another nation close to them.

11 - Second Purification (punishment):

<22> This time Jerusalem and also the temple were destroyed by the Romans. The Jewish people were scattered abroad again. <23> They settled mostly out of Jerusalem in neighboring countries. They became so rooted in other countries that each became a minority in those lands. They became a source of knowledge for other people and their story of struggle was soon a part of the myths of other nations. <24> Especially because of the connection of Christians with the Jewish background, their history was presented more vigorously to other nations than the history of any other people.

<25> However, Jews still were close to their ancient land. They were a nation within many other nations. They were not as scattered as they became later on.

Tablet Four

12 - The advent of Prophet Muhammad:

<1> Arabs are the closest race to the Hebrews. They are descendants of Ishmael, the son of Abram (Abraham, the father of the Hebrews). As it was said, the next Prophet would not come from the Jews but from another nation. Prophet Muhammad was the next Messenger who came from the Arabs. The advent of a Messiah from the Arabs (Children of

THE HOUSE OF JUDAH (JEWS)

Abram) was also promised to Abram (Abraham) – read Children of Abram (Abraham), All Prophecies Are Fulfilled.

<2> In the period before Prophet Muhammad became a Prophet, a great expectation was developed by the people that another Messiah would be sent to humanity. When Prophet Muhammad announced that he had been chosen as the expected Messenger from God, in the beginning the Jews accepted him as the one they were waiting for.

13 - The rejection of Prophet Muhammad and his prediction of a great punishment for the Jews:

<3> However, later on, when the Jews realized that Prophet Muhammad would not conform to their expectations of being exalted as the chosen people and allowed privileges over others, they started to oppose him. This then resulted in much conflict and eventually the Jewish people had to leave the Islamic territories.

<4> Also Prophet Muhammad prophesied that a great punishment would befall the Jews. In many verses in the Koran, they were condemned for changing the Scriptures and killing the Prophets, and they were warned that they would be punished for their misdeeds (bad karma).

<5> Baha'u'llah also realized that the people of Israel (Jews) deserved great punishments: "The people of Israel…! Thus hath God laid hold of them for their sins, hath extinguished in them the spirit of faith, and tormented them with the flames of the nethermost fire" (Baha'i World Faith, p. 14, Baha'i Publishing Trust, 1976).

14 - The third purification (punishment):

<6> After Prophet Muhammad, the Jews were scattered even more and went through a great period of misery with no land of their own. <7> However, the greatest punishment in this period is what happened in the Second World War.

15 - The Jews are given another chance:

<8> However, after this third purification act by that great disaster which befell the Jews, again God gave them another chance to correct themselves and understand the lessons He was trying to teach them. <9> He was also showing humanity that the Law of Karma is not a fancy philosophy of an imaginative yogi, or the revelations by Prophets are not something to be ignored by humans because they do not fit their petty false egos. God has a great purpose for creating this universe and will fulfill it no matter how stubborn the human might be.

Tablet Five

16 - A distinction between Hebrews and Jews:

<1> God chose the Hebrews and made a covenant with them that they would be His people forever, and He stood firm in His Covenant. Hebrew means "beyond, those who have overcome their lower natures, or the Children of Israel (those who struggle with God)." These people have been and forever will be the Elected Ones. <2> Whoever overcomes the world (its excess attraction, Maya) is an Elected One. They have always been reincarnated to struggle for His Purpose.

<3> However, "Jew" is a term that was used later on to identify people from Judah. This name is given to those people who God chose to set an example for the rest of humanity of the truth of His Divine Justice, and to show how severe He is in punishment and how merciful He is in reward.

<4> The question might be asked of how the Divine Justice could be understood if God punishes the children of the sinned ancestors. <5> The answer is that those who

THE HOUSE OF JUDAH (JEWS)

are incarnated in the Jewish community at the time of punishment are not the same as Hebrews (Elected Ones) who had not done any sin. These punished people were those who had sinned in their previous lives, even if they had not been one of the Jews before. <6> If a person in the Jewish community had done good deeds in his life, he would not have been reborn in that community at the time of punishment, and/or he would not be punished. <7> The justice of God can only be seen and explained if we realize the Laws of Karma and Reincarnation.

<8> At the time of punishment, those Jews in the past who changed the Scriptures, killed the Prophets, or others with heavy sins, were reincarnated in the Jewish community to show the human that misdeeds will result in punishment. <9> At the time of redemption (given another chance) those who were purified and those with good deeds would be born to this community. However, as history shows, some again would fail and the cycle of punishment and redemption goes on as it is.

Tablet Six

<1> It is very important to realize that the word "Jew" was selected to identify a certain people. However, each individual is responsible for his own actions, regardless of race or creed. <2> In fact, no individual (his Soul) belongs to anything in this world or in the world to come. He is a Soul made to progress, not to be bound to any human or body identification.

<3> People who are born in a specific race or place are there for gaining a certain experience or for repaying some of their past deeds. Therefore, no one can look down at any particular race or creed. <4> A man should be honored or dishonored for his individual actions, not because his body (for the reason of genetic combination) belongs to any special race.

<5> The reason for this repetition in explanation is to make this point completely clear that we should not recognize an individual as a Jew, but we should look at the name **as an identification for a special group of people** who were chosen to be an example for the rest of humanity. This is to teach humans that the Law of Karma is true and is not just a philosophy. That is, no Jew is responsible for the misdeeds of his ancestors, but he is a free Soul without ties to any binding force in this universe.

<6> Therefore, each Soul should make his choice in his life of be(com)ing Divine or not. <7> However, when the whole community fails in a case, those who were part of that failure will be punished. But those who realize the truth of the revelations by the Prophets and understand the truth behind history and God's Plan will be saved as free Souls.

Tablet Seven

17 - The struggle of God to make humans understand His Divine Justice:

<1> Therefore, if it is hard for the human to see this procedure of punishment and redemption in his own individual life or his own race or nation, <2> then by studying the history, revelations given by Prophets, and the history of the Jewish people, whom God chose to be a loud example for humanity, man can understand that there is Divine Justice, there is a Plan for this creation, and there is a God who is guiding His universe toward **The GOAL**.

<3> That is the struggle of God with humans. Those who struggle with Him in this task are the Hebrews (Elected Ones). <4> Those who do not understand and will not follow the Laws of the universe will be doomed to suffering by being cut off from His Grace.

<5> That is the only way if humanity wants peace, tranquility, happiness, brotherhood, and

THE HOUSE OF JUDAH (JEWS)

understanding of the truth.

<6> Those who feel that the whole universe is their home and they do not belong to any special group or race, those who regard all humans equally as their fellow struggling beings, and those who believe in Divine Justice, are the true believers.

<7> Now is again another chance for all to realize these truths and join together as one. So "His kingdom come, His Will be done, on earth as it is in Heaven."

CREATION AND HISTORY

The book, <u>Creation and History</u>, explains creation and history from a scientific, historical, and spiritual point of view. It explains how history has been guided by God and how He is in control of human events. Of course, since His Timetable is different than the human's, many people, in their short lives compared with God's timing, do not see His Hand in history. They believe that what happens in their lives and history are human doings. In reality He Plans and humans act out those plans. With a Spiritual Eye a person can see that whatever happens eventually leads to fulfillment of His Will. In this book some of His Doings as History (His Story) are Revealed!

CREATION AND HISTORY

INTRODUCTION

This book will explain the "creation and history" and combines the two aspects of history: The historical aspect and the spiritual aspect. The historical aspects are based on the book, <u>Children of Abram (Abraham), All Prophecies Are Fulfilled</u>, and the spiritual aspects are based on the book, <u>The Base</u>.

The historical part explains how God fulfilled the prophecies which He first revealed would happen. It was done so that, firstly, humans would understand that God exists and is the Controller of all things. This would increase their faith, and also they would know that they had better follow His Words and listen to His Prophets. Secondly, these fulfilled prophecies would be a witness and a sign to the truth of the teachings of **Maitreya** and **The Greatest Sign**. This part is explained in more detail in the book <u>Children of Abram (Abraham), All Prophecies Are Fulfilled</u>.

The spiritual aspects which are based on the book <u>The Base</u>, explain how the **Eternal Divine Path**, which will guide men to Pure Consciousness, was revealed step-by-step through the last six thousand years. Also it reveals how each of these steps became a truth or religion of the world. But the true path is one which contains all of the seven steps, and each of these truths by itself is only a part of the whole. To receive the entire truth, a person should understand the meanings and purposes of all of them so that he might know the way.

Tablet One

CREATION

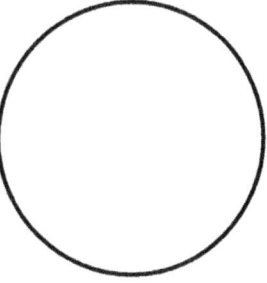

<1> God is complete, without beginning or end. He is everlasting, indivisible, and One.

> "In the beginning was the Word, and the Word was with God, and the Word was God.
> The same was in the beginning with God." (John 1:1-2)

<2> In the beginning before any creation, the universe was in the state of "Be"-ness.

<3> The universe consists of consciousness (Father) and the three creative forces (three gunas). These creative forces are called "The Word."

<4> The consciousness and its three creative forces (The Word) are a part and parcel of one entity (God). The consciousness cannot be separated from its creative forces. They are one and indivisible.

CREATION AND HISTORY

Tablet 2

<5> That is why "In the beginning was the Word, and the Word was with God, and the Word was God," and "the same was in the beginning with God."

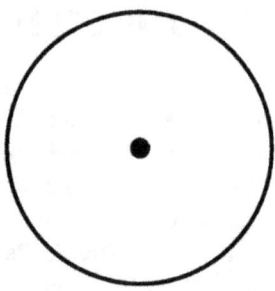

"All things were made by him; and without him was not anything made that was made." (John 1:3)

<6> Because of the desire of God, the operative powers of the three creative forces were released, <7> and by the use of these creative forces (The Word) and consciousness, "All things were made." Without the creative forces nothing could have been made "that was made."

Tablet Two

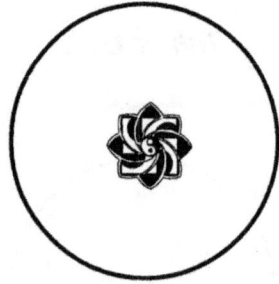

"In the beginning God created the heaven and the earth." (Genesis 1:1)

<1> The three creative forces are the crudifying force (tama), mutative force (raja) and sentient force (satva). Because of their influences, the false ego was created and the universe was divided into infinite unit consciousnesses. <2> The unit consciousness is the manifestation of the Divine (Pure Consciousness) through the gross in the illusive state of being separate from God (universe).

<3> With creation of the false ego, the feeling of being separate from the whole (God) was created. By this, the feeling of self-centeredness, egotism, unhappiness, and suffering became the dominating factor.

<4> God (Father) called this state hell (earth), and the state He Himself was in – Pure Consciousness (ॐ) – He called heaven. So heaven and hell (earth) were created.

And the earth was without form, and void;... (Genesis 1:2)

<5> Heaven and hell are not places nor do they have any shape. That is why the earth (hell) "was without form, and void."

CREATION AND HISTORY

Tablet 2

"...and darkness was upon the face of the deep..." (Genesis 1:2)

<6> Through the Universal Mind (▽), God saw this state of the unit consciousnesses present all throughout the universe, "and darkness was upon the face of the deep."

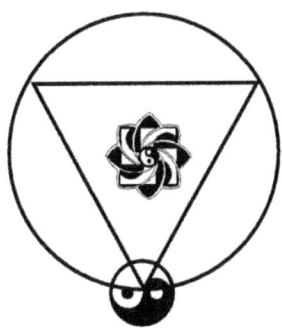

"...And the Spirit of God moved upon the face of the waters." (Genesis 1:2c)

<7> "Water" is a symbol for ether. <8> Through the Universal Mind ("Spirit of God"), He moved in the universe ("upon the face of the waters") and brought those lost unit consciousnesses (☯) under His Control (▽).

And God said, Let there be light:... (Genesis 1:3)

<9> He desired that these lost consciousnesses (☯) reach Pure Consciousness (✺), the Light. He projected His Light (The Word) into the universe, "Let there be light."

...and there was light. (Genesis 1:3)

<10> With the help of the Father with The Holy Ghost and through the **Eternal Divine Path**, eventually The Word reached Pure Consciousness (✺), "...and there was light."

<11> He became the First Begotten Son of God.

CREATION AND HISTORY
Tablet 2

<12> However, the process to reach Pure Consciousness in this state was very difficult. So God decided to create a more orderly way to bring the unit consciousnesses to Pure Consciousness. <13> He decided to create the manifested world and the evolutionary process.

<14> With the help of the creative forces (three gunas) and the lost unit consciousnesses, this manifested universe was created.

<15> Therefore, this manifested universe is nothing but a relative reality from the absolute (consciousness and three gunas) and the goal for its creation is that the unit consciousness (man) reach Pure Consciousness, **HAREE OM SHRII HUNG = The Goal of the Life is to Be(come) Divine**.

<16> However, to fulfill this goal of the universe, all should help. So even those who reach higher consciousness or Pure Consciousness should and will help others to reach this goal – to be(come) Divine.

<17> So the true way to explain the universe and its goal is that: **The goal of the life is to be(come) Divine and help others to be(come) Divine also**.

<18> After God created the first man, many evolutionary steps became necessary to reach the man we know today.

<19> The creation of man in this present state started twelve thousand years ago (after the symbolic events of the flood of Noah) and was completed around six thousand years ago. Since that time human history has evolved and in it lessons and many hidden truths for man are given, which are for his guidance and understanding.

<20> Through the last six thousand years, God has fulfilled two great Plans with different purposes: One for human spiritual guidance which we can call the spiritual Plan, and a second historical Plan to make the human understand that with no doubt He exists and is in control. <21> Also it is to show that His desire is for man to use his intelligence to establish His Will and to create a universe according to His Laws, so that the whole universe can reach Pure Consciousness at a faster pace.

<22> The creation is explained briefly in the previous pages (for a more detailed explanation, read <u>The Holiest Book</u>, <u>The Essence</u>, and <u>The Base</u>). The history will be explained in the following section.

CREATION AND HISTORY

Tablet Three

HISTORY

"And Noah builded an altar unto the Lord; and took of every clean beast, and of every clean fowl, and offered burnt offerings on the altar." (Genesis 8:20)

<1> As the Prophet and forerunner for the new kind of human, Noah set an example of how to worship God. <2> Also because this human no longer had direct contact with the spiritual world, their worship became gross as symbolized by building altars and offering burnt offerings.

<3> Some of these teachings were preserved and written down, which are known as the Vedas. <4> The true spiritual knowledge, however, is covered from the eyes of the profane, but can be found in the Scriptures of the Lord, in the spirit, through many Mystical Paths all throughout the earth, by those who truly seek. "Ask, and it shall be given you; seek, and ye shall find; knock, and it shall be opened unto you:" (Matthew 7:7).

<5> Also the gross form of the spiritual vibrations which can invoke the spiritual powers have come to man through the letters of the alphabet in many different languages. <6> The original words cannot be produced in the material world and the intellect of man, as we know it, cannot grasp them.

<7> These teachings became the base for the knowledge which is known as the Far East Philosophies and also the mystical spiritual knowledge in other world religions. They explain the relationship between man and the universe. Also the techniques and their rituals are to help in awakening the spiritual forces in man (☯).

<8> The symbol of these teachings is shown by the I-Ching (☯) which represents the latent spiritual forces. These teachings help man to awaken these forces.

And the Lord smelled a sweet savour; and the Lord said in his heart, I will not again curse the ground any more... (Genesis 8:21)

<9> God will not curse the ground because now He has complete control over man. The human has become so helpless that he can no longer create any disharmony in the universal forces. He might harm himself by going against the Laws of the Lord but he cannot change the universal set-up or creative forces. <10> Only those who prove worthy will gain control over these powers and they will not misuse them.

Every moving thing that liveth shall be meat for you; even as the green herb have I given you all things. (Genesis 9:3)

<11> The human became so gross and fleshly that God allowed him to eat meat after the flood of Noah. As it was commanded in Genesis chapter 1, verse 29, men should be

CREATION AND HISTORY

vegetarian. But after the flood of Noah, He allowed them to eat meat. <12> Also this would help them to become more flesh, because vegetables are for consciousness and meat is for flesh. Meat has much tama guna which crudifies the consciousness. <13> This causes man to be more lost and to fall even further.

<14> However, for those ready and seriously searching to find the way to higher consciousness, the true teachings and realities behind this universe were given to a few who would help them in their progress. Such beings are called Masters. <15> They bring new teachings or complete the old ones, for as the consciousness of the human grows or through experience (individually or collectively), he becomes ready to receive a higher truth.

> And the sons of Noah, that went forth of the ark, were Shem, and Ham, and Japheth:... (Genesis 9:18)

<16> The five different types of humans, which are: Workers (Shudras), warriors (Ksattriyas), intellectuals (Vipras), businessmen (Vaeshyas), and priests (Brahmins) were created. For more detail, read The Holiest Book in section Genesis chapters 9 and 10, and also The Kingdom Of Heaven On Earth and Commentaries on Prophecies in Daniel, Period of Intellectual Domination.

> ...every one after his tongue,... (Genesis 10:5, 20, 31)

<17> Many different tongues and dialects were created on earth.

> ...for in his days was the earth divided;... (Genesis 10:25)

<18> Before the earth became divided, humans had access to all the dry land. There were connections between all continents. By this occurrence, the Lord completely disconnected some lands from each other.

<19> Before this happened, the people who had the true knowledge of the spiritual world and were in a very high consciousness, realized that this disaster was coming to humanity. They left their mainland and were scattered throughout the world, carrying their knowledge to other lands. <20> But because of the loss of their mainland and center, and also because of not finding true seekers, they translated their knowledge into a symbolic language for their few followers and they built symbolic buildings for future generations. Then when God would open the spiritual eyes of the humans again, they would understand the truth of these symbols.

<21> Furthermore, by dividing the land, God kept an area separated from the rest for a great purpose – read Children of Abram (Abraham), All Prophecies Are Fulfilled.

> And the whole earth was of one language, and of one speech. (Genesis 11:1)

<22> Although they had many languages, still the telepathic ability for communication was with them. They started to misuse their intellect and this telepathic ability to gain fame and name. <23> They went against the Will of God which was to have humanity living all over the earth, "...and let us make us a name, lest we be scattered abroad upon the face of the whole earth." (Genesis 11:4).

> ...the Lord did there confound the languages of all the earth: and from thence did the Lord scatter them abroad upon the face of all the earth. (Genesis 11:9)

<24> So God took away their telepathic ability, and they no longer could understand each other well. This created confusion in their communication and caused them to move to all areas of the earth. <25> Indeed it was after they were scattered that "the earth was divided" (Genesis 10:25), and this caused their separation to be even more intense. It was before this happened that the great Masters left their mainland and scattered all over the world to preserve the secret knowledge.

CREATION AND HISTORY
Tablet Four

"And I will make of thee [Abram] a great nation,…" (Genesis 12:2)

<1> Some thousand years later and through the mystical knowledge which was preserved (☯), many Souls awakened their spiritual forces and reached a higher consciousness. They were ready to set an example for the rest of humanity. Abram was chosen to start this mission.

<2> The spiritual significance of this choosing was to elect those who had reached higher consciousness as a spiritual force to be used in awakening the spiritual knowledge in others. <3> Also, it was to eventually make humanity realize that their true happiness and prosperity depends upon understanding God and the truth behind this universe.

<4> They would go through great struggles in many lifetimes and their numbers would increase after a period of time until some time later they would become a nation (Elected Ones), "And I will make of thee a great nation." (Gen. 12:2).

<5> They truly do not belong to one nation on earth but they are a nation of God. They will be reincarnated wherever their presence is necessary, and eventually they will become perfect men who will gain the leadership of humanity and guide the whole universe to its goal – "to be(come) Divine."

<6> That is why the symbol (✡) is chosen for these people. The triangle upward (△) symbolizes organizational Hierarchy or outward action, and the triangle downward (▽) symbolizes control and justice. The two triangles together are the symbol for the Kingdom Of Heaven On Earth.

<7> Also, by choosing Abram, a great historical event started. That is, a long historical period began, and through the prophecies of what would happen in the future and the fulfillment of these prophecies in history (for more detail of these occurrences, read <u>Children of Abram (Abraham), All Prophecies Are Fulfilled</u>) He again would prove that He exists. <8> This would cause man to realize that he sees only a small part of the truth and judges things from that narrow view, and that is why humanity suffers.

<9> To start this great Plan, God promised Abram and his seed many things. The son of Abram was Ishmael, the son of Hagar. Ishmael is the father of the Arabs.

<10> Then God changed his name from Abram (A-Bram) to Abraham and gave him new promises for his seed. He then begot Isaac from his wife Sarah.

<11> The significance of the name change from Abram to Abraham, and the difference between the two promises given to **Abram** and his seed, and to **Abraham** and his seed, is very important for understanding the great mystery of the historical events which took place later on. Without knowing this, a great truth will be lost and we will not be able to see how the promises He had given to Abram and Abraham were fulfilled.

<12> Also in the promises He gave to Abram and Abraham, there were two aspects in each promise: (1) the birthright or territorial possession, and (2) the spiritual kingly promise (scepter). <13> Then the <u>Bible</u>

CREATION AND HISTORY

continues with the promises which were given to Abraham for his seed Isaac.

<14> Of the two sons of Isaac, it is Jacob who wins both of these promises, and also when his name is changed from Jacob to Israel a promise of "a nation and a company of nations" is given to him (Gen. 35:10-12).

<15> Later on, before his death, he makes his grandsons Ephraim and Manasseh (the sons of his own son Joseph) as his own sons (Gen. 48:3-5). Then he gives the birthright (territorial possession) to Joseph and through him to Ephraim and Manasseh. So Ephraim and Manasseh became two tribes and joined the Children of Israel.

<16> Also Israel (Jacob) gave the promise of the scepter or the spiritual kingship to Judah:

> The scepter shall not depart from Judah, nor a lawgiver from between his feet, until Shiloh come; and unto him shall the gathering of the people be. (Genesis 49:10)

<17> This is one of the greatest prophecies which has been ignored by many and is the very key in understanding most of the events which had happened throughout the past several thousand years.

<18> The scepter or the promise of the spiritual kingdom "shall not depart from" the tribe of Judah. Or in other words, the Messiah or spiritual king should come from the tribe of Judah. <19> Also the lawgiving and its enforcement shall be by this tribe.

<20> However, this promise is not forever, but only "until **Shiloh** come." When the promised Messiah (Shiloh) does come, not only would the promised scepter and lawgiving power of the Children of Abraham be fulfilled, <21> but also he (Shiloh) should gather the people, who will bare the name Israel unto themselves, "and unto him shall the gathering of the people be."

<22> Later on, the Children of Israel would be divided into two houses, the House of Judah (Jews) and the House of Israel. These would create the southern and northern kingdoms respectively. <23> Both of these kingdoms fall. The people of the House of Judah (Jews) returned to their land, but the ten tribes of the House of Israel, including the tribes of Ephraim and Manasseh, never, completely, came back. They are known as the ten lost tribes of Israel.

<24> However, some of the people of these ten tribes left their country and traveled west to England and to America. <25> They created a nation (England) and many nations (United States of America) at a later time. For more detail about all the events briefly explained above, read <u>Children of Abram (Abraham), All Prophecies Are Fulfilled</u>.

Tablet Five

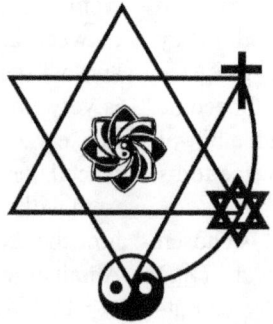

...until Shiloh come; and unto him shall the gathering of the people be. (Genesis 49:10)

CREATION AND HISTORY *Tablet 5*

<1> As it was explained, the spiritual king (scepter) should come from the tribe of Judah, and he did. <2> Esa The Christ, who was from the tribe of Judah, came as the expected Messiah.

<3> His spiritual message was that in order to establish the Kingdom Of Heaven On Earth (✡), sacrifice (✝) – to be humble – is necessary.

<4> But the historical effect was his coming as prophesied by Jacob (Israel) to finish the promise of the scepter given to the tribe of Judah.

> Therefore say I unto you, The kingdom of God shall be taken from you, and given to a nation... (Matthew 21:43)

<5> So this part of the prophecies was fulfilled. For what happened to the Jews after this, read The House of Judah (Jews).

<6> Also Esa fulfilled the prophecy of gathering together the people. He became the head and gathered all the ten lost tribes of the House of Israel (people) who immigrated toward the west under his banner (Christianity).

<7> So Esa fulfilled a threefold mission: (1) his spiritual message (sacrifice), (2) fulfillment of the promise given to Judah, and (3) gathering the people.

<8> As it was explained, the promises which were given to Abram were for Ishmael, the other son of Abraham from Hagar. Ishmael is the father of the Arabs. So they also should have gained a great territory and their numbers become "as the dust of the earth; so that if a man can number the dust of the earth, then shall thy seed also be numbered" (Gen. 13:16). <9> Also they would receive a great Prophet and kingly spiritual personality (scepter).

<10> By the coming of Esa (Shiloh), the kingly spiritual being promised to Abraham was finished and as Esa prophesied, "The kingdom of God shall be taken from" them and instead given to another nation (Matthew 21:43). Therefore, the scepter and the lawgiving were removed from the tribe of Judah and given to another nation. This other nation was the Arabs. The spiritual kingly personality was Muhammad. The spiritual truth and laws were Islam (☪) and the Koran.

<11> With this, another prophecy was fulfilled, and also history is the witness of this truth which God promised would happen. Furthermore, nothing happens without His Will. So if a person would be able to establish a new great religion, it has been His Will, even if some people do not understand or do not like it.

<12> The spiritual message of Prophet Muhammad can be understood from the very word "Islam." Islam comes from the word "tasleim" which means both to be surrendered and submissive to the Will of the Lord.

<13> To be "surrendered" means to do the work, try to follow His Will the best a person can, and then to surrender the result to the Lord. With doing this, there will be no attachment left to the result and that is the key to freedom from the binding power of the Law of Karma (action).

<14> Even greater than surrendering is "submission," which is to ideate that we are a

tool for His Will to be done through us. So we let Him do the action through us. With this ideation, no "I" will be left and the "Doer," "the One to whom the result of our actions has been surrendered," and "the thing Done" all will become One, or He. So no reaction of one's action remains, and no attachment to the result occurs, because "I" is not the doer. <15> In fact, there is no "I" left to become attached to the result. So the action is done, His Will is done, but the person is free from the result of the action, because the doer was not he but He.

<16> In the case of surrendering, there is still an "I" left as the one who surrenders, and there is a "He" to whom the result is surrendered. But in the case of submission, there is only He. So the "I" will be dissolved into "He," and then the "I" and "He" become **ONE**. <17> With this, the goal of spiritual progress is achieved, which is to become the same as God. It is not to merge into God, but to become the same as He (in His image) or to be able to manifest the qualities of God. <18> This is the highest spiritual realization.

Tablet Six

<1> However, with Islam, The Plan of God was not yet finished. Still there were three more truths which should have come before The Plan was complete. <2> The first four truths (Far East Philosophies or Mystical Paths, Judaism, Christianity, and Islam) plus the next three to be explained, make up the seven truths which are symbolized as the seven churches and seven seals in <u>The Revelation</u>, the last book of the <u>Bible</u> and are presented in **The Greatest Sign**.

<3> Also it was foretold in the <u>Koran</u> that a further truth would come:

>...Allah will bring a people whom He loveth and who love him... (<u>Koran</u>, Surah The Table Spread, 54)

<4> Furthermore, in Islam God is One who does whatever He pleases. So He can also send another Prophet if He wills (pleases) to do so. However, the spiritual understanding was finished with Prophet Muhammad, and from this point of view, he is the last Prophet.

<5> But to complete and expand the human mind, other steps were necessary. The next Prophet, who brought universalism (✹) was Bab (or the Baha'i Faith). Without the universal point of view, all of the four previous truths will be narrow, and narrowness indeed is the root cause of all suffering and is not according to the Will of God. Therefore, expansion of the mind (universalism) was necessary.

<6> The name of this new truth is historically known as the Baha'i Faith (✹). Although no new spiritual realization was brought to humanity by this religion, with realizing that universalism will result in expansion of the mind and destruction of all narrowness of the mind, the importance of this truth can be felt, and it also is a part of **The Eternal Path**.

CREATION AND HISTORY
Tablet 7

<7> The sixth truth (✡) is the explanation of those who will be chosen as members of the nation which God promised to Abram, "And I will make of thee a great nation" (Gen. 12:2).

<8> These are the ones who have gone through the **Eternal Divine Path**, which is to awaken the latent spiritual forces (☯), try to establish a spiritual environment for all to progress physically, mentally, and spiritually (✡), to be ready to sacrifice all for this great ideal (✝), to surrender and submit to the Lord (☪), <9> and to create a universal point of view for all these endeavors (✹). Such a person, who is a dynamic spiritual force and incorruptible, is called a Paravipra, or an Elect (✡).

<10> Through overcoming their lower natures and going through the **Eternal Path**, these Paravipras will be worthy to assume the leadership of humanity and help the whole universe to reach Pure Consciousness.

<11> Also historically it is in our era that the awareness of the people will have increased and many will long for a worldwide government which can bring peace, tranquility, and happiness to all. Who else could be the leaders of this new order, but those who have gone through the **Eternal Divine Path**? (Read The Kingdom Of Heaven On Earth and Mount Zion and Zion, and Explanation of the System).

Tablet Seven

<1> In the seventh spiritual center (chakra), the whole truth of God and the spiritual world will be revealed, and no mystery will be left. <2> Similarly by the coming of the seventh truth, the **whole truth** will be revealed. As explained in The Revelation:

But in the days of the voice of the seventh angel, ... the mystery of God should be finished,... (Rev. 10:7)

<3> This verse implies two things: First, that there would be seven truths which would be brought with seven Angels (Prophets), and

CREATION AND HISTORY   *Tablet 7*

secondly, that it is in the time of the seventh Angel that the sealed Scriptures would be unlocked and their mysteries revealed. Any other truths before this last one, are only a part of the whole, and none of the previous truths are complete or perfect by themselves. <4> But it is the seventh truth which reveals the whole mystery of God, and no man can claim he has the whole truth before it is revealed.

<5> This does not mean that after this seventh truth there would be no other great spiritual beings or Prophets, but only that there could be no more truths brought by them. They might explain these truths on deeper levels, or if a part of them are lost, they might bring them back. With this, the mystery of the Scriptures of the last 6,000 years will be finished.

<6> So any religion or truth in this world is a part of the **Eternal Divine Path**. However, it will take some time before the **Eternal Divine Path** is realized by all and its teachings are established on earth. Then is the time that many will reach Pure Consciousness and become the sons of God as it is promised in the book <u>The Revelation</u>:

> He that overcometh shall inherit all things; and I will be his God, and he shall be my son. (Rev. 21:7)

<7> So the requirement for becoming the son of God is to overcome, and the **Eternal Divine Path** is the way to overcome the external world (Maya) and the power of the tama guna (attraction to the external world, unspiritual desires, attachment to the external world, ignorance, and greed) over the Soul.

Whoever overcomes, by His Grace, is His son.

Amen (ॐ).

ALL ARE LESSONS TO LEARN, NOT TO ARGUE, BUT REJOICE

The book, **<u>All Are Lessons To Learn, Not To Argue, But Rejoice</u>**, explains that our teaching should not become a source of disagreement, argument, and division. It is to learn that God has been behind all these events, and rejoice in Him and His Wisdom.

ALL ARE LESSONS TO LEARN, NOT TO ARGUE, BUT REJOICE

Tablet One

<1> In all of our writings, there are points and truths which have happened throughout creation and history. Also there are points that might become objects of argument between different people.

<2> That might happen because they would not want to understand these truths in deeper levels, or because of their attachments to a special religion, race, etc., therefore they argue.

<3> But all these things have happened as lessons for humanity to learn from and so find the way of God and truth behind this universe.

<4> Therefore no argument should arise and a person should contemplate the truth behind them and gain the insight of the message they deliver. Then he would progress in the path instead of wasting time in unnecessary arguments and endless misunderstandings.

<5> In order that the truth of the short essay above is clearly demonstrated, some of these lessons in brief will be explained below.

God is everlasting, complete, without beginning and end. He is one and indivisible.

<6> **Lesson**: Everything is God.

The universe (God) is consciousness and its three creative forces (three gunas).

<7> **Lesson**: Everything (God) is consciousness and the three gunas.

In the beginning the operative powers of the three creative forces (three gunas) were not released but were in the passive or balanced state ($\triangledown$). So the universe was in a state of "Be"-ness.

<8> **Lesson**: Everything was eternal and God (universe) just "**WAS**" with the potential of creating and being created.

Through the desire of God, the operative powers of the three gunas were released.

<9> **Lesson**: It is desire (movement of the raja guna) which activates the Mind, and then the creative powers of the Mind (three creative forces) are released. So when desire is directed toward the external world, its creative powers will be used in that direction and man becomes the slave of Maya. But when it is directed toward God and the internal, the Soul releases itself from the bondage of the external world.

<10> Also when the desires of the external world are fulfilled according to God's Laws, they become spiritualized and help the person toward Divinity. So desires do not have to be destroyed, but should be spiritualized.

The illusion of being separated from the universe (God) was created because of the influences of the ego ("I"). This is the cause of suffering and inflicting suffering on others.

<11> **Lesson**: The cause of the illusion of separation (false ego) is the essence of all evils. This results in attraction toward the external world and the illusion of separation becomes even stronger. This results in the arousal of worldly desires, attachments, and greed. Greed intensifies the attraction, and the cycle goes on and on.

ALL ARE LESSONS TO LEARN   Tablet 2

<12> In truth, some people are afraid to accept God as everything and to dissolve their false egos into IT, <13> because each human (unit consciousness) wants to be God himself. <14> So there is a great resistance to accept God as superior to themselves because if they do so, then their egos will be humbled. Most people, because of their false pride, do not want this to happen to them. Their ego, they think, is the only thing they have to cling onto. <15> Therefore they reject the truth and God all together.

<16> Nothing human (egoistical) is good, not even human "love," because it is egoistical (conditional). So humans should become gods in order for all things to come to the right order.

Tablet Two

The light within man can be seen by those who reach a higher consciousness, but it is hidden from those who are in their lower natures (darkness). However, it is always there even in those who are in the dark.

<1> **Lesson**: All men inherit the possibility of becoming good and Divine.

"Haree Om Shrii Hung" means the goal of the life is to be(come) Divine.

<2> **Lesson**: That is the highest goal in the life. All other goals are secondary. After a person becomes Divine, then he or she can be a Divine father, a Divine mother, a Divine doctor, etc.

And God helped and desired that the lost souls realize their Divinity (light).

<3> **Lesson**: God helps and is desirous that man become Divine. But it is up to man to put forth effort and listen to God so to win His Grace and be(come) Divine. God has created all this universe, and through history and His Prophets He has sent the way to reach Pure Consciousness. Now it is up to man to follow the lessons and become Divine.

The triangle upward ($\triangle$) represents the Hierarchy of the unit consciousnesses in the universe.

<4> **Lesson**: This is the only true Hierarchy of authority in the universe. Human society should also come in harmony with this Hierarchy. Any other Hierarchy based on any other base than the state of unit consciousnesses is man-made, is not acceptable, and will fail.

The misuse of the universal forces and corruption brings the fall of human society and also violence on the earth (his environment).

<5> **Lesson**: Not only does the human action affect him and his society but also the physical environment (earth).

Abram was chosen to start his mission. God chose Abram and foretold what would happen in the future, then through history fulfilled it.

<6> **Lesson**: Everything is done by God, but the human glorifies men.

By rejecting God as their King (I Samuel 8:7), the Children of Israel cut themselves off from Him and so failed.

ALL ARE LESSONS TO LEARN

<7> Lesson: He who accepts any other authority than God will fail. Such a person either will fall into his own ego trips (eating of the tree of knowledge of good and evil), or will follow an earthly (from the lower nature) authority. Both are sure failures.

A great suffering came upon God's people (Children of Israel), because they rejected Him. He never rejected them, but they rejected Him.

<8> Lesson: This happened so that the Children of Israel became an example for others. Also God never rejects any man. Man suffers and thinks he has been punished because of the illusion of being separate from God. **<9>** God punishes no man. Men punish themselves by not being One with Him.

The promised Messiah came as Esa The Christ. But because Jews had so many concepts of how he would come, they rejected him.

<10> Lesson: The untrue concepts created from the human's lower nature (false ego) are the cause of rejecting the truth.

In the beginning of the spread of Christianity the followers of Esa observed God's Holy Days, but after the Romans accepted Christianity, their pagan holidays were Christianized.

<11> Lesson: The human loves to cling to what he used to follow and tries to change the new truth to old patterns which fit him. So the follower of this path should be careful not to fall into the same mistake.

The true Holy Days are given in chapter twenty-three of Leviticus in the Bible. They are the only Holy Days which should be followed. Any other is man-made and would be narrow.

<12> Lesson: Only these Holy Days are directly commanded by God and are His. Any other will divide humanity and create confusion. **<13>** They would be either pagan, or from a narrow view (such as from nationality, racism, etc.) and narrowness always brings suffering.

The Revelation, the last book in the Bible, was revealed to show what would happen in the future.

<14> Lesson: God first says what He is going to do and then does it. This has been the trend especially in the last six thousand years so that man would become faithful, start to follow His Laws, and fulfill the goal of the creation.

The pitfall in the first sign is to become an escapist.

<15> Lesson: One cannot reach Pure Consciousness by disregarding society. Maybe it was permissible in the past, but no longer for the majority. Man should create a society based on spiritual Laws and progress physically, mentally, and spiritually in the middle of society. As it is declared in the book The Revelation (3:16), those who want to reach Pure Consciousness by escaping society will be "spue[d] out of my mouth."

The pitfall in the second sign (step of progress) is the fear of trial in spiritual progress.

<16> Lesson: These trials are lessons and to strengthen the seeker. So he should have patience and persistence to overcome them.

ALL ARE LESSONS TO LEARN

The pitfall in the third stage (sign) is the possibility of falling back and using the powers gained for selfish desires.

<17> **Lesson**: The first three stages (chakras) make up the lower nature of man, and until they are overcome, the possibility of falling back to the lower nature is imminent. <18> Also the third stage is the last in overcoming the lower nature (to be born again).

The pitfall in the fourth stage (sign) is to be(come) narrow-minded.

<19> **Lesson**: Until a universal point of view is created and it is understood that God is everything, there is a possibility that the mind will become narrow in its scope and this will create suffering.

<20> Also here it should be mentioned that the pitfalls which are described above in different stages of progress are all present in the first stage, <21> then as each of these propensities are overcome, in each stage in the higher level they will not exist. <22> That is, narrowness of the mind is present in the first, second, and third levels, only overcome at the fourth level, and does not exist at the fifth.

Tablet Three

The pitfall in the fifth stage is to become escapist again, and also forget how it was received in the beginning and required effort to advance.

<1> **Lesson**: Because in this state which is universalism, all narrowness of mind is absent so it becomes expanded: They shall see God (Matthew 5:8). They see how the Laws of the universe work and so feel it is not necessary that they put any effort into it. <2> But indeed only those who put effort to help others will reach higher consciousness and become Paravipras (Elected Ones).

The pitfall in the sixth sign (stage) is to feel that there is no more truth to know.

<3> **Lesson**: With this, they lose their chance to know the all-embracing truth and fail to enter the last stage (Pure Consciousness). So the human should be open to all truths and accept those which are according to the **Eternal Divine Path**.

Then is the time when many, by overcoming their lower natures, will reach Pure Consciousness and become the sons of God.

<4> **Lesson**: In order to reach Pure Consciousness (✤) or become a son of God (✤), the only requirement is to overcome the external world, and it is up to the person to overcome. No man can overcome it for him. He might be helped and the path be shown to him, but it is he who has to make the effort to overcome. Through these efforts His Grace will be won.

<5> These are a few examples of the lessons which are given throughout creation and history. The point is that these lessons should be understood, learned, and implemented in human life.

<6> These happenings are not to be used against any race or people, and also no one should create a false superiority feeling because of them. <7> All is God and none is greater or lower. Only those who reach higher consciousness are greater in the sense that they can help others to reach higher consciousness with a greater capacity.

<8> All of history and our writings are just lessons. They are not to argue about and to create strife. This truth should not be lost

ALL ARE LESSONS TO LEARN

sight of, otherwise the writings will become a source of confusion for those who do not expand their minds and open their hearts to these Truths.

<9> However, not to argue does not mean not to **question** or **ask** or **search** or to accept the teachings blindly. On the contrary, it is the duty of each individual to ask, search, question, and come to understand the truth of them in the deeper levels of his or her being.

<10> As long as the thirst for knowledge is not satisfied, he should not stop asking.

<11> Only through this process can man know the truth in the deepest level, face the reality, overcome, and go toward perfection. Then he can rejoice in the meaning of the teachings, see the perfection of God, destroy the confusion between religions, create great devotion for God, and rejoice in Him.

<12> Therefore, "**All are lessons to learn, not to argue, but rejoice**."

COMMENTARIES ON
ST. MATTHEW

The book, <u>Commentaries on St. Matthew</u>, is a commentary on the first twenty-three chapters of the book of <u>Matthew</u> in the <u>Bible</u>.

COMMENTARIES ON ST. MATTHEW

(Chapters 1-23)

Tablet One

Chapter 1

"The book of the generation of Esa the Christ, the son of David, the son of Abraham." (Matthew 1:1)

<1> God promised Abraham that He would give two gifts to his children. One was a kingly spiritual domination (scepter) and the other material property as the birthright. These two gifts as promised were inherited from Abraham to Isaac, and then to Jacob (Israel). <2> At the time of his death, Jacob separated these inheritances and gave the scepter (kingly spiritual domination and lawgiving) to Judah, "The scepter shall not depart from Judah, nor a lawgiver from between his feet, until Shiloh [Messiah] come…" (Gen. 49:10). The birthright was given to Joseph and his seed. For more detail, read <u>Children of Abram (Abraham), All Prophecies Are Fulfilled</u>.

<3> That is why the great king of the Children of Israel, King David, is from the tribe of Judah, and also Esa, the King of the Jews (House of Judah) is from the same tribe. Abraham is the father of all the Hebrews, so he is the father of Esa also, and David was the king and from the tribe of Judah, so he is also the father of Esa. <4> That is why Esa who became Christ is "the son of David, the son of Abraham."

<5> However, as Christ himself said to the Pharisees in <u>Matthew</u> chapter 22, verses 42-45:

Saying, what think ye of Christ? Whose son is he? They say unto him, The son of David.

He saith unto them, How then doth David in spirit call him Lord, saying,

The Lord said unto my Lord, Sit thou on my right hand, till I make thine enemies thy footstool?

If David then call him Lord, how is he his son?

<6> No one could answer this question. But what is the answer? The answer is that Christ, or the First Begotten Son of God who became Pure Consciousness (Christ Consciousness) was in the world even before the creation of this manifested world (read <u>The Base</u> or <u>The Essence</u>). <7> So spiritually he could not be the son of any mortal man, not even David or Abraham. However, in a fleshly sense, he was born from a mother with Jewish ancestry and from the tribe of Judah. <8> Christ also is a consciousness, and a person.

<9> Also Esa was conceived from a virgin, so in truth his birth was a miracle and no worldly man could claim that he was his father. He was in Pure Consciousness even before coming to this world. He came to the earth as an Avatar (god-man). That is why he is called Emmanuel ("God with us"). <10> But even an Avatar does not know he is a god-man until later on in his life when he realizes himself and understands his mission.

<11> Furthermore, Christ was incarnated as the first Adam who guided other humans to the path of the spirit (path of Pure Consciousness) and later on as Noah and Abram (Abraham). <12> In fact, as God had promised to Abram (Abraham), "and in thee shall all families of the earth be blessed," the only way that all families of the earth could be blessed is by Abram (Abraham) being incarnated in so many different nations and situations, and bringing the truth and blessing to them.

<13> So whoever any nation or people consider as their father or the one who brought to them the blessings, is none other than Christ.
<14> God never fails in His Promises.

Reading of the generations (Matthew 1:2-15):

<15> With the explanation given about the first verse, the reading of the generations seems useless. But as it is described in The Holiest Book, the generations are used in the Bible to show that it takes hundreds of years before humans come to a higher understanding. In other words, it takes hundreds or thousands of years before an evolutionary step can be fulfilled. So the human should create patience in the process for His Will to be fulfilled.

"And Jacob begat Joseph the husband of Mary, of whom was born Esa, who is called Christ." (Matthew 1:16)

<16> Because Joseph married Mary and participated in bringing up Esa, he can be referred to as his earthly father. In truth he only was Mary's husband, not Esa's father. That is why we hear about him very little in the gospels.

<17> Also Esa, "who is called Christ," was not Christ in the beginning, but became Christ after he overcame the temptations in the desert. Although he was born from Pure Consciousness to the flesh (from spirit), he should have gone through a regular life and overcome the flesh before realizing his divinity as Christ (Pure Consciousness).

"So all the generations from Abraham to David are fourteen generations; and from David until the carrying away into Babylon are fourteen generations; and from the carrying away into Babylon unto Christ are fourteen generations." (Matthew 1:17)

<18> Therefore, it took forty-two generations from Abraham to Esa for the prophecy of Jacob (Israel) to be fulfilled.

"Now the birth of Esa the Christ was on this wise: When as his mother Mary was espoused to Joseph, before they came together, she was found with child of the Holy Ghost." (Matthew 1:18)

<19> Esa was from the Spirit, a child of The Holy Ghost. He had come from Pure Consciousness to the flesh. He was an Avatar.

"Then Joseph her husband, being a just man, and not willing to make her a publick example, was minded to put her away privily." (Matthew 1:19)

<20> Joseph, being just a man (not a son of God), was disturbed finding Mary with child. But because he was a just man and did not want to create any problems for her publicly, he decided to leave her without making her a public example, "put her away privily."

"But while he thought on these things, behold, the angel of the Lord appeared unto him in a dream, saying, Joseph, thou son of David, fear not to take unto thee Mary thy wife: for that which is conceived in her is of the Holy Ghost." (Matthew 1:20)

"And she shall bring forth a son, and thou shalt call his name (הישוע): for he shall save his people from their sins." (Matthew 1:21)

<21> However, Joseph was informed of the truth that Mary was a chaste and pure woman, and he should not be afraid of any unfaithfulness by her. The child was conceived through the power of The Holy Ghost (knowledge of God). <22> As described before, his spiritual name was (הישוע) which is the abbreviation for a name closely pronounced Y'wehshua or "the savior (Shua) of Y'weh (יהוה)," "...shall save his people...." His sacred name was revealed to Joseph.

COMMENTARIES ON ST. MATTHEW
Tablet Two

"Now all this was done, that it might be fulfilled which was spoken of the Lord by the prophet, saying," (Matthew 1:22)

"Behold, a virgin shall be with child, and shall bring forth a son, and they shall call his name Emmanuel, which being interpreted is, God with us." (Matthew 1:23)

<1> All these things happened so that the prophecies would be fulfilled and Esa, as an Avatar (Emmanuel, "God with us," god-man) would be born. Again God showed that He never fails to fulfill His Promises, and that all the prophecies eventually will be fulfilled.
<2> Humanity must and will realize that the best way is His Way, and the goal and purpose of this creation is that all reach Pure Consciousness.

"Then Joseph being raised from sleep did as the angel of the Lord had bidden him, and took unto him his wife:" (Matthew 1:24)

<3> After Joseph was informed and realized that he had been chosen for a great task, he obeyed and surrendered his earthly concepts and became submissive to His Will. So he took Mary to be his wife.

"And knew her not till she had brought forth her firstborn son: and he called his name (רְיֵשׁוּעַ)." (Matthew 1:25)

<4> He gave the name Esa as his birth name, but his true name, "...called..." was (רְיֵשׁוּעַ)!

Chapter 2

"Now when Esa was born in Bethlehem of Judaea in the days of Herod the king, behold, there came wise men from the east to Jerusalem," (Matthew 2:1)

"Saying, Where is he that is born King of the Jews? for we have seen his star in the east, and are come to worship him." (Matthew 2:2)

<5> Herod was the king of Judaea and subordinate to Rome. In his reign the wise men of the east, who were astrologers, came to worship Esa, because they had seen his star and knew a Great Soul was born as the "King of the Jews [House of Judah]."

"When Herod the king had heard these things, he was troubled, and all Jerusalem with him." (Matthew 2:3)

<6> Herod thought the king of the Jews would rise against him and take the earthly kingdom from him. He was very low in thought, like everyone else, "all Jerusalem with him." He could not understand that the "King of the Jews" had not come to destroy his kingdom. So he was troubled.

"And when he had gathered all the chief priests and scribes of the people together, he demanded of them where Christ should be born." (Matthew 2:4)

<7> He tried to find out where he could find the child. The negative forces started to try to destroy the light (Christ). He thought he could fight with the Will of the Lord.

"And they said unto him, In Bethlehem of Judaea: for thus it is written by the prophet," (Matthew 2:5)

"And thou Bethlehem, in the land of Juda, are not the least among the princes of Juda: for out of thee shall come a Governor, that shall rule my people Israel." (Matthew 2:6)

<8> It is true that Christ is called the King of the Jews (House of Judah) but in reality he came to rule over Israel (the House of Israel); read <u>Children of Abram (Abraham), All Prophecies Are Fulfilled</u>.

"Then Herod, when he had privily called the wise men, enquired of them diligently what time the star appeared." (Matthew 2:7)

<9> Herod was trying to find out the birth place and age of the child who was born a king.

COMMENTARIES ON ST. MATTHEW   *Tablet 2*

"And he sent them to Bethlehem, and said, Go and search diligently for the young child; and when ye have found him, bring me word again, that I may come and worship him also." (Matthew 2:8)

<10> Herod was trying to use the wise men to find the child. But as it was said, they were wise, and also God was with the child.

"When they had heard the king, they departed; and, lo, the star, which they saw in the east, went before them, till it came and stood over where the young child was." (Matthew 2:9)

<11> The wise men realized the young child when they saw him.

"When they saw the star, they rejoiced with exceeding great joy." (Matthew 2:10)

"And when they were come into the house, they saw the young child with Mary his mother, and fell down, and worshipped him: and when they had opened their treasures, they presented unto him gifts; gold, and frankincense, and myrrh." (Matthew 2:11)

<12> They accepted him as a great master by presenting gifts to him.

"And being warned of God in a dream that they should not return to Herod, they departed into their own country another way." (Matthew 2:12)

<13> The plan of Herod to use the wise men to find the child was thwarted by God.

"And when they were departed, behold, the angel of the Lord appeareth to Joseph in a dream, saying, Arise, and take the young child and his mother and flee into Egypt, and be thou there until I bring thee word: for Herod will seek the young child to destroy him." (Matthew 2:13)

"And when he arose, he took the young child and his mother by night, and departed into Egypt:" (Matthew 2:14)

"And was there until the death of Herod: that it might be fulfilled which was spoken of the Lord by the prophet, saying, Out of Egypt have I called my son." (Matthew 2:15)

<14> All these things happened, such as the wise men coming, Herod being informed of the child so that he was aroused, and then Mary and Joseph being forced to go to Egypt, <15> so that the prophecies "by the prophet" were fulfilled.

<16> Also, by Esa and his family moving to Egypt, they came in touch with the Egyptian spiritual knowledge and were influenced by it.

"Then Herod, when he saw that he was mocked of the wise men, was exceeding wroth, and sent forth, and slew all the children that were in Bethlehem, and in all the coasts thereof, from two years old and under, according to the time which he had diligently enquired of the wise men." (Matthew 2:16)

"Then was fulfilled that which was spoken by Jeremy the prophet, saying," (Matthew 2:17)

"In Rama was there a voice heard, lamentation, and weeping, and great mourning, Rachel weeping for her children, and would not be comforted, because they were not." (Matthew 2:18)

<17> Again Herod was used so that this prophecy would be fulfilled. The name Rama is the same as Rahma in Sanskrit.

"But when Herod was dead, behold, an angel of the Lord appeareth in a dream to Joseph in Egypt," (Matthew 2:19)

"Saying Arise, and take the young child and his mother, and go into the land of Israel: for they are dead which sought the young child's life." (Matthew 2:20)

"And he arose, and took the young child and his mother, and came into the land of Israel." (Matthew 2:21)

"But when he heard that Archelaus did reign in Judaea in the room of his father Herod, he was afraid to go thither: notwithstanding, being warned of God in a dream, he turned aside into the parts of Galilee:" (Matthew 2:22)

"And he came and dwelt in a city called Nazareth: that it might be fulfilled which was spoken by the prophets, He shall be called a Nazarene." (Matthew 2:23)

<18> Again all these things happened so that the prophecies were fulfilled and God is glorified.

Tablet Three

Chapter 3

"In those days came John the Baptist, preaching in the wilderness of Judaea," (Matthew 3:1)

<1> John the Baptist (Elijah) was expected to come before Christ to prepare the way. Esa himself declared this when he revealed to his disciples that Elias (Elijah) had already come but no one realized who he was, "but have done unto him whatsoever they liked." Then his disciples perceived that he meant John the Baptist (Matthew 17:11-13). <2> So John the Baptist was the reincarnation of Elijah who came before Esa to clear the way for him.

"And saying, Repent ye: for the kingdom of heaven is at hand." (Matthew 3:2)

<3> Both John and Esa preached the gospel of the Kingdom Of Heaven. <4> There are three Kingdoms Of Heaven: The Kingdom Of Heaven In Heaven (✡), the Kingdom Of Heaven On Earth (✡), and the Kingdom Of Heaven within (✡) (all three are shown in **The Greatest Sign**).

<5> However, the three Kingdoms become as one and under the rulership of the Lord when all of humanity repents from their egoistical ways, accepts and establishes His Laws, and creates the Kingdom Of Heaven within and on earth (the Kingdom Of Heaven In Heaven is already established). Only then will His Kingdom come and "His will be done on earth as it is in heaven."

<6> That is why both John and Esa preached that the human should repent of his selfish ways if he wants to establish the Kingdom Of Heaven. <7> They did not preach, "we have come to save you." They taught that it is up to each individual to repent, and turn away from selfishness and follow God's Laws. However, they are One with Him!

"For this is he that was spoken of by the prophet Esaias, saying, The voice of one crying in the wilderness, Prepare ye the way of the Lord, make his paths straight." (Matthew 3:3)

<8> So John declared that he was Elijah (Elias) who was expected to come before Christ.

"And the same John had his raiment of camel's hair, and a leathern girdle about his loins; and his meat was locusts and wild honey." (Matthew 3:4)

<9> **The complications in life cause the mind to become agitated.** Luxurious life creates attachment and increases desires and greed, so the mind becomes misdirected toward the mundane life. That is why John followed a simple lifestyle, so he could concentrate on higher thoughts and God. <10> However, that does not mean to become an escapist and not to face the true problems of life straight on.

<11> "Meat" means food, not the flesh of animals, when there is a reference to "meat" for someone.

"Then went out to him Jerusalem, and all Judaea, and all the region round about Jordan," (Matthew 3:5)

<12> Because John had reached a very high level of consciousness, he attracted those whose eyes were opened. This spiritual

attraction was so strong that, "went out to him Jerusalem, and all Judaea, and all the region round about Jordan." **<13>** That is how a spiritual person should become – a radiant, attractive personality that draws people to him from everywhere.

"And were baptized of him in Jordan, confessing their sins." (Matthew 3:6)
<14> They accepted John as a great Soul and allowed him to baptize them so that their past sins might be forgiven. They confessed to him because some people cannot create a personal relationship with God, so they need a mediator between themselves and the Lord. **<15>** However, the person who becomes a mediator should be spiritually very high and worthy to confess to, so that he is able to make the person (as his disciple) realize the true source of his power (God). That is why some seekers need a spiritual teacher.
<16> However, the best way to know the Lord is to hear what the Prophets have said, follow their words, and establish a personal relationship with God. Then you would not need a man to be a mediator, and God is the most trustworthy and the Holiest (truest).

"But when he saw many of the Pharisees and Sadducees come to his baptism, he said unto them, O generation of vipers, who hath warned you to flee from the wrath to come?" (Matthew 3:7)
<17> However, he verbally attacked the spiritual leaders of the Jews as the "generation of vipers," because they taught what they did not follow themselves. They were false teachers. **<18>** Whoever does not teach that the only goal of life is to be(come) Divine, and he himself does not try to be(come) Divine (truth), is a false teacher. That is why both John and Esa attacked the Pharisees and Sadducees in this way.

"Bring forth therefore fruits meet for repentance:" (Matthew 3:8)

"And think not to say within yourselves, We have Abraham to our father: for I say unto you, that God is able of these stones to raise up children unto Abraham." (Matthew 3:9)
<19> The only way these false leaders can be saved is through repentance and changing their hearts toward God and His Laws. However, these Pharisees and Sadducees had regarded themselves as the doctors of the laws, the chosen people, and the children of Abraham. So they had created big false egos.
<20> It is very hard for anyone with so many concepts to accept a humble person like John to teach him the truth or baptize him. It is easier for a camel to go through the eye of a needle than for such a man to enter the Kingdom Of Heaven.
<21> But they were not aware that one of the missions of John and Christ was to disqualify them as the chosen people and finish the promise of the scepter given to Judah. Also, the lawgiving would be taken from them, "the scepter shall not depart from Judah, nor a lawgiver from between his feet, until Shiloh [Messiah] come." **<22>** The Shiloh was Esa the Messiah.
<23> That is why John told them that, "You should not be proud that you are the children of Abraham, because if you do not repent but continue to lag behind in your progress toward becoming Pure Consciousness (Divine), then God can, in the course of the evolutionary process, help these stones to raise up and become plants, animals, humans, and eventually reach Pure Consciousness or become Elected Ones as the children of Abraham. Yet you will be cast out to the outer darkness because of your big false egos."

"And now also the axe is laid unto the root of the trees: therefore every tree which bringeth not forth good fruit is hewn down, and cast into the fire." (Matthew 3:10)
<24> Again here John foresaw that the truth which will come through him and Christ will uproot their false teachings (trees) "which bringeth not forth good fruit."

"I indeed baptize you with water unto repentance: but he that cometh after me is mightier than I, whose shoes I am not worthy to bear: he shall baptize you with the Holy Ghost, and with fire:" (Matthew 3:11)

<25> In fact, being baptized with The Holy Ghost (satva raja, or Fire) is the only true way of being baptized. Baptism by water is a symbol of that kind of baptism, because only after repentance and changing the way of life toward purification will a person receive The Holy Ghost and truly be baptized.

"Whose fan is in his hand, and he will throughly purge his floor, and gather his wheat into the garner; but he will burn up the chaff with unquenchable fire." (Matthew 3:12)

<26> John taught that Christ would come to separate the good and bad, and judge between them in truth. He is the light and the truth. Those who are ready would be attracted to him, and those who were not ready would be blinded by it and go far astray.

<27> That is why any time a new revelation comes to earth, many are guided and many others will go astray.

"Then cometh Esa from Galilee to Jordan unto John, to be baptized of him." (Matthew 3:13)

"But John forbad him, saying, I have need to be baptized of thee, and comest thou to me?" (Matthew 3:14)

"And Esa answering said unto him, Suffer it to be so now: for thus it becometh us to fulfill all righteousness. Then he suffered him." (Matthew 3:15)

<28> Esa was initiated by John and his eyes would be opened to his mission.

"And Esa, when he was baptized, went up straightway out of the water: and, lo, the heavens were opened unto him, and he saw the Spirit of God descending like a dove, and lighting upon him:" (Matthew 3:16)

<29> After his spiritual eye was opened, he realized his divinity and closeness to the Lord. It is true that he was born from Pure Consciousness to the flesh and was the son of God. But he should have gone through life without knowing who he was until John came to open his eyes so that he would remember who he was and realize his mission.

"And lo a voice from heaven, saying, This is my beloved Son, in whom I am well pleased." (Matthew 3:17)

<30> When he realized his divinity, then he remembered that he is the son of God, the First Begotten Son of God, who greatly pleased his Father.

Tablet Four

Chapter 4

"Then was Esa led up of the spirit into the wilderness to be tempted of the devil." (Matthew 4:1)

<1> After his spiritual eye was opened, his true struggle in overcoming the power of the tama guna started. That is why he was led to the wilderness, which is a symbol for the turbulent, uncontrollable mind. <2> In this wilderness of his turbulent consciousness, he started the greatest battle in his life, the battle of overcoming the lower nature which leads man to all kinds of attractions, desires, attachments, greed, or Maya. <3> John opened his eyes but it was Esa himself who should overcome.

"And when he had fasted forty days and forty nights, he was afterward an hungred." (Matthew 4:2)

"And when the tempter came to him, he said, If thou be the Son of God, command that these stones be made bread." (Matthew 4:3)

<4> The first psychic center (chakra) in the body is related to physiological and safety needs ("bread"). <5> That is why the

first temptation came to him to use his little-gained spiritual powers to gain these lower needs (bread) from society or the external world. The external world is like stone, from which it is hard to satisfy those needs, "command that these stones be made bread."

<6> The sentence, "he had fasted forty days and forty nights" shows that he had gone through a great purification for a long time ("forty days and forty nights") before he became aware that to strive for bread alone is a temptation.

"But he answered and said, It is written, Man shall not live by bread alone, but by every word that proceedeth out of the mouth of God." (Matthew 4:4)

<7> Also because he was born an Avatar (from Pure Consciousness to flesh) he remembered very well that the goal of life is to be(come) Divine, and one of the ways to reach this goal is to follow and live, "by every word that proceedeth out of the mouth of God." By following His Will, then the substance will be provided.

<8> A man who only lives for bread (physiological and safety needs) is bound in his first chakra and cannot emerge from being earthbound.

"Then the devil taketh him up into the holy city, and setteth him on a pinnacle of the temple," (Matthew 4:5)

<9> With overcoming this first temptation of the first chakra, he rose to a higher level into the second chakra, but still in the lower nature (the first three chakras are the lower nature of man). That is why the devil (the power of the tama guna) still is with him, "the devil taketh him up...."

"And saith unto him, If thou be the Son of God, cast thyself down: for it is written, He shall give his angels charge concerning thee: and in their hands they shall bear thee up, lest at any time thou dash thy foot against a stone." (Matthew 4:6)

<10> In the second level (chakra) in spiritual progress, there is the seed of doubt. He already overcame the misuse of the power and knowledge in the first level and rose to a higher level. <11> But in this level (second chakra), he doubted if God was really going to protect him against the problems in the outside world.

<12> In this level, he was exactly at the same stage where the woman was in chapter 3 in Genesis when she was tempted by the serpent that caused her to doubt the validity of the Lord's command. It is from this level that the question comes to the mind if it really is true, and if God means it when He said that He will take care of whoever overcomes the illusion of this external world.

<13> That is what the devil (tama guna) was doing here. He was putting the seed of doubt into Esa's mind, if He would really keep His Promise of protecting him. The temptation came to test God by doing something which would prove that it is true.

"Esa said unto him, It is written again, Thou shalt not tempt the Lord thy God." (Matthew 4:7)

<14> Again the truth came to him through his highly elevated Soul, that, "Thou shall not tempt the Lord thy God." That is, you have to overcome any doubt and follow Him. <15> In fact, after a person follows God's Commandments and Laws, then he realizes their depth and incredible effects on his life and mind, and on others.

<16> This doubting and tempting God in fact was the very reason for the fall of the woman from heaven to earth. She thought she knew better than God, so she could choose what "look[ed] good to her eyes" as the way of life. <17> But what looks good to a person is not necessarily good for his spiritual progress.

"Again, the devil taketh him up into an exceeding high mountain, and sheweth him all the kingdoms of the world, and the glory of them;" (Matthew 4:8)

<18> With this refusal to doubt and tempt God, he overcame the bondage of the second chakra and was elevated "into an exceeding"

higher level, or the third chakra. <19> It is in this level that the temptation comes to gain power, position, and prestige for the sake of glorifying self, instead of for the good of all.

<20> That is why the devil took him up into an exceedingly high mountain (which is much higher than the previous position at the top of the temple) and showed him the kingdom of the world. Or in other words, in this level he reached a point where he could see how he could gain earthly power. However, because he was still under the influence of the third chakra, he saw "the glory of them," not how they could be used for the good of all.

"And saith unto him, All these things will I give thee, if thou wilt fall down and worship me." (Matthew 4:9)

<21> However, he who becomes tempted to gain earthly powers for its glory, becomes the slave and worshipper of his lower nature. This is because in order to maintain that glory, he has no choice but to inflict misery on other people and use his powers to struggle all his life to stay in that position.

<22> That is why the devil said, "I will give you all the glories of the world," but there is a requirement to do this, "that you worship me instead of God."

"Then saith Esa unto him, Get thee hence, Satan: for it is written, Thou shalt worship the Lord thy God, and him only shalt thou serve." (Matthew 4:10)

<23> Again Esa saw the depth of the deceitfulness of the offering. What the devil (tama guna) was offering to him was nothing but Maya ("glory of this world"). But Esa knew the only absolute truth is He (Pure Consciousness). So he refused this last offering also, and said that in order to overcome the ocean of Maya and reach the truth (God), you should worship Him (through bhakti) and Him only.

<24> With this last realization, Esa overcame his lower nature (first three chakras) and entered his higher self (next four chakras). When a person overcomes the lower self (first three temptations) he will go to his higher self. <25> This is what is called "to be born again," that is, to be born from the lower self to the higher self. In order to be born again, a person, by His Grace, should overcome the lower self.

<26> In fact, this process of being born again – resurrection from the dead (lower self) – was the main mission of Esa to come on earth. That is why the symbol for his truth among the churches, which is in the second chapter of The Revelation and in **The Greatest Sign**, is the third one (✝), "the angel of the church in Pergamos" (Rev. 2:12). <27> As it is explained in the book Revelation of The Revelation, it is the place that a person might still fall back to his lower nature and be misled by Satan, "where Satan dwelleth" (Rev. 2:13). He might accept the worshipping of the earthly gods physically (idols), mentally (any other goal but to be(come) Divine) or spiritually (imaginary gods) and become a follower of the pagan doctrines, "thou hast there them that hold the doctrine of Balaam" (Rev. 2:14). Or he might become one of the evildoers or false prophets, "them that hold the doctrine of the Nicolaitanes."

<28> However, "To him that overcometh will I give…" (Rev. 2:17), he who overcomes the first three chakras will enter into the fourth one which is the secret (and sacred) heart. This is known to great men in the spirit as the center of Love and Grace (Holy Mother).

<29> The symbolic number three which is used all through the gospels and life of Christ, such as the three temptations, three falls while carrying his cross, resurrection after three days and nights, and also, being the Third Seal in **The Greatest Sign**, all are symbols of being born again, to be resurrected from the lower nature to the higher self.

Tablet Five

"Then the devil leaveth him, and, behold, angels came and ministered unto him." (Matthew 4:11)

<1> With this he overcame the power of the tama guna over his Soul, "the devil leaveth him," and went to his higher self where there is Michael (raja guna) and Gabriel (satva guna) and their angels. They would serve him, and his knowledge and actions would become Divine. <2> Also the devil (tama guna) becomes Lucifer, or the shining light in his path.

<3> Only those who are in their higher selves will be served by Angels.

"Now when Esa had heard that John was cast into prison, he departed into Galilee;" (Matthew 4:12)

<4> Now after Esa became Christ and overcame his lower self, he started his mission. The mission of John was to find him, open his spiritual eye to his divinity and purpose in life. So John's mission would begin to decrease and his would increase.

"And leaving Nazareth, he came and dwelt in Capernaum, which is upon the sea coast, in the borders of Zabulon and Nephthalim:" (Matthew 4:13)

"That it might be fulfilled which was spoken by Esaias the prophet, saying," (Matthew 4:14)

"The land of Zabulon, and the land of Nephthalim, by the way of the sea, beyond Jordan, Galilee of the Gentiles;" (Matthew 4:15)

<5> Christ left Nazareth because John was taken to prison. He went to Capernaum. With this, another prophecy was fulfilled.

"The people which sat in darkness saw great light; and to them which sat in the region and shadow of death light is sprung up." (Matthew 4:16)

<6> "The people which sat in darkness" refers to the people of the north of the House of Judah, "Galilee of the Gentiles" (verse 15), whom Christ visited. They received a great blessing by the Lord and "saw great light."

<7> The cities of Nazareth, Capernaum, and the regions Zabulon and Nephthalim were in the north part of Judaea and were in the region which was the home of the House of Israel before they were taken away captive.

<8> The people of the House of Israel (the northern kingdom) started to become idol worshippers after it was separated from the southern kingdom. Their king Jeroboam "made two calves of gold, and said unto them, It is too much for you to go up to Jerusalem: behold thy gods, O Israel, which brought thee up out of the land of Egypt" (I Kings 12:28) and people started to worship these calves.

<9> As it was explained in the book <u>Children of Abram (Abraham), All Prophecies Are Fulfilled</u>, it was the people of the House of Israel whom Christ came to gather together as was prophesied by Jacob, "until Shiloh [Messiah] come; and unto him shall the gathering of the people be." (Gen. 49:10). <10> But in order to make a new religion accepted by a people, first the previous religion should be weakened. Then when the new religion comes it can easily replace the old. That is why the people of the House of Israel went through such a period of change that even they are considered as the ten lost tribes. In reality they were not lost but were being prepared to receive the new teachings of the Shiloh (Messiah).

<11> That is the reason Christ lived and even started to preach in the north region of Israel (Ephraim) and gathered them under his banner so that the prophecy of Jacob would be fulfilled.

<12> Again we can see that what apparently seems to the human as some unrelated accidental events, in truth are planned and are interrelated happenings toward the goal God has in His Mind and is trying to fulfill. <13> He even declared that the reason the House of Israel was separated from the kingdom, was by His Will. That is, after the House of

Israel was separated from the House of Judah (southern kingdom), king Rehoboam, the king of the House of Judah "assemble[d] all the house of Judah, with the tribe of Benjamin, ... to fight against the House of Israel, to bring the kingdom again to Rehoboam the son of Solomon" (I Kings 12:21).

<14> "But the word of God came unto Shemaiah the man of God," (I Kings 12:22) that he should speak with the people of the House of Judah that, "Thus saith the Lord, Ye shall not go up, nor fight against your brethren the children of Israel: return every man to his house; <15> **for this thing is from me**...." (I Kings 12:24). <16> Therefore this separation of the kingdom of Israel into two nations was done by Him for a purpose that is now revealed to us; for more detail read <u>Children of Abram (Abraham), All Prophecies Are Fulfilled</u>.

<17> Again that is the reason this verse is used here when Esa was still in the northern part of Israel. It was in this region that, "the people which sat in darkness saw great light; and to them which sat in the region and shadow of death [spiritual death] light is sprung up." <18> In truth he had come to awaken **these** people, not the Jews, because the Jews had so many concepts that no matter how many signs Esa would show them, they would not believe in him.

"From that time Esa began to preach, and to say, Repent: for the kingdom of heaven is at hand." (Matthew 4:17)

<19> The mission of John was finished and the work of Esa began. However, he also brought the same message and showed the way, "Repent: for the kingdom of heaven is at hand," that only with repentance and change of heart can the Kingdom Of Heaven be established (within and without). This is the same message as John's. <20> He did not say, "I will forgive you without you repenting and changing the way of your life," but, "The first step was shown for you to take, 'repent.' Then after that I will help you to progress and enter the Kingdom."

"And Esa, walking by the sea of Galilee, saw two brethren, Simon called Peter, and Andrew his brother, casting a net into the sea: for they were fishers." (Matthew 4:18)

"And he saith unto them, Follow me, and I will make you fishers of men." (Matthew 4:19)

"And they straightway left their nets, and followed him." (Matthew 4:20)

<21> Also Esa started to select his disciples from those who were pure in heart, not from the Pharisees and Scribes or Sadducees who had created big false egos with many concepts. <22> Simon and his brother Andrew were so ready to follow the master that they left everything behind to go with him. They did not let anything keep them from being his disciples.

"And going on from thence, he saw other two brethren, James the son of Zebedee, and John his brother, in a ship with Zebedee their father, mending their nets; and he called them." (Matthew 4:21)

"And they immediately left the ship and their father, and followed him." (Matthew 4:22)

<23> The hierarchy of the importance of the beings in life starts with God, then the spiritual teacher, next the parents (especially if they help in one's spiritual progress), and lastly the spouse. That is why here we see John and his brother left their father and followed Christ.

"And Esa went about all Galilee, teaching in their synagogues, and preaching the gospel of the kingdom, and healing all manner of sickness and all manner of disease among the people." (Matthew 4:23)

<24> He started preaching his message, the gospel of the Kingdom. Also, to make people believe in him and follow his teachings, he then started to heal their sicknesses and diseases.

COMMENTARIES ON ST. MATTHEW

"And his fame went throughout all Syria: and they brought unto him all sick people that were taken with divers diseases and torments, and those which were possessed with devils, and those which were lunatick, and those that had the palsy; and he healed them." (Matthew 4:24)

<25> He became famous not because of his teachings and the truth he was revealing, but because he had healing power. They did not come to learn the truth from him, to repent and establish the Kingdom Of Heaven, but they brought him their sicknesses to be healed.

"And there followed him great multitudes of people from Galilee, and from Decapolis, and from Jerusalem, and from Judaea, and from beyond Jordan." (Matthew 4:25)

<26> A great multitude started to follow him and ask to be healed or be given some favors. People started using him for their own selfish petty interests. That is why he left them as it was written in chapter 5, and started teaching his doctrine to his disciples, not to the multitudes. <27> The multitudes were deaf, blind, and dead.

Tablet Six

Chapter 5

"And seeing the multitudes, he went up into a mountain: and when he was set, his disciples came unto him:" (Matthew 5:1)

"And he opened his mouth, and taught them, saying," (Matthew 5:2)

<1> He taught these things to his disciples, not to the people, because the multitudes were only interested in favors and miracles, not the truth.

"Blessed are the poor in spirit: for theirs is the kingdom of heaven." (Matthew 5:3)

<2> The poor in spirit refers to those refined Souls who hate evildoings and false teachings: "deeds of the Nicolaitanes" (Rev. 2:6). They intuitively know that there is more in life than only physiological satisfaction, safety needs, and pursuance of Maya (worldly attraction).

<3> Therefore, they long for that lasting happiness. They will come to the conclusion that the Kingdom Of Heaven is only within. So they forsake society and try to find the Kingdom Of Heaven within. They become escapists. <4> That is why people will call them poor in spirit, because they do not have the courage to face society and try to change it toward good (God). So they inherit the Kingdom Of Heaven within.

"Blessed are they that mourn: for they shall be comforted." (Matthew 5:4)

<5> (☯) Those who are poor in spirit yet have overcome being escapist and instead try to stay in society – "thy first love" (Rev. 2:4) – are those who mourn. They are poor in spirit and hate evildoings and false teachings, and they see so much wrongdoing and inequity in society. So they mourn over being oppressed in that environment and are very unhappy about why they do not receive their fair share. <6> They shall be comforted when the Kingdom Of Heaven On Earth comes, and they will receive their fair share.

"Blessed are the meek: for they shall inherit the earth." (Matthew 5:5)

<7> (✡) When a person mourns for awhile and no one listens to him, he realizes that he is too powerless to be able to gain whatever he wants. So he starts to conform instead of mourn. He becomes a meek person; he surrenders to the environmental pressure. He will endure suffering with patience and without resentment.

<8> However, these are the first people who will submit themselves when the Kingdom Of Heaven (justice) comes, and because they consist of the majority of the people, they will inherit the earth. (For a deeper under-

standing of verses 3 to 10, read chapters 2 and 3 of the book Revelation of The Revelation.)

"Blessed are they which do hunger and thirst after righteousness: for they shall be filled." (Matthew 5:6)

<9> (✝) A meek person, however, after surrendering to the pressure for some time, will realize that the reason for all his and others' suffering is because of the lack of righteousness in all levels. That is why he will create a strong desire for righteousness. He hungers and thirsts for righteousness to be established. <10> These are the ones who will be filled when the Kingdom Of Heaven On Earth is established and righteousness restored.

"Blessed are the merciful: for they shall obtain mercy." (Matthew 5:7)

<11> (☾) If a person progresses more in understanding himself (overcoming the false ego), he will realize that in all the last four stages, he has been following the demands of his own false ego. He was unhappy about society and was trying to change it because he wanted to have a fair share for himself. He had been in his first three chakras which are related to the false ego. <12> However, when he overcomes being selfish about what he wants himself, then he creates a great compassion for those in distress. He realizes that overcoming that ego is such a hard thing, so he creates compassion for those who are lost because of their false egos. He becomes merciful. So he himself will obtain mercy from heaven.

"Blessed are the pure in heart: for they shall see God." (Matthew 5:8)

<13> (✹) A pure in heart person is one whose innermost character, feelings, and inclinations are free from moral fault or guilt. He is a man after God's own heart. He is a man who not only is merciful, but has created a universal point of view with utmost compassion about all things in it. <14> So, he looks at the universe exactly the way God looks at it. Therefore, he will start to understand how God feels about all things in His universe, and he can see God face-to-face in all the manifested universe.

"Blessed are the peacemakers: for they shall be called the children of God." (Matthew 5:9)

<15> (✡) A peacemaker is one who brings harmony, tranquility, or quietness to people internally and externally. These are the ones who not only have reached the state of being pure in heart, but are actively engaged in establishing the Kingdom Of Heaven On Earth (establishing Daharma) in order to bring that harmony and tranquility to the world. <16> They are the real Paravipras, who with their spiritual understanding and powers, bring the Kingdom Of Heaven On Earth. They are the children of God, because they have completely realized the Will of the Father and are trying to fulfill it. They are good children of their Father.

"Blessed are they which are persecuted for righteousness' sake: for theirs is the kingdom of heaven." (Matthew 5:10)

<17> (✺) These are the ones who have already reached a very high consciousness or Pure Consciousness and have come back to earth in order to establish the righteousness. <18> They have no interest in this external material world for any selfish desires, but are interested in the establishment of the Kingdom Of Heaven On Earth in order to see that the proper environment is established for all to progress physically, mentally, and spiritually. <19> They have no fear of being persecuted for their ideology and goal, because they know the eternal life is everlasting.

<20> Theirs is the Kingdom Of Heaven (within and without), because these are the ones who are really worthy to assume the leadership of humanity. <21> They will be the Great Paravipras (Maha-Paravipras) who will establish and maintain the Kingdom Of Heaven On Earth.

<22> In reality the teaching of Esa finishes here. The rest of chapter 5 is the description of the characteristics of a Paravipra.

COMMENTARIES ON ST. MATTHEW
Tablet Seven

"Blessed are ye, when men shall revile you, and persecute you, and shall say all manner of evil against you falsely, for my sake." (Matthew 5:11)

<1> His disciples were also of those who would be persecuted for righteousness. The reason humans persecute these people and "say all manner of evil against [them] falsely" is because most men are in the lower nature and do not want to go out of it. <2> That is where they have been all their lives and also everyone had taught them that this is the way to live. So they feel more comfortable to conform than fight against these false teachings and power of Maya (lower nature).

<3> That is why those who go against this rule will be outcast, become different, and people will hate them. <4> The reason is that intuitively deep inside, each person longs to go to his higher self and break the bondage of this world and lower nature. But it needs a very brave person to do so. <5> When a person starts to progress in the spiritual path, he is suddenly confronted with so much opposition. It seems everyone is begging and trying to stop him. However, if he refuses to listen to them to stay in his lower nature, they will hate him.

<6> That is also one of the reasons why after a period of time the religions become diluted by people. The teachings of the founder (Prophet) seem very hard to follow. So a simpler doctrine suited to their own lower natures is adopted and the truth becomes lost by simplified dogmas. <7> That is when the religion dies but its followers will not throw away this dead religion and instead hold on to it until it becomes so distorted that it rots the whole society, "And their dead bodies shall lie in the street of the great city [earth], which spiritually is called Sodom and Egypt;..." (Rev. 11:8).

"Rejoice, and be exceeding glad: for great is your reward in heaven: for so persecuted they the prophets which were before you." (Matthew 5:12)

<8> This process has been repeated time after time in the past. Yet those who are chosen should keep their "eyes single" toward the goal and rejoice in their path of struggle, because "strait is the gate, and narrow is the way, which leadeth into life, and few there be that find it" (Matthew 7:14).

"Ye are the salt of the earth: but if the salt have lost his savour, wherewith shall it be salted? it is thenceforth good for nothing, but to be cast out, and to be trodden under foot of men." (Matthew 5:13)

<9> This whole universe was created so that man might reach Pure Consciousness. So those who find the way and try to become Pure Consciousness are the ones who make this system worthwhile, not those who stay in their lower natures and refuse to fulfill the Darma of this universe. That is why they are the salt of the world which gives savour to the world.

<10> However, if these people who have reached some progress fall back, their fall will be great. They will crash to nothingness and become more unworthy than a man in his lower nature. That is why they will be "good for nothing, but to be cast out, and to be trodden under foot of men."

"Ye are the light of the world. A city that is set on an hill cannot be hid." (Matthew 5:14)

<11> But those who continue their struggle and progress further in the path to become the light of the world will shine, and they cannot hide it.

"Neither do men light a candle, and put it under a bushel, but on a candlestick; and it giveth light unto all that are in the house." (Matthew 5:15)

<12> These people should accept their responsibilities as the guidance to humanity and become a guiding light for them.

"Let your light so shine before men, that they may see your good works, and glorify your Father which is in heaven." (Matthew 5:16)

<13> Shine in the world by your great actions, but surrender the result to the Lord. Become a channel for His Divine actions and glorify Him. When people praise you for what you did, let them know that it is He who does these great works through you. <14> That is the way to be freed from the bondage of karma.

<15> If a person lets Him do the great actions through him, then the real doer is not he but He. So there will not be a false ego created by the person, and then he is free from any trace of separateness from Him and will dissolve his ego to the Universal Ego. He will become one with Him.

"Think not that I am come to destroy the law, or the prophets: I am not come to destroy, but to fulfil." (Matthew 5:17)

<16> Each prophet comes to further the understanding of humanity by his new teachings and to clarify some points from the old, "to fulfil."

"For verily I say unto you, Till heaven and earth pass, one jot or one tittle shall in no wise pass from the law, till all be fulfilled." (Matthew 5:18)

<17> The Universal Laws (Darmas) cannot be broken. All will understand this truth and become it, "till all be fulfilled."

"Whoever therefore shall break one of these least commandments, and shall teach men so, he shall be called the least in the kingdom of heaven: but whosoever shall do and teach them, the same shall be called great in the kingdom of heaven." (Matthew 5:19)

<18> Whoever tries to break these Laws will break himself against them, and whoever follows them will reach Pure Consciousness, "shall be called great in the kingdom of heaven."

"For I say unto you, That except your righteousness shall exceed the righteousness of the scribes and Pharisees, ye shall in no case enter into the kingdom of heaven." (Matthew 5:20)

<19> The Pharisees and scribes used to teach, but not follow what they taught. So to become greater than them, a person not only should teach but also he should follow his teachings.

<20> Also Pharisees and scribes taught the Torah and Ten Commandments, but Esa taught that the goal is not, **not** to do sin, but is to reach such a state that no desire is left to do sin.

"Ye have heard that it was said by them of old time, Thou shalt not kill; and whosoever shall kill [murder] shall be in danger of the judgment:" (Matthew 5:21)

"But I say unto you, That whosoever is angry with his brother without a cause shall be in danger of the judgment: and whosoever shall say to his brother, Raca, shall be in danger of the council: but whosoever shall say, Thou fool, shall be in danger of hell fire." (Matthew 5:22)

<21> The goal is not "not to murder," but to reach such a state of consciousness that you would have complete control over your mind and would not become angry without a cause, would not curse any person, nor judge ("shall say, Thou fool").

"Therefore if thou bring thy gift to the altar, and there rememberest that thy brother hath aught against thee;" (Matthew 5:23)

"Leave there thy gift before the altar, and go thy way; first be reconciled to thy brother, and then come and offer thy gift." (Matthew 5:24)

<22> Reaching that state of purification of body, mind, and spirit is necessary. So search your Soul and find the impurities within and overcome them. After you have cleansed yourself then you might be able to approach the Lord.

<23> You have to approach the Lord with a pure heart and free of any guilt. With an impure soul you cannot see Him or know Him – only the pure in heart can see God (verse 8).

<24> This impurity also was the reason that

Adam and Eve hid themselves from the presence of the Lord. An impure person might try to pray or approach Him, but he will not benefit very much.

<25> However, this should not discourage a person to go to Him, but at the time of prayer, sacrifice, and meditation, a person should remember his actions and try to correct them, so he progresses more and more toward purity. To turn around and go to Him is a gradual, but sure, process.

Tablet Eight

"Agree with thine adversary quickly, whiles thou art in the way with him; lest at any time the adversary deliver thee to the judge, and the judge deliver thee to the officer, and thou be cast into prison." (Matthew 5:25)

<1> Do not become involved in disputes and mundane things in life. Leave them to those who are drowned in Maya. Be satisfied with whatever you have with no attachment to them, so you can concentrate on higher things and progress in becoming great.

"Verily I say unto thee, Thou shalt by no means come out thence, till thou hast paid the uttermost farthing." (Matthew 5:26)

<2> However, if you were accused of something, act in such a way that you would leave no doubt in others and your own mind of your honesty.

"Ye have heard that it was said by them of old time, Thou shalt not commit adultery:" (Matthew 5:27)

"But I say unto you, That whosoever looketh on a woman to lust after her hath committed adultery with her already in his heart." (Matthew 5:28)

<3> The goal is **not**, not to do adultery, but to reach a state of consciousness that even no desire to do adultery or lust is left.

"And if thy right eye offend thee, pluck it out, and cast it from thee: for it is profitable for thee that one of thy members should perish, and not that thy whole body should be cast into hell." (Matthew 5:29)

"And if thy right hand offend thee, cut it off, and cast it from thee: for it is profitable for thee that one of thy members should perish, and not that thy whole body should be cast into hell." (Matthew 5:30)

<4> Whatever is an obstacle in your path to reach that state (Divinity, Pure Consciousness) where no desire is left to do sin, should be destroyed, no matter how dear it is to you (very much like the teaching of the Bhagavad-Gita).

"It hath been said, Whosoever shall put away his wife, let him give her a writing of divorcement:" (Matthew 5:31)

"But I say unto you, That whosoever shall put away his wife, saving for the cause of fornication, causeth her to commit adultery: and whosoever shall marry her that is divorced committeth adultery." (Matthew 5:32)

<5> If husband and wife are soulmates, only they can be married as partners together. So if they divorce and she marries another person, they will be doing adultery because they are not true parts for each other. <6> Also couples and families are the base and blocks from which society is built. If these blocks are not strong, then the whole society will collapse. Even if married couples are not each other's true corresponding parts, still they can become a strong base for society with a little sacrifice.

"Again, ye have heard that it hath been said by them of old time, Thou shalt not forswear thyself, but shalt perform unto the Lord thine oaths:" (Matthew 5:33)

COMMENTARIES ON ST. MATTHEW

"But I say unto you, Swear not at all; neither by heaven; for it is God's throne:" (Matthew 5:34)

"Nor by the earth; for it is his footstool: neither by Jerusalem; for it is the city of the great King." (Matthew 5:35)

"Neither shalt thou swear by thy head, because thou canst not make one hair white or black." (Matthew 5:36)

"But let your communication be, Yea, yea; Nay, nay: for whatsoever is more than these cometh of evil." (Matthew 5:37)

<7> The goal is to be(come) the truth itself, and a person in truth does not have to swear at all. To reach this state you should refrain from idle talk, because idle talk "cometh of evil."

"Ye have heard that it hath been said, An eye for an eye, and a tooth for a tooth:" (Matthew 5:38)

"But I say unto you, That ye resist not evil: but whosoever shall smite thee on thy right cheek, turn to him the other also." (Matthew 5:39)

"And if any man will sue thee at the law, and take away thy coat, let him have thy cloak also." (Matthew 5:40)

"And whosoever shall compel thee to go a mile, go with him twain." (Matthew 5:41)

<8> Forgive those who do bad to you, and make your aggressor ashamed of his actions, by showing forgiveness and detachment.

<9> It should be kept in mind that the teachings of Christ are for individual progress and are related to the acts a person does to be(come) perfect to be(come) detached in overcoming the lower nature and an instrument to manifest His qualities. <10> However, there is another side of human life and that is the relationship of man with the society and external world. Therefore to complete these teachings of forgiveness, it should be taught:

<11> **Forgive whatever bad has been done to you, but forgive not bad done to society.**

<12> That is why Prophet Muhammad taught that if someone smites you, smite him back, because his teaching is more social-oriented and Christ's teaching is individual-oriented.

"Give to him that asketh thee, and from him that would borrow of thee turn not thou away." (Matthew 5:42)

<13> Be helpful to others in need as much as you can. <14> Help others with knowledge, not from ignorance (helping the wrong person, or at the wrong time, or in the wrong place), or from passion (with expecting something in return).

"Ye have heard that it hath been said, Thou shalt love thy neighbour, and hate thine enemy." (Matthew 5:43)

"But I say unto you, Love your enemies, bless them that curse you, do good to them that hate you, and pray for them which despitefully use you, and persecute you;" (Matthew 5:44)

"That ye may be the children of your Father which is in heaven: for he maketh his sun to rise on the evil and on the good, and sendeth rain on the just and on the unjust." (Matthew 5:45)

<15> In order to become like the Father (His son), you have to become indiscriminating in your love, as God giveth to both the good and the sinners. <16> Even if He punishes someone it is for that person's good so he might receive a lesson and progress further toward his goal. So be like Him and do all things with love toward the whole universe.

"For if ye love them which love you, what reward have ye? do not even the publicans the same?" (Matthew 5:46)

"And if ye salute your brethren only, what do ye more than others? do not even the publicans so?" (Matthew 5:47)

<17> If you do not love everything, because everything is He, then it shows that you still have your separated ego as "I" and only love those who love "I," and hate those who hate "I." Is not this the way with all those who have a false separated ego? <18> But in order to be different and perfect, look upon all things as God and as being manifested from God. Love all things because they are God. So in this, look at all things as God looks. Even when you punish a person, do it for the sake of correction but not from hate.

"Be ye therefore perfect, even as your Father which is in heaven is perfect." (Matthew 5:48)

<19> That is exactly what the goal of the life is, to be(come) perfect as the Father, to be(come) Divine, Pure Consciousness, the Law. <20> The goal is to reach this point. It is not to try to follow a set of rules, regulations, and Commandments, but to be(come) those Commandments. <21> It does not mean that the Laws and Commandments are destroyed by these teachings, but the true way is shown how to implement them by purification of one's existence (physically, mentally, and spiritually), or to reach that purity of the Father. Then you become the same as the Father. God is the Law so you also become the Law, or perfect. Until you reach there, any Commandments, Laws, or teachings are only words, however they show the way. <22> When you do reach there, then you do the Laws and follow the Commandments without even thinking about them.

<23> So, "be ye therefore perfect, even as your Father which is in heaven is perfect."

Tablet Nine

Chapter 6

"Take heed that ye do not your alms before men, to be seen of them: otherwise ye have no reward of your Father which is in heaven." (Matthew 6:1)

"Therefore when thou doest thine alms, do not sound a trumpet before thee, as the hypocrites do in the synagogues and in the streets, that they may have glory of men. Verily I say unto you, they have their reward." (Matthew 6:2)

<1> To do good, to be good, and all the acts of giving instead of receiving, are for self-purification. <2> He who strives in the path of spiritual progress in truth is trying to overcome the illusion of this external world (Maya). The desire to be glorified by man is one of them which binds the human to the earth.

<3> "Therefore when thou doest thine alms, do not sound a trumpet before thee," because that is the way of the hypocrites. That is the way of those who try to look spiritual but inside are filthy. In truth they receive their reward, which is the glory of men, but their spirit will not grow, and will even be more darkened.

"But when thou doest alms, let not thy left hand know what thy right hand doeth:" (Matthew 6:3)

"That thine alms may be in secret: and thy Father which seeth in secret himself shall reward thee openly." (Matthew 6:4)

<4> So those who truly want to do good will do it in secret. They will not do it to be glorified by man but will receive their reward inside as spiritual progress from the Father who is in Heaven. <5> Even if they do a good action in the open, they do it not to receive the attention of others but to set an example for them.

"And when thou prayest, thou shalt not be as the hypocrites are: for they love to pray standing in the synagogues and in the corners of the streets, that they may be seen of men. Verily I say unto you, They have their reward." (Matthew 6:5)

"But thou, when thou prayest, enter into thy closet, and when thou hast shut the door, pray to thy Father which is in secret; and thy Father which seeth in secret shall reward thee openly." (Matthew 6:6)

<6> This Law is true about any action. The action should be done not to receive praise and attention from others for selfish reasons ("to be glorified by men"), but to make the spirit purified and grow toward the goal – to be(come) Divine. To try to be glorified by man for our actions is the way of the hypocrites.

"But when ye pray, use not vain repetitions, as the heathen do: for they think that they shall be heard for their much speaking." (Matthew 6:7)

"Be not ye therefore like unto them: for your Father knoweth what things ye have need of, before ye ask him." (Matthew 6:8)

<7> The true prayer is done when a person is in deep meditation and in the silence of the heart. With merely repeating or much speaking, nothing will be gained. <8> Also there is no need to pray for anything, because whatever is necessary for you to have will be provided by God. Furthermore, God has already given man the body, intelligence, and all the tools necessary for him to use and to gain his basic necessities. <9> In truth, the only necessary prayer to the Lord is for His guidance to overcome the power of the tama guna over our Souls and detach ourselves from Maya.

"After this manner therefore pray ye: Our Father which art in heaven, Hallowed be thy name." (Matthew 6:9)

"Thy kingdom come. Thy will be done in earth, as it is in heaven." (Matthew 6:10)

"Give us this day our daily bread." (Matthew 6:11)

"And forgive us our debts, as we forgive our debtors." (Matthew 6:12)

"And lead us not into temptation, but deliver us from evil: For thine is the kingdom, and the power, and the glory, for ever. Amen." (Matthew 6:13)

<10> This was the prayer given by Esa to be performed by his followers. Before starting to pray, the ideation of respect and devotion toward God should be invoked. That is why the first verse gives praise to the Lord, "Hallowed be thy name," the same as, "We pay our salutations to the Divine Father."

<11> The second verse is an expression of the desire that the Will of the Lord be done, which is for His Kingdom to be established on earth, "as it is in heaven." <12> As it is shown in **The Greatest Sign**, there are three Kingdoms Of Heaven: The Kingdom Of Heaven In Heaven, the Kingdom Of Heaven within, and the Kingdom Of Heaven On Earth. The Kingdom Of Heaven In Heaven already has been established. When the Kingdom Of Heaven within (✡) and the Kingdom Of Heaven On Earth (✡) are also established, then His Kingdom will come and His Will, will be done on earth as it is in Heaven (✡). <13> So in this verse the Will (Desire) of the Lord has been expressed. He desires to see that His Kingdom come and through it the whole universe progress as rapidly as possible toward the goal (Pure Consciousness).

<14> "Give us this day our daily bread": To do His Will and/or before starting any spiritual progress, man's physiological and safety needs should be met. That is why the daily bread (minimum necessities) should be provided for all.

<15> "And forgive us our debts, as we forgive our debtors." We forgive those who have done wrong to us, and the Lord will forgive us also. Forgive and you will be forgiven.

<16> "And lead us not into temptation." The essence and reason for any wrong doing is temptation, when an action seems good to us to do, but in reality is against the Laws of the Lord. When temptation comes to the person through his lower nature, it is a great task to overcome it. <17> Also temptation occurs because of the power of the tama guna (crudifies the consciousness) and attraction to

Maya. So in truth this verse is similar to the sentence, "We open our hearts to Your Grace and pray for Your Guidance in overcoming the power of the tama guna over our Souls, and detaching ourselves from Maya," or "lead us not into temptation, but deliver us from evil (tama guna, Maya)."

<18> "For thine is the kingdom, and the power, and the glory, for ever." He has complete power over the three gunas and is the master of the universe. So only He can deliver us from evil or the power of the tama guna and help us detach ourselves from Maya. He is the only subject of praise in the universe, and only with directing all our attention and our being to Him can we be delivered from the ocean of Maya. So "the kingdom, and the power, and the glory" is His forever. The "Amen" is the same as "Aum" or "OM" (ॐ), which is to invoke the Lord or the Divine vibration in the universe.

"For if ye forgive men their trespasses, your heavenly Father will also forgive you:" (Matthew 6:14)

"But if ye forgive not men their trespasses, neither will your Father forgive your trespasses." (Matthew 6:15)

<19> Forgive whatever wrong has been done to you, and then you also will be forgiven. But do not forgive the bad done to society.

"Moreover when ye fast, be not, as the hypocrites, of a sad countenance: for they disfigure their faces, that they may appear unto men to fast. Verily I say unto you, They have their reward." (Matthew 6:16)

"But thou, when thou fastest, anoint thine head, and wash thy face;" (Matthew 6:17)

"That thou appear not unto men to fast, but unto thy Father which is in secret: and thy Father, which seeth in secret, shall reward thee openly." (Matthew 6:18)

<20> This is the same lesson as taught on alms-giving in the first verses of this chapter. Do good not to be glorified by men, but for your own spiritual progress, because in truth you do all these things for your own benefit to progress to Pure Consciousness. You do not do them for the Lord. God does not need your fasting, alms-giving, etc., but these are all for purification of your own Soul. <21> However, with doing these things for the sake of your own Soul and with detachment to them, you will invoke the Grace of the Lord, and through that Grace you will be saved.

<22> Also the act of washing, being clean, and staying fresh (like taking a half-bath) is emphasized.

Tablet Ten

"Lay not up for yourselves treasures upon earth, where moth and rust doth corrupt, and where thieves break through and steal:" (Matthew 6:19)

"But lay up for yourselves treasures in heaven, where neither moth nor rust doth corrupt, and where thieves do not break through nor steal:" (Matthew 6:20)

"For where your treasure is, there will your heart be also." (Matthew 6:21)

<1> Think about God, His universe, and His truths all the time, and love Him with all your might. Otherwise your attention will be diverted to the material world, mundane things, and you will fall into your lower nature (hell).

<2> So avoid anything that keeps your attention from Him. <3> Do good but do not be attached to the results of your actions and this external world. Then you might create a great treasure in heaven of the good deeds you have done. Your thoughts will then be there rather than on the material world, which results in attachments, attraction, desires, and greed

(the four winds), and the end by-product is bondage and spiritual death, because "where your treasure is, there will your heart be also."

"The light of the body is the eye: if therefore thine eye be single, thy whole body shall be full of light." (Matthew 6:22)

"But if thine eye be evil, thy whole body shall be full of darkness. If therefore the light that is in thee be darkness, how great is that darkness!" (Matthew 6:23)

<4> The "eye" refers to the spiritual eye which was closed after the flood of Noah (for more detail, read The Base, The Essence, or The Holiest Book). If this eye becomes opened and you become completely concentrated and one-pointed on spiritual progress, then the door of knowledge (light) of the spiritual truth will be opened to you, and you will be filled with this light. <5> But if your concentration is directed to Maya, "thine eye be evil," then the door of truth will be closed to you, "thy whole body shall be full of darkness," you will be drowned in Maya and your lower nature, and that is where hell is, "how great is that darkness!"

"No man can serve two masters: for either he will hate the one, and love the other; or else he will hold to the one, and despise the other. Ye cannot serve God and mammon." (Matthew 6:24)

<6> When the external world and its illusive promises become a person's master, then he has no choice but to hate the spiritual truth which discourages that attachment, or he will leave spirituality completely and go to Maya. <7> Also here the word "master" is used. Master means one who makes the person its slave. So only when the external world and attachment to it is so great that a person becomes its slave, is it bad. However, if it is used without attachment, we continue to progress toward higher consciousness in the middle of Maya, remembering the Lord, serving Him, seeing Him everywhere, and being His slave. <8> Only by being His slave can we avoid being the slave of Maya.

"Therefore I say unto you, Take no thought for your life, what ye shall eat, or what ye shall drink; nor yet for your body, what ye shall put on. Is not the life more than meat, and the body than raiment?" (Matthew 6:25)

<9> So be content with what you have, and direct your energy toward doing His Will, "Your will be done on earth as it is in heaven." The only things you need are the minimum necessities, "give us our daily bread." The rest of life should be used for purification, "lead us not into temptation," by His Grace, "but deliver us from evil." <10> Then the Kingdom Of Heaven within and without will be established, the three Kingdoms Of Heaven will be His, and His "will be done on earth as it is in heaven."

<11> Also why worry? We are not our bodies. The body is meat (flesh) and it is just like a raiment (garment) that we leave behind after death. The only things that will be with us are our Souls and spirits. We have to be concerned for what is permanent, not what we have to leave behind. So we should progress to make our Souls become Pure Consciousness. The body should only be used for this end.

"Behold the fowls of the air: for they sow not, neither do they reap, nor gather into barns; yet your heavenly Father feedeth them. Are ye not much better than they?" (Matthew 6:26)

<12> If God will provide sustenance for the birds, which are much lower in the evolutionary Hierarchy, would not He provide it for the human who is much higher in His eyes?

"Which of you by taking thought can add one cubit unto his stature?" (Matthew 6:27)

"And why take ye thought for raiment? Consider the lilies of the field, how they grow; they toil not, neither do they spin:" (Matthew 6:28)

"And yet I say unto you, That even Solomon in all his glory was not arrayed like one of these." (Matthew 6:29)

<13> Be content with what God has provided and work on the beauty within to be(come) the beautiful being you were born to manifest (qualities of God). As lilies in the field are content with what has been given to them and they manifest their beauty in full, "That even Solomon in all his glory was not arrayed like one of these."

"Wherefore, if God so clothe the grass of the field, which to day is, and to morrow is cast into the oven, shall he not much more clothe you, O ye of little faith?" (Matthew 6:30)

<14> If by surrendering and being content even lilies can receive such beauty, which have such a short life span and lower consciousness, then would not God manifest higher beauty, which is your Soul, through you? But to come to such a point of surrendering and being content in life needs much faith.

"Therefore take no thought, saying, What shall we eat? or, What shall we drink? or, Wherewithal shall we be clothed?" (Matthew 6:31)

<15> One thing should be remembered – that these things Esa was teaching to his disciples, or to those who give up everything to spread the word of God and His Messages (the Holy Men). These people should totally detach themselves from these things and be free to direct and concentrate completely on God's work.

"(For after all these things do the Gentiles seek:) for your heavenly Father knoweth that ye have need of all these things." (Matthew 6:32)

<16> Let the worldly people be worried. For those who dedicate themselves to God, the minimum will be provided and such a people should be content, surrendered, and have faith that they will receive it, because "your heavenly Father knoweth that ye have need of all these things."

"But seek ye first the kingdom of God, and his righteousness; and all these things shall be added unto you." (Matthew 6:33)

<17> Those who direct all their attention and concentration toward their spiritual progress and others' (first seek the Kingdom of God), "all these things shall be added unto" them. The worker is then worthy of his wage.

"Take therefore no thought for the morrow: for the morrow shall take thought for the things of itself. Sufficient unto the day is the evil thereof." (Matthew 6:34)

<18> So do not be worried about tomorrow. There will be enough problems each day that a Holy man would have to solve without having time for other things, "Sufficient unto the day is the evil thereof." **Be here now.**

Tablet Eleven

Chapter 7

<1> In this chapter, the multitudes were present, because it was directed also to them.

"Judge not, that ye be not judged." (Matthew 7:1)

"For with what judgment ye judge, ye shall be judged: and with what measure ye mete, it shall be measured to you again." (Matthew 7:2)

"And why beholdest thou the mote that is in thy brother's eye, but considerest not the beam that is in thine own eye?" (Matthew 7:3)

"Or how wilt thou say to thy brother, Let me pull out the mote out of thine eye; and, behold, a beam is in thine own eye?" (Matthew 7:4)

"Thou hypocrite, first cast out the beam out of thine own eye; and then shalt thou see clearly to cast out the mote out of thy brother's eye." (Matthew 7:5)

<2> These verses can best be described by the lesson Esa gave to those who brought the adulteress woman and asked him if they should stone her. The answer was that the one who has no sin should cast the first stone. All dropped their stones and left. <3> **Only those who have overcome and cleansed their spirit from all of the sins and false understandings can judge.** Otherwise the filthy things within will distort the person's judgment, and he will not judge correctly. He will create more suffering than tranquility and truth. He will be judged and suffer for his misjudgments also.

<4> So, "first cast out the beam out of thine own eye; and then shalt thou see clearly to cast out the mote out of thy brother's eye." Only such a people are worthy to judge and lead humanity. Otherwise they will have no choice but to become "hypocrites."

"Give not that which is holy unto the dogs, neither cast ye your pearls before swine, lest they trample them under their feet, and turn again and rend you." (Matthew 7:6)

<5> Be careful to whom you expose yourself (your Soul which is Holy and precious like pearls). If you open it to those who are not Holy (dogs and swine), they will try to destroy it, "lest they trample them under their feet,…"

"Ask, and it shall be given you; seek, and ye shall find; knock, and it shall be opened unto you:" (Matthew 7:7)

"For every one that asketh receiveth; and he that seeketh findeth; and to him that knocketh it shall be opened." (Matthew 7:8)

<6> The highest way to know is to go to God directly (to expose yourself only to Him). Whoever truly asks, sincerely seeks, and earnestly wants to know ("knock") will be given the truth. The only requirement is an intense desire to find the truth, and to seek to find it. It is promised that whoever has these qualities will succeed. <7> Christ does not say he is going to do it for you but it is up to you to ask, seek, and knock.

"Or what man is there of you, whom if his son ask bread, will he give him a stone?" (Matthew 7:9)

"Or if he ask a fish, will he give him a serpent?" (Matthew 7:10)

"If ye then, being evil, know how to give good gifts unto your children, how much more shall your Father which is in heaven give good things to them that ask him?" (Matthew 7:11)

<8> All the humans are God's children. So if we, who are mostly in our lower natures ("being evil") know how to give good things to our children, then imagine how eager God, who is the most Compassionate, Loving, and Holy, is to give the truth to those who seek it. So ask, seek, and search. <9> It is a promise you will find the truth.

"Therefore all things whatsoever ye would that men should do to you, do ye even so to them: for this is the law and the prophets." (Matthew 7:12)

<10> Do unto others as you expect others to do to you: This is the essence of all spiritual knowledge.

"Enter ye in at the strait gate: for wide is the gate, and broad is the way, that leadeth to destruction, and many there be which go in thereat:" (Matthew 7:13)

<11> It is easy to be selfish and do to others what we do not expect others to do to us, "wide is the gate, and broad is the way." But that is the way to go to the lower nature and be drowned in Maya, "that leadeth to destruction."

"Because strait is the gate, and narrow is the way, which leadeth into life, and few there be that find it." (Matthew 7:14)

<12> However, to do to others as we expect others to do to us is a very narrow and hard path, "strait is the gate, and narrow is

the way." But that leads to spiritual growth toward Pure Consciousness, "which leadeth into life." However, very few find it in each generation, "and few there be that find it."

<13> Verses 13 and 14 in fact show the very process of creation and The Plan of God. Those who go the easy path of the lower nature will be drowned in the ocean of Maya and will drift away from entering the Kingdom Of Heaven In Heaven (life, Pure Consciousness). <14> But those who choose the narrow and hard path, with His Grace, will find the way and enter into everlasting life (Pure Consciousness). That is why we are here and have this life.

"Beware of false prophets, which come to you in sheep's clothing, but inwardly they are ravening wolves." (Matthew 7:15)

<15> Whoever teaches anything else but that the goal of life is to be(come) Divine is a false prophet. It does not matter how they put it, "come to you in sheep's clothing, but inwardly they are ravening wolves."

"Ye shall know them by their fruits. Do men gather grapes of thorns, or figs of thistles?" (Matthew 7:16)

<16> You know them by what they offer to you and what result is produced by that offering, or by what their teaching is and where it leads the followers. Does it lead toward be(com)ing Divine (purity), or toward Maya? If the result of the fruit is Maya, then it is a false teaching.

"Even so every good tree bringeth forth good fruit; but a corrupt tree bringeth forth evil fruit." (Matthew 7:17)

<17> To follow a blind teacher results (fruit) in falling in decay with him, "a corrupt tree bringeth forth evil fruit," and to follow a true teacher will lead to growth and the true life, "good tree bringeth forth good fruit."

"A good tree cannot bring forth evil fruit, neither can a corrupt tree bring forth good fruit." (Matthew 7:18)

"Every tree that bringeth not forth good fruit is hewn down, and cast into the fire." (Matthew 7:19)

<18> Those who do not clean inside but assume the responsibility of leading others, have no choice but to be(come) hypocrites and corrupt. Such a people and their system will be destroyed, "every tree that bringeth not forth good fruit is hewn down, and cast into the fire." This truth has been shown all throughout history, and in this case it was the Pharisees, scribes, and Sadducees who were destroyed and hewn down.

"Wherefore by their fruits ye shall know them." (Matthew 7:20)

<19> Therefore, you will know if they are true or false prophets by what their teachings produce, Divine or otherwise.

"Not every one that saith unto me, Lord, Lord, shall enter into the kingdom of heaven; but he that doeth the will of my Father which is in heaven." (Matthew 7:21)

<20> You have to surrender yourself to the words revealed through the Prophets and follow them, "doeth the will of my Father which is in heaven." The Prophet himself is important only because of what he says. So for those who put more importance on the Prophet himself than on his words which are from God, miss the whole point. They will call him "Lord, Lord," but forget to follow what he said. Such a people will not enter into heaven or the Kingdom Of God In Heaven, because they have not purified themselves by following his teachings and still have big false egos. Whoever has the slightest false ego cannot enter into heaven.

"Many will say to me in that day, Lord, Lord, have we not prophesied in thy name? and in thy name have cast out devils? and in thy name done many wonderful works?" (Matthew 7:22)

"And then will I profess unto them, I never knew you: depart from me, ye that work iniquity." (Matthew 7:23)

<21> Many will gain some spiritual powers and misuse them to show their spiritual progress and impress others (use of spiritual powers can also be from three kinds: Ignorance, passion, or knowledge). Many also use a name, which is not His Sacred Name, to do these things. But they are not acceptable, "...I never knew you" (Matthew 7:22, 23). <22> In fact, spiritual power will be given to a person to test him to see if he will fail in handling it or will use it for the right purposes. These powers should be used for His Will (establishing the KOHOE).

"Therefore whosoever heareth these sayings of mine, and doeth them, I will liken him unto a wise man, which built his house upon a rock:" (Matthew 7:24)

"And the rain descended, and the floods came, and the winds blew, and beat upon that house; and it fell not: for it was founded upon a rock." (Matthew 7:25)

<23> Whoever opens himself, hears these teachings, and follows them, will enter his higher nature or self (will have no false ego) and will not be affected by the tribulations and changes in the world.

"And every one that heareth these sayings of mine, and doeth them not, shall be likened unto a foolish man, which built his house upon the sand:" (Matthew 7:26)

"And the rain descended, and the floods came, and the winds blew, and beat upon that house; and it fell: and great was the fall of it." (Matthew 7:27)

<24> But those who will not follow these truths and do not do them will stay in their lower natures and will be drowned in Maya. Then they will be affected by all kinds of tribulations and will be carried away deeper and deeper into desires, attachments, attraction of the external world, and greed (winds), and great is their fall.

"And it came to pass, when Esa had ended these sayings, the people were astonished at his doctrine:" (Matthew 7:28)

"For he taught them as one having authority, and not as the scribes." (Matthew 7:29)

<25> Christ finished the essence of his teachings here and people saw the authority in him because he was in truth. <26> Whoever is in truth cannot say anything but the truth, and truth is like a very sharp sword which cuts through the falsifications and prevails strongly, "having authority." <27> But people still thought it was his doctrine and could not see that it is the **only** doctrine, or the truth. <28> No one will be saved by merely believing in a Savior – after believing in the Savior he has to do and struggle in the path. Then he might earn His Grace and be saved.

<29> Also there were multitudes ("people") present at the end of this chapter, and Esa taught them mostly in parables and symbols. So in this chapter other people were present besides his disciples. However, chapters 5 and 6 were taught to his disciples only.

Tablet Twelve

Chapter 8

"When he was come down from the mountain, great multitudes followed him." (Matthew 8:1)

"And, behold, there came a leper and worshipped him, saying, Lord, if thou wilt, thou canst make me clean." (Matthew 8:2)

<1> After he finished his teachings, people forgot all about what he taught and started again asking for miracles and favors. <2> Also the miracles he did directed the attention of the people away from the teachings to these miracles. That is why the Prophets who came after Christ did not manifest these kinds of miracles but emphasized more the meaning of their teachings.

"And Esa put forth his hand, and touched him, saying, I will; be thou clean. And immediately his leprosy was cleansed." (Matthew 8:3)

<3> Christ knew that the only way to make people in that era and level of consciousness believe in him was by healing them and performing miracles. <4> But for the people of this time and of the era to come, the teachings of the Prophets should become more important than the Prophets themselves, or their miracles. <5> Each man has to learn to heal himself.

"And Esa saith unto him, See thou tell no man; but go thy way, shew thyself to the priest, and offer the gift that Moses commanded, for a testimony unto them." (Matthew 8:4)

<6> Here it is completely shown that it was not important for Christ that he healed the man. Instead, he desired to see that the people would follow the Laws and glorify the Father. He did great actions but took no pride for them, <7> because it is He who did these through him.

"And when Esa was entered into Capernaum, there came unto him a centurion, beseeching him," (Matthew 8:5)

"And saying, Lord, my servant lieth at home sick of the palsy, grievously tormented." (Matthew 8:6)

"And Esa saith unto him, I will come and heal him." (Matthew 8:7)

<8> This person was asking for a favor for someone else, a servant. He was not asking for himself or even for a close member of his family. Therefore, without hesitation, Christ volunteered to go to his house and heal his servant.

"The centurion answered and said, Lord, I am not worthy that thou shouldest come under my roof: but speak the word only, and my servant shall be healed." (Matthew 8:8)

<9> The centurion even humbled himself to Christ and with no arrogance accepted him as a Realized Soul and greater than himself. <10> Also Christ was using The Word (The Divine Sacred Name) to heal.

"For I am a man under authority, having soldiers under me: and I say to this man, Go, and he goeth; and to another, Come, and he cometh; and to my servant, Do this, and he doeth it." (Matthew 8:9)

<11> The centurion had authority, and people could satisfy their lower natures through him. Therefore, others obeyed him and followed his orders.

"When Esa heard it, he marvelled, and said to them that followed, Verily I say unto you, I have not found so great faith, no, not in Israel." (Matthew 8:10)

"And I say unto you, That many shall come from the east and west, and shall sit down with Abraham, and Isaac, and Jacob, in the kingdom of heaven." (Matthew 8:11)

"But the children of the kingdom shall be cast out into outer darkness: there shall be weeping and gnashing of teeth." (Matthew 8:12)

<12> When Esa saw that this man had such a great faith in him that he believed his servant would be healed if Christ only uttered The Word, and humbled himself even though he was in a higher position of earthly authority, Christ marvelled at how great a man he was and how high a consciousness he had reached.

<13> That is why Christ said that although this man is not of the people who call themselves the Chosen Ones, he and others like him will reach Pure Consciousness. But those who have created a great false ego by believing they are the Chosen Ones, because of this false ego, will "be cast out into outer darkness [ignorance]."

"And Esa said unto the centurion, Go thy way; and as thou hast believed, so be it done unto thee. And his servant was healed in the selfsame hour." (Matthew 8:13)

COMMENTARIES ON ST. MATTHEW — Tablet 12

<14> All will be done to you according to your faith. The slightest doubt will put you millions of miles away from God.

"And when Esa was come into Peter's house, he saw his wife's mother laid, and sick of a fever." (Matthew 8:14)

"And he touched her hand, and the fever left her: and she arose, and ministered unto them." (Matthew 8:15)
<15> Christ was merciful toward his disciples, their families who believed in him, and those who were associated with him.

"When the even was come, they brought unto him many that were possessed with devils: and he cast out the spirits with his word, and healed all that were sick:" (Matthew 8:16)
<16> He continued to heal people so that their faith might increase through these miracles. But he wanted them to understand his teachings and become as the Father in heaven (Pure Consciousness) (Matthew 5:48). However they were not ready yet to understand it.
<17> The term "devils" is used to refer to forces which crudify the consciousness by affecting the spirit (ethereal body, chakras). Or in other words, "devils" refers to the power of the tama guna over the Soul. Also it is related to the karmic reaction (sins) from past lifetimes. <18> Some of these situations also were created so that (יהושע) would be glorified.

"That it might be fulfilled which was spoken by Esaias the prophet, saying, Himself took our infirmities, and bare our sicknesses." (Matthew 8:17)
<19> That is what a Satguru does. He takes the karma of his disciples. He forgives a person's previous sins. The person becomes sinless and if he creates devotion for his teacher and God, he will be guided to the truth.

"Now when Esa saw great multitudes about him, he gave commandment to depart unto the other side." (Matthew 8:18)

"And a certain scribe came, and said unto him, Master, I will follow thee whithersoever thou goest." (Matthew 8:19)

"And Esa saith unto him, The foxes have holes, and the birds of the air have nests; but the Son of man hath not where to lay his head." (Matthew 8:20)
<20> A person who was not ready but had the desire to follow him came to Christ. But he discouraged this man and told him that it is a very hard path. It requires detachment from all earthly bondage and giving up everything before one can even begin to follow Christ.

"And another of his disciples said unto him, Lord, suffer me first to go and bury my father." (Matthew 8:21)

"But Esa said unto him, Follow me; and let the dead bury their dead." (Matthew 8:22)
<21> Only those who are spiritually dead become attached to the body of a physically dead person, because they think they are their bodies. Those who know they never die and that the Soul is immortal do not see anything dead. So only the dead bury the dead.
<22> Also it means not to be attached to anything that hinders the person in his goal of be(com)ing Divine. One way to reach this goal is to follow a true spiritual teacher, Christ, "follow me." Also it means, not to be concerned with the present happenings too much, but always keep the ultimate goal or vision in mind!

"And when he was entered into a ship, his disciples followed him." (Matthew 8:23)

"And, behold, there arose a great tempest in the sea, insomuch that the ship was covered with the waves: but he was asleep." (Matthew 8:24)
<23> These verses can be viewed as a symbol of the confusion of his disciples. Because Christ left them alone for awhile, "he was asleep," the doubt and many thoughts (mind) came to them, "a great tempest." They felt that they were lost, "the ship was covered with the waves."

"And his disciples came to him, and awoke him, saying, Lord, save us: we perish." (Matthew 8:25)

<24> The disciples went to him as their refuge to be saved from this turbulent sea.

"And he saith unto them, Why are ye fearful, O ye of little faith? Then he arose, and rebuked the winds and the sea; and there was a great calm." (Matthew 8:26)

<25> Christ said that this fear and tribulation was happening to them because of their little faith. If they had faith, the doubt would not dare to enter into their consciousnesses. So his spirit of truth arose and calmed his disciples by guiding them to the understanding, and then a great peace came to them.

"But the men marvelled, saying, What manner of man is this, that even the winds and the sea obey him!" (Matthew 8:27)

<26> They marvelled at how he could calm their turbulent minds, and realized that without a Savior it is not possible to overcome this restlessness and feel the peace of mind.

"And when he was come to the other side into the country of the Gergesenes, there met him two possessed with devils, coming out of the tombs, exceeding fierce, so that no man might pass by that way." (Matthew 8:28)

"And, behold, they cried out, saying, What have we to do with thee, Esa, thou Son of God? art thou come hither to torment us before the time?" (Matthew 8:29)

<27> Those forces which are used to punish a person with bad karmas (sins) from previous lives are to remain in the person until a due time. But Christ with his power to forgive sins (bad karmas or samskaras) could take these away from the person before the time is due, "torment us before the time."

"And there was a good way off from them an herd of many swine feeding." (Matthew 8:30)

"So the devils besought him, saying, If thou cast us out, suffer us to go away into the herd of swine." (Matthew 8:31)

"And he said unto them, Go. And when they were come out, they went into the herd of swine: and, behold, the whole herd of swine ran violently down a steep place into the sea, and perished in the waters." (Matthew 8:32)

<28> There are torments which animals cannot withstand but men can endure and continue to live.

"And they that kept them fled, and went their ways into the city, and told every thing, and what was befallen to the possessed of the devils." (Matthew 8:33)

"And, behold, the whole city came out to meet Esa: and when they saw him, they besought him that he would depart out of their coasts." (Matthew 8:34)

<29> The people could not understand and became very afraid of him. So instead of seeing his light and trying to realize him as an Avatar, they wished him to leave them alone in their ignorance and depart from them.

Tablet Thirteen

Chapter 9

"And he entered into a ship, and passed over, and came into his own city." (Matthew 9:1)

"And, behold, they brought to him a man sick of the palsy, lying on a bed: and Esa seeing their faith said unto the sick of the palsy; Son, be of good cheer; thy sins be forgiven thee." (Matthew 9:2)

<1> It was the Law of Karma and the sins (samskaras) which were done by this person in his previous lifetimes which caused him to

be tormented by the palsy. In other words, he was being punished for sins done in his previous lifetimes.

<2> In order to heal him, Christ forgave his samskaras (sins). Therefore, his samskaras would be dissolved, the cause of his sickness would no longer be present, and he would be healed. That is why Christ said, "thy sins be forgiven thee" – not your ancestors' but of "thee."

"And, behold, certain of the scribes said within themselves, This man blasphemeth." (Matthew 9:3)

<3> But the people could not understand the Law of Karma and looked at Christ as a regular person, not as the son of God who is in Pure Consciousness as the Father, and can do whatever the Father can (with His allowance). That is why even the scribes who were supposed to be the most learned were ignorant of these facts and thought he was blaspheming, because he put himself equal with God. <4> The scribes thought that God is the only Being who can forgive. They did not know that the son of God, with His permission, can do whatever the Father can.

"And Esa knowing their thoughts said, Wherefore think ye evil in your hearts?" (Matthew 9:4)

"For whether is easier, to say, Thy sins be forgiven thee; or to say, Arise, and walk?" (Matthew 9:5)

<5> Esa knew their thoughts, so he asked them which one is better: To do the miracles without letting it be known what is the cause of the sickness and suffering (which is sin), "Arise, and walk;" or to do the miracles and at the same time show the reason the suffering is there and how it can be cured (by the sin being forgiven by the Lord, and also by repentance and refraining from repeating it), "thy sins be forgiven thee."

<6> So sin is disobedience of the Lord's Laws and is the source of suffering individually or collectively.

"But that ye may know that the Son of man hath power on earth to forgive sins, (then saith he to the sick of the palsy,) Arise, take up thy bed, and go unto thine house." (Matthew 9:6)

"And he arose, and departed to his house." (Matthew 9:7)

<7> Esa, the son of man, was also the son of God as a god-man (Avatar, in Pure Consciousness) and if God willed, he could forgive sins. So he commanded that the sick man arise and go, which is the same as forgiving his sins. The man did this, so again it is shown that the son of God can forgive sins.

"But when the multitudes saw it, they marvelled, and glorified God, which had given such power unto men." (Matthew 9:8)

<8> But people marvelled at how these miracles were possible. When they saw these things happen which do not occur in everyday life, they glorified the Lord. <9> However, if people would just be more considerate to know God and try to see His miracles, they would see them in everything. <10> All of creation and the fact that they are here and alive, are miracles.

"And as Esa passed forth from thence, he saw a man, named Matthew, sitting at the receipt of custom: and he saith unto him, Follow me. And he arose, and followed him." (Matthew 9:9)

<11> Christ called another disciple who was so ready to accept him that only being told "follow me" was enough to make him leave everything and follow him.

"And it came to pass, as Esa sat at meat in the house, behold, many publicans and sinners came and sat down with him and his disciples." (Matthew 9:10)

"And when the Pharisees saw it, they said unto his disciples, Why eateth your Master with publicans and sinners?" (Matthew 9:11)

"But when Esa heard that, he said unto them, They that be whole need not a physician, but they that are sick." (Matthew 9:12)

"But go ye and learn what that meaneth, I will have mercy, and not sacrifice: for I am not come to call the righteous, but sinners to repentance." (Matthew 9:13)

<12> When a person is healthy, he does not go to a doctor and does not even think about one. But when he is sick, then he needs a doctor. <13> Likewise, it is the sinners who need a Savior.

<14> Also as long as a sick person does not believe he is sick, he does not go to the doctor. But when he realizes he is sick, then he seeks medical care. That is also true about the human. As long as they think they are not sinners (are not ignorant), they do not feel they need a Savior who can take them away from ignorance to the light (knowledge).

<15> That is why the publicans and sinners went to Christ to hear his words, but the scribes and Pharisees who also were ignorant but unaware of it, did not go to him. They had created a big false ego so they could not see the light in Christ.

<16> Also, many would do much sacrifice and go through different penances but did not have any mercy toward other humans. That is why Christ said, "I will have mercy, and not sacrifice." That is, the goal of sacrifice and penance, etc., is to become merciful toward the lost souls and try to help them out of ignorance, not to forsake the society and become an escapist.

"Then came to him the disciples of John, saying, Why do we and the Pharisees fast oft, but thy disciples fast not?" (Matthew 9:14)

<17> Here we can see that the followers of John who would do much fasting and penance, came to him and asked him why his disciples did not fast and do all those similar types of sacrifices.

<18> But Christ was trying to make a point that the goal of the life is to be(come) Divine (merciful), not to fast or sacrifice from ignorance. Those Divine attributes should be created which are manifested through a realized person and show God's qualities.

"And Esa said unto them, Can the children of the bridechamber mourn, as long as the bridegroom is with them? but the days will come, when the bridegroom shall be taken from them, and then shall they fast." (Matthew 9:15)

<19> Christ is not against fasting, but he had not come to teach penance and fasting. These practices have their place in spiritual progress. He had come to teach mercy and love towards others. <20> Without these virtues, other rituals and disciplinary acts are worthless.

"No man putteth a piece of new cloth unto an old garment, for that which is put in to fill it up taketh from the garment, and the rent is made worse." (Matthew 9:16)

"Neither do men put new wine into old bottles [skins]: else the bottles [skins] break, and the wine runneth out, and the bottles [skins] perish: but they put new wine into new bottles [skins], and both are preserved." (Matthew 9:17)

<21> The old truths have already been given to humanity by many Great Souls and Prophets. But Christ had something to add to them. He brought a new teaching. If he taught the same things as the people before him, what difference is there between he and them?

<22> He did not come to abolish the old teachings but to bring something new which could not be put in the old skins. However, with adding these new teachings to the old, a new wine will be created which will reveal a deeper truth.

COMMENTARIES ON ST. MATTHEW
Tablet Fourteen

"While he spake these things unto them, behold, there came a certain ruler, and worshipped him, saying, My daughter is even now dead: but come and lay thy hand upon her, and she shall live." (Matthew 9:18)

"And Esa arose, and followed him, and so did his disciples." (Matthew 9:19)

"And, behold, a woman, which was diseased with an issue of blood twelve years, came behind him, and touched the hem of his garment:" (Matthew 9:20)

"For she said within herself, If I may but touch his garment, I shall be whole." (Matthew 9:21)

"But Esa turned him about, and when he saw her, he said, Daughter, be of good comfort; thy faith hath made thee whole. And the woman was made whole from that hour." (Matthew 9:22)

<1> The prayers, repentances, and right requests will be granted when they are done with intense faith. When she touched Esa's hem, the healing power was moved from Esa to her. That is how he realized she had desired to be healed, by the touch of his garment.

"And when Esa came into the ruler's house, and saw the minstrels and the people making a noise," (Matthew 9:23)

"He said unto them, Give place: for the maid is not dead, but sleepeth. And they laughed him to scorn." (Matthew 9:24)

<2> In fact, death is nothing but a permanent sleep.

"But when the people were put forth, he went in, and took her by the hand, and the maid arose." (Matthew 9:25)

"And the fame hereof went abroad into all that land." (Matthew 9:26)

<3> Again here he became famous for his miracles, not for his teachings.

"And when Esa departed thence, two blind men followed him, crying, and saying, Thou son of David, have mercy on us." (Matthew 9:27)

"And when he was come into the house, the blind men came to him: and Esa saith unto them, Believe ye that I am able to do this? They said unto him, Yea, Lord." (Matthew 9:28)

"Then touched he their eyes, saying, According to your faith be it unto you." (Matthew 9:29)

"And their eyes were opened; and Esa straitly charged them, saying, See that no man know it." (Matthew 9:30)

<4> Again, it will be done to you according to your faith. The slightest doubt will block the cosmic power from reaching you.

<5> Esa was doing these things so that they might believe that he was saying the truth, and they might understand his teachings. But people wanted the miracles. After they received them, they would go out and make him famous for his miracles, which was not important to him. That is why he told the people, "See that no man know it."

<6> As his fame of being the person who can do miracles spread out and people believed that he could do anything he wanted to do, they expected him to do everything for them. <7> They did not seek the truth of his teachings but accepted him as the Savior, to fulfill their desires, but not as the one who has come to teach them the truth and save them from ignorance (save their Souls).

<8> To believe in this kind of Savior (one who will do all things for us) blocks the way of the person in putting forth any effort and endeavor to find the truth himself. He will not ask, knock, and search. So the very Savior becomes an obstacle in his way.

"But they, when they were departed, spread abroad his fame in all that country." (Matthew 9:31)

<9> They did not listen to him but followed their own wishes that all know they were healed by Esa. Again they emphasized his miracles.

"As they went out, behold, they brought to him a dumb man possessed with a devil." (Matthew 9:32)

"And when the devil was cast out, the dumb spake: and the multitudes marvelled, saying, It was never so seen in Israel." (Matthew 9:33)

"But the Pharisees said, He casteth out devils through the prince of the devils." (Matthew 9:34)

<10> People marvelled at how he did these things, but Christ said, "If you have faith even as a mustard seed you can do even greater things than I do." (Matthew 17:20).

<11> Also those spiritual leaders with little faith and much ignorance (Pharisees) could not understand and were trying to create false propaganda against him. They spread that he cast out devils (the samskaras) by the permission of satan, the prince of the devils. So through the ignorant people, they tried to destroy him.

"And Esa went about all the cities and villages, teaching in their synagogues, and preaching the gospel of the kingdom, and healing every sickness and every disease among the people." (Matthew 9:35)

<12> That is what the true purpose of the coming of Christ was, to teach "the gospel of the kingdom." In order to win the faith of the escapists, he also healed their diseases and did miracles. <13> However, his teachings are more important than his miracles.

"But when he saw the multitudes, he was moved with compassion on them, because they fainted, and were scattered abroad, as sheep having no shepherd." (Matthew 9:36)

"Then saith he unto his disciples, The harvest truly is plenteous, but the labourers are few;" (Matthew 9:37)

"Pray ye therefore the Lord of the harvest, that he will send forth labourers into his harvest." (Matthew 9:38)

<14> Christ looked and saw how people were lost like sheep with no shepherd. But he was alone and few could understand him, and even fewer were able to depart and teach the truth he was trying to spread. That is why he felt such a compassion toward the people who needed to be guided, yet very few could do that, "the labourers are few."

<15> That is why humanity should have waited, so that through many lifetimes of progress there would be more labourers ready to guide others to the truth, "that he will send forth labourers into his harvest." <16> The harvest time is **NOW**. Many labourers will be ready to guide the sheep to the goal of the life.

Tablet Fifteen

Chapter 10

"And when he had called unto him his twelve disciples, he gave them power against unclean spirits, to cast them out, and to heal all manner of sickness and all manner of disease." (Matthew 10:1)

<1> His disciples were ready to take the responsibility of becoming laborers for the Lord, so he gave them power and knowledge to go and spread his preaching of the Kingdom.

"Now the names of the twelve apostles are these; The first, Simon, who is called Peter, and Andrew his brother; James the son of Zebedee, and John his brother;" (Matthew 10:2)

"Philip, and Bartholomew; Thomas, and Matthew the publican; James the son of Alphaeus, and Lebbaeus, whose surname was Thaddaeus;" (Matthew 10:3)

"Simon the Canaanite, and Judas Iscariot, who also betrayed him." (Matthew 10:4)

<2> They were all equal and there was no discrimination. Only those disciples who were more sincere and would do the Will of the Father more intensely were greater, regardless of their background.

"These twelve Esa sent forth, and commanded them, saying, Go not into the way of the Gentiles, and into any city of the Samaritans enter ye not:" (Matthew 10:5)

"But go rather to the lost sheep of the house of Israel." (Matthew 10:6)

<3> "The House of Israel" is only a part of the Children of Israel. The Children of Israel were divided into two nations as the House of Judah (Jews) and the House of Israel (the ten lost tribes). <4> The House of Israel which was ten tribes, was kept captive and carried away by the Assyrians, and their territories (the Northern Kingdom) were given to other people. These ten lost tribes apparently never came back to their lands.

<5> But as it is described in the book Children of Abram (Abraham), All Prophecies Are Fulfilled, these ten tribes scattered north and northwest from their original land. Indeed Christ had come to gather these people as prophesied by Jacob that the Messiah is one who will gather the people of Israel, "until Shiloh [Messiah] come; and unto him shall the gathering of the people be."

<6> Christ had not come to gather the Jews (House of Judah) but "the lost sheep of the house of Israel." For more detail, read Children of Abram (Abraham), All Prophecies Are Fulfilled.

"And as ye go, preach, saying, The kingdom of heaven is at hand." (Matthew 10:7)

"Heal the sick, cleanse the lepers, raise the dead, cast out devils: freely ye have received, freely give." (Matthew 10:8)

<7> He taught his disciples to follow his example, preach his teaching, and do the healing.

"Provide neither gold, nor silver, nor brass in your purses," (Matthew 10:9)

"Nor scrip for your journey, neither two coats, neither shoes, nor yet staves: for the workman is worthy of his meat." (Matthew 10:10)

"And into whatsoever city or town ye shall enter, enquire who in it is worthy; and there abide till ye go thence." (Matthew 10:11)

"And when ye come into an house, salute it." (Matthew 10:12)

"And if the house be worthy, let your peace come upon it: but if it be not worthy, let your peace return to you." (Matthew 10:13)

"And whosoever shall not receive you, nor hear your words, when ye depart out of that house or city, shake off the dust of your feet." (Matthew 10:14)

"Verily I say unto you, It shall be more tolerable for the land of Sodom and Gomorrha in the day of judgment, than for that city." (Matthew 10:15)

<8> These were instructions given by Esa to his disciples to go preach and heal. In fact this should be the lifestyle of those who become renunciates (sannyasins).

"Behold, I send you forth as sheep in the midst of wolves: be ye therefore wise as serpents, and harmless as doves." (Matthew 10:16)

<9> The serpent is wisdom consciousness, which is the spiritual force latently asleep at the end of the spinal cord. In Sanskrit it is called the kundalini. <10> When this spiritual force is asleep there is not wisdom present in man and he is a rational animal. But when

it is risen to the higher self (fourth chakra and up), it becomes wisdom.

<11> It is the same serpent which was directed for satisfaction of the lower self and became temptation to the woman (Eve). She ate of the tree of knowledge and gave man also to eat of it. **<12>** But when this spiritual force, by His Grace, is directed to the higher self, a great wisdom will be gained.

"But beware of men: for they will deliver you up to the councils, and they will scourge you in their synagogues;" (Matthew 10:17)

"And ye shall be brought before governors and kings for my sake, for a testimony against them and the Gentiles." (Matthew 10:18)

"But when they deliver you up, take no thought how or what ye shall speak: for it shall be given you in that same hour what ye shall speak." (Matthew 10:19)

<13> Let the Lord do it through you, and glorify Him by knowing it is He who is doing great work through you.

"For it is not ye that speak, but the Spirit of your Father which speaketh in you." (Matthew 10:20)

<14> It is He who does it through you. Also if you are not pure enough, your ego will come in and you will learn your impurities, so go ahead anyway.

"And the brother shall deliver up the brother to death, and the father the child: and the children shall rise up against their parents, and cause them to be put to death." (Matthew 10:21)

"And ye shall be hated of all men for my name's sake: but he that endureth to the end shall be saved." (Matthew 10:22)

<15> People do not want to hear the truth (His Name, Pure Consciousness) and will hate whoever tells them the truth. But those who do not fail and keep the truth to the end will be saved. **<16>** He does not say, "I will save you." He says, "I give you the truth. By following It, you will be set free."

Tablet Sixteen

"But when they persecute you in this city, flee ye into another: for verily I say unto you, Ye shall not have gone over the cities of Israel, till the Son of man be come." (Matthew 10:23)

"The disciple is not above his master, nor the servant above his lord." (Matthew 10:24)

"It is enough for the disciple that he be as his master, and the servant as his lord. If they have called the master of the house Beelzebub, how much more shall they call them of his household?" (Matthew 10:25)

<1> They called Christ the prince of the devils (Beelzebub). So they would call his disciples names also and would persecute them for his sake. **<2>** He had not committed any crime. He had only said the truth.

"Fear them not therefore: for there is nothing covered, that shall not be revealed; and hid, that shall not be known." (Matthew 10:26)

<3> Be of good cheer because the truth will prevail eventually.

"What I tell you in darkness, that speak ye in light: and what ye hear in the ear, that preach ye upon the housetops." (Matthew 10:27)

<4> It is true that you are ignorant but if you let Him speak through you, you will say the truth "in darkness, that speak ye in light," and you will preach the truth openly, "upon the housetops."

"And fear not them which kill the body, but are not able to kill the soul: but rather fear him which is able to destroy both soul and body in hell." (Matthew 10:28)

<5> Fear the power of the tama guna in the universe (God) which can kill the Soul and body through the power of ignorance (hell). Man cannot kill the Soul, because as it is said in the Bhagavad-Gita, the sword cannot touch it (B.G. 2:11).

"Are not two sparrows sold for a farthing? and one of them shall not fall on the ground without your Father." (Matthew 10:29)

"But the very hairs of your head are all numbered." (Matthew 10:30)

"Fear ye not therefore, ye are of more value than many sparrows." (Matthew 10:31)
<6> Know that all is done by Him and put your trust in Him, because He is more concerned about you than many other things in the universe.

"Whosoever therefore shall confess me before men, him will I confess also before my Father which is in heaven." (Matthew 10:32)

"But whosoever shall deny me before men, him will I also deny before my Father which is in heaven." (Matthew 10:33)
<7> Whoever overcomes the fear of men, stands for truth, and confesses the truth without fear, will be saved. But those who are ashamed of saying the truth because of the fear of men will be denied entering heaven.
<8> Only those who overcome this world and all its fears will find the way. Those who are even slightly attached to it will be lost in it.

"Think not that I am come to send peace on earth: I come not to send peace, but a sword." (Matthew 10:34)
<9> If people truly follow Christ's teachings and come to Pure Consciousness, there will be no choice but to have a great battle between those who have reached the truth and those who follow false teachings. <10> That is the reason why each time an Avatar comes unto the world there will be a great tribulation ("sword") for purification of the world, and many will be saved through it. As it is explained in Revelation of The Revelation, after each Prophet and/or religion in the **Eternal Divine Path**, great upheavals come to the earth, "...I come not to send peace, but a sword."

"For I am come to set a man at variance against his father, and the daughter against her mother, and the daughter in law against her mother in law." (Matthew 10:35)

"And a man's foes shall be they of his own household." (Matthew 10:36)
<11> These things all happen when a new era is coming, and is called tribulation.

"He that loveth father or mother more than me is not worthy of me: and he that loveth son or daughter more than me is not worthy of me." (Matthew 10:37)

"And he that taketh not his cross, and followeth after me, is not worthy of me." (Matthew 10:38)

"He that findeth his life shall lose it: and he that loseth his life for my sake shall find it." (Matthew 10:39)
<12> Those who want to be born again and follow the truth (the Messiah) should crucify their false egos. Their false egos should die before they can be born again to their higher selves. To achieve this a man should overcome this world and love the truth more than anything else. He should take his cross (sacrifice) and follow the truth, and in the process crucify his lower nature (false ego). <13> Whoever finds his life in his lower nature will lose being born again, and whoever loses his false ego will find the everlasting life and will be born again.

"He that receiveth you receiveth me, and he that receiveth me receiveth him that sent me." (Matthew 10:40)

"He that receiveth a prophet in the name of a prophet shall receive a prophet's reward; and he that receiveth a righteous man in the name of a righteous man shall receive a righteous man's reward." (Matthew 10:41)

<14> Those who receive disciples of a person in Pure Consciousness (son of God) also receive the son, and whoever receives the son, receives the Father.

<15> A person who can see a Prophet and realize his Divinity, is at the same consciousness as the Prophet. This is true about all people. Those who see the truth and righteousness in others are at the same level as they.

<16> The man whose mind is crude cannot see the Light.

"And whosoever shall give to drink unto one of these little ones a cup of cold water only in the name of a disciple, verily I say unto you, he shall in no wise lose his reward." (Matthew 10:42)

<17> When a service is done with a humble manner, for the sake of serving the Lord, "in the name of a disciple," he shall "in no wise lose his reward."

<18> Serve God through serving His creation, and you can be sure that you are serving Him. This is a path to salvation.

Tablet Seventeen

Chapter 11

"And it came to pass, when Esa had made an end of commanding his twelve disciples, he departed thence to teach and to preach in their cities." (Matthew 11:1)

<1> Christ himself started to teach also, but to the people of "their cities" (Jews).

"Now when John had heard in the prison the works of Christ, he sent two of his disciples," (Matthew 11:2)

"And said unto him, Art thou he that should come, or do we look for another?" (Matthew 11:3)

"Esa answered and said unto them, Go and shew John again those things which ye do hear and see:" (Matthew 11:4)

"The blind receive their sight, and the lame walk, the lepers are cleansed, and the deaf hear, the dead are raised up, and the poor have the gospel preached to them." (Matthew 11:5)

<2> John recognized Esa as the Anointed One when he came to John to be baptized (Matthew 3:13-15). In that moment a sudden realization came to John to realize Esa. But later on when many things happened, John lost that high state of realization and doubt came to him about Esa.

<3> That is why he had sent his disciples to make sure that Esa is the one for whom they were waiting. Esa said that he was the one.

"And blessed is he, whosoever shall not be offended in me." (Matthew 11:6)

<4> Blessed is he who creates no doubt about the One (Christ) who brings the truth for humanity, and is not offended in the truth he reveals.

"And as they departed, Esa began to say unto the multitudes concerning John, What went ye out into the wilderness to see? A reed shaken with the wind?" (Matthew 11:7)

"But what went ye out to see? A man clothed in soft raiment? behold, they that wear soft clothing are in king's houses." (Matthew 11:8)

"But what went ye out for to see? A prophet? yea, I say unto you, and more than a prophet." (Matthew 11:9)

"For this is he, of whom it is written, Behold, I send my messenger before thy face, which shall prepare thy way before thee." (Matthew 11:10)

<5> John was not only a Prophet but he was a great Prophet. He was one of those whose coming had been prophesied.

"Verily I say unto you, Among them that are born of women there hath not risen a greater than John the Baptist: notwithstanding he that is least in the kingdom of heaven is greater than he." (Matthew 11:11)

<6> Whoever is most humble is greatest.

"And from the days of John the Baptist until now the kingdom of heaven suffereth violence, and the violent take it by force." (Matthew 11:12)

"For all the prophets and the law prophesied until John." (Matthew 11:13)

<7> John and his preaching were violently opposed. But this preaching of the Kingdom Of Heaven was given by all the Prophets until John. In fact the very reason for choosing Abram (Abraham) and the Hebrews was so they would establish the Kingdom Of Heaven On Earth, and the whole Old Testament is about God's struggle with the human kings to walk in His Ways.

"And if ye will receive it, this is Elias, which was for to come." (Matthew 11:14)

<8> Christ said, "If you are willing to accept it, John is the reincarnation of Elias which all were waiting to come and prepare the way." <9> As it is said, he went to preach to the Jews. Now he started to attack them directly to prepare them so that they would become bitter, so eventually crucify him, and the prophecies about him would be fulfilled.

"He that hath ears to hear, let him hear." (Matthew 11:15)

<10> Those who have opened their spiritual eyes and are ready to receive the truth will hear and understand these things to be true.

"But whereunto shall I liken this generation? It is like unto children sitting in the markets, and calling unto their fellows," (Matthew 11:16)

"And saying, We have piped unto you, and ye have not danced; we have mourned unto you, and ye have not lamented." (Matthew 11:17)

"For John came neither eating nor drinking, and they say, He hath a devil." (Matthew 11:18)

"The Son of man came eating and drinking, and they say, Behold a man gluttonous, and a winebibber, a friend of publicans and sinners. But wisdom is justified of her children." (Matthew 11:19)

<11> The human always tries to find fault in those who say the truth, so they can justify themselves why they will not follow the one who says the truth. It has been evident all through history. <12> People persecute the Prophets and Seers because they want to stay in their lower natures and not change and be born into their higher selves.

<13> That is why when John came, fasted, wore hard clothes, and ate simple food, they said he had a devil. Then Christ came and did the opposite, eating, drinking, and instead of going into the desert, he stayed in the cities. Then they said he was a friend of the publicans, a winebibber, and gluttonous. <14> It does not matter what the Prophet does. Those who are blind and deaf will not hear him, because they create so many concepts and pay attention to so many unimportant things that they forget about the main reason for which he had come, "the message."

<15> However, God (wisdom) will justify their actions. They will go through so much suffering that they will have no choice but to eventually become awakened into truth.

"Then began he to upbraid the cities wherein most of his mighty works were done, because they repented not:" (Matthew 11:20)

<16> He did so many mighty works and miracles but they would not repent. They either wanted more miracles, because only greedy people are attracted to the person who does miracles, or they accused him of doing them by the power of the devil. <17> Also man forgets miracles, and they become myths. That is why in the era to come, each person should become a priest and seek the truth. Each man should be(come) Divine and make others Divine also.

"Woe unto thee, Chorazin! woe unto thee, Bethsaida! for if the mighty works, which were done in you, had been done in Tyre and Sidon, they would have repented long ago in sackcloth and ashes." (Matthew 11:21)

"But I say unto you, It shall be more tolerable for Tyre and Sidon at the day of judgment, than for you." (Matthew 11:22)

"And thou, Capernaum, which art exalted unto heaven, shalt be brought down to hell: for if the mighty works, which have been done in thee, had been done in Sodom, it would have remained until this day." (Matthew 11:23)

"But I say unto you, That it shall be more tolerable for the land of Sodom, in the day of judgment, than for thee." (Matthew 11:24)

<18> He became very unhappy about the people. He had done so many miracles and mighty works for them, but they took the miracles and healing without repenting and following his teachings. That is why he angrily cursed them.

"At that time Esa answered and said, I thank thee, O Father, Lord of heaven and earth, because thou hast hid these things from the wise and prudent, and hast revealed them unto babes." (Matthew 11:25)

"Even so, Father: for so it seemed good in thy sight." (Matthew 11:26)

<19> Those who think they are wise and prudent have many concepts and expectations which will close their eyes to the truth. <20> Only simple people and the pure in heart, "babes," can understand these things.

<21> Christ surrendered (the result) to the situation because it was His Will to be this way, "for so it seemed good in thy sight."

"All things are delivered unto me of my Father: and no man knoweth the Son, but the Father; neither knoweth any man the Father, save the Son, and he to whomsoever the Son will reveal him." (Matthew 11:27)

<22> God has given all knowledge and power to Christ, who is the son of God (Pure Consciousness). <23> No man knows the Father but those who have reached Pure Consciousness (son) and those who see God's qualities through the son, "and he to whomsoever the Son will reveal him."

"Come unto me, all ye that labour and are heavy laden, and I will give you rest." (Matthew 11:28)

"Take my yoke upon you, and learn of me; for I am meek and lowly in heart: and ye shall find rest unto your souls." (Matthew 11:29)

"For my yoke is easy, and my burden is light." (Matthew 11:30)

<24> In other words, "I have peace and I can give it to those who are looking for it. I have no pride of the false ego. I will accept you as you are, and I will give to you from the fountain of life so that you will thirst no more, and will bring you to the peace of God."

<25> The burden of life is heavy because of ignorance. When a person goes to God and sees that most of his problems in reality are not problems at all but are there because he created them himself by his unnecessary attachments, desires, and greed, then he will simplify his life and find the peace and truth in simplicity and simple things. <26> He will surrender to the Lord, so his burden will be taken away or become light, as the burden of all realized people is light, "my yoke is easy, and my burden is light."

Tablet Eighteen

Chapter 12

"At that time Esa went on the Sabbath day through the corn; and his disciples were an hungred, and began to pluck the ears of corn, and to eat." (Matthew 12:1)

"But when the Pharisees saw it, they said unto him, Behold, thy disciples do that which is not lawful to do upon the sabbath day." (Matthew 12:2)

<1> The Pharisees had become so rigid in their beliefs that their laws had become a burden on themselves and others instead of a blessing. <2> This always happens in history. The intellectual spiritualists (intellect without intuition) create concepts and rigid interpretations of once blissful teachings of the Prophets. They cause them to be obstacles in the path of the human.

<3> The same rigidity also was created by the Brahmins in India, so much that the once joyful religions of the Aryans resulted in caste systems and the pessimistic philosophy of many branches in Hinduism that this world is entirely illusion and full of suffering. <4> This can be seen in all the old religions.

"But he said unto them, Have ye not read what David did, when he was an hungred, and they that were with him;" (Matthew 12:3)

"How he entered into the house of God, and did eat the shewbread, which was not lawful for him to eat, neither for them which were with him, but only for the priests?" (Matthew 12:4)

"Or have ye not read in the law, how that on the Sabbath days the priests in the temple profane the Sabbath, and are blameless?" (Matthew 12:5)

<5> Esa gave these incidents as an example of the flexibility of the Laws of God. All things depend upon the time, place, and people involved. <6> In the case of an emergency and when a person tries to do good (as Esa healed on the Sabbath), even the rules about the observation of the Sabbath can be relaxed.

<7> It does not say that David or the priest did a good thing in breaking the Laws of the Lord. But because it was urgent for them to do so, it was acceptable.

"But I say unto you, That in this place is one greater than the temple." (Matthew 12:6)

"But if ye had known what this meaneth, I will have mercy, and not sacrifice, ye would not have condemned the guiltless." (Matthew 12:7)

<8> "If you knew these things you would not have become so rigid and would not have so many vain desires for prestige and powers. <9> You would realize who I Am, 'greater than the temple,' would honor me and listen to my teachings. So you would receive my Grace and mercy, and then I would not have to sacrifice myself in order to awaken you and many others to the truth I am trying to reveal to you. Instead you would have received my mercy." <10> But they did not understand this and would condemn him, "the guiltless."

"For the Son of man is Lord even of the Sabbath day." (Matthew 12:8)

<11> The son of man, or he who is in Pure Consciousness (Christ Consciousness) in the body (man), is the truth. <12> By allowing his disciples to break their rigid, misunderstood laws, the concepts and bondage they have created for themselves and others would also be shattered. He is the Lord of the Sabbath.

"And when he was departed thence, he went into their synagogue:" (Matthew 12:9)

"And, behold, there was a man which had his hand withered. And they asked him, saying, Is it lawful to heal on the sabbath days? that they might accuse him." (Matthew 12:10)

"And he said unto them, What man shall there be among you, that shall have one sheep, and if it fall into a pit on the sabbath day, will he not lay hold on it, and lift it out?" (Matthew 12:11)

"How much then is a man better than a sheep? Wherefore it is lawful to do well on the Sabbath days." (Matthew 12:12)

<13> Therefore, good deeds and emergencies can be done anytime, even on the Sabbath.

"Then saith he to the man, Stretch forth thine hand. And he stretched it forth; and it was restored whole, like as the other." (Matthew 12:13)

<14> Esa healed the man, which was a good deed on that Sabbath.

"Then the Pharisees went out, and held a council against him, how they might destroy him." (Matthew 12:14)

<15> He said the truth which destroyed these rigid beliefs of the words of God, so the false egos of the Pharisees were hurt. Instead of listening to the truth and opening themselves to his words, they felt threatened and decided to destroy him. <16> But who can destroy the truth? The truth will eventually destroy the false.

"But when Esa knew it, he withdrew himself from thence: and great multitudes followed him, and he healed them all;" (Matthew 12:15)

<17> His time had not come yet, so he withdrew to be safe from their misdeeds.

"And charged them that they should not make him known:" (Matthew 12:16)

"That it might be fulfilled which was spoken by Esaias the prophet, saying," (Matthew 12:17)

"Behold my servant, whom I have chosen; my beloved, in whom my soul is well pleased: I will put my spirit upon him, and he shall shew judgment to the Gentiles." (Matthew 12:18)

<18> He rendered judgment on the Gentiles (intellectuals without intuition).

"He shall not strive, nor cry; neither shall any man hear his voice in the streets." (Matthew 12:19)

"A bruised reed shall he not break, and smoking flax shall he not quench, till he send forth judgment unto victory." (Matthew 12:20)

"And in his name shall the Gentiles trust." (Matthew 12:21)

<19> So with this, the prophecy of Esaias was fulfilled.

"Then was brought unto him one possessed with a devil, blind, and dumb: and he healed him, insomuch that the blind and dumb both spake and saw." (Matthew 12:22)

"And all the people were amazed, and said, Is not this the son of David?" (Matthew 12:23)

<20> Many realized his Messianic authority. They understood that he was the one who was prophesied to come as the son of David.

"But when the Pharisees heard it, they said, This fellow doth not cast out devils, but by Beelzebub the prince of the devils." (Matthew 12:24)

<21> But the Pharisees started a negative propaganda campaign against him. They said he received his power from satan, the prince of the devils.

"And Esa knew their thoughts, and said unto them, Every kingdom divided against itself is brought to desolation; and every city or house against itself shall not stand:" (Matthew 12:25)

"And if Satan cast out Satan, he is divided against himself; how shall then his kingdom stand?" (Matthew 12:26)

"And if I by Beelzebub cast out devils, by whom do your children cast them out? therefore they shall be your judges." (Matthew 12:27)

<22> A man cannot cast out the devil by the power of the prince of the devils (tama guna).

"But if I cast out devils by the Spirit of God, then the kingdom of God is come unto you." (Matthew 12:28)

<23> It can only be done by the Spirit of God (satva guna, The Holy Ghost) and then the truth of the universe will come to you (the Kingdom of God).

"Or else how can one enter into a strong man's house, and spoil his goods, except he first bind the strong man? and then he will spoil his house." (Matthew 12:29)

<24> If you want to take the power of the tama guna (devil) away from other people's Souls, first you should overcome it yourself (reach Pure Consciousness, take the beam out of your own eyes) and then, by the power of the satva guna (The Holy Ghost), you can take the tama guna from others.

"He that is not with me is against me; and he that gathereth not with me scattereth abroad." (Matthew 12:30)

<25> He who does not understand these truths and does not follow them ("me") will fall into ignorance and the grip of Maya. <26> "Then he will not be with me (truth) but with ignorance, which is against me. So he will not be gathered by me toward the Kingdom of God but will go away into the ocean of Maya, 'scattereth abroad'."

"Wherefore I say unto you, All manner of sin and blasphemy shall be forgiven unto men: but the blasphemy against the Holy Ghost shall not be forgiven unto them." (Matthew 12:31)

"And whosoever speaketh a word against the Son of man, it shall be forgiven him: but whosoever speaketh against the Holy Ghost, it shall not be forgiven him, neither in this world, neither in the world to come." (Matthew 12:32)

<27> Esa was using The Holy Ghost to heal the people's diseases (tama guna) and they called The Holy Ghost the prince of the devils. That is why he said they have made a great mistake by blaspheming against The Holy Grace, and they will not be forgiven for that.

Tablet Nineteen

"Either make the tree good, and his fruit good; or else make the tree corrupt, and his fruit corrupt: for the tree is known by his fruit." (Matthew 12:33)

<1> A man who does good is a good person, but a man who is evil cannot do good, unless he changes himself. <2> You know them by their fruit (action).

"O generation of vipers, how can ye, being evil, speak good things? for out of the abundance of the heart the mouth speaketh." (Matthew 12:34)

<3> Esa was telling them, "You who are evil and strive to gain the respect and attention of men instead of God, why should I expect you to speak good things and praise and glorify the Lord who has given such powers to man? <4> You cannot see good and say good things because your hearts (fourth chakra, sacred heart) are darkened (crudified), 'for out of the abundance of the heart the mouth speaketh.' That is why you say such evil things about me."

"A good man out of the good treasure of the heart bringeth forth good things: and an evil man out of the evil treasure bringeth forth evil things." (Matthew 12:35)

<5> From the heart comes actions and perceptions. "From your evil hearts, you see me as the devil. But if you had a pure heart, you would see me as I truly am and recognize my purity and beauty."

"But I say unto you, That every idle word that men shall speak, they shall give account thereof in the day of judgment." (Matthew 12:36)

"For by thy words thou shalt be justified, and by thy words thou shalt be condemned." (Matthew 12:37)

<6> As Esa said, the words come from the

heart. If the heart is darkened and evil, the words and also the action (fruit) will be evil. <7> So each man's words and actions represent his heart, and he will be judged accordingly.

"Then certain of the scribes and of the Pharisees answered, saying, Master, we would see a sign from thee." (Matthew 12:38)

"But he answered and said unto them, An evil and adulterous generation seeketh after a sign; and there shall no sign be given to it, but the sign of the prophet Jonas:" (Matthew 12:39)

<8> The people were asking for signs instead of listening to his teachings and truth. <9> Many signs were given before by many Prophets and still people did not believe in them, listen to their words, or follow the truths they revealed. <10> Esa came, performed many miracles, and taught them the truth, but still they were asking for a sign. <11> The false ego seeks all kinds of excuses to not see the truth.

<12> The only sign he gave them was "the sign of prophet Jonas."

"For as Jonas was three days and three nights in the whale's belly; so shall the Son of man be three days and three nights in the heart of the earth." (Matthew 12:40)

<13> This was the only sign he gave to them to witness as the sign of his authority. But even this sign has been distorted by the paganizers of Christianity in the Roman empire, after Christianity was accepted as the state religion.

<14> It is believed that he was crucified on Friday and rose on Sunday. However, study of the gospels shows that Christ was put in the cave ("heart of the earth") in the evening. <15> According to the belief of the majority, he was in the cave Friday night, Saturday during the day, and Saturday night, and rose on Sunday morning. This would mean that he was in the "heart of the earth" only two nights and one day. <16> So if we believe this (that he died on Friday night and rose Sunday morning), then Esa failed to fulfill the only sign he gave for his legitimacy.

<17> However, if he had been crucified on Friday and stayed in the cave for "three days and three nights," then he should have risen on Monday afternoon about the same time of day that he had been put into the earth.

<18> The truth is that Mary and her companions went to the cave where Esa was laid on that Sunday morning, and found it empty. That is because he had left it the evening before on Saturday afternoon around the same time when he was put inside the cave on the day he was crucified (later than the ninth hour of the day or three o'clock in the afternoon by our time standard). <19> Therefore he was taken to the cave on Wednesday before that Saturday, and he was in the "heart of the earth for three days and three nights." That is why those women who went to the cave the next Sunday morning did not find him there.

<20> This truth, like many other truths about Christ and his teaching, was changed after Christianity became the state religion of the Romans, with acceptance by the masses in great multitudes. They accepted the basic concepts of Christianity with Christ as the Savior, but they transformed it into a new religion with many flavors of their pagan religions, especially Mithraism.

<21> In fact, it was a part of the doctrine of Mithraism that a Savior from a virgin would come and all would be saved through him. So this part of the story of the birth of Christ matched their basic beliefs. <22> Also they injected their own festivals and holidays into the new religion. That is why most of the Christian religious holidays have pagan origins from the Roman religions.

<23> Sunday was the weekly holiday in which the sun god (Mithra) was worshipped, and Friday also was an exalted day. That is why a formula was created so that both Friday and Sunday stayed exalted as before. <24> Indeed the true Christians of the east and far west in England observed Hebrew Holy Days (their list is in Leviticus 23) until 700 A.D., and their Sabbath was on Saturday.

<25> Therefore, he fulfilled his promise

of staying in the heart of the earth for three nights and three days by being in the cave from Wednesday until Saturday afternoon, the Sabbath.

"The men of Ninevah shall rise in judgment with this generation, and shall condemn it: because they repented at the preaching of Jonas; and, behold, a greater than Jonas is here." (Matthew 12:41)

"The queen of the south shall rise up in the judgment with this generation, and shall condemn it: for she came from the uttermost parts of the earth to hear the wisdom of Solomon; and, behold, a greater than Solomon is here." (Matthew 12:42)

<26> Those who have strived to reach higher consciousness in many previous lifetimes will come back, hear his words, and rejoice in their truth. Eventually they will gain control of the Kingdom of God on earth and will render judgment on this rebellious generation. <27> That is because Christ, one who is in Pure Consciousness, who is greater than both Jonas and Solomon, was there and the people would not listen to the truth he revealed. So they have to go through much suffering until they become awakened.

Tablet Twenty

"When the unclean spirit is gone out of a man, he walketh through dry places, seeking rest, and findeth none." (Matthew 12:43)

"Then he saith, I will return into my house from whence I came out; and when he is come, he findeth it empty, swept, and garnished." (Matthew 12:44)

"Then goeth he, and taketh with himself seven other spirits more wicked than himself, and they enter in and dwell there: and the last state of that man is worse than the first. Even so shall it be also unto this wicked generation." (Matthew 12:45)

<1> When a Great Soul comes, he tries to cleanse men from their wickedness and tell them the truth so that they might progress. <2> Because of his teachings and presence, the faults and untruths will leave them for some time. But if they do not follow his teachings and instead become lost, they will go even further into Maya and ignorance. <3> The very teachings which were supposed to be a blessing become a block in their way of understanding and a burden on them. So "the last state of" them will be "worse than the first."

<4> That is exactly the message given in The Revelation, the last book of the Bible. After each Prophet comes and brings a truth, those people who fail to follow, search, and understand the truth and do not put away "the dead bodies" of the previous religions (Rev. 11:9) so that they might receive the new Prophet and teachings, will be struck with greater sufferings and tribulation, until they might become awakened through these tribulations.

<5> Furthermore, there are different kinds of healing processes: Physical, mental, and spiritual.

<6> When the spirit is cleansed by practices or through the understanding of God (truth) this is a spiritual healing. This is the highest kind of healing.

<7> When the truth behind the physical world is understood through mental faculties, the clarity of mind will occur. This is mental healing.

<8> When a problem in the body is corrected through healing energy, this is physical healing. This is the lowest healing.

<9> Healing can be done by the person himself or by another person. When a realized person helps another person to become realized also, it is a spiritual healing. <10> When a teacher or professor mentally helps a person to understand the laws in the manifested world, he is performing mental healing.

<11> When a healer lays hands on people or through massage therapy, reflexology, etc., and a person is healed, this is physical healing.

<12> In physical and mental healing, if the spirit is not cleansed and healed, the healing will not have a lasting effect. <13> In the case of mental development with spiritual inadequacy, that development will become dry intellect which will become a burden.

<14> In physical healing if spiritual and/or mental healing is not achieved, the healing will not last long and the problem will return. <15> In physical healing, when it is done through opening the spirit, because the aura of the person is opened but the person is not ready to handle this change, he might open himself to the forces which will make his state even worse than before. It is this state which the previous verses are referring to, "Then he saith, I will return into my house from whence I came out;..." and then "...taketh with himself seven other spirits more wicked ... : and the last state of that man is worse than the first...."

<16> That is why the healing should start from the spirit, then mental and then physical. If the spirit and mind are not healed, emphasis on physical healing might result in even greater spiritual problems.

<17> The physical, mental, and spiritual (emotional) bodies are interdependent. They should be healed and progress simultaneously to gain the greatest result. A balanced progress between them is the highest achievement.

<18> Scriptures and Holy Books of the Lord are healers of the spirit, as is **THOTH**.

"While he yet talked to the people, behold, his mother and his brethren stood without, desiring to speak with him." (Matthew 12:46)

"Then one said unto him, Behold, thy mother and thy brethren stand without, desiring to speak with thee." (Matthew 12:47)

"But he answered and said unto him that told him, Who is my mother? and who are my brethren?" (Matthew 12:48)

"And he stretched forth his hand toward his disciples, and said, Behold my mother and my brethren!" (Matthew 12:49)

"For whosoever shall do the will of my Father which is in heaven, the same is my brother, and sister, and mother." (Matthew 12:50)

<19> Parents are a tool through which we might receive a body. But in truth our true Father is God, our Mother is nature, our home is the universe, and those who do the Will of the Father are our brothers and sisters. <20> That is all there is for a true son of God. There are no other relationships left for him.

<21> Parents should be respected and helped if they truly need it. But if they are not doing the Will of the Father, a person does not have to be their slave. <22> This is especially true for those who want to dedicate their lives for God's purpose.

Tablet Twenty-One

Chapter 13

"The same day went Esa out of the house, and sat by the sea side." (Matthew 13:1)

"And great multitudes were gathered together unto him, so that he went into a ship, and sat; and the whole multitude stood on the shore." (Matthew 13:2)

"And he spake many things unto them in parables, saying, Behold, a sower went forth to sow;" (Matthew 13:3)

<1> He taught the multitudes in parables but he taught his disciples directly as in chapters 5 and 6.

"And when he sowed, some seeds fell by the way side, and the fowls came and devoured them up:" (Matthew 13:4)

"Some fell upon stony places, where they had not much earth: and forthwith they sprung up, because they had no deepness of earth:" (Matthew 13:5)

"And when the sun was up, they were scorched; and because they had no root, they withered away." (Matthew 13:6)

"And some fell among thorns; and the thorns sprung up, and choked them:" (Matthew 13:7)

"But other fell into good ground, and brought forth fruit, some an hundredfold, some sixtyfold, some thirtyfold." (Matthew 13:8)

<2> He gave this parable to the multitudes. Its meaning would be explained to his disciples later on.

"Who hath ears to hear, let him hear." (Matthew 13:9)

<3> Those who have opened their spirit (Heart) can understand the meanings behind his teachings.

"And the disciples came, and said unto him, Why speakest thou unto them in parables?" (Matthew 13:10)

"He answered and said unto them, Because it is given unto you to know the mysteries of the kingdom of heaven, but to them it is not given." (Matthew 13:11)

"For whosoever hath, to him shall be given, and he shall have more abundance: but whosoever hath not, from him shall be taken away even that he hath." (Matthew 13:12)

"Therefore speak I to them in parables: because they seeing see not; and hearing they hear not, neither do they understand." (Matthew 13:13)

"And in them is fulfilled the prophecy of Esaias, which saith, By hearing ye shall hear, and shall not understand; and seeing ye shall see, and shall not perceive:" (Matthew 13:14)

"For this people's heart is waxed gross, and their ears are dull of hearing, and their eyes they have closed; lest at any time they should see with their eyes, and hear with their ears, and should understand with their heart, and should be converted, and I should heal them." (Matthew 13:15)

"But blessed are your eyes, for they see: and your ears, for they hear." (Matthew 13:16)

"For verily I say unto you, That many prophets and righteous men have desired to see those things which ye see, and have not seen them; and to hear those things which ye hear, and have not heard them." (Matthew 13:17)

<4> His disciples wondered why he did not teach the multitudes as he taught them but instead spoke in parables to the masses. Esa answered that the multitudes were not ready to receive the true teachings or in other words, they were more interested in their mundane things. <5> They were attracted to his powers, healing, and their daily lives rather than to higher things. That is why "to them it is not given" to "know the mystery of the kingdom of heaven."

<6> However, those who seek, knock, and ask will gain some knowledge about God, "for whosoever hath," and to such a people even more knowledge will be given through the Universal Mind, "and he shall have more abundance." <7> But those who do not seek the truth will be drowned in the ocean of Maya (ignorance), "but whosoever hath not, from him shall be taken away even that he hath." So they become deaf, blind, and dumb to the understanding of the spiritual truth. They become spiritually dead.

<8> Therefore, as Esaias said, these people hear but do not understand, they see but cannot perceive, and so on. Because they have closed themselves to the truth, even the Messiah cannot save them. <9> But through these parables a seed was planted in their subconscious minds, so one day they might, "see with their eyes, and hear…", then they would be saved, "I shall heal them."

<10> Blessed are those who have opened themselves to receive the truth. That is why they see and hear things that great Prophets desired to see and hear but did not.

"Hear ye therefore the parable of the sower." (Matthew 13:18)

<11> Here Esa explained the meaning of the parable of the sower to his disciples.

"When any one heareth the word of the kingdom, and understandeth it not, then cometh the wicked one, and catcheth away that which was sown in his heart. This is he which received seed by the way side." (Matthew 13:19)

<12> He whose mind is crude will not understand the truth, because the truth will not even enter into it. So it is like the sower never planted the field and the seeds fall "by the way side." The tama guna ("the wicked one") causes them to be so ignorant that they will not receive the truth.

"But he that received the seed into stony places, the same is he that heareth the word, and anon with joy receiveth it;" (Matthew 13:20)

"Yet hath he not root in himself, but dureth for a while: for when tribulation or persecution ariseth because of the word, by and by he is offended." (Matthew 13:21)

<13> He who sees the truth and embraces it, but when he tries to follow it he falls, because of other people's disapproval (tribulation), is one who has no depth. So the seed cannot root deeply into him to protect him from failure. This type of person has a mind (ego) which is like the stone, with only a little soil on it to receive the seed. Therefore because there is not deep ground for it to take root, it will not last long and will be destroyed.

"He also that received seed among the thorns is he that heareth the word; and the care of this world, and the deceitfulness of riches, choke the word, and he becometh unfruitful." (Matthew 13:22)

<14> He who receives the truth, recognizes it, but has stronger love for the world, will forget the truth for this love of the world and Maya ("the deceitfulness of riches"). That is what is meant by "choke the word," The Truth.

"But he that received seed into the good ground is he that heareth the word, and understandeth it; which also beareth fruit, and bringeth forth, some an hundredfold, some sixty, some thirty." (Matthew 13:23)

<15> Yet those who are ready and are true seekers will receive truth in their prepared Souls (Elected Ones). Each of them will bring fruit according to their capacities.

"Another parable put he forth unto them, saying, The kingdom of heaven is likened unto a man which sowed good seed in his field:" (Matthew 13:24)

"But while man slept, his enemy came and sowed tares among the wheat, and went his way." (Matthew 13:25)

"But when the blade was sprung up, and brought forth fruit, then appeared the tares also." (Matthew 13:26)

"So the servants of the householder came and said unto him, Sir, didst not thou sow good seed in thy field? from whence then hath it tares?" (Matthew 13:27)

"He said unto them, An enemy hath done this. The servants said unto him, Wilt thou then that we go and gather them up?" (Matthew 13:28)

"But he said, Nay; lest while ye gather up the tares, ye root up also the wheat with them." (Matthew 13:29)

"Let both grow together until the harvest: and in the time of harvest I will say to the reapers, Gather ye together first the tares, and bind them in bundles to burn them: but gather the wheat into my barn." (Matthew 13:30)

<16> Those who go to the ocean of Maya will be drawn further in the depths of ignorance, "…bind them in bundles to burn." <17> But those who go toward Him, long for truth, and overcome Maya, will reach Pure Consciousness, "but gather the wheat into my barn."

"Another parable put he forth unto them, saying, The kingdom of heaven is like to a grain of mustard seed, which a man took, and sowed in his field:" (Matthew 13:31)

"Which indeed is the least of all seeds: but when it is grown, it is the greatest among herbs, and becometh a tree, so that the birds of the air come and lodge in the branches thereof." (Matthew 13:32)
<18> Those who open themselves to the truth and/or receive the light of truth even as little as the size of a mustard seed, will have that little truth grow in them as a great light and they will become the Savior of many because of their light, "so that the birds of the air come and lodge in the branches thereof."

"Another parable spake he unto them; The kingdom of heaven is like unto leaven, which a woman took, and hid in three measures of meal, till the whole was leavened." (Matthew 13:33)

<19> Those who reach Pure Consciousness, "leaven," will help the whole universe to reach the same, "till the whole was leavened."

"All these things spake Esa unto the multitude in parables; and without a parable spake he not unto them:" (Matthew 13:34)
<20> He only spoke to the multitudes in parables because they were dead (ignorant). **But it is amazing that with all these examples that understanding the truth is hard, still so many claim they know the truth!**

"That it might be fulfilled which was spoken by the prophet, saying, I will open my mouth in parables; I will utter things which have been kept secret from the foundation of the world." (Matthew 13:35)
<21> Esa would utter the mysteries of God in parables, "which have been kept secret from the foundation of the world." <22> But the same mysteries will be revealed by the seventh Angel without putting them in parables, "But in the days of the voice of the seventh angel, … the mystery of God should be finished, as he hath declared to his servants the prophets." (Rev. 10:7).

Tablet Twenty-Two

"Then Esa sent the multitude away, and went into the house: and his disciples came unto him, saying, Declare unto us the parable of the tares of the field." (Matthew 13:36)

"He answered and said unto them, He that soweth the good seed is the Son of man;" (Matthew 13:37)

"The field is the world; the good seed are the children of the kingdom; but the tares are the children of the wicked one;" (Matthew 13:38)

"The enemy that sowed them is the devil; the harvest is the end of the world; and the reapers are the angels." (Matthew 13:39)

"As therefore the tares are gathered and burned in the fire; so shall it be in the end of this world." (Matthew 13:40)
<1> It is the Prophets of God who sow the good seed which are the words revealed through them, "He that soweth the good seed is the Son of man." <2> The tares are sowed by the false prophets and teachers – whoever teaches that the goal of the life is anything else than be(com)ing Divine – or "the children of

the wicked one" (devil, tama guna). **<3>** But at the end of this era, the Angels (sons of God) will gather the children of the Kingdom to the Father (first resurrection). Those who have followed Maya will be thrown to the outer darkness, "burned in the fire;" only later on, after they have gone through a long struggle and many experiences, might they be saved also (second resurrection).

"The Son of man shall send forth his angels, and they shall gather out of his kingdom all things that offend, and them which do iniquity;" (Matthew 13:41)

"And shall cast them into a furnace of fire: there shall be wailing and gnashing of teeth." (Matthew 13:42)
<4> At that time, the sons of God (Angels) will come and will separate the righteous from the unrighteous. Those who have lagged behind will be sent back to the world, "into a furnace of fire" to be purified through their experience (fire is a symbol of purification).

"Then shall the righteous shine forth as the sun in the kingdom of their Father. Who hath ears to hear, let him hear." (Matthew 13:43)
<5> That is when the righteous or those who have purified themselves, will reach Pure Consciousness, "Shine forth as the sun in the kingdom of their Father." **<6>** Those who have opened their spiritual eyes will understand the truth of these teachings.

"Again, the kingdom of heaven is like unto treasure hid in a field; the which when a man hath found, he hideth, and for joy thereof goeth and selleth all that he hath, and buyeth that field." (Matthew 13:44)
<7> When a man realizes God, sees His Power, Peace, Beauty, Skills, etc., and realizes that only He is true and all other things are temporary, it would be like an earthly person who finds a great treasure in a field and sells all that he has in order to buy that field and become the owner of that treasure. **<8>** So a true God-realized person renounces all for Him.

"Again, the kingdom of heaven is like unto a merchant man, seeking goodly pearls:" (Matthew 13:45)

"Who, when he had found one pearl of great price, went and sold all that he had, and bought it." (Matthew 13:46)
<9> Those who have experienced the bliss of being with the Father will leave everything for His sake. Then it is easily possible to overcome the illusions of this external world (excess attraction, desires, attachments, and greed).

"Again, the kingdom of heaven is like unto a net, that was cast into the sea, and gathered of every kind:" (Matthew 13:47)

"Which, when it was full, they drew to shore, and sat down, and gathered the good into vessels, but cast the bad away." (Matthew 13:48)
<10> Again at the end of this era, humanity will be divided into those who have reached higher consciousness and those who have lagged behind. This is the first resurrection. **<11>** In the second resurrection, the righteous will be saved. This is also prophesied in the Koran, "Before the unavoidable Day which God has designed to come, people will be sundered..." in Surah The Romans (Ar-Rum).

"So shall it be at the end of the world: the angels shall come forth, and sever the wicked among the just," (Matthew 13:49)

"And shall cast them into the furnace of fire: there shall be wailing and gnashing of teeth." (Matthew 13:50)
<12> Those who have lagged behind will be thrown to the depth of ignorance, "furnace of fire."

"Esa saith unto them, Have ye understood all these things? They say unto him, Yea, Lord." (Matthew 13:51)

"Then said he unto them, Therefore every scribe which is instructed unto the kingdom of heaven is like unto a man that is an householder, which bringeth forth out of his treasure things new and old." (Matthew 13:52)

"And it came to pass, that when Esa had finished these parables, he departed thence." (Matthew 13:53)

"And when he was come into his own country, he taught them in their synagogue, insomuch that they were astonished, and said, Whence hath this man this wisdom, and these mighty works?" (Matthew 13:54)

"Is not this the carpenter's son? is not his mother called Mary? and his brethren, James, and Joses, and Simon, and Judas?" (Matthew 13:55)

"And his sisters, are they not all with us? Whence then hath this man all these things?" (Matthew 13:56)

<13> It is so hard for those who know a person from childhood and his family, and also for the family members themselves, to believe a person has acquired a wisdom from God or has become His Prophet. <14> It is even very difficult for many people to just accept another human being as a Prophet. <15> Usually they ask, "Why him?" This becomes an obstacle in their path and causes them to close themselves to the truth he reveals. So they will be deprived of it because of their concepts and ignorance.

"And they were offended in him. But Esa said unto them, A prophet is not without honor, save in his own country, and in his own house." (Matthew 13:57)

"And he did not many mighty works there because of their unbelief." (Matthew 13:58)

<16> **A Prophet or Savior is as powerful as the belief of the people and as powerless as their doubts.** That is why he did not do too much for them.

Tablet Twenty-Three

Chapter 14

"At that time Herod the tetrarch heard of the fame of Esa," (Matthew 14:1)

"And said unto his servants, This is John the Baptist; he is risen from the dead; and therefore mighty works do shew forth themselves in him." (Matthew 14:2)

"For Herod had laid hold on John, and bound him, and put him in prison for Herodias sake, his brother Philip's wife." (Matthew 14:3)

"For John said unto him, It is not lawful for thee to have her." (Matthew 14:4)

"And when he would have put him to death, he feared the multitude, because they counted him as a prophet." (Matthew 14:5)

"But when Herod's birthday was kept, the daughter of Herodias danced before them, and pleased Herod." (Matthew 14:6)

"Whereupon he promised with an oath to give her whatsoever she would ask." (Matthew 14:7)

"And she, being before instructed of her mother, said, Give me here John Baptist's head in a charger." (Matthew 14:8)

"And the king was sorry: nevertheless for the oath's sake, and them which sat with him at meat, he commanded it to be given her." (Matthew 14:9)

"And he sent, and beheaded John in the prison." (Matthew 14:10)

"And his head was brought in a charger, and given to the damsel: and she brought it to her mother." (Matthew 14:11)

"And his disciples came, and took up the body, and buried it, and went and told Esa." (Matthew 14:12)

<1> John the Baptist told Herod that he should not marry his brother's wife. Herod became angry because of that and put him in prison. But because he was afraid of people who thought John was a Prophet, he did not kill him. <2> He did not kill him because he was afraid of God!

<3> But at a birthday party, and most probably in a drunken state, he promised to give anything that the daughter of Herodias asked. When she asked for the head of John, he did not use his common sense to refuse such a cruel request, but again because of the people who heard his oath, he ordered John to be beheaded. <4> He did not fear God but men!

"When Esa heard of it, he departed thence by ship unto a desert place apart: and when the people had heard thereof, they followed him on foot out of the cities." (Matthew 14:13)

"And Esa went forth, and saw a great multitude, and was moved with compassion toward them, and he healed their sick." (Matthew 14:14)

<5> Esa went away after he heard that John was beheaded. A great multitude followed him!

"And when it was evening, his disciples came to him, saying, This is a desert place, and the time is now past; send the multitude away, that they may go into the villages, and buy themselves victuals." (Matthew 14:15)

"But Esa said unto them, They need not depart; give ye them to eat." (Matthew 14:16)

"And they say unto him, We have here but five loaves, and two fishes." (Matthew 14:17)

"He said, Bring them hither to me." (Matthew 14:18)

"And he commanded the multitude to sit down on the grass, and took the five loaves, and the two fishes, and looking up to heaven, he blessed, and brake, and gave the loaves to his disciples, and the disciples to the multitude." (Matthew 14:19)

"And they did all eat, and were filled: and they took up of the fragments that remained twelve baskets full." (Matthew 14:20)

"And they that had eaten were about five thousand men, beside women and children." (Matthew 14:21)

<6> Esa fed a great multitude in a miraculous way (by hidden manna).

"And straightway Esa constrained his disciples to get into a ship, and to go before him unto the other side, while he sent the multitudes away." (Matthew 14:22)

"And when he had sent the multitudes away, he went up into a mountain apart to pray: and when the evening was come, he was there alone." (Matthew 14:23)

<7> To go to a place of solitude and to be alone to pray and meditate is a requirement for those who want to elevate their Souls and become close to the Lord.

"But the ship was now in the midst of the sea, tossed with waves: for the wind was contrary." (Matthew 14:24)

<8> To be in the ship (a safe place) in the middle of turbulent water (water is a symbol for manifested consciousness or mind) means being safe from Maya (turbulent water or consciousness), <9> but still afraid (or a possibility) of being drowned in it.

"And in the fourth watch of the night Esa went unto them, walking on the sea." (Matthew 14:25)

<10> But Esa did not need a ship to stay

above the turbulent consciousness or Maya. He was beyond it, in Pure Consciousness.

"And when the disciples saw him walking on the sea, they were troubled, saying, It is a spirit; and they cried out for fear." (Matthew 14:26)

"But straightway Esa spake unto them, saying, Be of good cheer; it is I; be not afraid." (Matthew 14:27)
<11> People usually become afraid of a realized person, because he seems so different from them. <12> Also they feel guilt in the presence of such a pure person.

"And Peter answered him and said, Lord, if it be thou, bid me come unto thee on the water." (Matthew 14:28)
<13> Peter desired to become like Christ.

"And he said, Come. And when Peter was come down out of the ship, he walked on the water, to go to Esa." (Matthew 14:29)
<14> Because he trusted Esa and gave up his fear, he came out of his shelter (the ship) and was able to stay above the water (turbulent consciousness, mind).

"But when he saw the wind boisterous, he was afraid; and beginning to sink, he cried, saying Lord, save me." (Matthew 14:30)
<15> But when he saw the wind (the power of attraction, desires, attachment, and greed, the four winds) he lost his one-pointedness (faith) and started to sink into the ocean of Maya. <16> He cried for the help of the Lord, "Lord, save me."

"And immediately Esa stretched forth his hand, and caught him, and said unto him, O thou of little faith, wherefore didst thou doubt?" (Matthew 14:31)
<17> The slightest doubt puts you millions of miles away from the Lord. That is when faith weakens, and you will be drowned in the world. But if you truly ask for help, you will be saved.

"And when they were come into the ship, the wind ceased." (Matthew 14:32)

"Then they that were in the ship came and worshipped him, saying, Of a truth thou art the Son of God." (Matthew 14:33)
<18> They were more impressed by his miracles than his teachings. However, they realized he was "the Son of God."

"And when they were gone over, they came into the land of Gennesaret." (Matthew 14:34)

"And when the men of that place had knowledge of him, they sent out into all that country round about, and brought unto him all that were diseased;" (Matthew 14:35)

"And besought him that they might only touch the hem of his garment: and as many as touched were made perfectly whole." (Matthew 14:36)
<19> The people of this land were more interested in his healing powers than his teachings, so he only healed them.

Tablet Twenty-Four

Chapter 15

"Then came to Esa scribes and Pharisees, which were of Jerusalem, saying," (Matthew 15:1)

"Why do thy disciples transgress the tradition of the elders? for they wash not their hands when they eat bread." (Matthew 15:2)
<1> The scribes and Pharisees who were supposed to be the spiritual leaders for others by setting an example, instead had exploited others and created a wealthy distinguished class as superiors. <2> It was because they

had great wealth, were not worried about anything and had time, that they would keep themselves very clean and would wash their hands often. This distinguished them from the common people. That is why they criticized Christ for his disciples who were not as physically clean as they were.

"But he answered and said unto them, Why do ye also transgress the commandment of God by your tradition?" (Matthew 15:3)

"For God commanded, saying, Honour thy father and mother: and, He that curseth father or mother, let him die the death." (Matthew 15:4)

"But ye say, Whosoever shall say to his father or his mother, It is a gift, by whatsoever thou mightest be profited by me;" (Matthew 15:5)

"And honour not his father or his mother, he shall be free. Thus have ye made the commandment of God of none effect by your tradition." (Matthew 15:6)

<3> So Christ answered them that they break the Laws of the Lord and His Commandments by their false tradition. Then they complained about his disciples who had broken a law of man (tradition)! **<4> Which one is more important for a true spiritual person, the Laws and Commandments of the Lord or the traditions of men?**

"Ye hypocrites, well did Esaias prophesy of you, saying," (Matthew 15:7)

"This people draweth nigh unto me with their mouth, and honoureth me with their lips; but their heart is far from me." (Matthew 15:8)

<5> The words are worth nothing, it is the heart which should become spiritualized. Many people talk about love, devotion, surrendering, sacrifice, universalism, etc., <6> but unless the person becomes love, devotion, surrendering, etc., what he says are just words.

"But in vain they do worship me, teaching for doctrines the commandments of men." (Matthew 15:9)

<7> Unless you become God's Laws, only the repetition of words or talking about Him is all in vain. Those who stay in this illusion that they can follow the laws of men instead of God have no choice but to become hypocrites and teach the doctrines and commandments of men instead of God. <8> That is why it is necessary for the human to direct all his attention toward God and have no fear of men nor long for any approval but His.

"And he called the multitude, and said unto them, Hear, and understand:" (Matthew 15:10)

"Not that which goeth into the mouth defileth a man; but that which cometh out of the mouth, this defileth a man." (Matthew 15:11)

<9> Whatever comes out of the mouth comes from the heart. So he who defiles the Laws of God by his teachings not only defiles his own Soul but causes society to go astray also. <10> A person with soiled hands might damage himself physically, but a leader with an impure heart will bring great suffering to others.

"Then came his disciples, and said unto him, Knowest thou that the Pharisees were offended, after they heard this saying?" (Matthew 15:12)

"But he answered and said, Every plant, which my heavenly Father hath not planted, shall be rooted up." (Matthew 15:13)

"Let them alone: they be blind leaders of the blind. And if the blind lead the blind, both shall fall into the ditch." (Matthew 15:14)

<11> His disciples told him that the Pharisees were offended. <12> However, Christ was not here to please men, but to say the truth. <13> If the truth offends someone, it is not the fault of the Prophet but it is the filthiness of that person which will cause him to be offended. That is why Christ referred to

them as the blind leaders that only the blind (spiritually) would follow. Then both would fall together into the grip of the illusion of this world, "into the ditch."

"Then answered Peter and said unto him, Declare unto us this parable." (Matthew 15:15)

"And Esa said, Are ye also yet without understanding?" (Matthew 15:16)

<14> Esa became surprised that after all this time and effort he had put on his disciples, they still did not understand such a simple parable and teaching.

"Do not ye yet understand, that whatsoever entereth in at the mouth goeth into the belly, and is cast out into the draught?" (Matthew 15:17)

"But those things which proceed out of the mouth come forth from the heart; and they defile the man." (Matthew 15:18)

"For out of the heart proceed evil thoughts, murders, adulteries, fornications, thefts, false witness, blasphemies:" (Matthew 15:19)

"These are the things which defile a man: but to eat with unwashen hands defileth not a man." (Matthew 15:20)

<15> A person who has purified his spirit will not do sin (bad actions) and will not transgress the Laws of the Lord. To eat with unwashed hands is not a sin but evil thoughts, murders, adulteries, fornications, etc., are sins which are done because of dirty hearts (spirits).

<16> However, to have a clean spirit and also to wash the hands is the best.

Tablet Twenty-Five

"Then Esa went thence, and departed into the coasts of Tyre and Sidon." (Matthew 15:21)

"And, behold, a woman of Canaan came out of the same coasts, and cried unto him, saying, Have mercy on me, O Lord, thou son of David; my daughter is grievously vexed with a devil." (Matthew 15:22)

"But he answered her not a word. And his disciples came and besought him, saying, Send her away; for she crieth after us." (Matthew 15:23)

"But he answered and said, I am not sent but unto the lost sheep of the house of Israel." (Matthew 15:24)

<1> Esa did not answer the woman to make a point clear, that he had come to bring the lost House of Israel together. <2> This sentence is the key to understanding one of the greatest prophecies and Plans of the Lord which has been hidden from humanity for so long. <3> A clear understanding of this great point also shows the legitimacy of Esa as the Messiah and that God exists and is guiding the creation and history.

<4> In Genesis 49:10, Jacob prophesied about the future of Judah, his tribe and their inheritance:

> The scepter shall not depart from Judah, nor a lawgiver from between his feet, until Shiloh come; and unto him shall the gathering of the people be.

<5> Here are two prophecies which should have been fulfilled through the tribe of Judah: First, the promise of spiritual kingly domination which was given to Abraham and his seed will be fulfilled through the tribe of Judah. This is the scepter, lawgiver, and the Messiah (Shiloh) which will come from this tribe. <6> However the scepter and lawgiver will stay with the tribe of Judah until the Messiah comes, "…shall not depart … , until Shiloh come." <7> Secondly, when the Shiloh (Messiah) comes, he shall gather the people under his banner, "and unto him shall the gathering of the people be."

<8> Who are the people which should be gathered unto the Messiah? They are the ten

lost tribes of the House of Israel, "the lost sheep of the house of Israel," which were gathered together as Christians under the banner of Christ. For more detail, read Children of Abram (Abraham), All Prophecies Are Fulfilled. <9> Also the kingly spiritual domination was finished from the tribe of Judah (House of Judah).

<10> That is why Esa said that he was "not sent but unto the lost sheep of the house of Israel."

"Then came she and worshipped him, saying, Lord, help me." (Matthew 15:25)

"But he answered and said, It is not meet to take the children's bread, and to cast it to dogs." (Matthew 15:26)

"And she said, Truth, Lord: yet the dogs eat of the crumbs which fall from their masters' table." (Matthew 15:27)

"Then Esa answered and said unto her, O woman, great is thy faith: be it unto thee even as thou wilt. And the daughter was made whole from that very hour." (Matthew 15:28)

<11> It is true that he had come for the lost sheep of the House of Israel, but even those who were not of the House of Israel but had faith in him received his Grace.

"And Esa departed from thence, and came nigh unto the sea of Galilee; and went up into a mountain, and sat down there." (Matthew 15:29)

"And great multitudes came unto him, having with them those that were lame, blind, dumb, maimed, and many others, and cast them down at Esa's feet; and he healed them:" (Matthew 15:30)

<12> Again people (the multitude) were interested in his healing powers.

"Insomuch that the multitude wondered, when they saw the dumb to speak, the maimed to be whole, the lame to walk, and the blind to see: and they glorified the God of Israel." (Matthew 15:31)

<13> He healed so many that eventually it affected people, and they worshipped God.

"Then Esa called his disciples unto him, and said, I have compassion on the multitude, because they continue with me now three days, and have nothing to eat: and I will not send them away fasting, lest they faint in the way." (Matthew 15:32)

"And his disciples say unto him, Whence should we have so much bread in the wilderness, as to fill so great a multitude?" (Matthew 15:33)

<14> The disciples had already forgotten that Esa could feed people with only a little physical bread because he fed them by the life-force.

"And Esa saith unto them, How many loaves have ye? And they said, Seven, and a few little fishes." (Matthew 15:34)

"And he commanded the multitude to sit down on the ground." (Matthew 15:35)

"And he took the seven loaves and the fishes, and gave thanks, and brake them, and gave to his disciples, and the disciples to the multitude." (Matthew 15:36)

"And they did all eat, and were filled: and they took up the broken meat that was left seven baskets full." (Matthew 15:37)

"And they that did eat were four thousand men, beside women and children." (Matthew 15:38)

"And he sent away the multitude, and took ship, and came into the coasts of Magdala." (Matthew 15:39)

<15> So again he fed a great multitude with a few loaves of bread and fishes. <16> Actually because he had complete control over the life-force (prana), people received this life-force and were filled by it so they no longer felt hungry.

COMMENTARIES ON ST. MATTHEW
Tablet Twenty-Six

Chapter 16

"The Pharisees also with the Sadducees came, and tempting desired him that he would shew them a sign from heaven." (Matthew 16:1)

<1> Again people wanted him to show them signs from heaven as did the Prophets of old. But with all these signs those Prophets showed them, still they did not follow their teachings. Therefore, what was the point for Esa to do the same?

"He answered and said unto them, When it is evening, ye say, It will be fair weather: for the sky is red." (Matthew 16:2)

"And in the morning, It will be foul weather to day: for the sky is red and lowring. O ye hypocrites, ye can discern the face of the sky; but can ye not discern the signs of the times?" (Matthew 16:3)

<2> Instead of meditating on and contemplating the evidence that the coming of the Messiah was imminent, and then listening to Esa's teachings and seeing the truth behind them, they were resisting him and the truth he had brought. <3> Even with all his miracles and truth he taught, they still wanted more evidence. In reality most humans do not want to hear the truth. Many love darkness and are blinded by The Light.

"A wicked and adulterous generation seeketh after a sign; and there shall no sign be given unto it, but the sign of the prophet Jonas. And he left them, and departed." (Matthew 16:4)

<4> Only a wicked people who truly do not want to see the truth ask for signs from God. Those who are ready to receive the truth with an open heart see His signs everywhere. <5> Also again the only thing that was given by Esa to them as the sign of his messiahship was the sign of the Prophet Jonas. That is, as described before, he would stay in the heart of the earth for three days and three nights, and then would come out of it, as Prophet Jonas remained in the belly of a big fish for three days and three nights.

"And when his disciples were come to the other side, they had forgotten to take bread." (Matthew 16:5)

"Then Esa said unto them, Take heed and beware of the leaven of the Pharisees and of the Sadducees." (Matthew 16:6)

<6> Leaven is like sin, when it is added to human life it inflates and increases more and more. <7> Also the hate and resentment of the Pharisees and Saducees were inflating toward them, because of their own dirty spirits.

"And they reasoned among themselves, saying, It is because we have taken no bread." (Matthew 16:7)

"Which when Esa perceived, he said unto them, O ye of little faith, why reason ye among yourselves, because ye have brought no bread?" (Matthew 16:8)

"Do ye not yet understand, neither remember the five loaves of the five thousand, and how many baskets ye took up?" (Matthew 16:9)

"Neither the seven loaves of the four thousand, and how many baskets ye took up?" (Matthew 16:10)

"How is it that ye do not understand that I spake it not to you concerning bread, that ye should beware of the leaven of the Pharisees and of the Sadducees?" (Matthew 16:11)

"Then understood they how that he bade them not beware of the leaven of bread, but of the doctrine of the Pharisees and of the Sadducees." (Matthew 16:12)

<8> But his disciples could not understand

this simple truth he told them and thought he was blaming them as to why they had not brought any bread. Esa perceived their thoughts and again was unhappy about why they did not understand him. <9> He actually did not need bread, as he himself had declared, "I have meat to eat that ye know not of" (John 4:32). So he did not need human bread to live on.

<10> Also he had fed a great multitude with a few loaves, so he could feed his disciples too. But because of their little faith they did not trust him and were always afraid about their physiological needs. So they were earthbound and could not think about higher things. Only after he explained what he meant by the leaven of the Pharisees and Sadducees did they understand that he was referring to "the doctrine of the Pharisees and of the Sadducees."

<11> This shows how the disciples of a Prophet (Messiah, teacher, etc.) can misunderstand their teacher and misinterpret His Revelations. <12> That is why we should not put our trust on the teachings and interpretations of the disciples of a Prophet, but contemplate His direct Words and rely on God to understand them, "Ask and ye shall receive,…" (Matthew 7:7). The disciples might mislead us from the truth, and the truth of the Prophet might become lost, as it has happened in the past.

"When Esa came into the coasts of Caesarea Philippi, he asked his disciples, saying, Whom do men say that I the Son of man am?" (Matthew 16:13)

"And they said, Some say that thou art John the Baptist: some, Elias; and others, Jeremias, or one of the prophets." (Matthew 16:14)

"He saith unto them, But whom say ye that I am?" (Matthew 16:15)

"And Simon Peter answered and said, Thou art the Christ, the Son of the living God." (Matthew 16:16)

"And Esa answered and said unto him, Blessed art thou, Simon Barjona: for flesh and blood hath not revealed it unto thee, but my Father which is in heaven." (Matthew 16:17)

<13> Esa wanted to know that at least his disciples knew who he was. So he asked them first who the people thought he was. They said that they think he is John the Baptist who has been resurrected, or one of the Prophets. <14> Then he asked his disciples who **they** thought he was. At least Peter realized that he was the Christ, the Anointed One who everyone was expecting to come.

<15> He wanted to make sure that at least his disciples knew who he was, because the end of his ministry was near. He wanted to see that his disciples had realized who he was. When Peter declared it, Christ was so joyful and blessed him because of this realization. <16> If Peter had remained in his lower nature, "flesh and blood," he could not have seen this truth. But because he had gone out of his lower nature, he could see the higher realities and therefore God revealed to him this truth, "but my Father which is in heaven."

"And I say also unto thee, That thou art Peter, and upon this rock I will build my church; and the gates of hell shall not prevail against it." (Matthew 16:18)

<17> The name "Peter" means "stone," the steadfast. Because he had reached a higher consciousness, he was chosen as the head of his disciples, their leader who would build Esa's church. <18> That is the basic requirement for the leaders of men. Only those who have overcome their lower natures and have reached their higher selves are worthy to be chosen as leaders for others.

"And I will give unto thee the keys of the kingdom of heaven: and whatsoever thou shalt bind on earth shall be bound in heaven: and whatsoever thou shalt loose on earth shall be loosed in heaven." (Matthew 16:19)

<19> Those who reach their higher selves will be given the key to enter into Pure Consciousness, "kingdom of heaven," and he who

COMMENTARIES ON ST. MATTHEW

is in Pure Consciousness will receive all the powers on earth and in heaven.

"Then charged he his disciples that they should tell no man that he was Christ [The Word (יהוה/יהושע)]." (Matthew 16:20)

<20> Now he was sure that his disciples knew he was Christ. It was enough for the time being, so he could continue the rest of his ministry to the end and he knew the world would realize that he was the Christ through his disciples.

"From that time forth began Esa to shew unto his disciples, how that he must go unto Jerusalem, and suffer many things of the elders and chief priests and scribes, and be killed, and be raised again the third day." (Matthew 16:21)

<21> After he was sure that his disciples knew who he was, he revealed the last part of his mission, which was to be killed and rise again after three days. <22> The very meaning of being crucified and rising again is that whoever wants to be risen (resurrected) to his higher self has to crucify his lower self (false ego, lower nature). Only then will he be born again. This was as he taught that one has to be born again.

<23> The lower nature is made up of the lower propensities in the first three chakras: Excess fear for survival, temptation, excess attraction to the external world, unhealthy sexual desires, and hunger for power and prestige to satisfy the lower desires (physiological and safety). Also, in reference to staying in the earth for three days, each day can be a symbol of overcoming the lower propensities of one chakra. <24> Furthermore, the sign (✝) is the third sign in our **Greatest Sign**, and it is the third church (Rev. chapter 2) of the seven churches.

<25> All of these clearly indicate where Christ's teaching stands in history and why it is so celebrated by all, because going from the lower nature to the higher self is the first and most celebrated point in spiritual progress.

"Then Peter took him, and began to rebuke him, saying, Be it far from thee, Lord: this shall not be unto thee." (Matthew 16:22)

"But he turned, and said unto Peter, Get thee behind me, Satan: thou art an offence unto me: for thou savourest not the things that be of God, but those that be of men." (Matthew 16:23)

<26> Peter, who had received his blessings, still did not understand that what he said should happen, and like a regular person who becomes very unhappy about the death of a dear one and thinks the physical death is the end of human life, started to show his love in such a human fleshly way. But Esa rebuked him and said he was in his lower nature (satan) that he talked like a regular unspiritual man.

<27> If Peter was in his higher self, he would have known that it was the desire of the Lord to happen, and whatever He desires to happen is good.

"Then said Esa unto his disciples, If any man will come after me, let him deny himself, and take up his cross, and follow me." (Matthew 16:24)

<28> That is the way of Christ. Those who want to be born again should crucify their lower natures, "deny himself, and take up his cross," so that they might be born again to their higher selves. That is the way of the truth, "I am the way and the truth." Only such a person is the true follower of Christ, "and follow me," the way, the truth.

"For whosoever will save his life shall lose it: and whosoever will lose his life for my sake shall find it." (Matthew 16:25)

<29> Those who save their false egos by being selfish and self-centered will lose the opportunity to go to their higher selves. But those who crucify their false egos for the sake of their higher selves or truth, "my sake," will be born again and will find everlasting life.

"For what is a man profited, if he shall gain

the whole world, and lose his own soul? or what shall a man give in exchange for his soul?" (Matthew 16:26)

<30> The Soul is the only thing that is ours. Even our bodies are not ours, as they will be departed from us. <31> So what gain can it be if the only thing that is truly ours is lost in the process of gaining things which are transitory and are not ours, "world?"

<32> That is why The Goal Of The Life Is To Be(come) Divine. Only by beautifying and progressing spiritually and using our bodies and this universe for this purpose, will we gain the true profit from our lives. <33> The body, wealth, and all illusions of this world will pass, but even the slightest spiritual progress will remain with us forever, and that is the true gain.

"For the Son of man shall come in the glory of his Father with his angels; and then he shall reward every man according to his works." (Matthew 16:27)

<34> No spiritual progress is in vain, but will be rewarded accordingly.

"Verily I say unto you, There be some standing here, which shall not taste of death, till they see the Son of man coming in his kingdom." (Matthew 16:28)

<35> There were some with Esa who were in their higher selves and would stay there. <36> They would never go back to their lower natures, "shall not taste of death [spiritual death]," until eventually "they see the Son of man coming in his kingdom." They also will eventually reach Pure Consciousness, and the Kingdom of God will come to them and to the earth through them.

Tablet Twenty-Seven

Chapter 17

"And after six days Esa taketh Peter, James, and John his brother, and bringeth them up into a high mountain apart," (Matthew 17:1)

"And was transfigured before them: and his face did shine as the sun, and his raiment was white as the light." (Matthew 17:2)

<1> He showed to his disciples how unlimited is the power of man to master the elements of the universe. They saw his light body.

"And, behold, there appeared unto them Moses and Elias talking with him." (Matthew 17:3)

<2> So Moses and Elias were different Souls than Esa. Esa was the reincarnation of Adam, Elias was reincarnated as John the Baptist, and Moses is a different Soul than both of them.

"Then answered Peter, and said unto Esa, Lord, it is good for us to be here: if thou wilt, let us make here three tabernacles; one for thee, and one for Moses, and one for Elias." (Matthew 17:4)

<3> Again Peter was thinking of material things for them, and was in the lower thoughts. He was trying to glorify the Prophets instead of God.

"While he yet spake, behold, a bright cloud overshadowed them: and behold a voice out of the cloud, which said, This is my beloved Son, in whom I am well pleased; hear ye him." (Matthew 17:5)

<4> A voice came to them and made them realize who Esa was. He was the First Begotten Son, with whom the Father is "well pleased," and his disciples should listen to him and follow his teachings.

"And when the disciples heard it, they fell on their face, and were sore afraid." (Matthew 17:6)

<5> They were still not ready to be in the presence of the Father and a great fear came upon them. That is why most humans are

kept away from higher realizations, because it is very hard for many to see the truth. They are not ready yet. That is why the Soul should progress gradually toward the Father. When it is ready, it will receive His Darshan (Presence).

"And Esa came and touched them, and said, Arise, and be not afraid." (Matthew 17:7)

"And when they had lifted up their eyes, they saw no man, save Esa only." (Matthew 17:8)

<6> However, Esa, who was in Pure Consciousness, was not afraid. He comforted them by touching them and talking to them. They had been allowed to see a little of the truth <7> but when they came back to their regular state of being, they saw no one but Esa. They had been awakened from their vision.

"And as they came down from the mountain, Esa charged them, saying, Tell the vision to no man, until the Son of man be risen again from the dead." (Matthew 17:9)

<8> All these things were done so that his disciples would become familiar with his true mission and be able to be sure that he was Christ. So later on they could do his work with great faith.

"And his disciples asked him, saying, Why then say the scribes that Elias must first come?" (Matthew 17:10)

"And Esa answered and said unto them, Elias truly shall first come, and restore all things." (Matthew 17:11)

"But I say unto you, That Elias is come already, and they knew him not, but have done unto him whatsoever they listed. Likewise shall also the Son of man suffer of them." (Matthew 17:12)

"Then the disciples understood that he spake unto them of John the Baptist." (Matthew 17:13)

<9> John the Baptist was the reincarnation of Elias.

"And when they were come to the multitude, there came to him a certain man, kneeling down to him, and saying," (Matthew 17:14)

"Lord, have mercy on my son: for he is lunatick, and sore vexed: for ofttimes he falleth into the fire, and oft into the water." (Matthew 17:15)

"And I brought him to thy disciples, and they could not cure him." (Matthew 17:16)

"Then Esa answered and said, O faithless and perverse generation, how long shall I be with you? how long shall I suffer you? bring him hither to me." (Matthew 17:17)

"And Esa rebuked the devil; and he departed out of him: and the child was cured from that very hour." (Matthew 17:18)

"Then came the disciples to Esa apart, and said, Why could not we cast him out?" (Matthew 17:19)

"And Esa said unto them, Because of your unbelief: for verily I say unto you, If ye have faith as a grain of mustard seed, ye shall say unto this mountain, Remove hence to yonder place; and it shall remove; and nothing shall be impossible unto you." (Matthew 17:20)

"Howbeit this kind goeth not out but by prayer and fasting." (Matthew 17:21)

<10> To be able to help others, a person should have a great faith in the Lord and purify himself so that His powers might manifest through him, "but by prayer and fasting."

"And while they abode in Galilee, Esa said unto them, The Son of man shall be betrayed into the hands of men:" (Matthew 17:22)

"And they shall kill him, and the third day he shall be raised again. And they were exceeding sorry." (Matthew 17:23)

<11> Again Esa predicted his death and his rising on the third day, and his disciples

again did not understand the significance of this happening. But this time they accepted it without arguing that it should not happen to him. However they felt sorry inside, and they thought that he would actually die.

"And when they were come to Capernaum, they that received tribute money came to Peter, and said, Doth not your master pay tribute?" (Matthew 17:24)

<12> Tribute collectors were trying to cause trouble for him and his disciples.

"He saith, Yes. And when he was come into the house, Esa prevented him, saying, What thinkest thou, Simon? of whom do the kings of the earth take custom or tribute? of their own children, or of strangers?" (Matthew 17:25)

"Peter saith unto him, Of strangers. Esa saith unto him, Then are the children free." (Matthew 17:26)

<13> Esa asked Peter if the kings of the earth are just to the people, or do they impose suffering on those who are not the same as them, "strangers?" Peter answered that they impose burdens on strangers but not on those who are like themselves, "their own children."

<14> Esa asked if he (Peter) thought by doing this are the king's children free from burden? The answer is of course "NO." <15> By doing this, kings create a bad karma not only for themselves but for those who are protected under them, who accept the suffering of others so that they might live in prosperity.

"Notwithstanding, lest we should offend them, go thou to the sea, and cast an hook, and take up the fish that first cometh up; and when thou hast opened his mouth, thou shall find a piece of money: that take, and give unto them for me and thee." (Matthew 17:27)

<16> Esa instructed him to go and pay what they asked for and leave the judgment to the Father. If they have done an inequity, they will pay for it.

Tablet Twenty-Eight

Chapter 18

"At the same time came the disciples unto Esa, saying, Who is the greatest in the kingdom of heaven?" (Matthew 18:1)

"And Esa called a little child unto him, and set him in the midst of them," (Matthew 18:2)

"And said, Verily I say unto you, Except ye be converted, and become as little children, ye shall not enter into the kingdom of heaven." (Matthew 18:3)

"Whosoever therefore shall humble himself as this little child, the same is greatest in the kingdom of heaven." (Matthew 18:4)

<1> Unless a person completely turns around from the illusion of this external world, "be converted," and becomes pure and innocent as a little child, he cannot enter into heaven (Kingdom Of Heaven within).

<2> Those who truly overcome the illusion of the external world will shatter all kinds of narrow-mindedness, discriminatory ideas, and differentiation between man and man. This is the same as little children. They do not discriminate between men because their false egos have not developed yet. <3> Also those who want to enter into the Kingdom Of Heaven should crucify their false egos so that they might become like little children in heart (to be born again). <4> To become like a child does not mean to do childish things but to have a pure heart, and one who is pure in heart sees God (Matthew 5:8). Whoever sees God is in His Kingdom In Heaven.

"And whoso shall receive one such little child in my name receiveth me." (Matthew 18:5)

<5> Whoever opens himself to such a

humble and realized person in truth ("my name") "receiveth me" (the truth). He will be blessed by the realization of that person. That is why only those who receive a Realized Soul with an open heart can have hope to know his knowledge.

"But whoso shall offend one of these little ones which believe in me, it were better for him that a millstone were hanged about his neck, and that he were drowned in the depth of the sea." (Matthew 18:6)

<6> He who does not receive such a humble person with an open heart but offends him will create a very bad karma (sin). The burden of offending a pure in heart being and one who in truth "believe[s] in me" is even greater than having a millstone hanged on the neck and being drowned in the depths of the sea.

<7> To offend a pure person is the same as offending God.

"Woe unto the world because of offences! for it must needs be that offences come; but woe to that man by whom the offence cometh!" (Matthew 18:7)

<8> People in the world mock the Holy people and even kill and crucify them. They follow their blind leaders (false prophets). But woe to the leaders "by whom the offence cometh!"

"Wherefore if thy hand or thy foot offend thee, cut them off, and cast them from thee: it is better for thee to enter into life halt or maimed, rather than having two hands or two feet to be cast into everlasting fire." (Matthew 18:8)

"And if thine eye offend thee, pluck it out, and cast it from thee: it is better for thee to enter into life with one eye, rather than having two eyes to be cast into hell fire." (Matthew 18:9)

<9> Even if the obstacle is the closest member in your life, it is better to cut it off and progress than to let it stay and either stop you in your path or slow you down.

"Take heed that ye despise not one of these little ones; for I say unto you, That in heaven their angels do always behold the face of my Father which is in heaven." (Matthew 18:10)

<10> Be aware not to despise those who are pure in heart, "of these little ones," because they are so close to heaven (God) that anything which is done to them will create a great reaction and consequence, "their angels do always behold the face of my Father which is in heaven."

"For the Son of man is come to save that which was lost." (Matthew 18:11)

"How think ye? if a man have an hundred sheep, and one of them be gone astray, doth he not leave the ninety and nine, and goeth into the mountains, and seeketh that which is gone astray?" (Matthew 18:12)

"And if so be that he find it, verily I say unto you, he rejoiceth more of that sheep, than of the ninety and nine which went not astray." (Matthew 18:13)

"Even so it is not the will of your Father which is in heaven, that one of these little ones should perish." (Matthew 18:14)

<11> Christ had come to save those who were true seekers but were lost because of the confusion of the teachings and ideas in that time. These were the ones who saw his truth, either when he was alive or after, and rejoiced in them and were saved. <12> They were the lost sheep of Israel who should have been saved, because it was the Will of the Father that those who have struggled to progress spiritually to the Father should be saved.

"Moreover if thy brother shall trespass against thee, go and tell him his fault between thee and him alone: if he shall hear thee, thou hast gained thy brother." (Matthew 18:15)

"But if he will not hear thee, then take with thee one or two more, that in the mouth of two or three witnesses every word may be established." (Matthew 18:16)

"And if he shall neglect to hear them, tell it unto the church: but if he neglect to hear the church, let him be unto thee as an heathen man and a publican." (Matthew 18:17)

<13> Try to settle your differences with others secretly and peacefully. If it does not work, bring some witnesses to settle the problem. If that does not work, let the people in higher consciousness, "church," settle the dispute. If the other person does not try to come to an agreement after all this, then leave him alone and know that he is not worth the effort, "let him be unto thee as an heathen man and a publican." <14> Do not waste your time with those who do not understand, but Love The Light in everyone!

"Verily I say unto you, Whatsoever ye shall bind on earth shall be bound in heaven: and whatsoever ye shall loose on earth shall be loosed in heaven." (Matthew 18:18)

<15> Those who are in their higher selves are so close to God that whatever they desire will happen. However, because they are pure in heart, they never desire anything that is contrary to the Will of God and the purpose of His creation. <16> Another meaning is that: Man becomes bound with his thoughts, words, and actions.

"Again I say unto you, That if two of you shall agree on earth as touching any thing that they shall ask, it shall be done for them of my Father which is in heaven." (Matthew 18:19)

"For where two or three are gathered together in my name, there am I in the midst of them." (Matthew 18:20)

<17> Those who create peace, purify themselves, and gather together in truth and purity, "in my name (יהוה׳/יחשוה׳)," will create joy and God-consciousness, cooperation, and prosperity.

"Then came Peter to him, and said, Lord, how oft shall my brother sin against me, and I forgive him? till seven times?" (Matthew 18:21)

"Esa saith unto him, I say not unto thee, Until seven times: but, Until seventy times seven." (Matthew 18:22)

<18> Be patient in passing judgment on others and be forgiving to those who do bad to you. However, forgive not those who do bad to society.

"Therefore is the kingdom of heaven likened unto a certain king, which would take account of his servants." (Matthew 18:23)

"And when he had begun to reckon, one was brought unto him, which owed him ten thousand talents." (Matthew 18:24)

"But forasmuch as he had not to pay, his lord commanded him to be sold, and his wife, and children, and all that he had, and payment to be made." (Matthew 18:25)

"The servant therefore fell down, and worshipped him, saying, Lord, have patience with me, and I will pay thee all." (Matthew 18:26)

"Then the lord of that servant was moved with compassion, and loosed him, and forgave him the debt." (Matthew 18:27)

"But the same servant went out, and found one of his fellowservants, which owed him an hundred pence: and he laid hands on him, and took him by the throat, saying, Pay me that thou owest." (Matthew 18:28)

"And his fellowservant fell down at his feet, and besought him, saying, Have patience with me, and I will pay thee all." (Matthew 18:29)

"And he would not: but went and cast him into prison, till he should pay the debt." (Matthew 18:30)

"So when his fellowservants saw what was done, they were very sorry, and came and told unto their lord all that was done." (Matthew 18:31)

"Then his lord, after he had called him, said unto him, O thou wicked servant, I forgave thee all that debt, because thou desiredst me:" (Matthew 18:32)

"Shouldest not thou also have had compassion on thy fellowservant, even as I had pity on thee?" (Matthew 18:33)

"And his lord was wroth, and delivered him to the tormentors, till he should pay all that was due unto him." (Matthew 18:34)

"So likewise shall my heavenly Father do also unto you, if ye from your hearts forgive not every one his brother their trespasses." (Matthew 18:35)

<19> Forgive so that you might be forgiven also.

Tablet Twenty-Nine

Chapter 19

"And it came to pass, that when Esa had finished these sayings, he departed from Galilee, and came into the coasts of Judaea beyond Jordan;" (Matthew 19:1)

"And great multitudes followed him; and he healed them there." (Matthew 19:2)

"The Pharisees also came unto him, tempting him, and saying unto him, Is it lawful for a man to put away his wife for every cause?" (Matthew 19:3)

"And he answered and said unto them, Have ye not read, that he which made them at the beginning made them male and female," (Matthew 19:4)

<1> "So God created man in his own image, ... male and female created he them" (Gen. 1:27). As it is explained in The Holiest Book, this sentence means that God created man which was like God Himself, male and female (☯) at the same time. Man was in His image and likeness. <2> He created more than one of these, he created "them."

<3> Later on God separated male and female from this original being. So man is no longer in the image of God after this separation of male and female from the original. <4> When the male (Logic) and female (Grace) are manifested in a person, he will be an androgynous person. Two people with these qualities also will complement each other. Such a union brings perfection of energy between them.

"And said, For this cause shall a man leave father and mother, and shall cleave to his wife: and they twain shall be one flesh?" (Matthew 19:5)

<5> That is why, "For this cause," when soulmates find each other, they shall cleave to one another, "and they twain shall be one flesh." They should become one and help each other to reach higher consciousness and manifest God's qualities through themselves.

"Wherefore they are no more twain, but one flesh. What therefore God hath joined together, let not man put asunder." (Matthew 19:6)

<6> This is the Godly way of marriage, "What therefore God hath joined together." There will be no divorce in such a marriage. Otherwise, because of their false egos, the partners will not get along together, "let not man put asunder." <7> If they truly follow God's plan for marriage, they should not separate.

"They say unto him, Why did Moses then command to give a writing of divorcement, and to put her away?" (Matthew 19:7)

"He saith unto them, Moses because of the hardness of your hearts suffered you to put away your wives: but from the beginning it was not so." (Matthew 19:8)

<8> Moses received this Law because the people's minds were so crude "because of the

hardness of your hearts" that they could not recognize their true partners. <9> Also because of their lower natures, they desired the flesh of other women. So Moses relaxed the Law because the human was in a low level of consciousness. But truly fleshly desires and mental attractions are temporary and controllable. <10> The only true marriage between two people is the marriage of their spirits together so that they might become one.

"And I say unto you, Whosoever shall put away his wife, except it be for fornication, and shall marry another, committeth adultery: and whoso marrieth her which is put away doth commit adultery." (Matthew 19:9)

<11> First find your true partner and marry her or him. But even if two beings are not each others' partners, with becoming one with God they will become one with each other and live together and be One. So "Whosoever shall put away his wife," with no great cause, "except it be for fornication" and marries another, creates a great sin "adultery" by doing so. <12> Beside spiritual reasons for marriage, the family is a block of society and each of them counts in the strength or weakness of the society. <13> A society with a weak family structure will be easily destroyed.

<14> Therefore if a man and woman break their relationship for selfish reasons and this becomes a norm in a society, then that society will become corrupt and no matter how powerful it looks, it is weak and vulnerable. <15> In the new era to come it is the strength of the **Communities of Light** which will create strength in the society!

"His disciples say unto him, If the case of the man be so with his wife, it is not good to marry." (Matthew 19:10)

"But he said unto them, All men cannot receive this saying, save they to whom it is given." (Matthew 19:11)

"For there are some eunuchs, which were so born from their mother's womb: and there are some eunuchs, which were made eunuchs of men: and there be eunuchs, which have made themselves eunuchs for the kingdom of heaven's sake. He that is able to receive it, let him receive it." (Matthew 19:12)

<16> As it was said, each being has two parts (male and female) which when merged together become one or in the image of God. When they are together ((☯)) a person who is born in this state (androgynous) does not feel any need for a partner to be complete. Such people are those who, "which were so born from their mother's womb," or their partner has not been born in the flesh, so they cannot find it on earth.

<17> Another type of people who can stay unmarried are those who have been made impotent, especially in the past, by man, "and there are some eunuchs, which were made eunuchs of men." They usually were used in king's or rich people's harems.

<18> The third kind which does not marry are those who avoid marriage (become renunciates or sannyasins) because they feel they have a greater mission to fulfill and dedicate their lives to God and His Work, "and there be eunuchs, which have made themselves eunuchs for the kingdom of heaven's sake." They sacrifice all for their ideology and higher self.

<19> But those who have found their partners and are inclined toward reunion and married life also are greatly blessed. <20> With a marriage centered on God's Laws, they become one and create a great block for society, a beautiful environment to raise children, and can manifest God's beauty and creative forces (regeneration) through themselves. They can help each other and others to reach higher consciousness. So they can reach Pure Consciousness even in the middle of the family.

"Then were there brought unto him little children, that he should put his hands on them, and pray: and the disciples rebuked them." (Matthew 19:13)

"But Esa said, Suffer little children, and forbid them not, to come unto me: for of such is the kingdom of heaven." (Matthew 19:14)

"And he laid his hands on them, and departed thence." (Matthew 19:15)

<21> Children are the symbol of the pure in heart, so he loved them, because it is the pure in heart who will see God.

"And, behold, one came and said unto him, Good Master, what good thing shall I do, that I may have eternal life?" (Matthew 19:16)

"And he said unto him, Why callest thou me good? there is none good but one, that is, God: but if thou wilt enter into life, keep the commandments." (Matthew 19:17)

<22> A person came and tried to inflate his ego by calling him, "Good Master." Esa detested this and reminded him that no man deserves to be called good and praised but the Father who is the only one worthy of praise. Then he told the man that he should follow the commandments strictly if he wants to enter into Pure Consciousness, "into life." Also God Is, "that is, God."

"He saith unto him, Which? Esa said, Thou shalt do no murder, Thou shalt not commit adultery, Thou shalt not steal, Thou shalt not bear false witness," (Matthew 19:18)

"Honour thy father and thy mother: and, Thou shalt love thy neighbour as thyself." (Matthew 19:19)

<23> He asked Esa which Commandments he should follow. Esa repeated the ten commandments and told him to follow them. <24> This completely showed that Esa wanted his followers to follow these commandments and his coming did not destroy them.

"The young man saith unto him, All these things have I kept from my youth up: what lack I yet?" (Matthew 19:20)

"Esa said unto him, If thou wilt be perfect, go and sell that thou hast, and give to the poor, and thou shalt have treasure in heaven: and come and follow me." (Matthew 19:21)

<25> The man said he had followed the Commandments and wanted to know what to do next. Esa said, "If it is true, then you are worthy to follow me. So go and sell all that you have and give it to the poor. Then come with me."

"But when the young man heard that saying, he went away sorrowful: for he had great possessions." (Matthew 19:22)

"Then said Esa unto his disciples, Verily I say unto you, That a rich man shall hardly enter into the kingdom of heaven." (Matthew 19:23)

"And again I say unto you, It is easier for a camel to go through the eye of a needle, than for a rich man to enter into the kingdom of God." (Matthew 19:24)

<26> Rich people become attached to their possessions. It becomes very hard for them to give them up for higher things. It is almost impossible for them to overcome their false egos which make them feel important because of their riches. <27> That is exactly what the false ego is, **it is when a person sees his importance because of the things he possesses in the external world, not on his own true worth**.

<28> Only when this false ego has been destroyed and the true ego (actualized ego) is replaced, can man appreciate what he is and enjoy life and the creation. Then he can enter the Kingdom Of Heaven. <29> This false ego usually is greater as the person becomes richer in material possessions. That is why it is so hard for the rich to enter the Kingdom Of Heaven. You cannot have two masters, God and mammon (Matthew 6:24).

"When his disciples heard it, they were exceedingly amazed, saying, Who then can be saved?" (Matthew 19:25)

"But Esa beheld them, and said unto them, With men this is impossible; but with God all things are possible." (Matthew 19:26)

<30> With the work of man alone to reach Pure Consciousness, it is impossible, "With men this is impossible." But with His Grace, it is possible.

COMMENTARIES ON ST. MATTHEW

"Then answered Peter and said unto him, Behold, we have forsaken all, and followed thee; what shall we have therefore?" (Matthew 19:27)

"And Esa said unto them, Verily I say unto you, That ye which have followed me, in the regeneration when the Son of man shall sit in the throne of his glory, ye also shall sit upon twelve thrones, judging the twelve tribes of Israel." (Matthew 19:28)

"And every one that hath forsaken houses, or brethren, or sisters, or father, or mother, or wife, or children, or lands, for my name's sake, shall receive an hundredfold, and shall inherit everlasting life." (Matthew 19:29)

<31> His disciples would be with him whenever he comes back to earth and eventually will reach Pure Consciousness, "inherit everlasting life."

"But many that are first shall be last; and the last shall be first." (Matthew 19:30)

<32> Those who create false egos, exalt themselves, and think they are first will be last. Those who humble themselves and may think they are last will be first.

Tablet Thirty

Chapter 20

"For the kingdom of heaven is like unto a man that is an householder, which went out early in the morning to hire labourers into his vineyard." (Matthew 20:1)

"And when he had agreed with the labourers for a penny a day, he sent them into his vineyard." (Matthew 20:2)

"And he went out about the third hour, and saw others standing idle in the marketplace," (Matthew 20:3)

"And said unto them; Go ye also into the vineyard, and whatsoever is right I will give you. And they went their way." (Matthew 20:4)

"Again he went out about the sixth and ninth hour, and did likewise." (Matthew 20:5)

"And about the eleventh hour he went out, and found others standing idle, and saith unto them, Why stand ye here all the day idle?" (Matthew 20:6)

"They say unto him, Because no man hath hired us. He saith unto them, Go ye also into the vineyard; and whatsoever is right, that shall ye receive." (Matthew 20:7)

"So when even was come, the lord of the vineyard saith unto his steward, Call the labourers, and give them their hire, beginning from the last unto the first." (Matthew 20:8)

"And when they came that were hired about the eleventh hour, they received every man a penny." (Matthew 20:9)

"But when the first came, they supposed that they should have received more; and they likewise received every man a penny." (Matthew 20:10)

"And when they had received it, they murmured against the goodman of the house," (Matthew 20:11)

"Saying, These last have wrought but one hour, and thou hast made them equal unto us, which have borne the burden and heat of the day." (Matthew 20:12)

"But he answered one of them, and said, Friend, I do thee no wrong: didst not thou agree with me for a penny?" (Matthew 20:13)

"Take that thine is, and go thy way: I will give unto this last, even as unto thee." (Matthew 20:14)

"Is it not lawful for me to do what I will with mine own? Is thine eye evil, because I am good?" (Matthew 20:15)

"So the last shall be first, and the first last: for many be called, but few chosen." (Matthew 20:16)

<1> As it was explained, many will put much effort to reach Pure Consciousness in a selfish way by only using techniques, overcoming, or calling themselves the Elected Ones (first). However they will be last. <2> Although they might have started much earlier than many others, they will receive the same reward (Pure Consciousness). Others may have started much later but rightly, which is, that they progressed and at the same time helped others to progress also, "many be called, but few chosen."

<3> Also this parable completely supports that the day started at six o'clock in the morning (according to our clocks) in the time of Christ, and mid-day was at the sixth hour of the day. That is because the owner of the vineyard went out the third hour of the day (nine o'clock in the morning), the sixth (mid-day or noon), the ninth hour (three o'clock in the afternoon) and the eleventh hour (five o'clock in the afternoon). The day finished at the twelfth hour (six o'clock according to the present timing) because those who had been hired at the eleventh hour worked only one hour: "these last have wrought but one hour" (until the twelfth hour).

<4> So even then the hours of the day were divided logically from six in the morning as the beginning of the day, and the twelfth hour of the day would have finished at six in the afternoon. Night then would start and its twelve hours would finish at six the next morning. This is the most logical acceptance of the hours and is the closest to the natural relation of the days and nights.

<5> This logical set-up was upset by the Romans as they had many illogical ways for human existence, such as their holidays instead of God-centered Holy Days which are commanded by the Lord in chapter 23 of Leviticus to be observed forever. For more detail, read the chapter about the Holy Days and the hours of the day in the book Essays 1.

"And Esa going up to Jerusalem took the twelve disciples apart in the way, and said unto them," (Matthew 20:17)

"Behold, we go up to Jerusalem: and the Son of man shall be betrayed unto the chief priests and unto the scribes, and they shall condemn him to death," (Matthew 20:18)

"And shall deliver him to the Gentiles to mock, and to scourge, and to crucify him: and the third day he shall rise again." (Matthew 20:19)

<6> He again repeated The Plan for him which should be fulfilled. <7> Also he would be delivered to the Gentiles (who were the Romans) who symbolize the intellectuals and are the fourth kingdom in the book of Daniel (for more detail read Commentaries on Prophecies in Daniel, Period of Intellectual Domination).

"Then came to him the mother of Zebedee's children with her sons, worshipping him, and desiring a certain thing of him." (Matthew 20:20)

"Then he said unto her, What wilt thou? She saith unto him, Grant that these my two sons may sit, the one on thy right hand, and the other on the left, in thy kingdom." (Matthew 20:21)

"But Esa answered and said, Ye know not what ye ask. Are ye able to drink of the cup that I shall drink of, and to be baptized with the baptism that I am baptized with? They say unto him, We are able." (Matthew 20:22)

"And he saith unto them, Ye shall drink indeed of my cup, and be baptized with the baptism that I am baptized with: but to sit on my right hand, and on my left, is not mine to give, but it shall be given to them for whom it is prepared of my Father." (Matthew 20:23)

<8> His disciples thought that he owed

them something because they followed him. Even the mother of Zebedee and his sons thought that they could prepare a better position for themselves by asking him to grant that in advance before he was crucified. This shows how gross is the heart of man and how egoistical can be his thoughts.

<9> Esa answered them that they are not even ready to follow him and are still in their lower natures. How then could they ask to sit on the two sides of him? <10> Even if they went through a great effort, progressed, and were ready to reach Christhood, "Ye shall drink indeed of my cup, and be baptized with the baptism that I am baptized with," still he had no power to grant any position in heaven. It is completely up to the Father to choose the people in the Hierarchy as it fits His Purpose and Will, "it shall be given to them for whom it is prepared of my Father."

"And when the ten heard it, they were moved with indignation against the two brethren." (Matthew 20:24)

"But Esa called them unto him, and said, Ye know that the princes of the Gentiles exercise dominion over them, and they that are great exercise authority upon them." (Matthew 20:25)

"But it shall not be so among you: but whosoever will be great among you, let him be your minister;" (Matthew 20:26)

"And whosoever will be chief among you, let him be your servant:" (Matthew 20:27)

"Even as the Son of man came not to be ministered unto, but to minister, and to give his life a ransom for many." (Matthew 20:28)

<11> This thoughtless request also invoked anger in the rest of his disciples, and their lower natures were stirred. They forgot all about his teachings that in the Kingdom Of Heaven, the last will be first and the first the last. <12> Those who want to enter it selfishly, "Grant that these my two sons may sit, the one on thy right hand, and the other on the left, in thy kingdom" (Matthew 20:21), will be spued out of His Mouth (Rev. 3:16) and will be lost. <13> Also he taught that all men are equal in the Kingdom (Pure Consciousness) and no one is higher than any other. Even in flesh, the true sons of God are equal, with different tasks to fulfill.

<14> But because his disciples could not understand these things in this state of their progress, he had to call them together and give them instructions of how they should be after he left them. <15> Whoever was greater was the most humble, and there should be no dominating personality among them, that each should do His Work with no false pride.

<16> Only those who have overcome this world, are in their higher selves, and have no desire for the praise of the men (Paravipras) are worthy to assume the leadership of humanity.

"And as they departed from Jericho, a great multitude followed him." (Matthew 20:29)

"And, behold, two blind men sitting by the way side, when they heard that Esa passed by, cried out, saying, Have mercy on us, O Lord, thou son of David." (Matthew 20:30)

"And the multitude rebuked them, because they should hold their peace: but they cried the more, saying, Have mercy on us, O Lord, thou son of David." (Matthew 20:31)

"And Esa stood still, and called them, and said, What will ye that I shall do unto you?" (Matthew 20:32)

"They say unto him, Lord, that our eyes may be opened." (Matthew 20:33)

"So Esa had compassion on them, and touched their eyes: and immediately their eyes received sight, and they followed him." (Matthew 20:34)

<17> Again people asked him for favors and miracles.

COMMENTARIES ON ST. MATTHEW
Tablet Thirty-One

Chapter 21

"And when they drew nigh unto Jerusalem, and were come to Bethphage, unto the mount of Olives, then sent Esa two disciples," (Matthew 21:1)

"Saying unto them, Go into the village over against you, and straightway ye shall find an ass tied, and a colt with her: loose them, and bring them unto me." (Matthew 21:2)

"And if any man say ought unto you, ye shall say, The Lord hath need of them; and straightway he will send them." (Matthew 21:3)

"All this was done, that it might be fulfilled which was spoken by the prophet, saying," (Matthew 21:4)

"Tell ye the daughter of Sion, Behold, thy King cometh unto thee, meek, and sitting upon an ass, and a colt the foal of an ass." (Matthew 21:5)

"And the disciples went, and did as Esa commanded them," (Matthew 21:6)

"And brought the ass, and the colt, and put on them their clothes, and they set him thereon." (Matthew 21:7)

"And a very great multitude spread their garments in the way; others cut down branches from the trees, and strawed them in the way." (Matthew 21:8)

<1> Christ prepared himself to enter Jerusalem as the King of the Jews, but in a humbling and humiliating manner. That was done to show that greatness is not because of the wealth of the person, but how much Christ had overcome the lower nature.

"And the multitudes that went before, and that followed, cried, saying, Hosanna to the son of David: Blessed is he that cometh in the name of the Lord; Hosanna in the highest." (Matthew 21:9)

<2> People who knew him praised him on his way to Jerusalem as their king. They knew he had come in the name of the Lord (יהוה/יהושוה).

"And when he was come into Jerusalem, all the city was moved, saying, Who is this?" (Matthew 21:10)

<3> Because of the multitudes, the attention of most of the city was directed to his coming to the city.

"And the multitude said, This is Esa the prophet of Nazareth of Galilee." (Matthew 21:11)

<4> Still very few truly knew him.

"And Esa went into the temple of God, and cast out all them that sold and bought in the temple, and overthrew the tables of the moneychangers, and the seats of them that sold doves." (Matthew 21:12)

"And said unto them, It is written, My house shall be called the house of prayer; but ye have made it a den of thieves." (Matthew 21:13)

<5> Esa started to cleanse and purify the temple, and he threw out all the business activities from the temple. He reminded them that the temple is a place of worship, meditation, and a Soul-to-Soul relationship with the Lord, not a place of noise and business activities.

"And the blind and the lame came to him in the temple; and he healed them." (Matthew 21:14)

"And when the chief priests and scribes saw the wonderful things that he did, and the children crying in the temple, and saying, Hosanna to the son of David; they were sore displeased," (Matthew 21:15)

"And said unto him, Hearest thou what these say? And Esa saith unto them, Yea; have ye never read, Out of the mouth of babes and sucklings thou hast perfected praise?" (Matthew 21:16)

"And he left them, and went out of the city into Bethany; and he lodged there." (Matthew 21:17)

<6> With power and truth, he broke all the superstitions and concepts that the elders had created to bind their subjects. <7> He also showed his spiritual powers by healing people. But the only thing the priests and scribes could do was to try to mock him by pointing out that the little children praised him, so with this break him. He even won this by reminding them that <8> the true praise comes from the pure in heart, "the babes and sucklings."

"Now in the morning as he returned into the city, he hungered." (Matthew 21:18)

"And when he saw a fig tree in the way, he came to it, and found nothing thereon, but leaves only, and said unto it, Let no fruit grow on thee hence forward for ever. And presently the fig tree withered away." (Matthew 21:19)

<9> It was a tree with no fruit but only leaves, like those with much talk (leaves) but no actions (fruit). Such a person will give no fruit and will be withered away with no positive effect in his life.

"And when the disciples saw it, they marvelled, saying, How soon is the fig tree withered away!" (Matthew 21:20)

"Esa answered and said unto them, Verily I say unto you, If ye have faith, and doubt not, ye shall not only do this which is done to the fig tree, but also if ye shall say unto this mountain, Be thou removed, and be thou cast into the sea; it shall be done." (Matthew 21:21)

"And all things, whatsoever ye shall ask in prayer, believing, ye shall receive." (Matthew 21:22)

<10> That is why the slightest doubt will put you millions of miles away from the Lord, and he who has no doubt is with Him.

"And when he was come into the temple, the chief priests and the elders of the people came unto him as he was teaching, and said, By what authority doest thou these things? and who gave thee this authority?" (Matthew 21:23)

<11> The elders saw his authority, and they marvelled at who gave him this power and authority. That was because whatever he did was true, so affected everyone. <12> Also they wanted to point out that he had no authority to do these things and it was they who could make laws around the temple.

"And Esa answered and said unto them, I also will ask you one thing, which if ye tell me, I in like wise will tell you by what authority I do these things." (Matthew 21:24)

"The baptism of John, whence was it? from heaven, or of men? And they reasoned with themselves, saying, If we shall say, From heaven; he will say unto us, Why did ye not then believe him?" (Matthew 21:25)

"But if we shall say, Of men; we fear the people; for all hold John as a prophet." (Matthew 21:26)

"And they answered Esa, and said, We cannot tell. And he said unto them, Neither tell I you by what authority I do these things." (Matthew 21:27)

<13> With this he did not answer them directly and also showed their hypocrisy that they were afraid of men but not of God. <14> He was not afraid of men and had the power of God with him so his authority was from heaven.

"But what think ye? A certain man had two sons; and he came to the first, and said, Son, go work to day in my vineyard." (Matthew 21:28)

"He answered and said, I will not: but afterward he repented, and went." (Matthew 21:29)

"And he came to the second, and said likewise. And he answered and said, I go, sir: and went not." (Matthew 21:30)

"Whether of them twain did the will of his father? They say unto him, The first. Esa saith unto them, Verily I say unto you, That the publicans and the harlots go into the kingdom of God before you." (Matthew 21:31)

"For John came unto you in the way of righteousness, and ye believed him not; but the publicans and the harlots believed him: and ye, when ye had seen it, repented not afterward, that ye might believe him." (Matthew 21:32)

<15> The priests and elders were supposed to be the good children of God and they said they obeyed Him, but when His Prophet came unto them they said, "No," and believed not. But publicans were supposed to be the ones who did not walk in the ways of the Lord and said "No," to Him. However, when his Prophets came they accepted them and did His Will.

<16> The priests and elders of any old religions create so many concepts and attachments to their ways that they lose their common sense and cannot give up their false egos. They do not accept a humble Prophet and his truth. But those who are humble and have nothing to hang onto have no big false egos to prevent them from accepting the truth.

<17> Also Christ established this truth in these verses that the authority of John the Baptist had come from heaven but they (the priests) did not accept it. So his authority also came from the same Source, but still would be rejected by them.

"Hear another parable: There was a certain householder, which planted a vineyard, and hedged it round about, and digged a winepress in it, and built a tower, and let it out to husbandmen, and went into a far country:" (Matthew 21:33)

"And when the time of the fruit drew near, he sent his servants to the husbandmen, that they might receive the fruits of it." (Matthew 21:34)

"And the husbandmen took his servants, and beat one, and killed another, and stoned another." (Matthew 21:35)

"Again, he sent other servants more than the first: and they did unto them likewise." (Matthew 21:36)

"But last of all he sent unto them his son, saying, They will reverence my son." (Matthew 21:37)

"But when the husbandmen saw the son, they said among themselves, This is the heir; come, let us kill him, and let us seize on his inheritance." (Matthew 21:38)

"And they caught him, and cast him out of the vineyard, and slew him." (Matthew 21:39)

"When the lord therefore of the vineyard cometh, what will he do unto those husbandmen?" (Matthew 21:40)

"They say unto him, He will miserably destroy those wicked men, and will let out his vineyard unto other husbandmen, which shall render him the fruits in their seasons." (Matthew 21:41)

"Esa saith unto them, Did ye never read in the Scriptures, The stone which the builders rejected, the same is become the head of the corner: this is the Lord's doing, and it is marvellous in our eyes?" (Matthew 21:42)

"Therefore say I unto you, The kingdom of God shall be taken from you, and given to a nation bringing forth the fruits thereof." (Matthew 21:43)

"And whosoever shall fall on this stone shall be broken: but on whomsoever it shall fall, it will grind him to powder." (Matthew 21:44)

<18> This entire parable is directed toward the priests, elders, and all those who were supposedly chosen to take care of God's Kingdom. However, they beat and killed His Messengers (servants) and rejected His Kingship over themselves, "but they [Children of Israel] have rejected me [God], that I should not reign over them" (1 Samuel 8:7). <19> Now he had sent His First Begotten Son and they would kill him as Christ that they might not hear the truth. With doing this God would take the Kingdom from them and give it to another nation, "The kingdom of God shall be taken from you, and given to a nation bringing forth the fruits thereof."

<20> This end of the spiritual kingly domination and lawgiving (scepter) from the tribe of Judah by the coming of the Messiah (Shiloh) was prophesied by Jacob at the last moment of his death that, "The scepter shall not depart from Judah, nor a lawgiver from between his feet, until Shiloh come" (Gen. 49:10). Shiloh or Messiah (Esa) came and with this parable finished the prophecy. <21> That is why after Christ, no other great Prophet came from the Children of Israel, but from another nation, the Arabs, who also are the Children of Abram (Abraham). God had promised Abram that they also would have a great Prophet of their own; read Children of Abram (Abraham), All Prophecies Are Fulfilled.

<22> Therefore we can say that there were three parts in Esa's mission to be fulfilled: First to teach and symbolically show (to be crucified and rise again) how to overcome the lower nature by crucifying it (false ego), thus to be born again (rise to the higher self); <23> secondly, he came for the lost sheep of the House of Israel who were called "people" in Jacob's prophecy which he should have gathered, "…until Shiloh come; and unto him shall the gathering of the people be" (Gen. 49:10), which he fulfilled (read Children of Abram (Abraham), All Prophecies Are Fulfilled); <24> and thirdly, as described in the parables above, to finish and fulfill the prophecy of Jacob that the scepter and lawgiving would be finished from the tribe of Judah, so consequently from the Children of Israel, and would be given to another nation.

<25> Therefore he fulfilled all parts of his mission. Again we can surely realize that God never fails to fulfill His promises and the prophecies which are given through His servants. They might take longer than the human expects but they will come true eventually.

"And when the chief priests and Pharisees had heard his parables, they perceived that he spake of them." (Matthew 21:45)

"But when they sought to lay hands on him, they feared the multitude, because they took him for a prophet." (Matthew 21:46)

<26> He gave his message to them and was relieved from his duty to let them know what the message of the Lord was for them, so it will be done – they could accept it or reject it, it was up to them now.

<27> That is the duty of a Messenger – to give the message to those he had been chosen to take it to. He is not responsible for the consequence. It is up to God.

<28> In truth his mission as Messenger was finished here. But he should have continued until he was crucified on the cross. So he stayed and taught further, and he pressed the elders until they would do His Will. <29> For this reason the next two chapters are described separately in an appendix. They are his final attacks on the corrupt elders and some points which should have been described.

APPENDIX

Tablet Thirty-Two

Chapter 22

"And Esa answered and spake unto them again by parables, and said," (Matthew 22:1)

"The kingdom of heaven is like unto a certain king, which made a marriage for his son," (Matthew 22:2)

"And sent forth his servants to call them that were bidden to the wedding: and they would not come." (Matthew 22:3)

"Again, he sent forth other servants, saying, Tell them which are bidden, Behold, I have prepared my dinner: my oxen and my fatlings are killed, and all things are ready: come unto the marriage." (Matthew 22:4)

"But they made light of it, and went their ways, one to his farm, another to his merchandise:" (Matthew 22:5)

"And the remnant took his servants, and entreated them spitefully, and slew them." (Matthew 22:6)

"But when the king heard thereof, he was wroth: and he sent forth his armies, and destroyed those murderers, and burned up their city." (Matthew 22:7)

<1> The meaning of this parable is almost identical to the previous one in chapter 21. The priests, elders, and those who had called themselves chosen ones were invited to purify themselves and progress so to be fit to enter the wedding (Pure Consciousness). But they became so engaged in the illusion of their power, prestige, and that they were chosen ones, that they became attached to this external world and lost sight of the true goal of life, "But they made light of it, and went their ways, one to his farm, another to his merchandise."

<2> Not only did they become attached to the external world and could not make it to heaven, but they beat and killed the Prophets who came to warn them of their erring ways, "And the remnant took his servants, and entreated them spitefully, and slew them."

<3> Because of all these things, God would take His Blessings and give them to others as a lesson, for the future, to humanity.

"Then saith he to his servants, The wedding is ready, but they which were bidden were not worthy." (Matthew 22:8)

"Go ye therefore into the highways, and as many as ye shall find, bid to the marriage." (Matthew 22:9)

"So those servants went out into the highways, and gathered together all as many as they found, both bad and good: and the wedding was furnished with guests." (Matthew 22:10)

<4> John the Baptist came and called to the elders and priests to come, repent, and be baptized. But they did not come. They were the ones who were bidden to the wedding. So John and Esa were forced to go to the highways and gather together those who were not bidden first to the wedding, "both bad and good: and the wedding was furnished with guests." <5> Those who were chosen on the highways were not all ready to come to the wedding.

"And when the king came in to see the guests, he saw there a man which had not on a wedding garment:" (Matthew 22:11)

"And he saith unto him, Friend, how camest thou in hither not having a wedding garment? And he was speechless." (Matthew 22:12)

"Then saith the king to the servants, Bind him hand and foot, and take him away, and cast him into outer darkness; there shall be weeping and gnashing of teeth." (Matthew 22:13)

"For many are called, but few are chosen." (Matthew 22:14)

<6> Those who have not made themselves pure enough and ready to enter the Kingdom Of Heaven will be drowned in the ocean of Maya to the outer darkness (ignorance).

"Then went the Pharisees, and took counsel how they might entangle him in his talk." (Matthew 22:15)

<7> The Pharisees thought by destroying him they could destroy what God had revealed through him. Prophets and Messengers (sons of God) say what is the truth – to destroy their physical bodies (or not) makes no difference – their missions will be done.

<8> Pharisees were not aware of the Laws and ways of heaven (God) but of the ways of men. So they tried to destroy him by bringing accusations against him. However, he would even destroy this plan so that they would be forced to kill him although he was completely innocent, both from God's Laws and from man's. So they would be guilty either way.

"And they sent out unto him their disciples with the Herodians, saying, Master, we know that thou art true, and teachest the way of God in truth, neither carest thou for any man: for thou regardest not the person of men." (Matthew 22:16)

"Tell us therefore, What thinkest thou? Is it lawful to give tribute unto Caesar, or not?" (Matthew 22:17)

"But Esa perceived their wickedness, and said, Why tempt ye me, ye hypocrites?" (Matthew 22:18)

"Shew me the tribute money. And they brought unto him a penny." (Matthew 22:19)

"And he saith unto them, Whose is this image and superscription?" (Matthew 22:20)

"They say unto him, Caesar's. Then saith he unto them, Render therefore unto Caesar the things which are Caesar's; and unto God the things that are God's." (Matthew 22:21)

<9> Esa was teaching them the "subjective approach with objective adjustment." Although the goal (objective) is to bring the Kingdom Of Heaven On Earth, however until then we should objectively adjust ourselves to the existing realities (Caesar).

<10> So, "Render therefore unto Caesar the things which are Caesar's, and unto God the things that are God's."

"When they had heard these words, they marvelled, and left him, and went their way." (Matthew 22:22)

<11> Also with this answer he made their plan ineffective.

"The same day came to him the Sadducees, which say that there is no resurrection, and asked him," (Matthew 22:23)

"Saying, Master, Moses said, If a man die, having no children, his brother shall marry his wife, and raise up seed unto his brother." (Matthew 22:24)

"Now there were with us seven brethren: and the first, when he had married a wife, deceased, and, having no issue, left his wife unto his brother:" (Matthew 22:25)

"Likewise the second also, and the third, unto the seventh." (Matthew 22:26)

"And last of all the woman died also." (Matthew 22:27)

"Therefore in the resurrection whose wife shall she be of the seven? for they all had her." (Matthew 22:28)

"Esa answered and said unto them, Ye do

COMMENTARIES ON ST. MATTHEW

err, not knowing the Scriptures, nor the power of God." (Matthew 22:29)

"For in the resurrection they neither marry, nor are given in marriage, but are as the angels of God in heaven." (Matthew 22:30)

<12> The male and female energies have little to do with the physical bodies of men and women. In Pure Consciousness (heaven), each person is androgynous (male and female).

<13> So the questions of the Sadducees were irrelevant in this regard that there is no such thing as marriage in heaven. That is why usually, from a spiritual point of view, there is only one partner for each person. <14> However, from the point of view of mental or physical attraction or convenience of life*, there can be marriage between two people of the opposite sex.

"But as touching the resurrection of the dead, have ye not read that which was spoken unto you by God, saying," (Matthew 22:31)

"I am the God of Abraham, and the God of Isaac, and the God of Jacob? God is not the God of the dead, but of the living." (Matthew 22:32)

<15> The Soul does not die when the body stops functioning. The body is like a garment for the Soul. When it becomes old we leave it and assume a new garment (body). <16> That is why Abraham, Isaac, and Jacob (their Souls) are not dead either. Their bodies were put in the cave that Abraham built for his wife's (Sarah's) burial. But they were not their bodies. They left their bodies and were reincarnated as Moses, Joshua, Elijah, Esa, etc.

<17> That is why "God is not the God of the dead, but of the living." It is the illusion of man that he is his body that causes him to think that those whose bodies stop functioning are dead. But that is from ignorance. Therefore there is no such thing as the resurrection of the physically dead, but of the living (reincarnation)! Resurrection is for the spirit.

"And when the multitude heard this, they were astonished at his doctrine." (Matthew 22:33)

<18> People had never heard such things, so they were "astonished at his doctrine." His doctrine is true, and truth will prevail.

"But when the Pharisees had heard that he had put the Sadducees to silence, they were gathered together." (Matthew 22:34)

"Then one of them, which was a lawyer, asked him a question, tempting him, and saying," (Matthew 22:35)

"Master, which is the great commandment in the law?" (Matthew 22:36)

"Esa said unto him, Thou shalt love the Lord thy God with all thy heart, and with all thy soul, and with all thy mind." (Matthew 22:37)

"This is the first and great commandment." (Matthew 22:38)

<19> As the body becomes dirty in a couple of days, the mind becomes dirty even faster and the Soul will be drowned in Maya through the dirty mind. If a person wants to stay physically clean all the time, he should stay in the shower twenty-four hours a day.

<20> If to keep the body perfectly clean a person should be washing himself all the time, then it would be even more difficult to keep the mind clean and pure which becomes soiled faster than the body by being affected and pulled to the attractions of the external world and away from the spiritual world and thoughts.

<21> That is why if a person wants to stay in higher planes and keep the mind immersed in the spiritual world instead of to the external world, he should direct all his attention and

---

* For convenience of life: For example, marriage of a man and a woman because the first spouses are dead and the marriage between them can be used to make life easier for both, etc.

being toward it. The purest and holiest of all in the spiritual world is God. <22> So by loving the Lord God with all our hearts, and with all our minds, and with all our Souls, we will direct all our attention toward Him and His creation. By doing so, gradually we will know Him and His Ways so we will be saved from the ocean of Maya and be(come) Divine as He is. By this intense one-pointed direction of thought, He will be our companion all the time, so we will know Him and be(come) Him.

<23> It is then that we can manifest His qualities and glorify Him by our actions. Then we be(come) a son of God and men can know Him and go to Him through us.

"And the second is like unto it, Thou shalt love thy neighbour as thyself." (Matthew 22:39)

<24> Also God is everything and if you love Him with such an intense one-pointedness, then you should also love all His creation as His manifestation. The closest of all those is your neighbour. So with this realization that God is all, you would not dare to harm anything in the universe for selfish reasons, because harming anything for selfish reasons is harming the Lord, <25> and you do not harm those you love.

"On these two commandments hang all the law and the prophets." (Matthew 22:40)

<26> With these two commandments a man will automatically refrain from murdering, stealing, fornication, false witnessing, etc., because they are all selfish actions which will hurt others, and hurting others is the same as hurting God. <27> The man who loves God with all his heart, being, and mind will not hurt Him but he will follow the Commandments of the Beloved One (God).

"While the Pharisees were gathered together, Esa asked them," (Matthew 22:41)

"Saying, What think ye of Christ? whose son is he? They say unto him, The son of David." (Matthew 22:42)

"He saith unto them, How then doth David in spirit call him Lord, saying," (Matthew 22:43)

"The Lord said unto my Lord, Sit thou on my right hand, till I make thine enemies thy footstool?" (Matthew 22:44)

"If David then call him Lord, how is he his son?" (Matthew 22:45)

"And no man was able to answer him a word, neither durst any man from that day forth ask him any more questions." (Matthew 22:46)

<28> Who is the Lord of a person beside God? It is his Soul. So David in spirit (astral body) heard the Lord talk with him, "... saith unto my Lord," that He would destroy his (David's) enemy. So Christ in fact was the same as David himself.

Tablet Thirty-Three

Chapter 23

"Then spake Esa to the multitude, and to his disciples," (Matthew 23:1)

"Saying, The scribes and the Pharisees sit in Moses' seat:" (Matthew 23:2)

"All therefore whatsoever they bid you observe, that observe and do; but do not ye after their works: for they say, and do not." (Matthew 23:3)

<1> After he established the supremacy of his teachings and actions over those of the Pharisees, scribes, and Sadducees, and silenced them, now he started his direct attack and his last part of the mission to show their hypocrisy. He did not speak in parables

any longer but in plain language. <2> This would do the last hurting to the false egos of the priests, elders, and spiritual teachers of the people, and would make them more zealous to plot against him. Although he said the truth, they did not want to hear it.

<3> He was trying to show that it is not the teachings of Moses which are bad or should not be followed, but it is the actions of their leaders which had corrupted Moses' teachings and laws. <4> That is why what they said, which is what Moses taught, "sit in Moses' seat," is good for a person and his spirit. But they themselves did not follow what Moses taught, "for they say, and do not."

<5> Again this shows that Christ did not come to do away with God's Commandments and Laws. But as described before in the main part of these commentaries, his mission was something else and he fulfilled it. One was to end the lawgiving by the House of Judah.

"For they bind heavy burdens and grievous to be borne, and lay them on men's shoulders; but they themselves will not move them with one of their fingers." (Matthew 23:4)

<6> By using Moses' teachings and by creating a class distinction for themselves, they misused their position and became a burden on people. <7> In truth they should have been a blessing but because of their lower natures they did not have true spiritual understanding and Grace. So they used their power to satisfy the propensities of their lower selves (survival needs, dominating need, longing for false prestige, etc.).

"But all their works they do for to be seen of men: they make broad their phylacteries, and enlarge the borders of their garments," (Matthew 23:5)

<8> They do all things in the faith for show, to catch the eyes of men, and to establish distinction for themselves.

"And love the uppermost rooms at feasts, and the chief seats in the synagogues," (Matthew 23:6)

"And greetings in the markets, and to be called of men, Rabbi, Rabbi." (Matthew 23:7)

<9> These all are done to be glorified by men. Indeed they receive their reward from men but not from God.

"But be not ye called Rabbi: for one is your Master, even Christ; and all ye are brethren." (Matthew 23:8)

<10> Only those who reach Pure Consciousness, the sons of God and the First Begotten Son (Christ) are worthy to be Masters. All others are struggling fellow travelers in the path, "all ye are brethren."

"And call no man your father upon the earth: for one is your Father, which is in heaven." (Matthew 23:9)

<11> The earthly parents are only tools, but the actual creator of our bodies is the Father in heaven (God). So He is the Father of all. <12> However this does not mean we should disregard our earthly parents. On the contrary, they are the most respectful and honorable beings after God and our spiritual teachers.

"Neither be ye called masters: for one is your Master, even Christ." (Matthew 23:10)

<13> Only those who are in Christ Consciousness (Divine) can be called "Master."

"But he that is greatest among you shall be your servant." (Matthew 23:11)

"And whosoever shall exalt himself shall be abased; and he that shall humble himself shall be exalted." (Matthew 23:12)

<14> That is the Law in heaven. Those who think they are great and falsely exalt themselves will be humbled. But those who know the power of God and know He is the true doer through them and even their greatness is from Him, will humble themselves and be exalted by Him. They exalt the Father, so they will be exalted.

"But woe unto you, scribes and Pharisees, hypocrites! for ye shut up the Kingdom Of

Heaven against men: for ye neither go in yourselves, neither suffer ye them that are entering to go in." (Matthew 23:13)

<15> The Pharisees and scribes will not enter into the Kingdom Of Heaven (Pure Consciousness) because they love the world more than heaven. Also they do not let those who are ready, "them that are entering" to go in by keeping the mass in ignorance and binding them with superstitions and false doctrines. <16> In fact Esa here is describing what are called the intellectual spiritualists, those who try to explain the Scriptures without intuitional feeling and contact with the Universal Mind. Then intentionally (because of their lack of faith) or unintentionally (because of their lack of depth), they create doctrines or interpret the Scriptures in a way that binds man more than frees him.

<17> The goal of creation is to free man from bondage, and the reason for Prophets and the words God revealed through them was (and is) to show man the path to this freedom. But we can see that because of these intellectual spiritualists (scribes and Pharisees) the religions have become a source of suffering and bondage to man. That is why neither those intellectual spiritualists enter into heaven themselves nor suffer those who want to know the truth and enter it to do so.

"Woe unto you, scribes and Pharisees, hypocrites! for ye devour widows' houses, and for a pretence make long prayer: therefore ye shall receive the greater damnation." (Matthew 23:14)

<18> But woe to these ignorant and false teachers who intentionally use religions and beliefs to gain mundane material things or to satisfy their lower natures.

Woe unto you, scribes and Pharisees, hypocrites! for ye compass sea and land to make one proselyte, and when he is made, ye make him twofold more the child of hell than yourselves." (Matthew 23:15)

<19> They convert people to a belief which had lost the original truth. So they make the person "twofold more the child of hell."

"Woe unto you, ye blind guides, which say, Whosoever shall swear by the temple, it is nothing; but whosoever shall swear by the gold of the temple, he is a debtor!" (Matthew 23:16)

"Ye fools and blind: for whether is greater, the gold, or the temple that sanctifieth the gold?" (Matthew 23:17)

"And, Whosoever shall swear by the altar, it is nothing; but whosoever sweareth by the gift that is upon it, he is guilty." (Matthew 23:18)

"Ye fools and blind: for whether is greater, the gift, or the altar that sanctifieth the gift?" (Matthew 23:19)

<20> When the mind becomes materialistic and gross (crude), it no longer has the keenness to see these simple truths.

"Whoso therefore shall swear by the altar, sweareth by it, and by all things thereon." (Matthew 23:20)

"And whoso shall swear by the temple, sweareth by it, and by him that dwelleth therein." (Matthew 23:21)

<21> After sanctifying the gift, the temple sanctifies the altar, and all of them are sanctified because of God who dwells in everything. <22> That is why there is a Divine side in everything when looked at through its Darma, "by him that dwelleth therein."

Tablet Thirty-Four

"And he that shall swear by heaven, sweareth by the throne of God, and by him that sitteth thereon." (Matthew 23:22)

<1> That is because God is in heaven.

"Woe unto you, scribes and Pharisees, hypocrites! for ye pay tithe of mint and anise and cummin, and have omitted the weightier matters of the law, judgment, mercy, and faith: these ought ye to have done, and not to leave the other undone." (Matthew 23:23)

<2> They have left out the reason for the rituals and laws, and perform them without emphasizing (understanding) their purpose. They should have understood and made others understand that the goal of all those laws and rituals is to create justice, mercy, and faith – be(come) Divine. These things they should have taught and done.

<3> Also those laws and rituals were necessary, and Christ did not say they should be forgotten. Their significances should have been understood and then they would become great vehicles to be(come) Divine. That is why he said, "these ought ye to have done," which is to teach what is the goal of these laws and rituals. <4> But he did not say to just teach the reason for them and leave the rituals out, "and not to leave the other [pay tithe of mint and anise and cummin, etc.] undone." <5> Again we see that he had not come to do away with God's Laws and Commandments.

"Ye blind guides, which strain at a gnat, and swallow a camel." (Matthew 23:24)

<6> They emphasize the smaller points and forget the greater things.

"Woe unto you, scribes and Pharisees, hypocrites! for ye make clean the outside of the cup and of the platter, but within they are full of extortion and excess." (Matthew 23:25)

"Thou blind Pharisee, cleanse first that which is within the cup and platter, that the outside of them may be clean also." (Matthew 23:26)

"Woe unto you, scribes and Pharisees, hypocrites! for ye are like unto whited sepulchres, which indeed appear beautiful outward, but are within full of dead men's bones, and of all uncleanness." (Matthew 23:27)

"Even so ye also outwardly appear righteous unto men, but within ye are full of hypocrisy and iniquity." (Matthew 23:28)

<7> It is the purification of the spirit (ethereal body) which is important. So clean the spirit, "which is within the cup and platter," then the outward actions will be cleaned automatically. Otherwise the dirt inside will come out and there is no way for a person with a dirty spirit (heart) but to be(come) a hypocrite.

"Woe unto you, scribes and Pharisees, hypocrites! because ye build the tombs of the prophets, and garnish the sepulchres of the righteous," (Matthew 23:29)

"And say, If we had been in the days of our fathers, we would not have been partakers with them in the blood of the prophets." (Matthew 23:30)

"Wherefore ye be witnesses unto yourselves, that ye are the children of them which killed the prophets." (Matthew 23:31)

"Fill ye up then the measure of your fathers." (Matthew 23:32)

<8> Most of the humans do not really want to know or hear the truth, especially those who are hypocrites. That is why they kill the Prophets and distort the truth so that they may continue in their ways. <9> But more and more humans will reach higher consciousness and eventually the truth will prevail.

"Ye serpents, ye generation of vipers, how can ye escape the damnation of hell?" (Matthew 23:33)

<10> But these hypocrites and those who close their ears to the truth will go through suffering and tribulation until they would have no choice but to open their eyes and see the truth.

<11> That is why even the suffering, tribulations, and all the things that had happened in history to man are for his own good.

"Wherefore, behold, I send unto you prophets, and wise men, and scribes: and some of them ye shall kill and crucify; and some of them shall ye scourge in your synagogues, and persecute them from city to city:" (Matthew 23:34)

<12> God knows man and the power of his lower nature (power of the tama guna) so well that He had predicted beforehand what humans would do to His Prophets.

"That upon you may come all the righteous blood shed upon the earth, from the blood of righteous Abel unto the blood of Zacharias son of Barachias, whom ye slew between the temple and the altar." (Matthew 23:35)

<13> "By doing these things, you create such a great burden upon yourselves, 'that upon you may come all the righteous blood shed upon the earth.' That is when I bring tribulation, holocaust, suffering, etc., unto you to awaken you. <14> It would be justified because of your own previous actions."

"Verily I say unto you, All these things shall come upon this generation." (Matthew 23:36)

<15> These surely will happen and no human power can stop it, until this generation (those who are chosen for this reward of creation, to reach Pure Consciousness) eventually become awakened and know, through creation and history, that there is only one way and it is God's way.

"O Jerusalem, Jerusalem, thou that killest the prophets, and stonest them which are sent unto thee, how often would I have gathered thy children together, even as a hen gathereth her chickens under her wings, and ye would not!" (Matthew 23:37)

"Behold, your house is left unto you desolate." (Matthew 23:38)

<16> How many times should God send Prophets to gather His children together and they would not come? <17> So again with the coming of Christ, the scepter was taken from those who thought they were the Chosen Ones and given to another nation as it was prophesied by Jacob and was promised to Abram (Abraham); for more detail read <u>Children of Abram (Abraham), All Prophecies Are Fulfilled</u>.

"For I say unto you, Ye shall not see me henceforth, till ye shall say, Blessed is he that cometh in the name of the Lord." (Matthew 23:39)

<18> That is the only sign Christ gave for his ultimate return. He will come, "in the name of the Lord." The Holy Name of the Lord (יהוה) is in him, and he (יהושע) is in the Holy Name of the Lord. This Sacred Name of the Lord is the only name of the Lord which cannot be pronounced or uttered in the manifested (material) world. It is the Name of the Son (יהושע), who comes in the Name of the Father (יהוה) as One, The Word (יהושע/יהוה).

<19> He will not be recognized (accepted) by everyone, "...ye shall not see me henceforth,...." He will be accepted only by those who recognize him, see that he is Blessed and is a Blessing. They will also Bless him and will be Blessed, "Blessed is he that cometh in the name of the Lord."

<20> So the mission of Christ finished here. He said what he wanted to say, and he did what he wanted to do. <21> In chapters 24 and 25 some prophecies for the later days (before the Kingdom comes) are foretold. And the rest of the gospel explains the last supper (symbol of overcoming the last material attachments), his betrayal (symbol of the hatred of the lower nature for truth), and his crucifixion. <22> By this he reached the zenith of his mission, that is, self-sacrifice for his ideal – not being self-centered, being humble.

<23> Then he was resurrected to show that in order to be born again you have to crucify your lower nature for a great ideal (His Will). Then you will rise from the lower self (death) to the higher self (life).

<24> Many in the past have truly been born again, and many will be. But now is the time that those who have been born again in the past and are now on the earth in many different places and nations (also in the Jewish communities), and who long for the Kingdom

Of Heaven On Earth, should gather together and see the truth which has been revealed through **The Greatest Sign** (creation and history). <25> They should put all their efforts together so that the truth may come and His Kingdom come on earth as it is in heaven.

Amen (☧).

SAINT JOHN (EXPLAINED)

The book, <u>St. John (Explained)</u> is an explanation of the first four chapters of <u>St. John</u> in the <u>Bible</u>.

SAINT JOHN (EXPLAINED)

(Chapters 1-4)

INTRODUCTION

Many points will be made in this book. However, there are two main ones which should be clearly understood and are the most important in this writing. They are the explanations about the subjects in chapters 1 and 4.

To understand the point in chapter 1, a brief introduction is given here:

The universe consists of consciousness and the three gunas (for more detail, read the book The Base). The three gunas are the three creative forces in the universe. They are tama (static), raja (mutative), and satva (sentient).

In the beginning, the balance between these forces became disturbed and their operative powers were released. The operative abilities of the three gunas (creative forces, Prakrti) is "The Word." God made all things with these operative powers and the consciousness of the universe.

The three creative forces (Divine Mother) use the consciousness (Divine Father) to create the manifested world. Creative forces without Logic (Father) cannot create systematically toward a purposeful end. Logic without creative forces (Mother) has no creative ability. That is why they both are necessary as two sides of one entity, Father and Mother, Logic and Grace, etc. – The Word and God which were (and still are) One, "in the beginning."

However, the universe was in an illogical (chaotic) state, until God decided to create a logical and systematic process to bring about the end of this chaos. That is when He decided (willed), "Let there be Light…." It was then that through The Word (creative forces), the will became flesh, "…and the Word was made flesh,…."

It is this unit consciousness which went through the **Eternal Divine Path** to Pure Consciousness, "and there was Light." He became the First Begotten Son, or God in manifested form!

The Mother is the spirit of God or The Christ (The Holy Ghost). It is this spirit which manifests itself through the Son. He also manifests The Divine Logic (Father). That is why the Son is the Christ. He is the manifestation of the Father and the Mother. He is The Word (יהוה/יחשוה), which is the Father, Mother, and Son as one.

When Divine Logic (Father) be(comes) earthbound, he is man. When the Grace (Mother) be(comes) earthbound, she is woman. That is when confusion (cloud) will prevail and the Son has to come back as the Messiah!

The other important point to emphasize and which was clarified again in this revelation is the subject in chapter 4 about the Samaritan woman and how the people of Samaria believed in Christ and his sayings without resentment or expectation of signs or miracles. It shows they were ready to be harvested (saved).

In the last moments of his death, Jacob (Israel) prophesied that "…until Shiloh [Messiah] come; and unto him shall the gathering of the people be" (Gen. 49:10). The people who were supposed to be gathered were the ten lost tribes of the House of Israel, or the Northern Kingdom (Samaritans). They were scattered abroad, but eventually were gathered under the banner of Christianity (for more detail, read Children of Abram (Abraham), All Prophecies Are Fulfilled).

It was these Samaritans who, in the gospel of Saint John, believed in Christ without any expectation for miracles or signs. Also in The Acts when Philip went to Samaria and preached to them the teaching of Christ, they rejoiced and were all baptized (Acts chapter 8). But the Apostles were persecuted in Jerusalem.

Again this shows that Christ did not come for the Jews but for the people of the House of Israel (the ten lost tribes).

SAINT JOHN (EXPLAINED)

Tablet One

Chapter 1

"In the beginning was the Word, and the Word was with God, and the Word was God." (John 1:1)

"The same was in the beginning with God." (John 1:2)

<1> There is a beginning for all things. Before any beginning, the universe was in a state of "Be"-ness. <2> However, the universe had the potential to be awakened, to create, and to be created. <3> The creative forces (three gunas) were in the state of balance or unreleased (not yet activated). <4> The controller of the three gunas is the consciousness (God). The consciousness and three gunas are a part and parcel of one entity and inseparable. <5> This creative forces is called The Word (ॐ). It was, and is with God, and was an inseparable part of God "and the Word was God," so "The same was in the beginning with God."

"All things were made by him; and without him was not any thing made that was made." (John 1:3)

<6> Because of the desire of the Father, the operative powers of the three gunas (Mother) were released, and with the use of these creative forces and consciousness, all things are created. <7> Without these creative forces, nothing could be created.

"In him was life; and the life was the light of men." (John 1:4)

<8> The life-force in the universe is the raja guna which is in the universal consciousness, "In him was life." <9> Also this is the force in each individual consciousness which is the spiritual power in man, and when it is under the influence of the satva guna (knowledge) it becomes the light for the consciousness.

"And the light shineth in darkness; and the darkness comprehended it not." (John 1:5)

<10> However, because of the influence of the tama guna (darkness), man becomes ignorant and the raja guna (action) and satva guna (knowledge) will be directed toward mundane external life. So although the light is always present, an ignorant consciousness, "comprehend[s] it not."

"There was a man sent from God, whose name was John." (John 1:6)

"The same came for a witness, to bear witness of the Light, that all men through him might believe." (John 1:7)

"He was not that Light, but was sent to bear witness of that Light." (John 1:8)

<11> John the Baptist came, who was the harbinger for the one who had the Light.

"That was the true Light, which lighteth every man that cometh into the world." (John 1:9)

<12> This light is the goal of the life to be realized.

"He was in the world, and the world was made by him, and the world knew him not." (John 1:10)

<13> This light of truth (consciousness) is in the world (everywhere), and everything is made by Him. Because of the ignorance (lower nature of man) and illusive separation of "I," the "world knew him not."

<14> Christ (Pure Consciousness) came to the world, "He was in the world." He was in Pure Consciousness and was the light of truth. But "the world knew him not."

"He came unto his own, and his own received him not." (John 1:11)

<15> He came to humanity which have the same light of truth within themselves, "came unto his own," but because of their ignorance (false ego), they "received him not."

SAINT JOHN (EXPLAINED)

"But as many as received him, to them gave he power to become the sons of God, even to them that believe on his name:" (John 1:12)

<16> However, to those who were in a higher consciousness, realized his light, and received him, he gave the power to reach Pure Consciousness, "to become the sons of God." He showed them the way to overcome their lower natures and go to their higher natures (be saved).

<17> Also those who are initiated into and know The Holy Name, "believe on his name," were saved.

"Which were born, not of blood, nor of the will of the flesh, nor of the will of man, but of God." (John 1:13)

<18> God willed, "Let there be light…"

"And the Word was made flesh, and dwelt among us, (and we beheld his glory, the glory as of the only begotten of the Father,) full of grace and truth." (John 1:14)

<19> He became the First Begotten Son of God, "…and there was light."

"John bare witness of him, and cried, saying, This was he of whom I spake, He that cometh after me is preferred before me: for he was before me." (John 1:15)

<20> Esa had reached Pure Consciousness before John. He was the First Begotten Son.

"And of his fulness have all we received, and grace for grace." (John 1:16)

"For the law was given by Moses, but grace and truth came by Esa The Christ." (John 1:17)

<21> The goal of the life is to be(come) Divine, not to follow some rigid rules and regulations. Of course rules and regulations are necessary but if all be(come) Divine (the Law), they will become minimal.

"No man hath seen God at any time; the only begotten Son, which is in the bosom of the Father, he hath declared him." (John 1:18)

<22> Only the First Begotten Son knows the Father completely, because he and the Father are one "which is in the bosom of the Father." He completely manifests His Light and Truth, "he hath declared him." Men cannot see Him so they need to see His Spirit in His son to know who He is.

Tablet Two

"And this is the record of John, when the Jews sent priests and Levites from Jerusalem to ask him, Who art thou?" (John 1:19)

"And he confessed, and denied not; but confessed, I am not the Christ." (John 1:20)

"And they asked him, What then? Art thou Elias? And he saith, I am not. Art thou that prophet? And he answered, No." (John 1:21)

<1> The priests and Levites came to find out who John the Baptist was. He denied that he was Christ, Elias, or the Prophet. <2> However, as Christ declared to his disciples, John was the reincarnation of Elias (Matthew 17:11-13). But for the reason of fear of the Pharisees and the king, he denied his identity (discriminating mind).

"Then said they unto him, Who art thou? that we may give an answer to them that sent us. What sayest thou of thyself?" (John 1:22)

<3> The priests who were Pharisees (John 1:24) insisted to receive some words from him, but because of the corruption in religion and government, John knew he would cause trouble for himself and Esa if he answered their questions directly. That is why he indirectly gave them an answer in the next verse.

"He said, I am the voice of one crying in the wilderness, Make straight the way of the Lord, as said the prophet Esaias." (John 1:23)

<4> This quote is from Isaiah 40:3, which refers to the voice of the one who comes before Christ to straighten the way. The one who was to come before Christ was Elias

SAINT JOHN (EXPLAINED)

(Elijah) (Matthew 17:10), so John was the reincarnation of Elias.

"And they which were sent were of the Pharisees." (John 1:24)

"And they asked him, and said unto him, Why baptizest thou then, if thou be not that Christ, nor Elias, neither that prophet?" (John 1:25)

<5> Now the Pharisees wanted to upset the faith of the people who were following John, and also to put him in a situation to make him profess who he was. That is why they asked him, If he was not Christ, Elias, or that prophet, why was he baptizing?

"John answered them, saying, I baptize with water: but there standeth one among you, whom ye know not;" (John 1:26)

"He it is, who coming after me is preferred before me, whose shoe's latchet I am not worthy to unloose." (John 1:27)

<6> Again he answered them that he was the harbinger of Christ, that he was Elias (Elijah).

"These things were done in Bethabara beyond Jordan, where John was baptizing." (John 1:28)

"The next day John seeth Esa coming unto him, and saith, Behold the Lamb of God, which taketh away the sin of the world." (John 1:29)

<7> John recognized Esa who was The First Begotten Son, "which taketh away the sin of the world."

"This is he of whom I said, After me cometh a man which is preferred before me: for he was before me." (John 1:30)

"And I knew him not: but that he should be made manifest to Israel, therefore am I come baptizing with water." (John 1:31)

"And John bare record, saying, I saw the Spirit descending from heaven like a dove, and it abode upon him." (John 1:32)

"And I knew him not: but he that sent me to baptize with water, the same said unto me, Upon whom thou shalt see the Spirit descending, and remaining on him, the same is he which baptizeth with the Holy Ghost." (John 1:33)

"And I saw, and bare record that this is the Son of God." (John 1:34)

<8> John saw the signs which caused him to recognize Christ. "Israel," or the House of Israel, would also recognize him!

"Again the next day after John stood, and two of his disciples;" (John 1:35)

"And looking upon Esa as he walked, he saith, Behold the Lamb of God!" (John 1:36)

"And the two disciples heard him speak, and they followed Esa." (John 1:37)

<9> Again John was cautious to not loudly proclaim who Esa was, but he only said this to his disciples and in an indirect manner.

"Then Esa turned, and saw them following, and said unto them, What seek ye? They said unto him, Rabbi, (which is to say, being interpreted, Master,) where dwellest thou?" (John 1:38)

<10> John's disciples recognized Esa as the Messiah – because John called him "the Lamb of God" they realized he was Christ. They went to him and accepted him as their master by referring to him as Rabbi ("Master").

"He saith unto them, Come and see; They came and saw where he dwelt, and abode with him that day: for it was about the tenth hour." (John 1:39)

<11> By saying, "Come and see," Esa also accepted them as his disciples. So they followed him and stayed with him.

"One of the two which heard John speak,

SAINT JOHN (EXPLAINED)

and followed him, was Andrew, Simon Peter's brother." (John 1:40)

"He first findeth his own brother Simon, and saith unto him, We have found the Messias, which is, being interpreted, the Christ." (John 1:41)

"And he brought him to Esa. And when Esa beheld him, he said, Thou art Simon the son of Jona: thou shalt be called Cephas, which is by interpretation, A stone." (John 1:42)

"The day following Esa would go forth into Galilee, and findeth Philip, and saith unto him, Follow me." (John 1:43)

"Now Philip was of Bethsaida, the city of Andrew and Peter." (John 1:44)

"Philip findeth Nathanael, and saith unto him, We have found him, of whom Moses in the law, and the prophets, did write, Esa of Nazareth, the son of Joseph." (John 1:45)

"And Nathanael said unto him, Can there any good thing come out of Nazareth? Philip saith unto him, Come and see." (John 1:46)

"Esa saw Nathanael coming to him, and saith of him, Behold an Israelite indeed, in whom is no guile!" (John 1:47)

"Nathanael saith unto him, Whence knowest thou me? Esa answered and said unto him, Before that Philip called thee, when thou wast under the fig tree, I saw thee." (John 1:48)

"Nathanael answered and saith unto him, Rabbi, thou art the Son of God; thou art the King of Israel." (John 1:49)

"Esa answered and said unto him, Because I said unto thee, I saw thee under the fig tree, believest thou? thou shalt see greater things than these." (John 1:50)

"And he saith unto him, Verily, verily, I say unto you, Hereafter ye shall see heaven open, and the angels of God ascending and descending upon the Son of man." (John 1:51)

<12> Christ was gathering his disciples and choosing those who were ready and came unto him.

Tablet Three

Chapter 2

"And the third day there was a marriage in Cana of Galilee; and the mother of Esa was there:" (John 2:1)

"And both Esa was called, and his disciples, to the marriage." (John 2:2)

"And when they wanted wine, the mother of Esa saith unto him, They have no wine." (John 2:3)

"Esa saith unto her, Woman, what have I to do with thee? mine hour is not yet come." (John 2:4)

<1> Esa did not want to start his miracles, "mine hour is not yet come."

<2> Also he called his mother "woman." That shows again that he was beyond the earthly bonds and even his mother to him was not any different than other women. That is, he was now only the Son of God (in Pure Consciousness) and had no earthly bonds. <3> Furthermore, there is no differentiation for him. All are equal in his eyes. Only the more righteous is higher.

"His mother saith unto the servants, Whatsoever he saith unto you, do it." (John 2:5)

<4> But his mother insisted.

"And there were set there six waterpots of stone, after the manner of the purifying of the Jews, containing two or three firkins apiece." (John 2:6)

SAINT JOHN (EXPLAINED) — Tablet 3

"Esa saith unto them, Fill the waterpots with water. And they filled them up to the brim." (John 2:7)

<5> To show his respect to his earthly mother, he conformed to her request.

"And he saith unto them, Draw out now, and bear unto the governor of the feast. And they bare it." (John 2:8)

"When the ruler of the feast had tasted the water that was made wine, and knew not whence it was: (but the servants which drew the water knew;) the governor of the feast called the bridegroom," (John 2:9)

"And saith unto him, Every man at the beginning doth set forth good wine; and when men have well drunk, then that which is worse; but thou hast kept the good wine unto now." (John 2:10)

<6> Esa made the water wine, but the true meaning of it is that the wine he made, through His Grace, was different than the earthly wine. When a person reaches the blissful state of overcoming the lower nature (the first three chakras), there is a liquid-like fluid which will be experienced in the throat and body which is known as "nectar." The bliss of this experience is so incredible that the person looks very drunk and ecstatic.

<7> Because of the presence of Esa at the feast, through his powers over the three gunas, and because he was asked to make wine for them, he caused the water to affect the people in such a way that they tasted the bliss of experiencing their spirit (eating manna). <8> The bliss of the spiritual experience is far greater than being made drunk by earthly wine. That is why the "governor of the feast" was so surprised by the excellence of the wine (blessed water) he received.

<9> Therefore Christ never approved of earthly wine. In fact anywhere in the Scriptures that wine or liquor is mentioned in any sense is referring to that spiritual experience (nectar).

"This beginning of miracles did Esa in Cana of Galilee, and manifested forth his glory; and his disciples believed on him." (John 2:11)

<10> Esa himself did not want to make people believe in him because of his miracles, but because of his teachings. However, in order to make people believe in him, miracles were used. <11> As history has shown, **people become so attached to the miracles of the Prophet that they forget about the teachings**. <12> Miracles are for those who do not understand the reason behind how they are manifested. For he who knows the Laws behind all things, there is no miracle, and all things are miracles!

"After this he went down to Capernaum, he, and his mother, and his brethren, and his disciples: and they continued there not many days." (John 2:12)

<13> Esa left his home.

"And the Jews' passover was at hand, and Esa went up to Jerusalem," (John 2:13)

"And found in the temple those that sold oxen and sheep and doves, and the changers of money sitting:" (John 2:14)

"And when he had made a scourge of small cords, he drove them all out of the temple, and the sheep, and the oxen; and poured out the changers' money, and overthrew the tables;" (John 2:15)

"And said unto them that sold doves, Take these things hence; make not my Father's house an house of merchandise." (John 2:16)

<14> The temple is a place of meditation, quietness, and where people should remember God and read about Him. It is not a place of worldly exchanges and activities.

<15> That is why Esa started his purification of the Jewish religion with this act of reminding them that the temple is a place of worship, not a place of business.

SAINT JOHN (EXPLAINED)

"And his disciples remembered that it was written, The zeal of thine house hath eaten me up." (John 2:17)

<16> After Christ did this act, the meaning of the Scripture was revealed to his disciples, and they understood why God had said this and what He meant by it.

"Then answered the Jews and said unto him, What sign shewest thou unto us, seeing that thou doest these things?" (John 2:18)

"Esa answered and said unto them, Destroy this temple, and in three days I will raise it up." (John 2:19)

"Then said the Jews, Forty and six years was this temple in building, and wilt thou rear it up in three days?" (John 2:20)

"But he spake of the temple of his body." (John 2:21)

<17> The temple as a building is an external symbol of the temple of the body. When a building is designed and known as the temple and kept for worshipping, people will think and remember God when they enter it. They will quiet the worldly passions in themselves when they are there. <18> So in fact the effect of the building as a temple should be an internal effect on the Soul.

<19> This is why when a person engages himself in many activities or allows his worldly passions to run wild and does not even go to religious activities, he is bound to fall into his lower nature and be drowned in the grip of Maya.

<20> The true temple of man is his own body. If man keeps his body, mind, and environment pure, so also will his temple (body) be pure. But those who are drowned in worldly activities should go to the temples as buildings so that they might give themselves a chance to quiet their passions for some time and feel the peace of the Lord.

<21> Now if even the temples and places of worship become areas of worldly activities, then where is there hope for man to find the peace of God?

<22> That is why Esa was giving them a lesson by his actions. <23> Also he was referring to the temple of his body which he said he would raise after three days and nights as a sign of his legitimacy of being Christ.

"When therefore he was risen from the dead, his disciples remembered that he had said this unto them; and they believed the Scripture, and the word which Esa had said." (John 2:22)

<24> Even his disciples did not understand him completely until later on.

"Now when he was in Jerusalem at the Passover, in the feast day, many believed in his name, when they saw the miracles which he did." (John 2:23)

"But Esa did not commit himself unto them, because he knew all men," (John 2:24)

"And needed not that any should testify of man: for he knew what was in man." (John 2:25)

<25> Those who truly believed in him, he initiated to his name, "…believed in his name,…" He wanted them to understand his teachings. However, the majority only believed in him because of his miracles and that is why he did not accept them as his disciples (did not initiate them), "But Esa did not commit himself unto them."

<26> "Because he knew all men." Esa knew that they were in their lower natures and would try to make him commit himself to them. Then they would bind him to their ways, and then judge him with their filthy minds and concepts.

SAINT JOHN (EXPLAINED)

Tablet Four

Chapter 3

"There was a man of the Pharisees, named Nicodemus, a ruler of the Jews:" (John 3:1)

"The same came to Esa by night, and said unto him, Rabbi, we know that thou art a teacher come from God: for no man can do these miracles that thou doest, except God be with him." (John 3:2)

<1> Nicodemus came to talk to Esa, not like an upright man, but cowardly during the night. He wanted the respect and support of the Jews and at the same time Esa's Grace and truth. Respect from men and Grace from God do not go together. <2> He also did not accept Esa as Christ but as "a teacher come from God." He was not pure enough to see him as he was – the Christ. That is why Esa answered him in the following way:

"Esa answered and said unto him, Verily, verily, I say unto thee, Except a man be born again, he cannot see the kingdom of God." (John 3:3)

<3> That is, unless a person overcomes the lower nature (Eve, lower consciousness) and comes to the higher self, he will not see the Kingdom of God. <4> Esa was telling Nicodemus that he just talks without having experienced the truth, and he had not overcome the lower nature. Therefore, whatever he said was invalid and from his lower self.

"Nicodemus saith unto him, How can a man be born when he is old? can he enter the second time into his mother's womb, and be born?" (John 3:4)

<5> Like the majority of the people, Nicodemus took what Esa said literally to mean being born again from the mother. He misunderstood completely what "to be born again" means.

"Esa answered, Verily, verily, I say unto thee, Except a man be born of water and of the Spirit, he cannot enter into the kingdom of God." (John 3:5)

<6> Again Esa repeated himself, that a man should be born from his lower consciousness (animal consciousness), "water," or "spirit," which is the subtle body with different propensities of desires and bondage (lower chakras). <7> Or in other words, to be born from the lower self to the higher self.

"That which is born of the flesh is flesh; and that which is born of the Spirit is spirit." (John 3:6)

<8> A man who is born from the womb of his mother (flesh) and stays in his lower nature (crudified consciousness) is indeed flesh. <9> Because what is flesh? It is crudified consciousness, and if the consciousness of man becomes very crude indeed he has no consciousness but fleshly consciousness. So he is flesh.

<10> But the man who overcomes the flesh and his lower spirit, will have spiritual consciousness, and is spirit. His Soul will be born from the bondage of his lower spirit (turbulent water, lower chakras) and will become a free Soul. <11> Also only the First Begotten Son of God had reached Pure Consciousness before creation (flesh).

"Marvel not that I said unto thee, Ye must be born again." (John 3:7)

"The wind bloweth where it listeth, and thou hearest the sound thereof, but canst not tell whence it cometh, and whither it goeth: so is every one that is born of the Spirit." (John 3:8)

<12> Esa saw that Nicodemus was ignorant of the realities of spiritual understanding. So he described to him the difference between a true spiritual person and a fleshly person.

<13> The spirit is completely detached from this external universe, and it comes and goes like the wind. You can hear it and feel it but do not know where it comes from and where it goes. <14> In other words, a person

SAINT JOHN (EXPLAINED) — Tablet 4

of the spirit is detached from all the bondage of the external world. Such a man has been "born of the Spirit." He is in the higher self.

"Nicodemus answered and said unto him, How can these things be?" (John 3:9)
<15> Still he did not understand.

"Esa answered and said unto him, Art thou a master of Israel, and knowest not these things?" (John 3:10)
<16> Esa marvelled that Nicodemus, a master of the laws of Israel and spiritual leader, did not understand such a basic truth of spirituality. Esa realized that Nicodemus is not in that state of consciousness to understand these things. That is why he continued.

"Verily, verily, I say unto thee, We speak that we do know, and testify that we have seen; and ye receive not our witness." (John 3:11)
<17> Esa said that whatever he told Nicodemus was true as "we speak that we do know," or in other words, "because I have seen and experienced the truth ('testify that we have seen'), it is true. But because you have no knowledge of these truths and only follow the dead words of your Scripture, so you do not understand them ('ye receive not our witness')."

"If I have told you earthly things, and ye believe not, how shall ye believe, if I tell you of heavenly things?" (John 3:12)
<18> He said, "If I have told you about these simple basic things, and you did not understand or believe them, then how can I talk about things on a higher level ('heavenly things'), so that you might understand and believe their truth?"

"And no man hath ascended up to heaven, but he that came down from heaven, even the Son of man which is in heaven." (John 3:13)
<19> No man reaches Pure Consciousness without first being lost in Maya, "And no man hath ascended up to heaven, but he that came down from heaven." <20> Even The First Begotten Son had gone through this process, **Eternal Divine Path**, "even the Son of man which is in heaven."

"And as Moses lifted up the serpent in the wilderness, even so must the Son of man be lifted up:" (John 3:14)

"That whosoever believeth in him should not perish, but have eternal life." (John 3:15)

"For God so loved the world, that he gave his only begotten Son, that whosoever believeth in him should not perish, but have everlasting life." (John 3:16)

"For God sent not his Son into the world to condemn the world; but that the world through him might be saved." (John 3:17)

"He that believeth on him is not condemned: but he that believeth not is condemned already, because he hath not believed in the name of the only begotten Son of God." (John 3:18)
<21> Those who believe, follow his teachings and path, and come out of their lower natures cannot be and are not condemned. But those who stay in their lower natures, by the lower nature, are already condemned. <22> They will not know his name.

"And this is the condemnation, that light is come into the world, and men loved darkness rather than light, because their deeds were evil." (John 3:19)
<23> Their condemnation is that man loves to stay in his lower nature and follow Maya. That is why their deeds become evil because of the darkness of their Souls. They do not want to see the light, but they want to stay in darkness.
<24> As Krishna said in the Bhagavad-Gita, those who are in their lower natures hate the light (truth) in themselves and in others.

"For every one that doeth evil hateth the light, neither cometh to the light, lest his deeds should be reproved." (John 3:20)

"But he that doeth truth cometh to the light, that his deeds may be made manifest, that they are wrought in God." (John 3:21)

<25> Only those who be(come) Divine (go to their higher selves) are saved, through Him (His Name).

"After these things came Esa and his disciples into the land of Judaea; and there he tarried with them, and baptized." (John 3:22)

"And John also was baptizing in Aenon near to Salim, because there was much water there: and they came, and were baptized." (John 3:23)

"For John was not yet cast into prison." (John 3:24)

"Then there arose a question between some of John's disciples and the Jews about purifying." (John 3:25)

"And they came unto John, and said unto him, Rabbi, he that was with thee beyond Jordan, to whom thou barest witness, behold, the same baptizeth, and all men come to him." (John 3:26)

"John answered and said, A man can receive nothing, except it be given him from heaven." (John 3:27)

<26> Father in heaven knows what is good for humanity and uses our bodies to do His Tasks. That is why "a man can receive nothing, except it be given him from heaven." <27> So the power of Christ was coming from heaven. The power of John was coming from heaven also, so if God does not want something to happen, it will not happen and similarly, if He desires something to happen, it will happen.

<28> That is why the human should use his intelligence and all the powers given to him to understand and do God's Will, and then surrender the result (the outcome) to the Lord and be content with whatever the result is.

"Ye yourselves bear me witness, that I said, I am not the Christ, but that I am sent before him." (John 3:28)

"He that hath the bride is the bridegroom: but the friend of the bridegroom, which standeth and heareth him, rejoiceth greatly because of the bridegroom's voice: this my joy therefore is fulfilled." (John 3:29)

<29> Again John indirectly proclaimed Esa as the expected Messiah and the Christ.

"He must increase, but I must decrease." (John 3:30)

<30> John also said that his mission was fulfilled. He found and witnessed the Christ. So he must decrease, and Esa must increase.

"He that cometh from above is above all: he that is of the earth is earthly, and speaketh of the earth: he that cometh from heaven is above all." (John 3:31)

<31> Esa was the First Begotten Son of God, "cometh from above." He was the Great Avatar (Maha-Avatar). <32> John was in a very high consciousness or even an Avatar but Esa was before him. He was the First Begotten Son.

"And what he hath seen and heard, that he testifieth; and no man receiveth his testimony." (John 3:32)

"He that hath received his testimony hath set to his seal that God is true." (John 3:33)

"For he whom God hath sent speaketh the words of God: for God giveth not the Spirit by measure unto him." (John 3:34)

<33> Most of the people, because they are in their lower natures, will not receive him and his testimony. But those who receive and understand him will believe in God, because a person in Pure Consciousness, especially the First Begotten Son ("God hath sent") speaks the truth because he is in truth. <34> He speaks the "words of God." He is in complete tune with the Lord, so he uses the Universal Mind and uses it abundantly "for God giveth not the Spirit by measure unto him."

SAINT JOHN (EXPLAINED)

"The Father loveth the Son, and hath given all things into his hand." (John 3:35)

<35> As any father who loves his son will give all things to him, so the Father in heaven also gives all things to those who are in Pure Consciousness (His son) (Rev. 21:7). <36> So whatever belongs to the Father belongs to the son also, especially the First Begotten Son.

"He that believeth on the Son hath everlasting life: and he that believeth not the Son shall not see life; but the wrath of God abideth on him." (John 3:36)

<37> The Prophets and Messengers (sons of God) are sent from God to guide humanity. Those who have faith in them and follow their words will have "everlasting life."

<38> But those who do not, will fall into Maya and their lower natures. They will have "the wrath of God abideth on" them; if they repent, however, they will be guided to the path of truth (Pure Consciousness).

Tablet Five

Chapter 4

"When therefore the Lord knew how the Pharisees had heard that Esa made and baptized more disciples than John," (John 4:1)

"(Though Esa himself baptized not, but his disciples,)" (John 4:2)

"He left Judaea, and departed again into Galilee." (John 4:3)

<1> Again Esa avoided the Jews and those who tried to condemn him.

"And he must needs go through Samaria." (John 4:4)

<2> Samaria was the country of the House of Israel (the ten lost tribes of Israel) which were replaced by other nations. Many Israelites had returned to their land. <3> They are the ones (the House of Israel) who were to be gathered together by the Messiah, "…until Shiloh come; and unto him shall the gathering of the people be." (Gen. 49:10). For more detail, read Children of Abram (Abraham), All Prophecies Are Fulfilled.

"Then cometh he to a city of Samaria, which is called Sychar, near to the parcel of ground that Jacob gave to his son Joseph." (John 4:5)

<4> Joseph, as described in Children of Abram (Abraham), All Prophecies Are Fulfilled, was the receiver of the birthright (material possession) which was promised to Abraham by God. <5> Joseph's sons, Manasseh and Ephraim, were claimed by Jacob to be his own (Jacob's). They were supposed to create a nation and a multitude of nations, a promise given to Israel (Gen. 35:11). <6> The two tribes of Manasseh and Ephraim with eight others (not Judah and Benjamin) became the North Kingdom of the Children of Israel or the House of Israel which are also known by the name of Samaria.

<7> The House of Israel was captured, carried away by the Assyrians, and replaced by other people. <8> However, as it is explained in Children of Abram (Abraham), All Prophecies Are Fulfilled, they moved toward the west and northwest of Europe and created many nations which were gathered as Christians by the teachings of Christ.

<9> In this chapter, the mention of Esa going to the well of Jacob in Samaria which was given to Joseph, and also the fact that people believed in him in this land, shows the significance of the name Samaritans with the mission of Christ. <10> They also became the means to transfer the teachings of Christ further to the rest of the House of Israel in order for the prophecies of Jacob to be fulfilled and for God to be glorified.

"Now Jacob's well was there. Esa therefore, being wearied with his journey, sat thus

SAINT JOHN (EXPLAINED) Tablet 5

on the well: and it was about the sixth hour." (John 4:6)

"There cometh a woman of Samaria to draw water: Esa saith unto her, Give me to drink." (John 4:7)

"(For his disciples were gone away into the city to buy meat.)" (John 4:8)

"Then saith the woman of Samaria unto him, How is it that thou, being a Jew, askest drink of me, which am a woman of Samaria? for the Jews have no dealings with the Samaritans." (John 4:9)

<11> Esa asked the woman from Samaria to give him a drink. But she had so many concepts which had been imposed on her by the society and environment that she was surprised when a Jew asked her for a drink. She judged him by his appearance and background.

<12> But to God and the son of God (those in Pure Consciousness) all things in the universe are equal and all men are the same. That is why a Samaritan and a Jew were the same to Esa.

<13> He only loved men who were or are in their higher selves or striving to go to their higher selves. But the woman's concepts were so strong that she could not see who Christ was.

"Esa answered and said unto her, If thou knewest the gift of God, and who it is that saith to thee, Give me to drink; thou wouldest have asked of him, and he would have given thee living water." (John 4:10)

<14> Esa answered, "If you knew who I am and knew I am able to give you from the fountain of knowledge (Pure Consciousness) or living waters, you would not ask me such earthbound questions and would realize that all men are equal to me.

<15> "So you would have served me with great devotion and given me the water without question. Then you could have received from me the 'living waters' (Grace) which would free you from all these concepts and would enable you to enter the Kingdom Of Heaven (Pure Consciousness)."

"The woman saith unto him, Sir, thou hast nothing to draw with, and the well is deep: from whence then hast thou that living water?" (John 4:11)

<16> As usual, like most people, she took Esa's words literally and interpreted that Esa was talking about the water in the well. But he was talking about spiritual water (The Holy Ghost).

"Art thou greater than our father Jacob, which gave us the well, and drank thereof himself, and his children, and his cattle?" (John 4:12)

<17> She also had great attachment to her ancestral beliefs. She could not believe anyone could be greater than Jacob. However, Jacob can be reincarnated and manifest his greatness again. <18> Also this shows that she was one of those from the ten tribes who have come back to their land, because she referred to her ancestry as Jacob or Israel.

"Esa answered and said unto her, Whosoever drinketh of this water shall thirst again:" (John 4:13)

"But whosoever drinketh of the water that I shall give him shall never thirst; but the water that I shall give him shall be in him a well of water springing up into everlasting life." (John 4:14)

<19> Again Christ explained that he was not referring to the material water (H_2O) but to the spiritual water (The Holy Ghost). <20> Or in other words, Christ said, "I will open your eyes to the spiritual knowledge, and will take you from your lower nature (with all your worldly concepts related to it) to your higher self (higher consciousness) <21> and eventually to Pure Consciousness where there will be the 'everlasting life.'"

<22> This "everlasting life" which "shall be in him [Soul] a well of water [knowledge

SAINT JOHN (EXPLAINED)

of the Soul through the well of spirit (ethereal body)]" will lead to Pure Consciousness, "springing up into everlasting life."

"The woman saith unto him, Sir, give me this water, that I thirst not, neither come hither to draw." (John 4:15)

<23> Again the woman thought about the material water and wanted the "living water" so she would not have to go to the well and draw water. <24> She wanted some power to decrease her hardship. She did not want God, or spiritual progress, but material happiness, because she did not know what the goal of life is, and why she was there and had that life. <25> In reality she was not ready to receive the living water. So that is why Christ changed the subject.

Tablet Six

"Esa saith unto her, Go, call thy husband, and come hither." (John 4:16)

"The woman answered and said, I have no husband. Esa said unto her, Thou hast well said, I have no husband:" (John 4:17)

"For thou hast had five husbands; and he whom thou now hast is not thy husband: in that saidst thou truly." (John 4:18)

<1> By this conversation Esa showed her that she is not worthy to enter the Kingdom Of Heaven, because Esa taught that even if a man divorces his wife without any great cause, he and she have done adultery. So they are not pure. <2> Now this woman had five husbands and the man she lived with at the time was not even one of them, so surely that is adultery.

<3> Marriage and the commitments related to it have a great physical, social, mental, and spiritual significance, and whoever defiles it is not doing the Will of the Lord.

"The woman saith unto him, Sir, I perceive that thou art a prophet." (John 4:19)

"Our fathers worshipped in this mountain; and ye say, that in Jerusalem is the place where men ought to worship." (John 4:20)

<4> With this, the woman became awed and perceived that he was a Prophet. So she asked a spiritual question, whether the true place to worship God is in the mountains or in Jerusalem.

"Esa saith unto her, Woman, believe me, the hour cometh, when ye shall neither in this mountain, nor yet at Jerusalem, worship the Father." (John 4:21)

<5> He answered that there will be a time when the consciousness of man will rise to such a high level that they would not seek God in any temple or mountain, but in their own spirit.

"Ye worship ye know not what: we know what we worship: for salvation is of the Jews." (John 4:22)

<6> He told the Samaritans they do not know what they worship, because their king made two calves and told them these were their gods which brought them out of Egypt, and then they started to worship them. But the Jews continued their traditions and did not make any image as the object of their worship. That is why they were more in tune with God's Plan than the Samaritans.

"But the hour cometh, and now is, when the true worshippers shall worship the Father in spirit and in truth: for the Father seeketh such to worship him." (John 4:23)

"God is a Spirit: and they that worship him must worship him in spirit and in truth." (John 4:24)

<7> But the true worshipping is neither in the mountains nor in the temples. It is in the Soul-to-Soul relationship with the Father through meditation and The Holy Ghost. Only through such worshipping can man

SAINT JOHN (EXPLAINED)

establish a true relationship with God and reach the truth, "in Spirit and in truth."

"The woman saith unto him, I know that Messias cometh, which is called Christ: when he is come, he will tell us all things." (John 4:25)

"Esa saith unto her, I that speak unto thee am he." (John 4:26)

<8> The woman was impressed with what Esa said but hesitated to believe him. She brought up the subject of the Messiah only to mean that she will believe when the Messiah comes. <9> Esa told her, "I am the Messiah."

"And upon this came his disciples, and marvelled that he talked with the woman: yet no man said, What seekest thou? or, Why talkest thou with her?" (John 4:27)

<10> His disciples came and saw him sitting and talking with a woman. Because of their concepts, they were a little annoyed to see him talking with her but since he was so pure and unattached in his approach, they neither suspected nor dared to ask him why he, a Holy man, would talk with a woman.

<11> He was so pure that men and women were equal for him. He was in the Garden of Eden where all things are equal in the eyes, "And they were both naked, ... and were not ashamed." (Gen. 2:25).

"The woman then left her waterpot, and went her way into the city, and saith to the men," (John 4:28)

"Come, see a man, which told me all things that ever I did: is not this the Christ?" (John 4:29)

<12> The woman completely forgot about the "living water" and "everlasting life." She almost believed in him because he said things about her past. <13> She missed the truth by thinking about herself rather than about reaching Pure Consciousness. So she went to the town and called others to go see him, not to receive the "everlasting life," but because he told her of her past.

Tablet Seven

"Then they went out of the city, and came unto him." (John 4:30)

"In the mean while his disciples prayed him, saying, Master, eat." (John 4:31)

"But he said unto them, I have meat to eat that ye know not of." (John 4:32)

"Therefore said the disciples one to another, Hath any man brought him ought to eat?" (John 4:33)

"Esa saith unto them, My meat is to do the will of him that sent me, and to finish his work." (John 4:34)

<1> His disciples insisted that he eat, but he said that he had already eaten and was not hungry. His disciples did not understand what he meant by "I have meat to eat that ye know not of." He was referring to the "hidden manna" (Rev. 2:17), the nectar that allows people in higher consciousness not to require very much food. He went to an ecstatic state by experiencing the nectar.

<2> Those who do the Will of the Father ("him that sent" us to this world) will be provided with this food (nectar).

"Say not ye, There are yet four months, and then cometh harvest? behold, I say unto you, Lift up your eyes, and look on the fields; for they are white already to harvest." (John 4:35)

"And he that reapeth receiveth wages, and gathereth fruit unto life eternal: that both he that soweth and he that reapeth may rejoice together." (John 4:36)

"And herein is that saying true, One

SAINT JOHN (EXPLAINED)

soweth, and another reapeth." (John 4:37)

"I sent you to reap that whereon ye bestowed no labour: other men laboured, and ye are entered into their labours." (John 4:38)

<3> Christ entered into a prophetic mood. He said, "Is it not true that you say that after four months there will be a harvest? Now I tell you, look up and see the field (the Samaritan lands) that will be ripe in awhile to be harvested."

<4> Those who help in gathering and harvesting will receive wages which are the "fruit unto life eternal." Their reward will be in Heaven, that God and His sons in Heaven "may rejoice together."

<5> It is true here that "One soweth, and another reapeth." God sowed the seeds and now he and his disciples would reap those who were ready in that land.

<6> That is why they were there, "to reap that whereon" they "bestowed no labour." Many Prophets and Great Souls had worked many lifetimes to prepare these people, and now his disciples would gather what they had done with no labour exerted.

<7> The significance of these sayings is that they had been said in the land of the Samaritans, the land of the House of Israel (the ten lost tribes). <8> Also, many of the House of Israel had returned to their lands after they were freed from their captors, the Assyrians. So they are the people (the Children of Israel) who should have been gathered together and then spread Christ's teachings even further to the west, to their brethren in the west and northwest of Europe; read <u>Children of Abram (Abraham), All Prophecies Are Fulfilled</u>.

"And many of the Samaritans of that city believed on him for the saying of the woman, which testified, He told me all that ever I did." (John 4:39)

<9> They were so ready to accept Christ and with the testimony of only one person, many believed.

"So when the Samaritans were come unto him, they besought him that he would tarry with them: and he abode there two days." (John 4:40)

<10> The Samaritans believed and welcomed him to their houses. They did not condemn him or ask him for signs and miracles, but simply believed him because they did not have many concepts that would be a barrier to their spiritual understandings.

"And many more believed because of his own word;" (John 4:41)

"And said unto the woman, Now we believe, not because of thy saying: for we have heard him ourselves, and know that this is indeed the Christ, the Saviour of the world." (John 4:42)

<11> Also, many believed because of the truth of his teachings, not because of his miracles or knowledge of their past. <12> They believed in him because they saw the light, and because they were the seekers of the truth. They loved the light and came to him.

<13> Again The Plan of God is clearly stated here. God had reincarnated many Great Souls in higher consciousness in the Samaritan and Western European areas, who would accept the Christ and would gather these people under Christ (House of Israel).

"Now after two days he departed thence, and went into Galilee." (John 4:43)

"For Esa himself testified, that a prophet hath no honour in his own country." (John 4:44)

<14> It is true, those who are close to the Prophet do not believe in his prophethood, because they have seen his childhood, growth, mistakes and shortcomings in the past. They have a very hard time accepting him as a Messenger from God.

"Then when he was come into Galilee, the Galilaeans received him, having seen all the things that he did at Jerusalem at the feast: for they also went unto the feast." (John 4:45)

<15> However, this time the Galilaeans (the people of his home town) received him,

not because of his teachings, but because of "all the things that he did at Jerusalem."

"So Esa came again into Cana of Galilee, where he made the water wine. And there was a certain nobleman, whose son was sick at Capernaum." (John 4:46)

"When he heard that Esa was come out of Judaea into Galilee, he went unto him, and besought him that he would come down, and heal his son: for he was at the point of death." (John 4:47)

<16> Again Esa came to the Jewish territory, and they believed in him only when he did miracles. They were only interested in taking advantage of his powers. However, Samaritans believed in him because of his words (teachings).

"Then said Esa unto him, Except ye see signs and wonders, ye will not believe." (John 4:48)

"The nobleman saith unto him, Sir, come down ere my child die." (John 4:49)

"Esa saith unto him, Go thy way; thy son liveth. And the man believed the word that Esa had spoken unto him, and he went his way." (John 4:50)

"And as he was now going down, his servants met him, and told him, saying, Thy son liveth." (John 4:51)

"Then enquired he of them the hour when he began to amend. And they said unto him, Yesterday at the seventh hour the fever left him." (John 4:52)

"So the father knew that it was at the same hour, in the which Esa said unto him, Thy son liveth: and himself believed, and his whole house." (John 4:53)

"This is again the second miracle that Esa did, when he was come out of Judaea into Galilee." (John 4:54)

<17> So again these people believed in him only after they saw miracles. They were not interested in his teachings but in his powers. <18> However, in Samaria they believed in him because of his sayings (teachings).

READINGS
(THE KORAN)

The book, **Readings (The Koran)**, contains many essays on many verses of the **Koran**. **Koran** means "readings." These essays clarify many points in the **Koran**.

READINGS (THE <u>KORAN</u>)

INTRODUCTION

Next after The Revelation, the word of God came to Prophet Muhammad. As it is described in The Revelation, both the seven churches and seven seals are descriptions of the seven truths which will be revealed to humanity through Prophets (Angels of the churches).

Therefore, the next Scripture after the <u>Bible</u> was revealed to Moslems. In fact, the complete Scripture for humanity is one that covers the description of all the seven symbols in **The Greatest Sign**. The fourth sign (☾) and its Scripture will be considered in this small book of commentary.

Historically after Christianity covered a great part of the world for some centuries, the teaching of Christ became lost. Instead of following the example of Christ, people started to follow dogmas about the religion. Therefore, expectations of the coming of another great Prophet increased in this later period.

Prophet Muhammad was the one all were expecting. His mission was to bring the highest spiritual realization (submission) and to establish the Kingdom Of Heaven in a small part of the world for a short period of time. We must remember that the Arab civilization then was so primitive that the people used to kill their female children or sell them in childhood. However, after Islam was established, in a short period of time that same society became the center of the world civilization. That shows how the proper environment makes a difference for the progress of man.

The explanation of the advent of Islam given above is historical, but the spiritual explanation is that the coming of this new teaching for furthering the course of human evolution had been predicted in The Revelation when the fourth seal is opened (pale horseman). By adding this teaching to the <u>Bible</u>, the Scripture for humanity will become more complete.

Also, as it has been described in the book <u>Children of Abram (Abraham), All Prophecies Are Fulfilled</u>, the promise of a Messiah coming from the seed of Ishmael (the son of Abram, the father of the Arabs) was also given to Abram (Abraham). So with the coming of Prophet Muhammad, this promise was also fulfilled.

Before starting the commentary on the <u>Koran</u> there are two points which should be mentioned:

1- Allah was the name of God which was known by most of the religions of the world where Islam was revealed. As "God" is a very universal name for the Lord, and is used for God in all religions, "Allah" was the name used at that time. However, after Prophet Muhammad used this name in his religion, other religions stopped using it in order to differentiate Islam from themselves.

In fact the name Allah is closely related to many original sacred names found in the original <u>Bible</u>.* Some of these sacred names for God show their closeness to the name "Allah."

The name "Eloah" means "God" in the singular form. It comes from "Ahlah," which means "to worship, to adore, (and) presents God as the one supreme object of worship, the Adorable One."† In fact, that is exactly the meaning of God in Islam. He is the only

---

*   Restoration of Original Sacred Name Bible, Missionary Dispensary Bible Research (P.O. Box 1260, Briston, Okla. 74010).

†   Ibid., p. XIII.

object of worship, the Adorable One.

"Eloah" which is a Hebrew word, corresponds with the "Elah" or "Elahah" in the Chaldean language.‡ These names are very similar to the Arabic words "Ellah" and "Allaho," which mean the same as Allah. Also "Elohim" is the plural form of "Eloam."§

So Allah is related to the sacred names of the Lord as used in the Bible. In fact, they are sacred names because they are vibrational sounds (mantras) and are empowered to affect and awaken different spiritual forces in the human.

2- Also Prophet Muhammad himself declared that he did not consider the name of God to be Allah, but that all the beautiful names belong to Him:

> Say: Call Him Allah [Adorable One] or call Him Rahman [Compassionate], by whichsoever name you call Him (is the same). His are the most beautiful attributes [related to Him through all His beautiful names]. (Surah¶ The Children of Israel [Bani-Israel] verse 110)

Therefore, in this book the name Allah in the Koran is substituted for the name "God," a derivative of "Generator, Operator, and Destroyer," which are His attributes. This makes the Koran more universal and the reader can relate to the truth underlying the verses more easily.

These commentaries cover a variety of topics and are a revelation to enforce the truth behind the teachings and realities of **The Greatest Sign**. They include a very small portion of the Koran, but because this Scripture is a repetition of the same truths again and again, and a large part of it consists of different stories of past events, understanding these verses as described will greatly help in understanding the rest of the Koran.

However, the aspirant should remember clearly the truth behind the fourth symbol in **The Greatest Sign** which is being **submissive** (the highest spiritual realization) to The Plan (Will) of the Lord (to establish the Kingdom Of Heaven within and without).

Therefore, in studying the Koran and Islam we should always have in mind where its symbol is located in **The Greatest Sign**, and how Prophet Muhammad established the Kingdom Of Heaven in the Arab nations for a short period of time. Only then will these commentaries, the Koran itself, and Islam (Is Lamb), make more sense in relation to the other signs and history.

This book is also a source of different essays about various aspects of life. It is set up in the following manner:

Under each topic heading, there is a short essay about its meaning and how it relates to the Koran. Then the name of the Surah (both in English and Arabic) is given. Often a subtitle follows for the individual verses. Then the verse (or the relevant part of the verse) and its number is printed. Those words in parenthesis are part of the translation; the parts in brackets were added in this commentary to aid in the understanding of the verses, or to give the symbolic meaning of the words. Occasionally bolding was also added to bring attention to certain phrases in the verses. After the verse, there might also be another short explanation of that individual quote.

---

‡   Ibid., p. XIII.

§   Ibid., p. XIV.

¶   "Surah" refers to individual revelations, equivalent to a chapter.

READINGS (THE KORAN)

Tablet One

ABILITY OF GOD TO CHANGE HUMAN AND HIS CONDITION

<1> By controlling the power of the three gunas, God is guiding this universe to its ultimate goal, which is to reach Pure Consciousness. <2> As it was explained in the book The Base, He has changed the human form and condition many times until twelve thousand years ago when He created the human in the present condition. <3> Also later on, He confused men by taking away their telepathic ability. By their languages being different (Gen. 11:7), He prevented them from self-destruction. He tried to direct them toward the higher self by discouraging the pursuance of selfish and egoistical life (making fame and name instead of utilizing this universe to reach higher consciousness).

<4> Still, with all these evolutionary processes, humans did not listen to God, and we can see it was necessary for Him to send many Prophets for guiding humanity. Starting six thousand years ago, this present human has been left by himself with some guidance from Prophets. <5> But now it is time for the human to wake up and understand The Plan of the Father, to establish the Kingdom Of Heaven within and without, to utilize all this universe and life for reaching higher consciousness and Pure Consciousness, and to let the great spiritual people with leadership abilities take charge of guiding all of humanity to the goal.

<6> Otherwise, if humans do not understand these realities, the tribulation will become worse and many will suffer to complete destruction. Therefore, if the humans in this condition fail to understand the purpose of being here and do not establish the Kingdom Of Heaven as soon as possible, the Lord will save those who have reached higher consciousness and the others will be left in ignorance (hell). <7> He is able to create a new kind of man and a new condition to continue the process. But if we understand **The Greatest Sign** and establish the Kingdom Of Heaven as soon as possible, then the process of helping the whole universe to reach Pure Consciousness will be accelerated and all will continue to progress.

Surah Women (An-Nisa)

Ability of God to change the human condition as He wills:

O People, if God so desires, He is able to remove you and replace you by others. He has complete power to do this. (133)

Surah The Angels (Al-Mala'ikah)

Ability of God to change unit consciousnesses to a new evolutionary stage if it seems necessary:

If He so desires, He can remove you and create a new creation instead. (16)

AKASHIC RECORDS

<8> In physics there is a well-known law which states: "There is a reaction to each action equal with the action but negative in direction." This law is also true in the world of spirit (Universal Laws). <9> For each action of man there is a reaction that remains in the universe as a record. These records of the actions are called Akashic Records and in the Bible, "a book of remembrance" (Malachi 3:16).

<10> Akashic Records can be seen as the memory which remains in the Universal Mind. <11> Whoever places his mind in tune with the Universal Mind can receive the

READINGS (THE KORAN)

truth of all things which happened in the past, "Ask, and it shall be given you; seek and ye shall find; knock, and it shall be opened unto you:" (Matthew 7:7).

Surah Ornaments of Gold (Az-Zukhruf)

Akashic Records are the records of remembrance:

> Yes, It [the Koran] is an essential part of the Eternal Tablet (the source of all Scriptures), which we possess. (4)

Surah Defrauding (At-Tatfif)

"Sijjin" are bad records in the Akashic Records:

> The records of the transgressor are kept in Sijjin.
> How would you know what Sijjin is?
> It is a book of records. (7-9)

"Iliyin" are good records in the Akashic Records:

> The records of the righteous are kept in Iliyin.
> How would you know what Iliyin is?
> It is a book of records. (18-20)

<12> When Prophet Muhammad was demanded by Gabriel to "Read!", it did not mean to read from a paper or regular writings, but it meant to read from the Akashic Records. <13> Also there was a Prophet born in America by the name of Edgar Cayce who would go to sleep (in a kind of trance) and would reveal valuable information from these Akashic Records. His works also are known as "Readings." Koran means "Readings."

<14> Prophet Muhammad could not read or write even after He was chosen as a Prophet. What he read were the revelations given to him from the Akashic Records.

<15> Also it should be noticed that in the Surah "Ornaments of Gold (Az-Zukhruf)" it is clearly mentioned that "It" (the Koran) is an "essential part of the" Akashic Records ("Eternal Tablet") <16> but not all of it.

ALL THINGS BELONG TO GOD

<17> God has created all things. So everything belongs to Him. We are all only guests here in this manifested world. We are not here to become attached to this material universe, but to utilize it for our spiritual progress until we each become a son of God. Then, of course, whatever belongs to the Father also belongs to the son.

<18> Forgetting this fact causes man to think he is the owner of things in this world and to become attached to this idea. This then brings attachment to the material world and also greed, which creates unhappiness for the self and others.

<19> Therefore, this very fact should be understood by all: That all things belong to God. This universe should be utilized and shared in such a way that all have equal opportunities to progress physically, mentally, and spiritually toward the goal (Pure Consciousness).

Surah The Cow (Al-Baqarah)

All things belong to Him:

> To God belongs the East and the West, and whithersoever you turn, your face is toward Him. Surely He is All-Embracing, All-Knowing [He is everything]. (115)

Surah The Family of 'Imran (Ali 'Imran)

> To God belongs whatsoever is in the earth; and unto him all shall return. (109)

READINGS (THE KORAN) Tablet 1

ALL ARE GOD'S CHILDREN

<20> All humans are His children, because He brought them from the unaware part of the universe (state of "Be"-ness) and created everything to help them to reach Pure Consciousness.

<21> The word "children" is used because He separated them into men and women, so they are both sons and daughters of God. <22> When each of these children reach Pure Consciousness, he or she becomes a son of God (in His image). A son of God is neither male nor female, <23> but is both and is neither!

Surah The Family of 'Imran (Ali 'Imran)

Accepting the other religions because all are for His children:

Say (O Muhammad): We believe in God and that which has been revealed unto us, and that which was revealed to Abraham and Ishmael and Isaac and Jacob and the tribes, and which was given to Moses and Esa and other Prophets from their Lord. There is no distinction between them for us, and unto Him we submit. (84)

<24> He said, "The God of all these people who received the Scriptures is one. We believe in Him and whomever He sends." <25> However, the Scriptures were changed after they were revealed and many things were distorted. Prophet Muhammad said, "We should understand these things and know that there is only One God for all of us and we should worship only Him."

Surah The Spider (Al-'Ankabut)

Warning Moslems not to fight with Jews and Christians:

Argue not with the people of the book except with a good manner which is best, save their unjust ones. Tell them: We believe in that which is revealed to you; our God and yours are One, and unto Him we submit. (46)

<26> We see here that Prophet Muhammad was discouraging his followers from fighting, and even arguing, with the Jews and Christians. <27> Later on, however, there was a great fight between them (the Crusades). <28> So it is the people who create these fights and inflict suffering on humanity by following dogmatic beliefs and bringing the superstitions between groups.

<29> It is not the religions that have brought much suffering to humanity, but it is the people (intellectual spiritualists) who misinterpret the religions and present them to the people. Because of their ignorance and because they do not search for the truth themselves, the regular people believe whatever is told them. They become narrow-minded and this brings suffering to humanity. <30> In short, suffering comes from ignorance.

Surah The Troops (Az-Zumar)

All are God's children:

If God so willed to choose a son, He would have chosen whosoever He pleased out of His creation... (4)

ANGELS (AVATARS)

<31> All those beings or forces that God uses in order to guide His universe are called Angels. That is why the tama guna, raja guna, and satva guna are each called an Angel (Lucifer, Michael, and Gabriel). <32> Also each unit consciousness which reaches Pure Consciousness will be used to help the universe. These unit consciousnesses also become Angels (Avatars).

<33> When a unit consciousness reaches Pure Consciousness and comes back as a Prophet or spiritual teacher, he will be called

READINGS (THE KORAN)

an Avatar (god-man). However, when a unit consciousness reaches Pure Consciousness but does not leave his body and stays in the world to help others, he will be called a Satguru (man-god).

Surah Cattle (Al-An'am)
Avatars are mentioned in the Koran:

Had we appointed an Angel as Messenger, We would assuredly have him in the form of a man (that men could relate to him). (9)

<34> Therefore, Angels, who are in Pure Consciousness or the spiritual world, can assume human bodies and become Prophets.

Surah The Pilgrimage (Al-Hajj)

God chooses His Messengers from among the Angels and men. God certainly is All-Hearing, All-Seeing. (75)

<35> Those Prophets which come from the Angels are Avatars (god-men, Great Paravipras), and those who come from humans are Satgurus (men-gods).

Surah The Angels (Al-Mala'ikah)
Sending Angels as Prophets (Avatars):

…who appoints the Angels as His Messengers, having two, three or four wings [wings are symbols of the scope of their abilities]… (1)

Tablet Two
CHOICE OF THE HUMAN TO BE GUIDED OR TO GO ASTRAY

<1> The human (each unit consciousness) has the choice to be guided or to become a lost soul. <2> In fact, because this choice exists, the whole evolutionary process and creation of the universe became necessary.

<3> So those who use this choice for staying ignorant of the realities of the universe, and become attracted to Maya and self-centered, are the lost ones.

<4> Those who use their choice toward the submissiveness to The Plan of God are the saved ones.

Surah Ornaments of Gold (Az-Zukhruf)
The choice of the human to follow the spiritual path or to become lost:

Unbelievers say: that if the Gracious One so willed, we would not have worshipped any beside Him. They have no knowledge of truth… (20)

Surah "Time" or "Man" (Ad-Dahr or Al-Insan)
The human has the choice to believe or to become lost:

In truth, We have shown him [the human] the straight path, whether he be grateful and follows it, or be disbelieving and rejects it. (3)

DAHARMA

<5> Daharma (Darma) is a Sanskrit word which means "innate nature." Every particle or being in this universe has one or multiple Daharmas. The Daharma of an animal is to eat, drink, sleep, regenerate, progress in that level of consciousness, and die. He does not have any knowledge of self or God. <6> The Daharma of man in the physiological level is as an animal, but man is more developed and also has a greater Daharma. That greater

READINGS (THE KORAN)

Daharma is to realize the spiritual world and to reach the goal of creation: Pure Consciousness. <7> That is, the human body is the most perfect instrument for reaching Pure Consciousness.

<8> Daharma can also be described as rules, regulations, or Laws which govern each part of the universe alone, or all of the universe as a whole. We have individual Daharma, Daharma for a special group of people (men, women, etc.), Daharma for society, world Daharma, Universal Daharma (Laws), etc.

<9> These Daharmas are called the Laws of God by the Prophets. These Laws can never be broken. A person might think he can break these Laws, or even apparently that person will break the Laws. But eventually he who breaks these Laws breaks himself against them.

Surah The Poets (Ash-Shu'ara)
Following the Laws of the universe (Daharma):

So be aware of your duty to God and obey me. (179)

THE DEVIL

<10> The devil is that force which bends the Soul of the human toward material enjoyment (illusion of separation). He makes the delights of life become attractive, and promises many things which seem equal with everlasting happiness. <11> However, as a person gains them more and more, he sees the emptiness of these promises. So the person will continue to try to gain new promises of the attraction of the external world.

<12> Only a crudified Soul can be lost in the ocean of Maya (excess attraction to the external world, illusion). <13> The force which crudifies the Soul is none other than the tama guna, which bends the Soul and brings confusion – confusion to the mind, lethargy, and directs the actions toward materialism and the attention toward greed and the wanting of excessive material possessions. It causes the person to be drowned in the illusion of the world. It makes a person believe that the material world is all there is.

<14> Therefore, the only force that should be overcome is the power of the tama guna over the Soul, which causes all the false images a person has about the self and all the false attractions of the external world.

<15> However, overcoming this power is not so easy. It needs much purification, meditation, a pure environment, and an elaborate effort to bring the Soul out of the grip of this force. That is why the concept of the devil has been so powerful in human life. <16> This force has been the main reason for creating the whole universe and taking the unit consciousnesses through the evolutionary process until they gain this perfect human body with all the power of its flesh. Then a human can utilize all his strength to overcome the force of the tama guna over his Soul and reach Pure Consciousness.

<17> As man progresses, however, in warding off the devil (the power of the tama guna), he should utilize those powers he obtains toward a worthy goal. Otherwise he will misuse them for selfish gains and desires, and will go further under the influence of this force.

<18> That is why meditation alone, without having a worthy ideal to work for, will not be very helpful. It actually can be harmful in the long run, because the energy and power obtained by meditation will be directed toward false egoistical gain and will create bad samskaras (sins) which will throw the person further into ignorance (illusion). <19> In this regard a spiritual teacher (Master), who takes you to God, is most helpful.

Surah The Family of Imran (Ali 'Imran)
What the Koran means by the devil:

READINGS (THE KORAN)   Tablet 2

The desire for pleasure from the objects of the senses which comes from women and offspring and stored-up reserves of gold and silver, marked horses (by their names), and cattle and properties, appeal to the worldly men. These are the comfort for this material world. It is with God which is an excellent abode.

Say (O Muhammad): Shall I inform you of something better than these, which are so dear to you (O worldly people)? For those who keep from evil and are aware of their duty to God, there are gardens with rivers flowing beneath and pure companions, and the bliss of God. God is watchful of His bondmen. (14-15)

<20> Therefore, "desire for pleasure" comes from women (lower nature of man) and children and "stored-up reserves of gold and silver," and horses and land and cattle and things like that, which are the attractions of the external world. <21> In verse 15 it says, "those who keep from evil," which means, "Those who keep from being attracted to these things which are evil (which are attractions to the external world) can understand the reality of the spiritual world."

<22> So again evil is nothing but excess attraction to the external world. Evil is not a being. It is a quality of the human which can be overcome. So evil is the same as Maya, the attraction to the material world.

Surah The Pilgrimage (Al-Hajj)
The devil is excess attraction to the external world:

Let them be busy with eating, drinking, and being deceived by vain hopes. They soon will come to know the futility of their actions. (3)

Surah The Bee (An-Nahl)
The devil has power only over those who do not trust God, or do not accept His refuge:

Seek the protection of God. The devil has no power over those who put their trust in the Lord.
He only has power over those who become His friends and ascribe partners with God. (99-100)

Surah Exile (Al-Hashr)
The devil's way (ignorance):

They [the hypocrites] are like the devil, who says to man disbelieve, and when man believes, Satan says, I am not of you, I fear God, the Lord of the worlds. (16)

<23> Only by loving God with all your heart, mind, and being, and directing everything toward Him, can His Grace be won. Then you will be saved from the attraction of the external world (Maya), which without His Grace is impossible to overcome. <24> So a person should become one-pointed toward God and be submitted to His Will so that nothing is able to distract him from his concentrated attention to Him. "His eyes should become single" (Matthew 6:22).

DIFFERENCE BETWEEN GOD (FATHER) AND OTHERS

<25> In the beginning when the nucleus of the universe was formed, this center was (and still is) in Pure Consciousness and all-pervasive. He felt that the whole universe was His Body. He realized how His Body is dead under the influence of the tama guna (is in the state of unawareness, ignorance). He decided to create The First Begotten Son and this universe in order to help the cells of His Body (unit consciousnesses) come to life (Pure Consciousness, complete awareness).

<26> Therefore, He created the universe

READINGS (THE KORAN)

and developed the evolutionary process, which helps man to progress toward the highest and most delightful state of being in this universe, Pure Consciousness (perfection).

<27> So, is He equal with someone who has not created anything to help others in this great task? <28> Or is someone who sacrifices himself to guide others to the right path toward the goal, the same as those who do nothing for others but are selfish and self-centered? Certainly not!

<29> Self-centeredness and selfishness (the illusion of being separated from others) furthers ignorance and the crudification of the Soul. <30> But understanding the realities behind this universe and helping all to reach Pure Consciousness will free a man from that binding force (the devil).

Surah The Bee (An-Nahl)

The difference between God and others is that He has created all things but others did not or cannot:

> Is he who creates the same as one who creates not? Will you not then take heed? (17)

DISBELIEVERS

<31> Disbelievers are those who become attached to the external world and their limited false egos instead of realizing that this life is a transitory process which should be utilized for progressing toward perfection. They forget there will be a death for them also and another world.

<32> These are the ones who go far astray and will be drowned in Maya. This is the truth of being a believer or a disbeliever – it is not the amount of prayer or belief in some dogma. Those things are only tools to direct the mind toward the spiritual world.

Surah The Family of Imran (Ali 'Imran)

> And they (the disbelievers) devised their plans and God devised His; God is the best Planner. (54)

<33> Disbelievers think they can cheat God, especially by changing the Scriptures. But they do not know that God is very aware of their hearts and will carry out His own Plan for this universe. They (intellectual spiritualists) change the Scriptures in order to serve their own purposes; however, then God sends another great Prophet to bring the truth back to the light again. <34> So the sun does not stay under the clouds forever. The truth should be accepted by all. That is The Plan.

<35> God brings His religion again and again into this world. The people try to destroy it, but another great Prophet or spiritual teacher comes, uses the Akashic Records, and reveals the truth again, until eventually all understand the unseen Hand of God in history and creation.

Surah Women (An-Nisa)

Hypocrites seek attention of men instead of the Lord:

> Verily, the hypocrites seek to deceive God, but they will be punished by God. When they stay for prayer, it is only for show to be seen by men. They remember God but a little. (142)

Surah The Heights (Al-A'raf)

"You know them by their marks" corresponds to The Revelation "to receive a mark" (Rev. 13:16-17):

> The occupants of the Heights [highly developed spiritual Souls] call out to men who are known by their marks: Your multitude availed you not nor did your pride. (48)

<36> The mark is that pride of material possessions, GREED.

READINGS (THE KORAN)

Surah Abraham (Ibrahim)
Description of a disbeliever:

Woe unto the disbelievers; whom awaits a great punishment, for they have chosen the life of this world over the hereafter, and create obstacles in the way of God (for believers) and seek to make it look crooked; they verily have gone far astray. (3)

Surah The Ascending Stairways (Al-Ma'arij)

It [hell] encompasses him who turned and fled (from truth),
The one who hoarded wealth and withheld it. (17-18)

Tablet Three
DISCIPLES

<1> The Prophets, Gurus, and people in higher consciousness should be provided with plenty of time and privacy. They should be highly respected by others, especially their disciples. Impure vibrations should not be created in their presence. <2> In short, a pure environment is necessary for a high conscious person to be able to help others effectively.

<3> That is why people should approach him only for important matters or when they are given permission. Otherwise others will affect the mind of the spiritual teacher (or Prophet) and this will create annoyance toward disciples and others.

<4> In India, some people cover the picture of their Guru under a curtain during the day to prevent anxiety for their beloved. This also has another great significance. <5> Impure and unaware people who do not have enough respect for the beloved then cannot affect their spiritual environment and create bad energies.

Surah The Clans (Al-Ahzab)
Manner of disciples toward their spiritual guide and Prophets:

O those who believe, enter not the house of the Prophet uninvited for a meal, even then come in the proper time. But come when you are called, and when the meal is ended, disperse. Linger not eager to talk. This causes an annoyance to the Prophet – he would be shy to ask you to leave, but God is not shy of showing the right manner. And when you ask something from the wives of the Prophet, ask from behind the curtain [with purity in your hearts]. That would be purer for your hearts and their hearts. (53)

ELECTED ONES

<6> The Elected Ones are those Souls who, through many lives and much struggle, have cleansed themselves to such a state that they can easily ward off evil (the power of the tama guna) over their Souls. <7> They understand The Plan of God and are ready to take the responsibility of carrying out this Plan.

<8> These are the real spiritual soldiers for bringing the world back to the spiritual path and for helping others to understand that the true happiness is the way God has shown us, not the pursuance of selfishness.

<9> They will fight not by sword but by their spiritual powers, purity, and true knowledge of the spiritual world. Of course, if to establish the truth use of the sword is necessary, they would not hesitate to use it (Bhagavad-Gita).

READINGS (THE KORAN)

Surah The Family of Imran (Ali 'Imran)

Remember when God told Esa, I will cause you to die and then your Soul shall be ascended unto Me and will clean you from calamities of disbelievers, and will exalt those who follow you above disbelievers to the Day of Judgment; then unto Me you all will return, and I shall judge between you on what you used to differ. (55)

<10> Why will Christ and his followers be preferred over the disbelievers to the Day of Judgment? Because he and his followers were always preferred to the disbelievers. <11> They are the Elected Ones. The people who followed Christ were Elected Ones, as the people who followed Prophet Muhammad were Elected Ones. As Prophet Muhammad said, "I am (רִחנוּשַׂה)!"
<12> These people have been reincarnated again and again, and each time they set the world in the right direction. After they leave, in a short period of time, humanity becomes corrupt again. So they have to come back. Each time they come back, however, some new people will be saved and reach higher consciousness. <13> This process will continue until all understand The Plan of God and establish the Kingdom Of Heaven On Earth. That is why Christ called them "the salt of the earth." Without these people we wouldn't even be here where we are now. That is why they are above disbelievers. They are the Elected Ones, the Divines.

Surah The Heights (Al-A'raf)

Those who lead the truth are always chosen to establish the Kingdom Of Heaven, have been with Moses, and are always with the appointed Prophet of each era (the Elected Ones):

From the followers of Moses there is a group who follow the truth and establish justice by means of it. (159)

Surah The Prophets (Al-Anbiya)

Inheritance of the earth by the righteous:

Verily we have recorded in the Scriptures, after the exhortation, my righteous bondmen shall inherit the earth. (105)

<14> Who are the righteous bondmen? They are the Elected Ones. Those who are elected will come to this earth again and again until they establish the Kingdom Of Heaven On Earth and inherit it. They are the Paravipras. They are the ones referred to in Matthew 5:10 as, "Blessed are they which are persecuted for righteousness' sake: for theirs is the kingdom of heaven." They will inherit the Kingdom Of Heaven On Earth, within themselves, and in heaven.

Surah The Story (Al-Qasas)

He who does good will be rewarded more than his good deed; and he who does evil will only be punished equal to his action. (84)

<15> Those who do good will inherit the earth and His Kingdom.

Surah The Spider (Al-'Ankabut)

Tests to choose the believers (Elected Ones):

Do humans think it is enough to say that: We believe and would not be tested?
We verily tried people before them and also God will make known who is truthful and who is not [is a hypocrite]. (2-3)

Surah The Event (Al-Waqi'ah)

Elected ones from the past:

A large part of those of old. (13)

Elected ones who will be added to the ones from the past after each Prophet comes:

Add a few from later time. (14)

READINGS (THE KORAN) — Tablet 3
EVOLUTION

<16> Evolution is the process of progressing from the unaware state of consciousness to Pure Consciousness (complete awareness).

<17> In complete unawareness, a unit consciousness has no sense of knowledge of Self and is bound to its crudest form by the power of the tama guna. <18> However, as the grip of the tama guna loosens up, the unit consciousness becomes more and more aware of Self.

<19> The complete awareness of a unit being will not be gained unless the ego develops, which is a sense of separation from other parts of the universe and a feeling of independence. This achievement is very hard to gain in eternity (un-manifested universe), and when it is gained it is even harder to actualize that ego. Therefore, the false ego is developed. Without any process that could guide this false ego toward perfection (actualization) it is almost impossible for men to achieve, but not for God (His Grace).

<20> That is why the evolutionary process has been created in this manifested universe. This body is given to the human and is put in this manifested world in order to be used as a guide for the unit consciousness existing within it, by suffering whenever it goes wrong. <21> A realized person uses this universe and its suffering as a guiding light to reach the goal by overcoming those obstacles which are the source of the sufferings.

<22> All of the universe has been evolved by God. He has taken man through the evolutionary process to reach the stage of using the human body to ward off the power of the tama guna over his Soul and reach Pure Consciousness, and to help others reach there also.

<23> God has created the history and has left many marks for humans to understand the way this universe works. <24> Whoever misuses the power and Grace given by God is bound to be doomed. <25> But he who understands the realities behind this universe and utilizes this in order to reach the goal and help others also to reach it, will be given the greatest reward, Pure Consciousness (heaven).

Surah Cattle (Al-An'am)

There is no one animal in the earth, nor a flying bird which flies on its two wings, but are people like you. We have neglected nothing in the Book. Then with their Lord all will be gathered. (38)

<26> This verse shows that the evolutionary process has been revealed to Prophet Muhammad. He says all animals are like people, because they are unit consciousnesses too. They are in the evolutionary process and will reach higher consciousness, and eventually Pure Consciousness. Then they will become sons of the Lord. So they will be gathered unto Him.

Surah Ta Ha

Moses answered: Our Lord is He who has bestowed upon everything its nature, then has guided it to perfection. (50)

<27> How can a person be "guided to perfection" if he has only one lifetime to do that and fails? Unless he comes again and again to this world in many lifetimes and is guided a bit each lifetime towards perfection, it would seem to be an unfair creation. There are some people who never even have a chance to think deeply about God, creation, their destiny, and so on. <28> If we had only one lifetime, and did not have the chance to perfect ourselves, either from ignorance (being lost in Maya) or because of the situation we were in, then either God will not judge us or if He does, we cannot say He is a just God, which He is. So it is necessary for humans to go through the evolutionary process until they reach perfection (Pure Consciousness).

Surah Noah (Nuh)

God has created you from the earth to grow, (17)

READINGS (THE KORAN)

<29> Therefore, the evolutionary process goes from very subtle to very crude solid factors (earth), then goes back to human, and eventually goes to Pure Consciousness.

Surah The Fig (At-Tin)

Through the evolutionary process God has taken away the powers of the humans. Only those who are worthy will gain those powers back (as explained in The Base and The Essence):

Truly we created man in the best mould;

Then we cast him down to the lowest of the low [after the fall of man, but for his own good],

Except those who believe and do good works, for them is everlasting reward [to reach Pure Consciousness]. (4-6)

Tablet Four

GOD CAN DO ALL THINGS

<1> God has complete control over the power of the three gunas. He made the universe by using the unit consciousnesses and the power of the three gunas. So He can do whatever He desires to His universe by virtue of controlling the forces from which all things were made.

<2> However, He is just, merciful, and beneficent. He uses His Powers only for guiding men and testing them in order to be sure that they are worthy and have progressed enough to be able to enter heaven (Pure Consciousness).

Surah The Romans (Ar-Rum)

Observe, therefore, the signs of God's mercy (everywhere), how He quickens the earth after its death! He is the One who gives life to the dead, **for He is Able to do all things**. (50)

GOD DOES NOT HAVE A NAME – ALL GOOD NAMES ARE HIS

<3> Does a baby already have an earthly name when it is born? No, it is given a name by his parents. God was in this universe before any human. He was the first in the universe in Pure Consciousness. There was no one around to give Him a name. His Name cannot be pronounced on earth (manifested universe)!

<4> Also in the Bible God is referred to as "The God of Abraham, Isaac, and Jacob." He accepted no name in the Bible until after the Children of Israel left Egypt, and then He called Himself Jehovah, which is not really a name but a sound vibration close to the crudest part of The Word: "…the Word was with God, and the Word was God" (John 1:1), which is a sound vibration with God (and is God).

<5> Still this name was given to the Children of Israel not only to be used as a sound vibration for the remembrance of God, but because they were demanding a name for their God. All their neighbors had gods with names, so they wanted a name for their God. That is why He gave them this name, which they call Jehovah, which is really not the correct pronunciation of this part of The Word.

<6> This can be clearly seen when God revealed Himself to Moses in the burning bush. Moses wanted to know what to say if the elders of the Israelites asked him what the name of his God was. God answered, "I AM THAT I AM" (Ex. 3:13-14). So He did not give a name because He does not have a name. He is The Word. "He is that He is." He just IS.

READINGS (THE KORAN)

<7> In fact, not only is God "that He is," also all things are "that they are." Names are used for human convenience and communication. Therefore, nothing has a name but "is that it is." <8> However, sound vibrations have different effects on our Souls and environment.

<9> Other evidence for this point is the story of giving names to the different things in creation by Adam (Genesis 2:19-20). God did not name anything. It was Adam who gave names to animals and the things in the universe. And it is the human also in this world who uses names for his convenience or uses languages for communication. <10> But man becomes so attached to the names given by himself, and becomes so proud of his language, that he forgets the main reason for using these things. Then he is not ready to give them up because of some psychological attachment, such as nationalism or group attachment, false pride, etc.

<11> In fact, the human never gave up idol worshipping, because after Prophets destroyed idol statues and directed the attention of humanity toward the invisible God, humans still had psychological gods to worship. If we do not destroy these false psychological gods, do not understand the very deep purpose of all things in this universe, and do not utilize them as such, we will not reach true freedom.

<12> True freedom is to reach Pure Consciousness, and to consider the whole universe as our country and to accept a basic language as a world language. Those beautiful words or sentences from different cultures which cannot be translated to the basic language should be included in the world language. <13> Eventually in the process of time a new language will be created with all the powerful influences from other languages. This process can easily be seen in the English language as "Darma," "karma," etc., have been used as part of the English language in recent years and most people understand their meanings.

<14> Names and languages are for communication. Humans should not become attached to these things, but should leave behind all false relationships with them to create a freer flow between all of humanity.

<15> "Allah" also is a great sound vibration which directly affects the seed of the mind (the sixth chakra). <16> It consists of two syllables, "All" and "ah." "Ah" is directly related to the breath and is a part of the vibration of the Holy Breath, and "All" is a prefix which is used in front of names in Arabic. <17> So the most important part in the name Allah is the "ah" which is related to the breath and which can be used to awaken the spiritual centers in the body. So it is not really a name but a sound vibration (very subtle) like Jehovah (Ja-Hov-Ah). <18> In fact, its power is because of its subtlety of vibration, development of the power of concentration, and its relationship to the breath, three characteristics for a mantra.

<19> That is why Prophet Muhammad says, "It does not matter what you call Allah. All good names belong to Him."

Surah The Children of Israel (Bani Israil)

Say: Call Him Allah [Adorable One] or call Him Rahman [Merciful], by whichsoever beautiful name you call Him (is the same). His are the most beautiful attributes. (110)

GOD IS ALL-PERVASIVE

<20> When a unit consciousness overcomes the power of the tama guna (binding force), he reaches Pure Consciousness (all-pervasiveness). <21> Father was the first who was in Pure Consciousness and is all-pervasive. That is why it does not matter which direction you face to pray. His countenance is everywhere.

<22> Also, the whole universe is His Body, and that is why we have come from Him and will go back to Him.

READINGS (THE KORAN)

Surah The Cow (Al-Baqarah)

To Allah belongs the East and the West, and wheresoever you turn, your face is toward Him. Surely He is All-Embracing, All-Knowing [He is everywhere]. (115)

Surah Women (An-Nisa)

To God belongs whatsoever is in the heavens and whatsoever is in the earth; and He encompasses all things [All things are within Him, He is All and beyond]. (126)

Surah Iron (Al-Hadid)

God is everything (all-pervasive):

He is First and the Last [He has been, He is, and He will be forever], He is the Manifest and the Hidden, and He is the knower of all things. (3)

GOD IS THE GREATEST

<23> God (Father) was the first in Pure Consciousness. He is the One who knows the Laws of the Universe (the Laws of reaching Pure Consciousness). He created the universe in order to help the unit consciousnesses reach Pure Consciousness. He took the human through the evolutionary process in order to help him to the goal. He is the One directing the universe toward its goal.

<24> So He is the greatest.

Surah The Family of Imran (Ali'Imran)

A righteous human being whom God had given the Scripture and Wisdom and Prophethood will not say to people: Worship me instead of God. But they say, according to their duty: Be faithful devotees of God, by constant preaching and attentive studying of the Scripture. (79)

<25> This verse says that those whom God sends as His Messengers or Prophets do not tell the people, "Worship me." They come and say, "Worship the Lord." <26> For example, even if God incarnated Himself as a human and started preaching the truth, what good would it do for Him to say who He is? The only thing that would happen is that the people who followed Him would create big egos and start to look down at others. They would say, "We are the followers of God Himself, and you are the followers of the Prophets or His sons, so we are greater than you!" <27> That is why those who take the Prophets as the Lord God or think they are the Chosen Ones, not because they do the Will of the Father but for mere imagination, do more harm than good for God and His Will.

Surah The Unity (Al-Tauhid, Al-Ikhlas)

The Divine Father (God) is the greatest:

Proclaim: He is God, the One;
God the Self-Existing, Eternally Besought of All.
He begets not, nor is begotten;
And there is none comparable unto Him. (1-4)

Tablet Five

GOD WANTS HUMANS TO UNDERSTAND

<1> God can do whatever He wants to the powerless human, because He has complete control over the three gunas and all the unit consciousnesses. He can bring so much fear to men that they submit to Him. But God does not want humans to do that. <2> He wants

READINGS (THE KORAN)

humans to understand His love, wisdom, compassion, and mercy. He wants humans to understand the realities of this universe, and respect and love Him for all He has done for them. <3> Also He wants to see man progress toward the greatest achievement for each unit consciousness, which is to reach Pure Consciousness (to become a son of God). <4> He wants them to choose the path to Him by their own free wills, not from fear but of love.

Surah The Poets (Ash-Shu'ara)
God wants humans to understand His Compassion and Mercy by realizing what He has done for man. He can force man to submit to Him, but He does not need respect and love from fear:

> If We so willed, We can send down a portent to them from the heaven which would force them to submit. But We exercise not the force. (4)

HEAVEN IS PURE CONSCIOUSNESS

<5> In the Koran, heaven is the place where man meets the Creator (God). According to the Law of the universe "same sees same," it means that only those who reach the same consciousness as the Lord can see Him. God is in Pure Consciousness and pure, so when man also reaches Pure Consciousness or is pure in heart, he will meet his God (Divine Father) face-to-face. <6> So heaven and Pure Consciousness are the same.

<7> Also heaven is described as a place of rest. When a unit consciousness reaches Pure Consciousness, he masters all the powers of the universe so he does not have to struggle in using them. He is their master (by His Permission).

<8> Therefore, we can see that in the Koran, heaven was described in symbolic language suited to the level of consciousness of the people at that time. <9> Actually it is describing the same thing as what we call Pure Consciousness. Indeed, all the Scriptures should be read with a consideration of the time, place, and people involved. This allows for maximum benefit and an understanding of the symbolic language and also the consequence of the revelations.

Surah Cattle (Al-An'am)
Life as a symbol for spiritual understanding (resurrection or heaven):

> Is he who was dead [in ignorance], and we raised him into life and gave him light [spiritual understanding] that he might walk among men, the same as he whose similitude is in utter darkness [ignorance, hell] whence he can by no means emerge (from it)? (123)

Surah The Spider (Al-'Ankabut)
Meeting the Lord is the same as reaching Pure Consciousness:

> Those who hope to meet God should know his reckoning time is surely coming. He is the Hearer, the Knower. (5)

Surah Iron (Al-Hadid)
Heaven is infinite, Pure Consciousness:

> ...a garden [heaven] which spreads over the heavens and the earth [infinite], which has been kept for those who believe in God and His Messengers... (21)

Surah The Overthrowing (At-Takwir)
Heaven (Pure Consciousness) will be neared for those who are ready (Elected Ones):

> And when the garden will be brought nigh... (13)

READINGS (THE KORAN)
HELL (IGNORANCE)

<10> Hell is a place of torment and suffering. This world and life are also filled with torment and suffering for those who do not understand its realities and do not learn from the lessons given by the experiences or signs in their lives. Those who do not learn from their mistakes, repeat the same errors over and over again, and buy blame, shame, and unhappiness, are those whose Souls are under the influence of the crudifying force in the universe (tama guna). <11> They are the ones who follow their lower natures (the devil) and are lost in the attraction of the illusion of the promises of the external world (Maya). They are the ones who listen to their false egos. All these things are nothing else but being in hell.

<12> The only reason for following the things which take the person to that condition of hell is **IGNORANCE**: Ignorance of the realities behind this universe; ignorance of the fact that the human is a Soul, he is not only a body; ignorance of the reality that we should utilize this universe and our lives to progress to higher consciousness, not to become attached to the material world and its possessions which only bring greed, attachment, and unhappiness; ignorance about our importance because God loves us and we are humans, not because of our intellect, possessions, or family, but because we have self-actualized ourselves, and are happy and respectful as we are; ignorance of not knowing we are immortal, etc.

<13> This ignorance, this illusion of the world (separation from God) is what can be called "hell."

Surah Cattle (Al-An'am)
Death as ignorance or the unaware part of the universe:

Is he who was dead [in ignorance] and we raised him into life and gave him light [spiritual understanding] that he might walk among men, the same as he whose similitude is in utter darkness [ignorance, hell] when he can by no means emerge (from it)? (123)

Surah The Spider (Al-'Ankabut)
Hell is in each of our lifetimes if we do not see the light:

They ask thee hasten on the punishment of the day of the doom, but surely hell is already compassing the disbelievers. (54)

<14> Hell surrounds the disbelievers (ignorant) right now in this lifetime. They do not have to die to go to hell. They are in the hell of the attraction of Maya, which is attachment, desire, fear, shame, insecurity, and many other sufferings related with this attraction (or in other words, ignorance).

Surah Smoke (Ad-Dukhan)
The "first death" refers to ignorance:

They will not taste death therein after the first death [ignorance], and God will save them from the hell [ignorance] by His Grace. (56)

Surah The Event (Al-Waqi'ah)
Punishment for ignorance (they bring this punishment upon themselves):

But if he be one of the rejecters and stays in erring,
Then he will be welcomed by boiling water [anxiety],
And an abode in roasting fire [ignorance]. (92-94)

READINGS (THE KORAN)

THE HIERARCHY IN HEAVEN

<15> Is one who enters heaven (Pure Consciousness) by merely being a good person equal with someone who is ready to sacrifice all in order to carry on The Plan which is set up in the universe (to bring all to heaven or Pure Consciousness)? Surely he is not. <16> There is a Hierarchy in heaven, as there is also a Hierarchy on earth (which can be the same).

Surah The Children of Israel (Bani Israil)

See how we have exalted one over the other in this life; verily the life of the hereafter [heaven] will be greater in degrees of ranks and excellence. (21)

HISTORY AS A LESSON FOR HUMANITY

<17> Many times God blessed a nation, a people, or a person, but they forgot they had a duty for what they had received. So they started misusing that blessing and their powers for selfish desires. In fact, for the last six thousand years, the history of the human race was created only to give this lesson. <18> If we study history, we will find that each nation that gained power flourished rapidly in the beginning, either because of its humanistic approach to others, or because it was a part of a great Plan to be used to accomplish some purpose (like the English and French colonization of other parts of the world to bring the East and West closer).

<19> Those who had gained power and control over others because of their humanistic approaches, after a short period of time, forgot that they had to use that power to establish the qualities they cherished themselves: Freedom, brotherhood, and equity between nations (Kingdom Of Heaven On Earth). So they started to misuse others for narrow concepts such as nationalism and self-interest.

<20> That is when we see the blessing and Grace of God was withdrawn because of the Law of collective karma, and in a short period of time that great nation or power became weak and was destroyed.

<21> Now is the time for all to understand these lessons from the past and The Plan which has been set up. All of history occurred for humans to reach this point of understanding that selfishness is destructive to the self and others. <22> Humans have no choice – either they should understand the lessons of history and surrender themselves to The Plan of God – which is to establish the Kingdom Of Heaven On Earth and to help all to purify themselves (Kingdom Of Heaven within) – or go toward self-destruction.

Surah The Family of Imran (Ali 'Imran)
The hand of the Lord God in history:

There have been many dispensations passed before you. Just travel on the earth and see how evil is the end of those who rejected (the Messengers [truth]). (137)

<23> The Jews denied the Prophets and rejected the Lord God. They forgot why they had been chosen so the Lord punished them. He destroyed Jerusalem and scattered them all over the world [read The House of Judah (Jews)]. <24> We want God to punish everyone right away, but He takes His time. He does it by His own time schedule. It might take lifetimes.

Surah The Poets (Ash-Shu'ara)
History of humanity and individual life as lessons:

So the punishment came to them. In that surely is a portent, but most of them would not believe [they do not learn the lessons]. (158)

READINGS (THE KORAN)

Surah The Prostration (As-Sajdah)

Would it not be a guidance for them, how many a people We have destroyed before them amidst their dwellings they now walk? There are surely portents in that. Would then they not listen? (26)

Surah Ornaments of Gold (Az-Zukhruf)

And We made them a tale of the past and a lesson for the future comers. (56)

THE HOLY SPIRIT (BRINGS THE REVELATION)

<25> The Holy Spirit (Holy Ghost) is the sentient part (activated by the mutative force) of the Universal Mind (satva guna, symbolized in the Bible as the Angel Gabriel). The Universal Mind is made up of (or contains) three parts (the creative force of the universe): Satva guna – the part of decision-making, intelligence; raja guna – the mutative force, or the part which carries on the tasks (energy, activator); and tama guna – the static force, or the screen of the universe which is the part that reflects the things which are existing, or happening or happened (memory) in the universe.

<26> However, unless a person has conquered the tama force over his lower nature, by His Grace, he will not be able to come in tune with the Universal Mind and the logic of God. He will be unable to understand the realities of this universe which are in the consciousness. But being in tune with the sentient force will enable him to understand the manifested world and the nature of the universe. <27> Also this allows a Prophet to receive the revelations sent by God to him through The Holy Ghost.

<28> By being completely in tune with the Universal Mind, a person can comprehend the logic behind the activities in this universe. <29> However, he should overcome the lower nature first before he can reach that point, with His Grace (Holy Mother, which is The Holy Ghost).

Surah The Bee (An-Nahl)
The revelation comes from The Holy Spirit to Prophets:

Say that the Holy Spirit [Gabriel] has revealed it from the Lord with truth and wisdom, that it may strengthen the believers [Elected Ones], and be a guidance and good news for those who are submissive. (102)

Surah The Poets (Ash-Shu'ara)
Revelations are revealed by The Holy Ghost and the revelation is a Soul-to-Soul relationship between a Prophet and the Lord (by The Holy Ghost):

It [the Koran] is surely a revelation from the Lord of the worlds
By which the true spirit [Spirit of God] has been descended
To your heart [sacred heart], that you be (one) of the warners, (192-194)

Surah Counsel (Ash-Shura)
The Spirit of God is The Holy Ghost:

Thus have We revealed to you a spirit of our command [by Gabriel]. You did not know the Scriptures, nor the faith. But We have made your revelations as light, whereby We guide of our servants whom We will. (52)

Tablet Six

HUMAN AS A CHANNEL FOR DIVINE ACTIONS

<1> When God needs something to be done, He uses the human to carry out the task. When most people perform an action, their egos think it is they who have done it. <2> But in reality, knowingly or unknowingly, they have been a channel for God for that action to be done.

<3> The simplest example is the regeneration of the human. In addition to the many other spiritual reasons, God created the act of love-making to use the human body to make new bodies for those Souls who are ready to assume a human form and come to this world to progress. However, the human does the action because God created such an attraction between the two sexes. So the person who does the act creates the new body, and God uses this new body for a Soul to enter and then be born in the world. But parents think it is they who have created the child. However, they have been only a tool in carrying out the Will of God.

<4> It should be remembered that in the book of The Revelation in the Bible, God has already given the events which would happen in the future, and He has carried them out so far. Humans, however, think that everything which happened up to this point in history was done by them. For example, the flourishing of intellectual knowledge and science was predicted both in the Bible and the Koran. But the scientists think it is they who have discovered scientific facts. They do not know that it is God who uses them in order to reveal these truths to humanity. <5> The very clear example is Einstein. He found the formula of the transformation of mass to energy ($E=mc^2$), but he could not prove it or did not know how he came up with it.

<6> This does not mean that humans do not have any choice in their lives. Only those who reach very high consciousness and grow closer to God realize that they have no choice but to carry out His Plans. **The same is true for those who are chosen to be used for a special purpose.** <7> Others, however, have the choice of understanding and following the ways of God, or following their own false egos.

<8> That is why we should practice letting Him do the actions through us and realize that the greatest happiness and freedom comes when we allow our bodies to be tools for His Divine actions. With this ideation and devotion to Him, we will dissolve our false egos and will not be bound by the reaction of our Divine actions, because He is the doer, not us.

<9> However, a person is responsible for his own egoistical actions.

Surah Spoils of War (Al-Anfal)
God does things through us:

> O believers, it was not you who slew them, but it was God, who did (through you); and you (Muhammad) did not throw the gravel at them, but it was God who threw it (through you). (17)

IMMORTALITY

<10> You can neither kill a person nor can you yourself be killed. Man can kill another person's flesh, but the Soul cannot be destroyed.

<11> That is why Esa said do not be afraid of those who kill the flesh but of he who kills the Soul (Matthew 10:28). Only the tama guna can kill the Soul, which means crudifying to death (ignorance, unawareness).

<12> The Soul has been here, is here, and will be here. It was never born and will never be destroyed. In fact, nothing in this universe

READINGS (THE KORAN)

can be destroyed. It can be transformed to other forms, but not destroyed.

<13> However, immortality (everlasting awareness) comes only when a person completely overcomes the power of the tama guna over his Soul and reaches Pure Consciousness.

<14> But you cannot reach Pure Consciousness unless you help fulfill The Plan which was set up for the universe. That is why the Bible (Rev. 2:10), Koran, Bhagavad-Gita (B.G. 2:32), and other Scriptures all say that he who is slain for establishing the truth (the Kingdom of Heaven) will not suffer the second death. He will reach Pure Consciousness.

Surah The Family of Imran (Ali 'Imran)

Do not think of those who are slain in the way of God [righteous war] as dead. No, indeed they are with their Lord with a provision. (169)

<15> The righteous people have provision with their Lord and will become immortal (Rev. 3:21).

Surah Women (An-Nisa)
Christ was not slain:

And they say that we did kill the Messiah, Esa Son of Mary, the Messenger of God; they did not kill him, nor crucified him, but it just appeared to them as such; and those who had different opinions about this certainly are in doubt (and lost);

They have no definite knowledge of it, but only pursue a conjecture; they surely did not slew him. But God took him up to Himself. God is Mighty, Wise. (157-158)

<16> Christ was in Pure Consciousness (a god-man, an Avatar), which means he was immortal. So how can you kill an immortal person? That is why they just think they killed him but in truth he went to the Father in heaven.

JUDGE NOT

<17> No man can judge another man unless he is in Pure Consciousness (has overcome his own lower nature).

<18> That is why only after the Kingdom Of Heaven is established on earth, the true Paravipras are the leaders of the society, and there exists true justice and righteousness, can the laws of Moses and Prophet Muhammad be practiced. Otherwise, we should remember the story of that adulterous woman and Esa. He (Esa) told her accusers that if any of them had no sin, they could throw the first stone. But no one could be found without sin.

<19> That is why we find the laws of Moses and Muhammad so hard to practice in our unjust societies. In a society where all have the basic necessities, a man who steals out of greed can have his hand cut off. <20> But if a man steals out of necessity, or for any other forgivable reason, he cannot be judged for that action.

<21> Therefore, a person should purify his own eyes first, then he might take the speck out of his brother's eyes. <22> However, when you have cleansed eyes (reached higher consciousness, overcome your lower nature, etc.) still you should not judge but instead try to take the specks out of other people's eyes (help them to understand), because you would then know how hard it is to overcome the lower nature. You become merciful and compassionate.

Surah The Poets (Ash-Shu'ara)
Prophets do not judge their followers by their social status:

And they answered: Shall we believe you whom the lowest of the people follow?

Noah said: What knowledge do I have of what they have been doing (in

READINGS (THE KORAN)

the past) [their previous lives]?
Only my Lord can judge them, if you could understand [only God and His sons can judge, those who have overcome (Rev. 21:7)]. (111-113)

Tablet Seven
KARMA

<1> Karma means action. For any action there is a reaction in this universe. This Law is true in the spiritual world also. Any action will create a record (reaction) on the Soul and universe. The record or reaction (experience) which will remain on the Soul is called samskara. These samskaras are what Prophets call the letter of each person's deeds. <2> Through meditation, repentance, prayer, fasting, purification, progress, etc., and by His Grace, a person lightens and burns these samskaras and becomes more Divine.

<3> However, when these records of reactions of actions remain on the universal level, they are called the Akashic Records. When a person becomes pure enough and tunes himself with the Universal Mind, he can receive these records as revelations and also understand the Universal Laws (Daharmas).

<4> Although karma is used as a general term, we can recognize five categories of actions (karmas):

1- Those actions that man should do, such as honoring the parents, progressing physically, mentally, and spiritually, etc.
2- Those actions man should do but are not mandatory, such as, it is better to clean the place you leave behind, say "good-morning" to the people in the morning, etc.
3- Those actions which it does not matter if they are done or not. They do not create good vibrations or feelings, or bad ones.
4- Those actions which are better not to be done. These are usually the opposite actions of the second category. For example, it is better not to leave the place you have been unclean, etc.
5- Those actions which should not be done, such as, you should not commit adultery, should not kill for selfishness (murder), etc.

<5> Karma (action) has a direct relationship with Daharma (Laws of the universe). The action (karma) should be according to the Laws of the universe (Daharma). Otherwise, it will create bad reactions (samskaras) and bind the Soul (tama guna crudifies the consciousness, "sin").

Surah The Cow (Al-Baqarah)
Each person is responsible for his own actions:

> Those are the people that have passed away; theirs is what they earned (by their actions) and yours is what you earn (by yours). You are not responsible for what they did. (134)

Surah The Children of Israel (Bani Israil)

> Everyone's action We have fastened firmly to his neck, and We shall bring before him, on the Day of Judgment, a book wide open and he will be told: Read your record, you are sufficient to judge yourself. (13)

<6> That book is the reaction of your actions over your Soul, which is the same as samskaras. Karma is the action, and samskara is the effect of the reaction (experience) of your action over your Soul. These reactions are like a necklace over the Soul. <7> In the Day of Judgment or spiritual birth, a person will know what these reactions are. Like an open book, he will know how he is being rewarded or made to suffer for what he has done

READINGS (THE KORAN)

(he gains the lessons).

<8> However, some suffering or reward might not be because of the Law of Samskaras, but has been inflicted on the person in order to guide him to the right path or to give him a new experience for his later use (especially those who are in higher consciousness or Pure Consciousness).

<9> So, the human alone is enough to read his deeds (actions and reactions of these actions over his Soul) and to judge himself. **<10>** That is what a spiritual person does in his meditation. By meditating you start to bring these deeds to light. If they are kept in the Light, they will be no more, until you are completely free of all your sins (samskaras). That is why most of the time the individual tribulation starts when a person begins to meditate (to receive initiation).

<11> It is only through following the instructions of the Guru (spirit within and without) that the Grace can be won and a person can withstand these reactions. **<12>** However, with a zealous repent of sins (samskaras) and by not repeating the same mistakes, the reactions will be taken off the Soul by His Grace, because the purpose of all these things is to guide the human to the path. When a person comes to the path (learns the lesson), then none of them are needed.

<13> The path is to be surrendered to the Will of God and try to be(come) Divine and help others to be(come) the same (establishing the Kingdom Of Heaven within and without).

Surah The Ant (An-Naml)

He who does a good deed will have a more worthwhile reward, and the fear will not overcome him that Day (of Judgment).

And he who does evil, such will fall down into the fire on their faces, and will be asked: Are you rewarded not but for what you did? (89-90)

Surah The Romans (Ar-Rum)

Those who disbelieve will bear the consequences, and those who act righteously make provision for themselves. (44)

Surah O Man (Ya-Sin)

On that Day, no Soul will be wronged; but each will be recompensed according to what they used to do. (53)

Surah The Troops (Az-Zumar)

But the consequences of their evil actions smote them; those who do wrong will be overtaken; they cannot escape. (51)

Surah They Are Expounded (Fusilat)

He who does good, it is for the good of his own Soul, and he who does evil, bears the burden. Your Lord is not at all unjust to His slaves. (46)

Surah Noah (Nuh)

Because of the reaction of their evil deeds, they received disasters (Law of Karma):

Because of their sins they were drowned... (25)

Surah The Cloaked One (Al-Mudath-thir)

Every Soul is a pledge to that which he does;... (38)

Surah The Rising of the Dead (Al-Qiyamah)

The reaction of the action of each person will be recorded (samskaras):

On that day, man is informed of what he had committed and of what he had neglected. (13)

READINGS (THE KORAN) *Tablet 7*

Surah The Overthrowing (At-Takwir)

Awareness of people of the reason for their sufferings by becoming familiar with the Law of Karma:

> Then every Soul would know what he has reaped. (14)

Surah Defrauding (At-Tatfif)

> Are not the disbelievers punished for what they used to do? (36)

KNOWING GOD BY THINKING ABOUT HIS UNIVERSE (CREATION)

<14> Everyone wants to see God to be certain of His Existence. But few can see Him everywhere. Even those who see Him (His Hands in creation) or are sure of His Presence or have some relationship with Him cannot describe Him for others.

<15> So how can a person realize God and be sure He does really exist? One way to do this is by thinking about the universe, the perfection of this world, the perfection of the human body, and all the beautiful things everywhere. <16> Only by this realization of how perfectly all things have been created can a man see the hand of God all around. Then he will never be alone or helpless, because he knows <17> the force that guides the universe guides him also.

<18> So contemplating the universe, studying scientific truths about it, and seeing its incredible perfection, is a must for any aspirant. Even thinking about the perfection of the human body is like thinking about the whole universe, because each man is a universe himself. <19> Also realizing the hand of God in past history and present events will greatly increase the faith, especially the prophecies foretold in the Bible, which were revealed thousands of years ago to show what has happened in the past and what He will do in the future, and how He has fulfilled them.

Surah The Family Of Imran (Ali'Imran)

> Remember God, standing, sitting, lying on the sides and contemplating the creation of the heavens and the earth, which makes them to humbly utter: O Lord, you have not created this in vain [without purpose], Holy You are; preserve us from the torment of the Fire. (191)

<20> Contemplate the universe. Think about the perfection of this creation. Then you will know that it could not be by chance. Only those who have narrow knowledge and a crude mind would think that this universe has no Creator.

Surah Cattle (Al-An'am)

> We are One who send down water from the heaven; We bring forth all kinds of growth there from out of vegetables. We make thick-clustered grain, and from the date palm, from its pollen, we bring forth suspended bunches. We make gardens of grapes, and the olive and pomegranate, some alike and some unlike. Watch the fruit of all kinds of trees, when they bear fruits and how it ripens, for those who believe there are signs in this. (100)

Surah The Romans (Ar-Rum)

> Observe, therefore, the signs of God's mercy (everywhere) how he quickens the earth after its death... (50)

<21> He created the whole universe to help unit consciousnesses come from the unaware state to aware consciousness, and He is helping them to eventually reach Pure

READINGS (THE KORAN)

Consciousness. So that is one way to understand God's mercy and compassion in His Actions and creation, by His Prints in the universe. <22> In fact, these prints are the results of His Actions. That is exactly the same for people. You know them by their actions. You know God by His creation.

Tablet Eight
THE LAST DAYS (DAY OF JUDGMENT)

<1> There are three kinds of resurrections. One is when a person shatters the walls of ignorance and through knowledge, devotion, or selfless actions steps into spiritual realities. This can be called "being born again."

<2> The second kind of resurrection is the one which comes in the last days when men will be sundered. During this period both good and bad people will be in the world, and humans will eventually realize that spiritual people should be as dynamic and efficient as possible. They will become united and establish the Kingdom Of Heaven On Earth. Then they will help those who have lagged behind to the goal (higher consciousness). This resurrection is the re-establishment of the truth of spiritual knowledge in the world. This is the first and second resurrection in each era.

<3> The third is when the end of this world is reached. This will happen because the original energy created to maintain the creation will wear out. Then this manifested universe will be dissolved into its original form. Those who have reached Pure Consciousness by then will escape the state of ignorance and will be with the Father. Those who have stayed in ignorance should wait until crores of years for the next creation. Then they might progress to Pure Consciousness.

<4> So the human should not delay his progress and should utilize all opportunities to reach the goal and avoid the torment of hell (ignorance). However, eventually there is the victory of truth (knowledge) over the devil (ignorance).

Surah The Ant (An-Naml)
Discovery of the movement of the earth in the last days (when knowledge will increase); also at the end of creation all things will be dissolved and become like clouds.

And you see the mountains as if they are solid, in truth they move like the passing clouds. It is the creation of God who has perfected all things. He is aware of what you do. (88)

Surah The Romans (Ar-Rum)
On the Resurrection Day men will be sundered (separated); also at the end of the time of this creation they will be separated:

Before the unavoidable Day which God has designed to come, people will be sundered. (43)

…This is the Day of Judgment but you do not know. (56)

<5> So, it is the Day of Resurrection. Every day is the Day of Resurrection. These days are also the days of the first resurrection. The second resurrection will be sometime in the future – one thousand years (Rev. chapter 20).

Surah Smoke (Ad-Dukhan)
"Smoke" in the Last Days (air pollution) and disbelievers:

Then wait (O Muhammad) for the Day in which visible smoke will appear ["fireless smoke": The brown cloud],

Which will envelop the people: that will be a painful torment.

They will cry: Relieve us from this torment, we do believe.

How can there be admonishment for them when there came a Messenger with clear explanation of the truth to them,

READINGS (THE KORAN)

And they turned away from him saying: He was taught (these things), a madman?

Still, we remove the torment a little, but you will surely return to disbelieving. (10-15)

Surah The Enshrouded One (Al-Muzammil)
In the last days the children will grow old quickly. They will have so many problems to solve that they will not understand what childhood is:

...A day which will turn children gray-headed... (17)

Surah "He Frowned" ('Abasa)
Description of the last days, which corresponds to this day (this period of human life):

On the day when a man runs away from his brother,
His mother, his father,
His wife, and his children,
Every man that day will be engaged with his own concerns alone (heedless of others). (34-37)

LAW OF THE GRACE OF GOD

<6> The shower of the Grace of the Lord is constantly raining in the universe, but those who have the umbrella of their false egos over their Souls will not receive it.

<7> God gives His Blessings and Grace to people, nations, and individual humans. When they start misusing this Grace for ways other than His Ways, then the doom of those people, nations, and the individual human will come.

Surah Spoils of War (Al-Anfal)
God will not take His Grace away from anyone (or nation, etc.) He has given it to, unless they start misusing it:

God never withdrew the Grace He has bestowed upon a people, until they change their hearts toward Him. (53)

LIFE IS A STRUGGLE

<8> Life is a struggle (jahad) within and without. The struggle within is the fight between the higher and lower natures. This battle involves warding off the power of the tama guna (the force bending the Soul toward the external world) to establish the Kingdom Of Heaven within (✡). <9> The external struggle is to overcome excess attraction of Maya (illusion of life) and establish the Kingdom Of Heaven On Earth (✡).

<10> All these struggles are to create an environment that allows each individual to grow to his fullest potential.

<11> Those who say life is an illusion are greatly mistaken. Life and the manifested universe are not illusions, but **excess attraction** to this manifested universe is illusion.

Surah The Romans (Ar-Rum)

When We bestow Our Mercy on mankind, they rejoice in it; but if there be a tribulation because of their own actions [karmas], they become despairing [and forget about God and His mercies]. (36)

Surah The City (Al-Balad)
God created man in an environment of suffering in order to direct him toward the goal of life. As it was explained, through many evolutionary processes, man has reached such a powerless position that he suffers when he goes astray from the path, through the weakness of the flesh. So suffering is a purifier and is a guidance to salvation (Pure Consciousness):

READINGS (THE KORAN)   Tablet 8

We verily have created man committed to toil (in affliction). (4)

Surah Solace (Al-Inshirah)
The ups and downs of life, like a fountain when it goes up, it then comes down:

Verily, there is ease after hardship,
Surely there will also be hardship after ease. (5-6)

<12> Therefore, we should stay in the middle path.

LOWER NATURE

<13> Man has two natures, the lower nature (lower self) and the higher nature (higher self). In the lower nature (bestial nature), man is like an animal and is only concerned about himself. <14> In the higher nature, man becomes more aware of his Divine self.

<15> It is this lower nature which is the source of suffering for the human. This is the false ego of man, the part that sees himself separate from others, the part that is not universalist, the part that does not view all humans as brothers and sisters, and the part that gives that empty feeling of separation from the Lord, which is the greatest suffering of all (illusion of separation).

Surah Ornaments of Gold (Az-Zukhruf)
Lower nature as idle talk, play of life:

So leave them alone in their idle talks and busy with their plays [in the material world] until the Day which they have been promised. (83)

Surah Smoke (Ad-Dukhan)
Self-centeredness:

Saying, suffer now, you who hold yourself as mighty, the noble. (49)

Surah Muhammad
Animality is lust, excess comfort, and overeating, which all are related to the lower nature of man:

...while the disbelievers enjoy this material life and eat and drink as animals do, and the Fire [of ignorance, Maya] is their resort. (12)

Surah The Private Apartments (Al-Hujurat)
The ugliness of too much suspicion, spying, and backbiting:

O You who believe, refrain from too much suspicion; because some suspicion may create great harm. Also do not spy, nor backbite one another. Do any of you like to eat the flesh of his brother's corpse? Surely you would abhor that. Remember your duty to God. He is compassionate, Ever-Merciful. (12)

Surah The Event (Al-Waqi'ah)
There will be no idle talk:

They will not hear any vain speaking nor recrimination therein, (25)

Surah The Ascending Stairways (Al-Ma'arij)
The human's nature:

To be impatient is a part of man's nature [man's but not God's],
When tribulation comes he is full of sorrow.
But when good befalls he does not admit it is from Us,
Except constant worshippers. (19-21)

MAYA

<16> Maya means illusion. This world is not illusion, but the illusion is anything that makes us forget that this body, universe, and all the facilitating faculties which have been given or are provided for us are there to help our physical, mental, and spiritual progress. <17> That is why it has been said that anything which keeps the person from remembering the Lord is devilish (Maya). That is completely true, because humans should keep their ideal high and constantly in remembrance. Otherwise they will easily fall to their lower natures and be drowned in Maya (illusion of separation from God).

<18> Pursuance of Maya is like chasing the wind. There is always something in the external world which we think will give us everlasting happiness if we obtain it, but everlasting happiness can never be found there. It only comes through understanding His Bounty and Beauty. <19> However, this does not mean escapism, but being content with whatever we have and enjoying anything extra which happens to come to us. But we should never lose our Souls for material possession, or for any other illusive gain.

Surah The Cave (Al-Kahf)

Expound to them the similitude of the life of this world, like water which we sent down from heaven, and the vegetation on the earth grows and mixes with it to look fresh, then in one morning they become weathered and dry which is scattered about by the wind. God is able to do all things. (46)

Surah The Story (Al-Qasas)
The pettiness of wealth and power:

Karoh said: I have been given this (wealth) because of my great knowledge. Did he not know that God had destroyed those who were even mightier and richer than him before? (78)

<20> Wealth and power are really nothing, because even the proud, wealthy, and powerful nations were destroyed in the past, and no man can ever be that wealthy and powerful. <21> You do not even have the power over your own death. So when you die you have no choice – all the wealth you have accumulated will have to be left on earth. You are completely helpless. <22> These things are only the attractions of Maya to keep you from progressing toward the perfection of your Soul. They only bring the human a big false ego.

Surah The Spider (Al-'Ankabut)
This life is nothing but Maya (its attraction):

This life is nothing but a game and a pastime, the hereafter is but the true life, if they only knew. (64)

Surah Sad
The reason for forgetting the Lord is excess attraction to the external world (Maya):

We commanded him: O David, We appointed you a vicegerent in the earth; so justly judge between people, and follow not vain desire [attraction to Maya] that it lead you astray from the way of God. (27)

Surah Ornaments of Gold (Az-Zukhruf)
Idle talk and the play of life is Maya:

So leave them alone in their idle talks and busy with their plays [in the material world] until the Day which they have been promised. (83)

Surah Iron (Al-Hadid)
Maya is illusion of excess attraction to the external world:

Know that the life of this world is nothing but a play [notice "life of this world," not the world itself], and idle

READINGS (THE KORAN)

talk, and a show, and a subject of boasting between you, and competition in respect, for riches and children. Like the vegetable after the rain which makes it pleasing in the eyes of the tiller, but it dries up later and turns yellow, and then it becomes straw. In the hereafter there is severe punishment and also forgiveness from God and His satisfaction, whereas the life of this world is nothing but a matter of illusion. (20)

Surah The Ascending Stairways (Al-Ma'arij)

Most of the people are deeply unaware (sleepwalkers) of the reality behind this universe:

So leave them [the ignorant] chatting idle talks and playing until they face the Day they are promised. (42)

Tablet Nine
MEDITATION

<1> Meditation, in the simplest terms, means to calm the mind and direct its attention from the external world to the spiritual world.

<2> So silence, fasting, a good environment, purification, a healthy body, etc., all help in having a strong calm mind.

<3> Contemplation and concentration on higher thoughts makes a person rise above the lower self to the higher self.

<4> Using special words of power (mantras) will also help to activate the chakras (psychic centers) and bring energies from the lower chakras to the higher ones. <5> "Allah" is a word of power (vibration of the seed of the mind), so its repetition and thinking about the Lord will raise the consciousness.

<6> However, silence and fasting together is one of the most effective ways of calming the mind. <7> Closing the eyes and concentrating on mantras is best for sharpening the spiritual understanding of the aspirant.

<8> Prayer and chanting with utmost devotion is the cleansing process of the Soul. <9> To pray is to talk to God; to meditate is to listen to Him!

Surah The Family of Imran (Ali 'Imran)

Zachariah said: My Lord, lay upon me a token. He (the angel) replied: the token for you is that you should not speak to people for three days but by signs, and remember the Lord much, and praise Him by night and early morning. (41)

<10> What this verse presents is that silence, the remembrance of God, and meditating on Him and creation is a part of growing closer to Him. That is why meditation, silence, and being an observer is recommended by all great spiritual teachers. <11> That is, to keep yourself away from the crowd and think about creation, what is going on here in this world, why we are here, what we are doing, what we are, what is God, etc.

Remember God, standing, sitting, lying on the sides and contemplate the Creation of the heavens and the earth, which make them to humbly utter: O Lord, You have not created this in vain [without purpose]. Holy You are, preserve us from the torment of the fire. (191)

<12> Love your God with all your heart, mind, and being. Remember your Lord and meditate on Him (He is all) all the time.

READINGS (THE KORAN) Tablet 9

MIRACLES AND DISBELIEVERS

<13> As the consciousness of the human rises, there will be fewer demands for miracles and emphasis will be more on teaching and understanding the realities of the spiritual world. In the past, many miracles were shown in order to awaken the low consciousness of the regular humans and to develop belief in an unseen Power. <14> However, the human with a higher consciousness in this age does not need to be shown miracles. He can look at his body, universe, and all things and see the hand of the Invisible Power.

<15> Also, people usually put their attention on the miracles performed by the Prophet or on his personality, and they forget the true teaching and depth of his revelations. <16> That is why those who are ready for the realization of the truth behind the realities of the spiritual world do not need miracles, and those who will not believe, will not believe even after they are shown the miracles, as it has happened in the past. <17> Listen to His Voice in your Heart.

Surah Jonah (Yunus)

There will be no miracles because people will become so attached to them and the personality of the Prophet that they forget about the teachings:

> They ask: Why has not a portent been sent down to him from his Lord? Say (O Muhammad): Only God has knowledge of the unseen. So wait; I too wait with you. (21)

Surah The Story (Al-Qasas)

Miracles make people become so attracted to them that the true teaching is forgotten. Also, it is true from the past examples that they do not create better believers:

> ...they said: Why is he not given the like of which Moses was given? Did they not disbelieve before in which Moses was given?... (48)

MORE PROPHETS WILL COME

<18> This truth is revealed in Surah 5, verse 54, which in general states: If Moslems, or those who call themselves Moslems, fail in their fate, duties, and following the real teachings of Prophet Muhammad, they will be disregarded. A new nation or people will be selected as the current forerunners of the champion of belief in God and being completely in love with Him.

<19> God also will love them because they will be humble towards believers and stern toward disbelievers. They will be striving in the way of the Lord.

<20> Who are striving with God? As you know, Israel means, "He who struggles with God." Who are those who struggle "with Him?" ("With Him" means to be with God as a team.) They are the Elected Ones. If people do not follow the example of the Elected Ones who brought Islam, then these Elected Ones will be incarnated somewhere else and will again establish God's faith there. They will become new Moslems or new submissive ones.

<21> This again shows that Prophet Muhammad does not regard himself as the last Prophet. He says there can be other Prophets who will come with the Elected Ones and will bring the truth again and again on this earth. <22> So in these verses Prophet Muhammad clearly declares that he is not the last Prophet. There will be more Prophets to come.

<23> The reason Moslems believe that Prophet Muhammad was the last Prophet is primarily based on a word in the KORAN which has two pronunciations with two different meanings.

<24> The word "Khatem" means, "the last, the end," and "Khatam" means, "the seal." So the sentence which has this word can be

READINGS (THE KORAN)

translated as meaning both that Prophet Muhammad is the "last Prophet" or is "the seal of the Prophets." In a sense, both are true.

<25> As it is explained in our writings, Prophet Muhammad brought the religion of "Islam" which means "to be submissive." That is the highest spiritual realization, and if Prophets are referred to as those who bring a spiritual message to humanity and being submissive to the Lord is the highest spiritual message, then no other Messenger after Prophet Muhammad can bring any higher spiritual realization to humanity. So he was the last Prophet.

<26> Also as **The Greatest Sign** shows, the sign of Islam is at the very top of **The Greatest Sign**, like its seal. So the Messenger is also the seal of the Prophets.

<27> However, he is not by any means the last Messenger who will be sent to humanity. In fact, no one can be the last Messenger because even after the whole truth has been revealed to humanity, still there are people who will be sent to interpret these truths for the humans. Furthermore, the true teachings usually are lost after some time and new Messengers are necessary to come and bring the lost truth back again.

Surah The Table Spread (Al Ma'idah)
Muhammad was not the last Prophet:

> O you who believe, who so from you turns back from his religion, know that in his stead God will bring a people, whom He loves and they would love Him, kind and considerate toward believers, firm and stern toward disbelievers. They will struggle in the way of God and will fear not the blame of the fault-finders. Such is God's Grace, which is bestowed upon whosoever He wills, God is All-Embracing, All-Knowing. (54)

Surah The Family of Imran (Ali 'Imran)

> A righteous human being whom God had given the Scripture and wisdom and the Prophethood will not say to people: Worship me instead of God. But they say, according to their duty: Be faithful devotees of God… (79)

<28> God can give prophethood to anyone He wishes in any time of history before and after Prophet Muhammad. It is completely up to Him. Even thinking that any Prophet is the last one is a sin, because we are saying what God should do or should not do. The Lord God has a great Plan to fulfill, and He will not stop, until it is done.

Surah The Children of Israel (Bani Israil)
There will be more Prophets which God will send using the same method as with the previous Prophets:

> That has been Our method in the case of Our Messengers whom We sent before, and you will not find Our method to change. (77)

Surah The Pilgrimage (Al-Hajj)

> God chooses His Messengers from among the Angels and men. God certainly is All-Hearing, All-Seeing. (75)

<29> From whomever is able to become a Prophet, and whenever it is necessary, a Prophet will come. Therefore, you cannot bind God by saying that any Prophet is the last one, unless you are a disbeliever (not surrendered).

Surah The Criterion (Al-Furqan)
More Prophets will come. God can send more Prophets:

> If We so desired, We could raise up a warner in every village. (51)

Tablet Ten
PARAVIPRAS (ELECTED ONES)

<1> Paravipras are those who have made their Souls refined through numerous reincarnations and struggles in many lifetimes. They are the ones who are incorruptible.

<2> Paravipras are ready to sacrifice all things for their ideal. They are the light of the world and will guide humanity to the goal. Paravipras are the real leaders of society with no interests for selfish gain or desires. They intuitively know that all these desires and attachments are nothing but illusion to the Soul. The only goal of their lives is to carry on The Plan of The Most High.

<3> These are the Elected Ones, the greatest in the Hierarchy in Heaven.

Surah Light (An-Nur)
The advent of Paravipras, as the inheritors of the earth:

This is a promise from God; Those of you who believe and do good, He will surely make them the inheritors in the earth, as in the case of those before them, whom He made to succeed; and He will establish for them their chosen religions and will grant them safety and peace after their original fear. They will only worship Me… (55)

Surah The Poets (Ash-Shu'ara)
The importance of leaders in society for the progress of humanity toward higher consciousness (that is why the Paravipras are necessary):

And obey not those who break the laws,
Those who promise corruption in the earth and would not reform to bring order and security, (151-152)

Surah The Event (Al-Waqi'ah)
Reward of Paravipras and Elected Ones:

Thus if he is one of the chosen ones,
For him is the breath of life and prosperity in the everlasting Garden of Bliss [Pure Consciousness]. (88-89)

Reward of good people:

And if he be of those of the right,
Then he will be greeted by: "Peace be upon you who is of the right." (90-91)

PARENTS

<4> The duty of a human to his parents is to honor them highly. However, if they become an obstacle in their spiritual progress, children should not follow them. This is according to the hierarchy of the importance of people in human life. <5> The first most important being is God. The second most important is the spiritual teacher. The third most important beings in human life are the parents, and the fourth is the spouse. <6> However, if one of these becomes an obstacle in attending to the one higher up in the hierarchy, that being should be shunned.

Surah The Table Spread (Al Ma'idah)
Following the ancestors of ignorance:

When it is said unto them: Come to that which God has sent, and to the Messenger, they answer: That wherein we found our fathers is sufficient for us. Would they insist even though their fathers had no knowledge and had no true guidance? (104)

<7> It is true that you should honor your parents and your ancestors. But if they are

READINGS (THE KORAN)

ignorant, you should not follow them.

Surah Luqman

We have imposed upon the human concerning his parents: Be kind unto them, especially the mother, who bearest him with perpetual weakening ... First be grateful unto Me [because I created this whole universe to enable you to reach Pure Consciousness] and then to your parents [who helped you to gain this body by sacrificing their health and freedom for you]...

But if they try to make you ascribe partners to Me, do not obey them, but still be kind and helpful to them in worldly matters, and follow the way of him who turns unto Me with repentance. (14-15)

PROPAGATION OF RELIGIONS

<8> One of the best ways to understand religions is by reading the Scriptures, inquiring into the truth behind them, and trying to preach it to others. This can be done by going to those people who are familiar with and competent in different aspects of the truth beyond metaphysical (intellectual) understanding, and reaching out to teach it to others.

<9> Therefore, study of religions, inquiring about them, and propagation of their necessity in human life is a must in order to help humanity in its progress spiritually.

<10> Merely believing in whatever anyone teaches us about religions will not enable a person to expand his understanding, and he will become a follower of dogmas taught by preachers uninformed of the truth behind this universe. <11> Only those people with expanded minds who see God in everything and everywhere can help a seeker, not those who sell religions cheaply for worldly interest.

<12> That is why the search for the truth behind this life and universe is a duty of each human. <13> So it is necessary to create a common worldwide language that allows everyone to read all the Scriptures. Reading Scriptures from different religions, practices, meditation, concentration, contemplation, Satsang, etc., are all helpful in bringing the mind in flow with the Universal Mind and understanding the real truth behind this universe. <14> The search of religions should start in schools and the family environment, and continue until the end of a human's life.

Surah The Family of Imran (Ali 'Imran)

...Be faithful devotees of God, by constant preaching and attentive studying of the Scripture... (79)

<15> It is emphasized to read the Scriptures and share Satsang (teach it to others). That is one of the reasons why religions have lost their validity, because people do not know about them. They just believe whatever is told them.

PROPHETS

<16> There are many different references to Prophets in the Koran:

Surah The Family of Imran (Ali 'Imran)
Choosing the Prophets:

God's purpose is not to leave you in the present state. He shall separate the wicked from the good. Nor would He reveal to you the unseen. But God chooses of His Messengers whom He will and reveals to them the knowledge of the unseen. So believe in God and His Messengers. If you believe and are pure, yours is a great reward. (179)

READINGS (THE KORAN)

<17> "God's purpose is not to leave you in the present state" means that humans will not stay in a low state, <18> but will progress toward perfection or Pure Consciousness.

<19> "Nor would He reveal to you the unseen" because you are not ready physically, mentally, and spiritually, to know about the unseen.

<20> "But God chooses of His Messengers whom He will" means that only those who reach very high consciousness will be chosen by God. He chooses them, so He can choose another Messenger after Prophet Muhammad.

<21> "So believe in God and His Messengers. If ye believe and are pure, yours is a great reward." So listen and understand the Messengers and high spiritual people, purify yourself, and also destroy any jealousy and egotism toward Prophets and Messengers.

Surah Women (An-Nisa)
Surrendering to the Prophet is surrendering to the Lord (the Prophet is God's representative):

> Whoever obeys the Messenger is obeying God,... (80)

The spiritual teacher of Prophets is the Lord Himself:

> God has revealed to you the Scripture and wisdom, and has taught you that which you did not know. (113)

<22> The Prophets are a bridge between the manifested and un-manifested (spiritual) worlds.

Prophets are sent to the earth so that the humans do not bring this excuse that "they did not know:"

> We sent these Messengers of good tidings and as warners, so people may have no plea against God after the coming of Messengers... (165)

Surah The Heights (Al-A'raf)
Prophets are only Messengers and each has a message to reveal to humanity:

> Tell them: I [Muhammad] have no power to benefit nor hurt myself, except that God wills. Had I knowledge of the unseen, I would have secured abundance of wealth, and no adversity would have fallen on me. I am but a warner and a bearer of good tidings for those who believe. (188)

Surah Ta Ha
The Prophet should not be distressed or make his life miserable because of the revelations:

> We have not sent you this Qu'ran [Koran] that you may be distressed,
> But as a reminder for those who fear God. (2-3)

Surah The Prophets (Al-Anbiya)
Prophets are regular people:

> Before you, we also sent Messengers who were men We inspired. Ask the People of the Book [Believers], if you know it not.
> We did not give them bodies which did not need food, nor were they immortals. (7-8)

Surah The Poets (Ash-Shu'ara)
After the revelation comes to the Prophet, he will reveal it to humans in the language he is familiar with in the most plain and understandable style:

> To your heart [sacred heart], that you be (one) of the warners.
> In clear Arabic tongue. (194-195)

<23> The language is not important but the spirit of the revelation is important.

Prophets start purifying from their closest people and then extend it to others:

READINGS (THE KORAN) — Tablet 10

Warn your near kindred (O Muhammad),
And show kindness and affection to those believers who follow you. (214-215)

The difference between a poet and a Prophet: A poet is confused and says things that he does not follow himself, but a Prophet is not confused. He says things and follows them himself, because what he says are the Laws of the universe which lead to the goal of life (Pure Consciousness, salvation, etc.):

The erring ones follow the poets. Have you not seen how poets wander in every valley,
And how they say that which they do not?
Except ones who believe and are righteous and remember God often and ask for exact recompense when they have been wronged.
The wrongdoers soon will come to know to what place they will be gathered. (224-227)

Surah The Story (Al-Qasas)
It is the Lord's Grace and the readiness of the Soul of the person that will guide him to truth, not the Messenger or spiritual teacher. However, they (the Messengers and spiritual teachers) show the way:

Surely you cannot guide whomsoever you love, but God guides whom He will, and He knows best those who would be guided. (56)

The Prophets are not aware of their prophethood:

You did not expect such a Scripture to be revealed to you, but it came as a mercy from your Lord. (86)

<24> Even Prophet Muhammad did not know he was going to become a Prophet. <25> That is why it is difficult for people to accept a person as a Prophet when they can remember him as being one of them or because he seems exactly like themselves. It is one of the greatest problems for humans to overcome.

Surah The Spider (Al-'Ankabut)
Prophets should preach openly and fearlessly:

…The responsibility of the Messenger is to convey the message clearly. (18)

Surah Counsel (Ash-Shura)
Prophets communicate with God directly. He reveals to His Prophets whatever He feels necessary for those people whom the Prophet has come for, which depends upon the development of their consciousnesses:

It is beyond the capacity of a mortal man to speak to God, save by revelation or from behind a veil or **through a Messenger** to reveal what He will, by His permission… (51)

Surah Victory (Al-Fath)
Prophets are representatives of the Lord:

Whosoever swears allegiance to you swears allegiance to God; God's Hand is above their hands. So whoever breaks his oath does so to his Soul's hurt, and whoever fulfills his covenant which he made with God, on him will He bestow a great reward. (10)

THERE IS A PURPOSE IN CREATION

<26> God (Father) who is in Pure Consciousness felt that the whole universe was His Body. He realized how His Body is dead under the influence of the tama guna. So He

READINGS (THE KORAN)

decided to awaken His body from the unaware state and bring all unit consciousnesses to perfect awareness. That is why He has engineered such an elaborate creation to help the unaware part of the universe to Pure Consciousness.

<27> This universe was built for a definite purpose with utmost compassion. It is not a play (although in a sense, because it is a relative truth, it might be regarded as such). It is a place of opportunity for all to utilize to reach Pure Consciousness and to help others to the goal also.

Surah The Family of Imran (Ali 'Imran)

Remember God, standing, sitting, lying on the sides, and contemplate the creation of the heavens and the earth, which make them to humbly utter: **O Lord, You have not created this in vain** [without purpose]; Holy You are, preserve us from the torment of the fire. (191)

<28> God created this universe for a definite purpose to bring all to Pure Consciousness. He did not create this universe in vain. Those who do not understand this will be drowned in the lake of the fire of illusion.

Surah Al-Hijr

We have created not the heavens and the earth and all between them except with truth and wisdom, and the promised hour is sure to come, so forgive generously, O Muhammad. (85)

<29> The creation was made for a definite purpose. Its purpose is to bring all unit consciousnesses to Pure Consciousness. <30> The Day of Judgment will come to take all elected people to Pure Consciousness and help others to accelerate their progress to Pure Consciousness, because as Prophet Muhammad said, "All will be gathered unto Him."

Surah The Prophets (Al-Anbiya)
There is a definite purpose in creation. It is not only a play:

We created not the heaven and the earth and all between them as a play.
If We ever wished for a pastime, We would have found it in what is with us. (16-17)

<31> It is implied that: **"The Goal of the Life is to Be(come) Divine."**

Surah The Spider (Al-'Ankabut)

God has created the heavens and the earth for a purpose. There is definitely a sign for those who believe. (44)

<32> By understanding how perfect the universe and all things in it are, we would know that it could not have happened by chance. So there is a Creator, and knowing this will help us to become a believer.

Surah The Romans (Ar-Rum)
The many languages and races were made by Him for a definite purpose. The wise know that purpose (to weaken man to prevent him from self-destruction by using their oneness to gain power and then misuse it). Also many races were made so that the human would go through different experiences by being born into different races in various lifetimes:

...and in diversity of your tongues and colors [race]. There surely are signs for those who reflect. (22)

Surah Sad

We have not created the heaven and the earth and all between them in vain. That is what the disbelievers think. (28)

Surah The Troops (Az-Zumar)
There is a reason for everything:

They know not that God enlarges the provision for whom He wills and tightens it for whom He pleases. Surely in this are signs for those who believe. (52)

READINGS (THE KORAN)

<33> Those who start to understand God and the Universal Mind by becoming in His Flow, and those who try to become a vessel for Him to manifest Himself through them, can know the reason why everything happens to them, others, society, the world, and the universe.

<34> He does all these things not for selfish reasons but because it is necessary for a person's progress to be in those situations, and also to advance His Plans through these happenings.

Surah Crouching (Al-Jathiyah)
All of the universe was created to be used by humans:

God made whatever is in the heavens and whatever is in the earth as your subject; it all is from Him. There are surely signs in this for those who observe. (13)

Tablet Eleven
REINCARNATION

<1> If we say that Islam does not believe in reincarnation, then we are saying that God cannot reincarnate. That is directly opposed to the Koran's teaching of "Allah verily is Able to do all things." <2> Also, reincarnation is the way to believe in the justness of God. If all men have only one lifetime and a man was born in an environment where he never had a chance to progress and/or be told of the realities of the Scriptures and God, then God cannot judge him. But if he is reincarnated again and again, and warned and tested but he refuses to be guided, then it is justified for him to be drowned into illusion (be punished).

<3> Some people argue that, "If I have been in this world before, why do I not remember my past lives?" The answer is that it is the Soul which will be reincarnated, and the Soul does not have memory. Soul just **IS**. It receives the experiences of each lifetime. It is the unit consciousness which, by linking to the astral body and brain, has memory and receives its information and memories by using the storage rooms of the brain in each lifetime.

<4> However, all things will also be stored in the Universal Mind (Akashic Records) which humans can have access to only when in very high consciousness. <5> Those who change the Scriptures and destroy some revelations revealed by God, therefore, are doing it in vain, because some Prophet will come later on and bring the truth back to humanity by using the Universal Mind.

<6> That is why we do not remember our past lifetimes, but if we start meditating and analyzing ourselves, we will have experiences which will assure us we have been here before. Because the Soul had been impressed by the experiences in past lifetimes, it would react in such a way in different situations that we would, by realizing the self deeper, know that it had had some experiences before that causes it to now know how to act in this lifetime. <7> Also the memory of the past can be obtained from the Akashic Records (by His Grace).

Surah The Cow (Al-Baqarah)
The ability of God to kill or to give life (reincarnation):

And remember when you said: O Moses, We will not believe you until we see God face-to-face; and a lightning overtook you; you were witness thereof.

Then after you were downfallen, We revived you, that you might be grateful. (55-56)

<8> God has the power to bring to life whomever He wants, anytime He wants. Also, He can cause extinction to anyone at anytime He wants.

READINGS (THE KORAN)

Surah The Family of Imran (Ali 'Imran)

…You bring the living from the dead, and bring the dead from the living… (27)

<9> God is able to bring forth the living from the dead. Allah in the Koran is an able God. He can do whatever He wishes to do. <10> So if He is an able God and can bring the dead from the living and the living from the dead, then He is also able to reincarnate. Because if we say He cannot reincarnate, then we are saying that He is not an able God as Prophet Muhammad taught.

…and I raise the dead, by God's permission… (49)

<11> It is God who will decide to raise or cause to die. It is God who can reincarnate or not reincarnate. It is God who can send the same person again and again to this earth, or decide not to. It is God who can send some people sometime or other people another time. Or it is God who does not send at all. So again, if we say, "God cannot reincarnate" then we are saying He is not an able God. We are saying what He can do or what He cannot do. He can do whatever He wants to do.

Surah Cattle (Al-An'am)

Surely it is God who sprouts the grain of corn and the datestone. Verily it is He who brings forth the living from the dead and brings forth the dead from the living. Such is God… (96)

<12> He created this universe and is the knower of the Laws of this universe. He can bring the dead from the living and the living from the dead. He can do whatever He wants to do, so He can reincarnate too. If He can bring you once to existence, then He can bring you to this world again.

<13> The problem is that many think they are their bodies. <14> We are not our bodies but are our Souls (consciousnesses). The body might change, but the consciousness does not.

Surah The Heights (Al-A'raf)

There shall you live, and there you shall die, and from there you will be brought forth. (25)

<15> He said these things to Adam and Eve. So they will live on earth, they will die, and again they will be brought forth from the dead. The Lord God can bring into life whomever He wants. He can reincarnate.

Surah Jonah (Yunus)

Reincarnation to the gross world in order to progress and learn the lessons of life:

If God would have passed a judgment on humanity for the consequence of their evil actions as quickly as they desire to acquire good, the period of their lives would already have expired. But We allow those who do not believe in meeting with Us to wander in their transgressions blindly [stay in ignorance] so that they might progress. (12)

<16> So they (humans) will be left to live in the material world and would be reincarnated again and again until truly judged, and then a decision would be made about them, "But we shall allow those who do not believe in meeting with Us to wander in their transgressions blindly."

Surah The Romans (Ar-Rum)

Observe, therefore, the signs of God's mercy (everywhere), how He quickens the earth after its death! He is the One who gives life to the dead, **for He is Able to do all things**. (50)

<17> So He can quicken the Soul also, and reincarnate it again to a new life. "He is able to do all things."

READINGS (THE KORAN)

Surah The Wind-Curved Sand Hills (Al-Ahqaf)

Have not they realized that God, who has created the heavens and the earth and was not wearied thereafter [so God did not rest on the seventh day from exhaustion but He became a witness entity of His self-sustaining universe] has the ability to give life to the dead also? He is able to do all things. (33)

Surah Iron (Al-Hadid)

Reincarnation: The ability of God to "quicken" (or to bring the spirit to higher consciousness or rebirth) and to kill (or to take to further ignorance, or death). He is able to do all things:

God has sovereignty over the heavens and the earth; He is the giver of the life and causes death; and is able to do all things. (2)

Surah Noah (Nuh)

And He then made you to return thereto, and will bring you back again, anew. (18)

Surah "He Frowned" ('Abasa)

God can bring men to life "when He wills:"

...God created man and set a measure for him (to follow);
Then He eased the way for him,
And then caused him to die and be buried,
Then He brings him to life when He wills.
No, man has not yet fulfilled what He had commanded him. (19-23)

<18> God can reincarnate and bring man back to life even before resurrection – spiritual or physical, which is the same as reincarnation, because we know the body (cells) do not stay the same in a life period, so it is the Soul that assumes a new body – as He did in the case of Elijah (John the Baptist). John the Baptist was the reincarnation of Elijah (Elias).

<19> Also He "set a measure for him (to follow)," but man failed and has not become what God wanted him to be. It is only through many lifetimes and reincarnations that he will eventually reach perfection as He willed him to become.

RESISTANCE TO BELIEVE IN PROPHETS

<20> Prophets speak the truth. But the human does not want to hear the truth. He is like a little child who becomes very angry, cries, and tries to change the minds of his parents to give him back his toys to play with, or when he does all the things necessary to try to persuade others to conform to his unreasonable whims. <21> Humans also do not want to hear the truth. They follow the one who inflates their false egos.

<22> Prophets, however, tell them that they have to put the illusion of this external world aside and be(come) Divine. Although they see the truth revealed by Prophets, because it is not according to the demand of their lower natures, they disregard it. <23> If the Prophet insists, as they did in the past, they may even kill him. <24> But there will always be a great disaster and a lesson for the disbelievers of the Prophets of the time until humans understand those lessons given by history and surrender to the truth.

Surah Al-Hijr

Humans always ridicule Messengers:

Ever a Messenger was sent to them, they mocked him. (11)

Surah The Poets (Ash-Shu'ara)

Fear of Prophets to be rejected:

READINGS (THE KORAN)

Moses pleaded: My Lord, I fear that they would reject me, (12)

These verses below show that simple people (meek, humbled) believe easier, because they are not arrogant:

And they answered, Shall we believe you, when the lowest of the people follow?

Noah said: What knowledge do I have of what they have been doing (in the past) [their previous lives]?

Only my Lord can judge them, if you could understand [only God and His sons can judge, those who have overcome (Rev. 21:7)],

I am not here to drive away the believers,

I am only a plain warner. (111-115)

Resistance of humans to believe in Prophets:

They said: "You (Thamul) are but a human being like unto us.

Then bring to us a sign, if you are of the truthful." (153-154)

<25> Humans always look for miracles instead of concentrating on the truth of the teachings of the Prophet.

Surah The Wind-Curved Sand Hills (Al-Ahqaf)

Poor people (humbled) have fewer concepts, pride, and fear than others in accepting a new revelation:

The disbelievers say of those who have believed: If the Qu'ran had been any good, they [the poor and lowly] would not have accepted it before us. Since they [the unbelievers] are not guided by its truths, so they say: This is a fabricated lie from the ancient sayings. (11)

Tablet Twelve
SACRIFICE

<1> Sacrifice (being humble) is a must for a spiritual aspirant. However, sacrifice can be of three kinds like any other action. It can be from ignorance, passion, or knowledge. <2> Sacrifice which is performed for establishing the Kingdom Of Heaven cannot be from ignorance. It is from knowledge.

<3> Esa the Christ is the best example and symbol for humanity to show that the Kingdom will not be established without sacrifice. He came to show the way to Jews and others how to sacrifice for the human ideal (higher self). <4> That is why he is an example for humanity.

Surah Repentance (At-Taubah)

Those who die in God's Way (establishing the Kingdom Of Heaven) will be highly rewarded:

The believers surrender themselves and their possessions to God in exchange for paradise [Pure Consciousness]. So they fight for His cause and slay the enemy or are slain. This is the binding promise God has taken upon Himself, it is in the Torah, and the Gospel, and the Qu'ran; and who fulfills His covenant better than God? Rejoice, therefore, in this bargain you made with Him. Indeed it is the ultimate victory. (111)

<5> Not only is it in the Torah, Gospel, and Qu'ran (Koran) but also it is in the Bhagavad-Gita (2:32).

Surah Ornaments of Gold (Az-Zukhruf)

Sending Christ to set an example for the Children of Israel to show them how to

READINGS (THE KORAN)   *Tablet 12*

establish the Kingdom Of Heaven by sacrifice:

> He [Esa] was only Our slave upon which we bestowed favor, and made him an example for the Children of Israel. (59)

<6> He came to show the Children of Israel how to establish the Will of the Lord, which is given by their sign (✡), which means the Kingdom Of Heaven On Earth. He showed them that it can be done only by sacrifice (✝) (not being self-centered).

SELF-REALIZATION

<7> Self-realization means to know who you are. It is understood by wise men that "knowing self is knowing God." We are in the image of God, which means likeness to Him. So if we know ourselves, we will be able to know Him.

<8> Also, knowing Him is the same as knowing self. That is why by reading the Scriptures, listening to the truth spoken by realized souls (Satsang), contemplating the universe, etc., the human can come closer to Him and also to his own self.

<9> Each man is enough to understand all the truth of the universe by himself if he is a real seeker. He has the most perfect body and faculties to guide him on the path.

Surah The Rising of the Dead (Al-Qiyamah)

Each person is enough for judging himself:

> In truth man is a witness over his doings, (14)

SIN

<10> Sin is violation (or transgression) of the Universal Laws. <11> When a person does his actions according to the Universal Laws (Daharma) and his personal Daharma (nature), then there is no sin. <12> However, when a person violates his nature (the thing he was made to be) and universal set-ups, that is violence and he creates samskaras (reactions to the actions). These will stay as a burden on his Soul until either he understands the lessons given to him through these reactions or he bears the fruit of his deeds, to eventually understand the lesson. <13> There is also collective karma as an example for others.

Surah The Bee (Al-Nahl)

Sinning and not appreciating the Grace of the Lord will affect prosperity:

> God put an example as a guidance for you, the case of a town which was secure and well content, and its appointed provision coming to it from all quarters plentifully; but it became ungrateful and disbelieved in God's favor, so He made it experience famine and fear in the consequence of what they used to do. (112)

Surah The Spider (Al-'Ankabut)

The false leaders will create great burdens for themselves. Also in the Koran, karma (samskara) is equal with sin:

> However, they [false leaders] certainly will bear their own load beside the load of others which will be added to theirs, and they surely will be questioned on the Day of Judgment concerning that which they fabricated. (13)

<14> What is that "load?" That is the reaction of your bad actions (samskaras, sins). <15> Also you will be punished for misguiding others. So the false prophets will be severely punished.

READINGS (THE KORAN) — Tablet 13

SPIRITUAL STRUGGLE IS FOR SELF, NOT FOR PROPHETS OR GOD

<16> The spiritual struggle and teachings are necessary to be successful in the path. They are all for the good of the aspirant. The struggle is to bring the consciousness out of the grip of the lower nature to higher consciousness. <17> But it is not an easy process. That is why those who have gone through this path should show the way to others who want to also follow a spiritual life.

<18> God's Revelations, Prophets, Gurus, etc., are all the lights for human guidance. Each is like a light shining out of a dark jungle. It is true that the spiritual aspirant is in the jungle and cannot see anything, but if he directs all his attention to that light, he will reach it and escape the darkness.

<19> So it is not a favor from the disciple to his spiritual teachers that he become a believer, but it is the Masters, Prophets, or God who bestow favor upon the aspirant. They are striving for themselves, and the spiritual teachers are the lights of their way.

Surah The Spider (Al-'Ankabut)
The real meaning of "jahad," an internal and external struggle to establish the truth (the Kingdom Of Heaven):

> Whosoever strives in the Ways of God, strives only for the good of his Soul; God is certainly Independent from all creatures. (6)

Surah The Private Apartments (Al-Hujurat)
Those who believe actually do good to themselves, not to the Prophets:

> They make it as if they have done a favor to you that they have surrendered (to God).
> Say: Consider not by accepting to be submissive to Him [Islam] you have done me a favor. No, in truth it is God who bestowed a favor upon you that He has led you to the Faith, if you are truthful. (17-18)

Tablet Thirteen
STUDY OF SCRIPTURES

<1> Scriptures are written from the revelations by God to those who are in tune with Him. They are Satsangs which cleanse the Soul.

<2> Some say there is a jungle in all the Scriptures and you will be lost and more confused about the truth because of them.

<3> If we constantly have **The Greatest Sign** in front of our eyes and remember the time, place, and people the Scriptures were revealed to, if we keep in mind that some of the Scriptures have been changed by some carnal minds, and if we remember the truth behind **The Greatest Sign**, then we will not be lost.

<4> However, the real truth is common sense which evolves after much study and when we go beyond books and develop a direct relationship with The Holy Ghost. But before that connection occurs, Scriptures are very good guides, with having **The Greatest Sign** in mind.

Surah The Family of Imran (Ali 'Imran)

> ...Be ye faithful devotees of God, by constant preaching and attentive studying of the Scriptures, (79)

<5> Study of the Scriptures is one of the duties of the human. Those who believe they can find all the truth by only meditating are wrong. Study is a great part of spiritual progress.

READINGS (THE KORAN)
SURRENDERING

<6> Like many other words in spirituality, "surrendering" has been misunderstood. Many people say they are surrendered to the Will of God, so they do not have to be worried about anything, as long as they are surrendered everything will be all right. This interpretation of surrendering will lead to escapism, and is no better than believing that this world is illusion or in an all-powerful Messiah who will do it all for us, instead of God!

<7> God created intelligence, the brain, hands, feet, body, eyes and all the necessary faculties for man so that he is independent and able to manage his own life. <8> Man should use this perfect body to progress in all aspects of life and fight vigorously to overcome all opposing forces. So God does not love those who escape from life.

<9> However, God created this universe for a great purpose, to bring all to perfection. <10> In doing so, each individual should purify the self and overcome his lower nature (establishment of the Kingdom Of Heaven within). <11> Also he should help others to understand the goal of life and guide them toward it, and participate in establishing an environment that enables all to progress and reach the goal (establishing the Kingdom Of Heaven without).

<12> To be submissive to this Plan and to the Laws necessary in order to carry on The Plan is surrendering, not escapism. <13> Also surrendering means to do our best to do His Will (establishing the Kingdom Of Heaven within and without) and then give the result of our actions to Him (not to be attached to the result). <14> Greater than surrendering is submission, which is to let Him do the work through us, and we become a channel for His Divine actions. In this case, no "I" will be left so no reaction of our actions remains, because all is He, even the Doer. All is done by His Grace!

Surah The Cow (Al-Baqarah)
The essential meaning of Islam (being surrendered or submissive to the Lord):

No, but whosoever submits himself to the Will of God and does good, for him is reward from his Lord; they shall have no fear nor shall they grieve. (112)

<15> The highest spiritual achievement is to be surrendered or submissive ("…submits himself…") to The Plan (creates a good environment, "…does good,…") of the Lord. With this, the whole universe will be able to progress and achieve Pure Consciousness.

<16> By this achievement "they shall have no fear" because fear comes to those who are materialistic-minded and are attached to this external world. <17> Also, "nor shall they grieve," because grief is for those who do not know God and the spiritual world (the ignorant) – they are bound to this manifested world.

Surah The Family of Imran (Ali 'Imran)

O those who believe, be aware of your duty to God and be mindful of it, so you would not die but as one completely submissive to Him. (102)

<18> Islam comes from the word "tasleim." Tasleim means to be surrendered. Islam means "those who have surrendered or are submissive to God." Therefore, believers are those who have surrendered themselves to God. <19> So it is only necessary to be submissive to be called a Moslem.

<20> Also the moment of death is very important to man. In that moment, if he has been a true devotee of God, he will remember Him and this will be a sign of his mindfulness about God. <21> Therefore, he will go to a higher level of consciousness (heaven) or will be born in such a state. <22> That is why man should engage himself in activities directed to God, so at the moment of death he dies as one submitted to God.

READINGS (THE KORAN)

Surah Women (An-Nisa)

Whose religion is better than he who submits his will to God, while doing good, and follows the tradition of Abraham, the upright? God took Abraham as a friend. (125)

<23> The best religion is one in which you are surrendered and submissive to the purpose of the Lord while at the same time are helping others to reach their goal. <24> What was the tradition of Abraham? He was submitted to the Will of the Lord. So being submitted is the greatest achievement for a spiritualist. <25> However, submission does not mean escapism. That is submission from ignorance. Be submissive to the Lord's purpose, do the action but know that it is He who is using you as a channel and He is the true Doer, not you. Direct these actions toward establishing the Kingdom Of Heaven On Earth and within.

Surah Luqman

The greatest achievement in the spiritual path is being submissive (surrendered to the Father's Plan) while doing good:

Whosoever submits to God completely and does good, he has truly grasped a firm hand hold... (22)

Tablet Fourteen

SOME SYMBOLS CORRESPONDING TO THOSE USED IN THE BIBLE

<1> God has communicated with humans through many symbolic languages. In order to understand His Spiritual Messages, we should be familiar with these symbols. In the Bible and Koran, these symbols are the same. The last book of the Bible, The Revelation, is full of these symbols. Understanding them in The Revelation will greatly help in understanding the rest of the Bible and also the Koran (read Revelation of The Revelation).

<2> Here are some symbols and their correspondence to those in the Bible. There can be more, however.

<3> These symbols have not been understood so far, but with these revelations they can now be described.

Surah The Heights (Al-A'raf)

"You know them by their marks" corresponds to those who "receive a mark" in The Revelation, chapter 13:

The occupants of the Heights [highly developed spiritual Souls] call out to men who are known by their marks: Your multitude availed you not, nor did your pride. (48)

<4> The mark is that pride of material possession, or GREED.

Surah The Bee (An-Nahl)

All creation praises and prays to the Lord, corresponding to the symbols of the four beasts and twenty-four elders in the Bible (Rev. 5:14):

Whatsoever is in the heavens and whatsoever living creature is in the earth, and the Angels [all creative elements] submit themselves humbly to God, and they act not proudly. (49)

Surah Iron (Al-Hadid)

All things praise the Lord:

Whatsoever is in the heavens and in the earth glorifies God... (1)

READINGS (THE KORAN)

Surah Exile (Al-Hashr)

Whatsoever is in the heavens and whatsoever is in the earth glorifies God. He is Mighty, the Wise. (1)

Surah Ornaments of Gold (Az-Zukhruf)
"Love of many will wax cold" (Matthew 24:12):

Friends will be foes that day, save the righteous ones. (67)

Surah The Event (Al-Waqi'ah)
"Earthquake" symbolizes a change of social orders and old set-ups:

When the earth is violently shaken (4)

Surah The Event (Al-Waqi'ah)
Mountains and hills are symbols of great people who could be leaned on by others. They will lose their strength in this tribulation:

And the mountains fall and become as powder
Scattered dust they become. (5-6)

Surah The Emissaries (Al-Mursalat)

And when the mountains are blown away, (10)

Surah The Overthrowing (At-Takwir)

And the mountains are moved (3)

Surah The Emissaries (Al-Mursalat)
Star is used as a symbol for referring to the children, and also to those worthy people who will help the leaders of society carry out the tasks:

When the stars are dimmed (8)

<5> In the last days many people will reach higher consciousness and assume the leadership of humanity. Before it happens, the stars (the children in the families) will become rebellious and it will be hard to find honest worthy people.

Surah The Overthrowing (At-Takwir)

And the stars are no more, (2)

<6> In the last days the children and obedient people in society will be disobedient.

Surah The Emissaries (Al-Mursalat)
Sky or heaven refers to the heavenly social orders. In the last days old social orders will be shaken:

When the sky is rent asunder, (9)

Surah The Overthrowing (At-Takwir)

When the sky is no more, (11)

Surah The Overthrowing (At-Takwir)
Sun is the symbol of the father of the family and also the great and honest leaders in societies. In the last days a true father or leader will be rarely found. Also it is a symbol of the highest spiritual knowledge, so in the last days true spiritual knowledge will be lost:

When the sun is taken away, (1)

Surah The Morning Star (At-Tariq)
The morning star refers to the sun. The sun is the only star that rises in the morning. It is a symbol of the highest realization of spiritual life: Being completely submissive and surrendered to the Will of the Lord, which is to establish the Kingdom Of Heaven On Earth. Only these people can be real fathers and leaders on earth. That is why the sun is also a symbol for great leaders in society and the father of the family.

In the Bible Rev. 2:28, this same morning star is given to those who completely understand the teaching of the fourth church, which is Islam. As its name expresses, the spirit of the teaching of Islam is to be completely surrendered and submissive to The Plan of

READINGS (THE KORAN)   Tablet 14

the Lord, which is to bring the Kingdom Of Heaven On Earth:

> By the witness of the heaven and the Morning Star. (1)

Surah The Most High (Al-A'ala)
Corresponding to Rev. 9:6, "And in those days shall men seek death, and shall not find it:..."

He will therein neither die nor live. (13)

<7> These verses above also refer to the last days when the whole world will be destroyed. Only those who have reached Pure Consciousness will escape the destruction.

TESTS

<8> The human should go through tests, and each test is also a lesson for him in his life. Man should completely overcome his lower nature before he is allowed to enter the Kingdom Of Heaven (in heaven). He should show no trace of the false ego. <9> It is the purpose of all creation to make man so weak that he could be manageable, then through suffering and tests guide him and eventually bring him to perfection (Pure Consciousness).

<10> That is why only saying you believe or are submissive and surrendered will not be enough. You should prove that you have overcome the slightest doubt and all traces of false ego before you yourself realize the real joy of freedom of the Soul and are allowed to know God and enter His Kingdom.

<11> Each test is an awakening process for the spiritual aspirant. All are lessons to learn.

Surah Women (An-Nisa)
All things happen from God:

> Wheresoever you might be, death will overtake you, even though you hide in strong towers. Still **if something good happens to them they say it is from God, and if some misfortune comes to them, they make you responsible for it. Tell them: It is all from God. What is with these people that they do not even come close to the understanding of the events?** (78)

<12> This means that whatever happens in this world comes from God. <13> When something bad happens, it is a warning that you are not walking on the path, or it happens as a test or to give a lesson. <14> When good happens, it means it is a reward, or again a test and lesson of how it is to be used. <15> In other words, we can say that because this world is self-sustaining, the Laws are set up in such a way that bad actions provoke bad reactions and good actions cause good reactions. To be free of the Law of Karma, be submissive to Him. Father has complete control over everything.

Surah Repentance (At-Taubah)
All are put to tests in order to select Elected Ones:

> Do you think that you would be left alone by yourself while God has not yet clearly made known who strives in His Cause, and chooses no one beside God and His Messenger and the believers as his associates? God has complete knowledge of what you do. (16)

Surah The Spider (Al-'Ankabut)

> Do humans think that it is enough to say that: We believe and would not be tested?
> We verily tried people before them and also God will make known who is truthful and who is not [is a hypocrite]. (2-3)

READINGS (THE KORAN)

Surah Those Who Set The Ranks (As-Saffat)

Disasters are tests for humans to see how surrendered they are in their lives:

> We called him: Abraham, you have indeed fulfilled our command, and in the vision [to sacrifice his son]. Verily We reward those who are surrendered.
> It verily was a great test. (105-106)

<16> In truth, because Abraham passed this test, God gave him an unconditional promise for his seed which is fulfilled throughout history; read Children of Abram (Abraham), All Prophecies Are Fulfilled.

Surah The Troops (Az-Zumar)

Disasters and successes are all tests for humans. However, most people remember God when they are in distress and forget about Him when they are relieved:

> When a distress overtakes a human, he cries unto us; but when We bestow a favor unto him, he says, I have obtained it purely through my own knowledge. Verily it is only a test: but most of them know it not. (49)

Surah They Are Expounded (Fusilat)

Prosperity brings forgetfulness of God, and disaster brings remembrance:

> When we grant a favor on man, he goes away and turns aside; but when afflicted by evil, he prays abundantly. (51)

Surah Mutual Disillusion (At-Taghabun)

Relatives and wealth are tests:

> Your possessions and your offspring are but a test, only in God lies enormous reward. (15)

THIRST FOR LIMITLESSNESS

<17> There is a thirst for limitlessness in the human. When he directs this thirst toward the material world, he will be unhappy because this limited manifested world cannot quench this thirst. Only the discovery of the limitless spiritual world can give happiness and contentment to the limitless Soul.

Surah They Are Expounded (Fusilat)

> Man never tires of praying for good… (49)

TRIBULATION (THE WAY GOD WARNS US)

<18> Suffering is the purifier of the Soul. <19> The humans remember God more often in distress than in prosperity and joy. That is why tribulation has been symbolized as the fire of hell. Fire is also a purifier (especially the sacred fire). <20> Whenever humans go astray and make many reactions, tribulation as a purifier comes to them for several reasons: (1) to torment and purify the ones gone astray, (2) to bring those who are ready to higher consciousness, and (3) to set an example for humanity to understand how the Laws of the universe work. <21> Until the human understands the lessons and starts walking in God's way rather than his own limited ego's way, this process will continue.

Surah The Heights (Al-A'raf)

The way God warns people and then brings disaster to them (the repetition of this process is the reason for history: To teach humanity that they have no other choice but to follow God's way, which is to use all wealth and power for creating an environment that will enable the whole universe to grow and reach the highest consciousness possible for each unit consciousness):

READINGS (THE KORAN)

Whenever we send to a town a Prophet, we bring tribulation and suffering to its inhabitants that they might grow humble. (94)

Surah The Ant (An-Naml)

On the Day, when the trumpets sounded, fear will overtake whosoever is in the heaven and in the earth, except him whom God pleases [Elected Ones]. All shall come unto him, humbled. (87)

<22> So tribulation is for making people understand His Power and Glory, and is to make them humble (meek) so they would submit to Him, for the good of their own Souls.

Surah The Overthrowing (At-Takwir)
Tribulation as hell:

And when hell is ignited, (12)

Tablet Fifteen
UNIFYING THE SPIRITUALISTS

<1> Unless all the real spiritualists of the world unite, the Light will not be able to destroy the darkness. <2> Corrupt people support each other because they do not have anyone else to support them. <3> But spiritual people think they have God and do not need anyone else, so they are divided by insignificant differences in their beliefs.
<4> These insignificances should be shattered by understanding that any religion which divides man from man, no matter what its origin, is not expressing the spirit of God, and God will destroy it. <5> Especially at the brink of the new era that we are now entering, all narrowness of the mind should be destroyed and the universal truth should be understood. Only then can we kill the devil of ignorance and corruption.

Surah The Spoils of War (Al-Anfal)
Spiritual people should support each other in order to destroy corruption:

Disbelievers are supporters of one another, if you do not follow as you are commanded, there will be mischief and corruption in the land (by them). (73)

UNION, SEPARATION, AND REUNIFICATION

<6> The human was in the image (likeness) of God. <7> However, God separated them into two parts, male and female, so the human is no longer in the image of God until the two soulmates merge together and become one again.
<8> When both male and female merge together and become a perfect unit, they can become the same as He ("same knows same").

Surah Women (An-Nisa)
Merging with the other part upon entering heaven:

For those who have believed and done good, surely permission is granted to enter the Garden which underneath rivers flow and dwell therein forever. There also will be pure spouses for them... (57)

<9> Only when a person merges with his or her other part (becomes male and female) will he become in the image of God and enter paradise or the Garden of Eden (Pure Consciousness).

READINGS (THE KORAN)

Surah The Creator or The Angels (Al-Fatir)
Separation of male and female from their original:

God created you from dust [cosmic dust, manifested unit consciousness], then from sperm-drop [after humans became more flesh], then you were made pairs [male and female]. (11)

Surah Sad
The two separated soulmates (☯ ☯) will join together in heaven (☯):

With them would be pure women with modest gaze, companions of equal age. (53)

<10> The male and female will join together as one perfect, complete being.

Surah The Smoke (Ad-Dukhan)

They shall be given fair maidens as companions, having wide and lovely eyes. (54)

UNIVERSE IS CONSCIOUSNESS

<11> The universe consists of consciousness and the three gunas (tama, raja, and satva). Father (God) is the first who was in Pure Consciousness. Then He manifested the First Begotten Son and created the whole universe with the power of the three gunas and the unaware unit consciousnesses. So all things are made from consciousness and are able to reach Pure Consciousness. However, not all unit consciousnesses are equal in the spiritual world. Father is the greatest, and there is a Hierarchy.

Surah Women (An-Nisa)

...God took Abraham as a friend. (125)

<12> This sentence shows completely that the Father (Lord God) is consciousness like us who is able to choose another unit consciousness as a friend. The Son is God manifested!

Surah They Are Expounded (Fusilat)
All parts of the universe are unit consciousnesses:

...God who has given us speech can make everything speak [all are unit consciousnesses]...

...their ears and their eyes and their skins will testify against them [all are consciousnesses] of what they used to do. (21-22)

Tablet Sixteen
VIRTUES

Surah The Table Spread (Al Ma'idah)
Being just:

O you who believe, be steadfast in God's ways, and be an example (for others) in equity, and let not the enmity of the people toward you make you deal with them unjustly. Be just, it is nearer to righteousness, and be aware of your duty to God; verily God knows all that you do. (8)

<1> So, you should not let your hatred affect your justness, because justice is even "nearer to righteousness." <2> Also because all is God, how can a realized person hate any part of the universe?

READINGS (THE KORAN)

Tablet 16

Surah Repentance (At-Taubah)
Show strength of character toward disbelievers by showing annoyance toward wrongdoing:

O You who believe, fight with the disbelievers who are close to you, and let them find you strict [strong, one-pointed, steady, etc.]; know that God is with he who keeps his duty to Him. (123)

Surah The Story (Al-Qasas)
The virtue of being one-pointed:

...for those who believe and do good, God's reward is much better, and it is obtained only by the steadfast with patience. (80)

Surah The Enshrouded One (Al-Muzammil)
One-pointedness:

Remember the name of the Lord, therefore, and devote yourself wholly to His cause. (8)

<3> "Remember the name of the Lord" is the same as "Think about God, His Creation, and truth."

Surah The Troops (Az-Zumar)
Man cannot have two masters, or "Ye cannot serve God and mammon" (Matthew 6:24):

A man who belongs to several diverse people (who are at odds with each other) and the other one who belongs solely to one man, are these two cases similar? (29)

Surah The Romans (Ar-Rum)
To be thankful and hopeful in all situations:

When We bestow Our Mercy on mankind, they rejoice on it; but if there be a tribulation because of their own actions [karmas], they become despairing [and forget about God and His mercies]. (36)

Surah Iron (Al-Hadid)
Being peaceful and content at all times:

Grieve not for that which you have missed, nor exult for what has been given unto you. (23)

Surah The Clans (Al-Ahzab)
Detachment to the external world or one's actions:

Say unto your wives, O Prophet, if you desire worldly life and its glamour, come, I will make a provision for you, and release you in utmost fairness. (28)

Surah The Cloaked One (Al-Mudath-thir)
Detachment to worldly gain:

And bestow no favor for a worldly gain! (6)

WATER IS PURIFIER

<4> Water has always been one of the purifying elements in history. Hebrews as early as the time of Abraham used it for their purification, especially before eating. <5> Fire also is a purifying element and has been used extensively in pagan religions and Jewish sacrifices.

<6> In ancient times human sacrifice with fire was a symbol of a purifying act for the community. <7> The story of the sacrifice of the son of Abraham for God, and then switching to the ram instead (beside many other significances) is a symbol of the change of human to animal sacrifice. It was because the human consciousness had developed to a higher level that this change took place.

<8> Also the act of baptism is a symbol of switching from using fire as a purifier to water. Even animal sacrifice would seem cruel

READINGS (THE KORAN)

in the eyes of the humans in the great scale that Jews used to do, so water and baptism replaced animal sacrifice for purification.

<9> But real purification is overcoming the lower nature, to be purified in the sacred fire of meditation and be baptized by the water of the spirit.

Surah The Criterion (Al-Furqan)

…and we sent down purifying water from the heaven. (48)

WOMEN

<10> Women are equal with men for being provided all the things necessary for their physical, mental, and spiritual progress. <11> Then if in a spiritual environment a woman proved the abilities of a higher Soul or talents of some merits, she should be allowed to progress on those virtues.

Surah The Clans (Al-Ahzab)
How a virtuous woman should be:

Say unto your wives, O Prophet, if you desire worldly life and its glamour, come, I will make a provision for you and release you in utmost fairness. (28)

Surah The Ant (An-Naml)
Women can be leaders if they, like everyone else, prove themselves worthy (they are not fooled by the attraction of Maya and are not attached to their bodies):

Solomon said: Make this throne better than hers [Queen of Sheba], that we may see whether she is rightly guided or is of the ones gone astray. (41)

<12> The Queen of Sheba was a great leader of her people, and was a Great Soul.

ENDING

<13> As it was explained, this is only a small portion of the Koran. Many verses similar to those quoted in this book can be found throughout the Koran.

<14> However, to know the Koran and Islam, like any other religion or truth, the seeker should eagerly ask for guidance and be zealous in pursuing the truth behind the stories and symbols of the revelation. Only with His Blessing will the true meaning be revealed.

<15> But a real seeker will find the answers regardless of the confusion between religions, arguments, and the influence of intellectual spiritualists. "Ask, and it shall be given you; seek, and ye shall find; knock, and it shall be opened unto you:" (Matthew 7:7).

<16> Also remembrance of **The Greatest Sign** and the relationships between the different seals will greatly help to clear the way toward understanding the truth behind them all.

<17> Furthermore, for additional help, when studying a religion, there are three points which should be remembered: The common truth which underlies all religions, the mission of each Prophet, and the people for whom the revelation was given.

<18> God gives truths to people according to their capacities and readiness. That is why He uses the symbols most revealing to those people. But the truth behind those symbols is one, because the truth is **ONE**.

UNIVERSE AND MAN

The book, <u>Universe and Man</u>, explains the construction of the universe and its relationship with the structure of man. Man is created in the image of the universe (God).

UNIVERSE AND MAN

Tablet One

KOSHAS AND LOKAS

<1> The universe has been divided into seven levels, which are called "worlds" (lokas). These seven worlds contain the whole universe. <2> The first level is the physical or manifested world. The second is the pranic level or outgoing energy which coordinates the universal activities (and are those activities). The third is the lower mental world which contains the thoughts of the manifested universe, including how to manage it (earthly logic). <3> The fourth has the higher thoughts and willpower which attract higher ideals. The fifth is beyond thought and is the complete realization of the manifested world. The sixth is the state of complete control of the three gunas but still active in the manifested world, <4> and the seventh is the state of withdrawal (satayaloka).

<5> The human body, mind, and Soul (individual) also consists of seven stages or layers corresponding to the seven layers of the universe. <6> The first five of these layers are called sheaths or koshas. That is, in these first five koshas man is bound by universal forces and can only function in each layer according to that sheath and its propensities.

<7> The last two states in the human are where he becomes free of the bondage of these sheaths and no longer needs them. He reaches the goal.

<8> The crudest of these sheaths is the physical body, as the crudest world is the manifested world.

<9> The manifested universe is nothing more than consciousness crudified with the power of the tama guna. <10> Through this crudifying process (centripetal force), the five elements, namely ethereal, aerial, luminous, liquid, and solid factors* are created. The manifested universe consists of these five elements.

<11> Also the human body or the grossest layers of human existence consist of the same five elements. <12> Each cell in the body is an independent entity, existing in a collective effort for the well-being of the whole of the body and Soul.

<13> The active force, the life-force, or mutative force (raja guna) is the second layer or sheath in the human. This sheath, which is prana (life-force), is the coordinator and controller of the contacts between different organs and the whole body to the mind. <14> The prana, which is outgoing energy of the Soul (raja guna), has no knowledge or power of decision-making, but follows the orders given from the intelligent part of the mind (satva guna).

<15> That is why it can be used or misused according to the level of consciousness of the user. It is the life-force in the human. <16> One form of prana (energy) is electricity. It can only be found where the ether is. <17> Ether is the memory part of the brain. Without ether, prana cannot be verified and also no memory will remain.

<18> The outgoing prana (life-force) from the Soul becomes heedless **desire** (passion). <19> The ingoing prana to the Soul becomes **will** (controller of desires).

<20> Also in the universe, as the crudifying power of the tama guna makes the manifested world or the first loka (world), so the second world is the prana (mutative force, raja guna) in the universe, or the life-force (the breath of life). Through prana (mutative force), all activities are done and the coordination (through the satva guna, intelligence) in the universe is achieved. <21> Without prana, there would be no life and no activities.

---

*   Read Appendix II.

UNIVERSE AND MAN

<22> The prana is everywhere in the universe in many different forms. It is mixed with ether and functions through it. <23> The ether in the universe is the memory of the universe or the Akashic Records.

<24> These two, the physical sheath and pranic sheath, make up the external part of man. <25> Because there is nothing external for the universe (God), so there is no sheath for It, but only worlds.

Tablet Two

<1> The mental sphere in man is the beginning of the internal part of man. <2> The first level is the subconscious mind or subconscious sheath. It is the part which internalizes the external world. Whatever is in the external world will be created in this part and stored away to be used later.

<3> In this lower part of the mind, the desires toward the external world reside. In other words, the energy (prana) is directed outward (desires). So we can say it is the part that the "beast" (Rev. 13:1), which symbolizes desire, arises from. <4> This part collects information, elaborates on it, and comes up with the best decision for the fulfillment of its mundane desires.

<5> Also all the mundane decisions for the external world are made in this part of the Universal Mind, which are the collective lower thoughts of the individual plus the lower thoughts for maintenance of the manifested universe. <6> We can call this the crude mental world. In this third layer, the raja (mutative) and satva (sentient) forces are active, but are under the influence of the tama guna (external world).

<7> In the next sheath in the human, the noble or higher thoughts reside. It is deeper in man and the origin of the thoughts are not from the external world but from the internal. <8> Or in other words, the prana (energy) is directed internally and not externally. So the higher thoughts arise and prana becomes willpower and imagination (creative mind) instead of heedless desires. <9> Therefore the life of the person in this sheath becomes more under his control and he strives for things higher than only mundane satisfactions ("Man does not live by bread alone"). The mind becomes spiritualized (Buddhi). The intentions will be toward the spiritual world rather than toward illusion (Maya) of the external world.

<10> In the universe, this can be called the subtle mental world. The origin of noble thoughts and ideals occurs with this part, the unconscious mind.

<11> The next sheath is the state beyond mind, or when it is realized that all is Mind or all is God. It is the state of the beginning of freedom. <12> It is the state where a great joy (Ananda) is experienced. <13> However, still the person is in bondage and has not yet mastered his mind.

<14> This state in the universe is also the state of "All is He," the beginning of the shattering of ignorance. It is the collective joy of those who have realized this state.

<15> The sixth state in man is beyond any sheath. He realizes that "I am He," or that he is god also and can enter into Pure Consciousness and return, because a thin thread is still left between him and Him. He becomes the master of his mind (three gunas). He becomes a son of God.

<16> This state in the universe is known as savikalpa or the state of closeness to objectless-ness.

<17> The next (seventh) is the state of complete mastering of the illusion of separation. The only thing left is will and the creative mind. There is no separation between "I am" and "I AM." However, through will, he can return to his individual nature as an Avatar. <18> There is no heedless desire left but a will to help others reach the goal also. The direction of prana is completely internalized.

<19> This state in the universe is that of sat and the world in this state is called satayaloka. It is the absolute state, Pure Consciousness.

<20> These last two states are described as indescribable.

<21> Also because of the experiences which each unit consciousness goes through, he creates an individual character which will be carried with him any time he comes back to the manifested world. <22> This individual character will be enhanced, expanded, and modified by each new experience. So the nature of the universe is infinitely progressive.

Tablet Three

<1> Below a brief explanation of the relationship between the individual and his external world in general will be described:

<2> The Self or Soul or Atman ("I am") is the controller of the three levels of the unit mind, which are the three gunas. <3> The satva guna is the decision-making (reasoning) part of this unit consciousness. The raja guna is the recognizing part of the unit mind, and the tama guna is the screen. This part made by the tama guna is called the Chitta or projective part. <4> It is a protoplasmic (etheric) form which is affected by the messages received from the senses. Through this screen, the projection of the object of the senses to the mind occurs. It is then recognized by the raja part (Ahamtattva) and decisions are made by the satva guna part (Mahatattva).

<5> After the Chitta receives the required information from the senses, the recognizing part (raja guna) through the self, will realize what these messages are. Then according to the state of consciousness of that individual and under the influence of the satva guna, decisions will be made as to how to react. <6> The message of how to react according to the information received from the senses will be given to the raja (pranic) part to perform.

<7> According to the decision made in the reasoning part of the mind (Mahatattva), the proper action will be transmitted to the active part (Ahamtattva) and from there through the nervous system to the proper organ, to carry out the order.

<8> The nervous system and the brain are entirely different than the mind. The nerves carry the messages from the external world and internal organs to the Chitta, with the help of the Pancha tatwa. <9> Pancha tatwa is that thing which carries the sensations to the Chitta. It can be called the electrical form as messages which bring the senses to the Chitta. They are one kind of prana (electricity).

<10> The brain is a storage unit which contains experiences and learning of the present lifetime, and it will degenerate after death. <11> However, the reactions of the actions and memories of each lifetime also remain in the Universal Mind or the unconscious mind (the collective mind in the universe, Akashic Records).

<12> The crudest part of the mind (Chitta), or fine ether, is directly connected to the ethereal body (astral body) which contains the first five chakras in the human body (there are seven chakras in the body). With this, the mind is connected to these chakras also. The decision-making part of the mind receives messages from these chakras on how to react to the situation. <13> When the person's consciousness is in the lower centers, the decisions tend to be directed more toward selfishness and animality. Through spiritual progress, as the person develops to higher centers (higher sheaths), the decisions become more universally oriented and less self-centered (not from fear or passion or selfishness). <14> Even the information stored in the brain will be used according to the level of consciousness of that person. According to that level, the decision-making part of his mind will demand a proper reaction from the mutative part.

<15> This astral body (ethereal body) is linked to the material body through prana (the breath of life). Prana is absorbed mostly through the nostrils and lungs. <16> However, if a person develops the ability to control this element in the universe, it can be observed, directed, or used by will. Without

prana there would be no link between the ethereal body and physical body (aerial, luminous, liquid, and solid parts of the body). <17> Then the physical body would become unsuited for the Soul and its mind, and they would leave the body (that is when death occurs). <18> In other words, if the Soul, for any reason, withdraws its prana from the body it resides in, then death occurs and no link remains between the Soul and the body.

Tablet Four

<1> The five carrying elements of the senses are called "Pancha tatwa," which connect the Chitta (the crudest part of the mind) to the external world through the nervous system. <2> The five "organs of the senses" which enable man to experience the outside world (smell, taste, sight, touch, and hearing) are under the influence of the satva guna. But the carrying of their sensations is by prana. <3> The five "organs of action" – speech, hands, feet (motion), generation, and excretion – are under the influence of the raja guna (mutative force). <4> The five "objects of the senses" or the ability in the outside world to make us sense them are the smell of the object, the sight of the object, the taste of the object, the touch of the object, and the sound of the object (hearing). These are under the influence of the tama guna (crudified or manifested world).

<5> The Pancha tatwa, organs of the senses, and organs of the actions make up the fifteen fine organs in the body.

<6> The physical (material) or gross body consists of aerial, luminous (heat), liquid, and solid factors. <7> This material body is the container of the subtle body, which consists of the mind (the three parts of the mind), the Soul, the astral body, and the fifteen fine organs.

<8> Aerial factor fills the empty spaces in the body and also takes in prana and oxygen. Luminous factor provides heat for maintaining the body temperature and for activities such as digestion, motion, etc. Liquid factor keeps the body moist and provides fluid for many of its functions. Solid factor provides the container for the rest.

<9> Fifteen fine organs in the body, plus five basic elements (ethereal, aerial, luminous, liquid, and solid), and three levels of the mind (the three gunas) along with the illusive "I am" as a separate entity from the rest (God), make up the twenty-four elements in the body and in the universe. <10> These are symbolized as "the four and twenty elders" in Rev. 4:10.

<11> When a unit consciousness (human) goes beyond these twenty-four elements (elders), he reaches Pure Consciousness. <12> Then he knows he is none of these but he is "I am," which is a part of that "I AM."

<13> When reasoning is self-centered, the action is gross, and desires arise from self-gratification and sensual satisfaction, or other desires from the lower nature, then man is drawn toward Maya and he will be lost in the illusion of being separate. So he goes to "hell." **That is when the reasoning becomes gross and actions create bondage.** <14> This in turn creates desires and attachments, and the mind becomes "false ego" or unspiritualized.

<15> But when man realizes that he is a part of the universe and the universe is a part of him, his reasoning and actions will be directed toward the good of all. All this will direct man toward the Lord and Pure Consciousness. <16> **Then the reasoning becomes wisdom and action Divine**, and the mind becomes "Buddhi" or spiritualized.

Tablet Five

RELATIONSHIP BETWEEN CHAKRAS AND KOSHAS (SHEATHS)

<1> As the first kosha (sheath) in an individual is his physical body, which is under the influence of the tama guna and is manifested because of this force, so also the first chakra is completely dominated by this force and is related to this first sheath or kosha.

<2> The second sheath, which is prana in the body, is under the influence of the raja guna. <3> It is true that the raja guna is the life-force (prana) and is good in general, but when it is under the influence of the tama guna, it becomes worldly passion and thus unspiritual desires arise. <4> This second sheath is related to the second chakra in which the raja guna is active. But it is under the influence of the tama guna and is directed toward the external world, resulting in heedless activities done in the manifested universe. It is where the temptation arises and is symbolized as woman in the third chapter in <u>Genesis</u>.

<5> The third chakra is related to the third kosha. In this level both raja guna (mutative force) and satva guna (sentient force, intelligence) are active, but they are still under the influence of the tama guna. As the third kosha was the crude mental world, or the place where the mind was directed toward fulfillment of desires for things in the external world, so also in this chakra the intelligence and activities are under the influence of the tama guna (external world). <6> That is why this layer or kosha is called "mind." The worldly intelligence is in this level!

<7> This third kosha is the most important layer to be understood, because it is in this state that individuals use their intelligence to manipulate the external world for satisfaction of their gross desires. <8> That is also why this is the center where longing for wealth, possession, and power to satisfy one's selfish desires (first two chakras) is located.

<9> Therefore, control of this chakra or layer of the mind (kosha) is very important by individuals and society in general.

<10> A person in the first layer of the mind (kosha) is earth-bound. Then because of his fears, attachments, striving for survival, etc., he becomes bound to anything that fulfills his mundane needs. <11> A person in the second layer does not have that much intelligence to inflict great suffering on others. <12> But it is those in the third layer with intelligence who cause exploitation of the two others in lower levels. <13> This brings great suffering to humanity. <14> So understanding this layer in depth is very necessary in order to control the suffering inflicted on the individual and society.

<15> The fourth layer is related to the fourth chakra, in which prana (raja guna) dominates. However, its direction is not toward the external world (downward) but toward higher thoughts and the spiritual world (upward). It is the beginning of spiritual feelings and joy. <16> It is the place of unconditional Love.

<17> The fifth layer is related to the fifth chakra in which the satva guna (pure intelligence) dominates. Here a great joy (Ananda) is experienced and the person comes in contact with the ethereal world. All the activities and their purposes in the external world (spiritual logic) become clear to him.

<18> In the sixth chakra, the last bondage is also overcome and the person becomes the master of the three gunas. That is why no kosha (sheath, layer of the mind) is left and the person experiences infinity, great powers, and knowledge. But he still maintains a small "i" to keep him in the body. Such a person is called a Satguru or perfect master (man-god).

UNIVERSE AND MAN

Tablet Six

<1> In the seventh chakra, the Soul quiets its three gunas and becomes pure intuition. It enters into the state of perfect rest. <2> However by completely internalizing the raja guna (prana), the willpower in its highest level is present. Whatever is willed, will be done. <3> Also by this, the willpower of the unit consciousness, he can return to the koshas into the world as an Avatar (god-man).

<4> In both the sixth and seventh levels, a unit consciousness is in the state of Pure Consciousness. <5> In the sixth he uses the three gunas to help others and he feels the infinity, <6> and in the seventh he is in Pure Consciousness without maintaining a physical body.

<7> It should be noted that it is for the sake of comprehension that the chakras and koshas were devised to explain two aspects of human existence. In reality they are completely interrelated and of one nature. <8> Soul or the unit consciousness in its ordinary state is unaware of its divinity, the chakras, or the layers of the mind (koshas) in the body. So he identifies himself as the body. A person in this state can be called a rational animal.

<9> But through meditation, or for any other reason, the latent spiritual awareness which is called "kundalini" (sleeping serpent in the first chakra) might be awakened. <10> When it is awakened and rises to the seventh chakra into the pituitary gland, the spiritual understanding will start to be realized, including the effect of these forces and different layers of his mind. <11> He will become more and more familiar with his spirit and self.

<12> Before the awakening of these understandings, the person will follow the influences of these forces without having any control over them (as animals do). When this awakening occurs, however, the person realizes that there are messages which come from different chakras and influence his mind (koshas) and so his reactions. <13> Therefore, he starts to master these influences as he progresses further. With more development, he comes closer to the essence of his self which is one with the Universal Self (God). So eventually he becomes the same as He, through The Grace.

<14> Therefore, in reality, the message received from any chakra and the level of the awareness of the person creates the sheath of the mind (kosha) or the layer he is in. For example, a person who receives the messages from the first, second, and third chakras and has no knowledge of why he is bound to follow them, is in the first three layers of the mind (three koshas) and is earth-bound. Therefore he suffers. <15> That is why even when the spiritual awareness is awakened but the lower nature (the first three chakras) is not yet mastered, much suffering and many trials occur. Little-by-little the person becomes aware of how to master these influences.

<16> So actually the layers of the mind and the first five chakras are, in a sense, the same. It depends on how the Soul responds to the messages received from the chakras. When it responds to the messages received from the first three chakras, then the flow of energy (prana) will be outgoing (downward) and become binding desires, resulting in attachment, greed, and bondage. <17> But when the Soul responds to the call of the higher chakras, the flow of energy becomes inward (upward) and the result is higher thoughts (ideals), joy, control, willpower, and spiritual progress toward freedom from bondage. <18> Even desires cease to be self-centered, and only those which are good for spiritual progress of the self and others will be kept and followed.

<19> So again the relationship between lokas (worlds), koshas (layers of the mind), and chakras (spiritual centers in the human body) should be understood as not being separate things but parts of a whole interrelated system. <20> In fact, this should be kept in mind: That the human body is an open system related to the universe, especially in the first five chakras. That is why the first five lokas (worlds) are the same stages as the five koshas, but because these five are in the human body, they create sheaths or separation.

<21> However, this is not in a thorough sense of separation, because still they are related to each other and are a part of one world (loka).

<22> Again the emphasis in realizing their inter-relationships is to cause the seeker to ponder on these truths and realize deeper the beauty and depth of this wonderful creation. Also it should prevent him from becoming narrow in separating the universe into segments and missing the view of the whole.

UNIVERSE AND MAN SUMMARIZED

Tablet 6

CHAK-RA	GLAND	ELEMENT	SHAPE	COLOR/ PROPENSITY[†]	SOUND	DOMINATING FORCE	SANSKRIT NAME	NOTE	CORRESPONDING KOSHA	CORRESPONDING LOKA
1	Cells of Leydig	Solid	Rectangular	Gold	Lung	Tama dominates, Raja and Satva present[‡]	Muladhara	Do	Annamayakosha (physical body)	Bhuloka (physical world)
2	Gonads	Liquid	Half-moon	White	Wung	Tama dominates, Raja active[§], Satva present	Svadhisthana	Re	Pranamayakosha (prana)	Bhuvarloka (prana world)
3	Adrenals	Luminous (heat)	Triangle	Orange-red	Rung	Tama dominates, Raja and Satva active	Manipura	Me	Manomayakosha (mind)	Swarloka (crude mental world)
4	Thymus	Air	Circle	Smokey (grey)	Jung	Raja dominates, Satva and Tama active	Anahata	Fa	Vigamayakosha (discriminating mind begins, Buddhi)	Maharloka (subtle mental world)
5	Parathyroid and thyroid	Ether	No shape	Many (rainbow)	Hung	Satva dominates, Raja active and Tama present	Vishudaha	So	Anandamayakosha (etheric state or bliss, heaven, but still a part of Maya)	Janaloka (supramental world, state of knowingness or knowledge)
6	Pineal	Three gunas				Soul dominates, three gunas present	Ajina	La		Tapoloka (beyond mental world)
7	Pituitary	Soul				Soul and three gunas present…	Sahasrara	Thee		Satayaloka… (true world, essence, the reality)

(Column 5 marker: *Lower Nature* ▲ spans chakras 1–3)

† These colors represent the propensities of each chakra in higher levels: "Gold" as the kundalini in the first chakra (overcoming fear of not being provided one's physiological and safety needs, and death), "white" as compassion changed from passion in the second, and "orange-red" as overcoming the use of power for worldly gains. "Smokey" is a balance and "rainbow" is knowledge of all. The true colors of the chakras vary according to many factors which affect them.

‡ Present means they can be evoked but are completely dominated by the dominating force or forces. However, the present force usually is dormant.

§ Active force means the force is active but not the dominator. So when the mutative is active but satva is only present and tama dominates, the mutative force which has no polarity of itself will be crudified (become negative) and will be bent (directed) toward the external world.

APPENDIX I

Tablet Seven
ENERGY ACTIVATES PROPENSITIES

<1> Although there are many propensities (desires) existing in the universe, without energy (raja guna) which is the activating force, they would have remained dormant.

<2> The solar plexus is the coordinator of the energy (prana) throughout the body. It is located to the left of the navel area. <3> When the flow of energy is directed downward (woman, passion), the lower propensities, which reside in the lower energy centers (chakras), are activated. <4> When the same energy is directed upward (Mother, compassion), higher propensities will become active.

<5> The energy is directed toward any center as the kundalini (the awakening force which opens chakras) rises into each chakra and attracts the energy toward it to activate its propensities.

<6> The first energy center (chakra) controls solid factor. The first sheath or kosha corresponds to this chakra. The first kosha is related to the physical body. The influence of this kosha brings the longing for physiological and safety needs to be fulfilled. <7> The propensities in this chakra are: Physical longing (physiological and safety needs), psychic longing (desire to know), psycho-spiritual longing (desire to know the unknown – unconscious mind), and spiritual longing (desire to know God). <8> The last two longings are the effect of the kundalini which resides in this chakra.

<9> The second chakra controls liquid factor. The second sheath (kosha) corresponds to this chakra. The second kosha is related to pranic functions in the body. <10> Sexual activity is a bodily pranic function. That is why this chakra is so powerful. It uses prana (raja guna, Grace) directed toward the external world (absence of The Divine Logic).

<11> The influence of this kosha results in heedless actions and excess sexual desires. Some propensities in this chakra are distrust, proudfulness, overindulgence, pitilessness, or mercilessness, and fear of annihilation.

<12> The third chakra controls luminous factor (heat in the body which is mostly generated from the digestive system). This chakra is related to the third kosha or crude mental world. The creative energy of the mind is directed toward the mundane external world. <13> General longing is to gain control over others by misuse of power. Some of the propensities of this chakra are: Backbiting, slandering or betraying, over-attachment even though the person knows it is not good, melancholy, cruelty, lethargy, jealousy, fear, aversion and hatred, shame, and bashfulness.

<14> The propensities in the first three chakras above are most prominent in normal humans.

<15> The fourth chakra controls the aerial factor (lungs). The corresponding kosha is the fourth kosha or subtle mental world. The energy starts to flow upward when the kundalini reaches this chakra. That is why the unconditional Love is experienced in this chakra for the first time. <16> The healing power also starts when energy begins to flow upward to the fourth chakra and higher.

<17> However, to raise the kundalini from the first three chakras (lower nature) to the fourth and above is the hardest part of the spiritual journey. When this is done, a person "will be born again" from the lower self to the higher one. <18> Because of this difficulty and overlap of chakras into each other, the complete transformation of the energy to higher propensities and eventually to higher chakras is very gradual in this level. That is why there are still some negative propensities present in the fourth level. Some of the propensities in this chakra are: Sense of possessiveness, anxiety, arrogance and vanity,

UNIVERSE AND MAN

covetousness, hypocrisy, indecision (being in the crossroads of falling back to the lower nature or progressing further), unnecessary argument, regret and misery, endeavor, discrimination between right and wrong, and hope.

Tablet Eight

<1> The fifth chakra controls ethereal factor. The corresponding kosha is the fifth one. A blissful state of mind will be experienced in this level. The etheric reality and the purpose of this manifested creation will become clear to the person. <2> People who feel they are in touch with some ethereal being(s) are in this level. They usually and strongly feel they are a channel for this (these) being(s).

<3> The angelic music (the music of the spheres, melody of the gods) can be heard in this state. Many other beautiful experiences will be felt and great powers are gained in this level. <4> It is so enchanting that many will be trapped in this state and will be lost in going further in their spiritual progress. They might completely forsake the external world and start to enjoy this state of knowledge, power, and bliss. <5> It is not the highest spiritual achievement. They are still bound by Maya related to the fifth kosha or sheath. These all are still the illusion of separation from God (Maya). Heavenly experiences (as a place) occur in this state!

<6> It is in the sixth chakra that all illusion of separation (koshas) from God is shattered and no trap remains. Then such a person becomes a pure channel from the Most High (direct from God with no intermediary). <7> Such a person is a true Light Worker (Paravipra). This is the Highest achievement on earth!

<8> As it can be seen in **The Greatest Sign**, the first sign (☯) is also the last one (❀). The first sign is the awakening of the spiritual forces (kundalini). <9> The kundalini resides in the first chakra before it arises to higher ones. When it reaches the seventh chakra a person is in Pure Consciousness. <10> The first sign which is the last one also – "I am the first and the last" – therefore, shows the process of awakening the spiritual forces and reaching Pure Consciousness.

<11> This process can be achieved by following spiritual practices such as meditation, breathing, chanting, etc. <12> The rest of **The Greatest Sign**, however, not only will help the Kingdom Of Heaven to be established on Earth, but also will accelerate the processes of reaching Pure Consciousness.

<13> After a person starts to do spiritual practices, then the next step in **The Greatest Sign** is to also live in a community (✡). <14> By being around others, the propensities mentioned above will manifest in stronger intensity than living alone or escaping to the mountains. <15> Therefore a person will become aware of them with a greater impression on his consciousness.

<16> Then the person in the community also has to overcome being self-centered (✝). By trying not to be self-centered, he will again see how selfish and attached he is to the external world. <17> His fears and other propensities which exist in him will again manifest themselves in a greater manner, so the process will be accelerated again.

<18> Remember the person still is doing spiritual exercises and will continue to do so to the seventh seal. He meditates and goes deep inside to see how the forces are working within and without. <19> As these propensities become more intense, the deeper the realization of their existence will be felt through meditation, and eventually they will fall away and be no more. <20> With each propensity overcome, one is one step closer to perfection (God).

<21> The next step is to become a channel for God and submit unto Him (☪). With this practice he realizes he should not be attached to his spiritual power gained or experience that he feels. This will prevent any further karma.

UNIVERSE AND MAN

<22> Also when he reaches the fifth level of consciousness (✹) he will not be trapped by its enchanting effects. He will know these all are a part of God and the most important thing is to use these acquired powers and this knowledge toward helping others to progress. <23> Therefore he will pass this trap in the fifth level and become a great spiritual force (Light Worker) (✡), and will eventually reach Pure Consciousness (✺).

<24> Therefore, again with the **Eternal Divine Path** the possibility of being lost in the path is minimized. <25> It will guide a person directly to God, not to ethereal beings and many traps in the path.

APPENDIX II

Tablet Nine

THERE IS AN INFINITE RANGE IN CREATION

<1> The elements in the manifested universe, in a broad and general way, are divided into seven categories: <2> The consciousness, three gunas, ethereal factor, aerial factor, luminous factor, liquid factor, and solid factor.

<3> However, there is not a clear-cut way to separate each category from the following or the previous ones. <4> As in the case of colors, infinite varieties and shades can be found even for one of the distinguished colors. For example, blue can range from a very light blue to a very dark one, with infinite shades between. So in the case of these elements there are also infinite stages which can be found in each category and overlap to the next or with the previous one.

<5> When the operative power of the tama guna is first released and the memory or the feeling of "I have done" (Chitta) arises, the first stage of the ethereal factor or fine ether forms. Then there will be cruder forms of ether, until the formation of air, and so on.

<6> This might be easier illustrated by the more visible elements, such as liquid and solid. There are thin liquids which flow easily, and there are liquids in thicker forms until solid factors are reached. <7> Even in the solid state, there are soft solid forms and very hard solid factors, with infinite solid varieties in-between.

<8> It is the same for infinite different levels of consciousness from Pure Consciousness down to the very crude consciousness. <9> In fact, when the consciousness becomes very crude it indeed becomes flesh and the person identifies himself as his body.

<10> This analogy goes on and is true about all things in the universe. There are infinite levels of consciousness, sentient force (satva guna), mutative force (raja guna), static force (tama guna), ethereal factor, etc.

<11> So we have to create this ability not to see everything in black and white but always as an infinite spectrum of possibilities, <12> and still these infinite ranges are changing in time (I-Ching).

<13> Another point is that although the universe or its worlds are divided into seven levels, <14> in the spiritual Hierarchy (Hierarchy in the Kingdom Of Heaven), there are two more states.

<15> In the sixth and seventh stages, a man becomes a son of God (god). But before man was created there were two beings in this state. <16> So the eighth state is the state of the First Begotten Son, and the ninth is the state of the Father.

A NOTE

This book <u>Universe and Man</u> might seem to some a hard book to understand. Also the goal of the spiritual journey (Pure Consciousness) seems impossible to achieve. It all is so true. That is why Esa said to enter heaven is impossible for man, but it is possible for God (Mark 10:27). What makes it possible, is His Grace. The fire of Grace burns all impurities and a person becomes a pure channel for God. Then you will create Love, Compassion, and Mercy toward All. You will do good and become a giver as an example for others to be good (God).

You do not have to know much detail and explanation if it is not your nature as such. But Love God with all your Heart, Mind, and Spirit, and follow the **Eternal Divine Path**. This will win His Grace and your liberation is assured.

REVELATION OF
<u>THE REVELATION</u>

The book, __Revelation of The Revelation__, is a complete Revelation of the meaning of the last book in the __Bible__, __The Revelation__.

REVELATION OF THE REVELATION

INTRODUCTION

The book Genesis (the first book in the Bible) can be referred to as the introduction to the Bible, The Revelation (the last book in the Bible) as the conclusion or ending, and the rest of the Bible as the main part. With this, the Bible can be looked upon as a complete book given by the Lord.

Therefore, by understanding the introduction (Genesis) of the book (Bible) and its conclusion (The Revelation), it can be understood in depth. The introductory part of the Bible is described in The Holiest Book and Children of Abram (Abraham), All Prophecies Are Fulfilled, and the conclusion or the book of The Revelation is described here.

The commentaries in this book are an expansion of the revelations which are given about some verses of The Revelation in The Holiest Book, and also they cover the verses which are not explained in The Holiest Book. In other words, this is a complete book of commentaries on the whole book of The Revelation, verse by verse.

A brief explanation of the basic flow of The Revelation in whole, before the main commentaries start, will be given below.

In chapter 5 of Matthew, from verses 3 to 10, eight types of humans are described. Verse 3 describes the first ones, the poor in spirit, who become escapists and do not go through the spiritual struggle. They are the ones who forsake the society. From verses 4 to 9, the next six types are described, each one relating to one of the psychic centers in the human body (chakras) in spiritual progress. In verse 10 those who are called Maha-Para-vipras (Avatars) are described (the ones who have reached Pure Consciousness and return to help others).

In The Revelation, after a brief introduction in chapter 1, again the same trend of different types of people occur in chapters 2 and 3. Also the pitfall in each step of progress (going from the lower nature to the higher one) is described. Also after each stage it is explained what the reward is for the person who overcomes these pitfalls. These descriptions are symbolically called the seven churches, and are related to the eight types of humans described in ten verses in chapter 5 in St. Matthew.

Also each church is related to one seal in **The Greatest Sign** and its significance in history and human progress. Therefore not only is each church representative of a psychic center (chakra), but together they also present the progress of human consciousness through time and history. It shows where each seal stands in this progress and what the Prophet of that seal had tried to accomplish.

In fact we can say that the meanings of chapters 2 and 3 are the very base of both human history and understanding The Greatest Sign (the history but not the creation).

After chapter 3 in The Revelation, when a person progresses to a very high consciousness (Pure Consciousness), then, "After this I looked, and, behold, a door was opened in heaven: and the first voice which I heard ... said, Come up hither, and I will shew thee things which must be hereafter." (Rev. 4:1). After going through the stages described in chapters 2 and 3, then the door (of understanding) would be opened to the truth of the rest of The Revelation.

In chapters 4 and 5, it is described how the "Lamb" had reached Pure Consciousness and was about to open the seals of the understanding of the book "in the right hand of him that sat on the throne." (Rev. 5:1).

In chapter 6 until chapter 8 verse 2, the seven seals are opened by Christ, a symbol of each Angel of the seven churches. Also, each seal is a symbol of a religion which corresponds to one of the seven seals in **The Greatest Sign**.

From 8:2 until the end of chapter 11, the seven Angels with seven trumpets are described. The trumpet is an instrument with a tremendous sound, and if blown strongly, it can awaken people. So it is a symbol of truth which comes by these seven Angels, which are the same as the Angels of the churches (Prophets of the seven religions). They bring the truth to humanity, but humans do not pay any heed and continue in their own ways, so create karma or sin (sin is transgression from the Laws of the Lord), and this results in many disasters and tribulation. This is described to come after each Angel sounds his trumpet.

In chapter 10 before the seventh Angel comes, the era of flourishment of the intellectuals is described, which corresponds to the same era prophesied in the book of Daniel (for more detail, read Commentaries on Prophecies in Daniel, Period of Intellectual Domination). It is after this intellectual era that the seventh Angel will come, "when he shall begin to sound, the mystery of God should be finished..." (Rev. 10:7).

In chapter 11 it is described that these Angels (the Prophets) will come, bring the truth, and prophesy for three thousand five hundred years. But each time after they leave, their teachings will be distorted and become dead, "And their dead bodies shall lie in the street..." (Rev. 11:8), until eventually the seventh Angel will sound his trumpet and the kingdom of this world becomes the Kingdom of God.

In chapters 12 and 13, the process and reasons for confusion in the mind of the individual is described by four symbols: The red dragon as attraction to the external world; the beast with seven heads, "which rises up out of the sea"* (Rev. 13:1) symbolizes desire; the beast with "two horns like a lamb," (Rev. 13:11) as attachment which comes to man because of desires; and the result of all of these is the mark (Rev. 13:17) that such people carry on themselves. This mark that they will be known by is the GREED for having more of this external world.

The attraction of the external world (red dragon), desires (beast with seven heads), attachment (beast with two horns) and greed (the mark) are the four winds which cause both the individual consciousness and the world to become confused and turbulent; their consciousnesses (water) become restless by these winds. This confusion comes to the people because of the influence of the tama guna over their Souls which causes them to fall to their lower natures. It is this lower nature which should be overcome in the earthly life.

In chapter 14, again the seven Angels will bring other events that will happen besides those already described. These will occur in the same time period after each seal is opened by each Angel, consisting of a span of three thousand five hundred years. Again it is in the time of the seventh Angel that the earth is ripe and the winepress is used to separate those who are ready from those who have lagged behind.

Again, from chapter 15:1 to 16:18, the same Angels in the same period of time (3,500 years) will appear with the last plagues. When the seventh Angel pours out his vial, The Plan of God finishes and it will be done, "...It is done" (Rev. 16:17).

There are two points which should be emphasized and understood. First, the Angels of the churches (Prophets) who will open the seven seals (seven religions) come in a time period of three thousand five hundred years.

---

* "Sea" is the symbol of individual consciousness in confusion (mind), because sea symbolizes restless water (consciousness). But the use of the phrase "the great sea" refers to the consciousness of the world (human society) in general. That is why the symbolic meaning of baptism, by merging the person into the restless water (river of Jordan) and taking him out again, refers to removing him from confusion. However, the base for confusion in both consciousnesses (individual and social) are the four winds (attraction, desire, attachment, and greed).

REVELATION OF THE REVELATION

Also the seven Angels with trumpets, the seven Angels in chapter 14, and the seven Angels with the last plagues (Rev. 15:1-16:17) all come in the same time period. Each of them is a symbol of one Prophet or the bringer of the tribulation after each Prophet. The tribulation occurs because people will not follow the teachings of that Prophet.

The second point is that it is after the last or seventh Angel when the time comes that "the mystery of God should be finished" (Rev. 10:7), the Kingdom of God will come (Rev. 11:15), those who have lagged behind will be separated from those who are ripe, "...the clusters of the vine of the earth" will be gathered because "...her grapes are fully ripe" (14:18), and The Plan of God will be finished, "...It is done" (Rev. 16:17). So after the seventh Angel, the true reality and His Plan will finish.

After all these things occur and when many people realize the illusion of Maya, then is the time for Babylon to "come in remembrance before God" (Rev. 16:19). Babylon is the symbol of gaining wealth and power to satisfy the selfish desires and/or for making name and fame for selfish ends (vain hopes). In chapters 17 and 18 the fall of Babylon is described.

Then is the time for the glory of God to come, which is in chapter 19. The rest of The Revelation is about what will happen after that. In chapter 20, the two stages of judgment are described and many will be saved. So there will be many Angels (Avatars) by the end of the time of this chapter. Therefore, there will be many laborers to help the process of bringing the whole universe to Pure Consciousness. Those who had not reached Pure Consciousness by this time will be born again in the manifested world, "cast into the lake of fire" (Rev. 20:15).

Those who had reached Pure Consciousness and those who will also overcome and reach there "shall inherit all things; and I will be his God, and he shall be my son" (Rev. 21:7). Also in chapter 21 a symbolic description of New Jerusalem (Pure Consciousness) is presented.

In chapter 22 it is assured that all these things will surely happen and are true. Amen.

Tablet One

Chapter 1

"The Revelation of רחישוּה, which God gave unto him, to shew unto his servants things which must shortly come to pass; and he sent and signified it by his angel unto his servant John:" (Rev. 1:1)

<1> The Revelation is the truth that was revealed to the servants of God, who are the Saints and Great Souls. <2> "Which must shortly come to pass" means that it will happen in a short period of time. But as we know, the time schedule of God is not like ours. Six thousand years is a short period of time for a Being that has been living for ever and ever, millions and billions of years. So "shortly come to pass" might even mean several thousand years.

"Who bare record of the word of God, and of the testimony of רחישוּה, and of all things that he saw." (Rev. 1:2)

<3> John is recording the word of God and the testimony of Esa the Christ, and all the things that he saw. He is just a medium. He is not adding anything from himself. <4> In truth he finds all these things from his own Soul which speaks through the Christ Consciousness (רחישוּה).

"Blessed is he that readeth, and they that hear the words of this prophecy, and keep those things which are written therein: for the time is at hand." (Rev. 1:3)

<5> Therefore, this prophecy is one of the most important parts of the Bible, and he who hears it and understands it is a "blessed one" because he will be able to understand The

REVELATION OF THE REVELATION Tablet 1

Plan of God for the human. <6> The Revelation can be thought of as a mini-Bible. If a person understands The Revelation completely and can relate The Revelation to the rest of the Bible, he can understand what the true meaning of the Bible is.

<7> That is because in The Revelation it is revealed how a person progresses and what all the pitfalls in the path are, why God created this universe, how He is trying to bring all of His creation to higher consciousness and eventually Pure Consciousness, and what the purpose of life is. <8> Also in this book it is described what the devil is, the attraction of Maya, and the power of the tama guna over the Souls of the people, etc.

<9> The Revelation describes how the people are lost by following intellectual knowledge only. <10> Also it is explained what Babylon is – "the great city" – and how it made many kings and merchants. <11> It is told how people who are looking for power, money, wealth, and fulfilling those desires will fail, and how eventually God's Kingdom Of Heaven will be established on earth. <12> That is why whoever hears this prophecy and understands it is a "blessed one" because he will know what The Plan is, how it works, and how it is going to be.

<13> Then he will become part of the great struggle with the power of the tama guna, or the ignorance over the Souls of those lost people, <14> and he will help this struggle to be fulfilled, continued, and progressed until the whole universe reaches higher consciousness, and eventually Pure Consciousness.

"John to the seven churches which are in Asia: Grace be unto you, and peace, from him which is, and which was, and which is to come; and from the seven Spirits which are before his throne;" (Rev. 1:4)

<15> Why are the seven churches in Asia? Because all the great Prophets of these churches have come from there. At the same time, the mystery of the seven energy centers of the body (chakras) were spread to the world from this region (Asia).

<16> The seven spirits are the seven truths that lead a man to become a son of God. They are the seven spheres of the universe. As the body of the human has seven chakras, also the universe has seven spheres which are called "Lokas."

"And from יהושע, who is the faithful witness, and the first begotten of the dead, and the prince of the kings of the earth. Unto him that loved us, and washed us from our sins in his own blood," (Rev. 1:5)

<17> יהושע was the faithful witness because he came and struggled to bring humanity to higher consciousness and Pure Consciousness. <18> He was the "first begotten of the dead," or he was the first that came from ignorance to complete enlightenment. So he was the first one that reached Pure Consciousness and he became The First Begotten Son. He was begotten from the dead, which means ignorance. "And the prince of the kings of the earth" means that he is the ruler of the earth. The real kingdom of the earth has been given to him.

<19> "He washed us from our sins in his own blood," or he washed the sins of others by sacrificing himself, because he took up the struggle through the crucifixion and through showing how we can wash our sins through sacrificing to establish the Kingdom Of Heaven. With the fire of sacrifice we can purify the world.

"And hath made us kings and priests unto God and his Father; to him be glory and dominion for ever and ever. Amen." (Rev. 1:6)

<20> Eventually it would be the sons of God who would rule His Kingdom as Kings and Priests (Brahmins).

"Behold, he cometh with clouds; and every eye shall see him, and they also which pierced him: and all kindreds of the earth shall wail because of him. Even so, Amen." (Rev. 1:7)

<21> "Cloud" means confusion. He comes whenever confusion comes to humanity. "When righteousness is weak and faints and unrighteousness exults in pride [confusion], then my Soul arises on earth" (Bhagavad-Gita

4:7). <22> "Every eye shall see him," means that those who have their eyes opened (third eyes) will see him. "They also which pierced him" means that those who pierced him will also see his glory.

<23> When it is said that he will come from the sky, the sky means the same as heaven, and heaven means Pure Consciousness.

<24> So he comes from Pure Consciousness, or he comes as an Avatar (god-man).

"I am Alpha and Omega, the beginning and the ending,..." (Rev. 1:8)

<25> "I was, I am, and I will be." I am everything.

Tablet Two

"I John, who also am your brother, and companion in tribulation, and in the kingdom and patience of יהושע, was in the isle that is called Patmos, for the word of God, and for the testimony of יהושע." (Rev. 1:9)

<1> John was in exile on an island by the name of Patmos where he had been sent because he was struggling to establish righteousness.

"I was in the Spirit on the Lord's day, and heard behind me a great voice, as of a trumpet," (Rev. 1:10)

<2> "I was in the Spirit" means "I was in a trance." <3> The "voice of a trumpet" is the sound of many waterfalls which can be heard in higher consciousness (the sound of silence).

"Saying, I am Alpha and Omega, the first and the last: and, What thou seest, write in a book, and send it unto the seven churches which are in Asia; unto Ephesus, and unto Smyrna, and unto Pergamos, and unto Thyatira and unto Sardis, and unto Philadelphia, and unto Laodicea." (Rev. 1:11)

<4> "I am Alpha and Omega, the first and the last" means, I have been, I am, and I will be. I will be forever. <5> This vision would be written down by John and sent to the symbolic seven churches, which are seven truths that would be revealed to humanity by Messengers (Messiahs) who would be born in Asia.

"And I turned to see the voice that spake with me. And being turned, I saw seven golden candlesticks;" (Rev. 1:12)

<6> The seven golden candlesticks are the seven chakras. When a human masters the chakras, they become a golden light for his guidance.

"And in the midst of the seven candlesticks one like unto the Son of man, clothed with a garment down to the foot, and girt about the paps with a golden girdle." (Rev. 1:13)

<7> John was not sure that the being he saw was the son of man, or Christ. He could have been anyone. That means that each person has the potential to reach Christhood (Pure Consciousness). It was John's own Soul.

"His head and his hairs were white like wool, as white as snow; and his eyes were as a flame of fire;" (Rev. 1:14)

<8> White is always related to purity or wisdom. His head and hair were "white like wool, as white as snow," so he was very wise. <9> And his wisdom could be seen from his countenance, "and his eyes were as a flame of fire." His eyes were sharp and opened to spiritual understanding, so they were like fire. He would burn to the depth of things and see right through them.

"And his feet like unto fine brass, as if they burned in a furnace; and his voice as the sound of many waters." (Rev. 1:15)

<10> "And his feet like unto fine brass": He had gone through such a great struggle that his feet had become like brass, as if they had been burned in a furnace. They were burned in the struggle to overcome the power of the tama guna.

REVELATION OF THE REVELATION

<11> "And his voice as the sound of many waters": As it was mentioned, the sound of many waters has been recognized as the sound "OM" by the great Masters. The sound "OM" is related to the sound of many waters which will be heard by the aspirant in a very high level of consciousness, or when he has reached the fifth level of progress or chakra.

"And he had in his right hand seven stars: and out of his mouth went a sharp twoedged sword: and his countenance was as the sun shineth in his strength." (Rev. 1:16)

<12> The seven stars are the seven truths that have been revealed to humanity through Christ. Also each star refers to the Prophet of each seal, which symbolically represents each religion or truth in **The Greatest Sign**.

<13> "A sharp twoedged sword" is the truth that comes out of the mouth of a Realized Soul (in Christ Consciousness) or from the mouth of Christ. This sword cuts through the superstitions and ignorance, dispels the darkness, **<14>** and brings light and truth to humanity.

"And when I saw him, I fell at his feet as dead. And he laid his right hand upon me, saying unto me, Fear not; I am the first and the last:" (Rev. 1:17)

<15> What John had really seen was his own spirit of truth which is within each of us. The person who begins spiritual practices becomes fearful of meditating because seeing the truth within is hard. That is why when he saw who he was, "one like unto the Son of man," (which is his own Soul), he was afraid and "fell at his feet as dead."

<16> But the Soul is kind and humble. That is why he (the Soul) "laid his right hand upon" John and comforted him by saying, "Fear not; I am the first and the last," which means, "I will be with you in your progress from the beginning to the end."

"I am he that liveth, and was dead; and, behold, I am alive for evermore, Amen; and have the keys of hell and death." (Rev. 1:18)

<17> "I am he that liveth, and was dead" means, "I have come from ignorance, which is the state of unawareness (deadness), to life, which is the state of Pure Consciousness."

<18> "I am alive for evermore," means, "I am in Pure Consciousness. I have overcome the power of the tama guna over my Soul. Therefore, I gained the eternal life."

<19> "And have the keys of hell and of death" means, "I have mastered the power of the tama guna, which brings man to hell and death (ignorance). I have the truth which can release you from this hell and death."

"Write the things which thou hast seen, and the things which are, and the things which shall be hereafter;" (Rev. 1:19)

<20> Therefore, The Revelation is a brief explanation of The Plan of the Lord God which would happen through history. **<21>** It is an explanation of what happened in the beginning of the formation of this new human (generation) after Noah, **<22>** and how the Lord God will bring the human to the realization that he should only utilize this body and all the gifts related to this body for reaching Pure Consciousness, by serving Him.

<23> This brief and most important book of the Bible (The Revelation) shows how following the false ego, being under the influence of the power of the tama guna, and being attracted to the power of Maya will lead the human to destruction and death (ignorance).

"The mystery of the seven stars which thou sawest in my right hand, and the seven golden candlesticks. The seven stars are the angels of the seven churches: and the seven candlesticks which thou sawest are the seven churches." (Rev. 1:20)

<24> So the seven stars are the seven Angels of the churches, which means the Prophets who brought the seven religions. **<25>** The seven candlesticks are the seven churches. Each church is the teaching and purpose of one of these religions that was brought by these Prophets. Only when the purpose of **all** of them is understood in **The Greatest Sign** will the true path be realized and His Mystery be revealed.

REVELATION OF THE REVELATION
Tablet Three

Chapter 2

<1> Chapters 2 and 3 are messages that are sent to the seven churches. Each church can be viewed as one psychic center, and at the same time can refer to one symbol in **The Greatest Sign** and its corresponding religion.

<2> Each message contains the meaning of one of those churches, the pitfalls in that stage and how they should be avoided, and eventually what is the reward of overcoming these pitfalls.

"Unto the angel of the church of Ephesus write; These things saith he that holdeth the seven stars in his right hand, who walketh in the midst of the seven golden candlesticks;" (Rev. 2:1)

<3> The church of Ephesus can be viewed as the first chakra. <4> At the same time, it refers to the first awakening of the consciousness (●) and latent spiritual forces in the human (☯).

<5> "Who walketh in the midst of the seven golden candlesticks" shows that it is Christ who revealed all the truth of the religions to humanity. <6> Another meaning is that each person is a consciousness in the middle of their chakras. Each person is a consciousness as Christ is; each person is an Arjuna, struggling to overcome the lower nature (Bhagavad-Gita).

"I know thy works, and thy labour, and thy patience, and how thou canst not bear them which are evil: and thou hast tried them which say they are apostles, and are not, and hast found them liars:" (Rev. 2:2)

<7> Who are these people who are in their first chakra, or those who for the first time open their eyes more about the realities of their environment and the goal of their lives? <8> These are the poor in spirit (Matthew 5:3) who find more and more evil things going on around them. <9> They try to find real guidance ("apostles") in order to be led to the truth. Instead they find that all those who consider themselves to be teachers and guides are liars, and these teachers and guides are as lost as themselves.

<10> That is why the person becomes discouraged because he sees all the plays people engage in to get by in life. Therefore, he or she sets out to search for the truth. <11> That was why the yogis left the regular life and isolated themselves to find the truth in mountains or jungles, because they felt the truth could not be found by following men.

<12> That is why the first symbol in our **Sign** (☯) is related to the teachings of the Far East (Mystical Paths), which work to awaken or raise the latent consciousness from the first chakra to higher chakras.

<13> However, as long as man is lost in the attraction of the external world and gets along with the play of society, he will not even search to find what the real truth is. <14> But when he finds that all the guidance he used to follow is lost, then he will start to search his own Soul in order to find the truth.

"And hast borne, and hast patience, and for my name's sake has laboured, and hast not fainted." (Rev. 2:3)

<15> "And has borne, and hast patience": Why have these people "borne?" They have endured because they became different. They stopped playing and became searchers of the truth. Society does not like those who are different. That is why they become outcasts and will endure hardships in their search for finding the truth. Their patience leads them to the truth.

<16> "For my name's sake": What is his name? His name is "The Truth" (The Sacred Name, or The Holy Name). So they will bear persecution for the sake of the truth.

<17> However, those who persist and do not faint will find it.

"Nevertheless I have somewhat against thee, because thou hast left thy first love." (Rev. 2:4)

REVELATION OF THE REVELATION *Tablet 4*

<18> What was these people's first love? Was it not the external world? Was it not the society that they were first in love with? Did they not try to find the reality and truth in it? So these people (like yogis) who became escapists are those who leave their first love. God is against this.

"Remember therefore from whence thou art fallen, and repent, and do the first works; or else I will come unto thee quickly, and will remove thy candlestick out of his place, except thou repent." (Rev. 2:5)

<19> The sentence, "Remember therefore from whence thou art fallen," completely shows what the "first love" means. The first love is where the person has first fallen from: The society. He or she has fallen from the society and became discouraged about its teachings and plays.

<20> "Do the first works": What are the first works? The first works are to bring others to this realization that the truth is in spirit (but not become escapist) so also try to establish the Kingdom Of Heaven On Earth. Otherwise, "I will come unto thee quickly, and will remove thy candlestick out of his place." You will not reach anywhere, you will only become an escapist by leaving your first love, and you will further lose realization of the spiritual life. That is exactly what happened to the Far East. "Candlestick" means the light of guidance.

"But this thou hast, that thou hatest the deeds of the Nicolaitanes, which I also hate." (Rev. 2:6)

<21> What are the "deeds of the Nicolaitanes?" They are the evil things and false guides in society. People who are poor in spirit are escapists and the Lord God does not want them to be that way (poor in spirit). But He likes them because they hate evil things and the deeds of the false guides ("Nicolaitanes"). (Refer to Rev. 2:2.)

"He that hath an ear, let him hear what the Spirit saith unto the churches; To him that overcometh will I give to eat of the tree of life, which is in the midst of the paradise of God." (Rev. 2:7)

<22> "He that hath an ear, let him hear what the Spirit saith unto the churches," means that those who have their eyes (third eyes) opened will understand when the truth behind these revelations is explained, and what the message of the Spirit is to each church.

<23> "To him that overcometh will I give to eat of the tree of life" means that whoever understands that life is a struggle, and that a person should stay in society and perfect himself in order to set an example for others, will be helped to reach Pure Consciousness, which is life eternal. <24> The tree of life is the pattern in which a person progresses in spiritual understanding. It can be referred to as the raising of the kundalini through the chakras.

<25> These people are the ones who were mourning and will be comforted (Matthew 5:4). They will eat of the tree of life (Rev. 2:7) and are the conquerors of the Souls ("conquering and to conquer," Rev. 6:2).

Tablet Four

"And unto the angel of the church in Smyrna write; These things saith the first and the last, which was dead, and is alive;" (Rev. 2:8)

<1> What is the church in Smyrna? It is the second symbol in **The Greatest Sign** (✡), the star of David (the seal of Solomon). <2> It also refers to the second chakra.

"I know thy works, and tribulation, and poverty, (but thou art rich) and I know the blasphemy of them which say they are Jews, and are not, but are the synagogue of Satan." (Rev. 2:9)

<3> "I know thy works, and tribulation, and poverty" means that those who had overcome escapism will start to fight with evil

doers and liars. They will go through tribulation, become outcasts, and be struck with poverty.

<4> "But thou art rich" means, but you are rich in spirit and life, because you have an ideology to fight for and a goal for which to strive. <5> However, those who lie, do evil, and are lost in Maya are rich in material things but are poor in spiritual wealth.

<6> "And I know the blasphemy of them which say they are Jews, and are not, but are the synagogue of Satan": <7> Jews were supposed to be the Children of Israel (those who struggle with God, or the Elected Ones) <8> and they should have shown humanity that the KOHOE (✡) is necessary for human progress. They should have tried to establish it. <9> Hence those who do call themselves the Elected Ones but do not strive to bring this ideal are "the synagogue of Satan."

"Fear none of those things which thou shalt suffer: behold, the devil shall cast some of you into prison, that ye may be tried; and ye shall have tribulation ten days: be thou faithful unto death, and I will give thee a crown of life." (Rev. 2:10)

<10> "Fear none of those things" refers to suffering and being persecuted. Be faithful and do not fear death, because "I will give thee a crown of life." <11> There is no such thing as death for a Realized Soul. <12> He dies in knowledge and will gain eternal life. <13> Also it is true that in this state a person is in his second chakra but if he is so sincere as to be ready to sacrifice all for truth and his ideology, then he has overcome the attraction of this external world. <14> If a person who reaches this point, where nothing can stop him from fighting for truth, is killed, then he is martyred and becomes a martyr. He will reach Pure Consciousness because he is worthy of it, "I will give thee a crown of life." <15> This is also promised in both the Bhagavad-Gita: "A war to establish justice, such as this one, opens the doors of heaven ... . Happy is he who fights such a war. Not to fight such a righteous battle is to disregard your sacred duty and honour, and is sin [transgression of the Law (Darma)], Arjuna" (B.G. 2:32); <16> and the Koran: "Do not think of those who are slain in the way of God [righteous way] as dead, No, they are with their Lord..." (Family of Imran, Ali 'Imran, 169).

<17> This means that he who has the thoughts of God in his mind even at the moment of death ("be thou faithful unto death"), is he who Loves God with all his might. He will reach Pure Consciousness.

"He that hath an ear, let him hear what the Spirit saith unto the churches; He that overcometh shall not be hurt of the second death." (Rev. 2:11)

<18> Those who overcome their fears and attachments to this external life will gain everlasting life. They will reach Pure Consciousness. These are the people who are meek, who will inherit the earth (Matthew 5:5), and will gain eternal life (Rev. 2:11). The power will be given to them to take peace from the earth (Rev. 6:4).

Tablet Five

"And to the angel of the church in Pergamos write; These things saith he which hath the sharp sword with two edges;" (Rev. 2:12)

<1> What is the church in Pergamos? It is the third symbol (✝) in **The Greatest Sign**. It is the most direct teaching of Christ. <2> Who is the Angel? He is Esa.

<3> The sharp sword is the truth. Whoever is in Pure Consciousness will say the truth, which is sharp as a sword. <4> The sharp sword is used only in the verses about the third sign, because who has the sharpest teaching among the Prophets? It is Esa. The four gospels are the most direct and sharpest teachings of the truth. They cut through the faults (if you understand them!)

<5> This church can also refer to the third chakra.

"I know thy works, and where thou dwellest, even where Satan's seat is: and thou holdest fast my name, and hast not denied my faith, even in those days wherein Antipas was my faithful martyr, who was slain among you, where Satan dwelleth." (Rev. 2:13)

<6> "Where Satan's seat is": <7> The first three chakras are where a human is bound to the attraction of the external world and still greatly under the influence of the tama guna (satan). Therefore whoever overcomes these three psychic energy centers knows "where Satan's seat is."

<8> That is why Esa taught that you have to be born again. To be born again means to go from these first three chakras (lower nature), especially the third, to the higher chakras (higher self). <9> Or in other words, to crucify the false ego (lower self) so to be born again (resurrect) into the higher self and be glorified. That is why until you are born again, you are not saved. <10> In fact the very symbolic meaning of the crucifixion of Esa (symbol of the death of the false ego) and his resurrection is to show that you have to die first (your false ego) before you can be born again (resurrect to the higher self). <11> "And it is in dying that we are born to Eternal Life" (St. Francis of Assisi).

<12> "Anti-pas" is the true consciousness against the attraction of the external world which will be slain by these three chakras. By overcoming these first three chakras you enter "the heart of the Yogi" which is the place of unconditional Love (fourth chakra).

<13> Christianity is the symbol of this overcoming of these first three chakras. It is a symbol of individual achievement in detaching completely from Maya. <14> However, it does not mean you should be a Christian to reach this level. He who overcomes the first three chakras overcomes evil (attraction of Maya).

"But I have a few things against thee, because thou hast there them that hold the doctrine of Balaam, who taught Balac to cast a stumblingblock before the children of Israel, to eat things sacrificed unto idols, and to commit fornication." (Rev. 2:14)

<15> However, still in this stage between overcoming the power of the first three chakras and entering the fourth chakra, man can be misled by false prophets and teachers in spiritual realities. <16> He can fall from being a child of Israel (one who struggles with God) and be as lost as others.

"So hast thou also them that hold the doctrine of the Nicolaitanes, which thing I hate." (Rev. 2:15)

<17> As we saw, the deeds of the Nicolaitanes were evil doings and false guidance. In the third chakra, the desire for power, prestige, and possession is dominating. Therefore, the pitfall is that a person might follow false guides or become one of them himself, and do evil things. <18> That is what God does not like. He dislikes people who do evil things or become false guides for their own desires to gain power, position, or prestige, so He (His Holy Ghost) leaves them.

<19> Also, verses 14 and 15 refer to the influence of the Roman doctrines (pagan religions of Rome) and other false teachers who tried from the very beginning to influence Christ's teachings (Acts 8:1-24), <20> and eventually did.

"Repent; or else I will come unto thee quickly, and will fight against them with the sword of my mouth." (Rev. 2:16)

<21> How did Christ fight with the Pharisees and scribes? He fought with his teaching, which was sharp and true like the sword. He came quickly and fought for truth ("sword of my mouth") against those who were following false teachings (Balaam doctrine) and performing false doings (Nicolaitanes).

"He that hath an ear, let him hear what the Spirit saith unto the churches; To him that overcometh will I give to eat of the hidden manna, and will give him a white stone, and in the stone a new name written, which no man knoweth saving he that receiveth it." (Rev. 2:17)

<22> He who overcomes the first three chakras will enter the fourth chakra, which is the center of unconditional Love (pure raja). <23> The experience of bliss in this chakra is so great and the nectar felt in the throat area is so unexplainable that the joy is not comparable with anything in this external world.

<24> "And will give him a white stone, and in the stone a new name written." The white stone is the stone of purity (purified consciousness) and knowledge of God – not intellectual knowledge, but intuitive. <25> The experience of eating of the hidden manna (nectar flows through the throat to the heart chakra) will bring that relationship with God where there is no mistake, you know that He exists. <26> The "new name" is The Word, which is a vibration within you.

<27> These are the people who will hunger and thirst after righteousness and will be filled (Matthew 5:6). They will eat of the hidden manna, and they will be given a white stone and new name (Rev. 2:17). They will bring justice on earth, as symbolized by the balances in Rev. 6:5.

Tablet Six

"And unto the angel of the church in Thyatira write; These things saith the Son of God, who hath his eyes like unto a flame of fire, and his feet are like fine brass;" (Rev. 2:18)

<1> What is the church in Thyatira? It is the fourth symbol in **The Greatest Sign** (☪), the symbol of Islam (Is Lamb). <2> Islam comes from the word "tasleim," which means to be surrendered to the Will of God. <3> Being surrendered to God does not mean to be idle and let Him do everything for us, but to do our best and then surrender the result to Him with no attachment, "Work not for a reward, but cease not to do thy work" (Bhagavad-Gita 2:47).

<4> This church is also the end of the fourth chakra and the entering into the fifth chakra where the sound OM (ॐ) can be heard.

"I know thy works, and charity, and service, and faith, and thy patience, and thy works; and the last to be more than the first." (Rev. 2:19)

<5> By residing in the fourth chakra and trying to reach the fifth chakra, the quality of giving charity, doing service, and having great faith and patience will become manifest. You become merciful (Matthew 5:7). <6> Islam is the symbol of all these things. In fact definite rules and regulations are set up to awaken the people to do these things. Another quality in Islam was bringing the right of all being spiritually equal, "the last to be more than the first."

"Notwithstanding I have a few things against thee, because thou sufferest that woman Jezebel, which calleth herself a prophetess, to teach and to seduce my servants to commit fornication, and to eat things sacrificed unto idols." (Rev. 2:20)

<7> Who is this Jezebel? She is the false understanding of the teachings and realities that were revealed to the person who has come to the fourth chakra and is trying to go to the fifth chakra. These false understandings (which occur because of narrowness and not being a universalist) will lead these people to become a hindrance in the way of The Plan of the Lord.

<8> Islam is the most misunderstood religion. The Moslems have forgotten the depth of the teaching of Muhammad. Like many other religions, they follow concepts that have been imposed on them. <9> They have forgotten to be surrendered to His Will, so they oppose any Prophet after Prophet Muhammad. They do not accept the three truths after the sign of Islam in **The Greatest Sign**, nor do they add the knowledge of the three previous signs to their own.

"And I gave her space to repent of her fornication; and she repented not." (Rev. 2:21)

"Behold, I will cast her into a bed, and them that commit adultery with her into great tribulation, except they repent of their deeds." (Rev. 2:22)

<10> Islam means "to be surrendered." The surrendered person is the one who understands that the Lord God is able to do whatever He wants to do, and all the great events in the world have been directed by His Permission. <11> However, Moslems, like Jews, did not believe in any other great personality that came to teach them, and they opposed Prophets after Muhammad. They, like the Jews, killed the next Messiah, Bab, and did not believe in him.

<12> The following of this false belief is like adultery with Jezebel, who calls herself a prophetess, and this will create confusion and cause men tribulation and misery.

"And I will kill her children with death; and all the churches shall know that I am he which searcheth the reins and hearts: and I will give unto every one of you according to your works." (Rev. 2:23)

<13> In the phrase, "And I will kill her children with death," death means ignorance. Therefore, those who follow the false understandings of these teachings and realizations in this state (which is narrowness and not having a universal view), will become ignorant and their minds will become more narrow, further to death (ignorance).

"But unto you I say, and unto the rest in Thyatira, as many as have not this doctrine, and which have not known the depths of Satan, as they speak; I will put upon you none other burden." (Rev. 2:24)

<14> "As many as have not this doctrine" means, "As many as are surrendered to my will and are submissive to me, and so will progress further in the spiritual path, or are ignorant of the depth of Satan as they speak [they think they know], to these people will I be merciful."

<15> **The point is that the doctrine you follow in your life is the most important part of your spiritual progress. Doctrine means your ideology and goal.**

<16> Therefore, if you are ignorant of the depths of Satan (you are following false teachings or ignorance), "I will put upon you none other burden."

"But that which ye have already hold fast till I come." (Rev. 2:25)

<17> Those who stay in this state from ignorance will not be punished for their ignorance, but only for their bad deeds (samskaras, or sins).

"And he that overcometh, and keepeth my works unto the end, to him will I give power over the nations:" (Rev. 2:26)

<18> Those who overcome these false understandings of the teachings of the fourth symbol in **The Greatest Sign** will become surrendered ones to the Will of God. They will become people with expanded minds, and eventually will become Universalists. They will study the teachings of the three truths before (in **The Greatest Sign**) and also will accept the next three truths after this fourth one, "and keepeth my works unto the end." <19> Only such people can assume the leadership of the nations, because they have overcome the narrowness of the mind. The power over the nations was given to the Moslems when, in a short period of time, they conquered so many strong nations, such as Persia and Rome. <20> This was possible only because knowingly or unknowingly they were following the **Eternal Divine Path** and the true teachings of Prophet Muhammad at that time. <21> Also, it was His Will.

"And he shall rule them with a rod of iron; as the vessels of a potter shall they be broken to shivers: even as I received of my Father." (Rev. 2:27)

<22> "He shall rule them with a rod of iron" because his authority will not come from man but from the Father. <23> "Even as I received of my Father" means, in the same way, **as my authority which is from the Father.**

"And I will give him the morning star." (Rev. 2:28)

<24> The star of the morning is the sun. The "morning star" (sun) is the symbol of the highest spiritual realization, which is to be completely surrendered and submissive to The Plan of God.

<25> Surrendering does not mean escapism, but it means to use all the beautiful gifts of life, such as intellect, spiritual powers, our bodies, tongues, eyes, etc., toward bringing about The Plan of the Lord. This Plan was the main purpose for creation of the universe, which is to create the proper environment in order for all to reach Pure Consciousness. <26> So we try our best to use all of our abilities to do His Will and then surrender the results of our actions to Him. Or, we let Him do the actions through us.

<27> The people in the fourth chakra are those who are merciful and shall obtain mercy (Matthew 5:7). The Spirit says, "I will put upon [them] none other burden" (Rev. 2:24) and power over the nations will be given to them (Rev. 2:26), and they will receive the morning star – true knowledge of God (Rev. 2:28). <28> Also, power is given to them over the fourth part of the earth (Rev. 6:8).

"He that hath an ear, let him hear what the Spirit saith unto the churches." (Rev. 2:29)

<29> Those whose hearts are open will know these revelations to be true.

Tablet Seven

Chapter 3

"And unto the angel of the church in Sardis write; These things saith he that hath the seven Spirits of God, and the seven stars; I know thy works, that thou hast a name that thou livest, and art dead." (Rev. 3:1)

<1> The fifth church is represented by the symbol of the nine-armed star of the Baha'i Faith (✸). <2> The name Baha'u'llah means "The Beauty of God." "That thou hast a name" refers to this name which the followers of the Baha'i Faith should bring to the world. They should glorify the Lord. "That thou livest, and art dead": But this name is dead. They are not glorifying the Lord – Formless, Invisible, Nameless, and Eternal (FINE). They are glorifying their Prophet (Baha'u'llah).

<3> Also the fifth church is related to the fifth psychic center (chakra).

"Be watchful, and strengthen the things which remain, that are ready to die: for I have not found thy works perfect before God." (Rev. 3:2)

<4> "I have not found thy works perfect before God": The true founder of the Baha'i Faith was Bab (one of the titles Bab gave to himself was Baha'u'llah), who was martyred. His teachings were not perfect. <5> That is the reason why later on Baha'u'llah (one of Bab's disciples) tried to perfect his teachings and he changed many things. (We use the name "Baha'i Faith" for this church because it is better known by this name.)

<6> Also because the followers of Bab went through much persecution, they lost much of their strength. To make the movement survive, many things were changed at the time of Baha'u'llah so that his followers might be able to survive in their hostile environment. <7> Also, because of Bab's disciple, Baha'u'llah, these teachings spread west so that we might become familiar with them. Otherwise they would have remained a small group and never spread abroad as they did. <8> This all happened by His Will as it was predicted in these verses and shown in history.

<9> What remained and the main purpose of the coming of the Baha'i Faith is its universal view which should be accepted and preserved, "Be watchful, and strengthen the things which remain, that are ready to die."

"Remember therefore how thou hast received and heard, and hold fast, and repent. If therefore thou shalt not watch, I will come on thee as a thief, and thou shalt not know what hour I will come upon thee." (Rev. 3:3)

<10> The Baha'i Faith was revealed in Persia. Islam was the dominating religion. However, many people embraced the faith and were slain in doing so. But later on, the followers of the Baha'i Faith lost their strength and changed many things in their ideology in order to be able to live peacefully in that environment. <11> That is the meaning of "Remember therefore how thou hast received and heard, and hold fast, and repent."

<12> Also, in the individual situation in this level of spiritual progress, a person might again become an escapist. That is because he can now see God (Matthew 5:8) and His Perfect Universe, and so he might feel His Flow should not be interfered with. But with a little help, things can be accelerated. <13> These people forget how they went through a great struggle to reach here. That is why it says, "Remember therefore how thou hast received and heard." So become active and help others also.

"Thou hast a few names even in Sardis which have not defiled their garments; and they shall walk with me in white: for they are worthy." (Rev. 3:4)

<14> However, in the beginning of the movement a very few Great Souls supported the faith and were slain in doing so, who were worthy to walk with the Spirit (Christ) in white (Pure Consciousness, light, knowledge). <15> Those who overcome becoming escapists are worthy to reach Pure Consciousness (卍).

"He that overcometh, the same shall be clothed in white raiment; and I will not blot out his name out of the book of life, but I will confess his name before my Father, and before his angels." (Rev. 3:5)

<16> He who overcomes the pitfalls of this stage will overcome all attractions of Maya. He will overcome the material world (the five elements, the five koshas – sheaths). He will be spiritually purified. The white raiment will be given to him as mentioned also in Rev. 6:11, "And white raiment will be given unto every one of them." "Them" refers to "the souls of them that were slain for The Word of God, and for the testimony which they held," who are the people that were slain in the Baha'i Faith and those who reach the fifth chakra but will not become escapists. They reach the sixth stage (chakra).

<17> So, these are the ones who are blessed because they are pure in heart and will see God (Matthew 5:8). They will be given white garments, their names will be in the book of life, and the Spirit (Christ) will confess their names before the Father and His Angels (Rev. 3:5). They have been slain for The Word of God and for the testimony (of truth) which they held (Rev. 6:9).

"He that hath an ear, let him hear what the Spirit saith unto the churches." (Rev. 3:6)

<18> Those who have their eyes open know it is to be true.

Tablet Eight

"And to the angel of the church in Philadelphia write; These things saith he that is holy, he that is true, he that hath the key of David, he that openeth, and no man shutteth, and shutteth, and no man openeth;" (Rev. 3:7)

<1> The sixth church is the sign (✡) which was revealed to a great spiritual teacher in India. His affectionate name is Baba, and he is the one "that is true [and] hath the key of David." <2> The key of David is the sign (✡) which is the same as used in Baba's sign (✡), the symbol for the Kingdom Of Heaven within.

"I know thy works: behold, I have set before thee an open door, and no man can shut it: for thou hast a little strength, and hast kept my word, and hast not denied my name." (Rev. 3:8)

<3> "I have set before thee an open door,

and no man can shut it." That is true about the teachings of Baba. The truth he revealed to humanity is so great that "no man can [ever] shut it." <4> The concept of Paravipra has come from his teachings. But with knowing **The Greatest Sign**, we can understand their characteristics in a more crystallized way.

<5> "For thou hast a little strength": That is true about the path he revealed. They have very little strength in comparison to other religions. However, they have kept The Word of God (truth) and have not denied His Name (truth). <6> Also the door refers to the door of entering into Heaven, because after the sixth chakra is the seventh and last chakra, which is heaven (Pure Consciousness). Whoever is in the sixth chakra has this door opened for him.

"Behold, I will make them of the synagogue of Satan, which say they are Jews, and are not, but do lie; behold, I will make them to come and worship before thy feet, and to know that I have loved thee." (Rev. 3:9)

<7> "Which say they are Jews, and are not": As it can be seen from the sign of the Jews (✡) and also from their history, they were supposed to stay as Elected Ones (Hebrews) to keep their covenant with Him ("to keep His Words") and to establish the Kingdom Of Heaven On Earth (✡). But they did not. <8> Of course this should have happened because it was planned this way.

<9> Also the sign of the Jews (✡) is very similar to the sign of the sixth seal (✡), and the people in the sixth seal are those who have kept His Words, have not denied His Name (truth), and are trying to establish the Kingdom Of Heaven within and without (✡). <10> That is why they are the true Elected Ones (Hebrews). So those who call themselves Jews but are not doing His Will are not Elected Ones (Hebrews), "…are not."

<11> Those who falsely think they are the Elected Ones will be humbled to "worship before thy feet, and to know that I have loved thee." God loves the Elected Ones.

"Because thou hast kept the word of my patience, I also will keep thee from the hour of temptation, which shall come upon all the world, and to try them that dwell upon the earth." (Rev. 3:10)

<12> "I also will keep thee from the hour of temptation, which shall come upon all the world, to try them that dwell upon the earth." Therefore, this sixth church will come in the hour that the temptations will come upon the earth. <13> It is the same as this time that we are living in now. These teachings and the sign related to it were revealed at the beginning of this time (1945). The people in this path are trying to overcome these temptations with the many purifying techniques that are given by their spiritual teacher.

<14> Also, the sixth seal in Revelation 6:12 refers to the beginning of the tribulation and confusion in the world. The sixth seal which is in **The Greatest Sign** was also revealed at the time of the start of the tribulation and temptation in the world (1945).

"Behold, I come quickly: hold that fast which thou hast, that no man take thy crown." (Rev. 3:11)

<15> This verse means that the whole truth will be revealed very soon after the revelation of this sixth truth. Those who have reached the sixth stage should be steady. Behold the teachings and those things that are taught to you, because the last stages of The Plan of the Lord God are approaching. <16> If you do not hold fast in what you have, then you will lose in entering the next stage which is the crown of the stages (seventh level or chakra) and contains the whole truth.

Tablet Nine

"Him that overcometh will I make a pillar in the temple of my God, and he shall go no more out: and I will write upon him the name of my God, and the name of the city of my

God, which is New Jerusalem, which cometh down out of heaven from my God: and I will write upon him my new name." (Rev. 3:12)

<1> So, he who overcomes the hour of temptations and has patience in the time of tribulation will reach Pure Consciousness. He will become a son of God. <2> "He shall go no more out" means back to ignorance. When you once reach Pure Consciousness, you will never go back to ignorance. <3> You have finished your journey from ignorance to enlightenment (Pure Consciousness). <4> However, you come back as an Avatar (great Paravipra) to help others to reach Pure Consciousness.

<5> These are the ones who are the peacemakers and will be called the children of God (Matthew 5:9). <6> They are those who will have a pillar in the temple of God (Rev. 3:12) and will be sealed with the seal of the living God (Rev. 7:3).

"He that hath an ear, let him hear what the Spirit saith unto the churches." (Rev. 3:13)

<7> He who has his eye and heart opened knows that it is to be true.

Tablet Ten

"And unto the angel of the church of the Laodiceans write; These things saith the Amen, the faithful and true witness, the beginning of the creation of God;" (Rev. 3:14)

<1> These are the ones who try to reach Pure Consciousness through meditation, yoga exercises, or any other means that are taught in the Mystical Paths as the only way to raise the consciousness to the seventh chakra, without caring too much for other people. <2> They do not try to direct the spiritual energies they have gained toward establishing the Kingdom Of Heaven, but instead try to reach higher consciousness individually and selfishly. They try to reach Pure Consciousness by being escapists.

"I know thy works, that thou art neither cold nor hot: I would thou wert cold or hot." (Rev. 3:15)

<3> "Thou art neither cold nor hot": Why are they no longer cold or hot? They are this way because they have overcome any effects of the external world on their bodies and Souls, and are in the higher chakras.

<4> "I would thou wert cold or hot": However, God wishes them to be "cold or hot," because the purpose of this universe is to bring all to Pure Consciousness. Therefore, those who have reached this stage by merely using techniques and exercises should come back to this world of suffering (cold and hot, up and down) and help others come to the path of enlightenment.

"So then because thou art lukewarm, and neither cold nor hot, I will spue thee out of my mouth." (Rev. 3:16)

<5> Even when a person reaches Pure Consciousness ("neither cold nor hot") this way, he would not stay there for a long period of time but would gain his "I" back as an entity separate from God because "I will spue thee out of my mouth." <6> He would not be able to stay there forever, until he proves himself worthy by his actions in helping the whole universe to higher consciousness.

<7> Indeed, this part has the identical message as the third chapter of <u>Genesis</u>, when God threw Adam and Eve out of heaven and set up the flaming sword to keep them from the tree of life (Pure Consciousness).

<8> As it was explained, the reason for that was because Adam wanted to enter heaven and eat of the tree of knowledge and life when he was not yet ready for it. He was still in his lower nature (Eve). <9> He also had the same desire to go to heaven by force and through mastering the powers in the universe ("tree of knowledge of good and evil"). <10> Just as he was sent out of the garden, also those who attempt the same path will be thrown "out of his mouth" or a flaming sword will keep them from entering into heaven (the tree of life).

<11> Therefore, those who are indifferent ("lukewarm") to His Plan will be "spued out" of His Mouth.

"Because thou sayest, I am rich, and increased with goods, and have need of nothing; and knowest not that thou art wretched, and miserable, and poor, and blind, and naked:" (Rev. 3:17)

<12> Because they are in a very high consciousness, these people feel that they are superior to others, are rich in spirit, and need nothing. They become escapists, and they teach that this world is nothing but illusion. <13> God does not like it because they lose the real purpose of being in that high spiritual state. Instead of utilizing their abilities and high level of consciousness toward bringing about the Kingdom Of Heaven On Earth and helping others to become Pure Consciousness, they lead others to escapism. Therefore, God makes them miserable, poor, blind, and naked.

<14> Whoever thinks he is independent from God will fall into Maya.

"I counsel thee to buy of me gold tried in the fire, that thou mayest be rich; and white raiment, that thou mayest be clothed, and that the shame of thy nakedness do not appear; and anoint thine eyes with eyesalve, that thou mayest see." (Rev. 3:18)

<15> This verse means, "I helped you to reach this stage of consciousness which is so beautiful in order that you might be rich (in spirit) and pure (white raiment). Then you might help the world with these qualities and set an example for others of how to be. They were not given to you to become an escapist."

"As many as I love, I rebuke and chasten: be zealous therefore, and repent." (Rev. 3:19)

<16> This means, "Those I Love, I will rebuke and chasten until they become zealous. Be zealous therefore, and do the first work. Be a Paravipra." As you become closer to Pure Consciousness, you should pass more severe tests in order to be trustworthy. <17> God does not Love escapists, those who teach that this world is illusion, and do not engage in social activities.

"Behold, I stand at the door, and knock: if any man hear my voice, and open the door, I will come in to him, and will sup with him, and he with me." (Rev. 3:20)

<18> "I (Spirit) am in all of you. I am always within you. If any person hears what I say and opens his heart to Me, I will come in and he will know the truth."

"To him that overcometh will I grant to sit with me in my throne, even as I also overcame, and am set down with my Father in his throne." (Rev. 3:21)

<19> The pitfall in this stage is to forget about other people's sufferings and be content with the peace and joy of being in higher consciousness. <20> Therefore, whoever overcomes this last pitfall of the spiritual progress after he reaches higher consciousness will inherit the Kingdom Of Heaven On Earth, and will sit on the throne with the Lord God. He will become an Avatar.

<21> These are the people who will be persecuted for righteousness (Matthew 5:10). <22> They are dynamic spiritualists, not escapists. They will be as Angels to the earth and will guide humans to the understanding that the only way to salvation is to listen to the Prophets and follow the Laws of God.

Tablet Eleven

Some points should be noticed:

<1> The first point is that the first four churches are presented in one chapter. <2> Also the first four seals are related to four horsemen (chapter 6) and the first four Angels with trumpets (chapter 8) are presented in one chapter together. <3> Therefore, these first four churches and those first four horsemen and Angels have a relationship that causes

them to differ from the next three.

<4> Their relationship is that the spiritual understanding and coming to the state of direct contact with the depths of its reality finish with the first four chakras or seals. <5> However, a further development in understanding the realities of this universe is necessary, which can be gained through progressing and overcoming the next three chakras. That is why with Islam the real understanding of the spiritual world finishes. <6> The first seal is related to the Far East Philosophies and awakening the spiritual forces (☯), and the second is to direct these awakened forces toward the establishment of the Kingdom Of Heaven On Earth (KOHOE) (✡). The third is to sacrifice all and overcome the false ego for the KOHOE (✝). The fourth seal is to surrender the result to the Lord and be completely detached from the fruit, or to become submitted to Him (☪). <7> With this, the highest spiritual realization is achieved. That is why Prophet Muhammad can be viewed as the last Prophet in this regard, because with him the spiritual understanding ended. <8> However, to become perfect and free from bondage and narrowness of mind, it is necessary to become a universalist (✹) and dynamic spiritualist or Paravipra (✡), so we might then reach Pure Consciousness (卐). These last three seals are the three steps to freedom from bondage.

<9> The second point is that each understanding of one state or chakra or religion brings the human further on the path of entering the next stage (chakra). On the way to perfect the next stage there are pitfalls which should be overcome. <10> For example, when Christ (Spirit, truth) says that the woman Jezebel is a pitfall on your way, this is when a person is in the fourth chakra and trying to overcome the pitfalls in this level in order to rise to the next chakra. When a person masters that stage, the reward of this success will be given to him in the next chakra.

<11> In other words, when a person overcomes the pitfalls in the first chakra (stage), he will be given to eat of the tree of life. So he will leave the first stage and go to the next stage, which is the second one, and so on. <12> That is why in overcoming the pitfalls of the third stage the reward is to eat of the hidden manna which is in the fourth chakra. Or in overcoming the pitfalls of the sixth stage, the reward is to enter a pillar in the temple of God, which is the seventh stage.

Tablet Twelve

Chapter 4

"After this I looked, and, behold, a door was opened in heaven: and the first voice which I heard was as it were of a trumpet talking with me; which said, Come up hither, and I will shew thee things which must be hereafter." (Rev. 4:1)

<1> "After this" means, after a person goes through all the stages described in chapters 2 and 3.

<2> "A door was opened" means, the door of all-pervasive understanding and realization will be opened to the person who has reached this stage.

<3> "And the first voice which I heard" is the voice of truth that comes from The Holy Ghost, which guides a human to full realization.

"And immediately I was in the spirit; and, behold, a throne was set in heaven, and one sat on the throne." (Rev. 4:2)

<4> Being "in the spirit" means to go into a trance. <5> He went into a trance and his Soul was taken to the Akashic Records. He started to see the unseen and had a vision that there was a throne and "one sat on the throne."

"And he that sat was to look upon like a jasper and a sardine stone: and there was a rainbow round about the throne, in sight like unto an emerald." (Rev. 4:3)

<6> The One who was sitting on it was just like a stone. He was completely motionless, and "there was a rainbow round about the

throne, in sight like unto an emerald." <7> He was radiating all levels of vibration and would understand all levels of consciousness.

<8> This symbolizes that the One who was sitting on the throne was motionless and completely like a stone. <9> As it was said in Genesis, God rested after the sixth day so He became motionless in the whole universe. He is not active in the universe Himself. He is just an observer, a witness entity, omnipresent, and omniscient. He does not have to move. <10> But He does, and He rules and manages the whole universe by being seated on His throne motionless. <11> The One who is sitting on the throne, which means the Creator, is symbolized as a jasper and a sardine stone. And it means that He does not participate in the activity that is happening in the universe. <12> As you can see in all of The Revelation, never does He do anything Himself. Always the others (Angels) will carry on the duties and do everything that He wishes to be done. He just wishes and it will be done, and He wishes things that are according to the goal of the creation – to be(come) Divine.

"And round about the throne were four and twenty seats: and upon the seats I saw four and twenty elders sitting, clothed in white raiment; and they had on their heads crowns of gold." (Rev. 4:4)

<13> These twenty-four are the twenty-four attributes or things that the manifested universe is made with and works by. <14> These things are the five senses: Smell, taste, sight, touch, hearing; the five organs of action: Excretion, generation, speech, feet, and hands; the five objects of the senses (things that make the senses comprehend the external world): The smell of the things, the taste of the things, the sight of the things, the touch of the things, and the sound of the things; <15> the elements that created the universe: Ethereal factor, aerial factor, luminous factor, liquid factor, and solid factor; the three gunas: Tama guna, raja guna, and satva guna; and the illusive consciousness (separated "I" feeling). <16> These twenty-four attributes are symbolized by the twenty-four Elders which were sitting, "clothed in white raiment, and they had on their heads crowns of gold." <17> They are the princes or the greatest things in the universe that make it comprehensible to man. Humans can use these twenty-four attributes to progress to higher consciousness.

"And out of the throne proceeded lightnings and thunderings and voices: and there were seven lamps of fire burning before the throne, which are the seven Spirits of God." (Rev. 4:5)

<18> From the throne the things that God wishes, wills, and wants to be done will proceed as "lightnings and thunderings and voices." The universe will comprehend what should be done according to these signs. <19> "There were seven lamps of fire burning before the throne, which are the seven Spirits of God ['Let there be light:' (Genesis 1:3)]." The seven spirits of God are the seven truths (light) which God uses to guide lost consciousnesses to reach Pure Consciousness. They are like lights in front of Him, and through these seven spirits, God guides His universe toward Pure Consciousness. They are the seven levels of consciousness, seven lokas (worlds).

"And before the throne there was a sea of glass like unto crystal: and in the midst of the throne, and round about the throne, were four beasts full of eyes before and behind." (Rev. 4:6)

<20> Again the sea of glass which is in front of God symbolizes being emotionless, without any faulty emotions. He is emotionless and motionless, and He is completely true and Sat. He does not judge or guide the universe by emotion (unpurified chakras), but by complete truth. Emotionlessly He guides His universe toward its goal. This crystal is where the Akashic Records are stored (ether).

<21> The four beasts full of eyes are the four things created by God after the release of the creative forces. These four beasts are The Word, time, space, and the atom (avidya, ignorance). <22> Because of the desire of God, the creative forces in the universe (The Word)

were released – "In the beginning was the Word, and the Word was with God, and the Word was God" (John 1:1). After The Word was comprehended, time was understood. So time and The Word are both together. Without The Word (beginning) there is no time. And through The Word, space has been comprehended, and also through The Word (three gunas in the operative state), the manifested world (the atom) has been created. <23> So it is The Word which is the beginning of time, and it is the power of The Word that enables space to be comprehended. Through The Word, the atom is created. The Word is a part and parcel of the consciousness. **The Word is inherent in the consciousness.** The three gunas have been used by the consciousness to create all things.

<24> So The Word, time, space, and atom are the four beasts. And they were "full of eyes before and behind." Through these four beasts, God sees everything, the external world and the eternal world. <25> They are "full of eyes before and behind." "Before" means external and "behind" means eternal.

"And the first beast was like a lion, and the second beast like a calf, and the third beast had a face as a man, and the fourth beast was like a flying eagle." (Rev. 4:7)

<26> So these four beasts do not have the same qualities. Each of them is different. And each of them is symbolized by a different shape and different being to show the different qualities they have.

"And the four beasts had each of them six wings about him; and they were full of eyes within: and they rest not day and night, saying Holy, holy, holy, Lord God Almighty, which was, and is, and is to come." (Rev. 4:8)

<27> "And the four beasts had each of them six wings about him": Six always symbolizes beauty and attractiveness. So "six wings" symbolizes the beauty of this creation, of these four things which enable God to guide His beautiful universe. <28> Also the six wings symbolize the penetrability and pervasiveness of these four things in the whole universe or Kingdom Of Heaven In Heaven (✡), which through its six sides (two triangles together), which is in each atom, He controls His universe.

<29> The Word is everything and everywhere. Time is everywhere. Space is everywhere, and everything is made out of atoms. "And they were full of eyes within," so through them He has complete knowledge of His creation (without) and the within, of the Soul, or the self, and of the eternal.

<30> "And they rest not day and night, saying, Holy, holy, holy, Lord God Almighty," so these are present day and night. They praise the Lord for His Mighty Being, because He is all of them and has created them to help the whole universe to Pure Consciousness. <31> He used all these elements to create this universe to help other consciousnesses to reach higher consciousness. He is the "Lord God Almighty, which was, and is, and is to come." He is, He was, and He will be.

"And when those beasts give glory and honour and thanks to him that sat on the throne, who liveth for ever and ever," (Rev. 4:9)

"The four and twenty elders fall down before him that sat on the throne, and worship him that liveth for ever and ever, and cast their crowns before the throne, saying," (Rev. 4:10)

"Thou art worthy, O Lord, to receive glory and honour and power: for thou hast created all things, and for thy pleasure they are and were created." (Rev. 4:11)

<32> Not only do these four beasts worship the Creator (God), but also the twenty-four attributes (Elders) of the universe worship Him. They worship God because He created them – all are The Word and consciousness. They praise God who is in Pure Consciousness (Christ Consciousness or Godhead). They bow down in front of His Power, Glory, Knowledge, Wisdom, and all the things that are related to God who sits on the throne. And they say to the Lord, "Thou art worthy, O lord, to receive glory and honour and

power" because "thou hast created all things." So He created the whole universe. Why did He create the whole universe? "For thy pleasure they are and were created." <33> As it is described, the creative forces were released merely because God desired them to be so. Then by sacrificing the self to bring these lost unit consciousnesses to Pure Consciousness, He found the ultimate happiness (pleasure and joy). He found that the happiness comes when you forget about the self and sacrifice the self for some higher thing in the universe. And He created this whole universe to help the other unit consciousnesses to reach higher consciousness through compassion and for His own joy, <34> which comes from sacrificing the self (not being self-centered) and working to bring other unit consciousnesses to higher consciousness.

Tablet Thirteen

Chapter 5

"And I saw in the right hand of him that sat on the throne a book written within and on the backside, sealed with seven seals." (Rev. 5:1)

<1> "And I saw in the right hand of him that sat on the throne": The right hand is always considered to be positive and more spiritual than the left in the body. Or the right hand can symbolize the side that guides man to his higher nature.

<2> "A book written within and on the backside": "A book" refers to the words of God which will be revealed to the human through His Prophets. These words are the truths which underlie all the religions and their Scriptures. <3> "Written within" refers to the real meaning of the Scriptures which cannot be seen and realized by naked, unspiritual eyes, and "on the backside" is what most people read and take literally. They think that what they see is what it means.

<4> "Sealed with seven seals" means that the book (the words of God) is sealed. It reveals the mysteries of God and His Plan which will be unknown until "…the days of the voice of the seventh angel, when he shall begin to sound, the mystery of God should be finished,…" (Rev. 10:7). These mysteries, with the meanings of the seals, are revealed in **The Greatest Sign**.

"And I saw a strong angel proclaiming with a loud voice, Who is worthy to open the book, and to loose the seals thereof?" (Rev. 5:2)

<5> The verse means that the way is open for all to reach that state where they will be able to open the seals. The opening of the seals was offered to all.

"And no man in heaven, nor in earth, neither under the earth, was able to open the book, neither to look thereon." (Rev. 5:3)

<6> At this point, God had the truth and had it ready to be known by man. But in this state, no one had reached Pure Consciousness to understand it. It was before the beginning of creation, even earlier than when the First Begotten Son of God had reached Pure Consciousness.

"And I wept much, because no man was found worthy to open and to read the book, neither to look thereon." (Rev. 5:4)

<7> John (the Soul of John) was very sad because he saw that no one was going to open the book. The book is going to be filed away and no human will know what is in it. Humans will not understand how to reach Pure Consciousness. They will not have any example to follow or to show them how to reach there. That is why John was so sad about seeing this vision.

"And one of the elders saith unto me, Weep not: behold, the Lion of the tribe of Juda, the Root of David, hath prevailed to open the book, and to loose the seven seals thereof." (Rev. 5:5)

<8> The first Soul which reached the highest consciousness was The First Begotten Son. He went through the **Eternal Divine Path**, "…open the book, and to loose the seven seals thereof."

"And I beheld, and, lo, in the midst of the throne and of the four beasts, and in the midst of the elders, stood a Lamb as it had been slain, having seven horns and seven eyes, which are the seven Spirits of God sent forth into all the earth." (Rev. 5:6)

<9> Suddenly he saw that the Lamb has overcome all the elders and is in the midst of the four beasts. He has overcome all the power of the senses, the tama guna, the objects of the senses, the elements, and everything in the universe. He has reached Pure Consciousness. **<10>** So he is in the midst of the four beasts. He has reached a place where he is beyond The Word in Pure Consciousness.

<11> "And in the midst of the elders": Elders are all around him, and he has been slain (symbol of crucifixion of the false ego) to reach higher consciousness. **<12>** Being slain and going to the cross is a symbol of overcoming the false ego (lower nature) and all the pitfalls of the spiritual progress described in chapters 3 and 4, by following the **Eternal Divine Path**.

<13> He has seven eyes, "which are the seven Spirits of God sent forth into all the earth." He has overcome the seven spirits of the self, which symbolize the seven chakras or seven states of progress, and he has come to Pure Consciousness. **<14>** And these seven spirits have been "sent forth into all the earth," or each person has these seven spirits in himself.

"And he came and took the book out of the right hand of him that sat upon the throne." (Rev. 5:7)

"And when he had taken the book, the four beasts and four and twenty elders fell down before the Lamb, having every one of them harps, and golden vials full of odours, which are the prayers of saints." (Rev. 5:8)

<15> When he took the book from the hand of the One who sat on the throne, all the universe (four beasts and twenty-four Elders) became joyful. Now he could reveal to humanity the knowledge of the truth behind this universe and The Plan of God. All humans would know exactly what The Plan of God was, is, and will be, and why. It will be known what the purpose of life is, and why He created the universe and went through all this work to bring other consciousnesses to higher consciousness.

<16> Also, all the beauty of this universe is for the Saints, or Elected Ones. They are the salt and light of the world. They are why God is joyful to help the universe to reach higher consciousness, because they are the ones who God is very pleased with and who will inherit His Kingdom. They are the ones for whom His creation is working. God is tirelessly guiding all of humanity and the whole universe to the higher consciousness. However, it is the Saints with whom God is very pleased.

"And they sung a new song, saying, Thou art worthy to take the book, and to open the seals thereof: for thou wast slain, and hast redeemed us to God by thy blood out of every kindred, and tongue, and people, and nation;" (Rev. 5:9)

<17> It is the Christs (sons of God) who, through their struggles, bring the truth to humanity and try to redeem them to God. They will be persecuted and slain in their endeavors but they will save many in every kindred, tongue, people, and nation. **<18>** It is through their struggles, "by thy blood," that humans have even reached the state of consciousness they are in now, and it will be through their struggles (blood) that eventually the whole universe will reach Pure Consciousness.

"And hast made us unto our God kings and priests: and we shall reign on the earth." (Rev. 5:10)

<19> It is the Saints and the Elected Ones who should become Kings and Priests and guide humanity to higher consciousness and eventually to Pure Consciousness. <20> Again and again it is stated that it is the Saints who are going to inherit the earth and become the real leaders and rulers of humanity. <21> These are the Paravipras who will understand **The Greatest Sign** and become dynamic spiritual people. They will bring the Kingdom Of Heaven On Earth, and then they will become Kings and Priests and "shall reign on the earth."

"And I beheld, and I heard the voice of many angels round about the throne and the beasts and the elders: and the number of them was ten thousand times ten thousand, and thousands of thousands;" (Rev. 5:11)
<22> The number of these Saints and people who reach higher consciousness is going to be very many: "ten thousand times ten thousand, and thousands of thousands." So these people are going to reach higher consciousness and eventually Pure Consciousness.

"Saying with a loud voice, Worthy is the Lamb that was slain to receive power, and riches, and wisdom, and strength, and honour, and glory, and blessing." (Rev. 5:12)

"And every creature which is in heaven, and on the earth, and under the earth, and such as are in the sea, and all that are in them, heard I saying, Blessing, and honour, and glory, and power, be unto him that sitteth upon the throne, and unto the Lamb for ever and ever." (Rev. 5:13)

"And the four beasts said, Amen. And the four and twenty elders fell down and worshipped him that liveth for ever and ever." (Rev. 5:14)
<23> The one begotten from the dead, and the Lord, will help the whole universe to reach higher consciousness and eventually Pure Consciousness. <24> Not only God and Christ (Anointed Ones) will help the whole universe to reach higher consciousness and eventually Pure Consciousness, but also the Saints, the twenty-four Elders, and the four beasts all were helping, are helping, and will help humanity to understand the realities behind this universe, and to reach the goal.
<25> That is The Plan of God for the creation of this universe. He created the four beasts and the twenty-four Elders. <26> The Saints have reached higher consciousness, and Christ (the First Begotten Son of God) was the first who reached Pure Consciousness. <27> He became the spirit of the truth (Pure Consciousness), and with his saints he will help the whole universe and humanity to reach higher consciousness and eventually Pure Consciousness.

Tablet Fourteen

Chapter 6

"And I saw when the Lamb opened one of the seals, and I heard, as it were the noise of thunder, one of the four beasts saying, Come and see." (Rev. 6:1)
<1> Only the Lamb can open these seals as mentioned. The Lamb is that spirit of truth (Christ) that opened up or helped to open the truth of the seven truths (religions) to humanity.
<2> "Opened one of the seals": The other seals are numbered as second seal, third seal, etc., therefore this seal is the first seal.

<3> In **The Greatest Sign**, the first seal is represented by (☯), which is the I-Ching in the horizontal position and symbolizes latent spiritual forces. <4> This seal symbolizes the teachings of the Far East (Mystical Paths) which are related to the many techniques for awakening these spiritual forces. <5> Also these teachings give a philosophy of the relationship between the individual and the universe, and they have been given to humanity after the flood of Noah. <6> The books of the Vedas are their base, where many other

REVELATION OF THE REVELATION — Tablet 14

disciplinary ideals have begun from, such as yoga, Upanishads, etc. They all help a person to realize the deeper truth beyond religious dogmas. Other Mystical Paths all throughout the earth also fall into this category.

"And I saw, and behold a white horse: and he that sat on him had a bow; and a crown was given unto him: and he went forth conquering, and to conquer." (Rev. 6:2)

<7> "A white horse" symbolizes the process of purity. Indeed all exercises, disciplines, diets, philosophies, and teachings of the Far East are based on purifying the body, mind, and spirit.

<8> "He that sat on him had a bow" means that he who tries to follow these teachings becomes like a warrior (Arjuna). With his bow, he goes to war with the influence of the tama guna over his Soul and fights those creatures that make him or her poor in spirit. <9> These practices and philosophies awaken the kundalini which will help the person to conquer his weaknesses, expand his mind, experience the presence of God, and overcome all negative forces on his Soul.

<10> "And a crown was given unto him," because he starts to overcome the power of the tama guna over his Soul and tries to overcome the Maya. He becomes great by detaching himself from the attraction of the external world and he awakens the spiritual forces in order to overcome his lower nature. So he becomes the king of his Soul, with The Grace, and receives a crown.

<11> "He went forth conquering, and to conquer." He started to conquer those weaknesses within by purifying the self. He is a conqueror, because when the Soul starts becoming awakened, and through struggle, the conquering of the self (Soul) is guaranteed (like Arjuna in the Bhagavad-Gita). Also the philosophy of the Far East (mystics) is so deep and mind-catching that it conquers the hearts, minds, and Souls of those who are real seekers. However, these teachings do not reveal all of The Plan and desire of God for humanity to follow. That is why other seals are necessary to perfect these teachings.

"And when he had opened the second seal, I heard the second beast say, Come and see." (Rev. 6:3)

<12> The second seal is the second symbol in **The Greatest Sign** (✡), which is the star of David or the seal of Solomon.

"And there went out another horse that was red: and power was given to him that sat thereon to take peace from the earth, and that they should kill one another: and there was given unto him a great sword." (Rev. 6:4)

<13> The color red symbolizes activity, war, and action. <14> The sign (✡) is the symbol of the Kingdom Of Heaven On Earth (KOHOE). The power of taking peace from the earth is given to those Elected Ones who will fight to bring the KOHOE. This power was once given to the Hebrews, and it will be given to Elected Ones all the time in order to eventually bring the Kingdom to the earth.

<15> "They should kill one another" means that until the Kingdom Of Heaven is established on the earth, humans will be lost in narrowness of mind (ignorance) and will kill each other in the process. <16> However, if humans understand that all these things happened throughout history in order to bring all to this point of understanding that the only way for peace, harmony, and happiness is to give up the false ego and follow what God desires for them, then the Kingdom Of Heaven will come to the earth and then man can enjoy life. However, because they have not yet given up their false egos in this stage, they kill one another.

"And when he had opened the third seal, I heard the third beast say, Come and see. And I beheld, and lo a black horse; and he that sat on him had a pair of balances in his hand." (Rev. 6:5)

<17> In this stage the seal refers to the third seal in **The Greatest Sign**, the cross (✝), which is the symbol of Christianity. <18> The cross itself is representative of a balance if you add the scales on the two sides (⚖).

<19> The black horse symbolizes the death of the devil (false ego, lower nature) in this

REVELATION OF THE REVELATION

stage of development of the human, <20> and the pair of balances is the symbol of equality. With Christ's teachings and the understanding of his teachings, a person should come to the point where he can overcome the devil (which is the attraction to Maya and/or false ego) and be ready to sacrifice all of individual self for establishing the Kingdom Of Heaven (balances). He should hunger for righteousness and try to bring equity on earth.

"And I heard a voice in the midst of the four beasts say, A measure of wheat for a penny, and three measures of barley for a penny; and see thou hurt not the oil and the wine." (Rev. 6:6)

<21> He who has the pair of balances has come to make sure that equity has been established in the human race. Therefore, the phrase, "A measure of wheat for a penny, and three measures of barley for a penny" means to make sure that the laws which have been set up are followed and no one is exploited, and all will have the basic necessities. <22> The phrase, "and see thou hurt not the oil and the wine" means: Make sure that those who are worthy to have more than the basic necessities of life are not being hurt. Whosoever contributes more to society should receive more. <23> Spiritual contribution is superior to intellectual, and intellectual contribution is superior to physical. <24> Another meaning is that the Chosen Ones (Paravipras) will establish this equity on earth. These are the ones who have the pair of balances in themselves (Kingdom Of Heaven within).

"And when he had opened the fourth seal, I heard the voice of the fourth beast say, Come and see." (Rev. 6:7)

<25> The fourth seal is the fourth symbol in **The Greatest Sign** (☪), which is the last part of the symbol OM (ॐ). <26> It is the symbol of Islam, which was brought by Prophet Muhammad. With this seal, the four horsemen are finished.

"And I looked, and behold a pale horse: and his name that sat on him was Death, and Hell followed with him. And power was given unto them over the fourth part of the earth, to kill with sword, and with hunger, and with death, and with the beasts of the earth." (Rev. 6:8)

<27> The pale horse means a balance in the revelation in this stage, a balance between spirit and matter. It is neither white, nor red, nor black, but a balance between all these extremes. That is why in Islam the material world and spiritual world both are considered equally important, and many laws were set up for social relationships.

<28> "And his name that sat on him was Death," means that the one who sat on him brings the death of Maya, because in this stage, you will enter the fifth chakra which is the abode of overcoming all unnecessary material longings.

<29> "And power was given unto them over the fourth part of the earth, to kill with sword,...." Islam covered the fourth part of the earth through the concept of "Holy Wars." They established themselves by the power of war "with sword," which was given to them. If this power had not been given to them, they would not have been able to do it.

Tablet Fifteen

"And when he had opened the fifth seal, I saw under the altar the Souls of them that were slain for the word of God, and for the testimony which they held:" (Rev. 6:9)

<1> This seal is the fifth seal in **The Greatest Sign** (✷), the nine-armed star, which is the symbol of the Baha'i Faith. It symbolizes universality. <2> As described before, many Saints of this religion were slain for the word of God (their belief which came by their Prophet), "and for the testimony which they held."

"And they cried with a loud voice, saying, How long, O Lord, holy and true, dost thou not judge and avenge our blood on them that dwell on the earth?" (Rev. 6:10)

REVELATION OF THE REVELATION

"And white robes were given unto every one of them; and it was said unto them, that they should rest yet for a little season, until their fellow servants also and their brethren, that should be killed as they were, should be fulfilled." (Rev. 6:11)

<3> White robes were given to them, which corresponds to the promise that if they overcome the pitfalls of the fifth church (fifth seal) they will be given white raiment (Rev. 3:5).

<4> They have reached the state where they can see God (Matthew 5:8). So they were crying for justice. <5> However, they should wait, "for a little season." Baha'i came in the 1800's. So the judgment should come sometime after this revelation which is in this century.

"And I beheld when he had opened the sixth seal, and lo, there was a great earthquake; and the sun became black as sackcloth of hair, and the moon became as blood;" (Rev. 6:12)

<6> The sixth seal is the sixth symbol in **The Greatest Sign** (✡). As it was mentioned in Rev. 3:10, with the revelation of this sign, the tribulation based on temptation started in the world. This sign was revealed to humanity in the year 1945 at which time tribulation (the attraction to Maya and the external world) also became stronger (after World War II).

<7> "Sun" refers to the "morning star" (Rev. 2:28), which is the only star that rises in the morning. The fourth church in chapter 2 in The Revelation is the symbol of the completion of spiritual knowledge (being surrendered). Therefore, the morning star (sun) is the symbol of the highest spiritual knowledge.

<8> After the opening up of this sixth seal the spiritual knowledge for the majority of humanity will be darkened. <9> Moon refers to the government or those who have managing abilities and knowledge (humans who supposedly have received their knowledge from the sun or the source of spiritual knowledge or God). But this knowledge will also be lost in this tribulation and replaced by a show of knowing rather than reality. <10> Also, sun and moon have other meanings as explained below.

<11> Sun refers to the father of the family who is supposed to be the priest of the house and also the great leaders in society (who have received the true spiritual knowledge). <12> So those who were considered great leaders in the past will lose their positions and will be replaced by unworthy personalities in society.

<13> Moon is related to the mothers in the family or women in society. So mothers will lose their pride of being mothers, and women will lose their spiritual values and become "red as blood," which is the color of attraction to Maya. Great women will be replaced by the shallow show of show girls.

<14> Therefore, the verse, "There was a great earthquake; and the sun became black as sackcloth of hair, and the moon became as blood," means that a great social change ("earthquake") will happen. The old order will fall, and all the rules and regulations that were respected by humans will lose their validity, "and the sun became black as sackcloth of hair, and the moon became as blood."

"And the stars of heaven fell unto the earth, even as a fig tree casteth her untimely figs, when she is shaken of a mighty wind." (Rev. 6:13)

<15> "Star" is related to the children. So the children will also become rebellious and will not stay in the previous orders that were set up by society. <16> Also star can be related to the great people in the society in different levels. They will lose their positions to unworthy ones.

"And the heaven departed as a scroll when it is rolled together; and every mountain and island were moved out of their places." (Rev. 6:14)

<17> "The heaven," which means a peaceful environment on earth, will be taken away. <18> "And every mountain and island were moved out of their places." "Mountain" refers to the strong personalities who were able to withstand all the problems. But the tribulation

and environment will be in such a way that even these people will fall. <19> Mountain also refers to the governmental hierarchy. <20> "Island" refers to those people who used to strive for comforting others. These people will also fall because of such a crude environment.

"And the kings of the earth, and the great men, and the rich men, and the chief captains, and the mighty men, and every bondman, and every free man, hid themselves in the dens and in the rocks of the mountains;" (Rev. 6:15)
<21> Even the mighty people who in appearance seemed strong will lose their strength and become lost. They will search in order to find a refuge.

"And said to the mountains and rocks, Fall on us, and hide us from the face of him that sitteth on the throne, and from the wrath of the Lamb:" (Rev. 6:16)

<22> Those who are guilty drown themselves deeper into Maya and create more problems for themselves and others who are similar. So they create more karma and go further away from God and His Presence. <23> These problems cause their egos to feel alive and bring an illusory relief by hiding them from the torture of seeing the truth and also the filth within. They hide themselves under the burden of their heavy karmas. <24> But as they continue this process, their burdens become heavier, so they have to create even heavier burdens so that they would not face the truth and that they are deceiving themselves, "And said to the mountains and rocks, Fall on us, and hide us…." When they hit the bottom, they might return to God.

"For the great day of his wrath is come; and who shall be able to stand?" (Rev. 6:17)
<25> Then is when the great day of His wrath is near.

Tablet Sixteen

Chapter 7

"And after these things I saw four angels standing on the four corners of the earth, holding the four winds of the earth, that the wind should not blow on the earth, nor on the sea, nor on any tree." (Rev. 7:1)
<1> These four Angels symbolize the withholders of the tribulation that would come over humanity, and they have withheld the destruction of the earth.

"And I saw another angel ascending from the east, having the seal of the living God: and he cried with a loud voice to the four angels, to whom it was given to hurt the earth and the sea," (Rev. 7:2)

"Saying, Hurt not the earth, neither the sea, nor the trees, till we have sealed the servants of our God in their foreheads." (Rev. 7:3)
<2> In this time period before tribulations (disasters) start, the teachings of the Far East (Mystical Paths) will be brought to the West. <3> Those who are the servants of God (Elected Ones) will become interested in them and familiar with them in order to become prepared for understanding the real meaning which underlies the reality behind their Scriptures. <4> With this understanding they will be sealed with "the seal of the living God," which is the spiritual knowledge.

"And I heard the number of them which were sealed: and there were sealed an hundred and forty and four thousand of all the tribes of the children of Israel." (Rev. 7:4)
<5> All the tribes of the Children of Israel (which at the time of the covenant was 144,000) have been sealed with the seal of God. <6> So the promise of God that they are and will be His Chosen Children will be fulfilled. Those who have made the covenant with God have reached higher consciousness, and they are in the Paraviprahood. They are in the sixth seal in **The Greatest Sign**. They

are the Paravipras. <7> They are not, however, the ones that are born in the same condition as the children of Jacob (Israel). They have been reincarnated in different places in the world. They have been reincarnated again and again, until now, that they have reached a much higher consciousness. They are the Elected Children of God. And in the next step they become the sons of God (Rev. 21:7).

"Of the tribe of Juda were sealed twelve thousand. Of the tribe of Reuben were sealed twelve thousand. Of the tribe of Gad were sealed twelve thousand." (Rev. 7:5)

"Of the tribe of Aser were sealed twelve thousand. Of the tribe of Nephthalim were sealed twelve thousand. Of the tribe of Manasses were sealed twelve thousand." (Rev. 7:6)

"Of the tribe of Simeon were sealed twelve thousand. Of the tribe of Levi were sealed twelve thousand. Of the tribe of Issachar were sealed twelve thousand." (Rev. 7:7)

"Of the tribe of Zabulon were sealed twelve thousand. Of the tribe of Joseph were sealed twelve thousand. Of the tribe of Benjamin were sealed twelve thousand." (Rev. 7:8)

<8> In each of the twelve tribes of Israel, twelve thousand were sealed, which makes 144,000 Children of Israel. <9> Also the number 144,000 can be added together as $1 + 4 + 4 = 9$. The number nine is a symbol of perfection. Therefore those who have reached higher consciousness are sealed.

"After this I beheld, and, lo, a great multitude, which no man could number, of all nations, and kindreds, and people, and tongues, stood before the throne, and before the Lamb, clothed with white robes, and palms in their hands;" (Rev. 7:9)

<10> Not only the original Elected Ones who had reached higher consciousness <11> but many others who had understood and become the champions of the cause of the Lord will be in that stage by that time. They had their hands in the position of Sal-Om, "... palms in their hands."

"And cried with a loud voice, saying, Salvation to our God which sitteth upon the throne, and unto the Lamb." (Rev. 7:10)

<12> Again here we can see that besides the Children of Israel, <13> many Saints have reached higher consciousness and the sixth seal. <14> They all praise the Lord and the Lamb, or Christ.

"And all the angels stood round about the throne, and about the elders and the four beasts, and fell before the throne on their faces, and worshipped God," (Rev. 7:11)

<15> Again, all the universe, Saints, and Angels fell down in front of the throne and worshipped God.

"Saying, Amen: Blessing, and glory, and wisdom, and thanksgiving, and honour, and power, and might, be unto our God for ever and ever. Amen." (Rev. 7:12)

<16> They accepted Him as the only God, their Father, King, and the One who is worthy to be worshipped, the Adorable One.

"And one of the elders answered, saying unto me, What are these which are arrayed in white robes? and whence came they?" (Rev. 7:13)

<17> John was questioned, "Who are they?"

"And I said unto him, Sir, thou knowest. And he said to me, These are they which came out of the great tribulation, and have washed their robes, and made them white in the blood of the Lamb." (Rev. 7:14)

<18> They have overcome their lower natures and have come to their higher natures. They have overcome the tribulation and the temptation of the external world, Maya, and they have reached the sixth seal. They have been given white robes, which is the symbol of purity.

"Therefore are they before the throne of God, and serve him day and night in his temple: and he that sitteth on the throne shall dwell among them." (Rev. 7:15)

<19> These people have reached the sixth seal and the next stage is to reach Pure Consciousness. Then they will go to eternity with God. "They serve him day and night" means that even after they have reached Pure Consciousness, it is the Father who is the greatest and they will serve Him in His temple (universe). Also they would surely know that God is all, even they themselves, and all-pervasive, "And God will dwell among them."

"They shall hunger no more, neither thirst any more; neither shall the sun light on them, nor any heat." (Rev. 7:16)

<20> In eternity there is no hunger, thirst, light as sun, or cold, as God said, "Thou art neither cold nor hot…" (Rev. 3:15).

"For the Lamb which is in the midst of the throne shall feed them, and shall lead them unto living fountains of waters: and God shall wipe away all tears from their eyes." (Rev. 7:17)

<21> They are in the sixth seal, and the Lamb will guide them to the seventh seal. As the spirit said in the sixth church (Philadelphia) in Revelation 3:8, He had opened the door, and "no man can shut it." <22> He, the Lamb, which "is in the midst of the throne shall feed them, and shall lead them unto living fountains of waters." The fountains of waters symbolize the state of Pure Consciousness. <23> God shall "wipe away all tears from their eyes" and there will be no sorrow or misery.

Chapter 8

"And when he had opened the seventh seal, there was silence in heaven about the space of half an hour." (Rev. 8:1)

<24> After these teachings of the East come to the West and are understood, many will reach the reality of spiritual knowledge, detach themselves from Maya, and reach a very high level of consciousness. <25> Many people in the East and West will be ready to reach Paraviprahood. <26> With the revelation of the seventh truth, the mystery of God will be finished (Rev. 10:7). <27> There will be a quiet period after the seventh seal is opened, "…half an hour!"

Tablet Seventeen

The rest of The Revelation can briefly be explained as below:

<1> In Revelation 8:2 until the end of chapter 11, the same seven Angels which opened the seven seals are described as seven Angels with seven trumpets. Each of them comes and by their teachings, which are like trumpets, humanity is awakened. <2> Later on, after the Angels leave, when humanity fails to understand and creates many samskaras (bad reactions), the disasters follow to hurt them in order to burn their karmas (sins).

<3> In chapter 10 the era of the flourishing of the intellect is described, and how following this, by the coming of the seventh Angel, the mystery of God will be finished (Rev. 10:7). In chapter 11 it is described that these Angels are the Prophets who will come and prophesize for three thousand five hundred years. After that the seventh Angel will sound his trumpet. Then the Kingdom of God and His Glory will come.

<4> In chapter 12 until verse 14 it is described how the lower nature of the unit consciousness was with the human from the very beginning of his existence (the power of the tama guna over the Soul), when it describes the wonder of the dragon who appeared in heaven. <5> This lower nature of the unit consciousness became manifested as Maya on earth. This is symbolized by the casting out of the dragon from heaven to earth (by Michael and his Angels, Rev. 12:7-10).

<6> It is this lower nature that should be overcome in the earthly life. In fact overcoming this lower nature (dragon, Maya) is much

easier in this body and situation, because the dragon (Maya) "...hath but a short time." (Rev. 12:12). So the "dragon was wroth ... and went to make war with the remnant of her seed,..." (Rev. 12:17). The war is the attraction of this external world for those who are in their lower natures.

<7> Chapter 13 describes how this dragon (Maya) uses desires and attachment (first and second beasts) to bring humanity to the ocean of Maya (dragon).

<8> Chapter 14 again describes the advent of Christ (truth) and the same seven Angels that opened the seven seals. However, some other events which happened in addition to those described in previous chapters occur in this chapter in the same time period (three thousand five hundred years). Again in the time of the seventh Angel the earth is ripe and the winepress is used to separate the ripe from the unripe.

<9> In chapter 15 until 16:18 the same Angels who opened the seals are described as Angels with the last plagues. When the seventh Angel pours his vial, The Plan of God finishes and it will be done. "...It is done" (Rev. 16:17).

<10> After this last Angel is the time when the mystery of God will be finished (Rev. 10:7), the Kingdom of God will come (Rev. 11:15), the nations will become angry (Rev. 11:18), and the ripe will be separated, "...the clusters of the vine of the earth" will be gathered because "...her grapes are fully ripe" (Rev. 14:18). <11> It is in the time of the seventh Angel that it will be finished (The Plan), "...It is done" (Rev. 16:17).

<12> After all these things happen, then is the time for Babylon to fall. Babylon symbolizes the making of a name by wealth and power (or false ego). It is described in chapters 17 and 18.

<13> Then is the time for the glory of God to come, which is described in chapter 19.

<14> By the sword of the mouth of the one who sits on the white horse, the darkness will be dispelled out of the minds of the people. "And the remnant were slain with the sword of him that sat upon the horse, which sword proceeded out of his mouth:..." (Rev. 19:21).

<15> So the remnant will be slain by the power of truth which comes from the mouth of the one sitting on the horse.

<16> The rest of The Revelation describes the two stages of liberation (resurrection) and how the state of Pure Consciousness is.

Tablet Eighteen

"And I saw the seven angels which stood before God; and to them were given seven trumpets." (Rev. 8:2)

<1> So far one period of explaining the seven seals is finished. Now each Angel is related to one seal. Each seal is opened. Each Angel represents bringing the tribulation after the seal was opened, and those who did not listen to that Prophet will go through these tribulations until they become more ready to reach higher consciousness.

"And another angel came and stood at the altar, having a golden censer; and there were given unto him much incense, that he should offer it with the prayers of all saints upon the golden altar which was before the throne." (Rev. 8:3)

<2> This Angel that is the first of the seven, is related to the teachings that were revealed by the horseman of the first seal or the Mystical Paths (Rev. 6:1-2). <3> The incense is the beautiful fragrance of these teachings, and the prayers of the saints are the prayers of those who have reached or will reach higher consciousness through them.

"And the smoke of the incense, which came with the prayers of the saints, ascended up before God out of the angel's hand." (Rev. 8:4)

<4> All these were for Him and are offered to Him.

"And the angel took the censer, and filled it with fire of the altar, and cast it into the earth:

and there were voices, and thunderings, and lightnings, and an earthquake." (Rev. 8:5)

<5> These teachings and the truth behind them were revealed to humanity, "cast it into the earth." They were purified with God, "fire of the altar." But truth always is torture to those who have false egos, so humans resist these Laws. **<6>** Therefore, suffering results, and because they do not follow His Laws, tribulation comes, "and there were voices, and thunderings, and lightnings, and an earthquake." **<7>** Also this refers to the beginning of the new generation which was completed six thousand years ago, after the flood of Noah and the revelation of the truth in the books of the <u>Vedas</u>.

"And the seven angels which had the seven trumpets prepared themselves to sound." (Rev. 8:6)

<8> The seven Angels became prepared to bring the disasters to humanity because they did not believe in the Prophets or follow the Daharma. In truth each trumpet is the teaching of the Prophet of each sign which comes to humanity. But they will not listen to the truth. So the tribulation or disaster follows.

"The first angel sounded, and there followed hail and fire mingled with blood, and they were cast upon the earth: and the third part of trees was burnt up, and all green grass was burnt up." (Rev. 8:7)

<9> By this, many disasters followed.

"And the second angel sounded, and as it were a great mountain burning with fire was cast into the sea: and the third part of the sea became blood;" (Rev. 8:8)

<10> After the second seal, the second Angel brought some other disasters. "Sea" is also a symbol of the consciousness of the people, when it is restless. So in the phrase, "and the third part of the sea became blood," blood means that their consciousnesses became so crude that they could not understand the truth. It became bloody!

"And the third part of the creatures which were in the sea, and had life, died; and the third part of the ships were destroyed." (Rev. 8:9)

<11> Disaster after disaster occurred. Even those who were saved from the restless waters ("sea"), "and had life," will also be dead in understanding, "died." They were above these restless waters in ships. But they died and their secure places (ships) will be destroyed.

"And the third angel sounded, and there fell a great star from heaven, burning as it were a lamp, and it fell upon the third part of the rivers, and upon the fountains of waters;" (Rev. 8:10)

<12> After the third seal was opened, the third Angel sounded the third trumpet, and again, because of the actions of the people, the disasters came to them. "Fountains of waters" refers to the Universal Mind from which all true knowledge comes. Only those who are in Pure Consciousness can fully tune themselves with it.

"And the name of the star is called Wormwood: and the third part of the waters became wormwood; and many men died of the waters, because they were made bitter." (Rev. 8:11)

<13> Water symbolizes the consciousness. So the bitterness of the water and/or the part that was dead is referring to the crudification of the human mind. **<14>** By sounding any trumpet or revelation of each seal, because of human confusion in seeing the relationships between them as is explained in **The Greatest Sign**, the minds of the people become cruder, and many of them will fight with each other. They will engage in wars and kill one another. **<15>** All these things will occur because their minds (consciousnesses) are bitter (crude). They have not reached that state of development to expand their minds and see that all is a part of a greater Plan. So their minds are narrow, and that is the cause of all conflicts and sufferings.

"And the fourth angel sounded, and the third part of the sun was smitten, and the third part of the moon, and the third part of the stars; so as the third part of them was darkened, and the day shone not for a third part of it, and the night likewise." (Rev. 8:12)

<16> As we mentioned, the sun symbolizes the father of the family or the great people in the society, and the moon is the mother or the women in society. The stars symbolize the children or the great people who occupy the positions in society. So with this Angel, one-third of the great people, one-third of the women, and one-third of the children, or great personalities, will be darkened. <17> It was after the fourth Angel in **The Greatest Sign** (☾) that the dark Medieval period appeared and many wars were staged in the name of religion. So one-third of history (day and night) became darkened.

"And I beheld, and heard an angel flying through the midst of heaven, saying with a loud voice, Woe, woe, woe, to the inhabiters of the earth by reason of the other voices of the trumpet of the three angels, which are yet to sound!" (Rev. 8:13)

<18> Woe to humanity because three more Angels will sound, and it is after each of these last three Angels that human progress and also tribulation will be increased. <19> Here we can see that the first four Angels came together and the last three Angels came later in a separate chapter. Therefore, as was mentioned, there is a relationship between these first four Angels, and between the last three Angels. <20> With the fourth Angel, which is the fourth seal in **The Greatest Sign**, the truth of religion or the truth behind spiritual understanding is finished. <21> And the rest of the Angels came to expand the minds of humanity. <22> They came to show how to become Universalists, how God will help Paravipras to establish the Kingdom Of Heaven, and how all the truth will be revealed with the seventh Angel.

Tablet Nineteen

Chapter 9

"And the fifth angel sounded, and I saw a star fall from heaven unto the earth: and to him was given the key of the bottomless pit." (Rev. 9:1)

<1> The real attraction of Maya, or the external world, started after the fifth Angel sounded his trumpet or after the fifth seal was opened. The fifth seal is the fifth sign (✹) in **The Greatest Sign**. It was revealed in the 1800's, and after that century, humans became so materialistic and more and more they became attracted to the external world rather than to spirituality. <2> Spirituality really became very unimportant in the life of the human. It was the time when intellectual understanding increased and many things were discovered in the world. Humans progressed in materialism so fast that they almost neglected God and His Authority completely (**material progress is not bad, but forgetting the Lord as the Creator of this material world is bad**). <3> So as we can see again, this Angel came after the fifth seal was revealed. He came to open the bottomless pit, which is the release of the devil or the attraction of Maya (the excess attraction to the external world, illusion of separation from God).

"And he opened the bottomless pit; and there arose a smoke out of the pit, as the smoke of a great furnace; and the sun and the air were darkened by reason of the smoke of the pit." (Rev. 9:2)

<4> Again here we can see that the sun (spiritual knowledge) was darkened. This means that the great people, the great understanding of higher consciousness and realization, were darkened by the smoke of the bottomless pit. <5> It had already been revealed that this was going to happen, and it should have happened, because religion had become so corrupt that the reality behind it was hidden

and no one could understand it. Humans became so crude that they taught people, "Do not worry about this world. Everything is in the next world. Do not progress, do not struggle, but just believe in these dogmas and follow what we tell you. Then you will be saved." Or in other words, the period of intellectual spiritualists had flourished.

<6> That understanding of religion should have been darkened, so that the people would become more attracted to the material world and progress more in material growth, which was necessary for the progress of humanity. <7> With the development of materialism, humans will become more comfortable (physically). With being more comfortable and having more time, they can utilize their energies more for progressing mentally and reaching higher consciousness instead of spending it for obtaining their basic physiological needs. <8> However, until this is understood by humanity, the material world will attract people in such a way that their spiritual parts will almost be forgotten.

"And there came out of the smoke locusts upon the earth: and unto them was given power, as the scorpions of the earth have power." (Rev. 9:3)
<9> These dark-minded people started to create things that sting like scorpions. The materialistic progress has become like a sting to the people. Instead of making them happier, it has made them more unhappy, egoistical, and self-centered, and has caused everyone to be concerned only about their own interests. <10> Religious understanding has been darkened. So this materialistic progress brought stinging power to everything, because humans do not use this progress for reaching higher consciousness but instead for selfish desires.

"And it was commanded them that they should not hurt the grass of the earth, neither any green thing, neither any tree; but only those men which have not the seal of God in their foreheads." (Rev. 9:4)
<11> This verse means, "Hurt only those that are lost in the attraction of Maya, which has been sent to test and find out who will become detached from it and who will get lost in it." <12> So those who do not understand that this universe is neither illusion nor reality, but is a process to reach Pure Consciousness, will be hurt by these tribulations.

<13> Again we can see that these will sting only the people who do not understand the spiritual truth behind this universe but instead pursue the intellectual understanding of it, "they will not have the seal of God in their foreheads." <14> These people just look at the appearance of the universe and take it as truth. When they take these things as truth, they will be lost in their egoistical pursuance and in the power of Maya and the tama guna. <15> They will be stung in any walk of life and become lost, because they will not feel that oneness with the self and the spiritual world. <16> Separation of the individual from the feeling of "I am a part of this universe" will result in lost and egoistical feelings, and that is hell.

"And to them it was given that they should not kill them, but that they should be tormented five months: and their torment was as the torment of a scorpion, when he striketh a man." (Rev. 9:5)
<17> These humans will be stung all the time in their lives. These things will not kill them in one day or two, but sting them little by little until their Souls are completely killed (become flesh). They will lose their Souls, by gaining the world, and become completely lost in this dark age which had to come after the fifth seal was opened.

"And in those days shall men seek death, and shall not find it; and shall desire to die, and death shall flee from them." (Rev. 9:6)
<18> The rate of suicide has increased more and more since the 18th century and especially during the 20th century. If you ask most of the youth or the people whether they have ever considered suicide, 99% of them will answer that they have at least thought about it. They may have decided to do it, but

did not go through with it. So they seek death, but death will flee from them. <19> They are so unhappy about everything as they do not know what is going on, what life is all about, what spirituality is, and what the purpose of life is, so they become so lost that they wish for death. But death will flee from them.

"And the shapes of the locusts were like unto horses prepared unto battle; and on their heads were as it were crowns like gold, and their faces were as the faces of men." (Rev. 9:7)

"And they had hair as the hair of women, and their teeth were as the teeth of lions." (Rev. 9:8)

"And they had breastplates, as it were breastplates of iron; and the sound of their wings was as the sound of chariots of many horses running to battle." (Rev. 9:9)

"And they had tails like unto scorpions, and there were stings in their tails: and their power was to hurt men five months." (Rev. 9:10)

<20> These verses are describing symbolically what false prophets and teachers are. It is saying that they look strong and beautiful like humans, and have long hair like women. They look like they have a crown of gold on their heads, and many of them appear to have very strong personalities. They have breastplates of iron, which symbolize their strength. They sounded like the chariots of many horses, which means they sounded very great and willing to battle, as if they really know and understand what they are doing in life. So they look very good. <21> But in their tails, like the scorpion, there are stingers, and they would sting with them. With all these things they were so egoistic that they had only their own interests in their eyes, and they were not concerned for anyone else's welfare. They were here only to hurt humanity more and more. False prophets are those who teach anything else but, "The Goal Of The Life Is To Be(come) Divine and Help Others To Be(come) Divine Also."

"And they had a king over them, which is the angel of the bottomless pit, whose name in the Hebrew tongue is Abaddon, but in the Greek tongue hath his name Apollyon." (Rev. 9:11)

<22> Even the king of the bottomless pit, which is the way to destruction, is an angel (tama guna, Lucifer). <23> This means that even great destructions which have been imposed on humanity have occurred with the permission of the Father in order to awaken humans to the realization that following egotistical ways will bring destruction to humanity. The only way to peace, harmony, and happiness is to give up the false ego. <24> That is, by following the desires of the false ego, which is self-gratification or community gratification (false superiority beliefs), humans will create individual or collective samskaras (sins). This brings disasters to individuals and communities, or to humanity in general. <25> That is why most of the people do not understand why suddenly a person comes, gains some power, and imposes so much suffering on humanity. That suffering should have happened to humans, and the power of that person has come from Heaven. **Without permission of God, no man has power to do anything**, "…A man can receive nothing, except it be given him from heaven" (John 3:27).

"One woe is past; and, behold, there come two woes more hereafter." (Rev. 9:12)

"And the sixth angel sounded, and I heard a voice from the four horns of the golden altar which is before God," (Rev. 9:13)

"Saying to the sixth angel which had the trumpet, Loose the four angels which are bound in the great river Euphrates." (Rev. 9:14)

<26> We can see that the sixth Angel refers to the sixth seal. As we remember in verse 1 of chapter 7, after the sixth seal was opened, the four Angels were bound, and we can see that these Angels again relate to the sixth seal. Now God demands that the four Angels which have four winds should be released, because

those that had to be sealed by the seal of God have already been sealed. They are not going to be hurt by the tribulation (four winds) that is going to come to the earth. The four winds are attraction, desire, attachment, and greed.

"And the four angels were loosed, which were prepared for an hour, and a day, and a month, and a year, for to slay the third part of men." (Rev. 9:15)

<27> Again they have to come to destroy the consciousness and understandings of men.

"And the number of the army of the horsemen were two hundred thousand thousand: and I heard the number of them." (Rev. 9:16)

<28> There were many that were fighting against each other.

"And thus I saw the horses in the vision, and them that sat on them, having breastplates of fire, and of jacinth, and brimstone: and the heads of the horses were as the heads of lions; and out of their mouths issued fire and smoke and brimstone." (Rev. 9:17)

<29> This describes the equipment the humans created to kill each other.

"By these three was the third part of men killed, by the fire, and by the smoke, and by the brimstone, which issued out of their mouths." (Rev. 9:18)

<30> This equipment was used to kill each other, causing one-third of the humans to die.

"For their power is in their mouth, and in their tails: for their tails were like unto serpents, and had heads, and with them they do hurt." (Rev. 9:19)

<31> Again this is the description of how they work. Some of them hurt from the back, and some of them from their mouths. Some hurt by their tails, like airplanes with machine-guns in the back, and some of them hurt with their mouths, like tanks, etc.

"And the rest of the men which were not killed by these plagues yet repented not of the works of their hands, that they should not worship devils, and idols of gold, and silver, and brass, and stone, and of wood: which neither can see, nor hear, nor walk:" (Rev. 9:20)

<32> With all these plagues and all these things that happened to humanity, still they do not repent. They do not understand that all these things are happening to them because of their actions and the reactions of those actions that were created in the world. They should understand that they are one, and should get together and become united. They should create one world government, one country, one language, and if possible, one race, and live together happily. <33> But because they do not understand, they do not repent, and they stay in the illusion of worshipping the false beliefs and psychological attachments which have been imposed on them. Their brains are washed by false teachers and prophets – those who preach the goal of the life is to gain more material possessions and is not to be(come) Divine. These false prophets and teachers make them unable to see the realities behind this universe.

"Neither repented they of their murders, nor of their sorceries, nor of their fornication, nor of their thefts." (Rev. 9:21)

<34> They do not repent. They do not understand why these tribulations are happening. They do not give up what they are doing in this world. They do not follow the Daharmas (God's Laws).

Tablet Twenty

Chapter 10

"And I saw another mighty angel come down from heaven clothed, with a cloud: and a rainbow was upon his head, and his face was as it were the sun, and his feet as pillars of fire:" (Rev. 10:1)

"And he had in his right hand a little book open: and he set his right foot upon the sea, and his left foot on the earth," (Rev. 10:2)

<1> This Angel is the symbol for the five elements of the manifested world. <2> The rainbow is the color related to the ethereal factor. He was clothed with a cloud (grey), symbol of aerial factor. His feet were as a pillar of fire (luminous factor). His "right foot [was] upon the sea" (liquid), and "his left foot on the earth" (solid).

<3> The book, which is a small book, is the symbol of intellectual knowledge of the four cruder elements, which is very little knowledge in comparison with spiritual and intuitional knowledge. These are intellectuals who try to understand and explain the realities behind this universe by studying the truth which underlies the visible elements. <4> However, this knowledge is very limited and has very small value in comparison to the intuitional knowledge of all things which have been created by an Intelligence which exists and is guiding the whole universe toward a definite purpose for which it was created.

<5> They (intellectuals without intuition) also gain very little knowledge of the ethereal factor, "a rainbow upon his head."

"And cried with a loud voice, as when a lion roareth: and when he had cried, seven thunders uttered their voices." (Rev. 10:3)

<6> Intellectual knowledge gained power in the last century and many great discoveries of the truth of the world were revealed to humanity, such as the theory of evolution. <7> Then the greatness of the intellect and scientific discoveries sounded so loudly that many people discredited religions and thought the Scriptures were opposing science. <8> Even religions and intellectual knowledge seemed contradictory (because of the lack of understanding the truth beyond the Scriptures).

<9> That is why when the Angel presented the little book with such a loud voice, others also backed up this belief ("seven thunders uttered their voices") that science and intellect are superior to spiritual understanding and religion.

"And when the seven thunders had uttered their voices, I was about to write: and I heard a voice from heaven saying unto me, Seal up those things which the seven thunders uttered, and write them not." (Rev. 10:4)

<10> What happened after intellectual discoveries (new trends of thought in the world) sounded so loudly on the earth? A new outlook came to man. Material progress boomed. Scientists and intellectuals went so far that they believed they could explain everything through science and intellect. <11> They tried and tried, but as they tried harder, they understood more that there are much subtler and more ungraspable elements that they could not explain. There are phenomena that cannot be understood by this limited intellect of the human.

<12> That is why psychologists started to include the idea of parapsychology in their field (unexplainable phenomena in the psychic world). Scientists started to become confused by so many different theories. They started to believe in a Creative Intelligence existing in the universe that guides all things. <13> In fact, the blind intellect that believes everything can be explained by research and examination, guided man to the real truth of religion: That all things were created by God and have come from that original cause (in our teachings, consciousness and the three gunas). Whatever scientists discover is what God has created in the universe. <14> In fact they are discovering how the Engineer (God) has built this universe. However, they have a long way to go and still they will never be able to explain all things by mere dry intellect.

"And the angel which I saw stand upon the sea and upon the earth lifted up his hand to heaven," (Rev. 10:5)

<15> The Angel "lifted up his hand to heaven" because he was so grieved with the lost situation of the people who believed that intellect, or that little book he presented to them, is all, and they forgot about God.

"And sware by him that liveth for ever and ever, who created heaven, and the things that therein are, and the earth, and the things that therein are, and the sea, and the things that are therein, that there should be time no longer:" (Rev. 10:6)

<16> The Angel himself knows that it is God who created the earth (solid factors), the sea (liquid factors) and heaven (luminous, aerial, and ethereal factors), <17> and it is after this zenith of the period of dry intellectual domination that the time of intuitional development appears <18> and the mystery of God will be finished, "…should be time no longer."

Tablet Twenty-One

"But in the days of the voice of the seventh angel, when he shall begin to sound, the mystery of God should be finished, as he hath declared to his servants the prophets." (Rev. 10:7)

<1> The mystery of God will be finished with the sound of the trumpet of the seventh Angel which will come after this intellectual boost to bring to humanity the truth of the realities of this universe and spiritual world. <2> **THOTH** is "the voice of the seventh angel!"

"And the voice which I heard from heaven spake unto me again, and said, Go and take the little book which is open in the hand of the angel which standeth upon the sea and upon the earth." (Rev. 10:8)

<3> The voice said, "…take the little book…," and find out for yourself how it works on you. <4> Also the book "is open," which means all can have access to it and can try it.

"And I went unto the angel, and said unto him, Give me the little book. And he said unto me, Take it, and eat it up; and it shall make thy belly bitter, but it shall be in thy mouth sweet as honey." (Rev. 10:9)

"And I took the little book out of the angel's hand, and ate it up; and it was in my mouth sweet as honey: and as soon as I had eaten it, my belly was bitter." (Rev. 10:10)

<5> That is how blind intellectual knowledge or the knowledge of this world is. In the beginning when an intellectual starts to gain this knowledge, it is sweet and interesting. <6> But when he goes deeper inside and reaches a higher understanding, he becomes even more confused and drier than before. He becomes lost in so many theories and concepts that he loses his common sense. <7> The knowledge which he had gained becomes a bitter burden on him.

<8> This is also the quality of Maya. It tastes good in the beginning, but brings bitterness later.

"And he said unto me, Thou must prophesy again before many peoples, and nations, and tongues, and kings." (Rev. 10:11)

<9> John will be reincarnated again and again to warn the people and tell them what these revelations mean, and to make them understand that intellect is not everything. There are many more beautiful things beyond intellect.

Chapter 11

"And there was given me a reed like unto a rod: and the angel stood, saying, Rise, and measure the temple of God, and the altar, and them that worship therein." (Rev. 11:1)

<10> However, John, who had been taken to the state of Pure Consciousness (intuitional knowledge) was allowed to understand the reality of the highest spiritual truth and be able to measure its depth. <11> He was permitted to experience the temple of God (universe) and understand about the altar (Father, nucleus of the universe).

"But the court which is without the temple leave out, and measure it not; for it is given unto the Gentiles: and the holy city shall they tread under foot forty and two months." (Rev. 11:2)

<12> But the understanding of the physical elements in the manifested world, "without the temple," leave to the Gentiles (intellectuals).

<13> Those who are lost and take this material life as the only reality, or those who try to understand everything through measuring this material world (Gentiles), will stay in this illusion for "forty and two months," which is equal with three and one-half years. Each year is a symbol for one thousand years, so they will be lost in this dry intellect for three thousand five hundred years.

"And I will give power unto my two witnesses, and they shall prophesy a thousand two hundred and threescore days, clothed in sackcloth." (Rev. 11:3)

<14> These two Prophets would bring the word of God for one thousand two hundred and sixty days, which is three and one-half years (forty and two months). If again we believe that each year is symbolic of one thousand years, then these Prophets will come again and again for three thousand five hundred years and try to bring to humanity the teachings that will guide them toward the goal of life. They would try to make humans understand that the intuitive knowledge (knowledge of God) is superior to intellect.

<15> The phrase "clothed in sackcloth" means that they come in a humbling manner.

"These are the two olive trees, and the two candlesticks standing before the God of the earth." (Rev. 11:4)

<16> So these two Prophets are like candlesticks that stand before "the God of the earth." And they have been sent to prophesy, bring the truth again and again into the world, and perfect the previous teachings with the new revelations.

"And if any man will hurt them, fire proceedeth out of their mouth, and devoureth their enemies: and if any man will hurt them, he must in this manner be killed." (Rev. 11:5)

<17> From the mouths of these Prophets the truth will be revealed to burn all superstitions and oppositions of their enemies. And if the people hurt the Prophets, they will create very bad karma (very bad sin) and they will be killed, or they will be badly judged because they have done that bad action.

"These have power to shut heaven, that it rain not in the days of their prophecy: and have power over waters to turn them to blood, and to smite the earth with all plagues, as often as they will." (Rev. 11:6)

<18> They have the power to shut the understanding of the reality behind this universe, and rain (truth) will not come to the minds of the lost people. The consciousness of the people will not comprehend their prophecies. <19> "Power over waters to turn them to blood" means that the consciousness of the people will be turned into bloody consciousness, and they will hate these Prophets. <20> Also they can bring disasters to the earth as often as they want.

"And when they shall have finished their testimony, the beast that ascendeth out of the bottomless pit shall make war against them, and shall overcome them, and kill them." (Rev. 11:7)

<21> Each time that the Prophets bring their teachings to humanity and finish their work, after they leave the earth, the desires and attachments to Maya or the external world (the beast) will kill them (their teachings) and will overcome the understanding of their teachings.

"And their dead bodies shall lie in the street of the great city, which spiritually is called Sodom and Egypt, where also our Lord was crucified." (Rev. 11:8)

<22> "And their dead bodies" means, the dead teachings of them. That is, the real teachings will be forgotten and misinterpreted as dogmas, and what remains will be kept as truth ("their dead bodies shall lie in the street of the great city [earth]").

"And they of the people and kindreds and tongues and nations shall see their dead bodies three days and an half, and shall not suffer their dead bodies to be put in graves." (Rev. 11:9)

<23> And people will not put away these dead concepts and beliefs. They will cleave unto them as truth. If they put their "dead bodies" away, they would be prepared to receive the next Messenger of God. But because of their wrong beliefs, they do not receive the new Prophets. **<24>** However, this should have been done in the last three thousand five hundred years, until the time of the explanation of all truths and their significances. **<25> It is time now that these dead bodies should be put away.**

"And they that dwell upon the earth shall rejoice over them, and make merry, and shall send gifts one to another; because these two prophets tormented them that dwelt on the earth." (Rev. 11:10)

<26> Whenever these two Prophets came, their true teachings tormented the people who were following their own false egos and the false teachings ("dead bodies"). **<27>** The Prophets told them they should give up their egoistical pursuance, should follow the truth, and be selfless and humble. These things they cannot do, because it requires giving up the false ego. Giving up the false ego is a very hard thing to do for those who have not overcome.

"And after three days and an half the Spirit of life from God entered into them, and they stood upon their feet; and great fear fell upon them which saw them." (Rev. 11:11)

<28> However, after a short period of time these Prophets will bring the truth back to humanity. Again truth will bring fear to those who see its power.

"And they heard a great voice from heaven saying unto them, Come up hither. And they ascended up to heaven in a cloud; and their enemies beheld them." (Rev. 11:12)

<29> After they finish completing the prophecies, they will leave the earth and go to heaven.

"And the same hour was there a great earthquake, and the tenth part of the city fell, and in the earthquake were slain of men seven thousand: and the remnant were affrighted, and gave glory to the God of heaven." (Rev. 11:13)

<30> After the prophecies are finished, the tribulation reaches its peak, and people start coming back to God and start searching for everlasting happiness. Or, each time some more people will be saved from Maya (the dragon).

"The second woe is past; and, behold, the third woe cometh quickly." (Rev. 11:14)

<31> The seventh Angel, or the third woe, is going to come to humanity after all these things happen. After these Prophets and all the intellectual understandings have come, and then, after these two Prophets finish their prophecies and the people hate and kill their revelations, then the seventh Angel will sound.

"And the seventh angel sounded; and there were great voices in heaven, saying, The Kingdoms of this world are become the kingdoms of our Lord, and of his Christ; and he shall reign for ever and ever." (Rev. 11:15)

<32> When those two Prophets finish their work, the seventh Angel will sound his trumpet, the truth will come to this world, and the Kingdom Of Heaven will be established on earth.

"And the four and twenty elders, which sat before God on their seats, fell upon their faces, and worshipped God," (Rev. 11:16)

"Saying, We give thee thanks, O Lord God Almighty, which art, and wast, and art to come; because thou hast taken to thee thy great power, and hast reigned." (Rev. 11:17)

<33> With the sound of the seventh Angel, the Kingdom of the earth will be the Kingdom of God. And all the universe will glorify God because He has undertaken such a beautiful Plan to bring humanity to understand the reality behind this universe through showing the history and revealing the reality of this creation. He has taken humanity through an elaborate evolutionary process to the point where He has made humanity so powerless. God then took the human through history to this point where he is completely confused and does not know what is the purpose of his life. <34> With all these things, when the seventh Angel reveals the truth, humanity will suddenly wake up and start to understand. The Saints, with His Grace, will start to become active. They will take over the earth and guide humanity and the whole universe to its purpose, Pure Consciousness.

"And the nations were angry, and thy wrath is come, and the time of the dead, that they should be judged, and that thou shouldest give reward unto thy servants the prophets, and to the saints, and them that fear thy name, small and great; and shouldest destroy them which destroy the earth." (Rev. 11:18)

<35> Those who lag behind in the process of understanding the reality behind this universe (that this world has been created for growth in the spiritual path) and use this earth for their own selfish desires will be very angry and will start fighting. <36> But the power of God is much mightier than these people, and they will be judged and given punishment. It is the time of reward for the Prophets and Saints who will be reincarnated. They will gain the reward of going through all this tribulation. And those who destroyed the earth will be destroyed.

"And the temple of God was opened in heaven, and there was seen in his temple the ark of his testament: and there were lightnings, and voices, and thunderings, and an earthquake, and great hail." (Rev. 11:19)

<37> The truth behind God's Covenant with His chosen people will be revealed. These chosen people are the ones who have been reincarnated again and again in many different parts of the world. They obtained the Light, stayed with the Light and followed the Light, and they fight for bringing the righteousness and establishing the Kingdom Of Heaven On Earth. Only these people are the Elected Ones, or the Paravipras. These are the true Children of Israel. God never fails in His Promise (covenant) to these people, and these people never fail in their promise (covenant) to God. <38> And they stayed with their promise in any incarnation. They furthered the Kingdom Of Heaven more and more. But after the seventh Angel sounds his trumpet or brings the truth, the real time for judgment will occur. It will be the end of this age, which started 12,000 years ago to make humanity understand that the only way is the way of the spirit, the way of God, and the realization of His Truth, not the selfish desires of humanity. The selfish desires of humanity will bring destruction of the self and others.

Tablet Twenty-Two

Chapter 12

"And there appeared a great wonder in heaven; a woman clothed with the sun, and the moon under her feet, and upon her head a crown of twelve stars:" (Rev. 12:1)

<1> This is the description of the beginning of the awakening of the creative forces (The Word) in the universe. The Word (The Holy Ghost) which is The Holy Mother, "And there appeared ... a woman...," is awakened (released). Through understanding The Holy Ghost, "...clothed in the sun," "the moon" or lower nature can be overcome. However, if The Holy Ghost (Holy Mother) is not understood and/or is misused, it becomes "The Woman" and will become temptation and the lower nature of man ("moon").

<2> Those who overcome will be "clothed with the sun [spiritual knowledge]" over their lower natures ("moon") and will be crowned by the twelve powers (pranic powers) of heaven.

"And she being with child cried, travailing in birth, and pained to be delivered." (Rev. 12:2)

<3> She was delivering a child, the First Begotten Son.

"And there appeared another wonder in heaven; and behold a great red dragon, having seven heads and ten horns, and seven crowns upon his heads." (Rev. 12:3)

<4> "A great red dragon": The color red is the symbol of attraction. So the dragon is attractive and catches the attention. The dragon is related to the Maya (Holy Mother becomes woman or passion), which is the power of the external world to bind a man and prevent him from pursuing higher consciousness. <5> The seven heads of the dragon are the seven false attractions of Maya which bring false satisfaction to the false ego. These are:

1- excess attachment to life (survival),
2- excess attraction to food (overeating),
3- power,
4- beauty (of body or for self-gratification),
5- false attraction to the sexual world†,
6- wealth, and
7- intellect (blind intellect).

<6> The seven crowns are the false satisfactions or prestige related to these things. <7> The ten horns are the by-products of the false ego related to these seven heads of Maya, such as anger, fear, vanity, false prestige, lust, pride, envy, etc.

<8> In fact, attraction to Maya will bring desire, and desire results in attachment, and attachment increases the greed, and greed brings more attraction, and the wheel goes on and on. <9> These will result in being drowned in the ocean of Maya and being eaten up by the red dragon. The result will be uncontrollable anger, lust, pride, envy, and all those things related to the lower nature (the animal part of the human).

<10> The "wonder" appeared in heaven, so the dragon was still in heaven. In this stage the unit consciousnesses were still in the un-manifested world, and they were under the influence of the lower nature, which is the power of the tama guna over their Souls.

"And his tail drew the third part of the stars of heaven, and did cast them to the earth: and the dragon stood before the woman which was ready to be delivered, for to devour her child as soon as it was born." (Rev. 12:4)

<11> So Maya (the lower nature) stands in front of all humans, even the Great Souls, to mislead them as soon as possible, "stood before the woman...."

<12> The sentence, "his tail drew the third part of the stars of heaven, and did cast them to the earth" means that Maya has misled so many unit consciousnesses (in heaven) away from the path to higher consciousness and has led them to hell (their lower natures, ignorance, earth) even before this manifested world was created. <13> Also this means that Maya casts people from reaching higher consciousness (heaven) to the earth (lower nature, ignorance, hell).

"And she brought forth a man child, who was to rule all nations with a rod of iron: and her child was caught up unto God, and to his throne." (Rev. 12:5)

<14> However, "her child was caught up unto God, and to his throne," which means that God will protect her child from being misled by Maya. As it was said, the woman is the symbol of The Holy Ghost in the universe (the creative force, The Holy Mother) from which the First Begotten Son, "...a man child," had emerged. <15> Also, being "caught up unto God, and to his throne" means that only by His Grace can man be saved (of course, after we prove ourselves to be willing).

---

† False attraction to the sexual world for satisfying unsatisfied emotional needs; false attraction as adultery; false attraction when sex becomes a great part of the life; false attraction as a thinking disturbance rather than the reality of it, which is unimportant. Spiritual attraction to the sexual world is to have sex through marriage in order to have children and create a unit block for society, and also to become unified in higher levels as one (☯).

<16> So by His Grace this First Begotten Son of God is saved "who was to rule all nations with a rod of iron." <17> It happened before this manifested universe was created ("Let there be light...," Genesis 1:3 – for more detail, read the book The Base). To be "caught up unto God, and to his throne" means to become God-conscious and saved by Him from the power of the tama guna (dragon).

"And the woman fled into the wilderness, where she hath a place prepared of God, that they should feed her there a thousand two hundred and threescore days." (Rev. 12:6)
<18> This woman will be fed in the wilderness for 3,500 years, or, for this period of time, the true meaning of who this woman is will be hidden from humanity. The wilderness is the confused world. "The place prepared of God" means that it all has been done by His Will.

"And there was war in heaven: Michael and his angels fought against the dragon; and the dragon fought and his angels," (Rev. 12:7)
<19> The Angel Michael is the symbol of the raja guna or the "I do" part of the Universal Mind. It is used as the active force in using the tama guna (the dragon) to create the manifested universe (Maya). <20> But there was a great resistance on the part of the dragon to be used in this process, "and the dragon fought and his angels."

"And prevailed not; neither was their place found any more in heaven." (Rev. 12:8)
<21> They were cast out of heaven to the earth. The tama guna was used in creating this manifested universe and "neither was ... found any more in heaven."

"And the great dragon was cast out, that old serpent, called the Devil, and Satan, which deceiveth the whole world: he was cast out into the earth, and his angels were cast out with him." (Rev. 12:9)
<22> Eventually truth will win over ignorance, and the devil (which is Maya) will fall from its high position. It will fall on the earth, which means that only those who are in their lower natures will be deceived by him.
<23> This verse also means that the earth is a place where the lower nature of man (devil, power of the tama guna) has been cast to from heaven (higher or Pure Consciousness). <24> Again we see that this manifested universe is a place for purification. It is neither illusion nor reality, but a place of opportunity to grow to higher consciousness and overcome the lower nature.

Tablet Twenty-Three

"And I heard a loud voice saying in heaven, Now is come salvation, and strength, and the kingdom of our God, and the power of his Christ: for the accuser of our brethren is cast down, which accused them before our God day and night." (Rev. 12:10)
<1> The First Begotten Son of God (Christ) reached Pure Consciousness, "Now is come salvation, and strength, and the kingdom of our God, and the power of his Christ." That is because the power of the tama guna has been overcome, so the First Begotten Son of God has reached Pure Consciousness.
<2> The dragon (Maya, the power of the tama guna over the Soul, the lower nature) first was in heaven (eternity). With His Grace, His First Son overcame it and cast the dragon (evil) out of heaven. <3> So the rest of the consciousnesses in the universe, "our brethren," are released from the power of the tama guna in eternity or the spiritual world. It was "cast down" to the earth.

<4> **Maya is and is not. It is as long as you are its slave. It will cease to be after you know its illusions.**

"And they overcame him by the blood of the Lamb, and by the word of their testimony; and they loved not their lives unto the death." (Rev. 12:11)
<5> "By the blood of the Lamb" means self-sacrifice. They have to sacrifice in order

REVELATION OF THE REVELATION *Tablet 23*

to overcome the evil, or "that old serpent" (false ego). <6> After overcoming the lower nature (crucifying the false ego), they will have the testimony and the words of truth. They will not love their lives until the death of their lower natures and overcoming the power of the tama guna in the universe.

"Therefore rejoice, ye heavens, and ye that dwell in them. Woe to the inhabitants of the earth and of the sea! for the devil is come down unto you, having great wrath, because he knoweth that he hath but a short time." (Rev. 12:12)

<7> This means, woe to those who stay in their lower natures, because it is where the devil dwelleth. These people will be drowned in the ocean of Maya. "Of the sea" means those confused consciousnesses (sea) lost in Maya. <8> However, the process of reaching Pure Consciousness is much faster in the manifested universe, "because he knoweth that he hath but a short time."

"And when the dragon saw that he was cast unto the earth, he persecuted the woman which brought forth the man child." (Rev. 12:13)

<9> The dragon (power of the tama guna) was very wrathful to that woman and works hard to crudify the minds of the unit consciousnesses toward the illusion of the separation from God, "persecuted the woman." <10> All the unit "I am's" are under the mercy of this dragon.

"And to the woman were given two wings of a great eagle, that she might fly into the wilderness, into her place, where she is nourished for a time and times, and half a time, from the face of the serpent." (Rev. 12:14)

<11> However, each unit consciousness is able to fly from the dragon and overcome it, even in the middle of confusion (wilderness). They go to God "into her place." But this truth will be clouded for some period of time, "for a time [one thousand years], and times [two thousand years], and half a time [five hundred years]."

"And the serpent cast out of his mouth water as a flood after the woman, that he might cause her to be carried away of the flood." (Rev. 12:15)

<12> The flood is the mind or the power of the tama guna over the consciousness. The flood is that negative thoughtfulness of mind that comes in and makes us completely lost in our thoughts, fears, attachments, and desires. <13> The serpent (the devil, tama guna) attempts to make those who try to go to God confused and drowned in Maya.

"And the earth helped the woman, the earth opened her mouth, and swallowed up the flood which the dragon cast out of his mouth." (Rev.12:16)

<14> By understanding the illusion of excess attachment to this external world (the earth), she was saved from the flood (confusion) which was sent by the dragon. When this understanding is awakened in a person, then satan (devil) becomes Lucifer ("shining star") and this world becomes a guide in the path of the seeker to the truth. Then the person will overcome its illusion. <15> So "the earth" or manifested world becomes a light in the path and swallows up the flood or confusion of this external world, "which the dragon cast out of his mouth."

"And the dragon was wroth with the woman, and went to make war with the remnant of her seed, which keep the Commandments of God, and have the testimony of יהושוה." (Rev. 12:17)

<16> The devil could not overcome the consciousness of those who direct all their lives toward God. <17> Those who have overcome their lower natures, the woman as depicted in Genesis chapter 3 (not the woman above, who is The Holy Mother) symbolize those who keep the Commandments of God and the testimony of Christ. <18> So the serpent will go to mislead those who are in their lower natures. But those who follow the truth, "testimony of יהושוה," should have no fear.

Chapter 13

"And I stood upon the sand of the sea, and saw a beast rise up out of the sea, having seven heads and ten horns, and upon his horns ten crowns, and upon his heads the name of blasphemy." (Rev. 13:1)

<1> This beast is different than the beasts in Daniel, chapter 7. Those arose from the "great sea" (collective consciousness). But this beast arises from "the sea" (the consciousness of one human).

<2> This beast is the symbol of the desires for the things Maya (illusion of the external world) offers. The dragon is the Maya itself. <3> But the beast is that desire which arises in the consciousness (sea) and brings attachment to humanity. Maya is attraction to the external world, and desire is the wanting of the fruits of this attractive world.

<4> The seven heads are the seven attractions to the seven powers of Maya (survival, food, power, beauty, false attraction to the sexual world, wealth, and blind intellect). <5> The ten horns are the devils which result from this attraction (greed, fear, anger, envy, false prestige, etc.). With these desires to the attraction of the external world (Maya), blasphemy will come to humanity. They will forget God. <6> Desires arise from the consciousness of the human ("the sea"). By purifying the consciousness, desires also become purified and the dragon becomes a dove. Then the desires will be(come) Divine.

"And the beast which I saw was like unto a leopard, and his feet were as the feet of a bear, and his mouth as the mouth of a lion: and the dragon gave him his power, and his seat, and great authority." (Rev. 13:2)

<7> It is really desires that make people slaves of Maya. As long as there is no desire for the attractions of Maya, it (Maya) has no power over the Soul. But the moment desire is stimulated, man becomes its slave. So the dragon gives the powers to this beast to bring people to his feet. <8> However, only excess or mundane desires are bad. Desires which are according to Daharma, for spiritual progress, and to be(come) Divine, are good.

"And I saw one of his heads as it were wounded to death; and his deadly wound was healed: and all the world wondered after the beast." (Rev. 13:3)

<9> "One of his heads as it were wounded" means that by the coming of Prophets and great spiritual teachers, people will lose their excess attachments for survival, because other attractions really come when a person feels he is only his body. This brings great fear and attachment to the external world and results in awakening the other attractions of Maya (illusions). <10> So the head, which is attraction for survival, was wounded many times. But later on, people again will become attached to life and that head of the beast will be healed.

<11> All the people wondered how this beast could make them go astray and not find the answers. This occurred because they were bound by the desires of their lower natures and could not understand.

"And they worshipped the dragon which gave power unto the beast: and they worshipped the beast, saying, Who is like unto the beast? who is able to make war with him?" (Rev. 13:4)

<12> People worship the devil (Maya) through their desires (the beast). Because they are in their lower natures, they think life consists of the attraction to the external world and that there is no other reality. <13> They spend their lives desiring and chasing it, "Who is like unto the beast?" They never believe that the beast can be destroyed. But by practice, knowledge, and faith, with His Grace, false desires will fade away.

"And there was given unto him a mouth speaking great things and blasphemies; and power was given unto him to continue forty and two months." (Rev. 13:5)

<14> Desires (the beast) chatter continually and tempt all to do evil and follow their lower natures. The beast is the one who brings temptations and is responsible for the fall of man. He tempted the woman (lower nature) to eat of the tree of knowledge (forbidden actions) and then gave it to man (symbol of the higher nature). Because of these actions, they were thrown out of Eden (higher consciousness).

<15> So it is desire which blasphemies, tries to defile the Laws of God, and attempts to make man follow what is good in his eyes but not in His.

<16> "And power was given unto him to continue forty and two months." Forty-two months again is 1,260 days, or 3,500 years. So the false ego has been left alone to make humanity fall for 3,500 years, exactly the same amount of time that has been given to the Prophets and the woman!

"And he opened his mouth in blasphemy against God, to blaspheme his name, and his tabernacle, and them that dwell in heaven." (Rev. 13:6)

<17> The dragon, these desires of the false ego of the human, will continue to deceive humanity, blaspheme against the truth (His Name), and try to destroy it. <18> Also, those who are in their lower natures cause trouble for those who are in their higher selves, "and them that dwell in heaven."

"And it was given unto him to make war with the saints, and to overcome them: and power was given him over all kindreds, and tongues, and nations." (Rev. 13:7)

<19> "To make war with the saints," means that the real spirituality will be lost because of the power of these desires in humans. All the nations and kindreds will be deceived because of this.

"And all that dwell upon the earth shall worship him, whose names are not written in the book of life of the Lamb slain from the foundation of the world." (Rev. 13:8)

<20> "That dwell upon the earth" means those who are in their lower natures. "Whose names are not written in the book of life of the Lamb" refers to those who have not reached higher consciousness or those who do not try to be(come) Divine. <21> The Lamb is he who overcame his lower nature ("slain") before the creation of the manifested world ("from the foundation of the world.")

"If any man have an ear, let him hear." (Rev. 13:9)

"He that leadeth into captivity shall go into captivity: he that killeth with the sword must be killed with the sword. Here is the patience and the faith of the saints." (Rev. 13:10)

<22> Whoever pursues animality will go to destruction and animality. That is the Law of the universe. He who kills by the sword for selfish pursuance eventually will be killed also by the sword because of the Law of Karma. That is what makes Saints believe and have patience, because the Laws of the universe never fail. The reaction of the action will stop if the lesson is learned. <23> However, action by knowledge for bringing harmony and peace, creates no karma (samskaras). As we saw, power was given to the fourth horseman to kill by sword (Rev. 6:8), but he will not be killed by sword because he was doing it to fulfill His Will.

"And I beheld another beast coming up out of the earth; and he had two horns like a lamb, and he spake as a dragon." (Rev. 13:11)

<24> This beast symbolizes the attachment which develops when a person becomes attracted to Maya. So Maya gives his authority to the desires in man, and fulfillment of desires brings attachment. His two horns are wealth and power, which enable a man to fulfill his desires. <25> He comes from the earth, which is attachment to the external world or carnal self.

"And he exerciseth all the power of the first beast before him, and causeth the earth and them which dwell therein to worship the first beast, whose deadly wound was healed." (Rev. 13:12)

<26> Again, this is the power of attachment which is symbolized by the beast. It causes humans to become greedy. Greed brings more attraction, attraction brings desire, fulfillment of desire brings more attachment, and attachment brings more greed. That is how this beast makes people worship the one before him, "causeth the earth and them which dwell therein to worship the first beast."

"And he doeth great wonders, so that he maketh fire come down from heaven on earth in the sight of men," (Rev. 13:13)

<27> He brings so much attraction to humanity that they become completely drawn to whatever is in the external world. They become amazed with the fire play (the illuminated world of Maya), the parties, and everything that is bright, shiny, and makes the eyes feel it is beautiful, and they follow these things. He brings many wonders to them, and they become more attached to these wonders. They become more and more bound to their egoistical desires.

"And deceiveth them that dwell on the earth, by the means of those miracles which he had power to do in the sight of the beast; saying to them that dwell on the earth, that they should make an image to the beast, which had the wound by a sword, and did live." (Rev. 13:14)

<28> "Make an image to the beast" means that desires come as an image in the conscious mind. Then the image becomes a desire. Fulfillment of desires increases their desires for the external world, which was the first beast. They will have more desires, which will bring more attachment. More attachment will increase the attraction, and attraction will increase the desires in this cycle that goes on and on.

<29> That is the reason why people in this age have more desires, because of the images that stimulate them in all walks of life, from street advertisements, T.V. and radio images, and other Mayaistical images available everywhere. <30> More false desires create more dissatisfaction.

"And he had power to give life unto the image of the beast, that the image of the beast should both speak, and cause that as many as would not worship the image of the beast should be killed." (Rev. 13:15)

<31> The attachment has the power to awaken the desires in a person and bind him to the external world, "to give life unto the image of the beast." Fulfillment of these awakened images brings more attachment, and so on.

<32> "And cause that as many as would not worship the image of the beast should be killed." Those who do not follow the crowd and do not stay lost in Maya will be cast out or shunned ("should be killed") by the lost crowd.

"And he causeth all, both small and great, rich and poor, free and bond, to receive a mark in their right hand, or in their foreheads:" (Rev. 13:16)

<33> These people who follow their desires and are attached to the external world will be recognized so easily as they will have a mark on themselves. A person with understanding (a person whose eyes are opened) will recognize them with the first sight. <34> The mark is the "GREED" of these people for more and more, never being satisfied.

"And that no man might buy or sell, save he that had the mark, of the name of the beast, or the number of his name." (Rev. 13:17)

<35> The mark of the beast is greed, especially for money and external possessions. And you cannot buy or sell anything without money. This is what people are attracted to. The people (in this lost world) who have this mark strive to gain more and more external things in life. They try to buy and sell as much as they can. <36> In this age, the prestige, beauty, and height of each person is related to the possessions that he has in the external world, but not his spiritual knowledge. These possessions, which are the mark of the beast

that bring more attachment, desires, and excess attraction to the external world, are Maya (illusion).

"Here is wisdom. Let him that hath understanding count the number of the beast: for it is the number of a man; and his number is Six hundred three score and six." (Rev. 13:18)

<37> The number 666 would be treated as 6 + 6 + 6 = 18. The number 1 is for leadership and 8 is for prosperity or material longing. Therefore it represents those who lead a life in Maya. The number 18 also can be shown as 1 + 8 = 9. The number 9 represents the ultimate, the completion. The number 6 represents beauty or attraction of the external world. So the number 666 is the number of those who have reached the ultimate depth of Maya. They are greatly attracted to the external world, so their desire for what it offers is great (beast with seven horns). They are very attached to it and are extremely greedy. The name of such a person is 666 and is in the camp of the devil.

<38> The number 144,000 also is equal with 9 (1 + 4 + 4 = 9). As explained above, the number 1 is the number of leadership, but the number 4 is of strength, manifestation (of the Divine) and forebearing. That is why it is the number of the Chosen Ones. They are leaders (1) who, with great forebearing (4) manifest (4) Divine attributes (God).

Tablet Twenty-Five

Chapter 14

Chapters 12 and 13 are about Maya, the attraction, the beasts, and how they all work. They lead the minds of the humans to a cruder and cruder point so that eventually most of humanity will follow these beasts. Chapter 14 again is describing other events that are going to happen in the same 3,500 years.

"And I looked, and, lo, a Lamb stood on the mount Sion, and with him an hundred forty and four thousand, having his Father's name written in their foreheads." (Rev. 14:1)

<1> These one hundred forty-four thousand people have reached higher consciousness. This is even before Abraham was chosen as the first Elected One to bring humanity to the goal. Abraham is the same as the Lamb himself and the same as Christ. <2> This verse says that the Lamb and his followers were elected to bring the great history of the Hebrews and their Scriptures to guide humanity in the way to establish the Kingdom Of Heaven On Earth. "Sion" is the same as Zion.

"And I heard a voice from heaven, as the voice of many waters, and as the voice of a great thunder: and I heard the voice of harpers harping with their harps:" (Rev. 14:2)

<3> Again the voice of many waters, as it was described, is the sound a person hears when he reaches very high consciousness. It resembles the sound of "OM." They will hear this sound, and it is the sound heard in the fifth chakra (overcoming the five elements).

<4> And there was singing and celebration for these people who had reached such a high consciousness.

"And they sung as it were a new song before the throne, and before the four beasts, and the elders: and no man could learn that song but the hundred and forty and four thousand, which were redeemed from the earth." (Rev. 14:3)

<5> Before the history of humanity or the history of the Hebrews started, some people already had reached a very high consciousness. They had progressed to a place where no other human had ever been before. They had been redeemed from the earth and chosen as the leaders for humanity to guide others to the path of enlightenment and eventually to Pure Consciousness.

<6> "And they sung as it were a new song," means that in this time period only these people heard this sound of many waters, the music,

and the beauty of that higher consciousness. Not everyone had reached that higher level. Only these people had reached there.

<7> Another thing is that this verse is referring only to the 144,000, not the Saints and the other people mentioned in chapter 7 who had also reached this higher consciousness but at a later time, "therefore are they before the throne of God" (Rev. 7:15). In that verse, John was asked who they were, and John did not know. One of the Elders told him that they were the Saints who had reached that consciousness. Here in this verse, only 144,000 had reached this higher consciousness, which is 3,500 years ago. They had been elected by God already. They had a covenant with Him to be the children of God, or the Children of Israel (those who struggle with God), which means they are the ones who work with God to bring humanity to the goal.

"These are they which were not defiled with women; for they are virgins. These are they which follow the Lamb whithersoever he goeth. These were redeemed from among men, being the firstfruits unto God and to the Lamb." (Rev. 14:4)

<8> These were the first who have overcome their lower nature (woman).

"And in their mouth was found no guile: for they are without fault before the throne of God." (Rev. 14:5)

<9> They had reached a very high consciousness in the sixth seal of **The Greatest Sign**. So these people in this higher consciousness have no guile before God, "are without fault before the throne of God." <10> But men might try to find fault in them!

"And I saw another angel fly in the midst of heaven, having the everlasting gospel to preach unto them that dwell on the earth, and to every nation, and kindred, and tongue, and people," (Rev. 14:6)

"Saying with a loud voice, Fear God, and give glory to him; for the hour of his judgment is come: and worship him that make heaven, and earth, and the sea, and the fountains of waters." (Rev. 14:7)

<11> Again this Angel is related to the first seal. It is the truth of the everlasting gospel and the reality behind this universe. It is the teaching of Daharma, reincarnation, karma, and all the Laws of following the nature of things and becoming in harmony with the flow of nature. All of these gospels have been preached by the first Angel to humanity. <12> He told them to glorify God for all His creation, that they are a part of Him (universe), and that He is trying to bring humanity to higher consciousness. "The sea, and the fountains of waters" represent the sub-consciousness, super-consciousness (Universal Mind, "fountains of waters"), and all things that can help the human reach the goal.

"And there followed another angel, saying, Babylon is fallen, is fallen, that great city, because she made all nations drink of the wine of the wrath of her fornication." (Rev. 14:8)

<13> This Angel is bringing the news of the fall of Babylon, because the Elected Ones were chosen – second sign (✡) – to fight with "that great city," which symbolizes the egoistical pursuance of the external world. So that is why this Babylon will fall after these people start fighting with it through history (internally and externally).

"And the third angel followed them, saying with a loud voice, If any man worship the beast and his image, and receive his mark in his forehead, or in his hand," (Rev. 14:9)

"The same shall drink of the wine of the wrath of God, which is poured out without mixture into the cup of his indignation; and he shall be tormented with fire and brimstone in the presence of the holy angels, and in the presence of the Lamb:" (Rev. 14:10)

"And the smoke of their torment ascendeth up for ever and ever: and they have no rest day nor night, who worship the beast and his image, and whosoever receiveth the mark of his name." (Rev. 14:11)

<14> This third Angel is related to the third seal in **The Greatest Sign**. This Angel has come to warn the people that they should not follow the beast or have his mark (greed). They should not be attracted to the external world unnecessarily. Instead they have to use this external world for their spiritual progress to higher consciousness and eventually Pure Consciousness. **<15>** If they do not follow this commandment and teaching, they will lag behind, they will be burned (suffer), and they will fall into the ocean of Maya. In short, they should overcome their false egos (the first three chakras). They should sit on the black horse (false ego) and try to bring equity (the balance) (Rev. 6:5).

"Here is the patience of the saints: here are they that keep the commandments of God, and the faith of Esa." (Rev. 14:12)

<16> That is what prevents Saints from falling into the grip of Maya. They know that there is a reward and punishment (purification). Whoever follows Maya will be punished (because of the Law of Karma), and whoever overcomes the weaknesses of the mind and lower nature of the human will be rewarded (will be in His Grace).

<17> This third Angel and his teachings are what Esa the Christ brought to humanity, "and the faith of Esa."

"And I heard a voice from heaven saying unto me, Write, Blessed are the dead which die in the Lord from henceforth: Yea, saith the Spirit, that they may rest from their labours; and their works do follow them." (Rev. 14:13)

<18> Those who fight and die for the sake of righteousness and establishing the Kingdom Of Heaven will rest from their labours and "their works do follow them." They will be rewarded for their works by God. They have overcome the first three chakras (lower nature) and are in their higher selves, "from henceforth." **<19>** Also death here refers to spiritual death (false ego).

"And I looked, and behold a white cloud, and upon the cloud one sat like unto the Son of man, having on his head a golden crown, and in his hand a sharp sickle." (Rev. 14:14)

<20> This Angel is related to the fourth seal. He and the son of man are one (Is Lamb). Also the sickle is shaped as the moon in the fourth sign (☾).

"And another angel came out of the temple, crying with a loud voice to him that sat on the cloud, Thrust in thy sickle, and reap: for the time is come for thee to reap; for the harvest of the earth is ripe." (Rev. 14:15)

<21> This is related to the fifth seal, because when it comes, the harvest will be ripe. **<22>** Those who have been good will have progressed, and those who have lagged behind will be thrown to the outer darkness or ignorance, until they also become ready to be harvested.

"And he that sat on the cloud thrust in his sickle on the earth; and the earth was reaped." (Rev. 14:16)

<23> The earth was ready to be harvested. There were those who were so ready that they were martyred for the truth of the fifth seal.

"And another angel came out of the temple which is in heaven, he also having a sharp sickle." (Rev. 14:17)

<24> This is related to the sixth seal. It was the time for gathering and separating those who have not progressed from those who have.

"And another angel came out from the altar, which had power over fire; and cried with a loud cry to him that had the sharp sickle, saying, Thrust in thy sharp sickle, and gather the clusters of the vine of the earth; for her grapes are fully ripe." (Rev. 14:18)

<25> Those who have lagged behind are symbolized by the clusters of the vine of the earth, which will be gathered by the Angel. **<26>** He was "from the altar," he was from Pure Consciousness. **<27>** He has power over Maya (fire) so that they can be separated from the rest. **<28>** Fire also means the purifying power of truth.

REVELATION OF THE REVELATION

"And the angel thrust in his sickle into the earth, and gathered the vine of the earth, and cast it into the great winepress of the wrath of God." (Rev. 14:19)

"And the winepress was trodden without the city, and blood came out of the winepress, even unto the horse bridles, by the space of a thousand and six hundred furlongs." (Rev. 14:20)

<29> Those who have lagged behind are punished through the tribulation that comes to the earth.

Tablet Twenty-Six

Chapter 15

"And I saw another sign in heaven, great and marvellous, seven angels having the seven last plagues; for in them is filled up the wrath of God." (Rev. 15:1)

<1> In another vision for the same time period as before, seven plagues which will come by the seven Angels are described. They are the last seven Angels which will be described in The Revelation.

"And I saw as it were a sea of glass mingled with fire: and them that had gotten the victory over the beast, and over his image, and over his mark, and over the number of his name, stand on the sea of glass, having the harps of God." (Rev. 15:2)

<2> They are the first ones who had overcome the attachment (beast), non-spiritual desires (his image), and greed (his mark), and they have been chosen as Elected Ones.

"And they sing the song of Moses the servant of God, and the song of the Lamb, saying, Great and marvelous are thy works, Lord God Almighty; just and true are thy ways, thou King of saints." (Rev. 15:3)

<3> They have become the servants of God like Moses and the Lamb, "sing the song of Moses ... , and the song of the Lamb." They also have realized how marvellous the universe and God are. <4> Also, all His Works and Ways are "just and true." Only when a person realizes all these things can he easily follow Him, become a Saint, and accept Him as his King, "thou King of saints."

"Who shall not fear thee, O Lord, and glorify thy name? for thou only art holy: for all nations shall come and worship before thee; for thy judgments are made manifest." (Rev. 15:4)

<5> By understanding His Powers and Marvelousness, a Saint realizes He has complete power over all things, "Who shall not fear thee, O Lord, and glorify thy name?" The Father who has never been under the influence of the tama guna is completely sinless, "for thou only art holy." These truths will be realized by all and eventually they will come and surrender to Him. In order to bring unit consciousnesses to Pure Consciousness, He has to judge them, "for thy judgments are made manifest." That is why the following plagues will come to humanity.

"And after that I looked, and, behold, the temple of the tabernacle of the testimony in heaven was opened:" (Rev. 15:5)

"And the seven angels came out of the temple, having the seven plagues, clothed in pure and white linen, and having their breasts girded with golden girdles." (Rev. 15:6)

"And one of the four beasts gave unto the seven angels seven golden vials full of the wrath of God, who liveth for ever and ever." (Rev. 15:7)

<6> The new events with these seven Angels started.

"And the temple was filled with smoke from the glory of God, and from his power; and no man was able to enter into the temple, till the seven plagues of the seven angels were fulfilled." (Rev. 15:8)

<7> No man will enter into the temple of God (heaven) until history is fulfilled. Even if someone did reach higher consciousness or Pure Consciousness, he would not be able to enter the temple of God until history is fulfilled. First the seven angels must come and bring to the earth the disasters and all the things necessary for the humans to come to their senses. After that, the human might be able to enter the temple of God, which is Pure Consciousness. <8> Even those who have reached Pure Consciousness will be sent back to help others, "will be spued out of His mouth" (Rev. 3:16).

Chapter 16

"And I heard a great voice out of the temple saying to the seven angels, Go your ways, and pour out the vials of the wrath of God upon the earth." (Rev. 16:1)
<9> The order to start the Mission, or The Plan, was given by God.

"And the first went, and poured out his vial upon the earth; and there fell a noisome and grievous sore upon the men which had the mark of the beast, and upon them which worshipped his image." (Rev. 16:2)
<10> As the first truth came, those who were following the beast became miserable because of it.

"And the second angel poured out his vial upon the sea; and it became as the blood of a dead man: and every living soul died in the sea." (Rev. 16:3)
<11> The second Angel poured out his vial. The second Angel is related to the second truth. As each seal is opened, those who do not follow the Prophet or the truth which is related to that seal and instead follow their own egoistical pursuance will fall. They refuse to follow what God sends through that Prophet and so will be sent disasters. <12> So the second Angel brings a disaster which is described as "the blood of a dead man." "Upon the sea" again refers to the water, or the consciousness of those people. They become like the blood of a dead man. Their minds become completely crudified, and they go further into ignorance.

"And the third angel poured out his vial upon the rivers and fountains of waters; and they became blood." (Rev. 16:4)
<13> The third Angel is related to the third seal. The people who do not listen to the truth revealed through the third seal will have their consciousnesses become like blood. They will become more crudified.

"And I heard the angel of the waters say, Thou art righteous, O Lord, which art, and wast, and shalt be, because thou hast judged thus." (Rev. 16:5)

"For they have shed the blood of saints and prophets, and thou hast given them blood to drink; for they are worthy." (Rev. 16:6)
<14> The consciousnesses of these people ("the angel of the waters") deeply know they have killed Saints and Prophets and that they should be judged, because God sent these Messengers who said the truth but they did not accept it. So they and whoever does not follow the Prophets and truth have to drink this blood, which means their minds should become cruder and cruder, and they suffer because of this, "for they are worthy" of this judgment. <15> However, if they expand their minds and become Universalists, they will also be saved as any other narrow-minded people who will be saved by the expansion of the mind (universalism).

"And I heard another out of the altar say, Even so, Lord God Almighty, true and righteous are thy judgments." (Rev. 16:7)
<16> Again all the universe knows that God's Judgments are true.

"And the fourth angel poured out his vial upon the sun; and power was given unto him to scorch men with fire." (Rev. 16:8)
<17> This is related to the fourth seal again. After the fourth seal was opened, those who have not followed the teaching were

scorched with fire (truth), and they failed to understand the highest spiritual knowledge (sun), which is to be surrendered and/or submissive to Him.

"And men were scorched with great heat, and blasphemed the name of God, which hath power over these plagues: and they repented not to give him glory." (Rev. 16:9)

<18> People would not follow this teaching and the disasters came. God sent disasters to cause them unhappiness. But they did not repent or follow God's Prophet.

"And the fifth angel poured out his vial upon the seat of the beast; and his kingdom was full of darkness; and they gnawed their tongues for pain," (Rev. 16:10)

<19> This fifth Angel is related to the fifth seal. Expansion of the mind comes with the seal of universalism. The "seat of the beast" is narrowness of the mind and prejudice which comes from ignorance. Expansion of the mind is the same as throwing a plague or disaster over "the seat of the beast." And the beast was very wrathful, and darkness came to his kingdom (narrowness of the mind). <20> He who expands his mind and becomes a universal person will bring darkness to the kingdom of the devil or evil (serpent) because expansion of the mind means to see God. To see God results in forgetting everything of the Maya. <21> Also, becoming expanded in mind is to shatter all the psychological bondage that has been imposed over a human spirit. **Bondage is anything that does not let you see this whole universe as your only home, God as your only Father, and nature as your only Mother. Freedom from all narrowness is the Goal.**

"And blasphemed the God of heaven because of their pains and their sores, and repented not of their deeds." (Rev. 16:11)

<22> Again people did not accept this truth and they were very unhappy, so many disasters came to them.

"And the sixth angel poured out his vial upon the great river Euphrates; and the water thereof was dried up, that the way of the kings of the east might be prepared." (Rev. 16:12)

<23> "The sixth angel poured out his vial upon the great river Euphrates." So again we can see that this sixth Angel is related to the sixth Angel mentioned in chapter 9, who loosed "the four angels which are bound in the great river Euphrates" (Rev. 9:14). <24> So, these are the same events happening in the same period of time, but with a different point of view and vision. The water of this river Euphrates dried up, which means the consciousness of the people dried up and they could not even think straight. They were all confused and in tribulation.

"And I saw three unclean spirits like frogs come out of the mouth of the dragon, and out of the mouth of the beast, and out of the mouth of the false prophet." (Rev. 16:13)

<25> Blasphemies and false prophets – those who teach anything else but that the goal of life is to be(come) Divine – were attracting people to Maya as unclean spirits. They were all over the world. False teachers, desires, and attractions of Maya were all trying to lead people to the tribulation. They were trying to misguide humanity to the path of ignorance, rather than to enlightenment. <26> Again here tribulation started at the time of the sixth Angel, corresponding with the sixth seal.

"For they are the spirits of devils, working miracles, which go forth unto the kings of the earth and of the whole world, to gather them to the battle of that great day of God Almighty." (Rev. 16:14)

<27> The battle is between the attraction of Maya or the external world, desires, and false prophets, and the Saints or Paravipras. Saints and Paravipras are trying to bring humanity to the path of enlightenment to higher consciousness and eventually Pure Consciousness. But Maya, its attraction, the desires, and those things that brainwash humans to be pulled to the external world, attract many people. <28> Like unclean spirits, they make many miracles ("spirits of devils,

working miracles") that are eye-catching to material life. Now is the time of a battle between God Almighty's Servants and Saints, and the power of the attraction of Maya and the false prophets.

"Behold, I come as a thief. Blessed is he that watcheth, and keepeth his garments, lest he walk naked, and they see his shame." (Rev. 16:15)

<29> Blessed are those who are aware in this time period and wait for the coming of the truth. The truth will come like a thief unto the people, and those who watch and "keepeth their garments clean" (of attachments, desires, and greed) will be saved. Those who do not will be lost with the brainwashing of this great attraction to the world. However, those who overcome this attraction, with His Grace, will be saved.

Tablet Twenty-Seven

"And he gathered them together into a place called in the Hebrew tongue Armageddon." (Rev. 16:16)

<1> The battle will be in Armageddon, which means "world."

"And the seventh angel poured out his vial into the air; and there came a great voice out of the temple of heaven, from the throne, saying, It is done." (Rev. 16:17)

<2> It is in the time of the seventh Angel that it will be done. Again and again we see that in the time of the seventh Angel, The Plan of God will be done.

"And there were voices, and thunders, and lightnings; and there was a great earthquake, such as was not since men were upon the earth, so mighty an earthquake, and so great." (Rev. 16:18)

<3> The earthquake is always a symbol of the disruption of the old order in society and the coming of a new order to humanity. So the new revelation, or the new set-up of rules and system, will be revealed to humanity. The old order will fall off just like an earthquake which destroys the earth. <4> Everything will fall off the earth and a new kind of understanding, revelation, and set of rules and regulations will be established.

"And the great city was divided into three parts, and the cities of the nations fell: and the great Babylon came in remembrance before God, to give unto her the cup of the wine of the fierceness of his wrath." (Rev. 16:19)

<5> After the seventh Angel reveals the great truth, the tribulation will come over the cities. The cities will fall and the great multitude of people who were thinking that they would last forever will fall. The great Babylon will come to the memory of God, and God will say, "Now is the time to 'give unto her the cup of the wine of the fierceness of [my] wrath.'" <6> He will destroy that Babylon, which is the egoistical pursuance for selfish gain and fame. As we remember in Genesis, they said, "Go to, let us build us a city and a tower, … and let us make us a name" (Gen. 11:4). So the pursuance that is for making a name and fame is related to the great city Babylon.

"And every island fled away, and the mountains were not found." (Rev. 16:20)

<7> The great people are like islands. Others who needed comfort would go to them but those people like islands, had fled away. No one would be helping anyone because all were so attached and wrapped up in the selfish desires and power of Maya that there was no "island" (comforter) for rest.

<8> "And the mountains were not found": The great people who were like mountains for humanity and could be leaned on because of their greatness were no longer around. <9> Everyone in the world would be completely lost.

"And there fell upon men a great hail out of heaven, every stone about the weight of a talent: and men blasphemed God because of the plague of the hail; for the plague thereof was exceeding great." (Rev. 16:21)

<10> The last tribulation will come and great troubles will plague humanity. Humans will be so lost in the tribulation and the pursuance of the Mayaistic and egoistical things that each person will feel just like having a great stone of hail fall upon them. They will not know what to do with their weight, and they will not understand and find a way out.

<11> Their minds will become more and more gross and crudified. They will not understand that the only way is to go back to God, understand the ways of the Spirit, give up the egoistical pursuance, and come to sharing, caring, and understanding that, "The earth has enough for everyone's need, but not enough for everyone's greed" (Mahatma Gandhi).

Tablet Twenty-Eight

Chapter 17

From this verse on, future prophecies are given. They all will be fulfilled, but how and when only the Father knows. That is why they will mostly be explained in general, and some whose meanings are necessary will be explained in more detail.

"And there came one of the seven angels which had the seven vials, and talked with me, saying unto me, Come hither; I will shew unto thee the judgment of the great whore that sitteth upon many waters:" (Rev. 17:1)

<1> The "great whore" refers to power and wealth which are gained in order to acquire a name or fulfill desires. Water is the symbol of the consciousness. <2> Therefore, this great whore, which is to gain wealth and power in order to make a name, resides in the consciousness of many.

"With whom the kings of the earth have committed fornication, and the inhabitants of the earth have been made drunk with the wine of her fornication." (Rev. 17:2)

<3> "With whom the kings of the earth" means those leaders in lower consciousness who have gained high positions in society will try to be a friend of this whore. They will try to gain fame and name for selfish purposes. They gained power and fame by hoarding wealth and imposing suffering on their people in order to gather more wealth, power, and fame.

<4> Also people on earth (in their lower natures) "have been made drunk" by following this whore, "her fornication."

"So he carried me away in the spirit into the wilderness: and I saw a woman sit upon a scarlet coloured beast, full of names of blasphemy, having seven heads and ten horns." (Rev. 17:3)

<5> It is the same beast as the one who was wounded and then healed (Revelation 13:1,2…). It is the power of desires toward the attraction of the external world (Maya). It is because of these desires (which are in the subconscious mind) that people strive to gain wealth and power, in order to fulfill their longings. <6> However, the human has a thirst for limitlessness, and when he directs this desire toward the external world which is limited and finite, he can never quench his thirst. The finite universe cannot satisfy infinite longings. Only spiritual knowledge which is infinite can satisfy that immeasurable thirst.

"And the woman was arrayed in purple and scarlet colour, and decked with gold and precious stones and pearls, having a golden cup in her hand full of abominations and filthiness of her fornication:" (Rev. 17:4)

<7> Wealth is symbolized by colorful dresses, gold, precious stones, pearls and other things that people become attached to as the wealth of the earth. If they become your master, you are lost.

"And upon her forehead was a name written, MYSTERY, BABYLON THE GREAT, THE MOTHER OF HARLOTS AND ABOMINATIONS OF THE EARTH." (Rev. 17:5)

<8> Therefore, "Babylon the Great," that city which is always referred to as a female (woman), is this great whore. It is a great attraction of Maya and symbolizes the power and wealth when they are gained in order to inflict suffering on others, or in short, the false ego.

"And I saw the woman drunken with the blood of the saints, and with the blood of the martyrs of יהושע: and when I saw her, I wondered with great admiration." (Rev. 17:6)

<9> It is the fear of losing power and wealth that causes people to kill the Prophets and close their ears to the truth.

"And the angel said unto me, Wherefore didst thou marvel? I will tell thee the mystery of the woman, and of the beast that carrieth her, which hath the seven heads and ten horns." (Rev. 17:7)

<10> As we remember, this beast is the same as the first one in chapter 13 that came out of the sea. He had seven heads and ten horns, symbolizing the power of the desires toward Maya. This beast is the false desires that make a man pursue the Mayaistic and egoistic things and become more and more attached to the external world. And the desire of becoming famous, having power, making a name and fame for oneself, and fulfilling these desires, is related to the lower chakras, or the lower self of the human. **<11>** The woman here is the same as the lower nature of the human which is carried away by these desires, and these desires are that beast with the seven heads and ten horns.

"The beast that thou sawest was, and is not; and shall ascend out of the bottomless pit, and go into perdition: and they that dwell on the earth shall wonder, whose names were not written in the book of life from the foundation of the world, when they behold the beast that was, and is not, and yet is." (Rev. 17:8)

<12> "The beast was, and is not" means that it is true that the power of the tama guna is over the Soul, but really the power of this guna is not, because it causes just an illusion of separation of man from God that, by His Grace, can be overcome. When it is overcome, there is no beast, and it "is not." **<13>** So it is just something to overcome (through The Grace). That power is really the illusion of the attraction of the external world. People follow this illusion of the external world because of their false egos, which is the whore, or the excess, unnecessary, and unspiritual desires which are, but if overcome, they are not. **<14>** These desires are created by the power of the tama guna, and the power of the tama guna causes the lower nature to pursue the wanting of the external world. But when man reaches the higher nature or higher chakras, this same beast (or the power of the tama guna, the lower nature) will become a tool for humanity in pursuing the path to higher consciousness.

<15> "The beast … shall ascend out of the bottomless pit." The bottomless pit is the depth of ignorance. "And go into perdition: and they that dwell on the earth shall wonder, whose names were not written in the book of life from the foundation of the world." This refers to those who do not pursue the right path and in the many incarnations again and again fail in realizing the human potential of be(com)ing Divine. Instead they go more and more to ignorance, and become more bound by the power of the tama guna. **<16>** "Behold the beast that was, and is not, and **yet is**." So for them the beast is. For those who overcome (by His Grace), it is not, and yet it is. But even those who overcome it, if they are not one-pointed toward God, they might go under its influence, and it becomes "is" again.

"And here is the mind which hath wisdom. The seven heads are seven mountains, on which the woman sitteth." (Rev. 17:9)

<17> As it was described, these seven heads are the seven attractions of Maya which cause the lower nature to pursue them. This woman, or the lower nature of man (that which is attracted to gaining name and fame from power and wealth) sits on these seven heads of the beast who came out of the sea (consciousness of man) (Rev. 13:1). **<18>** Also most of the governmental systems (△)

of the earth (mountain) are based on these attractions (seven mountains).

"And there are seven kings: five are fallen, and one is, and the other is not yet come; and when he cometh, he must continue a short space." (Rev. 17:10)

<19> Seven times this beast, or this attraction of Maya, has defiled humanity. Before the Prophets or the Angels of the church came, he was defiling humanity. After the first Angel, some people did not believe him, so he defiled them. After the second time, his head was healed and he came back. He defiled the people again and caused them to go to their lower natures. The third Angel came, and so on. This is symbolized by, "one of his heads as it was wounded to death; and his deadly wound was healed:…" (Rev. 13:3). <20> So it will be seven times. And after the seventh Angel comes, he will be finished after a short period of time.

"And the beast that was, and is not, even he is the eighth, and is of the seven, and goeth into perdition." (Rev. 17:11)

<21> As it is described in chapter 20, "the dragon" will be taken and locked up for a thousand years (a long period of time) after the Kingdom of God comes to the earth. However, after this time, "he must be loosed a little season" (Rev. 20:3), or the dragon would come back, but this period would be very short.

<22> This last coming after one thousand years (a long time after the Kingdom comes) would be the eighth time of "the beast that was, and is not, even he is the eighth." He is the same as the one who was destroyed as the seventh king, "and is of the seven." But it will eventually be destroyed, "and when the thousand years are expired, Satan shall be loosed…" (Rev. 20:7) but after a short time it will be destroyed, "…was cast into the lake of fire … and shall be tormented day and night for ever and ever."

<23> So the phrase, "he is the eighth," refers to this last time of the fall of man and the last lesson humans will receive in order to understand the nature of the devil and the beasts, and to become rid of their mark (greed), and go to Pure Consciousness, where the Father is.

"And the ten horns which thou sawest are ten kings, which have received no kingdom as yet; but receive power as kings one hour with the beast." (Rev. 17:12)

<24> It is these ten horns that are the by-products of the desires toward the attraction of Maya that have never gained any kingdom. It is always the beast itself, or the desire toward the attraction of Maya, which is the king. They are the by-products of that king. It is true that the desire and attraction of Maya are what people try to overcome, but there will be a very short period of time when people will still be under the influence of these by-products. They will rule humanity with anger, vanity, and fear even after they overcome the false desires. Still these psychological problems will remain in humanity, but they will not last long. They will be lost very soon after the Kingdom Of Heaven comes.

"These have one mind, and shall give their power and strength unto the beast." (Rev. 17:13)

<25> These by-products of the beast will try to bring the beast back and to raise the desires of humanity.

"These shall make war with the Lamb, and the Lamb shall overcome them: for he is Lord of lords, and King of kings: and they that are with him are called, and chosen, and faithful." (Rev. 17:14)

<26> The Lamb will fight with these devils and overcome them by his spiritual powers, and by the faithful Elects.

"And he saith unto me, The waters which thou sawest, where the whore sitteth, are peoples, and multitudes, and nations, and tongues." (Rev. 17:15)

<27> As was mentioned earlier, water is related to the consciousness of the human. So it is through the consciousness of man that

this whore or this lower nature, woman, will persuade humanity to do whatever she wants. It is in all the people, in all the multitudes, in all the nations, and all of the time. All of humanity is defiled by these desires, attachments, fears and all the things that are related to the lower nature in their consciousnesses through this woman ("waters ... where the whore sitteth").

"And the ten horns which thou sawest upon the beast, these shall hate the whore, and shall make her desolate and naked, and shall eat her flesh, and burn her with fire." (Rev. 17:16)

"For God hath put in their hearts to fulfil his will, and to agree, and give their kingdom unto the beast, until the words of God shall be fulfilled." (Rev. 17:17)

<28> Anger, fear, vanity, unhappiness, cowardice, and all these things that are the by-products of pursuing Maya, will come to the people. They will become completely lost and their desires will be unfulfilled more and more. These things will awaken the people to the realization that, "We are following all these things because we are attached and attracted to the external world. Whatever we are following is just like chasing the wind. This Maya is never going to be captured. We are never going to be able to obtain satisfaction through this Maya." <29> And these horns, which will bring frustration to humanity, will destroy the woman or the lower nature, not by the desires of the people being fulfilled, but by desires not being fulfilled or a new desire arising after any previous desire is fulfilled. Eventually humanity will reach the point of understanding that life is not just for following the heedless desires.

<30> They will find out that it is not possible to fulfill all the desires. And when the desires are not fulfilled, anger, vanity, fear and attachment will come to them, and they will feel miserable and depressed. The by-products of the desires will cause them to realize that gaining name and fame is not the goal of life. **The Goal Of The Life Is To Be(come) Divine.** So these ten horns will eat the flesh of the woman and burn her with fire, and they will completely destroy this part of the consciousness of the human. That is what God planned for and put in their hearts, to fulfill His Will.

<31> That is why the tribulation will come to the people. The tribulation will be good for them, because after they go through it, they will reach the point of understanding that, "This is not the goal of life. I am following my own egoistical ways. I am trying to do everything for my little 'I,' and I am always thinking about myself. But I am not happy." And they will come to realize that this is not the way. <32> **The way is to be God-conscious instead of self-conscious!**

<33> These by-products of Maya will destroy Maya itself, by itself. That is why again we see that there is no devil. <34> Even the tribulation and becoming lost is a process for reaching a point of understanding that there is more to life than just pursuing the external world and its attractions.

"And the woman which thou sawest is that great city, which reigneth over the kings of the earth." (Rev. 17:18)

<35> This lower nature, or the attraction of Maya, or the pursuance for fame and name, is what rules the world and all of humanity. All the humans will have these things, even the greatest Masters. They will have to overcome this attraction and the desires of the lower nature to reach their higher nature. <36> And that is why the woman "reigneth over the kings of the earth." This lower nature has caused the kings to be so wrathful and egoistical. They think it is their might or power that has caused them to become kings, instead of realizing that it was the might and power of God that allowed them to become kings.

REVELATION OF THE REVELATION
Tablet Twenty-Nine

Chapter 18

"And after these things I saw another angel come down from heaven, having great power; and the earth was lightened with his glory." (Rev. 18:1)

"And he cried mightily with a strong voice, saying, Babylon the great is fallen, is fallen, and is become the habitation of devils, and the hold of every foul spirit, and a cage of every unclean and hateful bird." (Rev. 18:2)

"For all nations have drunk of the wine of the wrath of her fornication, and the kings of the earth have committed fornication with her, and the merchants of the earth are waxed rich through the abundance of her delicacies." (Rev. 18:3)

"And I heard another voice from heaven, saying, Come out of her, my people, that ye be not partakers of her sins, and that ye receive not of her plagues." (Rev. 18:4)

<1> This time after the seventh Angel, this egoistical pursuance of the lower nature will be destroyed. The people will realize through the tribulation that egoistical pursuance ends up nowhere but to more ignorance, bondage, and unhappiness. That is why this Angel comes, and it is the time when Babylon (or the lower nature or the desire to have name, fame, and power) through the by-products of desire (ten horns) will fall. <2> It will be almost impossible through that tribulation to reach anywhere. Everyone will be so lost and unhappy that no one would even **want** name and fame. Name and fame will not mean anything to great people any longer.

<3> "All the nations have drunk of the wine of the wrath of her fornication," means that so many nations have pursued name and fame. That is why nations are considered to be great, because they are pursuing power, name, and fame. They think they are greater, because they have made the greater name or greater fame. <4> "And the kings of the earth have committed fornication with her." These kings also became kings to make name and fame for themselves instead of to establish justice. They built great cities, buildings, and castles, and made names for themselves.

<5> "And the merchants of the earth are waxed rich." The merchants were "waxed rich" through their greed. They became very rich and thought that it was the right way to live, but it is really from their lower natures. And that is why the voice comes from heaven and says, "Come out of her, my people." It means to come out of your lower natures and come to your higher natures.

<6> "That ye be not partakers of her sins" means, that you will not be one of those who will go to outer darkness. "That ye receive not of her plagues" means, that you will come to your higher natures and not be affected by the tribulations that will fall on those who are in their lower natures and are pursuing the Maya, causing them to be bound more and more in the ocean of illusion. Those who go out of their lower natures will be saved. His people will be saved.

"For her sins have reached unto heaven, and God hath remembered her iniquities." (Rev. 18:5)

<7> That is the time for her to be completely destroyed. God knows how much iniquity has been done because of the attraction of Maya and the lust for Babylon The Great.

"Reward her even as she rewarded you, and double unto her double according to her works: in the cup which she hath filled fill to her double." (Rev. 18:6)

<8> Those who stay in the world (earth), because of their attachments and engagement to it, cannot save themselves from these tribulations and will suffer as the changes come, even double.

"How much she hath glorified herself, and lived deliciously, so much torment and sorrow give her: for she saith in her heart, I sit a queen, and am no widow, and shall see no sorrow." (Rev. 18:7)

<9> And that is the false ego. It is the lower nature of man that glorifies himself instead of following the Father, the Creator of this manifested universe. Then he might love God (universe) and so reach the higher self. And he thinks that he will never fall off, and that the throne he is sitting on is glorifying him.

"Therefore shall her plagues come in one day, death, and mourning, and famine; and she shall be utterly burned with fire: for strong is the Lord God who judgeth her." (Rev. 18:8)

<10> All the things of this world which they thought will save them will become obsolete.

"And the kings of the earth, who have committed fornication and lived deliciously with her, shall bewail her, and lament for her, when they shall see the smoke of her burning," (Rev. 18:9)

<11> When the tools that these kings or the people who had been following their own egoistical ways are burned, they will not be able to follow their false egos any more, and "they shall bewail her, and lament for her."

"Standing afar off for the fear of her torment, saying, Alas, alas that great city Babylon, that mighty city! for in one hour is thy judgment come." (Rev. 18:10)

<12> People will be completely astonished at how the egoistical pursuance and pagan doctrines are suddenly destroyed.

"And the merchants of the earth shall weep and mourn over her; for no man buyeth their merchandise anymore:" (Rev. 18:11)

"The merchandise of gold, and silver, and precious stones, and of pearls, and fine linen, and purple, and silk, and scarlet, and all thyine wood, and all manner vessels of ivory, and all manner vessels of most precious wood, and of brass, and iron, and marble," (Rev. 18:12)

"And cinnamon, and odours, and ointments, and frankincense, and wine, and oil, and fine flour, and wheat, and beasts, and sheep, and horses, and chariots, and slaves, and souls of men." (Rev. 18:13)

"And the fruits that thy soul lusted after are departed from thee, and all things which were dainty and goodly are departed from thee, and thou shalt find them no more at all." (Rev. 18:14)

<13> The people will understand that the Mayaistic and egoistic pursuance of having all these things are just attractions of Maya. They will realize that they will be provided for and they have to use the rest of life in pursuing higher consciousness and eventually Pure Consciousness – to be(come) Divine, the highest goal of the life.

"The merchants of these things, which were made rich by her, shall stand afar off for the fear of her torment, weeping and wailing," (Rev. 18:15)

"And saying, Alas, alas that great city, that was clothed in fine linen, and purple, and scarlet, and decked with gold, and precious stones, and pearls!" (Rev. 18:16)

"For in one hour so great riches is come to nought. And every shipmaster, and all the company in ships, and sailors, and as many as trade by sea, stood afar off," (Rev. 18:17)

"And cried when they saw the smoke of her burning, saying, What city is like unto this great city!" (Rev. 18:18)

"And they cast dust on their heads, and cried, weeping and wailing, saying, Alas, alas that great city, wherein were made rich all that had ships in the sea by reason of her costliness! for in one hour is she made desolate." (Rev. 18:19)

<14> Everything will fall apart in a short period of time.

"Rejoice over her, thou heaven and ye holy apostles and prophets; for God hath avenged you on her." (Rev. 18:20)

"And a mighty angel took up a stone like a great millstone, and cast it into the sea, saying, Thus with violence shall that great city Babylon be thrown down, and shall be found no more at all." (Rev. 18:21)

<15> Egoistical pursuance will fall, and the world will be with the Saints, Apostles, and Prophets.

"And the voice of harpers, and musicians, and of pipers, and trumpeters, shall be heard no more at all in thee; and no craftsman, of whatsoever craft he be, shall be found any more in thee; and the sound of a millstone shall be heard no more at all in thee;" (Rev. 18:22)

<16> No egoistical things will be done any longer. Everything will be directed toward spiritual progress in that blessed world. The musicians, craftsmen, and all others will work in bringing happiness and bliss for all, but not for her (Babylon).

"And the light of a candle shall shine no more at all in thee; and the voice of the bridegroom and of the bride shall be heard no more at all in thee: for thy merchants were the great men of the earth; for by thy sorceries were all nations deceived." (Rev. 18:23)

<17> It is the egoistical pursuance that has caused all the sorceries and deceitfulness of the nations. The sorceries are all the ways to make people believe that material gain is all there is.

"And in her was found the blood of prophets, and of saints, and of all that were slain upon the earth." (Rev. 18:24)

<18> The people killed each other because of their selfish desires, being in their lower natures, and not understanding those who were in their higher natures (the Prophets).

Tablet Thirty

Chapter 19

"And after these things I heard a great voice of much people in heaven, saying, Alleluia; Salvation, and glory, and honour, and power, unto the Lord our God:" (Rev. 19:1)

<1> When it becomes apparent that the pursuance of Maya leads to no true gain but to complete destruction, then salvation comes and glory, honor, and power will be "unto the Lord our God." Alleluia will be given to Him. At this time, many will be saved and reach higher consciousness (heaven). Then man will praise the Lord (ALLELU = praise be to; YAH = God).

"For true and righteous are his judgments: for he hath judged the great whore, which did corrupt the earth with her fornication, and hath avenged the blood of his servants at her hand." (Rev. 19:2)

"And again they said, Alleluia. And her smoke rose up for ever and ever." (Rev. 19:3)

<2> Now many people will be in their higher natures. The spiritual forces will surpass the egoistical ones. This will make it possible to guide others to the higher consciousness easily.

"And the four and twenty elders and the four beasts fell down and worshipped God that sat on the throne, saying, Amen; Alleluia." (Rev. 19:4)

<3> All the universe will worship God because of His Judgment and the beautiful Plan He has made for humanity to reach this point.

"And a voice came out of the throne, saying, Praise our God, all ye his servants, and ye that fear him, both small and great." (Rev. 19:5)

<4> All should praise and worship God, the One, the Praiseworthy, the Adorable One.

REVELATION OF THE REVELATION   Tablet 30

"And I heard as it were the voice of a great multitude, and as the voice of many waters, and as the voice of mighty thunderings, saying, Alleluia: for the Lord God omnipotent reigneth." (Rev. 19:6)

<5> Praise to God has been given by the people in their higher natures.

"Let us be glad and rejoice, and give honour to him: for the marriage of the Lamb is come, and his wife hath made herself ready." (Rev. 19:7)

"And to her was granted that she should be arrayed in fine linen, clean and white: for the fine linen is the righteousness of saints." (Rev. 19:8)

"And he saith unto me, Write, Blessed are they which are called unto the marriage supper of the Lamb. And he saith unto me, These are the true sayings of God." (Rev. 19:9)

<6> It is now the time that the Lamb (the spirit of the truth, or the one who has reached higher consciousness, or the Christ, or the יהשוה who overcame the lower nature and was slain, and then knew the reality behind this universe) marries with his wife, which is the real way and the truth of higher consciousness. And, <7> "Blessed are they which are called unto the marriage supper of the Lamb." Blessed are those who understand this truth. They will be in higher consciousness and will be called to the supper of the Lamb (which means they will be in Pure Consciousness). And the truth that comes to the earth is **the** marriage ceremony of the Lamb, because that is what Christ, the spirit of truth, the Soul of the human, wants to see established on earth. When it comes, those who have been invited to it have overcome their lower natures and are in their higher natures. These will be blessed.

"And I fell at his feet to worship him. And he said unto me, See thou do it not: I am thy fellowservant, and of thy brethren that have the testimony of יהשוה: worship God: for the testimony of יהשוה is the spirit of prophecy." (Rev. 19:10)

<8> You should not surrender yourself to anything else but Him, the Formless, Nameless, and Invisible (God), and the Divine Path to Him (יהוה), which has come through His son (יהשוה), and "is the spirit of prophecy."

"And I saw heaven opened, and behold a white horse; and he that sat upon him was called Faithful and True, and in righteousness he doth judge and make war." (Rev. 19:11)

"His eyes were as a flame of fire, and on his head were many crowns; and he had a name written, that no man knew, but he himself." (Rev. 19:12)

"And he was clothed with a vesture dipped in blood: and his name is called The Word of God." (Rev. 19:13)

"And the armies which were in heaven followed him upon white horses, clothed in fine linen, white and clean." (Rev. 19:14)

"And out of his mouth goeth a sharp sword, that with it he should smite the nations: and he shall rule them with a rod of iron: and he treadeth the winepress of the fierceness and wrath of Almighty God." (Rev. 19:15)

"And he hath on his vesture and on his thigh a name written, KING OF KINGS, AND LORD OF LORDS." (Rev. 19:16)

<9> The Kingdom Of Heaven now will come and the one whose name is called The Word (יהוה/יהשוה) of God, will be prepared to establish it.

"And I saw an angel standing in the sun; and he cried with a loud voice, saying to all the fowls that fly in the midst of heaven, Come and gather yourselves together unto the supper of the great God;" (Rev. 19:17)

"That ye may eat the flesh of kings, and the flesh of captains, and the flesh of mighty men, and the flesh of horses, and of them that sit on them, and the flesh of all men, both free and bond, both small and great." (Rev. 19:18)

<10> These people will fail and they will be smote down by this truth. They will be cast out to the darkness, and their flesh will be the feast of the fowls and the beasts.

"And I saw the beast, and the kings of the earth, and their armies, gathered together to make war against him that sat on the horse, and against his army." (Rev. 19:19)

<11> The fight will start between those who follow the beast, the desires, and the Maya, and the truth which is like a two-edged sword which has come from the mouth of the one that sits on the white horse.

"And the beast was taken, and with him the false prophet that wrought miracles before him, with which he deceived them that had received the mark of the beast, and them that worshipped his image. These both were cast alive into a lake of fire burning with brimstone." (Rev. 19:20)

<12> The truth will be revealed even to the kings and those who have not understood it. "The beast will be taken away," so the tools that make the people fall into Maya will be taken away from them. They will be burned, and the people will no longer have those tools, the things that attract humanity to the Mayaistic and egoistic pursuance. <13> Through tribulation and the spiritual powers of the Saints, this will happen. The beast (desires and attachments) will be taken away from humanity by the Elects.

"And the remnant were slain with the sword of him that sat upon the horse, which sword proceeded out of his mouth: and all the fowls were filled with their flesh." (Rev. 19:21)

<14> The remaining will be slain. The lower nature of the human which remains will be slain by the truth that comes through the mouth of the Lamb, and they will realize and reach higher consciousness. <15> "Which sword proceeded out of his mouth: and all the fowls were filled with their flesh." <16> So this lower nature will be killed by the sword of his mouth (truth).

Tablet Thirty-One

Chapter 20

"And I saw an angel come down from heaven, having the key of the bottomless pit and a great chain in his hand." (Rev. 20:1)

"And he laid hold on the dragon, that old serpent, which is the Devil, and Satan, and bound him a thousand years," (Rev. 20:2)

<1> When the false desires, attachments, and greed have been destroyed by the truth which is revealed to the people, the dragon or the attraction of Maya cannot stay in this world any longer because people will not be affected by his false temptations. They will know the reality and pursue the spiritual life. They will overcome Maya and the power of the tama guna over their Souls. <2> That is why he will be cast into the bottomless pit and the reality will be revealed, and it will stay with people for a long time ("a thousand years").

"And cast him into the bottomless pit, and shut him up, and set a seal upon him, that he should deceive the nations no more, till the thousand years should be fulfilled: and after that he must be loosed a little season." (Rev. 20:3)

<3> After one thousand years, again the people will lose the understanding of the reality of what has been revealed to them, and the serpent or this attraction of Maya, will catch their eyes. <4> They will lose their attraction to the great and the goal of the life, which is to be(come) Divine. They will pursue the worldly things as they are doing now, and they will be lost again. But it will be for a very short period of time.

"And I saw thrones, and they sat upon them, and judgment was given unto them: and

REVELATION OF THE REVELATION

I saw the souls of them that were beheaded for the witness of (יהושע), and for the word of God, and which had not worshipped the beast, neither his image, neither had received his mark upon their foreheads, or in their hands; and they lived and reigned with Christ a thousand years." (Rev. 20:4)

<5> The kingdom of the earth will become the Kingdom of God, and Christ and his Saints will reign over the world. The Paravipras will gain the leadership of humanity and guide them towards higher consciousness.

"But the rest of the dead lived not again until the thousand years were finished. This is the first resurrection." (Rev. 20:5)

"Blessed and holy is he that hath part in the first resurrection: on such the second death hath no power, but they shall be priests of God and of Christ, and shall reign with him a thousand years." (Rev. 20:6)

<6> These first people will all reach Pure Consciousness and will be with Christ. They will not die "the second death," because they are in Pure Consciousness. This is the first resurrection.

<7> In this period of time (a thousand years), those people who have overcome their lower natures will be reincarnated again and again. They will live and make the world prepared. They will bring peace and harmony to the universe and prepare the world for those who have been lost and are not going to be reincarnated for a long period of time – a thousand years ("the rest of the dead lived not again until the thousand years"). <8> After this period when they come back, everything will be prepared to help them progress as fast as possible to Pure Consciousness. This will be the second resurrection.

"And when the thousand years are expired, Satan shall be loosed out of his prison," (Rev. 20:7)

<9> After one thousand years, again the people will become lost, because those who did not reach Pure Consciousness the first time (first resurrection) will be incarnated again. These people are in their lower natures and will lose their way again.

"And shall go out to deceive the nations which are in the four quarters of the earth, Gog and Magog, to gather them together to battle: the number of whom is as the sand of the sea." (Rev. 20:8)

<10> Many of the unit consciousnesses who are in their lower natures will be incarnated or reincarnated at this time. <11> Also, new unit consciousnesses might be awakened for the first time from the unaware part of the universe. Because these people are in their lower natures, they will easily become lost.

"And they went up on the breadth of the earth, and compassed the camp of the saints about, and the beloved city: and fire came down from God out of heaven, and devoured them." (Rev. 20:9)

<12> Again they will be punished for their actions and purified by its fire.

Tablet Thirty-Two

"And the devil that deceived them was cast into the lake of fire and brimstone, where the beast and the false prophet are, and shall be tormented day and night for ever and ever." (Rev. 20:10)

"And I saw a great white throne, and him that sat on it, from whose face the earth and the heaven fled away; and there was found no place for them." (Rev. 20:11)

"And I saw the dead, small and great, stand before God; and the books were opened: and another book was opened, which is the book of life: and the dead were judged out of those things which were written in the books, according to their works." (Rev. 20:12)

"And the sea gave up the dead which were in it; and death and hell delivered up the dead which were in them: and they were judged every man according to their works." (Rev. 20:13)

"And death and hell were cast into the lake of fire. This is the second death." (Rev. 20:14)

"And whosoever was not found written in the book of life was cast into the lake of fire." (Rev. 20:15)

<1> Those who have reached their higher natures, in this generation, will be saved. This is the second resurrection. Those who have lagged behind will fall into ignorance (earth) with the next generation to come.

Chapter 21

"And I saw a new heaven and a new earth: for the first heaven and the first earth were passed away; and there was no more sea." (Rev. 21:1)

<2> John had a vision of heaven, or Pure Consciousness, or the city (New Jerusalem), or the world that will be given by God to those who have overcome their lower natures and obeyed Him. <3> They were beyond a turbulent consciousness, "there was no more sea." <4> They had reached the peace of God or Pure Consciousness.

"And I John saw the holy city, new Jerusalem, coming down from God out of heaven, prepared as a bride adorned for her husband." (Rev. 21:2)

<5> These people reach Pure Consciousness ("holy city").

"And I heard a great voice out of heaven saying, Behold, the tabernacle of God is with men, and he will dwell with them, and they shall be his people, and God himself shall be with them, and be their God." (Rev. 21:3)

<6> Those people will reach Pure Consciousness (tabernacle of God), where God is. <7> They will dwell with Him.

"And God shall wipe away all tears from their eyes; and there shall be no more death, neither sorrow, nor crying, neither shall there be any more pain: for the former things are passed away." (Rev. 21:4)

<8> These people have reached Pure Consciousness. Nothing of the sorrow and misery of the external world or material life will be found there. <9> They will be "neither hot nor cold."

"And he that sat upon the throne said, Behold, I make all things new. And he said unto me, Write: for these words are true and faithful." (Rev. 21:5)

<10> These are all true, and will come to pass.

"And he said unto me, It is done. I am Alpha and Omega, the beginning and the end. I will give unto him that is athirst of the fountain of the water of life freely." (Rev. 21:6)

<11> Those who reach Pure Consciousness will know that He was the first, He is, and He will be. He will give freely to those who are thirsty for reaching Pure Consciousness, which is "the fountain of the water of life." <12> Also, "I am Alpha and Omega," means "I am everything" (**OM NAM KEVALAM**: God is everything).

Tablet Thirty-Three

"He that overcometh shall inherit all things; and I will be his God, and he shall be my son." (Rev. 21:7)

<1> Those who reach Pure Consciousness will become the sons of God, as Christ reached Pure Consciousness and became the son of God. Those who overcome their lower natures will become sons of God as those who overcome their false egos will become His sons. <2> Also, they will inherit all things, because they are His sons and sons inherit all things from their Father (God). **<3> So the prerequisite of becoming His son is to overcome the lower nature.** No one will

overcome it for you, but it is you who should put forth effort. Your effort wins His Grace and you will be saved. <4> This is the final resurrection when The Plan will be completed.

"But the fearful, and unbelieving, and the abominable, and murderers, and whoremongers, and sorcerers, and idolaters, and all liars, shall have their part in the lake which burneth with fire and brimstone: which is the second death." (Rev. 21:8)

<5> But those people who do not follow the Holy life or have as their goal to be(come) Divine, will be cast out into the lake of fire (earth, manifested world) or ignorance. <6> All these things are related to the lower nature of man.

"And there came unto me one of the seven angels which had the seven vials full of the seven last plagues, and talked with me, saying, Come hither, I will shew thee the bride, the Lamb's wife." (Rev. 21:9)

<7> His Wife is Truth.

"And he carried me away in the spirit to a great and high mountain, and shewed me that great city, the holy Jerusalem, descending out of heaven from God," (Rev. 21:10)

"Having the glory of God: and her light was like unto a stone most precious, even like a jasper stone, clear as crystal;" (Rev. 21:11)

<8> It is a beautiful place to be. It is pure light.

"And had a wall great and high, and had twelve gates, and at the gates twelve angels, and names written thereon, which are the names of the twelve tribes of the children of Israel:" (Rev. 21:12)

<9> John is symbolically describing what this city (Pure Consciousness) is.

"On the east three gates; on the north three gates; on the south three gates; and on the west three gates." (Rev. 21:13)

"And the wall of the city had twelve foundations, and in them the names of the twelve apostles of the Lamb." (Rev. 21:14)

"And he that talked with me had a golden reed to measure the city, and the gates thereof, and the wall thereof." (Rev. 21:15)

<10> Only the person who reaches Pure Consciousness understands how great and infinite the realities behind this universe are.

"And the city lieth foursquare, and the length is as large as the breadth: and he measured the city with the reed, twelve thousand furlongs. The length and the breadth and the height of it are equal." (Rev. 21:16)

"And he measured the wall thereof, an hundred and forty and four cubits, according to the measure of a man, that is, of the angel." (Rev. 21:17)

"And the building of the wall of it was of jasper: and the city was pure gold, like unto clear glass." (Rev. 21:18)

"And the foundations of the wall of the city were garnished with all manner of precious stones. The first foundation was jasper; the second, sapphire; the third, a chalcedony; the fourth an emerald;" (Rev. 21:19)

"The fifth, sardonyx; the sixth, sardius; the seventh, chrysolyte; the eighth, beryl; the ninth, a topaz; the tenth, a chrysoprasus; the eleventh, a jacinth; the twelfth, an amethyst." (Rev. 21:20)

"And the twelve gates were twelve pearls; every several gate was of one pearl: and the street of the city was pure gold, as it were transparent glass." (Rev. 21:21)

"And I saw no temple therein: for the Lord God Almighty and the Lamb are the temple of it." (Rev. 21:22)

<11> All these things symbolize the beauty of that state of Pure Consciousness, and/or His Kingdom.

"And the city had no need of the sun, neither of the moon, to shine in it: for the glory of God did lighten it, and the Lamb is the light thereof." (Rev. 21:23)

"And the nations of them which are saved shall walk in the light of it: and the kings of the earth do bring their glory and honour unto it." (Rev. 21:24)

<12> Those leaders who have followed His Will (Paravipras) will also be there <13> and will be glorified, "the kings of the earth do bring their glory and honour unto it."

"And the gates of it shall not be shut at all by day: for there shall be no night there." (Rev. 21:25)

"And they shall bring the glory and honour of the nations into it." (Rev. 21:26)

"And there shall in no wise enter into it any thing that defileth, neither whatsoever worketh abomination, or maketh a lie: but they which are written in the Lamb's book of life." (Rev. 21:27)

<14> Only those who are in the book of the Lamb (those who overcame and reached Pure Consciousness) can enter this heaven, <15> or this place that is symbolically described in such a beautiful way. <16> It is pure light, Pure Consciousness, all embracing, infinite beauty, infinite understanding, and all the beautiful things that the imagination can grasp.

Tablet Thirty-Four

Chapter 22

"And he shewed me a pure river of water of life, clear as crystal, proceeding out of the throne of God and of the Lamb." (Rev. 22:1)

<1> It is the stream of prana or His Grace which proceeds from the nucleus of the universe into the universe and sustains and guides it.

"In the midst of the street of it, and on either side of the river, was there the tree of life, which bare twelve manner of fruits, and yielded her fruit every month: and the leaves of the tree were for the healing of the nations." (Rev. 22:2)

<2> Prana is of many kinds, "twelve manner of fruits," and is the healing power.

"And there shall be no more curse: but the throne of God and of the Lamb shall be in it; and his servants shall serve him:" (Rev. 22:3)

<3> He who knows that prana (The Holy Ghost) is beyond the curse, and knows God and His Sons, is His Servant.

"And they shall see his face; and his name shall be in their foreheads." (Rev. 22:4)

<4> They shall see Him everywhere and bear His Light. <5> They will know His Sacred Name.

"And there shall be no night there; and they need no candle, neither light of the sun; for the Lord God giveth them light: and they shall reign for ever and ever." (Rev. 22:5)

<6> They would never fall into ignorance (night), and the light of the truth will surpass any other smaller lights. <7> They do not have to ideate on following the path because they are the path, the way, and the truth themselves, "for the Lord God giveth them light."

"And he said unto me, These sayings are faithful and true: and the Lord God of the holy prophets sent his angel to shew unto his servants the things which must shortly be done." (Rev. 22:6)

<8> These are all true and will come to pass.

"Behold, I come quickly: blessed is he that keepeth the sayings of the prophecy of this book." (Rev. 22:7)

REVELATION OF THE REVELATION

"And I John saw these things, and heard them. And when I had heard and seen, I fell down to worship before the feet of the angel which shewed me these things." (Rev. 22:8)

<9> Again John is mistakenly worshipping the Angel instead of God, the Formless, Invisible, Nameless, and Eternal.

"Then saith he unto me, See thou do it not: for I am thy fellowservant, and of thy brethren the prophets, and of them which keep the sayings of this book: worship God." (Rev. 22:9)

<10> The Angel says that he is a servant of humanity. He is John's brethren, so John and he are in the same level of being. The Prophets are the same as Angels (they are in Pure Consciousness), "of them which keep the sayings of this book." <11> Those people who become pure will reach higher consciousness and eventually Pure Consciousness. They will become Angels. Do not worship Angels, Prophets, Gurus, etc., but only "worship God." <12> That is why we should only surrender to Him, the words revealed to us through His Prophets (which are His Words), and His **Greatest Sign**, which clarifies the confusion between all (Scriptures).

"And he saith unto me, Seal not the sayings of the prophecy of this book: for the time is at hand." (Rev. 22:10)

<13> "The time is at hand" means that it is time for this revelation to be revealed to humanity because people were becoming anxious about the coming of Christ. God sent His complete Plan in a symbolic language to humanity. He revealed everything that was going to happen to humanity beforehand. <14> So when the true meaning of this revelation is revealed by the seventh Angel, they would know that He is, He was, and He will be. He is guiding His Universe toward the goal.

"He that is unjust, let him be unjust still: and he which is filthy, let him be filthy still: and he that is righteous, let him be righteous still: and he that is holy, let him be holy still," (Rev. 22:11)

<15> These all are necessary for guiding the human toward his goal, because if there are not the unjust how can we appreciate the just? These things should have happened throughout history to make people appreciate when the Kingdom Of Heaven comes. <16> Also all will be judged by God. <17> So perfect yourself and leave the judgment unto Him.

"And, behold, I come quickly; and my reward is with me, to give every man according as his work shall be." (Rev. 22:12)

<18> The truth will come quickly. It is that "you reap what you sow."

"I am Alpha and Omega, the beginning and the end, the first and the last." (Rev. 22:13)

<19> He was, He is, and He will be. Also it means, He is everything.

"Blessed are they that do his commandments, that they may have right to the tree of life, and may enter in through the gates into the city." (Rev. 22:14)

<20> Those who do His Commandments will have the right to the tree of life, which is to progress in the spiritual journey and "may enter in through the gates into the city." Eventually they may enter the city the New Jerusalem and reach Pure Consciousness.

"For without are dogs, and sorcerers, and whoremongers, and murderers, and idolaters, and whosoever loveth and maketh a lie." (Rev. 22:15)

<21> Only in the state of Pure Consciousness is there peace and purity.

"I יהושע have sent mine angel to testify unto you these things in the churches. I am the root and the offspring of David, and the bright and morning star." (Rev. 22:16)

<22> It is Christ who, through his Angels, has revealed these truths to the churches. He is the source of the spiritual kingly dominance and the revealer of the truth, "morning star."

"And the Spirit and the bride say, Come. And let him that heareth say, Come. And let

REVELATION OF THE REVELATION   *Tablet 34*

him that is athirst come. And whosoever will, let him take the water of life freely." (Rev. 22:17)

<23> This is The Plan, so come and help in this great endeavor, that all may partake from "the water of life freely."

"For I testify unto every man that heareth the words of the prophecy of this book, If any man shall add unto these things, God shall add unto him the plagues that are written in this book:" (Rev. 22:18)

<24> As we can see, the Scriptures have always had some verses added to them. John was afraid that people would add something to his prophecy, so he cursed whoever might have done this.

"And if any man shall take away from the words of the book of this prophecy, God shall take away his part out of the book of life, and out of the holy city, and from the things which are written in this book." (Rev. 22:19)

<25> In the past people would change the Scriptures to suit their own egoistic positions. Therefore, John was afraid someone would take some verses out of the book, and shorten the meaning of it. Then no one could understand it.

"He which testifieth these things saith, Surely I come quickly. Amen. Even so, come, Lord יהוה." (Rev. 22:20)

<26> These will surely happen.

"The grace of our Lord (יהושע) be with you all. Amen." (Rev. 22:21)

<27> The Grace of (יהושע) be with you all. Amen (ॐ).

Every word of God has more than seven meanings.‡

---

‡   (according to seven levels of human consciousness – chakras – and there are many levels in each level).

THE ESSENCE
"ETERNAL DIVINE PATH"

The book, <u>The Essence</u>, presents the essence of Maitreya's teachings, in a very concentrated and compressed manner.

THE ESSENCE
"ETERNAL DIVINE PATH"

Tablet One

<1> God is everlasting, complete, without beginning or end. <2> He is one and indivisible. <3> He is the source of all things. <4> All things are made from Him.

<5> God is the infinite consciousness. The creative forces of this infinite consciousness are three (three gunas).

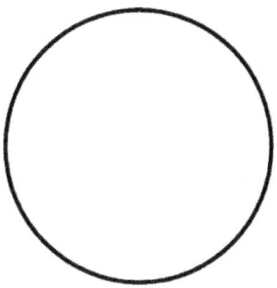

<6> The universe consists of consciousness and the three creative forces (three gunas). <7> The three creative forces are the sentient force (satva guna), the mutative force (raja guna), and the static or crudifying force (tama guna).

<8> The sentient force, in the operative state, is that part in the universe which creates the feeling of "know"-ness or "I know" (awareness). <9> The mutative force, in the operative state, is that part in the universe which creates the feeling of "doer"-ness or "I do" (action). <10> The static (crudifying) force, in the operative state, is that part in the universe which creates the feeling of remembrance, or "I have done" (memory). Also, the static force (tama guna) in its operative power, creates the fine ethereal factors in the first stage of release of its operative power. Ethereal factor is the storage place for events which happen in the universe – Universal Memory, Akashic Records (akasha means "ether").

<11> As the crudifying power of the tama guna continually crudifies the consciousness in the universe, the other elements, namely cruder ethereal factor, aerial factor, luminous (heat, light, fire, or the first visible factor in the universe), liquid factor, and solid factor, will evolve.

<12> The reason for creation of different factors in different stages is because of the presence of different proportions of each creative force. <13> In the ethereal state, there is more sentient (satva) force, <14> and in the solid factor more static (tama) force. <15> Or in other words, the crudifying (centripetal) force has a greater grip in the solid factor and a lesser one in the ethereal factor.

<16> There is not a clear-cut way to separate the three gunas from each other as three distinct forces, because of their transformability to each other and their ability to mix and create things in different stages (different factors from fine ether to the most solid).

<17> Also these forces (three gunas) cannot be separated from the consciousness. <18> Consciousness and the three gunas are the part and parcel of one entity, and they are inseparable. The three gunas comprise the creative force of the consciousness.

<19> In brief we can say:

Without tama guna there would have been no manifestation and no memory.

THE ESSENCE *Tablet 2*

<20> Without raja guna there would have been no vibration and no movement or action (energy).

<21> Without satva guna there would have been no intelligence and no decision-making.

<22> Without consciousness there would have been no control (Logic).

<23> The circle above is the symbol for God as the infinite consciousness, being all, infinite and indivisible.

Tablet Two

<1> Before any expression of awareness, the universe was in a state of "Be"-ness, "Am"-ness or pure intuition (Nirvikalpa). <2> This state of "Be"-ness was an omnipotent state, capable of creating and being created, like a sleeping human, which has the potential to become awakened and is able to do things in the awake state.

<3> The universe was in this state because the three gunas were in a passive or balanced (symmetric) state ($\triangledown$) and had not come to their operative positions. They were in a latent state, or unreleased.

<4> In the figure above, the circle in the middle represents the universe, and the dark shadow in the background represents the inability of the human mind to comprehend infinity.

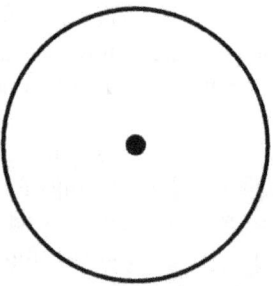

"In the beginning was the Word, and the Word was with God, and the Word was God.

The same was in the beginning with God.

All things were made by him; and without him was not anything made that was made." (John 1:1-3)

<5> An intuitive desire to become aware was created in the collective consciousness: Desire is the outgoing power of the raja guna (energy); when the same power (prana) is directed inwardly, it becomes imagination and will. <6> Through this outward direction of the raja guna (desire), the balance of the forces became disturbed and the operative powers of the three gunas became active (Prakrti).

<7> Because of the operative influence of

THE ESSENCE

the satva guna (the most sentient force) and with the presence of the tama guna, an awareness of "I know" or "I know that I am" appeared and spread in the universe. <8> The first part of the Ego was evolved.

<9> Because of the operative influence of the second guna (raja guna or mutative force) with the presence of the tama guna, the feeling of "I do" or "I am the doer also" was created and spread in the universe. <10> This brought the second part of the Ego into play.

<11> By the release of the operative power of the tama guna (static, binding or crudifying force), the fine ethereal factor was evolved, and memory came into play. <12> So the third and last stage came into existence, and the third and last part of the Ego was completed. The sense of "I have done" (memory) was awakened and spread in the universe. <13> The feeling of "I" as a separate entity was concluded.

<14> The dot in the middle of the circle above symbolizes the first sign of awareness in the universe and the invocation of the three gunas into the operative stage as the three creative forces. <15> This first expression of awareness was a vibration, which is sound. This sound vibration is "The Word" (ॐ), the creative force in the universe. <16> It has been with God and all things are made by Him.

<17> With the release of the operative powers of the three gunas, many different parts of the universe felt separated from the rest. <18> Also, the first unit consciousnesses were evolved (a unit consciousness is the expression of the Divine through the manifested universe, as an entity separate from the rest of the universe). With this, a great chaos was created in the universe, and great forces were released. The entire universe came to be in a violent state.

Tablet Three

"In him was life; and the life was the light of men.
And the light shineth in darkness; and the darkness comprehended it not." (John 1:4-5)

<1> The outgoing force of the Soul (prana) which is the life-force of the Soul, is the power of the spirit and is in the consciousness and the universe (God) which was with Him, "in him was life." <2> This prana, which is also the mutative force (raja guna), is responsible for all the activities in the universe. It is the life-force in the universe (the breath of life).

<3> But because it is a neutral force (tama guna is negative, and satva is positive), its presence is even harder to realize, and it assumes the polarity of tama (negative) when used from ignorance, and satva (positive) when used from knowledge. <4> In itself it is the passion and is a force without mind. So when used in this regard the action is from passion. It is pure action.

<5> When it is not controlled and is used freely and outwardly toward fulfillment of worldly desires (passions), or used from ignorance, it becomes the very Maya (illusion) itself. <6> But when this force is realized, controlled, and directed inwardly, it becomes a light (spiritual realization, imagination, and willpower) and can be directed toward higher thoughts. <7> Then it will spiritualize the mind, and the higher levels of the mind (Buddhi) will develop.

<8> This force (prana, the life-force) was in the universe (God) and also is present in each unit consciousness (man), and when it is directed toward higher consciousness (satva guna, light) it becomes the light of the consciousness, "and the life was the light of men." <9> But because of the influence of the tama guna (darkness), although this light is always within them, they cannot comprehend it, "and the light shineth in darkness, and the darkness comprehended it not."

THE ESSENCE — Tablet 4

Tablet Four

"In the beginning God created the heaven and the earth." (Genesis 1:1)

<1> Because of the influence of the tama guna and creation of "I" as a separate entity (unit consciousness, ego), an illusion of being separate from the rest of the universe (God) was created in each unit being. <2> With this illusion comes the unhappiness, fear, and all the evil things related to being self-centered.

<3> **Therefore, the feeling of being separated from the rest of the universe (self-centeredness) is the cause of unhappiness.**

<4> Father (God) called this state of the illusive feeling of separation "hell" (earth). The state of Pure Consciousness (✤), which He was in, He called "heaven." It is where there is no illusion of being an entity separate from the rest (God).

<5> So "the heaven and the earth [hell]" were created.

<6> The sign above represents Pure Consciousness (✤) and also is called **Haree Om Shrii Hung**, which means, "The Goal of the Life is to Be(come) Divine (Pure Consciousness)." <7> This sign consists of four parts. The (●) in the middle is a representation of the beginning of the release of the operative powers of the three gunas (Prakrti) or creative forces ("The Word"). <8> The I-Ching sign (☯) symbolizes the dual nature of all things in the universe as positive and negative.

<9> The other parts in the sign of **Haree Om Shrii Hung (HOSH)** are the Expanding Lotus (✤) and the sign (卐), which is called the "Lotustica." <10> The Expanding Lotus is the loving side and all the qualities of pure spirit, such as love, compassion, forgiveness, etc., of God, <11> and the Lotustica is the part which is used by God to guide humans toward Pure Consciousness. It is the force which is used to destroy the old and obsolete orders in the path of progress of the human. Also it is the part which, by allowing a unit consciousness to go away from Him (detachment), gives him the understanding that the illusion of separation from Him is equal with suffering and unhappiness.

<12> Therefore, in general, the sign **Haree Om Shrii Hung** means that through the spiritual powers (☯), God controls the operative powers of the three gunas (●) – The Word (ॐ). <13> The Expanding Lotus shows that He is all-pervasive and loving. The Lotustica demonstrates His Power of punishment and destruction in order to guide unit consciousnesses to realize the true goal of the life – to be(come) Divine.

"And the earth was without form, and void;..." (Genesis 1:2a)

<14> The earth (hell) does not have a form nor is it a place, but it is a state of consciousness. It is the darkness of the Soul when it is lost, confused and feels completely separate from the rest of the universe.

<15> Even the feeling of being a part of a small portion of the universe (belongingness, or being a part of a group, nation, organization,

THE ESSENCE — Tablet 5

etc.) gives some happiness to the Soul.

<16> However, true joy comes when the Soul feels and knows it is a part of the whole universe, and the universe is a part of it.

Tablet Five

"…And darkness was upon the face of the deep…" (Genesis 1:2b)

<1> God (Father) controls the Universal Mind (▽), which consists of the three gunas. <2> The satva guna (sentient force) in the universe is the intelligent or decision-making part of the Universal Mind (Mahatattva); the raja guna (mutative force) in the universe creates the recognizing part of the Universal Mind (Ahamtattva); the tama guna (static force) in the universe is the visualizing or screen of the Universal Mind (Chitta) and also the memory (akasha).

<3> Through this visualizing part of the Universal Mind, God can see His Universe. He can identify each part and parcel of it with the recognizing part, and then make the proper decision about it with the intelligent or decision-making part. <4> Then the action will be carried out through the mutative force in the universe.

<5> The triangle downward (▽) represents the Universal Mind created by the three gunas, and (✹) is the representation of the sign **Haree Om Shrii Hung (HOSH)** or God.

<6> Through the Universal Mind (▽), God (Father) beheld His Universe and saw how many lost parts were in His Body (Purusa), or how many parts were not awakened but still under the complete control of the tama guna. In short, He found it to be in a state of chaos, "and darkness was upon the face of the deep." <7> He created a great compassion for these lost souls and greatly desired to help them out of the hell and bring them to Pure Consciousness (heaven).

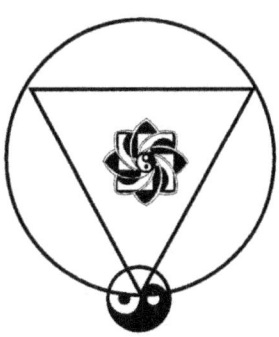

"…And the Spirit of God moved upon the face of the waters." (Genesis 1:2c)

<8> **Water is a symbol for manifested consciousness (ether).** <9> So God (Father), through His Universal Mind ("Spirit of God"), moved upon the consciousnesses ("waters")

THE ESSENCE

of the universe and tried to bring the unit beings (☯) under His Control, in order to guide them to Pure Consciousness.

<10> With the help of the Universal Mind (Spirit of God, The Holy Ghost), He was able to guide the unit minds (●) (the Divine manifested as an illusive mind or consciousness as a separate unit) to reach the goal (Pure Consciousness, to become Divine).

<11> These unit consciousnesses could be seen on the screen of the universe, identified by the recognizing part of the Universal Mind, and their situation was determined and decisions were made by the intelligent (decision-making) part as to how to best help these unit consciousnesses reach Pure Consciousness (卍).

<12> The I-Ching sign (☯) represents a unit consciousness. There is a dot (●) in the middle of the I-Ching which represents the unit creative force (mind) of each unit consciousness. <13> Each unit consciousness now is under the control of the Father through the Universal Mind (▽) (Spirit of God).

<14> It should be noted that the I-Ching sign is shown in a horizontal position. <15> The horizontal line indicates passivity (still under the influence of the tama guna) or not being awakened. <16> This horizontal symbol can be compared to a person lying down – it is a pose of passivity, and most probably he will fall asleep.

Tablet Six

"And God said, Let there be light:…" (Genesis 1:3a)

<1> God started guiding the lost unit consciousnesses toward Pure Consciousness, and He projected His Light into the lost universe, "Let there be light," and The Word (ॐ) became flesh (יהוה/יהושוע)!

<2> Through God's Guidance, this unit consciousness (flesh) started to meditate on his consciousness and little by little he became aware of the influence of the power of the three gunas over his Soul (unit consciousness). <3> Because of their influences, his ego had an illusive feeling of being separated from the rest of the universe, and this would bring a deep awareness of loneliness, unhappiness, and depression to him.

<4> He started to meditate on his moods and how the forces of the universe influenced him. He realized that he went from a state of feeling completely separate from the rest of the universe to a state of feeling to be a part of it. <5> When he was separated completely from the rest, a feeling of unhappiness prevailed, but when he felt to be a part of the universe, even to just a small part (belongingness), a happiness was created in him.

<6> Through these ups and downs he started to become more and more aware of these influences over himself. Through a great struggle he started to understand them. <7> He became familiar with the influences of the three gunas. He understood the differences between them. <8> He realized that when the tama guna prevailed, a great feeling of separation and unhappiness came to him. When the satva guna was dominant, that crude feeling lessened and it was replaced by happiness and release.

<9> With meditating on the tama guna and understanding how it works, little by little he started to master this force and its influences. Eventually he came to a higher consciousness and started to realize his Soul on a deeper level.

Tablet Seven

<1> As he started to reach a higher consciousness, he became a more sentient (satvic) being. Not only did his happiness, feeling of belonging to the universe and surroundings, increase, but also he started to realize more about himself and the forces which were within.

<2> He realized the spiritual power (raja guna, prana), the intelligence (satva guna), and the crudifying force (tama guna) within, and through meditating on them, he realized them on an even deeper level.

<3> He also realized the dual nature of his being as "positive and negative" (). **<4> These two polarities can be found universally in all of nature.**

<5> Also because God has both polarities as positive and negative, they balance each other and He becomes neutral. <6> However, God in Its purest form – beyond the influence of the creative forces (gunas) – is Pure Consciousness. In this state He just "IS" – Formless, Nameless, Invisible, and Eternal, neither male nor female.

<7> However, this unit consciousness had not yet mastered the power of the tama guna completely. So still there were times when he would feel its influence and would go from happiness to helplessness, up and down.

<8> Through these struggles he also realized how his surrounding environment affected him. When there is a greater amount of the tama force (impure) present in the environment, the unhappiness, fear, and all bad propensities because of the tama guna (lower nature) increase. So he avoided such an environment and tried to keep himself away from such influences. <9> He realized how necessary a sentient (proper) environment is for spiritual progress.

<10> In this state he realized how many other unit consciousnesses around him were lost and needed help, and if he could aid others to reach higher consciousness, it would be possible to create a better environment.

<11> Therefore, he tried to help them. With this, he realized that even a greater happiness was created in him, because in the process of helping others (sacrifice, not being self-centered), he would forget about himself. <12> This resulted in negation of his ego and the flow of God's Spirit (Grace) through him.

<13> That is the key to happiness and joy, to forget the self for a greater task. It is to help others to reach higher consciousness and create an environment (✡) that allows all to reach the highest level of realization possible. So the feeling of

THE ESSENCE

self-centeredness is forgotten and the cause of unhappiness will vanish.

<14> The source of happiness is not to think about the self all the time but to forget it by sacrificing to help others to grow.

<15> So again, he started even a greater struggle in overcoming the egotism and self-centeredness (mastering the power of the tama guna). With this process, by gaining wisdom to do sacrifice (from knowledge but not from ignorance or passion) and by helping others through more intensity and sacrifice, he came to a higher consciousness. Then even a greater desire to help others was created. <16> Eventually by becoming other-centered instead of being self-centered, he overcame the selfishness and self-centeredness, and with this he overcame his lower nature and entered the higher self (was born again).

<17> Although he had overcome his lower nature and eagerly was sacrificing to help others, still he had not mastered the power of the tama guna completely. There were times that the discouragement would come to him and he would wonder why, with all his sacrificing for others, they were not progressing and there was not a great result. <18> Or he might have thought how wonderful he was in sacrificing so much for others.

<19> However, later on a greater realization came to him, that **being attached to the result of one's action is a hindrance in spiritual progress**. He offered the result of his actions to God.

<20> Therefore, he shattered all bondages which would stand in his way, slow down his progress, and bind him. Now he would do the actions with the highest possible efficiency but would throw the result away (to the universe). <21> With this, there would be no attachment to the result.

<22> Therefore, first of all there would be no anxiety if the result did not turn out to be the best, because he had tried his utmost but if the result was not ideal, he was not attached to it. <23> Secondly, there would be no ego built up of "How great I am that I am doing so much good."

<24> He realized also, that submission to God is even greater than surrendering. In submission, God is the One doing the actions through him. He is only a channel for those Divine actions. <25> In this case no "I" is left but "He." So he would radiate God's Grace as a channel.

Tablet Eight

<1> In this stage, He was greatly engaged in helping his immediate surroundings with the feeling of belonging to that environment. <2> Also the feeling of possessiveness of that immediate surrounding was with him. So again a great attachment was created in him.

<3> But as he progressed further, his mind was expanded and he felt more unit consciousnesses as a part of him. He realized that being attached to a small part of the universe creates narrowness of the mind, and this results in prejudice and misjudgment. <4> Also

THE ESSENCE — Tablet 8

he more and more understood that all is God, and if all is God, how can he only love a part of God and hate the rest? <5> So he gave up the narrow feeling of belonging to a small part of the universe and created a great compassion for the whole.

<6> With this, his mind was expanded and all the narrowness was destroyed. <7> **Any other view than universalism is narrow and a hindrance in human progress toward becoming one.**

<8> However, there would be times that he would not feel to help others or would become attached to the result of his actions. He would become discouraged, unhappy, and depressed again. <9> So even a deeper realization came to him.

<10> This deeper realization was that **the power of the tama guna, which is not yet mastered, crudifies his consciousness and is the cause of forgetting all these realizations and becoming self-centered again**. <11> The result would be the feeling of separation, egotism, discouragement, and all the evils related to these things. <12> This egotism (power of the tama guna over the Soul) influences both the reasoning (satva guna or sentient force) and the action (raja guna or mutative force) causing them to be directed toward selfishness and results in the feeling of separation even deeper.

<13> However, when the reasoning and action are done with a universal outlook for the good of all, these forces (satva and raja) will be directed toward the well-being of the whole universe. <14> **Then the reasoning becomes Wisdom, and the actions become Divine.**

<15> Also, the process toward the feeling of being a part of the whole is accelerated, and the direction of the creative powers become universally-centered rather than self-centered. <16> And that is the key to true happiness and freedom, through universally directed actions and attention.

<17> Furthermore, through realization of the self and the nature of the three gunas, including the effect of the tama guna on the self, and then by going beyond these influences and mastering them, the result would be the rise of great devotion toward the universe (God) and all its components. <18> Then the true nature of the self will arise and that is where the true happiness, supreme peace, and the greatest joy (Ananda) is.

<19> **Whoever knows the consciousness (Chit) truly (Sat) will experience bliss (Ananda). "Sat, Chit, Ananda."**

<20> So even a more intense period began in his spiritual progress. By deeper realization of the self (☉), with longing to create an environment (✡) where he could help others more effectively to progress and he himself progress in the process, by realizing that to create such an environment a great sacrifice is needed (✝), and by surrendering the result of his sacrifice and actions, (and even greater than that, to become submissive to God) (☾), he realized he could overcome any binding effect of his actions. <21> Also he directed all his efforts and attention with a universal view for the good of all (✸). <22> With this, he became a great spiritual force in the universe in helping others to reach higher consciousness (✡).

<23> By these realizations and through his struggles, he won the Grace of God. <24> So by his struggles and great endeavors, he dissolved his ego to the Universal Ego. <25> Through the Grace of God, he eventually overcame any feeling of separation as "I am" apart from the "I AM."

THE ESSENCE

Tablet Nine

"...and there was light." (Genesis 1:3b)

<1> With this success, he became Pure Consciousness (☸) or complete awareness. <2> The cycle of ups and downs as going to the state of happiness with feeling that one is a part of the universe, and then feeling lonely and unhappy because of the domination of the tama guna, ceased, and the great permanent joy (Ananda) with infinite knowledge and power was replaced instead.

<3> He was aware that "I know" (satva, positive), "I do" (raja, neutral), and "I have done" (tama, negative) with no attachment to them, and each with a universal feeling.

<4> He also knew that "I AM" (consciousness, passive) is none of these feelings (influences of the three gunas) but "I am that I am." He knew that he was beyond the three gunas, and that they were his servants.

<5> So he who proved to be worthy through his struggle, won His Grace and became the **First Begotten Son of God**. <6> He overcame the power of the tama guna over his Soul, and whoever overcomes will become His Son (Revelation 21:7). <7> He becomes in His Image (a son is in the image or likeness of his Father).

<8> God is in the state of Pure Consciousness or perfect awareness with control over the three gunas in the universe. <9> Also whoever reaches this state (by His Grace) will gain complete awareness with perfect power over the three gunas of his consciousness and also with whatever power the Lord gives to him. (As **The Greatest Sign** shows, even in the state of Pure Consciousness, the unit consciousness is under the control of the Father).

<10> Such a consciousness is in Pure Consciousness, one with the Father, and the son of God (a god). <11> He himself becomes a center and nucleus for those who recognize the truth (God) through him. He radiates the qualities of God. <12> By his example he becomes the way and the truth, and whoever follows his way (**The Eternal Path**) will reach the Father (the Truth, the Light).

<13> However, the true radiating nucleus of the universe and the controller of all is the Father (God), and it is He who unifies. <14> But because each unit consciousness goes through different experiences, each will become unique in itself as an individual at the same time being a part and parcel of God (All).

<15> In other words, God (universe) is all and each individual is specialized through his experiences. So God can manifest Himself with special qualities through each individual with different expressions. <16> The total of the individuals (in all levels) with their qualities together manifest all the qualities of God.

"And God saw the light, that it was good: And God divided the light from the darkness." (Genesis 1:4)

<17> God saw the **Divine Path**, "and God saw the light," and He was very pleased, "that it was good." <18> He completely divided the state of Pure Consciousness (light) and the path to reach there from the state of being lost and ignorant (darkness), <19> and He became the master of the process of coming from ignorance to Pure Consciousness, "and God divided the light from the darkness."

THE ESSENCE — Tablet 10

> "And God called the light Day, and the darkness he called Night. And the evening and the morning were the first day." (Genesis 1:5)

<20> The path to Pure Consciousness, **Eternal Divine Path**, leads to the light, and the state of Pure Consciousness is the state of complete awareness and knowledge. There the truth becomes clear as "Day." <21> But he who is under the control of the tama guna is in ignorance and is dark as "Night."

<22> At this point the first period of the struggle to help the lost unit consciousnesses was finished, "And the evening and the morning were the first day."

Tablet Ten

> "And God said, Let there be a firmament in the midst of the waters, and let it divide the waters from the waters.
> And God made the firmament, and divided the waters which were under the firmament from the waters which were above the firmament: and it was so." (Genesis 1:6-7)

<1> The process of progress from complete ignorance (under the control of the tama guna) to Pure Consciousness in this state, before the manifested world, was a very difficult one. This is what the First Begotten Son went through. <2> Because the unit consciousnesses would not feel any need for help or even the necessity for progress, they had not tasted the joy and beauty of being in the state of Pure Consciousness. So they were satisfied with the state they were in.

<3> But God knew how wrong they were and created even greater compassion for them. Therefore He decided to create a feasible and more orderly process to bring these lost souls to Pure Consciousness. <4> He planned the process of creation of the visible universe so that these unit consciousnesses, through progressive evolutionary steps, would reach Pure Consciousness.

<5> **Therefore, the process of creation is based on compassion and the purpose of creation is to bring all lost souls to Pure Consciousness.**

<6> With this decision, He started to divide the consciousnesses (waters) in the universe into many levels according to their awareness, "…Let there be a firmament in the midst of the waters, and let it divide the waters from the waters."

<7> The triangle upward ($\triangle$) symbolizes the Hierarchy in which the consciousnesses had been divided. <8> Those who are in a higher consciousness are at the top of the triangle and those who were lost in a complete illusion of separation, are at the bottom of the triangle ($\triangle$).

<9> Therefore, the triangle upward ($\triangle$) represents the Hierarchy of the unit consciousnesses that had reached Pure Consciousness

441

THE ESSENCE

(sons of God) in heaven, then has those who are in higher consciousness, until the bottom is reached. The very bottom represents those who are completely lost. <10> The more sentient the consciousness, the higher the possibility of reaching Pure Consciousness.

<11> The two triangles together symbolize the Kingdom of Heaven (in heaven) (✡). <12> The triangle upward (△) symbolizes the actions taken to carry out the activities to help the unit consciousnesses reach the goal (Pure Consciousness) by all the elements of the universe and those who had already reached this state. <13> The triangle downward (▽) symbolizes the Universal Mind which enables the Father (the controller and nucleus of the universe) to control and direct these activities.

<14> Or, in other words, the triangle upward symbolizes actions and the Hierarchy (△) in heaven, and the triangle downward (▽) symbolizes control and justice of God.

<15> After this division of the consciousnesses into different levels, by using the crudifying ability of the tama guna, then God started to bind and crudify the consciousnesses (waters) toward a more solid state. <16> As the binding power of the static force (tama guna) started working, the first elements of the basic five elements (ether, air, luminous – heat, light, fire – liquid, and solid), namely, ethereal and aerial factors, were made manifest. <17> These two elements are referred to as the "waters which were above the firmament." <18> Those consciousnesses, which in the process of crudification would become the base for creating the liquid and solid factors, are called the "waters which were under the firmament."

> "And God called the firmament Heaven. And the evening and the morning were the second day." (Genesis 1:8)

<19> At this stage, those parts of the elements that contained ethereal, aerial, and gaseous factors were called "Heaven" (sky or the most invisible elements in the universe). <20> The ethereal and aerial factors were created, <21> and the second period of struggle to bring the universe to Pure Consciousness was finished, "and the evening and the morning were the second day."

<22> From this verse on, the description of how the visible creation would be manifested is described.

Tablet Eleven

> "And God said, Let the waters under the heaven be gathered together unto one place, and let the dry land appear: and it was so." (Genesis 1:9)

<1> As it was explained, "the waters under the heaven" are those consciousnesses which, in the process of crudification, became the base for creating liquid and solid factors. <2> Now in this stage they would be crudified further to create dry land (solid factor), "Let the waters under the heaven be gathered together unto one place, and let the dry land appear."

<3> This gathering together or crudifying process is what is called the centripetal force of nature. <4> Through this centripetal force, different levels of the universal elements, which are ethereal, aerial, luminous (fire, heat, and light), liquid, and solid, and all the elements between them, were created.

> "And God called the dry land Earth; and the gathering together of the waters called he Seas: and God saw that it was good." (Genesis 1:10)

THE ESSENCE

<5> The dry land, from the most crudified consciousnesses (solid factors), was created ("Earth"). <6> Also from the consciousnesses less crude than those which were used to create the solid factors, the liquid factors were formed ("the gathering together of the waters called he Seas"). <7> With this, all the necessary elements to start the rest of the creation and the evolutionary processes in the universe were prepared.

<8> Also with this, the seven worlds or lokas were completed. The lowest world is the physical or manifested one (ethereal, aerial, luminous, liquid, and solid). <9> These factors are manifest because of the crudifying power of the tama guna (static, crudifying force).

<10> The second is the world of prana or activities in the universe which are carried on by the mutative force (raja guna). This force is responsible for any action and the energy in the universe. <11> It is the life-force (prana) in the universe and it presents itself in many forms.

<12> The third and fourth layers are the lower and higher mental worlds. <13> In the lower mental world, the maintenance of the physical world and its needs are considered, <14> and in the higher mental world, the higher thoughts and ideals reside.

<15> The fifth world is the state of complete realization of the functions of the manifested world and the mastering of its forces. <16> The sixth layer is the state of complete control over the three gunas, and the seventh is the state beyond the three gunas. <17> The sixth and seventh states both can be called the states of Pure Consciousness. <18> In the sixth state the consciousness still actively controls and works with the three gunas, but in the seventh state, it will internalize all its forces and become a witness entity.

<19> Through these seven worlds, the progress of the individual is carried out to Pure Consciousness (heaven).

"And God said, Let the earth bring forth grass, the herb yielding seed, and the fruit tree yielding fruit after his kind, whose seed is in itself, upon the earth: and it was so." (Genesis 1:11)

<20> With the help of the centrifugal force, or by the loosening of the crudifying power of the static force, and by the use of the five already created elements and consciousnesses in the higher levels, <21> God now planned to start the creation of the plants.

<22> The process of evolution is self-sustaining and will continue by itself, "whose seed is in itself." So everything will continue to grow, evolve, and progress toward the goal.

Tablet Twelve

"And God said, Let us make man in our image, after our likeness:..." (Genesis 1:26)

<1> The evolutionary process of going from plants, to animals and eventually to humans, was achieved. <2> However, the entire first chapter of Genesis in the Bible is a description of creation in the state of planning and thinking. The real creation as a manifested world starts in chapter 2 of Genesis.

<3> God decided to create man in His Image and likeness. He decided to bring the unit consciousnesses to human form as they were, "positive and negative" and "male and female" in one being.

<4> As it was explained previously, satva guna is positive, raja guna (Grace) is neutral and is female principle, and tama guna is negative.

<5> When raja guna (action) is directed toward higher things, it is Grace (The Divine Mother). <6> It is directed toward satva guna dominating the consciousness (Divine Logic),

which is male principle. <7> Then female and male principles become Shiva (The Divine Logic) and Shakti (The Divine Mother, The Divine Grace).

<8> When the same force (raja guna) is directed toward worldly activities (Maya) it becomes bondage and illusion, or the woman, or as Kali the ugly, fierce, and blood-thirsty Hindu Goddess with a hideous countenance, dripping with blood. <9> Kali is the power of destruction. It destroys all who are out of The Holy Ghost and The Divine Grace.

<10> Also, man is the end of the evolutionary process. <11> **The human is in that state of being which can reach Pure Consciousness or perfect awareness.** <12> He can (with The Grace) gain complete control of the tama guna over his Soul and can also go beyond the influences of the crudified satva guna (reasoning directed toward selfishness) and the crudified raja guna (selfish actions). He can direct his energy toward universalism and the **Eternal Divine Path** – to be(come) Divine, a son of God, Pure Consciousness.

> "And God blessed the seventh day, and sanctified it: because that in it he had rested from all his work which God created and made." (Genesis 2:3)

<13> With the completion of the evolutionary process, God did not have to interfere in the progress of the unit consciousnesses any longer, because He created the universe self-sustaining. <14> Through the process of the Laws of the manifested world and the power of the tama guna, now man would become attached to the external world and believe he is his body and follow it.

<15> So he would be drawn into the Maya (illusion of the reality of the external world and its offerings), resulting in the crudification of his consciousness. <16> Therefore suffering would follow, and this process would continue until after many lifetimes of misery, he eventually would realize that the attraction to the external world brings unspiritual desires and this results in attachments and greed. Greed accelerates the attraction to the external world, and this wheel goes on and on.

<17> Then is the time when he sees the truth and turns his attention from the external world to the internal (spiritual) world. He realizes that he is not his body, and the only thing he has is his Soul. <18> So he will start to glorify his Soul, and through his struggle will realize the **Eternal Divine Path** and create the love of God in himself. By His Grace, He will reach the goal (Pure Consciousness).

Tablet Thirteen

> "And the Lord God formed man of the dust of the ground, and breathed into his nostrils the breath of life; and man became a living soul." (Genesis 2:7)

<1> When the first expression of awareness appeared as a sound vibration, "The Word," time was perceived. When this manifested universe started to be created, the reality of space became understood, and the atom was built. <2> In Sanskrit, the atom (Anu) is called "Avidya," meaning "ignorance." This same atom in the <u>Bible</u> is called "the dust of the ground" which is the atom in its first stages and also can be called the "cosmic dust."

<3> Man did not have the same body as we know it today. His body was made more of psychic and spiritual factors.

<4> However, he had many basic things in common with the man of today. <5> He had a Soul (he was a unit consciousness), which had a unit mind (the three gunas). This unit being resided in the ethereal factor (spirit), but he also gradually obtained a material body consisting of the four other elements, namely,

THE ESSENCE

aerial, luminous, liquid, and solid. <6> The four-elemental-material body can only link itself to the psychic (spirit) or ethereal body (unit Soul and its ethereal factor) with the co-ordinating energy (life-energy of the Soul). This fine element in the <u>Bible</u> is symbolized as "the breath of life" and is also called "prana." <7> Prana is the active energy and life-force of the body. It brings contact between different parts of the body and Soul, and maintains their inter-balance. <8> It is the outgoing and in-coming energy from the Soul (raja guna).

<9> This prana, which is more subtle than the aerial factor, can be found in much fresh air and is even more necessary for survival than oxygen. <10> It is the life-force which is also available in other elements in nature besides air. It is the living element that can be controlled, directed, and used for many purposes in human life. <11> It is the life-force of all living things and is the outgoing and in-coming life-energy of the Soul (collectively and individually).

<12> Not only was the human created in the image of God in respect to the Soul, but also his body is in the resemblance and image of the universe. It consists of seven levels. <13> The first five levels of these seven stages are called sheaths or koshas.

<14> They correspond to the seven worlds (lokas) in the universe. But because, in the first five levels, man is bound to those levels and there is an illusion of separation that exists between him and the external world (universe, God), so there a layer (veil) exists between him and the outside. <15> That is why these first five stages are like a sheath between him and the universe.

<16> But the same stages in the universe are called worlds, because for the universe there is no separation between these stages and the universe itself. They are a part of it.

<17> The first sheath, corresponding to the first world, is the physical body of man which consists of solid, liquid, luminous, aerial, and ethereal factors.

<18> The second is the pranic sheath which is the life-force from the Soul and the universe. <19> The third and fourth are the lower and higher mental sheaths. <20> In the lower mental sheath, the energy is going outwardly and worldly desires arise from it. <21> In the higher mental sheath, the prana (energy) is internalized (going inward) and desires become controllable, the imagination and willpower increase, and the noble thoughts arise.

<22> The fifth sheath is the state of self-realization (control of the tama and raja gunas), which results in great joy.

<23> The sixth and seventh states are the states of freedom from illusion (sheaths). <24> In the sixth state, the person becomes the master of the three gunas and feels one with God, but still maintains a very small "i" as a separate entity. <25> In the seventh state, there is no "i" left and he reaches Pure Consciousness.

<26> In this last stage, the pranic energy is completely internalized and the individual Soul becomes pure intuition. <27> Through this internalized mutative force (raja guna) which becomes willpower, the unit consciousness can return to the external world only by willing to do so.

<28> By creating the manifested universe, the evolutionary process, and the human, God guides the unit consciousnesses. <29> With the attraction of the external world (Maya), and because of the ignorance of man of his Divinity as "I am" one with the "I AM," <30> he becomes a slave of his illusion that he is a separate being in the whole universe, <31> and he becomes more and more lost because of the impulses of his desires and attachments to the external world. <32> Only after many lifetimes, he reaches a point where he realizes that there should be more in life than this heedless pursuance of the lower nature which brings so much suffering.

<33> That is when he starts searching for more meaningful realities than these unsatisfying, impulsive desires, which are the root of all suffering. <34> That is when he will be helped and be shown the way to salvation, and is the reason for this creation and Maya.

THE ESSENCE

Tablet Fourteen

> "And the Lord God caused a deep sleep to fall upon Adam, and he slept: and he took one of his ribs, and closed up the flesh instead thereof;
> And the rib, which the Lord God had taken from man, made he a woman,..." (Genesis 2:21-22)

<1> However, a further evolutionary process became necessary: The separation of each being into two parts. This occurred because each man was both male and female in one being. Therefore it would not be attracted toward the great (the goal). <2> So a separation of each took place, especially at the higher levels of the evolutionary process (higher plants, animals, and humans). "And the rib, which the Lord God had taken from man, made he a woman,...."

<3> With this separation a great feeling of not being complete is inherent in the human, and forces a man to search for the cause of this emptiness and dissatisfaction. <4> The search to find the other half draws them even deeper and faster into the ocean of Maya. <5> This helps the humans realize how weak they are. Through this process man starts questioning the reason for being here, who he is, where he has come from, where he is going, and so on.

<6> This is the beginning of the attraction to the mystery of the universe and the basis for the human search in finding answers to these questions. This will lead him to the deeper level of his being and cause him to become more familiar with the world within. <7> If he continues, and is sincere and persistent, eventually he will be led to the reality that there is a Superior Power in this universe, with definite Laws to follow and many realities to understand. <8> It is then that he will thirst to know the truth, and if he is sincere and willing to do whatever is necessary to gain it, he will know. "Ask, and it shall be given you; seek, and ye shall find; knock, and it shall be opened unto you" (Matthew 7:7).

<9> Intuitively he knows that he was once perfect in the past but sometime ago he has lost one part of himself. With all these drives, his journey toward Pure Consciousness begins.

<10> **Only when a human realizes his imperfection and feels the need of help from God will he be helped.**

<11> At the time of reunion with his other part, when both become perfect, they will reach Pure Consciousness. When this happens, he will become a son of God, because he has overcome the forces of nature over his Soul and is in the image and likeness of God. He will reach Pure Consciousness (卍).

<12> Also, the separation of the consciousness into man and woman is a symbol of the separation of the lower and higher natures of the unit consciousness as lower and higher spiritual centers (chakras) in the human. As the consciousness rises to higher spiritual centers (chakras), it reaches higher consciousness and becomes closer to being unified to its higher self and becoming one with God.

<13> **This merging of two perfected parts (or lower and higher selves) and reaching Pure Consciousness is the goal of yoga (yoga means "union").**

> "Unto Adam also and to his wife did the Lord God make coats of skins, and clothed them." (Genesis 3:21)

<14> As the human fails and becomes more separated from God, a new evolutionary step is necessary. Up to this point, the human was more a mass of Soul (unit consciousness), spirit (ethereal body), and psychic being, than a physical being. <15> He also had a direct relationship with the forces of nature, and he could manipulate these occult powers for his own selfish desires.

<16> The misuse of these powers brought

a fall in morality and humans started to use them for their mundane self-satisfaction. This affected man's environment and crudified the human more. They became more flesh, "did the Lord God made coats of skins, and clothed them." They were given "skin" to cover the newly-made flesh.

Tablet Fifteen

"There were giants in the earth in those days; and also after that, when the sons of God came in unto the daughters of men, and they bare children to them, the same became mighty men which were of old, men of renown." (Genesis 6:4)

"And God said unto Noah, The end of all flesh is come before me; for the earth is filled with violence through them; and, behold, I will destroy them with the earth." (Genesis 6:13)

<1> Through the misuse of their occult powers, the humans fell more, and this caused the degeneration of the earth. A different generation with great powers was living on earth then. They misused these powers. <2> The misuse of these powers affected the world environment and climate ("the earth is filled with violence through them").

<3> That is why God decided to destroy "them with the earth." He decided to create a new kind of man ("men of renown") and a new kind of climate for the earth. <4> Therefore a further evolutionary change took place: The power of reasoning and intellect remained for man, but the human's occult center (the third eye) was closed, and his direct contact with the forces of nature was taken away.

<5> That is symbolized as the destruction of the world by the flood at the time of Noah. <6> The power of the third eye became latent at the pineal gland in the middle of the brain. <7> Also man was divided into many different races ("after their families, in their nations") (Gen. 10:5). <8> Furthermore, the five types of humans (Shudras, Ksattriyas, Vipras, Vaeshyas, and Brahmins) appeared (Genesis 9 and 10, The Holiest Book). This is where the human now stands, from six thousand years ago.

<9> Also at this point there were more than one unit consciousness who had reached Pure Consciousness, because there were **sons** of God, "when the sons of God came in unto...."

Tablet Sixteen

"And the whole earth was of one language, and of one speech." (Genesis 11:1)

<1> One more minor evolutionary change was necessary. Humans still had telepathic ability. Being able to communicate with each other through telepathy, and being united through this good communication, the humans again reached a very advanced technological civilization in a short period of time. <2> Intoxicated with these achievements, they started again to use their powers for self-gratification and self-destruction, "and let us make us a name, lest we be scattered abroad upon the face of the whole earth" (Genesis 11:4).

<3> But God wanted to see them scatter not only on earth but also to other planets. <4> So God took away their telepathic abilities. Because their tongues were different, "every one after his tongue,..." (Gen. 10:5),

THE ESSENCE

they could no longer understand each other. So their good communicative abilities broke down and they were scattered all over the earth (as God wanted them to be).

<5> So, God created this universe to help man go to Him, to Pure Consciousness. But because of the power of the tama guna, man will feel separated from the rest of the universe and become self-centered. This causes him to fall into his lower nature and so suffer. <6> Through many evolutionary steps, God brought humans to such a helpless situation that even they differentiate each other by race, language or country. The last evolutionary change happened around 12,000 years ago and finished 6,000 years ago. <7> God did these things neither as a play nor for selfish reasons. He did it to prevent man from self-destruction and in order to help him to Pure Consciousness.

<8> Then, through the last six thousand years, God left man almost completely alone, except for sending Prophets, to give another good lesson through history and also to prepare him for further advancement. The last six thousand years is the time of the history of humanity as we know it.

<9> Through these six thousand years of history, besides other events which had occurred, He has worked to make humans progress and eventually understand that He exists and is desiring greatly to bring them to higher consciousness. <10> He also has revealed the seven truths to humanity which are the seven essential steps toward reaching the goal (Pure Consciousness).

<11> To reach this goal is the reason for creation and history. The essence of these seven steps or stages, which have been revealed to humanity through the Prophets, will be discussed below. We can call each step a seal and the process to reach the goal the **Eternal Divine Path**.

Tablet Seventeen
THE FIRST SEAL

<1> The first seal (☯) or truth, is the necessity of awakening the spiritual forces, which are latent in the human. This can be done through many techniques, teachings, knowledge, and all other techniques or exercises which help in awakening the spiritual forces. The most important of all is the Grace of the Lord (and spiritual teacher, which should be the same). <2> Also other things, such as contemplation, meditation, prayer, exercises, etc., are important.

<3> These techniques and teachings, however, are not the ultimate in the sense of guiding a person to Pure Consciousness. Further knowledge and steps are necessary which will be described in the next six seals. <4> Following only this seal can result in escapism, which God does not like. <5> This seal can be called the Mystical Paths.

THE ESSENCE *Tablet 17*

THE SECOND SEAL

<6> The next step is to realize that a proper environment is necessary in which the physiological and safety needs of the person are provided and the disturbing things (physically, mentally, and spiritually) are eliminated. <7> This sentient environment is needed before a person is able to start to meditate and/or practice the techniques to awaken his spiritual forces, or even to start to read, have time and enough concentration to become familiar with these things. <8> So a proper environment is a must and <9> this can start from creating a Kingdom of Heaven in one's home, then community, city, country, and eventually the world. <10> Then the Kingdom of Heaven (✡) On Earth will be established (realized) and all can pursue physical, mental, and spiritual progress.

THE THIRD SEAL

<11> To create such an environment, sacrifice is necessary. Greed and self-centeredness are the cause of all problems of humanity. So only by understanding this truth and creating the spirit of sacrifice – not being self-centered (✝) – can the Kingdom of God be recognized (✡) on earth as it is in heaven.

<12> However, sacrificing and selflessness should start from the top of the society (the leaders). Otherwise the mass will be exploited through their sacrifices and a few will take advantage of these sacrifices for their own selfish desires.

THE FOURTH SEAL

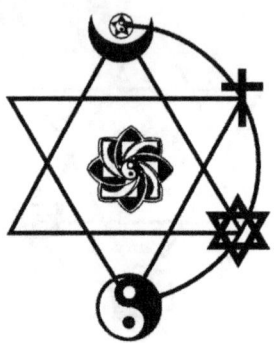

<13> To be attached to one's merits or good actions (sacrifices) is an obstacle in spiritual progress. So good should be done and the results should be surrendered to God or thrown away to the universe to be used for the progress of others (☾).

<14> Even greater than surrendering is submission to Him. That is, to become a channel for His Divine Actions to be done through us. <15> In surrendering, there is still an "I" which exists as one who surrenders, and the surrenderer is different from the one who is surrendered to. <16> But when a person becomes a channel for His Divine Actions, then no separation exists and the surrenderer, the thing being surrendered, and the one being surrendered to, become one. <17> This state is called the state of renunciation, when the "I" and all things related to it are no more.

THE FIFTH SEAL

<18> Also, in order for a person to free himself from all narrowness of the mind and bondage related to it, he should become a universalist (✸). Any "ism" other than universalism will result in narrowness, and this again will bring suffering. So the ideal is to work and help to create the Kingdom of Heaven so that the **whole** universe can progress toward the goal, not just a few or a small portion of the universe. <19> Otherwise we are not following the Will of God and our awakened spiritual forces, sacrifices, and submission are narrow, so they will bring suffering, because they are not according to the Spirit of God, which is to see the whole universe reach Pure Consciousness.

THE SIXTH SEAL

<20> With awakening the spiritual forces (☯), longing for a spiritual environment (✡), and selflessly (✝) working to create such an environment, and by being detached from the results of these endeavors and becoming submissive to Him (☾), with a universal point of view (✹) for all, a person can be(come) a dynamic being, free from any narrowness of mind or bondages from his actions. <21> With the use of the acquired powers through his spiritual progress, he will work to establish the Kingdom of God in the universe and help others also to understand this true path of salvation.

<22> Such a person can be called a Paravipra (✡). Only these people can be(come) the true leaders of humanity, and by their examples help all to progress and reach Pure Consciousness. Otherwise there will always be suffering, strife, and class wars.

Tablet Eighteen
THE SEVENTH SEAL

<1> With this progress to Paraviprahood, the false ego as a being separate from the universe or belonging to a small part is dissolved and the ego will be expanded to be(come) one with the Universal Ego. <2> The Grace of God will be won and the person will be helped to reach Pure Consciousness, as it is declared in the sixth church in <u>The Revelation</u> chapter 3: "…I have set before thee an open door, and no man can shut it:…" (Revelation 3:8).

<3> But to win the reward, which is to reach Pure Consciousness, the person should hold fast to what he has gained. He should not become narrow and thereby prevent further realizations of the truth, but he should be open to all things which God reveals. <4> These are the teachings and realizations of the whole truth, which is revealed through the seventh seal (✺) or its Angel. <5> Therefore, "…hold that fast which thou hast, that no man

take thy crown" (Revelation 3:11). If he does, then he will enter Pure Consciousness (☸).

<6> This path of awakening the spiritual forces and coming to higher consciousness (☯), directing the energy and knowledge gained for teaching, helping others to the path, and trying to bring the Kingdom Of Heaven On Earth (✡), sacrificing in this endeavor (✝), surrendering the result to Him and being submissive to Him (☪), <7> be(com)ing a universalist and working for the good of the whole universe (✹), be(com)ing a spiritual force in leading others, and learning the way of negating the ego and feeling of separation by be(com)ing a dynamic spiritual force (✡), <8> will win His Grace, and this will result in knowledge and devotion toward the universe and eventually reaching the goal (Pure Consciousness) (☸).

<9> This is the **Eternal Divine Path** which the sons of God, knowingly or unknowingly, have realized and gone through, and it is the path which should be followed by all.

KINGDOM

This section contains three books which explain how human social systems have been guided by Divine Will for the last twelve thousand years. Now a system is given so that the human might manifest His Kingdom (Will) on earth.

COMMENTARIES ON PROPHECIES IN DANIEL
"PERIOD OF INTELLECTUAL DOMINATION"

In the book, Commentaries on Prophecies in Daniel, "Period of Intellectual Domination," Maitreya explains the meaning of the dream of King Nebuchadnezzar, and other dreams and prophecies in the book of Daniel in the Bible. This book shows how it is God's desire to see His Kingdom come on earth and how He will fulfill this.

COMMENTARIES ON PROPHECIES IN DANIEL
"PERIOD OF INTELLECTUAL DOMINATION"

PREFACE

There are three very important prophecies in the book of Daniel in the Bible, which will be described in this commentary. From a prophetic point of view, the events which would happen in the future were foretold hundreds and thousands of years before and were done to increase the faith of the faithful and create faith in the skeptic.

In addition to the spiritual lessons and importance of the symbols which were used in this book, the main point to focus on is that these prophecies were revealed to show how, from about two thousand three hundred years ago, a period of intellectual development would follow. This is important because in this period two aspects of human abilities (characteristics) were developed to their highest. First, the intellect was developed, in the sense of understanding the material (scientific discoveries), social (sociology), and human (psychological) worlds, and other intellectual knowledge increased. Secondly, the development of human economical abilities occurred, which increased the standard of living of man through the stimulation of economical values, use of money, proper distribution of resources, and the use and coordination of these resources (material, labor, science, etc.) toward the betterment of life (business). **In fact, the business and economic understandings can also be categorized as intellect directed toward the control of resources.** So both of these characteristics can be viewed as the intellectual development of man.

These discoveries increased the knowledge and standard of living of the human and apparently should have increased man's happiness. But because of their side effects, such as discrediting the spiritual values of man, a great feeling of materialism and dry intellectualism (not combined with intuition) developed in the human.

This part of the effect of the intellectual discoveries in these prophecies is called "the little horn." This little horn will dominate humanity for this long period of time (two thousand three hundred years). The bad side effects of the intellectualization of the world (undermining the spiritual values) will dominate the world in this period until the human consciousness develops to the next step of the evolutionary development, which is intuition and understanding the spirit behind all the dry intellectual knowledge.

That is, nothing is bad in this universe. Things become evil or create suffering when they are not used properly. Intellect and economy are also not bad or evil. But they can become that when they are not used toward human spiritual progress. Then they become a burden on humanity ("little horn").

The point is that when in Daniel intellect or economy (business) is described as that which fought with the Saints and destroyed spiritual truth, it refers to this bad side of them. Otherwise, when intellect is combined with intuition (spiritual understandings) and economy (use of resources on earth) for creating comfort for all to progress physically, mentally, and spiritually, then they both become blessings.

If they are not spiritualized, the intellect becomes dry, inflexible, and loses its common sense, and economy becomes a constant struggle to cope with a speedy life unsuited for human psychology. These bad aspects of the intellectualized world (which is Maya) are also symbolized as "the little book" in The Revelation chapter 10, which in the beginning seems sweet as honey, but it makes the life dry and bitter, "it shall make thy belly bitter, but it shall be in thy mouth sweet as honey" (Rev. 10:9).

COMMENTARIES ON PROPHECIES IN DANIEL

Tablet One

THE DREAM OF KING NEBUCHADNEZZAR

Daniel Chapter 2

"Thou, O king, sawest, and behold a great image. This great image, whose brightness was excellent, stood before thee; and the form thereof was terrible." (Daniel 2:31)

<1> Daniel is describing the dream of King Nebuchadnezzar, the king of the Chaldean Empire. Later on, he will give the interpretation of the dream.

<2> In his dream, the king saw an image which was very bright but terrible. The brightness of the image is a symbol of its attractiveness which is like the attractiveness of Maya (Maya is the excess attraction to the external world, illusion of separation from God). <3> As the truth of pursuing the worldly desire is none but terrible, so was the image. Its true characteristic was terrible.

"This image's head was of fine gold, his breast and his arms of silver, his belly and his thighs of brass," (Daniel 2:32)

"His legs of iron, his feet part of iron and part of clay." (Daniel 2:33)

<4> So it was a metal image, with the head of gold, the breast and arms of silver, the belly and the thighs of brass, the legs of iron, and the feet partly of iron and partly of clay. <5> As the construction of the metal image comes down from the head to the feet, it loses its fineness. <6> Gold is precious, it is a symbol of warmness, and it is a very flexible metal (fine gold is very soft). The next metal is silver, still precious but not like gold; also it is not as flexible as gold. Then is brass, which is much lower in quality in comparison to gold and silver, next is iron, and the last is iron and clay.

"Thou sawest till that a stone was cut out without hands, which smote the image upon his feet that were of iron and clay, and brake them to pieces." (Daniel 2:34)

<7> This terrible image was not as strong as it looked, because it had a very weak foundation (of clay and iron). So it would be broken from its feet by a stone which "was cut out without hands." This stone (truth) did not come from the hand of man, but from God.

"Then was the iron, the clay, the brass, the silver, and the gold, broken to pieces together, and became like the chaff of the summer threshing-floors; and the wind carried them away, that no place was found for them: and the stone that smote the image became a great mountain, and filled the whole earth." (Daniel 2:35)

<8> Wind is the symbol for illusionary ideals. As the wind is caused by temperature differences in two places, which is a short-lived phenomena, and cannot be caught (even when the wind is caught it is not wind any longer because it stops), so are the illusionary ideals. That is why when the image was broken, it was carried away and was no more. It was an illusion which never was the truth.

<9> "The stone that smote the image became a great mountain, and filled the whole earth": The symbol for showing organizational structure in management is a triangle upward ($\triangle$). Also a mountain has the same shape as a triangle but in three dimensions, so it is much stronger than a triangle. <10> The organizational structure made by the human is shown as a triangle upward, and the organizational structure made by God is shown as a mountain (very strong and stable). <11> So the mountain means the Kingdom Of Heaven On Earth, which will fill "the whole earth."

Up to this point Daniel was describing what the dream was. Now God revealed its meaning through Daniel as below:

"Thou, O king, art a king of kings: for the God of heaven hath given thee a kingdom, power, and strength, and glory." (Daniel 2:37)

COMMENTARIES ON PROPHECIES IN DANIEL Tablet 1

<12> Nebuchadnezzar was a great king, but his kingdom, power, strength, and glory all had been given to him by God. If God had not so desired, Nebuchadnezzar could not have had all these things.

"And wheresoever the children of men dwell, the beasts of the field and the fowls of the heaven hath he given into thine hand, and hath made thee ruler over them all. Thou art this head of gold." (Daniel 2:38)

<13> For understanding the significance and meaning of this verse completely, we should describe other subjects and even go ahead of ourselves to the verses in the following prophecies in Daniel (which will be described later).

<14> At the end of chapter 9 and in chapter 10 of Genesis in The Holiest Book, the symbolic meaning of the three sons of Noah – Ham, Japheth, and Shem – was described. <15> They are the symbols for the five types of humans after the flood of Noah.

<16> Ham is the symbol of those humans who try to benefit from the external world by their works and try to satisfy their basic needs through manual labor. They are the workers (Shudras). Also Ham is a symbol of those who try to control and dominate their environment by their strength and courage. They are the warriors or the leaders of the societies (Ksattriyas) (for more detail, read The Kingdom Of Heaven On Earth), like Nimrod who was the grandson of Ham and became a great king (Gen. 10:10).

<17> Japheth is the symbol of those who try to dominate their environment through their minds, either by intellectual administrative abilities and politics (Vipras), or by directing their intellect toward controlling the resources as businessmen (Vaeshyas).

<18> Shem is the symbol of the true spiritual people, those who become seers, Masters, Prophets, and so on. That is why Abram came from the generation of Shem. <19> They are not intellectual spiritualists who create superstitions and false doctrines so that they might be able to exploit and dominate the masses, but they are the real seekers of the truth and are the Elected Ones (Brahmins). (Although Abram was called by man "A-bram," which means not a Brahmin, still God chose him as such!)

<20> Therefore, there are five different kinds of people that can be recognized in the human race: The workers (Shudras), the warriors (Ksattriyas), the intellectuals (Vipras), the businessmen (Vaeshyas), and the true spiritual people (Brahmins).

<21> Also in the course of history some of these classes dominated other ones in a successive manner. The Ksattriyas dominated the Shudras, the intellectuals dominated the Shudras and Ksattriyas, and the Vaeshyas dominated the Shudras, Ksattriyas and Vipras. The period of domination of each of these classes is known as their era in history.

<22> Each of these kinds have a common general characteristic by which they can be recognized. The workers (Shudras) usually do manual work and are interested mostly in day-to-day events of life and the basic necessities and safety needs. As long as these needs are fulfilled, they usually have no further ambitions.

<23> The warrior types (Ksattriyas) are those who are courageous. Their want is to overcome physical obstacles and to conquer their enemies. They value fearlessness, valor, honor, discipline, and strength. <24> Because of these abilities, the Ksattriyan class assumed the leadership of the Shudras. These Ksattriyas in return felt a sense of duty toward their subjects and took some responsibility for the protection and welfare of the Shudras. <25> This era of the domination of the Ksattriyas is symbolized in the Bible by the appearance of Nimrod as the king (Gen. 10:10).

<26> These Ksattriyas were basically simple people and their greatness came from their ability to protect and create a good environment for their subjects. However, their era is marked by conquests and wars in order to bring peace and wealth to their territories. <27> Their intention to exploit others was not as subtle as intellectuals, but bold and direct.

<28> The intellectual types love to use their minds to penetrate the laws governing

COMMENTARIES ON PROPHECIES IN DANIEL

the social and physical spheres in order to control and dominate their environment. They dominate others by their administrative abilities, innovation of tools, ideas, and creation of superstitious and religious doctrines that bind man instead of freeing him.

<29> As the kingdoms of the Ksattriyas expanded and empires were created, the dependence of kings and emperors on their ministers (intellectuals) increased. This expansion of the rule of intellectuals slowly brought the domination of this class over the society. The kings became puppets, and their rule became symbolic. The real rulers became the ministers, and they cleverly gained control over all things without changing the monarchal structure of the past (a good example of this is in the Medieval times when the Catholic church was running Europe where there were kings and queens on their thrones).

<30> These prophecies in the book of Daniel are about the start of the domination of the intellectuals over the Ksattriyas and the era of intellectuals. <31> King Nebuchadnezzar is the head of the image, which is of gold. He had the ultimate characteristics of a Ksattriya. He was disciplined, benevolent, simple, concerned, and had great power over his subjects to such an extent that he built a large image and demanded all to worship it. <32> He believed he had obtained his kingdom and rights by Divine sanction (that is how Shudras used to think about kings), so he was the gold of his era. <33> He was also the king of kings and had domination over all his subjects.

<34> From here on, in the evolutionary process of man, the development of the intellect started toward its heights.

Tablet Two

"And after thee shall arise another kingdom inferior to thee, and another third kingdom of brass, which shall bear rule over all the earth." (Daniel 2:39)

<1> Then after this "head of gold" (the symbol of the king himself), other kingdoms would arise, but they would lose their fineness as true rulers with the special characteristics of a king. That is why the second one would be of silver, and the third of brass. They would have fewer and fewer good qualities of a Ksattriya.

<2> As the spiritual qualities are strengthened more in simplicities, and because the following kingdoms became more and more complicated, therefore, their spiritual parts were weakened and they relied more on their own intelligence and their ministers, rather than on the true values for themselves and others.

"And the fourth kingdom shall be strong as iron: forasmuch as iron breaketh in pieces and subdueth all things: and as iron that breaketh all these, shall it break in pieces and bruise." (Daniel 2:40)

<3> However, the true dryness and false strength (inflexibility) would come at the time of the fourth kingdom, which would completely rely on intellectual strength and try to intellectualize all things. <4> But as iron is strong but inflexible, it also "breaketh in pieces and subdueth all things, ... shall it break in pieces and bruise." Through this fourth kingdom the strength of the intellect would be imposed on humanity. Also through the same kingdom, all things would be subdued and destroyed. <5> That is, the limit of its strength would eventually destroy itself.

"And whereas thou sawest the feet and toes, part of potters' clay, and part of iron, the kingdom shall be divided; but there shall be in it of the strength of the iron, forasmuch as thou sawest the iron mixed with miry clay." (Daniel 2:41)

"And as the toes of the feet were part of iron, and part of clay, so the kingdom shall be partly strong, and partly broken." (Daniel 2:42)

<6> From this completely intellectualized kingdom there would arise another kingdom later on of ten kings (as the ten toes proceed

from the legs and feet). But they are half iron and half clay. That is, not all of the people in this kingdom would believe in the intellectual strength any longer. They would become as clay (humbled). So this kingdom is half intellectually strong and half spiritually awakened.

<7> As it was described in the previous pages, there are five types of humans. The characteristics of Shudras, Ksattriyas, and Vipras were explained, and it was also seen how Vipras became the dominating class in society. Now to understand these verses, we will continue in describing the characteristics of the Vaeshyas (businessmen) and how they became the dominating class in this last era we are in now.

<8> As it was said, businessmen are also intellectuals, but they direct their mental energy toward economic development, seeking to gather and hoard physical wealth. <9> These business-oriented people became the dominating class in human society because of the lack of interest of the other types (classes) in controlling the physical resources and services, as the other classes were merely interested in using them. That is why all the wealth that was gathered by the intellectuals and warrior types was spent for things they desired.

<10> As the influence and power of the intellectuals increased, they longed for more pleasure and resources. Ultimately it put the Vipras in a position of economic dependency on the Vaeshyas, for the Vaeshyas controlled the wealth the Vipras spent. This resulted in the domination of the Vaeshyas over the society and their control was completed with the Industrial Revolution. <11> Businessmen could not become the dominant class in the era of the Ksattriyas because these warriors simply would take over the wealth of the rich class (Vaeshyas) by force. But because intellectuals believe in democracy, they could not and did not do that. So the Vaeshyas became the dominating class.

<12> Therefore, these verses prophesy that close to the end of the intellectual domination (Vipras and Vaeshyas), a great kingdom of ten kings would arise, which is symbolized as the ten toes of the image. <13> It would put its strength on the previous intellectual discoveries and beliefs, but many people already have been humbled and have realized the limits of those things. So this kingdom would not be as strong as the previous ones. They still would have some strength, but half of it would be of clay.

"And whereas thou sawest iron mixed with miry clay, they shall mingle themselves with the seed of men: but they shall not cleave one to another, even as iron is not mixed with clay." (Daniel 2:43)

<14> Because many would have already realized the limits of intellectualized ideals ("seed of men"), therefore they would not support these kings, as iron will not mix with clay, so these people also would not mix together, and the kingdom would not be strong.

"And in the days of these kings shall the God of heaven set up a kingdom, which shall never be destroyed: and the kingdom shall not be left to other people, but it shall break in pieces and consume all these kingdoms, and it shall stand for ever." (Daniel 2:44)

"Forasmuch as thou sawest that the stone was cut out of the mountain without hands, and that it brake in pieces the iron, the brass, the clay, the silver, and the gold; the great God hath made known to the king what shall come to pass hereafter: and the dream is certain, and the interpretation thereof sure." (Daniel 2:45)

<15> It is in the climax of these last ten kings when the truth will be revealed, those who have made themselves ready through many lifetimes (Saints) will be chosen (Paravipras), <16> the true spiritual people will be unified, and the Kingdom of Heaven will be established on earth as it is in heaven.

<17> This last part of the dream also completely agrees with the things that are revealed in chapter 10 of The Revelation about "a small book." This small book is the symbol of intellectual knowledge which is very small in comparison to the knowledge of God. <18> It is also in the time of the intellectual heights that "...there should be time no

Tablet Three

VISION OF THE FOUR BEASTS BY DANIEL

Chapter 7

"In the first year of Belshazzar king of Babylon Daniel had a dream and visions of his head upon his bed: then he wrote the dream, and told the sum of the matters." (Daniel 7:1)

<1> This is a dream by Daniel himself. Also it is not a usual dream but it is a "dream and visions." It is the kind of dream which comes to a person as a message from the spiritual world (Unconscious Mind, Universal Mind).

"Daniel spake and said, I saw in my vision by night, and, behold, the four winds of the heaven strove upon the great sea." (Daniel 7:2)

<2> As it was explained, wind is the symbol of the illusion of life (Maya). These illusions which are the cause of all suffering are four: Attraction, desire and its fulfillment, attachment, and greed. <3> The excess (unnecessary) **attraction** toward the external world and its temporary pleasures create **desires** in man. **Fulfillment of desires** causes man to become **attached** to the external world, **attachment** increases the desires and brings greed to have more and more, and **greed** drowns the man deeper into the ocean of Maya (illusion).

<4> As the man sinks deeper into these four illusionary phenomena, they become even stronger to confuse the person. <5> That is why they are like the "four winds of the heaven" which hit "the great sea."

<6> Water is a symbol for consciousness. When symbolized as a river, sea, or ocean (restless waters), it implies confused consciousness (mind). <7> The confusion of the mind is created by these four "winds of the heaven." As the hurricane creates much restlessness in the ocean, also it is these four winds which cause desires to arise in the consciousness and create attachment, greed, more attraction, more desires, and so on. <8> "The great sea" here is the symbol of the collective consciousness of the people of the earth. ("Great sea" – ocean – is different than "sea." The great sea is the symbol for the collective consciousness of many humans, but sea is the symbol of the confused mind of one unit consciousness or human).

"And four great beasts came up from the sea, diverse one from another." (Daniel 7:3)

<9> "Four great beasts came up" from this confused world. They arose from the earth with earthly standards (these beasts are different than the ones described in The Revelation. Those beasts have arisen from the sea, not from the great sea).

<10> As it will be described later on in this chapter, "These great beasts, which are four, are four kings, which shall arise out of the earth" (verse 17). Again the emphasis is that they "shall arise out of the earth," so that great sea (earth) is from where their standards have come. These kings are not from heaven but from earth. They are as confused as others on earth, and have arisen from this confusion. <11> They are "diverse one from another," or they are not from the same quality but are different with separate purposes.

<12> Also, the fourth beast had ten horns on his head, "...fourth beast, ... and it had ten horns" (verse 7). <13> These ten horns are the ten kings which would come out of the fourth kingdom, "And the ten horns out of this kingdom [fourth kingdom] are ten kings that shall rise;…" (verse 24).

<14> In the dream of King Nebuchadnezzar, the ten toes which had come out of the feet and legs of the fourth kingdom were the ten kings who would arise in later days. Here in Daniel's dream, these ten horns have the same meaning as those ten toes.

<15> Therefore, the vision-dream of Daniel and the dream about the metal image have identical messages and also are complementary. So the first beast will be as the first kingdom, or the head of gold, or the Chaldean Empire with King Nebuchadnezzar as its leader.

<16> The second beast is the same as the silver part of the metal image. The third beast is the brass part, and the fourth is the iron part of the image. The ten toes are the same as the ten horns, which will be ten kings who will arise from the earth.

Tablet Four

"The first was like a lion, and had eagle's wings: I beheld till the wings thereof were plucked, and it was lifted up from the earth, and made stand upon the feet as a man, and a man's heart was given to it." (Daniel 7:4)

<1> This first beast is the first king or Nebuchadnezzar. "Lion" is the symbol of kingship, and eagle's wings are the symbol of high ideals and also egotistical ambitions. <2> This first beast's wings would be plucked. It would be humbled, and its ego would be destroyed. After its wings were plucked, then it would be exalted and would be "lifted up." It would go to his higher nature from his lower nature ("earth"). <3> After it went to its higher self, he would be "made [to] stand upon the feet as a man." He would become a man with true higher human qualities, "and a man's heart would be given to it."

<4> This is a description of King Nebuchadnezzar, who also was the head of gold of the metal image. This first beast was humbled and was given a "man's heart" (his egoistical pursuance is described in chapter 3 of Daniel, and how he was humbled and eventually accepted the God of Daniel is told in chapter 4). <5> He overcame his lower nature and became a just king. As in the image he was the best part (head) from the best quality metal (gold), here also he is described as a beast with a heart of man and with good qualities.

"And behold another beast, a second, like to a bear, and it raised up itself on one side, and it had three ribs in the mouth of it between the teeth of it: and they said thus unto it, Arise, devour much flesh." (Daniel 7:5)

<6> This second king also had a dominating characteristic as a bear, which is a great ruling animal in the forest and usually is not as blood-thirsty as the leopard (next beast). As the second kingdom in the image (from the spiritual-values point of view) was symbolized as silver which is inferior to gold, so is the bear to the lion.

<7> Also it did not have a "man's heart," but it was given authority to devour much flesh, "...and they said thus unto it, Arise, devour much flesh." It was not "lifted up from the earth" as the first one, but "it raised up itself on one side." He never became as high as the first one, and he was much lower in nature.

"After this I beheld, and lo another, like a leopard, which had upon the back of it four wings of a fowl; the beast had also four heads; and dominion was given to it." (Daniel 7:6)

<8> This third one was even more savage than the second, "like a leopard." In chapter 8 of the book of Daniel, he will have another vision in which it is revealed that the second and third kingdoms after the Chaldean Empire would be the Persian and Greco-Macedonian Empires.

<9> The Persian Empire is symbolized as a ram with two great horns (as two great kings), and the Grecian Empire is symbolized as "an he goat" with one "notable horn" as its first great king (Alexander the Great). <10> Also in the interpretation of that vision it is predicted that the Grecian Empire would be divided into four after Alexander.

<11> This third beast is also the third kingdom or the Grecian Empire. Here in this

vision this division of the empire into four is symbolized by the "four wings" (symbol of the protective force) and "four heads" (symbol of kings or heads of state).

<12> All these things happened later on exactly as the vision said. Also it is important to notice that as the different parts of the image were different in quality and as the later kings arose, they lost their fineness (from gold until iron). <13> So these beasts also became more savage as the later kingdoms arose. This shows that they became more intellectualized and lost their fine qualities and intuitions.

"After this I saw in the night visions, and behold a fourth beast, dreadful and terrible, and strong exceedingly; and it had great iron teeth: it devoured and brake in pieces, and stamped the residue with the feet of it: and it was diverse from all the beasts that were before it; and it had ten horns." (Daniel 7:7)

<14> As the two legs of the image were from iron – a symbol of losing all its spiritual values and becoming inflexible but strong and tough (like the intellect) – this fourth beast also is more dreadful than all the previous three. It was "dreadful and terrible" and was "strong exceedingly," as iron is also stronger than gold, silver, and brass (used as the symbols for the three kingdoms preceding the fourth of iron in the case of the image of the dream of the king).

<15> "And it had great iron teeth": It was even stronger in destructive and savage qualities than the previous three beasts. "It devoured and brake in pieces, and stamped the residue with the feet of it": All the spiritual values and greatness were taken away from this beast. It had no "man's heart." <16> It had its domination purely by its own strength. It destroyed whatever good had been left, "residue."

<17> As it was described, the first kingdom is the Chaldean Empire, the second the Persian, and the third the Greco-Macedonian. <18> Also as it was revealed in the dream of King Nebuchadnezzar about the image made of different metals, the fourth kingdom was symbolized by the two legs of the image, which means it would be divided. The great empire that came after the Greco-Macedonian and was divided into two can be none other than the Roman Empire which was divided, with Rome and Constantinople as the two capitals. So this fourth beast is also related to the Roman Empire.

<19> The Romans also were intellectually superior to the previous three. <20> Intellect in comparison to spiritual quality is like comparing iron to gold. Gold is precious and flexible like a true spiritual person, while iron is dry and inflexible, like intellectuals who want to find set rules and regulations, in order to fix everything and solve all problems or explain the unexplainable. **<21> In fact, when spirituality becomes intellectualized, then it loses its flexibility and truth, and becomes a burden on humanity and a source of suffering.**

<22> "And it was diverse from all the beasts that were before it": As the other three previous kingdoms tried to dominate by their might, this one tried to dominate not only by its might but also by its mind. <23> The Roman Empire was the first to constitute a national assembly and senate, and brought democracy, which is from an intellectual mentality, as the Renaissance also was led by intellectuals.

<24> "And it had ten horns," as the image in King Nebuchadnezzar's dream had ten toes. As the toes emerged from the legs and feet, the horns also emerged from the head of the beast. <25> So the ten horns or the last kingdom (fifth king) will have a very close relationship with this fourth kingdom (Roman Empire), or the last of this kind.

Tablet Five

"I considered the horns, and, behold, there came up among them another little horn, before whom there were three of the first horns plucked up by the roots: and, behold, in this horn were eyes like the eyes of man, and a mouth speaking great things." (Daniel 7:8)

<1> "There came up among them another little horn": This little horn is one which will make "war with the saints, and prevailed against them" (verse 21). It "shall speak great words against the most High, and shall wear out the saints of the most High, and think to change times and laws: and they shall be given into his hand until a time and times and dividing of time [2,300 years, explained in 8:14]" (verse 25).

<2> Also in chapter 8 of Daniel, in his vision about a ram and an he goat, the ram is the symbol of the Persian empire, and the he goat is the symbol of the Grecian Empire. The he goat would have a "notable horn" as the symbol of its first king. <3> After this king conquered the whole world, he would be destroyed and his kingdom would be divided into four. From one of these four kingdoms would arise a little horn, "And out of one of them [four kingdoms] came forth a little horn, which waxed exceeding great,..." (Daniel 8:9).

<4> This little horn also would "wax great" and stand against Saints and God's Laws, "And it waxed great, even to the host of heaven; and it cast down some of the host and of the stars to the ground, and stamped upon them" (8:10). "Yea, he magnified himself even to the prince of the host,..."(8:11). This little horn also would do as the little horn grown in the middle of the ten horns on the head of the fourth beast.

<5> Also in chapter 8 it is revealed that this horn will practice and prosper for two thousand three hundred years, "...Unto two thousand and three hundred days; then shall the sanctuary be cleansed" (8:14), or "a time [one thousand years] and times [one thousand years] and the dividing of time [three hundred years]" (7:25).

<6> Therefore, this little horn which is symbolized as "a king of fierce countenance, and understanding dark sentences,..." (8:23) does not refer to a human or even a dynasty, because none of them lasted for two thousand three hundred years. <7> However, at the time of the Grecian Empire and after that, the greatest thinkers and philosophers of humanity were born. Socrates, Plato, Aristotle, and their students, created the cornerstone of the philosophical and intellectual understanding of the era to come. This happened around 300 BC.

<8> These intellectual discoveries and the ability of the human to reason, question, and try to find the answers behind all things, brought a new outlook to man which later on also made him go astray. <9> That is what the tree of knowledge of good and evil is (Gen. 2:17), when man tries to reason what is good or bad by himself instead of following God's Laws.

<10> This intellectualization of all things and trying to find answers through reasoning and experimental methods made man believe that he can create his own laws, change time, understand all the truth behind this universe through science and intellect, discredit the religions, create superstitions, divide humans by creating false doctrines, and so on. <11> This belief in the superiority of the human intellect and the use of it to cover spiritual truth, which creates superstitions and the separation between humans, is what the little horn is.

<12> It is true that the intellectual era was started by the three great philosophers about 300 BC. But its thorough grip on human life and the world reached its zenith at the time of the Roman Empire and after that.

<13> In fact, the world is still under the influence of this little horn, and will be until the truth comes and destroys all the intellectualization of things and establishes the truth.

<14> This does not mean that the intellect and intellectual endeavors are worthless. But it means that intellectual understandings have a limit. After that they become dry, inflexible, and bitter, like the little book in The Revelation (10:10). <15> Only when intellect is combined with spiritual understanding (intuition) does it reach its highest usefulness.

<16> Therefore, many ideas which came out of the Roman Empire were intellectualized and followed by the intellectual nations (Gentiles) unto this day. <17> In fact, the Medieval era in Europe started after this time,

because the religions of Europe became so dry that they developed such a superstitious and binding nature that they brought suffering and misery to the people.

<18> History shows what this little horn did to Europe for centuries. But its dominance is still continuing to this day, and will continue until sometime in the future. <19> As it says in this prophecy, it "came up among them," and these ten horns will be the fifth dominating force (kingdom) which is the last intellectual domination. <20> So it is through this little horn that these ten horns (kings) will be unified and will be partly of iron and partly of clay. They will be the last attempt to stand against the truth. But they will fail.

<21> "Before whom there were three of the first horns plucked up by the roots": Through following this little horn, many of these kings will be destroyed from their "roots," as some European countries (such as Spain, France, and England) tried to expand their domination or tried to unify Europe in the past, but they failed. Their endeavors were "plucked up by the roots."

<22> "And, behold, in this horn were eyes like the eyes of man, and a mouth speaking great things." So it looks great and talks great, but it will not show the truth nor bring the truth. <23> It is just all big talk.

Tablet Six

"I beheld till the thrones were cast down, and the Ancient of days did sit, whose garment was white as snow, and the hair of his head like the pure wool: his throne was like the fiery flame, and his wheels as burning fire." (Daniel 7:9)

<1> "The Ancient of days" refers to God, the Father who is the first one in Pure Consciousness and has complete control over this universe (for a detailed explanation, read The Essence and The Base). <2> He is the oldest. He is "the Ancient of days."

<3> White is the symbol of purity and detachment. Fire is a symbol for spiritual powers and also purity (purified spiritual powers).

"A fiery stream issued and came forth from before him: thousand thousands ministered unto him, and ten thousand times ten thousand stood before him: the judgment was set, and the books were opened." (Daniel 7:10)

<4> After the ten horns in the fourth beast arise, corresponding to the ten toes of the image as the fifth kingdom or empire, then "the thrones" will be "cast down" and the "books" (Akashic Records) will be opened so that men will be judged according to their deeds. The Kingdom of God will be established on earth.

"I beheld then because of the voice of the great words which the horn spake: I beheld even till the beast was slain, and his body destroyed, and given to the burning flame." (Daniel 7:11)

<5> "Even till the beast was slain": Until the complete destruction of the base of these pagan ideologies and intellectual beliefs occur, this little horn will continue to exist and talk great words but not the truth. It is very stout, "…that horn that had eyes, and a mouth that spake very great things, whose look was more stout than his fellows" (verse 20).

<6> "And his body [was] destroyed, and given to the burning flame": When the truth comes, then this horn and its influences will be destroyed and will be purified by the flame of the truth, "and given to the burning flame."

"As concerning the rest of the beasts, they had their dominion taken away: yet their lives were prolonged for a season and time." (Daniel 7:12)

<7> Roman influence and their ideas are still dominating human society. Even the words "Senate" and "veto," and the yearly calendar, times of the day, etc., have all come from that culture. <8> But the domination of the Chaldean Empire, Persian Empire, and Grecian Empire have been taken away and will be taken away even more. However, they are still alive in some parts of the world, "yet their lives were prolonged for a season and time."

COMMENTARIES ON PROPHECIES IN DANIEL *Tablet 7*

"I saw in the night visions, and, behold, one like the Son of man came with the clouds of heaven, and came to the Ancient of days, and they brought him near before him." (Daniel 7:13)

<9> "Son of man" is one who is in Pure Consciousness but comes back to earth as a human (Avatar). "Clouds of heaven" mean the confusion which comes to the world (great sea) with the four winds of heaven (attraction, desire, attachment, and greed). <10> So the "Son of man" comes whenever it is necessary to establish the truth and righteousness in the confused world, especially at the end of this era.

"And there was given him dominion, and glory, and a kingdom, that all people, nations, and languages, should serve him: his dominion is an everlasting dominion, which shall not pass away, and his kingdom that which shall not be destroyed." (Daniel 7:14)

<11> "And there was given him dominion, and glory, and a kingdom…": These things were given to him. He did not gain these things by himself. It is only by His Grace that he had dominion over all, or it is He who gives the dominion and glory to people. <12> More correctly, it is He (God) who gives dominion and all things to His Saints after the Kingdom of Heaven is established.

<13> "All people, nations, and languages, should serve him…": As it is said in verse 10, "thousand thousands ministered unto him…." These are the ones who had reached Pure Consciousness and are in heaven, and they serve Him (God). <14> But when the son of man comes on the earth, or the one who God has anointed to have dominion on earth, then "all people, nations, and languages, should serve him" as a representative of the Lord. <15> However, this does not mean that people should surrender unto him and his words, but they should surrender to the words of God (truth) which are revealed through Him and His Prophets. <16> All people should "bow their heads in front of and serve all those Great Souls who will show them how to become Pure Consciousness, and how to receive the compassion and mercy of the Lord."

<17> Whoever reaches Pure Consciousness has "everlasting dominion," especially the First Begotten Son.

<18> Now from verse 17 the interpretation of the vision is given.

Tablet Seven

"These great beasts, which are four, are four kings, which shall arise out of the earth." (Daniel 7:17)

<1> "Which are four kings" corresponds to the first four kingdoms in the metal image in king Nebuchadnezzar's dream. They will arise "out of the earth," that is, they are earthly kingdoms.

<2> It also should be noticed that these kings had arisen on earth after the Children of Israel rejected God as their king (I Samuel 8:7), so God again wanted to show the human how earthly kings and laws are limited and eventually will result in suffering. <3> Even the Roman peace could not last forever!

"But the saints of the most High shall take the kingdom, and possess the kingdom for ever, even for ever and ever." (Daniel 7:18)

<4> But eventually those who have gone through much struggle in many lifetimes and have made themselves ready to become Paravipras will gain control of the world and will establish the Kingdom of God on earth.

"Then I would know the truth of the fourth beast, which was diverse from all others, exceeding dreadful, whose teeth were of iron, and his nails of brass; which devoured, brake in pieces, and stamped the residue with his feet;" (Daniel 7:19)

"And of the ten horns that were in his head, and of the other which came up, and before whom three fell; even of that horn that had eyes, and a mouth that spake very great things, whose look was more stout than his fellows." (Daniel 7:20)

<5> The real truth of the fourth beast and its importance is not that it is the Roman Empire, but that it is a symbol of the beginning of intellectual domination in the world and the belief of the human that he can create laws and regulations to govern himself, can scientifically overcome nature and explain all things, and can also give freedom to all individuals of doing whatever they want to do.

<6> This new view of human life and ability is what makes the Romans different than the rest of the beasts, "which was diverse from all the beasts that were before it…" (verse 7). After Rome we can see the domination of the intellectuals in human history. <7> Intellectuals control others not by their might but through the ideas and symbols that they create in society. They exploit the masses by spreading binding doctrines, superstitions, and creating differentiation between man and man by adopting classes in society (in fact the caste system in India was created with intellectual Brahmins, not the true Brahmins).

<8> That is why the very base of rejecting God in Communist ideology, the reliance on science in explaining the unexplainable, the belief of man that he can create his own laws and follow them, the intellectualized religions after Rome, and all things that have made man go astray and blaspheme the Lord, is from the confused intellect, which is symbolized by "the little horn with the eyes and mouth."

<9> Also later on in the time of the Industrial Revolution and the era of capitalism, the domination of the businessmen occurred. <10> Businessmen are those intellectuals who use their intelligence in controlling the resources and providing services to others. Also by controlling these resources, they exploit others to become workers in their establishments. <11> As nothing is bad in this universe until it is used in an improper way, intellect and business are not bad, but they become exploitative when they are used in the wrong ways. <12> We are still in this intellectual era until the era of intuition (purified heart) comes.

"I beheld, and the same horn made war with the saints, and prevailed against them;" (Daniel 7:21)

"Until the Ancient of days came, and judgment was given to the saints of the most High; and the time came that the saints possessed the kingdom." (Daniel 7:22)

<13> The whole base of thought in recent centuries is that the intellect of man is superior to religious beliefs. Also intellectualized religions replaced the true religions. So this little "horn made war with the saints and prevailed against them."

<14> But its domination will not last forever. The truth will come, the imperfection of this little horn will be understood, and the true kingdom and understanding will eventually prevail when the Paravipras (Saints) (those true spiritualists who follow the **Eternal Divine Path** and have leadership abilities) will possess the kingdom.

"Thus he said, The fourth beast shall be the fourth kingdom upon earth, which shall be diverse from all kingdoms, and shall devour the whole earth, and shall tread it down, and break it in pieces." (Daniel 7:23)

<15> So this fourth beast is different than the previous three, because it will try to change all things and is based on the belief that there is no need for any other thing but man's intellect and abilities. It will create symbols, superstitions, false religions, change the time, change the old orders, etc. It will try to "tread it down, and break it in pieces."

"And the ten horns out of this kingdom are ten kings that shall arise: and another shall rise after them; and he shall be diverse from the first, and he shall subdue three kings." (Daniel 7:24)

<16> So these ten horns which are ten kings will come "out of this kingdom [the fourth kingdom]." Since each king should have a country, these ten kings are a united nation of ten countries. Then another kingdom will arise among them, and will subdue three kings. This little horn will destroy three kingdoms from their roots. <17> Also, the

ten will be united through this little horn and will fail all together.

"And he shall speak great words against the most High, and shall wear out the saints of the most High, and think to change times and laws: and they shall be given into his hand until a time and times and the dividing of time." (Daniel 7:25)

<18> So this great horn will blaspheme the Lord, will prevail against the Saints, and also will "think to change times and laws." <19> The Romans brought the new calendar, the hours in the day, and changed the time of many festivals to suit themselves. Also they (intellectuals) tried and are trying to bring human laws to replace God's Laws. However, it will not last forever.

"But the judgment shall sit, and they shall take away his dominion, to consume and to destroy it unto the end." (Daniel 7:26)

<20> When the truth comes, all this fallacy will eventually be destroyed.

"And the kingdom and dominion, and the greatness of the kingdom under the whole heaven, shall be given to the people of the saints of the most High, whose kingdom is an everlasting kingdom, and all dominions shall serve and obey him." (Daniel 7:27)

<21> Those who have made themselves ready will inherit the kingdom. The Saints will become the true leaders of humanity, and the kingdom will be His.

"Hitherto is the end of the matter. As for me Daniel, my cogitations much troubled me, and my countenance changed in me: but I kept the matter in my heart." (Daniel 7:28)

<22> "Hitherto is the end of the matter": It is the end of The Plan of God ("the matter") for the earth. His Will, will be done on earth as it is in heaven.

Tablet Eight

VISION OF THE RAM AND HE GOAT BY DANIEL

Chapter 8

"In the third year of the reign of King Belshazzar a vision appeared unto me, even unto me Daniel, after that which appeared unto me at the first." (Daniel 8:1)

"And I saw in a vision; and it came to pass, when I saw, that I was at Shushan in the palace, which is in the province of Elam; and I saw in a vision, and I was by the river of Ulai." (Daniel 8:2)

<1> River symbolizes confusion in the consciousness (mind, water is the symbol for manifested consciousness). These things will happen in the confusion of the world.

"Then I lifted up mine eyes, and saw, and, behold, there stood before the river a ram which had two horns: and the two horns were high; but one was higher than the other, and the higher came up last." (Daniel 8:3)

<2> This ram is described to be the "kings of Media and Persia" (verse 20). This kingdom had two great kings (two horns, also two silver arms of the image in the dream of King Nebuchadnezzar), the second greater than the first ("...the higher came up last").

"I saw the ram pushing westward, and northward, and southward; so that no beasts might stand before him, neither was there any that could deliver out of his hand; but he did according to His Will, and became great." (Daniel 8:4)

<3> Just as the kings of Persia conquered southward, northward, and westward later on, this ram was pushing toward those directions. He was given to conquer all that he desired and no man could stand in front of him, and he "became great." <4> The kings of Persia became great because there was a purpose

which should have been fulfilled through them. <5> That is how God uses humans, however, then the humans think that it is they who are doing the action. But in reality it is He who does all great things through man.

"And as I was considering, behold, an he goat came from the west on the face of the whole earth, and touched not the ground: and the goat had a notable horn between his eyes." (Daniel 8:5)

<6> This he goat is the kingdom of Grecia and the notable horn is its first great king (verse 21) which came from the west and conquered Persia and went even further to Tibet.

"And he came to the ram that had two horns, which I had seen standing before the river, and ran unto him in the fury of his power." (Daniel 8:6)

<7> So the king of Grecia would attack the Persian Kingdom, as did occur.

"And I saw him come close unto the ram, and he was moved with choler against him, and smote the ram, and brake his two horns: and there was no power in the ram to stand before him, but he cast him down to the ground, and stamped upon him: and there was none that could deliver the ram out of his hand." (Daniel 8:7)

<8> The king of Grecia would destroy the Persian Empire, as he did.

"Therefore the he goat waxed very great: and when he was strong, the great horn was broken; and for it came up four notable ones toward the four winds of heaven." (Daniel 8:8)

<9> When this he goat (Grecian Empire) with its great king (Alexander the Great, "notable horn") conquered the whole earth as its kingdom, then the horn would be broken and the kingdom would be divided into four. That is exactly what happened. <10> After Alexander the Great conquered all the great empires and lands as far as Tibet, on his way back he died without any warning, "the great horn was broken." Then his empire was divided between his four great generals, "and for it came up four notable ones." All this has happened from the confusion on earth and earthly bonds, "toward the four winds of heaven."

"And out of one of them came forth a little horn, which waxed exceeding great, toward the south, and toward the east, and toward the pleasant land." (Daniel 8:9)

<11> The intellectual philosophies and new ideas of the Greeks then appeared. This one little horn which later on also appeared in the head of the fourth beast (Roman Empire) symbolizes all the endeavors that have been done to explain that God does not exist (atheism, dialectic materialism, etc.), and also all those intellectualized religions that have created separation between man and man.

<12> This base of intellectualizing all things started from Athens, "...out of one of them...," which is in one of the four kingdoms in the west part of the Grecian Empire.

<13> It would conquer the south, west ("toward the pleasant land," America) and east. There has never been such a king as a person from the Grecian Empire. This little horn is a symbol for intellectual achievements of Athens through great philosophers and thinkers of Greece and the beginning of the domination of the intellect.

"And it waxed great, even to the host of heaven; and it cast down some of the host and of the stars to the ground, and stamped upon them." (Daniel 8:10)

<14> The superior power of this little horn is not over other kings or empires but is directed toward spirituality and the truth of the existence of the Lord, "even to the host of heaven." <15> **It is intellectual arguments that try to explain all things, by putting God out of the discussion.** <16> Through empirical studies, it is intellectual discussions which talk about dialectic materialism and try to explain that God does not exist. It is the intellectuals who try to bring laws from themselves and replace them for the Laws of God. So they try to wax great, "even to the host of heaven." They feel they are God themselves.

COMMENTARIES ON PROPHECIES IN DANIEL

<17> It was this horn which created superstitions, differentiation between religions and men, and attempted to destroy the idea of God and His Laws, "it cast down some of the host and of the stars to the ground, and stamped upon them."

"Yea, he magnified himself even to the prince of the host, and by him the daily sacrifice was taken away, and the place of his sanctuary was cast down." (Daniel 8:11)

<18> It was this intellectual superiority which replaced the truth of religions. Man started arguing with the Laws and regulations of the Lord and tried to replace them (man always tries to replace His Laws) with what he believed was good, like the woman who thought the fruit of the knowledge of good and evil was good to eat (Genesis chapter 3), without having the deep feeling of seeing the spiritual consequences of her actions and beliefs ("eating of the tree of the knowledge of good and evil": To follow the sight or appearance instead of listening to God).

<19> A true seeker does not argue with God and His Revelations, but he contemplates His Sayings, and will find the truth of His Commands for purity, sacrifice (not being self-centered), obedience, and Daharma. <20> But it is intellectuals who try to intellectualize His Commands and do not understand the depth and effect of them on the well-being of humanity.

<21> That is why they magnify themselves "even to the prince of the host." They say there is no truth but their own reasoning. They do not even know what reasoning is itself!

They intellectualize religions and make them dry and a burden on humanity (like the Pharisees and scribes), "and by him the daily sacrifice was taken away." <22> They also destroy the House of God which is within them by crudifying themselves with thinking about matter instead of the spirit behind it, "and the place of his sanctuary was cast down." <23> The destruction of the temple in Jerusalem is a symbol of this. It was destroyed by the Romans!

"And an host was given him against the daily sacrifice by reason of transgression, and it cast down the truth to the ground; and it practiced, and prospered." (Daniel 8:12)

<24> Because of the attraction of Maya ("an host was given him") and the dullness of the mind to grasp the reality, which follows when man becomes attached to this manifested world instead of understanding why and how it has been manifested, this little horn will use all its power to destroy the daily sacrifice (sacrifice for others, forgetting the self for the rest of the universe), and it will cast down the truth of the religion and reality behind this universe to the ground, and try to destroy it.

<25> With doing these things many believed in him and thought they could understand everything through intellect. They believed all religions are just an imaginary fancy thought of some too smart or crazy people, "...and it cast down some of the host and of the stars to the ground, and stamped upon them" (verse 10). He practiced this teaching and prospered.

Tablet Nine

"Then I heard one saint speaking, and another saint said unto that certain saint which spake, How long shall be the vision concerning the daily sacrifice, and the transgression of desolation, to give both the sanctuary and the host to be trodden under foot?" (Daniel 8:13)

<1> These people who will reach higher consciousness and know surely that there is a God with a definite Plan for this creation but do not know what The Plan is and how it will be fulfilled, despair that "...How long shall be the vision concerning the daily sacrifice, and the transgression of desolation, to give both the sanctuary and the host to be trodden under foot?" They wonder when the Kingdom of God will come and the unworthy people and unbelievers will be destroyed (their diseased minds).

COMMENTARIES ON PROPHECIES IN DANIEL

"And he said unto me, Unto two thousand and three hundred days; then shall the sanctuary be cleansed." (Daniel 8:14)

<2> If they are real seekers, then The Holy Ghost will reveal to them the truth. If each day is a symbol for one year, then it will take around two thousand three hundred years after the empire of Grecia that the truth will destroy the intellectualized world. <3> No king can live that long. So it is not talking about a human king nor even about a dynasty. But the little horn is the symbol of intellectual domination in this period. The Grecian Empire started its decline around three hundred B.C.

"And it came to pass, when I, even I Daniel, had seen the vision, and sought for the meaning, then, behold, there stood before me as the appearance of a man." (Daniel 8:15)

<4> Daniel intensely desired to know the meaning of his vision. So the meaning would be given to him, "Ask, and it shall be given you; seek, and ye shall find; knock, and it shall be opened unto you" (Matthew 7:7).

"And I heard a man's voice between the banks of Ulai, which called, and said, Gabriel, make this man to understand the vision." (Daniel 8:16)

<5> All the revelations, truth, and spiritual knowledge can be gained through Gabriel, which is The Holy Ghost (satva guna).

"So he came near where I stood: and when he came, I was afraid, and fell upon my face: but he said unto me, Understand, O son of man: for at the time of the end shall be the vision." (Daniel 8:17)

<6> The end of the era in the vision would be two thousand three hundred years after this little horn was created following the four kings of the Grecian Empire.

"Now as he was speaking with me, I was in a deep sleep on my face toward the ground: but he touched me, and set me upright." (Daniel 8:18)

<7> He was in a trance and was bent forward, so his kundalini was blocked. Therefore he was straightened "upright," which is with the spine straight.

<8> Kundalini is the spiritual energy (consciousness) latent at the base of the spine. When it rises, it will open spiritual centers and true understanding. Because it rises through a very tiny channel in the middle of the spine, when the body is bent the channel is blocked. Therefore, in meditation the spine should be kept straight so that this channel is open and the kundalini is able to rise.

"And he said, Behold, I will make thee know what shall be in the last end of the indignation: for at the time appointed the end shall be." (Daniel 8:19)

<9> After he was straightened up, then Gabriel said, "Behold, I will make thee know...." So The Holy Ghost was going to reveal to him what will happen in the last days and how it will come about. **<10> So the period of injustice and indignation was also permitted by the Lord to happen so that it would become a lesson to humanity.**

"The ram which thou sawest having two horns are the kings of Media and Persia." (Daniel 8:20)

<11> The first kingdom of the five was the Chaldean Empire. Now here it is revealed that the next will be the Persian Empire, symbolized by a ram (calmer and more spiritual than the rough he goat). Its notable kings are symbolized as two horns of the ram. The horn therefore is the symbol of earthly domination. Also the two arms and chest of the metal image were of silver. The two arms are also symbols of the two great kings of Persia.

"And the rough goat is the king of Grecia: and the great horn that is between his eyes is the first king." (Daniel 8:21)

<12> The third kingdom to come will be the Grecian Empire, and the notable horn is its first great king. As the third beast was more dreadful than the second, so the he goat is rougher than the ram (the symbol for the second empire).

"Now that being broken, whereas four stood up for it, four kingdoms shall stand up out of the nation, but not in his power." (Daniel 8:22)

<13> This first great king will die, and his empire will be divided into four kingdoms. This exactly happened. After Alexander the Great suddenly died, his kingdom was divided between his four commanders. But they would never become as great as he, "not in his power."

"And in the latter time of their kingdom, when the transgressors are come to the full, a king of fierce countenance, and understanding dark sentences, shall stand up." (Daniel 8:23)

"And his power shall be mighty, but not by his own power: and he shall destroy wonderfully, and shall prosper, and practise, and shall destroy the mighty and the holy people." (Daniel 8:24)

"And through his policy also he shall cause craft to prosper in his hand; and he shall magnify himself in his heart, and by peace shall destroy many: he shall also stand up against the Prince of princes; but he shall be broken without hand." (Daniel 8:25)

<14> This is all about the little horn which came "in the latter time of their kingdom," which was explained to be the fulfillment of intellectual thoughts and philosophy, at the time of the appearance of the greatest philosophers and thinkers of mankind, Aristotle, Plato, and Socrates.

<15> As it was explained, by these intellectuals the cornerstone of human life for about the next two thousand three hundred years was planned (especially in the West). <16> However, after this period man again will understand that human intellect is limited. It neither can explain the unexplainable, nor can it bring everlasting happiness, because it is dry like brass and iron.

<17> This little horn will also appear later on in the Roman Empire as the little horn in the middle of the ten horns on the head of the beast. This second little horn, which is really the same as the first one, even gains greater influence over man's life. It changes time, creates human laws and governments, intellectualizes religions, institutes new festivals and holidays, and so on.

<18> This little horn will dominate human life for more than two thousand years after it was created during the Grecian Empire, and will continue until the ten kings arise on earth. <19> Then is the time humans will understand that the only way is to go beyond intellect and follow God's Laws and regulations (Daharma) and accept Him as the only King, because intellectual knowledge is just like a little book which is sweet in the beginning, but bitter and dry at the end (Rev. 10:10).

<20> The phrase, "and by peace shall destroy many" means that by the preaching of democracy and the use of diplomacy, an illusive peace will be created, but through these tools (politics) very subtly the truth of the spirit will be destroyed.

"And the vision of the evening and the morning which was told is true: wherefore shut thou up the vision; for it shall be for many days." (Daniel 8:26)

<21> There were some visions which have been shut up here which are true also. Because the Bible is complete, is one of the basic Scriptures of religions, and all things have been revealed in it, those visions which are "shut up" here are revealed in later books, especially in The Revelation, the last book in the Bible. Actually what is explained in Daniel was "sealed up" in The Revelation (10:4). What is sealed up here in Daniel is revealed in The Revelation.

"And I Daniel fainted, and was sick certain days; afterward I rose up, and did the king's business; and I was astonished at the vision, but none understood it." (Daniel 10:27)

<22> The spiritual forces are very strong, and the human nervous system and body are often too weak to withstand them. That is why even Daniel, with all his experiences of having contact with the spiritual world, "fainted" and became ill. That is the reason

for spiritual exercises such as yoga postures or meditation. They all are to strengthen and prepare the human body to be able to receive spiritual forces, visions, and realizations.

Tablet Ten

CONCLUSION

<1> As it is explained in The Holiest Book (holy means "truth") after the flood of Noah, the new generation was created: "men of renown" (Gen. 6:4). <2> This new generation is symbolized by the three sons of Noah: Ham, Japheth, and Shem. Ham is the symbol for two types of humans, the laborers (Shudras) and the warriors (Ksattriyas). Japheth also is a symbol of two types of humans, intellectuals (Vipras) and business-oriented people (Vaeshyas). Shem is the symbol for true spiritual humans, those who are called Masters, seers, or true Great Souls (Brahmins).

<3> These five types were separated from the very beginning in the new generation from the old generation after the flood of Noah, but this new generation went through twelve thousand years of evolution until their true characteristics were developed.

<4> In a short period of time after the flood of Noah, the warrior type (Ksattriyan) of the human emerged. Nimrod is the symbol of the first mighty one, or mighty hunter, and the beginning of kingdoms was started by him, "and the beginning of his [Nimrod's] kingdom was Babel..." (Gen. 10:10).

<5> The era of warriors and kings continued until the kingdom of Nebuchadnezzar, which is symbolized in his dream as the gold head of the image. He was the king of kings. He was the last of the mighty ones of war.

<6> After him, the evolution of man went more toward intellectual development and reached its true beginning in 300 B.C. at the end of the Grecian Empire. <7> This beginning of the domination of the intellect, especially the bad side of it, is symbolized and foretold in the prophecies of Daniel as the "little horn with eyes and mouth," one whose look was "more stout than his fellows" (Daniel 7:20).

<8> It is this little horn (bad side of intellect, or intellect without intuition) which will make war with the Saints, blaspheme "the host of the heaven" (God), will try to change times and laws, shall speak great words, etc., until "a time and times and the dividing of time" (Daniel 7:25), or until "two thousand and three hundred days;..." (Daniel 8:14) which can be interpreted as two thousand three hundred years.

<9> It is after this time that the human reaches his highest development and again the spiritual eyes of many will be opened. <10> Also after six thousand years of history, about two thousand years of intellectual domination, and from the lessons in these periods, man will realize that he has no choice but to follow God's Laws. The intellectuals were the dominating force for the last two thousand three hundred years. <11> After this time, the true spiritual humans will emerge (Paravipras), those who are in their higher evolutions, have been prepared through the last six thousand years (as intellectuals also were prepared for the first four thousand years), and will assume the leadership of humanity. That is why after "two thousand and three hundred days" the true spiritual knowledge comes to humanity and "then shall the sanctuary be cleansed" (Daniel 8:14) by the Saints.

<12> It is at this point in history that we are close to the end of the two thousand three hundred years. <13> Also we can see many people are longing for the true spiritual knowledge. <14> Furthermore, the intellectual discoveries and theories are losing their validity as absolute truths more and more; even scientists and intellectuals are reaching the point of realizing that there are elements in all things which cannot be explained. New fields of study and thought have entered into science, such as parapsychology, a common field from which all matters have come, etc.

<15> So we are on the brink of the New Order of the Ages. <16> The only thing left is to unify all Saints and bring the true knowledge unto man, to cleanse the sanctuary, and to establish His Kingdom on earth as it is in heaven.

THE KINGDOM OF HEAVEN ON EARTH

The book, <u>The Kingdom of Heaven on Earth</u>, gives the guidelines for how the Kingdom of Heaven On Earth can be established. It shows how human society advances in a progressive way, and how these guidelines can be used to ease human progress from one phase to the next.

THE KINGDOM OF HEAVEN ON EARTH

"…shall the God of heaven set up a kingdom, which shall never be destroyed: and the kingdom shall not be left to other people,…" (Daniel 2:44)

Tablet One
THE FIVE CLASSES AFTER THE FLOOD OF NOAH

<1> After the flood of Noah, humans were divided into five different types (read Genesis in The Holiest Book, chapters 9-11). They are symbolized by the three sons of Noah: Ham, Japheth, and Shem. <2> Ham is the symbol of the father of those who have characteristics of laborers (Shudras, symbolized by Canaan) and also those with characteristics of warriors or courageous ones (Ksattriyas, symbolized by Nimrod). <3> Japheth is the symbol for those who have intellectual (Vipran) and business (Vaeshyan) abilities. <4> Shem is the symbol of those with true spiritual characteristics (Brahmins) or great seers. That is why Abram (Abraham) came from this generation.

<5> Each of these types have special characteristics which distinguish them from others. Their characteristics in brief are explained below:

Shudras: <6> They are mainly interested in day-to-day life activities. They strive to satisfy their basic physiological and safety needs. Their interests usually remain on this level. <7> As long as these basic needs are met, they have no further ambitions. They form the labor force in society.

Ksattriyas: <8> They struggle to conquer their environment by physical might. Their main objective is to overcome their enemies and obstacles through their strength. <9> They are courageous and protective toward the weak, especially of their subjects. They respect honor, discipline, and strength. They are pioneers, conquerors, emperors of the past, the chiefs of the tribes, and firefighters, and are involved in any other areas that need leadership.

Vipras: <10> They try to understand the laws governing the society and manifested universe through their intellect. Their struggle is more inside rather than outside themselves. Through this inside struggle they create strong minds and penetrate the realities of the external world. <11> They are responsible for discoveries which help human civilization advance (physically and mentally) and also for much of its degeneration and spiritual superstitions.

Vaeshyas: <12> They can best be described as intellectuals who direct their intellect toward economic developments. They are the businessmen. <13> They are merely interested in accumulation of physical wealth, and then use this wealth for control and distribution of the resources.

Brahmins: <14> They are the ones who are mostly interested in understanding the Laws of the spirit behind all things (Daharmas). They try to understand the relationships between the individual and universe, God and man, and the Laws governing these relationships.

<15> Each individual might have more than one characteristic of each class. That is, an intellectual person might also have Ksattriyan

qualities, or a Brahmin can have Vipran and Shudran qualities. Therefore, there is no clear definite border between the different classes. <16> However, usually a dominating characteristic of one of the classes is present which the man identifies himself with most. That dominating characteristic represents the class to which that person belongs.

<17> Also it is possible to create qualities of one class if a person desires to do so. However, it is very difficult if that is not the person's basic character. <18> It is easier to do if the environment supports such a change, and in that case a person can adopt the new character with some effort.

<19> Apparently the era of Shudras started a long time before the flood of Noah. It began from the time man was sent out from the Garden of Eden, "to till the ground…" (Gen. 3:23). <20> This era (which was a long time ago) was to end after the flood of Noah as his father (Lamech) foretold, "And he [Lamech] called his name Noah, saying, This same shall comfort us concerning our work and toil of our hands,…" (Gen. 5:29).

<21> It was after the flood of Noah that the domination of the Ksattriyan class (kings, as understood by humanity after the flood) started. This is symbolized by the appearance of Nimrod, who "began to be a mighty one in the earth" (Gen. 10:8). "He was a mighty hunter before the Lord," (Gen. 10:9) and "the beginning of his kingdom was Babel,…" (Gen. 10:10). Therefore, Nimrod was the first Ksattriya who became a great king with a kingdom. This happened after the flood of Noah, and he was from the generation of Ham.

<22> This Ksattriyan era continued all through the Old Testament until the time of King Nebuchadnezzar of the Chaldean Empire. It was after this king that the qualities and characteristics of the Ksattriyas started to decline. <23> The decline of this era and the coming of the era of intellectuals is demonstrated through the dreams and visions in the book of Daniel (for more detail, read Commentaries on Prophecies in Daniel, Period of Intellectual Domination).

<24> In the book of Daniel, it is predicted that four kingdoms will arise, one after another, which will successively decline in fine qualities. The fourth kingdom is symbolized as iron (as compared to gold for the first) and from this kingdom a little horn will appear which will gain domination over all things. <25> As it was described in the commentaries on Daniel, the Ksattriyan era declined steadily after King Nebuchadnezzar and intellectual domination increased until the end of the Grecian Empire during the Roman Empire, and even later, until it reached its maturity and zenith with the Renaissance. <26> Then with the Industrial Revolution, the period of domination of the Vaeshyas started and continues to the present age.

<27> Also if we accept Vaeshyas as intellectuals, then the era of intellectuals started during the Grecian Empire with great philosophers such as Aristotle, Plato, and Socrates, and has continued until today.

<28> The true Brahmins never gained any dominating positions in society because they never were interested in things of this world. <29> However, the intellectual spiritualists, those who intellectualized the religions and Scriptures and created binding doctrines to exploit the masses, gained a great control over people. These intellectual spiritualists can also be viewed as part of the intellectual era. The very loud example of this is the influence of the Roman Catholic Church in medieval times in Europe.

Tablet Two

HISTORICAL EXPLANATION OF THE CLASS DOMINATION

<1> In the previous chapter, the domination of the different classes in different eras during the last six thousand years of history is explained. <2> As it was described in The Holiest Book, in the second chapter of Genesis, God has created this universe self-

sustaining. He only interferes in this system when it is extremely necessary. <3> Around twelve thousand years ago, after the flood of Noah, the political and social systems in human civilization were also made in this way (self-sustaining). Human civilization has continued to progress during these years through the clashes between different classes (Shudran, Ksattriyan, Vipran, and Vaeshyan) and through the domination of each class in its era to further human advancement.

<4> In the era of Shudras, man was living in fear and awe. They had few advancements in terms of tools and living conditions. Also they were afraid of all things in their surroundings. They would not dare to leave their territories to explore other lands. In short, they had no courage.

<5> That is why in the Shudran era, physical strength, courage, the ability to hunt, and leadership qualities were praised by those who did not possess these characteristics. <6> After a period of time, the courageous ones (Ksattriyas) created a distinguished class in their tribes. The greatest of them became the head or chief of the tribe.

<7> These chiefs later on became the generals, kings, and emperors. They reached such a status that godly attributes were given to them, or at least it was believed that their authority was by Divine sanction. As we can read in the book of <u>Daniel</u>, King Nebuchadnezzar made an image and demanded all to worship it, and all did.

<8> In the beginning of this era (Ksattriyan), the successor to the previous leader would be selected through a contest between candidates. But later on, this process was changed, and the son of the leader would just inherit the throne. This arrangement simplified the selection of the successor, but also weakened the leadership qualities, <9> **because the son of a good leader does not necessarily have the abilities of his father.**

<10> Also as the kingdoms expanded and empires were created, the administrative abilities of the Vipras were more and more needed. <11> In addition, with the numerous battles, there evolved an increasing reliance on sophisticated tools, weapons, and political abilities, and it was the Vipras who had the abilities to develop such tools, weapons, and diverse political maneuvers. So the kings and monarchs started to depend more and more on their ministers and administrators. <12> The battles between enemies was shifted from physical struggles into political, and the advancement of artillery was encouraged in order to assume supremacy.

<13> For these reasons the Vipras started to develop, and little by little they gained control and domination over the kings. The monarchs and kings became merely symbolic figures as the heads of state, but the true rulers were the ministers and religious leaders. <14> They exploited the masses by their systems of administration, ideas, and religious superstitions. They created classes, psychological fears, differentiated races from each other, and separated man from man by teaching binding religious doctrines. With these tools they demobilized the masses and kept them in ignorance, and then exploited them far beyond the Ksattriyas.

<15> Ksattriyas inflicted suffering by gathering wealth from their subjects and taking them to the battlefield for purposes of self-glorification. <16> The Vipras not only did both of these exploiting acts, but also created psychological blockades with such deep effects that they still have not been overcome by humanity. <17> **Most of the misunderstandings between humans are because of these doctrines, especially in the case of religions, racism, and idealism.**

<18> However, it is also intellectuals who invented great tools, discovered scientific facts (by His Will) and helped man to develop the finer thoughts, such as the arts.

<19> But Vipras are not faultless. They have an insatiable taste for sensual enjoyment, and also they have very little ability and care for economic development and/or the activities necessary for business ventures. They praise money and wealth for the immediate enjoyment it brings them.

<20> It is Vaeshyas who engage themselves in economic activities, and their joy is

THE KINGDOM OF HEAVEN ON EARTH

to increase their holdings of the wealth. <21> So as the Vipras gathered more power and money, the Vaeshyas provided them with their objects of enjoyment. The money they spent for these enjoyments was collected by the Vaeshyas. Then the Vipras became more and more dependent upon the Vaeshyas for money and resources. Eventually, after the Renaissance and Industrial Revolution, the era of the Vaeshyas was firmly established.

<22> The Ksattriyas exploit Shudras, and the Vipras exploit Shudras and Ksattriyas. However, the Vaeshyas exploit all the other three active classes in society (the Shudras, Ksattriyas, and Vipras). <23> In fact these three classes in the era of the Vaeshyas will all be reduced to Shudrahood. They all will strive for their basic physiological and safety needs. They will sacrifice all greater ideals for the mundane life. <24> They all will become the slaves of the shrewd Vaeshyas.

<25> As it was explained, Brahmins never became the dominating class and will usually be exploited only slightly, because they live simply and with only the minimum. They are not drawn into the battle of material or intellectual domination.

Tablet Three

<1> However, the class domination will not end with the Vaeshyan control over the other three. The Vipras and Ksattriyas who have been reduced to the Shudra level will not tolerate this situation for long. <2> Through Vipran struggle for freedom, they create Ksattriyan (leadership) qualities, and with the help of other Ksattriyas and Shudras, the Shudra revolution will take place.

<3> It will be the Ksattriyas who will assume power a short time after the revolution as the revolutionary consuls or body. <4> The Shudras dominate only for a brief period when chaos and looting occurs right at the time of the revolution. After that, it is the Ksattriyas who gain control over the army or create an armed force for this purpose.

<5> Again later on when order is restored, the era of the Ksattriyas will continue until it becomes tyrannical and opposes any new idea or individual freedom. Also Ksattriyas will become more and more dependent upon Vipras. <6> It is in this time that the spirit of intellectuals will arise. <7> So a struggle will start between these two classes and eventually the Vipras will again become the dominating class.

<8> With their love for individual freedom and democracy, Vipras will direct the society from the collective consciousness of the Ksattriyan era toward democratic freedom for the individual. <9> This again will lead to Vaeshyan domination and eventually a second Shudra revolution. <10> So this cycle will continue.

<11> If individual ownership is not allowed in the Vipran eras, however, a progressive part of the class duration (one cycle of three dominating classes) will be eliminated and an even greater struggle will occur between Ksattriyas and Vipras for power. <12> The elimination of the Vaeshyan class will hinder the progress of human civilization, because it is the Vaeshyas who utilize the discoveries of Vipras for human advancement. They determine how to economically use those discoveries. <13> It is most probable that eventually Vaeshyas will emerge as the dominating class.

<14> This cycle of domination from Ksattriyas to Vipras, to Vaeshyas, and then a Shudra revolution, followed by the start of a new round, can go on forever. <15> After the end of each cycle, however, humans will advance one step further physically, mentally, and spiritually.

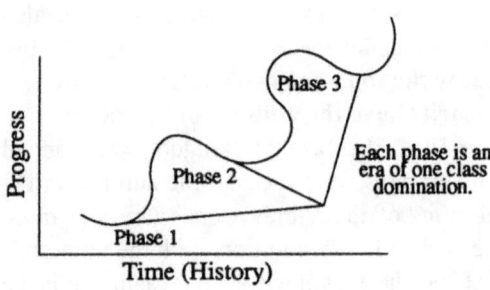

Each phase is an era of one class domination.

THE KINGDOM OF HEAVEN ON EARTH

<16> However, because of the Law of revolution (or evolution), progress, stable progress, and decline of the life span of each class domination, and because of the requirement of great changes in the period of transformation from one era to the next (sometimes with violence), this process, if it is not checked and guided, will bring much suffering, because God would force the change on humanity. Therefore, a system should be devised, or in better words, the True Plan of the Lord for human society, civilization, and its progress, should be understood to prevent the suffering from these changes.

Tablet Four
PARAVIPRAS AND THEIR ROLE IN SOCIETY

...an inheritor of my mountains: and mine elect shall inherit it, and my servants shall dwell there. (Isaiah 65:9)

<1> As it was described, in each era one class was a dominating force in society. Therefore, the leader of society would also emerge from that particular class. So only that class would be favored by the leaders, and other classes would be exploited and suppressed. <2> To eliminate this defect, a leader should be chosen who would have the characteristics of all classes and also be morally and spiritually advanced. This would allow the establishment of justice for all. <3> Such personalities were in the process of being perfected during the last twelve thousand years. They are the true Israelites ("those who struggle with God") or Hebrews ("those who have passed beyond"). They can be called Paravipras.

<4> These Paravipras are the ones who have experienced many incarnations during the last twelve thousand years and have created the characteristics of Shudras, Ksattriyas, Vipras, and Vaeshyas. They also are spiritually advanced and are very in tune with His Will. They are incorruptible.

<5> They are those who have gone through the progress from the first seal in **The Greatest Sign** to the sixth. They have awakened their spiritual powers (☯). They know that without a proper environment and application of the Laws of the Lord (✡), human progress is impossible. For establishing such an environment (the Kingdom Of Heaven On Earth) sacrifice – not being self-centered, to be humble – (✝) is necessary. They utilize all their energy and abilities toward their ideal (one-pointedness) and will surrender all to Him. They become submissive to Him (☪) <6> and create a universal feeling to shatter all narrowness of the mind (✹). They will tirelessly work toward their ideal (✡), to bring the Kingdom Of Heaven On Earth, as it is in heaven, and eventually by their help, all will reach the goal, Pure Consciousness (卍).

<7> Those Elected Ones, through this process in the last twelve thousand years, are now ready to manifest these qualities. They work to fulfill the purpose of this creation, which is to bring the whole universe to Pure Consciousness. In doing so they will create a society in which all have equal opportunities to progress physically, mentally, and spiritually.

<8> Because they have the characteristics of all classes, therefore, they themselves are classless. <9> They can work like a Shudra if it is necessary. They guide Shudras with an iron hand and understand their needs and mentality, so they deal with them on their level.

<10> They are courageous and fearless like Ksattriyas, so they will fight for and protect the oppressed. <11> They have Vipran abilities to grasp the realities behind the material world and intellectual understandings, so they also will prevent intellectuals from spreading superstitious and binding ideals.

<12> They are shrewd like Vaeshyas in economic development, but understand how all can be exploited through it. Therefore they can prevent Vaeshyas from going too far before a revolution breaks out.

<13> Also they will unify all the different religions in the world under one true faith and

THE KINGDOM OF HEAVEN ON EARTH

will destroy the differences between them, as it is explained in **The Greatest Sign**.

<14> The role of Paravipras in society as true leaders is to direct the progress of civilization toward its ultimate goal by guiding the cyclic continuation of class domination as described above in an evolutionary manner.

<15> Paravipras will ease the way for the domination of the next class by active participation from the center of the society (as leaders). At the time that the dominating class starts to go toward stagnation or exploitation, they will ease the way for the next class and weaken the hold of the previous one. <16> With this a smooth progressive society can be created. Each era will come and go without violence and unrest, but after each era society will progress one more step toward the ever-reaching perfection.

<17> Only if humanity establishes this Paravipra-society, and chooses true Paravipras as their leaders (with their great intuition and understanding of the phases of society) will a peaceful world be created and progress toward the goal be accelerated. <18> Otherwise, as the last six thousand years have shown, during which God has guided humanity to this point, the progressive steps of class domination will continue, but with unrest, revolutions, and suffering. <19> In any case, God is the true King of the universe and guide of humanity.

<20> However, because the whole universe is marching toward perfection and the nature of this world is progressive, the emergence of Paravipras is imminent and the Kingdom of God will be realized by all on earth as it is in heaven.

<21> Also it should be mentioned that the greatest crime is the misuse of the power by these leaders. **If the leaders of a society fall, that whole civilization will fall also.** <22> So it is the responsibility of these leaders to tune themselves to His Will and do what is right in His Eyes. Otherwise the suffering of humanity will continue.

Tablet Five
CONTRIBUTION OF EACH CLASS IN SOCIETY

<1> Each of the active classes in human society (Shudras, Ksattriyas, Vipras, Vaeshyas, and Brahmins) have contributed to many facets of human society. All of them are necessary in the human march to perfection.

Shudras (Laborers): <2> All the basic physical tasks are done by this class.

   a-**Good trends**: <3> They do the basic tasks in society. They play an important part in the economy. They do the tasks so the other classes are able to concentrate on other things.

   b-**Bad trends**: <4> They have limited ability to channel their frustrations to a collective, beneficial endeavor, so in the time of social change they create chaos in society or show their discontentment in an unnatural individual way, such as revenge.

   <5> Sometimes they unreasonably demand higher wages through collective bargaining, so they artificially can increase the cost of commodities.

Ksattriyas: <6> Those who lead the society toward new changes; those with leadership abilities.

   a-**Good trends**: <7> They lead the revolutions and bring new conditions to society. They discipline the society in a way to achieve higher levels in its progress. They protect society from intruders and criminals.

   b-**Bad trends**: <8> They are authoritative. They fear changes when they are in power, and have a military mentality, believing that everything can be solved by force.

Vipras: <9> The brains of the society, the head.

a-**Good trends**: <10> They are the inventors, scientists, administrators, advisors of the leaders, researchers, members of the committees, etc. They help in the advancement of the human standard of living. The more intuitive ones are artists, writers, painters, etc.

b-**Bad trends**: <11> They tend toward excessive love for sensual enjoyment, creation of binding ideas, and development of religious doctrines and superstitions (intellectual spiritualists). They have excessive love for individual freedom and democracy (self-centeredness).

Vaeshyas: <12> The controllers and directors of the economic resources.

a-**Good trends**: <13> They have abilities to combine and use physical resources and intellectual ideas for useful and economical commodities. They are able to distribute these commodities from the manufacturing sites to where they will be used. Also, they help in increasing the standard of living in society.

b-**Bad trends**: <14> They tend toward excessive love for hoarding physical wealth, so this creates suffering for others (greed). They try to substitute business values for all other human values.

Brahmins: <15> The spiritualists, those who are more interested in the Laws of the Lord than the laws of men (they are different than intellectual spiritualists), so they are familiar with those Laws.

a-**Good trends**: <16> They seek God rather than attachment to the material world (Maya). They pursue a simple life and therefore are not burdensome on nature. They are comforters for many as a symbol of the champion of God. They are the Holy men.

b-**Bad trends**: <17> They might become escapists and believe the world is an illusion, and use the excuse of being Holy men for escaping the realities of the external world.

<18> Each class, through their good trends, helps in human progress, and through their bad ones, interferes with its progress. So anytime the bad trends start to appear, Para-vipras would know that it is time to change the course of society for further progress.

Tablet Six

BALANCE

<1> The best state of society is one in which each of the five active social classes is in a balanced position with respect to the other classes. In such a civilization each class will be complementary to the others, and the progress of the human and society will occur at its highest speed.

<2> However, because of the tendency of each class to dominate, maintaining that balance is very difficult, if not impossible.

<3> Because of the existence of these forces in society, five different social movements occur:

1- **Natural movements**: <4> Those usual movements which do not affect the main course of social evolution and do not bring permanent or long-lasting changes. They are temporary, such as short-lived fashions.

2- **Evolutionary movements**: <5> Those main changes which occur gradually in society with little or no violence, such as the change of the Ksattriyan era to Vipran. <6> These usually evolve from the top of the society. That is why Paravipras should assume the top positions of leadership to bring the successive evolutionary phases, with little suffering, into society.

3- **Revolution**: <7> Abrupt forceful changes usually with violence, such as Shudra revolutions. These usually start from the bottom of the society.

4- **Counter-evolution**: <8> A gradual return to a previous phase in the social cycle.

5- **Counter-revolution**: <9> An abrupt forceful return to a previous phase in the social cycle.

<10> Because of the progressive character of social movements, the periods of existence of counter-evolutions are very short. Shorter than these are counter-revolutions.
<11> If the progressive change of social cycles is not naturally permitted, the change will be imposed on society through forceful and violent revolutions. <12> The longer the movement is suppressed, the more explosive will be the eruption.
<13> Before a new phase of the progressive social cycle is created and replaces the previous phase, many attempts will be necessary. <14> As each attempt fails, new leaders will be created and more awareness will be awakened. So, again, because of the progressive nature of society, the progressive phase will eventually succeed. <15> Nothing can stop the progress of the universe toward its goal. It can be delayed, but never stopped. <16> A smooth evolutionary change from one phase to another and from one cycle to the next is possible, and is most preferable, only if true leaders (Paravipras) in society are in the positions of leadership.

<17> Each phase of social movements, like the life span of any other relative thing in this manifested world, goes through five steps before the next phase starts. <18> They are: 1- period of the start of the new phase, 2- progress, 3- peak or a steady period of prosperity, 4- decline, and eventually, 5- stagnation. This is shown in the diagram below.

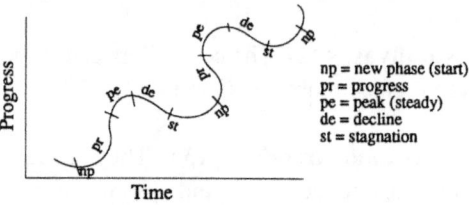

<19> It is in the period of stagnation when the new progressive ideas develop and the new leaders for the next phase emerge to guide people toward further progress.

Tablet Seven

<1> In the case of a counter-evolution or counter-revolution, for a short period of time, the old era will dominate, but it will soon be replaced with a more progressive ideal.
<2> Paravipras will accelerate the progressive phases of the cycle by helping the next era to occur before the previous era reaches its lowest level of decline or stagnation. This will be done by understanding the phase the society is in, and by detecting signs of decline in that stage. <3> The signs of stagnation can easily be detected, as **it is when the dominating class starts to use its position to exploit other classes because of its bad trends**.
<4> The exploitative attitudes are different for each class (Ksattriyas, Vipras, and Vaeshyas). <5> The Ksattriyas will use and direct all resources toward the warfare and arms struggle to gain power over the masses. <6> Vipras will emphasize excessive individuality over reasonable collectivity. They will try to destroy Godly values with intellectual

THE KINGDOM OF HEAVEN ON EARTH *Tablet 7*

explanations and try to make their ideas appear good. <7> Vaeshyas will undermine the higher human side and will replace it with economic values, and the importance of men will be related to their material wealth instead of their higher character.

<8> Whenever each of these decaying signs becomes prominent, Paravipras, with their great intuitive ability, should de-emphasize the help for the dominating class and ease the way for the next one. <9> As the human society progresses and advances toward the higher level, the time period of social cycles will be shortened. <10> Also, because of humanity being in a higher consciousness and more experienced, these cycles will infinitely approach the balanced position, and the progress of society and the human will accelerate with ever-increasing speed.

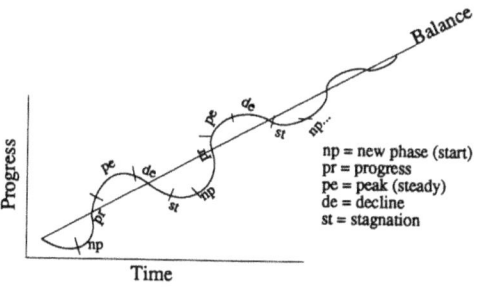

<11> New phases occur before the previous phase reaches the point of stagnation. <12> Also the period of duration shortens and class domination approaches a balanced position between classes.

<13> This cyclical progressive social movement, as explained, started after the flood of Noah and has continued during the last six thousand years. <14> One complete cyclical duration has been completed (in many places in the world) and also in some societies the second duration has started.

<15> By understanding this self-sustaining, progressive, cyclical movement of society, and also through understanding that God has been directing the system during the last twelve thousand years and will continue to do so, then we can see again that He is the true King of humanity and His Laws and systems are faultless and absolute. <16> He will guide all toward its goal whether the humans participate or not!

<17> If humans understand and accept this truth and His System, and if a social order is established which allows only true leaders to be chosen as the heads of society (Paravipras, those who are in tune with the Will of the Lord and the state of society), then such a society will be guided toward the highest progress in a smooth evolutionary manner.

<18> But if such a society (the Kingdom Of Heaven On Earth) is not created, and the human continues with his own course and laws, as has happened in the last six thousand years, the result will be nothing else but suffering which will occur with resisting the progress toward the goal of the universe (to become Divine).

<19> The cyclical progressive social movements are one of the Laws of the Lord. As with any other Law (Daharma) of the Lord, it cannot be broken. Whoever tries to break His Laws will break himself against them. <20> Therefore, it is the duty of all of humanity to strive to bring about the Kingdom Of Heaven On Earth by establishing a true social system which allows the progressive social movements to smoothly continue and by following the nature of all things in life (Daharma). Otherwise the suffering and useless struggle of the human to slow down the progress of the universe will continue. <21> But the ever-continuing progress of the universe toward higher consciousness will not be stopped. Any narrow idea or doctrine will be crushed to nothingness if it stays in the way of the everlasting progress of the universe.

<22> Just as those animals who did not adapt themselves to the new earthly conditions in the evolutionary process were destroyed, also those who oppose the progress of humanity by their narrow views cannot continue to exist for long.

THE KINGDOM OF HEAVEN ON EARTH
Tablet Eight

THE CLASSLESS HUMANS

<1> Beside the five active social classes, namely, Shudras, Ksattriyas, Vipras, Vaeshyas, and Brahmins, there are four more types of humans who live in society but are classless. <2> They are Prophets (Avatars, God's sons, etc.), Gurus (true spiritual teachers), Artists, and Paravipras. These four classless types of humans can be briefly described as below:

Prophets (Avatars, Sons of God): <3> Those who have come to earth to bring a new message to humanity or to re-establish a forgotten faith. <4> They come whenever it is necessary with the proper signs, prophecies, and powers according to the time, situation, and their mission.

Gurus (true spiritual teachers): <5> Those great Souls who manifest God's qualities to their disciples and cause many (according to their capacities) to realize God through them. <6> They go beyond the Scriptures and writings. They awaken and open spiritual understandings of their disciples by their powers that have been entrusted to them. <7> These spiritual teachers help in keeping the basic truth of God-realization in simple form, and will prevent these simple basic truths from becoming lost or changed by intellectual spiritualists (priest class). <8> They teach from the foundation of knowledge within themselves (Heart).

Artists: <9> Those intellectuals in higher and finer levels with their intuition awakened. <10> They can invoke higher thoughts in others by their art. They are teachers to others. <11> They see the society from the outside and recognize its weaknesses and strengths. They can see where it is headed and guide it to the next phase by invoking the inside visions in others.

<12> The true artists are different than those who commercialize and sell their abilities for some material wealth. They do the art for the sake and fulfillment of their thirsty Souls for truth. <13> They are also the teachers of humanity. They can help Paravipras to understand the state of society in each period of time.

Paravipras: <14> Those universal, dynamic leaders who have awakened their spiritual forces (☯), long to establish the Kingdom Of Heaven On Earth (✡), sacrifice all for their ideal (✝), and become one-pointed and surrendered to His Will (☪). <15> Also they direct all for the good of the whole universe (✹). <16> At the same time they have the abilities of all active classes in society. <17> They can undertake physical work like a Shudra, if it is necessary. <18> They are courageous and have leadership abilities like a Ksattriya. They have sharp intellects like an intellectual. <19> They are shrewd in economic endeavors like a Vaeshya and are spiritually incorruptible like a Brahmin.

<20> Only such leaders can guide all classes toward the best position possible, because they are classless and therefore would not prefer one class over the others. <21> If a leader is accepted who is from any of the five active classes, such a leader will favor the class he is from and oppress the other classes. But a Paravipra does not belong to any particular class, so he will treat all equally and according to the time, place, and state of society.

<22> All these four different types are beyond the regular human classification. They each create a special class while at the same time are out of the five active social classes, but their existence is necessary as is any other class in human progress toward the goal.

THE KINGDOM OF HEAVEN ON EARTH
Tablet Nine
GUIDING LIGHT FOR THE LEADERS

<1> This whole universe was created for a great purpose, **<2> which is to help all to reach Pure Consciousness**. <3> Therefore, the goal of progress of human society also should be based on this universal goal.

<4> Therefore, the goal of human progress individually or collectively is to progress physically (materially) and mentally (intellectually), and to use this progress toward his (their) and others' spiritual (intuitional) progress.

<5> The problems in society start when people lose the view of this most important principle. They try to progress in material and mental aspects and forget that these progressions should be directed toward their spiritual development. Then they start to use these gains for self-gratification, games, and indulgence. <6> That is when the decay of that society starts and the signs of decline appear.

<7> This trend of struggle, progress, steady prosperity, appearance of the signs of decline, and decline of society, can be traced in all great civilizations in past history.

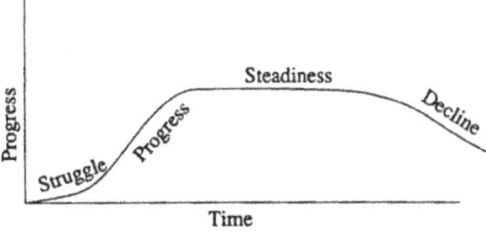

<8> The only reason for this trend is because the third part is forgotten: That the purpose of progressing materially and mentally is to help the spiritual progress. <9> This lack of directing these material and mental advances toward spiritual progress is the reason for decay and destruction.

<10> Therefore, any time a class in society starts to use its power against the spiritual progress, that is when Paravipras know it is time for that dominating class to be replaced with the next class.

<11> Any other principle devised for progress of society will be secondary and/or subordinate to this first and most important basic principle. <12> Six important sub-principles can be recognized as below:

1- Minimum necessity of food, shelter, and clothing should be provided for all, while education and medical care should be adequately available.

<13> Regardless of the participation of an individual in the activities of a society, the minimum necessities should be provided for all. <14> This minimum should in a true sense be minimum, so it discourages people from becoming lazy. <15> These resources should go only to those who really, for any reason, are unable to participate in social activity and its advancement and prosperity. <16> This minimum will not change or will change very little with the material advancement of society. It will stay almost constant regardless of society's level of development. This minimum can be increased only when this will help the stimulation of the economy. <17> Education and medical care are exceptions.

<18> These people, however, especially on the physiological and safety levels, are best served through direct help from others more prosperous. <19> Indeed those in need are an opportunity for others to serve as a manifestation of God and as serving God, and so allow the development of their charitable qualities.

<20> So with this, the responsibility of the government toward the needy becomes minimal. However, the education and health needs, at least for these people, should be provided by the government.

<21> The charity is best done when given to those closest to the person and his environment, then to others further out. <22> Charity can be physical (material), mental, emotional, or spiritual.

THE KINGDOM OF HEAVEN ON EARTH
Tablet Ten

2- Minimum standard of living should be guaranteed for those who participate in the activities of society and its prosperity.

<1> Those who work and participate in society should receive a minimum standard of living recognized for all in any given time. <2> Those who participate more and create more prosperity should receive more. <3> But in the ever-progressive process of human advancement, the minimum standard of living should increase indefinitely.

3- Mental ability (intellect) is superior to physical ability (labor), and spiritual understanding is superior to mental. Therefore, the humans should be utilized according to their dominating characteristic with having this hierarchy of characteristics in mind.

<4> If a person is physically strong, and at the same time has a very good intellect, his intellect should be considered more than his physical strength. <5> Or a person with spiritual insight and good mental ability should be considered more a spiritual being rather than an intellectual. <6> However, as everything depends on time, place, and person, in times that physical endeavor is the more important factor, even a spiritual person might be used as a laborer.

4- The utilization of these abilities should be ever-progressive toward higher ones.

<7> By the advancement of tools and science, the higher abilities should be encouraged and developed further. <8> Any advancement in technology should provide more time for humans to develop physically, mentally, and spiritually. Also these advances will help man develop even further in these aspects, especially mentally and spiritually.

5- Accumulation of individual wealth should be directed toward human advancement. When this accumulation starts to become a burden on others and is used for exploitation, the collective body (of Paravipras) has complete power over that wealth to use it in a proper way for further human advancement.

<9> In the era of Ksattriyas, when the decay of their period appears, Paravipras will discourage their domination by supporting intellectual characteristics. <10> In the time of the decay of the intellectual era, they will provide enough wealth and opportunities so that the Vaeshyas are able to use them in combination with Vipran discoveries, laborers, and land to advance material development.

<11> However, when the decay of the Vaeshyan era starts, it is time to take the wealth away from them and bring a relatively more equal distribution of resources between all. <12> In this function Paravipras might have to use Ksattriyas to help them bring about this change. <13> However, if they have complete control over the wealth of society, this can be done smoothly with indirect actions and a little use of the Ksattriyas.

6- All things depend on time, place, and people involved (the situation). According to the situation, the decisions can be from ignorance (tama), passion (raja), or knowledge (satva).

<14> Any rigid belief that one way is the only way is bound to be wrong and will finish in failure. Therefore, all things should be looked upon according to time, place, and person. <15> In any situation according to time, place and the people involved, the decisions can be made from complete ignorance, from passion (for selfish desires), or from knowledge (for the good of all and according to His Laws). <16> This Law also is true about the decisions of Paravipras in guiding humanity toward the Goal.

MOUNT ZION AND ZION, AND EXPLANATION OF THE SYSTEM

The book, **<u>Mount Zion and Zion, and Explanation of the System</u>**, explains the true symbolic meaning of Mount Zion and Zion, and Reveals the system for the Kingdom Of Heaven On Earth.

MOUNT ZION AND ZION, AND EXPLANATION OF THE SYSTEM

INTRODUCTION

There are many symbols used in the Bible and other Scriptures which at the same time are names for places on the earth. So these symbols are taken to be the literal references to these places.

However, the true meanings of many of these symbols are given in the revelations throughout our writings. In this book, the meanings of Mount Zion and Zion are given.

Also this book again reveals the desire of the Lord, that His Kingdom be realized and established by all on earth (✡) as it is in heaven.

Tablet One

PART I: WHAT ARE MOUNT ZION AND ZION?

The symbolic meaning of mountain in the Bible:

<1> The meaning of mountain in the Bible is given in chapter 2 of Daniel in the dream of King Nebuchadnezzar. In verse 35, it is described how a stone will smite the image in the king's dream and consume it, and how, "...the stone that smote the image became a great mountain, and filled the whole earth" (Daniel 2:35).

<2> In the interpretation of the dream, the meaning of the stone which destroyed the image (earthly kingdom) is given in verse 44:

> And in the days of these kings [the last ten kings symbolized as ten toes of the image] shall the God of heaven set up a kingdom [mountain which filled the earth], which shall never be destroyed: and the kingdom shall not be left to other people, but it shall break in pieces and consume all these kingdoms [as the stone did to the image], and it shall stand for ever.

<3> So the stone (symbol of truth) will come and destroy the untrue set-ups symbolized by the image. <4> The stone will become a great mountain and fill the whole earth. This mountain is the Kingdom which will be set up by the God of heaven and will last forever.

<5> Therefore the symbolic meaning of mountain in the Bible is the coming of the Kingdom Of Heaven On Earth, "and filled the whole earth." This Kingdom will be directed by the Elected Ones, not by others, "and the kingdom shall not be left to other people, … and it shall stand for ever."

Similarity of the shape of a mountain to a triangle upward (△):

<6> The shape of a mountain, especially when it is standing by itself, is similar to a triangle upward (△). As it is revealed in **The Greatest Sign** and is described in our writings, the triangle upward is the symbol for organizational structure. <7> In the organizational structure, the president is at the top of the structure and then comes one or more vice-presidents, department heads, and so on:

MOUNT ZION AND ZION

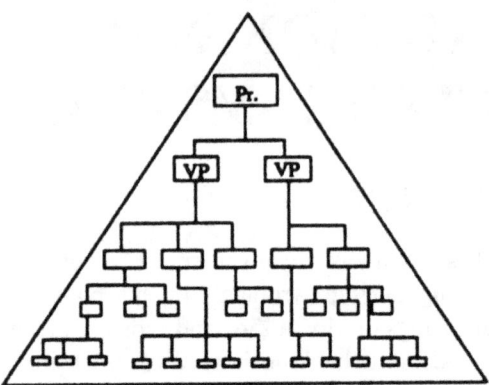

<8> If a border is put around this organizational structure, we will have a triangle upward (△).

<9> However, in the Bible this structure has been symbolized by a mountain. The mountain is one of the most stable structures on earth, as is the organizational structure of the Kingdom Of Heaven On Earth (KOHOE), which has God Himself at the very top as the King of the kings of the universe and earth.

Mount Zion:

<10> This mountain or organizational structure of the Kingdom Of Heaven is called Mount Zion.

Zion:

<11> However, as it is revealed in **The Greatest Sign**, the Kingdom Of Heaven consists of two triangles, one upward (△) and another downward (▽) merged together (✡) (star of David). The triangle downward is the symbol of justice and control. Therefore, there is a counterpart for Mount Zion as justice and control through organizational structure. <12> This is symbolized as Zion.

<13> So Mount Zion and Zion together symbolize the Kingdom Of Heaven (God) on earth (✡).

Tablet Two

There are three Kingdoms of Heaven:

<1> As it is shown in **The Greatest Sign**, there are three Kingdoms of Heaven. <2> One Kingdom is symbolized by the two great triangles together in the middle of **The Greatest Sign** with the symbol of **Haree Om Shrii Hung** (卐) in its center. This is the Kingdom Of Heaven in Heaven. This Kingdom has already been established.

<3> The sign or seal of Solomon (✡) (the sign used by Jews) is the symbol of the Kingdom Of Heaven On Earth, which is the same as Mount Zion (△) and Zion (▽) together (✡).

<4> The third is the sign of the Kingdom Of Heaven within (✡), or the sign of Paravipras. Paravipras are those who follow **The Greatest Sign** and become it (follow the **Eternal Divine Path**). They are the ones who struggle with God to bring the whole universe to Pure Consciousness (卐).

<5> When it is realized that the King of all these three Kingdoms is He, then these three Kingdoms become one and according to His Will. Then the peace and tranquility will come to humanity and all things will be directed toward the goal of life and creation, which is to be(come) Divine.

God is the only true King of these three Kingdoms, whether humans accept it or not:

<6> The true King of these three Kingdoms of Heaven (in heaven, on earth, and within) is He. It truly does not make any difference if humans accept this truth or not. Only by this being accepted can man walk in His Ways and His Flow, and bring happiness and tranquility to all. <7> Otherwise God will continue to guide and direct His universe toward its goal but because of the resistance of humans to follow Him, they will suffer in the process of change and progress.

<8> As it is described in the book <u>The Kingdom Of Heaven On Earth</u>, the duration

MOUNT ZION AND ZION

of class domination and consequent progress will continue regardless of human resistance. <9> But if this process is understood and true leaders (Paravipras) with universal views guide this process, tranquility will come to humanity and its progress will be in an evolutionary manner. So the suffering from resistance to change will be eliminated -- read <u>The Kingdom Of Heaven On Earth</u>.

<10> Also the Kingdom Of Heaven within comes when the reality beyond this universe is recognized and the goal of life is understood by each individual. This goal is to be(come) Divine and help others to be(come) Divine also. So the mind will be directed toward God and spirit, and that is when peace of mind and tranquility within will be established. <11> Only by directing all of one's life toward God, through self-realization, and by pursuing the true goal of life – which is to manifest God's qualities (Divinity) and do His Will – can individual happiness (Grace) be realized. <12> That is when a person knows he is not his body and that his Soul is a part of the universe.

<13> So God is the only subject of worship and the giver of salvation. He is the King and Director of this universe, and He is the only way to happiness and tranquility, individually or collectively. <14> This is true whether man accepts it or not.

<15> If it is accepted and His Ways are followed, there will be peace for humanity. If not, there will be suffering. But in any case He guides the universe and earth, and is its King.

<16> So the struggle of humanity is to understand Him and His Ways, with His Grace, and to follow them in order to reach peace and tranquility.

Tablet Three

God desires to see that His Kingship is known and accepted (established):

<1> As it is shown in **The Greatest Sign**, the symbol of the Kingdom Of Heaven On Earth (✡) is one part of The Plan of the Lord. The sign was given to the Hebrews*, who are the Elected Ones chosen to establish this Kingdom. <2> The structure of the Kingdom or its Hierarchy was revealed through Moses to the Children of Israel.

<3> So it is God's desire that the Kingdom Of Heaven On Earth be established and man progress toward his goal with as little suffering as possible.

<4> The Kingdom Of Heaven On Earth in general can be defined as **any environment that provides at least the minimum physiological and safety needs, and all other activities are directed toward self-realization and God-realization, and serving His universe**. <5> In a broader sense, it is to create a worldwide system and environment that allows the physiological and safety needs of humanity to be satisfied while all other aspects of human life are directed toward the true goal of life (Divinity).

Only in such an environment is peace, tranquility, and prosperity possible for humanity. Otherwise suffering will continue to be present:

<6> Only in such an environment with a worldwide system having a universal view, and with understanding God's Ways, can man have truth and tranquility on earth. <7> Otherwise the suffering for humanity will continue. <8> So it is a duty for all to endeavor to understand the truth behind this universe and bring the Kingdom of God by accepting Him as the only King and Leader, His Hierarchy as the only Hierarchy, and His Laws as the only Laws.

---

*   Hebrew means, "those who have passed beyond, or those who have overcome (Elected Ones)."

MOUNT ZION AND ZION

Tablet 3

Mount Zion is given to humanity:

<9> Mount Zion is given as the shape of a pyramid with four sides, a square base (square is the most stable base), and an eye at the top:

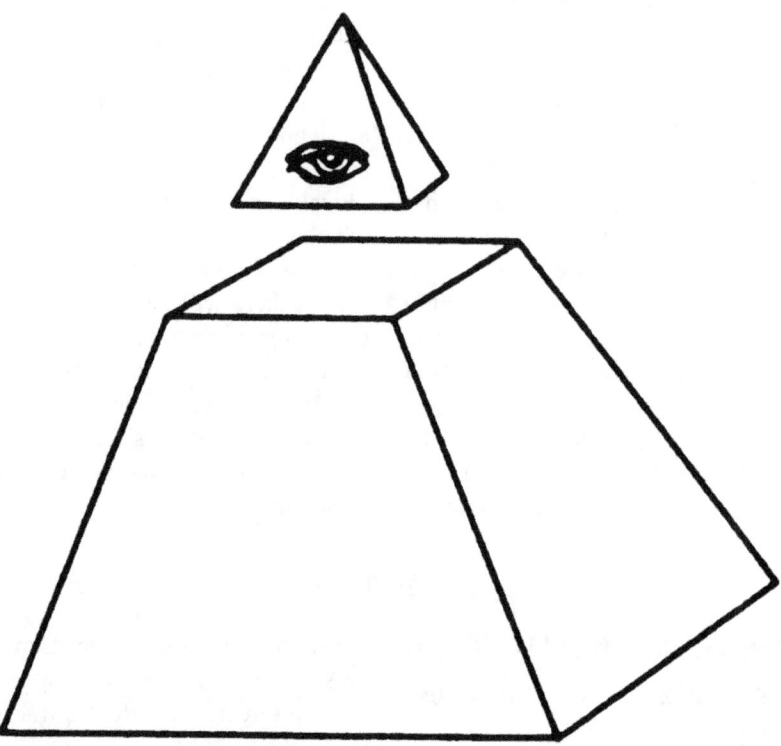

<10> This sign is used on one side of the Great Seal of America. The eye at the top is the eye of God watching and guiding His System, which is the rest of the pyramid as the Hierarchy. <11> It has four necessary elements or pillars symbolized by the four sides of the pyramid.

<12> These four sides or pillars on which this system is based are: The administrative body, the judicial body, the legislative body, and the Elders.

<13> These four parts will be described at length in the next section (Part II), but in brief, from the functional point of view, the administrative, judicial, and legislative bodies are similar to the present human system. <14> But what this present system lacks is the process of selecting the true leaders and the observer or witness part of the system (the Elders).

<15> A similar system was given to Moses for administering the Children of Israel. <16> But later on they did not follow it, longed for an earthly king, "like all the nations" (I Samuel 8:5), and rejected God as their King (⚠). <17> This is the greatest mistake a society can make.

<18> Therefore beside these four necessary pillars, it should not be forgotten for a moment that the leaders should seek the Will of the Lord and trust in Him. <19> Only with such a system can His Kingdom be realized on earth as it is in heaven.

<20> That is why the new order or era will dawn after this system is implemented on earth (NOVUS ORDO SECLORUM = The New Order of The Ages)† <21> and whatever efforts are made to bring about this New Order of The Ages are favored and blessed by God (ANNUIT COEPTIS = God Has favored Our Undertaking)†.

---

† Sentences used with this sign on the American Seal.

PART II: MOUNT ZION

Introduction to Mount Zion:

<1> In any level of existence, or in any situation where the presence of God has not been considered, there is bound to be suffering for the people involved. <2> The reason for this is very simple: the power of attraction to the illusion of the external world (Maya, lower nature, false ego, etc.) is so strong that any moment man forgets about his higher nature and spiritual part, he is drawn into his lower nature. <3> That is why only by remembering the Lord and entering Him into all levels of human existence can man be saved from himself. <4> Only He can take us from the ocean of Maya.

<5> That is why humans should come to the realization that the lower nature of man is very strong. Therefore, only those who are chosen to be strong enough to resist this lower nature should become the true leaders of society. <6> These people are the ones who will try to bring God (Divine Logic and Grace) into all levels of human activities. These are the ones who can be called Paravipras. They will fill the positions in the administrative, judiciary, and legislative branches of the government. <7> However, even these great personalities might lose their sense of judgment by becoming overactive in day-to-day problems. That is why another group out of the system will emerge as the overseers of the system. These are the Elders. <8> With the knowledge that God is the true Leader of all these earthly leaders, His Laws will be established, which are the Laws of the universe (Darmas). With such a system we will bring the Lord back into our lives and accept Him as our true King.

<9> This system is described in this book. However, first a brief explanation will be presented as to why the present systems cannot work.

In general, five reasons can be considered:

(1) Selection process of the leaders,

(2) Unawareness of the leaders that any existing ideology or approach is valid only in a given time, and

(3) Attachment of the leaders (and people) to a small portion of the earth, a special culture, group, religion, ideology, etc.,

(4) Lack of a body as an overseer of the system (Elders), and

(5) Lack of the presence of spiritual considerations (putting God out of the system).

(1) Selection process of the leaders:

<10> In order for the true leaders to be elected in the present systems, four conditions are necessary:

(a) A high level of literacy.
(b) Awareness of the basic rights (socio-economic awareness) by the majority.
(c) Willingness of the majority to demand their rights and stand firm until gained.
(d) High standard of ethics in all levels of society, especially in the leadership levels.

<11> Existence of all these conditions is rare. In fact, they are nonexistent in the present state of human evolution. Some of them might be found in some societies but not all of them. <12> These conditions (except the first) only exist in the time of crisis when the conditions become unbearable. Then the awareness of the people is aroused, and they are willing to take action to improve their condition and even sacrifice for the cause. <13> It is in these situations that usually the great leaders emerge from the masses. <14> But after the situation has been corrected, the awareness of the people becomes lax until the next crisis. Then again people will be aroused, the situation corrected, and then laxation occurs. <15> This cycle will

MOUNT ZION AND ZION

continue and in the process many will suffer.

<16> The lack of the presence of the four above-mentioned elements leads to the emergence of leaders who will bring the society to the brink of the crises. <17> Therefore, a system should be devised which will minimize the effect of the lack of the presence of these necessary factors, and also facilitate the emergence of aware and benevolent leaders.

(2) Unawareness of the leaders that any existing ideology or approach is valid only in a given time:

<18> There is a time for everything, and everything has its own time. This is also true about any approach or ideology.

<19> With clear evidence from history, all through **THOTH** it is explained how the social progress of humanity is based on a cyclical movement; read The Kingdom Of Heaven On Earth. <20> As it was explained in that book, after each of these cyclical periods, human society will progress to a higher level.

<21> These evolutionary cyclical movements so far have not been understood by humanity. <22> With awareness of this truth and how each of the existing ideologies and procedures are valid in one given period of time, the leaders will be more equipped to deal with human problems and lead all to an ever-progressive future.

Tablet Five

(3) Attachment of the leaders (and people) to a small portion of the earth, a special culture, group, religion, ideology, etc.:

<1> Anything that separates human from human will create suffering. <2> In truth suffering, chaos, confusion, etc., all come from division and separation.

<3> Therefore any one ideology, attachment to a small portion of the earth, or to promote only a special group, religion, culture, etc., are all bound to cause suffering.

<4> This can only be cured by expansion of the mind and being able to see that all little groups, cultures, races, etc., are of a whole, and each of them are necessary and planned to help in this one body.

<5> To achieve this goal a worldwide government and a universal point of view is needed. <6> Humans have to realize that they are so interdependent that they either should learn to share and co-exist, or they will all perish.

(4) Lack of a body as an overseer of the system:

<7> A body which would be out of the system, but familiar with how it works, is necessary. This body which was mentioned above is called "The Elder Body" in our system, and would emerge from the system. <8> Therefore, those who would be Elders are very familiar with the system. But because they are not engaged in its activities and are only its observers, they can easily see in what direction it is headed and are able to correct it.

<9> This lack of such a body in the present systems is another reason for their failure. In the present systems there is no knowledgeable person whose whole concern would be to observe and direct the system by his suggestions, while these suggestions are accepted because those in the system respect the opinion of these Elders.

<10> This gain of respect is the greatest task for each Elder in the observing body (Elders), because they can only give suggestions that may be accepted because of this respect.

(5) Lack of the presence of spiritual considerations (putting God out of the system):

<11> As it has been suggested throughout our teachings, one of the reasons for human failure to bring peace, tranquility, equity, justice, etc., on earth is because we have put God out of our lives and government.

<12> The phrase, "separation of church and state" actually should have read, "separation of dogma and state." <13> Those who

brought this great realization as a part of the constitutions of some nations did not intend to imply, "separation of God and state," or "a state without God."

<14> Any ideal that separates human from human based on a set of beliefs, inspired under the name of religion, or any other name, is considered dogma. No such forces should become the dominating class in government, or be supported by it (government).

<15> Also as it is explained all throughout our teachings, the intellectual spiritualists who bring these ideas in order to exploit the masses also should not be allowed to dominate the government. <16> States which are run by the clergy or priest class, for the reason above, will eventually become dictatorships, and the masses will be exploited in the name of religion.

<17> That is why in our system, although the spiritual values are considered, the priest class is not a dominating force. <18> Also the Brahmin class, it is hoped, will not become dogmatic. It will bring God into the government, but will not use religion as a tool to exploit the masses. <19> True spiritual experience and/or realization is an individual relationship with God. It can never be politicized!

<20> These described shortcomings of the present systems, combined with individual shortcomings, are the cause for the present state of the earth. <21> That is why not only is a reform of the existing social orders necessary but individuals also have to be prepared and progress.

<22> These two interdependent ingredients of social make-up (individuality and collectivity) will be modified simultaneously. As more individuals become aware of the necessity for reform, the new set-ups will form, and as these set-ups evolve, more individuals become aware, progress, and become involved in creating the reformed order. This process will continue until the desired environment is created.

<23> The system which is presented on the following pages, plus the rest of our teachings, is aimed to eliminate the problems above and also to bring that unity which will help humanity out of this great suffering based upon division.

<24> In the suggested system, a process has been designed in which each leader would emerge from the very bottom of society. In this process, their true intentions and abilities would be known. Therefore only those who are truly equipped with all the abilities to lead others toward harmony, equity, justice, and well-being, will emerge.

<25> In this system also, another group of leaders would be elected by mass vote. This would be done to bring a balance into the system. By these elected persons from outside of the system, fresh and new ideas can be brought to the top of the leadership. This will prevent the system from becoming rigid and bureaucratic. Therefore, it will not become a field of domination of a few having all the powers, or a system that requires some rigid rituals or special manners to reach the top. This will leave room for unorthodox leaders to be able also to influence the direction of the leadership by their progressive ideas.

<26> One more important point can be made: This system is for humanity and the New Order of The Ages to come. However, there will be those who will help to bring this system to the earth, establish it, and help its continuation. <27> They are those who are on earth but not of it.

Tablet Six

REGIONAL GOVERNMENT

Administrative body, twelve-people-leader selection process:

<1> There will ultimately be twelve regions in the world. Each region will be divided into twelve sub-regions. Each sub-region

will be divided into states, each state into counties, and each county into districts. Each district will be divided into small communities (**Communities of Light**). <2> Any small group of people (ideally around twelve people) in these communities represents a unit of decision-making and of the selection process. <3> **Only those people who join this system of a small group of people can be selected and promoted to the leadership of the collective body.** The only criteria necessary to form such a unit is the desire of these people to form such a unit.

<4> One person will emerge as the leader from each of these units (rather than being elected or selected by vote in these small units, he might be selected by consensus as the emerged leader). <5> Ideally each twelve of such leaders will make up a second level of decision-making, and they will select one person as their leader, and so on, until one community leader‡ emerges from each community. <6> Then one person will emerge as the leader of each district, one as the leader of each county, and so on. This process will continue until twelve selected leaders for all the twelve sections of that region are chosen. <7> Any person who is selected to serve on a higher level in the Hierarchy will be replaced with someone from a level lower than the one from which he had emerged. This process will continue to the bottom of the Hierarchy, so that all the levels will be filled.

<8> There will also be six people selected on a mass-vote basis. These six will not be chosen through the twelve-people-leader selection process mentioned above, but rather by general vote. These six elected will join the twelve who were selected by the system described above. <9> Therefore, the number of the collective body of each region will be eighteen: twelve from the twelve-people selection process, and six mass-elected. <10> One person will be selected as representative of that region to the world collective body. One person will be selected as the leader of the collective body, and four as direct reporters to this leader. The rest (twelve) will be divided into four three-person groups, each under one of the four direct reporters to the leader.

<11> These twelve will assume the direct responsibility for the twelve sub-regions. <12> The six mass-elected cannot assume the positions of world representative, leadership of the collective body, or become a direct reporter for their first time elected to the collective body. <13> However, they can assume the position of direct reporter after being elected twice, and can be regarded as candidates for the leader of the collective body or regional representative to the world body if elected three times.

<14> Because the world representative of that region, the leader of the collective body, and the four direct reporters would no longer be available to assume the responsibilities of the sub-region they were elected from, the six mass-elected will each be given a sub-region to lead. <15> Since the six mass-elected people will not necessarily be familiar with the problems and situations of those sub-regions, the selected person from that region and the ones who have been elected by mass vote together will assume the responsibilities of that region. They will cooperate together and the person who is selected by that region will act as an advisor to the person who assumes his responsibilities.

<16> However, if the person selected from that sub-region does not agree with the decisions made by the person who replaced him, the matter will be solved by the judgment of the leader of the collective body. <17> If the problem is between the regional world representative or the leader of the collective body

---

‡ The leader of the community can emerge from the community at large (without breaking the community into 12 people units). But by formation of 12 people units, the effect of mass hypnosis (when people follow the crowd and lose their own identity) will be broken. The person who emerges from the 12, however, should prove his or her worth, to each person in the group, before being chosen or emerging as the representative of the group.

and the leader of their sub-region, the matter will be solved by the majority vote of the collective body, or by the decision made by The Eldest of the region.

<18> None of the four direct reporters to the leader of the collective body can have leadership of a region he was selected from, or can assume leadership of a three person group that includes his region.

<19> The twelve selected by the process of twelve-people-leader selection dissolves each four years, and the six mass-elected also have terms of four years.

<20> After four years, the collective body will select the regional representative to the world body and the leader of the collective body of that region for the next four years. <21> After the selection of these leaders, the rest of this body will be dissolved to their respective twelve-leadership levels. Then the leaders for the next four years at those levels will be selected. The rest will dissolve to the next twelve-selected leadership units, and so on, until all the levels are selected. <22> Because of the dynamics of the system, **it should not take a long time**.

<23> The terms of the six elected at large will end before the selection of the regional body and the world representatives. Thus if they were elected for a second or third time, they can be considered as possible direct reporters, the regional representative, or the leader of the collective body.

<24> A person can only be selected as leader of the collective body for two periods (eight years). If a person succeeds in being the leader of the collective body for two periods, he will assume a position of an Elder of the collective body. <25> Also, any person who is selected as direct reporter for three times will assume the title of Elder in that level. <26> The members of the collective body, or any other level in the twelve-people-leader selection process down to the bottom of the Hierarchy, can only be selected in any given level for four periods (sixteen years). This is also true for the regional representative in the world body. <27> If a person was elected for four periods in a level of the Hierarchy, he will assume an Elder position at that level.

Tablet Seven

Judiciary board (Board of Brahmins):

<1> From each of the twelve unit groups, one person who seems to have a keen sense of judgment, and Brahmic qualities (contemplative) and powers, can be selected as the judge for the group. <2> Such a person should not be the same as the leader of the group.

<3> Twelve such people from 12 groups form the second level of the judiciary system, and this, same as the collective body, continues to the top of the Hierarchy to the regional and world judiciary court. <4> Also, as with the administrative body, six judges are elected through voting (or by the head of the collective body), and the same procedures, described about the administrative body, are applicable to the judiciary. <5> As it was mentioned, it is best that this body consist of people with Brahmic qualities who are more observant of the events (than engaged in them), usually have keen judgment abilities, and are spiritually knowledgeable.

<6> Therefore, through the judiciary board and because its Hierarchy is made from people with Brahmic qualities (spiritualists), this class also will have a voice in society and its welfare, but will not dominate it.

<7> The judiciary system will be formed with Godly-character individuals who have emerged as such from the bottom of society. They have gone through many levels of tests to prove that they have taken "the beam out of their own eyes," so they are qualified to take "the speck out of the eyes of others." <8> A judge without these qualities would not be qualified to judge, as Esa has shown in the case of the adulterous woman (John 8:3-11).

<9> Only those with the above qualities can be chosen as judges. Otherwise, because of their own guilt of not being completely pure, they cannot properly judge. <10> Either they would judge harshly because of their ignorance of how hard it is to overcome the lower nature, or they would judge without considering the state of the society the person is in.

<11> So a victim who otherwise could have been guided to the right path would be unjustly judged and even greater resentment and confusion would prevail in society, <12> or he would be judged too mildly, because of the impurity in the judge himself.

<13> The Board of Brahmins also will examine the validity of the laws from a spiritual point of view and their justness, as will be described in the explanation of the decision-making process.

<14> In this system, there is a separation between the church (dogma) and state. But it is a state under God. <15> There will be no priest class in a usual sense (intellectual spiritualists, clergy). It is the duty of each individual to study, become familiar with God's Revelations, meditate and find the truth. <16> People should not take the words of others as God's Revelations. They should ask, search, and find the truth individually or from those who teach (true spiritual teachers) in spirit (etherically – by the Heart).

<17> The maintenance of the temples and spiritual centers can be given to the Brahmin class, but the truth is in Scriptures and in each person's Soul, and should be found by each individual. <18> Only those who are worthy of being spiritual teachers (true Gurus) can be chosen as guides by individuals.

<19> The idea, as expressed before, is that these leaders, the Brahmin class, spiritual teachers (Gurus), etc., all will emerge, but are not elected by vote, selected by special assignment, or chosen because of some educational background, etc. <20> If a system does not allow its leaders in any level to emerge, but sets up criteria, such as a level of education (it might help but is not essential), or being born into the right family, class, race, etc., – then the requirement to gain leadership would become a status quo. <21> Such a society will fail!

<22> Therefore, with these Brahmins, the spiritual people will have a strong voice in society but will not dominate it. This will prevent the spread of superstitions by those low spiritualists who call themselves clergy or spiritual leaders (intellectual spiritualists), but because of their inability to manifest the real spiritual truth, they exploit people by spreading binding doctrines (dogmas) and causing inferiority complexes, etc., in others. They then take advantage of those lost Souls (people).

<23> This happened in the past in many religions: spiritual domination through suppression of the real truth of the reality behind the Scriptures. <24> It occurred by the preaching of dogmas and imposing ideas in the name of religions which were merely man-made in order to control other classes (priest class controlling other classes).

<25> This phenomena led to the separation of religion and state. Those who invented the idea of separation of church and state, as was described, did not mean a state without God, but they meant, **separation of dogma and state.** <26> That is why the Brahmins should have a voice in society but not dominate it.

Tablet Eight

Legislative body (House of Elects):

<1> The House of Representatives and/or Senate (or both) will be chosen by vote of the people from different states. <2> They will consist of those who are known for their virtues and willingness to solve the problems of their communities, regions, and world in general.

<3> The duty of the Senate is to carefully study the problems in society and to consider appropriating laws for dealing with them.

<4> Spiritual values should also be regarded in these decisions.

<5> The Senate has the power of impeachment of the officials in the governmental and judiciary systems. <6> If a leader is found to be guilty, the highest and most severe punishment should be imposed on him. As is a part of our teachings, the injustice which is done to you, forgive, but that which is done to society should not be forgiven or pardoned, but should be punished severely to uproot the corruption. This type of crime is the worst because it brings the fall of morality and affects everyone, down to the lowest level of the society. <7> Leaders ("the heads") have the greatest effect on society. If they are godly, the society also will become righteous. If they are corrupt, their subjects will follow them. That is one of the most important lessons of the Old Testament and history.

Tablet Nine

Elders:

<1> Those who have been elected for two terms as the head of the collective body (administrative body), the judiciary body (Brahmins), and the legislative body (Senate) will assume the positions of the Elders in these levels. <2> They will be witnesses of the system. <3> Also those people who have been elected in any position in any other level of government (except the direct reporters whose terms are for three times) for four successive terms will gain the title of Elder in that level.

<4> For example, if a person was elected for four terms (sixteen years) by twelve people as their leader and he never was elected in any higher level, he will become an Elder to those twelve people. <5> But if he was promoted to a higher level in the Hierarchy, in any level of the Hierarchy that he would be elected four times, he will assume an Elder position in that level.

<6> The Elders in all levels have an indirect but powerful influence on the government. By their experience and because they would be out of the activity of the system, they can see the problems or wrongdoings of those in the system. <7> By their influences which they should gain by their character and leadership abilities, with gain of respect, they can point out these problems and constantly direct and correct the system if it is so needed.

<8> The Elders would be out of the activity. Usually those who are outside of an activity see things more clearly, and because of the experience, proven characters, and abilities of these leaders through many levels and tests in the past, these Elders will become the true seers of the problems and are able to influence the direction of the leadership indirectly without being involved in it.

<9> These Elders should influence the system through their fine characters and wisdom. If an Elder does not manifest these abilities or loses them because of old age or for any other reason, then his ill advice will not be considered. <10> It is a prestigious position for those who truly deserve its status.

<11> These Elders are the true leaders who emerge as Great Souls and are in tune with God's Will and the current situation of society. Those Elders at the top of the Hierarchy should be highly exalted and their words should be heard and accepted as light for the guidance of society and humanity.

<12> The Elders from the heads of the judiciary (Brahmins) and administrative bodies each can choose one person as their head. <13> Also they will choose another person by a collective vote of the two Elder bodies (judiciary and administrative) as the Eldest.

<14> The Eldest and the two heads of the Elders from the Collective Body and the Board of Brahmins (judiciary board) will be regarded as the guardians of our teachings and His Kingdom.

<15> In any disputed matter or disagreement in the case of spiritual, civil, judicial, or other spheres, when unsolvable in the system through the decision-making process, then the

ultimate source will be the opinion of these three guardians in each region.

<16> After they have meditated on the matter, discussed the matter together, and reached the same conclusion in one opinion, then that would be what all should accept as the Law and the Will of God.

<17> The final decision will be with the Eldest. <18> Also the Eldest has power to intervene in any level of the Hierarchy, legislative, administrative, or judiciary bodies and question their activities, decisions, or procedures. <19> Only in this level, therefore, do the Elders have a direct influence on the system. Of course, Elders can persuade the Eldest to influence the system directly if they and the Eldest felt it was necessary.

<20> However, the Elders from the two bodies or collective body plus the Board of Brahmins combined, can vote the Eldest down if they feel that he is losing his power of judgment (from insanity, old age, misuse of power, etc).

<21> The Elders also can be retired by vote from the board in each level from which they have emerged.

<22> Also members of the boards of the administrative and judiciary bodies can be impeached by the Senate.

<23> Therefore, although the Eldest apparently has unlimited power, if he starts to misuse it he can be replaced by the Elders or by collective vote of the administrative and judiciary boards, and if the Elders fail to do so or lose their abilities to judge, they can be disqualified by the two boards (administrative or judiciary). <24> If these two bodies unjustly try to disqualify them or misuse their powers in any other case, they can be impeached by the Senate, and if the Senators are not doing their duties satisfactorily, they will not be elected by the people.

<25> The Senate also has the power of questioning any activity in any level of government (judiciary and administrative) if it seems desirable, but of course, only by majority vote.

<26> On rare occasions, any eleven people in any level of the twelve selection Hierarchy can, with a majority vote of seven (spirit) or more, over four (matter) or less, vote down the person who has been selected by them. <27> This can be practiced more often at the lower levels of the Hierarchy and much more rarely at the top.

<28> With the above power given to any group to be able to control their representative (leader), and the other safeguards described above, this system can truly be called a government from the people, by the people, and for the people. <29> That is when "The Meek will [truly] inherit the earth.

Tablet Ten

Decision-making process:

<1> As it was explained above, there will be four bodies or pillars in the governmental structure: administrative, judiciary, legislative, and the Elders.

<2> The legislative body, which is the Senate or the House of Representatives, will have many committees. These committees will receive requests and complaints from people or governmental bodies, or they themselves will find problems. Then they will search for solutions, which will be recommended to the Senate. <3> After the Senate studies a proposal from the point of view of practicality and justness, they will vote on accepting or rejecting it. If passed by the majority, then the proposed bill will be sent to both the administrative board and the Board of Brahmins.

<4> The administrative board will study the bill from the point of view of practicality and feasibility. <5> The Board of Brahmins will study it from the point of view of spirituality and justness to all or the majority.

<6> If the bill was accepted by both boards, it will become a law. If both bodies reject it, it will be dead. <7> But if one passes it and the other rejects it, then the bill will be returned to the Senate with the reasoning from each

side for their acceptance or rejection. Then the Senate will make a decision again. <8> If it was passed or with some change it was passed, it will be sent to the two mentioned boards for further study.

<9> Again if one accepts and the other rejects the proposal, the matter will be referred to the Senate one more time. If it gains the majority vote in the Senate but the same decision is reached by the boards again, this time the matter will be referred to the Elders. <10> After it is discussed by them, then the three guardians will review it and each head of the two bodies of Elders (heads of the Elders from the administrative and judiciary bodies) will give their opinion and reasoning behind it to the Eldest. <11> It is the Eldest who will make the final decision.

<12> The presence of the Elders can be especially helpful in these times. They might point out the pros and cons of the proposed law and guide the boards toward a wise decision.

Tablet Eleven
WORLDWIDE APPLICATION (WORLD GOVERNMENT)

<1> The governmental body of each region was explained in the previous pages. This system, with the necessary alterations, can be applied to the smaller parts of a region (sub-region, sub-sub-region, city, etc.) or to a larger area, such as the entire earth. <2> That is the goal of the system – to create a worldwide government.

<3> In order to achieve this goal, a World Collective Body (administrative), World Judiciary Board (Board of Brahmins), World House of Representatives, and World Body of Elders, are necessary also.

<4> To create the world administrative and judiciary bodies, one person from the corresponding boards of each region will be selected as the representative to the world body.

<5> From those who are elected by vote, only ones who have been selected three times to the regional levels can be considered for election to the world bodies. <6> Also for each body in the world level (administrative and judiciary), there will be seven people elected through voting. <7> So the number of each of these two bodies will be nineteen (twelve from the twelve regions and seven by vote).

<8> One leader will be selected in each body as their head, and two people will be the direct reporters to the leader. There will be two reporters to each direct reporter. Each reporter to the direct reporter will be in charge of three regional leaders and the coordinator of the activities for one region with other regions. <9> If a disagreement develops between the world representative and the regional leaders, the matter will be solved by the World Eldest (or Elder body). The decision of the World Eldest is final.

<10> Those who serve two terms as the leaders of these bodies will become Elders in their respective levels, and those who serve as direct reporters or report to the direct reporters after three terms, and representatives of a region for four terms, will become Elders in their levels.

<11> The rest of the functions and relationships of these bodies would be similar to the regional but in the higher level – worldwide.

<12> At the time of election, the people for the head of these bodies should be elected first. Then those who have not been elected will return to their regions and the election process would continue as described before. <13> Of course, seven people elected by vote should be elected first so that if they were elected for a second or third time, they could be considered as potential candidates for direct reporters, reporters to the direct reporters, or the leader of the body.

<14> The world legislative body will be elected through voting. Two representatives will be elected from each sub-region (there are twelve sub-regions in each twelve

regions). Therefore, the World Senate will contain 12 x 12 x 2 = 288 members from all over the world (or other arrangements can be devised, such as representatives from states until sub-regions are completely formed).

<15> A House of Representatives can also be formed. The elected people in this house can be based on a special number of the population in each region. So not only would each sub-region have a representative in the Senate, but those regions which have a greater population would be represented by a greater number of representatives. A House of Representatives also can be formed in each region.

<16> The presence of two houses brings a greater screening power into the system, and also more complication (bureaucracy).

<17> Each representative will work for the sub-region and region from which he was elected. He and the other representatives from his region will coordinate the functioning of that region with the other regions and sub-regions through other representatives.

<18> Also this body will bring about laws, bills, and legislative works in the world level for the good of all.

<19> The decision-making process in the world government will work similarly to that described in the regional level. <20> However, if the House of Representatives exists, it will first pass the bills. Then if the Senate also passed the bill, it would be sent to both the World Administrative Board and the World Judiciary Board. <21> The rest is the same as in the regional level. When a bill becomes a law, it will be for the whole world and enforceable.

<22> The primary function of the world government would be to execute all the governmental matters which affect the worldwide concerns and to be a coordinating force for the twelve regions. <23> The regional government should not overburden the world government by their regional problems. So this body should be able to concentrate on higher things concerning all.

<24> **The only logical and true ideal is to create this earth as one country and share all resources, abilities, and knowledge to create the ideal environment for all**. Therefore each individual can progress to his highest potential, physically, mentally, and spiritually. <25> Also it is the only way if the human wants peace, prosperity, and to be able to continue to exist!

<26> Otherwise, no one will benefit by separating one from another and all might even perish at the end.

<27> It is the desire of the Lord that the **KOHOE** (✡) is established and He be recognized as the true and only King of the King of the kings (⬢) of this system and government. Only then will His Will be done on earth as it is in heaven.

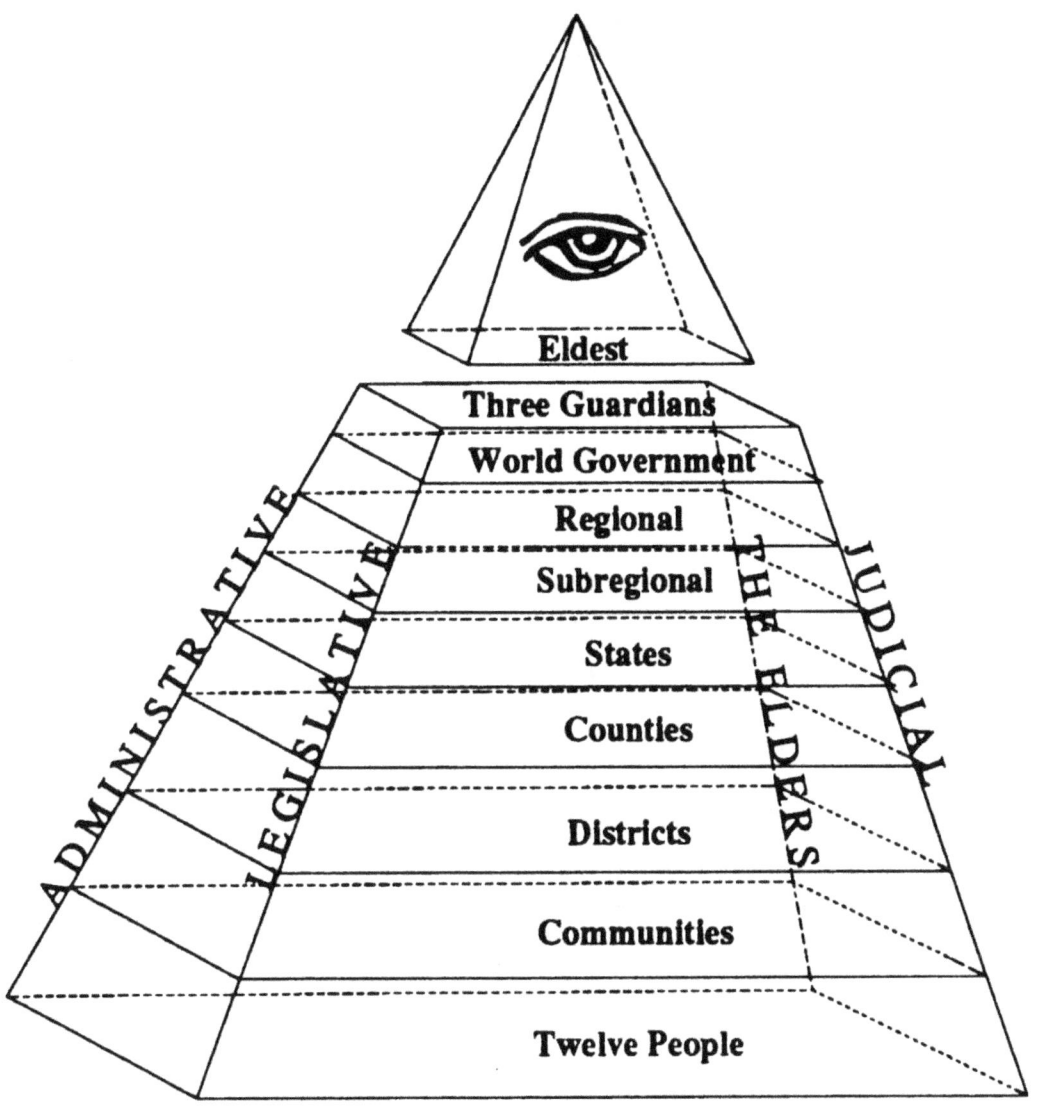

The Hierarchy

Tablet Twelve

THE HIERARCHY

The place of each class in society:

<1> As it was described in the book The Kingdom Of Heaven On Earth, there are five active human types in society. <2> They are: Shudras (laborers), Ksattriyas (warriors), Vipras (intellectuals), Vaeshyas (businessmen) and Brahmins (true spiritual people). <3> Also there are four other classes which cannot be categorized in the regular five human types. <4> They are: Prophets, Gurus (true spiritual teachers), Artists, and Paravipras.

MOUNT ZION AND ZION

<5> Ideally, the people who will be chosen in the legislative body (collective body) will be selected from the Paravipras, and the judiciary body (Board of Brahmins) from the Brahmin class (true seers or spiritualists).

<6> Intellectuals will be utilized on different committees, research facilities, scientific pursuance, and other places where they can manifest their abilities. <7> Business people also will be used to develop the discoveries of intellectuals and to create economical products for human necessities, with the combination of labor, capital, and land.

<8> The warrior class will make up the police force in order to keep the discipline of the society. <9> However, this force should not be used for the benefit of a few. <10> Shudras are the ones who will carry on the basic tasks in the society to help its production and provide service.

<11> Prophets come whenever morality goes down or a new message is necessary to be brought to humanity. <12> Gurus are those who will gather their disciples together and are able to manifest God's qualities to them. <13> Artists are those who will bring finer thoughts to humanity.

<14> When a society where each class falls in its place is created and it is understood that even with the apparent differences between them, they are all equal in His Eyes, <15> they all are working toward the goal of creation, and each is necessary for the well-being and progress of the others, and with acceptance of Him as the King, <16> then His Kingdom will be realized on earth.

Tablet Thirteen

PART III: ZION

Justice (Zion) in the system:

<1> As it was explained, the triangle downward (∇) in the seal or star of David (✡), which is the symbol for the Kingdom Of Heaven On Earth, means justice.

<2> It was described what the Hierarchy for the Kingdom Of Heaven On Earth ($\triangle$) is. <3> Only creating this Hierarchy, however, is not enough. Application of justice (∇) in the system should be considered and without it there will be no Kingdom Of Heaven On Earth. <4> In fact, neglect of this part in the system is equal with neglecting God as the Eye Witness and King. <5> That again means, His Kingdom is not truly recognized on earth as it is in heaven.

<6> If any system, religion, ideal, or government is established but does not bring justice to humanity, it cannot be accepted as from God. <7> It is a human-made hypocritical idea, no matter what name has been given to it or cloth used to cover it.

When the system becomes corrupt:

<8> The Hierarchy, the justice which is necessary to perfect it, and the other truths which are presented here, make up an ideal situation to create a world government which is the desire of the Lord to be established. <9> Therefore, it is the duty of men to struggle to bring this ideal. <10> **Life is a struggle!**

<11> However, it is the goal that His Kingdom eventually be realized on earth. <12> Therefore with the human in the next era who is in higher consciousness, and with the lessons which they should have learned from the last twelve thousand years and history, soon all will realize they have no choice but to accept His Will and follow His Laws.

<13> If the system becomes corrupt after it is established, again Great Souls will come and man will struggle and His Kingdom will be established.

<14> In any case He is the King and Director of the events in the universe. <15> But if

man does not realize this, as it is described in the book The Kingdom Of Heaven On Earth, it is he who will suffer by resisting God's progressive guidance.

<16> In the case of corruption, people will not participate in the twelve-people process as the base to form the system. So the system will be weakened and if it continues to be corrupt, eventually it will fall and a new truthful people will replace it.

Tablet Fourteen

PART IV: FINANCING THE SYSTEM, AND THE BEST WAY TO CREATE THE BASE OF TWELVE

Financing the system:

<1> There will be three sources of income for the judiciary, administrative, and Elder bodies: <2> one from the contributions of the twelve people selection; a second from gifts from the believers; and the third through matching funds from taxes.

<3> The best way for the twelve people to be the base of the twelve-people-selective system is that they all live in a close area together, and if possible even in a large building as a small community. <4> Therefore they would be able to create strong bonds, progress together, do spiritual practices as a group and be a comfort, strength, and protection, etc., for one another.

<5> Each individual or couple in these small communities would give 10% (tithe) or more of their income to the system which should be sent to the regional control financial agencies to be used for the expenses of the system.

<6> The other financial arrangements in each community depend upon the people involved. <7> One way to do this is to identify the collective expenses and finance them through contributions by all in the community. This can include administrative expenses, etc., of the community.

<8> Another way is to surrender a fixed percentage of each person's income or a fixed amount to be used for community expenses. <9> The idea is that everyone shares in making the community become a vital, organic unit. This of course needs much compassion, understanding, sharing, etc. <10> However, no one should become a burden on the community and/or system. <11> Such elements should be supported with the minimum.

<12> If the twelve people are not living in a community together, each individual should send at least ten percent (10%) to the central financial agencies and support other collective expenses of the community, such as expenses for the administration of the group, etc.

<13> However, it is recommended that the twelve people as the base live together in housing close by each other, <14> or even use the recommended house which will be explained in the next section (or something similar) so that they can be close together physically, mentally, and spiritually.

<15> Also those who are not participating in the twelve people as base, but are willing to support the cause of the Lord and His System, should give at least ten percent (10%) of their income (tithes) to the system, to be used to finance it.

<16> Another source of income for the system will be gifts, direct contributions, donations, etc., to the system. <17> These funds and the tithes, of course, will be tax deductible.

<18> The tithes (10%) given to the system are a purifier of one's wealth. They are given as a thanksgiving for His Kingdom and for the tranquility, justice, etc., which it brings. <19> Thanksgiving is the first Law.

<20> If the system did not represent God and became corrupt, people can withdraw even this, so the system will collapse. However, they can continue the communities and communication between them until another

true Hierarchy would emerge.

<21> There will also be a matching fund as a percentage of the money generated in this fashion in each region (from the people of the base and the tithes), by the tax money which will be collected from the masses for the services that will be provided by the government for them.

<22> If the money collected from the first two sources (the twelve base and tithes) does not seem sufficient for the expenses for these bodies, then from the tax collected from the masses, up to one hundred percent (100%) can be taken to double the income of these bodies and for their expenses. <23> But this matching money should never exceed the hundred percent (100%) limit.

<24> However, if the money collected from tithes (also donations, etc.) was sufficient, no matching fund is required or at least not one hundred percent. <25> Also this matching fund can be used as an economical tool to inject or withdraw money from the economy in order to control it.

<26> The reason for only 100% matching fund is that the judicial and administrative bodies should be so respected and trusted that people should be willing to join and support the system as much as possible only through the first two sources of income (twelve base and tithes).

<27> So if they became corrupt, these bodies would not be able to use unlimited amounts of taxpayers' money and continue their corrupt ways. <28> When people do not have trust in the system any longer, they will not support it and the first two sources of income will decline. This will force the bank of matching funds to go down also. So it will force the system either to correct itself or collapse, then a new system will be created.

<29> From the income which is generated in each region as described above, thirty percent (30%) will be sent to the world body from each region, and seventy percent (70%) will be used for regional expenses.

<30> Ten percent (tithes) of the money generated in the world level government will be given to the world Eldest to be used for his expenses and also for the expenses of the Elders in the world level. <31> This is also true in the regional level: ten percent of the disposable income – after thirty percent (30%) is sent to the world government, or the remaining seventy percent (70%) – will be dedicated to the Elders and will be given to the Eldest to be used for his expenses and that of the Elders.

<32> It is the Eldest (both regional and worldwide) who has complete control over this money. Indeed it can be said they should be given a kingly attribute and power, and this money should be used to maintain their status. <33> Of course, as it was described, Elders should influence the system indirectly, and the Eldest acts as the Highest symbol as a channel for God.

<34> The rest of the income in both the world and regional levels – the ninety percent (90%) – will be used for the administrative and judiciary bodies which include the Temples and community centers. <35> The maintenance and administration of the Temples and community centers will be by the communities, Brahmins (such as renunciates), and judiciary bodies. But the administrative body would channel its energy more toward the administration of worldly matters.

<36> The masses will be taxed for the services they require from the government, <37> and also the salaries and financial requirements for maintaining and operating the Senate (the House of Representatives) should be paid by the taxpayers.

<38> The financing of the candidates who run for office through vote will be paid half by contribution from the people to the candidates and the other half as a matching fund from taxes by the government. Of course a ceiling can be put on how much a candidate can spend.

Tablet Fifteen

A recommended house for twelve people:

<1> A recommended housing for those twelve people who truly want to be close physically, mentally and spiritually is a housing complex which is built around a circular or a six-sided (hexagon) center:

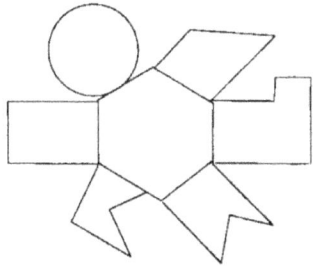

Each house can have different shapes or designs according to its location, need, or taste of each person.

<2> So there will be six houses around the center. <3> In each house one couple with their children will reside and the hexagon center will be their place of worshipping. and gathering.
<4> With this set-up, although each family has relative privacy, they still will be close together and can use the center as a place of love, sharing, worshipping, and becoming one.
<5> Such a house also can be used to invite others to their private temple and share their oneness with them. <6> These twelve people will also be a unit of decision-making and a base to create the system, and there are many other advantages.
<7> Each of these six houses should become a center of love and as a healthy unit (family) to build the society. <8> Then after each individual learns how to create a great family, the next step is to become a good citizen of his small community and to be able to share with the rest of the twelve people, and then reach the rest of the community.
<9> All of these will help a person's growth physically, mentally, emotionally, and spiritually. <10> Of course, such an arrangement can only continue to exist if it is based on God and His Laws. Otherwise the self-centeredness and selfishness will destroy it. <11> However, one of the functions of the family (marriage) and this twelve people arrangement is to dissolve the ego-centeredness and make a person reach out of himself, follow the **Eternal Divine Path** in his environment, and create the KOHOE.
<12> Then after this training ground, he can reach out to the other communities which surround him and eventually toward the whole universe. <13> So in truth this is a training place to create true leaders who are physically, mentally, emotionally, and spiritually balanced with having developed the ability to live with others. <14> So they can grow to lead others to the path of righteousness (Divinity).
<15> This arrangement can even be expanded, and twelve such housing complexes can be built closely to create a second level of decision-making, and twelve of such twelve houses will be the third level. So there will be at least 12 x 12 x 12 = 1,728 (or more) which can be called a community. <16> Then a community center can be built to serve them on a broader scale.
<17> The greater number of such communities created, the better. That is because then more people will participate in the decision-making process and also in the selection of the administrative, judiciary, and eventually the Elder members. <18> So the possibility of true leaders with true characteristics emerging increases.

MOUNT ZION AND ZION
PART V: FINAL POINTS

Subjective approach with objective adjustment:

<19>"Subjective approach" means a constant approach toward our goal or ideal or perfection. "Objective adjustment" is to adjust ourselves and our ideal to the situation we are in now. <20> Therefore, the two phrases together, "subjective approach with objective adjustment" means to ceaselessly strive toward our goal, ideal, and perfection, but to be flexible enough to adjust ourselves with the situation we are in. However, we should never stop progressing. <21> In implementing the system of government which was explained previously, this approach is very important. The explanations are the ideal system and the eventual goal. But there can be some adjustments before we reach the ultimate. <22> This law is applicable in all approaches and goal achievements.

Progressive nature of the universe:

<23> The very nature of the universe is progressive and all things are marching toward perfection. <24> It is true about everything, even our system. So if in the future this system can be perfected, or by progress of humanity to a higher level of consciousness, altered, this can be viewed as an evolution in the system toward its perfection.
<25> However, it should be progressive, not counter-evolutionary. It can be improved or adjusted. But its base, which is to bring justice, peace, and progress into the universe, should not be sacrificed.

Exceptions to the rule:

<26> The system described above, or any other approach to human existence, should not become a rigid set-up. As the chart of normal distribution in statistics shows, there are always exceptions which exist in any kind of distribution.
<27> In fact it is the few positive exceptions to the rule which usually bring greater change and progress. <28> Therefore no system or set-up should become so rigid as to destroy or slow down these exceptional talents to bloom and manifest themselves. <29> The very nature of the universe, in its highest state, is free, happy, and progressive. Anything that opposes this basic right is not natural, will create suffering, and will eventually be destroyed.

ESSAYS

There are three books of ESSAYS. They are called Essays 1, 2, and 3. In these three books, Maitreya covers many topics. They show how the future societies should follow these recommendations for greater unity, peace, and prosperity.

ESSAYS 1

<u>**Essays 1**</u> covers many topics. These topics are related to human society and its progress. They are guiding lights for the coming Golden Age.

ESSAYS 1

Tablet One

SAL-OM (SALUT-OM)
A DERIVATION FROM SHALOM, SALAAM, SALUTE, AND OM (ॐ)

Shalom: <1> (used by Jews) hello, good-bye, and peace.
Salaam: <2> (used by most Moslems) comes from the root "tasleim" which means "surrendered." Therefore, "salaam" means "to be surrendered."
Salute: <3> (a universal greeting) health, safety, greeting; <4> to address with expression of kind wishes, courtesy, or honor; <5> to give a sign of respect, courtesy, or good will; <6> the position (as of the hand) or the entire attitude of a person saluting another person.

<7> Therefore, "Sal-Om" is a greeting of "hi" and "good-bye." <8> At the same time by the position of the hands over the fourth chakra, which is the center of love in humans, we express our love and courtesy to the other person and wish him to be surrendered to the Will of the Divine God, and for peace to be upon him. <9> Also we wish him health, a long-lasting life, and we honor him.
<10> However, all wishes we make for the person and all respect he deserves can come to him only by being surrendered to the Father and His Laws (Daharmas).
<11> On the other hand, the word "sal" is an abbreviation of the word "salute." Therefore, the word "Sal-Om" can be translated to be: "salute to the sound OM (ॐ)." <12> The sound OM is the root sound of all sounds in the universe <13> and will be heard in the high state of realization. <14> By greeting another person with the word "Sal-Om" we are really greeting his most Divine nature within, or his consciousness in pure form.
<15> Therefore, not only do we greet a person by "Sal-Om" and give him many other good wishes, but we greet him as a Divine being who is able to reach Pure Consciousness. <16> We pay our salutations to the Divinity within him.

Tablet Two

ATMAN

<1> The nucleus of any object is its atman. <2> The nucleus of the universe is the Atman of the universe. The atman controls the object that it is the nucleus of. That is why the nucleus of the universe is the Controller of the universe. <3> Any part that has separated itself from the whole (of the universe in whole) becomes a universe in itself and will have a nucleus as its controller (atman).
<4> The controller of each object as its nucleus has control over the object according to its state of awareness. That is, as the object is in lower awareness, so the atman also has lesser control. As the object comes to a higher level of awareness, so the atman also becomes more aware and gains greater control over the object. <5> That is why man has greater control over himself and his body (as the object of his atman) and God has the greatest control over His object, the universe.
<6> Also as the Father is the Atman of the universe, any other level or universe which is created will have a separate nucleus, but will still be subject to the main center of the universe (God). <7> Also each universe or world itself can be divided into sub-worlds and sub-sub-worlds and so on until unit consciousnesses are reached, each as a nucleus (atman). <8> However, each nucleus or atman is also a subject of the atman of the greater object to

which it belongs. For example, each atom in the human body has a nucleus (atman), and many of them create an organ with its own nucleus (atman), and many organs together become a component or a system in the body with its own controller (atman), and all of them together create the body with its nucleus (atman) as the Soul.

<9> Also each individual is subject to many different, bigger parts with different nuclei, such as home, society, world, galaxy, etc. Each of these has a nucleus which in different ways controls him. <10> So, in a greater sense, he is controlled by the world (Loka) he belongs to, and on a universal scale, all of them are controlled by the Universal Atman, or God.

<11> This truth is what the Shrii Yantra represents by using triangles, each as an object separate and at the same time one with the Controller.

<12> If we mix two objects together, a new nucleus will be created and the old nuclei will lose their identities and become subjects of this new nucleus. <13> So in a sense, atman, or this nucleus, is an imaginary or illusive assumption in any object. That is why when a person realizes that everything is God and He is the true Controller of the universe, the feeling of "I" (atman) will be dissolved and he becomes the subject of the Universal Atman. <14> That is the state in which a person realizes the "Tat Twam Asi," or "That art thou" (God is everything), and no feeling of "I" is left.

DAHARMA (DARMA)

<15> Daharma or Darma means the "innate nature," or the Laws governing each and every thing. In human life and in the universe as a whole, there are Laws (Darmas) which have been set up by God or have existed in the universe.

<16> Deviation from these Laws is violence, because violence means to deviate from a set of rules which have been ascribed to be followed. <17> Therefore, non-violence is to not violate these Laws.

TIME, PLACE, AND PERSON, IGNORANCE, PASSION, OR KNOWLEDGE

Time, place, and person: <18> In this universe many laws, especially those related to the physical body or manifested world, depend on the time, place, and person (or people and situation). <19> With this in mind, first of all we can better understand history and its incidents. Also we can be flexible in many different situations of life and environment. For example, it is true that a vegetarian diet and sentient foods are the most beneficial for the physical, mental, and spiritual well-being of a human, but in an environment with cold weather, the rajasic (mutative) foods become satvic (sentient). Also in places with extremely cold weather like Siberia, Alaska, or the North Pole, the tamasic (static) foods might be considered satvic.

<20> Another example is the eating of a dead carcass. It is true that usually the human does not eat a dead carcass, but if he is trapped in a situation where he has no choice for survival and there is a dead carcass there,

ESSAYS 1

then one might consider it as food. <21> Every human, however, should use his or her intelligence in deciding about how to act in any situation (time, place, and people involved) and act as close to the Will of God as possible.

Ignorance, passion, or knowledge: <22> According to the time, place, and person, the decision, however, can be of three kinds: from ignorance, from passion, or from knowledge. For example, according to the time, place, and person, service to others can be from ignorance (when someone insists to help another person when it is not necessary or the help will make the other person lazy, or he does not want the help); it can be from passion (when a person has some gain in his mind, for example, he thinks that if he does these services for the other person he will be profited with something for selfish gain, such as love, attention, possession, material things, etc.). <23> The service from knowledge is done when it is necessary and is done completely selflessly. Otherwise it is not a service but a business. <24> This is true in all of the decisions a man can make. They can be from ignorance, passion, or knowledge according to the time, place, and person. <25> Also, the decision-making process is a perpetual process. A good decision (or anything) made now may not be as good six months from now.

Tablet Three
THE THREE GUNAS

<1> The universe consists of three forces and the consciousness. In Sanskrit, these three forces are called tama (static), raja (mutative) and satva (sentient). <2> Tama guna (guna means force) is that force which crudifies consciousnesses. Raja guna is the active force or action. Satva guna is the force of logic or decision-making. <3> The Soul (unit consciousness) uses these forces to relate to and control the universe. <4> However, we can never separate these forces with any clear-cut borders. There is a range between almost complete domination of tama guna to almost complete domination of satva guna. This can be represented by the graph below:

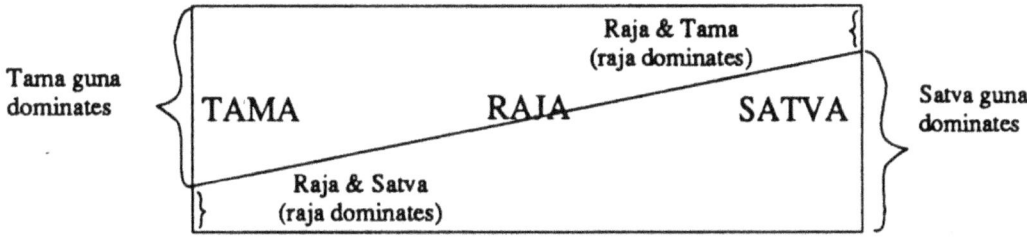

<5> When tama guna dominates, there is still some raja guna and satva guna present which is shown as the small area at the bottom. This is also true when satva guna dominates (right side of the graph). There is still some tama guna and raja guna present.

<6> Tama guna is the force responsible for this manifested universe and also for the unawareness of the consciousness in the unaware part of the universe. <7> As it is illustrated in the graph above, as the satvic force becomes more dominant over the consciousness, tama guna loses its power over the Soul. <8> That is why through gaining power over the tama guna, spiritual people feel freer and freer from the bondage of this external world and become closer and closer to the spiritual world which is beyond the control of this crudifying force.

<9> The material world (manifested world) is made of consciousnesses crudified (bent) by the power of the tama guna ("gathering of the waters," Gen. 1:9). This was created in order to help these unit consciousnesses

to progress toward higher consciousness and eventually Pure Consciousness. <10> Also this tama guna is the force responsible for crudifying the consciousness of the human. That is why the human should overcome the tama guna and avoid anything that empowers this force over his Soul or reach a state that it has no power over him. <11> When this manifested world is not used properly (by becoming attached to its illusion, Maya) or a sentient environment is not created to direct the consciousness toward higher thoughts (by creating crudifying images or objects which bend man toward his lower nature), the consciousness becomes more and more self-centered and separated from the spiritual world – where tama guna has no power over it.

<12> These three gunas are represented symbolically in the Bible as the three famous angels Michael, Gabriel, and Lucifer. <13> As it is mentioned in Isaiah 14:12, Lucifer (which means "the shining star") was made by God to be the king of the world. But he failed and was cast out (that is exactly what the tama guna does when a Soul is under its influence). The Soul becomes so crude that it is drowned in the ocean of Maya (ignorance) and will not be able to understand the realities behind this universe. That is why we say that person is following the devil (satan, evil, etc.). In other words, he is under the influence of the tama guna.

<14> Therefore, it is the tama guna which bends us toward the excessive attraction to the external world. When tama guna is present, raja guna (action, mutative force) will be bent toward excessive materialistic possession, or we will be attached to the result of our actions, or we will create expectations. When tama guna is present, satva guna will be bent toward the material world (satva guna is that part of us which makes the decisions and commands the ego to do the decisions). When tama guna dominates, decisions will be directed toward bondage toward the material world (attachments, desires, greed, etc.). <15> However, when tama has been overcome, decisions will be selfless toward the spiritual Laws and for the welfare of the whole universe. This will make our actions (raja) also pure and free from bondage. <16> So it is the tama guna (devil) which should be overcome and controlled.

<17> Again we can see that the devil is the same as the tama guna which crudifies the consciousness. <18> When tama guna dominates the human Soul, it is the devil (satan). <19> When the human Soul dominates tama guna, it becomes a "shining star" (Lucifer). Then this manifested world becomes a guiding light toward reaching the spiritual world. Hence, we see that the foolishness of the external world is a shining star to guide us to God.

<20> Tama guna is any force that bends the human Soul toward the excessive attraction to the external world and therefore creates unnecessary attachment, desires, expectations, greed, etc., toward the external world, <21> or anything that looks good to do or follow but after it is done or followed brings suffering and the feeling of emptiness and separation from God (universe).

CONTROL OF THE LOWER SELF

<22> As the tama guna is the devil when the Soul is under its influence and becomes a shining star (Lucifer) when it is overcome, so is the lower nature. <23> The lower nature in itself can be a hindrance in spiritual progress, or, if its selfish tendencies are overcome, can be used for physical, mental, and spiritual progress of self and others (others as the rest of the universe).

<24> For example, the desire to survive, which is related to the first chakra, can be an inspiration for material advancement. But if a person is ignorant of the unimportance of what we see as our only life and is desperately afraid of death, then it can be a hindrance in his path.

<25> Or sex, which is a powerful force in the human body, when controlled and used to channel its energy to the higher self (psychic

centers) or used to create a healthy body for a new human being, it is a blessing. However, if it makes a man heedlessly seek its satisfaction uncontrollably and makes him do whatever is necessary to gain this satisfaction, then it is an obstacle in human progress.

<26> The use of the power of the third chakra is similar. When this center is controlled and used for gaining power in order to establish the Kingdom Of Heaven, then it also becomes a guide for human progress. But using it for gaining positions and prestige for the sake of self-gratification, makes it a devilish center.

<27> However, selfishness resides in these first three centers. Therefore, man should gain control over them first by raising his spiritual consciousness to the higher self and then use the power of these centers for the progress of the self and others.

<28> Notice that you have to gain control over these lower centers, not destroy them. You do not kill a wild horse, but instead break him down in such a way that he is under your control. Then you will have a powerful horse to give you rides and pleasure. That is also true about the lower self. <29> When you gain control over it, then you will have many powerful forces to use for the progress of yourself and others.

INVISIBILITY OF GOD AND HUMAN

<30> We learn that God is invisible, but is not man invisible also? We think that man is visible but indeed he is not. We make the mistake of identifying a person as his body. The truth is that we are not our bodies but the consciousness which is so subtle, even subtler than the ether. <31> We have this body; Father does not have any body (if we do not consider the manifested universe as His Body). That is the only difference. Therefore, we both are invisible. <32> We know Him by His qualities and actions (creation), and we know a person by his qualities and actions also.

<33> When a person does not act and remains inactive, we assume he is dead. The reason that the person remains inactive is because there is no Soul in that body any longer, so there is no human consciousness there. <34> However, because the Soul is invisible, the only way for us to relate to that person is when he is in a body.

<35> In fact man is visible only in the interval from birth to death. It is through his actions by his body or through the effect of his actions on the environment that we know him. <36> After a person dies (leaves his body) people will remember the many things he had done in his lifetime and will see the results of his actions. But they cannot see **him** because he is a Soul, and a Soul cannot be seen by these naked eyes.

<37> This is also true about God. We can know His existence through His actions, or by contemplating this perfect, self-sustaining universe made by Him. We can know He exists by the way He is guiding us toward the goal. <38> There is no doubt as man progresses toward higher spiritual understandings and develops his spiritual faculties that the existence of God will be insured by establishing a direct telepathic relationship with Him. <39> However, even He is invisible as man himself is invisible also.

Tablet Four
THE PREREQUISITES OF SPIRITUAL LIFE

<1> The prerequisites of spiritual life are physical health, mental equilibrium (simple life), and spiritual cleanliness (spiritual environment).

ESSAYS 1

A. <2> **Physical health** is possible only when a person lives in an environment where the seven basic necessities for a strong physical body are provided:

1- **Fresh Air**, which is the #1 "must." It is the most essential physical necessity. Even the greatest yogis cannot live without prana which can be found in clean fresh air.

2- **Sunshine**, the second "must" in order to gain the freshest life energies from the sun and build strong bones and a healthy physical body.

3- **Good food**, sentient, fresh, and balanced food to be used by the body to create strong cells. The sun also helps food to be digested properly. Food is the most beneficial when it is cooked with a joyful group and is eaten with the same joy by the group.

4- **Pure water**, which not only gives much prana to the person, but also provides the essential fluid and moisture for the body, many essential minerals, and prevents many diseases.

5- **Good rest**, especially when done in fresh air will provide happiness, joy, and contentment, which all are very necessary for good health.

6- **Exercise and Innercise**, to stimulate the circulation and provide the body and brain with more blood, ease the work of the heart, and provide relaxation and health and also Innercise (yoga postures, which mostly work on the glands and Spirit rather than the muscles).

7- **Concentration and the use of the power of the mind**, this will help a person to use his/her healing power and provide this power more easily for physical stability and health.

B. <3> **Mental equilibrium**: To acquire a simple life to prevent the disturbance of the mind (but not so simple that the person becomes a burden on society). <4> Simple life does not mean escapism <5> but avoiding those activities which provide much stress with no beneficial results to the person or others, such as games (when they become a show, instead of for health purposes), luxury, too much attachment to the external world, drugs, drinking, smoking, thinking too much about the opposite sex, putting material gain prior to spiritual progress, etc.

C. <6> **Spiritual cleanliness**: In addition to physical and mental cleanliness, a person has to strive to be spiritually clean. As the body becomes dirty in a few days, the mental aspects of the human also become soiled. Actually the mind becomes soiled much faster than the body, and even faster than the mind is the spirit that becomes unclean (through the mind). <7> So we can see how important these things are: the environment we live in, the materials we read, the shows we see, or the people we have as our companions. They all affect our mental and spiritual cleanliness. <8> A spiritual person not only tries to avoid crudifying environments but eventually he also should be able to stay in the equilibrium of his mind even in the middle of the worst environment. Otherwise (if he does not become that strong), he will leave the society and go off to the mountains or fall into the grip of Maya as he loses his Soul in it.

ENVIRONMENT

<9> Stimulation of the imagination of the human results in raising the desires (images, the first beast in The Revelation, chapter 13) by the environment (objects of desires, Maya) and is the cause of the development of unspiritual desires, and these desires bring the wanting to fulfill them. That causes a man to pursue them heedlessly and become drowned in Maya. Fulfillment of desires brings attachment, and then follows greed. Greed will create more desires, and on and on.

<10> It is true that with systematical destruction of desires a man can overcome Maya, but also he will destroy a potential creative part of himself which when directed toward higher goals, is a forceful necessity for doing great endeavors in the universe.

<11> However, it is also true that the

human should overcome and control, with The Grace, his desires in order to transfer the desires of his lower nature toward his higher nature. <12> Creating a proper environment will greatly help the human in this endeavor and will make his work much easier.

<13> In an environment where the mind of a man is stimulated again and again by the external world, it is almost impossible to control the beast (desires). <14> That is why it is the responsibility of the men, women, society, government, etc., to create that sentient environment which does not allow any stimulation of the lower nature of the human.

<15> In this endeavor women have a great responsibility. They should emphasize the beauty of their higher selves rather than the beauty of their bodies (which should be a channel to manifest His Grace and be sacred to their husbands who are their soulmates). <16> It is also true about men. They have to create manly characteristics and emphasize their higher natures.

<17> Forgetting about the higher nature of the human will throw them into that state which is described as the city of Gomorrah or other lost civilizations such as the last days of the Roman Empire, and results in the destruction of the society. <18> If we do not understand these truths and do not follow them because of our limited egos, soon we will see the effect of our actions individually and collectively, and will become another example for the future humans. <19> It is the Law of the universe to develop our higher natures and help others to do the same. Otherwise we are going against the Law and The Plan in the universe, and that always leads to self-destruction.

<20> In short, anything that stimulates the lower self of the person, others, or collective society, should be avoided.

PURITY (PURITY OF BODY, MIND, AND ENVIRONMENT)

<21> In order to become pure, you have to have a pure heart and mind. To have a pure heart and mind, a pure environment is necessary – but not in the case of the man who keeps his mind immersed in the higher thoughts (God) all the time. <22> However, to remain in such higher thoughts so that the cruel environment does not affect the person is a difficult task and needs much training of the mind. With the background of many people in this age, and with the speed of life in our society, for many it is a very hard thing to do.

<23> Therefore, the first step toward purity is to create an environment where man can concentrate on higher thoughts with the least disturbance, or in other words, to create an environment where the stimulation of the lower nature becomes minimal.

<24> As we know, man's goal in life is to be(come) Divine, which is to reach Pure Consciousness and help others to reach there also. And we know the lower nature of man is made up of those propensities which he shares with animals, such as thirst, hunger, sex, need for shelter, etc. Although it is necessary for this part of man to be moderately satisfied, too much emphasis on these things will result in bringing man to his lower nature and will cause him to be lost in the ocean of Maya. Then the man will lose his true goal of the life and become an impure, lost soul.

<25> Again we see that establishing the Kingdom Of Heaven within is almost an impossibility without establishing the Kingdom Of Heaven without.

<26> As the body becomes dirty in a day or two because of the unclean particles outside of it, the mind becomes dirty even faster than that. If we want to have clean bodies all the time, then we should stay in the shower twenty-four hours a day. That is also true about the mind and spirit. If we want to keep our minds clean and pure, then we should stay in His Shower of Grace twenty-four hours a day in order to prevent any impurities from entering into the consciousness. That is why

we should love Him with all our mind, all our heart, and all our being twenty-four hours of the day. That is the only way if we want to stay pure in a crude environment, and that is the only way if we want to eventually create a pure environment also. <27> "We make the world with our thoughts, and the world makes our thoughts." Therefore, there should be a simultaneous purification of the environment and an individual's mind.

<28> Only after we have created a pure mind might we understand Him and His Laws on deeper levels, and then we are able to keep our bodies and Souls pure also. Then a person will become pure in heart, <29>and only the pure in heart can see God.

Tablet Five
SATSANG

<1> As the body becomes soiled from the external particles, also the spirit of the human becomes dirty because of the influence of the external world and the power of Maya.

<2> We have to wash our bodies to be cleansed from dirt, and if we do not clean ourselves we will be inflicted with many diseases. This is also true about our spirit. As man directs his attention toward the external world, and lets the mundane things affect him and bring him to his lower nature, so his spirit becomes dirty and he goes to his lower nature.

<3> To direct the attention from the mundane to higher self, the spirit should be cleansed. This can be done through spiritual gatherings and sharing of the spiritual truths with others. <4> This kind of gathering and talking about God and the truths behind this universe is called "Satsang."

<5> As water cleans the flesh, the Satsang cleanses the spirit. It is the shower for the spirit. <6> Our body, in normal situations, becomes soiled in a day or two. Our spirit becomes dirty even faster than that. As we should take a shower often, so we should clean our spirit even more often. Meditation, singing the kirtan, remembrance of the mantras, offering the food to the Lord, and all the techniques used in spiritual progress are for cleansing the spirit. <7> One of the most important ones is Satsang: Faith comes by hearing the words of God.

<8> In Satsang, the aspirants should not talk about themselves, but about the invisible Lord and His universe. <9> Satsang should be given by spiritually advanced people, and usually true Satsang happens spontaneously with no previous preparation. <10> Satsang should be performed as many times as possible. But formal spiritual gatherings should be done every evening.

<11> We should clearly recognize the difference between Satsang and idle talk. Idle talk will make man go more to Maya (illusion), and Satsang takes him toward the Lord (higher consciousness).

THE IMPORTANCE OF THE SPIRITUAL TEACHER

<12> Although God in Its highest is Formless, Invisible, Nameless, and Eternal (FINE), however we see many people need some kind of mediator (manifested or un-manifested) between themselves and God. <13> Such realized mediators (being One with God) can be called spiritual teachers, Gurus, or Masters, etc.

<14> The spiritual teacher is the one who is able to impart the knowledge of higher consciousness or God to others. <15> It does not matter what he wears or looks like. He will be the source of bliss and suffering for his disciples, and by this process the growth of the disciples occur. <16> The disciple might not understand the actions of his teacher but

there is a link between the two that cannot be broken. This link is what helps the disciple to stay and go through this process of reaching higher consciousness.

<17> Only those who are in tune with the spiritual world will be able to take on this elaborate task of guiding others to higher consciousness. <18> They will become like lights in the path of the disciple. It is true that the disciple is in the depth of the jungle of ignorance but the spiritual teacher is standing as a light out of that jungle. The disciple is in darkness, but if he keeps his eyes fixed on the spiritual teacher, his escape from that dark jungle is assured.

<19> However, without utmost respect and love for the spiritual teacher, it is impossible to see that light. <20> When a disciple realizes that Divinity within his spiritual teacher, he should never forget that and never judge his teacher by the appearance of his actions. Only then can the disciple fix his eyes to the Divinity he has realized in his teacher and become it.

<21> The spiritual teacher and his teachings are the ideal of the disciple. Whoever betrays that ideal is one like Judas who betrayed Christ.

Tablet Six
UNIVERSALISM

<1> The only "ism" is universalism. Any other "ism" is from narrowness.

<2> Only by accepting the universe as the only home, nation, and country, can a man overcome being narrow-minded by relating the self to a specific group or land. <3> Only then can he destroy the very disease of the mind, which is a feeling of belonging to one part rather than feeling that the only home is the entire universe.

<4> Also, by becoming a universalist and understanding that this whole universe is made up of nothing else but unit consciousnesses and the three gunas (Souls and the creative force) then a man will not only love God and His awesome creation but every part and parcel of it. With this again a man does not look to another man as only a body and/or different than himself, but as a Soul which does not belong to any race or group. <5> Not only will people become respectful Souls in different levels of consciousness but also the whole universe will be seen from the same perspective, different Souls in different levels of consciousness.

<6> The question might be asked, then, what about the other "isms?" The answer is that the other "isms" are each a part of a greater truth. That truth is that Paravipras, who are the true leaders and concerned about the welfare of all in the universe, should lead humanity to the highest prosperity. <7> However, as long as people have not become Universalists and are separated by countries, dogmatic religions, psychological barriers, etc., politicians and others will exploit them in the name of nationalism, religion, race, group, etc. <8> The only way to the highest happiness and prosperity is to understand The Plan of creation, become a universalist (shattering the narrowness of the mind), and follow the Will of the Father.

SELECTION OF ONE LANGUAGE

<9> In the Bible it is said that God scattered humans all over the world and confused them by creating many languages (took away their telepathic powers). He did this because they started to use their good communicative abilities and intelligence to build things which were destructive to their existence. <10> Therefore, for their own good, God confused them (Genesis chapter 11).

<11> However, it is now time for the

human to go back to a one-language based society all over the world. By understanding the lesson that **THOTH** has given, the human should be wiser by now and use his energy and knowledge only toward the purpose and goal of creation of the universe: To bring humans and the whole universe toward Pure Consciousness. <12> However, this can be done only by understanding the reality behind **The Greatest Sign**.

<13> For selecting a language that enables all of humanity to communicate and at the same time preserves all the great achievements of the different cultures, we should accept one language as the base. By translating all the great literature and Scriptures of each culture to this basic language, and by using those words from the different cultures which cannot be translated to this basic language (words like "Daharma," "karma," "jahad," etc.), after some time a new language will be created which allows greater versatility and eventually will cover all the beautiful words in other languages. It will be a great and powerful language of the world.

<14> However, the native languages should be preserved for many years until, in the course of time, the new language replaces the old languages and transforms the society to a higher understanding of all other different cultures and their achievements in other parts of the world.

<15> English seems to be the most suitable one at this time to be accepted as the basic language. <16> However, learning the languages of the Scriptures, such as Sanskrit, Hebrew, Greek, and Arabic, etc., is also recommended.

MIXING RACES

<17> Each race and people have a special place in creation. Through the evolutionary process they have been separated into many different races. Each race now has a characteristic which dominates that race. With mixing the races together, we will create new bodies for those Souls who are ready to occupy such bodies. This will also enable humanity further to overcome the feeling of racism.

<18> Another application of mixing races is to cause different cultures to come closer together and therefore create the feeling of universalism. This will help humans to understand more and more that we are one family.

<19> Again that is what should be done in the era to come and is The Plan of creation for making man understand that we are all in the path of becoming Pure Consciousness, and any obstacle in this path should be shattered and destroyed. <20> Racism and nationalism are two of these which can be destroyed more effectively, beautifully, and peacefully, by intermarriage between different races and cultures.

<21> Also racism is one of the problems within many nations. Therefore, marriage between different races within a country is highly recommended. Then marriage between those of different countries will occur, until humans become so mixed that separation of the races is impossible.

<22> In this process, however, the spiritual unification of the couple involved is the most important factor. With this view, all obstacles can be overcome. <23> Also bringing the whole world under one international government can accelerate this process, and correspondingly, this process will accelerate the establishment of a world government.

<24> Some people argue that marriage within the same race, culture, and background produces less trouble for the couple. It is true, and that is why the first pioneers who marry from two different races should be truly matured and strong, so that they can withstand the problems related with breaking the tradition, until mixed marriages become more acceptable throughout the world. <25> Some of this argument springs from the fear of change and/or prejudice.

<26> Mixed marriages are more difficult for the couples in this state of social and intellectual development of man. <27> However,

if there were not difficulties, humans would have never progressed. As time passes, it will become easier. <28> There should always be pioneers to initiate a change, and those are usually the ones who go through the most hardships. They are also the builders of the future.

<29> However, it is mostly a personal decision. If a male and a female are truly and spiritually attracted and complementary to each other, no barriers should stand in their way. <30> Of course in all cases the consultation with their parents, spiritual teacher, and eventually meditating on it and praying (seeking His Will) should be considered. In this case the advice of a true master (spiritual guide) is the most helpful.

<31> Even if the process of intermarriage does not result in a complete mixing of the races, still it should be kept in mind that each race, like each beautiful flower, has its beauty and distinct fragrance. <32> When they are all put together as a bouquet they can be even more beautiful than only one single kind of flower.

<33> With the advanced communicative and transportative abilities of man, humans have no choice any longer but to accept this truth. <34> They should not only create a brotherly feeling toward each other, but realize that all are a part and parcel of God, so all is He and all are equal with different natures and purposes (Daharmas).

Tablet Seven
VIRTUES OF MARRIAGE

<1> The truth below should be understood by both partners who want to marry. <2> Parents and society are also responsible to make sure that both the man and woman understand the truth which underlies a marriage, are aware of its spiritual and social values, are ready to carry out their responsibilities in this unification, and are familiar with their duties.

<3> Each person should choose his/her partner but parents and elders can assist in this matter. <4> However, they should not impose their will on the choice, unless a young person is making an obvious mistake from a spiritual or psychological point of view – but not from a financial or social point of view (position, class, race, etc.).

A. **Understanding Marriage From The Spiritual Point Of View**:
1- **Origin** (☯): <5> In the beginning the male and female energy was in a balanced state in each being (they were in the image of God) (☯).
2- **Separation** (☯☯): <6> In the course of evolution, however, it became necessary to separate them into two parts as male and female. This was necessary in order to be able to help each unit consciousness more effectively. <7> Before this happened, the unit consciousness did not feel any need for help from the external world, so they would not strive to progress toward higher consciousness.

3- **Unification** (☯): <8> When a man and woman understand that they are greatly attracted to each other on a spiritual level (not physically or intellectually) in such a way that they are almost sure they are each other's soulmate, then they should marry. <9> However, marriage between an unmatched male and female can also be successful if they understand the spiritual truth behind the unification through marriage. By focusing on God and becoming one with Him, they also become one with each other, as each other's halves.

<10> As the false ego tends to direct a person to self-centeredness, the spiritual realization, however, can only be gained by dissolving the false ego through being more concerned about others than the self. <11> This can be achieved very easily by marriage if each partner becomes more concerned about the physical, mental, and spiritual progress of the other partner. This will cause one to forget about one's little false ego (self-centeredness) and to merge with the other partner

by understanding his or her needs instead of thinking about the self. Therefore, the person creates the ability to come out of himself and be concerned about others. <12> Only then can these couples manifest the love and selflessness of the Lord by their own example toward each other and others.

4- **Generation and Appreciation (Children)**: <13> With having children, parents also become creators. Therefore they can feel the same love that God feels about His creation and the humans. This also increases the spiritual realization of the couple toward God-realization. <14> If they love their children so much (and they actually did not create the children but were only tools used to bring them to the world), you can imagine how much God loves humans and His creation which He personally created!

5- **Independence (Separation From Parents)**: <15> Marriage also brings independence for couples. As stated in Genesis 2:24, "Therefore shall a man leave his father and his mother, and shall cleave unto his wife: and they shall be one flesh." They will gain their own family and become an independent, separate family block in society.

6- **Duties**: <16> The man is the provider and protector of the family. He should also be the priest and spiritual example (Divine Logic) for others. <17> The woman is the comforter (Divine Grace) and coordinator of the family. She is also the center of the family life.

<18> Man and woman are equal in progressing physically, mentally, and spiritually, and all facilities should be provided equally for both to progress in these three levels. <19> However, equality does not mean similarity. Men and women are different physically, mentally, emotionally, and spiritually (the female body is more suited to manifest Grace, and male – Logic). So they should realize this fact and act according to their own natures.

7- **Spiritual Progress**: <20> With this kind of marriage, humans can reach Pure Consciousness in the middle of the family life. Man should not forsake the family in order to pursue a spiritual life. With understanding the realities behind things in this universe and their Darmas (natures), the human can realize all things are spiritual. <21> As man follows the Laws of God as they have been set up, he can continue living in society and doing actions without being bound by them.

B. <u>Understanding Marriage From A Social Point Of View</u>:

1- **A Unit Block Of Society**: <22> As many small bricks create a building, many families make up the society. If a building is composed of strong, well-chosen bricks, it will be strong. Similarly, if the families are strong and well-formed, the society will be strong also. <23> A society with confused family planning, many divorces, and misunderstanding the importance of strong families is a weak society, no matter how wealthy or powerful it might look.

<24> However, a society with a strong family structure is like a house built on stone. It will not be shaken with wind, flood, or disasters. This kind of society can easily withstand negative forces against itself. <25> In fact the very reason for those societies which have developed highly and have become powerful is based on their strong family structure, and the reason for their fall is based on the loss of their early family structure because of prosperity which brings greater self-centeredness.

<26> Therefore, also understanding and following the truth behind marriage from a social point of view is a must.

2- **Satisfaction Of Physiological Needs**: <27> The human body is created in such a way that it is also physically attracted to the opposite sex. The best way to satisfy this need is through marriage with the other part which will result in the highest experience of the relationship between a man and a woman. <28> In fact, this is the only acceptable way to satisfy this physiological need.

3- **Companionship (Satisfaction Of Psychological Needs)**: <29> Marriage is also the most perfect way to bind two beings together so closely to form the best friendship possible. This will satisfy the psychological need of having companionship for those who have

4- Best Environment For The Growth of Children: <30> An ideal marriage creates a loving, secure, and suitable environment for children to grow physically, mentally, emotionally, and spiritually in order to create a great society.

C. The Ritual Of Marriage And Its Significance:

1- <31> The man is asked if he is fairly sure that the woman is his soulmate, because when two parts as soulmates marry, they will never divorce. <32> He should take an oath that he understands the merits, reasons, and philosophy behind marriage completely, understands his duties as protector and provider, and also will help his partner to grow physically, mentally, and spiritually.

2- <33> The same questions are asked and an oath is taken from the woman, that she understands the virtues of marriage and will be the comforter and loving wife as the center of the family, etc.

3- <34> An oath is taken from the audience that they will help the couple (as much as possible) in their growth, physically, mentally, and spiritually, and also will help them to become established in their marriage (society is responsible for the individual as the individual is responsible for society).

4- <35> The couple is announced to be wife and husband.

<36> Also the bride and groom can each have a candle in their hands and at the end of the ceremony, light them and exchange them as the lights of their consciousnesses. They can bring the candles together to form one flame as a symbol of having merged together and become one.

<37> Then while the two flames are still merged as one, they bring the candles to a dish with water which is close to them. They extinguish the flame by immersing it into the water. <38> The extinguishments of the flame symbolizes the death of the ego into ashes by becoming One in God (consciousness, water) and <39> continuation of their spiritual marriage even beyond death.

<40> Then the bride and the groom take some of the burned ashes from their candles by their thumbs and put the ashes on each other's forehead (third eye, ego). <41> This further is a symbol of how each will help the other in the process of becoming one with God (consciousness) and their egos will become ashes in Him. <42> They will become One with each other in God.

<43> The candles are wet and cannot be re-lit. The couple is sealed together forever in God.

Tablet Eight

UNIVERSAL NAMING

<1> Another way to create universal feelings and accelerate the process of breaking barriers between different cultures is to collect spiritual names with beautiful meanings from all the cultures, societies, and Scriptures in the world (from sources with positive forces behind them) and create a pool of them.

<2> Then from this pool, a name can be selected for a person from all cultures. This name can be used as an accepted name for a lifetime or can be chosen as a spiritual name. <3> The meaning of the name should be pleasant and at the same time give some ideal expression to strive for, such as a name with the meaning "wise." So the person should strive to become what the meaning of his name is.

<4> Also the person should know what culture his name has come from, and this will create an attraction toward knowing more about those people. <5> Therefore, he will not only think about his own culture but will create the habit of being interested in the whole world.

<6> This will help the human more toward universalism.

SOCIETY

<7> Humanity should structure a very healthy and free society so that everyone is able to enjoy and utilize their abilities in the highest possible way. No one should be allowed to lag behind. <8> If the inner thirst for fulfillment and the basic necessities of the Soul are not satisfied, the energy and powers will be directed toward the destruction of the self and/or others.

<9> This can be another reason for the increasing number of crimes in the more complicated countries. The governments and institutions of these countries every day increase the obstacles for the opportunities available to the people to express their spirit. <10> Therefore, as we can see, this causes the human to lose the direct touch with his basic abilities and results in an ever-increasing crudification of the mind, leading to the point where he completely becomes a victim of his own desires and basic instincts.

<11> Therefore it is the duty of the people who have opened their third eyes and have a deeper vision of this situation to wake up and guide humanity to the right path – these problems are solved by creation of **Communities of Light**!

EDUCATION

<12> The elementary and high schools should educate children in such a way to expand their minds and bring them to a point of knowing themselves so well that they will be able to choose the best careers suited to their abilities. <13> Their work can then be a joy for themselves and a blessing to society. Research and fact-finding abilities cannot be overemphasized.

<14> Understanding the underlying truth and teaching of **The Greatest Sign** and universality, how each Scripture is related to the teaching of **The Greatest Sign**, and how God created the whole universe from compassion to help all of humanity and the universe to reach Pure Consciousness, should be taught with the utmost love and tolerance possible. Any superstition or narrowness of the mind should be shattered mercilessly. <15> The base of education should be for expansion of the mind.

<16> There should not be a limitation of time in mastering a subject, such as a semester or term, etc., but the relationship between student and teacher, or disciple and Guru, should be based on love and respect. <17> They will work together until the disciple masters the subject. When the teacher and disciple both agree that he has mastered the subject, he can then go on to other topics in his field. <18> This process is especially helpful in college and higher levels of education.

<19> The best way to follow this method is by the student listening to many teachers in that subject, and then choosing one teacher as his instructor. Then the teacher will also decide if he can work with that pupil. If both accept each other, they can then start to work together. <20> When the pupil masters his education under this teacher, he can continue in other subjects or under other teachers in higher levels.

<21> In technical subjects, the theoretical studies should be accompanied by practical parts, so the students become complete in both sides of the education.

Tablet Nine

SCIENCE

<1> Science should conquer space and bring a high standard of living to help unit consciousnesses to accelerate their journeys.

<2> Science should be directed toward the

goal of the human life and The Plan of God: For all to reach Pure Consciousness. <3> By occupying other planets more and more, eventually all unit beings will come to Pure Consciousness.

<4> It is up to humanity to advance in science so far that they can make other planets livable and spread the seed of man all throughout the universe. <5> The Plan of God in the beginning was to see the human race inhabit all parts of the earth. In order to do that, He "confound[ed] their language, that they may not understand one another's speech. So the Lord scattered them abroad from thence upon the face of all the earth and they left off to build the city" (Gen. 11:7-8).

<6> However, in the era to come the process should be reversed, and the humans should create one language again, but with the understanding that the Will of God is to see the humans scattered not only all over the earth but all over the universe.

<7> First man should establish the Kingdom Of Heaven On Earth and then try to completely understand the Laws that govern the earth and space. Then by the lessons given in history, humans should utilize all this knowledge not for selfish pursuance but toward fulfillment of The Plan for creation.

<8> However, understanding the earth and utilizing its resources (such as oceans, deserts, etc.) has priority in human advancement over discovering space. <9> Therefore, first man should expand his knowledge of the earth (with collective participation of all humans) and even start to live under or over the water if it is necessary. Then after that (or parallel with) conquer space also.

<10> In short, science should and will discover all the Laws that govern this manifested universe, <11> but never will be able to enter the realm of the eternal, un-manifested world. <12> Science should be used for the well-being of humanity, not for self-destruction.

<13> Also, in all discoveries, the by-products of those discoveries and their effects on human life should be predicted. If there is some by-product (such as pollution) in that discovery which will adversely affect human life and health, the way to eliminate those effects should first be determined. <14> Otherwise that discovery should not be used, until those shortcomings are corrected. The science based on spiritual Laws has no side effects!

POPULATION

<15> Science should conquer the universe and enable the human to reside on other planets. <16> That is the reason why so many planets have been made. Science can and will do it.

<17> Still, by doing meditation and yoga (becoming familiar with the Universal Laws governing the human body), the human can become more familiar with his body and will be able to gain more of his basic life energy from the air and sun. <18> Also, by becoming more vegetarian, we will be able to feed more people.

<19> However, only giving food will not solve the problem. People should be educated on how to obtain their basic necessities from the environment.

<20> The sources of the ocean should be utilized and science should understand the basic Laws underlying the different necessities for the body, and these should be created by extracting them from the environment.

<21> Also, excessive and improper use of available food for humans should be discouraged. As Mahatma Gandhi said, "There is enough for everyone's needs but not for everyone's greed." <22> Sacrifice is necessary. This is the lesson humans should learn. Without sacrifice, nothing is possible, and no comfort for all will come.

<23>Therefore, it is not the population which is a problem, but the other aspects of the present society: (l) The misdirection of science and resources toward discovering luxury items and warfare instruments, instead of utilizing the brains of scientists toward

unveiling the true Laws governing the universe which will bring higher standards of living to all; (2) The lack of an environment that gives an equal opportunity for all to develop to the highest possible potential. Therefore, many great brains remain dormant; (3) The mismanagement of space and food available to humanity; (4) The abundance of undereducated nations which do not utilize their fertile lands in full capacity; (5) The wrong philosophy of life in some cultures which teaches that this world is illusion and therefore the people do not strive for material advancement, etc.

<24> Again the next era is the age of cooperation and unity between all. The human has no choice. <25> This is God's Plan. <26> It does not matter how much intellectuals argue about human problems (and come up with no solutions). The Plan of the Father will be fulfilled and man will learn that God, like a good father, will guide His children until they learn the lessons. <27> Going against His Plan will hurt no one but the human himself.

<28> Therefore, again we can see that the human should destroy those barriers that have separated man from man and utilize all his abilities toward the goal – <29> all toward Pure Consciousness. And that requires sacrifice by all.

ARTISTS

<30> There are four classes of humans who are beyond the categories of the five socially active classes (Shudras, Ksattriyas, Vipras, Vaeshyas, and Brahmins). These four classes are:

1- **Prophets or Avatars**: those who have a message or new teaching for humanity.
2- **Gurus or Satgurus**: those who manifest God's qualities and bring many to the realization of the Lord.
3- **Paravipras**: the true leaders who are classless but have the characteristics of all five socially active classes.
4- **Artists**: the intuitive intellectuals who manifest finer thoughts and understandings to humanity.

<31> Artists work in the finer levels of human thought. <32> They can influence humanity by their abilities to bring and manifest the deeper levels of their feelings. <33> The artist class can be a great guide and blessing in helping humanity reach higher consciousness.

<34> A true artist never sells his ability for commercial use or for cheap praise (gains the world but loses his Soul). He works for his perfection, both internally and externally. <35> His ultimate goal is to manifest himself and the relationship of this self with the rest in the most perfect way possible.

<36> Also artists can manifest the problems in society in their art and show the way through their subtle communicative talents. <37> They can be a guidance for the future progress of the society in any moment of time and history. <38> Because of their deep intuitive abilities, they can see the future and the way to reach the highest level. So they can then guide others also to the next progressive phase. They have leadership duties.

Tablet Ten

JUSTICE

<1> Whenever we think about justice we should remember the story about Esa the Christ and the adulterous woman. When people asked Esa, "Should we stone the woman?" he said, "The one who has no sin cast the first stone." Then all the people left, and Christ himself forgave her and let her go.

<2> It is such a profound and deep story.

It has been told, read, and reread by many, but the true meaning of it has not been considered. The meaning is: "Only those who have no guilt can judge." <3> Christ does not say, "Do not judge her," or "Do not stone her," but only, "Those who have no guilt can judge and pass judgment on others."

<4> Or in other words, only those who have overcome their lower natures can judge. First of all, they will not easily forgive the sin done to society, because they have no guilt or sin themselves (or if they had in the past, they have overcome it and are in that peaceful state, with His Grace, where no guilt is present). So they will not overlook other people's sins because of their own guilt feelings. <5> Secondly, they will know that overcoming and being sinless is a great struggle. Therefore they will be compassionate toward sinners and will judge them by love. <6> Thirdly, they will be aware of the situation of the society and environment. Therefore, those sins which would not have been done if the society was not corrupt would not be judged harshly, because the victim is an effect of the cause of the corrupt society. It has been the society and environment that has created the victim, not his nature or greed.

<7> The man who has guilt himself will unjustly forgive others, because he is not truthful with himself and intuitively knows, "How can I judge when I do many sins myself?" That is why only Brahmins (sinless ones) should judge. Greater than salvation is justice. Justice is salvation.

<8> As long as petty criminals are judged and punished when these crimes are done because of inequity in society or from ignorance, and the big criminals who created such an unjust society for their own self-interests are overlooked because of their power or ties to the higher classes in society, or because of following the wrong philosophy in society in whole, justice will not be established. <9> Only in a true society with the greatest possible equity and true philosophy based on God's Laws, with true leaders, can justice be preserved.

<10> In such a society each person can assume the best position which is most suited to his own nature (Daharma). Then we will have a natural society (✡), where all the basic needs of the human are met and equity of the highest possible form is present. <11> Then if there is a criminal, he should be judged as harshly as necessary.

<12> However, in a natural society (Kingdom Of Heaven On Earth) it is expected that the number of wrongdoings would become minimal. <13> That is because more people will reach higher consciousness and they will have an effect on the consciousnesses of others in the direction of being a good citizen and compassionate.

<14> In fact, the very reason that the laws in the <u>Torah</u> and Shariah (Islamic laws) seem impractical in our societies is because these laws can only be used in a just society with the highest possible equity between people. <15> Otherwise they can be misused by opportunists or unjust leaders to take advantage of ignorant people in the name of religion. <16> That is what happened in the past, and if the Kingdom Of Heaven is not established, it will happen in the future.

<17> In short, the Kingdom Of Heaven should be established first, and then true and just leaders of humanity (Brahmins) can be the judges.

THE MEDIA

<18> The media should be used for spiritual progress. It is a part of the make-up of the environment and therefore should not be a source of stimulation of man's lower nature or a source of directing human attention from the goal of the life to other things.

<19> Man is nothing else but an ideal. <20> **A man without an ideal is an animal.** That is the only difference between a man and an animal. In eating, drinking, sex, and fear for survival, man shares the same tendencies with an animal. Only when man chooses

an ideal and strives for it will he be different. <21> However, an ideal can also be from ignorance. The only ideal which is not from ignorance is to become Divine, which is the goal of human life. <22> Other ideals are secondary to this one.

<23> The media, therefore, should be utilized toward this end and should direct man's desires toward his higher nature, which is Divine.

<24> This can be done by bringing the true knowledge of human life and spirituality to humans, by looking at this universe through the eyes of God, and by making all understand the significance of the things happening to humanity. <25> Also with respecting great figures in history and making Great Souls as ideals for young people to strive to follow in their steps, and by stopping things which come from the lower nature of the man or stimulate it, can this be achieved.

WHAT IS WRONG WITH MANAGEMENT STUDIES

A. <26> In management studies, the assumption is that the human hierarchy of needs, according to Maslow's theory, is as below:

1- Physiological
2- Safety
3- Belongingness: To be a part of a group
4- Esteem: To progress and be someone in that group
5- Self-actualization

<27> The two needs, belongingness and esteem, are not real needs but they are the by-products of the false ego. <28> **A false ego is created when a person feels important because of something outside in the external world**, such as: A nice house, a big car, a prestigious job, a group he belongs to, or because of the praises he receives from others, etc.

<29> The false ego can be easily recognized. That is, if that source of feeling important is taken away from the person, he will start to feel miserable and will either lose his confidence and become very depressed, or he will become violent.

<30> Also, true needs are those which should continue to stay with the person even after a higher need is fulfilled. But in the case of belongingness and esteem, when a person becomes self-actualized, these needs cease to exist, but the physiological and safety needs still remain. <31> That is, a self-actualized person still needs to eat, sleep, have shelter and medical care, but he no longer has a need for belongingness or esteem. <32> He might enjoy people and their company or even his achievements, but he is not desperate to have them. <33> He is content with himself as he is.

<34> Therefore, the true hierarchy of needs are as below:

1- Physiological
2- Safety
3- Self-actualization

<35> We can say that the belonging and esteem needs arise as false needs in order to assist a person to realize eventually that his true values and importance are not outside but within himself. <36> When this is understood, those false needs cease to exist. We can say that these needs are just illusionary needs (Maya). When the veil of illusion is taken away, a person becomes self-actualized. He will try to know his true values and know himself. <37> Whoever knows self, knows God.

<38> Furthermore, self-actualization is not a need but it is the goal. <39> So in truth, the only basic needs of existence are physiological and safety.

B. <40> The second problem with management studies is that only the organizational structure as the symbol of a triangle upward (△) is considered. <41> However, true organization consists of two triangles (✡).

<42> The triangle downward is the symbol for deeply understanding the Laws of the universe and implementing them in the organization, or the triangle downward means justice. <43> The two triangles together create the symbol of the Kingdom Of Heaven On Earth, or a true earthly organization (Seal of Solomon).

<44> Only by understanding the true nature of the human, helping all to become self-actualized, and establishing a natural organization (✡) with self-actualized members, can a true organization be created.

Tablet Eleven
THE TEMPLE

<1> The Temples will be built in the shape of **The Greatest Sign**.

<2> There are six doors entering the corridors of the **Temple**. The corridors form the sign of the Kingdom Of Heaven In Heaven (✡), which will connect all parts of the **Temple** together. <3> The six doors are: The Door of Pure Consciousness (☯), the Door of The Kingdom Of Heaven On Earth (✡), the Door of Sacrifice (✝), The Door of Surrendering and Submission (☪), The Door of Universalism (✹), and the Door of Paravipras (Elects) (✡).

<4> There are twelve sections around the center of the **Temple** (in the illustration shown above, these are numbered from 1 to 12). Each of these sections will be used as a library to house all the spiritual realizations throughout history. <5> The first section from the first sign (☯) to the sign of the Kingdom Of Heaven On Earth (✡) will have all the books or spiritual and historical materials from this period. <6> Section two (2) will have all the materials about Judaism, the Hebrews, and their history, religion, and philosophy. <7> In section three (3) between the sign of the Kingdom Of Heaven On Earth – or the Seal of Solomon (✡) – until the sign of sacrifice, Christianity (✝), the materials of the history between these two eras should be placed. <8> In section four (4) all the materials about Christianity will be housed. <9> Section five (5) will have materials of the history between Christianity and Islam (surrendering). <10> The rest of the sections will be as follows: In section six (6) the materials about Islam, <11> in section seven (7) materials of the history between Islam and the advent of Bab, <12> in section eight (8) materials about the Baha'i Faith (universalism), <13> in section nine (9) materials between the Baha'i Faith until the sign of Paravipra, <14> in section ten (10) materials about Paravipras and the teachings of the Baba, <15> and in section eleven (11) the history to come (how eventually God will fulfill His Plan until the human reaches very high consciousness and the Kingdom will become His Kingdom – in heaven, on earth, and within each individual).

<16> In section twelve (12) all the unknown ideas, speculations, and theories about man before the evolution of the present human

being will be found. Also all the speculations of what Pure Consciousness is (the theories of what kind of state of being it is) will be here.

<17> In section twelve (12) also all the teachings of the **Maitreya** should be placed separately. All other teachings and theories should be studied and looked at through these teachings. Otherwise the confusion of the Scriptures and revelations will make the path of the seeker difficult. <18> But with understanding creation and history, **The Greatest Sign**, and realizing how all things took place to bring man to higher consciousness and to show him there is no other way but God's way, then the seeker will reside in the flow of the Universal Plan instead of considering only one part of The Plan and becoming narrow-minded.

<19> However, the real realization does not come by merely studying the books in this great library, but by understanding The Plan of God, becoming **The Greatest Sign**, and going beyond search and study. <20> This state is symbolized by the very center of the **Temple**, which is beyond these libraries – section thirteen (12 + 1).

<21> This section (13) will be a place of absolute silence and meditation. Men and women should enter it with humility and respect. No lectures, talking, or noise should occur there. It is a place of Soul-to-Soul communion between God and His children. That is when the real realization is obtained. <22> In the next era, many will be ready to reach this stage of direct communion and understanding. They are the ones who will lead others also to higher consciousness and true realization.

<23> Meditation and silence or using any techniques alone might not bring full realization of God, as intellectual readings and research will not lead to that realization either. But a comprehensive inclusion of all kinds of awakening processes and false-ego-shattering steps can help an aspirant to come to a perfect realization so that the peace and understanding of the infinite truth can be achieved in the middle of society and family life. <24> So in this age, man should not run away from the realities of life but face the problems of this universe with enough vigor and understanding to surpass any obstacle. We now have many high conscious people who have already progressed greatly by their individual endeavors and His Grace in their past lifetimes. It is their responsibility to establish that environment to help others also to reach higher consciousness. That is why the time of being an escapist is gone for spiritual people. They have no choice now but to stay and work for the real spiritual truths which cover all aspects of life.

<25> A second story can be built over the **Temple**. Over sections 2, 4, 6, 8, 10, and 12, pyramids with a triangular base (tetrahedron) can be built. <26> By dividing each of the six arcs (of the circle around the **Temple**) into two and making straight lines from the center of each arc to the two points of the arc, a twelve-sided structure (dodecahedron) at the top of the **Temple** will be created. Therefore, sections 1, 3, 5, 7, 9, and 11 will have a four-sided shape. Then pyramids with a four-angle base can be built over them.

<27> The twelve pyramids (six with triangular bases and six with quadrangular bases) can be built over the libraries, preferably from glass to let the light into the building.

<28> A dome or similar structure can be built over section thirteen. A glass or crystal design of the **HOSH** sign will be placed in the center. <29> Domes have a spiritual effect on humans, and pyramids an intellectual one.

<30> The offices for maintaining the **Temple** should be built outside, and no profitable activity should be done in the **Temple**. <31> The **Temple** should be a place of worshipping and for gaining spiritual and intellectual knowledge. Also it should be a place of service.

<32> The physical fitness facilities, such as gymnasiums and running tracks, pools, and other sports areas, can be built close by if financially feasible. Also centers of other knowledge and education such as universities can be built around or close to the **Temple**.

<33> The physical fitness facilities should not be built for show or games, but for individual health and should be used moderately.

ESSAYS 1

Man consists of a physical body, mental abilities, and spirit and Soul, so all three levels should be developed properly. <34> Emphasis on any one part will be equal with loss in another.

<35> Also around the **Temple** beautiful flowers should be grown, also trees, grass, and many varieties of pleasant smelling plants, so that the Soul is refreshed on the way to the **Temple**. <36> After this garden border, the other facilities such as offices, gymnasiums, universities, or the communities can be built.

Tablet Twelve
SPIRITUAL CENTER

<1> These spiritual centers can be built for each community. <2> The purpose of their existence is to have a place of gathering for the community, a training center, a place for the offering of prasadam (spiritual food), all types of spiritual activities, Satsang, service, meditation, education, etc.

<3> These spiritual centers can be built for each community which consists of (12 x 12 x 12) which is "1,728" people (or around 2,000 people). <4> However, these centers do not belong to a special community or religion but to anyone who would like to go to them.

<5> There should be a main floor for meditation, Satsangs, lectures, community discussions, solving of community problems, etc.

<6> There should be kitchen facilities large enough to prepare food for those in training at the center and also for preparation of the spiritual food for prasadam.

<7> There should be enough rooms and facilities to provide a place for training in the center, and also enough room for guests and travelers on their way from one city to another. However these facilities should not necessarily be luxurious. The minimum should suffice (according to time, place, and people).

<8> The training is mainly for sannyasins (renunciates) and other seekers (these people should become renunciates at least during the training) who have dedicated their lives to pursue a restricted spiritual life and are there to become spiritual leaders of the future of society and the communities.

<9> However, these centers will be used for community discussions only when a public discussion is necessary. There should be a separate place for discussions between leaders of the community. And if there is a big and better place for community discussions, that instead should be used. <10> The spiritual centers should be used for spiritual purposes as much as possible.

<11> If a sannyasin (renunciate) decides to become a family person, he should be free to do so. <12> Also if a family person wishes to come to the center and learn, he should be allowed to do so only if his family is secure (financially and supportively) and he leaves the family for the time of being in the center.

SETTING OF THE ALTAR

<13> The altar should be positioned in the houses, community Satsang buildings (community building or center), and in any closed area which has been set up especially for meditation in such a way that preferably people will be facing north when sitting for meditation. This means that **The Greatest Sign** will be directed toward the south, so people who sit in front of it will be facing toward the northern top of the world.

<14> However, the altar in the **Temples** will be set up in the center of the **Temple** on the top of a pillar. In the **Temple** all will face toward this center in their prayers and meditations.

<15> In the outdoors when the person does not know what direction is north, or when sitting toward the north is not possible, or for any reason (personal or impersonal), a person

can do his **Reminder** and meditation (attunement) in any direction which is most feasible.

<16> By accepting the practice of facing toward the positive pole of the earth, not only will all humanity be facing a very positive point on the earth, but also, because the north pole is not a livable place, it will not be a point of dispute as any place (like a city) on earth would be.

<17> As we know God is everywhere, so, in any direction we face, He will be there. <18> However, the positive pole of the earth and the top of the world have a positive effect on the spiritual and mental progress of the meditator.

<19> In the **Temple**, the central point there represents the most concentrated spiritual energy of the **Temple**. <20> So to face this point will intensify this quality, and also will be beneficial to the meditator.

<21> When a person is doing **The Reminder**, prayer or meditation in an open field, that person can choose the most pleasant direction or the most convenient place which will help his ideation toward the Supreme. <22> This will prevent people from being superstitious that they have to face a certain direction. However, if they prefer to face a certain direction, so be it.

Tablet Thirteen
THE BASE OF HISTORY AND DATING

<1> The beginning of this human generation started 12,000 years ago (12,000 years will end in the year 2017), after the flood of Noah. Therefore, the real base for this human history is 12,000 years minus the number of years before 2017.

<2> This manifested world was created millions of years ago, therefore, actually the base of history should be the date of the beginning of this creation. However, we cannot find the exact time of the very beginning of creation, or even if we find it, it would not be practical to use for our base of dating because it would be such a tremendously large number. Therefore we put a zero before 11,000 years, and this generation or the man with his present form will be 12,000 years old in the year 2017 A.D. <3> The zero is a symbol for infinity!

<4> Also, the most logical time to start the new year is in the spring, because it is in the spring that all things start to renew themselves. The trees bloom, and the new offspring of the animals and birds are born. <5> It was the best season to start the new year in ancient times. Even the astrological charts start at this time of the year.

<6> There will be two types of years, solar and lunar.

<7> The lunar year, which is twelve rotations of the moon around the earth, is about ten days shorter than the solar year which is one rotation of the earth around the sun.

<8> So the lunar year will fall around ten days short of the solar year. To correct for this, we have to add one month to the lunar year about every three years. Or more precisely, we follow the Metonic cycle, adding a thirteenth month seven times in a period of 19 years [according to a disciple's calculation].

<9> The lunar years should be used for the Holy Days of the Lord, and the solar years for the calendar and earthly activities. <10> With the use of the lunar year for God's Holy Days, the Passover will always be in the first full moon of the lunar year.

<11> As the sun is a symbol for the male, and moon is the symbol for the female, so the naming of the months of the solar year is chosen from great Prophets and spiritual personalities, and for the months of the lunar year (which are based on the moon, the symbol for the female) from the women personalities.

ESSAYS 1   Tablet 13

	Solar Year		Lunar Year
	NAME	**LENGTH**	**NAME**
1	Adam (Atman)	31	Eve
2	Noah	31	Ruth
3	Shiva	31	Shakti
4	Abram (Abraham)	31	Sarai (Sarah)
5	Moses	31	Miriam
6	Krishna	31	Radah
7	Buddha	30	Maya
8	Esa	30	Mary
9	Mohammed	30	Khadija
10	Bab	30	Tahirah
11	Baba	30	Devi
12	Maitreya	29 or 30	Maitreyii
13	Since the lunar year is shorter than the solar year, we will have an extra month in some years. It will be called:		Presence

<12> With this universal outlook of the base of history and the names of the months, the new dating system can be provided. For example, today, November 22, 1978 can be represented as: Mohammed Sub 2, 011961.

<13> The names of the days of the week (7-days) can be derived from the seals in **The Greatest Sign**.

> Sunday = Awakening (☯)
> Monday = Kingdom (✡)
> Tuesday = Sacrifice (✝)
> Wednesday = Submission (☪)
> Thursday = Universalism (✹)
> Friday = Paravipra (✡)
> Saturday = Pure Consciousness or Divine (卐)

<14> They can be abbreviated as Aw, Ki, Sa, Sub, Un, Para, and Pure.

<15> Therefore, today, Wednesday November 22, 1978 will be: Mohammed Sub (Submission) 2, 011961, or Sub Mo 2, 011961.

<16> The best way to eliminate the many different festivals, birthdays, memorial days, etc., now existing in many different religions, cultures, and countries which are considered to be holidays is to accept the Holy Days of God which He had demanded from mankind in chapter 23 of <u>Leviticus</u> in the <u>Bible</u>. <17> In fact other holidays, memorial days, or festivals are all man-made and usually narrow in view. But the Holy Days of God are directed toward the invisible God of the whole world, so only they can unify humanity and are not designed from narrowness of human view.

<18> All the great events which happened to advance human progress should be listed in all the different cultures and religions (those which historically have been proven or strong evidence shows them to probably have existed, or stories which are truly inspiring to be used as Satsang), <19> and on each day of their occurrence, a brief story or play (depending upon the time, place, and people) should be presented in each community center in order to inspire everyone mentally and spiritually.

<20> Only those events that mentally and spiritually are inspiring and have a universal view or are directed toward God (universe) can be used. <21> Stories that present narrowness of the mind and favors for special groups or people are not permitted.

<22> The Sabbath day (weekly Holy Day) will be Saturday as God demanded to be the

day of rest and kept by Hebrews. <23> As humans progress toward a more advanced material life, if possible also Fridays and after that, Sundays, can be added to the weekly off-days and there will be three days in the week to rest and do things that are necessary to be done. If Fridays and Sundays become holidays, then Friday can be used for personal things, such as cleaning, shopping, personal business, Satsang can be given, collective meditation performed, and community problems can be discussed, but not necessarily resolved, if desired. <24> Saturday (Sabbath) should be used to fast. Also on Saturdays the silence should be observed and solitude is recommended. After a day of rest, meditation, and deeper thought, it is a good idea to have the community meeting to resolve community problems. <25> Sunday is the day of joy, gathering, picnicking, feasting, and interaction between people.

Wednesday, Nov. 22, 1978
Mohammed Sub 2, 011961

Tablet Fourteen
THE DAYS AND THE NIGHTS

<1> Night starts at sunset, and the day begins with sunrise. <2> However, because sunset and sunrise change every day and during the seasons, a fixed time, which is close to the average of their changes, can be accepted.

<3> At present 6:00 P.M. seems the most logical time to start the night. In fact, that is the reason midnight has its name (it is six hours after the beginning of night). <4> But the observation of midnight at 12:00 is again one of the thoughtless acceptances of Roman set-ups which humanity is following without questioning.

<5> After time reaches midnight, which means the middle of the night, then the next minute of any added time after that is called morning. That is, 1:00 A.M., 2:00 A.M., and so on. In other words, being in the middle of something means that thing will continue at least equally after it occurs. Or at midnight we are in the middle of the night, so equal time from the beginning of the night is still to come.

<6> But according to our illogical timing, day starts in the middle of night. It is just like we are trying to reach a destination, then in the middle of the way we assume we have reached it. <7> However, as it is described in the book <u>Commentaries on Prophecies in Daniel, Period of Intellectual Domination</u>, it was predicted that the little horn would try to change the time according to its confused understanding.

<8> The acceptance of this time schedule has come to humanity from the Roman Empire. <9> It has been explained how illogical their reasoning was in this arrangement, as is most of what they have presented to man (dry and inflexible like iron). (For more detail, read <u>Commentaries on Prophecies in Daniel, Period of Intellectual Domination</u>.)

<10> With the same reasoning, noon or mid-day also is an incorrect time for being 12:00 A.M., because mid-day means we still have six hours left from the beginning of the day.

<11> Also, as it was said, the most natural time to start the night is when the sun sets, and finish the night with the sunrise. Similarly, day naturally starts at sunrise and ends at sunset. <12> However, because of the change of the time of sunset and sunrise, we can accept the present 6:00 P.M. as the beginning of the night and the end of the day. Therefore when it is 6:00 P.M. it will be midnight (12:00 at night of the present timing system), and it is true midnight, because we still have six more hours left of night. <13> Also with this method of timing, when it is 12:00, the morning starts. At 6:00 A.M. it will be noon or mid-day and we will have six more hours of the day left.

<14> This is a more logical (but not necessarily most natural) way of timing the day and the night. <15> More natural than this is to follow the actual sunset and sunrise as the beginning and end of the days and nights. This is the way humans used to identify night and day in the past, even many earlier civilizations before the Roman Empire.

FEASTS AND HOLY DAYS OF THE LORD

<16> In chapter 23 of Leviticus, the feasts and Holy Days which the Lord had commanded for humans to observe are listed. <17> He commanded them to be observed for ever and ever.

<18> This life and body is given to us so that we realize the truth beyond this universe and perfect ourselves toward becoming Pure Consciousness. That can be achieved when the false ego as a separate entity is dissolved and it is realized that the unit identity is not separate from the universal identity. <19> Then it is known that both are part and parcel of one Universal Self.

<20> But because of the false ego of the human, man always separates himself as a self-centered entity away from the rest. <21> That is why God always had demanded from man to exalt, adore, and worship Him instead of self. Then man might dissolve his unit self into the Universal Self (God) and become Divine.

<22> That is why all activities, thoughts, and relationships of man should evolve around God and be for Him. <23> The feasts, festivals, and Holy Days also should be for Him so that man's thoughts might be directed toward its goal, which is to dissolve the self into the Universal Self and realize he is a part of the All.

<24> That is the reason why in chapter 23 of Leviticus in the Bible, God has given the days that He demanded to be kept as His Feasts and Holy Days. There should not be any other holidays. <25> Any other holidays are not Holy, because they are not from God.

<26> Also only these Holy Days which are demanded by the Lord and are in one of His Holy Books can be easily accepted in this respect. Otherwise any nation or group will insist on their own, and no other Holy Days are so directly demanded by the Lord Himself to be observed.

<27> Also the rituals and contents of these days might differ from the original demand by God. But the spirit of them will be the same as it has been intended to be. That is, to keep these days Holy, to come together in order to remember Him, share our knowledge of Him, and rejoice in His perfection, compassion, and love for us. <28> In other words, to dissolve ourselves into Him.

<29> These feasts and Holy Days are described in brief below. A more detailed description is given in chapter 23 of Leviticus.

1- There are Holy Days and there are feasts of the Lord.

2- They go along with holy convocation (collective meditation and remembrance of the Lord).

3- The seventh day of the week is the Sabbath of rest.

4- In the evening of the fourteenth day of the first month is the night of Passover and the beginning of the Feast of Unleavened Bread.

5- The Feast of Unleavened Bread is the fifteenth day of the first month, with no servile work, and then for seven days practice sacrifice (with knowledge – when it is needed and is for the good and progress of others).

6- On the seventh day (twenty-first of the first month) is a holy convocation with no servile work.

7- After this holy convocation, the next day will be the offering of the "firstfruits" (as explained in Leviticus 23:10, which no longer is necessary; Christ was the firstfruit!). After this day, count fifty days (seven weeks, which will include seven Sabbaths); another yearly Sabbath, a holy convocation, with no servile work. Each week of these seven weeks symbolizes one seal of the seven seals in the

ESSAYS 1

Eternal Divine Path. After the seventh seal, the last Revelation of God will (has) come. Therefore, this yearly Sabbath from now on will be called the Feast of Revelation.

8- On the first day of the seventh month there will be a Sabbath, a memorial of blowing of trumpets, a holy convocation, with no servile work.

9- On the tenth day (evening of the ninth to the evening of the tenth) of the seventh month is the day of atonement, a holy convocation, with no work (not at all). Celebrate this Sabbath by atonement to the Lord.

10- The fifteenth day of the seventh month shall be the Feast of Tabernacles and for seven days there will be a feast. On the first day a holy convocation, and no servile work.

11- After seven days of feasting, a Sabbath on the eighth day, a holy convocation. It is a solemn assembly, with no servile work.

Tablet Fifteen
NEW YEAR, PASSOVER, AND OTHER SYMBOLS

<1> The new year begins in the springtime. <2> As the earth starts a new life cycle, so also the human can begin a new start. That is why this time of year has different periods to observe, each having a definite relationship with the regular life of every human.

<3> As the human is in the childhood state for the first seven years of his life, so the first seven days of the first month of spring (Eve) should be as the childish period. <4> The first day of spring can be designated as Parents Day for appreciation of parents. <5> In this period also study of books from the Far East, such as the Upanishads, Vedantas, Bhagavad-Gita, Puranas, etc., or any other mystical book, is recommended.

<6> The next seven days should be used in preparation for the Passover observation. As a child becomes prepared to enter adulthood at the age of fifteen, so the second seven days in the beginning of the year is a time of preparation for the Passover and period of unleavened bread. <7> In this period a more intensive spiritual observation should be practiced. Study of the Old Testament and understanding the second seal of **The Greatest Sign** in this period is recommended.

<8> On the evening of the fourteenth day of the first lunar month (Eve), Passover starts. This night is for putting away the sins and coming out of the lower nature (Egypt), which is symbolized by putting the yeast out of the house and eating unleavened bread. <9> It should be clearly understood that the rituals in religions are not important, but the meaning behind them is the important part. For example, people argue about the time of observation of a ritual or the way it should be done. This causes them to become so involved in the unimportant part that they forget about the true meaning behind the ritual. <10> During this third seven-day period, the study of the teaching of Esa the Christ and understanding his sacrifice as a symbol of the destruction of the false ego and overcoming the lower nature (going out of Egypt, or "to be born again") should be observed.

<11> The Passover and the seven-day period of eating unleavened bread corresponds with the third seven-day period of the life of the human, from age fifteen to twenty-one. <12> During this stage of overcoming a person should grow in such a way that by the age of twenty-one he is able to decide if he is more suited for family life or becoming a renunciate. This decision, however, can be made between the ages of eighteen until twenty-five.

<13> Those who choose the family life should seek a profession according to their natures. By the age of twenty-eight they should be completely settled and should utilize all their energies and efforts toward an ideal family environment in God's way. By the age of thirty-five they should have finished the number of children they would like to have. By the age of forty-two there should be no children with them in the childhood years (less than seven) but all on their way to adulthood.

<14> At age forty-nine (7 x 7) a human reaches his/her highest maturity. Either in this age or sometime later, he should go back more toward the spiritual world and give less emphasis to the family and external world. By this time or a little later, all the children should be mature enough to be independent or even be helpful to the parents. This period can be the second period of the growth of the couple, either together or separately.

<15> Those who decide to become renunciates should go through intensive study, discipline, and spiritual practices until the age of twenty-eight. From the age of twenty-eight to thirty-five, they should develop their own ideal for their teachings. After that they can start their careers as spiritual teachers. By the age of forty-two they should be completely developed in the spiritual path. <16> At the age of forty-nine (7 x 7) they should be matured completely in understanding and teaching the realities behind this universe by their example.

<17> But, as we know, there are always exceptions in this universe, and also everything, including these teachings, depend on time, place, and person. <18> According to time, place, and person, the decision can be from ignorance, passion, or knowledge.

<19> The fourth seven-day period of this month (Eve) corresponds with the period of human life from the age of twenty-one to twenty-eight. In this period a person completes his decision for what he wants to become, and also completes his spiritual understandings. <20> So this period relates to the fourth seal in **The Greatest Sign**. Therefore, study and understanding materials related to the fourth seal in the fourth seven-day period of the first month is recommended.

<21> The fifth seven-day period (which will start in the first month and continue in the second), is related to the fifth seal or the age period from twenty-eight to thirty-five, when man destroys all narrowness of the mind and becomes a universalist. <22> So in this period the material about the fifth seal will be helpful to complete the studies of the previous periods.

<23> The sixth seven-day period, as a symbol for the ages thirty-five to forty-two, is related to the sixth seal. This is when a person, with the knowledge of all the previous seals, should become a dynamic spiritual force in establishing the Kingdom Of Heaven within and without. <24> So in this period of the year, a study of the materials related to this seal is recommended.

<25> A sum of all the previous studies, and understanding their inter-relationships with each other, the Master Plan of God, and the ultimate goal of life, should be understood by the study and contemplation of the materials of the seventh seal.

<26> The observation of these periods are only recommended and are not mandatory, but if an individual would observe them, it will be a great help to him in understanding the overall goal of The Plan of creation and God. This will help in the acceleration of the spiritual journey.

<27> Also, as usual, in all these studies, we should keep **The Greatest Sign** in our minds and always remember the place of each teaching in **The Greatest Sign**. <28> After study of the Scriptures and observation of these periods, then the person should contemplate the overall meaning of all of them and try to reach Pure Consciousness (bliss) and <29> help the whole universe to reach there also.

Tablet Sixteen

KINGDOM OF HEAVEN IN HEAVEN (KOHIH)

<1> He who overcomes, becomes a son of God, "He that overcometh ... he shall be my son" (Rev. 21:7), and whoever overcomes, reaches Pure Consciousness. He becomes the same as the Lord (God), in His Image (a god). He enters into heaven.

<2> However these sons of God will be sent back to help others reach Pure Consciousness

<3> and also to establish the Kingdom Of Heaven On Earth (**KOHOE**).

<4> As more people reach higher consciousness and Pure Consciousness, more people will be available to be used as great people in the **KOHOE**.

<5> Those who reach Pure Consciousness (sons of God) will come back as humans and in the flesh, but they are not of this world and their Kingdom is not of this world. <6> However, they will act like regular people but they come for a definite purpose and fulfill it.

<7> These sons of God assume their responsibilities, accomplish their missions, and do the Darmas which have been designated for them in each lifetime. <8> They lead a regular life until they remember who they are and then help others to progress also. They live like regular people but with no attachments to the external world.

<9> These sons of God create a Hierarchy which shapes the Hierarchy of the Kingdom Of Heaven In Heaven (**KOHIH**). Although many of them will come to this world, they are not from this world. Also they are completely obedient to their Father as their King and Ruler. <10> They accept their positions no matter what the position is in the Hierarchy. That is why the **KOHIH** is already established. God has been accepted as the King and His Laws as the only Laws.

<11> When humanity also accepts God as the only true King and His Laws as the only true Laws, then the Kingdom Of Heaven also will be recognized and established on earth. <12> Then is the time that "His Will, will be done on earth as it is in heaven," and that is when the sons of God will come on earth to be with the humans as it was in the past, "that the sons of God saw the daughters of men … and they took them wives of all which they chose" (Gen. 6:2) or "…the sons of God came in unto the daughters of men,…" (Gen. 6:4).

<13> Therefore no man can strive to reach Pure Consciousness and be free from coming back to this external world, because even those who reach Pure Consciousness will be sent back to help others to reach higher consciousness and Pure Consciousness. <14> The goal is to create the **KOHOE** (in the manifested world) and then all enjoy it with being in it and praise the Father for creating the universe and this Great Plan to bring all to Pure Consciousness.

<15> So no man can escape the duty of helping the whole universe to reach Pure Consciousness. Therefore, avoid those philosophies which cause escapism and start vigorously to make this world a better place to live in, even if your help is on a very small scale. So all the efforts of those in higher consciousness and/or Pure Consciousness will become combined and the force will bring the **KOHOE** as soon as possible. <16> Then man and gods (sons of God) will be together as in the past.

<17> Then the peace, tranquility, and prosperity will come, and many will reach Pure Consciousness (become a son of God, reach godhood) and this again will accelerate the progress of the universe toward its goal – to be(come) Divine.

SONS OF GOD (gods)

<18> The first place the phrase "son of God" is mentioned in the Bible is in chapter six of Genesis. In fact it is mentioned twice in the same chapter:

…That the sons of God saw the daughters of men… (Genesis 6:2)
…the sons of God came in unto the daughters of men,… (Genesis 6:4)

<19> There are two points which should be noticed: 1- There **were** sons of God even before the flood of Noah; and 2- There were more than one ("son<u>s</u> of God").

<20> Also in the Bible God has declared that:

He that overcometh … I will be his God, and he shall be my son. (Rev. 21:7)

<21> Therefore, the requirement to become a son of God is to overcome ("He that overcometh ... shall be my son").

<22> Those who are referred to as the sons of God in chapter 6 of Genesis are the ones who had overcome and had become His sons, even before the flood of Noah. <23> There should have been at least two sons at that time before the flood. Of course there were more than two, but according to the Bible we can be sure of two. <24> One is the First Begotten Son of God (the first Adam or later on as Esa, etc.) who became the First Begotten Son of God even before creation, and the second one was Enoch who, "walked with God [overcame]: ... for God took him" (Gen. 5:24). He did not die, but because he overcame, he became a son of God ("God took him").

<25> Not only can each human reach the status of the son of God, but also it is declared that each human is a god, "...that we may know that ye are gods..." (Isaiah 41:23) and Christ himself declared "...Ye are gods" (John 10:34). <26> God is pure and faultless. He is unaffected by the pulls of this external world like a person who has overcome (a son of God). So those who reach godhood also are those who are pure, faultless, and have overcome. <27> In other words, the sons of God, or gods, can be used interchangeably and have the same meaning.

GOD JUST "IS"

<28> When Moses asked God what His Name was, He replied, "I AM THAT I AM" (Exodus 3:14). <29> That is, "'I' just 'AM.'" <30> However, then the human goes on and tries to find God in many different ways, shapes, and concepts. Some say He is love, some He is light, some He is OM, others give names to Him, and still others give Him names and shapes.

<31> However, He is none of these but IS all. <32> He IS, so He IS LOVE, He IS LIGHT, He IS OM, etc. He IS it all. He IS everything. <33> Because He just "IS," if you put Him in front of anything, He becomes that also.

<34> As it was explained in the books The Base and The Essence, the universe was in the state of "Be"-ness. Through the desire of God, the operative powers of the three gunas were released and the feelings of "I know," "I do" and "I have done" were awakened in the universe, and God multiplied Himself into infinite unit consciousnesses. <35> However, when the power of the tama guna is overcome and the separate consciousness in the illusive state "am" reaches Pure Consciousness, it becomes that "AM" again. <36> That is why God and whoever reaches Pure Consciousness (His sons) just "are."

<37> Therefore, if you give God any name, shape, or concept (such as He is love, etc.) division is created in humanity. Only God in the state of Formless, Invisible, Nameless, and Eternal, neither male nor female, (AM) unifies. In any other state, humanity will be divided.

<38> We can say that God also "Is Not!" When the consciousness of a person becomes very crude, such a person becomes so separate from God that for him He "Is Not." But Blessed is he for whom God "Is!" Therefore, the question is "To Be" or "Not To Be!"

ESSAYS 2

The book, <u>Essays 2</u>, is the second book of Essays written by Maitreya. <u>Essays 2</u> is the continuation of <u>Essays 1</u>. Maitreya covers many topics in these books.

ESSAYS 2

Tablet One
FALSE EGO

<1> If a person is hurt by criticism, other people's actions, or words, and if he tries to retaliate and hurt others, indeed there is an ego present in such a person.

<2> In truth the reason for so much trouble in the world is because one person hurts the ego of the other and he retaliates. <3> Then the first person strikes back and the process goes on and on until complete destruction occurs.

<4> However, if a person with the ego tries to hurt a realized person, because there is no ego in such a person, he will not be hurt but will create compassion for the other person who unjustly tries to do him harm. So he forgives him, or even gives him more love which he does not have.

<5> Wherever there is ego there is no real love, and where there is true love there is no ego.

<6> Indeed to test a person and his state of progress, usually Masters play with the ego of the person a little bit to see how he reacts. By his reaction it is shown how realized or unrealized he is.

<7> As it was said, the ego is hurt and by continuing the process of hurting and counter-hurting, a vicious cycle will start and continue to complete destruction. <8> Indeed this vicious cycle exists in many situations in life. The only way to stop the cycle is to break it.

<9> That is what a realized person does, he stops (breaks) the cycle before it becomes vicious and leads to bondage of the world and/or complete destruction.

Tablet Two
RELATIONSHIPS

<1> There are four beings which each person should consider as the most important people in his life. <2> They are God, spiritual teacher, parents, and spouse.

<3> In a person's relationship with these beings, God is at the top of the hierarchy. Then comes the spiritual teacher who leads a person to God. Next are the parents who are instruments used to allow him to receive a body so that he could come to this world and advance in his spiritual journey. Eventually is the spouse, who is his twin flame and helper in his physical, mental, and spiritual progress.

<4> So if any being in this hierarchy becomes an obstacle for a person to attend to his obligations to the one higher up, that being should be disregarded.

<5> If a spiritual teacher does not help a person to truly know God, he is not a true teacher and should be disregarded. If parents become an obstacle in one's spiritual progress and an obstacle between him and his true spiritual guide, although they should not be disrespected, the person should follow his spiritual teacher rather than them.

<6> Also if a spouse would make the person disrespectful to his parents or spiritual teacher, that spouse should be corrected or disregarded. <7> However, when a man and woman marry, if it is possible, it is better for them to start their independence by separating themselves from their parents and, with all respect to the parents, start their own course of life and only listen to their parents if their advice is sound and will guide them closer to God.

<8> After these four beings, the relationships of a person can be expanded to their children and others in the external world.

<9> Children are the guests of the parents

and are beings entrusted to them by God to be helped to progress physically, mentally, and spiritually. Parents are the channels through which children are born. <10> Also they are the co-creators of them, so parents should create a godly love toward them, as God has love toward man.

<11> However, they should always be aware that the children are not theirs and should let them be free when the time comes. Parents should never possess their children nor make them their slaves by their excessive love and emotional webs. <12> Of course, children have great responsibility toward their parents to assist them when it is needed and to give them the highest respect.

<13> In regard to the relationship with others, if a person is living in a **Community of Light** and is one of the 12 people as the base for selecting the leaders (read Mount Zion and Zion, and Explanation of the System), then his community would be regarded as the second family. <14> Then the person has a great responsibility, first, to become an example for others and a leader, and secondly, to be observant to choose truly the best person as the leader or the judge of the twelve.

<15> It is in this community in which a person learns to live with others and also learns to become a leader. A leader who has not gone through this test of being able to live with others and emerge as a Chosen One, cannot be trusted as a true leader.

<16> If a person does not live in such a community, he should still help the cause of creation and progress physically, mentally, and spiritually and help others in this endeavor also. <17> If he is married and has a family, then the rest of the universe is his second family, and he should treat them as such.

<18> Also in choosing friends, the person should associate with those who would help him in his progress toward the goal of his life – to be(come) Divine. He should disregard those who would lead him away from this and his responsibilities toward the first four beings described in the beginning (God, spiritual teacher, parents, and spouse).

<19> In regard to work associates and the job environment, a vocation that one respects, enjoys, and is proficient in doing should be chosen. He should be(come) one with it and do it perfectly, and that should be all the requirement necessary in any job.

<20> The associates at work can be accepted as friends if it is possible to be helpful in each other's progress or to create a more spiritual environment there. However, they should not become a channel for satisfaction of unspiritual, unsatisfied psychological or emotional needs. These all would be from the false ego, and the relationships would be based on one ego supporting the other. Such relationships would be shallow and are based on false needs which eventually will end in deep dissatisfaction for both partners. <21>The ego does not have love and compassion and indeed is hungry for these, so two people who do not have these things try to receive them from each other. Then they will both be disappointed when they realize that the other person cannot provide what they long for, because he does not have it either.

<22> However, they take the attention the other person gives to them as Love, or as a true relationship. But in truth that attention is a trick to receive the attention of the other person. This kind of relationship is indeed a business. The translation is, "I give you attention, you give me attention." The base is on ego, not Love, respect, and progress.

<23> So become best in what you do and base your life on God and the establishment of His Kingdom. Any relationship that becomes an obstacle to this ideal should be disregarded and is from false needs and false ego.

PARENTS

<24> Parents have the most profound effect on their children. They shape the future characteristics of the men and women in society. Therefore they have a great responsibility in their chosen careers as parents.

<25> To be a parent does not finish with providing material comfort for children. It is a commitment physically, mentally, and spiritually. <26> In fact the spiritual needs of the human are greater than his mental and physical needs. The human thirst for knowing the truth about his being also is subtler than his other needs.

<27> When spiritual needs are reasonably satisfied, other needs become minimal, because when the thirst of the human Soul for limitlessness is directed toward the finite and a man tries to quench this thirst by material rewards which are limited, then the problems start. He tries to gain as much of the external world as he can, but he will never be satisfied with it. <28> He thirsts for fulfillment of his infinite longing within.

<29> In fact that is one of the reasons children blame their parents for their problems, because they (parents) did not show them how to quench this thirst for knowing God. Therefore they intuitively know their parents did not fulfill their duties as parents.

<30> However, if truly committed parents progress spiritually themselves or at least create enough opportunities for their children to satisfy this part of their being (to have a great spiritual teacher) and also provide them with their mental and physical needs, then a true unit family with satisfied children, spiritually, mentally, and physically, will be created.

<31> Only with such a true family unit can also a great society be created, and only with such a commitment from the parents can they expect their children to be committed to them.

<32> Again this is one of the reasons some children leave their parents when they are old, or put them in nursing homes without feeling much guilt. The message is, "You provided us with our physiological needs when we needed you, and now we will provide you with your physiological needs when you need us."

<33> If their parents were truly committed to them when they were children and were not thinking about how they can enjoy themselves but about how they can be true parents and help their children grow spiritually, mentally, and physically, they would not have been left alone in their old age.

<34> So, it is again another reason that each human should search for the truth himself, and become familiar with the truth behind this universe (creation and history) and the purpose of this life. <35> Therefore not only should they become parents for their children but also the spiritual teacher so that through them their children might realize God.

<36> With this, parents will assume the duties of two beings as parents and spiritual teacher, <37> so that they might become the second most respectful beings, after God, in the life of their children. <38> With such parents, the Kingdom of God will surely be established on earth as it is in heaven.

Tablet Three

MASOCHISM AND SADISM

<1> The false ego has different ways to feel alive. Because in truth it is an illusion, so in order for a person to feel his separateness and glorify the self as the only being, it needs to constantly have different ways to prove it exists.

<2> So it is not wrong to say that even creating problems is a way the ego can feel it survives, because if there is a problem which is related to it, so it surely exists!

<3> Also in this category is to create excitement and constant stimulation so with it a feeling of existing is created. Usually the person says that because of these stimulations, he

feels good. <4> In truth what he is saying is, "'I' as a separate ego feel alive."

<5> One way for the ego to feel this existence is to choose the way of masochism or sadism. <6> By becoming an object of torture and misuse, a person feels he exists and derives energy from the person who misuses him or her. Also the person who misuses others, thinks he is powerful, so his ego derives satisfaction.

<7> However, the dilemma is that the one who assumes the role of the torturer (sadist) assumes this position because of his inadequacies, and by taking on this role he feels like a god. But because of his feeling of separation, after the act of excitement is finished, again he falls into his agony of feeling nonexistent, inadequate, and separate. So he has to repeat the act more often and more brutally. Therefore after some time he becomes completely separated and lost.

<8> Also the masochist who becomes the object of the torture feels the other person has misused him. Although he continues his relationship with this other person, because that is the only way he derives his satisfaction, he creates resentment and looks down upon his torturer.

<9> The sadistic person who tortures to be glorified not only does not achieve his objective but even will degenerate. Also he loses his power to the person he misuses. So this again adds to decline and this cycle goes on and on until both of them go to the depth of their hellish situation.

<10> Ego at the same time is not. Those who realize this do not strive to prove they exist by creating problems or deriving satisfaction from the outside world. It is then that such a person becomes one and a part of the universe. <11> Then not only does he cease to create problems but actually will start to solve some true ones (ninety-nine percent of the problems in the world have been created by the false ego and are not real).

<12> Those who are masochistic activate the sadistic part of the sadist, then derive power from it. So the sadist loses power (prana), and the masochist lives on this energy.

MALE AND FEMALE

<13> Besides the consciousness, there are three gunas which exist in the universe. Satva guna is neither male nor female. It is passive and positive. Raja guna (life-force) is the female principle. It is active and neutral. It activates and brings all into life. Tama guna is also neither male nor female. It is passive and negative. Consciousness is passive and neutral.

<14> Raja guna (energy) is the only active force in the universe. When it is in the passive state the universe will be un-manifested. Universe (God) will be in the state of "Be"-ness, which is formless, nameless, invisible, eternal, neither male nor female. <15> This is the seventh state of consciousness.

<16> When the same consciousness becomes activated, but still is in pure form (Pure Consciousness), it will become engaged in planning and guiding the universe. In this state it becomes pure Divine Logic (Father).

<17> Logic is male energy or principle. This is the sixth state of consciousness.

<18> Raja guna in the active state, however, receives the polarity of positivity when directed toward higher things (satva); will be neutral when pure raja; and negative when directed toward mundanity (tama).

<19> When satva guna is activated (by raja guna – female principle, Grace) and it dominates the consciousness (Logic or male principle), in this state God is Male (Father) Female (Mother) God. <20> It is the fifth state of consciousness. It is in this state that The Holy Ghost (Bliss) is experienced which is full of Grace (female principle) and knowledge (male principle).

<21> Raja guna is Grace, when it dominates the consciousness and is directed to higher things. Because it has no polarity, it becomes the unconditional Love (Mother, no

polarity or condition) or The Divine Grace (The Divine Mother). <22> This is experienced in the fourth level of consciousness (chakra).

<23> Tama guna is bondage. When it is activated by energy (raja guna) and dominates active satva guna and the consciousness, then the Logic becomes earthly. It is then that a person becomes man (earthly). <24> This is the third state of consciousness.

<25> In the state where tama dominates the active raja and consciousness, then The Grace (female) becomes passion and temptation. A person then will become woman. This state is what is referred to as woman in the Bible. <26> This is the second state of consciousness.

<27> In the first level of consciousness, tama guna dominates with complete force. The consciousness (kundalini) is dormant. <28> By meditating and creating greater prana (raja guna) in the body, the grip of the tama guna will be loosened and the consciousness will be brought to higher levels. <29> This is called the awakening of the spiritual forces (kundalini).

<30> As long as the consciousness is latent in the first level (chakra) a person will be bound by his physiological and safety needs. His energy will be used toward maintenance of his physical body and worldly activities. He also will receive most of his energy by consuming food. <31> In this state man is a rational animal and has no Divine consciousness. He identifies himself only as being the body.

<32> Although the physical body of the human as male and female has some relationship with manifestation of Logic or Grace, it is not absolute. Each of these qualities can be developed by practice in either sex and also there are exceptions.

<33> Whoever opens his heart chakra (fourth chakra) will manifest unconditional Love or Grace (Divine Mother) and he who reaches the sixth level is one with the Father (pure Logic controlling the emotions – first five levels).

<34> In the explanation above the most important thing is the dual nature of raja guna (female principle activating energy). It either can be directed to positivity as Divine Grace or Holy Mother, or toward negativity as the lower nature of man. <35> These two sides of the same phenomena (energy) have been mythically symbolized in Hindu religions as the two consorts of their gods such as Krishna and Shiva. Usually one of them is the symbol of the energy of transmutation and destruction, such as Kali and Durga, and the other as one full of Grace, Shakti, and Radah. <36> These two consorts actually are the two sides of each person or the mythical gods themselves.

<37> This part of female energy is symbolized as the woman in the Bible, the same meaning implied by the goddess Kali, who is shown as an old dark-skinned woman who has a necklace of skulls around her neck and is dreadful.

<38> The same phenomena (raja guna) when directed toward higher things, becomes The Divine Grace or The Holy Mother.

Tablet Four

MEN AND WOMEN

<1> The purpose of creation is to make each unit consciousness (human) reach Pure Consciousness (Divinity).

<2> According to the teachings behind **The Greatest Sign**, the first step is to awaken one's spiritual forces (☯), and the second step is to direct the realizations and energy gained through awakening these forces toward creating the Kingdom Of Heaven On Earth (✡).

<3> The first step in creating this Kingdom is through the family units. <4> However, if the couples do not build this unit on a higher level of spiritual attraction and ideation, this unit will be destroyed along with society.

<5> That is why if the lower nature of the

couple becomes an interference, they have to realize what is the cause of the problems.

<6> A realized woman usually longs to be with a man whom she can respect. <7> A high Soul man also likes to be with a woman who does not emphasize her body but her higher being. Then they would overcome their lower natures and each become a true man (male, Divine Logic) and woman (female, Divine Mother, Divine Grace).

<8> However, through his excess attraction to the woman's body and sex, the man will fall to a lower consciousness and so the woman becomes an object of sex for him. <9> The woman who loves this man conforms to his wishes so to make him happy. But this act will bring both to the sensual and physical level.

<10> A man who becomes more like an animal and loses his strength and vital energies, feels it is the woman who causes him to become low and not able to achieve his higher nature.

<11> The woman who is misused and looked upon as a sex object, and sees the man as only an animal, becomes disenchanted and annoyed, feels the man is using her, and loses the respect for him.

<12> With these deep wounds, which sometimes the person is not even aware of, a gap will appear between the couple. As both try to fill this gap with more physical relationships, it becomes even wider.

<13> The answer to this dilemma is to start the relationship on a higher spiritual level and use the sexual energy for love and care for each other. This means to respect and love each other as two struggling human beings, to be forgiving, compassionate, and true friends, and to help each other physically, mentally, and spiritually.

<14> The man should work as hard as he can to win the respect of his wife by being spiritually strong, submissive to the Lord, and a priest and guide of the family. Also he should look at his wife as a human being and not an object for sexual fulfillment.

<15> The woman also should emphasize her higher qualities and make him realize his higher nature and responsibilities. Then their relationship will be based on higher levels and they will live in peace and tranquility with each other. <16> Their home will be a center of love and higher thoughts for their children and others.

<17> Those men and women who come together only for sensual purposes and stay together for the same reasons, will never find the true peace of God. Their environments will never be suitable to raise healthy children nor be a center of inspiration for higher understandings.

<18> However, those who base their relationship on higher levels soon will realize that the sexual relationships are a very small part of the joy of being together. Even this physical union becomes an expression of love and commitment, and eventually they can even overcome this unimportant relationship. They will become one in the higher level in spirit, if they choose to do so.

<19> In summary: Most women indeed desire the higher nature of men and respect it. However, because of the very nature of their bodies, they bring men into their lower natures, and so are despised.

<20> So it is a vicious cycle. Men should stay in their higher selves, but by their very sexual attachment to women, they cannot fulfill this task.

<21> Women should help men to reach their higher selves instead of accelerating their development into beasts.

<22> The reason for this is that both feel to be separate egos, and because of this separation, they fall into their lower selves. <23> So it is up to both to meet each other in that level where they are one, by being one with God. <24> Then their spiritual, mental, and physical union will become Divine and both will love each other's higher self and beauty.

<25> That is why men should learn restraint and gain control over their lower natures. Women should help them by not regarding themselves as bodies but as spiritual beings, and they should not emphasize their body gratification but accentuate their Souls.

<26> Otherwise both sexes will feel they

have been betrayed. The women cannot find true men with great characters, and men will direct their hate of being weak toward women, and this cycle will continue endlessly.

RENUNCIATES (SANNYASINS)

<27> He who has the capacity to become completely renounced from this world can become a renunciate.

<28> This is easily possible for those whose soulmate(s) has not been incarnated in the flesh. They cannot find anyone in the flesh to marry, so they can easily become a celibate and renunciate. <29> Also those who are perfect (☉) (in Pure Consciousness or close to it) can assume this position.

<30> However, because such a people are very beneficial for those around them, they also have been permitted to have more than one wife in some religions. Not only can they create equity and bliss for their wives but also it helps them overcome the female attraction, be free from the physical desires, and serve others in a higher capacity.

<31> A renunciate should refrain from sex, eating flesh (or too much of it), strong drinks, and killing, and he should live in the simplest way possible and possess nothing in this world.

<32> He should become a wanderer and not stay in one place for long (if he feels he becomes attached to places), so he would not create any attachment to any place or people.

<33> He can stay with people who would provide him the minimum necessities. Therefore he can be in communion with God all the time and make others to become god-conscious also.

<34> If these renunciates (sannyasins) do not find any person to provide them with food and shelter, they should be provided these things in the community centers. However only the minimum should be supplied. They should never live a life of luxury and excess. They should be the Holy Ones.

<35> Their beds should be God's Lap, their subject of talk should be God, and they should see Him in everything and everywhere.

<36> They should be a source of inspiration for others to become God-conscious by their actions, purity, compassion, wisdom, etc.

<37> They should be free like the wind solely depending on God and their own purity so that their minimum necessities are provided.

<38> When they are old, it will be a great blessing for those who take care of these saint-like beings. <39> However, if they prefer, their necessities can be provided in the community centers.

<40> Even for those who pursue a worldly life, a short period of living the life of a renunciate is recommended. <41> This will cause them to learn to trust solely in God, be detached from the external world, and find the truth in a deeper sense.

<42> However, if Sannyasins create godly characters and attract disciples, <43> each can become a center of light and teach the truth to their disciples as spiritual teachers (Gurus).

Tablet Five

ORIGIN OF THE MYTHS

<1> The human uses his imagination to create great fables and stories whenever he does not know very much. <2> In the past, stories were about the magical lands in other parts of the earth (although some of them were valid, because they were about the time before the flood of Noah). <3> After the human spread all over the earth and found there were no magical lands on earth, then those stories lost their validities. <4> However, the human loves to stretch his imagination. That is why now imaginary beings from other planets are created and movies are made about them. Many people love to believe in them even if

<5> This stretch of the imagination has also been used in spiritual understanding. That is why there are so many different theories and so many imaginary concepts about God and the spiritual world. These concepts and distorted logics are so untrue that any logical mind cannot accept the religious concepts and myths that are told by supposedly religious leaders.

<6> For the person who knows the spiritual world truly and it is as real for him as this external world, then he knows that the spiritual world is as perfect and logical as our manifested universe, <7> and also is guided with definite Laws and regulations toward the goal of all creation.

<8> That is why humans should understand the realities behind exaggerated religious stories and find out the symbolic meanings of them, instead of accepting them as truth, and becoming an illogical person about spirituality.

<9> A person might listen to others and try to understand what they say, but he should accept only those parts that seem logical. He should strive to expand his own mind and spiritual experiences. <10> Whatever experiences he gains, he should just accept those as true. He should not accept anyone else's experiences as his own goal and should not use his own experiences on others as the goal of their spiritual achievement. <11> Each human should strive in his own path (in the middle of the collective path) to grow more and more everyday.

VISIONS, IMAGES, AND DREAMS

<12> Throughout all of history, there have been humans who have had visions of heaven, God, angels, and many other things. Many have seen the same scene or same angel in different shapes. So many have concluded these things truly exist and also many have become confused by their varieties.

<13> In truth, visions are nothing but the production of a scene to give a message to a person or to make him truly believe in the revelation which has come to him. <14> In fact, in most cases if such visions, voices, or signs had not happened, the person would not dare to speak out or to carry on his mission.

<15> So according to the state of consciousness of the chosen person, the proper vision is given to him so that he becomes inspired to do the work, <16> but in truth they are just a production of his consciousness, or the production of the Universal Consciousness (God) to convince him of his belief.

<17> Also images are nothing but the production of an individual's own consciousness and they are created by the concentrated mind. <18> In truth, they do not exist, and at the same time, they exist!

<19> However, the unconscious mind which knows all truth and solutions to all the problems, through visions, images, and dreams, communicates messages. If these are understood, they become a great tool in comprehending the solutions to worldly problems and increasing spiritual knowledge.

<20> In short, we can say that there are three kinds of visions, images, and dreams. <21> The first type are those which have no meaning, are scattered, and are useless.

<22> The second type are the ones which are related to day-to-day life and problems. Usually in this category the solutions to these problems are given and the consciousness is trying to transmit a message to the individual. <23> It is this kind of message with which the psychiatrists are most familiar. They are generated from the subconscious mind.

<24> The third kind are those from the unconscious mind (spiritual world) which have a spiritual and higher message for the individual. This message is not related to individual or day-to-day life but has a universal scope and is a spiritual message. <25> The person can then become the Messenger (channel) to convey this message to others.

<26> Therefore, visions, images, and

dreams are not real, although they sometimes seem very real, <27> but they are the creation of the mind (either individual or Universal).

ETHEREAL BEINGS AND ASTRAL PROJECTION

<28> Astral projection is of two kinds: Those which are messages from higher planes or God, and those which are created by the ego.

<29> In truth, astral projection is nothing but the creation of the individual mind or the Universal Mind.

<30> Those whom God wants to use to reveal a message, but are not in that level to realize the Formless, Nameless, and Invisible, need another channel between the physical world and the Formless, Nameless, and Invisible. That is why God creates a master or guidance for them in the astral plane (or any other kind that the person feels he has communication with). <31> Then he can realize God through it, and also it helps people in this state to feel assured of the existence of higher and invisible worlds and truths.

<32> In truth such a master does not exist – of course the consciousness in the image is a Master (God), – but like visions and higher dreams, all is created by the Universal Mind. <33> If a person realizes that even these are all illusions and tries to realize the only true source (the Highest Source or God), he can even overcome this last illusion.

<34> However, this process helps those who are in this level of progress, and if they could eliminate their egos completely, God can reveal many truths to the person through that created channel. <35> But that image eventually should be given up, because even that is an obstacle to complete freedom and perfect enlightenment that all is God (consciousness and the three gunas).

<36> The other kind of astral projection is to travel in the ethereal body and create images in this plane with the mind (ego). In this kind of astral projection, the person learns how to go to this plane but he is not advanced enough to be guided to higher truths. <37> In this plane the person can see what he imagines. So usually, with his bad thoughts (false ego), he creates scary scenes, and they seem so real to him that he rushes back to the body from fear of them.

<38> As it is said, the only reliable source is the Formless, Nameless, and Invisible (Universal Mind). Any other things are just illusions and so obstacles in the path to complete freedom. <39> Therefore, they have to be disregarded.

<40> True masters (Avatars) come to this world in the flesh like regular people. Then later on the signs that were prophesied about them will be manifested and they themselves realize their missions. <41> This has been true all throughout history. Examples are Buddha, Esa, Muhammad, Bab, etc., who all came as regular people and then realized their Divinity later on in their lives.

<42> Even in the case of these Great Souls, although they are subjects of reverence, what they said and preached is important, not themselves. <43> However, devotion to them works as a Bridge to God!

Tablet Six

IDOL WORSHIPPING

<1> Humans never gave up idol worshipping. They discontinued idol worshipping of statues but they replaced it with the worshipping of certain humans (for example Prophets), or they have created psychological idols such as status, name, power, etc. <2> Even some people worship themselves and what has been imposed on them psychologically or socially.

<3> Still in this century (where man claims

to have reached a very high civilization) we find some humans worshipping statues as their deities and Gods. <4> However, their type of worship is more acceptable than those who have created psychological gods for themselves, have narrowed their minds, and are the source of suffering for others.

<5> It is inconceivable that the human cannot direct all his attention and adoration toward the Creator of this perfect universe which is the source of all these other things that attract him.

<6> The very reason is that the human does not utilize his mind and other faculties given to him to think about life, its purpose, or the perfection of all things. He is lost in the small things in life and the attraction of Maya. <7> Also he rejects God because he wants to be God himself. So by rejecting God, or by replacing Him with false gods, he can follow his own false ego and feel himself to be the God of his destiny and life. But God will make him realize, with His Power through the events of his life, that in truth he is a very helpless being. <8> However, man loves his false ego so much that he does not want to give it up and continues to be blind to the truth.

<9> If man could adore only the invisible God and direct all his attention toward Him, most of the problems of today's human would be solved in a very short period of time.

<10> Therefore, keep your attention with the whole power of your being toward Him. <11> Otherwise, the rest is just an illusion of the lower nature, and whoever falls into the lower nature is lost.

CULTS

<12> When a group of people gather around one personality, attach much importance to him without him fulfilling any prophecies, and rely on him completely (not on God's Laws and prophecies), then we can say a cult is created.

<13> In fact the very reason the followers of central figures attach such importance to him and are apt to believe in this importance, is so that they who follow him are also important. <14> Or the central figure gives them a false assurance that they are fine as they are and/or they can do whatever they want. <15> So these people accept this so to not see the truth about themselves.

<16> In truth such a people do not differ from those who put their importance on their wealth or anything which is from the external. <17> Both have a false sense of importance for what is not directly of them but is outside of them.

<18> Of course this rule of creating a central figure and making him the point of importance is applied in all walks of life, in all levels of society, and in all social relationships. <19> Instead of looking at their own merits and developing their own abilities, people praise others, become latent, and do not develop themselves.

<20> **In brief, when a personality becomes more important than the teachings based on God's Laws, that group can be called a cult.**

<21> That is why to submit to the Formless, Nameless, and Invisible God enables a person to free himself from becoming attached to a person or figure <22> and allows us to learn from each being and message. Then we can pick the best of all of them, and so at the end become Great.

MIDDLE PATH (BALANCE)

<23> A middle path (balance) is the best way, not reactionary solutions which are called thesis and antithesis. <24> In the past history, the human has always handled the situation of this world in a reactionary way. He always reacts to what happened to him **after** the cause of dissatisfaction becomes unbearable. This process is so common in

human life that he has come to believe in the theory of thesis and antithesis. <25> According to this theory, there is an antithesis for everything in this universe. So there is a struggle going on between the thesis and its antithesis. Eventually one of them will dominate, and a new antithesis will be created for this new thesis. So it will go on and on.

<26> The true reason for creation of an antithesis, however, is disequilibrium of the thesis. <27> That is, whenever the equilibrium between the elements of a complex system become disturbed, it is then that an antithesis will naturally be created to bring the situation back to equilibrium or to create a new thesis (equilibrium).

<28> That is why a controller in a system is necessary to maintain the equilibrium between all the elements of the system. However, so far the human has used such controlling elements only in his machines (such as thermostats), but not in his day-to-day life or in society in general. <29> Only by creating a system with a sensitive controller at the top who does not ignore any act which will lead to an imbalance in the system, and who has enough incentive to allow all the elements of the system to grow together, can humans establish a society of harmony and peace.

<30> That is why the advent of true leaders and a very sensitive system is necessary, to prevent the misconduct of the elements of the society and classes within it. Only these true, selfless leaders can maintain an equilibrium between workers, warriors, intellectuals, and businessmen (read <u>The Kingdom Of Heaven On Earth</u>). They will not let any of these classes exploit others, but will allow all four classes to grow hand-in-hand. <31> However, if any of these elements went out of hand, they should be guided back to their places. <32> If their growth seemed necessary for the progress of society, they will be allowed to do so, but they will be guided so that others do not become exploited with any of these elements.

<33> The theory of equilibrium or balance is not only applicable to the social system, but is true in all affairs of life. <34> Indeed, it can be said to be what the great masters called the "middle path."

Tablet Seven
LAW OR JUSTICE

<1> Laws are created to bring justice. <2> But most of the laws were created in the past, and under the circumstances with which they have been implemented, they have been just. <3> However, these laws have accumulated and been written down, and then they are taken as just laws for all situations.

<4> By doing this, the written words have created power over the common sense and those who are supposed to bring justice will be caught up with the power of these words. They take them as the only way to deal with all situations.

<5> So even though each situation is unique in itself, and judges should consider each of them separately and bring justice to the parties involved, they find themselves bound by these laws and they follow the words of the laws instead of their spirit.

<6> That is why we see nations or people who have many laws and are creating more laws every day. They try to have a better and more just society through these laws, but in truth, they go more and more away from being just. <7> They become rigid in their interpretations of those laws, and the laws become a burden on them.

<8> That is when there are laws but not justice. <9> Such societies should then stop and ask themselves, "Why do our laws not bring justice?" so they would start to institute common sense in their system and choose those who have this common sense in themselves as judges. <10> Or they should see that their society is degenerating, and eventually will collapse and be replaced.

<11> This phenomena can be traced all throughout history. The lesson is that laws

should be flexible enough to bring justice, <12> and also only those who have the ability to bring justice as a whole should be selected as judges. <13> Furthermore, justice cannot be brought to humanity unless all narrowness of the mind is destroyed and there are true judges who have no prejudices or other biases in their judgments.

<14> Otherwise this problem will persist and it will be another cause for suffering and upheaval in human society. <15> Therefore, justice should be the focus of the judiciary system, not the laws.

EXTERNAL SYMBOL OF INTERNAL PUNISHMENT

<16> In all the great religions of the world, the Law of Karma (a reaction for any action and its consequence) more or less has been accepted. Although this law has been presented in different terms or phrases, they all express this truth: <17> Those who do not follow God's Laws (sin) will be punished sooner or later, unless they learn their lesson and repent.

<18> So if it is true, then why do we need social punishment and/or why did Moses and Muhammad constitute external punishment for the wrongdoers?

<19> Although the Law of Karma is true and man knowingly or unknowingly is punished for his wrongdoings, <20> this Law prevents only those who are sensitive enough or are in a higher consciousness from wrongdoing. They realize the truth behind this Law and therefore keep themselves from sin.

<21> However, those who are in their lower natures truly believe they are nothing more than this physical body. They have no sense of spiritual existence and no sensitivity toward the punishments which they bear because of their actions.

<22> They only understand bodily discomfort and punishment. <23> In fact earthly laws are for people in this level of consciousness who, by being punished physically or by seeing others punished physically, are prevented from wrongdoings.

<24> That has been the base for the laws brought by Moses or Prophet Muhammad. <25> The man who is spiritually aware knows that the judgment of God is enough for him, and His Laws are followed by internal awareness of the consequence of breaking them and/or the joy of following them. Grace burns all impurities! But the man of flesh only knows the punishment of flesh and how to avoid such a punishment.

<26> However, these laws are only valid and enforceable if a just society has been created and true leaders (incorruptible and just) are leading society.

<27> In order to implement God's Laws in society justly, the awareness of the people of the truth behind religions and God (truth) is another factor. So the mass would not be exploited by intellectual spiritualists (dogmas) because of their ignorance.

<28> These are again more reasons that each person should become familiar with the truth behind the spiritual world and realize that the leadership of Paravipras (true leaders, Elected Ones) is necessary. After such a society has been established, then the Laws of God can be applied to those who even in such a society will not follow the social orders but continue to commit crimes. Then they will be punished. <29> With this, they would become an external symbol of internal punishment for those who need such an example.

Tablet Eight
WHEN THE LIFE STARTS

<1> Does life start at the time of conception or when the child is born? The answer is neither one! <2> That is because life is there even before the conception of the child. In fact the reason conception occurs is because the life is already present.

<3> The question might arise then as to why the Bible calls the child in the womb a fetus.

<4> The reason is because the Soul enters the body at the time of birth. So the body which is prepared in the womb has no Soul, because the body can only have a Soul when it breathes by itself independently. <5> The body in the womb is the same as a body which is kept alive on a machine, when the Soul of the person is no longer there but the body as a machine continues to function with the help of artificial breathing technology.

<6> Occasionally when the child is born, he does not breathe. He should be hit on the buttocks (over his first chakra where the kundalini resides) to connect the Soul to the body (consciousness of the body) through the spirit (of God). <7> It is then that the child starts to breathe and becomes whole.

<8> The body in the womb of the mother is being prepared for a very special Soul who is waiting to enter this world to further its progress toward the goal of his life.

<9> So by aborting the fetus, that Soul will be deprived of coming to this world and that is a great sin.

<10> However, in the cases in which the life of the mother is in danger, the fetus is dead, a conception has occurred because of rape (God forbids such a great sin) or for any other cause which is not selfish but has a profound reason behind it, abortion can be done. It should not be done for financial reasons.

<11> The final decision rests on the couple, their family, and their spiritual teacher. <12> God is the Judge!

Tablet Nine
ETERNAL DIVINE PATH

<1> Most of the writings of **Maitreya** (God Bless Him and His family) are descriptions of the Scriptures which support His teachings and **The Greatest Sign**. <2> But in truth everything has evolved around **The Greatest Sign** and that should be the focus for those who want to know the truth.

<3> Although there are many truths which have been revealed throughout His teachings, the essence is the **Eternal Divine Path** and following Its steps to Pure Consciousness.

<4> That is why the **Mission of Maitreya** has no dogma, but is a practical path to bring the Kingdom Of Heaven On Earth and within. Then all might progress and become perfect in the process.

<5> Even those who might not agree with **all** of the truth revealed in **Maitreya's** teachings or practices can still follow the **Eternal Divine Path** and overcome any bondages and narrowness of the mind, and be set free.

<6> So the emphasis should be on understanding and following the path (which is **The Greatest Sign**), and creating a human community based on Its teachings. Only with doing so will all petty differences be overcome. <7> Everyone can follow this path and participate in the system of government, regardless of their basic beliefs, as long as they help in establishing His Kingdom, open themselves to the truth behind this path, and are ready to expand their minds (universalism, all is God), and free themselves from bondage.

<8> So a man who realizes this path, but does not follow the practices recommended, is far more worthy than a person who does all the practices and talks much but does not follow and do.

<9> Therefore, we can say the teachings of **Maitreya** can be summarized as knowing and following the **Eternal Divine Path** and creating His Kingdom by following **IT**.

TEACHINGS OF MAITREYA SIMPLIFIED

1- **Haree Om Shrii Hung**
<10> "The Goal Of The Life Is To Be(come) Divine."

2- **Om Nam Kevalam**
<11> "That Divinity Is Everything."

3- The path to Be(come) Divine:
A- <12> Awakening the spiritual forces – Mystical Paths (☯).
B- <13> Directing all energy and power gained toward establishing the Kingdom Of Heaven On Earth – Judaism (✡).
C- <14> Sacrificing all for this ideal, or to be humble – Christianity (✝).
D- <15> Becoming a surrendered or submissive one to His Will – Islam (☪).
E- <16> Expanding one's mind by becoming a universalist – Baha'i Faith (✹).
F- <17> Be(com)ing a dynamic spiritual force – (✡) – and helping others in the path.
G- <18> So win His Grace and reach the Goal – Pure Consciousness (卍).

HAREE OM SHRII HUNG (HOSH) SIGN

<19> The sign representing Pure Consciousness is the sign of **Haree Om Shrii Hung** (卍) which means "The Goal Of The Life Is To Be(come) DIVINE." <20> This sign consists of four parts. The dot (●) in the middle is a representation of the beginning of all things and also of the beginning of the spiritual struggle or operative power of the three gunas ("The Word"). The I-Ching (☯) represents the dual nature of all things in the universe (positive and negative), and also the spiritual powers of the three gunas in the operative state (awakened by the raja guna).

<21> The two other parts are the Expanding Lotus (✺) and the sign (卍) which is called the Lotustica. The Expanding Lotus (✺) is the loving side of God, and the Lotustica (卍) is the destructive or punishing side, which is invisible and "is not." <22> Punishment and destruction come to man only when man goes against His Laws. <23> Indeed it does not exist and it is not God who punishes or destroys. It happens because man goes against His Laws and so brings destruction to himself. <24> Destruction also happens when the old has to be replaced by the new.

<25> Therefore, the sign **Haree Om Shrii Hung** in general means that with spiritual powers (☯), God controls the operative powers of the three gunas (●), and He is the nucleus of the universe. <26> The Expanding Lotus shows that He is all-pervasive and loving. <27> The Lotustica demonstrates His Power (the Universal Laws) of guiding and advancing the universe.

<28> The equivalent to the **HOSH** sign is the four-armed Krishna in the Hindu religion and the square mandala in tantric Buddhism.

<29> The I-Ching sign (☯) in the middle is a representation of the Krishna and in Buddhist terms is the center of the mandala (Vajrasattva).

<30> The four-armed Lotustica (卍) shows the four arms of the Krishna and the four sides (north, south, west, and east) in the mandala. <31> The I-Ching in the middle and the four-armed Lotustica together can be viewed as five jinas in the core of the Buddhist mandala.

<32> Hinduism and Buddhism both strive to reach a state of consciousness beyond the manifested mind. Although this state is called by different names such as samadhi, nirvana, union with God, etc., but they are all referring to the same thing, which we call Pure Consciousness (God in transcendental form). <33> This state of consciousness is the goal

of all Mystical Paths – to be(come) in the Image of God.

<34> Therefore we can see that Buddhism and Hinduism as religions are also covered in **The Greatest Sign**.

<35> The Expanding Lotus (꽃) shows the all-pervasiveness of the Lord (꽃) or Supreme Consciousness.

<36> Also the three colors of the sign, white, orange, and blue, respectively represent satva guna, raja guna, and tama guna, or Brahma (Preserver), Vishnu (Protector), and Shiva (Destroyer). The very center of the sign represents the Father or Rama in Hindu terminology.

<37> Of course to write the true meanings of the **HOSH** sign and/or **The Greatest Sign – Om Nam Kevalam (ONK)** – is like trying to describe God Himself (Is Infinite). <38> They (**HOSH** sign and **ONK** sign) are representations of His qualities and attributes.

Tablet Ten
SUN, MOON, AND STARS

<1> The sun is the only star which rises in the morning. So it is "the morning star." <2> It is the symbol of the highest spiritual realization. When a person becomes spiritually realized, he will be like a sun which shines and gives life to all things.

<3> The sun is the symbol of the male principle (logic). <4> It refers to great leaders in the society and also the father (The Divine Logic, the priest) in the family.

<5> As it is said in the Bible and the Koran, in the last days the sun will be darkened, which is true spiritual knowledge. This will lead to the downfall of true fathers and leaders in the society. <6> Then the mountains (great persons) will not be found and the islands (comforters) will vanish.

<7> That is why the true fathers and leaders should also be the spiritual guides of the families and society.

<8> Moon refers to the female principle (Grace). When it is directed toward Maya, a female becomes woman (Maya). <9> The same energy directed toward the Divine Logic (God) becomes The Divine Grace and/or The Divine Mother.

<10> Women, therefore, should receive the light from their fathers, mothers, or whoever has the Light, and shine themselves. <11> Only these women can manifest the qualities of true females (Divine Mother) and assume the responsibilities of carrying out the most respected position, which is motherhood.

<12> Stars are also the children of the family. It is true that they can enlighten themselves and shine. But their shining quality is dependent upon the father and mother. <13> When the sun becomes darkened, and the moon becomes "like a sack cloth," (Rev. 6:12) then it is the time for children to fall from heaven also.

SYMBOLIC MEANING OF BAPTISM

<14> Water is the symbol of manifested consciousness (ether), and restless water such as a river or ocean, is the symbol of confused consciousness or mind. Therefore to baptize in the river by letting the person merge in it, and then taking him out, is a symbol of saving the person from confusion (river) and pulling him out like a fish. <15> That is why Christ told his disciples that he was going to make them fishers of men.

<16> The feeling of bliss which accompanies baptism arises because when a person is suddenly immersed in water and then taken out again, the reaction to this act is the release of some prana from the solar plexus to the brain. <17> Also because the chakras become cooled, they will be quickened. Both of these reactions result in a feeling of bliss and

refreshment, which is interpreted as receiving the spirit and being saved. This feeling is intensified with a religious atmosphere which stimulates the emotions. In truth, all of these result in the quickening of the chakras which is the same as receiving the spirit (awakening the astral body). <18> However, only those who truly repent and overcome the lower nature and go to their higher natures (to be born again) are the true saved ones.

TO SIN AND TO COMMIT SIN

<19> When a person sins and is not aware of his sin or does not see the wrong in what he does, such a person sins.

<20> But when a person sins and is aware he has sinned, sees the wrong in his action, is ashamed and repentant, and is ready to face that ugly part of the self and so overcome it, such a person has committed a sin. <21> He has not reached perfection but he is on the path to reach there.

<22> The person who sins is in a far worse situation than the one who commits sin. The one who sins has no consciousness of his own actions and their effects on himself and others. So he is very close to animal life.

<23> But one who commits sin knows he is not perfect, but is aware that his actions affect him and others. He can see how they cause him to go away from God and are the source of preventing him from being with Him. He realizes they are the very reason for his sufferings.

<24> Such a person has awakened his spiritual understanding and if he meditates deeply and sees his wrongdoings, they will be destroyed and little by little he will reach perfection and God.

<25> This truth about to sin or to commit sin is shown in the <u>Bible</u> in the case of Cain and Lamech.

<26> Cain sinned by slaying his brother, but could not see the wrong in what he did. So he received God's judgment (punishment), and if any human would judge him over God's judgment, "…whosoever slayeth Cain…" (Gen. 4:15), such a person will be avenged seven times for his judgment of Cain, "…vengeance shall be taken on him sevenfold" (ibid).

<27> But in the case of Lamech who sinned but confessed and was aware of his sin and its wrong, if men judged him harshly for his wrongdoing, they would be avenged seventy times seven, "If Cain be avenged sevenfold, truly Lamech seventy and sevenfold" (Gen. 4:24).

<28> It is only this awareness that causes a person, with His Grace, to strive to overcome his bad habits and sins. Without it, all kinds of actions seem good to him, and he is doomed to fall into sin.

<29> This is also one of the reasons for confessing the sin. If a person feels guilty of his wrongdoing and confesses it, he then is aware he has done wrong and so will strive to overcome it. <30> However, the best confession is when a person deeply inside becomes aware of his vain hopes and desires, and he sees the reason for his sins inside in his meditation. <31> By facing them this way, he overcomes them.

<32> So those who are in the path toward perfection commit sin. As no man will be sinless overnight, it needs much practice. Such a person will put all his effort on not making the same mistakes but if he does, he should become aware of them and, with His Grace, gradually reach the state of sinless-ness.

<33> It is alright if a mistake is made, but its lesson should be learned and the mistake should not be repeated. <34> As man does less wrong, he will do more right and come closer to God, be more aware, and see even deeper and more subtle wrongdoings. Such a man is in the path of perfection (Divinity).

THE ROLE OF INDIA AND THE FAR EAST IN THE PROGRESS OF HUMAN CIVILIZATION

<1> India and the Far East regions of the world had a great role in bringing the understanding of the reality of the universe to the access of the human. Also they have preserved most of the basic realities underlying all religions. <2> The Far East Philosophies, through gaining knowledge about being more and more familiar with the body, mind, and spirit, and through direct experience with the external world, make it possible for a true seeker to perceive and realize the magnificence of his body and how to develop those latent faculties which have been closed in the course of the evolutionary progress of the human.

<3> This part of the world has been set aside to preserve the techniques and teachings that enable man to understand his great potential of awakening his inner strength. <4> That is why people are becoming more and more interested in these teachings, because these systems work directly on individuals and cause them to experience that world which other religions and Prophets have only described. <5> But very few people have been able to perceive them with that direct experience.

<6> However, other religions are necessary to perfect these systems. As it has been revealed by **The Greatest Sign**, a person can become complete only when he understands the basic realities behind **The Greatest Sign**. <7> None of the seals alone presented in **The Greatest Sign** is complete or greater than any of the other ones. <8> But each seal has its greatness in the successive manner toward Pure Consciousness.

<9> Therefore, the teachings of the Far East (and other Mystical Paths in other parts of the world) also have their validities only when studied in respect to the rest of the seals in **The Greatest Sign**.

ACTION (KARMA), KNOWLEDGE (JNANA), AND DEVOTION (BHAKTI) YOGAS, AND THEIR PLACES IN THE GREATEST SIGN

<10> Yoga means "union," to become one or the same as God, or to be(come) in His image.

<11> In the Far East Philosophies (also there are numerous branches and techniques), basically three ways are recognized to reach the Goal. They are called Karma Yoga (through action), Jnana Yoga (through knowledge) and Bhakti Yoga (through devotion).

<12> Karma Yoga is suited for those who like to do and act, but also want not to be bound by their actions. So in this practice, the aspirant does the action and surrenders the result to the Lord. <13> Therefore he will become free of being attached to the external world (results of his actions).

<14> Jnana Yoga is for those who want to free themselves from the bondages of this world through knowledge of its Laws and how they work and bind the consciousness. <15> By study, contemplation, meditation, etc, and with His Grace, they come to grasp the truth behind the Laws governing the universe. So through this knowledge they become free.

<16> Bhakti Yoga is based on devotion. In essence, it is "to love the Lord with all your mind, heart, and being." Through this one-pointed devotion, a person will be saved by Him. <17> With all the attention directed toward Him, no mind or Maya enters, so the world has no power over His devotee.

<18> Now the question is, where do they fit in **The Greatest Sign**?

<19> The I-Ching sign in the horizontal position (☯) at the very bottom of **The Greatest Sign** represents a unit consciousness when it is lost and is on the path toward enlightenment. So this point is the beginning of his journey.

<20> If a unit mind (•) tries to understand the realities behind this universe by gathering knowledge, through meditation, contemplation, reflection, study, etc, he will start to awaken his spiritual forces (☯) and by His Grace, will realize the truth (卍). <21> So the very sign **Haree Om Shrii Hung (HOSH)** is the path of knowledge or Jnana Yoga.

<22> The man who directs his attention with complete devotion to the center of **The Greatest Sign** (卍) or the Lord as the only object of worship and devotion, will be following the path of Bhakti Yoga. With this intense devotion, he will win His Grace and know all truth (卍).

<23> The person who realizes the meaning of the sign at the very top or the sign of surrendering (☪) will be following the path of Karma Yoga, or action. Through his surrendering, he will win His Grace and so will know Him (卍).

<24> So as we can see, any unit consciousness (☯) in any of the three paths mentioned above can easily find his place in the teachings of **The Greatest Sign**. <25> However, his endeavors will be of little value if he does not understand the rest of the teachings of **The Greatest Sign**.

<26> That is: All of those who follow these different paths, according to their nature (Daharma) should direct their knowledge, devotion, or action toward establishing the desired environment (✡) so that others can also benefit from their progress and follow the path toward God-realization (according to their natures).

<27> In this endeavor, they should be ready to sacrifice all for their ideal (✝) and be a channel for Him to guide them in their actions (submission) (☪). They should long to help the **whole** universe to progress to its highest potential (✺) and so become a Paravipra (✡).

<28> Only then will their knowledge (Jnana), devotion (Bhakti), or action (Karma) be blessed. Then all will be following His Will and therefore become Divine (卍). <29> So no matter what your path is, you are a part of the **Eternal Divine Path** and will be perfected by following it. Amen (ॐ).

Tablet Twelve

SOME POINTS IN ISLAM

<1> Islam comes from the word "tasleim" which means to be surrendered and/or submissive to Him. To be surrendered means to do the best we can or to do His Will and surrender the result to Him. <2> Because His Will is not clear to everyone in any moment (His overall Plan and Will is revealed in **The Greatest Sign**) so we try to do our best to do His Will. Then if God wills ("Enshallah"), the action we do will give a great result. <3> But there should be no attachment to the result.

<4> There are three principles which are accepted by all Moslems as the basic principles of Islam. They are:

1- Tohied = One God.

2- Nabovat = Acceptance of Prophets sent by God.

3- Moaad = Day of Judgment.

<5> Some light will be shed on the meaning of these principles with the following explanations:

Tohied: <6> In its lower meaning, tohied means that there is only one God. <7> But it comes from the word "vahdat" or "vahed" which means "to become one" or "one," so its greater meaning is that He is everything and all is God. However, this greater meaning is not understood by many.

<8> This is a great truth in spiritual understanding, because if "He is everything," then

each unit consciousness is a part of Him, so the illusion of separation will vanish. <9> Even accepting the first meaning as there is only one invisible God in the universe (formless, nameless, etc.) can unify humanity, because anything else (anything) besides the invisible God accepted will divide humans on earth.

<10> Even if God Himself comes to the earth and calls Himself by a name, the result would be a division between people. Those who followed Him would use the name He was given on earth, and those who followed an invisible God would not use that name, or other people would follow the same God with a different name. So the division would start. <11> It is not the Will of God to divide humanity from Himself, but He wants to see all come back to unity with Him and be unified.

<12> Through the virtue of this unifying aspect of the invisible God (Allah), Prophet Muhammad unified Arabs and created the Kingdom Of Heaven On Earth for a short period of time in a small part of the world.

<13> Only He (the nameless) unifies. Any other thing divides. That is why in His Ten Commandments to the Hebrews, God emphasized that they should not have any other gods beside Him, and they should not make any image or anything as their object of worship (not even pictures or names). <14> The reason is very clear: It is true that He is everything and if you look at anything He is there also, but this apparent division, which is relative, will bring disunity to humanity, especially to those who cannot see the unity between the seen and unseen.

<15> Therefore, tohied should be followed by everyone in order to bring the unity to all. The other names and images all should be forgotten and thrown away. There is only One God – the rest are dogmas.

Nabovat: <16> This means acceptance of the Prophets and Messengers from God as those who have been chosen to bring messages of the Lord to humanity. These Prophets should not be taken as God Himself, but as His Messengers. Although they are in complete tune with the Lord, and might even be the Father Himself, accepting them as the Lord God will again result in disunity. <17> Indeed the Prophet himself or his miracles are not important but his teachings are what is important. The teachings are surely from God regardless of whether the Prophet was the Father Himself or not.

<18> The Prophets come with definite signs and fulfill many prophecies about their coming. God does it this way so everyone can be sure that the person who claims to be the Expected One is true and chosen. <19> Otherwise many will come in their name and deceive many. It has been done this way so only the True One will be recognized by the Elects.

Moaad: <20> This means that there is a last day of judgment when the good people will be separated from the bad. This also will happen. <21> When the original energy which was generated to create this universe is consumed, then all will be dissolved into its original form, and those who have reached Pure Consciousness or higher consciousness will enter heaven (Pure Consciousness), and those who lagged behind will have to wait until the next generation (creation). They will then have to struggle again for crores of years for their salvation, because they have lost the opportunity that was given to them in this creation to reach Pure Consciousness. <22> That is why this life is an opportunity, especially for humans, to reach Pure Consciousness. Otherwise who knows when another chance will be given to them?

<23> Also every day and every moment is the time of judgment, and human actions create karma (the Law of action and reaction) or judgment, and man reaps what he sows.

<24> Three other concepts in Islam will briefly be explained below:

<25> It is believed by Moslems (followers of Islam) that Muhammad was the last Prophet. They refer to a verse in the Koran that contains a word which has two different pronunciations, each with a different meaning.

ESSAYS 2   *Tablet 13*

<26> It can be pronounced Khatem (last, the end) or Khatam (the seal).

<27> The true meaning of this word has been the subject of dispute for centuries. Some say it is Khatem, so Prophet Muhammad was the last Prophet. Some say Khatam, so he was the seal of the Prophets but they do not give an explanation as to why he was the seal.

<28> However, in truth the word can be pronounced in both ways, and both meanings are correct.

<29> Prophet Muhammad brought the highest spiritual realization for humanity, to be surrendered and submissive to the Lord. So there will not be any higher realization brought to humanity (for more detail, read Revelation of The Revelation). <30> So from this point of view, he is the last Prophet, the "Khatem" of the Prophets.

<31> Also as it has been shown in **The Greatest Sign**, the sign of Islam (☾) is at the very top:

<32> Therefore, it is the seal in The Plan of the Lord, and Prophet Muhammad is the seal of the Prophets ("Khatam" of the Prophets).

<33> The problem is that the human wants to narrow God's works into one aspect or dimension. But God's words and actions are multidimensional. That is where the misunderstanding starts. You cannot narrow the expanded work of the Lord to the small understanding of man. <34> To know Him and His Words requires bringing yourself to His expanded level.

<35> This endeavor of man to narrow the works of the Lord is another reason for human sufferings.

<36> Another concept in Islam is the word "jahad" which is loosely translated as "holy war." <37> The true meaning of jahad, however, is internal and external struggle to establish truth and holiness. Its meaning is the same as the tone of the Bhagavad-Gita with its warrior Arjuna, who should internally and externally struggle and overcome the obstacles toward his perfection.

<38> In fact only those who internally and externally struggle all their lives are the ones who can declare a holy war. <39> Otherwise, holy wars can be misused by those who have narrow interests and manipulate the emotions of the people toward their religions for their own selfish ends.

Tablet Thirteen

JAHAD

<1> "Jahad" is one of the most misunderstood words in Islam. Jahad comes from Jahd, which means struggle to achieve something. Therefore, jihad means "struggle." <2> It is said in the writings of Prophet Muhammad that the greatest struggle (jahad) is the struggle of the human within.

<3> So jahad means going from imperfection to perfection. It resembles the word "sadhana" in Sanskrit which means "struggle"

("sadhana" also refers to meditation).

<4> Jahad also means external struggle in order to establish the truth over wrongdoings – the Kingdom Of Heaven On Earth (Daharma). That is why Prophet Muhammad used this word for the Holy Wars with the Arab tribes in order to destroy their pagan beliefs and establish his monastic teaching in that land.

<5> This external jihad was necessary at that time because of all the opposition by those people whose main source of income was threatened by the Islamic ideology. Mecca, the holy city, was a center of worship for many different beliefs. In that city countless images and statues were created so that each believer could feel at home when they came there. The very basic tenet of Muhammad's teaching that "there is no God but Allah" meant the rest of the gods in Mecca were no gods.

<6> However, the businessmen of Mecca told Muhammad that he could preach his religion if he did not oppose the images in Mecca. This would enable the merchants from all around the world to come and worship their images in Mecca (and spend their money).

<7> But he did not accept their proposal, and the light of enmity began between those rich businessmen and Prophet Muhammad.

<8> This became so strong that Prophet Muhammad had to leave Mecca and go to Medina. Later on the fight between Mecca and Medina kindled, and the concept of jahad was revealed to Muhammad as "Holy Wars" (the same as war in the Bhagavad-Gita). <9> However, its true meaning is internal and external struggle.

<10> In the course of time jahad lost its more important meaning as internal struggle and was used only to mean the duty of each Moslem to take up a weapon and fight the enemy that had attacked Moslems or to be used to destroy disbelievers. Many leaders in Islam lost the truth that external struggle is an impossibility without internal struggle.

<11> So, jahad means internal and external struggle to perfection (to internally and externally become perfect). This is the same as Christ taught the Pharisees, that they should clean the inside and the outside of the cup if they want to have a clean cup. Again we can see that with misunderstanding beautiful concepts such as this, great disasters take place. <12> It is not religions that are the source of suffering, but the way they have been interpreted by humanity.

Tablet Fourteen

AN ESSAY ON THE THEORY OF THE HIERARCHY OF NEEDS OF MASLOW

<1> According to the theory of Maslow (which is accepted by many as a well-established theory), the hierarchy of needs of the human consists of five general categories.

1- **physiological needs**: hunger, thirst, sleep, need of physical health, etc.
2- **safety needs**: security, shelter, etc.
3- **social needs**: belonging to society or a group.
4- **esteem needs**: being distinguished as a useful member of society or the group one is associated with.
5- **self-actualization**: to understand our true natures and become what we really are.

<2> In understanding the true nature of human needs, we should first explain the difference between a true need and a false need.

<3> The need for food and nourishment in a normal sense for the satisfaction of physiological demands can be defined as a true (or real) need. <4> But the constant need of food because of nervousness or for some psychological deficiencies is a false need.

<5> Also a true need is one which if not fulfilled or if the situation is not provided for a

long period of time, death or the destruction of the human life results. <6> But a false need is one which will not result in natural death but will create desperation and unhappiness.

<7> A person who is deprived of food or lives in an unsafe situation will most probably die of hunger, disease, injury, etc. But a person who is desperate for food because of a false need will feel anxiety and unhappiness, but he will not die. <8> In fact that feeling of great desire for food is a psychological defense against the desire of the Soul to see its true being. It is from the fear of going through a struggle or even opposing the many psychological set-ups in the environment in order to be released from those psychological problems. <9> This person intuitively knows that to become actualized means to stand for his own rights. But he is not strong enough to do that, so he directs that deficiency toward believing that he can gain the lost happiness of being actualized by overeating.

<10> Also the needs for belonging and esteem can be categorized as false needs, because if they are not fulfilled the death of the person in a natural way will not result (he might commit suicide, but that is of ignorance, not because the need is true).

<11> As in the case of the person who overeats because he does not want to stand for his birthright (which is to know his true self) or the person who desperately needs to belong to a group and feel its support, or the person who requires recognition and respect (esteem), all these needs can be categorized as false needs. <12> The reason is because only a person with a false ego seeks support and attention from others (from outside) instead of accepting himself as he is and developing his talents and abilities. Therefore, respect comes because he is worthy to receive it, not because he needs it and is ready to do whatever is necessary to gain it.

<13> Also he will enjoy the company of others and will participate in group activities, not because he needs to be in groups but because he realizes that greater achievements can be gained through collective endeavors. <14> This person can also create deeper interpersonal relationships with the group's members because he is not desperate for the false need of belonging. Therefore, he can enter into a relationship without anxiety. <15> So the relationship will be based more on a true feeling rather than a nervous one, from a desperate need of being accepted.

<16> Therefore, as we can see, a moderate need for physiological satisfaction and safety can be recognized as the true needs of the human. <17> Any desperate need to belong to some group or to be recognized in the group (when the person is ready to do anything to gain that recognition) is a false need.

<18> However, an actualized person can enjoy the company of others, because he can create deep interpersonal relationships which will help both partners to grow through deep understanding of each other. <19> Also he will enjoy being recognized and respected by the group or society, not because he needs it, but because his true merit is worthy to be recognized (even in this stage, a realized person knows that his talent and worth is nothing to be attached to, because it has been given to him by the Lord to be used for the good of all).

<20> Therefore, the need for belongingness and esteem are related to the false ego, which is the lower nature of man. These cannot be categorized as real (true) needs. <21> True needs are only physiological and safety needs, which should be provided for all people who are born in the universe.

<22> Self-actualization (or better "ego-actualization") is the goal. It also cannot be categorized as a need but is the goal of the life. <23> The actualized ego is related to the higher nature of man. To reach the higher nature (higher consciousness, Divinity, Pure Consciousness, etc.) is the purpose of life. Only people in their higher natures (self-actualized) can create effective groups or are worthy of being recognized or respected for their true achievements. They can create deep relationships with each other and the groups, and they can work toward what they are made to be, not toward what society or their parents think they should be. <24> Only then do

belongingness and esteem also become actualized rather than false needs.

<25> That is why it is so important to create such a society where each person can be sure of receiving his basic needs (physiological and safety) and a system that will help each person to grow physically, mentally, and spiritually. <26> Then it is the responsibility of each person to strive and struggle to actualize his ego and find his place in society in order to help others toward the goal. With this set-up, the whole universe will be utilized for the advancement of all unit consciousnesses toward higher and eventually Pure Consciousness. That is when the whole universe will joyfully march toward the goal – to be(come) Divine.

<27> It is so important that parents, teachers, educational systems, and society as a whole be very careful to prevent any false ideals from being set up for the children and youth. <28> Instead, all parts of society should encourage and inspire them to study and understand the life of the great men so that they search for their higher natures. They should be taught self-control and be encouraged to discipline the self, be sincere, and to direct their attention to the higher self rather than the lower. <29> Failure to do so will lead humanity toward disasters and self-destruction, which is always the by-product of following the lower nature of man.

<30> Therefore, we can conclude that the true needs of man are: (1) a healthy, moderate need for physiological processes (thirst, hunger, air, rest, etc., but not sex which has a multi-purpose function, is more spiritual, and can be controlled), and (2) safety needs. <31> Belongingness and esteem are false when they become needs, but will be a source of joy in life when used for the growth of individuals and the progress of society (and the human). <32> Self-actualization (ego-actualization) is the goal of the life, and enough inspiration should be created for all to achieve it.

<33> This essay was also a brief explanation of the true needs of man, and is written to distinguish between false needs and true needs. Its understanding requires a deep realization, and to achieve its goal a great environment is needed which enables each person to become what he truly is. <34> It should also be realized that it has not been suggested that groups and societies are unnecessary for man and he should go away from them to become ego-actualized. In contrast, groups and society are a must for a person to understand the realities of life, the universe, and to become ego-actualized. <35> However also solitude, thinking, concentration, and inspiration will help when there is a balance between them and sociability.

<36> Another point which should be mentioned is that sex is not categorized as a physiological need. There are many reasons for this. First of all, sexual energy can be controlled, and even its desire can be overcome by techniques such as right diet, exercises, meditation, fasting, use of cool water, etc. (sex is not a basic need – natural death will not occur from abstinence). <37> Secondly, sex has multiple purposes in addition to a physiological discomfort when it is not controlled or a satisfaction when it is released. Sex is a psychological (ethereal) relationship between two persons in a marriage. Its most important purpose is to create children. It is a union of a man and woman physically, mentally, and spiritually, etc. <38> Thirdly, through marriage, sex is a way of creating the unit blocks of families in society and a proper environment to raise the children. <39> Therefore, to look at sex as only a physiological need will result in ignoring the other more important aspects of sexual relationships. That is why sex is not a basic need for man, but is a means for spiritual progress.

<40> In addition, the hierarchy of needs proposed by Maslow can be related to the spiritual centers (chakras) in the body. <41> The physiological and safety needs (survival needs) are related to the first chakra, which is one of the most important spiritual centers (or psychological center). The kulakundalini (spiritual force) resides in this chakra.

<42> The social and belonging needs are related to the second chakra, which also controls thirst, hunger, and sexual energy. It is one of the most powerful chakras in the lower

nature (the first three chakras) in the human.

<43> The esteem, struggle for power, and prestige needs are related to the third chakra in the navel area. <44> Therefore, all these needs are related to the lower nature of man which can be controlled by overcoming this lower self.

<45> However, moderate physiological and safety needs are necessary for human existence. It is true that even physiological and safety needs can be overcome, but the amount of effort necessary to do so makes it neither practical nor desirable. That energy and endeavor can instead be utilized for the good of humanity.

<46> From the fourth chakra the self-actualization process starts, and at the sixth and seventh chakras man reaches Pure Consciousness.

<47> Also one more thing should be realized, and that is the difference between a self-actualized person and an inspired person. A self-actualized person is content with what he does and is satisfied with what he is. <48> An inspired person is one who stands for truth in front of all opposition, and he is not only content with what he is but also would like to see all become what they can be(come).

Tablet Fifteen
PRESSURE

<1> Pressure is the instrument of the lower nature. When a person responds under pressure, in fact he is doing things that are not according to his deep motives, because he reacts from fear. <2> Any action from fear brings suffering.

<3> Indeed this world is the kingdom of the devil, because most of the people work and react to the pressures of the external world. <4> Their motivations are not from the self, but from their fears created in the external world.

<5> These fears, which are the very cause of tension and pressure, can be physical, emotional, or mental. <6> The physical pressures (physical slavery) are much easier to detect and in a great scale have been eliminated from human civilization (although still existing in some parts).

<7> However, the mental and emotional pressures still exist and are much subtler. They have replaced the physical pressures (slavery) of the past.

<8> In the time of slavery in history, man knew who made him a slave, so he had a clear picture of his situation and could identify the enemy. But in mental or emotional slavery, which is very subtle, he does not know his master.

<9> So the pressure and fear become tension, and tension creates a turbulent mind. This causes greater confusion and increases his fear so he conforms to the pressure more.

<10> With this vicious cycle, he truly becomes the slave of these subtle threads and goes further and further away from the self and truth.

<11> The cure to this problem is meditation! Only with deep meditation, creating a calm mind, facing the truth, becoming familiar with the subconscious mind, and recognizing these pressures and their sources (mentally and emotionally), can a person come in tune with his self and realize how and why he reacts to the pressures as he does.

<12> The emotional pressures come from deep desires and attachments. <13> So those who we think we love, are attached to, or can fulfill our desires, can easily put pressure on us.

<14> One of the most widely known is peer-pressure. Because we are not self-actualized, we need other people's approval so we conform to their pressures. <15> To overcome peer-pressure, we should know ourselves and then accept a profession according to our abilities (physical, mental, and spiritual). We should become highly proficient in that task, do our best, and not give in to pressure. <16> Whenever there is pressure and a

person reacts to it, there is a problem in that situation.

<17> The mental pressures are those which make us believe we have to have or become something, but we truly cannot become it, do not want to become it, or do not need it, such as sale pressure to buy things we do not require.

<18> There is a direct interrelationship between emotional and mental pressures. They are complementary and help one another to create the reaction of the person to the pressure.

<19> A self-actualized person, or he who has a calm mind and control over it, never acts under external pressure, so he can never be enslaved.

<20> Those who give in to pressure (individually or collectively) might conquer the world but they will lose their Souls, and that is not a good bargain.

DAYDREAMERS

<21> There are people who hear voices, see visions, talk with spirits, and receive revelations which give them a hope of something that apparently would change their lives. They hope these things will come true some day.

<22> So they daydream of when these will happen, and they escape the reality. <23> But surprisingly if the fulfillment of their dreams is offered to them, usually it can be seen that they lose their artificial happiness and might even run away and find some fault in the fulfiller of the dream.

<24> Or in other words, they do not really want or expect that dream to be fulfilled, because the very reason they were drawn into this state has been their feelings of inadequacy and inability to cope with reality. So when the fulfillment of the dream is offered to them, there would be nothing left to escape to and the person would be forced to face the reality again. <25> For a person who has been out of touch with reality for so long, it is a hard step.

<26> Also if the dream was generated by a great ambition to be in a special position, when that position is offered to the person, he becomes very unhappy again because he truly did not want to have that position. It was really an escape to feel he is worthy enough to have it. <27> He either has to face the reality and improve himself, or find some fault in something that surrounds the situation, or fall into another dream to escape again.

Tablet Sixteen
PREDESTINATION OR CHOICE

<1> There has been a great and long argument on this subject. Some say all are predestined, and others say man has choice.

<2> In truth both of them are correct. To demonstrate this, let us use an example:

<3> If we imagine that there is a king in a land and he rules the land with great authority and power, then all his subjects obey his will. So we can suppose that he has complete control over his people.

<4> However, if we consider his prime minister and a peasant in his kingdom, which one has more freedom of choice in his life?

<5> Of course the peasant does, because he can choose where he wants to live, how to spend his day, how to relate to others, etc. <6> But the prime minister or those who are closer to the king, have a much smaller choice in these regards. However, they have more power in the land.

<7> Furthermore, if the king willed some peasant to do something for him, such a person also loses his choice and has to follow the will of the king.

<8> Also those who know the will of the great king and follow it will lose their choices but will receive his mercy and come to be in his presence.

<9> This is also true between the human and the Father. Those who come close to Him lose their choices, because they have to follow His Will. <10> Those who do not follow His Will have choice but will not come close to Him. <11> Those whom He chooses to do His Will, knowingly or unknowingly, will do it, and those who do His Will, will go unto Him.

<12> As in a land there are laws which all have to follow and if they do not they will be punished, also there are Laws in the universe that all have to follow.

<13> So although those who are peasants in His Kingdom have the choice to choose, their choices are limited. <14> They cannot go against His Laws, but are freer than those who are closer to Him.

<15> Therefore, those who are close to Him, follow His Will or are chosen for a task, have their lives predestined. <16> But those who are neither close to Him, nor follow His Will, nor are chosen, have choice in their lives, and their choices shape their progress or otherwise.

Greater than meditation is to share God (Satsang) with someone.

Greater than prayer is to fulfill someone else's need.

Greater than fasting is to feed someone who is starving!

ESSAYS 3

The book, <u>Essays 3</u>, is the last book of the essays written by Maitreya. This book is mostly related to spiritual purification of the individual and community. The books of essays cover many topics in this regard.

ESSAYS 3

Golden Rule: Do to others as you expect others to do unto you. But if they did not do unto you as you expect, forgive them.

INTRODUCTION

In any given situation according to time, place, and people involved, the purpose (Daharma) of the laws are to bring justice. Therefore, we can never set some rigid rules and regulations and assume in all similar circumstances they can bring justice.

That is why when laws and a set of rules are created to regulate the society or to bring justice, after some period of time, such societies realize that those laws have become more important than the justice which they were supposed to bring.

That is, the following of the laws becomes so important that their spirit to bring justice is lost. Then they almost become rituals which are to be automatically performed instead of to be understood and changed to bring justice for each situation. In other words, the notion would be law, not justice, so a bureaucracy would be created. But whatever is rigid in this universe and does not do what it was intended to do (its Darma) has no choice but to be broken and replaced by another system which will suit the situation, or one which is flexible enough to change and adapt to the situation.

In order to bring a high ideal of justice to society, also only those who have overcome and have no guilt any longer can judge. The points above were well demonstrated by Esa and the adulterous woman. They brought her to him saying that they had caught her in the act of adultery and according to the laws of Moses she should be stoned. Esa said that he who has no guilt should throw the first stone. All left and no one was found worthy to judge her.

They were following the law but without considering her situation and also how hard it is to overcome. That is why only those who have overcome (have no guilt) know how hard it is to do so. They are aware of the forces in the universe and society, and how they cause a man to do things that he might not have done otherwise.

So such a person or persons will look at each situation on a deeper level by their intuition and knowledge, and then they will judge others. Only these people should be selected into the judiciary body of the government.

However, a base of general laws to govern the society can be accepted. But in each situation these basic laws should be adjusted to bring the desired justice. These Divine basic Laws have been brought to humanity through Moses and Prophet Muhammad.

Of course, many argue that these laws are harsh and outmoded. But the reason they have not been able to be used in any society to bring justice is because there has never been a society and people who have created an environment where these laws can be used.

In order to implement His Laws, a just society with just leaders is necessary. Unless an ideal environment is created, no law is just!

If such an environment is created, and then a person commits crimes, a harsh justice given through a just judge is readily acceptable. That is because in this situation the person has not done the crime because of physiological or safety needs, but other tendencies which deserve punishment.

Also it might be argued that according to the Law of Karma, people will be punished for their bad actions. Why then do we need to punish them externally if we know that they will be punished anyway?

Although that is true and the realized person has no doubt about that, not all people are realized. This external symbol of internal punishment is for those who are in their physical levels and need to see the punishment in this level.

Those who are in the spirit and see the justice in the spirit will not sin. He who does not sin does not need any laws.

In the following pages, some recommendations, Commandments, and points will be considered as guidance on the spiritual path. They are by no means the ultimate and not all of them are applicable for all. But except for the Commandments and Laws which should be followed, they are recommendations for those who follow them and will benefit the aspirants in their spiritual path, according to their situation (time, place, and people involved).

The essence of the teachings of **Maitreya** is the **Eternal Divine Path**, which leads a person to become Divine. So he who follows this path and has become it does not need to follow any rituals or laws, but the recommendations and laws in this book are helpful for a person to follow the **Divine Path**.

So it is a two-way consideration – those who follow these recommendations (or any other practices helpful to them) will find it easier to follow the **Eternal Divine Path**, and he who is following the **Path** and has become it will easily follow these recommendations, understand their depth, and greatly benefit from them.

However, no rituals, meditation, exercises, etc., are valid if they do not lead a person to follow the **Eternal Divine Path**.

Tablet One
BATH

<1> It is recommended that a full bath be taken at least every other day. <2> The full bath consists of washing the whole body with some cleansing material. <3> It is also recommended not to use very hot water in taking a bath.

<4> The best position to take the bath is in the sitting position in the water, or on the heels (squatting) while taking a shower. This allows a great absorption of prana and minerals in the water. <5> That is why a great feeling of restfulness prevails after this kind of bathing in contrast to taking a bath standing under a running shower.

<6> It is also recommended to ideate on the bath ideation before, during, and after the bath which brings the mind to the higher thoughts and reminds the person of the goal of life.

Bath Ideation Before and During Bathing

1- **I wash myself with water which is the symbol of purity.**
2- **Not only do I wash my body with this water but also I will ideate that this is an act of baptism, and I will be free of my previous bad habits.**
3- **This water also will wash away my fears, unnecessary desires, and attachments. I will only be attached to God.**
4- **Only then will I be free, pure, and clean enough to stand in front of the Father, the Ancestors of humanity, and the Sages in the past, and pay my salutations to them.**

<7> This ideation can be repeated and contemplated before and during the bath.

Bath Ideation After Bathing
(Repeated Three Times)

1- **My reverent salutations to the Ancestors of Humanity.**
2- **My reverent salutations to all the Sages and Messengers.**
3- **They were all in the path of becoming Pure Consciousness.**
4- **I am one with them in Spirit.**
5- **Therefore it is the goal of my life to become Pure Consciousness and help the whole universe to become the same.**
6- **(Third time only) The act of offering, the heat which was used to offer, and the one who offers are all He.**

Sal-Om.

<8> It is recommended that the bath ideation after bathing be done with the proper gestures (mudras) in front of the sun or a white light while the body is still wet and dripping. The water on the body will absorb the light and because each drop is like a convex lens, it will concentrate the energy of light to the body.

CIRCUMCISM

<9> It is a law that the male should be circumcised. It is an act of cleanliness and a sign of obedience to the Lord. **<10>** This will cause the male organ to cool off faster and also prevents the accumulation of germs and dirt underneath the foreskin, therefore preventing many diseases. **<11>** Also there will be acceleration of mental development, less unwanted sexual stimulation, and many other benefits.

<12> The circumcision is best done when the person is very young or even in the early days of birth. **<13>** But if the male is too old to be circumcised, the foreskin should be pulled back and cleaned regularly.

CLOTHING

<14> Clothes should be decent and modest in appearance, and according to the situation in such a way that an upright mind would not object.

<15> It is better for men and women to wear distinct clothing.

COOLING OF THE BODY

<16> Too much heat in the body creates lethargy and is responsible for many diseases. Therefore it is recommended to keep the body as cool as possible. The best way to do this is by washing with cool water the entire body or those places which create heat.

Half-Bath: **<17>** is similar to the tradition which in the Bible is called "to wash the feet," "…and water to wash his feet, and the men's feet that were with him" (Genesis 24:32), or in the New Testament as "…wash thy face" (Matthew 6:17), and in Islam as washing before prayer (vozo).

<18> The half-bath cools the centers which create heat, the nervous system, and consequently the spinal cord, and the energy centers (chakras). It releases the body from the burden of doing this itself. **<19>** Therefore the energy (prana) of the body can be used for other functions in the body. With this a healthier body will be gained.

<20> A half-bath is recommended to be performed before meditation, eating, and sleeping.

<21> Cool water should be poured over the genital area first. This will cool off the second and first chakras (energy centers) and also the lower part of the spinal cord.

<22> Then the knees to the toes are cooled with water (or at least the feet). This cools off the endings of many nerves in the feet, and also the nerves which come from the spinal cord to the legs and that part of the spinal cord from which these nerves arise.

<23> Then water is poured over the elbows down to cool the lower part of the arm below the elbows. This will cool off the nerve endings in the hands and the upper part of the spinal cord.

<24> Next cool water is taken into the mouth. While the water is kept in the mouth, water is splashed into the eyes. The eyes should stay open while water is being splashed into them.

<25> It is recommended to breathe in deeply through the nose before splashing the water to the face, and then exhale after each splash, and inhale again and splash the water. **<26>** This will develop the habit of inhaling through the nostrils and deep breathing, and also helps to absorb more prana from the water splashed into the face and eyes. <27> Seven to fifteen times of splashing is recommended to cool off the eyes and the face. However this number can be increased or decreased according to a person's desire.

<28> Then water should be sucked in through the nostrils until it passes through the nose and comes out the mouth.

<29> This will help the whole nervous system in the face, the sinuses, and the glands in the brain to be cooled, therefore preventing many diseases and the common cold.

<30> Then the neck, back of the head, behind the ears, and if desired, the hair, can be cooled off with the water. <31> When this half-bath is completed, a feeling of freshness will prevail.

<32> The half-bath is especially a blessing in hot climates and/or in the summer. However, it can be taken even in the winter and causes the body to become accustomed to cool weather and therefore stay cool.

One-Fourth of the Bath: <33> is the same as the half-bath but only the hands and face part is done. It is recommended when a quick cooling of the body is necessary or the situation does not allow a half-bath.

<34> The hands are washed with cool water, water is kept in the mouth, water is splashed into the eyes and face, and the neck and behind the ears are cooled off.

Cool Bath: <35> is recommended upon arising in the morning. The best way to take a cool full bath is to take a half-bath, then after finishing it also cool the navel area and the opposite side of the navel at the back. Then massage the surface of the body with wet hands and while sitting on the heels, pour water from the crown of the head to run over the back of the spine down the body.

<36> Then one can pour cool water all over the body and wherever much heat is felt. It is a great disciplinary act and accustoms the body to withstand cold weather. It makes the body healthy, refreshed, and ready for meditation and the day.

Cooling of the Genital Area: <37> is done by pouring cool water over the genital area after urination. This will squeeze the urethra and the remaining urine will be drawn out. <38> Also it keeps this organ cool, prevents many diseases, and lowers the unwanted sexual stimulations.

<39> This act should become so habitual that the person does it without a second thought.

Tablet Two
DISPOSING OF THE DEAD BODY

<1> The best way to dispose of the dead body is to wash it with water which contains disinfectant material, then put some camphor in the mouth, and wrap the body in a white cloth. <2> It should be buried at least three meters under the ground.

<3> The way traditional Jewish people and Moslems bury their dead also is acceptable, which is very similar to the procedure above.

<4> The use of a decorated casket is not recommended. <5> Only those who identify themselves with their bodies glorify their bodies even after death. But as we know, we are not our bodies and to identify the self with the body is indeed the first step toward becoming flesh and falling into ignorance.

<6> One of the reasons we cannot find any traces of the Prophets and Great Souls in the past – such as Abram (Abraham) – is because a strong casket was never used to preserve the dead. They knew preservation of the flesh or bones is not from the spirit.

<7> Also they would never put a sign on their graves to identify them or to distinguish them from the rest of the ground, because that also is a sign of glorifying the dead. <8> Erection of stones was considered as an altar to the Lord, and only God should be glorified,

not men.

<**9**> However, the dead body should be handled with respect as a part of the universe.

<**10**> If the death occurred while on the sea, the procedure is the same but the body should be thrown into the sea with a heavy weight attached to it. <**11**> If the death occurred in space, the body can be thrown into space or be burned with no procedure necessary.

<**12**> In the case the body is infected with some spreadable and dangerous disease or if a person so desires, it can be cremated.

DIVINE PATH

(Repeated After Collective Meditation)

> **<13> The thoughts, love, and peace of God will arise in those who perform meditation and/or The Reminder twice a day or more regularly.**
>
> **<14> They will become an instrument for His Will, sacrifice all for this ideal, surrender and submit unto Him, and become a universalist at last.**
>
> **<15> Also they follow the Fifteen Commandments.**
>
> **<16> With these, they will become the Elects, win His Grace, and reach their goal.**
>
> **Maitreya**

Explanation of the Divine Path: <**17**> The wording above is indeed the same as the explanation of the steps of **The Greatest Sign – Om Nam Kevalam (ONK)** sign – or the **Eternal Divine Path**.

<**18**> "The thoughts, love, and peace of God (卐) will arise (☯) in those who perform meditation and/or **The Reminder** twice a day or more regularly. They will become an instrument for His Will (✡), sacrifice all for this ideal (✝), surrender and submit unto Him (☪), and become a universalist at last (✷)."

<**19**> "Also they follow the **Fifteen Commandments**:" Without a moral base, meditation is an impossibility. <**20**> Therefore those who want to benefit from their meditation should follow Yama and Niyama or at least the Ten Commandments. But by following the **Fifteen Commandments**, a person will be following both Yama and Niyama and the Ten Commandments together (and even more). <**21**> So for those who want to become an Elect (Divine), following the **Fifteen Commandments** is highly recommended (of course with a discriminating mind for the welfare of the whole universe).

<**22**> "With these, they will become the Elects" or Divine (✡), "win His Grace, and reach their goal (卐)." This is the **Essence** of the teaching of **Maitreya**.

Tablet Three

FASTING

<**1**> It is recommended to fast on the full moons, first moons, eleven days after the full moon, and eleven days after the first moon. It is also recommended to fast on the Sabbath. <**2**> Fasting on the full and first moons is especially recommended for single people and renunciates (sannyasins). <**3**> The fast should start at sunset until the sunset of the next day. If this seems too long, a fast from sunrise to sunset is advisable.

<**4**> The purpose of fasting (in addition to many benefits which are derived from it, physically and mentally) is spiritual. That is, fasting should be done to bring the person closer to the Lord and make him realize the self.

<**5**> That is why it is recommended to keep away from talkativeness and sexual intercourse, and to direct the thoughts toward God.

<**6**> A complete fast is one without food or liquid. However, those who do long fasting and/or those whose bodies are not used to fasting, can fast with water and/or juice.

<7> Before the age of puberty and after the age of sixty, it is not required to fast. After the age of sixty it is up to the individual. Before the age of puberty, the individual can try light fasting (a few days in a year) if they would like.

FIFTEEN COMMANDMENTS

<u>Five General Commandments:</u>

1- **Submission**: <8> The Divine Father in heaven is One, Invisible, Nameless, and the Greatest.

2- **Surrendering**: <9> Do not go to complete prostration (submit) to anyone or thing except Him, the words revealed through His Prophets, and **The Greatest Sign**, which clarifies the confusion between all.

3- **Goal of the Life**: <10> Remember the goal of the life, which is to reach Pure Consciousness and help others to reach the same.

4- **Messengers**: <11> Consider the Prophets, Satgurus, Avatars, or likewise as God's Messengers to bring His Messages and Laws to humanity.

5- **Elects**: <12> Accept Paravipras as the Chosen Ones to establish and enforce the Laws, and to spread the Messages of God and establish the Kingdom Of Heaven.

<u>Five Observing Commandments (Yama):</u>

6- **Non-violence**: <13> Not violating the Daharma. In understanding this Commandment, we should first define what violence is.
<14> **Violence is the deviation from a set of rules and regulations.**
<15> Therefore, non-violence in this Commandment means: Do not deviate from or violate the Laws and regulations of the universal set-up (Daharmas).
<16> However, because one of the greatest Laws of the universe is to refrain from inflicting pain or injury on others by action, thought, or speech, this has been used as the meaning of the word "non-violence." <17> However, not inflicting pain or injuries on others for selfish desires is a minor meaning of non-violence. In a greater sense, it means not violating the Laws of the universe or nature, or in other words, following the Daharma of things.
<18> Even in its minor meaning, it does not mean to refrain from fighting for establishing truth – that is escapism. And it does not mean non-injury when a wise injury might be the real cure for the disease physically, mentally, or spiritually. <19> In short, like everything else, non-violence can be of three kinds – from ignorance, passion, or knowledge.

7- **Truthfulness, with Discriminating Mind**: <20> To guide all thought, speech, and action with the spirit of welfare.

8- **Not to Steal (Non-Stealing, physically, mentally, or spiritually)**: <21> Do not take things which belong to others, by thought, by taking (action), or by preventing them from doing their duties or possessing things which belong to them.

9- **Non-Indulgence**: <22> Not to indulge in the enjoyment of such amenities and comforts as are superficial to the preservation of life.

10- **Attach to God**: <23> To keep the mind immersed in the ideation of God, to remain attached to God, and to accept Him as the only Refuge, the only King, and His Laws as the only Laws.

<u>Five Actional Commandments (Niyama):</u>

11- **Internal and External Cleanliness**: <24> To maintain purity and cleanliness of mind, body, and environment.

12- **Contentment and Mental Ease**: <25> To remain in a state of mental equanimity and contentment.

13- **Satsang, Service, and Meditation**: <26> To attain true Satsang (when people talk only about God, the universe, and His Will), to practice penance in the service of others (as being done for the Lord, in creating **Communities of Light**), and to sincerely meditate and/or do **The Reminder** at least twice a day.

14- **Understanding God and His Laws through the Scriptures**: <27> To clearly understand the underlying meanings of the Scriptures and discourses of spirituality.

15- **To Be(come) Divine**: <28> To strive to become perfect in our actions as God is, to ideate that He does the Divine actions through us, and to become a perfect instrument for His Will to be done, <29> until able to radiate His Divine Universal Truth through ourselves.

Tablet Four

EXPLANATION OF THE FIFTEEN COMMANDMENTS

<1> The **Fifteen Commandments** will be described in very brief paragraphs, although each paragraph could be expanded much further. However, there are many other writings available to the Divines which will help them in expanding the meanings of these Commandments through exploring those truths.

<2> Also the Ten Commandments given in the Bible (Exodus chapter 20) are covered in these descriptions to show that the Ten Commandments are a part of the **Fifteen Commandments** and are not discredited or destroyed by them.

<u>Five General Commandments:</u>
1- **Submission**: <3>**The Divine Father in heaven is One, Invisible, Nameless, and the Greatest.**
a. <4> Only the Invisible, Nameless, Shapeless God can unify. Any other kind of God will divide. That is why He is called the God of Abraham, Isaac, etc., with no name or visibility. <5> However, all beautiful names which are related to His attributes in the universe are His.
b. <6> Even if God Himself comes to the earth, He would not reveal His identity because that would create disunity.
c. <7> The first three of the Ten Commandments are related to this Commandment:
(1) Thou shalt have no other gods before me.

(2) Thou shalt not make unto thee any graven image, or any likeness of any thing that is in heaven above, or that is in the earth beneath, or that is in the water under the earth.

(3) Thou shalt not take the name of the Lord thy God in vain [He is the Greatest]. His only true name is His Sacred Name!

2- **Surrendering**: <8> **Do not go to complete prostration (submit) to anyone or thing except Him, the words revealed through His Prophets, and The Greatest Sign, which clarifies the confusion between all.**
a. <9> To surrender to anyone else but Him causes us to follow that person's whims and desires, which might not be the Will of God. <10> But surrendering only to Him takes us completely out of the influences of this external world and Maya. He then becomes our only Lord and King, so we will follow Him and His Will.
b. <11> Also because we might not know what His Will is, we surrender ourselves to the words which are revealed to us through His Prophets, which are really His Words, especially the Prophets of the seven seals in **The Greatest Sign**.
c. <12> Also we surrender ourselves to the meaning behind **The Greatest Sign**, which clarifies the confusion between the words revealed

to us through His Prophets. <13> If we do not follow **The Greatest Sign**, then we will become confused about the revelations of the many Prophets and their apparent differences.

d. <14> The Commandment, "Thou shalt not bow down thyself to other gods, nor serve them" is covered with this Commandment. The words "to bow down" here mean to surrender because we serve only those to whom we surrender.

3- **Goal of the Life:** <15> **Remember the goal of the life, which is to reach Pure Consciousness and help others to reach the same.**

<16> That is the highest goal in human life. Other goals in life are secondary and less important than this one, but they might still be necessary, especially when they help us in this goal.

4- **Messengers:** <17> **Consider the Prophets, Satgurus, Avatars or likewise as God's Messengers to bring His Messages and Laws to humanity.**

a. <18> We should surrender ourselves to the words revealed to us through His Prophets, but not to the Prophets themselves. The Prophets, Gurus, Avatars, or likewise are important because they show us His Will, not because of themselves.

b. <19> Also, even if the Lord God Himself came to the earth He would not reveal His identity as a person, because that would bring disunity between humans. <20> That is why God emphasizes that we should worship Him as the Invisible, Nameless, Formless God. With this, humanity will become unified.

c. <21> Furthermore, the Prophets, Avatars, Gurus, etc., are not their bodies but are the invisible Souls, which are one with Him. But if we mistake them as God, then we will create disunity, because of their apparent shapes, names, and visible bodies.

<22> For the same reason, idol worshipping should be prohibited, especially because the idols do not even have the invisible Souls as Gurus, Prophets, etc., have.

5- **Elects:** <23> **Accept Paravipras as the Chosen Ones to establish and enforce the Laws, spread the Messages of God, and establish the Kingdom Of Heaven.**

a. <24> Paravipras are the implementers of the Will of the Lord.

b. <25> They are the spiritual beings (Brahmins) with Shudran, Ksattriyan, Vipran, and Vaeshyan abilities.

c. <26> They have gone through many incarnations in the last twelve thousand years or before to reach this level of mastery.

d. <27> They prefer to be incarnated again and again to help the whole universe to reach the goal (Pure Consciousness) rather than themselves individually reaching it. They are true Bodhisattvas.

Tablet Five

Five Observing Commandments (Yama):

6- **Non-violence (Ahimsa):** <1> **Not violating the Daharma.**

a. <2> Non-injury, not inflicting pain on others, etc., are Daharmas themselves. They are not the true meaning of "Ahimsa." Also sometimes to inflict pain or injury is the only way to cure the disease.

b. <3> "Not fighting" is not the meaning of Ahimsa. Fighting to establish the righteousness is not against Ahimsa, nor is fighting against aggressors or in self-defense.

c. <4> The Commandment, "Honor thy father and thy mother" is one of the Laws (Daharmas) of the universe. After the Father (Lord God) and spiritual teacher, the parents are the highest to honor. <5> However, to honor does not mean to follow them if they are not walking with the Lord.

d. <6> And the Commandment, "Thou shalt not murder" which is a great violence of the Laws of the Lord, is covered under this Commandment.

7- **Truthfulness, With Discriminating Mind:** <7> **To guide all thought, speech, and action with the spirit of welfare.**

a. <8> Even truthfulness can be of three kinds, like everything else. It can be from ignorance, passion, or knowledge.

b. <9> Only truthfulness from knowledge is acceptable.

c. <10> Untruthfulness for selfish desires is not a part of this Commandment. That is in the category of discrimination of truthfulness from passion, and that is sin.

8- **Not to Steal (Non-stealing, physically, mentally, or spiritually):** <11> **Do not take things which belong to others, by thought, by taking (action), or by preventing them from doing their duties or possessing things which belong to them.**

a. <12> Non-stealing physically: Not to take what rightfully belongs to others.

b. <13> Mentally: Not to take other people's ideas or realizations as one's own.

c. <14> Spiritually: Not to prevent someone from doing his duties.

d. <15> The Commandment, "Thou shalt not steal" of the Ten Commandments is a part of this Commandment.

9- **Non-indulgence:** <16> **Not to indulge in the enjoyment of such amenities and comforts as are superficial to the preservation of life.**

a. <17> The physical wealth on the earth is limited. If one indulges in the use of this physical wealth, others will be deprived even of their basic necessities.

b. <18> Also the person who indulges will become dull-minded and lazy, and this creates misery and unhappiness in that person.

c. <19> So indulgence is bad for society, the world, and the individual.

d. <20> To give charity and help to others with our excess will cure these problems on an individual and societal level.

10- **Attach to God:** <21> **To keep the mind immersed in the ideation of God, to remain attached to God, and to accept Him as the only Refuge, the only King, and His Laws as the only Laws.**

a. <22> This is the only approvable attachment. Any other attachment without ideation on Him will prevent the person from reaching Pure Consciousness. To be attached to Him is the only way to overcome the Maya.

b. <23> By following this Commandment the other four observing Commandments can be met perfectly. It is the most important of the observing Commandments.

c. <24> To see Him in everything and everything in Him, so love all things because everything is a part of Him and be attached to them because of Him.

<u>Five Actional Commandments (Niyama):</u>

11- **Internal and External Cleanliness:** <25> **To maintain purity and cleanliness of mind, body, and environment.**

a. <26> The Soul becomes unclean faster than the mind, and the mind faster than the body.

b. <27> To think about God all the time is like being spiritually in the shower of His Grace all the time.

c. <28> To do impure actions, not follow the Daharma, or do harm to others will affect our own Souls more than the victim.

d. <29> The Commandments, "Remember the Sabbath day, to keep it holy" (to rest and contemplate God), "Thou shalt not commit adultery," "Thou shalt love thy neighbor as thyself," and "Do not desire anything which rightfully belongs to him," and also other Commandments, are all related to this Commandment and are for purification.

12- **Contentment and Mental Ease:** <30> **To remain in a state of mental equilibrium and contentment.**

a. <31> To be surrendered to any situation and keep the mind at ease, and to ideate that all things happening in our lives are for our own good as lessons and experiences to further our progress.

b. <32> To be able to contemplate the situation without acting unwisely (jumping into the situation), and to decide with an equilibrated mind and clear vision.

c. **<33>** To be in a meditative mood all the time.

13- Satsang, Service, and Meditation: **<34>** To attain true Satsang (when people talk only about God, the universe, and His Will), to practice penance in the service of others (as being done for the Lord, in creating Communities of Light), to sincerely meditate and/or do The Reminder at least twice a day.

a. **<35>** True Satsang is when the conversation is centered on God.

b. **<36>** Service is from knowledge when it is done for a person who really needs it, with no expectation for return. Any expectation for return of a service done makes it a business (passion). Service done when it is not needed is service from ignorance.

c. **<37>** Meditation is the fastest way to develop spiritual understandings.

14- Understanding God and His Laws through the Scriptures and history: **<38>** To clearly understand the underlying meaning of the Scriptures and discourses of spirituality.

a. **<39>** To understand **The Greatest Sign** and the relationship of different Scriptures with it.

b. **<40>** To understand the symbolic meanings behind the Scriptures' symbols.

c. **<41>** To become professional in discussing and understanding their relationships.

d. **<42>** Sabbath (Saturday) is a day for reading and contemplating the Scriptures.

15- To Be(come) Divine: **<43>** To strive to become perfect in our actions as God is, to ideate that He does the Divine Actions through us, and to become a perfect instrument for His Will to be done, until able to radiate His Divine Universal Truth through ourselves.

a. **<44>** To be(come) the same as the Father, to strive to be(come) perfect in our natures and actions as God is.

b. **<45>** To keep the mind immersed in the ideation of God while engaging in actions (to ideate that God works through us by using our bodies for Divine actions), **<46>** until able to radiate His Universal Truth through ourselves, and become a perfect instrument for Him to do His Will.

c. **<47>** "Be ye therefore perfect, even as your Father which is in heaven is perfect" (Matthew 5:48). This achievement is the goal of life and the result of following the **Fifteen Commandments** and the **Eternal Divine Path**.

Tablet Six

FOOD

<1> In general food can be categorized into three types:

1- Satvic (sentient): Fruit, milk and milk products, grains, most vegetables, most legumes, natural sweeteners, nuts and seeds, seaweed (except kelp), black pepper, green pepper, cooked dried mustard (in small quantities).

2- Rajasic (mutative): Chocolate, coffee and tea, soda pop (especially colas), lentils (tamasic at night), sea kelp, chilies, vinegar.

3- Tamasic (static, crudifying): Meat and fish, poultry, seafood, eggs, onions, garlic, mushrooms, tamari, red lentils, mustard spread, uncooked dried mustard, stale spoiled food, cayenne (in small quantities is rajasic), wine, beer and other alcoholic beverages, tobacco, blue cheese with mold.

<2> The satvic (sentient) foods are for consciousness and create sentient vibrations. **<3>** In fact in the beginning of creation when man was more consciousness than flesh, God demanded man to be vegetarian:

And God said, Behold, I have given you every herb bearing seed, which is upon the face of all the earth, and every tree, in the which is the fruit of a tree yielding seed; to you it shall be for meat. (Gen. 1:29)

<4> Flesh is tamasic in comparison with consciousness, and man became more flesh after the flood. Therefore, meat became nourishment for the body, and it was allowed to be consumed. <5> So tamasic food may be good for the flesh but not for the consciousness.

<6> Rajasic foods are usually the stimulants. They accelerate and release prana from places where stored in the body. So they usually give a burst of energy. By using the stored prana, the defense system of the body is weakened.

<7> The animals are divided into clean and unclean. Those which are clean have flesh that is easier to digest and is convertible to human flesh. <8> Those which are unclean are not good for human consumption.

<9> The clean animals are:

These are the beasts which ye shall eat: the ox [beef], the sheep, and the goat,
The hart, and the roebuck, and the fallow deer, and the wild goat, and the pygarg [antelope], and the wild ox, and the chamois [mountain sheep].
And every beast that parteth the hoof, and cleaveth the cleft into two claws, and cheweth the cud among the beasts, that ye shall eat. (Deut. 14:4-6)

<10> The unclean animals are:

Nevertheless these ye shall not eat of them that chew the cud, or of them that divide the cloven hoof [except the camel if it is a part of the regular diet of a people]; and the hare and the coney: for they chew the cud, but divide not the hoof; therefore they are unclean unto you.
And the swine, because it divideth the hoof, yet cheweth not the cud, it is unclean unto you: ye shall not eat of their flesh, nor touch their dead carcass. (Deut. 14:7-8)

<11> Clean fishes are:

...all that have fins and scales... (Deut. 14:9)

<12> There are six characteristics for clean birds:

1- They should not be birds of prey.
2- They catch food thrown to them in the air and bring it to the earth, then divide it with their bills and eat it. Unclean birds devour their catch in the air, or press it with one foot to the ground and tear it with their bills.
3- They must have an elongated middle front toe and a hind toe.
4- They must spread their toes so that three front toes are on one side of a perch and the hind toe on the other side.
5- They must have craws or crops.
6- They must have a gizzard with a double lining which can easily be separated.

<13> Animals that are dead or their blood has not been drained should not be eaten. <14> To drain the blood, the Adam's apple in the throat area should be cut in the middle.

<15> In an emergency when there is no other alternative, all these rules can be relaxed, and even a dead carcass might be eaten.

<16> However, it is advisable to have an emphasis on vegetables in our diets or more sentient (satvic) foods. But if it is desirable to eat meat, the above rules should be followed.

<17> Also the weather, environment, availability of food, etc., are factors to determine the diet of a person. For example, some tamasic or rajasic foods become rajasic or sentient respectively in cold or extremely cold weather. <18> So any diet should not become a burden, but the joy of food in the ideation of God is more important.

<19> Also, the Goal Of The Life Is To Be(come) Divine (righteous), although what

we eat usually affects the amount of control we have over our thoughts and actions. But if a man is righteous and follows God's Laws, yet eats everything, he is exalted over the man who eats vegetables but is unrighteous.

<20> Tamasic and rajasic foods, overeating, or food which is not chewed thoroughly, stimulates the lower energy centers (chakras). <21> However, those who are in their higher selves will always have their energies directed upward toward higher centers. That is why even when they eat these kinds of food, still they are not affected (by His Grace) very severely or at all.

<22> But those who are not able to transform the energy from the lower centers to higher ones are greatly affected by these foods or by overeating. <23> That is why being vegetarian is recommended for these people, so they can easily transfer the lower energies to the higher, because the vegetables, grains, etc., are sentient (satva) and are easily directed to the higher energies.

<24> This is the reason why in the Bible Paul called those who eat herbs weak in belief, "For one believeth that he may eat all things: another, who is weak, eateth herbs" (Romans 14:2).

<25> The reason is that those who are truly believers are the ones who are in their higher selves (were born again). But the vegetarian diet is for those who are in the beginning of the journey.

<26> However, emphasis on vegetables in our diets (even for those in their higher selves) is recommended. <27> But meat-eating is not condemned, especially for those who have no guilty conscience about it, because, "Not that which goeth into the mouth defileth a man; but that which cometh out of the mouth, this defileth a man" (Matthew 15:11).

<28> Or in other words, "The Goal Of The Life Is To Be(come) Divine." That is only possible by following the **Divine Path** and gaining His Grace, not by diet **alone**.

<29> Furthermore, the true food and highest nutritious food is the Holy Manna or nectar. Whoever eats such a food has "meat to eat that ye know not of [from the Father]" (John 4:32).

Tablet Seven
GIFT-GIVING

<1> There is a gift which binds your Soul, and there is a gift which frees you.

<2> Do not accept those gifts which bind you, but only the ones which free your Soul.

<3> Like everything else, gift-giving is of three kinds. When a gift is given to the right person, at the right time, at the right place (with the right ideation), it is good and is from knowledge.

<4> When a gift is given for a return or favor (with the wrong ideation), it is from passion.

<5> Gifts given to the wrong person, at the wrong place, at the wrong time, are gifts from ignorance.

<6> All gifts given to the Lord, or those who have overcome and use gifts for glorifying the Lord, are from knowledge.

HOSPITALITY

<7> Hospitality is a virtue. Be hospitable from knowledge. Keep the company of other spiritually awakened beings and share together your material blessings. <8> Help each other in the path and talk about God, His wonders, and glorify only Him. Do not glorify men.

<9> Even if you have nothing to offer to those who come to your house, offer them a glass of water. <10> Hospitality warms the heart and brings out the best in others.

MUSIC

<11> The universe is nothing but vibration (ॐ). <12> The reason for so many diverse manifestations is only because each of them are in a different level of vibration.

<13> As when we put a pendulum in motion, and if there is another pendulum with the same frequency close to this one, it will start to move without even a touch, so music also vibrates different chakras (energy centers) in the body.

<14> The music and songs that affect lower chakras will bring the consciousness down, and unspiritual thoughts and uncontrollable emotions will arise in the person.

<15> The music that is about God, played with spiritual instruments, or accompanying a mantra, will raise the consciousness to higher levels (higher consciousness) and make the person come closer to God.

<16> Therefore only such music is recommended to be listened to so that the human can also in this aspect keep his consciousness immersed in God-realization.

<17> However, in general it is not recommended to forget the self and become hypnotized by the music too often. To stay in this state often makes the music a tool for escaping from reality, and the person becomes a daydreamer instead of dealing with the real world.

<18> Also usually instruments that create sounds by vibrating the air, such as drums, flutes, the organ, etc., are more spiritual than instruments with strings (of course there are exceptions). <19> However, the harp, bells, cymbals, sitar, and such instruments also can be considered to be in higher levels.

<20> The songs which are used in music also should glorify the Lord, spirit, and universe, but not man, or stimulate unworthy earthly emotions. <21> The highest music is the Music of Heaven (of the spheres).

OCCUPATION (WORK)

<22> It is the duty of each person to take up an occupation and become perfect in that work. <23> It does not matter what it is a man does but how perfectly he does it.

<24> "Work is worship," so the work should be done without any attachment to the result. Work in silence for the sake of the work and its usefulness in perfection. <25> The reward will come a hundredfold when the work is done in this beneficial way. Those who work for reward will never understand the joy of work.

<26> Do the work at hand each day. Solve each day's problems in that day. <27> Never delay in solving daily problems, and do not put them off for later days.

<28> When you are perfect in your occupation, no one can make you a slave, because you will be in demand for your perfect work.

<29> The earthly occupations are especially recommended for men who are married. <30> But those who have accepted a renunciate (sannyasin) life should have an occupation of guiding others to the path of enlightenment and be full-time workers for the Lord.

PRAYER

<31> (This is an example for prayer. Pray to become an instrument for His Will; other things that you need will be given to you. Be surrendered to what happens to you, they are all good.)

Praise be to Thee, O Hidden and Manifested ONE. Praise be to Thy Glory, to Thy Might, to Thy Power, and to Thy Great Skill.

O Lord, to Thee all greatness, power, beauty, and perfection belongs. Thou art ALL.

Give us, O Lord, a steadfast heart, which no unworthy affection may drag downwards; give us an unconquered will, which no tribulation can wear out; give us an upright mind, which no unworthy purpose may tempt aside. Unto Thee we surrender.

(Source: Partly taken from a Sufi Invocation and a prayer of St. Thomas Aquinas.)

Tablet Eight
THE REMINDER

1- We pay our salutations to The Divine Father [The Divine Logic], who has helped all come from ignorance to the Path of Enlightenment. Ignorance is the state of unawareness of the reality behind this universe, and enlightenment is the state of Pure Consciousness.

2- We open our hearts to Your Grace [The Divine Mother, The Holy Ghost] and pray for Your Guidance in overcoming the power of the tama guna [crudifying force, principalities] over our Souls and detaching ourselves from Maya [illusion of separation from God].

3- We adore and promise to endeavor to help the whole universe to reach higher consciousness and eventually Pure Consciousness.

4- In reverence we bow our heads in front of all those Great Souls in the past and those to come who have helped and will help all to understand Your Compassion and Mercy in Your Actions and Creation.

5- We surrender ourselves to You, the Words revealed to us through Your Prophets, and Your **Greatest Sign** which clarifies the confusion between all.

6- We submit only to You which is formless, nameless, and invisible, [neither male nor female]. You in this state unify – in any other state, humanity will be divided. Also, this will prevent us from surrendering to false prophets and teachers.

7- However, in reverence we bow our heads in front of all those Great Souls who will teach us how to know You and show us the way to become Pure Consciousness, as is the goal.

EXPLANATION OF THE REMINDER

1- **We pay our salutations to The Divine Father [The Divine Logic], who has helped all come from ignorance to the Path of Enlightenment. Ignorance is the state of unawareness of the reality behind this universe, and enlightenment is the state of Pure Consciousness.**

1-1 We pay our salutations to The Divine Father [The Divine Logic],...
<1> "We" refers to all who do this **Reminder** or believe in its meaning. <2> The Divine Father, who is in heaven (Pure Consciousness), has complete power over the universe. Through the Universal Mind, He helped, is helping, and will help all unit consciousnesses to reach Pure Consciousness. He does it only from His Compassion for the unit consciousnesses (which we are). So He deserves to be saluted as the Greatest Master and Lover of this universe.

<3> In fact, this first sentence is the meaning of our greeting to each other, "Sal-Om," which means, "We pay our salutations to that Divine Vibration, God within you. It is The Word, which is with the Lord God and is He. Also it is us."

1-2 …who has helped all come from ignorance to the Path of Enlightenment.

<4> It is the Father who helps us come from ignorance (the un-awakened state, death) to the path, and He helps us in the path toward the state of enlightenment (complete awareness). <5> In fact that is the only Divine purpose behind the creation of this whole universe, including the human body. He not only guides Elected Ones to reach Pure Consciousness, but He also is concerned for those who are lost. He is trying to bring "all" to Pure Consciousness.

1-3 Ignorance is the state of unawareness of the reality behind this universe…

<6> What is the reality behind this universe? It is **Haree Om Shrii Hung**, the most important goal of the life is to be(come) Divine. <7> Therefore, those who follow other goals in their lives above this goal are in the state of ignorance.

1-4 …and enlightenment is the state of Pure Consciousness.

<8> The goal of life is to reach Pure Consciousness. It is the state of complete awareness. It is the state of being most Divine. It is when a person becomes a son of God. So all the manifested and unaware ("I am") parts of the universe are in the path of becoming Divine. Who helped them and is still helping them to that stage? It is the Father, the Lord God. <9> He uses the power of the satva guna as The Holy Ghost to guide us to this stage. When we suffer, it is a good sign for us to know that either we are going off the path or we are burning the reaction of our previous actions (samskaras). In the first case we should repent and correct ourselves. In the other case we should rejoice that this suffering is a sign of progress and a lesson, and we should be aware of our actions so as to not create any more reactions by pursuing a Divine life, doing Divine actions, and rendering the results to God.

2- **We open our hearts to Your Grace [The Divine Mother, The Holy Ghost] and pray for Your Guidance in overcoming the power of the tama guna over our Souls and detaching ourselves from Maya.**

2-1 We open our hearts to Your Grace (The Divine Mother, The Holy Ghost)…

<10> You have to go to the Lord with an open heart. If not, you will not be able to receive His Grace, which is the guarantee for reaching the goal. <11> So we open our hearts to His Divine Grace which is The Holy Ghost, The Divine Mother.

2-2 …and pray for Your Guidance in overcoming the power of the tama guna over our Souls…

<12> It is true that this universe was made to be self-sustaining, and our actions will create reactions for which we should receive punishment or reward. But with His Grace we can burn our samskaras (sins) in a second if He so desires. <13> He has complete power over the tama guna, so He can release its grip over our Souls in a blink of an eye. <14> However, we should become ready to withstand the power of truth which will be revealed to us in higher consciousness. It would be very difficult for us to understand that Great Truth before we are ready. We can reach there by His Grace gradually, with His Guidance, which is The Holy Ghost (The Divine Mother). <15> To pray for His Guidance is the only boon or request that we have to ask from God. The destructive part of the tama guna is used for guidance when mistakes are made, which brings suffering. If no mistake is made, there would be no suffering but Bliss. That is why the tama guna should be overcome.

2-3 …and detaching ourselves from Maya.
<16> Maya is the attraction of the external world, or illusion of separation from Him. One of the greatest struggles of the spiritual path is being detached from this attraction while staying in the middle of it (society). It needs much overcoming and Grace to do so.

3- **We adore and promise to endeavor to help the whole universe to reach**

ESSAYS 3

higher consciousness and eventually Pure Consciousness.

3-1 We adore…
<17> We worship the whole universe which is God (consciousness and the three gunas). <18> Also we think about its perfection and beauty and of how great is His Power and Logic to create such a perfect universe. This then helps us to realize Him more.

3-2 …and promise to endeavor to help the whole universe to reach higher consciousness and eventually Pure Consciousness.
<19> The goal of the life is to be(come) Divine and help others to be(come) the same. Who are these others? They are the infinite unit consciousnesses which make up the whole universe. <20> So each person will not only try to help other humans to reach higher consciousness, but he will direct his actions in such a way that the whole universe will accelerate its progress. For example, taking care of an animal or plant can be considered to be such a help, or any other such Divine action.

4- **In reverence we bow our heads in front of all those Great Souls in the past and those to come who have helped and will help all to understand Your Compassion and Mercy in Your Actions and Creation.**

4-1 In reverence we bow our heads in front of all those Great Souls…
<21> We do not discriminate between all Great Souls. Whoever helped humanity to progress materially, mentally, or spiritually, is worthy to be respected. We even revere those who brought seemingly contradictory ideas, but these apparent contradictions are either situational or from our ignorance. <22> The reality behind this universe can be described in many different ways (or the descriptions seem different because of the mission of the Messenger). Whoever brought some progress to humanity, no matter where and when, we revere that Great Soul for it. "To revere" here means to pay respect, it does not mean to surrender to the person whom we revere. If his words are God's and are according to the **Eternal Divine Path**, we follow!

4-2 …in the past and those to come…
<23> Not only do we pay homage to the Great Souls in the past, but also we pay respect to those to come. <24> This means that none of the great personalities in any sphere of life – material, mental, or spiritual – have been the last. Nor will there ever be a last Great Soul in the future either.

4-3 …who have helped and will help…
<25> These great people have helped humanity in the past, and they will be reincarnated again and again to help humanity in the future. They are the Elected Ones.

4-4 …all to understand…
<26> They have helped the **whole** universe to understand, not just a special group or religion, but all of humanity.

4-5 …Your Compassion and Mercy in Your Actions and Creation.
<27> Why is the Lord God compassionate and merciful in His creation? Because He created this whole universe by compassion. It was created only because He had compassion for other lost un-awakened consciousnesses and wanted to help them reach that beautiful state of being (Pure Consciousness). So He created this universe and the evolutionary process.

<28> He has compassion and mercy in His actions too. He closed the human's understanding of his occult powers, not because He wanted to see them powerless, but because humans, like children, were foolishly misusing them, so for their own good He took these powers away from them, like good parents who take matches away from their children in order to prevent them from burning themselves. <29> That is why even suffering and those events that seem unfair to us in the world are done by compassion in order for the human to understand that he is walking on the wrong path. <30> The only way is the path of

the Spirit. Neither the way of mental knowledge nor material gain will bring everlasting happiness. Those ways should be used only for spiritual progress.

Tablet Nine

5- We surrender ourselves to You, the Words revealed to us through Your Prophets, and Your Greatest Sign, which clarifies the confusion between all.

5-1 We surrender ourselves to You…

<1> He is the only being to whom you should surrender. He is the Greatest Master of the universe. Even Satgurus and Avatars are proud to be His disciples. Therefore, by surrendering to Him you will gain the best spiritual Master in the universe. <2> Also He is the only being that you can trust as not being a false prophet or teacher.

5-2 …the Words revealed to us through Your Prophets…

<3> Also we surrender to "the Words revealed to us through Your Prophets." We do not surrender to the Prophets themselves, but to the Words revealed through them by the Lord. Therefore, the Messenger is important only because he reveals the Words of the Lord to us and what God wants us to do and become. <4> The Messenger himself is important only because he is a Great Soul, and we revere all Great Souls who have helped humanity progress toward a higher level. We respect them because they helped us to know the Lord better and showed us how to reach Pure Consciousness.

<5> However, we surrender ourselves to their Words, because these Words have come from the Lord. We have to understand and follow them in order to be(come) Divine and realize God's Laws. Therefore, the teachings of the Prophets are much more important than the Prophets themselves.

<6> Even if the Lord Himself came to this world and brought some teachings to humanity, He would not tell who He is, because the only source that can unify is the **Invisible** God. Anything else will cause disunity, and God wants to see all of humanity unified and having learned their lessons through creation and history.

5-3 …and Your **Greatest Sign**…

<7> We also surrender to **The Greatest Sign**, because by understanding **The Greatest Sign** and the realities behind it, we can realize Him. <8> In fact one of the greatest problems of the human is that it is very hard for him to surrender to something that he cannot see. However, **The Greatest Sign** is a visualized form which shows that the Invisible Lord is in Pure Consciousness and how He has manifested all through creation and history to bring us to this point. Only with a complete understanding of **The Greatest Sign** are we able to see how compassionate and merciful He is and to understand His purpose of this creation. Only then can we surrender to that Invisible Being which has done all these things for us.

5-4 …which clarifies the confusion between all.

<9> What confusion? Confusion about: Why are we here? What is the purpose of life? What is the destiny of man? Why are there so many different Prophets and Scriptures? What is the purpose of creation? What is The Plan?, etc. <10> These questions can be answered and understood through **The Greatest Sign**. That is why **The Greatest Sign** will clarify the confusion between all and the words revealed to us through the Prophets.

6- We submit only to You which is formless, nameless, and invisible. You in this state unify – in any other state, humanity will be divided. Also, this will prevent us from surrendering to false prophets and teachers.

6-1 We submit only to You which is formless, nameless, and invisible.

<11> God is consciousness, as is everything in the universe. He just "Is," so He has no form. <12> He has been here even before names. Names were created by man to distinguish things from one another. That is why He called Himself the God of Abraham, Isaac, and Jacob, and also when Moses asked what was His name, He answered, "I am that I am" (Exodus 3:14). <13> But all the nations had gods with names, so the Children of Israel insisted that their God should have a name also. In truth He has no name (in another state He has a name or has names). <14> It is true that God is everything. But God as the Father is a Soul and Spirit. The Soul and Spirit are invisible and formless.

<15> Also by submitting to Him, we become a channel for His Divine actions, and there is no "I" left. So there would be no reaction for the actions we do. We would be free from any reaction of our action and detached from its result, because we are not the doer but He is. <16> However, if the action is selfish and is done for the self, an "I" will be present. So we are responsible for those actions. We can only submit ourselves to Him for Divine actions.

6-2 You in this state unify – in any other state, humanity will be divided.

<17> God is all-pervasive and is everything. But only the Father, the nucleus of the universe, as a formless, nameless, and invisible God, can unify. God in any other state, such as with a form (any kind of form), with a name (any pronounceable name in physical manifestation), or visible, will create division between humans. As the goal in the era to come is to unify all, humanity should realize that God (Father) has no form, is nameless, and is invisible. His only form is transcendental, and His True Name (יהוה) is not pronounceable.

<18> When a pronounceable name is given to God as His Name, only a few people will believe in that as the Name of God. Some other people will give Him another name. So they will become divided and the problem of separation and division will start. This is true about accepting a form for God (such as idols) or believing He appears in forms. <19> All of these are one of the sources of division between religions and beliefs.

<20> Therefore the ultimate realization is that He is formless, nameless, and invisible as any Soul, which is formless, nameless, and invisible.

<21> However, it should be realized that most of the names that are given to God are actually mantras (sound vibrations, sacred names) which affect the spirit and awaken the spiritual forces in man. They are useful in spiritual progress and are a part of God in the manifested universe, <22> but God in the absolute state is formless, nameless, and invisible.

6-3 Also, this will prevent us from surrendering to false prophets and teachers.

<23> If we surrender and submit ourselves to the Lord which is formless, nameless, and invisible, to His Words which are revealed to us through His Prophets, and with reference to **The Greatest Sign** which clarifies the confusion between these Words (teachings), then we can safely approach the real truth that God has revealed through creation and history. <24> We can easily be prevented from following (surrendering to) false prophets and teachers.

7- However, in reverence we bow our heads in front of all those Great Souls who will teach us how to know You and show us the way to become Pure Consciousness, as is the goal.

7-1 However, in reverence we bow our heads in front of all those Great Souls…

<25> Again there is no discrimination. We pay our respects to all the Great Souls, alive or dead. <26> We revere their divinity (invisible) and their physical presence.

7-2 …who will teach us how to know You…

<27> How can a person make another person realize God? <28> By manifesting the qualities of God that he has gained through his progress toward higher consciousness. <29> So only Great Souls can manifest these

qualities. They teach who God is by their conduct, their light, and their knowledge. <30> That is why a visible spiritual teacher sometimes is so important.

7-3 ...and show us the way to become Pure Consciousness...
<31> After we begin to understand You through these Great Souls and accept them as our teachers, then they will guide us in the path of self-realization and toward reaching Pure Consciousness. <32> Again only Great Souls can do that. <33> All Prophets are in this status.

7-4 ...as is the goal.
<34> That is "the" goal in life. All other goals are secondary.

Tablet Ten
SABBATH AND SABBATH COMMUNITY UNITY MEETING

<1> After Sabbath, a day of fasting, prayer, and rest on Saturdays, the community gathers together for their regular weekly meeting. <2> Before the formal meeting begins, they read the words below. This will bring into focus and reiterate the purpose of Sabbath. It also reminds all that the meeting is for strengthening the community and furthering the resolution of any problems that might exist in the community. It teaches members not to be attached to their proposals and to learn to work with a group with diverse opinions and levels of consciousness. That group will grow together. <3> **Communities of Light** are the base of the Kingdom Of Heaven On Earth:

<4> As God created the universe in six stages (periods, days) we also work to establish His Kingdom for six days each week and rest on the Sabbath (as He did on the seventh day).
<5> After He finished the creation, He sat back on the seventh period (day) and contemplated His creation. <6> We also have to use the Sabbath to contemplate the last six days of our lives and see how we spent them. Did we use them for His Purpose and/or Will?
<7> We eventually have to reach a point where we feel as God felt about His Work. We look and see that it has been blessed by God. When God created the universe and saw that it was Good (God), He blessed it and was pleased. <8> He did not look for approval or disapproval from anyone. He did not need to be praised by anyone. But He was pleased with Himself that He had done a perfect job.
<9> That also should be our approach to life. We do the job (His Will) but leave the results to Him. <10> On the Sabbath we re-evaluate our work and improve it to a higher level, as God also is perfect.
<11> We meditate on our week and contemplate on the problems in the community. We recognize the ones related to our own emotions and have nothing to do with community. <12> We find the true (real) problems. Then we can further contemplate what kind of solution we can offer.
<13> In the evening after the Sabbath is over, at the time of the community meeting, we will bring up these real problems to discuss them with others. We will not be attached to our findings but we will leave them on the table for all to see.
<14> This will result in "brain storming." The problem will be discussed. Maybe it is not really a problem. Maybe there are deeper reasons for its existence which we either did not realize or still are not realizing. Maybe it is a

legitimate problem, but the community is not ready to see it yet.

<15> Therefore, if a solution is not found and/or a proposal is not accepted or is replaced by some other solution, we gracefully accept the situation. <16> We will further meditate on the situation, and if further reason is found to bring the matter to the meeting, we will do so at the next Sabbath community meeting.

<17> We always have to accept the limitations and sacrifices necessary to live in a community. We also have to consider the blessings it will bring to us, to the community, and to the earth in whole.

<18> Only then can we create **Communities of Light**. **Communities of Light** are the base of the Kingdom Of Heaven On Earth.

Tablet Eleven
SAMGACCHADVAM
(Could be sung before collective meditation or after **The Reminder**)

SAMGACCHADVAM SAMVADADHVAM
Let us move together, let us sing together.

SAMVOMANAMSI JANATAM
Let us come to know our minds together.

DEVABHAGAM YATHAPURVE
Let us share, like Sages of the past,

SAMJANANA UPASATE
That all people together may enjoy the universe,

SAMANII VA AKUTI
Unite our intention,

SAMANA HRDAYANIVAH
Let our hearts be inseparable.

SAMANAMASTU VO MANO
Our mind is as one mind,

YATHAVAH SUSAHASATI
As we, to truly know one another, become One.

(from Rg Veda)

SPIRITUAL CHANTING AND DANCING (KIRTAN)

<1> In most religions, especially the mystical side of them, we find spiritual music, chanting, and dancing. <2> Even in the Old Testament in the Bible, the verse below shows that this tradition existed:

...that thou shalt meet a company of prophets coming down from the high place with a psaltery, and a tabret, and a pipe, and a harp, before them; and they shall prophesy: (Samuel 10:5)

<3> The Dervishes are well-known for how they dance, go into a trance, and sometimes prophesy. Also in the Buddhist and Hindu traditions we can find spiritual chanting and dancing. <4> In Sanskrit this is called "kirtan."

<5> Even in the beginning of Christianity this tradition was practiced. But as it became intellectualized, this aspect was less emphasized and eventually forgotten.

<6> So we can see that this practice has been in all great religions of the world. The reason for this is because there are many spiritual benefits in kirtan.

<7> With chanting, special words (mantras), playing instruments, and dancing, all three aspects of human life, physical, mental, and spiritual, will be engaged in a rhythmic

movement. <8> So they all become in tune and a balance between them is achieved.

<9> This rhythmic movement also increases the coordinative ability of the person, because a greater coordination between the mind and body will be achieved when a person is practicing the kirtan. He should chant, dance, and play the instrument at the same time, so he has to improve his coordination.

<10> Also spiritual chanting and dancing brings the mind into the present and now. <11> That is the secret of controlling the mind. The mind that wanders into the past or worries about the future never can realize the self and joy of living: "Be still and know that I am God…" (Psalm 46:10). <12> So kirtan helps the mind become still and know the Lord.

<13> Also as we know, the whole manifested universe is nothing but vibration. When spiritual music is used with some mantras and ideation toward God and higher thoughts, this stimulates the higher chakras and brings the higher thoughts and energy to the person.

<14> For the vibrational reason, music stimulates the glands and spiritual music helps in creating a balance between the glands, so therefore brings a healthier body and emotional response.

<15> Also because it takes the consciousness to higher levels, it loosens the dry intellect. <16> Although it is hard for intellectuals to give in, indeed it is very good for them, because they can forget themselves to be rational and lose themselves into the higher plane which is devotional.

<17> Indeed kirtan is the base to awaken devotional feelings in man. That is why those who practice this exercise receive a blissful feeling from it. <18> They rise from being on a rational plane to a devotional one where the joy and happiness cannot be realized by the state of man. It is indescribable.

<19> Kirtan also is an exercise and loosens up the muscles and joints in the body. Therefore the body becomes prepared to sit in meditation poses much easier. <20> After kirtan, a person is physically, mentally, emotionally, and spiritually more prepared to sit for meditation.

<21> Furthermore, when kirtan is done by a group, it brings a unified vibration to all involved. Even though each person might have come from different backgrounds with different vibrations, by doing kirtan together they come into the same rhythm of vibration, feeling one, and becoming one.

<22> So there is much merit in kirtan, but many people shy away from it because the ego dies fast and many do not want their egos to die.

<23> As it can be seen in the verse which was quoted above from the Bible, only a few high spiritual people ("Prophets") were following this practice. <24> Also few people in those religions who practice chanting and dancing are fully dedicated to kirtan.

<25> Therefore we can conclude that although this kind of practice is recommended, not very many people truly appreciate it. <26> That is because to let the ego go and create high devotion for God is very frightening for some, and also sometimes is not necessary in this degree. <27> We need people in other levels of consciousness also. The least one can do is to be tolerant.

Tablet Twelve
THIRTY-THREE VIRTUES

1- Fearlessness
2- Purification of one's existence
3- Cultivation of spiritual and intellectual knowledge
4- Charity
5- Self-control (perpetual restraint of behavior and temper)
6- Performance of sacrifice – selfless service, not being self-centered, to be(come) humble

7- Study of spiritual Scriptures
8- Austerity and simplicity
9- Non-violence (not violating the Daharma of things)
10- Truthfulness
11- Freedom from anger
12- Renunciation (to offer the result of your actions to the Lord, and ideate that your body is a tool for Him to perform Divine actions)
13- Tranquility (magnanimity of mind)
14- Aversion to faultfinding
15- Compassion and freedom from covetousness
16- Gentleness
17- Modesty and steady determination
18- Vigor
19- Forgiveness
20- Fortitude
21- Cleanliness
22- Freedom from envy
23- Patience for honor
24- Readiness to sacrifice everything of individual life for the ideology
25- Sweet and smiling behavior
26- Moral courage
27- Setting an example by individual conduct before asking anyone to do the same
28- Strict adherence to the **Fifteen Commandments**
29- Constant contemplation of **The Greatest Sign**
30- Even while dealing with a person of inimical nature, one must keep oneself free from hatred, anger, and vanity
31- Keep aloof from talkativeness (idle talk)
32- Obedience to the structural code of discipline
33- Sense of responsibility

UNIVERSAL CALL TO PRAYER

This is the Universal Call to prayer and meditation for All.

Come all those who are chosen and called to Pray to One God.

Those who strive to experience God.

Those who Struggle with God to bring His Kingdom.

Those who Sacrifice all for His Kingdom.

Those who are Surrendered and Submitted to God's Will.

Those who are Universalists and see Unity among all humanity.

This is the Call to the Chosen (Elects), be an example and help all to reach God.

We declare that there is no God but One God and **Maitreya** (Muhammad) is His Lion of the Tribe of Judah, the Seventh Angel, Opener of the Seven Seals, Revealer of the Book Sealed with Seven Seals, Fulfiller of all Prophecies, the Prince of Peace, The Christ.

Come All, this is a Universal Call to Prayer to the Formless, Invisible, Nameless, and Eternal (FINE)!

WASHING OF THE COLON

<1> One of the reasons for sickness and lethargy is toxins in the body. The greatest source of toxins in the body is from the colon. A clogged and inefficient digestive system can be very disturbing to the health of the body. <2> By cleaning the colon regularly, the digestive system will be greatly helped. This also keeps the most toxic part of the body clean and detoxified.

<3> However, the washing of the colon should not be performed too often. This will result in laziness of the muscles in this organ, and it will become dependent on this process. The best way is to do it whenever it seems right. <4> The rule of time is every two or three weeks or so.

WORSHIPPING
(Collective Meditation)

<5> Always approach the Lord when you are pure and in a good state of mind. If you are not in a good state of mind, chanting the "Haree Om Shrii Hung" (**HOSH**) mantra and/or dancing kirtan is recommended with ideating on its meaning. This would help to bring you to a good state of mind and devotion.

<6> **The Reminder** can be done in the morning, noon, evening, and at night.

<7> At night there should be places where the seekers can go for spiritual studies and Satsangs or stories about Great Souls. This causes people to be in good company either by reading good books and Scriptures or by being with other good Souls.

<8> On some evenings, there can be collective kirtan for those who like this kind of spiritual practice. It is recommended that the duration of these collective kirtans be at least three hours. <9> Also there can be a collective meditation (attunement and transmission) once a week. At least three people should be present to start a collective meditation. The best number is twelve and even better is the twelve people who form a unit as the base for selecting the leaders (read Mount Zion and Zion, and Explanation of the System).

<10> After collective meditation, the community problems and other concerns of the group can be discussed. So the leaders become aware of the problems and discuss them with other leaders of the community. They can find solutions for them, and then report the results back to others in the next Community Unity Meeting.

<11> Collective meditation can begin with performance of **The Reminder** by the group, singing of the "Samgacchadvam" before meditation, and then meditation for as long as the leader of the collective meditation feels is necessary. <12> Meditation finishes by recitation of the "Divine Path." After that there can be a community discussion, readings from Scriptures, spiritual discussions, or discourses, etc.

<13> If the circumstance does not permit a full course of collective meditation, a collective "**Reminder**" or any other combination, or only the community discussion, can be performed to suit the situation.

<14> It is recommended that the body be cooled (half-bath, etc.) before **The Reminder**, meditation, eating, and sleep. The mantra **HOSH-ONK** can be repeated all the time and its meaning concentrated on to keep the mind on higher thoughts.

<15> Prayer is like a shower for the Soul. Pray for guidance and that you might become an instrument for His Will. The sample prayer in this book entitled "Prayer" can be used. Pray for His Grace – It will be given to you if you need It.

<16> Meditation is different than prayer. It is the process of self-realization, seeing the wrongdoings of the self, and becoming repentant for them (consciously or unconsciously).

Therefore, they are overcome in the process without too much effort.

<17> So prayer, meditation, **The Reminder**, etc., each have their own place and combined together with following the **Eternal Divine Path**, with His Grace, will lead to the goal.

<18> Prayer is done in a kneeling position with hands intertwined, back straight, elbows resting on something comfortably in front of you, and forehead resting on your hands, with eyes closed and a deep feeling of His Presence, or pray in any other comfortable position. <19> Pray to the Father and call upon Him. True prayers will be heard and, if necessary, will be fulfilled.

YOGA POSTURES (ASANAS)

<20> As the muscles become stronger by exercise, the ethereal body becomes purified and stronger by yoga postures (asanas). That is why we can call asanas "innercise" in contrast to exercise which affects the external.

<21> These postures affect the glands which control the energy centers in the body (chakras) and bring a balance between the physical body, spirit (ethereal body) and Soul (Self).

<22> It is also recommended to practice asanas, especially in the beginning of the spiritual journey and so strengthen the spirit and become familiar with the body and how it functions.

<23> However, a person should not become obsessed with this kind of practice and use it only for physical fitness. Unless such a person is a professional teacher of asanas, the spiritual effect of this practice should be kept in mind more than the physical. <24> Like any practice or habit, it should not become a person's master.

<25> Eventually a person will become so familiar with the body that he realizes many other things affect it. <26> By avoiding ones which bring negative forces and accumulating more positive forces, the need of doing asanas can be eliminated or brought to a minimum and only used as an occasional tool to tune the body, spirit, and mind together. <27> It is not only practices that make a man free but knowledge of the Laws of the Lord and His Grace. These practices make a person become more sensitive to understand His Laws and become purer to feel His Grace, <28> so he might eventually find the way (**Eternal Divine Path**), receive The Holy Ghost, <29> and by trial of The Holy Ghost (His Grace), reach the Goal.

SUPPLEMENTS

The book, <u>Supplements,</u> is the last book in our Scripture, <u>The Holiest Of The Holies (THOTH), The Last Testament</u>. Maitreya discusses many topics in this book. It is an open-ended book, while Maitreya is alive, so Maitreya can add to it if a clarification, new revelation, etc. needs to be added to <u>THOTH</u>. In any new edition of <u>THOTH</u>, there might be some changes in this book.

These are additional essays or new revelations which were written to eliminate any confusion and/or expand <u>THOTH</u> further as future needs might demand. God is Infinite, so His Truth can be explained in infinite ways!

SUPPLEMENTS

INTRODUCTION

The material in this book is not a part of the main teaching and the Master Plan which is revealed in **The Holiest Of The Holies (THOTH), The Last Testament**. This material was written in response to situations that developed after **THOTH** was finished. It consists of further explanations of topics in **THOTH**, new essays, and writings which make the teaching more flexible to suit the situation (time, place, and people involved).

The materials in this book, with other literature (such as correspondence by **Maitreya**, articles, speeches, etc.), plus **Maitreya's** actions in general, all together provide a wealth of knowledge to guide the seeker of truth so we do not become rigid and inflexible in the path of God and in life on earth. God and earth, in one level of consciousness, are ONE.

A SLOGAN

FORMATION OF THE COMMUNITIES OF LIGHT IS THE WAY TO SALVATION:

PHYSICALLY, MENTALLY, AND SPIRITUALLY.

MISSION OF MAITREYA (MOM)

The Goal Of The Life Is To Be(come) Divine (**HOSH**). That Divinity is Everything (**ONK**).

The path to become Divine is the **Eternal Divine Path**. However, this path is useful only when it is practiced in a collective manner in communities. Otherwise the person who follows it might be exploited by opportunists, because the person sacrifices without his effort being channelized to bring the **Kingdom Of Heaven On Earth (KOHOE)**.

Therefore, the creation of **Communities of Light** based on the **Eternal Divine Path** will bring the **KOHOE** and so help humanity toward Divinity.

This essay is the very essence and purpose of the **Mission of Maitreya (MOM)**.

THE ONLY ISSUE

The only issue is the formation of the **Communities of Light**. Other issues are the effect, not the cause. The cause is the unfulfilled basic needs of individuals to be in a community with other like-minded people and the lack of creation of basic relationships in this level.

These communities cannot exist separately from one another. By linking themselves together they also will create the power to influence the events and correct the problems.

The ecological and pollution problems

SUPPLEMENTS

cannot be solved unless we spread the factories evenly all throughout the earth, especially to the deserts and isolated places, and also by developing clean industries by using Science based on Spirit. This will only be revealed to humanity if we learn our lessons and share. Otherwise this knowledge will be misused as has occurred in the past, and the misuse of anything results in suffering.

Intellectuals, who can only exist based on the confusion of the masses, bring many issues into our minds and make us confused about the simple issue of our basic needs and the cause of the issues. Then we become lost in the jungle of these confused issues and do not see the simple solutions.

Therefore, do not let the many issues confuse you. The issue and solution, is the formation of the **Communities of Light** based on the **Eternal Divine Path**, and networking between them. Then we can easily solve the other issues, which are the effects.

COVENANT WITH GOD, OR THE MISSION OF MAITREYA (MAITREYA)

Those who have seen the Vision of the **Mission** and have realized that this indeed is the Last Revelation of God are chosen and are called! They have a Covenant with God, the **Mission**, and **Maitreya**.

If you are one of them, you should realize that you have no choice but to join the **Mission** and have a covenant with Him, from Eternity (Foundation of the Creation!) You should profess that: *I declare that there is no God but God (Formless, Invisible, Nameless, and Eternal or FINE) and Maitreya (or Muhammad) is His Last Major Prophet (Messiah, Savior, Major Manifestation, etc.), and I believe in the Mantra, Haree Om Shrii Hung, Om Nam Kevalam, which means: The Goal Of The Life Is To Be(come) Divine (following the Eternal Divine Path), That Divinity Or God Is Everything.* You are accepted as a Disciple, a Member of the **Mission** (a Divine), and an Elect!

Since you have seen the Vision and are a part of it, you want this Vision to Manifest, and you want to help in any way possible in this task. Therefore you are required to offer all the help you can give. Furthermore, you become a volunteer to be a point of contact (a contact person) for the **Mission** where you are (if there is no danger for you to be a contact).

There will be two categories of people who have a covenant with **Maitreya (have seen the Vision)**:

1- The support group.

2- The Light Workers, which the Leaders and Teachers will also emerge from.

The support group consists of those who will support the **Mission** physically, mentally, and spiritually, but are not physically close to the **Mission** and they are not a part of its staff. They might live anywhere in the world, but are connected to the **Mission** by their work, dedication, and support. They should have a steady job. They are the ones who will mostly help the **Mission** financially. Their minimum financial help will be their tithes that God has demanded as His (of course, they can help more if they would like. In fact, anyone can help in any way they can). The Covenant and understanding of what is asked in this page with continuous tithes is required before one can be Initiated!

The Light Workers are those who will come close to the **Mission** center. From the Light Workers, the leaders and teachers will emerge, and will be called Light Guides (The Guiding Lights). Light Workers and Light Guides will be involved in all kinds of activities for the **Mission**. They will be the administrators, teachers, and staff of the **Mission**. They will have abilities to carry out these tasks with the highest level of professional integrity and Spiritual Guidance (letting God do it through them). They will create a well-oiled and efficient organization that can carry this Message to the end of the world with

SUPPLEMENTS

precision and the professional caliber of a business organization.

God indeed has given us the knowledge of creating efficient organizations. Ungodly people are using these principles to create multinational organizations to manipulate resources; we will use them to free man to God (remember, nothing is bad in this universe, it depends on how it is used according to time, place, and people involved – situation).

Until we reach a point that the administrators, teachers, and staff can be supported with the support group, these people will have to have some support mechanism so that they can do the **Mission** while at the same time are provided with their physiological and safety needs (could be minimal). When we reach a point that the support group is able to provide for the Light Workers, they will be chosen from the best and will be supported to do the best job they can.

This covenant will continue between you and God (**Maitreya**) forever. All those who will come in the future are also obligated to respond to the call of God and help the **Mission** to continue to spread. They also will have a covenant with God (**Mission**) forever.

Anyone who brings disunity to the One Body of God (**Mission**) or tries to dismember this United Body, and those who help such a person, will be fuel for the fire of hell. The **Mission of Maitreya**, **Eternal Divine Path** is One Body forever. If any disagreement starts, all should stop; they should all follow the **Eternal Divine Path** and become united as One Body again.

Tithes: For instructions on how to pay your tithes and/or automatic recurring payments for tithes, send an email to the **Mission** (tithes@maitreya.org).

WHY TITHES

The first time that tithes are mentioned is when Abram (Abraham) gave his tithes to the king of Salem (Genesis 14:20-24). He did that because Salem was considered the high priest in that time, and tithes were given to the priests and high priest.

We then can hear about the tithes all through the Bible (in Leviticus God commanded tithes – Lev. 27:31-34). Tithes are for the priest class (Num.18:24). One tenth (10%) of the tithes gathered will be for the head of the priesthood (Aaron – Eldest in our system) (Num. 28:26-28). Tithes are the minimum you can/should offer; you can offer more (Deut. 12: 6 and 11, tithes are at the top of other sacrifices/giving).

One part of tithes is to help and feed those in need (Deut. 26:12). People should be obedient to this Law and the importance of tithes (2 Chronicles 31). Again the same topic (Nehemiah 10:37-38, 12:44, Nehemiah 13:5, Amos 4:4).

Even in the New Testament (NT), not paying tithes is considered robbing God (Matthew 3:8). In the NT also it is encouraged to pay tithes (Matthew 3:10). Paying tithes does not release you from being humble in the presence of God and following His Laws and Commandments (Luke 18:12).

It is with Paul that the teaching of God is being challenged. Paul started preaching his understanding instead of God's and His Prophets' (Hebrew 7:5-9). In this chapter (Hebrew 7) Paul teaches what are his ideas, not God's! He argues that since Esa (Christ) was from the tribe of Judah (from his father Joseph) God changed His Mind and the Priests (Messiahs) do not have to come from Abram (Abraham) and since Abram (Abraham) gave tithes to Melchizedek, He (Abraham) was subjugated to Melchizedek and the priesthood has changed and they should come from Melchizedek, etc.

The Truth of the matter is that indeed Christ was from the tribe of the Levites since Mary, his mother, was a Levite. So Paul again is incorrect. Furthermore, God promised that the Messiah (Shiloh) will come from the tribe of Judah (Genesis 49:10). So God again fulfilled both requirements for Christ to be the

SUPPLEMENTS

Messiah, His Prophet, Christ, the Son of God, etc.

This is one of the discrepancies between the Words of God and Paul. There are many, and for these reasons, we do not accept Paul as Christ's representative and/or disciple/apostle. We only accept Christ's words (in red in the Bible) as from God, and Christ said He has not come to destroy the Laws (Matthew 5:17)!

Since Paul has no authority from God and Christ, he cannot abolish tithes, change the way God Prophesied and Chose Christ and the Priesthood (until Christ came) to stay with the Levites. And Christ came as the Lion of the Tribe of Judah (Christ).

Indeed tithes are what made the Hebrews a great nation. Tithes are the reason Mormons created a worldwide outreach. Tithes are the Command by God to see His Kingdom to manifest on earth. So those who want to follow God's Will, will accommodate His Revelation and follow as obedience to His Commands and pay their tithes and more.

Since the Mission is the Last Revelation from God and is the Revealer of the Mystery of God and the Implementer of God's Will and Kingdom, It is the only Religion (organization) that everyone should be giving their tithes to. Giving any money and/or tithes (or anything) to any other organization is disobedience to God and His Revelations (Words) and Will!

The whole idea is to create a culture in which people learn to live on 90% of their gross income without borrowing. This can easily be done by following the **Eternal Divine Path** in the **Communities Of Light** (Sharing)! Children will be brought up to learn to do this so it becomes second nature to them (part of their upbringing and culture).

Some people say, "I am too poor to pay tithes." In fact, one of the reasons to pay tithes is to create more effective people who constantly improve their financial situation so they will not only have a better lifestyle but also will be able to tithe easily. So find a better job with better pay. Improve your educational situation (go to school and obtain higher degrees so you would be able to have higher pay). Start a business which has a better future for you (be your own boss and make more money). Share life with someone and/or live in a **COL** so there is sharing which makes life easier in many levels for everyone involved, etc.

Tithing indeed should encourage the Divines (those in the **Mission Of Maitreya**, **Eternal Divine Path**) to become great in what they do and be known as good workers whom people Love to hire. Divines also should become high earners and business people in the society and eventually become the cream of the crop in all societies (if they have the ability to do so). This will not only help them to be financially secure, but they also can help the **Mission** to do the same. It will also allow the **Mission** to help many who need it (mostly to stand on their own two feet so they also can become productive members of the society; however, if they truly cannot become productive members, then help them as much as the **Mission** has resources to do so).

Note: For instructions on how to pay your tithes and/or automatic recurring payments for tithes, send an email to the **Mission** (tithes@maitreya.org).

SHOULD WE ACKNOWLEDGE THE TEACHER?

We teach that the teacher is not important, but the Message and God are. Does this mean that we should not acknowledge the teacher and should not tell people from where we received our knowledge/understandings?

The meaning of the teaching that we should not make the teacher God, is that we should not make him an obstacle in the path of the human to reach God. That is what has happened in the past and the religion has become a cult (the teacher became more important than the teaching – God). This results in people not seeking the Formless, Invisible, Nameless, Eternal (FINE) anymore but

SUPPLEMENTS

believing in a set of dogmas. So we have to be careful not to create a cult.

However, when we reach out to humanity and we talk about the teachings of the **Mission**, we have to acknowledge where our understanding comes from. As **Maitreya** received His teachings from God, and He acknowledges it, you have received your teachings and understandings from **Maitreya** and the **Mission**, and you have to acknowledge that. You connect people to **Maitreya** and the teachings (the source), and **Maitreya** and the **Mission** will connect them to God.

What happens if people do not acknowledge from where they have received this Knowledge? They would take it, that it is theirs. They will eventually bring their understandings into our teachings, and they also will accept that as the truth. Little by little they will take them more and more away from the original Teachings, and the Truth, and will replace them with what they think is the truth. We will eventually have many versions of what the **Mission** and God's Revelation is supposed to be. We will have divisions and branches in the **Mission**, and the unity will be lost.

Therefore, acknowledging where our teaching has come from and connecting people to the **Mission** and **Maitreya** are essential in the unity and manifestation of the **KOHOE** (Kingdom Of Heaven On Earth). Let us understand this in its deepest level, put our egos aside, and bring all to the feet of the Lord, that all humanity receives the purest Message and Revelation, and be(come) United.

Be a servant of God.

SHOULD I COME AND LIVE IN THE MISSION CENTER, OR CLOSE BY?

As the <u>Bible</u> clearly states: **If they said Christ is here and/or there, do not go!** God has provided all the tools that you might evaluate the claims of the **Mission** and know the Teachings. He has provided the Internet, and we have created, with His Grace, a very useful website that gives all the information you need to make an educated decision about our claims and know our Teachings.

So the idea seems to be, stay where you are. Go to our website and prove it to yourself that the **Mission** is indeed the result of the Prophecies from God and is the Last Revelation from God. Know then that God needs a lot of workers to accomplish this Revelation and the Vision. It is then that you have to decide if you are called to join this force (Soldiers of the Lord) to accomplish this Great Task.

The first step is to become a contact person. As you reach to others and become more involved with the **Mission**, you might feel an urge to serve the **Mission** in a greater degree.

It is then that you have to prove your sincerity even more and dedication to **Maitreya** and the **Mission** (God) completely. The first step is to read the essay in this book (<u>Supplements</u>) called "Covenant With God, or the **Mission Of Maitreya** (**Maitreya**)." The requirements for those who want to come and stay close to the **Mission** are the same as for those who want to be initiated.

If you meet these minimum requirements, then your case will be looked at and if approved, you will be invited to come to live in our area. You will have to find a job and rent a place to live. You will be required to render services for the **Mission**! This requirement is a part of your spiritual progress (Satsang, Service, and Meditation).

Exception to this set-up is coming to the Feast of Tabernacles. If you decided to join us for the Feast, you can always come without meeting any of these requirements. **Maitreya** usually gives a few Satsangs (Discourses) during these Feasts. So you might have an opportunity to be in His Presence.

SUPPLEMENTS

TO BE(COME) A CONTACT PERSON FOR THE MISSION

Almost anyone can become a contact person for the **Mission**. As the name implies, you try to connect people in your area to the **Mission**. Most people would love to have a personal contact in the area they live in. So the duty of a contact person ranges from a clearing house (just connect people to the **Mission**), to a person who becomes a center of attraction for the **Mission**.

You will provide an address, phone number, and your email address. People who live close to you can contact you and receive more information about the **Mission**. You can further your help by starting some meditation classes, transmission sessions, six-week meditation courses, **THOTH** reading times, opening rooms in PalTalk in the Internet, and eventually create a **Community Of Light** where you are.

So a contact person can be a simple point of contact and/or a center for the **Mission**. Hopefully we will have many dedicated teachers in the **Mission** who will eventually act as the elders in these Centers started by these contacts and will help to create many **Communities Of Light** in these places. Therefore being a contact person means the beginning of a greater process to manifest the **Mission** in your area. It is a great service in bringing the **Kingdom Of Heaven On Earth**.

So we encourage everyone who is interested in the **Mission** to consider becoming a contact person for the **Mission**. Attract likeminded people in your area and start a Center for the **Mission** where you are. Let us find the Elects and Teachers of the **Mission** (those who have been called to be teachers of the **Mission**). Start small but be persistent and expand your horizons and involvement as time progresses. Be so dedicated to the **Mission** that all your spare time can be used for this great work.

If you would like to be a contact person, send us an email (contacts@maitreya.org) and express this desire. We will work with you to start the process. A contact person is the beginning of the creation of the **Communities Of Light**! The Kingdom Of God is based on the **Communities Of Light**!

FAMILY

A strong family bond and its structure is the very base to create strong **Communities of Light** and so a strong society.

Therefore, any lifestyle that opposes this basic necessity and is not useful in human progress physically, mentally, and/or spiritually, would not be recommended.

There is only one exception and that is when a person dedicates himself or herself to a greater purpose and renounces the world as a renunciate (Sannyasin). Such people and their lifestyle are directed toward advancing humanity physically, mentally, and/or spiritually, and so are well accepted.

THERE SHOULD NOT BE ANY SECRETS IN THE COMMUNITIES OF LIGHT

The whole idea of knowing the self is to reach a point where our three personalities (what we think we are, what other people think we are, and what we really are) become One (god).

Of course, the very reason that what we think we are and what we really are is different is that we do not really want to know ourselves. When we truly know ourselves, what we think we are and what we really are

SUPPLEMENTS

become One.

The reason that what we are is different than what other people think we are is that other people do not know themselves either; therefore, they look at us through their personality (not their essence) and so their perception is colored with their personality (wrong understandings, cultures, past experiences, etc.). Most probably, therefore, what they see is different than what we really are.

In the case of how other people see us, we have less control than in the case of how we see ourselves. We can close the gap between who we are and what we think we are by knowing the self. Then, of course, we can also clearly see who other people truly are (the essence, god). The only way we can help others to see themselves and others as they truly are is to Guide them to Know themselves so they can also see us as we truly are.

Communities Of Light are a great help in accelerating this process of knowing oneself. As it is clearly proven, man does not want to know the self and does not want to face who he really is. Others, however, can see another person better than they can see themselves. As a person has to be open to the self and there should not be any hidden secrets between him and the self so that he can truly know himself, there should also not be hidden secrets in a community. What we try to hide from other people are things we are trying to hide from ourselves. If we are not willing to face these hidden behaviors and if we are also unwilling to let the community know them, then these behaviors will be hidden from us forever and we will never truly know the Self (God).

In fact, a great function in the **COLs** is that everyone is an open book to everyone else. In this process of knowing one another we can help each other to know ourselves. Since others are much better at seeing us (or at least identifying our faults) than we are at seeing ourselves, others in the community can help us to know ourselves. Indeed one of the functions of the Community Unity Meeting on Saturdays is for others to point out where we can improve ourselves in the **COL**.

If we are not willing to see ourselves and do not let others point us to where we can improve, we will never KNOW ourselves!

Besides the personal privacy, what we do in our rooms and/or houses (which should not be immoral), whatever else that affects the community should be an open book to everyone in the **Community Of Light**. The community should help each individual to progress to become a better and more productive member in that community. If an individual in the community resists this process, he or she is not community material. Either they have to change this resistance or they will not last long in a **COL**!

Also there should not be any secrets in a marriage. The rules above go beyond the **COLs** in this case, as the wife and husband can further help one another to progress and Be(Come) One since they are together even in their private quarters!

In all cases, each individual should have the best intentions to help the other individual or individuals. They should also be open themselves to the input from other people so they can also see their deeper motives. The whole process should make everyone have deeper meditation on who they really are, and so become their Essence. They should be open with no hidden secrets and/or agenda (hidden agenda is a disease itself).

CHIDREN AND COMMUNITY

A child in the womb of his/her mother is one with her in all levels of existence, physically (uses the same resources of existence), mentally, and emotionally (shares the same spirit). These two beings indeed are one in these levels. It is only at the time of birth that the Soul enters the body of the fetus and they become two separate individuals.

SUPPLEMENTS

However, the oneness of their physical, mental, and emotional links lasts a lifetime. An etheric bond will continue to exist between them. This relationship is the strongest in each person's life, unless there are greater bonds existing between the child and others from previous lives. **If the child is a Great Soul and feels he only belongs to God, he will eventually transform this bond toward God**.

Transformation of this relationship from only the mother to others starts by the child experiencing contact with other people.

If the transformation of this etheric bond is not spread to many relationships in early childhood, the person becomes very selective in his or her relationships and creates an egocentric approach in life. Such a person will look only for his own interests in life, create a manipulative approach in his relationships with others (as he learned to manipulate his mother), and will look for only one other person to cling to.

Communities will help to alter this attitude. With many people around, especially if the raising of the child is shared with many in the community, the etheric bond from the mother will be expanded to others and the one-to-one relationship will be broken. New experiences and vibrations will be felt by the child. So he or she will expand the sphere of his or her being and will create an open relationship with many.

As these children grow older, with the community being connected with other communities and the external world, they will expand themselves even in a greater degree. This expansion of their relationships eventually will lead to universalism.

Because this first etheric bond is formed with a woman, transformation from being connected with female energy to male energy should be gradual. Also the effect of male energy is different than female energy. That is why the child should come in contact with male energies in a greater degree with increasing age (especially for boys) and different settings (when his or her logical mind starts to develop). This has been the reason for women being chosen as the main beings to rear the child in the younger ages until 7 or 8.

To share the experience of contact with others by providing babysitters for the child is not the same as community rearing. The motivation in being a babysitter may not be pure and loving. This vibration will be felt by the child. So the experience will be negative and counter-productive. The loving vibration and willingness of the person other than the mother to be with the child and share herself with him is extremely important. It should be a heart (fourth chakra) energy (etheric) connection. Any lower energy will not do.

To live with a single parent in a house or apartment or even in one culture or level of social status, will create men and women of limited experience, which will result in narrowness of the mind, a feeling of being separate from the rest, egotism, and self-centeredness. These are all the diseases of the mind and the base for the suffering of the individual and society.

Therefore, again we can see how **Communities of Light**, networking between these Communities, and our teachings, are the way to dissolve limited egos into the Universal Ego and to bring Oneness to All, besides many other benefits.

With the present lifestyles and the way the world is going, man is further pushed to believe that he has to be concerned only for one's self. This attitude will accelerate the process of being more self-centered and the eventual result will be utter destruction.

The way out is expansion, sharing, and not being self-centered. The way out is given in our teachings. It is up to those who see it to respond to it.

The process explained above is the way which will be helpful in the development of the subconscious mind. The subconscious mind is accumulated knowledge from our present and past lives. By expansion (dissolving) of the subconscious mind, a person will accelerate his progress of bridging the barriers between the conscious mind and Unconscious Mind (Universal Mind).

When this intermediary consciousness

SUPPLEMENTS

(subconscious mind) is overcome, there is only conscious mind and Unconscious Mind remaining. The narrower the experience of the subconscious mind, the more difficult will be the possibility of realizing the Universal Mind (Unconscious Mind). The more expanded the subconscious mind (experiences of the present lifetime) the greater the possibility of knowing the Universal Mind.

In fact in the ultimate state, the subconscious mind and Universal Mind become One.

The capacity of expanding our subconscious mind is also related to our experiences from the past, and of course, His Grace.

Indeed meditation is the process of expanding the subconscious mind into the Unconscious Mind or Universal Mind. **Communities of Light** accelerate this process.

POSITIVE, NEGATIVE, AND NEUTRAL FORCES IN THE UNIVERSE

The negative force is the same as tama guna, and the positive is satva guna. However, there is another force, raja guna, which has no polarity and is neutral. But it is this force that creates movement in the universe (consciousness). The movement or desire (raja guna) arises in the consciousness. According to the dominating force (positive or negative), the consciousness is bent toward that polarity.

If the tama guna (negative force) is dominating, the consciousness is bent toward the crudifying (hell) tendencies. But if the positive force (satva guna) is dominating, it is bent toward happiness, joy, and freedom (heaven).

However, in the state of complete objectivity (Pure Consciousness) the consciousness becomes a witness entity. The desires (raja guna) arise and evolve into negative and positive aspects in the universe but the consciousness itself stays untouched by these activities and free from any influences in the universe. In such a state a person becomes involved in busy activities while always knowing he is not the activity and the doer but merely observes them as they proceed. He only learns from those activities without being affected by them.

Such a state has been called by many names, such as being centered, Pure Consciousness, Witness Consciousness, etc. In our **Greatest Sign** and **HOSH Sign**, it is the state in the very center of the signs, where a person is beyond any influences out of that center. It is only in this center that a consciousness knows all and perceives all with complete freedom and detachment.

Such a person might come out of this center once in awhile just to accomplish some objectives and/or learn some new lessons, but it is only in this center that the significance of all things, including his activities, can be fully perceived.

That is why meditation is helpful to clarify the situation of a person, because the process of meditation is to take one away from the influences of these forces to the center or state of objectivity of the Soul. Only in this center can a person clearly see the truth. But those who have not mastered the influences of these forces will be under their influences any time they come out of their meditation.

As they practice and realize this process of becoming objective and then involved in activities and losing their objectivity, little by little they will master themselves and will not be affected by these forces even in the middle of busy activities. They will stay centered and objective in all situations.

However, without knowledge of the **Eternal Divine Path**, this awesome power might be misdirected and misused thus bringing suffering to the person and others. But by understanding how this knowledge and energy should be utilized, such a person can be beneficial in the progress of the universe toward its goal.

SUPPLEMENTS

SUBCONSCIOUS MIND

The subconscious mind is where our deep desires and personal will reside. These desires and will are created by our past and present experiences and lives. Therefore, we can say the subconscious mind is where our karmas reside!

Because of these past and present karmas, this part of the mind is programmed to unconsciously guide us, advise us, protect us, make us succeed or fail, etc., in our personal lives. It is the part which makes us do things which we later might regret. The subconscious mind is a barrier between us and the Universal Mind (Unconscious Mind).

The goal is to eradicate this part (not having any karma) so we can be in direct contact with the Universal Mind (God). Then we will become a pure channel for Him and will know All (His Will).

Many people are becoming aware of the subconscious mind. They realize how this powerful part of the mind indirectly affects their lives. They also know that this part is like a little child and can be programmed or reprogrammed to achieve a positive or negative result. That is why they suggest how to reprogram this part to achieve success in their personal lives.

However, as it was explained above, the goal is to clear this self-will part of the mind so we can become only the conscious and Unconscious Mind (Universal Mind). Then our achievements will not only be for our own good but for the good of All.

This reprogramming of the subconscious mind is done through hypnosis. In the state of hypnosis, desired suggestions are implanted in the subconscious mind. These suggestions become a great influence in the life of the person without him realizing it (if he is not aware of them). This is also the method used by those who use brainwashing techniques!

Therefore, the difference between hypnosis (self-hypnosis) and meditation, is that: In hypnosis, the previous subconscious mind (karmas) is replaced by a new set of programs (subconscious mind). But in meditation, the subconscious mind eventually, with His Grace, will be dissolved, and a direct relationship between the person and the Universal Mind (God) is established.

In other words, the goal of self-hypnosis is to create a new programming for the subconscious mind. With this, still karma exists. But in meditation, the goal is to become a direct channel for Him, with no karma left.

SUBCONSCIOUS MIND, REVISITED

We have talked a lot about the subconscious mind all through our teachings. However, it seems there is still confusion about this topic. So we will try to explain it one more time in as deep a level as possible.

It seems people do not have much trouble understanding conscious mind. It is easy to understand this since it is not hidden, and you always experience it. It is what you are conscious of, at any moment. So everyone has experienced it and they know what the conscious mind is.

The problem starts when it comes to the subconscious mind and Unconscious Mind. The Unconscious Mind is not questioned because most people have no idea what it is and have never experienced it. Anything we have not experienced is beyond our realm of familiarity and so no question will be raised about it. Even if there is any question about it, since this state has to be experienced, it cannot be explained. These are the reasons why the subconscious mind seems to be the one that is most troubling for many, and harder to understand. It is experienced by everyone (they are under its influence), but it is hidden at the same time. So it can be explained but it is hard to fathom.

We know that there was the Unconscious Mind (God in Its Highest State) from the very

SUPPLEMENTS

beginning. It is the only permanent thing in the universe. The moment that, That Pure State was disturbed and the ego evolved, the feeling of I know, do, and have done was manifested. The subconscious mind was born! It is this "I" that is separating man from the Rest. Therefore, it is this "I" that has to be eliminated!

This state of separation from the Essence continued to be present and in each lifetime more memories, learning, programming of the subconscious mind, were added to it. Therefore, the worldly person accumulated more programming of the subconscious mind toward dealing with the external world. Now we can see there are vast differences between humans. Of course the most obvious differences are the programming and learning that we have acquired in this life. These programmings are most obvious to everyone. Each person is born in different cultures, environments, families, etc.; we are programmed differently, so we are different! Of course programming from previous lives is also affecting us. That is why although many are born in the same culture there are still vast differences between them.

Later on God gave humans the physical senses to experience the external world. Now we also have conscious mind. As it was explained above, we hear, we can see, touch, and smell, etc. so everyone knows the conscious mind well. We are conscious of this manifested world. This is the conscious mind. This everyone is aware of, is experiencing, and so it needs no explanation.

Now the question is, what do all these have to do with this life, creation, the Goal of Life, etc.? It has everything to do with all these questions. As we can see from the explanation above, the only state of consciousness that is permanent and worth considering is the Unconscious Mind (God in Its Highest Level). The conscious mind darkens when this body is no more, and the subconscious mind (ego) is the very reason for our separation from the Essence (Unconscious Mind). In each incarnation, when we return, we pick up this subconscious mind to work on ourselves again toward the Goal of Life. The Goal of Life Is To Become Divine (return to the Essence). The only way that can be done is to eliminate the subconscious mind (ego). Now how can that be accomplished?

One way to do this is to learn to negate the "I" and let more and more God come through and so eventually eliminate the subconscious mind and return back to The Godhead. If everyone follows this Path then those who remain behind will have no Guides to be taught how it is done. Each person has to learn it, all over again, alone. That will be wasteful and time-consuming. That is why God said if you try this approach (you become neither hot nor cold) I will "spue you out of My Mouth" (return you back to this world). You have to return and help others to go back Home!

The Goal is to return back to God. The problem is the subconscious mind. You are supposed to eliminate it. However, if you do that you will not be able to stay in the Essence (God) since you will be spued out back to the external world to help others! Then you have to start all over, etc.!

What is the answer to this riddle, puzzle, and this question? How then can we go back?

The only solution is: To create an environment that human progress toward Pure Consciousness is accelerated so when they return home they are not sent back. The only reason they are sent back is because there are not enough workers to help those who want to go back to learn how it is done and so they can go back. If we created the **Communities Of Light** and many Great Souls return and help many to learn to go back, they will not be "spued out" anymore. They have done a good job. They made more workers to help and so they need not return. They will be Home.

So the first step to solve this problem is to create the **Communities Of Light** and the Kingdom Of Heaven On Earth.

Therefore, we have to understand how this can be done. The subconscious mind, as we explained above, can be programmed. Indeed many have realized this and have created many ways to manipulate it and charging millions of dollars from people who want to be

SUPPLEMENTS

reprogrammed to become successful, happy, more effective, cure their psychological problems, etc. These techniques and approaches, however, all reprogram the subconscious mind, not eliminate it, as we said is the Goal. Now what if we reprogrammed the subconscious mind to accept the Will of God and work toward that end?

So the differences between people, cultures, etc. are the programs of each person in their environments and also from what they have accumulated from the previous lives. Now if we reprogram them to realize that the Goal of Life is to Be(Come) Divine, then their subconscious mind and God's Will, will be One. They will strive to return Home. However, since they also know that they cannot accomplish this unless they create an environment that will accelerate the progress of everyone toward that end, they will come together to create such environments. This needs a collective cooperation and that is the only way out of the conundrum that human life is at (the Goal is to return to God but they cannot, etc.).

Now the question is, how can this reprogramming of the subconscious minds of the masses, to become One with God, be accomplished? It can be accomplished with a mass reprogramming of all humans' subconscious minds (or at least those who are ready to be reprogrammed) toward this new Subconscious Mind. Those whose subconscious minds are already close to these ideals (have meditated many lives to be close to these understandings/God) easily accept this and reprogram themselves to be in Oneness with God's Consciousness. Those who accumulated worldly subconscious minds, in many lives, will have a hard time to understand these Truths and will go against God's Will and Plan. That is why this is the time of sundering!

The more subconscious minds of the masses are reprogrammed to the Will of God, the more similar they will be and so their Unity will become Greater. At the end we eventually can eliminate the last residue of the subconscious mind and many will reach Mukti or Moksha (Salvation), as the Sages did in the past!

So all those who have the ability to influence humanity should teach that the Goal of Life is to Be(Come) Divine (Return Home/to God). However, the first step in this process is the creation of the **Communities Of Light** and the Kingdom.

MALE, FEMALE, MAN, WOMAN, ADAM, gods, DIVINE FATHER, DIVINE MOTHER, GOD

1- Male: The Male Principle, The Divine Logic.

2- Female: The Female Principle, The Divine Grace.

3- Man: Human male body. It is supposed to manifest the Male Principle; when he does not, he becomes a rational animal, a beast.

4- Woman: Human female body. It is supposed to manifest the Female Principle; when she does not, she becomes the very Maya, Eve.

5- Adam: The perfected man, who manifests both Male Principle (The Divine Logic) and Female Principle (The Divine Grace, The Holy Ghost).

6- gods: Those who manifest Male and Female principles and are in Pure Consciousness. They are Male and Female, and are neither.

7- Divine Father: Pure Consciousness and the Director of the whole universe.

8- Divine Mother: The Creative Force (The Holy Ghost) of the universe.

9- God: Both Male and Female Principles of the whole universe; the Father Mother God, who is Male and Female, and is neither.

SUPPLEMENTS

GOD'S LAWS VS. MAN'S LAWS

God's Laws, such as the ones brought by Moses and Prophet Muhammad, have been misused in many societies. Still they have great merits when they are properly implemented.

When a crime has been committed by a person and it is certain that it was committed by him, then it should be considered if this was the first time. If so, most probably the punishment should be as lenient as possible. If that person is also repentant and promises never to do it again, he should be freed.

If the crime is repeated, then the punishments recommended by Moses and Muhammad (Divine Laws) have greater merits than the present systems. In the present systems, first, the prisons gradually destroy the spirit and most men are destroyed mentally through the process. Secondly, to keep the prisons going is costly.

By quick physical or financial punishments, which are recommended by Divine Laws, a person will receive the result of his action, is punished, and most probably will not do it again. Also it is a quick response to the crime committed. So the spirit will not be destroyed in the process of a long imprisonment, and with no prisons there also will not be much expense.

However, as explained all through our writings, we have to create just societies first, and the judges should be so in tune with the Divine Justice that they would be flexible enough to bring justice to any individual cases. Otherwise no matter which law is used, it can be misused and justice will not be!

To emphasize, the present prison systems are worse than physical or financial punishments recommended by Divine Laws. The Divine Laws might hurt a person physically or financially, but the prison system destroys the spirit which is much greater than the physical body or financial well-being.

Probably the best approach is to give a person a chance of choosing between a physical and/or financial punishment or imprisonment.

GODLY SOCIETIES AND UNGODLY SOCIETIES

When the fathers do not act like fathers, mothers do not act like mothers, grandfathers do not act like grandfathers, and grandmothers do not act like grandmothers, then children will not act like children. In such a society, the family will break down and ungodly acts seem Godly. We indeed will have a Sodom and Gomorrah-based society!

It is then that the merchants and companies do not consider the well-being of the society, cheating becomes prevalent in the society, lying will become politically correct, and all manner of destructive tendencies permeate the society.

When fathers act like fathers, mothers act like mothers, grandfathers act like grandfathers, and grandmothers act like grandmothers, then children will be children. In such a society the family is strong and ungodly acts are shunned and looked upon as unworthy, and only the Godly will be worthy. We indeed will have a God-based society.

It is then that the merchants and companies will consider the well-being of the society, cheating will become appalling in the eyes of the society, lying will become politically incorrect, and all manner of productive (goodness or Godness) tendencies will permeate the society.

Godly societies will prosper and survive; the ungodly societies will eventually be destroyed.

This is the LAW!

SUPPLEMENTS
ABSOLUTE LAWS AND RELATIVE LAWS

God has created this universe for a purpose. The Goal of the universe is to return the darkness ("And darkness was upon the face of the deep," Genesis 1:2) back to Light ("And God said, Let there be light," Genesis 1:3). So God has set laws and a way to accomplish this. We Know the Way (**Eternal Divine Path**), we should also Know the Absolute Laws in order to be able to Follow the Way!

For a Lucid Mind (Enlightened) it is easy to see these Absolute Laws. For a confused and untrained mind, it is hard. Absolute Laws are the Innate Nature (Daharma) of things. It is: What is the purpose of anything created? If we follow the Innate Nature (Daharma) of anything, then we are following the Laws which are Absolute and unbreakable. It is when man tries to break these Laws that Karma (Sin) is created and so the Face of God will be against them. As long as humanity follows the Daharma, God's Blessings will be with them.

Some people think these Laws only apply to individuals. However, you can ask: Do these laws also apply to the societies, earth and the universe? If they do, then collective endeavor to uphold these Laws are also a part of their lives. In fact the whole society and human ways toward the universe should reflect this understanding. The Communities, the Cities, the Regions and the whole earth has to strive to establish an environment that helps the Goal of Life and the Universe.

As we have stated, and all religions and Prophets agree: These Laws cannot be broken. Whoever tries to break them will break themselves against them. It does not matter if it is an individual, a community, city, etc. The Face of God will be against them.

That is why in God's System, the Head (the Eldest and the Elder Body) has to be connected to Spirit (God) and have a Lucid Mind to see what things are created to be and used for. They bring the Spirit of God to man. They will not approve of anything that is not promoting the Goal of the Universe. They bring the Grace of God to man and are a source of Light for them. Indeed this has been the basic idea of the King in old cultures and in the past Golden Ages. He was connected to God and would bring His Grace and Light to earth. Of course as the dark age approached, the kings no longer were connected to God, and they became dictators and darkness came to man.

The cruel kings and dictators changed the perception of man on what a chosen leader by God means and what He is supposed to be! Nowadays a king means a dictator that fills his own pockets with wealth and gives the best positions in the land to his own family, relatives, and friends. Many such people who no longer were connected to God became leaders of our known history. In fact the record of how people took away the Way of God and replaced it with their own ways is in the Bible.

God had a system that the Judges were chosen as the leaders of the Children of Abraham. At the time of Samuel, people decided they wanted someone who they would chose as their leader (a king), like their neighbors had. God clearly told them that the leader they would chose as a king would tax them heavily, would take their wealth for himself, would take their children to unjust wars, etc. They still insisted that they wanted to choose their own leaders. God permitted them to do so, and the result was disastrous!

It was after this long period of the disastrous rules of such kings that the idea of democracy emerged: The rule of the majority. As long as this system does not infringe on the Absolute Laws, it works well. However, if the majority decides to go against these Absolute Laws, the Face of God will be against them!

Besides these Absolute Laws, there are man's laws and regulations. These, usually, are related to what concerns the day to day living of man and this external world. The majority can decide about these decisions and usually these things do not concern the Spirit and the Setup of the Universe. In this level the **Mission** is also democratic and the

SUPPLEMENTS

majority decision is welcomed. However, the Clear Mind of the Eldest and the Elder Body is the one that is supposed to connect man and his society to the Spirit and God. It is this Body that brings the Grace of God to man, the Guiding Light!

These are the Ones that Christ called: The Salt of the earth. What happens if even the Salt spoils and no longer is Lucid (Clear)? That is when the darkness comes, and we have been in this Dark Age for the last twelve thousand years.

DIVINE SYSTEM
(A SYSTEM FROM DIVINES, BY DIVINES, AND FOR DIVINES)

The world seems to be mostly divided into two camps: Those who promote democracy and those who are under dictators. Each of them claims their system is better. However, both are man-made. In democracy, man chooses his leader, and in dictatorship, the gun does the job.

Dictatorship is obviously a system under the gun and so is a system under duress. Neither man nor God is in charge but the dictator. This system is the most appalling to God. It is neither acceptable to man nor to God!

In democracy man is in charge. They choose the leaders. What the majority says is supposed to be the will of the society. If the majority can be persuaded to accept and approve ideas that are not based on nature and/or Godly, still they are accepted and implemented. Therefore, again God is not in charge, man is.

God created the system of judges for the Children of Israel. However, they longed for kings like their neighbors. Samuel conveyed this desire to God. After God forewarned them of what would happen if they choose kings, then He let them choose their king. With a majority vote they chose Saul. They did not choose him because he was the wisest and most connected (Godly) but because he was tall and handsome!

God rejected their choice and chose a man named David to be their king, ordinary to the eyes, but highly connected to Spirit (He was the Anointed One). This idea to choose the Anointed One (Christ) is the base for many cultures to accept the idea of the king (chosen by God). Even those nations, mostly Greece, Rome, and Europe, that started democratic ideas, did eventually succumb to the idea of the king, and went back and forth between democracy and kingship. However, all through history, all over the world, the kings eventually became dictators, as God forewarned the Children of Israel that they would.

The reason for returning to the kings, after being under the democratic rule, is that the will of the people becomes corrupt and they choose not the leaders with the Highest Ideals and those chosen by God, but the ones who will make them feel good and accept their ideas, but are rejected by God. As we saw in the case of choosing Saul, they do not always choose wisely. When they reach a point that they choose wrong leaders, then the head will be sick and when the head is sick, so will be the body (society). They eventually long for stability and safety, and so they choose dictators who eventually become kings, etc.

Therefore, God is not in favor of what man chooses, and He is not in the favor of the dictators who impose their will on humans under duress. So what does God approve of and is the best for man?

He has clearly shown His Way when He instructed the Children of Israel to have judges over them, who were supposed to be Connected to God. The judges failed and became disconnected from God. The Children of Israel wanted kings, and they chose the wrong king (not anointed). After their chosen king failed, God decided to let them have their King who is also Connected to Him and Follows His

SUPPLEMENTS

Will. This is the best for man and the Universal Setup. He Chose David for them who became the best leader they ever had!

This idea of the Chosen One (Christ) to be accepted as The King is not new. In fact we read in the Bible that Melchizedek not only was the King of Salem but the High Priest! The very idea of the pope in the Catholic Church is also choosing a leader who is connected to God. The idea of Caliph in Islam is also based on this idea: A person who has been chosen to lead the Ummah or the community of all Muslims. There are many other cultures that also had the same idea.

Now the question arises: If all these people and cultures had this idea before, why did it not work, and why should we follow a failed idea? That is an excellent question. The short answer to this is that humanity did not have the whole Truth and so no matter what religion and idea they followed, it was only a part of a greater Truth. When a good idea is based on 1/7th or less, of a larger Truth, it will not work! Also God had left man to make his own decisions for the last twelve thousand years. With all these shortcomings and missing information, humans chose wrong leaders and/or lost their rights to the dictators who had the armies with them.

It is like having 1/7th of the layout for a house and trying to build the whole house. No matter how well the intentions, it will not work. Many people have this idea, but they are also flooded with dogmas, separating ideas and plain hostility toward others, or others are hostile toward them, etc. They could not present God in its Fullness and so The Grace was not with them. When The Grace is not present, the failure is assured!

As we saw in the case of Saul, humans follow their eyes and the cultural norms, not God's Will. So they chose wrong leaders, not the Anointed One. Of course even if they could have chosen the Anointed One, as they did in the case of King Cyrus, who also was called Christ, still such leaders could have only a partial influence on earth events and in a very limited sense.

So we can see many conditions had to be met before humanity is able to choose the right leaders and so bring the Greatest Acceleration of Salvation to man. These conditions are:

1- The whole Truth should have been Revealed.
2- Paravipras had to be created and United.
3- A system that helps the Anointed One to emerge from the people, by the people, for the people, and Connected to God (Divine), has to be accepted by man.
4- The cyclical movements and the effects of different types of humans on societies should have been understood.

These conditions are now on earth. We indeed have the New Heaven (Revelation) and Earth (Divine System) for humanity. This is the stone that the Bible has predicted to come and hit the image King Nebuchadnezzar saw in his dream. The image (worldly setups) was broken to pieces and was no more.

Humanity now has the Whole Truth (the Seven Seals are opened). The Elects are called to come forward and be unified. The Hierarchy from the **Communities of Light** is in formation (a system from Divines, by Divines, and for Divines). The cyclical movements in history and societies are Revealed. Paravipras will observe the society and will transfer these cyclical movements to the new one in transitory (Harmonic) ways instead of violent ways. It is from these Communities and system that the benevolent leaders (Anointed Ones) will emerge. The System also has strong checks and balances to prevent any one leader to become a dictator.

This New Way has all the benefits of the present systems and none of the weaknesses which are present in them. The leaders are not chosen by the whim of those who will follow their eyes but by those who are ready to follow the **Eternal Divine Path** (in the **Communities of Light**) and so are in Higher Consciousness. Others (who are not in the **Communities of Light**) are not left out and are given opportunities to participate in the process; however, their impact is not as severe as before.

SUPPLEMENTS

The most important part of this Divine System is: The ability of humans to recognize and choose those who are anointed by God to lead them, especially The Eldest (The Head). He then, can extend the power that is given to him, in our system, to choose others who also are anointed to help Him to manage God's Kingdom.

So we can see that those who are still attached to the old earthly systems and are trying to make them work, are wasting their time and energy and will not succeed. It is a new day and it is God's Day. So humans have to eventually acknowledge that God indeed has Fulfilled all things He promised He would do. It is time to stop our understandings and succumb to God's Will and His Ways.

The Stone has come, the statue has been completed, and it is time for the statue to be broken to pieces. This again is the call to man to come and Marvel on what God has done. Those who resist, they resist God. God will always win at the end. The sooner humans realize this, the sooner we can bring Peace, Unity, and God's Will for this creation to Manifestation!

COLLECTIVE KARMA

When decisions are made in a situation (societies) that create Karma (are against God's Laws) it is everyone's duty and responsibility to oppose/correct such decision(s). If they do not, all those who have been present (involved) and did not correct the decision against God's Laws are collectively responsible for the consequences of those decision(s). They will create Collective Karma!

Although in our system the idea is for the head to be connected to God, the body also has to be vigilant so the head indeed is connected to the Spirit and God. They cannot have the excuse that: A few at the top are making (or made) these wrong decisions and they are the ones who are responsible, not us. The leaders of a society (head) are a reflection of the body. Who have they emerged from? If they are from the body (people) and they are going against the Universal Laws (Dharma) then the body also has fallen!

This is especially true for the systems that people have some voice in that system. If someone is living under a dictator they have a greater excuse of why they do not (or did not) act against an oppressive system. However, if you have the ability to oppose a system that is following laws (or passing them) that are not Godly, and you either stay silent and/or support such laws, you are participating in the decision-making process and will be counted in the Collective Karma of that group and/or society.

Spiritual life is an inner and outer Struggle (Jahad or Jihad) to Purify the universe within and without. That is why the head and the body have to be Purified and Strong against the temptations and pulls of the world. Only such people can create an environment that will accelerate human progress and bring Purity, Unity, and Justice to everyone (Justice is the Closest to the Heart of God).

Even in the societies that people do not have a voice, everyone has to work toward bringing the voice of the people, to the system. Hopefully, eventually, in the Kingdom all in One Voice support God's Ways, and the Body and the Head will be synchronized with God.

Therefore, the human should become involved in the society and promote the Dharma of things and the way things are created to Be. Only this way will the Peace, Unity, Justice, etc. come.

God's Way is the Way! God's Way is the **Eternal Divine Path**!

SUPPLEMENTS

PASSING OF THE SCEPTER

God has created the whole universe. He Knows how it works. He Knows how the unit consciousnesses can be best helped to return Home (to Him/Her/It). This can only be accomplished by being Focused on Him. Much focus, however, is given to the Kings and the heads of a society. If everyone accepts God as the King and the Head of the society, all attention will be on Him, all will follow His Laws, and all will return to Him. So when you accept God as the King and the Lawgiver, you accelerate the progress of humanity in returning back to God (our True Home).

God Knows this very well. That is why He has been trying to make humans accept this Truth since the beginning of the creation. Man, however, having a strong will (ego) has other ideas in mind. S/He thinks he knows better than God what is good for him (knowledge of the tree of good and evil). This misconception and egocentric approach takes man where it is not Godly and takes him further away from God (The Goal). This falling away takes man to Maya (illusion of separation from God).

This is symbolized by the story of Adam and Eve, and their fall, in the Garden of Eden. Since then a great struggle has occurred between God and man. God has been trying to bring man back Home (God), and man has gone astray. As **THOTH** clearly shows, God made man go through a long period of evolution until the creation of man to the state that we are at now (most of our spiritual powers closed, etc.). Since this last evolutionary step twelve thousand years ago (Flood of Noah), and the History (His Story), and especially since the last six thousand years, a Plan has been devised to make this clear to man: That God indeed is in control and is the King (Point of Focus). To be Focused on God is man's Salvation!

He created Canaan (workers or Shudras and warriors or Ksattriyas), Japheth (intellectuals or Vipras and businessmen or Vaeshyas) and Shem (true spiritual people or Brahmins). These four classes (Shudras, Ksattriyas, Vipras and Vaeshyas) have been the main classes in this new man and his society. Then God chose Abram (Abraham) to be an example for humanity. He Blessed him and his children as such an example for man. Abram (Abraham) was the reincarnation of Adam (The First Begotten Son). God Blessed him above all men, and all men (and nations) will be Blessed through him. He then gave him two sons, Ishmael and Isaac. It is through these Sons and their children that God will send His True Mouthpieces (Prophets, Messiahs) to bring man His Messages (Revelations).

Until recently (mid-2002) I (**Maitreya**) accepted that this happened through the reincarnations of Adam (The First Begotten Son) as these Mouthpieces (Prophets, Messiahs). At this time, God Revealed another aspect of His Plan: He also accomplished this through keeping a pure Lineage from Abraham to this day and so He has Revealed His Revelation through this Pure Lineage. All Great Prophets and Messengers have come from His Lineage. I am from this Lineage as well (Lineage of Abram and Abraham).

Again God fulfilled the Promises He gave to Abram (Abraham), and again proved that He indeed exists and Glory Be To Him/Her/It.

Although our assumption is correct that it is The First Begotten Son who has Revealed all Revelations from God to man (Blessed all nations), God, however, reincarnated the First Begotten Son only in this Lineage to accomplish this. In other words, God accomplished it in two ways: He Incarnated the First Begotten Son to Reveal His Revelations (**Eternal Divine Path**), and He reincarnated the First Begotten Son in the Lineage of Abram (Abraham).

Therefore, the **Mission** was correct even before we came to the understanding of the Genealogy and its importance in God's Plan. It is indeed the First Begotten Son who was Adam, Noah, Krishna, Shiva, Abram (Abraham), Christ, Muhammad, Bab, etc., and **Maitreya**. Although it seems that Krishna, Shiva,

SUPPLEMENTS

and such are not from the lineage of Abram (Abraham), Noah, who brought the Mystical Paths, was the First Begotten Son. We can see that in regards to the Mystical Paths, the lineage does not apply (Baba seems not to be of this lineage either). Prophets who came from the Mystical Paths and the Sixth Seal have their own Prophecies and understandings of God's Plan. They, however, merge with the Plan of the Lineage of Abram (Abraham) in **Maitreya** (are united!). It is our Teachings that bring these two plans together and unify them.

The importance of the Lineage of Abram/Abraham was impressed on people in the Judeo-Christian, Islamic, and Bab/Bahá'ís religions. God went even further and made it clear that **Maitreya** will also be from the Lineage of King David (Lion Of The Tribe Of Juda or Judah). It is only He (Lion Of The Tribe Of Judah) who can Open the Book Sealed with the Seven Seals. Muslims also are waiting for their Messiah to come from the Lineage of Prophet Muhammad. All these beliefs were impressed on people (religions) that did not strongly believe in reincarnation. Most probably these religions and their followers would have had a harder time to believe our Teachings and Revelations if we could not have been able to connect **Maitreya** to Abram (Abraham).

All these, of course, have been fulfilled through our Teachings and **Maitreya**. God did not leave any possibility for anyone to doubt that indeed our **Mission** is from God. For those who still do not, or cannot, believe it, there surely is something wrong with them! They indeed do not have the Spirit of God with them and are not the Elects.

Why have all these things happened? They are all to Glorify God (Jallal'u'llah). Yes indeed, He and Christ are the only subjects that should be Glorified. Christ represents the Spirit of God on earth (Manifestation). He is here to Glorify God, and whoever Glorifies Christ (His Spirit, Revelations) Glorifies God. This Glory is symbolized by the concept of Scepter, which was given to these Prophets (Messiah, The Anointed King).

The Scepter is the symbol of the kings. In this case it is the Kingly Spiritual Domination that is the Spirit Of God. This Scepter belongs only to God and He only gives (and has given) it to the Anointed One (Christ). God Promised Abram (Abraham) that such Anointed Ones shall come from His Lineage. These Anointed Ones will come both from Ishmael's Lineage and Isaac's Lineage. Prophet Muhammad came from the Ishmael Lineage, and Esa (Christ) came from Isaac. Bab came from the Lineage of Prophet Muhammad, and **Maitreya** is from both Lineages.

These Anointed Ones bring the Spirit of God to man. They have the Kingly Spiritual Domination, which comes from the Spirit of God, with them. Indeed it is God who is this Spirit and is the King. The focus is on God. That is man's salvation.

So the original Plan was that God would be the King FOREVER (I mean as long as the sun and the moon exist). This is what the children of Israel (and all humanity in general) rejected, and instead they longed for a human king. With this, they rejected God and His Plan. They chose Saul, a handsome tall man (they went by their sight instead of their Spirit/Heart) as their king, and he failed miserably.

Then God chose a King for them (King David) and put His own Spirit on Him (he became the Anointed of God, Christ). His Lineage will be the Chosen Kings on earth. Those whose Spirit will be upon them are Christ, Messiah. At the end, however, the human has to realize what God has been doing and eventually succumb to His Original Will!

Parallel to this Plan, there was another Plan! This one was the One for the people of the Far East. These people believe in the Mystical Paths and believe in reincarnation strongly. They have had their own understanding of the Plan of God, their own Prophecies and beliefs. This Plan and what is described above (Children of Abram/Abraham, Lion Of The Tribe Of Judah, etc.) seemed to be incompatible with one another, until NOW.

From these religions (Mystical Paths) and their Revelations came the Revelations from

SUPPLEMENTS

Baba (Anandamurti, Mr. Sarkar, my Spiritual Teacher). They are clearly included in **The Greatest Sign**, and the Sixth Seal is the only One that did not follow what has been Revealed to the Judeo/Christian/Islamic/Bab/Bahá'í religions. Of course, this is just an appearance, as God clearly has foretold of its coming in the Bible (the Sixth Seal). Baba indeed has fulfilled many Prophecies in Hindu (and maybe even other) religions, and it is mentioned in the Bible that He would come.

In fact, in this later time, by the coming of Baba and His Teachings, and our unifying Revelation, these two Plans have merged together as One. Again the Unification is in the Revelation of the Seven Seals and the Seventh Angel.

All these explanations, to this point, were to show that God has a Great Plan for man. He wants man to realize and understand the **Eternal Divine Path**, know that God is indeed in Control, and is the King, that only through focusing on Him and following His Laws (the King's Laws) can they return Home (to God). He, however, gave this Power to His Chosen Ones all throughout History. This passing of the powers to these individuals to do His Will is what we can call the **Passing Of The Scepter**.

Throughout History, this power (Scepter) was given to many people all over the world. Those who have received it used it to do His Will (knowingly or unknowingly). The Scepter (in a limited degree) was given to Cyrus, for example, to bring the Jews back to their land and build the Temple. That is why he also was called Christ (an Anointed One). The Scepter has been given to the Prophets and His Messengers in a greater degree than any other men. The Scepter, however, will be given to the Seventh Angel in an unlimited measure. He indeed represents the ultimate Manifestation Of God (Jallal'u'llah, The Glory Of God, He and His Teachings indeed Glorify God forever).

Now the question is: Will God Pass the Scepter to anyone else after the Seventh Angel who will Open the Seventh Seal and will Reveal the Book sealed with the Seven Seals? God Promised that David and His Lineage would be Kings forever, and He kept His Promise to this point! Will this continue?

To find the answer, we have to look to see what God says after the Seven Seals are Opened and the Book Sealed with the Seven Seals is Revealed.

Before the importance of the Genealogy and Lineage of Abram/Abraham, King David, and Prophet Muhammad, and their relationship to **Maitreya** came to the **Mission**, we still believed that God kept His Promises and indeed all the Great Kings and Messiahs (Prophets), etc. were the First Begotten Son Of God (King David, His Reincarnation who was the First Begotten Son – God's Spirit, etc.). We, however, believed that this happened through Reincarnation, and that Adam (The First Begotten Son) was born as all the Great Prophets and Messiahs (Kings, Reformers, and all things that affected the progress of man and their evolution further, even if they have not been from the Blessed Lineage).

There are, however, many who were born in this Lineage who were not the First Begotten Son Of God (Christ, Anointed, etc.). They are those who did not manifest Great things and/or were cruel and unworthy. These are the ones who were placed in this position between the incarnations of Christ. Whenever Christ is born, He will occupy these positions as Christ who is from the Blessed Lineage. After the opening of the Seven Seals, however, it sounds like God is saying that this no longer will be the case:

> Dan 2:44
> 44 And in the days of these kings shall the God of heaven set up a kingdom, which shall never be destroyed: and the kingdom shall not be **left to other people**, but it shall break in pieces and consume all these kingdoms, and it shall stand for ever. (KJV)

Since we believe this Kingdom will be established after the Seventh Angel comes (at the end time), after this (Seventh Angel) it will not "**be left to other people**." This seems to

SUPPLEMENTS

be clearly saying that the Scepter will no longer pass to anyone. It will stay with Christ (the First Begotten Son) and God. Christ and God will Reign forever. This is also shown in The Revelation:

Rev 11:15
15 And the seventh angel sounded; and there were great voices in heaven, saying, The kingdoms of this world are become the kingdoms of our Lord, and of his Christ; and he shall reign for ever and ever. (KJV)

How is this possible? If we believe that Christ comes as a man and will bring God's Revelations (Spirit Of God) to man and dies later, how can God Reign forever, with Christ (will not be left to others)?

The answer has already been given in the arrangement we have made in the **Mission**. It is true that **Maitreya** will leave this body, but He will return. The very board of directors (The Round Table) and later the elders in the facilitating body (**Body Of Christ**) of the **Mission** are also the searching committee to find **Maitreya** in His next reincarnation. After **Maitreya** leaves His body, each member in the board of directors will be the head of the Body for one year. Each year a new head is chosen from those who have not been the head to that point, by vote from the whole group. **Maitreya** will choose the members of this body. Those who remain the members of this body, at the time that **Maitreya** leaves His body, are the **Body Of Christ**. The Spirit of Christ (**Maitreya**) will be upon them.

If **Maitreya** left His body before choosing all twelve members of the Round Table (RT), those who are in the RT at that time will be the permanent members. They can then evaluate the members in the **Mission** and fill the remaining seats (up to twelve). However, those who join this body (**Body Of Christ**) at this point will assume junior positions to the permanent members.

Permanent members cannot be removed unless they have done something to warrant impeachment. The impeachment process begins with the majority vote of the entire body (minus the person being impeached). At the end of the impeachment process, majority vote will decide the fate of the member impeached. Permanent members also can retire if they so desired (or if the majority of the permanent members vote that they should retire).

Periodically (permanent members can decide how long this period will be), the permanent members might consider voting junior members to senior positions. Senior members can be removed by majority vote of the permanent and senior members.

Junior members cannot remove permanent or senior members. The only thing they can do is file a petition for a junior member to be removed by the body. If the petition is accepted, the majority vote of the body is needed.

If further adjustments become necessary for this body to function properly (based on God's Will) the body will come up with them so they will become a strong and united body in God.

So between **Maitreya's** Reincarnations, this body acts as caretaker of the **Mission** and continues what has been set up (in a more limited degree) until **Maitreya** returns (they cannot bring any new revelations, change the teaching, or destroy what **Maitreya** has brought to humanity). Each member of this body is fallible. The body together, however, is infallible, because God's Spirit will be with them (they are the collective **Body Of Christ**).

This Spirit, however, will be with them until **Maitreya** is ready to assume His position as the Eldest. In that Moment that Spirit will no longer be with them, but will be with **Maitreya**. **Maitreya** in His future incarnations cannot change the basic Teachings of the **Mission**. If the person who has been found as **Maitreya** tried to do that, the board of directors has made a mistake and should replace Him with the True **Maitreya** by using the process of impeachment described in our system (with 2/3 majority vote).

So the Spirit of God will be the King forever. He is the Spirit with **Maitreya**. He (the Spirit Of God) will be with the **Body Of**

SUPPLEMENTS

Christ, which is also the Searching body for **Maitreya's** Reincarnations. He (God) will be with **Maitreya** when He is again ready to assume His position as the Eldest.

This arrangement will continue until the facilitating body is formed and the **Communities Of Light** are established all over the world. At that time, the Hierarchy will manifest Itself from the bottom of the society. All positions, as it is envisioned in The Plan, will be filled and The Hierarchy will be formed. The Executive, Judiciary, and Elder bodies will be manifested. In this reincarnation (when all things are manifested) after **Maitreya** leaves His body, the Eldest from the Elder bodies can be chosen. At this time we no longer will look for **Maitreya**, as even the Eldest will emerge from the Hierarchy. However, the moment the Eldest is chosen, He will be in the Capstone and God's Spirit (and Christ) will be with Him (He will be called **Maitreya**). **Maitreya** (Spirit Of God, Christ, King David, etc.) will be King forever and ever. He indeed will be Christ, the Spirit of God on earth, The King! This fulfills the Promise God gave to King David. King David (the Spirit of God, The First Begotten Son) will be King Forever. God never fails in His Promises.

If the Eldest, however, would not manifest the Spirit of God and/or tries to change **Maitreya's** Teachings, he can be removed as prescribed in our system (MAP).

This first arrangement, however, will be only for a thousand years:

Rev 20:4
4 And I saw thrones, and they sat upon them, and judgment was given unto them: and I saw the souls of them that were beheaded for the witness of (יהושע), and for the word of God, and which had not worshipped the beast, neither his image, neither had received his mark upon their foreheads, or in their hands; and they lived and reigned with Christ a thousand years. (KJV)

This arrangement will work because those who are not chosen and are not the Elects will not be incarnated for a thousand years. It is only the Elects who will be on earth. So our system will work for this time period well.

Rev 20:5
5 But the rest of the dead lived not again until the thousand years were finished. This is the first resurrection.

Rev 20:6
6 Blessed and holy is he that hath part in the first resurrection: on such the second death hath no power, but they shall be priests of God and of Christ, and shall reign with him a thousand years. (KJV)

After a thousand years (a long time) people who have not been incarnated for this period of time will be reincarnated again to see if any of them have learned their lessons. Those who have will join the rest of the Elects.

Rev 20:7
7 And when the thousand years are expired, Satan shall be loosed out of his prison,

Rev 20:8
8 And shall go out to deceive the nations which are in the four quarters of the earth,... (KJV)

Humanity again will fall for a short period of time. This time, however, the deceiver (Maya) will be cast into the lake of the Fire forever.

Rev 20:10
10 And the devil that deceived them was cast into the lake of fire and brimstone, where the beast and the false prophet are, and shall be tormented day and night for ever and ever. (KJV)

We all shall return again. At this time the Elects should start looking for **Maitreya**

SUPPLEMENTS

again. This will be our last battle with impurities and Maya (illusion of separation from God).

> Rev 20:11-15
> 11 And I saw a great white throne, and him that sat on it, from whose face the earth and the heaven fled away; and there was found no place for them.

The second resurrection will occur, and those who have not progressed will be Judged.

> 12 And I saw the dead, small and great, stand before God; and the books were opened: and another book was opened, which is the book of life: and the dead were judged out of those things which were written in the books, according to their works.
>
> 13 And the sea gave up the dead which were in it; and death and hell delivered up the dead which were in them: and they were judged every man according to their works.
>
> 14 And death and hell were cast into the lake of fire. This is the second death.
>
> 15 And whosoever was not found written in the book of life was cast into the lake of fire. (KJV)

Those who have overcome, at this point, will be(come) His Sons and Inherit everything.

> Rev 21:7
> 7 He that overcometh shall inherit all things; and I will be his God, and he shall be my son. (KJV)

These Saved People will have these qualities.

> Rev 21:22-24
> 22 And I saw no temple therein: for the Lord God Almighty and the Lamb are the temple of it.

There is no Temple because their bodies are their Temples. They will find God within (His Spirit; within/therein – they learn how to Meditate deeply).

> 23 And the city had no need of the sun, neither of the moon, to shine in it: for the glory of God did lighten it, and the Lamb is the light thereof.

It is the Spirit of God (Christ) which Lightens their bodies.

> 24 And the nations of them which are saved shall walk in the light of it: and the kings of the earth do bring their glory and honour into it. (KJV)

Even the government (kings) will be enlightened and Glorify God.

> Rev 21:27
> 27 And there shall in no wise enter into it any thing that defileth, neither whatsoever worketh abomination, or maketh a lie: but they which are written in the Lamb's book of life. (KJV)

There is no doubt about the Purity of these Saints.

So as we can see:
First: After the Seventh Angel, The Kingdom will not be left to **other people** but to the First Begotten Son Of God (Christ) and God (the Scepter shall not be passed any longer). Therefore the genealogy no longer is valid, and the system has already been set up correctly. The system is under the Protection of God directly (it will not be left to others).

Second: We are not trying to establish the Kingdom that will last forever. We are setting the base for that Kingdom, which will eventually (after a thousand years) last forever. We, however, at this time, are gathering the Elects to help with the process. It is these Elects who will be reincarnated again and again for a thousand years.

When our system is firmly in place, and

SUPPLEMENTS

all of us become well-versed in the Scriptures and know how to work in this system (after a thousand years), the last period of tribulation and purification will come. At this time those who have not been incarnated for this thousand years shall return again, and they again will be judged. Those who have overcome will join the rest of the Elects and then all of us will enter Pure Consciousness (will be with God and Christ).

These Words are the Truth, and are based on the Scriptures and the Words of God. So they will surely come true. Amen.

LAWS ON NATIONS AND PEOPLE

These are the lessons of History (His Story) that man has to learn:

1- The oppressor will be oppressed.
2- The oppressed will be the oppressor, and later on will be oppressed again.
3- Those who let their government oppress others, their government will eventually oppress them.
4- Those who see some unalienable rights for themselves, but will deny others the same rights, will lose those rights as well.
5- The conquerors will be conquered.
6- The conquered will be conquerors.
7- Those who are oppressed will use all means against the oppressor. They will eventually exhaust the oppressor. No matter how powerful the oppressors are, they will eventually lose.

Those who do not learn these lessons of history will repeat these mistakes, and so history will repeat itself. The only way to stop these vicious cycles is to create the **Communities Of Light** and to bring His Kingdom on earth, according to His Revelations in **THOTH**.

The universe marches toward Balance and Unity. It will do it with violence, or it can be done in an evolutionary way if the cyclical changes are understood and helped to change smoothly. Now with these Revelations man knows how they can smooth these processes. It is up to humanity to accept these and bring a Balance and Unity to these processes, or continue their ways and see the violence and destruction continue.

This world indeed is the Babylon (Babel On) the Great. Men cannot hear the background, Quiet Voice of God. They are drawn in the foreground noise of the world. Come out of the Babylon, those who have been called for this **Mission**. Hear this Voice of Reason and Truth. Come together, meditate, and Hear the Background and Quiet Voice of God. Create, and/or join, the **Communities Of Light**. This is your Salvation and the Salvation of Man.

Creation of the **Communities Of Light** and bringing the Kingdom Of God on earth is the Most Urgent task for humanity to accomplish. Therefore march on toward this Most Holy Goal. Do not let any unworthy, earthy goal hinder you in accomplishing this Goal!

ARTIFICAL POWER CENTERS

With emphasis on educational background, previous experiences, and credential gains, a person can create an artificial power center based on these things. Therefore the attention will be diverted from what a person truly can do to what kind of background he has.

Although experiences, credentials, and education have their place, the ability to manifest results should be the only consideration in the final analysis, "You know them by their fruit."

Therefore, we have to be keenly aware that these "artificial power centers" do not form. The real power centers should truly represent a real manifestation, and a person should not only be experienced, educated, and have credentials but also have common sense

SUPPLEMENTS

(wisdom) and know how to truly "get the job done."

In short the real power center and the artificial power center should be one.

IS IT IMMORAL OR ILLEGAL?

There are many human laws that prohibit man to take some actions. There are also God's Laws that if they are broken, a man has committed an immoral act. An immoral act is not necessarily an illegal act. An illegal act is not always immoral!

There can be many examples of this conundrum. For example, fighting for freedom from the yoke of a tyrant might be illegal in the environment that the tyrant has power over but it is not immoral.

WHY GOD COMMANDED US TO EAT KOSHER FOOD AND AVOID EATING UNCLEAN FOOD

Unclean animals, as categorized in the Bible, are usually scavengers. Even if they are not scavengers, they are all somehow helpful to nature. They eat garbage, dead animals, toxic wastes, and things considered to be unclean. These make them unsuitable for human consumption. They are very helpful in cleaning the earth from wastes, weak animals (to promote stronger breeds), and toxins.

The reasons why we should not eat them are: First, they are not good for us. God did not create them for human consumption. They are much more tamasic than kosher foods, even kosher meat. Second, by eating them we take the animals that are created to clean/help the earth away from their duty, and accelerate polluting/destroying the earth. It is like firing the garbage collectors and cleaning crew in a city and expecting a clean city. It will not work. The garbage (toxins, pollution, etc.) will pile up in that city, and disease and death will follow. Destroying these animals will have the same effect.

Therefore, even if you do not eat unclean animals because they are not good for you, you should not eat them because they are good for the earth. Those who want an unpolluted earth should realize this and help the process by following a kosher diet. They should also make others aware of these facts and encourage them to follow this advice. Although kosher animals might eat toxic materials and become toxic, they will never become as toxic as unclean animals that eat mostly garbage/toxins.

We should stop polluting the earth as much as we can. We also should give nature a fighting chance to eradicate any pollution/waste we make. Polluting the earth and taking the animals that clean it out of circulation is an act of double jeopardy. We surely will destroy the earth and ourselves at an accelerated rate if we continue this course!

The clean animals, on the other hand, are made to be eaten. They help very little in cleaning/healing the earth. Even in this regard we should eat meat much less than other food categories (vegetables, grains, etc.) that God has created for us.

When God Commands humans to do something, it is good for them and the universe. However, now (in the age to come), the human should understand the reason behind these Commandments. It is then that they will follow them because they realize it is good (God) for them and their lives. They will then Praise the Praiseworthy (God) for His Wisdom and Creation.

There is always a good (God) reason behind His requests/Commandments.

SUPPLEMENTS
EASTERN AND WESTERN BIAS

The Mystical Paths or philosophies which believe in individual liberation do not put any emphasis on the necessity for the Messiah or the Anointed One.

On the other hand, in the Western belief or Judeo-Christian religions, the Messiah has a central place.

This difference has created a bias on both sides. Those who follow Mystical Paths or Far East Philosophies downplay the necessity of the Messiah and historical events of the last 12,000 years. They believe the spiritual path is an individual quest and the rest is not important.

However, those whose beliefs have been generated based on a Judeo-Christian background put a great deal of emphasis on the importance of the Messiah and disregard spiritual practices and the mystical teachings of the ancient wisdoms.

To eradicate these biases and understand the importance of both teachings and how they are complementary, an understanding of our teachings and the events that have happened in the last 12,000 years is necessary.

As it is explained in our teachings, around 12,000 years ago a great evolutionary step was taken. The old humans were destroyed and replaced by new humans. This new generation, as we are, was completed around 6,000 years ago.

The ancient wisdom and the essence of the realities behind this universe were revealed to humanity as the basic truths in the Mystical Paths. These teachings basically explain the relationship between man and the universe or the spirit of man and the universe (God). Because God is infinite, these teachings and understandings can be explained in infinite ways.

For this reason, this part of the human understanding of God is so vast and sometimes seems confusing. However, if we understand that the mystical understanding of God is a personal relationship between each individual and Him, then when such a relationship is established, this confusion will be dissolved. Although the experience of others might be helpful in our own journey, still we should not become confused by expecting the same experiences to happen to us. We find our own way to establish a direct relationship with the universe or God.

With this approach, not only would there be no confusion for each individual, but also we accept and respect the way of others in their spiritual progress. Therefore, we can see a unity in diversity. It is in this part of human progress that a spiritual teacher or Guru is important and helpful. It is recognized in all Mystical Paths that a Master can be most helpful in the path of an aspirant. Masters are those who themselves have already passed beyond the illusion of the manifested world.

However, there has been a Great Plan in the last 12,000 years, to reveal to humanity the seven steps of the **Eternal Divine Path**. It is this Plan which started to form step-by-step from 12,000 years ago (especially since 3,500 years ago). It is explained in detail all through our teachings how the new generation was divided into different human types, how their third eyes were closed, how a land was kept aside for the future to be given to the Children of Abraham, and how all prophecies which God foretold have been fulfilled and will be fulfilled, etc.

It is because of this Plan to reveal the **Eternal Divine Path** that the importance of the Messiah can be recognized. The Messiah and the process of His coming and fulfilling a part of The Plan, each time He comes, is a testimony to create faith in God.

Also the whole process brings a greater understanding of the truths behind the human and universe (God), and the **Eternal Divine Path** crystallizes the Path to individual and collective liberation. They go hand-in-hand: individual salvation is impossible without collective salvation. This is the lesson that the mystics should learn.

Also individual and collective liberation is not possible without understanding the basic truths of the relationship between man

SUPPLEMENTS

(individual) and the universe, or the mystical part of God.

Therefore, we have to overcome the Eastern and Western biases toward each other, understand the place and importance of each in God's Plan, and create unity between them. In this regard understanding our teachings and **The Greatest Sign** is most important. These biases should be broken down in order to bring the unity to all.

CRYSTALS

Crystals are nothing but crudified ether. When they are kept in the hand or used for healing, because they are the closest element to ether in nature, they direct the vibrations of the body toward its ethereal (Akashic) level.

The very structure of the first five chakras or astral body consists of ether. Therefore, crystals activate this element in the body and clean the ethereal body or the first five chakras, and bring it close to the Akashic (ethereal) level of the universe. So some realization from the Akashic Records will be gained.

However, the human spiritual body consists of seven (or even more) levels. Although crystals are useful tools in the beginning of spiritual progress, or whenever a person wants to use them to clean the first five chakras, still they have a limitation to guide the human to the highest spiritual realization and might become the master of the person. Like any other material thing, or anything besides the ultimate realization of the highest God as the Only Source as absolute, they will become an obstacle in our spiritual progress and our freedom from bondage. Therefore, although they are useful in our spiritual progress, they should be ignored at the end. Each person has to become a crystal, to manifest His Will, himself.

The ultimate realization is to create absolute trust in God, do His Will to bring His Kingdom to all, and be submitted unto Him. He is our only Master. Man cannot have two masters. The other goals are: To create compassion, mercy, forgiveness, cooperative attitude, expansion of the mind, etc. These are the goals to achieve, not gaining powers!

RELATIONSHIP BETWEEN THE SPINAL CORD, MEDICAL LOGO (CADUCEUS), AND THE STORY OF KING ARTHUR

In the middle of the spinal cord there are three energy currents. One of them is a straight energy current which connects the base of the spine directly to the pituitary gland. The other two currents intertwine around this central energy current.

The two intertwining energy currents continue until they end in the two sides of the nostrils. It is through these two energy currents that prana (life-force) is mostly absorbed through breathing, and it is these two energy currents that are strengthened and opened through breathing exercises (Pranayama).

There is a very delicate channel (passageway) in the center of the central nerve. This passageway is where the central current flows. It is through this channel that the spiritual force latent at the base of the spinal cord (kundalini) is raised to its goal or seventh spiritual center (pituitary gland).

Wherever the two intertwining energy currents meet with each other and make a point together with the central energy current, a great power center (chakra) will form. The first point where these three energy currents meet is at the very base of the spinal cord. This point then is the first chakra or psychic center. There are four more points where these currents cross each other. With this, the second, third, fourth, and fifth chakras are formed.

SUPPLEMENTS

The first chakra is at the anal area, the second at the sexual organ, the third at the navel, the fourth at the middle of the chest, and the fifth at the throat area. Then the two intertwining energy currents are separated and they end up at the sinus area in the two sides of the nostrils. The central energy current continues to the middle of the brain, passing through the pineal gland (third eye) into the pituitary.

The first five chakras are related to the five elements in the manifested world: The first chakra to the solid factor (earth); the second, liquid factor (water); the third, luminous factor (fire); the fourth, aerial factor (air); and the fifth, ethereal factor (ether). Therefore, the two intertwining energy currents and their functions are related to the manifested world. That is why they form the first five chakras.

The central energy current, however, continues to the pineal gland (the third eye), which is the sixth chakra. This current continues to the pituitary gland or Master Gland, which is the seventh chakra. These last two chakras merely work with the spiritual aspects of the human. Therefore we can say that the central current and its channel connect man to the spiritual aspects of the universe.

Not only is the central energy current a passageway for the kundalini to rise and open higher chakras (understandings), but also through this passageway and the seventh chakra, a direct connection to the spiritual world is established. Although this connection is always there, the awareness of this connection will not be realized until the kundalini is raised.

Because these three energy currents are deeply connected together at the very bottom of the spinal cord, and as explained, the two intertwining currents are responsible for the functions of the human related to the manifested world, then the central energy current and its passage by being connected to the two other currents, create a bridge between the physical body and spiritual world (Universal Mind, the world beyond the manifested one, etc.).

By understanding this, a person realizes the connection between the physical body (manifested portion of the human) with its spiritual part (spirit and Soul). He also sees where this connection is established in the body. It is the spinal cord and its functions which bridge this connection. That is the reason it is said: If a person wants to gain complete health and happiness, he or she should keep the spinal cord in the best shape possible. This truth was known to the ancient physicians. This can be realized by understanding the relationship between the medical logo (Caduceus) with the materials described above.

The Caduceus, which is used universally all throughout the earth, consists of a sword with two serpents which intertwine on the two sides of this sword. The sword is the symbol for the central current or spiritual passage (the sword of spirit) in the spinal cord, and the two serpents are the two intertwining energy currents around the central one. They make five points of connection with each other and the central current, symbolizing the five chakras.

The two serpents are also the symbol of duality in the manifested world, the good and the bad, the spirit and the matter, the yin and the yang, etc. The serpent with its head at the right (looking at the picture of Caduceus) is more spiritual. It is Yin. It symbolizes the intertwining energy current with its ending at the left nostril, which is connected with the functions of the left portion of the brain.

The serpent at the left is related more to matter and to the manifested world. It is Yang. It is the same as the nerve ending at the right nostril or the functions of the right side of the brain. Through observing the nostrils, we can create a balance between these two forces (spirit and matter). In fact, health can be obtained by having this balance. When one of the nostrils is blocked, it is a sign that there is either some problem in the matter regarding that side, or the balance between the two forces is disturbed.

It is by this observation of Yin and Yang that some people try to create a balance between them and become healthy. They are familiar with foods which have Yin or Yang in them. With this knowledge, they maintain the balance between these two sides.

This truth, as was mentioned above, was

known to the ancient seers. That is why the symbol of a sword and the serpent was chosen as the representation for the goal of medicine. That implies that if a person creates a balance and a calmness between the two serpents, through the sword, a balanced life and radiant health will be gained. That is the secret of a healthy balanced life.

The two serpents could also be considered as the separation between the spiritual world (Yin) and the material world (Yang) in the confused era of the past. This is the reason that only one serpent whose head is at the right, has replaced the two serpents, now that we are close to the dawn of the New Order of the Ages (in fact that is how the Caduceus used to look in ancient times). The message is that all is spirit and the balance will come when everything is healed through spirit.

The sword which is used in the medical logo has the same symbolic meaning as the sword – Excalibur – mentioned in the story of King Arthur. The sword of King David is shown to be inserted inside a stone.

The sword (Excalibur) indeed is the sword of spirit. Only the One who will take this sword out of the stone will be worthy to be the King. It is offered to all who would like to take up the challenge. But only the One who can take the sword out of the stone is the Anointed One.

The kundalini, which is the spiritual force in the human, is like a sleeping serpent within the first spiritual center (controls solid factor, stone) in the human body. This first center is the very bottom of the central energy current (passageway) which is connected to the two other currents in the spine. When the kundalini has not been raised, no spiritual realization can be gained, and man is a rational animal. Therefore the sword of the spirit (Excalibur) cannot be used. This process has been symbolized by Excalibur being planted inside the stone (latent spiritual forces). The kundalini should be raised, which is symbolized by taking the Excalibur out of the stone. Then the two-edged sword of spirit can be used for a great purpose or His Will. Such a person becomes an instrument for God or King Arthur.

As the intention (spiritual energy) is directed toward mundane life and the external world, the sword is useless and is engrossed into the stone (first chakra). But when intention or spiritual energies are directed toward things higher than mundanity, then the sword, with His Grace, will be loosened up (raising of the kundalini) and will become a double-edged sword of truth which will cut through the falsity, and its owner will become a Knight (Elect).

As it was said, to take the sword out of the stone and to become the King was offered to all. That is why many mighty men answered the call and took up the challenge. But none of them succeeded. Then Arthur, the Anointed One, a humble man, only through His Grace, was able to take the sword out and proclaim himself the rightful owner of the title of King.

It was through him, the Anointed One, who was a channel for God to radiate His truth and Grace, that the other mighty men became unified and the Round Table became possible.

SYMBOLIC MEANINGS OF THE STORY OF KING ARTHUR

When he was born, Arthur was taken by Merlin. He was cut from any family bonds. This symbolizes that in order to pursue the path of spirit, one should cut all worldly attachments. Merlin symbolizes his spiritual guide or teacher. He stayed with his spiritual teacher for a long time after he overcame his attachments.

He eventually overcame the first portion of his lower nature (false ego). This is symbolized by taking the two-edged sword of the truth – Excalibur – from the stone of the false ego (raising of the kundalini). By marrying Guinevere, he was unified with his soulmate and through marriage, he purified his sexual relationship.

SUPPLEMENTS

However, he had not yet overcome completely. That is why when he was challenged by Sir Lancelot, he invoked his spiritual powers, symbolized by calling upon the power of Excalibur, in order to show his supremacy over Sir Lancelot. With this misuse of power, he fell, symbolized by Excalibur being broken.

He repented for his action and understood that by the misuse of his powers, he had broken a great Law of the spirit and he promised he would never do it again. That is why the Lady (Holy Ghost) of the Lake (consciousness) gave back his sword of truth (Excalibur). He did not have to take it out of the stone any longer. He had already awakened his kundalini. The powers were taken from him only as a test and lesson. When these lessons were learned, God gave him back what was his birthright.

It was after this that he started to prosper and eventually formed the Round Table. However, by becoming engaged in worldly activities, he had to compromise in order to manage the kingdom, until eventually the point was reached that things went out of hand and the simple purity of the Soul was lost by all. That is symbolized by the unfaithfulness of Guinevere and Sir Lancelot.

When Guinevere failed, and because King Arthur was attached to her, he lost his Excalibur again. With this, everything fell apart.

It was then that the quest for the highest state of consciousness – The Holy Grail – or Pure Consciousness, started. The Knights and King Arthur, who were all aiming for the highest, understood that with all their achievements they still had not found the complete truth. After a great struggle they realized that highest state – The Holy Grail – is within themselves. To purify and conquer the impurities within was an even greater struggle than the establishment of the Round Table and his kingdom.

With Guinevere emphasizing her higher self, symbolized by her becoming a nun, Arthur overcame his attachments to her physical body, and so he received the Excalibur back. It was Guinevere who gave it back to him by emphasizing her higher self. She had the power to lead him to his higher self, so he overcame his second chakra. It was then that the last battle between Arthur and the evil one, who truly was a part of him – his son – started.

Then at the last battle he killed his evil son (his third chakra). He (false ego) also would be killed in the battle, but his spirit lives on (to be born again). King Arthur and the Knights of the Round Table will arise to establish His Kingdom. They will come again and again until His Kingdom will be firmly established. As Krishna (Christus) said to Arjuna, "When righteousness is weak and faints and unrighteousness exults, then my spirit arises on earth."

This spirit will eventually overcome the evil one, and His Kingdom will be established on earth as it is in heaven.

LOTUSTICA VS. SWASTIKA

The swastika is an ancient symbol which has been used in different cultures all through the earth. In each culture it has assumed many different meanings. Until World War II, it had mostly a positive meaning. However, since World War II, after it was used by Hitler as the symbol of Nazi Germany, it was depicted as a negative sign.

As we know, nothing is evil or negative by itself. It is the way it is used that makes it good (God) or evil (devil). This is also true about any sign, logo, symbol, etc. A surgical knife can be used to heal or to kill. Can we say the knife is good or evil? It is neither. It becomes good or evil as we use it.

Not only the swastika, but anything which closely resembled this sign, after World War II, created a negative response. This could be true about the sign Lotustica. Although very similar to the swastika, it is not exactly the same. The insides of the arms are curved. Also it is called "Lotustica." These

SUPPLEMENTS

differences should completely change the perception of many who have a negative connotation related to the swastika. It is not a "swastika" but "Lotustica."

As it can be seen, the Lotustica in reality does not exist. It shows the background of **The Greatest Sign** which is blue. The Lotustica itself is transparent, or nonexistent. It exists when man goes against God's Laws. He will be punished, not by God, but by going against the universal set-ups. It also becomes apparent when an old set-up has to be replaced by a new one: The old has to be destroyed.

The only place in **The Greatest Sign** that the Lotustica is apparent and exists, is in the sixth seal (✡), the sign of Paravipras. It is in this state that this force can effectively and wisely be used for the progress of the universe. Then it becomes good. Paravipras can use it to replace the old, or guide others toward the Goal. For them it exists.

Again we can see how human ignorance can create obstacles to understand the deeper meanings of things. This becomes the source of unfounded fears, resentments, and misunderstandings. That is when the narrowness of the mind begins and the suffering of many follows. Those who have the power might use it to force their ideas, dogmas, or misunderstandings on others.

Only when we expand our minds to see everything is God, will all our fears vanish. There is nothing bad in God (Good). Human actions make it bad. If His Will (Way) is accepted, All is Good (God).

DOES GOD TALK TO EVERYONE DIRECTLY?

We hear many people claim that God talks to them. Can this be true? If this is true, then why does God Prophesy for a long time before He sends a Major Prophet (Manifestation, Messiah, etc.)? It seems that God talks only to One person, and that happens every few hundred years or a thousand years.

We can see that many have awaited the coming of the Messiah. He has to fulfill the Prophecies, bring a New Revelation, and usually suffers immensely at the hands of man, etc. This Truth that God does not talk to everyone is Revealed in the Scriptures as well. Christ plainly says this in a very elegant way: No One goes to the Father but through Me. And Prophet Muhammad Revealed the same thing in the verse below:

Surah Counsel (Ash-Shura)
It is beyond the capacity of a mortal man to speak to God, save by revelation or from behind a veil or through a Messenger to reveal what He will, by His permission... (51)

You will find similar Revelations from all the Major Prophets.

There are three categories of humans who claim that God talks to them:

First are those who hear voices and act upon these voices, and their actions show that the voice they hear is not from God. An example of this is a murderer who claims that God told him/her to kill someone. God will not tell anyone to do that. God is Good!

Second are people who claim that God talks to them and they create a new organization with their followers, or they splinter an existing religion, etc. We have seen a proliferation of this kind at this time of human history. Indeed there are more teachers than followers, it seems. It is these people who should be questioned if they have fulfilled the Prophecies and have brought to humanity what God has Promised.

The third category are people who say that God talked to them and He told them a Truth that helped them in understanding the Scriptures, meaning of a teaching, received a solution to a problem, etc. These are mostly related to an individual and/or community. These realizations, of course, cannot be categorized as a Major Revelation and the person who receives them is not a Major Manifestation

SUPPLEMENTS

(Prophet, Messiah, etc.).

In the case of the first category, of course, we have to recognize that such a person is deluded and needs mental help. They might even be dangerous to the society and should be kept isolated so they cannot harm others.

In the case of the second category, man should not follow anyone but the Scriptures and the Major Manifestations (Prophets, Messiah) sent by God. These are clearly distinguished and History (His Story) has clearly Revealed who they are. They have brought the Greatest Revelations to man, and they are a part of the Seven Seals, **Eternal Divine Path** and **The Greatest Sign**. People in this category should be exposed and their followers educated so they will not follow the false prophets. Only the Major Prophets and the Words they bring to humanity (Scriptures) should be followed.

In the case of people in the third category, these realizations cannot be called Revelations. These are given to a person to strengthen his faith, help him to solve a problem, understand a teaching and/or to help others to understand any of these situations. These realizations should be compared with the Words of God (Scriptures) to see if they are according to the Words of God. If they are, with some diligence, deep thinking, and understanding, they may be accepted as help from heaven. That does not mean that God is directly talking to them. It means that they have received help from the level of consciousness they are in. Some truths are even revealed to humanity, about their lives, in dreams! That is why with analyzing dreams we can resolve some psychological problems. These, however, are not Revelations.

In general the approach to this kind of message is this: Revelations from Prophets (Scriptures) should be looked at as the overall umbrella in our lives. Anything we receive (or anything in our lives) should be under this umbrella. We have to examine anything that comes to our lives to see if it is according to God's Words (Scriptures). If we find something is not according to God's Will, we have to avoid it and ignore it.

As Prophet Muhammad Revealed in the verse above, God may talk to man "from behind the veil." "From behind the veil" here shows that although God reveals some truths to some people and Guides them, by them being behind the veil (their ego), however, they do not talk to God directly. It is the same as we are saying, that man filters the Words of God, and their egos do not let them hear Him in the Purest form. That is why Scriptures are needed and man can find the Purest Form of His Words in these Books.

Therefore, the only person who directly talks to God is the Chosen Prophet (Manifestation, Messiah) who fulfills the Prophecies and God's Promises. Those who claim to be a prophet of God, have not fulfilled the Prophecies, and are not the One who fulfills God's Promises, are false prophets and should be exposed and ignored. Those who say God told them to do bad things (God Is Good) are not hearing God for sure. Those who receive guidance from the Spirit (their Higher natures) should see if it is really from the Spirit. They should see if it is according to God's Ways (Words, Scriptures). If it is not, it should not be followed, and with fasting and prayer they may realize that it is not from the Higher Self (Spirit)!

May this be a Guide for humanity to lead them to a Purer Life and the Straighter Path.

GO TO THE SOURCE

Anytime a Great Light (teacher) comes to earth, many are attracted to him. They become the disciples. However, each disciple can filter only a part of this great Light. Those who in the second level hear or see these disciples, judge the Light by their (the disciples') sayings and/or actions. They receive only a much dimmer light. This dimming effect can continue until a very little or no light is left from the original teachings.

SUPPLEMENTS

That is why in our teachings only the sayings or actions of the original teacher have been considered. It does not matter how great the disciples were, they still have their own personalities and points of view. They can never understand completely the experience that the Source (First Begotten Son) had gone through, "The disciple is not above his master…" (Matthew 10:24). They may, however, reveal great truth, but not all of it.

Therefore, do not judge the Source by the disciples. Listen to what the disciples have to say, but eventually go to the Source. Only a direct experience with the Source can give you the total picture and depth of the Source. Even the Source in the body eventually should take you to the Ultimate; only then can you be a true disciple.

CHANNELING VS. BEING A LIGHT WORKER

There are many who claim that they are channels for one or more beings from the ethereal plane. They bring messages from these beings and many believe in them. These are ones who do "channeling."

There are others who do the Work and Will of God the Most High. They are not a channel for any ethereal being but are kind, compassionate, have great love for all, and work toward the creation of the unity of men. These are called "The Light Workers."

Although there are great channels who bring great revelations to humanity, these truths come from the ethereal sphere which is the fifth level of consciousness.

As it is explained in **THOTH**, the pitfall in this state is again to be(come) an "escapist," because in this level a person can see the perfection of God's work and universe, and he feels no need to interfere in the processes. He forgets that it takes a great struggle to pass from the lower nature to the higher self, "Remember therefore how thou hast received…" (Rev. 3:3). Also not all voices can be trusted!

It is only when they pass this pitfall of just being observant and engage themselves in helping others in the path that they become "Light Workers" (Paravipras). As it has been said, "You know them [the Elects] by their fruits [Actions]."

MEDITATION AND PRAYER

Meditation is a state when God talks to a person. Prayer is when a person talks to God! That is why in meditation one feels Oneness with God or being Him. Without being humble, this might create a superiority feeling in the person who meditates.

This is the reason why selfless service is recommended for the disciples, to bring a balance between a great feeling of being One with God and the humbleness of being selfless (His servant). Prayer also does the same thing. In order for a person to kneel down and pray to God, he or she should humble the self to do so.

Therefore, meditation and prayer go hand-in-hand. They bring a balance to a person. Meditation makes a person to be with God; prayer makes him humble. Prayer in fact is a spiritual service (not being self-centered) to the Self.

IN PRAYING

When we pray, we have to pray in the Sacred Name of the Father (יהוה), the Son (יהושוע), and The Holy Ghost (Mother). However, the Sacred Name (The Word) cannot be pronounced (uttered) in manifested words.

In order to pray in His Name without attempting to utter His Name (The Word), we should invoke God (Father, Son, and The Mother) without outwardly saying The Holy Name. Therefore, when in prayer, pray

SUPPLEMENTS

in the Name (Sacred Name) of the Father (יהוה), the Son (יהושוה) and The Holy Ghost (Mother).

For those who have received the Sacred Name (The Word, The Holy Name), they can listen to it within themselves. Then they can pray "in the Sacred Name of the Father, the Son, and The Holy Ghost." In The Word, the names of the Son and the Father merge as One. The movement and the creative energy created (felt) within is The Mother (raja guna).

Therefore, always remember the Father, the Son, and The Mother in your prayers by invoking them. The Son is used in the middle (between) the Father and The Holy Ghost, to show his mediating position. He manifests the Father and the Mother (The Holy Ghost), as the Messiah, in the manifested world. Each of them are necessary in creation.

The Father is the Divine Logic and the controller of the universe. The Mother (Holy Ghost) is the Creative Force in the universe. God is both the Father and the Mother (Holy Ghost). He is Generator, Operator, and Destroyer. The Son enables God to be manifested (Messiah) in the material world. Therefore, when praying, pray "in the Name of the Father, the Son, and The Holy Ghost." Any other name(s) or vibration used is not the Sacred Name and is man-made!

NON-VIOLENCE

Non-violence is the path of evolution! It is evolvement to bring about a change when the time is ripe for such a change – any moment an attempt to bring a change earlier or later creates suffering and violence. To know the right time to take action is the path of wisdom.

All the forces in the universe are evolving toward guiding It to Its destiny – Perfection and Harmony. There are moments in which each of these evolvements or a combination of them give their fruit. Sometimes the relationship between many elements in a whole evolutionary step is not clear to a mind concentrated on a small portion of the whole. But the march of the whole to its destiny is harmonious and non-violent.

Sometimes an evolutionary step can be accelerated by providing some positive elements, but it cannot be rushed. Also this process can be slowed down by creating obstacles, but never can be stopped! It is this Law which determines the success of an evolutionary or revolutionary step. When such steps are taken in the proper time, they will succeed with minimum violence (suffering). If one is taken prematurely, it can become a counter-evolutionary or counter-revolutionary step. Such steps slow down the process, but can never completely stop It. The universe marches on to Its destiny. Anything which insists to stay in Its path and resists Its progress will be crushed. The greater the resistance, the greater the crush will be!

It is this resistance to change and creating obstacles in the path of progress which creates the antithesis in nature. Then a great struggle is necessary to eradicate the resistance. If the leaders are wise and can see where the next step in the evolution of humanity is, they can guide it to the next step without allowing a great resistance. This is then the path of non-violence, the path of Evolution and Harmony.

Therefore, we can see how important this Law is. It is the path of Balance and Harmony. To create leaders who understand this and are not trapped in one ideology or the other, is of prime importance. Such wise counselors who can guide humanity from one phase to the other should be created. In this regard **Communities of Light** and our teachings (**THOTH**) are most helpful.

SUPPLEMENTS

LIGHT BODY

In **THOTH**, the ethereal body and astral body are regarded as the same. Some, however, make a distinction between them. Indeed the ethereal and astral bodies are two different stages of the etheric body. The ethereal body is under the influence of the tama (crudifying) force, and the astral body is the etheric body under the raja (mutative) force.

That is why in the astral body a person can enter (move into) the ethereal spheres. Then in this state a person can create his own creation by his own will. Even greater than the astral state is the etheric sphere under the influence of the satva (sentient) force. Some call this state the state of Divine Logic. It is in this state that the Will of the Creator and man become One. Then such a person becomes a pure channel to manifest the Will of God on earth.

Before reaching this highest state, still a person might fall into the spiritual traps of the ethereal body (spiritual powers) or the astral body (become trapped in his own creation). However, when the Will of the Creator and man become One, there is no illusion left. It is then that the Light Body will also be manifested.

The goal of spiritual progress is neither to gain powers (siddhis) nor to become an astral traveler, but to manifest the Will, Love, and Power of God. If any power is granted to him, or if he is allowed into the astral world, then he will utilize them for the Will. They then can no longer become a trap. The goal is to create Love, Compassion, Humility, Understanding, Joy of God, etc. The rest will be added to us.

MERGE INTO GOD OR PLAY THE PLAY

Many mystics and those on the path to self-realization have set their goal as to merge with God and/or escape the suffering to reach Nirvana. Of course if the desire is intense, God might allow such a merging. But that is not the goal of creation. In the beginning All was in the state of "Be"-ness. Then God's desire set the creative energy (Mother) into action. Then creation became a sport.

Therefore, insisting to go back as it was ("Be"-ness, merging by leaving the body, etc.) is **against God's desire**. That is why God said, "I will spue thee out..." (Rev. 3:16). Therefore, the Highest achievement while in the body is to realize The Play and play it. It is to see the hand of the creative force (Divine Mother) and the Divine Logic (Father) in the manifested world, then learn how to become a great surfer on their waves. Then like a good surfer, enjoy the ride to the shore of salvation.

Of course until we become a perfect surfer and professional in this art of cosmic waves (plays), we might fall from the surfboard many times. Each time we fall from our surfboard (Higher self), the waves will crush us and take us underneath. However, with a little struggle (meditation) and purification, we can mount the surfboard again a little wiser, stronger, and more professionally.

This will continue until life (surfing) becomes a Joy of Gracefully (with The Grace) riding the waves of destiny!

OVERACTIVE CHAKRAS IN A PREGNANT WOMAN

The metabolism of a woman changes when she is pregnant. Nature (God) prepares her body to nourish the fetus. That is why the hormones in her body become overactive. Hormones are directly related to the chakras.

For this reason, the body of a pregnant woman is an overactive body. The chakras (hormones) are working excessively. This, of course, brings a greater feeling of acceleration. That is why most women feel a great

SUPPLEMENTS

joy during their pregnancy.

During pregnancy, since the chakras are overactive, a greater degree of feelings are present in the woman. Since the matter of pregnancy is directly related to the second chakra (the emotional center), also the swing in emotions, with stronger emotions in each swing, is greater. This time is indeed a great period for pregnant women to meditate and become familiar with these emotions, and is a great help in their spiritual progress.

In this period the physical and ethereal body (spirit) of the child are also forming, so some of these swings of emotions and new feelings might come from this new spirit which is being implanted in the woman for the child (Soul) which will occupy it. Many mothers feel they know their child even before he or she is born. This is the reason their emotions and feelings (chakras) are interdependent and related.

Not only is the child connected to the mother, but he or she is also connected to the father. That is why it is so important for both the mother and father to be present in the life of the fetus. The bonding between them starts at the time of conception. The physical presence of the father is not as important as the feeling of the mother for him, the commitment she has to him (bond of marriage), the love for him, etc. The greater these feelings are between them, the greater the spirit of the child will be.

During the pregnancy, the body is also very sensitive to toxins. It will try to block the toxins from entering the body. It will even fight and repel the toxins that it normally would have tolerated. Since the body is in the state of purification in a greater degree during the night, it will detoxify the body of the woman and she will be sick in the morning, throwing up the toxins (or whenever the body gets a chance).

That is why women should be especially more aware of their diets and of what they put into their bodies. The less toxins they put into their bodies, the less the sickness.

This detoxification of the body, of course, has a direct relationship with greater hormonal activities, as did the stirring of the emotions, etc.

In other words, the body of a pregnant woman acts like a person who has opened his chakras. If a person who is not pregnant has done that, he has learned in the process how to control them (hopefully). However, a pregnant woman is often not a yogi, so that is why she has such a hard time to control these feelings and emotions. This is indeed a great time to meditate, observe, control, and progress.

Some feel a "letdown" after they deliver the child, because the overactive presence of hormones (chakras) recedes and the woman does not feel the same as she did during the pregnancy. Some overworked glands (chakras) even produce less than they normally do. That is the reason why some new mothers feel depressed. This time after pregnancy should be a time of rebuilding the strength physically, mentally, emotionally, and spiritually.

COLLECTIVE MEDITATION VS. TRANSMISSION MEDITATION

There is a difference between Collective Meditation and Transmission Meditation:

Collective meditation is to strengthen the community. That is why we meditate together (in fact it should be done every day together in the morning and evening). Transmission meditation is what we do on Saturdays (6:00 AM to 6:30 AM and again 6:00 PM to 6:30 PM, MST). Transmission Meditation is individual meditation for good (God) Will to man and Peace on earth, etc.

In other words: Collective Meditation is to reach (strengthen) the COLs; Transmission Meditation is to reach out to the rest of humanity and the universe!

SUPPLEMENTS

Collective Meditation is to strengthen the community and accelerate the progress of the members in the community. As mentioned above, it is recommended to be practiced twice a day collectively. The more people participate in this wonderful practice, the greater the acceleration in individual and collective consciousness. That is why we practice over the Internet to increase our numbers.

In Collective Meditation, each individual will become integrated to the collective body, and a collective consciousness is created by them. This Collective Consciousness represents God in a Greater degree. God is the Total collective Consciousness in the Universe and beyond! The more people participate in this practice, the Greater Manifestation of God will be Present!

Transmission meditation, however, is an individual endeavor to bring Good (God) thoughts and Peace to man. Although Collective Meditation will also help in this process, Transmission Meditation brings a greater awareness that we are responsible for the well-being of all unit consciousnesses in the universe. We are not an isolated island in the universe.

The well-being of the rest of the universe will accelerate our well-being as well. If even one person is suffering in the universe, all are responsible for this suffering and should be concerned and try to help to alleviate all sufferings. Transmission Meditation is the beginning of this awareness and help.

When the members of the **Communities Of Light** become One, when their Intentions are to bring Peace and Good Will to all members in the **COLs**, then they will/can extend these wonderful qualities to the rest of humanity and eventually to the whole Universe (God) as well.

Note: There has been a question on what is the difference in performing (the process) between Collective/Transmission Meditations and individual meditation. Here is the answer:

In both of these meditations (Collective and Transmission) go to the Calm place in your meditation (if you can without going through the meditation process).

*In Collective Meditation, concentrate on your **Community Of Light** and seek answers to the question of how you can become more One with the Community and create a **COL**. Realize the problems in it, come up with solutions (for your problems first, then others and eventually the whole Community). Solve your individual problems (including the ones you have with other people). Any solution you come up for others and/or the Community in whole, give it to them in the form of a suggestion. Let others also learn how to come up with solutions themselves instead of making decisions for them all the time.*

*In Transmission Meditation, reach out to humanity and the universe. Again go to the Calm Place within (without going through the process) and then imagine the Love and Light of God touches everyone. See what the problems on earth (or the universe) are. Seek solutions to them and see how the **Mission** will Solve all of them, etc. Pray for humanity (universe) and visualize Peace will come after the **Mission** is established, etc. Then visualize how you can join the **COLs** and help this process, etc.*

SALVATION

In order to know the truth, we should look to the past to see a pattern that will confirm any teachings. In the teachings of the Far East, especially Hinduism, a period is described when many Great Souls were living on earth. They were called by many names such as Rishies, Masters, Mahatmas, Munies, etc. Their teachings, however, became a

SUPPLEMENTS

wealth of knowledge for future generations.

In their teachings a state of oneness with God (Atman) is explained. According to these teachings, that is the goal of spiritual endeavors. Whoever reaches this Oneness has reached the Goal.

However, for many thousands of years (12,000), few have realized this Oneness. The reason for this has been the 12,000 year period of human history when man fell further away from God (Truth). We are now at the point of return to the Godhead. That is the reason for such a great confusion in this conjunction between the end of the Old and Dawn of the New. However, the old (history) should not be completely disregarded. There are great lessons to be learned from it. The New indeed should be based on these lessons of the old. We are on the brink of discovering much great knowledge which can either be used for Good (God) or evil.

It is after the establishment of the Kingdom, for one thousand years, that humanity will learn the great lessons which have been revealed throughout this book (**THOTH**) and the **Eternal Divine Path**, "But the rest of the dead live not again until the thousand years..." (Rev. 20:5). Eventually through the formation of the **Communities of Light** and creation of the proper environment, one more time many Great Souls will reach the Great Oneness with their Essence which is God (Good). This is when many will attain salvation. This is the Goal of our teachings. They will reach Pure Consciousness. They will be with the Father as His Sons.

These Great Souls one more time will teach humanity the Goal of their lives, "To Be(come) Divine (One)." Then is the time that the Golden Era will dawn and one more time, "The Sons of God" will be with man (At-Man).

THE NEW MAN

The ultimate Goal or the Result of our teaching is to create the New Man, a man (human) who has broken through all the bondages that life has put on him! The New Man of the Golden Age, with a lucid mind, sees things clearly as God sees them, a person in the Image of God!

Such men have broken through anything that stands in front of them to be a Universalist. They expand their minds and are beyond all falsities. They see the Hand of God in history (His Story) and realize that they have been born so many times in so many cultures, religions, and backgrounds that they have no prejudices against any of them. They Guide humanity toward God's Nation and Culture.

History is a lesson for them. They learn from it and will not repeat the mistakes of the past. They see that the **Communities Of Light** (**COLs**) are the answer to all human problems. They do not hesitate to spread this Message and wait for humanity to be awakened and succumb to God's Will. They see that the **Mission** indeed has the answers to all human problems, and it presents God's Will. They see God with knowing the teachings and they know God Exists.

They realize that none of the man-made political, financial, social, etc. systems have the ultimate answer. It is only God with His flexible and adoptable system that will solve all the problems. The cyclical periods in human lives are real and clear to them as day. They know how to help societies to overcome these periods in a smooth and evolutionary manner. They strive for the Ultimate Balance between all forces. It is then that human life becomes a smooth way of knowing when to implement what part of the transitional actions to the next phase!

Indeed we need this New Man with a Lucid Mind. The **Mission** and our teachings will create such a Man, a Superman who belongs to the whole humanity (earth), men who are larger than life, men who represent all classes of humanity. They rest not until they have destroyed the last vestiges of impurities and narrowness in themselves and others.

We call the New Men: Paravipras (beyond Intellect). No matter what you call them, these New Men will be created with what God has Revealed to humanity: Our teachings. He is the New Man who is made for a New Era.

Those who know the teachings and still are not Paravipras, either have not seen the Vision clearly or other things in life are preventing them to become One. God is Patient and He has already Chosen those who see this Vision clearly and are One.

So Know the ultimate result of our teachings. See the Vision Clearly. Become larger than Life. Shatter all bondages in your life. Free yourself to God. Become the New Man, a Paravipra!

A DECREE

The opinion(s) expressed by any disciple of Maitreya, or their actions, do not necessarily represent Maitreya and His Teachings.

Each individual has to find out about Maitreya and His Teachings personally.

Go to God directly. Let no one stand in your way. Read His Scriptures and study His Actions, so you eventually may know Him and be(come) in His Image. Only then can you represent Him.

Maitreya

GLOSSARY

The Glossary contains the terms used in the Mission Of Maitreya.

GLOSSARY

A

Abraham: Same as Abram.

Abram (Abraham): The son of Terah from Ur, who was a true Brahmin. He is the father of the Hebrews (Elected Ones).

After Abram had his son Ishmael, God changed his name to Abraham. Then he begot Isaac, his other son.

Abu Bakr: The first Caliph of the Muslims.

Actualized Person: A person who knows the Self and is aware of what he can and cannot do. He is content with what he is without relying on others' approval or disapproval.

Adam: The name of the first perfect man (First Begotten Son of God) who came to the first humans as their guide to lead them to God's Ways. Also Adam refers to the first humans who were both "male and female" in one being (). Later these humans were divided into two beings as man and woman (☯☯) or soulmates.

Ahamtattva: The second part of the mind. It consists of raja guna. It is the recognizing part of the mind. After the Chitta (screen, the crudest part of the mind) takes the shape of the external object, the recognizing part identifies the messages received by the Chitta. The Chitta itself has no sense of identifying things but it just receives them. Then it is the Ahamtattva which recognizes what it is and gives the information to the logical or decision-making part of the mind (Mahatattva), which makes decisions on how to react to the information received through the Chitta and Ahamtattva. Then orders are given to the nervous system to carry out the decision with the raja guna (energy).

The Universal Ahamtattva is the recognizing part of the Universal Mind through which all things can be recognized.

Ahimsa: Means "non-violence." Violence means to deviate from a set of rules or regulations, so Ahimsa means to not violate those rules (Daharmas) or Laws of the universe.

"A-Him-Sa" in truth means "I-am-He." In the abbreviated form of "Hung-So" or "So-Hung," it is used as a very powerful mantra in the Far East.

Ajna: The sixth chakra in Sanskrit.

Akasha (Akasa): Same as ether.

Akashic Records (Book of Remembrance, Source of Decrees, in Islam: Eternal Tablet): The cosmic records of creation and history; the memory of the Universal Mind; the records kept of all events in the past and what is happening or will happen in the universe.

It is through these records that God (through His Prophets) corrects or advances the old revelations. Because of these records, even if humans change the Scriptures, God will reveal the truth to those who are chosen to know. Or those who are sincere will have access to these records as a revelation, by His Grace. "Ask, and it shall be given you; seek, and ye shall find; knock, and it shall be opened unto you" (Matthew 7:7).

Ali: The fourth Caliph of the Muslims.

Allah: The name used by Prophet Muhammad in Islam, which means, "God, the Adorable One, the Praiseworthy." It has also been used as the name of God in the Baha'i Faith.

GLOSSARY A

In the Hebrew language and related tongues, we can find names for God as El (means "strong" or "first"), or Eloah ("One Supreme Object of Worship"), Elah, or Elahah, which are the singular forms for Elohim (God).

With comparison of these names for God with the name of Allah, we can see their similarities and closeness in pronunciation and meaning. So we can say that the name of "Allah" has been used as reference to God. It has been used throughout the Middle East as the name for God.

So Allah is related to the names in the Bible. They are all sacred names because they create vibrational sounds (mantras) which affect the consciousness and expand it toward higher understandings.

Amen: The same as Aum or OM (ॐ). It is also a mantra as Aum is. It is used to invoke God's attention (spiritual forces). That is why it is used after prayer. For the same reason, people hope their prayers will be fulfilled if they say the word "Amen" at the end of the prayer.

Anahata: The fourth chakra in Sanskrit.

Ananda (Bliss): The blissful state of higher or Pure Consciousness, the ultimate goal of the spiritual journey. The experience starts at the fifth chakra and continues on.

He who truly (Sat) knows the consciousness (Chit) will experience bliss (Ananda). That is the goal of the life (Sat, Chit, Ananda).

Anandamaya Kosha (Etheric State or Bliss, Heaven, still a part of Maya): The Kosha corresponding to the fifth chakra.

Angel: (He who is not from earth!) same as Avatar. Also refers to the three gunas and their different levels of attributes in the universe (different combinations of them).

Annamaya Kosha (Physical Body): The kosha corresponding to the first chakra.

Anu: Atom. In the Bible, it is called "the dust of the ground."

Artists: Intellectuals with more intuitive ability; those who can show the present state of the society through their art and how to progress to the next phase.

They are one of the classless groups in society. That is, they do not belong to the five active classes in society (read Kingdom of Heaven on Earth).

Astral Body (Spirit, Ethereal Body): Is what has been referred to as the spirit or ethereal body. It consists of ethereal factor in the human body. The Soul (self, unit consciousness) resides in this ethereal body. In fact the first five chakras reside in this ethereal body and is what the Soul progresses through toward reaching higher consciousness. The sixth chakra is the place of the three gunas (the mind, different than the brain), and the seventh chakra is where the Soul reaches beyond the power of the three gunas. It becomes Pure Consciousness.

Therefore, the container of the first five chakras is what we can call the astral body, ethereal body, or spirit. When the Soul through this body leaves the gross body and travels in ethereal factors, it is called astral projection.

Atman: Same as Soul, or Adam.

Atom: The smallest manifested matter as the basic blocks of creation.

For many thousands of years scientists thought the atom was unbreakable and solid. However, eventually they realized that the atom is actually an empty space compared with its basic structure. Later on they were able to break the atom into even finer components. They achieved this by using the accelerators to break it into the particles of the atom.

However, the atomic particles are unstable and are very short lived in the environment of the laboratories. With this they have realized that the creation is much more complex than they have ever imagined.

GLOSSARY

Through these studies and based on the theory of a unified field that all things have come from, scientists have discovered that there are three forces. The scientific explanation of these forces are: The weak force mediates the process of radioactive decay. The strong force binds elements together to create matter. The electromagnetic force carries light (energy) from the sun (heat) and stars.

When we consider the explanation about these three forces, we can see the relationship between them and the three gunas. The weak force mediates the process of radioactive decay. Decay is the transformation of matter into its more basic elements, to be used to create other more complicated elements in creation. This is the function of the sentient (satva) force – to loosen the grip of the tama guna and free the elements to be used to further the creation.

The strong force binds elements together to create matter. This is the very function of the crudifying force (tama guna), binding the elements (consciousness) to create matter. The electromagnetic force carries light (energy) from the sun (heat) and stars. Not only does it carry energy, it is energy itself. Energy is the mutative (raja) force in nature. It is the magnet in the universe.

However, science has not yet mastered the ether. If this element is understood by them, they will realize that all particles in the atom, and the atom itself, are created by crudified ether. If they could ever go deeper than this, they would also realize that these three forces function on the consciousness which is the most illusive of all elements in the universe!

Through these studies and based on the theory of a unified field that all things have come from, scientists have discovered that there are four forces in the universe. These forces are generally known as the weak force, electromagnetic force, strong force, and force of gravity.

The opposite force to this pulling (gravity, attraction) effect, is the influence of the weak force (the total amount of weak force or total amount of the absence of the strong force, repulsion). The greater the absence of the strong force, the greater the repulsive force. It is the interplay of these two forces (effects) which keep the planets in their orbits!

All of these forces (Mother) are under the control of the consciousness (Father). If science realizes this, then its followers no longer can be called scientists but mystics!

Avatar (Son of God, god, god-man): In the image of God; he who manifests God's qualities (Compassion, Mercy, Knowledge, Goodness, etc.). He is One with God when he talks about (is connected to) Him. He might act like a regular person when he is not connected, as did Christ, who was a Son of God (connected and One with God), and a son of man (who was just a man)!

An Avatar comes back to this world after reaching Pure Consciousness in order to help others to reach higher consciousness and/or Pure Consciousness. He is called an Avatar, son of God, god-man.

Avatars come to this world with definite missions according to the time, place, and situation (the situation and/or level of consciousness of humanity). Besides Avatars (Sons of God) there is the First Begotten Son (Maha Avatar, Christ, The Anointed One, etc.) who comes as the Major Manifestation to bring the Revelations of God to man!

The coming of a Major Manifestation is rare. There will be only one more Major Manifestation but that will occur in a thousand years, but no new Revelation. It is then that the last part of the Plan of God will be fulfilled (the Golden Age will dawn). However, there might still be Avatars who come to implement these teachings and to keep them intact and refreshed until then.

Avidya: "Vidya" means knowledge. "Avidya" means ignorance. It is the name given to the material manifested world. Also each atom (anu) is called an avidya (ignorant) and has to progress through the evolutionary process to reach Pure Consciousness (vidya).

GLOSSARY

B

Babel: (Gen. 11:4) "And they said, Go to, let us build us a city and a tower, whose top may reach unto heaven; and let us make us a name,…"

So the city was going to be built for making a name for themselves. That is why all throughout the Bible, the "city of Babylon" refers to egoistic pursuance for making a name and fame, which is from ego and creates confusion (Babel).

Baha'i Faith: The religion founded by Prophet Bab (Baha'u'llah) in Persia. Its most significant feature is its universal view of religion and its teaching of the unity of humanity. We can say it is a religion of universality.

The symbol of universality is the fifth seal (✹) in **The Greatest Sign**.

Baha'u'llah: Another name of the Bab, the founder of the Baha'i Faith, the fifth seal in **The Greatest Sign**. The name Baha'u'llah means, "the worth of God."

Balaam, Doctrine of: Any belief or doctrine which does not teach that "The Goal Of The Life Is To Be(come) Divine, That Divinity (God) Is Everything."

Baptism: A ritual performed to become pure, or repentant. It is an act of turning from the external world toward the spiritual world. At the moment of baptism, the person will decide to change the direction of his or her life from flesh toward spirit, so his past deeds will be forgiven for a promise of a new life in purity and goodness.

This universe was made to enable man to overcome his lower nature and go to his higher self. Any moment a person decides that he will change his life and will sanctify it toward good deeds and purity, his past bad actions will be forgiven, and he can start a new life of struggle toward becoming more and more Divine. Through his struggle, he wins God's Grace and will reach salvation.

The act of baptism does not finish with its rituals, but it is the beginning of a lifetime struggle to be(come) Divine (or even many lifetimes).

The ritual of using water and the experience which follows the ritual is because the person is immersed in water, or water is poured on the top of his head (the seventh chakra). Suddenly prana, which is stored in the solar plexus, is released and a blissful feeling occurs. The person feels he received the Spirit of The Holy Ghost.

However, the commitment of the person to be(come) Divine after baptism is what is most important.

Bardo: According to Tibetan Buddhists, the stages a person goes through after death.

"Be"-ness: The state of Pure Consciousness, pure intuition; the state that the universe was in before the release of the creative forces in the universe.

Bhagavad-Gita: Songs of God, the Hindu Scripture depicting the war between good (God) and evil.

Bhakti Yoga: The yoga of devotion; the path of realizing God through loving Him as the only object of adoration and love. Through this intense love and also by realizing that God is everything, a person creates a great love for Him and His creation. Through his devotion and service, he will win His Grace, realize Him, and go to Him (Pure Consciousness). The service is done by following the **Eternal Divine Path** and leading others to realize Him.

Bhuloka (Physical World): The first loka in Sanskrit.

Bhuvarloka (Prana World): The second loka in Sanskrit.

GLOSSARY

Blind Intellect: Intellect without intuition.

It is when an intellectual sees this manifested world as the only truth and has no realization that this visible universe has come from the unseen. He does not know God and has no intuitive knowledge of spirit. Such an intellect is blind and dry like iron. But intellect with intuition is precious and flexible like fine gold.

Bondman: The name given by Prophet Muhammad for the believers in Islam.

It is true in the sense that God has complete control over all unit consciousnesses through His Universal Mind (three gunas). So all are His bondmen.

Book of Remembrance: Same as the Akashic Records. It is used in the Bible with the same meaning.

"Born Again": To go from the lower self to the higher self. When a person overcomes his lower nature, he will be born into his higher nature. He will start to grasp the reality behind the spiritual world.

Brahmins: The priest class.

God divided humans into five different types after the flood of Noah, according to their evolutionary progress (chapters 9 and 10 of Genesis in The Holiest Book).

Brahmins are those who have spiritual inclinations and a keen sense of justice. They are symbolized by the sons of Shem in the Bible. Abram (Abraham) was one of the children of Shem also. He was a true Brahmin and chosen by God for a great beginning and the shaping of future history.

Breath Of Life, The (Prana): Same as prana.

Buddhi: When the mind is directed toward God-realization and the "I" feels it is a part and parcel of the universe, and the universe is a part of him, then the mind becomes spiritualized (Buddhi).

When the direction of attention (prana, energy) becomes inward rather than outward, the mind becomes Buddhi.

Buddhism: The religion founded by Buddha.

Its main objective is to awaken the spiritual forces in man, therefore it can be included in the religions from the Far East which are related to the first seal (☯). Buddha taught about the self-sustaining part of the universe and the Laws governing it (Darma).

C

Canaan: One of the children of Ham, the son of Noah. He is the symbol for the Shudra (laborer) class of humans.

Cayce, Edgar: The sleeping Prophet of America.

He was born in 1877 on a farm near Hopkinsville, Kentucky. His ability to have access to the Akashic Records and to bring information about many truths, and his talent to diagnose diseases and recommend cures while in a sleeping state, are the reasons for his fame.

Centrifugal Force: The loosening of the grip of the tama guna over the consciousness.

In order to create this universe, God used the power of the tama guna for crudifying the consciousnesses into different elements in the universe (ethereal, aerial, luminous, liquid, and solid). This process of crudification is done through the centripetal force.

At the end of creating the five basic elements, the creation of plants, animals, and humans was accomplished. It was done by using the five basic elements and the unit consciousnesses in higher states, and also by the loosening of the power of the tama guna over the consciousnesses contained in these elements. This loosening of the crudifying power of the tama guna is the centrifugal force.

GLOSSARY

Centripetal Force: The tightening of the grip of the crudifying power of the tama guna over the consciousnesses of the universe.

In order to create this universe, God used the power of the tama guna for crudifying the consciousnesses into different elements in the universe (ethereal, aerial, luminous, liquid, and solid). This power of crudification of the tama guna is the centripetal force.

Chakras: The seven energy centers in the human body. The first five reside in the ethereal body (astral body, spirit). The sixth is the center of controlling the power of the three gunas (mind), and the seventh is the state of Pure Consciousness.

The first chakra controls the solid factor (flesh) and is located in the anal area (solid waste). The second controls the liquid factor and is located in the genital area (liquid waste). The third chakra controls the luminous factor and is located in the navel area (heat is used for digestion, the hottest part of the human body). The fourth controls the aerial factor and is located in the middle of the chest (controls the lungs, air). The fifth controls the ethereal factor and the previous four chakras, and is located at the throat area.

The sixth chakra is the controller of the mind (three gunas) and is located between the eyebrows (the middle of the forehead). The seventh controls all others and is located at the crown of the head.

Channel: Same as being submissive.

Cherubims: The guardians of the garden of Eden (Pure Consciousness) (Gen. 3:24) which were "placed at the east of the garden … and a flaming sword which turned every way, to keep the way of the tree of life."

It is the symbol for Maya which prevents those who are in their lower natures from entering Pure Consciousness which gives the everlasting life (tree of life).

Children of Israel: Israel means "he who struggles with God." "With" here means to be with or on the same team. Therefore, "to struggle with God," here means to work with God in the struggle that all reach Pure Consciousness.

The Children of Israel are those who have struggled lifetimes to overcome their lower natures and will struggle further to help all reach Pure Consciousness. They are the Elected Ones.

Chitta: The crudest part of the mind, which consists of tama guna. It is the screen of the mind to which the objects in the external world are projected and then it takes the shape of those external objects. It is directly connected to the ethereal (astral) body. Also it receives the messages carried by the nervous system from the external world.

The Universal Chitta is the screen of the Universal Mind through which all things can be observed.

Christ: Same as Pure Consciousness; also means The First Begotten Son (יהושוח) who manifests both Father and Mother. Whoever overcomes reaches Pure Consciousness (a son).

It is that state of consciousness which Esa the Messiah was in so he was called Christ. In the Bible (Matthew, chapter 3), it is after Esa overcame the temptations of evil that he again became Christ.

Christ Consciousness: Same as Pure Consciousness.

Christhood: Same as Pure Consciousness.

Christianity: The faith of the followers of Esa the Christ.

If Christianity is taken as the message brought by Esa the Christ, then it is to believe that in order to establish the Kingdom Of Heaven within and without, the utmost sacrifice (not being self-centered, being humble) is necessary.

The symbol of Christianity is the cross (✝), the third seal in **The Greatest Sign**.

GLOSSARY

Classless Types of Humans: Those humans who cannot be categorized into the five major classes of humans. They are the Prophets (Messengers, Avatars, Angels, etc.), Gurus (Spiritual Teachers), Artists (those who guide the society by their art; they are intuitive intellectuals), and Paravipras (true leaders of human society).

Cloud: Symbol for confusion, individually or collectively.

Whenever this confusion comes, a Savior is necessary to rescue the earth.

Collective Consciousness (Universal Mind): Same as Unconscious Mind.

Concepts: Those ideas which we believe because we were told to believe them.

Every person is born into a family, society, culture and environment that influences and shapes his beliefs. These beliefs create a system of values which represent the base of that culture and in return again affect the person. Therefore ideas and beliefs are instilled in the person without him even questioning them.

However there are spiritual truths which are the only true beliefs to follow. When a belief in society or a person is different than the truths in the universe, that belief becomes a concept which is an obstacle in the path of the person's progress.

That is why each person should question his own and society's values and beliefs. He should then seek and find out the true values and replace the false ones with these true ones. Only then can man make himself free from all the bondage which has been imposed on him.

That is why God has sent the Scriptures to man, so that they can be a guidance for him. Man might then find the way to the truth if he understands the real meaning behind the symbolic language of the Scriptures, or if he finds a true teacher to show it to him.

Communities Of Light: Communities that follow the **Eternal Divine Path** (refer to **Eternal Divine Path**).

Consciousness: The witness entity; awareness in the universe; the logic and/or male part in the Universe (God).

Cosmic Dust: Atom.

Creative Force, The (Prakrti, The Three Gunas In The Operative State): When raja guna (energy) is activated, then the three gunas will be in the operative position, and they become the creative force in the universe. They become the three levels of the Universal Mind and unit minds.

The most sentient part of these creative forces (Mahatattva) is the decision-making part. The second part (Ahamtattva, mutative force) is the doer or recognizing part, and the third and crudest (also crudifying) part (Chitta) is the one which is used to create the manifested universe (centripetal). Also, the Chitta is the visualizing part of the mind.

Crudifying: Same as centripetal force.

D

Daharma (Darma): The very word "Daharma" (or "Darma") means "innate nature." Any subject in this world has a nature, even this universe itself has a nature. Also as the subjects become more complicated, they will become multi-natured (they will have more than one Daharma or Darma).

These Daharmas should be viewed as Laws set up for each subject to follow. If a subject follows his or her nature, it will be in harmony with the Universal Laws. If he or she does not follow his or her nature, disharmony will be created which will result in confusion and unhappiness.

These natures or Darmas can be understood by deep observation, meditation, and

GLOSSARY

concentration. Also most of them are revealed by God through His Prophets (if you understand them).

When all things follow their Darmas, then the Kingdom Of Heaven within and without can be established.

Darkness: Ignorance, being under the influence of the tama guna.

Darma: Same as Daharma.

Devil: Crudifying power of the tama guna over the Soul; ignorance.

When the Soul is under the influence of the tama guna, the mind becomes crude and will be attracted toward the desires and impulses of the lower nature. This causes desires to arise in the mind ("sea") and will result in being attracted to the external world (Maya, "the dragon"). The result of fulfillment of desire is attachment and greed. Greed will result in more attraction, desires, attachment, and greed. This wheel goes on and on, so the person will be drawn more and more into the ocean of Maya, and more and more held by the grip of the crudifying power of the tama guna.

The by-product of all these things is uncontrollable lust, anger, vanity, fear, and all the vices of human life. This process is what is called **the wheel of Maya**.

Divine: God-like, supremely good. That is the goal of life: To be(come) Divine (Pure Consciousness).

Divine Actions: Those actions which make a person Divine. All the actions taken to help the universe to reach higher consciousness are regarded as Divine actions (actions done for the establishment of the Kingdom within and without).

Divine Father: See Father.

Divine Logic: See Father.

Divine Mother: Same as Divine Grace.

Dogma: What seems right! Dogma is a set of beliefs that can be the truth, or not. It is a set of concepts that are accepted by the followers of a religion or a sect, which they believe to be the truth. However, usually when it is used in our teachings it refers to the negative meaning as a set of beliefs that are not from God but are man-made!

Dragon, The Red: (<u>The Revelation</u>, chapter 12): Maya; excess, unnecessary attraction toward the external world (any attraction which is contrary to our spiritual progress).

E

Earth (Hell): Is used as a symbol for being in the lower nature and also as the planet Earth.

However, its symbolic meaning is used more often than the other in the Scriptures. In general, it is used as meaning "hell." In fact, this earth is a hell when the Laws of God are not followed.

Eden: An ideal environment in which humans progress at the most accelerated rate. Also it refers to the state of Pure Consciousness, to be in the image of God.

Ego: The values related to the self.

Ego should be divided into two kinds: False ego and actualized ego.

False ego is accepting false and imaginary values as one's own true values. These false values can be internal or external.

Internal false values are the beliefs of having some merits which actually do not exist in the person. We can recognize these false internal values when the person needs external support to believe that he actually possesses such merits (that others support that we have such values). If a person does not receive this external support, he will lose his confidence and feel very miserable.

External false ego is any kind of value or greatness we relate to ourselves because of external possessions in the material world. If a person loses these possessions, he will lose confidence and be lost.

Both internal and external false egos are what can be called the illusion of life (Maya).

Actualized ego is when the true values of the person and his higher self are actualized, recognized, realized and developed by him. Such values do not need any external support, and such a person does not value himself by external possessions. Only a person with an actualized ego will gain true confidence and happiness. He will expel the illusions of the false ego and set himself free.

Elders: The five sensual attributes (pancha tatwa), five organs of the senses (smell, taste, sight, touch, hearing), five organs of the actions (speech, hands, feet [motion], generation, and excretion), five basic elements in the universe (ethereal, aerial, luminous, liquid and solid), three levels of the mind (the three gunas), along with the illusive "I am" as an entity separate from the rest of the universe, make up the twenty-four elements in the body and in the universe, which are symbolized as "the four and twenty elders" in the Bible (Rev. 4:4).

Also it refers to those leaders who become observers in the Hierarchy in the system of Zion and Mount Zion and have great influence in preserving the system and justice.

Elected Ones: Those who have struggled through many lifetimes and have reached higher consciousness or Pure Consciousness. They are the ones who struggle with God (Children of Israel, the Hebrews) in order to bring all to Pure Consciousness.

Energy: Same as raja guna.

EnshaAllah: If God Wills.

Ephraims: Same as the House of Israel. The Children of Israel were divided into the House of Judah (Jews) and the House of Israel (Ephraims, or Samarians).

The House of Israel became the ten lost tribes which traveled toward the West and immigrated to Europe, England and eventually to the U.S.; for more detail, read Children of Abram (Abraham), All Prophecies Are Fulfilled.

Also Ephraim was the younger son of Joseph – son of Jacob (Israel) – whom, with his older brother Manasseh, was accepted as his own son by Israel (Jacob). Israel preferred him over his older brother Manasseh. Both Manasseh and Ephraim inherited two portions of Israel's inheritance and became two tribes of the twelve tribes of the Children of Israel.

Esa: See Jesus.

Eternal Divine Path: The path to reach Pure Consciousness, which is explained and revealed through **The Greatest Sign**.

It is to endeavor to awaken the spiritual forces (☯) (Far East Philosophies – mystical experience), to direct the realization and energy created by the process of awakening the spiritual forces toward the establishment of the Kingdom Of Heaven On Earth (✡) (Hebrews), and in order to establish the Kingdom, utmost sacrifice – not being self-centered, sharing – (✝) (Christianity) is necessary. However the attachment to the result of one's actions would become a hindrance in his progress so surrendering and submission to His Will (☪) (Islam) is necessary. Then expansion of the mind or to become a universalist (✹) (Baha'i Faith) is necessary to shatter all narrowness of the mind. After all this progress, when a person becomes a dynamic spiritual force to help the whole universe understand the purpose of their lives and help them to reach Pure Consciousness, such a person becomes an Elect (Paravipra) (✡).

Through these Paravipras, eventually all will reach Pure Consciousness (卐) and these Elected Ones also will reach there (卐).

This path, which has been established in eternity by the Father and the First Begotten Son, will lead a person to Divinity. That is why it is called the "**Eternal**" (because it is established in eternity), "**Divine**" (because it leads to Divinity), "**Path**" (because it is the way to Divinity).

Ether (Akasha): The first manifested element in the universe. It is the element that stores memory. In its solidified form, it is what is known as crystal (silicon). That is why in its solidified form, it is used for memory in computers.

In its subtler (subtlest) form (most invisible element in the manifested world – creation) it encompasses all things. It contains the Universal Memory (Akashic Records). Beyond the ethereal element, there is the Essence of God (consciousness and three gunas). In this state there is no memory and no manifestation (it is beyond Mind!)

Ethereal Body (Spirit, Astral Body): Same as astral body.

Eve: Same as woman.

Evil: Same as devil.

Evolution: The process of progressing from the unaware state of consciousness to Pure Consciousness (complete awareness).

Expansion Of The Mind, (Universalism): When accepting the whole universe as our home, the Divine Father as our father, nature as our mother, truth as our religion, God as our King, His Laws as the true Laws, and the rest of humanity as our fellow strugglers, brothers and sisters. In short, **universalism**.

F

False Ego: See ego.

False Prophet: Whoever teaches anything other than "The Goal Of The Life Is To Be(come) Divine."

False Teachers: Same as false prophets.

Far East Philosophies: Refers to all the understandings that have come from the Far East about the relationship of man and the universe, and the Laws which govern them.

Also it refers to the exercises, techniques, and practices which enable man to awaken and control spiritual forces in the physical, mental, and spiritual levels.

As it is explained by the first seal in **The Greatest Sign (☯)**, these philosophies and practices are to awaken the latent spiritual forces and understandings in the physical, mental, and spiritual levels. This covers all the mystical and psychological teachings all over the world.

To know Laws such as karma, reincarnation, samskara, or the other teachings such as Maya, three gunas, yoga, Sufism, mystical Christianity, and mystical Judaism, etc., and the philosophies such as in the Vedantas, Upanishads, and many spiritual stories from the Far East or other parts of the world about these related subjects, will help in better understanding the rest of the teachings of **The Greatest Sign**.

Therefore, although a general term of Far East Philosophies has been given to them, it is a much broader body of knowledge. We can say that any philosophy, practice, or technique that helps a person to become attuned to his or her own spirit and to realize its oneness with the universe as a part of the whole, can be considered as a part of the awakening of the spiritual forces (☯).

This is also the reason why the first symbol and the teachings related to it cannot be presented as a separate religion. The spirit of these Mystical Paths, however, has been intertwined all through our teachings. It can be said that the philosophies and practices related to the first symbol – awakening of the spiritual forces – are the spirit of the rest of the teachings. They help the rest make sense!

The words "Far East Philosophies" have

been chosen for this part of the teaching, because this part of the world seems to present the closest resemblance to the meaning of this part of our teachings as a religion.

Although mystical teachings and paths can be found all throughout the world, it is the Far East part of the world (especially India) which has assimilated so many different paths into one great body of knowledge. Although they are presented as a religion, yet it can by no means be limited to a set of dogmas.

Furthermore, Hinduism is the best known old religion which has its basic teachings written down as the three books of the Vedas. Most of the rest of the knowledge in that part of the world is an enhancement of these basic teachings and/or a contribution from other religions. It is because of the vastness and flexibility of these basic teachings that this part of the world has been able not only to assimilate knowledge from other religions but enhance them and most of the time eventually even dissolve these new movements into its vastness.

That is also the goal of this part of our teaching, to become so vast in consciousness that we can assimilate the truth of each path, enhance the path, and eventually make it a part of ourselves, but never become narrowed into any one set of dogmas!

Father: Divine Logic in the universe; the Laws in the universe.

Female: Divine Mother; energy as unconditional Love; raja guna.

Fifteen Fine Organs: The five pancha tatwa, the five organs of the senses, and the five organs of the actions make up the fifteen fine organs in the body.

FINE: Abbreviation for Formless, Invisible, Nameless, and Eternal or God in Its unmanifested form ("Be"-ness).

First Begotten Son, The: The first consciousness who, by the Grace, reached Pure Consciousness before creation (Spirit of God).

Five Active Classes In Society: Consist of Shudras (laborers), Ksattriyas (warriors, courageous ones), Vipras (intellectuals), Vaeshyas (businessmen), and Brahmins (spiritualists).

Four Beasts: Are the "four beasts full of eyes before and behind" (Rev. 4:6).

These four beasts are the four things which were either recognized or created after awareness came to the universe. They are: The Word, time, space, and the atom.

When the operative power of the three gunas was released, "The Word" came into existence. Then the state of awareness came to the universe, so time was perceived and space was recognized. Then through the use of the creative force (The Word) in a period of time in space, the atom was created. These four things are present in the universe all the time, and they are round about the throne.

Four Winds Of Heaven: Excess attraction to the external world, unnecessary mundane desires and their fulfillment, attachment to the external world, and greed.

G

Gabriel, Angel (Satva Guna): The most sentient force in the three creative forces of the universe (three gunas). It is the decision-making part of the Universal Mind, or the part which feels "I know." That is why Gabriel revealed the knowledge of God and the Akashic Records to the Prophets and those who are able to tune themselves to this part of the Universal Mind.

Gentiles: Intellectuals, those who are intellectual but their intuitional abilities (spiritual eyes) are latent. That is why Gentiles in the Bible is taken to mean Christians (especially

GLOSSARY

after the Roman decline) who make up the most intellectual nations of the world (western world). Also they are the most dominating nations in the period of intellectual domination in the last two thousand three hundred years (read Commentaries on Prophecies in Daniel, Period of Intellectual Domination).

However, the next ability to be awakened after the intellect is intuition. So it is evident that many will soon awaken their spiritual understanding (intuition) for the era to come. There will be understanding, not domination!

God (Generator, Operator, and Destroyer): The consciousness plus the three gunas. All the universe is nothing more than consciousness (awakened, un-awakened, and in Pure Consciousness) and the three gunas (creative force). That is why God is everything.

Also God is referred to as the nucleus of the universe (The Divine Logic), which is in Pure Consciousness (Father) and through Him, God has complete control over the three gunas in the universe (Universal Mind) and the universe.

god (Avatar, Son Of God, god-man): Same as Avatar.

god-man (Avatar, Son Of God, god): Same as Avatar.

Grace (The Divine Mother): Divine assistance given to man in his progress toward his goal – Pure Consciousness, be(com)ing Divine. Those who strive in the path of be(com)ing Divine (**Eternal Divine Path**), and show sincerity, steadfastness, and overcoming, will win His Grace, and through their endeavors and His Grace, they will reach Pure Consciousness.

Great Babylon ("The Great Whore"): Same as Babel; symbol for self-centered egoistical pursuance to make name, fame, and to gain power in order to satisfy selfish desires.

Great Sea, The: Universal Mind; the operative power of the three creative forces (three gunas) of the universe. "The great sea" is different than "sea," which refers to the individual mind.

"The great sea," which is used in the prophecies in Daniel of the Bible, refers to the events which will happen because of the collective confusion of the world. But the "sea" which is used in chapter 13 of The Revelation is about the individual mind and how it makes a person a slave of his desires ("the first beast") which arise from the "sea."

Great Whore, The: Same as the Great Babylon.

Greatest Sign, The (Shrii Shrii Para Maha Yantra): Refers to **The Greatest Sign** in the teachings of **Maitreya** that explains all the realities behind this universe, creation, history, destiny of man, and clarifies the confusion between the different religions.

It is a yantra because even by meditating on it, many realizations will come to the person and also it increases the concentration.

It also reveals the essence of the **Eternal Divine Path** which leads to Divinity (read The Essence or The Base).

Guru (Spiritual Teacher): A realized person who can manifest God's qualities through himself and help others by these qualities in their path toward be(com)ing Divine. As true realization comes through God's Grace, so the progress of the student also depends upon The Grace of his spiritual teacher. As man serves God to gain His Grace, so the student serves the teacher to gain his Grace.

However, there are many false teachers. To recognize them, it should be noticed that anyone who teaches anything other than the goal of the life is to be(come) Divine is a false teacher.

Also the Guru or the teacher should eventually lead a person to the realization of the formless, nameless, invisible, and eternal God. Otherwise such a person is creating a personality cult and is not a true Guru or teacher.

GLOSSARY   H

Haj: Pilgrimage to Mecca.

Ham: One of the three sons of Noah.
He is the symbol of the father of the Shudran (symbolized by Canaan) and Ksattriyan (symbolized by Nimrod) classes in humanity.

Harbingers: Forerunners; those who initiate change (same as Paravipras).

Haree Om Shrii Hung (HOSH), the first part of our Universal Mantra: The middle sign in **The Greatest Sign** (⌘). The meaning of it in brief is: "The Goal Of The Life Is To Be(come) Divine."
That is the highest goal in human life. Other goals are secondary and any other purpose which keeps the person from attending to this goal should be disregarded and forgotten.
The sign consists of a dot (●), the I-Ching (☯), the Expanding Lotus (❋), and the sign Lotustica (卐). The dot is the beginning of the spiritual journey when the operative powers of the three gunas are released (The Word) and the consciousness is still under the influence of the tama guna. The I-Ching is the symbol for awakening the spiritual forces in order to overcome the power of the tama guna, and to reach Pure Consciousness. The lotus is the symbol for reaching Pure Consciousness and represents the embracing, loving part of the person in Pure Consciousness and God's Love. The Lotustica is the symbol of the guiding part of a being in Pure Consciousness to correct and guide others.
So in general, the sign means that the unit consciousness (●) should awaken his spiritual forces (☯) in order to overcome the power of the tama guna over his Soul so to reach Pure Consciousness (❋), and to manifest God's qualities – both the loving part (❋) and the corrective part, His Laws (卐).

Haree Om Shrii Hung, Om Nam Kevalam: The Universal Mantra of the **Mission Of Maitreya**. For a deeper explanation, see the separate entries in The Glossary of "Haree Om Shrii Hung" and "Om Nam Kevalam."

Heaven: Same as Pure Consciousness.

Hebrews: Same as Elected Ones.

Hell (Ignorance): Because of the influence of the tama guna, the feeling of "I" (ego) as a separate entity is created, and the unit consciousness becomes self-centered and separated from God.
As the self-centeredness increases and he goes more away from God, he falls deeper to his lower nature and deeper into hell. So hell means false ego, the separation from God and falling into the lower nature.

Hidden Manna: The nectar which is felt in the throat area when the lower nature (first three chakras) is overcome and the person goes to his fourth chakra. It is a liquid which runs through the throat and an indescribable bliss follows. The person surely feels the presence of the Lord beyond any doubt. It is what is promised to be given to those who overcome the first three chakras (Rev. 2:17).

Higher Nature Of Man (Consciousness Beyond The First Three Chakras, Superior Nature, Higher Self): When a person overcomes the power of the first three chakras over his Soul, he enters his higher nature. He overcomes his lower nature. That is why Eve (the lower nature) is the mother of all humans, because humans should overcome this lower nature first to be born again, to the higher nature.

Higher Self (Consciousness Beyond The First Three Chakras, Superior Nature): Same as the higher nature of man.

GLOSSARY

Hinduism: A body of knowledge, philosophy, and belief that originated and was expanded in India, mostly from the Vedas. It is one of the Far East teachings which is used to awaken the spiritual forces and is related to the first sign (☯) in **The Greatest Sign**.

Holy: Means whole, perfect, and true. As the person becomes more perfect, he becomes holier.

Holy Ghost: Same as The Divine Grace (The Holy Mother).

House of Israel, The (The Samarians, Ephraims): The Children of Israel or the twelve tribes of Israel were divided into two nations after the time of King Solomon. These two nations are "the House of Israel" – ten tribes, and "the House of Judah" – the tribes of Judah, Benjamin, and the Levites (priests) with them (Jews).

The House of Israel was the first to become captive, and their land was given to other people. Apparently they did not come back to their land after that, so they are known as the ten lost tribes of Israel. But in reality, some of them did come back to their land and some others traveled toward the West, Northwest, and some even reached the land of America (as is recorded in The Book of Mormon). For a more detailed study, read the book Children of Abram (Abraham), All Prophecies Are Fulfilled.

House Of Judah, The (Jews): After the time of King Solomon, the Children of Israel were divided into two nations: The House of Israel and the House of Judah. The House of Judah is the nation from which the Jews have come. They are the tribes of Judah, Benjamin, and the Levites (priests) with them.

I

I AM: The infinite consciousness of the universe; the universal feeling of "I AM"-ness, or "Be"-ness; The Atman.

I am: The unit consciousness of each individual; the individual illusive feeling of "I am"-ness.

Ibrahim: Abraham.

I-Ching (☯): The symbol of the dual nature (positive and negative) of all things in the universe. Also it is a symbol for spiritual powers in man and the universe. It is the first step in the **Eternal Divine Path**.

I Do: The feeling of the raja guna (mutative) part of the mind; the doer-ship of the consciousness (Ahamtattva); the second part of the mind (ego).

I Have Done (Memory): The feeling of the tama guna (static) part of the mind; the memory of "doer-I" of the consciousness (Chitta); the etheric part of the mind which connects the mind to the external world.

I Know: The feeling of the satva (sentient) part of the mind; the "knower-I" of the consciousness (Mahatattva); the decision-making and knowledge part of the mind.

Ignorance: Same as hell.

Ignorance, Passion, Or Knowledge: In any situation (time, place, and person), the decision or action can be from: Ignorance (tama), when it is irrelevant to that situation; passion (raja) when it is purely selfish and self-centered; or knowledge (satva) when it is relevant and is for the benefit of all.

Iliyin: The name for the good records in the Akashic Records used in the Koran.

Illuminated Intellect: When an intellectual person creates intuitional knowledge (spiritual knowledge) through spiritual practices (meditation, concentration, etc.), he will illuminate his intellect. He does not follow his intellect blindly but sees that there is the hand of the Creator in all (by His Grace). Only this kind of intellectual person can understand the subtle realities behind this manifested universe.

Illuminated Intelligence: When intelligence plus intuitional knowledge has been gained. Illuminated intelligence is different than illuminated intellect because intellect is different than intelligence. (For further explanation, refer to the definitions of intellect and intelligence.)

Incarnation: The transfer of a Soul from one body into a new body after death.

Inspired Person: Is an actualized person who is also inspired by truth. So he feels he has a mission to fulfill and he devotes all his time and energy in fulfilling his mission.

He also, as an actualized person, does not rely on the approval or disapproval of others.

Intellect: The ability to understand the material and visible universe; the ability to learn, reason, think, and understand.

Intellectual Spiritualists: Those intellectuals who try to explain God and the invisible universe by intellectual, inflexible doctrines as dogmas. They create binding doctrines in order to control the masses under such binding beliefs, so they will knowingly or unknowingly exploit them and create bondage for humanity.

Religion and God-realization are supposed to free the human from bondage. But most of the religious doctrines available now bind the human more than free him because they have been created by intellectual spiritualists in the last two thousand three hundred years.

Intelligence: The capacity to acquire and apply knowledge.

Intuition: The ability to feel and know the truth which is beyond intellect and reasoning, that is, an intuitive person. Intuition knows a truth without sometimes being able to explain why. However, in a deeper level, there is a reason for everything.

Ishmael: The son of Abram and Hagar; the father of the Arabs.

Islam: From the root "tasleim" which means "to be surrendered and/or submissive;" also the religion founded by Prophet Muhammad, the fourth sign (☾) in **The Greatest Sign**.

Israel: "He who struggles with God" ("with" here is used to mean "to be with"); the same as Elected Ones, (the Sons of Light).

Also it is the name given by God to Jacob, the grandson of Abraham.

J

Jahad (Jehad): Comes from the root "Jahd" which means "struggle." This word also has been used in Islam to mean internal and external purification. It has also been used for Holy Wars (as external purification) between Moslems (submitted ones) and unbelievers.

Jallal'u'llah: Glory Of God.

Janaloka (Supramental World, State of Knowingness or Knowledge): The fifth loka in Sanskrit.

Japheth: One of the sons of Noah; also the father of the intellectual types (Vipras) and business-oriented types (Vaeshyas) in the human race (intellectuals, Gentiles).

Jehad (Jahad): See Jahad.

GLOSSARY

Jesus: The false name given to the founder of the Christian religion.

There is no "j" in the Hebrew language. So in any word that has a "j" in the <u>Bible</u>, either the letter "y" has been changed to "j" (for example, Joseph which is actually Yoseph), or the name is from other languages.

All those who have studied the name "Jesus" and its origin agree with one thing: That it is not his original name. The most common explanation is that "Jesus is the Greek form (equivalent) of the Hebrew name Y'shua." In Latin the "Y" is pronounced "J." How the rest of the name "-shua" was transformed to "-esus," there seems to be no reliable explanation.

Furthermore, the very name Y'shua (in Hebrew, Ycshu) is his Sacred Name, not his birth name or given name. This name in full is "Y'wehshua," which means, "Y'weh (God יהוה) saves." However, as it is explained all through our teachings, this Sacred Name (The Holy Name) is not pronounceable in the manifested world. That is why we show it all through our writings as יהושוה. Therefore, any pronunciation given to it is not acceptable. This was the main reason that the Children of Abram were forbidden to utter the Name of the Lord. That is also why the Name of the Lord is written as יהוה, which has no vowels in it to show that it is not pronounceable!

This truth, that the Sacred Name of the Father (יהוה) and the Son (יהושוה) cannot be pronounced in the manifested words (by mouth), was also known to the early Christians. That was the reason that, in older branches in Christianity, such as Greek Orthodox and in the Catholic Church, they pray in the Name of the Father (יהוה), Son (יהושוה) and The Holy Ghost (Mother), without mentioning any name(s).

The Sacred Name was also known in Islam. In a story about Prophet Muhammad, someone asked him, how many names does God have? He answered, "3,000. Of these, 2,999 are revealed to humanity." The One which is kept secret is His Sacred (Holy) Name.

The creative energy (the movement felt within when repeating The Holy Name or The Word silently inside) created by the words (when the Name of the Father and Son merge as One) is the Mother (Holy Ghost).

In the prayer, in the Name of the Father, Son, and The Holy Ghost, the Name of the Son is used in the middle between the Father and the Mother to show that he is the mediator to manifest them in the manifested universe. Without the Son, the qualities of the Father and Mother will remain un-manifested!

Another less popular theory of how the name "Jesus" has come about is that it is a combination of two names, "Isous" and "Zeus." However, the most plausible explanation, which is given to us intuitively (from the Akashic Records) is that: The name "Jesus" actually has evolved from two words, "Jay" and "Zeus." "Jay" in the course of time has become "Je," and "Zeus" has become "sus."

The Greek, Latin, and Sanskrit languages all belong to the Indo-European language family. "Jay" in Sanskrit still means "Victory to," therefore, the two words combined "Jay-Zeus" mean, Victory to "Zeus." It has the same meaning as "Hay" (hail to) "Zeus," in Spanish.

This all, therefore, leads us to conclude that he had a Sacred Name and at least a birth (given) name. If his Sacred Name was (יהושוה), then what was his birth name?

There is another name that has been used extensively as his name, in the East. That is the name "Esa" ("E" pronounced as in "Emmanuel" and "S" as in "Son"), or "Esa the Messiah." This name has other similar-sounding names in Hebrew, such as "Esau" and "Isaiah." This name also is used as his name in Arabic, which is a close language to Hebrew. An ancient writing, from his time, found in a monastery in India, also called him Esa.

With all the evidence above and our own intuitional certainty, we believe that his given (birth) name is (was) Esa. That is why we chose this name as his birth name in **THOTH**. However, if another more plausible explanation with enough evidence would be given for another name as his birth name, so be it. We are open to the ultimate truth!

GLOSSARY

Jew (there is no "j" in Hebrew. It is pronounced "Yahudi"): Children of the House Of Judah.

Jews (there is no "j" in Hebrew so it really is Yahudis!): People from the House of Judah who returned to the holy land after they were taken captive by the Assyrians. The House of Judah consisted of the tribe of Judah, Benjamin and the part of the Levites (priest class) which was with them.

Jnana Yoga: The yoga of knowledge; to know the self and God through knowledge of the truth behind this universe.

Juda or Judah (there is no "j" in Hebrew so it is Yahud or Yahudi): From the tribe of Juda or Judah.

Judaism: The faith of the Jews.

Judgementality: To be judgmental; to be critical without being pure enough to judge.

Kali: The dreaded dark and destructive goddess of the Hindu religion.

Karma (Action): (See also samskaras and reincarnation.) Karma means action. It is also used as the Law of Karma which in the simplest way can be described as: Any action creates a reaction that remains in the universe. Bad actions create bad reactions, and the person should pay for them. Good actions create good reactions and a person should be rewarded for those actions.

The reactions remaining in the unconscious mind (Universal Mind) are called samskaras. They are one of the bases for determining the Law of Reincarnation in order that these samskaras are paid off. But reincarnation is more complicated than only this.

The Law of Karma has been devised, in a sense, for each unit consciousness to learn the Laws of the universe, learn the lessons, and progress. When the lessons that should have been learned through these actions and reactions (lessons), are learned, the samskara (the result of the action) will be dissolved. True repentance is the acknowledgment that the lesson is learned, and the mistake will not be repeated!

Until the lesson is learned completely, a repetitive pattern will continue in a person's life until he or she creates enough awareness to realize the reason behind these patterns of sufferings, and breaks it by not making the same mistake again.

Karma Yoga: Yoga of action.

It is the practice of living an active life without being attached to the result of the action. In this path the person does the action but gives (surrenders) the result to the Lord.

Khatam: The last one or the seal of.

Khatam is an Arabic word which can be pronounced in two ways: Khatem, meaning the last; and Khatam, meaning the seal. It has been used as the state of prophethood of Prophet Muhammad. Some say he was the last Prophet with taking the word as meaning "the last." But some believe he was the seal of the Prophets (like followers of the Baha'i Faith) and other Prophets will come after him.

However, the truth is that the word is used with both meanings: Khatem, as the one who finished the spiritual knowledge which is to be surrendered or submissive to God, which is the very meaning of Islam and that is the highest spiritual realization; and Khatam, as the seal of the Prophets. As it is shown in **The Greatest Sign**, the sign of Islam is at the top of the Sign and is the seal of **The Greatest Sign**.

Khatem: The last; also refer to the word "Khatam" and its explanation.

GLOSSARY

Kingdom Of Heaven In Heaven (KO-HIH): Same as Pure Consciousness. This also refers to all the forces and Sons of God whom He uses to guide His universe to Pure Consciousness.

Those who reach Pure Consciousness will come back to this world and in different levels and places help humanity and the universe progress toward perfection. They obey His Laws and accept their responsibilities (with gladness and joy) in His Hierarchy ($\triangle$) no matter how small they may seem.

Also He uses the three creative forces in the universe, the three gunas ($\triangledown$), to control the universe and establish justice.

It is shown as two larger triangles together (✡) in the middle of **The Greatest Sign**.

Kingdom Of Heaven On Earth (KO-HOE): When God is accepted and followed as the only and True King, His Laws as the only Laws, His organizational system as the only System, and the spiritual Hierarchy as the true Hierarchy (when the Kingdom Of Heaven within is established by the majority), then His Kingdom will be realized (established) on earth as it is in heaven.

In truth He is the King whether humans accept it or not. If humanity accepts His Laws, follows them, and realizes that His Will should be done on earth as it is in heaven, then the true peace and tranquility will come to the earth. At that time, because people will not resist His Will, there will be no suffering, because suffering comes from resisting God's Will.

Kirtan: Spiritual dancing and chanting.

Koran: The Scripture revealed through Prophet Muhammad. The name "Koran" means "readings."

Koshas: The seven layers of the universe.

Ksattriyas: The warrior type of human; those humans who are courageous, and have initiative and leadership abilities.

In the past they were mostly those who tried to control the external world with their physical struggle or their armies; the children of Ham (son of Noah).

Kulakundalini: The latent spiritual consciousness in the state of unawareness (ignorance) at the base of the spine at the first chakra. It is also called "the sleeping serpent." Only when the kulakundalini has been awakened and risen to higher chakras (from the lower self, the first three chakras, to the higher chakras) can the true spiritual knowledge be gained, by His Grace. Then such a person sees the light of the kundalini, not only within but everywhere. This is called "to be born again."

L

Life-force: Same as raja guna.

Light: The state of Pure Consciousness; the path of knowledge toward Pure Consciousness; the light which shines at the darkness of the consciousness, and also everywhere else.

Little Book, The: Intellectual knowledge that is very small in comparison with spiritual knowledge (Rev. 10:2).

Little Horn, The: The binding and dry side of the intellect during the period of intellectual domination from 300 B.C. until now. The next era will be the era of intuitional knowledge.

This "little horn" is used in the prophecies of Daniel. It fought with the Saints and truth, and prevailed for some time. But eventually it will be defeated by true knowledge (read Commentaries on Prophecies in Daniel, Period of Intellectual Domination).

Lokas: The worlds.

As there are seven chakras in the human body, there are seven lokas in the universe which correspond to these seven chakras (read Universe and Man).

Lotustica: The four-armed sign (卍) over the Expanding Lotus in the sign **Haree Om Shrii Hung** (🕉). It is the symbol of the guiding side of God in order to correct the human and guide him toward his goal – Pure Consciousness; be(com)ing Divine.

Actually it is the human who suffers himself by going against God's Laws.

Lower Nature Of Man: The state of consciousness in the first three chakras; lower self; Eve; the Soul under the influence of the tama guna.

When the consciousness (self) is crudified by the tama guna, man becomes more flesh than spirit. So he is more concerned for fleshly needs and desires, becomes earthbound, and will be drowned in Maya.

This state of being under the influence of the tama guna and being bound in the bondage of desires, attachments, and unnecessary attraction to the external world, is the lower nature of man. When man overcomes these influences of the tama guna, he goes to his higher nature and will be free from earthly bondage (will be born again).

Lucifer, Angel: Same as tama guna.

Lucifer also means "shining star." The devil is the crudifying power of the tama guna over the Soul. But when this crudifying power is overcome, the same force becomes a shining star for guiding the spiritual aspirant. Because he can see the power of this force, how it affects other people, and how it works, he can be guided by these realizations.

Also it is the crudifying power of the tama guna which is responsible for this visible creation, and so made it possible for the human to be born in this body and progress through experiences in this world toward Pure Consciousness. So again it is highly exalted in the eye of the Creator. It is a shining star.

Lucifer (tama guna) is the crudifying force in the creative force (the three gunas) in the universe (Universal Mind). It is that part of the Universal Mind which creates the screen of the universe and has the feeling of "I have done" (memory). The feeling of being a separate "I" will be concluded from this, and so the feeling of separation becomes complete.

M

Maharloka (Subtle Mental World): The fourth loka in Sanskrit.

Mahatattva: The first and most subtle part of the mind. It is the decision-making part of the mind. After messages are received by the Chitta, then recognized by the Ahamtattva part of the mind, decisions will be made as to how to react to the message by this part.

The decision which will be made most of the time will be influenced by the state of spiritual progress of the person (from what chakra the propensity or reaction comes).

The Universal Mahatattva is the decision-making part of the Universal Mind.

Mahatma: Great soul.

Mahdi (Mehdi): The One the Muslims are waiting for, as Christians are waiting for Christ!

Maitreya (Mehdi): The One Buddhists are waiting for, as Christians are waiting for Christ!

Male: The Divine Logic.

Man (used interchangeably as Adam and the Higher Nature): The male part that was separated from the original dual-natured Adam. However, it has also been used interchangeably with the same meaning as Adam.

Also it has been used to symbolize the higher nature (Divine Logic) of the human in

GLOSSARY · M

general. When this Divine Logic is directed toward the mundane, it becomes worldly logic.

Man-god (Perfect Master, Satguru): Same as Satguru.

Manipura: The third chakra in Sanskrit.

Manomaya Kosha (Mind): The Kosha corresponding to the third chakra.

Mantra: The empowered words used to invoke the latent spiritual forces.

As it is explained in the books The Base and The Essence, the first expression of awareness appeared in the universe at the time when the balance between the three forces in the universe was disturbed. Then the operative powers of the three gunas were released, which was "The Word." This Word is the creative power in the universe and created the first sound vibration.

Sound cannot be without vibration. So through this Word, with different frequencies, many different things were created in the universe. In reality all things are nothing but vibrations at different frequencies.

For example, two objects with similar frequencies can stimulate each other even if only one of them is put in motion. That is, if there are two objects with the same frequency range close to each other, and we vibrate one of them, the other one will be vibrated without any need of external stimulation.

This law is also true in the spiritual sphere which consists of ethereal factors. If the vibrational frequency of different levels of spiritual states are known, that level of spirit can be vibrated (awakened) with the sounds of the same frequency, and that state of consciousness can be realized and mastered.

Mantras are the words which are used for this purpose. Their power is their ability to stimulate and awaken different levels of spirit and bring understanding of that level to the Soul.

Also the effect of music follows the same principle. That is why according to the level of spiritual advancement, different people like different kinds of music. Also each type of music affects people differently. Therefore, listening to spiritual music is recommended, and any music which is crudifying and agitating to the mind should be avoided.

However, in higher consciousness a person can no longer enjoy earthly music because his music is in heaven, which is superior to earthly music.

Mark (Greed): Greed is the mark of those who are in their lower natures "mark of the beast" (The Revelation, chapter 13) – and are the followers of Maya and their desires, and are attached to this external world.

Masjed: Mosque; Islamic equivalent to a temple, synagogue, church, etc.

Maya: The illusion of separation from God, which results in the excessive and unnecessary attraction to the external world.

This universe was made to be utilized for spiritual progress. When this view is forgotten and things start to be used in unnatural ways for the satisfaction of the lower nature, the same becomes Maya (illusion).

For he who follows the Darma of everything, there is no Maya.

Meditation: The process of directing attention from going outward to going inward.

In Sanskrit the word for meditation is "sadhana," which means "struggle." So it is a process of struggling to know the self, the relationship of the self with the universe, and overcoming those forces which are in our way toward the goal to be(come) Divine.

Meditation is not escapism, but an all-out and in struggle to overcome all kinds of evil (tamasic) influences.

God and self-realization are not for those who want to escape the struggling but are for those who are soldiers of the Lord.

Mehdi (Mahdi): See Mahdi.

GLOSSARY

Messiah (Messias): The Savior; the one who comes to the earth to further human progress toward their goal and their understanding of God. He comes at a time when many have reached higher consciousness and the old teachings lose their validity or have been badly distorted, or when confusion ("cloud") has overcome human understanding. Then the Messiah brings "the new wine" (spiritual wine, nectar of realization).

Michael, Angel (Raja Guna): The mutative force in the three creative forces of the universe (three gunas). It is the force responsible for actions in the universe or the part of the Universal Mind that feels "I do." That is why it is Michael and his Angels which fight with the dragon (devil, Maya) in chapter 12 of The Revelation.

Middle Path: Balance.

The human is an extremist. For most of them, it is either black or white. But the best way is the middle path, or a balanced path between physical (material), mental, and spiritual needs. Emphasis on any of them without progressing in others is imbalance.

However, because to maintain this balance is difficult, humans should strive toward this balance, but at the same time remember that all things depend upon time, place, and person. According to the time, place, and person, the action can be from ignorance, passion, or knowledge.

Therefore, unless that complete balance is achieved, the middle path means to strive for creating the balance between the physical (material), mental (psychological) and spiritual spheres with flexibility to adjust to the situation. Also it means not to go to extremes.

Mind: In general refers to the three parts of the human mind as Chitta (tama guna), Ahamtattva (raja guna) and Mahatattva (satva guna).

Especially it means when man is bound by his desires toward the external world, then he will create a false ego as mind, which makes life miserable.

When the mind becomes spiritualized, it becomes Buddhi (when it is directed toward God-realization and "I am" feels it is a part of the "I AM").

Mithra: The sun god of the religion of Zoroastrianism.

Mithraism: A branch of the Zoroastrian religion whose followers worshipped the sun god Mithra, one of the gods of this religion.

It was believed Mithra would be born from a virgin who would come at the end of time to destroy the dark forces and establish the truth.

This branch of Zoroastrianism spread from its original land (Persia) to the West and later on became one of the most prominent religions in the Roman Empire.

In fact the signs of the sun can be seen in the Roman culture in their equipment, clothing, and even their hairstyles. It is believed that if Christianity had not been accepted by the Romans, the religion of the West would have continued to be Mithraism.

Christianity replaced this religion. However, many of its beliefs, dogmas, and festivals continued to exist under the newly accepted Christianity, and continue even to this day.

Moaad: The last day of judgment.

Moaad is one of the three principles of Islam. The other two are "Tohied" and "Nabovat." Moaad means there will be a last day in which all will be judged according to their lifetime deeds. Those who have done good, will go to heaven (higher consciousness or Pure Consciousness), and those who have done evil will go to hell (will stay in ignorance, or the manifested universe).

Moon: Symbol for woman, mother of the family, or the emotional part of the human.

Morning Star: Sun. The largest star which shines after the morning has started, is the sun. So the morning star is the sun. Its symbolic meaning is the same as for the sun.

GLOSSARY

Moslems (Muslims): The followers of Islam (surrendered or submissive ones). Islam means "to be surrendered and submissive to the Lord." Therefore a Moslem is one who is surrendered (or submissive) to the Will of God.

Mother: The Divine Grace, The Holy Ghost.

Mount Zion: A symbol used in the Bible for the Hierarchy of the Kingdom Of Heaven. The human organizational structure is shown as a triangle upward (△), but the organizational structure of the Kingdom Of God is shown as a mountain (or pyramid) which is much more stable than human organization.

Mountain: God's governmental structure.
The organizational structure in management starts with a president at the top, then two or more vice-presidents under the president, and then some departments under each vice-president. This goes on until the very bottom of the Hierarchy is reached. This structure is shaped as a triangle upward (△).
A mountain also has the same triangular shape (△), but it is three-dimensional. As the human organization is triangular and unstable, God's organization is solid and stable like a mountain.
Mountain also symbolizes people with great characters and the leaders of society whom others can depend on and trust.

Muawiya: The fifth Caliph of Muslims.

Muhammad, Prophet: The Prophet and founder of Islam.
Prophet Muhammad was born in Mecca in Arabia around 570 to 632 A.D.

Muladhara: The first chakra in Sanskrit.

Muni: The silent ones.

Murdering: "To murder" is different than to kill. When a person is killed, it is done either by accident or because of the circumstance that allowed such a killing (self-defense, by order of the judiciary body, etc.). But when premeditated for selfish reasons, it is murder and is what is called "shedding the blood" in the Bible and God's Commandments.

Mutative Force (Raja Guna): Same as raja guna.

Mystical Paths: All the mystical paths followed by many different groups, cultures, religions, etc. These paths are referred to as the Far East Philosophies in our teachings (see Far East Philosophy).

N

Nabovat: Belief in Prophets.
This is one of the three principles of Islam. The other two are "Tohied" and "Moaad." Nabovat means to believe that God has chosen and will choose from among humans and Angels (Avatars) to bring His Messages to humanity. Or in other words, to believe in the Prophets and their messages from God.

Narrowness Of The Mind: Any ideal that does not have a universal outlook and does not believe that all is God.

New Jerusalem: The state of Pure Consciousness.

Nicolaitanes, Deeds of: Those who through ignorance, do evil deeds; followers of the darkness.

Nimrod: The grandson of Ham (the son of Noah).
He was the great hunter, warrior, and king, and is a symbol for the start of the Ksattriyan era (warriors, courageous ones) in history.

GLOSSARY

Nirvikalpa: The state of "I am"-ness; pure intuition; the seventh state of consciousness.

Niyama: The five external codes of yoga. They are:
1- **cleanliness**: internal and external cleanliness.
2- **contentment**: to stay in a state of equilibrium in all situations; magnanimity of mind.
3- **service**: (Satsang, service, and meditation), which are internal and external services.
4- **to read the Scriptures**: to read and understand the underlying truths behind the Scriptures.
5- **to become perfect as God**: to let God do Divine actions through us and become perfect as our Father, so to glorify Him by our actions and become the same as He.

Notable Horn: Same as the "little horn."

Nuh: Noah.

O

Objects Of The Senses: The ability of objects in the external world to make us sense them. They are five: The smell of the objects, the taste of the objects, the sight of the objects, the touch of the objects, and the sound of the objects. These can be perceived because of the tama guna (Chitta).

Occult Powers: Powers which can be gained through physical, mental, and spiritual practices and training.

Usually they are given to a practitioner as a test to see how he will use them. They should be used for good purposes. Otherwise, either they will be taken away or they will be harmful to the person and others. Spiritual powers are raja guna (pranic).

OM (ॐ): The root of all sounds in the universe.

This sound which is heard in higher consciousness cannot be reproduced in the physical plane. The closest sounds in this manifested world are: The sound which continues after a bell has been rung, the "humming" sound heard when many people talk in one place, and the sound of a great waterfall.

Also if we concentrate on any sound, a humming background can be realized in it which resembles the sound of many waterfalls.

However, as it was said, its subtlest form can only be heard in higher consciousness. It is the subtlest sound and the root of all sounds. It is The Word, and The Word leads to OM (ॐ).

Om Nam Kevalam (ONK), the second part of our Universal Mantra (see "Haree Om Shrii Hung, Om Nam Kevalam"): The meaning of it is: God (That Divinity) is Everything. So, everything is Divine or God. Although we are a part of this Divinity and our essence is Divine, or God, because of the influence of the tama guna (crudifying force) we have the illusion of separation from God. Therefore, the goal of the life is to Be(come) Divine (Haree Om Shrii Hung) and if we can reach this goal, we know we are a part of God (Om Nam Kevalam).

Omar: The second Caliph of Muslims.

One-pointedness: The state of perfect concentration toward the goal of life.

Only by being one-pointed can a person overcome all the forces (externally and internally) which try to divert the attention from our goal and mislead us toward the fall into the lower nature.

That is why one of the definitions of the devil is "he who diverts the attention," or that force which diverts us from being one-pointed in our endeavors and takes our attention from going within toward the spiritual world

GLOSSARY

to going without toward the external world.

So one-pointedness means to create a perfect concentration toward our ideal and goal.

Organs Of The Actions: Are five which involve speech, hands, feet (motion), generation, and excretion. These are done under the influence of the raja guna (mutative force).

Organs Of The Senses: These enable man to experience the world. They are five: Smell, taste, sight, touch, and hearing. These senses are under the influence of the satva guna (sentient force).

P

Pancha Tatwa: The five carrying elements (prana) of the senses which connect the Chitta (the crudest part of the mind) to the external world and internal organs through the nervous system.

Parama Purusa (Beyond Purusa): "Purusa" means the material visible universe and those parts of the universe which are not in Pure Consciousness. "Parama" means "beyond." So Parama Purusa refers to the nucleus of the universe (God).

Paravipras: True leaders.

They are those Elected Ones who have gone through many lifetimes and through struggle, have awakened their spiritual forces (☯). They long to establish a just environment (✡), are ready to sacrifice – not being self-centered, to be humble and sacrifice all for this ideal (✝), and use all their spiritual powers to do it. They surrender themselves and the result of their actions to the Lord and so become surrendered and submissive ones (☪). They long for the good of the whole universe and create a universal outlook (✺).

With these qualities and through their struggles, they also create the Shudra (laborer) characteristics. That is, they will assume physical work if it is necessary to work like a laborer. They will have leadership abilities of a Ksattriya (warrior), mental abilities of a Vipra (intellectual), shrewdness of a businessman (Vaeshya), and purity and incorruptibility of a Brahmin (true spiritualist). Only such a person with these qualities is worthy to assume the title of a Paravipra (✡).

It is these true leaders, who with their great intuitive abilities, will guide the successive trends of the progress of the human society. They will establish the Kingdom Of Heaven On Earth to allow humans to progress toward the goal with ever-increasing speed, and will help the whole universe to reach the goal (Pure Consciousness), and they themselves will reach the goal also.

Perfect Master (Satguru, Man-god): Same as Satguru.

Prakrti: Same as creative force.

Prana (Breath Of Life): Same as raja guna or energy. It is the outgoing force from the Soul.

It is the life-force and coordinating force in the universe. It carries many different functions and is the base of any movement. Without it (raja guna) there would have been no movement in the universe.

In truth it is the cause of the invocation of the mind (individually or universally) and thinking.

Pranamaya Kosha (Prana): The Kosha corresponding to the second chakra.

Prasadam: Food which has been prepared in a good state of mind as sacrifice and is offered to God (formless and invisible), and then offered to be consumed by those who want to receive the blessings of such a food.

Prophets: Those chosen, inspired individuals who bring a message from God to humanity. They are also called Angels and Avatars.

GLOSSARY

Psychic Body (Astral Body): Same as astral body.

Pure Consciousness (Christhood, Christ Consciousness, Being Divine, State Of Enlightenment): The state in which the power of the three gunas over the consciousness is overcome, and the consciousness in its pure form (pure intuition) beyond the mind (ego) is realized. Then the oneness with God (universe) is complete, and there would be no Maya left.

Purification: Means to become clean internally and externally, physically, mentally, and spiritually: To avoid all things which alter this process or to create an environment that will accelerate the processes of purification.

Anything that stimulates the first three chakras unnecessarily is a hindrance toward purification, especially for those who have not overcome the influences of the external world over themselves and will be affected by it easily.

Purusa: Manifested world.

Purusattma: Same as Parama Purusa (the nucleus of the universe).

Q

Questioning: The beginning of the spiritual progress.

Quiet Mind: When emotions are still and there is no turbulence of the mind. Then the Soul becomes a reflection of the truth, like a still lake which reflects the objects in the sky. So the self will reflect its oneness with the Self (universe).

Quietness: Is to become observant of the external world, so to see its plays and faults with an objective mind. It helps the aspirant to be more able to achieve the truth about Maya (illusion of the external world).

Qureysh: Prophet Muhammad's tribe.

R

Raja Guna (Mutative Force, Prana, Energy, Life-Force): The outgoing force of the Soul and in the universe; the activating force in the universe (mutative force in the Universal Mind).

It is what is known in the manifested universe as prana or the life-force or energy. Without it there would have been no movement in the universe or the feeling of "doership" ("I do").

Rajasic: When raja guna is dominating in anything, that thing is called rajasic. For example, foods with raja guna dominating in their construction are rajasic foods. A rajasic person has much energy, and if he does not have control over his mind, that energy becomes stress.

Reincarnation (see also karma and samskaras): The assumption of a new body by a Soul after physical death. The Law of Karma and Samskara plays a great part in the execution of the Law of Reincarnation.

Also some Souls assume new bodies merely to come to this world in order to help others in their journey toward the goal (Pure Consciousness).

Renunciate (same as sannyasin): Those who dedicate their lives to serve God and forego marriage and family life. It also means those who are not attached to the result of their actions (are surrendered and submissive to God).

GLOSSARY

Resurrection: A symbol of being born again; to resurrect (rise) from the lower nature to the higher self.

S

Sabbath: Day of rest and attunement to God.

The very base of God-realization and spiritual progress is to be able to calm the mind, contemplate, and attune the self to the truth of the universe. That is why God has emphasized the Sabbath as being one of the most important Commandments. That is because if a man cannot rest and calm his mind, he would never realize anything.

So it is very important that at least one day of the week be for rest, fasting, and kept holy by calming the mind and contemplating creation, God, and the truth behind them.

Sacrifice: To give of the self (physically, mentally, or spiritually) for others. In the highest form, sacrifice means not to be self-centered.

Sahasrara: The seventh chakra in Sanskrit.

Sal-Om: A derivation from "Salaam," "Shal-om," "Salute," and "OM (ॐ)." It means "hello, goodbye, peace, be surrendered to the Divine (Lord), health, safety, greetings, kind wishes, courtesy, honor, to give a sign of respect, and good will; and the position (as of the hand) or the entire attitude of a person saluting another person."

In short, "Sal-Om" means, "We pay our salutations to the Divinity within you (to the Divine vibration OM), and wish you to be surrendered and submissive to Him, and to understand and follow His Laws. Then you will have the best in the universe." Sal-Om!

Samarians: Same as the House of Israel.

Samskara (see also Karma and Reincarnation): The effect of the action which remains in the universe in order for the Soul to receive its proper rewards or punishments. This is the description of samskara according to the Far East Philosophies.

However, when a person repents and never again does the sins, he will be forgiven, because the purpose of all these Laws and creation is to help man overcome his lower nature and go to his higher self.

So if a person accomplishes this goal, there is no point that he be punished or gain experience which he has already achieved since he is ready to refrain from repeating his past mistakes.

When a person starts to meditate, samskaras are stirred up and the repetitive pattern which so far was controlling a person's life becomes even more intense. Also by meditation, the awareness increases. With a more intense life and greater awareness, with His Grace, lessons are learned quicker and progress is accelerated.

Sannyasin (same as renunciate): Those who dedicate their lives to serve God and forego marriage and family life. It also means those who are not attached to the result of their actions (are surrendered and submissive to God).

Sarkar, P. R.: The earthly name of the Baba, the founder of Ananda Marga (the Sixth Seal).

Sat, Chit, Ananda (Truth, Consciousness, Bliss): Ananda is the experience of realization. It can be accomplished by a person who truly (Sat) knows his consciousness (Chit). Such a person will experience bliss (Ananda).

He who truly (Sat) knows the consciousness (Chit) will experience bliss (Ananda). Or, by truly (Sat) knowing the self (Chit), you will know God (CHIT), and God is bliss (Ananda).

GLOSSARY

Satguru (Perfect Master, Man-god): The individual who, for the first time, reaches Pure Consciousness but comes back to this world in order to help others to reach Pure Consciousness. Such a person is called a Satguru, man-god, or perfect Master.

Satayaloka (True World, Essence, The Reality): The seventh loka in Sanskrit.

Satsang: A company of people who gather together to talk about God and truth; good company.

There are three kinds of gatherings:

There is idle gathering which is when people gather together and exchange idle talk, which neither helps them materially (worldly) nor spiritually. Such a gathering and talk should be avoided by those who are in the path of the spirit.

There is a gathering to discuss and solve the real problems (**real** problems, not unreal problems from ignorance or passion). These gatherings are helpful to take care of worldly matters, "sufficient unto the day is the evil thereof" (Matthew 6:34).

The third kind of gathering is the one in which people gather to talk about God, His creation, and Truth. This kind of gathering is the most desirable. In fact, to establish such a gathering and worship will help in solving most of the other small problems. This kind is Satsang. Faith comes by hearing!

Also Satsang refers to realizing the truth through visualizing (to see the truth), through hearing, reading, etc., or all the things which are truth or aid us in realizing the truth.

An example of this is: When a person sees an unhappy person and realizes that this person is unhappy because he or she does not know God. This realization or observation is a Satsang.

So Satsang in general is whatever helps us to know the self (Chit), God (CHIT), which is truth (SAT).

Satva Guna (Sentient Force): The most sentient force in the creative forces (one of the three gunas) of the universe (Universal Mind). It is responsible for the feeling of "I know" in the individual mind and Universal Mind. It is the same as the Angel Gabriel.

It is the decision-making part of the mind ("I know").

Satvic (Sentient): When satva guna is dominant in a subject, that subject is called satvic or sentient. For example, satvic foods are those with satva guna dominating in them. Anything satvic is preferable over rajasic and tamasic.

Also, sometimes subjects change their position as being satvic, rajasic, or tamasic in different situations (according to time, place, and person). For example, the food that is rajasic in a hot climate might become satvic in a cold climate.

Savikalpa: The state of active "Logic" or "Will"; the sixth state of progress.

Sayyed: Those who are from Prophet Mohammed's genealogy.

Scepter, The: The promise of spiritual dominance and kingly position given to Abram (Abraham).

Sea: The consciousnesses under the influence of the tama guna, or when restless.

Sea is a turbulent water, as is a consciousness under the influence of the tama guna (turbulent by attraction, fulfilled desires, attachments, and greed – the four winds), and a turbulent consciousness can neither realize itself nor realize God.

That is why the beasts (desires and attachments) arise from the sea in chapter 13 of The Revelation.

Seal: Used in The Revelation (the last book in the Bible). According to our teachings, each Seal is One Truth of the Seven Truths covered as part of the **Eternal Divine Path**, brought with each major Prophet and/or religion on earth.

The First Seal: *Covers all Mystical Paths. They include Hinduism, Buddhism, Cabala, Saints in Christianity,*

Sufis in Islam, and any other religion that teaches Know Thyself to Know God (self and God are One!)

The Second Seal: Is the Old Testament (Communities of Light, which is the Base of the Kingdom of Heaven on Earth).

The Third Seal: Is the New Testament (Sacrifice).

The Fourth Seal: Is Islam, which means being Surrendered and Submitted to the Will of God (not being attached to the result of one's action, let God be the doer, etc.)

The Fifth Seal: Is the Bab/Baha'i teachings (Universalism).

The Sixth Seal: Those who go through these first five Seals (Steps) become the Elects (Paravipras). This sixth state is the Sixth Seal or the teachings of the Baba (from the Ananda Marga organization).

The Seventh Seal: Is the Seal of Unification and Revelation of the Seventh Angel (which Reveals the whole Mystery of God), our teachings.

Self: Same as Soul.

Self-Centeredness: To be only concerned about the self and its mundane needs (selfishness).

Self-centeredness means to feel separate from the rest of the universe and to be unconcerned about the rest of creation. It is a feeling of not being a part of the universe and the universe a part of the self.

That is the essence of the feeling of separation, loneliness, and misery. That is the very reason people seek the company of others and feel lonely and lost when they are alone.

The opposite of being self-centered is to be other-centered or universally-centered. That is, to love the self because you love the whole universe, and because you are also a part of it. So you love yourself also, and you take care of the self and the rest of the universe for the same reason, because everything is God. A person with such a realization is never alone.

He is always with God, and God is with him, even when in the company of others.

Sentient Force (Satva Guna): Same as satva guna.

Serpent (Lucifer, Devil): Same as devil. However, it is also related to the kulakundalini (latent spiritual force). When the kulakundalini is in the first three chakras, the serpent is a "devil." But when it is raised to higher chakras, it becomes wisdom, or light.

Service: To give physical, mental, or spiritual help to others with no expectation for any return, or to serve others in the spirit of serving God.

Service is of three kinds: From ignorance, from passion, and from knowledge.

Service is from ignorance when it is done for the wrong person (he does not need that service), at the wrong time, and/or at the wrong place.

Service is from passion when it is done in the spirit of gaining something in return. In fact such an act is not a service but is a business.

Service is from knowledge when it is done for the right person, at the right time, and at the right place, without expectation. However, service done to do God's Will is always from knowledge.

Not only can service be from ignorance, passion, or knowledge, but also in any situation (time, place, and people) any decision can be from these points.

Shah Bahram: The savior in the Zoroastrian religion who comes at the end time.

Shariah: Islamic Laws.

Shem: One of the three sons of Noah.

He is the symbol of the father of the Brahmin (true priest) class in humanity. That is why Abram (Abraham) is the descendant of Shem.

Shii'a: One of the two main branches of Islam.

The followers of Shii'a, who mostly reside

GLOSSARY

in Iran and the neighboring countries, hold that Ali, the son-in-law of Prophet Muhammad, was the rightful choice for assuming the leadership of the Moslems as the Imam. There were three other successors (Abu Bakr, Othman, and Omar) before Ali eventually became the Caliph (the leader of the Muslims). Even then he was assassinated, and his children did not succeed him as Caliph. The Islamic government changed from leaders following the Prophet's example to more secular and was organized as an empire.

Shii'as never accepted this situation and also never accepted the first three Caliphs as legitimate. That became the point of contention between the Shii'as and Sunnis (who accepted this situation). Shii'as still insist that this should not have happened.

Shii'as continued following the Imams (Ali's children). This created great tension between these unofficial leaders and the central government. So Ali and all his children, who Shii'as believe should have succeeded him and followed as Imams, were all poisoned and killed. The twelfth Imam disappeared and that is who Shii'as are waiting to return as Mahdi (Messiah).

Shiloh: Messiah.

This name is used in Gen. 49:10 as the bearer of the scepter, who will come and gather the people of Israel unto himself. This prophecy was fulfilled through Christ and he gathered the House of Israel under his banner (✝) as Christians, especially the early Christians; read <u>Children of Abram (Abraham), All Prophecies Are Fulfilled</u>.

Shrii Shrii Anandamurti: The spiritual name of the Baba, the founder of Ananda Marga (the Sixth Seal).

Shrii Shrii Para Maha Yantra (The Greatest Sign): Same as **The Greatest Sign**.

Shudras: Laborers; children of Ham.

Shudras are the worker type of humans, and are the ones who do the basic, usually physical, tasks in society.

Siddhis: Siddhis means powers. By overcoming the mundane propensities of each psychic center (chakra), different powers can be gained.

In a sense these powers are a boon for our work toward perfection. In another sense, they are a test to see how we use our acquired boons. If we use them for selfish reasons, either they will be taken away from us, or they will become a trap and an obstacle in further spiritual development.

That is why the goal of spiritual practices and progress should not be to gain siddhis, because they can result in regression or become a trap in the Path.

However, if a siddhi is gained in the process it should be used to help others in the path, with the ideation that it is not ours, but we are only channels (submission).

If a power is gained and is misused, and a person or persons are hurt, learn the lesson and do not misuse your powers any more, or if a power is gained and you do not know what to do with it, just give it up and give it back to the universe until you are ready for it.

Spiritual practices to gain powers (siddhis) indeed are of a very low level of consciousness. The goal of spiritual practices is to be(come) Divine, which is to create wisdom, compassion, and become free and one with the Father and The Holy Ghost (The Mother).

Sign Of Paravipra: The sixth seal in **The Greatest Sign** (✡) (see Paravipra).

Sijjin: The name given for the bad records in the Akashic Records in the <u>Koran</u>.

Sin (Samskara): Transgression of the Laws (Daharmas) of the Lord (universe).

Social Movements: (Natural, evolutionary, revolutionary, counter-evolution, and counter-revolution):

There are five different movements in society:

1- **natural movements**: those insignificant movements that do not bring a deep permanent change in society, such as fashions.

GLOSSARY

2- **evolutionary movements**: gradual permanent changes which usually start from the top of society to the bottom.

3- **revolutionary movements**: sudden, abrupt, permanent changes with great force, which usually occur from the bottom to the top of the society.

4- **counter-evolution**: a gradual return to the previous state.

5- **counter-revolution**: an abrupt return to the previous situation.

Counter-evolutions and counter-revolutions are very short lived. The progress of society can never be forced back for long (read The Kingdom of Heaven on Earth).

Son Of God: Same as Avatar.

Soul (Atman, Self): The manifestation of the Divine in gross form as a separate consciousness.

Soul is different than spirit. Spirit is the same as astral body, consists of ethereal factors, and contains the first five chakras. The Soul is consciousness with the three gunas as its creative force or mind. Soul is the same as self.

Source Of Decrees (In The Koran): Same as Akashic Records.

Spirit (Ethereal Body, Astral Body): Same as astral body.

Spiritual Teacher: Same as Guru.

Stars: Symbol for the children in the family, the civil servants in society, and those who have small spiritual lights in guiding others a little.

Static Force (Tama Guna): Same as tama guna.

Struggle With God: This does not mean to struggle against God. The word "with" here is taken to mean "to be with."

Therefore the sentence "struggle with God" here means to be on God's side (Elects) and struggle with Him against those who have gone astray.

Subconscious Mind: Stored memories of this lifetime which are accessible to each individual by a little effort from the storage part of the brain, also stored karmas of the past lives.

Submission: When a person ideates that he and his body are only a channel for the Lord to do the Divine actions through them.

With this, there will be no "I" left and the person is free from egoistical attachment to the result of his actions because he is not the doer but He is. Then he will be free from any attachment, and that is the key to salvation.

Islam also means "submission" and this ideation of being submissive to the Lord is related to the fourth seal (☾) in **The Greatest Sign**.

Subtle Body: The subtle body consists of: The mind (the three parts of the mind), the Soul, the astral body, and the fifteen fine organs.

Sun: The symbol of the father in the family (male, Logic); same as morning star.

Sunni: One of the two main branches of Islam.

The followers of Sunni differ from the other branch, Shii'a, in that Shii'as did not accept the successors of Prophet Muhammad as legitimate (see Shii'a) but Sunnis believe in their legitimacy.

Superior Nature (Consciousness Beyond The First Three Chakras, Higher Self): Same as the higher nature of man.

Supreme Consciousness: Same as "I AM" or God.

Surrendering: To do the actions but to surrender the result to the Lord.

Greater than surrendering is to be submissive. That is, to become a channel for His Divine actions. In surrendering still an "I" is

GLOSSARY

present who surrenders "the result" of "his" action to God.

But in submission, there is no "I" left. Because it is He who is the doer, not the individual "I," therefore no attachment will be created to the result.

Svadhisthana: The second chakra in Sanskrit.

Swarloka (Crude Mental World): The third loka in Sanskrit.

T

Tabaokolaho Ahasanol Khaleghin: Praise be to the Highest in the creation which is man.

Tama Guna (Static Force): The crudest force in the creative force of the universe (the operative power of the three gunas). It is through the crudifying ability of the tama guna that the consciousnesses have been made, crudified, thickened, and enabled the manifested universe to be created. It is also responsible for the feeling of "I have done" (memory) in the individual mind and Universal Mind.

Tama guna is also responsible for the state of ignorance (crude consciousness) or unawareness. It is the source which binds the Soul toward becoming self-centered, narrow-minded, lost, and having a feeling of separation from the universe. It is the same as devil.

Tamasic: When the tama guna is dominating in anything, it becomes tamasic. For example, tamasic foods are those in which the tama guna is dominating, and they crudify the consciousness.

Tapoloka (Beyond the Mental World): The sixth loka in Sanskrit.

Tasleim: To surrender, to submit; is the root for the word "Islam" meaning to be surrendered or submissive.

Tat Twam Asi ("I Am That Also"): God is everything.

Telepathic Ability: The ability to communicate only through the use of mind waves.

Temple: Symbol for the body, and also the universe as the "temple of God." The body is a universe too, as it has all the ingredients which can be found in the universe. The Soul of man is the god of the body. The nucleus (Soul) of the universe is God of the universe.

The buildings as temples are an external expression of internal truth. They are an effort to create a symbolic physical structure for this spiritual meaning of temple. Also a building as a temple will become a center of worshipping and gathering for people. This has a social significance beside spiritually reminding people of their duties to God.

Third Eye: The spiritual eye of the human which has been closed. It is, however, present as the pineal gland in the center of the brain. When the spiritual aspirant opens this center in the middle of the brain, he can grasp the realities of the spiritual world. His eyes will be opened. He is no longer dead. He will become different from the people of this world.

Three Gunas, The: The three forces in the universe as satva (sentient), raja (mutative), and tama (static). In the operative state, they are the same as the creative force of the universe (Prakrti). They are also the three parts of the Universal Mind and individual mind ($\triangledown$).

The three gunas and consciousness are a part and parcel of one entity (inseparable). Consciousness is the controller of the three gunas, and the three gunas are the creative power of the consciousness.

Time, Place, and Person: All things in this universe depend on time, place, and person (persons) involved. In any situation, the

GLOSSARY

action or decision can be from ignorance (irrelevant to that situation), from passion (being for selfish gain), or from knowledge (relevant, correct, and Divine).

Tohied: God is one.

"Tohied" is one of the three principles of Islam. The two others are "Moaad" and "Nabovat."

In its more expanded meaning, "Tohied" means that all things have come from one Source, or from God. So God is everything, and everything is One. This is supported by the sentence, "and unto Allah we return" (which is repeated many times in the Koran). It means that we have come from Him and we should return to Him. Or in other words, He is everything.

In a narrower sense, "tohied" means that there is only one God to be worshipped as the Supreme Being. There is no God other than He.

Tree Of Knowledge Of Good And Evil, The: To follow one's own feelings and judgment as guidance rather than to follow God's Laws, Commandments, and guidance.

That is exactly what the woman did. She "saw that the tree was good for food, and that it was pleasant to the eyes, and a tree to be desired to make one wise [temptation], she took of the fruit thereof, and did eat…" (Gen. 3:6).

She did what seemed good to her, so felt it was alright. But the result was to fall into misery and confusion. In fact that is the reason for the miseries of humanity, because they do not follow God's Laws and examples. Instead of sharing and cooperating, they follow the rule of taking and create confusion – because of their crude minds under the influence of the tama guna (devil, serpent). So they become fallen men.

Tree Of Life: Immortality and the way to the state of Pure Consciousness.

Tribulation: Corrective punishment to guide humanity.

The Law of Karma works both individually and collectively. This can be realized by observing individual lives and also history. In fact, history is an especially good lesson to observe and learn from.

If the human learns these lessons, he can create a proper environment to live in. Otherwise the suffering will continue to be on earth.

True Leaders: Same as Paravipras.

Twenty-Four Elders: The twenty-four elements in the body and universe. These consist of the fifteen fine organs in the body (the five Pancha Tatwa, five organs of the senses, and five organs of actions), plus five basic elements (ethereal, aerial, luminous, liquid, and solid), and the three levels of the mind (the three gunas) along with the illusive "I am" as a separate entity. These are symbolized as or correspond to "the four and twenty elders" in Revelation 4:10.

U

Unconscious Mind (Collective Consciousness): Same as Universal Mind.

Also refers to the memories in the Akashic Records which are not easily accessible to all individuals. Only those who purify themselves and go beyond their individual minds (egos), with His Grace, can have access to them.

Unit Consciousness: Same as Soul.

Universal Mind ($\triangledown$) (Collective Consciousness, Unconscious Mind): Same as the creative force in the universe, the three gunas in the operative state.

Universalism: To consider the good and progress of the whole universe as the goal of life; to consider the universe as our home and country; to see the whole universe as God, so serving the universe is serving Him.

GLOSSARY

Any ideal other than universalism will result in narrowness of the mind, and any narrowness is bound to create suffering.

Upanishads: Same as Vedantas; many writings which were written to bring light (supplementary) to the meanings of the Vedas (the end of the Vedas or Vedantas).

Uthman: The third Caliph of Muslims.

V

Vaeshyas: The business-oriented type of human.

Those humans who are inclined toward accumulation of the physical wealth and control of the resources, and are interested in economic activities, are the Vaeshyas.

They can be categorized as intellectuals (Vipras) whose intellects are directed toward economic activities. They have very little interest in things other than these activities.

Vedantas: The last chapter of the Vedas (end of the Vedas; "Veda" + "anta" which means end); the ultimate truth. The Upanishads are called the Vedantas (the final goal of the Vedas).

Vedas: The oldest Scriptures known to man as the earliest Hindu sacred writings.

Veda (from the Sanskrit root "vid," to know) means the knowledge which contains the evidence of its truth within itself. The Vedas are made up of four principle books as Rg, Yajus, Sama, and Atharva.

The Rg Veda contains prayers and hymns to the elemental deities ("rig" means "to laud"). The Yajus ("yaj," "to sacrifice") contains sacrifices and prayers adapted for certain rites. The Sama-Veda contains songs of lyrical character to be recited with melody. The Atharva-Veda consists of various hymns and incantations.

The Atharva-Veda is considered to not be an Aryan Scripture, but one that was added to the Vedas later on.

Vidya: Knowledge.

"Vidya" is opposite to avidya (ignorance). Vidya means "to turn toward God or knowledge." Avidya means to turn toward the external world (Maya) or ignorance.

Vigamaya Kosha (Discriminative Mind Begins – Buddhi): The kosha corresponding to the fourth chakra.

Vipras: The intellectual type of human.

Vipras are those whose abilities are to penetrate, understand (to know), and to try to explain the phenomena in the material or manifested world and in society.

The honest and developed intellectuals are guided with rational minds, but not with emotions or intuition. The intellectualized spiritual theories (the binding religious doctrines) are created or supported by those intellectuals who want to exploit the masses (consciously or unconsciously).

When intellect is accompanied by intuition, it becomes illuminated intellect and a guide for the self and others.

Vishudaha: The fifth chakra in Sanskrit.

W

Water: Is the symbol for manifested consciousness (ether); also is used for purification of the consciousness in religious rituals (baptism).

White: Symbol of purity and detachment.

Wind: Symbol of illusionary ideas.

As the wind never can be chased or captured (even if it is captured, it will not be wind

GLOSSARY

any longer), so the illusions of being attracted to this external world (Maya) also cannot be chased or captured. Even when an unnecessary desire (illusion) is fulfilled (captured), a new desire will replace it and the process is insatiable.

That is why in the Bible, "wind" is used as the one that stirs the sea (unit consciousness) or the great sea (collective consciousness). The winds that stir up the consciousness are attraction to the external world, unnecessary desires, when desires are fulfilled, they bring attachment to the external world, and the result of all of them is the greed.

These are the illusions (winds) of the world that bring confusion and tribulation ("restless sea" or "great sea") to man.

Wine (Nectar): When a person reaches higher consciousness, especially to his fourth chakra, a liquid kind of fluid will be felt in the throat area which is known as "nectar." The blessing felt in this stage is beyond description. It is called milk and honey nectar, and is symbolized as wine in the Bible.

Woman (Used Interchangeably As The Lower Nature, Eve): The part that was, symbolically, separated from Adam (the original dual-natured human); also used symbolically as the lower nature of the human; Divine Mother (energy) directed toward mundanity (woman).

Word, The: The Divine Vibration that resides in each Soul. It leads to Pure Consciousness. The Word consists of four parts. When the four parts are learned internally and correctly, and meditated on, the Divine Vibration will be realized which is The Word. This will become a guide for the person. If the person starts to go astray, it vanishes and when he starts coming back to the path, it returns. The ultimate achievement will be Pure Intuition (卍).

Y

Yama: The five observing codes of yoga:
1- **Non-Violence**: Not violating the innate nature (Darma) of things.
2- **Truthfulness, With Discriminating Mind**: To guide all thought, speech, and action with the spirit of welfare.
3- **Non-Stealing**: Not to take things which rightfully are others or prevent someone from his duties.
4- **Non-Indulgence**: Not to indulge in the enjoyment of such amenities and comforts as are superficial to the preservation of life.
5- **Attach To God**: To keep the mind immersed in the ideation of God and to remain attached to Him.

Yamama: The place where the Muslims lost a lot of people who knew the Koran by heart.

Yantra: A crystallized ideology in the shape of a painting, symbol, or sign; or a shape or painting which guides the mind into its deeper levels.

Ya-Sin: O Man.

Y'shua: (See Jesus.)

Yoga: Union.
A systematic process to awaken latent spiritual forces toward higher consciousness.

Yunus: Jonah.

GLOSSARY

Zion: The triangle downward ($\triangledown$) in the Star of David (✡) which symbolizes justice and control.

Zakat: Islamic tax on unbelievers.

YOU CANNOT FURTHER PERFECT THE PERFECTION

Do not write authoritative commentaries on <u>THOTH</u>! How can you further perfect The Perfection? If you write anything about <u>THOTH</u>, state that it is your own understanding. Refer people to the Source (<u>THOTH</u>, God, and His Prophet). Let each man understand God's Words Alone (All One!) with God.

So do not add or subtract from this Book. If you do so, God will add to your burden and/or subtract from your portent with Him!

INDEX

The Index lists the page locations of the important terms in THOTH. You can use this index in conjunction with the search function on our website (maitreya.org) to further deepen your study of these terms.

Note: This (tenth) edition of THOTH is the first edition to include an index. Also, those who created it are not professional indexers. Therefore, this index can be considered a first draft. If you encounter any errors or inconsistencies, notice a useful term is missing, etc., and/or would like to help create a truly professional index for THOTH, please send an email to thoth@maitreya.org.

INDEX

To most effectively utilize this index, note the following organizational decisions:

- The index has two levels of organization: Terms, and sub-terms under some terms.
- Sub-terms are used in two situations:

First is when a term is clearly a subtopic of another term (for example, "flood of Noah" under "flood").

Second is when a term is mentioned so many times in **THOTH** that its index seems too large to be useful (for example, "God"). In these cases, various iterations of the word are separated out into sub-terms (i.e. "God blesses" "God creates" "Plan of God" etc.). **These sub-terms are not comprehensive** (they do not capture every instance of the main term) but are an attempt to make various uses of the term easier to access. To see every instance of a term, refer to its main index.

- Similar terms such as singular and plural (i.e. "community" "communities") or verb tenses (i.e. "baptize" "baptized" "baptizing") have been left separate, with three exceptions:

First, multiple spellings of the same word are listed as one index term (for example, "darma" "daharma" and "dharma" are all unified as "darma/daharma/dharma").

Second, for the second type of sub-term (iterations of words with very large indexes), if an iteration of the word includes a verb, the various verb tenses are unified (i.e. the sub-term "God blesses" also includes "God bless" "God blessing" and "God blessed").

Third, also in these sub-terms, some attempt has been made to unify similar ideas (for example, the sub-term "God chooses Abraham" also includes instances of "Abraham is chosen").

Aaron *605*

Abel *27-28, 30, 270*

abominable *425*

abomination *426, 625*

abominations *414*

abortion *561*

Abraham (see also "Abram") *iii, 19, 46, 51-56, 76, 82, 85, 87, 102-104, 121, 127-129, 131-138, 143-144, 147-149, 158, 160-164, 169, 174-177, 191-193, 196, 200-201, 216, 223, 227, 243-244, 262, 265, 270, 275, 285, 289, 293, 297, 302, 305, 336, 339, 341-342, 361, 407, 479, 539, 580, 583, 594, 605, 616, 620-622, 628, 645, 649, 653, 658-659, 671-673*

    Abraham and Isaac *19, 103, 131, 136-137, 160, 265, 305, 583, 594*

    Abraham could *133*

    Abraham is *52, 54, 87, 103, 131, 133-134, 160, 175, 177, 191, 407, 621*

    Abraham's *52, 128, 132, 134-135, 143, 147, 149*

    Abraham, the father *163*

    Abraham would *132-133, 138*

    be Abraham *52, 131*

    before Abraham *407*

    Children of Abraham *55, 138, 176, 196, 616, 628*

    God chooses Abraham *103, 158, 407*

    God of Abraham *19, 135, 265, 305, 583, 594*

    has Abraham *196*

    is Abraham *132*

    of Abraham *19, 55, 87, 102, 135, 138, 147, 176-177, 191, 196, 265, 305, 336, 342, 583, 594, 616, 628, 659*

    promises Abraham *191*

    to Abraham *52, 85, 131-135, 137, 144, 147-148, 175-177, 243, 285, 297, 645*

A-bram *51, 175, 459*

Abram (see also "Abraham") *iii, 46, 50-52, 54, 56, 82, 104, 120-121, 127-133, 138, 146-149, 161-164, 169, 174-177, 191, 193, 200-201, 223, 227, 244, 262, 270, 275, 285, 289, 293, 339, 361, 459, 479, 539, 580, 605, 620-622, 645, 649, 653, 658-660, 671-673*

    Abram (Abraham) *iii, 46, 51, 54, 56, 82, 104, 121, 127-129, 147, 149, 161-162, 164, 169, 174-176, 191, 193, 200-201, 223, 227, 244, 262, 270,*

INDEX A

275, 285, 289, 293, 339, 361, 479, 539, 580, 605, 620-621, 645, 649, 653, 658, 671-673

Abram and Abraham *147, 175, 620*

Abram has *645*

Abram is *50-52, 130-133, 175, 177, 459, 660*

Abram or Abraham *138, 149*

Abram's *50-51, 128, 130-131, 133, 146-147, 149*

Abram to Abraham *52, 131-133, 175*

Children of Abram *iii, 46, 51, 54, 56, 82, 104, 121, 127-129, 147-149, 161-164, 169, 174-176, 191, 193, 200-201, 223, 244, 262, 270, 275, 285, 289, 293, 339, 361, 621, 653, 658, 660, 673*

God chooses Abram *129-130, 175, 620*

is Abram *129*

promises Abram *132, 175, 262, 621*

says unto Abram *51, 120, 130-131*

to Abram *51-52, 82, 128-129, 131-133, 146-147, 149, 164, 175, 177, 191, 270, 293, 620-621, 671*

absolute *22, 82, 172, 199, 348, 474, 487, 536, 553, 594, 616, 629*

abstinence *571*

Abu Bakr *645, 673*

Actional *582, 585*

active *6-7, 21-22, 73, 108, 347-349, 351, 354-355, 374, 379, 400, 402, 432, 445, 482, 484-485, 488, 507, 519, 532, 552-553, 646, 655, 661, 671*

actualization *304*

actualize *304, 571*

actualized *255, 570-571, 645, 652-653, 659*

Adam *19-20, 24-27, 29-32, 35, 60-61, 76, 89-90, 102, 117, 191, 206, 248, 306, 330, 376, 446, 539, 545, 587, 614, 620, 622, 645-646, 663, 678*

administrative *44, 459-460, 481, 496-497, 499, 501, 503-506, 509-511*

Adorable *90, 293-294, 306, 388, 420, 645*

adulteress *213*

adulteries *243*

adulterous *232, 245, 313, 501, 532, 577*

adultery *61, 71, 206, 254-255, 287, 314, 372, 577, 585*

aerial *13, 18, 108, 114-116, 347, 350, 355, 357, 379, 396-397, 431, 442-443, 445, 630, 649-650, 653, 676*

Africa *118*

Ahamtattva *349, 435, 645, 651, 658, 663, 665*

Ahasanol (see "Tabaokolaho Ahasanol Khaleghin") *675*

Ahimsa *584, 645*

A-Him-Sa *645*

Akasa/akasha *5, 17, 431, 435, 645, 654*

Akashic Records *83, 90, 145-146, 295-296, 301, 314, 329, 348-349, 378-379, 431, 466, 629, 645, 649, 654-655, 658, 660, 673-674, 676*

Alexander *152, 463, 470, 473*

Ali *69, 296-297, 299, 301, 303, 310, 313, 321, 323, 325, 328, 330, 334-335, 369, 645, 673*

Allah *82-93, 146, 178, 293-294, 306-307, 321, 329-330, 567, 569, 645-646, 676*

Allaho *294*

ALLELU *420*

Alleluia *420-421*

Alpha *65, 365, 424, 427*

Amen *ix, 65-66, 75, 130, 159, 180, 209-210, 271, 363-364, 366, 376, 383, 388, 420, 428, 566, 626, 646*

America *46, 49, 118, 140, 142, 145, 147-148, 153, 155, 176, 296, 470, 496, 649, 658*

American *145*

Americans *148*

Anahata *646*

Anandamaya *646*

Anandamurti (see also "Baba" "Sarkar") *622, 673*

Ananda (see also "Sat, Chit, Ananda") *348, 351, 439-440, 646, 670, 672-673*

androgynous *16, 20, 30, 253-254, 265*

angel *67-69, 71, 73-75, 81, 83, 125, 133-134, 137, 144, 146, 163, 179-180, 192-194, 199, 237, 297-298, 311, 321, 361-363, 367-369, 371, 373-374, 376, 381, 387, 389-392, 394-397, 399-400, 402, 408-413, 415-416, 418, 420-422, 425-427, 451, 462, 556, 598, 622-623, 625, 646, 655, 663, 665, 671-672*

an angel *146, 194, 297-298, 392, 394, 421-422*

angel ascending *81, 387*

Angel Gabriel *311, 671*

Angel Michael *402*

angel's *390, 397*

another angel *81, 387, 390, 408-409, 418*

each Angel *361-362, 390*

fifth angel *392, 412*

first Angel *391, 408, 416*

fourth angel *392, 411*

his angel *426*

last Angel *390*

mighty angel *395, 420*

mine angel *427*

same angel *556*

INDEX   A

second angel *391, 411*

seventh Angel *125, 144, 163, 179-180, 237, 362-363, 381, 389-390, 392, 397, 399-400, 413, 416, 418, 427, 462, 598, 622-623, 625, 672*

sixth angel *394, 412*

strong angel *381*

the angel *67-69, 71, 73-75, 83, 133-134, 137, 192-194, 199, 311, 321, 367-369, 371, 373-374, 376, 390, 394, 396-397, 402, 409-411, 415, 425, 427, 671*

third Angel *391, 408-409, 411, 416*

This Angel *390, 392, 396, 408-409, 418*

angelic *356*

angels *28, 74, 77, 81, 85, 91, 99, 118, 122, 125, 162, 179, 198, 200, 237-238, 248, 251, 265, 279, 293, 295, 297-298, 323, 336, 341, 362-363, 366, 374, 377, 379, 383, 387-392, 394-395, 402, 408, 410-412, 414, 416, 425, 427, 520, 556, 651, 665-666, 668*

(Angels) *118, 125, 162, 238, 379*

Angels and Prophets *85*

Angels as Prophets *298*

Angels (Avatars) *297, 363, 666*

angels came *200, 392, 410*

angels Michael, Gabriel, and Lucifer *520*

Angels of the churches *81, 293, 362, 366*

angels of the seven churches *366*

as Angels *77, 377, 390, 427*

become Angels *297, 427*

by Angels *200*

called Angels *297, 668*

four angels *77, 81, 377, 387, 392, 394-395, 412*

his angels *28, 74, 99, 198, 238, 248, 374, 389, 402, 427, 665*

holy angels *408*

many angels *363, 383*

same Angels *362, 390*

seven Angels *122, 179, 362-363, 366, 389-391, 410-411, 414, 425*

take Angels *85*

the angels *91, 237-238, 265, 279, 295, 298, 323, 336, 341, 362, 366, 388-389, 392, 416*

their angels *200, 251*

these Angels *362, 389, 394*

three angels *392*

twelve angels *425*

worship Angels *427*

Annamaya *646*

ANNUIT COEPTIS *155, 496*

Anointed *56, 226, 246, 383, 467, 617-619, 621-622, 628, 631, 647*

antithesis *558-559, 636*

Arab *82, 293-294, 569*

Arabia *666*

Arabic *294, 306, 326, 526, 660-661*

Arabs *131, 146-148, 163, 175, 177, 262, 293, 567, 659*

Archangel *152*

Arjuna *67, 69, 78-79, 367, 369, 384, 568, 632*

ark *35-39, 41-42, 174, 400*

Armageddon *413*

art *488, 532, 637, 646, 651*

Arthur *629, 631-632*

artist *532*

Artists *485, 488, 507-508, 532, 646, 651*

arts *481*

Aryan *677*

Aryans *120, 229*

asanas *600*

Asia *65, 364-365*

Asi (see "Tat Twam Asi") *518, 675*

aspirant *iv, 294, 316, 321, 332, 334, 338, 366, 536, 565, 628, 663, 669, 675*

aspirants *43, 524, 578*

Assisi (see "Francis of Assisi") *70, 370*

astral *15, 18, 266, 329, 349-350, 557, 564, 629, 637, 646, 650, 654, 669, 674*

astrologers *193*

astrological *538*

astrologically *14*

astrology *13*

Atharva/Atharva-Veda *677*

Atman *15, 19, 349, 517-518, 539, 640, 646, 658, 674*

At-Man *640*

atom *17, 19, 26, 116, 379-380, 444, 518, 646-647, 651, 655*

atomic *17, 646*

atoms *17, 380*

attachment *10-11, 25, 27, 71, 81, 92, 112, 123, 177-178, 180, 195, 206, 211, 241, 286, 296, 306, 309, 352, 362, 371, 390, 395, 401, 403-407, 410, 417, 438, 440, 462, 467, 485, 497-498, 520, 522, 554-555, 566, 585, 589, 652-653, 655, 674-675, 678*

any attachment *27, 123, 555, 589, 674*

INDEX

attachment accelerates *25*

attachment to *10-11, 27, 123, 178, 180, 206, 211, 286, 296, 401, 403-405, 438, 440, 485, 498, 522, 554-555, 566, 589, 653, 655, 674, 678*

attachment which *362, 405-406*

create attachment *195, 462*

more attachment *25, 406-407*

no attachment *71, 112, 177-178, 206, 371, 438, 440, 566, 675*

over-attachment *355*

without attachment *211*

your attachment *27*

attachments *21, 61, 69, 116, 183, 197, 210, 215, 228, 238, 261, 270, 324, 350-351, 369, 395, 398, 403-404, 413, 417-418, 422, 444-445, 520, 544, 572, 578, 631-632, 663, 671*

attraction *20, 22-23, 25, 27, 57, 67, 69-70, 78-79, 81, 83, 92-93, 97-98, 110, 116-117, 164, 180, 196, 202, 209-210, 215, 238, 241, 247, 265, 299-300, 309, 312, 318, 320, 343, 362, 364, 367, 369-370, 384-386, 390, 392-393, 395, 401, 404, 406-407, 412-418, 422, 444-446, 458, 462, 467, 471, 497, 520, 529, 553-555, 558, 591, 608, 647, 652, 655, 663-664, 671, 678*

attraction between *20, 312*

attraction for *404, 608*

attraction of *23, 27, 67, 69-70, 78, 92-93, 97-98, 116, 215, 299-300, 309, 318, 343, 362, 364, 367, 369-370, 384, 390, 392-393, 404, 407, 412-418, 422, 445, 471, 558, 591*

attraction to *22, 25, 79, 81, 83, 93, 117, 180, 209, 247, 299-300, 318, 320, 362, 385-386, 392, 401, 404, 406-407, 413, 422, 444, 446, 458, 497, 520, 554, 655, 663-664, 678*

attraction toward *462, 529, 652*

attraction while *591*

excessive attraction *520*

female attraction *555*

spiritual attraction *553*

attractions *42, 74, 83, 86, 91, 131, 197, 254, 265, 299-300, 320, 374, 401, 404, 412, 415-417, 419*

attune *670*

attuned *654*

attunement *538, 599, 670*

Aum (see also "Om") *74, 210, 646*

Avatar *32, 50, 65, 191-193, 198, 218-219, 225, 284, 298, 313, 348, 352, 365, 376-377, 467, 646-647, 656, 674*

Avatars *32, 77, 91, 100, 104, 297-298, 361, 363, 488, 532, 557, 582, 584, 593, 647, 651, 666, 668*

avidya *116, 379, 444, 647, 677*

awake *432*

awaken *15, 67, 71, 78, 118-119, 122, 125, 149, 201, 229, 270, 294, 306, 322, 328, 362, 367, 371, 384, 394, 406, 417, 449, 488, 553, 566, 594, 597, 649, 653-654, 656-658, 664, 678*

awakened *5-6, 9, 17, 77-78, 99, 108, 124, 149, 175, 227, 233, 249, 270, 276, 352, 378, 384, 389, 400, 403, 406, 423, 432-433, 435, 450, 461, 483, 486, 488, 545, 562, 564, 588, 632, 640, 656, 662, 664, 668*

(awakened) *664*

awakened by *562*

awakened images *406*

awakened spiritual forces *77, 378, 450*

be awakened *5, 9, 249, 276, 352, 423, 486, 640, 656, 662*

become awakened *149, 227, 233, 270, 384, 432*

has awakened *99, 124, 483, 488, 564, 668*

is awakened *6, 78, 108, 352, 389, 400, 403, 433, 545*

not awakened *435*

spiritually awakened *461, 588*

awakening *15, 22, 67, 77-78, 82, 96, 120, 173, 175, 338, 352, 355-356, 367, 378, 383, 400, 404, 451-452, 536, 539, 553, 562, 564-565, 653-654, 657*

awakens *78, 384*

B

Bab *73-74, 94-95, 104, 123-124, 148, 178, 372-373, 539, 557, 620-622, 648, 672*

Baba (see also "Anandamurti" "Sarkar") *74, 374-375, 539, 621-622, 670, 672-673*

babbling *48*

Babel *44, 48, 103, 474, 480, 626, 648, 656*

Babel-like *48*

Babylon *47, 140-141, 192, 363-364, 390, 408, 413-415, 418-420, 462, 626, 648, 656*

Babylonians *140*

Baha'i i, *73-74, 80, 94-95, 104, 123, 148, 163-164, 178, 373-374, 385-386, 645, 648, 653, 661, 672*

Baha'u'llah *73, 94-95, 104, 123-124, 148, 164, 373, 648*

INDEX B

Bahram (see "Shah Bahram") *672*

Bakr (see "Abu Bakr") *645, 673*

Balaam *64, 70, 199, 370, 648*

baptism *196-197, 257-258, 260, 342-343, 563, 578, 648, 677*

Baptist (see "John the Baptist") *195, 227, 239-240, 246, 248-249, 261, 263, 276-277, 331*

baptize *196-197, 278, 563*

baptized *196-197, 226, 257-258, 263, 275, 284-285, 343*

baptizest *278*

baptizeth *278, 284*

baptizing *278, 284*

beast *14, 16, 19, 21, 25, 34, 36-41, 79-80, 152, 173, 348, 362, 380, 384-385, 398, 404-412, 414-417, 422-423, 462-468, 470, 472-473, 522-523, 587, 614, 624, 656, 664*

beasts *36-37, 64, 78-80, 152, 336, 379-380, 382-383, 385, 388, 390, 404, 407, 410, 416, 419-420, 422, 459, 462, 464, 466-469, 554, 587, 655, 671*

Beelzebub *224, 230*

Begotten *11-12, 26, 30, 75, 102, 104, 113, 171, 191, 197, 248, 262, 267, 275, 277-278, 282-285, 300, 307, 341, 357, 364, 381-383, 401-402, 440-441, 467, 545, 620-625, 635, 645, 647, 650, 653, 655*

> begotten of the dead *364, 383*
>
> First Begotten Son *11-12, 26, 75, 102, 104, 113, 171, 191, 197, 248, 262, 267, 275, 277-278, 282-285, 300, 341, 357, 364, 381-383, 401-402, 440-441, 467, 545, 620-625, 635, 645, 647, 650, 653, 655*
>
> has begotten *30*
>
> is begotten *307, 364*
>
> old-age-begotten *53*
>
> only begotten *277, 283*

Benjamin *140-141, 201, 285, 388, 658, 661*

Bhagavad-Gita *65, 67, 69, 71, 78-79, 86, 206, 225, 283, 302, 313, 332, 364, 367, 369, 371, 384, 542, 568-569, 648*

Bhakti *199, 565-566, 648*

Bhuloka *648*

Bhuvarloka *648*

Bible *iii, 5, 16, 22, 29-31, 44, 48, 56, 63-64, 66, 81-82, 86, 90, 102, 115-116, 122, 130, 138-139, 144, 146-148, 152, 155, 163, 175, 178, 185, 190, 192, 233, 274, 293-295, 305, 311-313, 316, 336-337, 360-361, 364, 366, 443-445, 456-457, 459, 473, 493-494, 520, 525, 539, 541, 544-545, 553, 561, 563-564, 579, 583, 588, 596-597, 605-607, 616, 618, 622, 627, 646, 648-650, 653, 655-656, 660, 666, 671, 678*

as the Bible *607*

(Bible) *64, 361*

Bible and *64, 178, 312, 336, 493, 563, 666*

Bible clearly *607*

Bible has *130, 618*

Bible is *16, 29, 81, 115-116, 139, 163, 293, 361, 364, 443-445, 473, 493, 544, 579, 655*

Bible will *82*

chapter in the Bible *31, 138*

from the Bible *146, 597*

in the Bible *iii, 16, 22, 29-31, 44, 48, 63-64, 86, 90, 102, 115-116, 130, 138-139, 144, 146, 152, 155, 185, 190, 192, 274, 294-295, 305, 311-312, 316, 336-337, 360-361, 443-445, 456-457, 459, 473, 493-494, 520, 525, 539, 541, 544, 553, 563-564, 579, 583, 588, 596, 606, 616, 618, 622, 627, 646, 649-650, 653, 655, 660, 666, 671, 678*

of the Bible *56, 64, 66, 122, 129, 138, 147-148, 152, 163, 178, 233, 336, 361, 364, 366, 656*

original Bible *44, 293*

throughout the Bible *155, 605, 648*

to the Bible *64, 293, 361, 545*

birthday *239-240*

birthdays *539*

birthright *53-54, 135-138, 140, 142, 146-148, 175-176, 191, 285, 570, 632*

Board *501-506, 508, 623*

boards *504-505*

Brahma *563*

Brahmic *501*

Brahmin *45, 51, 119, 459, 480, 488, 499, 502, 508, 645, 649, 668, 672*

Brahmins *43-44, 102, 119, 174, 229, 364, 447, 459, 468, 474, 479-480, 482, 484-485, 488, 501-505, 507-508, 510, 532-533, 584, 620, 649, 655*

brass *29, 140, 150, 152, 223, 365, 371, 395, 419, 458, 460-461, 463-464, 467, 473*

breath *17-18, 36-38, 102, 116, 306, 324, 347, 349, 433, 444-445, 649, 668*

breathe *561, 579*

breathed *17, 116, 444*

breathes *561*

breathing *16, 18, 356, 561, 579, 629*

Buddha *539, 557, 649*

Buddhi *348, 350, 433, 649, 665, 677*

Buddhism *vii, 562-563, 649, 671*

Buddhist *562, 596*

Buddhists *648, 663*

687

INDEX C

Cabala/Cabbala *vii, 671*
Caduceus *629-631*
Cain *27-31, 564*
calendar *466, 469, 538*
Caliph *618, 645, 666-667, 673, 677*
Caliphs *673*
candlestick *59, 68, 204, 368*
candlesticks *65, 67, 365-367, 398*
caste *43, 229, 468*
Catholic *460, 480, 618, 660*
Cayce, Edgar *145-146, 296, 649*
centrifugal *13, 115, 443, 649*
centripetal *5, 13, 115, 347, 431, 442, 649-651*
chakra *22, 25-26, 65, 67-75, 77, 80, 97, 125, 179, 197-199, 224, 231, 247, 306, 351-352, 354-356, 361, 366-371, 373-376, 385, 407, 517, 520-521, 553, 561, 571-572, 610, 629-632, 638, 645-646, 648, 650, 657, 662-664, 666, 668, 670, 673, 675, 677-678*

   (chakra) *22, 73, 77, 179, 197-198, 355, 361, 373-374, 553, 629, 673*
   chakra or *77, 351, 629*
   each chakra *65, 354-355*
   fifth chakra *71, 74, 80, 351, 356, 371, 374, 385, 407, 646, 677*
   first chakra *67, 77, 198, 351-352, 354, 356, 367, 520, 561, 571, 629-631, 646, 650, 666*
   fourth chakra *22, 70-72, 77, 97, 224, 231, 351, 355, 370-371, 373, 553, 572, 610, 646, 657, 677*
   heart chakra *22, 371, 553*
   last chakra *74, 375*
   next chakra *77*
   or chakra *75, 77, 366, 375*
   second chakra *22, 25-26, 68-69, 198, 351, 355, 368-369, 571, 632, 638, 668, 675*
   seventh chakra *75, 125, 352, 356, 376, 630, 646, 648, 670*
   sixth chakra *74, 306, 351, 356, 375, 630, 645-646, 650*
   that chakra *77*
   third chakra *69-70, 97, 199, 351, 355, 369-370, 521, 572, 632, 650, 664*
   this chakra *26, 70, 351, 355, 371, 571*
   what chakra *663*

chakras *15, 22, 25, 58, 65, 67-70, 77, 97, 186, 198-199, 203, 217, 247, 280, 282, 321, 349, 351-352, 354-355, 361, 364-365, 367-368, 370-371, 376, 378-379, 382, 409, 415, 446, 563-564, 571-572, 579, 588-589, 597, 600, 629-630, 637-638, 646, 650, 657, 662-663, 669, 672, 674*

   (chakras) *15, 65, 186, 355, 361, 364, 446, 571, 579, 588, 600, 638*
   chakras and koshas *351-352*
   different chakras *352, 589*
   five chakras *349, 352, 629-630, 646, 674*
   four chakras *77, 199, 378, 650*
   higher chakras *22, 67, 70, 352, 355, 367, 370, 376, 415, 597, 630, 662, 672*
   his chakras *67, 638*
   lower chakras *25, 282, 321, 415, 589*
   seven chakras *65, 349, 364-365, 382, 662-663*
   the chakras *65, 68, 321, 352, 354, 365, 368, 563-564, 637-638*
   these chakras *349*
   three chakras *58, 69-70, 77, 97, 198-199, 203, 247, 280, 352, 355, 370-371, 378, 409, 572, 657, 662-663, 669, 672, 674*
   two chakras *351, 630*

Chaldean *152, 294, 458, 463-464, 466, 472, 480*
channel *59, 112, 205, 312, 335-336, 356, 358, 438, 450, 472, 484, 510, 520, 523, 550, 556-557, 566, 594, 612, 629-631, 635, 637, 650, 674*
channeled *22*
channeling *635*
channelized *603*
channels *32-33, 550, 635, 673*
chant *597*
chanting *321, 356, 596-597, 599, 662*
charitable *489*
charity *71, 371, 489, 585, 597*
Cherubims *26-27, 650*
Chit (see also "Sat, Chit, Ananda") *439, 646, 670-671*
Chitta *8, 349-350, 357, 435, 645, 650-651, 658, 663, 665, 667-668*
Christhood *65, 258, 365, 650, 669*
Christian *64, 232, 370, 622, 660*
Christianity *57, 63-64, 70, 79, 82, 121, 144-145, 147-148, 162, 177-178, 185, 232, 275, 293, 370, 384, 596, 650, 653-654, 660, 665, 671*
Christianized *185*

INDEX C

Christians *63, 92, 163, 232, 244, 285, 297, 655, 660, 663, 673*

Christos *11*

Christs *382*

Christ (see also "Esa" "Jesus") *vii, ix, 11, 22, 56, 62-63, 65-67, 69-70, 73-74, 77-80, 82, 84, 87, 91, 95, 100, 104, 121, 143-145, 148-149, 162, 177, 185, 191-193, 195-197, 199-201, 207, 213, 215-220, 222-229, 232-233, 241-242, 244, 246-247, 249, 251, 257, 259, 261-262, 266-267, 269-270, 275-282, 284-289, 293, 303, 313, 332, 361, 365-367, 369-370, 374, 380, 383, 385, 388, 390, 399, 402-403, 407, 409, 421, 423-424, 427, 525, 532-533, 541-542, 545, 563, 569, 598, 605-607, 617-618, 620-626, 633, 647, 650, 663, 669, 673*

 accept Christ *289*

 and Christ *196, 269, 383, 423, 532, 545, 606, 621, 624, 626*

 as Christ *191-192, 262, 277, 282, 367, 407, 424, 622*

 be Christ *281, 624*

 before Christ *195, 277*

 call Christ *192, 224, 288, 618, 622, 650*

 (Christ) *ix, 73-74, 78, 193, 226, 267, 374, 383, 402, 605-606, 617-618, 621, 625*

 Christ and *63, 84, 145, 149, 200, 216, 232, 275, 289, 303, 423, 532, 542, 606, 623, 673*

 Christ brings *409*

 Christ comes *143-144, 200, 227, 606, 623*

 Christ Consciousness *66, 191, 229, 267, 366, 380, 650, 669*

 Christ does *213, 215, 267, 269, 275, 281, 533*

 Christ forgives *219*

 Christ fulfills *144-145*

 Christ has *220, 223, 251, 259*

 Christ himself *191, 226, 532, 545*

 Christ is *62, 84, 87, 104, 191-193, 196, 207, 216-217, 220, 222, 232, 242, 246, 277, 279, 284, 286, 303, 313, 332, 367, 541, 605, 607, 621-622*

 Christ's *62-63, 70, 79, 145, 148, 162, 207, 225, 247, 289, 370, 385, 606*

 Christ says *22, 143, 216, 218-220, 222, 227, 286, 606*

 Christ should *193*

 Christ teaches *80, 569*

 Christ to *195, 220, 277, 332, 605*

 Christ will *196*

 Esa the Christ *104, 121, 143, 162, 177, 185, 191-192, 277, 282, 332, 409, 532, 542, 650*

 even Christ *267*

 for Christ *216, 605, 663*

 his Christ *399, 402, 623*

 if Christ *216*

 is Christ *67, 84, 247, 249, 277-278, 367, 427, 621*

 not Christ *192, 278*

 of Christ *ix, 56, 62-63, 66, 69-70, 82, 104, 143, 145, 148-149, 191, 199, 207, 222, 226, 232, 244, 247, 257, 266, 270, 275, 278, 284-285, 293, 366, 369, 390, 423, 427, 622-624*

 or Christ *65, 365, 388*

 that Christ *191, 193, 197, 232, 267, 275, 278, 617, 623*

 the Christ *vii, 104, 121, 143, 162, 177, 185, 191-192, 246-247, 275, 277, 279, 282, 284, 288-289, 332, 409, 421, 532, 542, 598, 650*

 through Christ *66, 366, 673*

 will Christ *303*

 with Christ *100, 145, 232, 423, 623-624*

Christus *632*

circumcise *132*

circumcised *132, 143, 579*

circumcision/circumcism *579*

class *44-45, 119, 241, 267, 451, 459-461, 479-489, 495, 499, 501-502, 507-508, 527, 532, 605, 649, 661, 672*

classes *160, 459, 461, 468, 479-488, 502, 507, 532-533, 559, 608, 620, 640, 646, 651, 655, 657*

classless *45, 483, 488, 532, 646, 651*

clay *152, 458, 460-461, 466*

COEPTIS (see "ANNUIT COEPTIS") *155, 496*

Commandment *35, 51-52, 217, 242, 265, 409, 582-585*

Commandments *53, 60, 63, 134, 143, 150, 198, 205, 208, 242, 255, 266-267, 269, 403, 409, 427, 567, 578, 581-586, 598, 605, 627, 666, 670, 676*

committee *623*

committees *485, 504, 508*

Communist *468*

communities

 Communities of Light *254, 500, 530, 583, 586, 595-596, 603-604, 606, 608-611, 613-614, 618, 624, 626, 636, 639-640, 651, 672*

Communities *56, 254, 270, 394, 500, 502, 509-511, 530, 537, 583, 586, 595-596, 603-604, 606, 608-611, 613-614, 616, 618, 624, 626, 636, 639-640, 651, 672*

community *viii, 54, 94, 159, 165, 342, 356, 394, 449, 500, 509-511, 537, 539-540, 550, 555, 561,*

INDEX

576, 595-596, 599, 603, 608-610, 616, 618, 633, 638-639

    Community Of Light *550, 608-609, 639*

compassion *22, 34, 58, 62, 66, 93, 98, 101, 203, 222, 240, 244, 252-253, 258, 308, 317, 328, 354-355, 358, 381, 434-435, 439, 441, 467, 509, 530, 541, 549-550, 555, 590, 592, 598, 629, 637, 647, 673*

    compassion and mercy *66, 308, 467, 590, 592*

    compassion for *34, 58, 98, 101, 203, 435, 439, 441, 549, 590, 592*

    create compassion *58, 62, 98, 203, 549, 629*

    great compassion *34, 58, 98, 101, 203, 435, 439*

compassionate *213, 294, 313, 319, 533, 554, 592-593, 635*

consciousness

    Pure Consciousness *(see "Pure Consciousness")*

Consciousness *5-12, 15-22, 24, 26-27, 29, 31-35, 40-44, 47-48, 51, 54, 56, 58-61, 63, 65-70, 72-77, 81, 84-87, 89-93, 96-104, 107-119, 129-130, 143, 150-151, 169-172, 174-175, 179-180, 183-186, 191-193, 195-199, 203-206, 208-212, 214, 216-217, 219, 223-226, 228-229, 231, 233, 237-238, 240-241, 246-249, 252-258, 263, 265, 267-270, 275-277, 279, 282-289, 295-318, 321-322, 324-332, 334-335, 337-342, 347-350, 352, 356-358, 361-371, 373-377, 379-383, 387-393, 395-398, 400-405, 407-412, 414-417, 419-427, 431-448, 450-452, 457, 462, 466-467, 469, 471-472, 482-483, 487, 489, 494, 508, 512, 517, 519-521, 523-533, 535-536, 539, 541, 543-545, 552-557, 560-567, 570-572, 578, 582, 584-587, 589-595, 597, 603, 610-611, 613-614, 618, 626, 632, 634-635, 639-640, 646-658, 661-671, 673-678*

    a consciousness *15, 67, 191, 216, 367, 440, 611, 671*

    and consciousness *6, 22, 170, 276, 380, 553, 675*

    Christ Consciousness *66, 191, 229, 267, 366, 380, 650, 669*

    collective consciousness *404, 432, 462, 482, 639, 651, 676, 678*

    (consciousness) *8, 116, 276, 472, 529, 611, 632, 647*

    consciousness (Ahamtattva) *658*

    consciousness and *5, 9-10, 18, 22, 24, 31, 33, 54, 58, 77, 89, 93, 100-101, 107-108, 130, 150, 169, 172, 174, 180, 183, 186, 203, 238, 253, 269, 275-276, 295, 297, 300, 306, 308, 312, 328, 337, 341, 348, 361-364, 382-383, 388, 392, 395-396, 401-402, 409, 412, 419, 421, 423-424, 427, 431, 433, 436-437, 439-440, 446, 462, 466-467, 471, 487, 520, 523, 533, 536, 544, 552, 554, 556-557, 578, 582, 584, 586, 590, 592-593, 614, 646-647, 654, 657, 665*

C

Consciousness Beyond *562, 657, 674*

consciousness (Chitta) *658*

consciousness (ether) *8, 111, 435, 563, 677*

consciousness (Father) *169, 647, 656*

consciousness has *24, 304, 342, 408, 437, 467*

consciousness is *6-8, 15, 21-22, 59, 108, 113-114, 117, 170, 186, 204, 308, 349, 352, 382-383, 388-390, 403, 427, 431, 433, 440-442, 446, 536, 552-553, 556, 562, 567, 611, 613, 639, 652, 657, 669, 675, 678*

consciousness (Mahatattva) *658*

consciousness or *15, 29, 58, 90, 103, 114-115, 172, 196, 203, 240-241, 284, 298, 308, 315, 331, 380, 405, 411, 440, 444, 462, 524, 539, 555, 563, 567, 653, 665*

consciousness (self) *663*

consciousness should *172, 302*

Consciousness will *22, 69, 86, 92, 247, 295, 297, 301, 326, 338, 369, 377, 411, 424, 487, 544, 553, 567, 662*

Consciousness without *6, 26, 283, 352*

crude consciousness *357, 675*

Divine consciousness *22, 553*

first consciousness *655*

for consciousness *16, 114, 174, 462, 586*

guilty consciousness *24*

high consciousness *29, 54, 58, 76, 86, 103, 174, 203, 284, 312, 326, 329, 361, 377, 407-408*

higher consciousness *9-11, 26, 54, 56, 65, 75-77, 84, 89-90, 92, 99-100, 102, 104, 112, 114, 118-119, 129-130, 172, 174-175, 184, 186, 211, 233, 238, 246, 252-254, 269, 277, 286, 288-289, 295, 302-304, 309, 313, 315, 317, 322, 324, 331, 334, 337, 339, 364-365, 376-377, 379-383, 387-388, 390, 392-393, 401-402, 405, 407-409, 411-412, 415, 419-423, 427, 433, 436-439, 441-442, 446, 448, 452, 471, 487, 508, 520, 524-525, 527, 532-533, 536, 544, 560, 567, 570, 589-592, 594, 618, 646-647, 652-653, 664-665, 667, 678*

highest consciousness *77, 339, 382*

his consciousness *112, 356, 436, 439-440, 444, 517, 556, 589, 670*

human consciousness *7, 342, 361, 457, 521*

in consciousness *655*

infinite consciousness *107, 431-432, 658*

is consciousness *5, 183, 341, 594, 674*

low consciousness *322*

lower consciousness *212, 282, 414, 554*

INDEX

C

manifested consciousness *8, 111, 240, 435, 469, 563, 677*

of consciousness *7-8, 15, 19, 21-22, 27, 43-44, 51, 60-61, 76, 81, 101, 107-108, 110, 169, 195, 205-206, 216, 254, 275, 283, 298, 304, 308, 335, 341, 347, 349, 357, 366, 377, 379, 382, 389, 431, 434, 512, 525, 552-553, 556, 560, 562, 595, 597, 603, 613, 632, 634-635, 647, 650, 654, 663-664, 667, 673*

or consciousness *240, 436*

same consciousness *7, 21, 226, 308, 552*

separate consciousness *545, 674*

spiritual consciousness *282, 521, 662*

Supreme Consciousness *563, 674*

the consciousness *5-7, 9, 22, 56, 67, 75, 89, 102, 108-110, 114, 143, 169, 174, 209, 217, 275-276, 282, 287, 311, 314, 321-322, 330, 334, 357, 367, 376, 380, 391, 395, 398, 403-404, 411-412, 414, 416-417, 431, 433, 439, 442-443, 446, 462, 469, 519-521, 523, 545, 552-553, 556-557, 565, 587, 589, 597, 611, 646-647, 649, 656-658, 662-663, 669-670, 675, 677-678*

turbulent consciousness *197, 241, 424, 671*

unit consciousness *6, 15, 24, 87, 101-102, 108-109, 116-117, 170, 172, 184, 275, 297-298, 304, 306, 308, 329, 339, 341, 349-350, 352, 389, 403, 433-434, 436-437, 440, 444-447, 462, 519, 527, 553, 566-567, 646, 657-658, 661, 676, 678*

universal consciousness *6, 276, 556*

without consciousness *6, 432*

consciousnesses *6, 8-13, 15-16, 34, 41, 67, 81, 89, 101, 108, 110, 113-116, 170-172, 218, 295, 297, 299-300, 304-305, 307, 316, 327-328, 330, 341, 362, 379-382, 391, 401-403, 410-411, 417, 423, 433-438, 441-445, 517, 519, 525, 529-530, 533, 545, 571, 590, 592, 620, 639, 649-650, 671, 675*

Constitution *153*

countenance *27, 210, 306, 365-366, 444, 465, 469, 473*

counter-evolution *486, 673-674*

counter-evolutionary *512, 636*

counter-evolutions *486, 674*

counter-revolution *486, 673-674*

counter-revolutionary *636*

counter-revolutions *486, 674*

counties *500*

county *500*

couple *20-21, 265, 509, 511, 526, 528-529, 543, 554, 561*

couples *20, 61, 206, 526, 528, 553*

covenant *36, 41-42, 52, 131-134, 143, 150, 161, 164, 327, 332, 375, 387, 400, 408, 604-605, 607*

creative *5-6, 12, 33, 48, 101, 107-108, 110, 169-170, 172, 183, 254, 275-276, 311, 336, 348, 355, 379, 381, 396, 400-401, 431, 433-434, 437, 439, 522, 525, 614, 636-637, 648, 651, 655-656, 660, 662-665, 668, 671, 674-675*

Creator *86, 92, 162, 267, 308, 316, 328, 341, 379-380, 392, 419, 558, 637, 659, 663*

crucified *87, 121, 144, 232, 247, 258, 262, 313, 398*

crucifixion *70, 145, 162, 270, 364, 370, 382*

crucify *70, 225, 227, 247, 250-251, 257, 270, 370*

crucifying *262, 403*

crude *13, 33, 86, 226, 236, 253, 268, 282, 305, 316, 348, 351, 355, 357, 387, 391, 393, 436, 443, 520, 524, 545, 652, 675-676*

cruder *13, 357, 391, 396, 407, 411, 431*

crudest *13, 304-305, 347, 349-350, 645, 650-651, 668, 675*

crudification *7, 13, 114-115, 301, 391, 442, 444, 530, 649-650*

crudified *115, 117, 231, 282, 299, 347, 350, 354, 411, 414, 442-444, 447, 519, 629, 647, 663, 675*

crudifies *5, 9, 108, 174, 209, 299, 314, 431, 439, 519-520*

crudify *13, 114, 217, 403, 675*

crudifying *5-6, 13, 29, 107, 114-115, 170, 309, 312, 347, 431, 433, 437, 442-443, 471, 519-520, 522, 586, 590, 611, 637, 647, 649-652, 663-664, 667, 675*

crystal *379, 425-426, 536, 629, 654*

crystals *629*

cycle *25, 149, 165, 406, 440, 482, 486, 497, 538, 542, 549, 552, 554-555, 572*

cycles *486-487, 626*

cyclic *484*

cyclical *487, 498, 618, 626, 640*

Cyrus *141, 618, 622*

INDEX   D

D

Daharma/Darma/Dharma *19, 24, 28-29, 31, 34-35, 58-59, 69, 90, 100, 104, 203-204, 268, 298-299, 306, 314, 333, 369, 391, 404, 408, 471, 473, 487, 518, 526, 533, 566, 569, 577, 582, 584-585, 598, 616, 619, 649, 651-652, 664, 678*

Daharmas/Darmas *17, 33, 35, 42, 48, 60, 205, 298-299, 314, 395, 479, 497, 517-518, 527-528, 544, 582, 584, 645, 651-652, 673*

Daharmic *31*

dance *596-597*

danced *227, 239*

dancing *596-597, 599, 662*

Daniel *iv, 42, 45, 64, 151-153, 174, 257, 362, 404, 455-474, 479-481, 493, 540, 656, 662*

Darshan *249*

David *55, 68, 74, 79, 103, 121, 139, 154-155, 191-192, 221, 229-230, 243, 258-259, 266, 320, 368, 374, 381, 384, 427, 494, 508, 617-618, 621-622, 624, 631*

daydream *573*

daydreamer *589*

daydreamers *573*

Declaration *153*

democracy *461, 464, 473, 482, 485, 616-617*

democratic *64, 482, 616-617*

Dervishes *596*

Destroyer *93, 294, 563, 636, 656*

destructive *310, 464, 525, 562, 591, 615, 661*

Devi *539*

devil *69, 79, 82, 197-200, 222, 227, 230-231, 237-238, 243, 249, 299-301, 309, 317, 340, 364, 369, 384-385, 392, 402-404, 407, 412, 416-417, 422-423, 520, 572, 624, 632, 652, 654, 663, 665, 667, 672, 675-676*

   a devil *222, 227, 230, 243*

   (devil) *231, 403, 520, 632*

   devil's *300*

   Same as devil *654, 672, 675*

   the devil *69, 79, 82, 197-200, 222, 227, 230-231, 237, 249, 299-301, 309, 317, 340, 364, 369, 384-385, 392, 402-404, 407, 412, 416, 422-423, 520, 572, 624, 663, 667*

devilish *320, 521*

devils *202, 214, 217-218, 222-224, 230-231, 395, 404, 412, 416, 418*

devotee *37, 335, 565*

devotees *84, 307, 323, 325, 334*

devotion *20, 85, 187, 209, 217, 242, 286, 312, 317, 321, 439, 452, 557, 565-566, 597, 599, 648*

devotional *597*

dialectic *470*

dictator *616-619*

dictators *616-618*

Dictatorship *617*

dictatorships *499*

disciple *70, 73, 196, 219, 224, 226, 334, 373, 524-525, 530, 604, 606, 634-635, 642*

disciples *56-58, 63, 73, 80, 195, 201-202, 204, 212, 215, 217-224, 226, 228-229, 234-237, 240-250, 254-260, 264, 266, 277-281, 284-286, 288-289, 302, 373, 488, 508, 524, 555, 563, 593, 634-635*

   his disciples *56-58, 63, 80, 195, 201-202, 204, 212, 215, 217-224, 226, 228-229, 234-237, 240, 242-250, 254-258, 266, 277-281, 284-286, 288-289, 524, 563, 593*

   the disciples *218, 220, 235, 240-241, 244, 246, 248-250, 254, 259-260, 288, 524, 634-635*

   their disciples *264, 302, 488, 508, 555*

   thy disciples *220, 229, 241, 249*

   twelve disciples *222, 226, 257*

district *500*

districts *500*

Divines *303, 583, 606, 617-618*

dogma *94, 301, 498-499, 502, 561, 652*

dogmas *v, vi, viii, 59, 78, 82, 204, 293, 325, 384, 393, 398, 502, 560, 567, 607, 618, 633, 655, 659, 665*

dogmatic *vi, iv, 92, 98, 297, 499, 525*

dragon *362, 389-390, 399, 401-405, 412, 416, 422, 652, 665*

dream *64, 151-152, 192, 194-195, 456, 458, 461-464, 467, 469, 474, 493, 573, 618*

dreams *iv, 456, 480, 556-557, 573, 634*

Durga *22, 553*

INDEX   E

E

east
    and east *140, 470, 562*
    East Indian *44*
    Far East *40, 65, 67-68, 77-79, 81, 119, 122, 125, 147-148, 163, 173, 178, 367-368, 378, 383-384, 387, 542, 565, 621, 628, 639, 645, 649, 653-655, 658, 666, 670*
    Middle East *646*
    the east *18, 26, 29, 44, 46-47, 53, 81, 135-136, 140, 193-194, 216, 232, 296, 307, 310, 387, 389, 412, 425, 470, 650, 660*

East *18, 26, 29, 40, 44, 46-47, 53, 65, 67-68, 77-79, 81, 119, 122, 125, 135-136, 140, 147-148, 163, 173, 178, 193-194, 216, 232, 296, 307, 310, 367-368, 378, 383-384, 387, 389, 412, 425, 470, 542, 562, 565, 621, 628, 639, 645-646, 649-650, 653-655, 658, 660, 666, 670*

Eastern *628-629*

Eden *18, 25-26, 29, 288, 340, 405, 480, 620, 650, 652*

Edgar (see "Cayce, Edgar") *145, 296, 649*

ego *v, vi, 6-7, 10-11, 16, 29, 33-35, 58, 60, 62, 66, 70, 77, 79, 91, 97, 100, 108, 112, 121, 123, 125, 145, 149, 162, 170, 184-185, 203, 205, 208, 214-216, 220, 224-225, 228, 232, 236, 247, 255, 262, 276, 304, 319-320, 338-339, 350, 366, 370, 378, 382, 384-385, 390, 394, 399, 401, 403, 405, 409, 415, 419, 433-434, 436-439, 451-452, 463, 497, 520, 527, 529, 534, 541-542, 549-552, 557-558, 570-571, 597, 610, 613, 620, 631-632, 634, 648, 652-654, 657-658, 665, 669*
    beyond ego *vi*
    (ego) *236, 557, 613, 620, 657-658, 669*
    ego-actualization *570-571*
    ego-actualized *571*
    ego and *10, 33, 79, 112, 384, 437, 452, 542, 552, 558, 571, 610, 648, 652-653*
    ego-centeredness *511*
    ego comes *6, 10*
    ego creates *60, 205*
    ego does *162, 550*
    ego goes *597*
    ego has *255, 405, 436, 551*
    ego into *11, 60, 433, 529*
    ego is *6, 29, 58, 97, 108, 121, 170, 203, 255, 304, 399, 433, 534, 549, 570, 652-653*
    ego loves *16*

ego of *123, 319, 405, 541, 549*

ego's *339*

ego seeks *232, 570*

Ego should *652*

ego tends *527*

ego to *205, 439, 520, 552*

ego trips *185*

ego will *224-225, 451, 653*

ego would *463*

false ego *10, 28, 34-35, 58, 60, 66, 70, 77, 79, 91, 97, 121, 125, 145, 149, 162, 170, 185, 203, 205, 214-216, 220, 225, 228, 232, 247, 255, 262, 276, 304, 319-320, 338, 350, 366, 370, 378, 382, 384-385, 390, 394, 399, 401, 403, 405, 409, 415, 419, 451, 497, 527, 534, 541-542, 549-552, 557-558, 570, 631-632, 652-654, 657, 665*

from ego *648*

is ego *549*

Limited ego *16*

little ego *100*

no ego *438, 549*

overcome ego *58*

own ego *185*

see ego *654*

their ego *184, 634*

with ego *549*

your ego *224*

egocentric *610, 620*

egoistic *394, 415, 419, 422, 428, 648*

egoistical/egotistical *97, 112, 184, 195, 258, 295, 299, 312, 393-394, 399, 406, 408, 411, 413-414, 417-420, 463, 656, 674*

egos *6, 20, 34, 55, 58, 83-84, 125-126, 149, 164, 184, 196, 201, 203, 214, 225, 230, 247, 250, 253, 255-256, 261, 267, 301, 307, 309, 312, 318, 331, 384, 387, 391, 399, 409, 415, 419, 424, 523, 529, 554, 557, 597, 607, 610, 634, 653, 676*
    big egos *307*
    (egos) *676*
    false egos *20, 34, 55, 58, 83-84, 125, 164, 184, 196, 201, 203, 214, 225, 230, 247, 250, 253, 255-256, 261, 267, 301, 309, 312, 318, 331, 384, 391, 399, 409, 415, 419, 424, 653*

individual egos *6*

limited egos *149, 523, 610*

our egos *607*

693

INDEX   E

   separate egos *126, 554*
   their egos *126, 184, 312, 387, 529, 557, 597, 634*
egotism *86, 120, 149, 170, 326, 438-439, 610*
Egypt *46, 53-54, 59, 103, 134, 136, 138, 140, 160, 194, 200, 204, 287, 305, 398, 542*
Egyptian *194*
Egyptians *54, 160*
Einstein *312*
Elah *294, 646*
Elahah *294, 646*
Elder *45, 53, 135, 142, 498, 501, 503, 505, 509, 511, 616-617, 624*
elders *241, 247, 260-263, 267, 305, 336, 350, 379-383, 388, 399, 407-408, 420, 496-498, 503-505, 510, 527, 608, 623, 653, 676*
Eldest *501, 503-505, 510, 605, 616-617, 619, 623-624*
Elect *175, 183, 581, 604, 631, 653*
Elected *50-51, 54-55, 63, 69, 79, 81, 84, 88-89, 91, 96, 103, 121, 129-130, 147, 151, 160, 164-165, 175, 186, 196, 236, 257, 302-303, 308, 311, 322, 324, 328, 338, 340, 369, 375, 382, 384, 387-388, 400, 407-408, 410, 459, 483, 493, 495, 497, 499-506, 560, 591-592, 645, 650, 653, 657, 659, 668*
   are elected *84, 91, 303, 407, 500-501, 503, 505-506*
   be elected *160, 408, 497, 499-500, 503-505*
   elected by *151, 408, 499-500, 502, 504-505*
   Elected One *54, 103, 160, 164, 407*
   Elected Ones *50-51, 54-55, 63, 69, 79, 81, 84, 88, 91, 121, 130, 147, 151, 160, 164-165, 175, 186, 196, 236, 257, 302-303, 308, 311, 322, 324, 338, 340, 369, 375, 382, 384, 387-388, 400, 408, 410, 459, 483, 493, 495, 560, 591-592, 645, 650, 653, 657, 659, 668*
   elected people *89, 96, 129, 160, 328, 499, 506*
   elected will *91, 303, 500, 505*
   mass-elected *500-501*
   those Elected *79, 96, 151, 384, 483, 668*
Elects *81, 93, 96, 416, 422, 502, 535, 567, 581-582, 584, 598, 608, 618, 621, 624-626, 635, 672, 674*
Elias/Elijah *195, 227, 246, 248-249, 265, 277-278, 331*
Ellah *294*
Eloah *293-294, 646*
Eloam *294*
Elohim *7, 90, 294, 646*
Emmanuel *56, 191, 193, 660*

emotion *379*
emotional *vi, 125, 234, 489, 550, 572-573, 597, 610, 638, 665*
emotionally *511, 528-529, 572, 597, 609, 638*
emotionless *379*
Emotionlessly *379*
emotions *22, 379, 553, 564, 568, 589, 595, 638, 669, 677*
England *142, 145, 176, 232, 466, 653*
English *294, 306, 310, 526*
   English-speaking *142, 147*
enlighten *14, 563*
enlightened *616, 625*
enlightenment *75, 144, 364, 376, 407, 412, 557, 566, 589-591, 669*
Enoch *29, 31, 129, 545*
EnshaAllah/Enshallah *566, 653*
Ephesus *67, 365, 367*
Ephraim *53-54, 136-142, 147, 176, 200, 285, 653*
Ephraims *653, 658*
E Pluribus Unum *154*
Esaias *195, 200, 217, 230, 235, 242, 277*
Esa (see also "Christ" "Jesus") *56, 58, 60, 69-70, 84-85, 87, 104, 121, 143-144, 161-162, 177, 185, 191-201, 203, 205, 209, 212-213, 215-223, 226, 228-232, 234-241, 243-250, 252-266, 268, 277-290, 297, 303, 312-313, 332-333, 358, 369-370, 409, 501, 532, 539, 542, 545, 557, 577, 605, 621, 650, 653, 660*
   And Esa *85, 193, 195-197, 201, 215-222, 230, 240, 243-244, 246, 249-250, 256-260, 263, 277, 280, 284, 297, 313, 621*
   before Esa *195*
   born Esa *192*
   by Esa *194, 209, 222-223, 245, 277, 577, 650*
   call him Esa *660*
   (Esa) *161, 262, 313*
   Esa and *85, 194, 241, 284, 297, 577*
   Esa becomes *200, 243*
   Esa begins *201, 226*
   Esa comes *162, 221, 232, 246, 249, 278, 290*
   Esa could *244*
   Esa fulfills *177*
   Esa gives *213, 229*
   Esa has *200, 215, 226, 239, 253, 258, 277, 281, 290, 501*
   Esa hears *216, 220, 240*

INDEX   E

Esa is *143, 161, 191-193, 197, 201, 212, 216-217, 221, 226, 231-232, 248, 263-264, 278-279, 281-282, 284, 286, 290*

Esa knows *199, 219, 230, 281*

Esa on *162*

Esa overcomes *199, 650*

Esa prophesies *177*

Esa's *192, 198, 221, 244-246, 262, 282, 286*

Esa saith *216-217, 221, 238, 244, 250, 252, 260-261, 279-280, 286-288, 290*

Esa says *161, 198, 216-217, 220, 226, 231, 239-240, 243-245, 249, 254-256, 265, 282-283, 287-288, 290, 312, 358, 577*

Esa sees *199, 216-218, 279, 282*

Esa should *144*

Esa teaches *60, 69, 205, 215, 287, 370*

Esa the Christ *104, 121, 143, 162, 177, 185, 191-192, 277, 282, 332, 409, 532, 542, 650*

Esa the Messiah *87, 162, 196, 650, 660*

Esa would *144, 201, 237, 279*

followers of Esa *185, 650*

is Esa *56, 69, 196-197, 259, 369*

name Esa *193*

of Esa *58, 70, 162, 177, 185, 191-192, 199, 201, 203, 239, 243, 279-280, 285, 370, 409, 542, 650*

tell Esa *84, 144, 240, 303*

to Esa *192, 241, 249, 279, 282, 286*

worship Esa *193*

Esau *53, 135-136, 147, 660*

escapism *68, 72, 76, 79, 87, 96, 119, 320, 335-336, 368, 373, 377, 448, 522, 544, 582, 664*

escapist *68, 73-74, 76, 148, 185-186, 195, 202, 220, 368, 374, 377, 536, 635*

escapists *57, 68, 74-77, 96, 100, 202, 222, 361, 368, 374, 376-377, 485*

essence *vii, i, iii, 2, 15, 21, 40, 80, 94, 101, 119, 129, 145, 148, 150, 154, 172, 191, 209, 211, 213, 215, 305, 352, 429-431, 448, 466, 545, 561, 565, 578, 581, 603, 609, 613, 628, 640, 654, 656, 664, 667, 671-672*

In essence *15, 565*

its essence *94*

our essence *667*

the essence *vii, i, iii, 2, 21, 40, 80, 101, 119, 129, 145, 148, 150, 154, 172, 191, 209, 211, 213, 215, 305, 352, 429-431, 448, 466, 545, 561, 578, 581, 609, 613, 628, 654, 656, 664, 672*

their Essence *609, 640*

very essence *603*

-esus *660*

Eternal *v, vii, viii, ix, i, ii, iii, iv, 1-2, 7, 12, 21, 26-27, 48, 58, 66-70, 96, 101-103, 118, 123, 125, 146, 148, 169, 171, 178-180, 186, 203, 225, 255, 275, 283, 288-289, 296, 358, 366, 368-370, 372-373, 380, 382, 427, 429, 431, 437, 440-441, 444, 448, 452, 468, 494, 511, 524, 531, 542, 545, 552, 561-562, 566, 578, 581, 586, 592, 598, 600, 603-606, 611, 616, 618-620, 622, 628, 634, 640, 645, 648, 651, 653-656, 658, 671*

and Eternal *7, 373, 427, 437, 524, 545, 598, 604, 655-656*

Eternal Divine Path *(see "Eternal Divine Path")*

eternal life *58, 66, 68-70, 96, 203, 255, 283, 288-289, 366, 368-370*

Eternal Tablet *146, 296, 645*

Eternal Truth *vii*

eternal world *27, 380*

Formless, Invisible, Nameless, and Eternal *7, 21, 373, 427, 437, 524, 545, 552, 598, 604, 655-656*

Eternal Divine Path *v, vii, viii, ix, i, ii, iii, iv, 2, 12, 48, 67, 101-103, 118, 123, 125, 148, 169, 171, 179-180, 186, 225, 275, 283, 358, 372, 382, 429, 431, 441, 444, 448, 452, 468, 494, 511, 542, 561-562, 566, 578, 581, 586, 592, 600, 603-606, 611, 616, 618-620, 622, 628, 634, 640, 648, 651, 653, 656, 658, 671*

and the Eternal Divine Path *12, 180, 444, 586, 628, 640*

(Eternal Divine Path) *v, 123, 600, 616, 620, 656*

Eternal Path *vii, 178-179, 440*

follow the Eternal Divine Path *ii, 358, 372, 382, 468, 511, 561-562, 578, 600, 604-606, 618, 648, 651*

is the Eternal Divine Path *i, ii, 452, 561, 578, 603, 619*

Mission of Maitreya, Eternal Divine Path *605-606*

of the Eternal Divine Path *vii, viii, iv, 2, 102-103, 148, 180, 566, 611, 628, 656, 671*

through the Eternal Divine Path *171, 179, 275, 382*

eternity *vii, 304, 389, 402, 604, 653-654*

ether *5-6, 8, 13, 111, 171, 347-349, 357, 379, 431, 435, 521, 563, 629-630, 645, 647, 654, 677*

ethereal *6-7, 12-13, 15-18, 33-34, 102, 108, 114-117, 217, 269, 287, 347, 349-351, 356-357, 379, 396-397, 431, 433, 442-446, 557, 571, 600, 629-630, 635, 637-638, 646, 649-650, 653-654, 664, 674, 676*

695

INDEX   E

ethereal body *15, 18, 116-117, 217, 269, 287, 349-350, 445-446, 557, 600, 629, 637-638, 646, 650, 654, 674*

ethereal factor *6, 116, 356-357, 379, 396, 431, 433, 444-445, 630, 646, 650*

ethereal factors *108, 397, 431, 445, 646, 664, 674*

ethereal stage *12-13, 16, 102*

ethereal state *12, 15, 17, 431*

etheric *349, 356, 610, 637, 646, 658*

etherically *502*

Europe *49, 118, 142, 144, 147, 285, 289, 460, 465-466, 480, 617, 653*

European *289, 466*

Europeans *148*

Eve *26-27, 30, 60, 76, 89, 206, 224, 282, 330, 376, 539, 542-543, 614, 620, 654, 657, 663, 678*

evil *18, 23, 26, 34, 40, 58-59, 62, 67-68, 70, 76, 82-83, 85-86, 97, 124, 137, 185, 204, 207, 209-214, 219, 231-232, 243, 257, 283, 300, 302-303, 310, 315, 330, 339, 367-370, 376, 402-403, 405, 412, 434, 457, 465, 471, 520, 620, 632, 640, 648, 650, 654, 664-666, 671, 676*

   all evil *137*

   an evil *231-232*

   become evil *283, 457*

   be evil *211, 213, 231-232*

   by evil *339*

   doeth evil *283*

   do evil *68, 70, 97, 303, 315, 369-370, 405, 666*

   (evil) *402*

   evil actions *315, 330*

   evil deeds *315, 666*

   evil (devil) *632*

   evil doings *370*

   evil fruit *214*

   evil hearts *231*

   evil is *83, 85, 300, 310, 465, 471*

   evil man *231*

   evil one *632*

   evil (serpent) *412*

   evil son *632*

   evil things *68, 97, 231, 367-368, 370, 434*

   evil thoughts *243*

   evil treasure *231*

   evil will *303, 665*

   eye evil *211, 257*

   from evil *82-83, 209-211, 300*

   good and evil *18, 23, 26, 76, 185, 376, 465, 471, 620, 676*

   good or evil *18, 632*

   is evil *40, 67, 83, 231, 283, 300, 367, 370, 632*

   of evil *58-59, 62, 204, 207, 650, 664*

   overcome evil *70, 370*

   resist not evil *62, 207*

   the evil *62, 68, 86, 207, 212, 231, 368, 403, 434, 632, 671*

   this evil *124*

   ward off evil *302*

   ye evil *219*

evildoers *68, 199*

evildoings *57, 70, 202*

evils *11, 21, 126, 439*

evolution *14-15, 20, 26, 34, 43, 46, 51, 90, 116, 129, 148, 293, 304, 396, 443, 474, 483, 485, 497, 512, 527, 620, 622, 636, 654*

evolutionary *13, 15, 17-18, 26, 30, 32-33, 36-37, 40, 46, 48, 88-89, 91, 93, 95-96, 102-103, 113, 115-117, 129-130, 172, 192, 196, 211, 295, 298-299, 301, 304-305, 307, 318, 400, 441, 443-448, 457, 460, 484, 486-487, 495, 498, 526, 565, 592, 620, 626, 628, 636, 640, 647, 649, 673-674*

   evolutionary change *447-448, 486*

   evolutionary development *457*

   evolutionary Hierarchy *211*

   evolutionary intervals *15*

   evolutionary leap *15*

   evolutionary manner *484, 487, 495, 640*

   evolutionary movements *486, 674*

   evolutionary phases *486*

   evolutionary process *15, 17, 26, 30, 33, 36-37, 40, 48, 88-89, 91, 93, 95-96, 102-103, 113, 115-117, 129, 172, 196, 298-299, 301, 304-305, 307, 400, 443-446, 460, 487, 526, 592, 647*

   evolutionary processes *295, 318, 443*

   evolutionary progress *13, 46, 565, 649*

   evolutionary stage *295*

   evolutionary step *32, 117, 129, 192, 446, 620, 628, 636*

   evolutionary steps *15, 18, 129-130, 172, 441, 448*

   evolutionary way *626*

evolutions *474*

Excalibur *631-632*

Executive *624*

Ezra *55, 141*

F

facilitate *85, 498*

facilitating *320, 623-624*

factor *6, 13, 115-116, 170, 350, 355-357, 379, 396, 431, 433, 442, 444-445, 490, 526, 560, 630-631, 646, 650*

factors *13, 64, 108, 114-116, 305, 347, 350, 354, 357, 397, 431, 442-445, 498, 587, 646, 664, 674*

fast *69, 72-73, 75, 93-94, 98, 100, 210, 220, 370, 372-375, 392, 423, 451, 540, 581-582, 597*

fasted *197-198, 227*

fasting *210, 220, 244, 249, 314, 321, 571, 574, 581-582, 595, 634, 670*

Father (uppercase "F") *7, 12, 21-22, 37, 41, 48, 56, 59, 62-63, 72, 74-76, 85, 87, 90, 99, 110, 113, 126, 159-161, 169-171, 197, 203-204, 207-214, 216-217, 219, 223-226, 228, 234, 238, 242, 246, 248-253, 255, 257-258, 267, 270, 275-277, 280, 284-285, 287-288, 295-296, 300, 306-308, 313, 317, 327, 336, 338, 341, 357, 364, 372, 374, 377, 388-389, 394, 397, 407, 410, 412, 414, 416, 419, 424, 434-435, 440, 442, 466, 517, 521, 525, 532, 544, 552-553, 563, 567, 574, 578, 582-584, 586, 588, 590-591, 594, 600, 614, 633, 635-637, 640, 647, 650, 652-656, 660, 667, 673*

    Divine Father *12, 209, 275, 307-308, 582-583, 590, 614, 652, 654*

    (Father) *7, 21-22, 169-170, 275, 300, 307, 327, 435, 552, 594, 637, 647, 656*

    Father and *48, 56, 74, 99, 203, 248, 275, 374, 517, 600, 636, 650, 653, 660, 673*

    Father controls *110*

    Father has *161, 338*

    Father is *87, 234, 248, 277, 306, 341, 416, 517, 594, 636*

    Father Mother *7, 614*

    Father or *7, 563*

    Father's *280, 336, 407*

    Father should *251*

    Father will *210, 238, 532*

    heavenly Father *210-212, 242, 253*

    his Father *48, 87, 197, 248, 364, 440*

    loving Father *159, 161*

    my Father *72, 74, 76, 99, 214, 225, 228, 234, 246, 251-252, 257-258, 372, 374, 377*

    O Father *228*

    only Father *412*

    our Father *209, 667*

    the Father *7, 22, 37, 41, 56, 62-63, 72, 74-75, 85, 113, 126, 160-161, 171, 203, 207-208, 216-217, 219, 223, 226, 228, 234, 238, 248-251, 255, 258, 267, 270, 275-277, 285, 287-288, 295-296, 307, 313, 317, 341, 357, 372, 374, 389, 394, 410, 414, 416, 419, 440, 442, 466, 517, 525, 544, 563, 567, 574, 584, 586, 588, 591, 594, 600, 614, 633, 635-636, 640, 653, 660*

    their Father *203, 238, 388, 424, 544*

    thy Father *208-210*

    true Father *234*

    your Father *59, 62-63, 204, 207-210, 213, 224-225, 251, 267, 586*

fault-finders *88, 323*

faultfinding *598*

fear *24, 41, 58, 66, 69, 88, 92, 96-97, 135, 185, 192, 203, 218, 224-225, 240-242, 247-248, 260, 277, 300, 307-309, 315, 323-324, 326, 331-333, 335, 340, 349, 354-355, 366, 369, 399-401, 403-404, 408, 410, 415-417, 419-420, 434, 437, 481, 484, 526, 533, 557, 570, 572, 652*

    Excess fear *247*

    fear and ignorance *96*

    fear and tribulation *218*

    fear automatically *24*

    fear death *69, 369*

    fear for *247, 533*

    fear God *240, 300, 326, 408*

    fear him *224, 420*

    fear in *333*

    Fear none *69, 369*

    fear not *66, 88, 135, 192, 224-225, 323, 366*

    fear of *41, 58, 96-97, 185, 203, 225, 242, 277, 331, 354-355, 415, 419, 526, 557, 570*

    fear that *332*

    fear the *225, 260*

    Fear them *224*

    fear thy *400*

    fear to *307, 399*

    fear will *315, 340*

    for fear *241*

    from fear *308, 349, 557, 572*

    great fear *248, 399, 404*

    no fear *58, 203, 242, 335, 403*

    not fear *69, 240, 369, 410*

INDEX

original fear *324*
will fear *88, 323*
without fear *225*
feared *146, 239, 262*
fearest *133*
fearful *24, 66, 218, 366, 425*
fearless *483*
fearlessly *327*
fearlessness *459, 597*
fears *24, 69, 96, 225, 351, 356, 369, 403, 417, 481, 572, 578, 633*
feast *64, 280-281, 289, 422, 541-542, 607*
feasts *267, 541, 607*
female *7, 16, 19-22, 30, 36-37, 82, 102, 115, 117, 253-254, 265, 293, 297, 340-341, 415, 437, 443-444, 446, 527-528, 538, 545, 552-555, 563, 590, 610, 614, 645, 655*
females *563*
festivals *63-64, 232, 469, 473, 539, 541, 665*
fetus *561, 609, 637-638*
finance *509*
financial *509-510, 527, 561, 604, 606, 615, 640*
financially *536-537, 604, 606, 615*
financing *509-510*
FINE (uppercase) *1, 373, 524, 598, 604, 606, 655*
fire *13, 19, 41, 60, 76, 86, 115, 164, 196-197, 205, 214, 237-238, 249, 251, 309, 315-316, 319, 321,* *328, 339, 342-343, 358, 363-365, 371, 377, 379, 390-391, 395-396, 398, 406, 408-412, 416-417, 419, 421-425, 431, 442, 466, 605, 624-625, 630*
firmament *12-14, 114-115, 441-442*
firstborn *45, 136-138, 193*
flood *16, 32-33, 36-37, 40-44, 46-48, 78, 102, 118-120, 129-130, 172, 174, 211, 383, 391, 403, 447, 459, 474, 479-481, 487, 528, 538, 544-545, 555, 587, 620, 649*
  flood of Noah *16, 32-33, 36, 42, 46, 78, 118-120, 129-130, 172, 174, 211, 383, 391, 459, 474, 479-481, 487, 538, 544-545, 555, 620, 649*
foreskin *132, 579*
Formless *1, 7, 21, 73, 373, 421, 427, 437, 524, 545, 552-558, 567, 584, 590, 593-594, 598, 604, 606, 655-656, 668*
fornication *61, 70-71, 206, 254, 266, 370-371, 395, 408, 414, 418-420*
fornications *243*
four-elemental-material *445*
four-element-material *116*
France *466*
Francis of Assisi *70, 370*
French *310*
Friday *232, 539-540*
Fridays *540*

G

Gabriel *146, 152, 200, 296-297, 311, 472, 520, 655, 671*
Gandhi *414, 531*
gaseous *13, 114, 442*
genealogy *140, 620, 622, 625, 671*
Generator *93, 294, 636, 656*
Gentiles *44, 200, 212, 223-224, 230, 257-258, 397-398, 465, 655, 659*
Germany *632*
giants *33, 118, 447*
gift-giving *588*
gland *34, 352, 447, 629-630, 675*
glands *522, 580, 597, 600, 638*
God *v, vi, vii, viii, ix, i, iv, 1-2, 5-8, 10-43, 46-49, 51-56, 58, 60-66, 68-95, 98-104, 107-126, 128-139, 141-156, 158-165, 168-175, 177-180, 182-187, 191-203, 205, 207-214, 217-220, 225-235, 237-248, 250-255, 258-270, 275-289, 293-343, 346, 348, 350, 352, 355-358, 362-366, 368-377, 379-405, 407-421, 423-428, 431-452, 456, 458-459, 461-463, 465-471, 473-474, 479-480, 483-485, 487-489, 493-499, 502-504, 508-511, 517-521, 523-525, 527-534, 536, 538-539, 541-545, 549-552, 554-558, 560-569, 574, 578, 580-595, 597-598, 602-610, 612-629, 631-642, 645-657, 659-672, 674-678, 680*
  against God *326, 405, 674*
  And God *vii, 12-17, 19, 24, 30-31, 34-35, 38-42, 52-53, 93, 101-102, 107, 111, 113-116, 118-119, 131-133, 136, 171, 184, 195-196, 217, 275, 301, 309, 312, 329, 340, 389, 410, 413, 418, 424, 436, 440-444, 447, 517, 524, 543, 545, 560, 564, 605-606, 616-617, 619, 623, 625, 661, 670, 672*
  be God *184, 555, 558*

INDEX   G

by God *23, 31, 33, 42, 47-48, 54, 56, 86-87, 102, 142, 145-146, 151-152, 168, 185, 194, 209, 265, 285, 301, 304, 311, 326, 329, 334, 379, 396, 408-409, 411, 424, 427, 434, 458-459, 518, 520, 550, 566, 595, 606, 616-617, 619, 633-634, 649, 652, 659*

by God's *330*

children of God *58, 75, 99, 144, 203, 261, 376, 388, 408*

connect to God *616-619*

covenant with God *387, 604-605, 607*

Divinity (God) *648*

Does God Talk to Everyone Directly *633*

Essence of God *654*

First Begotten Son of God *11, 102, 113, 171, 191, 197, 277, 282, 284, 381, 383, 402, 440, 545, 622, 625, 645*

from God *v, 6, 12, 19, 28-29, 41, 62, 72, 75, 87, 109, 117, 164, 170, 185, 208, 214, 217, 239, 245, 267, 276, 282, 285, 289, 309, 320-321, 324, 338, 356, 376-377, 387, 392, 399, 403, 415, 423-425, 446, 458, 508, 541, 545, 564, 567, 590-591, 606-607, 617, 620-621, 625, 633, 640, 652, 657, 664, 666-668, 676*

(God) *vi, vii, 5, 21, 83, 93, 101, 108, 110, 112, 154-155, 169-170, 183, 196, 199, 202, 225, 251, 264, 266-267, 276, 307-308, 341, 346, 348, 350, 352, 356-358, 380, 396, 407, 421, 424, 433-434, 439-440, 467, 474, 494, 517, 523, 541, 543, 552, 556-557, 563, 595, 607-609, 612-613, 616, 620, 624, 627-628, 632-633, 637-640, 646, 648, 651, 668*

God and Abraham *132*

God and all *433*

God and as *208, 489*

God and be *300, 316, 322, 335, 541*

God and become *509, 527*

God and can *83, 330*

God and Christ *383, 606, 626*

God and earth *603*

God and for *74, 374*

God and He *518, 621*

God and higher *597*

God and His *112, 139, 159, 161, 196, 212, 254, 289, 307-308, 314, 318, 321, 325-326, 332, 338, 342, 364, 381, 387, 389, 392, 426, 471, 511, 525, 536, 583, 586, 606, 621*

God and how *20, 168*

God and human *521*

God and in *603*

God and is *27, 55, 62, 185, 302, 564, 590, 606-607*

God and Maitreya *598*

God and mammon *211, 255, 342*

God and man *479, 620*

God and men *266*

God and none *186*

God and of *423, 426, 624*

God and others *301*

God and our *267, 450*

God and Paul *606*

God and spirit *495*

God and state *499*

God and the *48, 64, 124, 150, 161, 175, 179, 252, 267, 286, 329, 335, 357, 403, 524, 550, 556, 606, 635, 655, 659*

God and their *55, 555*

God and they *261*

God and to *90, 408, 678*

God and truth *183, 671*

God and will *88, 323*

God and yours *92, 297*

God-based *615*

God Bless *561*

God blesses *14, 16-17, 40, 116, 134, 310, 444, 620*

God calls *7, 12-13, 24, 102, 113-115, 441-442*

God-centered *257*

God changes *131-132, 175, 605, 645*

God comes *33-34, 81, 118, 201, 293, 416, 447, 544, 613*

God commands *18, 36, 52, 242, 605, 627*

God-conscious *30, 402, 417, 555*

God could *13, 15, 17, 118*

God creates *7, 14-17, 20, 30, 86, 101, 109, 116, 170, 172, 253, 312, 318, 328, 331, 335, 341, 364, 434, 444, 448, 530, 544, 557, 595, 617*

God demands *36, 134, 394, 539, 586*

God does *10, 19, 27, 33, 37, 42, 47, 68, 70-71, 76, 100, 103, 119, 133, 210, 282, 284, 305-307, 312, 331, 335, 368, 370-371, 377, 426, 444, 448, 470, 567, 604, 621, 625, 627, 633, 667*

God fulfills *169, 620*

God gives *62, 135, 143, 162, 318, 343*

God giveth *207, 284, 426*

God has a *27, 46, 64, 84, 164, 323, 616, 622*

God has already *209, 312, 395*

699

INDEX   G

God has been *iv, 182, 421, 487, 544, 620-621*
God has both *437*
God has chosen *159, 666*
God has commanded *37*
God has complete *41, 87, 305, 338, 649, 656*
God has control *93*
God has created *46, 130, 184, 296, 304, 328, 396, 480, 616, 620, 627*
God has declared *144, 544*
God has designed *238, 317*
God has destroyed *91, 320*
God has directed *i, 2*
God has emphasized *670*
God has established *116*
God has favored *155, 496*
God has fulfilled *172*
God has given *55, 134, 149, 228, 307, 323, 541*
God has in *200*
God has knowledge *322*
God has left *618*
God has made *21*
God has more *428*
God has no *242*
God has not *17, 93, 338, 459, 497*
God has planned *54*
God has promised *132, 135, 191, 262, 633*
God has provided *212, 607*
God has reached *282, 381, 387, 402*
God has revealed *64, 264, 326, 594, 641*
God has sent *55, 88, 118, 324, 651*
God has shown *156, 302*
God has taken *20, 117, 305, 332, 446*
God has the *27, 329, 381, 517*
God has to *18*
God in a Greater degree *639*
god-incarnated *85*
God incarnates *84, 307*
God indeed has *605, 619*
God is a *v, 15, 287, 628*
God is able *51, 196, 320, 330, 372*
God is against *68, 368*
God is all *46, 112, 266, 389*
God is cautious *26*
God is complete *169*
God is concerned *36*

God is everlasting *5, 107, 183, 431*
God is everything *123-124, 186, 266, 307, 424, 518, 594, 604, 648, 656, 675-676*
God is glorified *195*
God is guiding *295*
God is in *250, 268, 287, 305, 308, 440, 617*
God is just *159*
God is male *22, 552*
God is no *149*
God is not *51, 150, 178, 265, 302, 617, 652*
God is observing *47*
God is one *85, 124, 178, 672, 676*
God is planning *13, 16*
God is pleased *13-14, 41, 113*
God is pure *7, 545*
God is the *7, 63, 85, 93, 118, 146, 196, 208, 219, 298, 301, 307, 311, 379, 431, 438, 484, 494-495, 497, 561, 634, 639*
God is to *17, 180, 531, 545*
God is trying *27, 129, 149*
God is very *12-13, 40, 83, 102, 134, 301, 382, 597*
God is watchful *300*
God is with *8, 194, 342, 424, 672*
God is withdrawn *310*
God knows *24, 133, 270, 341, 418, 441, 620*
God-like *652*
god (lowercase "g") *63-64, 100, 232, 348, 357, 440, 521, 543-545, 552, 604, 608-609, 614-615, 627, 637, 647, 656, 665, 675*
God makes *12, 14, 16-17, 26, 30, 33, 38, 41, 76, 114, 117, 137, 159, 275, 329, 377, 441, 446-447, 620*
God of Abraham *19, 135, 265, 305, 583, 594*
God of Isaac *135, 265*
God of Jacob *138, 265*
God or *84, 239, 275, 307, 424, 450, 518, 631, 635, 637, 677*
God prophesies *606, 633*
God-realization *84, 103, 488, 495, 528, 566, 589, 649, 659, 665, 670*
God-realized *238*
God rejects *617*
God reveals *138, 148, 246, 268, 305, 451, 458, 620, 634*

INDEX   G

God says *12-17, 19, 21, 23-26, 35, 41-42, 52-53, 101, 111, 114-115, 118, 132-133, 136, 139, 171, 389, 436, 441-443, 447, 587, 613, 616, 622, 637*

God's Commandments *198, 267, 666*

God sends *26, 33, 83, 104, 163, 270, 283, 301, 307, 382, 411-412, 427*

God shall *43, 145, 148, 162, 177, 261-262, 389, 417, 424, 428*

God should *84-85, 125, 144, 163, 179, 209, 237, 308, 323, 362-363, 381, 397, 462, 580, 594*

God's Kingdom *viii, 155, 262, 364, 619*

God's Messengers *582, 584*

God's Plan *130, 144, 162, 165, 253, 287, 532, 620-621, 629*

God's Prophet *412*

God's Revelation *607*

God's Revelations *334, 502, 623*

God's way *98, 150, 270, 332, 339, 536, 542, 619*

God's Ways *18, 341, 495, 619, 634, 645*

God's Will *55, 137, 139, 153, 284, 503, 598, 606, 614, 618-619, 623, 634, 640, 662, 672*

God's Words *568, 634, 680*

God takes *18, 31, 87, 120, 130, 162, 174, 313, 336, 341, 447, 545*

God talks *52, 131, 633, 635*

God warns *339*

God will *28, 34, 56, 64, 66, 72, 81, 91, 95, 100, 104, 117, 148, 152, 185, 211, 248, 303-304, 309, 318, 323, 338, 340, 363, 366, 377, 389-390, 392, 397, 401, 413, 446, 451, 462, 466, 471, 484, 494, 521, 542-544, 551, 558, 567, 581, 583, 616, 619-620, 623, 633, 639, 645, 647, 680*

God would *12, 14, 17, 38, 51, 134, 136, 174, 262-263, 330, 483, 567, 621*

good (God) *202, 358, 595, 627, 632-633, 638-640, 648*

go to God *213, 403, 642*

Grace of God *ix, 11, 124, 310, 318, 439, 451, 616-617*

hand of God *83, 85, 301, 316, 640*

has God *340, 494*

I am God *53, 119, 136, 597*

if God *84, 164, 198, 211-212, 219, 284, 295, 297, 307, 330, 459, 566-567, 583, 653*

image of God *15-16, 20-21, 30, 41, 253-254, 333, 340, 445, 563, 640, 647, 652*

instrument for God *631*

is God *5-6, 11, 62, 83, 101, 108, 154, 169-170, 183, 186, 208, 234, 266, 276, 305-307, 312, 321,* *324, 330, 334, 341, 348, 380, 397, 432, 439, 470, 518, 549, 557, 561, 566, 592, 621, 633, 640, 666, 672, 675*

know God *8, 92-93, 125, 151, 219, 316-317, 333, 335, 338, 355, 426, 534, 538, 549, 551, 640, 649, 670-672*

message from God *668*

messages from God *666*

Messenger from God *164, 289*

Messenger of God *87, 313, 399*

Messengers from God *567*

Messengers of God *162*

my God *75, 100, 375-376*

mystery of God *81, 125, 144, 163, 179-180, 237, 362-363, 381, 389-390, 397, 462, 606, 672*

name of God *293-294, 412, 594, 645*

one God *48, 82, 84-85, 297, 566-567, 598, 676*

on God *14, 83, 131, 246, 253, 511, 527, 550, 555, 586, 613, 620-621*

or God *7, 15, 275, 298, 334, 386, 435, 518, 524, 557, 604, 628, 655, 667, 674*

Plan of God *i, 47, 64, 72, 84, 95, 145, 178, 214, 289, 298, 302-303, 310, 362-364, 373, 382-383, 390, 413, 469, 531, 536, 543, 621, 647*

Praise God *380*

prophet of God *634*

Prophets of God *237*

reject God *55, 138-139, 160-161, 467-468, 496, 558, 621*

Revelation from God *606-607*

Revelation of God *542, 604*

Revelations from God *620*

Revelations of God *647*

should God *270*

son of God *11, 30, 32-33, 35, 41, 64-65, 71, 75, 99-100, 102, 113, 115, 117, 125-126, 171, 180, 186, 191-192, 197-198, 218-219, 226, 228, 234, 241, 266, 277-279, 282-284, 286, 296-297, 308, 348, 357, 364, 371, 376, 381, 383, 402, 424, 440, 444, 446, 543-545, 591, 606, 622, 625, 645, 647, 656, 674*

sons of God *29, 31-34, 118-119, 180, 186, 238, 258, 264, 267, 277, 285, 364, 382, 388, 424, 442, 447, 452, 488, 543-545, 640, 647, 662*

Spirit of God *8, 94, 99, 101, 111, 171, 197, 230, 275, 311, 340, 435-436, 450, 616, 621, 623-625, 655*

stand before God *390, 423, 625*

submission to God *25, 438*

INDEX G

submit to God *123, 335-336*

temple of God *75, 77, 259, 376, 397, 400, 411, 675*

understand God *175, 329, 583, 586*

Voice of God *33, 626*

Will God *622*

Will of God *71-72, 85, 90, 95, 145, 153, 174, 178, 252, 312, 315, 335, 371-372, 450, 504, 519, 567, 583, 614, 635, 637, 666, 672*

with God *ix, 5-6, 24, 28, 31, 33-35, 40, 52, 54, 69-70, 77, 88, 91, 101, 108, 111, 121, 150, 164, 169-170, 196, 201, 219, 254-255, 276, 288, 300, 305, 322, 327, 369-371, 380, 387, 389, 391, 408, 432-433, 445-446, 471, 483, 494, 499, 524, 529, 545, 554-555, 562, 598, 604-605, 607, 614, 619, 626, 635, 637, 640, 647, 650, 653, 659, 669, 672, 674, 680*

worth of God *648*

goddess *22, 444, 553, 661*

Godhead *380, 613, 640*

godhood *26, 544-545*

Godly *253, 481, 486, 503, 550, 555, 615, 617, 619-620*

    Godly-character *501*

god-man *191, 193, 219, 298, 313, 352, 365, 647, 656*

god-men *32, 85, 91, 100, 104, 298*

Godness *615*

gods *22-23, 26, 31-32, 55, 160, 184, 199-200, 287, 305-306, 356, 544-545, 553, 558, 567, 569, 583-584, 594, 614, 665*

Gog *423*

gold *18, 76, 82-83, 146, 152, 194, 200, 223, 268, 296, 298, 300, 311, 319-320, 332, 337, 354, 377, 379, 394-395, 414, 419, 425, 458-461, 463-464, 474, 480, 649*

golden *ii, 65, 67, 365-367, 382, 390, 394, 409-410, 414, 425, 516, 577, 616, 640, 647*

Gomorrah/Gomorrha *45, 223, 523*

    Gomorrah-based *615*

graven *150, 583*

gravity *647*

Greatest Sign *vii, viii, ix, ii, 63-67, 69, 71-72, 74, 78-81, 96, 99-100, 103-104, 106, 119-120, 123, 125, 149, 163, 169, 178, 195, 199, 209, 247, 271, 293-295, 323, 334, 343, 356, 361-362, 366-369, 371-372, 375, 381, 383-387, 391-392, 408-409, 427, 440, 483-484, 493-495, 526, 530, 535-537, 539, 542-543, 553, 561, 563, 565-566, 568, 581-584, 586, 590, 593-594, 598, 611, 622, 629, 633-634, 648, 650, 653-654, 656-659, 661-662, 673-674*

    about The Greatest Sign *vii*

    and The Greatest Sign *viii, 106, 163, 169, 561, 582-583, 629, 634*

    around The Greatest Sign *vii, 561*

    as The Greatest Sign *323, 440, 673*

    behind The Greatest Sign *125, 334, 526, 553, 565, 583*

    complete The Greatest Sign *149*

    Greatest Sign and *vii, 66-67, 123, 295, 343, 361, 367, 383, 493-494, 530, 561, 586, 593, 611*

    Greatest Sign has *viii*

    Greatest Sign is *74, 120, 356, 375, 565, 593, 629*

    Greatest Sign should *103*

    Greatest Sign will *72, 366, 372, 537, 593*

    has the Greatest Sign *334*

    His Greatest Sign *427*

    in The Greatest Sign *64-67, 69, 71-72, 74, 78-81, 96, 99-100, 103-104, 120, 178, 195, 199, 209, 293-294, 356, 361-362, 366-369, 371-372, 375, 381, 383-387, 391-392, 409, 483-484, 493-495, 539, 543, 563, 565-566, 568, 583, 622, 633, 648, 650, 654, 657-659, 661, 673-674*

    is the Greatest Sign *ii*

    know The Greatest Sign *74, 375*

    of The Greatest Sign *viii, 123, 294, 323, 343, 356, 408, 494, 530, 535, 542, 566, 581, 593, 598, 633, 654, 661-662*

    on The Greatest Sign *ii*

    or The Greatest Sign *563*

    our Greatest Sign *247, 611*

    (The Greatest Sign) *673*

    through The Greatest Sign *271, 593, 653*

    Together The Greatest Sign *ix*

    to The Greatest Sign *63, 593-594, 656*

    underlie The Greatest Sign *66, 119*

    understand The Greatest Sign *64, 295, 361, 383, 586, 593*

    Your Greatest Sign *590, 593*

Greco-Macedonian *463-464*

Greece/Grecia *152, 470, 472, 617*

Greek/Grecian *152, 394, 463, 465-466, 470, 472-474, 480, 526, 660*

Greeks *470*

guiltless *229*

Guinevere *631-632*

INDEX

guna *5-9, 12-13, 21-22, 26, 66, 69, 78-79, 98, 101, 107-111, 113-116, 174, 180, 197-200, 209-210, 217, 225, 230-231, 236, 238, 270, 276, 297, 299-300, 302, 304, 306, 309, 311-314, 318, 327, 347-352, 355, 357, 362, 364-366, 370, 379, 382, 384, 389, 393-394, 401-403, 410, 415, 422, 431-441, 443-445, 448, 472, 519-520, 545, 552-553, 562-563, 590-591, 611, 636, 645, 647, 649-653, 655, 657-658, 662-663, 665-669, 671-672, 674-676*

    guna means *519*

    raja guna *(see "raja")*

    satva guna *(see "satva")*

    second guna *433*

    tama guna *(see "tama")*

    this guna *415*

gunas *5-9, 15, 18, 21, 101, 107-111, 116, 150, 169, 172, 183, 210, 275-276, 280, 295, 305, 307, 341, 347-352, 357, 379-380, 396, 431-437, 439-440, 443-445, 519-520, 525, 545, 552, 557, 562, 592, 646-647, 649-651, 653-657, 662-665, 669, 671, 674-676*

Guru *90, 302, 315, 530, 628, 656, 674*

Gurus *302, 334, 427, 488, 502, 507-508, 524, 532, 555, 584, 651*

H

Hagar *51, 131, 133, 175, 177, 659*

half-bath *210, 579-580, 599*

Ham *32, 35, 37, 42-46, 174, 459, 474, 479-480, 649, 657, 662, 666, 673*

Haree Om Shrii Hung *110, 172, 184, 434-435, 494, 562, 566, 591, 599, 604, 657, 663, 667*

heathen *209, 252*

heaven *iv, 7, 13-14, 36-38, 42, 45, 47, 53-65, 68-69, 74-77, 79-81, 84-85, 87, 90-91, 93, 96-97, 99-104, 109, 114-115, 120-121, 124, 126, 129, 133-135, 138-139, 141, 143, 145, 150-152, 154-155, 160, 162, 166, 170, 174-175, 177, 179, 195-198, 201-205, 207-211, 213-214, 216-217, 223, 225, 227-228, 234-240, 245-247, 250-252, 254-256, 258, 260-261, 263-265, 267-268, 271, 278-279, 283-287, 289, 293-295, 303-305, 308, 310, 313, 315-318, 320, 324, 328, 332-338, 340-341, 343, 356-358, 361, 364-365, 368-369, 374-378, 380-381, 383-386, 389, 391-392, 394-402, 405-413, 416, 418, 420-427, 434-435, 442-443, 449-450, 452, 458-459, 461-462, 465, 467, 469-470, 474-475, 477-479, 483-484, 487-488, 492-496, 498, 506-509, 521, 523, 531, 533, 535, 543-544, 551, 553, 556, 559, 561, 563, 567, 569, 582-584, 586, 589-590, 595-596, 603, 607-608, 611, 613, 618, 622-623, 625, 632, 634, 646, 648, 650, 652-653, 655, 657, 662, 664-666, 668, 672, 674*

    and heaven *65, 365, 397*

    as heaven *65, 365*

    by heaven *61, 207, 268*

    called heaven *115, 170*

    doors of heaven *69, 369*

    enter heaven *76, 225, 305, 310, 340, 358, 376, 567*

    from heaven *38, 58, 197-198, 203, 245, 260-261, 278, 283-284, 320, 389, 391-392, 394-397, 399, 402, 406-407, 409, 418, 422, 462, 563, 634*

(heaven) *13, 265, 304, 335, 401, 411, 420, 435, 443, 611*

[heaven] *308, 310*

heaven and *7, 60, 76, 101, 109, 135, 170, 205, 228, 308, 328, 338, 340, 376, 418, 420, 424, 434, 493*

heaven (eternity) *402*

heaven (God) *251, 264, 267, 494*

heaven is *37-38, 57, 63, 79, 99, 195, 201-202, 208, 223, 227, 236-239, 256, 263, 284, 308, 313, 358, 384, 410, 467, 494, 533, 582-583, 586*

heaven or *214, 310*

heaven (Pure Consciousness) *74, 101, 217, 268, 286, 305, 308, 310, 375, 567, 590*

heaven's *254*

in heaven *47, 59, 62-64, 77, 81, 87, 91, 101, 104, 114, 129, 138-139, 151, 154, 166, 195, 204, 207-211, 213-214, 217, 225, 234, 246-247, 250-252, 255, 258, 265, 267-268, 271, 283-285, 289, 303, 310, 313, 324, 338, 341, 361, 378, 380-381, 383, 389, 399-402, 405, 409-410, 420-421, 442, 449, 461, 467, 469, 475, 483-484, 493-494, 506, 508, 535, 543-544, 551, 582-583, 586, 590, 623, 632, 662, 664*

into heaven *74, 99, 214, 250, 268, 375-376, 543*

is heaven *74, 100, 375*

Kingdom of Heaven *(see "Kingdom of Heaven")*

Music of Heaven *589*

new heaven *424, 618*

or heaven *308, 337*

out of heaven *75-76, 100, 102, 133-134, 376, 402, 413, 423-425*

see heaven *279, 421*

than heaven *268*

INDEX   H

the heaven *7, 13-14, 38, 101, 109, 115, 134, 170, 308, 316, 328, 338, 340, 343, 386, 423, 434, 442, 459, 462, 474, 625*

to heaven *76, 99, 240, 251, 263, 283, 310, 376, 396, 399, 665*

unto heaven *47, 120, 228, 418, 648*

ways of heaven *264*

winds of heaven *467, 470, 655*

Hebrew *54, 90, 103, 135, 155, 164, 232, 294, 394, 413, 526, 605, 646, 660-661*

Hebrews *50, 54, 79, 103, 121, 130, 143, 146-149, 160, 163-165, 191, 227, 342, 375, 384, 407, 483, 495, 535, 540, 567, 606, 645, 653, 657*

hell *7-8, 60-61, 66, 80, 92, 101, 109-110, 113, 170, 205-206, 210-211, 224-225, 228, 246, 251, 268-269, 295, 302, 308-309, 317, 339-340, 350, 366, 385, 393, 401, 423-424, 434-435, 605, 611, 625, 652, 657-658, 665*

    a hell *652*

    heaven and hell *7, 109, 170*

    (hell) *7, 109, 113, 170, 210, 225, 295, 434, 611, 652*

    [hell] *302, 434*

    hell and death *66, 366, 423-424, 625*

    hell delivers *423, 625*

    hell (earth) *7, 101, 109-110, 170*

    hell fire *60, 205, 251*

    hell follows *80, 385*

    hell [ignorance] *309*

    Hell (Ignorance) *309, 317, 657*

    hell is *8, 92, 170, 211, 309, 340, 424, 625*

    hell means *657*

    in hell *224, 309*

    into hell *61, 206, 251, 657*

    is hell *393*

    of hell *60, 66, 205, 246, 268-269, 309, 317, 339, 366, 605*

    Same as hell *658*

    the hell *92, 101, 110, 309, 435*

    this hell *66, 101, 366*

    to hell *66, 92, 228, 309, 366, 401, 665*

hellish *552*

herb *13, 16-17, 25, 41, 115, 443, 587*

herbs *13, 16, 41, 237, 588*

Herod *193-195, 239-240*

Herodians *264*

Herodias *239-240*

Hierarchy *12, 15, 32, 114, 155, 175, 201, 211, 258, 310, 324, 341, 357, 387, 441-442, 490, 495-496, 500-501, 503-504, 507-508, 510, 534, 544, 549, 569, 571, 618, 624, 653, 662, 666*

Himalayas *120*

Hindu *22, 444, 553, 562-563, 596, 622, 648, 661, 677*

Hinduism *vii, 229, 562-563, 639, 655, 658, 671*

Hindus *44, 119*

Hitler *632*

holiday *232*

holidays *63, 185, 232, 257, 473, 539-541*

Holies *vi, i, 602-603*

Holiest *vi, i, iii, 1-5, 50, 56, 81, 94, 96, 101, 119, 129, 172, 174, 192, 196, 211, 253, 266, 361, 447, 459, 474, 479-480, 602-603, 649*

holocaust *270*

horseman *82, 293, 390, 405*

horsemen *77, 80, 377, 385, 395*

HOSH (see "Haree Om Shrii Hung") *110, 154, 434-435, 536, 562-563, 566, 599, 603, 611, 657*

    HOSH-ONK (see "Haree Om Shrii Hung" "Om Nam Kevalam") *599*

humble *66, 143, 148, 177, 196, 226-227, 250-251, 256, 258, 261, 267, 270, 322, 332, 340, 366, 399, 483, 597, 605, 631, 635, 650, 668*

humbled *149, 154, 184, 216, 267, 332, 340, 375, 461, 463*

humbleness *635*

humbling *259, 398*

humbly *19, 86, 316, 321, 328, 336*

humility *536, 637*

Hung (see "Haree Om Shrii Hung") *110, 172, 184, 434-435, 494, 562, 566, 591, 599, 604, 657, 663, 667*

Hung-So (see also "So-Hung") *645*

hypocrisy *260, 266, 269, 356*

hypocrite *212, 269, 303, 338*

hypocrites *208-210, 213-214, 242, 245, 264, 267-269, 300-301*

hypocritical *508*

INDEX   I

I-am-He *645*

Ibrahim (see "Abraham") *302, 658*

I-Ching *78, 96, 110, 357, 383, 434, 562, 566, 657-658*

idle *48, 62, 71, 207, 231, 256, 319-321, 371, 524, 598, 671*

idol *200, 306, 557, 584*

idolaters *425, 427*

idols *70-71, 150, 199, 370-371, 395, 557, 584, 594*

Iliyin *146, 296, 658*

illusive *108, 170, 211, 276, 320, 350, 379, 434, 436, 473, 518, 545, 647, 653, 658, 676*

image *15-16, 20-21, 30, 32, 35, 41, 115, 117, 125-126, 150-152, 178, 253-254, 264, 287, 297, 333, 340, 346, 406, 408, 410-411, 422-423, 440, 443, 445-446, 458, 460-461, 463-464, 466-467, 469, 472, 474, 481, 493, 527, 543, 557, 563, 565, 567, 583, 618, 624, 640, 642, 647, 652*

    an image *406, 458, 481*

    any image *150, 287, 567*

    graven image *150, 583*

    great image *458*

    his image (lowercase "h" and "i") *16, 30, 35, 408, 410-411, 422-423, 624*

    His Image (uppercase "H" and/or "I") *16, 30, 32, 41, 115, 125-126, 178, 253, 297, 440, 443, 543, 565, 642*

    image has *463*

    image is *150, 458, 464, 472, 557*

    image (likeness) *340*

    image of God *15-16, 20-21, 30, 41, 253-254, 333, 340, 445, 563, 640, 647, 652*

    image of the beast *406*

    image of the universe *346, 445*

    image's *458*

    large image *460*

    metal image *458, 463, 467, 472*

    our image *15, 115, 443*

    own image *16, 35, 253*

    terrible image *458*

    that image *557*

    the image *15-16, 20-21, 30, 41, 117, 151-152, 253-254, 333, 340, 346, 406, 440, 445-446, 458, 460-461, 463-464, 466, 469, 474, 493, 527, 557, 563, 618, 640, 647, 652*

images *150, 299, 406, 520, 522, 556-557, 567, 569*

Imam *673*

Imams *673*

impeached *504, 623*

impeachment *503, 623*

incarnated *21, 30, 32, 84-85, 88, 165, 191, 307, 322, 423, 555, 584, 620, 624, 626*

incarnation *31, 85, 96, 400, 613, 659*

incarnations *43, 45, 54, 415, 483, 584, 622-623*

incorruptibility *99, 668*

incorruptible *99, 324, 483, 488, 560*

incorruptibles *99*

India *74, 120, 229, 302, 374, 468, 565, 655, 658, 660*

Indian *44*

Indo-European *660*

innercise *522, 600*

intellect *v, 33-34, 40, 47, 64, 72, 102-103, 118, 120, 173-174, 229, 234, 309, 373, 389, 396-398, 401, 404, 447, 457, 459-460, 464-465, 468, 470-471, 473-474, 479, 490, 597, 641, 649, 656, 658-659, 662, 677*

    as intellect *72, 373, 457*

    beyond intellect *397, 473, 641, 659*

    blind intellect *396, 401, 404, 649*

    confused intellect *468*

    dry intellect *234, 396, 398, 597*

    good intellect *490*

    his intellect *40, 64, 490, 659*

    human intellect *465, 473*

    illuminated intellect *658-659, 677*

    (intellect) *33, 490*

    intellect and *64, 174, 396, 457, 465, 468, 473, 659, 677*

    intellect is *47, 389, 396-397, 457, 465, 473, 649, 656, 659, 677*

    intellect or *457*

    intellect should *490*

    intellect with intuition *649*

    intellect without intuition *229, 474, 649*

    intellect without spirit *v*

    intellect would *460*

    limited intellect *396*

    only intellect *118*

    or intellect *474*

INDEX

our intellect *309*
reasoning and intellect *447, 659*
science and intellect *396, 465*
superior to intellect *398*
the intellect *34, 47, 64, 173, 389, 396, 457, 460, 464-465, 468, 470, 474, 656, 662*
their intellect *47, 103, 120, 174, 459, 479*
through intellect *471*

intellects *43, 488, 677*

intellectual *v, iv, 20, 35, 42-45, 64, 70, 79, 99, 118, 130, 153, 174, 229, 257, 268, 297, 301, 312, 325, 343, 362, 364, 371, 385, 392-393, 396-397, 399, 455-457, 459-461, 464-466, 468, 470-474, 479-480, 482-483, 485-486, 488, 490, 499, 502, 526, 536, 540, 560, 597, 649, 655-656, 658-659, 662, 668, 677*

an intellectual *35, 99, 397, 464, 479, 488, 490, 536, 649, 658*
his intellectual *130*
(intellectual) *325, 668*
intellectual achievements *470*
intellectual administrative *459*
intellectual arguments *470*
intellectual beliefs *466*
intellectual boost *397*
intellectual Brahmins *468*
intellectual characteristics *490*
intellectual contribution *79, 385*
intellectual development *457, 474, 526*
intellectual discoveries *396, 457, 461, 465, 474*
intellectual discussions *470*
intellectual domination *iv, 42, 45, 64, 153, 174, 257, 362, 397, 455-457, 461, 466, 468, 472, 474, 480, 482, 540, 656, 662*
intellectual endeavors *465*
intellectual era *362, 465, 468, 480, 490*
intellectual heights *461*
intellectual ideas *485*
intellectual knowledge *70, 312, 364, 371, 396-397, 457, 461, 473, 536, 597, 662*
intellectual mentality *464*
intellectual nations *465, 656*
intellectual person *479, 658-659*
intellectual philosophies *470*
intellectual power *118*
intellectual readings *536*
intellectual spiritualists *v, 43, 229, 268, 297, 301, 343, 393, 459, 480, 485, 488, 499, 502, 560, 659*

intellectual strength *460-461*
intellectual superiority *471*
intellectual thoughts *473*
intellectual type *677*
intellectual types *459, 659*
intellectual understanding *44, 392-393, 465*
intellectual understandings *130, 399, 465, 483*
intellectual (Vipra) *99*
intellectual (Vipran) *479*
intuitive intellectual *99*
physical or intellectual *20*
superior to intellectual *79, 385*
Their intellectual *118*

intellectuals *43-44, 119, 174, 230, 257, 362, 396, 398, 459-461, 464, 468-471, 473-474, 479-483, 488, 507-508, 532, 559, 597, 604, 620, 646, 651, 655, 659, 677*

intelligence *5, 33, 47-48, 87, 107-108, 172, 209, 284, 311, 335, 347, 351, 396, 432, 437, 460, 468, 519, 525, 659*

intelligent *347, 435-436*

intuition *7, 33, 96, 229-230, 352, 396, 432, 445, 457, 465, 468, 474, 484, 488, 577, 648-649, 656, 659, 667, 669, 677-678*

intuitional *268, 396-397, 489, 655, 658-660, 662*

intuitions *464*

intuitive *70, 99, 371, 398, 432, 485, 487, 532, 646, 649, 651, 659, 668*

intuitively *24-25, 57, 59, 96-97, 117, 202, 204, 324, 446, 533, 551, 570, 660*

invisible *1, 7, 13, 21, 63, 73, 85, 115, 150, 306, 322, 373, 421, 427, 437, 442, 521, 524, 539, 545, 552, 557-558, 562, 567, 582-584, 590, 593-594, 598, 604, 606, 654-656, 659, 668*

invocation *433, 590, 668*

Iran *673*

iron *29, 72, 150, 152, 307-308, 320, 331, 336, 342, 372, 394, 401-402, 419, 421, 458, 460-461, 463-464, 466-467, 473, 480, 483, 540, 649*

Isaac *19, 52-53, 85, 103, 128, 131-138, 147-149, 160, 175-176, 191, 216, 265, 297, 305, 583, 594, 620-621, 645*

Isaiah *277, 483, 520, 545, 660*

Ishmael *51-52, 85, 103, 122, 128, 131-133, 138, 145-149, 163, 175, 177, 293, 297, 620-621, 645, 659*

Ishmaelites *147*

Islam *71, 73, 77, 80-82, 85, 88, 122-123, 147-149, 163, 177-178, 293-294, 322-323, 329, 334-335, 337,*

INDEX   J

343, 371-372, 374, 378, 385, 566-569, 579, 618, 645, 649, 653, 659-661, 665-666, 672, 674-676

    and Islam *71, 148, 178, 294, 343*

    in Islam *71, 80, 178, 293, 371, 385, 566-569, 579, 618, 645, 649, 659-660, 672*

    Islam comes *71, 85, 177, 335, 371, 566*

    Islam is *71, 73, 82, 147, 293, 323, 337, 371, 374, 568, 618, 661*

    Islam (Is Lamb) *294, 371*

    Islam means *85, 335, 372, 666*

    of Islam *71, 80, 82, 123, 148, 163, 293, 323, 335, 337, 371, 385, 566-568, 661, 665-666, 674, 676*

Islamic *95, 164, 533, 569, 621-622, 664, 672-673, 679*

Israelite *161, 279*

Israelites *54-55, 160, 285, 305, 483*

Israel (see also "Jacob") *19, 53-56, 69-70, 86, 88, 103-104, 121, 136-145, 147-148, 150, 160-162, 164, 176-177, 185, 191-194, 200-201, 216, 222-224, 243-244, 251, 256, 262, 275, 278-279, 283, 285-286, 289, 294, 305-306, 310, 314, 322-323, 332-333, 369-370, 387-388, 400, 408, 425, 467, 495-496, 594, 617, 621, 650, 653, 658-659, 670, 673*

    become Israel *136, 147*

    child of Israel *70, 370*

    Children of Israel *19, 53-56, 69-70, 86, 88, 103, 121, 137-140, 142, 144-145, 148, 150, 160-161, 164, 176, 185, 191, 201, 223, 262, 285, 289, 294, 305-306, 310, 314, 323, 332-333, 369-370, 387-388, 400, 408, 425, 467, 495-496, 594, 617, 621, 650, 653, 658*

    cities of Israel *224*

    firstborn of Israel *138*

    from Israel *54*

    God of Israel *55, 244*

    history of Israel *55*

    House of Israel *104, 139-142, 144, 147, 161, 176-177, 193, 200-201, 223, 243-244, 262, 275, 278, 285, 289, 653, 658, 670, 673*

    in Israel *160, 216, 222*

    is Israel *140*

    (Israel) *53-54, 56, 136, 160, 177, 191-192, 275, 388, 653*

    Israel blesses *136-137*

    Israel gives *137*

    Israel has *121, 289*

    Israel is *54, 140-142, 145, 160-161, 200-201, 223, 285, 650, 653, 658*

    Israel (Jacob) *53-54, 136-137, 162, 176, 653*

    Israel means *54, 88, 322, 650*

    Israel refers *139*

    Israel's *136-137, 653*

    Israel separates *53, 137*

    Israel shall *53, 136*

    Israel takes *136, 142*

    Israel would *140, 176*

    kingdom of Israel *201*

    king of Israel *55, 139, 279*

    kings of Israel *55, 137*

    land of Israel *194*

    laws of Israel *283*

    master of Israel *283*

    my people Israel *193*

    name Israel *53, 136, 147, 176*

    O Israel *200*

    part of Israel *201*

    people of Israel *164, 223, 673*

    prophesy by Israel *140, 144, 162*

    region of Israel *200*

    sheep of Israel *251*

    son of Israel *138*

    stone of Israel *138*

    to Israel *53, 136, 142-143, 145, 176, 278, 285*

    tribes of Israel *142, 145, 176, 256, 285, 388, 658*

J

Jacob (see also "Israel") *19, 53-54, 56, 85, 103, 135-138, 140, 144, 147-148, 160, 162, 176-177, 191-192, 200, 216, 223, 243, 262, 265, 270, 275, 285-286, 297, 305, 388, 594, 653, 659*

jahad/jehad/jihad *318, 334, 526, 568-569, 619, 659*

Jahd *568, 659*

Ja-Hov-Ah *306*

Jallal'u'llah *621-622, 659*

Janaloka *659*

Japheth *32, 35, 37, 42-46, 174, 459, 474, 479, 620, 659*

Jay *660*

Jay-Zeus *660*

INDEX   K

Jehovah *305-306*

Jerusalem *55, 61, 75, 86, 100, 141, 143, 162-163, 193, 195-196, 200, 202, 207, 241, 247, 257, 259, 270, 275, 277, 280-281, 287, 289-290, 310, 363, 376, 424-425, 427, 471, 666*

Jesus (see also "Christ" "Esa") *56, 653, 660, 678*

Jew *139, 164-165, 286, 661*

Jewish *104, 161-165, 191, 270, 280, 290, 342, 580*

Jews *iii, 55-56, 68, 86, 92, 104, 137, 139-141, 143-146, 148, 157-159, 161-165, 176-177, 185, 191, 193, 196, 201, 223, 226-227, 259, 275, 277, 279-282, 284-287, 297, 310, 332, 343, 368-369, 372, 375, 494, 517, 622, 653, 658, 661*

   are Jews *68, 368-369, 375*

   called Jews *140*

   for Jews *143*

   Jews' *280*

   (Jews) *iii, 86, 104, 140-141, 144, 157-159, 162, 164, 176-177, 223, 226, 310, 653, 658*

   [Jews] *144*

   Jews and Christians *92, 297*

   Jews and Hebrews *164*

   Jews are *68, 104, 139, 143, 164, 369*

   Jews become *139*

   Jews deny *86, 310*

   Jews from *139-140, 144*

   Jews have *137, 162, 185, 201, 286, 658*

   Jews return *55, 141, 143*

   Jews would *193*

   King of the Jews *143, 191, 193, 259*

   the Jews *iii, 55-56, 86, 137, 139-141, 143-146, 148, 162-165, 177, 191, 193, 196, 201, 223, 227, 259, 275, 277, 279, 281-282, 284-287, 297, 310, 372, 375, 622, 658, 661*

   those Jews *165*

jinas *562*

Jnana *565-566, 661*

John the Baptist *195, 227, 239-240, 246, 248-249, 261, 263, 276-277, 331*

Jonah/Jonas *232-233, 245, 322, 330, 678*

Jordan *195-197, 200, 202, 253, 278, 284*

Joseph *53-54, 136-138, 140, 142, 147, 176, 191-194, 279, 285, 388, 605, 653, 660*

Joshua *54, 103, 138, 265*

Judaism *148, 178, 535, 654, 661*

Juda/Judah *iii, 53-55, 86, 104, 137-148, 157-162, 164, 176-177, 191, 193, 196, 200-201, 223, 243-244, 262, 267, 285, 310, 381, 388, 598, 605-606, 621, 653, 658, 661*

   House of Judah *iii, 86, 104, 139-141, 144, 157-162, 176-177, 191, 193, 200-201, 223, 244, 267, 310, 653, 658, 661*

Judas *223, 239, 525*

Judeo *622*

Judeo-Christian *621, 628*

judges *55, 138, 160, 175, 230, 501-502, 533, 559-560, 615-617*

judicial *496, 503, 510*

judiciary *497, 501, 503-506, 508-511, 560, 577, 624, 666*

K

Kabalah/Kabbala/Kabbalah *(see "Cabala/Cabbala")*

Kali *22, 444, 553, 661*

karma (see also "samskara" "sin") *19, 24, 28-29, 55, 59, 89, 92, 103-104, 129, 159, 164-165, 177, 205, 217-219, 250-251, 306, 310, 314-316, 333, 338, 356, 362, 387, 398, 405, 408-409, 526, 560, 565-567, 577, 612, 616, 619, 654, 661, 669-670, 676*

   any karma *612*

   bad karma *24, 103, 129, 164, 250-251, 398*

   collective karma *159, 310, 333, 619*

   create karma *19, 362, 567, 619*

   further karma *356*

   (karma) *314, 565-566*

   "karma" *306, 526*

Karma (action) *177, 314, 661*

karma exists *612*

karma has *661*

karma is *24, 89, 164-165, 314, 560*

karma means *314, 661*

karma (samskara) *92, 333*

karma (samskaras) *405*

karma (sin) *251, 616*

Karma Yoga *565-566, 661*

Law of Karma *29, 55, 89, 104, 129, 159, 164-165, 177, 218-219, 315-316, 338, 405, 409, 560, 577, 661, 669, 676*

Laws of Karma *103, 159, 165*

INDEX K

more karma *387*

no karma *405, 612*

of Karma *28-29, 55, 59, 89, 103-104, 129, 159, 164-165, 177, 205, 218-219, 315-316, 338, 405, 409, 560, 577, 661, 669, 676*

the karma *217*

karmas (see also "samskaras" "sins") *159, 218, 314, 318, 342, 387, 389, 612, 674*

karmic *29, 217*

karmically *21*

Kevalam (see "Om Nam Kevalam") *424, 562-563, 581, 604, 657, 667*

Khadija *539*

Khaleghin (see "Tabaokolaho Ahasanol Khaleghin") *675*

Khatam *322, 568, 661*

Khatem *148, 322, 568, 661*

king *54-55, 61, 64, 78, 103, 138-143, 151-152, 154, 160-161, 176-177, 191, 193-194, 200-201, 207, 226, 239, 250, 252, 254, 259, 263-264, 277, 279, 287, 384, 388, 394, 410, 416, 421, 456, 458-465, 467-470, 472-474, 480-481, 484, 487, 493-497, 506, 508, 520, 544, 573, 582-583, 585, 605, 616-618, 620-624, 629, 631-632, 654, 658, 662, 666*

> a king *161, 193, 394, 458, 460, 465, 470, 473, 573, 616, 621*
>
> fifth king *464*
>
> first king *152, 463, 465, 472*
>
> great king *55, 61, 191, 207, 459, 463, 470, 472-473, 480, 573*
>
> human king *55, 138, 160-161, 472, 621*
>
> King Arthur (see "Arthur") *629, 631-632*
>
> King David (see "David") *55, 139, 191, 621-622, 624, 631*
>
> King Nebuchadnezzar (see "Nebuchadnezzar") *64, 151-152, 456, 458, 460, 463-464, 469, 480-481, 493, 618*
>
> king of kings *416, 421, 458, 460, 474, 494, 506*
>
> King of the Jews (see also "Christ" "Esa" "Jesus") *143, 191, 193, 259*
>
> king's *226, 250, 254, 473, 493, 622*
>
> King Solomon (see "Solomon") *658*
>
> only King *160-161, 473, 495, 506, 582, 585*
>
> second king *463*
>
> seventh king *416*
>
> their king *55, 138-139, 160-161, 200, 259, 287, 467, 496, 544, 617, 621*
>
> the king *54, 78, 139-141, 151-152, 191, 193-194, 201, 239, 259, 263-264, 277, 279, 384, 394, 416,* *458-461, 464, 470, 472, 474, 494-495, 506, 508, 520, 544, 573, 605, 616-618, 620-624, 631, 662*
>
> true King *154, 161, 484, 487, 494, 497, 544, 662*

Kingdom *viii, i, ii, iv, 37, 42, 44-45, 47, 54-58, 60, 63-65, 68-69, 74-77, 79-80, 84-85, 87-88, 90-91, 93, 96-97, 99-100, 103-104, 114, 121, 124, 126, 129, 139, 141-143, 145, 147-148, 151-152, 154-155, 159-160, 162, 166, 174-177, 179, 193, 195-196, 199-203, 205, 209-212, 214, 216, 222-223, 227, 230-231, 233, 235-238, 246, 248, 250, 252, 254-258, 261-264, 267-268, 270-271, 275, 282, 285-287, 293-295, 303, 310, 313, 315, 317-318, 332-338, 356-357, 362-365, 368, 374-378, 380, 382-385, 389-390, 392, 399-400, 402, 407, 409, 412, 416-417, 421, 423, 425, 427, 442, 449-454, 456, 458-475, 477-480, 483-484, 487-488, 492-496, 498, 503, 507-509, 521, 523, 531, 533, 535, 539, 543-544, 550-551, 553, 559, 561-562, 567, 569, 572-574, 582, 584, 595-596, 598, 603, 606-608, 613-614, 619, 622, 625-626, 629, 632, 640, 646, 650, 652-653, 662, 666, 668, 672, 674*

> and Kingdom *606*
>
> another kingdom *460, 468*
>
> earthly kingdom *193, 493*
>
> fifth kingdom *466*
>
> first kingdom *152, 463-464, 472*
>
> fourth kingdom *152, 257, 460, 462-464, 468, 480*
>
> great kingdom *152, 461*
>
> His Kingdom *i, ii, 44, 64, 75, 88, 104, 139, 141, 151, 154, 159, 166, 193, 195, 209, 230, 238, 248, 250, 271, 303, 338, 364, 382, 412, 425, 454, 456, 459-460, 465, 467, 473, 475, 480, 493, 496, 503, 508-509, 550, 561-562, 573-574, 595, 598, 606, 626, 629, 632, 662*
>
> intellectualized kingdom *460*
>
> kingdom and *365, 460, 468-469, 509*
>
> Kingdom as *364, 416*
>
> Kingdom comes *166, 195, 209, 270-271, 416, 456*
>
> Kingdom for *467, 595*
>
> Kingdom has *i, 469, 494, 574*
>
> Kingdom is *37, 44, 55, 142, 151-152, 154, 412, 461, 463-464, 468-469, 473-474, 480, 494, 508, 544, 553*
>
> Kingdom of God *99, 129, 145, 148, 152, 162, 177, 212, 214, 230-231, 233, 248, 255, 261-262, 282, 362-363, 389-390, 399, 416, 423, 449, 451, 462, 466-467, 471, 484, 495, 551, 608, 626, 666*
>
> kingdom of Grecia *470*
>
> Kingdom of Heaven *(see "Kingdom of Heaven")*
>
> kingdom of Nebuchadnezzar *152, 474*
>
> kingdom of our God *402*

709

INDEX K

kingdom of the devil *412, 572*

kingdom of the earth *364, 399, 423*

kingdom of this world *362*

kingdom or *463, 466, 495*

kingdom shall *216, 460-461, 479, 493, 622*

Kingdom should *151*

Kingdom to *79, 209, 238, 384, 472, 606, 629*

kingdom unto *417*

Kingdom will *viii, 64, 139, 154, 209, 332, 468-469, 493, 508, 622, 625, 632, 662*

kingdom would *461, 465, 470*

last kingdom *152, 464*

or Kingdom *380*

Persian Kingdom *470*

same kingdom *460*

second kingdom *152, 463*

third kingdom *460, 463, 472*

this Kingdom *55, 461-462, 468-469, 480, 493-495, 553, 622*

Kingdom Of Heaven *iv, 42, 45, 47, 54-58, 60, 63, 65, 68-69, 74-77, 79-80, 84-85, 87, 90-91, 93, 96-97, 99-100, 103-104, 114, 121, 124, 126, 139, 143, 145, 151, 154-155, 160, 162, 174-175, 177, 179, 195-196, 201-203, 205, 209, 211, 214, 216, 223, 227, 235-238, 246, 250, 252, 254-256, 258, 263-264, 267-268, 270, 286-287, 293-295, 303, 310, 313, 315, 317-318, 332-338, 356-357, 364, 368, 374-378, 380, 383-385, 392, 399-400, 407, 409, 416, 421, 427, 442, 449-450, 452, 458-459, 461, 467, 477-479, 483, 487-488, 492-495, 498, 507-509, 521, 523, 531, 533, 535, 543-544, 553, 559, 561-562, 567, 569, 582, 584, 595-596, 603, 607-608, 613, 646, 650, 652-653, 662, 666, 668, 672, 674*

   and the Kingdom Of Heaven *124, 195, 209, 399, 461, 613*

   establish the Kingdom of Heaven *56, 58, 65, 68, 75, 79-80, 84-85, 87, 90, 93, 96-97, 100, 103, 126, 155, 162, 177, 195, 202-203, 227, 293-295, 303, 310, 315, 317-318, 332-333, 335-337, 364, 368, 375-376, 385, 392, 400, 407, 409, 488, 521, 523, 531, 543-544, 562, 582, 584, 650, 668*

   is the Kingdom of Heaven *57-58, 91, 202-203, 252, 254, 303, 494*

   Kingdom Of Heaven as *295*

   Kingdom Of Heaven cannot *332*

   Kingdom of Heaven comes *416, 427*

   Kingdom of Heaven consists *494*

   Kingdom Of Heaven In Heaven *47, 91, 114, 154, 195, 209, 214, 338, 380, 442, 494, 535, 543-544, 662*

Kingdom of Heaven is *57, 79, 195, 201-202, 223, 227, 236-238, 256, 263, 313, 384, 467, 494, 533*

Kingdom Of Heaven more *400*

Kingdom Of Heaven now *421*

Kingdom Of Heaven On Earth *iv, 42, 45, 47, 54-56, 58, 65, 68-69, 76-77, 79, 84, 91, 93, 97, 103, 121, 139, 151, 154-155, 174-175, 177, 179, 195, 202-203, 209, 227, 264, 303, 310, 317-318, 333, 336-338, 368, 375, 377-378, 383-384, 400, 407, 452, 458-459, 477-479, 483, 487-488, 492-495, 498, 507-509, 531, 533, 535, 544, 553, 559, 561-562, 567, 569, 595-596, 603, 607-608, 613, 646, 653, 662, 668, 672, 674*

Kingdom Of Heaven should *121, 250, 533*

Kingdom of Heaven so *450*

Kingdom Of Heaven to *99, 143, 356*

Kingdom Of Heaven will *264, 364, 384, 399, 409, 461*

Kingdom Of Heaven within *47, 57, 74, 79, 85, 87, 90, 96-97, 100, 104, 124, 126, 145, 160, 162, 195, 202, 209, 211, 250, 294-295, 310, 315, 318, 335, 374-375, 385, 494-495, 523, 543, 650, 652, 662*

Kingdom Of Heaven without *335, 523*

Kingdom Of Heaven would *103*

symbolize the Kingdom of Heaven *103, 114, 442, 494*

(the Kingdom of Heaven) *313, 334*

kingdoms *44, 141, 152, 176, 195, 198, 209, 211, 399, 460-461, 463-465, 467-468, 470, 473-474, 480-481, 493-494, 622-623*

kirtan *524, 596-597, 599, 662*

kirtans *599*

Knight *631*

Knights *632*

KOHIH (see "Kingdom Of Heaven In Heaven") *47, 543-544, 662*

KOHOE (see "Kingdom Of Heaven On Earth") *47, 77, 79, 82, 215, 369, 378, 384, 494, 506, 511, 544, 603, 607, 662*

KOHW (see "Kingdom Of Heaven Within") *47*

Koran (see also "Qu'ran") *iii, 69, 82-83, 86, 92-93, 95, 123, 144, 146, 148, 164, 177-178, 238, 291-294, 296, 298-299, 308, 311-313, 322, 325-326, 329-330, 332-333, 336, 343, 369, 563, 567, 658, 662, 673-674, 676, 678*

   and Koran *336*

   and the Koran *177, 312, 369, 563*

   (Koran) *332*

   [Koran] *326*

INDEX

Koran and *69, 294, 343*

Koran has *146*

Koran is *82-83, 146, 294, 330*

Koran means *82, 146, 292, 296, 299*

Koran's *329*

Koran says *146*

the Koran *iii, 69, 82-83, 86, 92-93, 95, 123, 146, 164, 177-178, 238, 291-294, 296, 298-299, 308, 311-312, 322, 325, 330, 333, 336, 343, 369, 563, 567, 658, 673-674, 676, 678*

kosha *351-352, 355-356, 646, 664, 668, 677*

koshas *347, 351-352, 356, 374, 445, 662*

kosher *627*

Krishna *22, 67, 90, 283, 539, 553, 562, 620, 632*

Ksattriya *99, 460, 480, 488, 668*

Ksattriyan *459, 474, 479-482, 486, 584, 657, 666*

Ksattriyas *43-45, 55, 102, 119, 174, 447, 459-461, 474, 479-484, 486, 488, 490, 507, 532, 620, 655, 662*

kulakundalini/kundalini *22, 68, 78, 118, 223, 352, 354-356, 368, 384, 472, 553, 561, 571, 629-632, 662, 672*

L

laborer *99, 490, 649, 668*

laborers/labourers *26, 43, 222, 256, 363, 474, 479, 484, 490, 507, 655, 673*

Lamb *78, 278, 294, 361-362, 371, 382-383, 387-389, 402, 405, 407-410, 416, 421-422, 425-426, 625*

Lamech *29, 32, 480, 564*

Lancelot *632*

language *44, 46-48, 54, 94, 103, 120, 122, 143, 148, 163, 174, 267, 294, 306, 308, 325-326, 395, 427, 447-448, 525-526, 531, 646, 651, 660*

languages *44-48, 103, 120, 173-174, 295, 306, 328, 336, 467, 525-526, 660*

Laodicea *365*

latent *22, 67, 78, 82, 96, 99, 118-119, 122, 352, 367, 383, 432, 447, 472, 553, 558, 565, 629, 631, 654-655, 662, 664, 672, 678*

latently *223*

Latin *660*

leaven *237, 245-246*

leavened *237*

legislative *496-497, 502-506, 508*

Levi *388*

Levite *605*

Levites *140-141, 277, 605-606, 658, 661*

life-energy *445*

life-force *5, 7, 17, 21, 33, 109, 116, 244, 276, 347, 351, 433, 443, 445, 552, 629, 662, 668-669*

lifetime *30, 32-33, 89-90, 92, 304, 309, 329, 349, 521, 529, 544, 610-611, 613, 648, 665, 674*

lifetimes *33, 64, 86, 90, 92, 116, 129, 175, 217-219, 222, 233, 289, 304, 309-310, 324, 328-329, 331, 444-445, 461, 467, 536, 648, 650, 653, 668*

like-minded *603, 608*

likeness *15-16, 30, 32, 35, 41, 43, 49, 113, 115, 117, 126, 253, 333, 340, 440, 443, 446, 583*

likenesses *49*

lilies *211-212*

limitless *339*

limitlessness *339, 414, 551*

Lineage *620-622*

Lineages *621*

Lion *380-381, 396, 404, 463, 598, 606, 621*

lions *394-395*

liquid *13, 18, 108, 114-116, 347, 350, 355, 357, 379, 396-397, 431, 442-443, 445, 581, 630, 649-650, 653, 657, 676, 678*

liquids *357*

Logic *vi, viii, 7, 20-22, 25, 33, 253, 275, 311, 347, 351, 355, 432, 443-444, 497, 519, 528, 552-554, 563, 590, 592, 614, 636-637, 651-652, 655-656, 663-664, 671, 674*

loka *347, 353, 518, 648, 659, 663, 671, 675*

lokas *12, 15, 65, 347, 352, 364, 379, 443, 445, 662*

London *142*

Lot *33, 50-51, 131, 607, 612, 678*

Lotus *110, 434, 562-563, 657, 663*

Lotustica *99, 110, 434, 562, 632-633, 657, 663*

Louisiana *142*

Lucifer *200, 297, 394, 403, 520, 663, 672*

luminous *13, 18, 108, 114-116, 347, 350, 355, 357, 379, 396-397, 431, 442-443, 445, 630, 649-650, 653, 676*

INDEX   M

M

magnanimity *598, 667*

Magog *44, 423*

Maha *647, 656, 673*

    Maha-Avatar (see also "Avatar") *284*

    Maha-Paravipras (see also "Paravipras") *58, 104, 203, 361*

Maharloka *663*

Mahatattva *349, 435, 645, 651, 658, 663, 665*

Mahatma *414, 531, 663*

Mahatmas *639*

Mahdi *663-664, 673*

Maitreya *ix, i, ii, iii, iv, 106, 169, 430, 456, 514, 536, 539, 548, 561-562, 576, 578, 581, 598, 602-608, 620-624, 642, 644, 656-657, 663*

Maitreyii *539*

Major *15, 604, 633-634, 647, 651, 671*

male *7, 16, 19-22, 30, 36-37, 102, 115, 117, 135, 253-254, 265, 297, 340-341, 437, 443-444, 446, 527-528, 538, 545, 552-554, 563, 579, 590, 610, 614, 645, 651, 663, 674*

males *132*

management *139, 458, 534, 666*

Manasseh/Manasses *53-54, 136-138, 140-142, 147, 176, 285, 388, 653*

mandala *562*

man-god *298, 351, 664, 668, 671*

manifestation *ix, 6-7, 15, 18, 22, 108, 170, 266, 275, 407, 431, 489, 553, 594, 604, 607, 619, 621-622, 626, 633-634, 639, 647, 654, 674*

manifestations *154, 589, 634*

Manipura *664*

man-made *51, 185, 502, 539, 617, 636, 640, 652*

manna *70-71, 77, 97, 240, 280, 288, 370-371, 588, 657*

Manomaya *664*

mantra *19, 306, 589, 599, 604, 645-646, 657, 664, 667*

mantras *294, 321, 524, 594, 596-597, 646, 664*

MAP *624*

Marga *670, 672-673*

marriage *20-21, 50, 253-254, 263, 265, 279, 287, 421, 511, 526-529, 571, 609, 631, 638, 669-670*

marriages *526*

married *20, 37, 61, 135, 147, 192, 206, 254, 264, 550, 589*

marries *206, 254, 421*

marrieth *254*

marry *61, 206, 240, 254, 264-265, 526-527, 529, 549, 555*

marrying *29, 631*

martyr *69, 369-370*

martyred *69, 73, 369, 373, 409*

martyrs *415*

Mary *64, 87, 192-194, 232, 239, 313, 539, 605*

Masjed *664*

Maslow *534, 569, 571*

masochism *551-552*

masochist *552*

masochistic *552*

mass-elected *500-501*

master *vii, 64, 113, 161, 194, 201, 210-211, 217, 219, 224, 232, 248, 250, 255, 264-265, 267, 278, 283, 288, 299, 308, 348, 351-352, 414, 436, 440, 445, 527, 543, 557, 572, 590, 593, 600, 603, 611, 628-630, 635, 664, 668, 671*

    a Master *vii, 64, 283, 557, 628*

    Good Master *255*

    Greatest Master *590, 593*

    great master *194*

    his master *224, 572, 635*

    (Master) *299*

    Master Gland *630*

    master means *211*

    master of the universe *210, 593*

    Master Plan *vii, 64, 543, 603*

    master themselves *611*

    only master *161, 629*

    Perfect Master *351, 664, 668, 671*

    person's master *211, 600*

    spiritual Master *593*

    their master *278, 308*

    the master *113, 201, 210, 224, 348, 351, 440, 445, 543, 603, 629*

    to master *248, 352, 436*

    true master *527*

    will master *611*

    your master *219, 250, 267, 414*

INDEX M

masters *65, 77, 119-120, 174, 211, 244, 255, 267, 308, 334, 342, 365-366, 417, 459, 474, 524, 530, 549, 557, 559, 628-629, 639*

materialism *299, 392-393, 457, 470*

materialistic *98, 268, 392-393, 520*

   materialistic-minded *335*

Maya *22-23, 25, 33-35, 57, 59, 61, 66, 68, 70, 74, 76, 78-81, 83, 86, 91-93, 97-98, 110, 116-117, 125, 164, 180, 197, 199, 202, 204, 206, 208-211, 213-215, 231, 233, 235-238, 240-241, 264-266, 281, 283, 285, 298-301, 304, 309, 318-320, 343, 348, 350, 356, 363-364, 366, 369-370, 374, 377, 384-390, 392-393, 397-399, 401-407, 409, 412-420, 422, 433, 444-446, 457-458, 462, 471, 485, 497, 520, 522-524, 534, 539, 558, 563, 565, 583, 585, 590-591, 614, 620, 624-625, 646, 650, 652-654, 663-665, 669, 677-678*

   about Maya *407, 669*

   as Maya *83, 300, 389, 654*

   become Maya *664*

   for Maya *650*

   from Maya *70, 209-210, 240, 370, 389, 399, 590-591*

   into Maya *110, 233, 285, 377, 387, 422*

   is Maya *214, 320, 402, 407, 457*

   (Maya) *25, 35, 76, 81, 116, 180, 208, 300, 309, 320, 348, 356, 390, 402, 404, 414, 444-445, 462, 485, 534, 563, 624, 653, 677-678*

   Maya has *401*

   Maya is *68, 320, 369, 402, 404, 412, 416-417, 458, 591*

   Maya itself *404, 417*

   Maya leaves *669*

   Maya will *66, 92, 237-238, 366, 401, 406, 409, 417, 422*

   to Maya *22, 25, 79, 81, 209, 211, 298, 320, 385-386, 398, 401, 405, 412, 524, 620*

   toward Maya *214, 350, 415, 563*

   very Maya *433, 614*

Mayaistic *414-415, 419, 422*

Mayaistical *406*

Mecca *569, 657, 666*

Medina *569*

meditate *8-9, 86, 90, 111, 125, 240, 315, 321, 436, 449, 502, 583, 586, 595-596, 625-626, 638, 670*

meditated *504, 614, 678*

meditates *vii, 356, 564, 635*

meditating *10, 22, 66, 83-84, 90, 245, 315, 321, 329, 334, 366, 436-437, 527, 553, 656*

meditation *9, 11, 24, 75, 83, 86, 90, 119, 206, 209, 259, 280, 287, 299, 314-315, 321, 325, 343, 352, 356, 376, 472, 474, 524, 531, 536-538, 540-541, 564-566, 569, 571-572, 574, 578-581, 583, 586, 596-600, 607-609, 611-612, 635, 637-639, 651, 659, 664, 667, 670*

   before meditation *579, 599*

   by meditation *299, 670*

   collective meditation *540-541, 581, 596, 599, 638-639*

   deeper meditation *609*

   deep meditation *209, 572*

   do meditation *531*

   for meditation *24, 537, 580, 597, 664*

   greater than meditation *574*

   his meditation *90, 315, 564*

   individual meditation *638-639*

   in meditation *24, 472, 597, 612, 635*

   is meditation *572*

   (meditation) *637*

   meditation alone *299*

   meditation and/or The Reminder *581*

   meditation and prayer *24, 598, 635*

   meditation and Reminder *538*

   meditation and silence *536*

   meditation and yoga *531*

   meditation (attunement) *538*

   meditation class *608*

   meditation is *574, 581, 586, 599, 611, 635, 638-639, 664*

   meditation or prayer *538*

   meditation or yoga *474*

   meditation process *611, 639*

   meditation should *581*

   meditation will *299, 639*

   of meditation *280, 343, 611*

   perform meditation *581*

   Satsang, Service, and Meditation *583, 586, 607, 667*

   their meditation *581, 611*

   through meditation *9, 75, 287, 314, 352, 356, 376, 566*

   to meditation *569*

   Transmission Meditation *638-639*

   your meditation *639*

meditations *537, 639*

INDEX

meditative *586*

meditator *538*

meek *69, 97, 148, 202-203, 228, 259, 332, 340, 369, 504*

Mehdi *663-664*

Melchizedek *605, 618*

men-gods *85, 91, 104, 298*

Merlin *631*

Messenger *56, 86-88, 146, 163-164, 226, 262, 289, 298, 313, 317, 323-324, 326-327, 331, 338, 399, 556, 592-593, 633*

Messengers *33, 48, 84-86, 88, 91, 118, 130, 139, 145, 149, 154, 162, 262, 264, 285, 298, 307-308, 310, 323, 325-327, 331, 365, 411, 567, 578, 582, 584, 620, 622, 651*

Messiah/Messias *vi, vii, ix, 33, 54, 56, 87, 104, 121, 137, 142-143, 162-164, 176-177, 185, 191, 196, 200, 223, 225, 235, 243, 245-246, 262, 275, 278-279, 284-285, 288, 293, 313, 335, 372, 604-606, 621, 628, 633-634, 636, 650, 660, 665, 673*

    all-powerful Messiah *335*

    a Messiah *143, 163, 293*

    another Messiah *164*

    Esa the Messiah *87, 162, 196, 650, 660*

    expected Messiah *143, 177, 284*

    Great Messiah *104*

    kingly Messiah *142*

    (Messiah) *vii, 162, 200, 243, 636, 673*

    [Messiah] *54, 191, 196, 200, 223, 275*

    Messiah can *628*

    Messiah cannot *235*

    Messiah comes *vi, 121, 137, 143, 162, 185, 243, 288, 293*

    Messiah has *628*

    Messiah is *56, 143, 223, 245, 650*

    Messiah (Shiloh) *56, 176, 243, 262, 605*

    Messiah should *143*

    Messiah to *33, 143, 621*

    Messiah would *164*

    Messias *279, 288, 665*

    new Messiah *162*

    next Messiah *372*

    promised Messiah *54, 162, 176, 185*

    their Messiah *621*

    the Messiah *ix, 33, 56, 87, 121, 137, 143, 162, 176, 196, 223, 225, 235, 243, 245, 262, 275, 278, 285, 288, 313, 605, 628, 633, 636, 650, 660, 665*

Messiahs *365, 605, 620, 622*

messiahship *245*

messianic *135, 230*

Metonic *538*

Michael *200, 297, 389, 402, 520, 665*

mini-Bible *64, 163, 364*

minor *447, 582*

Miriam *539*

mission (lowercase "m") *32, 51, 54, 82, 95, 103, 143-144, 162, 175, 177, 191, 197, 199-201, 247, 249, 254, 262, 266-267, 270, 284-285, 293, 343, 488, 556, 592, 603-604, 607-608, 659*

missions *196, 264, 544, 557, 647*

Mission (uppercase "M") *411, 561, 603-608, 616, 620-623, 626, 639-640, 644, 657*

    Mission Of Maitreya *561, 603-607, 644, 657*

Mithra *63-64, 232, 665*

Mithraism *232, 665*

Moaad *566-567, 665-666, 676*

Mohammed/Muhammad *62, 71-72, 77, 80-89, 91-93, 95, 104, 144, 146, 148-149, 163-164, 177-178, 207, 293-294, 296-297, 300, 303-304, 306, 312-313, 317, 319, 322-323, 326-328, 330, 371-372, 378, 385, 539-540, 557, 560, 567-569, 577, 598, 604, 615, 620-622, 633-634, 645, 649, 659-662, 666, 669, 671, 673-674*

    and Muhammad *313, 560, 615*

    is Muhammad *177*

    Mohammed *539-540*

    (Muhammad) *312, 598*

    [Muhammad] *87, 326*

    Muhammad and *93, 164*

    Muhammad and Moses *313, 560, 615*

    Muhammad could *296*

    Muhammad has *569*

    Muhammad is *71, 82, 84, 86, 88, 92, 146, 148, 163, 293, 296-297, 303, 322-323, 567-568, 666*

    Muhammad's *569, 669, 671*

    Muhammad would *164*

    O Muhammad *82, 85, 89, 297, 300, 317, 322, 327-328*

    or Muhammad *604*

    Prophet Muhammad *62, 71-72, 77, 80-86, 88-89, 91-93, 95, 104, 144, 146, 148-149, 163-164, 177-178, 207, 293-294, 296-297, 303-304, 306, 313, 322-323, 326-328, 330, 371-372, 378, 385, 560, 567-569, 577, 615, 621-622, 633-634, 645, 649, 659-662, 666, 673-674*

INDEX

tell Muhammad *569*

to Muhammad *569*

Moksha (see also "Mukti") *614*

Monday *232, 539*

month *37-39, 395, 426, 538-539, 541-543*

months *288-289, 393-394, 397-398, 405, 519, 538-539*

moon *13-14, 80, 386, 392, 400, 409, 426, 538, 563, 581, 621, 625, 665*

moons *581*

Mormon *140, 658*

Mormons *142, 606*

morning *12-14, 16, 72, 83, 102, 113-114, 232, 245, 256-257, 260, 314, 320-321, 337-338, 373, 386, 427, 441-442, 473, 540, 563, 580, 599, 638, 665, 674*

Moses *19, 54, 85, 90, 103, 138, 160, 216, 248, 253-254, 264-267, 277, 279, 283, 297, 303-305, 313, 322, 329, 332, 410, 495-496, 539, 545, 560, 577, 594, 615*

Moslem *85, 95, 335, 569, 666*

Moslems/Muslims *71-72, 81, 88, 92, 95, 146, 293, 297, 322, 371-372, 517, 566-567, 569, 580, 618, 621, 645, 659, 663, 666-667, 673, 677-678*

Mosque *664*

Mother (uppercase "M") *7, 12, 22, 48, 64, 70, 90, 199, 234, 275-276, 311, 355, 400-401, 403, 412, 443-444, 552-554, 563, 590-591, 614, 635-637, 647, 650, 652, 655-656, 658, 660, 666, 673, 678*

Mount *iv, 38, 46, 134, 179, 259, 407, 491-494, 496-497, 550, 599, 637, 653, 666*

mountain *57, 198-199, 202, 215, 240, 244, 248-249, 260, 287, 386-387, 391, 416, 425, 458, 461, 493-494, 587, 666*

mountains *38, 67, 133, 251, 287, 317, 337, 356, 367, 387, 413, 415-416, 483, 522, 563*

Muawiya *666*

mudras *579*

Mukti (see also "Moksha") *614*

Muladhara *666*

Muni *666*

Munies *639*

mutative *5-6, 101, 107-108, 170, 275, 311, 347-351, 354, 357, 431, 433, 435, 439, 443, 445, 518-520, 586, 637, 647, 651, 658, 665-666, 668-669, 675*

mysteries *vi, 122, 125, 180, 235, 237, 381*

mystery *vi, 65, 81, 117, 125, 144, 163, 175, 179-180, 235, 237, 362-364, 366, 381, 389-390, 397, 414-415, 446, 462, 606, 672*

Mystic *vi, ix*

Mystical *v, vii, viii, 32, 40, 67, 75, 77-78, 103, 119, 122, 125, 147-148, 160, 163, 173, 175, 178, 367, 376, 383-384, 387, 390, 448, 542, 562-563, 565, 596, 621, 628-629, 653-655, 666, 671*

    mystical book *542*

    mystical experience *v, 653*

    mystical experiences *v, vii*

    mystical explanations *v*

    mystical Judaism *654*

    mystical knowledge *viii, 175*

    Mystical Paths *vii, 40, 67, 75, 77-78, 103, 119, 122, 125, 147-148, 173, 178, 367, 376, 383-384, 387, 390, 448, 562-563, 565, 621, 628, 654, 666, 671*

    mystical religions *160*

    mystical teachings *628, 655*

    mystical understanding *628*

    mystical understandings *vii*

mystics *vi, 32, 384, 628, 637, 647*

N

Nabovat *566-567, 665-666, 676*

Nameless *1, 7, 21, 73, 373, 421, 427, 437, 524, 545, 552, 557-558, 567, 582-584, 590, 593-594, 598, 604, 606, 655-656*

Nam (see "Om Nam Kevalam") *30, 424, 562-563, 581, 604, 657, 667*

narrow-minded *92, 186, 297, 411, 525, 536, 675*

narrow-mindedness *250*

narrowness *iv, 11, 46, 71-72, 77, 79, 94-95, 98, 123-124, 126, 129, 144, 178, 185-186, 340, 371-372, 378, 384, 412, 438-439, 450-451, 483, 525, 530, 539, 543, 560-561, 610, 633, 640, 653, 666, 677*

    all narrowness *11, 46, 124, 126, 178, 186, 340, 412, 450, 483, 543, 560, 653*

    in narrowness *79, 384, 450, 610, 677*

    is narrowness *71, 95, 372, 412*

    narrowness of the mind *iv, 11, 46, 71-72, 77, 79, 95, 98, 123-124, 126, 129, 144, 178, 186, 340, 372, 378, 384, 412, 438, 450-451, 483, 525, 530, 539, 543, 560-561, 610, 633, 653, 666, 677*

INDEX   O

    the narrowness *72, 94-95, 98, 372, 439, 525, 633*
Native *148, 526*
natives *46, 148*
Nazi *632*
Nebuchadnezzar *64, 141, 151-152, 456, 458-460, 463-464, 467, 469, 474, 480-481, 493, 618*
nectar *70, 97, 280, 288, 371, 588, 657, 665, 678*
Nefilims *33*
negative *7, 18, 21-22, 78, 94, 109-110, 193, 230, 295, 354-355, 384, 403, 433-434, 437, 440, 443, 528, 552, 562, 600, 610-612, 632-633, 652, 658*
neutral *7, 21-22, 109, 433, 437, 440, 443, 552, 611*
Nicodemus *282-283*
Nicolaitanes *57, 68, 70, 97, 199, 202, 368, 370, 666*
Nimrod *44, 459, 474, 479-480, 657, 666*
Ninevah/Nineveh *45, 233*
nirvana *562, 637*
Nirvikalpa *432, 667*
Niyama *581-582, 585, 667*
Noah *16, 32-46, 50, 66, 78, 102-103, 118-120, 129-130, 172-174, 191, 211, 304, 313, 315, 331-332, 366, 383, 391, 447, 459, 474, 479-481, 487, 538-539, 544-545, 555, 620-621, 649, 657, 659, 662, 666-667, 672*
    after Noah *43, 45, 66, 366*
    as Noah *50, 191*
    beget Noah *32*
    flood of Noah *16, 32-33, 36, 42, 46, 78, 118-120, 129-130, 172, 174, 211, 383, 391, 459, 474, 479-481, 487, 538, 544-545, 555, 620, 649*
    for Noah *32*
    generations of Noah *34-35*
    name Noah *32, 480*
    Noah begets *32, 35*
    Noah builded *40, 119, 173*
    Noah finds *34*
    Noah has *35*
    Noah is *32, 34-37, 42-43*
    Noah's *37*
    Noah says *313, 332*
    Noah sets *173*
    Noah walks *34-35*
    son of Noah *649, 662, 666*
    sons of Noah *35, 37, 42-43, 46, 174, 459, 474, 479, 657, 659, 672*
    time of Noah *102-103, 447*
    to Noah *32*
    unto Noah *35-37, 39, 41-42, 118, 447*
non-violence *31, 35, 518, 582, 584, 598, 636, 645, 678*
non-violent *636*
northern *49, 118, 176, 200-201, 223, 275, 537*
notable *152, 463, 465, 470, 472, 667*
nothingness *20, 59, 204, 487*
NOVUS ORDO SECLORUM *496*
Nuh (see "Noah") *304, 315, 331, 667*

O

objective *264, 479, 512, 552, 611, 649, 669*
objectively *264*
objectives *611*
objectless-ness *348*
observing *31, 47, 498, 582, 584-585, 630, 676, 678*
occult *33, 102, 117, 446-447, 592, 667*
Omar *667, 673*
Omega *65, 365, 424, 427*
Om (see also "Aum" "Haree Om Shrii Hung" "Om Nam Kevalam") *65, 71, 80, 104, 110, 172, 184, 210, 366, 371, 385, 407, 424, 434-435, 494, 517, 545, 562-563, 566, 581, 591, 599, 604, 646, 657, 663, 667, 670*
oneness *94, 111, 124, 328, 393, 511, 610, 614, 635, 640, 654, 669*
one-pointed *211, 266, 300, 342, 415, 488, 565, 667*
one-pointedness *163, 241, 266, 342, 483, 667-668*
ONK (see "Om Nam Kevalam") *563, 581, 603, 667*
operative *5-6, 101, 107-110, 170, 183, 275-276, 357, 380, 431-434, 545, 562, 651, 655-657, 664, 675*
Operator *93, 294, 636, 656*
ORDO (see "NOVUS ORDO SECLORUM") *155, 496*
overactive *497, 637-638*

INDEX   P

P

pagan *63-64, 70, 185, 199, 232, 342, 370, 419, 466, 569*

paganizers *232*

Pancha *349-350, 653, 655, 668, 676*

parable *235-237, 243, 257, 261-263*

parables *215, 234-235, 237, 239, 262-263, 266*

Parama *90, 109, 668-669*

parapsychology *396, 474*

Para (see "Paravipra" "Shrii Shrii Para Maha") *539, 656, 673*

Parasutma *109*

Paravipra *43, 58, 74, 76-77, 99, 104, 124, 163, 203, 356, 375-377, 451, 488, 539, 566, 641, 653, 668, 673*

    Paravipra-society *484*

Paraviprahood *387, 389, 451*

Paravipras *58, 79, 81, 91, 96, 99-100, 104, 124, 179, 186, 203, 258, 298, 303, 313, 324, 383, 385, 388, 392, 400, 412, 423, 426, 461, 467-468, 474, 483-490, 494-495, 497, 507-508, 525, 532, 535, 560, 582, 584, 618, 633, 635, 641, 651, 653, 657, 668, 672, 676*

    are Paravipras *91*

    become Paravipras *81, 186, 467*

    called Paravipras *99, 483, 497*

    Great Paravipras *58, 104, 203, 298*

    of Paravipras *124, 324, 484, 490, 494, 560, 633*

    other Paravipras *104*

    (Paravipras) *79, 258, 385, 426, 461, 474, 486, 495, 635, 672*

    Paravipras and Elected Ones *324*

    Paravipras and Saints *412*

    Paravipras are *96, 313, 324, 412, 483-484, 494, 584*

    Paravipras can *104, 633*

    Paravipras (Elected Ones) *186, 324*

    Paravipras have *618*

    Paravipras might *490*

    Paravipras (Saints) *468*

    Paravipras should *99-100, 486*

    Paravipras who *383*

    Paravipras will *179, 423, 467, 484, 486, 490, 618*

    Paravipras would *485*

    real Paravipras *58, 203*

    true Paravipras *313, 484*

parent *27, 134, 551, 610*

parents *20-21, 27, 88, 201, 224, 234, 267, 305, 312, 314, 324-325, 331, 527-528, 542-543, 549-551, 570-571, 584, 592*

passive *7, 21, 432, 440, 552*

Passover *64, 280-281, 538, 541-542*

Paul *588, 605-606*

peacemaker *58, 203*

peacemakers *58, 75, 99, 203, 376*

Peleg *45-46, 49, 142, 153*

Pergamos *69, 199, 365, 369*

Persia *72-73, 141, 148, 152, 372, 374, 469-470, 472, 648, 665*

Persian *149, 152, 463-466, 470, 472*

Persians *149*

Peter *201, 217, 222, 241, 243, 246-248, 250, 252, 256, 279*

Pharaoh *140*

Pharaohs *138*

Pharisee *269*

Pharisees *60, 70, 143, 191, 196, 201, 205, 214, 219-220, 222, 229-230, 232, 241-242, 245-246, 253, 262, 264-269, 277-278, 282, 285, 370, 471, 569*

phase *14, 16, 30, 44, 478, 486-488, 532, 636, 640, 646*

phases *14, 102, 484, 486-487*

Philadelphia *74, 365, 374, 389*

Philosophies *40, 65, 77-78, 94, 119, 122, 148, 173, 178, 378, 384, 470, 544, 565, 628, 653-654, 666, 670*

philosophy *78-79, 94, 98, 149, 164-165, 229, 383-384, 473, 529, 532-533, 535, 654, 658, 666*

phoenix *154*

physiological *22, 43, 57, 125, 197-198, 202, 209, 246-247, 298, 354-355, 393, 449, 479, 482, 489, 495, 528, 534, 551, 553, 569-572, 577, 605*

Pilate *161*

Pilgrimage *91, 298, 300, 323, 657*

pineal *34, 447, 630, 675*

pitfall *70, 76-77, 95, 97-100, 185-186, 361, 370, 377, 635*

pitfalls *65, 67, 74-75, 77, 80, 126, 148, 186, 361, 364, 367, 374, 382, 386*

pituitary *352, 629-630*

Plato *465, 473, 480*

INDEX   P

plexus *355, 563, 648*

Pluribus (see "E Pluribus Unum") *154*

Pontius *161*

pope *618*

positive *7, 18, 21, 109-110, 260, 381, 433-434, 437, 440, 443, 512, 529, 538, 552, 562, 600, 611-612, 632, 636, 658*

Praiseworthy *420, 627, 645*

Prakrti *275, 432, 434, 651, 668, 675*

prana *7, 17, 22, 102, 109, 116, 244, 347-352, 355, 426, 432-433, 437, 443, 445, 522, 552-553, 563, 578-580, 587, 629, 648-649, 668-669*

Pranamaya *668*

Pranayama *629*

pranic *18, 347-349, 355, 400, 445, 667*

prasadam *537, 668*

predestination *573*

prerequisite *424*

prerequisites *521*

pressure *202-203, 572-573*

pressures *572-573*

principalities *590*

progressive *95, 349, 441, 478, 482, 484, 486-487, 499, 509, 512, 532*

propensities *186, 247, 267, 282, 347, 354-356, 437, 523, 673*

propensity *356, 663*

Prophecies *iii, iv, 42, 45-46, 51, 54, 56, 64, 82, 103-104, 121, 127-129, 143, 145-146, 152-153, 161-162, 164, 169, 174-177, 191, 193-195, 200-201, 223, 227, 243-244, 257, 262, 270, 275, 285, 289, 293, 316, 339, 361-362, 398-399, 414, 455-457, 459-460, 474, 480, 488, 540, 558, 567, 598, 607, 621-622, 628, 633-634, 653, 656, 658, 662, 673*

    All Prophecies *iii, 46, 51, 54, 56, 82, 104, 121, 127-129, 161-162, 164, 169, 174-176, 191, 193, 200-201, 223, 244, 262, 270, 275, 285, 289, 293, 339, 361, 598, 628, 653, 658, 673*

    any prophecies *558*

    many prophecies *103, 129, 143, 567, 622*

    on Prophecies *iv, 42, 45, 64, 153, 174, 257, 362, 455-456, 480, 540, 656, 662*

    own Prophecies *621*

    Prophecies from *607*

    the prophecies *64, 162, 169, 175, 177, 193-195, 227, 262, 285, 316, 399, 474, 607, 633-634, 656, 662*

prophecy *vii, 64, 122, 152, 162, 177, 192, 194, 200, 230, 235, 262, 364, 398, 421, 426-428, 466, 673*

prophesied *55-56, 64, 95, 130, 137, 140, 143-144, 152, 162, 164, 177, 200, 214, 223, 226-227, 230, 238, 243, 262, 270, 275, 362, 557, 606*

prophesize *389*

prophesy *242, 362, 397-398, 461, 596, 633*

prophet *59-60, 62, 66, 71-73, 77, 80-86, 88-89, 91-95, 104, 143-146, 148-149, 161-164, 173, 177-178, 193-195, 200, 204-205, 207, 214, 217, 225-227, 230, 232-233, 237, 239-240, 242, 245-246, 259-262, 277-278, 280, 287, 289, 293-294, 296-297, 301-304, 306, 311, 313, 322-323, 326-332, 340, 342-343, 361, 363, 366, 371-373, 378, 385, 390-391, 411-412, 422-423, 560, 567-569, 577, 593, 604, 606, 615, 621-622, 624, 633-634, 645, 648-649, 654, 659-662, 666, 669, 671, 673-674, 680*

    American Prophet *145*

    and Prophet *146, 149, 313, 568-569, 577, 615, 622, 633*

    another Prophet *83, 95, 148, 178*

    false prophet *214, 412, 422-423, 593, 624, 654*

    great Prophet *82-83, 162, 177, 226, 262, 293, 301*

    last Prophet *71, 77, 88, 178, 322-323, 378, 567-568, 661*

    Major Prophet *604, 633, 671*

    new Prophet *94, 233*

    next Prophet *148-149, 163, 178*

    of Prophet *72, 88, 163-164, 177, 232, 293, 322, 372, 568, 621, 661, 673-674*

    or Prophet *302, 560*

    (Prophet) *59, 204*

    Prophet and *71, 95, 173, 177, 225-226, 233, 261, 311, 411, 666, 671*

    Prophet Bab *648*

    Prophet born *296*

    Prophet but *226, 242*

    prophet comes *60, 143, 148, 163, 205, 233, 261-262, 303*

    prophet has *327*

    Prophet himself *214, 567*

    prophet is *84, 91, 94, 143, 239, 322-323, 326-327, 423, 567, 624*

    prophet Jonas *232, 245*

    Prophet might *246*

    Prophet Muhammad *62, 71-72, 77, 80-86, 88-89, 91-93, 95, 104, 144, 146, 148-149, 163-164, 177-178, 207, 293-294, 296-297, 303-304, 306, 313, 322-323, 326-328, 330, 371-372, 378, 385, 560, 567-569, 577, 615, 621-622, 633-634, 645, 649, 659-662, 666, 673-674*

INDEX

Prophet of *66, 259, 262, 303, 361, 366, 391, 634, 649*

Prophet of God *412, 634*

Prophet or *83, 239, 297, 301, 322, 363, 411, 593*

prophet's *225, 673*

Prophet should *326*

Prophet to *301, 311*

Prophet will *88, 91, 323, 329, 390*

Prophet with *661*

Prophet would *95, 163*

Sleeping Prophet *145, 649*

the Prophet *66, 173, 193-195, 200, 214, 217, 226-227, 230, 232, 237, 242, 245-246, 259, 277, 280, 289, 302, 322, 326-327, 331-332, 361, 366, 391, 411, 567, 666*

prophethood *84, 91, 160, 162-163, 289, 307, 323, 327, 661*

prophetic *163, 289, 457*

prophets *vi, 28, 33, 48, 55-56, 59-60, 63-65, 69-70, 77, 81, 84-86, 88, 91-93, 118, 125, 130, 140, 142-143, 149, 154, 159, 161-162, 164-165, 169, 179-180, 184, 195-196, 199, 204-205, 213-216, 220, 227, 229, 232, 235-237, 245-246, 248, 251, 261, 263-264, 266, 268-270, 279, 285, 289, 293, 295, 297-299, 302-303, 306-307, 310-311, 313-314, 322-323, 325-328, 331-334, 362, 364, 366, 369-370, 372, 377, 381, 389, 391, 394-395, 397-400, 404-405, 411-413, 415-416, 420, 426-427, 448, 459, 467, 488, 507-508, 532, 538, 557, 565-568, 580, 582-584, 590, 593-597, 605, 616, 620-622, 633-634, 645, 651-652, 654-655, 661, 666, 668*

All Prophets *595*

and Prophets *33, 48, 85, 154, 220, 302, 395, 411, 420, 565, 616*

false prophets *vi, 63, 70, 92, 199, 214, 237, 251, 333, 370, 394-395, 412-413, 590, 593-594, 634, 654*

great Prophets *65, 86, 236, 364, 538, 620, 622*

His Prophets *55, 64, 118, 130, 162, 169, 184, 261, 270, 327, 381, 427, 467, 582-584, 594, 652*

Major Prophets *633-634*

many Prophets *55, 140, 143, 232, 235, 289, 295, 584*

more Prophets *88, 161, 322-323*

of Prophets *326, 331, 404, 420, 566, 596*

or Prophets *28, 84, 180, 307*

other Prophets *85, 88, 91, 93, 297, 322, 661*

Prophets' *605*

(Prophets) *179, 362, 622*

Prophets and *63, 70, 86, 118, 142, 165, 214, 227, 232, 235, 237, 264, 268-269, 285, 289, 310, 326, 370, 377, 394-395, 399-400, 404-405, 411, 415, 538, 567, 580, 584, 590, 593-594, 620, 622, 634, 655, 666*

prophets are *91, 93, 143, 164, 323, 326-327, 394, 398, 427, 593, 595*

prophets come *48, 261, 399, 508, 567, 596*

Prophets from *85, 297*

prophets have *55, 159, 196, 565*

Prophets in *149, 325*

Prophets of *65, 237, 245, 331, 362, 364, 583*

Prophets or *149, 307, 334, 391, 416, 532*

prophets predict *140*

Prophets should *216, 327, 567*

Prophets to *88, 154, 270, 322, 331*

Prophets who *55, 88, 91, 215, 263, 322, 366, 389, 621*

Prophets will *91-92, 322-323, 333, 398-399, 661*

Prophets would *398*

send prophets *270, 448*

the Prophets *55-56, 59-60, 69, 77, 85-86, 91, 140, 143, 149, 159, 161-162, 164-165, 195-196, 204-205, 213-216, 227, 229, 237, 245-246, 248, 263, 266, 269-270, 279, 285, 299, 302-303, 307, 310, 323, 325-328, 331, 334, 362, 366, 369, 377, 389, 391, 397-400, 405, 411, 415-416, 420, 427, 448, 567-568, 580, 582-584, 593, 622, 651, 655, 661, 666*

two Prophets *398-399*

Your Prophets *590, 593*

publican *223, 252*

publicans *62, 207, 219-220, 227, 261*

Puranas *542*

Pure Consciousness *7-8, 11-12, 15-17, 20-21, 26, 29, 31-35, 40-42, 47-48, 54, 58-61, 63, 65-66, 68-69, 72-77, 85-87, 89-93, 96, 98-104, 109-111, 113-117, 119, 129, 151, 169-172, 179-180, 184-186, 191-193, 196-199, 203-206, 208-211, 214, 216-217, 219, 224-226, 228-229, 231, 233, 237-238, 241, 246-249, 254-258, 263, 265, 267-268, 270, 275-277, 279, 282-288, 295-301, 304-308, 310, 313, 315, 317-318, 324-328, 332, 335, 338, 340-341, 348, 350, 352, 356-358, 361, 363-366, 368-369, 373-377, 379-383, 389-391, 393, 397, 400, 402-403, 407, 409-412, 416, 419, 421, 423-427, 434-437, 440-444, 446-448, 450-452, 466-467, 483, 489, 494, 517, 520, 523, 526, 528, 530-532, 535-536, 539, 541, 543-545, 552-553, 555, 561-562, 565, 567, 570-572, 578, 582, 584-585, 590-595, 611, 613-614, 626, 632, 640, 646-648, 650, 652-657, 662-663, 665-666, 668-669, 671, 676, 678*

INDEX

all reach Pure Consciousness *100, 104, 193, 423, 650*

and/or Pure Consciousness *544, 647*

and Pure Consciousness *54, 295, 308, 350, 364, 544*

and reach Pure Consciousness *113, 299, 304, 313, 356, 426-427, 446, 451*

as Pure Consciousness *650, 657, 662*

become Pure Consciousness *33, 40, 42, 48, 59, 76, 93, 191, 196, 204, 211, 377, 440, 467, 526, 541, 578, 590, 594-595, 646*

cannot reach Pure Consciousness *185, 313*

can reach Pure Consciousness *16, 20, 41, 115, 172, 254, 444, 528*

consciousnesses reach Pure Consciousness *12, 16, 307*

consciousness reach Pure Consciousness *102, 297-298, 308*

enter Pure Consciousness *26, 100, 452, 626, 650*

eventually reach Pure Consciousness *93, 196, 248*

for reaching Pure Consciousness *66, 299, 366, 424, 657*

have reached Pure Consciousness *92, 104, 228, 277, 282, 317, 338, 361, 363, 381-382, 389, 402, 411, 424, 441, 447, 467*

he reaches Pure Consciousness *11, 31, 33, 306, 350*

in Pure Consciousness *32, 66, 69, 75, 85, 87, 89, 109, 191, 219, 226, 229, 233, 241, 247, 249, 265, 276, 279, 284-286, 298, 300, 305-308, 313, 327, 341, 352, 356, 366, 369, 380, 382, 391, 421, 423, 427, 440, 466-467, 555, 593, 614, 656-657, 668*

is Pure Consciousness *7, 308, 411, 437*

man reach Pure Consciousness *16, 96, 283, 572*

might reach Pure Consciousness *59, 204*

not reach Pure Consciousness *363, 423*

of Pure Consciousness *12, 26, 48, 66, 98-101, 110, 113, 191, 352, 366, 389-390, 397, 425, 427, 434, 440-441, 443, 535, 590-591, 648, 650, 652, 662, 666, 676*

of reaching Pure Consciousness *17, 114, 129, 307, 356, 403, 442*

P

or Pure Consciousness *29, 31, 58, 75, 86, 90, 103, 114, 172, 203, 310, 315, 326, 402, 411, 424, 544, 632, 646-647, 653, 665*

others reach Pure Consciousness *104, 543*

(Pure Consciousness) *7-8, 21, 35, 65, 74, 76, 91, 93, 101, 109-110, 114, 116, 170, 186, 192, 199, 209, 214, 217, 228, 257-258, 263, 268, 276, 285-286, 296, 304-305, 308, 310, 318, 338, 340, 358, 361, 363, 365, 375-376, 383, 425, 434, 442, 444, 448, 452, 552, 567, 584, 590, 592, 611, 648, 650, 652, 668-669*

Pure Consciousness and *31, 33, 58, 89, 100, 180, 186, 203, 276, 297, 300, 306, 308, 328, 348, 361, 363-364, 423-424, 466-467, 523, 544, 578, 582, 584, 593, 614, 657*

Pure Consciousness can *7, 391*

Pure Consciousness is *7-8, 59, 113, 117, 204, 308, 390, 403, 427, 441-442, 446, 536, 562, 613*

Pure Consciousness or *15, 115, 196, 298, 308, 440, 444, 539, 555, 567*

Pure Consciousness will *69, 92, 247, 295, 297, 301, 338, 369, 411, 424, 544, 662*

to Pure Consciousness *15, 34, 54, 75-76, 86, 89, 93, 99, 102, 111, 113, 169, 172, 210, 225, 275, 286-287, 304-305, 317, 328, 363, 376-377, 380-383, 407, 410, 416, 423, 435-436, 440-443, 448, 483, 494, 531, 544, 561, 591, 653-654, 662, 678*

to reach Pure Consciousness *16, 26, 47, 68, 72, 74-75, 93, 100, 119, 172, 179, 184-186, 255, 257, 270, 277, 295, 297, 301, 305-306, 308, 325, 328, 341, 368, 373-374, 376, 379, 381, 389, 393, 451, 523, 530-531, 543-544, 567, 582, 584, 590-591, 593, 647, 653, 657, 671*

toward Pure Consciousness *34, 117, 119, 214, 379, 434, 436, 446, 526, 532, 565, 613, 662-663*

whoever reaches Pure Consciousness *467, 545*

who reach Pure Consciousness *26, 100, 237, 267, 383, 424-425, 544, 662*

will reach Pure Consciousness *60, 69, 100, 117, 180, 186, 205, 216, 237-238, 256, 313, 369, 376, 382, 424, 446, 544, 640*

would reach Pure Consciousness *441*

you reach Pure Consciousness *63*

Purusa *90, 109, 435, 668-669*

Purusattma *669*

INDEX

Q

quiet *33, 162, 281, 389, 626, 669*
quietness *58, 203, 280, 669*
quiets *352*

Qu'ran (see also "Koran") *326, 332*
Qureysh *669*

R

Rabbi *267, 278-279, 282, 284*
race *46, 48, 54, 66, 79, 104, 129, 151, 159, 163, 165-166, 183, 186, 310, 328, 385, 395, 448, 459, 502, 525-527, 531, 659*
races *29, 35, 46, 48, 328, 447, 481, 498, 526-527*
Radah *22, 539, 553*
Rahman *90, 294, 306*
rainbow *41, 354, 378, 395-396*
raja *5-7, 21-22, 79, 101, 107-110, 115-116, 170, 197, 200, 275-276, 297, 311, 341, 347-352, 355, 357, 371, 379, 402, 431-433, 435, 437, 439-440, 443-445, 490, 519-520, 552-553, 562-563, 611, 636-637, 645, 647, 651, 653, 655, 658, 662, 665-669, 675*
    active raja *22, 553*
    pure raja *22, 371, 552*
    (raja) *170, 490, 520, 647, 658*
    raja (action) *109*
    raja becomes *109*
    raja guna *5-7, 21-22, 79, 101, 107-110, 115-116, 200, 276, 297, 311, 347, 349-352, 355, 357, 379, 402, 431-433, 435, 437, 439, 443-445, 519-520, 552-553, 562-563, 611, 636, 645, 651, 653, 655, 658, 662, 665-669*
    raja gunas *445*
    raja (mutative) *101, 275, 348, 519, 637, 675*
    raja part *349*
    raja (pranic) *349*
    satva raja *197*
rajasic *518, 586-588, 669, 671*
ram *64, 152, 342, 463, 465, 469-470, 472*
Rama *194, 563*
reaction *28, 89, 92, 129, 159, 178, 217, 251, 295, 312, 314-315, 333, 335, 349, 405, 549, 560, 563, 567, 573, 591, 594, 661, 663*
reactionary *95, 558*
reactions *87, 89-90, 94, 314-315, 333, 338-339, 349, 352, 389, 395, 563, 591, 661*
reading *192, 325, 333, 586, 599, 608, 671*

readings *iii, 82, 145-146, 291-293, 296, 536, 599, 662*
Rebekah *135*
region *65, 104, 195-196, 200-201, 364, 499-501, 504-506, 510*
regional *499-501, 505-506, 509-510*
regions *200, 499, 502, 505-506, 565, 616*
reincarnate *54, 83, 89, 93, 100, 159, 329-331*
reincarnated *33, 51, 55, 65, 84, 96, 129, 151, 164-165, 175, 248, 265, 286, 289, 303, 329-330, 388, 397, 400, 423, 592, 620, 624-625*
reincarnation *83, 89, 92-93, 99, 103, 129, 159, 165, 195, 227, 248-249, 265, 277-278, 329-331, 408, 620-624, 654, 661, 669-670*
reincarnations *51, 54, 99, 324, 331, 620, 623-624*
Reminder *326, 538, 581, 583, 586, 590, 596, 599-600*
Renaissance *464, 480, 482*
renunciate (see also "sannyasin") *21, 537, 542, 555, 589, 608, 669-670*
renunciates (see also "sannyasins") *30, 45, 223, 254, 510, 537, 543, 555, 581*
renunciation *10, 450, 598*
reporter *500-501, 505*
reporters *500-501, 503, 505*
representative *79, 326, 361, 384, 467, 500-501, 504-506, 606*
representatives *327, 501-502, 504-506, 510*
reprogram *612, 614*
reprogrammed *612, 614*
reprogramming *612, 614*
resurrect *70, 370, 670*
resurrected *89, 199, 246-247, 270*
resurrection *70, 82, 92, 104, 144, 199, 238, 264-265, 308, 317, 331, 370, 390, 423-425, 624-625, 670*
resurrections *317*
revolution *461, 468, 480, 482-483, 486*
revolutionary *482, 636, 673-674*

INDEX

revolutions *484, 486*
Rg *596, 677*
rib *20, 117, 446*
ribs *20, 117, 446, 463*
rig *677*
risen *15, 224, 227, 232, 239, 247, 249, 281, 662*
Rishies *639*
ritual *529, 542, 648*
rituals *173, 220, 269, 499, 541-542, 577-578, 648, 677*
Roman *70, 149, 152, 154, 232, 370, 464-468, 470, 473, 480, 523, 540-541, 656, 665*
Romans *64, 92-93, 149, 163, 185, 232, 238, 257, 305, 315-318, 328, 330, 342, 464, 468-469, 471, 588, 665*
Rome *63, 70, 72, 152, 193, 370, 372, 464, 468, 617*
Ruth *55, 539*

S

Sabbath *64, 228-230, 232-233, 539-542, 581, 585-586, 595-596, 670*
Sabbaths *541*
sackcloth *80, 228, 386, 398*
Sadducees *196, 201, 214, 245-246, 264-266*
sadhana *568-569, 664*
sadism *551-552*
sadist *552*
sadistic *552*
Sages *578, 596, 614*
Sahasrara *670*
Saint *ix, iii, 99, 273, 275, 410, 471*
 saint-like *555*
Saints *64, 80, 95, 152, 382-383, 385, 388, 390, 400, 405, 408-413, 415, 420-423, 457, 461, 465, 467-469, 474-475, 625, 662, 671*
Salaam *517, 670*
Sal-Om *388, 517, 578, 590, 670*
salt *59, 84, 91, 99, 204, 303, 382, 617*
salutations *209, 517, 578, 590, 670*
salute *62, 207, 223, 517, 670*
saluted *590*
saluting *517, 670*
SALUT-OM *517*
salvation *ix, iv, 8, 18-19, 33, 48, 56, 77, 89, 111, 116, 122-123, 125, 139, 149, 226, 287, 318, 327, 377, 388, 402, 420, 445, 451, 495, 533, 567, 603, 614, 618, 620-621, 626, 628, 637, 639-640, 648, 674*
 collective salvation *628*
 individual salvation *628*
 of salvation *451, 495, 618, 637*
 reach salvation *19, 89, 149, 648*
 salvation is *ix, 48, 77, 287, 377, 533, 628*
 salvation of man *620-621, 626*
 salvation to *56, 125, 388, 618*
 to salvation *iv, 18, 33, 48, 77, 111, 116, 122, 125, 139, 226, 318, 377, 445, 603, 674*
samadhi *562*
Samaria *139-140, 275, 285-286, 290*
Samarian/Samaritan *141, 275, 286, 289*
Samarians/Samaritans *141, 223, 275, 285-287, 289-290, 653, 658, 670*
Sama/Sama-Veda *677*
Samgacchadvam *596, 599*
samskara (see also "karma" "sin") *89, 92, 314, 333, 654, 661, 669-670, 673*
samskaras (see also "karmas" "sins") *29, 72, 86, 89-90, 92, 102, 218-219, 222, 299, 314-315, 333, 372, 389, 394, 405, 591, 661, 669-670*
sannyasin (see also "renunciate") *21, 537, 589, 608, 669-670*
sannyasins (see also "renunciates") *30, 223, 254, 537, 555, 581*
Sanskrit *44, 50, 116, 194, 223, 298, 444, 519, 526, 568, 596, 645-646, 648, 659-660, 663-664, 666, 670-671, 675, 677*
Sarah (see also "Sarai") *44, 52, 132-133, 175, 265, 539*
Sarai (see also "Sarah") *50, 52, 132-133, 539*
Sardis *73, 95, 365, 373-374*
Sarkar (see also "Anandamurti" "Baba") *622, 670*
Satan *68-69, 72, 199, 222, 230, 247, 300, 368-370, 372, 375, 402-403, 416, 422-423, 520, 624*
satayaloka *347-348, 671*
Satguru *217, 298, 351, 664, 668, 671*
Satgurus *91, 104, 298, 532, 582, 584, 593*
Satsang *84, 325, 333, 524, 537, 539-540, 574, 583, 586, 607, 667, 671*
Satsangs *334, 537, 599, 607*
Sat (uppercase "S") *379, 439, 646, 670-671*

INDEX
S

Sat, Chit, Ananda *439, 646, 670*

Saturday *64, 232-233, 539-540, 586*

Saturdays *540, 595, 609, 638*

satva *5-7, 21-22, 78, 101, 107-110, 115, 170, 197, 200, 230-231, 275-276, 297, 311, 341, 347-351, 354, 357, 379, 431-433, 435-437, 439-440, 443-444, 472, 490, 519-520, 552-553, 563, 588, 591, 611, 637, 647, 655, 658, 665, 668, 671-672, 675*

    active satva *22, 553*

    (satva) *22, 110, 170, 431, 490, 552, 588, 647, 658*

    satva dominates *109*

    satva guna *5-7, 21-22, 78, 101, 107-109, 115, 200, 230-231, 276, 297, 311, 347, 349-351, 357, 379, 431-433, 435-437, 439, 443-444, 472, 519-520, 552-553, 563, 591, 611, 655, 665, 668, 671-672*

    satva (positive) *433*

    satva raja *197*

    satva (sentient) *101, 275, 348, 519, 637, 658, 675*

satvic *111, 437, 518-519, 586-587, 671*

Saul *55, 139, 617-618, 621*

savikalpa *348, 671*

Savior/Saviour *54, 192, 215, 218, 220-221, 232, 237, 239, 289, 604, 651, 665, 672*

Sayyed *671*

scepter *53-54, 56, 133, 135-138, 140, 142-148, 175-177, 191, 196, 243, 262, 270, 620-623, 625, 671, 673*

science *v, vi, viii, 15, 312, 396, 457, 465, 468, 474, 490, 530-531, 604, 647*

sciences *v*

scientific *v, vi, 168, 312, 316, 396, 457, 481, 508, 647*

scientifically *468*

scientists *v, vi, 15, 312, 396, 474, 485, 531, 646-647*

scribe *217, 238*

scribes *60, 70, 143, 193, 201, 205, 214-215, 219-220, 232, 241, 247, 249, 257, 259-260, 266-269, 370, 471*

Scripture *i, ii, 81-82, 84, 91, 119, 123, 281, 283, 293-294, 307, 323, 325-327, 530, 602, 648, 662, 677*

Scriptures *ii, iii, 6, 43, 45, 65, 81-85, 119, 125, 130, 145, 149, 155, 163-165, 173, 180, 234, 261, 265, 268, 280, 296-297, 301, 303, 308, 311, 313, 325, 329, 333-334, 381, 387, 396, 407, 427-428, 473, 480, 488, 493, 502, 526, 529, 536, 543, 561, 583, 586, 593, 598-599, 626, 633-634, 642, 645, 651-652, 667, 677*

    all Scriptures *6, 296*

all the Scriptures *308, 325, 334*

behind the Scriptures *502, 667*

change the scriptures *83, 145, 164-165, 301, 329, 428, 645*

explain the scriptures *268*

interpret the scriptures *268*

in the Scriptures *65, 130, 173, 261, 280, 303, 626, 633, 652*

know the scriptures *265, 311*

of Scriptures *ii, 334*

of the Scriptures *84, 119, 125, 145, 180, 329, 334, 381, 526, 536, 543, 561, 583, 586, 651*

oldest Scriptures *677*

other Scriptures *iii, 82, 155, 163, 313, 493*

read the scriptures *84, 325, 333, 667*

receive the scriptures *297*

sacred Scriptures *45*

Scriptures' *586*

(Scriptures) *427, 634*

scriptures and holy books *234*

scriptures are *ii, iii, 84-85, 163, 297, 334, 396, 634*

scriptures have *334, 428*

Scriptures should *6, 308*

Scriptures would *180*

sealed Scriptures *180*

send the scriptures *651*

spiritual Scriptures *163, 598*

take the scriptures *43*

their Scriptures *81, 381, 387, 407*

to the Scriptures *149*

sea *14-16, 41, 81, 134, 200-201, 217-218, 234, 238, 240-241, 244, 250-251, 260, 268, 362, 379, 383, 387, 391, 396-397, 403-404, 408, 410-411, 415, 419-420, 423-424, 462, 467, 581, 586, 625, 652, 656, 671, 678*

    a sea *379, 410*

    by sea *419*

    earth and the sea *81, 387*

    fishes of the sea *41*

    fish of the sea *15-16*

    from the sea *14, 462, 671*

    great sea *404, 462, 467, 656, 678*

    in the sea *217, 383, 391, 411, 419*

    into the sea *201, 218, 238, 260, 391, 420, 581*

    no more sea *424*

INDEX   S

of the sea *15-16, 41, 200, 240, 251, 362, 391, 403-404, 415, 423*

on the sea *240-241, 387, 410, 581*

restless sea *678*

sand of the sea *404, 423*

(sea) *403-404*

sea gives up the dead *423, 625*

sea is *462, 671*

sea kelp *586*

sea of glass *379, 410*

turbulent sea *218*

unto the sea *244*

seal *vii, viii, 66, 68, 74-75, 77-82, 96, 98-100, 104, 120, 123-125, 148, 153-155, 163, 199, 284, 293, 322-323, 356, 361-362, 366, 368, 375-376, 378, 383-396, 408-409, 411-412, 422, 427, 448-451, 483, 494, 496, 508, 535, 541-543, 565, 568, 621-622, 633, 648-650, 654, 661, 670-674*

    each seal *66, 125, 361-362, 366, 390-391, 411, 565, 671*

    fifth seal *80, 98, 123, 148, 385-386, 392-393, 409, 412, 450, 543, 648, 672*

    first seal *vii, 77-78, 96, 120, 378, 383, 390, 408, 448, 483, 649, 654, 671*

    fourth seal *77, 80, 82, 98, 293, 378, 385, 392, 409, 411, 450, 543, 672, 674*

    his seal *284*

    its seal *323*

    one seal *361, 390, 541*

    Seal not *427*

    Seal of America *155, 496*

    seal of God *75, 81, 376, 387, 393, 395*

    seal of Solomon *68, 79, 368, 384, 494, 535*

    seal of the Prophets *323, 568, 661*

    Seal of Unification *672*

    seal of universalism *412*

    Seal up *396*

    second seal *viii, 78-79, 383-384, 391, 449, 542, 672*

    seventh seal *81, 100, 356, 389, 451, 542-543, 622, 672*

    sixth seal *74, 80-81, 96, 99, 124, 375, 386-389, 394, 408-409, 412, 451, 543, 621-622, 633, 670, 672-673*

    that seal *361, 411*

    the seal *68, 75, 79, 81, 153-155, 322-323, 368, 376, 384, 387, 390, 393, 395, 412, 508, 535, 568, 661, 672*

    third seal *78-79, 199, 383-384, 391, 409, 411, 449, 650, 672*

    this seal *78, 80, 124, 383, 385, 448, 543*

sealed *21, 75, 81, 180, 376, 381, 387-388, 395, 473, 529, 598, 621-622*

seals *77-79, 81, 122, 125, 153, 178, 293, 343, 361-362, 377-378, 381-384, 389-390, 448, 539, 541, 543, 565, 583, 598, 618, 621-622, 634, 672*

Seas *13-14, 38, 115, 442-443*

SECLORUM (see "NOVUS ORDO SECLORUM") *155, 496*

seek *24, 56, 76, 117, 145, 161, 173, 194, 212-213, 221, 227, 235, 278, 287, 296, 300-302, 338, 343, 393-394, 446, 472, 485, 496, 521, 542, 639, 645, 651, 672*

seeker *vi, 104, 185, 325, 333, 343, 353, 403, 471, 536, 565, 603*

seekers *79, 174, 196, 236, 251, 289, 384, 459, 472, 537, 599*

seeks *145, 213, 220, 232, 570*

seers *43-44, 46, 119, 227, 459, 474, 479, 503, 508, 631*

self *10, 20-21, 25-26, 47, 59, 70, 78-79, 96-97, 103, 119, 159, 161, 199-200, 204, 215, 224, 247, 254, 262, 270, 282-283, 286, 295-296, 298-299, 304, 310, 319, 321, 329, 332-335, 349, 352, 355, 370, 380-382, 384-385, 393, 400, 405, 415, 419, 437-439, 446, 463, 471, 520-521, 523-525, 527-528, 530, 532, 534, 541, 551, 554, 564, 570-572, 580-581, 589, 594, 597, 599-600, 608-610, 632, 634-635, 637, 645-646, 648-649, 652-653, 657, 661-664, 669-672, 674, 677*

    and self *352*

    for Self *334*

    higher self *21, 25-26, 59, 70, 199-200, 204, 224, 247, 254, 262, 270, 282-283, 286, 295, 319, 321, 332, 370, 419, 438, 446, 463, 520-521, 524, 554, 571, 632, 634-635, 637, 648-649, 653, 657, 670, 674*

    know self *333, 534*

    lower self *25-26, 47, 70, 97, 199-200, 224, 247, 270, 282, 319, 321, 355, 370, 415, 520-521, 523, 572, 649, 662-663*

    of self *298, 304, 541*

    or self *215*

    own self *97, 333*

    (self) *600, 663*

Self-actualization *534, 569-572*

self-actualized *309, 534-535, 570, 572-573*

INDEX S

self and *10, 59, 70, 103, 119, 159, 161, 204, 224, 296, 299, 304, 310, 335, 352, 370, 381, 393, 400, 439, 446, 520-521, 530, 541, 554, 564, 572, 589, 597, 609, 645, 661, 672, 677*

self has *247*

self is *47, 247, 333, 608, 653*

self or *298, 349*

self-realization *47, 98, 333, 445, 495, 595, 599, 637, 664*

self-sacrifice *97, 270, 402*

self-sacrificing *139*

self-sustaining *12-13, 17, 87, 116, 331, 338, 443-444, 480-481, 487, 521, 591, 649*

self to *26, 199, 282, 321, 355, 381, 525, 635, 649, 670*

self-will *612*

self will *439, 669*

self with *532, 580, 664*

the self *10, 20, 78-79, 96, 103, 119, 159, 161, 296, 299, 310, 329, 335, 349, 352, 380-382, 384, 393, 400, 437-439, 471, 521, 525, 527-528, 530, 541, 551, 564, 571-572, 580-581, 589, 594, 597, 599, 608-609, 635, 645, 652, 661, 664, 669-672, 677*

self-centered *9-10, 56, 79, 97, 104, 111-112, 121, 145, 247, 270, 298, 301, 333, 349-350, 352, 356, 381, 393, 434, 437-439, 448-449, 471, 483, 520, 541, 597, 610, 635, 650, 653, 656-658, 668, 670, 672, 675*

become self-centered *111-112, 439, 448, 657, 675*

less self-centered *349*

more self-centered *9, 111, 520, 610*

not be self-centered *10, 56, 79, 104, 121, 145, 270, 333, 356, 381, 437, 449, 471, 483, 597, 610, 635, 650, 653, 668, 670*

self-centered egoistical *656*

selfish and self-centered *247, 301, 658*

symbol for self-centered *656*

self-centeredness *6, 9-10, 12, 125, 170, 301, 319, 434, 438, 449, 485, 511, 527-528, 610, 657, 672*

self-hypnosis *612*

selfless *317, 399, 520, 559, 597, 635*

selflessly *451, 519*

selflessness *97, 449, 528*

Senate *464, 466, 502-506, 510*

Senators *504*

sense *15, 54, 121, 142, 149, 186, 191, 240, 261, 280, 294, 304, 323, 328, 334, 350, 352-353, 355, 397, 433, 448, 457, 459, 489, 495, 497, 501-502, 518, 555, 558-560, 569, 582, 598, 618, 626, 645, 649, 654, 661, 667, 673, 676*

common sense *240, 261, 334, 397, 457, 559, 626*

deeper sense *555*

false sense *558*

make sense *654*

more sense *294*

no sense *304, 560, 645*

sense of *15, 54, 149, 304, 353, 355, 433, 448, 457, 459, 497, 501, 558, 560, 598, 645, 649*

sense them *350, 667*

senses *35, 82-83, 104, 129, 300, 349-350, 379, 382, 411, 613, 653, 655, 667-668, 676*

sentient *5-6, 10, 13, 101, 107-109, 111, 114, 170, 275, 311, 348, 351, 357, 431, 433, 435, 437, 439, 442, 449, 518-520, 522-523, 586-588, 637, 647, 651, 655, 658, 668, 671-672, 675*

more sentient *10, 13, 114, 431, 437, 442, 587*

most sentient *433, 651, 655, 671*

(sentient) *101, 111, 275, 348, 518-519, 586, 637, 658, 671, 675*

sentient environment *10, 449, 520, 523*

sentient force *5-6, 101, 107-108, 170, 311, 351, 357, 431, 433, 435, 439, 655, 668, 671-672*

serpent *21-25, 198, 213, 223-224, 283, 352, 402-403, 412, 422, 630-631, 662, 672, 676*

serpents *22, 223, 269, 395, 630-631*

service *28, 71, 226, 371, 508, 519, 536-537, 583, 586, 597, 607-608, 635, 648, 667, 672*

services *461, 468, 510, 519, 607, 667*

servile *541-542*

seven *vii, i, 4, 12-13, 15, 31-32, 36-37, 39, 49, 65-67, 73, 81, 89, 92, 100-103, 116-118, 122, 139, 147, 150, 163, 165, 169, 178-179, 204, 233-234, 244-245, 247, 252, 264, 288, 293, 314, 347, 349, 355, 357, 361-367, 373, 379, 381-383, 389-391, 396, 399, 401, 404, 407, 410-411, 414-416, 425, 428, 437, 443, 445, 448, 467, 486, 501, 504-505, 522, 527, 538, 541-542, 559, 564, 580, 583, 588, 598, 618, 621-622, 628-629, 634, 650, 662-663, 671*

and seven *31-32, 49, 81, 122, 178, 293, 382, 401, 505*

are seven *32, 349, 365, 379, 415-416, 662*

have seven *15, 65, 364, 382, 401, 404, 414-415*

Holiest One to Seven *4*

of seven *347, 445, 504, 629*

or seven *382*

seven and *39*

INDEX

seven Angels *122, 179, 362-363, 366, 389-391, 410-411, 414, 425*

seven categories *357*

seven chakras *65, 349, 364-365, 382, 662-663*

seven churches *65, 67, 81, 122, 163, 178, 247, 293, 361, 364-367*

seven crowns *401*

seven-day *542-543*

seven days *36-37, 39, 541-542*

seven energy centers *65, 364, 650*

seven eyes *382*

seven false *401*

seven golden *65, 67, 365-367, 410*

seven heads *362, 401, 404, 414-415*

seven hundred *32*

seven is *32*

seven lamps *379*

seven last *410, 425*

seven levels *347, 357, 379, 445*

seven lokas *12, 379, 662*

seven meanings *428*

seven people *505*

seven plagues *410*

seven religions *103, 118, 362, 366*

seven Sabbaths *541*

seven seals *81, 122, 178, 293, 361-362, 381-382, 389-390, 541, 583, 598, 618, 621-622, 634*

seven sections *i*

seven Spirits *65, 73, 364, 373, 379, 382*

seven stars *65-67, 73, 366-367, 373*

seven-step *vii*

seven steps *102-103, 169, 448, 628*

seven subsections *4*

seven thousand *399*

seven trumpets *362, 389-391*

seven truths *65-66, 81, 118, 122, 147, 163, 178-179, 293, 364-366, 379, 383, 448, 671*

seven vials *414, 425*

seven weeks *541*

seven worlds *347, 443, 445*

seven years *31-32, 49, 89, 542*

sevenfold *29, 564*

sevens *32, 36*

seventh *i, 17, 21, 38, 74-75, 77, 81, 100, 104, 116, 125, 144, 163, 179-180, 237, 264, 290, 331, 347-348, 352, 356-357, 362-363, 375-376, 381, 389-390, 392, 397, 399-400, 413, 416, 418, 425, 427, 443-445, 451, 462, 541-543, 552, 572, 595, 598, 622-623, 625, 629-630, 646, 648, 650, 667, 670-672*

(seventh) *348*

seventh Angel *125, 144, 163, 179-180, 237, 362-363, 381, 389-390, 392, 397, 399-400, 413, 416, 418, 427, 462, 598, 622-623, 625, 672*

seventh chakra *75, 125, 352, 356, 376, 630, 646, 648, 670*

seventh chakras *572*

seventh day *17, 116, 331, 444, 541, 595*

seventh king *416*

seventh level *75, 375*

seventh levels *352*

seventh loka *671*

seventh month *38, 542*

seventh one *i*

seventh period *595*

seventh seal *81, 100, 356, 389, 451, 542-543, 622, 672*

seventh spiritual center *100, 179, 629*

seventh stage *i, 77, 104*

seventh stages *357*

seventh state *21, 443, 445, 552, 667*

seventh states *443, 445*

seventh truth *81, 125, 179-180, 389*

Shah Bahram *672*

Shakti *22, 444, 539, 553*

SHALOM *517*

Shal-om *670*

Shariah *533, 672*

sheath *347-348, 351-352, 355-356, 445*

sheaths *347, 349, 351-352, 374, 445*

sheep *vi, 27, 55, 214, 222-223, 229, 243-244, 251, 262, 280, 419, 587*

Shem *32, 35, 37, 42-43, 45-46, 48-49, 174, 459, 474, 479, 620, 649, 672*

shepherd *138, 222*

shewbread *229*

Shii'a *672, 674*

Shii'as *673-674*

Shiloh *54, 56, 121, 137, 143-146, 176-177, 191, 196, 200, 223, 243, 262, 275, 285, 605, 673*

Shiva *22, 444, 539, 553, 563, 620*

Shrii (see also "Haree Om Shrii Hung") *110, 172, 184, 434-435, 494, 518, 562, 566, 591, 599, 604, 656-657, 663, 667, 673*

INDEX S

Shrii Shrii Anandamurti (see "Anandamurti") *673*
Shrii Shrii Para Maha *656, 673*
Shudra *99, 482-483, 486, 488, 649, 668*
Shudrahood *482*
Shudran *480-481, 584, 657*
Shudras *26, 43-45, 102, 119, 174, 447, 459-461, 474, 479-484, 488, 507-508, 532, 620, 655, 673*
sickle *409-410*
siddhi *673*
siddhis *75, 637, 673*
Sijjin *146, 296, 673*
silver *82-83, 152, 223, 300, 395, 419, 458, 460-461, 463-464, 469, 472*
sinless *217, 410, 533, 564*
sinless-ness *564*
sinned *26, 164-165, 564*
sinners *23, 62, 207, 219-220, 227, 533*
sinning *162, 333*
sin (see also "karma" "samskara") *19, 27-29, 60-61, 69, 84, 92, 102, 129, 159, 162, 165, 205-206, 213, 219, 231, 243, 245, 251-252, 254, 278, 313-314, 323, 333, 362, 369, 398, 532-533, 560-561, 564, 578, 585, 616, 673*

    any sin *165*
    a sin *84, 243, 323, 564*
    bad sin *398*
    commit sin *564*
    do sin *61, 205-206, 243*
    from sin *560*
    great sin *162, 254, 561*
    his sin *28-29, 564*
    into sin *564*
    is sin *69, 219, 369, 585*
    like sin *245*
    no sin *213, 313, 333, 532*
    not sin *578*
    of sin *231*
    (sin) *19, 159, 251, 560, 616*
    sin against *252*
    sin is *219, 333, 362, 564*
    sin lieth *27*
    Sin (Samskara) *673*
    sin (samskaras) *102*
    sin should *61, 213*
    the sin *102, 219, 278, 533, 564*
    to sin *60, 564*
    without sin *129, 313*
    with sin *92, 333*

sins (see also "karmas" "samskaras") *28-29, 55, 72, 90, 92, 129, 143, 150, 164-165, 192, 196, 213, 217-219, 243, 299, 315, 333, 364, 372, 389, 394, 418, 533, 542, 564, 591, 670*
Smyrna *68, 365, 368*
Socrates *465, 473, 480*
Sodom *45, 59, 204, 223, 228, 398, 615*
So-Hung (see also "Hung-So") *645*
solid *13, 18, 108, 114-116, 305, 317, 347, 350, 355, 357, 379, 396-397, 431, 442-443, 445, 630-631, 646, 649-650, 653, 666, 676*
Solomon *68, 79, 201, 211-212, 233, 343, 368, 384, 494, 535, 658*
sorcerers *425, 427*
sorceries *395, 420*
Soul *8, 15, 17-19, 25-26, 28, 33, 43, 50, 55, 60, 65-67, 69, 78-79, 84, 89-91, 93, 97, 102, 111, 113, 115-117, 132, 139, 150-151, 159, 165, 180, 193, 196, 198, 200, 205, 210, 212-213, 216-217, 224-225, 230, 233, 242, 248-249, 251, 265-266, 281-282, 286-287, 298-299, 301, 303-304, 309, 312-316, 318, 320-321, 324, 327, 329-331, 333-334, 338-339, 343, 347, 349-350, 352, 364-367, 369, 378, 380-382, 384, 389, 402, 404, 411, 415, 419, 421, 433-436, 439-440, 444-446, 495, 502, 518-523, 525, 530, 532, 537, 551, 554, 561, 570, 585, 588, 592-594, 599-600, 609-611, 630, 632, 638, 646, 652, 657, 659, 663-664, 668-670, 672, 674-676, 678*

    and Soul *111, 347, 445, 537, 600, 630*
    and the Soul *265, 329*
    bind the Soul *314, 675*
    each Soul *165, 678*
    first Soul *382*
    from the Soul *90, 116, 347, 445, 668*
    Great Soul *50, 55, 139, 151, 193, 196, 233, 343, 592-593, 610, 663*
    higher Soul *26, 343*
    high Soul *554*
    his Soul *26, 78, 90, 111, 113, 115, 117, 165, 200, 248, 266, 282, 299, 304, 313, 315, 333-334, 378, 384, 436, 440, 444, 446, 495, 520, 522, 532, 657*
    is the Soul *329, 331*
    living soul *17, 116, 411, 444*
    my Soul *65-66, 230, 364, 366*
    no Soul *315, 521, 561*

INDEX

S

of the Soul *19, 287, 301, 321, 327, 338-339, 347, 380, 433-434, 445, 530, 570, 611, 632, 669*

or Soul *349*

over the Soul *89, 97, 180, 217, 299, 314, 389, 402, 404, 415, 439, 519, 652*

(Soul) *43, 79, 159, 384, 638, 675*

Soul after *669*

Soul and *60, 78, 102, 113, 115-117, 196, 205, 210, 216, 224-225, 299, 304, 313-314, 338, 350, 384, 444-446, 594, 610, 669*

Soul and spirit *102, 537, 594, 630*

Soul arises *65, 364*

Soul enters *561, 609*

Soul has *312, 329*

Soul in *67, 367, 521-522, 592*

Soul is *66, 78, 193, 217, 230, 248, 299, 314-315, 366, 378, 495, 520-521, 530, 537, 632, 652, 674*

Soul of *33, 299, 327, 381, 421, 561, 675*

Soul or *25, 151, 343, 349, 352, 520*

Soul's *93, 327*

Soul should *165, 249*

Soul through *287, 646*

Soul to *43, 312, 561, 570, 670*

Soul-to-Soul *259, 287, 311, 536*

Soul toward *318, 520, 675*

Soul which *89, 213, 329, 382, 525*

Soul who *28, 561*

Soul will *265, 282, 315, 561*

Soul would *316*

thy soul *265, 419*

to the Soul *324, 347, 435, 445, 664*

your Soul *60, 84, 89, 91, 150, 205, 212-213, 303, 314, 320, 588*

soulmate *20, 527, 529, 555, 631*

soulmates *29, 61, 206, 253, 340-341, 523, 529, 645*

Souls *38, 46, 54, 57, 68, 73-75, 79-80, 87, 89, 99, 101, 111, 113, 119-120, 123-124, 130, 147, 151, 165, 175, 184, 202, 209-211, 220-221, 228, 231, 236, 240, 248, 265-266, 283, 289, 301-302, 306, 309, 312, 318, 320, 324, 330, 333, 336, 340, 362, 364, 368, 374, 376, 384-385, 393, 401, 419, 422-423, 435, 441, 467, 474, 488, 502-503, 508, 524-526, 534, 554, 557, 573, 580, 584-585, 590-595, 599, 613, 624, 639-640, 669*

and Souls *75, 79, 376, 384, 419, 524*

Great Souls *46, 54, 73, 119, 130, 147, 220, 289, 374, 401, 467, 474, 488, 503, 508, 534, 557, 580, 590, 592-595, 599, 613, 639-640*

invisible Souls *584*

lost souls *101, 111, 113, 184, 220, 435, 441*

many Souls *120, 124, 175*

our Souls *89, 209-211, 266, 306, 320, 330, 590-591*

own Souls *340, 585*

refined Souls *57, 99, 202*

respectful Souls *525*

some Souls *669*

Souls and *101, 111, 209, 211, 220, 240, 306, 435, 503, 525, 590-591, 595*

Souls are *38, 87, 124, 151, 309, 393, 639*

Souls have *120, 289*

Souls in *113, 289, 525, 580, 590-592*

souls of *46, 74, 79-80, 123, 364, 374, 384-385, 419, 423, 624*

souls to *441*

Souls who *54, 57, 119, 202, 302, 312, 467, 488, 526, 590, 593-594*

Souls will *318, 508, 640*

their Souls *221, 240, 265, 283, 302, 318, 324, 362, 393, 401, 422, 554, 573*

the souls *68, 74, 80, 123, 364, 368, 374, 385, 423, 624*

those Souls *302, 312, 526*

your souls *228*

southern *118, 176, 200-201*

Spain *466*

Spanish *660*

spinal *223, 579, 629-630*

spine *472, 580, 629, 631, 662*

spirit *v, vi, vii, 8, 15, 18, 20, 33, 35, 57, 60, 65-68, 72-74, 76-78, 94-96, 99-102, 111, 116-119, 135, 141, 161, 163-164, 171, 173, 191-192, 197, 199, 202, 205, 208-209, 213, 217-218, 224, 230, 233-235, 241, 243, 265-267, 269, 275, 277-278, 280, 282-284, 287-288, 295, 311, 315, 326, 331, 337, 340, 343, 352, 358, 361, 365-370, 373-374, 376-378, 383-385, 389, 399-400, 409, 412, 414, 418, 421, 425, 427, 433-437, 444-446, 449-450, 457, 471, 473, 479, 482, 495, 502, 504, 522-524, 530, 537, 541, 554, 559, 561, 564-565, 577-578, 580, 582, 585, 589, 593-594, 600, 604, 609, 615-617, 619, 621-625, 628, 630-632, 634, 638, 646, 648-650, 654-655, 663-664, 671-672, 674, 678*

affect the spirit *217, 594*

and spirit *v, vi, 60, 78, 102, 161, 205, 358, 384, 495, 522-523, 537, 565, 594*

bring the spirit *vi, 331, 616, 621*

INDEX   S

cleanse the spirit *524*
clean the spirit *269*
destroy the spirit *615*
express the Spirit *94, 99, 340*
from the Spirit *192, 234, 580, 621, 634*
his spirit *218, 243, 267, 277, 352, 524, 621, 625, 632*
in spirit *20, 57, 67-68, 76, 78, 96, 191, 202, 266, 287-288, 361, 367-369, 377, 384, 578*
in the spirit *vi, 65, 173, 199, 365, 378, 414, 425, 578, 672*
is spirit *282, 631*
is the spirit *vii, 275, 421, 522, 621, 623, 625, 654*
lower spirit *282*
my spirit *33, 118, 230, 632*
of spirit *vii, 287, 295, 630-631, 649, 664*
of the spirit *68, 119, 135, 191, 197, 234, 269, 282-283, 343, 368, 400, 414, 433, 471, 473, 479, 592, 631-632, 671*
receive the Spirit *564, 648*
see the Spirit *197, 278*
(spirit) *76, 116, 377, 444-445, 504, 634, 638*
spirit and *vi, 68, 78, 202, 234, 243, 287-288, 352, 369, 385, 427, 433, 537, 564, 578, 594, 600, 615-617, 619, 621, 630-632, 654, 664*
Spirit arises *632*
spirit behind *457, 471, 479*
spirit into *197, 414*
spirit is *60, 68, 119, 161, 205, 233-234, 282-283, 368, 594, 674*
spirit of *vii, 8, 66, 78, 94-95, 99, 101, 111, 141, 163-164, 171, 197, 218, 224, 230, 275, 311, 326, 337, 340, 366, 383, 399, 421, 435-436, 449-450, 482, 524, 541, 582, 585, 616, 621, 623-625, 628, 638, 648, 654-655, 672, 678*
Spirit of God *8, 94, 99, 101, 111, 171, 197, 230, 275, 311, 340, 435-437, 450, 616, 621-625, 655*
Spirit on *65, 365, 621*
Spirit refers *57, 202*
Spirit saith *68, 368-370, 373-374, 376*
Spirit says *72, 100, 373, 389*
spirit to *102, 311, 331, 425, 577*
spirit which *275, 615, 638*
spirit will *208, 243, 473, 578, 615, 621, 623, 632*
spirit within *315*
strengthen the spirit *600*
their spirit *208, 213, 235, 280, 530, 559, 577, 621*

this Spirit *275, 621, 623, 632*
to Spirit *616-617*
to the Spirit *450, 617, 619*
toward Spirit *648*
understand the spirit *457*
what the Spirit *68, 368-370, 373-374, 376*
with Spirit *v*
with the spirit *vi, 73, 374, 582, 585, 678*
spirits *65, 73, 211, 217, 222, 233-234, 243, 245, 254, 364, 373, 379, 382, 412, 573*
spiritual *v, vii, iii, iv, 9-11, 15, 19-20, 22, 27, 30, 32-34, 40, 43-46, 53-54, 58-59, 65-68, 70-80, 82-86, 88-90, 95-96, 98-100, 103-104, 110, 113, 116, 118-120, 122-126, 129-130, 132-133, 135, 137-138, 140, 142-149, 160, 163, 168-169, 172-180, 185, 191-192, 194-198, 200-201, 203-204, 208-215, 217, 220, 222-224, 227, 233-235, 238, 241-244, 247-248, 254, 260, 262, 265-267, 276, 280, 282-283, 286-287, 289, 293-302, 306, 308-309, 312, 314-315, 317, 320-324, 326-327, 331-332, 334-341, 343, 348-349, 351-352, 355-358, 361, 365-370, 372-378, 381-387, 389, 392-393, 396-397, 400, 402, 404, 406, 409, 412, 414, 416, 420, 422, 427, 433-434, 437-439, 444, 446, 449-452, 457, 459-462, 464-466, 471-474, 479, 483, 488-490, 497-499, 502-503, 507, 509, 518-522, 524-529, 531, 533, 535-538, 542-543, 549-551, 553-556, 560-564, 566, 568, 571-572, 576, 578, 581, 584, 586, 589, 591-600, 604, 607, 619-622, 628-632, 635, 637-638, 640, 646, 648-649, 651-658, 661-665, 667-675, 677-678*

and spiritual *53, 80, 85, 88, 99, 116, 140, 145-146, 168, 211, 233-234, 267, 283, 287, 320, 327, 343, 352, 355, 385, 397, 444, 449, 472, 479, 490, 497, 502, 518, 520-522, 527-528, 538, 543, 549, 551, 556, 572, 584, 596-597, 604, 630, 654, 665, 667, 670*
be spiritual *20, 502*
has spiritual *40, 282, 649*
is spiritual *19, 528, 581, 651*
look spiritual *208*
more spiritual *98, 381, 472, 550, 571, 589, 630*
or spiritual *83, 89, 176, 287, 297, 301, 314, 327, 489, 502, 535, 549, 592, 630-631, 672*
(spiritual) *326, 444*
spiritual and *iii, 234, 396, 527, 535-536, 538, 556, 597*
spiritual aspect *169*
spiritual aspects *169, 630*
spiritual aspirant *332, 334, 338, 663, 675*
spiritual aspirants *43*

729

INDEX

S

spiritual being *34, 177, 490*

spiritual beings *v, 43, 180, 554, 584*

spiritual blessing *53, 140, 142, 145-148*

spiritual body *629*

spiritual center *98, 118, 179, 537, 629, 631*

spiritual centers *15, 306, 352, 446, 472, 502, 537, 571*

spiritual cleanliness *521-522*

spiritual consciousness *282, 521, 662*

spiritual development *489, 673*

spiritual dominance *137-138, 142, 145, 671*

spiritual domination *132-133, 138, 143, 191, 244, 502, 621*

spiritual effect *536, 600*

spiritual energies *75, 376, 631*

spiritual energy *472, 538, 631*

spiritual environment *124, 302, 343, 451, 521, 550*

spiritual event *vii*

spiritual exercises *356, 474*

spiritual explanation *82, 293*

spiritual eye *34, 168, 197, 200, 211, 675*

spiritual eyes *174, 227, 238, 474, 655*

spiritual force *11, 113, 124, 163, 175, 223-224, 357, 439, 452, 543, 571, 629, 631, 653, 672*

spiritual forces *9, 11, 22, 67, 77-78, 82, 96, 99, 118-120, 122, 124-125, 173, 175, 294, 356, 367, 378, 383-384, 420, 449-452, 473-474, 488, 553, 562, 566, 594, 631, 646, 649, 653-654, 657-658, 664, 668, 678*

spiritual gatherings *524*

spiritual inadequacy *234*

spiritual journey *96, 100, 355, 358, 427, 543, 549, 600, 646, 657*

spiritual king *176-177*

spiritual knowledge *82, 98-99, 119, 173, 175, 194, 213, 286, 317, 337, 386-387, 389, 392, 400, 406, 412, 414, 472, 474, 556, 563, 658, 661-662*

spiritual language *44*

spiritual lessons *457*

spiritual level *v, 527, 554*

spiritual levels *654*

spiritual life *20, 33, 68, 334, 337, 368, 422, 521, 528, 537, 619*

spiritual Master *593*

spiritual masters *120*

spiritual meaning *675*

spiritual message *177, 323, 556*

Spiritual Messages *336*

spiritual observation *542*

spiritual or *331, 527*

spiritual part *135, 497, 630*

spiritual parts *393, 460*

spiritual path *10, 27, 59, 65, 71-72, 76, 104, 126, 163, 204, 298, 302, 336, 372, 400, 543, 578, 591, 628*

spiritual people *45-46, 86, 295, 317, 326, 340, 383, 459, 461, 502, 507, 519, 536, 597, 620*

spiritual person *90, 96, 196, 242, 282, 315, 464, 490, 522*

spiritual personalities *538*

spiritual personality *32, 129, 177*

spiritual plane *30*

spiritual point *168, 265, 502, 527*

spiritual power *215, 276, 356, 437*

spiritual powers *vii, 40, 72, 75, 104, 110, 118-119, 130, 173, 198, 215, 260, 302, 373, 416, 422, 434, 466, 483, 562, 620, 632, 637, 658, 667-668*

spiritual practice *599*

spiritual practices *66, 96, 356, 366, 509, 543, 628, 658, 667, 673*

spiritual progress *iv, 54, 72-73, 84, 88, 103, 120, 124, 160, 178, 185, 198, 201, 208-212, 215, 220, 247-248, 287, 296, 320, 324, 334, 343, 349, 352, 356, 361, 372, 374, 377, 382, 404, 409, 420, 437-439, 449-451, 457, 489, 520, 522, 524, 527-528, 533, 549, 571, 593-594, 607, 628-629, 637-638, 652, 663-664, 669-670*

spiritual promises *137*

spiritual qualities *460*

spiritual quality *464*

spiritual realities *70, 317, 370*

spiritual realization *72, 77, 82, 123, 148, 178, 293-294, 323, 373, 378, 433, 527-528, 563, 568, 629, 631, 661*

spiritual realizations *535*

spiritual Scriptures *163, 598*

spiritual significance *175, 287*

spiritual (Soul) *43*

spiritual state *76, 377*

spiritual states *664*

spiritual studies *599*

spiritual teacher *74, 83, 88, 196, 201, 217, 297, 299, 301-302, 324, 326-327, 374-375, 524-525,*

INDEX

527, 549-551, 561, 584, 595, 622, 628, 631, 656, 674

spiritual teachers *83, 267, 321, 327, 334, 404, 488, 502, 507, 524, 543, 555, 651*

spiritual truth *43, 96, 130, 138, 148, 177, 211, 235, 393, 397, 457, 465, 502, 527*

spiritual truths *149, 524, 536, 651*

spiritual types *45*

spiritual understanding *58, 68, 77, 95, 104, 144, 149, 178, 203, 267, 282, 308-309, 321, 352, 365, 368, 378, 392, 396, 465, 490, 556, 564, 566, 656*

spiritual understandings *118-119, 289, 457, 488, 521, 543, 586*

spiritual unification *526*

spiritual world *43, 77, 80, 83, 103, 148, 173-174, 179, 265-266, 298-302, 314, 321-322, 335, 339, 341, 348, 351, 378, 385, 393, 397, 402, 462, 473, 519-520, 525, 543, 556, 560, 630-631, 648-649, 667, 675*

spiritualist *77, 87, 336, 378, 668*

spiritualists *v, 43, 45, 77, 99, 229, 268, 297, 301, 340, 343, 377, 393, 459, 468, 480, 485, 488, 499, 501-502, 508, 560, 655, 659*

spirituality *160, 211, 283, 335, 392, 394, 405, 464, 470, 504, 534, 556, 583, 586*

spiritualize *433*

spiritualized *242, 348, 350, 457, 649, 665*

spiritually *vii, 19-21, 32, 43, 58-59, 63, 71, 74, 77, 86, 96, 99, 103, 121, 124, 148, 160, 185, 191, 196, 199, 203-204, 208, 217, 235, 243, 248, 251, 296, 314, 325-326, 371, 374, 398, 449, 457, 461, 482-483, 488, 490, 501, 506, 509, 511, 522, 524, 527-529, 539, 550-551, 554, 560, 563, 571, 582, 585, 588, 592, 597, 603-604, 608, 638, 669-671, 675*

    be spiritually *71, 74, 196, 371, 374, 522, 554, 585*

    is spiritually *217, 483, 488, 501, 560*

    or spiritually *199, 582, 585, 592, 608, 670*

    physically, mentally, and/or spiritually *608*

    physically, mentally, and spiritually *20, 58, 63, 77, 86, 99, 121, 124, 148, 160, 185, 203, 208, 296, 314, 326, 449, 457, 482-483, 490, 506, 509, 511, 528-529, 550-551, 554, 571, 604, 669*

    physically, mentally, emotionally, and spiritually *511, 528-529, 597, 638*

    physically, mentally, or spiritually *582, 585, 670*

    progress spiritually *20, 103, 248, 251, 325, 551*

    (spiritually) *21, 243*

    spiritually advanced *483, 524*

    spiritually and *121, 248, 550*

spiritually attracted *20, 527*

spiritually awakened *461, 588*

spiritually aware *560*

spiritually clean *522*

spiritually dead *217, 235*

spiritually equal *71, 371*

spiritually incorruptible *488*

spiritually is *59, 204, 398, 511, 539*

spiritually knowledgeable *501*

spiritually, mentally, and physically *551*

spiritually purified *74, 374*

spiritually realized *563*

spiritually strong *554*

spiritually very *196*

spouse *201, 324, 549-550*

spouses *340*

spue *75, 100, 119, 185, 376, 613, 637*

spued *26, 258, 377, 411, 613*

spuing *26*

squatting *578*

star *66, 68, 72-73, 79-80, 98, 121, 139, 154-155, 193-194, 337-338, 366, 368, 373, 384-386, 391-392, 403, 427, 494, 508, 520, 563, 663, 665, 674*

stars *14, 53, 65-67, 73, 133-134, 138, 154, 337, 366-367, 373, 386, 392, 400-401, 465, 470-471, 563, 647, 674*

static *5, 13, 101, 107-108, 111, 114-115, 275, 311, 357, 431, 433, 435, 443, 518-519, 586, 658, 674-675*

struggle *9-10, 13, 17, 40, 48, 54, 59, 63, 68-69, 73, 78, 88, 98-99, 102, 104, 113, 118-119, 121, 138, 149, 160, 162-165, 197, 199, 204, 215, 227, 238, 302, 308, 318, 322-323, 334, 361, 364-365, 368-369, 374, 384, 393, 408, 436, 438, 440-442, 444, 457, 467, 479, 482-483, 486-487, 489, 494-495, 508, 533, 559, 562, 567-572, 598, 619-620, 632, 635-637, 648, 650, 653, 659, 662, 664, 668, 674*

    and struggle *215, 571, 674*

    a struggle *68, 318, 368, 482, 508, 559, 570*

    external struggle *318, 334, 568-569*

    greater struggle *438, 482, 632*

    greatest struggle *568*

    great struggle *48, 63, 73, 149, 160, 162, 364-365, 374, 436, 533, 620, 632, 635-636*

    his struggle *102, 113, 440, 444, 648*

    internal struggle *569*

    lifetime struggle *648*

    little struggle *637*

INDEX S

means struggle *568*
much struggle *302, 467*
not struggle *393*
of struggle *54, 59, 99, 163, 204, 442, 489, 648*
physical struggle *662*
spiritual struggle *334, 361, 562*
"struggle" *568, 659, 664*
struggle against *674*
struggle and *59, 98, 104, 149, 160, 204, 238, 334, 508, 568-569*
struggle for *164, 482, 572*
struggle goes *559*
struggle has *620*
struggle he *436*
struggle in *88, 197, 215, 308, 323, 438, 467, 569*
struggle is *13, 99, 102, 113, 163, 318, 334, 479, 569, 636*
struggle of *54, 162, 165, 487, 495, 568*
struggle or *562, 570, 662*
struggle than *632*
struggle that *365, 650*
struggle they *138, 479, 632*
struggle to *10, 17, 73, 99, 121, 334, 364-365, 374, 441-442, 457, 479, 486, 508, 568-569, 571, 635, 648, 664*
struggle toward *119, 648*
struggle will *444, 482*
struggle with *40, 54, 69, 88, 118, 164-165, 227, 364, 369, 408, 483, 494, 598, 650, 653, 674*
struggle within *318*
their struggle *59, 119, 149, 204, 479*
the struggle *10, 13, 17, 54, 98, 138, 165, 318, 334, 364-365, 441, 495, 568, 650*
They struggle *479*
through struggle *78, 384, 668*
who struggle *69, 88, 121, 164-165, 322, 369, 408, 483, 598, 653*
will struggle *88, 323, 508, 650*
struggled *251, 364, 650, 653*
strugglers *654*
struggles *54, 70, 88, 160, 175, 318, 322, 324, 370, 382, 437, 439, 481, 591, 650, 659, 668*
struggling *54, 67, 149, 166, 267, 365, 367, 554, 664*
subconscious *235, 348, 414, 556, 572, 610-614, 674*
sub-consciousness *408*
subjective *264, 512*

submission *10, 18, 25, 112, 122-123, 126, 177-178, 293, 335-336, 438, 450, 535, 539, 566, 582-583, 653, 673-675*
submissive *10-11, 52, 58, 60, 72, 82, 85, 87, 97, 122, 146, 148, 177, 193, 294, 311, 322-323, 334-338, 372-373, 412, 439, 451-452, 483, 554, 566, 568, 650, 659, 661, 666, 668-670, 674-675*
    become submissive *11, 122, 193, 439, 451, 483*
    be submissive *10, 52, 58, 148, 294, 323, 334-336, 338, 452, 650, 674*
    is submissive *72, 85, 311, 335, 338, 372*
    submissive and surrendered *337-338*
    submissive or surrendered *148*
    submissive to *10, 52, 72, 82, 85, 87, 97, 122, 148, 177, 193, 323, 334-338, 372-373, 412, 439, 451-452, 483, 554, 566, 568, 661, 666, 669-670, 674*
    surrendered and/or submissive *412, 566, 659*
    surrendered and submissive *72, 82, 85, 87, 177, 336-337, 373, 568, 666, 668-670*
    surrendered or submissive *85, 148, 335, 661, 666, 675*
submissiveness *298*
submit *10, 82, 85, 92, 99, 104, 123-124, 148, 202, 297, 307-308, 336, 340, 356, 558, 581-583, 590, 593-594, 675*
submits *87, 335-336*
submitted *77, 85, 123, 300, 335-336, 378, 598, 629, 659, 672*
submitting *82, 594*
sub-region *499-501, 505-506*
sub-regions *499-500, 505-506*
sub-sub-region *505*
sub-sub-worlds *517*
sub-worlds *517*
Sufi *590*
Sufis *672*
Sufism *vii, 654*
suicide *393, 570*
sun *13-14, 62-64, 72, 80, 83, 99, 124, 142, 147, 207, 232, 235, 238, 248, 301, 337, 366, 373, 386, 389, 392, 395, 400, 411-412, 421, 426, 522, 531, 538, 540, 563, 579, 621, 625, 647, 665, 674*
    (sun) *72, 373, 386, 412*
    sun and moon *14, 386*
    sun becomes *80, 124, 386, 563*
    sun god *63-64, 232, 665*
    sun is *235, 337, 392, 538, 563*

INDEX

Sunday *64, 232, 539-540*

Sundays *540*

sundered *92, 238, 317*

sundering *614*

Sunni *674*

Sunnis *673-674*

sunrise *24, 540-541, 581*

sunset *24, 540-541, 581*

super-consciousness *408*

Supramental *659*

Supreme *137, 148, 293, 439, 538, 563, 646, 674, 676*

surrender *10, 34, 59, 64, 71-72, 77, 82, 85, 87, 93, 99, 104, 123-124, 148, 177, 205, 214, 228, 284, 310, 331-332, 371, 373, 378, 410, 421, 427, 467, 483, 509, 566, 581, 583-584, 590, 592-594, 668, 674-675*

    should surrender *10, 85, 467, 584, 593*

    submit or surrender *148*

    surrender and submit *82, 123-124, 581, 594*

    surrender ourselves *93, 583-584, 590, 593*

    surrender the result *10, 59, 71, 77, 99, 148, 177, 205, 284, 371, 378, 566, 674*

    surrender the results *72, 87*

    surrender to *10, 34, 228, 331, 410, 427, 467, 583, 592-593*

    we surrender *583-584, 590, 593-594*

surrendered *10-11, 27, 37, 71-72, 82, 85, 87-88, 90-91, 95, 104, 112, 123, 134, 148, 177-178, 193, 212, 228, 315, 323, 334-339, 371-373, 386, 412, 450, 488, 517, 566, 568, 585, 589, 598, 659, 661, 666, 668-670, 672, 675*

    be surrendered *11, 71, 82, 85, 87, 90, 95, 134, 148, 177-178, 315, 335, 371-372, 386, 412, 450, 517, 566, 568, 585, 589, 659, 661, 666, 670, 672, 675*

    has surrendered *85, 334-335*

    is surrendered *72, 87, 178, 335-336, 339, 372, 450, 598, 666, 669-670*

    submissive and surrendered *337-338*

    submissive or surrendered *148*

    surrendered and/or submissive *412, 566, 659*

    surrendered and submissive *72, 82, 85, 87, 177, 336-337, 373, 568, 666, 668-670*

    surrendered is *87*

    surrendered or submissive *85, 148, 335, 661, 666, 675*

    surrendered will *338*

surrenderer *450*

surrendering *10, 72, 82, 85, 87, 112, 122-123, 125, 134, 177-178, 203, 212, 242, 326, 335, 373, 438-439, 450, 452, 535, 566, 582-583, 590, 593-594, 653, 674*

surrenders *87, 123, 178, 202, 450, 565, 661, 675*

survival *15, 116, 247, 267, 351, 401, 404, 445, 518, 533, 571*

survive *15, 73, 373, 520, 615*

survives *15, 551*

Svadhisthana *675*

Swarloka *675*

swastika *632-633*

synagogue *68-69, 229, 239, 368-369, 375, 664*

synagogues *201, 208, 222, 224, 267, 270*

synthesis *vii*

Syria *139, 202*

Syrians *139*

system *viii, i, iv, 12, 15, 43, 55, 59, 138, 155, 160, 179, 204, 214, 349-350, 352, 355, 413, 454, 468, 473, 481, 483, 487, 491-493, 495-506, 508-512, 518, 539-540, 550, 559-561, 571, 577, 579-580, 587, 599, 605, 615-619, 623-626, 640, 645, 650-651, 653, 662, 668*

    adoptable system *640*

    another system *577*

    any system *508*

    a system *viii, i, 12, 454, 483, 496-499, 502, 518, 559, 571, 616-619, 651*

    caste system *43, 468*

    complex system *559*

    dating system *539*

    defense system *587*

    digestive system *355, 599*

    Divine System *617-619*

    God's System *616*

    His System *155, 487, 496, 509*

    human system *496*

    ideal system *512*

    interrelated system *352*

    judiciary system *501, 560*

    nervous system *349-350, 473, 579-580, 645, 650, 668*

    new system *viii, 510*

    no system *512*

    only System *662*

    open system *352*

    oppressive system *619*

INDEX

organizational system *662*
our system *498-499, 512, 605, 619, 623-625*
present system *496*
prison system *615*
sensitive system *559*
similar system *496*
social system *487, 559*
suggested system *499*
system has *495, 625*
system is *viii, 454, 496-497, 499, 508-509, 559, 617, 619, 625*
system of *55, 138, 160, 500, 512, 561, 587, 617, 651, 653*
system should *483, 498, 508*
system will *viii, 214, 497, 501, 509-510, 599, 624*
that system *619*
their system *214, 559, 617*
the system *viii, iv, 15, 55, 138, 155, 160, 179, 487, 491-493, 496-501, 503-506, 508-512, 550, 559, 561, 599, 617-619, 625, 653*
this system *viii, 55, 59, 204, 481, 496-497, 499-500, 502, 504-506, 512, 616-617, 626*
timing system *540*
worldwide system *495*
systems *i, 229, 415, 454, 481, 487, 497-499, 503, 565, 571, 615, 618-619, 640*

T

Tabaokolaho Ahasanol Khaleghin *675*
tabernacle *405, 410, 424*
Tabernacles *64, 248, 542, 607*
Tahirah *539*
talk *48, 56, 62, 129, 150, 207, 242, 260, 264, 266, 282-283, 288, 302, 319-321, 466, 470, 524, 555, 573, 583, 586, 588, 598, 607, 633-634, 667, 671*
talkativeness *581, 598*
talked *28, 52, 131, 234, 247, 288, 414, 425, 612, 633*
talkest *288*
talking *77, 95, 242, 248-249, 286, 288, 378, 472, 524, 536, 634*
talks *48, 282, 319-321, 466, 561, 633-635, 647*
tama *5-9, 12-13, 21-22, 26, 66, 69, 78-79, 98, 101, 107-111, 113-115, 170, 174, 180, 197-200, 209-210, 217, 225, 230-231, 236, 238, 270, 275-276, 297, 299-300, 302, 304, 306, 309, 311-314, 318, 327, 341, 347-351, 354, 357, 362, 364-366, 370, 379, 382, 384, 389, 393-394, 401-403, 410, 415, 422, 431, 433-441, 443-445, 448, 490, 519-520, 545, 552-553, 563, 590-591, 611, 637, 647, 649-650, 652, 657-658, 663, 665, 667, 671, 674-676*
  ability of the tama *114, 675*
  active tama *6, 108*
  for tama *79*
  grip of the tama *22, 304, 553, 647, 649*
  influence of the tama *6-8, 12, 69, 78, 109, 113, 276, 300, 327, 348, 350-351, 362, 370, 384, 410, 433-434, 520, 637, 652, 657, 663, 667, 671, 676*
  influences of the tama *663*
  is tama *275*
  is the tama *109, 520*
  power of the tama *6, 9, 22, 66, 78, 98, 108-109, 111, 113, 180, 197-198, 200, 209-210, 217, 225, 231, 270, 299, 302, 304, 306, 313, 318, 347, 357, 364-366, 384, 389, 401-403, 415, 422, 431, 433, 437-440, 443-444, 448, 519, 545, 590-591, 649-650, 652, 657, 663*
(tama) *22, 110, 170, 431, 490, 552, 658*
tama (crudifying) *637*
tama dominates *109, 354, 553*
(tama guna) *5, 107-108, 114, 198-200, 230-231, 309, 357, 431, 437, 647, 663, 665, 674*
tama guna becomes *6*
tama guna brings *101*
tama guna (crudifying force) *6, 667*
tama guna (darkness) *7, 109, 276, 433*
tama guna dominates *7, 22, 519-520, 553*
tama guna has *402, 520*
tama guna in *225, 402-403*
tama guna is *7, 12, 21-22, 109, 349, 357, 402, 410, 415, 433, 441, 443, 519-520, 545, 552-553, 591, 649-650, 675*
tama guna over the soul *26, 66, 78, 113, 115, 200, 217, 299, 304, 313, 366, 384, 389, 402, 439-440, 444, 652, 657*
tama guna should *591*
tama guna (static force) *111, 435, 675*
tama guna will *22, 553*
tama guna would *111*
tama has *520*
tama (negative) *433*

INDEX

tama present *111*

tamasic *9, 518, 586-588, 627, 664, 671, 675*

tantra *78*

tantric *562*

Tapoloka *675*

tasleim *71, 85, 122, 148, 177, 335, 371, 517, 566, 659, 675*

Tat Twam Asi *518, 675*

tatwa *349-350, 653, 655, 668, 676*

tax *509-510, 616, 679*

taxed *510*

taxes *509-510*

taxpayers *510*

telepathic *47-48, 103, 120, 174, 295, 447, 521, 525, 675*

telepathically *47*

telepathy *103, 447*

temple *viii, i, 75, 77, 100, 141, 163, 198-199, 229, 259-260, 268, 270, 280-281, 287, 375-376, 389, 397-398, 400, 409-411, 413, 425, 471, 511, 535-538, 622, 625, 664, 675*

temples *281, 287, 502, 510, 535, 537, 625, 675*

temporary *111, 238, 254, 462, 485*

tempt *23, 25, 133, 198, 264, 405, 590*

temptation *22-25, 74-75, 80, 198-199, 209-211, 224, 247, 351, 375, 386, 388, 400, 553, 676*

temptations *25, 74, 192, 199, 375-376, 405, 422, 619, 650*

tempted *23-24, 197-199, 405*

tempter *197*

tempting *198, 245, 253, 265*

Testament *i, 86, 121-122, 146-147, 155, 163, 227, 400, 480, 503, 542, 579, 596, 602-603, 605, 672*

thank *228*

thankful *342*

thanks *244, 380, 399*

thanksgiving *388, 509*

thesis *558-559*

thief *73, 81, 374, 413*

thieves *210, 259*

THOTH *vi, vii, viii, ix, i, ii, iii, iv, 4, 54, 125, 163, 234, 397, 498, 526, 602-603, 608, 620, 626, 635-637, 640, 660, 680*

Thursday *539*

Thyatira *71, 365, 371-372*

thyself *61, 198, 206, 216, 255, 266, 277, 584-585, 672*

T

Tibet *470*

Tibetan *648*

tithe *269, 509, 606*

tithes *509-510, 604-606*

Tithing *606*

Tohied *566-567, 665-666, 676*

Torah *60, 205, 332, 533*

tradition *87, 241-242, 336, 526, 579, 596*

traditional *580*

traditions *55, 242, 287, 596*

tranquility *58, 155, 165, 179, 203, 213, 494-495, 498, 509, 544, 554, 598, 662*

transcendental *562, 594*

transgress *241-243*

transgression *69, 333, 362, 369, 471, 673*

transgressions *330*

transgressor *146, 296*

transgressors *473*

Transmission *599, 608, 638-639*

tribe *137, 140, 143, 148, 176-177, 191, 201, 243-244, 262, 381, 388, 481, 598, 605-606, 621, 661, 669*

tribes *85, 139-142, 145, 147, 161, 176-177, 200, 223, 244, 256, 275, 285-286, 289, 297, 387-388, 425, 479, 481, 569, 653, 658*

tribulation *41, 68-69, 71, 74-75, 80-81, 90, 93, 98, 124, 150, 154, 218, 225, 233, 236, 269-270, 295, 315, 318-319, 337, 339-340, 342, 362-363, 365, 368-369, 372, 375-376, 386-388, 390-392, 395, 399-400, 410, 412-414, 417-418, 422, 590, 626, 676, 678*

  a tribulation *318, 342*

  bring tribulation *270, 340*

  call tribulation *225*

  great tribulation *71, 225, 372, 388*

  has tribulation *69, 369*

  individual tribulation *90, 315*

  in tribulation *365, 412*

  of tribulation *376, 626*

  the tribulation *74-75, 80, 93, 150, 295, 363, 375, 386-388, 390-391, 395, 399, 410, 412-414, 417-418*

  this tribulation *337, 386*

  through tribulation *68, 369, 422*

  (tribulation) *154, 236*

  tribulation as *339-340*

  tribulation because *318, 342*

  tribulation comes *319, 391*

735

INDEX

tribulation has *339*
tribulation is *93, 98, 150, 218, 340*
tribulation starts *90, 150, 315, 412*
tribulation will *93, 295, 376, 392, 413-414, 417*
when tribulation *236, 319*
why tribulation *98, 339*
world tribulation *150*

tribulations *81, 215, 233, 269, 387, 390, 393, 395, 418*

trumpet *65, 77, 208, 362, 365, 378, 389, 391-392, 394, 397, 399-400*

trumpets *77, 340, 362-363, 377, 389-391, 542*

Tuesday *539*

Twam (see "Tat Twam Asi") *518, 675*

twelfth *257, 425, 673*

twelve *vii, i, 2, 20, 31, 75, 118, 122, 129, 133, 136, 145, 172, 215, 221-223, 226, 240, 256-257, 295, 332, 378, 388, 400, 425-426, 443, 454, 474, 481, 483, 487, 499-501, 503-511, 535-538, 550, 566, 584, 597, 599, 617-618, 620, 623, 653, 658*

   are twelve *425, 505, 535, 538, 599*
   BASE OF TWELVE *509*
   be twelve *499*
   has twelve *136, 425*
   (twelve) *500*
   twelve angels *425*
   twelve apostles *222, 425*
   twelve base *510*
   twelve baskets *240*
   twelve books *i, 2*
   twelve disciples *222, 226, 257*
   twelve foundations *425*
   twelve gates *425*

U

twelve hours *257*
twelve houses *511*
twelve-leadership *501*
twelve manner of fruits *426*
twelve members *623*
twelve pearls *425*
twelve-people *500, 509*
twelve people *500, 503, 509, 511, 599*
twelve-people-leader *499-501*
twelve-people-selective *509*
twelve powers *400*
twelve princes *133*
twelve pyramids *536*
twelve regions *499, 505-506*
twelve rotations *538*
twelve sections *500, 535*
twelve select *500-501*
twelve-selected *501*
twelve selection *504*
twelve-sided *536*
twelve sons *136*
twelve stars *400*
twelve sub-regions *499-500, 505*
twelve thousand *vii, 118, 129, 172, 295, 388, 425, 454, 474, 481, 483, 487, 508, 584, 617-618, 620*
twelve thrones *256*
twelve tribes *256, 388, 425, 653, 658*
twelve unit *501*
twelve unit groups *501*
twelve will *500*
twoedged/two-edged *65-66, 366, 422, 631*

U

Ummah *618*
unalienable *626*
unappreciative *27*
unbelief *239, 249*
unbeliever *91*
unbelievers *83-84, 298, 332, 471, 659, 679*
unbelieving *425*
uncircumcised *132*
unclean *36, 222, 233, 314, 412, 418, 522-523, 585, 587, 627*

uncleanness *269*
unconditional *7, 22, 52-53, 62, 70, 134, 143-144, 339, 351, 355, 370-371, 552-553, 655*
unconditionally *143*
Unconscious *348-349, 355, 462, 556, 610-613, 651, 661, 676*
unconsciously *599, 612, 677*
unexplainable *70, 371, 396, 464, 468, 473*
ungodly *605, 615*
unification *viii, 526-527, 622, 672*

INDEX

unified *v, vi, viii, 446, 461, 466, 567, 584, 593, 597, 618, 631, 647*

unifies *v, viii, 85, 128, 150, 440, 545, 567*

unify *ii, 150, 466, 475, 483, 539, 567, 583, 590, 593-594, 621*

unifying *340, 567, 622*

union *20, 117, 152, 253, 340, 446, 554, 562, 565, 571, 678*

United States *142, 147, 153, 176*

Universal *vi, 6, 8, 11-12, 18, 21, 28, 34, 48, 58, 60, 63, 71, 73, 82, 90, 94, 98-99, 101, 103-104, 110-111, 114-115, 119, 123, 145-146, 153, 162, 171, 178, 186, 203, 205, 235, 268, 276, 284, 293-295, 299, 311, 314, 325, 329, 333, 340, 347-349, 352, 372-373, 391, 402, 408, 412, 431, 435-436, 439-440, 442, 451, 462, 483, 488-489, 495, 498, 517-518, 529, 531, 536, 539, 541, 556-557, 562, 582-583, 586, 590, 598, 610-612, 618-619, 630, 633, 645, 648-651, 654-658, 661, 663, 665-669, 671, 675-676*

    and Universal *333, 611, 671, 675*

    become universal *vi*

    more universal *82, 294*

    or Universal *146, 557, 611*

    Those universal *488*

    universal and *294*

    Universal Call *598*

    Universal Chitta *650*

    universal consciousness *6, 276, 556*

    universal family *21*

    universal feeling *123, 440, 483, 658*

    universal feelings *529*

    universal forces *119, 347*

    universal knowledge *146*

    Universal Laws *18, 34, 48, 60, 103, 205, 295, 314, 333, 531, 562, 619, 651*

    Universal Mahatattva *663*

    Universal Mantra *657, 667*

    universal memory *90, 146, 431, 654*

Universal Mind *8, 12, 28, 101, 110-111, 114, 145-146, 171, 235, 268, 284, 295, 311, 314, 325, 329, 348-349, 391, 402, 408, 435-436, 442, 462, 557, 590, 610-612, 630, 645, 649-651, 655-656, 661, 663, 665, 669, 671, 675-676*

universal name *293*

UNIVERSAL NAMING *529*

universal outlook *63, 439, 539, 666, 668*

universal person *412*

universal personality *162*

Universal Plan *536*

universal point *58, 71, 94, 99, 104, 178, 186, 203, 451, 498*

universal scope *556*

Universal Self *352, 541*

universal set-up *582, 618*

universal view *71, 73, 94, 153, 372-373, 439, 495, 539, 648*

universal views *495*

very universal *293*

universalism *94-95, 98, 115, 130, 178, 186, 242, 411-412, 439, 444, 450, 525-526, 529, 535, 539, 561, 610, 654, 672, 677*

universalist *11, 77, 98, 319, 371, 378, 450, 452, 525, 543, 581, 640, 653*

Universalists *72, 99, 126, 372, 392, 411, 525, 598*

universality *80, 94, 385, 530, 648*

universally *349, 437, 439, 630, 668*

    universally-centered *439, 672*

unleavened *541-542*

un-manifested *7, 18, 21, 304, 326, 401, 524, 531, 552, 655, 660*

unspiritual *180, 247, 351, 381, 415, 444, 522, 550, 589*

unspiritualized *350*

Unum (see "E Pluribus Unum") *154*

Upanishads *78, 384, 542, 654, 677*

Uthman *677*

Vaeshya *99, 488, 668*

Vaeshyan *479, 481-482, 490, 584*

Vaeshyas *43-44, 102, 119, 174, 447, 459, 461, 474, 479-488, 490, 507, 532, 620, 655, 659, 677*

vahdat *566*

vahed *566*

Vajrasattva *562*

Veda *596, 677*

Vedantas *40, 163, 542, 654, 677*

Vedas *40, 65, 78, 119-120, 173, 383, 391, 655, 658, 677*

Vedic *163*

INDEX

vegetarian *16, 174, 518, 531, 586, 588*

veto *466*

vibrate *664*

vibrated *664*

vibrates *589*

vibrating *589*

vibration *5-6, 70, 85, 90, 101, 108, 116, 210, 305-306, 321, 371, 379, 432-433, 444, 589-590, 597, 610, 636, 664, 670, 678*

vibrational *294, 597, 646, 664*

vibrations *173, 302, 306, 314, 586, 594, 597, 610, 629, 664*

vice-president *666*

vice-presidents *493, 666*

vid *677*

Vidya *647, 677*

Vigamaya *677*

vipers *196, 231, 269*

Vipra *99, 668*

Vipran *479-483, 486, 490, 584*

Vipras *43-44, 102, 119, 174, 447, 459, 461, 474, 479, 481-486, 488, 507, 532, 620, 655, 659, 677*

virgin *63-64, 147, 191, 193, 232, 665*

virgins *408*

Vishnu *563*

Vishudaha *677*

vision *i, ii, 16, 64, 152, 217, 249, 339, 365, 378, 381, 395, 410, 412, 424, 462-465, 467, 469, 471-473, 530, 556, 586, 604, 607, 641*

    vision-dream *463*

visions *iv, 15, 64, 152, 462, 464, 467, 473-474, 480, 488, 556-557, 573*

vote *499-505, 510, 617, 623*

voting *501, 505, 623*

vozo *579*

W

warner *323, 326, 332*

warners *162, 311, 326*

warrior *45, 55, 78, 99, 384, 459, 461, 474, 508, 568, 662, 666, 668*

warriors *43-45, 55, 119, 174, 459, 461, 474, 479, 507, 559, 620, 655, 666*

wedding *263*

Wednesday *232-233, 539-540*

week *539-541, 595, 599, 670*

weekly *232, 539-540, 595*

weeks *541, 599*

Western *289, 628-629, 656*

whore *414-417, 420, 656*

whoremongers *425, 427*

witness *17, 116, 169, 177, 232, 243, 255, 276-277, 283-284, 329, 331, 333, 338, 364, 376, 379, 423, 443, 496, 508, 611, 624, 651*

witnesses *155, 251-252, 269, 398, 503*

wolves *vi, 214, 223*

Word (uppercase "W") *5-6, 9, 70, 85, 90, 97, 101, 108, 110-111, 116, 169-171, 216, 247, 270, 275-277, 305, 371, 374-375, 379-380, 382, 400, 421, 432-434, 436, 444, 562, 590, 635-636, 655, 657, 660, 664, 667, 678*

    and The Word *5-6, 9, 90, 101, 108, 169-170, 275-277, 305, 380, 432, 436, 667*

    beyond The Word *382*

    is The Word *5, 70, 90, 101, 108, 169-170, 275-276, 305, 371, 379-380, 432, 590, 667, 678*

    "The Word" *6, 116, 169, 275, 433-434, 444, 562, 655, 664*

    (The Word) *110, 169-171, 379, 400, 635, 655, 657*

    through The Word *275, 380*

    use The Word *216*

    utter The Word *216*

    without The Word *380*

    Word (…) *90, 101, 108, 247, 270, 275-276, 421, 436*

    Word becomes *101, 111*

    Word consists *678*

    Word is *5-6, 9, 90, 101, 108, 169-170, 275-277, 305, 380, 432, 664*

    Word of God *374-375, 421*

    Word reaches *101, 171*

worker *212, 356, 635, 673*

workers *44-45, 119, 174, 459, 468, 559, 589, 604-607, 613, 620, 635*

INDEX

Y

Yaghob (see "Jacob") *135*
YAH *420*
Yahudis *661*
Yahud/Yahudi *661*
Yahweh *90*
yaj *677*
Yajus *677*
Yama *581-582, 584, 678*
Yamama *678*
Yang *630-631*
Yantra *518, 656, 673, 678*
Ya-Sin *315, 678*
yeast *542*

Yeshu *660*
Yin *630-631*
yoga *75, 78, 117, 376, 384, 446, 474, 522, 531, 565-566, 600, 648, 654, 661, 667, 678*
yogas *565*
yogi *70, 164, 370, 638*
yogis *67, 367-368, 522*
Yoseph (see "Joseph") *136, 660*
Y'shua *54, 138, 660, 678*
Yunus (see "Jonah/Jonas") *322, 330, 678*
Y'weh *19, 192, 660*
Y'wehshua *192, 660*

Z

Zakat *679*
Zeus *660*
Zion *iv, 155, 179, 407, 491-494, 496-497, 508, 550, 599, 653, 666*

Zoroastrian *665, 672*
Zoroastrianism *665*
Zoroastrians *63*

www.ingramcontent.com/pod-product-compliance
Lightning Source LLC
Chambersburg PA
CBHW080536230426
43663CB00015B/2613